COMPARATIVE PUBLIC ADMINISTRATION: THE ESSENTIAL READINGS

RESEARCH IN PUBLIC POLICY ANALYSIS AND MANAGEMENT

Series Editor: Lawrence R. Jones

Recent Volumes:

RESEARCH IN PUBLIC POLICY ANALYSIS AND MANAGEMENT
VOLUME 15

COMPARATIVE PUBLIC ADMINISTRATION: THE ESSENTIAL READINGS

EDITED BY

ERIC E. OTENYO
Northern Arizona University, USA

NANCY S. LIND
Illinois State University, USA

United Kingdom – North America – Japan
India – Malaysia – China

Emerald Group Publishing Limited
Howard House, Wagon Lane, Bingley BD16 1WA, UK

First edition 2006

Reprints and permission service
Contact: booksandseries@emeraldinsight.com

British Library Cataloguing in Publication Data
A catalogue record for this book is available from the British Library

ISBN: 978-0-7623-1359-4
ISSN: 0732-1317 (Series)

Awarded in recognition of Emerald's production department's adherence to quality systems and processes when preparing scholarly journals for print

INVESTOR IN PEOPLE

CONTENTS

v

PERMISSIONS AND ACKNOWLEDGEMENTS

Andersen, K. V. (1999). Reengineering public sector organizations using information technology. In: R. Heeks (Ed.), *Reinventing government in the information age international practice in IT-enabled public sector reform* (pp. 312–330). New York: Routledge. (Reprinted with permission.)

Bellamy, C., & Taylor, J. A. (1994). Introduction, exploiting IT in public administration: Towards the information polity. *Public Administration, 72,* 1–12. (Reprinted with permission.)

Bowornwathana, B. (2003). Transforming bureaucracies for the 21st century: The new democratic governance paradigm. *Public Administration Quarterly,* 294–308. (Reprinted with permission.)

Brinkerhoff, J., & Brinkerhoff, D. W. (1999). International development management in a globalized world. *Public Administration Review, 59*(4), 473–506. (Reprinted with permission.)

Caiden, G. E. (2005). The administrative state in a globalizing world: Some trends and challenges. ECOSOC, United Nations Organization, New York, September 2004, p. 25.

Caiden, N. (2006). Budget issues in developing countries. In: E. E. Otenyo & N. S. Lind (Eds), *Comparative public administration: The essential readings.* London: Elsevier.

Chang, S. Y., & Jones, R. A. (1992). Approaches to privatization: Established models and a U.S. innovation. *Government Finance Review, 8*(4), 17–22. (Reprinted with permission.)

Conyers, D. (April/June, 1983). Decentralization: The latest fashion in development administration. *Public Administration and Development, 3*(2), 97–109. (Reprinted with permission.)

Deva, S. (1979). Western conceptualization of administrative development: A critique and an alternative. *International Review of Administrative Sciences, 45*(1), 59–63. (Reprinted with permission.)

Donk, W. B. H. J. Van de., & Tops P. W. (1992). Informatization and democracy: Orwell or Athens, A review of the literature. *Informatization and the Public Sector, 2,* 169–196. (Reprinted with permission.)

Esman, M. (1980). Development assistance in public administration: Requiem or renewal. *Public Administration Review, 40*(5), 426–431. (Reprinted with permission.)

Farazmand, A. (1994). The new world order and global public administration: A critical essay. In: J-C. Garcia-Zamor & R. Khator (Eds), *Public administration in the global village* (pp. 61–81). Westport, CT: Praeger. (Reprinted with permission.)

Gant, G. (1979). The concept of development administration. *Development administration: Concepts, goals, methods* (Ch. 1, pp. 3–31). Madison, University of Wisconsin Press.

Garcia-Zamor, J-C. (1994). Neoteric theories for development administration in the new world order. In: J.-C. Garcia-Zamor & R. Khator (Eds), *Public administration in the global village* (pp. 101–120). Westport: Praeger. (Reprinted with permission.)

Gayle, D. J., & Goodrich, J. N. (Eds). (1990). Exploring the implications of privatization and deregulation. *Privatization and deregulation in global perspective* (Ch. 1, pp. 1–23). New York: Quorum Books. (Reprinted with permission.)

Gray, A., & Jenkins, B. (1995). From public administration to public management: Reassessing a revolution? *Public Administration, 73*(Spring), 75–99. (Reprinted with permission.)

Heady, F. (1995). *Public Administration: A comparative perspective* (Ch. 1, pp. 1–70). New York: Marcel Dekker. (Reprinted with permission.)

Henry, N. (2006). Resuscitating good government: Democracy, honesty, and competency. (Written exclusively for this volume.)

Jones, L., & Kettl, D. (2003). Assessing public management reform strategy in an international context. *International Public Management Review, 4*(1), 1–19. (Reprinted with permission.)

Jreisat, J. (2006). The field of comparative administration through the years. (Written exclusively for this volume.)

Kickert, W. J. M., Stillman, R. J. II., Chevallier, J., Seibel, W., Pollit, C., & Jorgensen, T. B. (1996). Changing European states: Changing public administration [France, Germany, UK, Netherlands, Scandinavia]. *Public Administration Review, 56*(1) (January/February), 65–104. (Reprinted with permission.)

La Palombara, J. (1967). An overview of bureaucracy and political development. In: J. La Palombara (Ed.), *Bureaucracy and Political Development* (2nd. ed., pp. 1–39). (Reprinted with permission.)

Leonard, D. K., & Marshall, D. R. (1982). Analyzing the organizational requirements for serving the rural poor. *Institutions of rural development for the poor: Decentralization and organizational linkages* (Ch. 1, pp. 1–39). Berkeley: Institute of International Studies, University of California.

Loveman, B. (1976). The comparative administration group, development administration, and anti-development. *Public Administration Review* (November/December), 616–621. (Reprinted with permission.)

Lynn, L. E., Jr. (2002). The new public management as an international phenomenon: A skeptical view. *Presentation at the conference on the new public management in international perspective* (pp. 11–13). St. Gallen, Switzerland. (Reprinted with permission.)

Montgomery, J. (1980). Administering the poor if we can't help rich dictators, what do we do for the poor? *Public Administration Review, 40*(5), 421–426. (Reprinted with permission.)

Rice, E. (1992). Public administration on post-socialist Eastern Europe. *Public Administration Review, 52*(2), 116–125. (Reprinted with permission.)

Riggs, F. W. (1964). The prismatic model. *Administration in developing countries: The theory of prismatic society* (Ch.1, pp. 3–49). Boston: Houghton Mifflin. (Reprinted with permission.)

Riggs, F. W. (1998). *Global perspective on comparative and international administration.* (This comment has been prepared for use at a mini-symposium on the future of comparative and international administration sponsored by the Section on International and Comparative Administration of the American Society for Public Administration, held at Seattle, May 1998. Reprinted with permission.)

Rondinelli, D. A. (2003). Government decentralization and economic development: The evolution of concepts and practices. (Not previously published. Printed with permission.)

Savoie, D. (1995). What is wrong with the new public management? *Canadian Public Administration, 38*(1), 112–121. (Reprinted with permission.)

Seitz, J. (1980). The failure of US technical assistance in public administration: The Iranian case. *Public Administration Review, 40*(5), 407–413. (Reprinted with permission.)

Sigelman, L. (1976). In search of comparative administration. *Public Administration Review, 36*, 621–625. (Reprinted with permission.)

Thompson, V. A. (1964). Administrative objectives for development administration. *Administrative Science Quarterly, 9*, 91–108. (Reprinted with permission.)

Toonen, T. (1993). Analyzing institutional change and administrative transformation: A comparative view. In: J. J. Hesse (Ed.), *Administrative transformation in Central and Eastern Europe towards public sector reform in post-communist societies* (pp. 151–168). Cambridge: Blackwell. (Reprinted with permission.)

Van Wart, M., & Cayer, J. N. (1990). Comparative public administration: Defunct, dispersed, or redefined? *Public Administration Review, 50*(2), 238–248. (Reprinted with permission.)

Waldo, D. (1964). *Comparative public administration: Prologue, problems and promise.* American society for public administration comparative administration group, Sybil stokes papers special series, No. 2. (Original work published 1963; Reprinted with permission.)

Waterston, A., Martin, C. J., Schumacher, A. T., & Steuber, F. A. (1965). *Development planning: Lessons of experience* (Ch. 1, pp. 1–7). Baltimore: Johns Hopkins Press. (Reprinted with permission.)

PERSONAL ACKNOWLEDGEMENTS

This book has benefited immensely from the support of Jamal Nassar, chair of the Department of Politics and Government, and Gary Olson, dean of Arts and Sciences at Illinois State University. We wish to thank Larry Jones, the series editor, for his helpful advice throughout the preparation of this volume. We wish to thank those who provided encouragement and suggestions for improving this volume.

We would like to express deep appreciation to the two icons in the field, Fred Riggs and Ferrel Heady, for their endorsement of this project and for their willingness to stay involved in the field of Comparative Public Administration. We sincerely thank each of the authors and publishers who generously granted rep\rint permission for the inclusion of their works as well as the authors who penned new ideas for this book.

We are grateful to our graduate students, Jeri-Anne Hose-Ryan, Kate James, and Anthony Bolton at Illinois State University, and Mai Wakisaka at Northern Arizona University. These students deserve appreciation for contributing to the research and scanning the documents. We would also like to show our appreciation to the production team of Macmillan India Limited, for checking all the citations and making helpful editorial suggestions.

We have long lists of persons who have supported us in our careers, space doesn't allow us to mention their names, but we thank them all. Finally, we acknowledge the support and understanding of our respective families. We dedicate this volume to them.

Eric E. Otenyo
Nancy S. Lind
Editors

INTRODUCTION: ESSENTIAL READINGS IN COMPARATIVE ADMINISTRATION

Comparative public administration is a branch of public administration that focuses on comparative analysis of administrative processes and institutions. The comparative approach has been around since the inception of government. As a specialized field of interest, the significance of comparison cannot be accurately traced to a single event or country. What we know is that early scholarly work in the parent field drew upon knowledge and perspectives with cross-national origins. For example, Ferrel Heady reminds us that pioneers in the study of American public administration, including Woodrow Wilson and Frank Goodnow, made full use of lens' provided in European scholarship (Heady, 2001, p. 6). Likewise, past and recent non-western scholarship has drawn substantial inspiration from European and American models. The reasons for this are easy to discern. At least three can be advanced. First is the colonial experience – with most countries in the southern hemisphere having derived a large part of their bureaucratic structures from their former colonizers, the importance of comparative approaches cannot be overemphasized. Second is the increased flow of information worldwide has made it easier for scholars to compare notes on administrative systems in different countries. Third are domino effects of human development, including deliberate attempts by various international bodies to encourage development via adoption of institutional and administrative models that have proven to enhance the quality of life. In fact, coincidentally, sustained comparative analysis in public administration occurred at the end of the World War II when many organizations with a global outreach emerged.

It is hardly an exaggeration to say that the comparative method is central to both practical and academic aspects of public administration. Scholarship that informs practice can hardly be adjudged as scientific if it lacks a comparative dimension. Unfortunately, the evolution of comparative public administration has not been dynamic in terms of consistency in scholarship.

There have been concerns that, much like its parent discipline, comparative administration lacked a focus and was disjointed. What passed as comparative works were analysis of single-country administrative processes, institutions, and systems. In the past, analyses borrowed more than a leaf from the sociological functionalist approaches. Comparison was hinged upon functional equivalence of the various administrative apparatus and processes. Importantly, cross-cultural scholarship has been in short supply (Jreisat, 2002, p. 4). Yet, happily, the interest and enthusiasm in the comparative method is growing rather than dwindling. In a recent article, Jamil Jreisat stated that Comparative Public Administration is back in, prudently (Jreisat, 2005, p. 231).

We believe it is important to continue to expand the empirical base of public administration by placing in perspective the centrality of the comparative approach. Hence we need to continue to eliminate the semantic confusion arising from the perception that comparative public administration means foreign administration. Fred Riggs said it well, "All Political Science and any scientific understanding of Public Administration needs to be comparative" (Riggs, 2002). He added,

> Actually, all systems of government require comparative analysis if we are to understand cause/effect relationships and achieve predictability. This applies as much to the study of American government as any other. Whenever we want to focus our attention on any country, we can easily use geographic terms to specify the context – e.g. public administration in Asia, Africa, Latin America, Europe, or the U.S. (2002).

Have the recent works in comparative public administration shed enough light on the evolution and salience of comparative administration as a central part of public administration? Probably not, if we lack a systematic organization of the seminal and essential readings that guide our understanding of contemporary administrative processes worldwide. Many of the new works are taken as givens. They are accounts of changes in society showing the contributions of administrative processes but not the basic works upon which new studies are built. Having a book with well-selected classics and essential readings is a starting point for continuing to advance the subfield of comparative administration. That is the rationale for this present edition: to present the most influential works in the field in a convenient volume. It may well be that some of the articles selected are archaic, but they still have staying power and provide general and specialized readers the vocabulary and essence of comparative administration.

The basic threads in the comparative analysis of administration are relatively constant. Comparative administration is still contextual. The analysis of administrative systems cannot be carried outside of the political, social, technological, and economic settings in which it exists. An historical presentation of influential works in this book validates that assertion. Of course it also enables the reader to gain a sense of the development of the main thoughts in the field. The readings are products of research carried out globally as opposed to a single country and, therefore, purposefully affirm and refine the essence of generic administration. No doubt, then, these writings contribute to the intellectual understanding of the field at large.

CRITERIA FOR SELECTION

The editors of *Comparative Public Administration: The Essential Readings* seek to provide key classic and influential readings on comparative administration. The objective is to introduce readers to underpinnings in the field's evolution and growth. The selected readings have been classified as "essential" because they are among the most enduring in the field. Some of the works present the field's seminal frameworks and contributions of enduring value. For the most part, they are the most frequently cited and are rich in conceptual and theoretical content. Most of the selected readings provide the generic vocabulary for understanding public administration in a globalizing world.

Selecting a field's essential articles is a potentially contentious issue. The editors make no pretense to have selected all the important works. Indeed, many articles with a higher impact on the field's development were not selected. Others from related social sciences were perhaps subconsciously omitted. Likewise, only portions of many of the selected articles appear in this volume. We did not mean to minimize this scholarship but rather sought to reproduce articles not readily available. We placed a considerable emphasis on the thematic relevance of the selected articles. Finally, there were also issues of readability, work recency, method, and backgrounds of the authors. This present volume is deliberately written to have a wide appeal to all students and practitioners of comparative public administration regardless of their stations in life.

The readings are grouped into four broad topics, which reflect the field's growth and evolution, shifting paradigms and interests, and contemporary concerns. The first part plumbs the definition, evolution, and distinctiveness of the comparative administration approach. It examines the emergence of the field and its methodological rigor or lack of it. Two distinct divisions can be discerned, the first historical and the second conceptual and contextual frameworks for understanding public administration anywhere. The first building block for reading comparative administration is its ecology. Therefore, this part places emphasis on the relevance of the environment of administration and the unique history of bureaucratic developments globally.

The second part deals with the rise of administrative development and development administration. These subsets of comparative administration emerged as a result of the proliferation of new nations and their desire to establish administrative institutions to meet the challenges of development in the 1960s and 1970s. This section considers the key literature on the development of administrative ministries to respond to the needs of emerging nations. There is also considerable discussion on the prospects and perils of development administration.

The third part of this book focuses on particularly enduring debates in the field of administration. Three questions are addressed. First, do administrative institutions matter? Second, was planning as a managerial device essential to achieving success in administrative processes? And, third, does decentralization and strengthening of local jurisdictions deliver on its promise? The selected works raise questions about managing institutions in mostly developing areas. Issues of capacity building and planning for development were once the most-defining tools for administration in developing areas. The section reflects on the lessons learned from these experiences. Next, while urbanization has continued to be an important feature of all societies, the world has yet to see an end to debates about rural development. Rural communities continue to exist even in the most developed parts of the world, and how they are administered must be of interest to public administrators.

Importantly, contemporary interest in deregulation and privatization cannot be understood outside the context of debates on power of the state. Subsequently, interest in understanding the logic of state-owned enterprises and their reform is a worldwide phenomenon. This section deals with the culture, development, and decline of state-owned enterprises (SOEs) and privatization as a strategy for administrative reforms.

Part four zeros in on basic issues of the trendy global adoption of "new public management" (NPM). NPM, as Savas notes, is the "latest manifestation of the never-ending process of government reform, and it is taking place at all levels of government." (Savas, 2005, p. 4). It is characterized by actions such as rightsizing of government, application of market principles, embracing new technologies, decentralization and focusing on management, and reverting to core functions of government. To the extent that the applications of these approaches produce different results, they merit our closer analysis, from a comparative perspective. The final subset in this part treats the attendant question of globalization and its impact on administrative processes. The selections in this part elucidate reform and *change* themes in the new millennium.

To guide the reader, we have written brief introductory essays explaining our reading of the themes. Besides, new notes are introduced to enliven the discourse and to update many of the earlier assumptions and data. The primary goal remains to explain public administration in a comparative perspective. The values for doing so go beyond theory building to allow for sharing of ideas between practitioners from different countries and cultures.

It is reasonable to conclude that there is no agreed upon way of studying comparative administration. Of course, there is also no best way to organize themes central to the study of any subset of public administration. The salience of any one theme selected is really a matter of the assumptions made by the editors. Indeed, an examination of a sample of undergraduate- and graduate-level course syllabi in universities across the globe shows considerable differences in approaches to studying comparative administration. What is common to all approaches is the desire to provide a framework for understanding public administration in a wide range of countries.

REFERENCES

Heady, F. (2001). *Public administration a comparative perspective*. New York: Dekker.

Jreisat, J. E. (2002). *Comparative public administration and policy*. Boulder, CO: Westview Press.

Jreisat, J. E. (2005). Comparative public administration is back in, prudently. *Public Administration Review*, 65(2), 231–242.

Riggs, F. W. (2002). The exceptional American bureaucracy as explained by Paul Van Riper. Paper presented as the ASPA Conference, Van Piper Symposium, The State of the Public Service, Phoenix, Arizona, March 23, 2002. Available at http://webdata.soc.hawaii.edu/fredr/phoenix.htm accessed September 9, 2005.

Savas, E. S. (2005). *Privatization in the city success, failures, lessons*. Washington, DC: Congressional Quarterly Press.

Eric E. Otenyo
Nancy S. Lind
Editors

PREFACE: THE FIELD OF COMPARATIVE ADMINISTRATION THROUGH THE YEARS

I

Comparative Public Administration (CPA) attained its greatest intellectual influence during the post World War II era, although it was utilized much earlier. In 1887, for example, Woodrow Wilson's article, considered the first articulation of public administration as a field of study, clearly emphasized the comparative approach as the foundation of developing administrative principles. Wilson argued for "putting away all prejudices against looking anywhere in the world but at home for suggestions" in the study of public administration. He emphasized that "nowhere else in the whole field of politics … , can we make use of the historical, comparative method more safely than in this province of administration" (Wilson, 1887).

During the early part of the 20th century, Max Weber also differentiated and compared three types of authority system: traditional, charismatic, and legal–rational, producing in the process one of the most influential conceptualizations in social sciences the bureaucratic model. To underscore the attributes of the bureaucratic rational model of administration, Weber compared it to other systems that were prevalent in other times and places. What matters here is that the comparative approach was central to Weber's theory on authority systems throughout history.

The post WWII advance and expansion of comparative administration scholarship was stimulated by contributions from scholars whose intellectual pursuits reached beyond the national boundary of one country, and who managed to bridge the divide between administration and politics. Actually, in 1953, the American Political Science Association had a committee on comparative administration, before the American Society for Public Administration created the Comparative Administration Group

(CAG). This group evolved into what is now ASPA's Section on International and Comparative Administration (SICA).

In the early years of the CAG, Fred W. Riggs provided leadership, managed the group, attracted more recruits to the comparative approach, and contributed significant writings that set new directions in comparative research. Many lasting contributions are included in this volume, *Essential Readings in Comparative Administration*. Some of these readings included in the collection have been foundation blocks in the evolution of the comparative public administration approach, and have been utilized in public administration courses at universities across the country and internationally.

The growth of CPA was also induced by the collapse of the colonial order and the emergence of many newly independent nations. This reality generated huge demands for competent public service organizations. Developing the administrative capacity in these emerging societies was crucial for successful implementation of their national development plans. Steadily, the quest for tried and tested processes of administrative reform and organizational capacity building became almost universal.

In the 1960s, CPA focused on promoting empirical analysis and gathering applied evidence in order to serve the main premises of the comparative perspective. Riggs and others called for cross-cultural empirical data as the essential building blocks for redirecting research and scholarship from *ideographic* (distinct cases) toward *nomothetic* approaches (studies that seek explicitly to formulate and test propositions). At the same time, another pronounced shift of emphasis advocated moving away from a predominantly non-ecological to an ecologically based comparative study (Heady & Stokes, 1962, p. 2). Thus, the early period emphasized priorities of the CPA in terms of refining concepts and defining processes that have wider application, beyond Western systems of governance.

Utilizing advances in the study of comparative politics and administration, a growing number of scholars became engaged, particularly those trained in the continental administrative law tradition. Even if rigorous cross-cultural comparison was tangential in many of the early single-case studies,[1] the net results were significant. These studies expanded empirical knowledge, incorporated ecological variables in the analysis, and provided better understanding of the anomalies of administration and politics in the emerging nations. Overall, the early contributions helped to define, articulate, and suggest solutions to perennial problems of public administration in developing countries.

II

The primary purpose of CPA has been the development of administrative knowledge through comparisons of administrative experiences in different contexts. From early years, one of the driving forces of the momentum for cross-cultural administrative studies was the search to discover patterns and regularities from which generalizations can be established to enhance theory construction and reform application. Context (ecology or environment) refers to social, political, economic, and historical factors that influence public administration. A greater specificity of contextual relations is decisive for resolving issues surrounding administrative change, particularly the role of culture, which has increasingly received recognition in organization and management studies (Almond & Verba, 1989; Schein, 1985; Hofstede, 1980). Whereas the concept of culture remains without a precise definition, it evokes shared values and patterns of interaction among social groups over long periods of time. Culture includes language, religion, institutions, morals, customs, history, and laws that are passed from one generation to another, shaping attitudes, perceptions, and behaviors of individuals. Thus, cross-cultural comparisons essentially seek to formulate more reliable generalizations about administrative theory and process. The frequent unit of analysis has been the national bureaucracy, despite its real and potential conceptual and methodological limitations.

The search for administrative patterns and regularities cross-culturally afforded the CPA to show diversity of the human experience as well as the amazing uniformity within any given country or civilization. Students learn from comparisons how to explore, reflect, and understand the whole human experience, not to be confined to an ethnocentric perspective. The examination and analysis of what is often regarded as novel or unfamiliar systems would certainly open up the range of inquiry to include learning about similarities and differences that could balance outlooks and reduce internalized biases build over years of parochial learning.

Certainly, the comparative method, applied to intra- or inter-cultural situations, provides higher confidence in the generalizations and conclusions reached. "Comparison is so central to good analysis that the scientific method is unavoidably comparative" (Collier, 1991, p. 7). Similarly, social scientists regard the comparative approach as "the methodological core of the humanistic and scientific methods" (Almond et al., 2000, p. 33). As a requirement of the scientific investigative process, the comparative approach has been consistently emphasized in public administration literature for over a century. Indeed, the "comparative study … propels us to a level of conceptual methodological self-consciousness and clarity rarely found in non-comparative studies of public administration" as Rockman and Aberbach (1998, p. 437) point out.

The comparative approach, also, is often employed in studies of administration within one culture and in units smaller than the nation-state. Practices in cities, regions, and various public organizations have been compared within one society. Cities and counties are subjects of numerous comparative studies that evaluate, describe, classify, characterized, compare to a benchmark, and rank these units in enumerable ways. Comparative performance measurement at all levels of government, in the U.S. and internationally, has been used to identify differences in performance and the reasons for these differences. This is helpful for learning how to improve agencies and their operations (Morley, Bryant, & Hatry, 2001) but also illustrates the indispensability of the comparative approach for developing reliable generalization. Administrative functions are compared in different organizational contexts, such as law enforcement, budgeting, employment, or training in the same geographical area or internationally.

The CPA has been remarkably committed to administrative change and reform in its cross-cultural search for discovering the best practices or for differentiating practices that work from those that do not. Proven practices, then, can be designated as most worthy patterns and generalizations to be applied or benchmarked for improvements worldwide. This reformist commitment ultimately would improve the general efficacy of public administration as a field of study. Comparative research was often centered on characteristics and conditions of administrative systems associated with "good" performance.

As an outgrowth of the tendency to build administrative capacity in emerging nations, a cluster of concepts and applications evolved into what became known as "development administration." The conventional practices for building administrative capacity included creation of instruments that can define and champion improvements of administrative performance. Today, comparative and development administration often appear closely affiliated. Development administration has been promoting the creation of its own instruments of action in developing societies, such as institutes of public administration, development-oriented universities, national planning councils, international technical assistance agreements, and hiring foreign consultants. Development-oriented training programs for public employees became virtually an appendage to most proposed reform measures.

One cannot adequately discuss the early development administration without referring to Fred W. Riggs' pioneering work. In 1964, Riggs published *Administration of Developing Countries*, which laid the foundation for the forthcoming scholarship in this area. Riggs recognized the increasing global interdependence and the unique opportunities it offers for comparative and development public administration. The emerging global linkages call for transforming previously confined scholarly interests into a forefront field of creative contributions. Today, knowledge is regularly crossing cultural boundaries in important areas such as finance, technology, and corporate management. The global economic revolution is breathtaking and world's political boundaries are giving in to free movement of people, goods, information, and even cultural values. The "search for excellence" in American management stimulated interest in managerial processes of other countries. During the past few decades, we noticed a great deal of interest in Japanese management in particular, but also explorations were continuous for identifying relevant practices that could improve performance in the public as well as the private sectors.

III

Perhaps, one of the greatest challenges to CPA scholarship at the present is how to deal with the pervasive global influences on governance. Whereas the comparative perspective would have the effect of "deprovincializing" the field of Public Administration, it has to extend its realm, utilizing unprecedented accessibility to various countries, and deal with new and different problems of governance in the global context (Jreisat, 2004). The examination of administrative processes of other societies permits us to see a wider range of administrative behaviors and actions, identify a variety of problems, and, simultaneously, improve understanding of the shortcomings and limitations of our own administrative systems.

Current globalization trends stress the need for expanding the international thrust of comparative administration and for imaginative reformulation of traditional concepts and practices of organization and management. In the global context, public managers can hardly manage effectively in total disregard of global influences, limitations, and opportunities. Whether dealing with policies of healthcare, education, travel, trade, finance, or national security, today's public managers cannot ignore factors and conditions outside their boundaries. Comparative data and methods serve the practitioners by expanding their horizons of choice and their capacity to observe, learn, and improve performance. The current information revolution, facilitated by various communication tools that were not available only few years ago, should make the processes of cross-cultural learning and adaptation easier and more attainable.

True, the CPA has not successfully reached all its objectives. The literature conveys many real and imagined shortcomings. Perhaps, expansion of comparative research output in many cultures generated less information and knowledge on the inner working of administrative systems of other countries than expected. It is also hard to determine who benefited from managing public policies and who did not, or to ascertain how accountable are the administrative actions and methods of enforcement. Certainly, improvement of relevance and synthesis of comparative studies largely depends on developing generalizations from an aggregate of particular facts that have been reliably established and without ignoring the concreteness and distinctiveness of the case being investigated. This is why knowledge of the operating attributes of the system is crucial not only for developing generalizations but also to ensure that the relationship between the particular (the operating system) and the general (the context) is complimentary and coherent. These limitations of the comparative approach should not conceal the more significant contributions and accomplishments.

The effects of the collapse of communist systems and the failure of the Soviet bureaucratic edifice to produce promised outcomes did not help the promotion of cross-cultural administrative studies. During the 1980s and after, public bureaucracy in general has been widely disparaged as ineffective, corrupt, and self-serving. The negative image undermined the traditional attitude toward "public service," augmented by political distortions of relationships between citizens and their governments. One result was that funding for comparative research declined, and the quality of scholarship suffered from numerous poorly executed research projects.

In addition, developing countries did not perform as instructed by international consultants or in accordance with foreign aid blueprints. These countries have not lumbered their way faithfully through Western-designed schemes of administrative reform. Granted, researchers find administrative reform increasingly intractable, despite all earnest efforts. This is not to say, however, that no societal change has occurred. In developing societies, dynamic forces have been at work, altering every aspect of life in these systems and not always in the preferred way or direction. The assumption in many modernization prescriptions that to modernize is to move toward the side of the continuum inhabited by Western systems, proved to be questionable.

In brief, the quest for reliability of existing concepts and practices has been a primary moral and intellectual justification for the pertinence of the cross-cultural approach to the study of public administration. Perhaps, the contributions were not always self-evident nor fairly demonstrated. Nevertheless, cross-cultural comparisons profoundly benefited education, adding to students' capacities to make better judgments about an increasingly shrinking global context. Cross-cultural analysis improved students' knowledge and appraisal of world affairs. Having a sense of space, time, size, and cultures of this world invariably stimulates desires and capacities for exploration and reflection. Knowledge of other systems is the best medium for achieving a balance of perspective and for reducing myopic views of the others.

NOTES

1. Examples (not exhaustive listing) to illustrate such case studies include: Ralph Braibanti, 1966. *Research on the Bureaucracy of Pakistan*; Robert T. Dalan, 1967. *Brazilian Planning: development Politics and Administration*; Fred Riggs, 1966. *Thailand: the Modernization of Bureaucratic Polity*; Milton J. Esman, 1972. *Administration and Development in Malaysia*.

REFERENCES

Almond, G. A., et al. (2000). *Comparative politics today* (7th ed.). New York: Longman.

Almond, G., & Verba, S. (Eds). (1989). *The civic culture revisited.* Newbury Park, CA: Sage.

Collier, D. (1991). The comparative method: Two decades of change. In: D. A. Rustow & K. P. Erickson (Eds), *Comparative political dynamics.* New York: HarperCollins.

Heady, F., & Stokes, S. L. (Eds). (1962). *Papers in comparative public administration.* Ann Arbor, MI: Institute of Public Administration, University of Michigan.

Hofstede, G. (1980). *Culture's consequences: International differences in work-related values.* Beverly Hills, CA: Sage.

Jreisat, J. (2004). Comparative public administration back in, prudently. *Public Administration Review, 65*(2), 231–242.

Morley, E., Bryant, S., & Hatry, H. (2001). *Comparative performance measurement.* Washington, DC: The Urban Institute Press.

Rockman, B., & Aberbach, J. D. (1998). Problems of cross-national comparison. In: D. E. Rowat (Ed.), *Public administration in developed democracies: A comparative study* (pp. 419–440). New York: Marcel Dekker.

Schein, E. H. (1985). *Organizational culture and leadership.* San Francisco, CA: Jossey-Bass.

Wilson, W. (1887). The study of administration. *Political Science Quarterly, 2*(June), 197–222.

FURTHER READING

Heady, F. (2001). *Public administration: A comparative perspective* (6th ed.). New York: Marcel
    Dekker.
Riggs, F. W. (1964). *Administration in developing societies*. Boston: Houghton Mifflin.

Jamil E. Jreisat

FOREWORD

There was a time, not long ago, when the study of comparative public administration had nearly slipped off the academic agenda. Interest in the administration of colonies by major powers evaporated, and concern about development administration slipped. A handful of scholars, led by many of the luminaries who have contributed to this book, kept the field alive. They rightly remained convinced of its importance, but many other experts pushed it aside.

That changed with the rise of the "new public management" in the late 1970s and early 1980s. The scope of comparative public administration broadened, from a focus on knowledge transfer from developed to developing nations to embrace efforts to help develop nations transform themselves. New Zealand's efforts to shrink the size of its government and radically transform its administrative structure caught the attention of the world. As the movement spread, to the United Kingdom, to other nations with a Westminster style of government, and then to other nations as well, recurring themes emerged. Just what is this "new public management"? Was it a fad, or was there something more enduring at work? And from the experiences of the vast global experimentation in government reform, could we learn deeper lessons about governance?

Comparative public administration reemerged, attracting a new generation of scholars and focusing on an even richer collection of issues. The classic issues – just what is comparative public administration, and how can we sensibly make comparisons? – became the foundation for a new set of puzzles – what is the relationship between administration and the state, and how can we transform public administration to improve public governance? Debates in the field became far livelier and drew in a far broader array of participants.

Students of public administration came to realize that any study of a single nation's administrative apparatus had to include a comparative dimension. That analysis provides the bright light that identified what was truly interesting and distinctive about the system, and how it might be changed. Students of comparative politics came to realize, even more fundamentally, just how important the administrative system was to the way governments operated.

Meanwhile, students of the broad issues of government came to see in the rejuvenated analysis of comparative public administration truly fundamental questions about public affairs in the 21st century. Is it possible to support the welfare state, whether the large welfare apparatus of the Scandinavian nations or the far smaller welfare programs of the United States – at a time when citizens have increasingly grown distrustful of government and opposed to paying taxes? Can administrative reform help restore public trust in government? Can it reduce the need for seeking ever-higher levels of taxation by increasing government's productivity? And, most broadly, what is the relationship between governmental institutions and the other institutions in society – nonprofit and for-profit – that increasingly share responsibility for pursuit of the public interest.

The deeply rooted study of comparative public administration framed all of these questions decades ago. When many students of politics lost the lessons, key scholars kept the flame alive. This book not only celebrates their enduring contribution, but also some of the very best and most exciting issues in the field today. No one can claim to be a literate student of public policy or public administration without delving deeply into the issues they examine here.

And, given the inescapable pressures of expanding public expectations for services, diminishing public appetites for paying the bill, growing pressures for finding new and more productive ways of delivering public services, and discovering new strategies for enhancing democracy, the issues in this lively book are sure to remain fresh and vibrant for a very long time to come.

Donald F. Kettl

PART I

COMPARATIVE PUBLIC ADMINISTRATION: GROWTH, METHOD, AND ECOLOGY

Eric E. Otenyo and Nancy S. Lind

Comparative public administration is a branch of public administration. As an approach, it considers the workings of government in different socio-economic and cultural settings. Much like public administration, comparative administration covers a wide variety of activities. Scholars employing the comparative approach focus on a wide variety of issues including public policy making and implementation in both the developed and developing areas. Comparative administration seeks to strengthen our understanding of broader public administrative processes by trying to expand the empirical basis of the field. By taking a keen look at administrative processes in all socio-economic and ecological settings, we have a more holistic view of the larger field.

Persuasive justifications for the comparative method are well documented (Heady 2001, p. 6). In brief, formulating general principles of administration requires a larger pool of cases and hence the need to study diverse administrative institutions and processes. To dismiss or minimize administrative processes in areas populated with more than two-thirds of the world's population is to have a narrow frame of reference in the larger public administrative enterprise. Statistically, theory building benefits from including analyses from a wide variety of cases. Although the comparative method has

Comparative Public Administration: The Essential Readings
Research in Public Policy Analysis and Management, Volume 15, 1–7
Copyright © 2006 by Elsevier Ltd.
All rights of reproduction in any form reserved
ISSN: 0732-1317/doi:10.1016/S0732-1317(06)15049-6

obvious strengths, it has serious flaws as well. Chiefly, ecological, historical, and cultural conditions determine lens through which we view other societies (Rowatt, 1988; Rockman & Aberbach, 1998).

Comparative administration has the fundamental problem of finding objects of focus. There are substantial problems making value comparisons such as how efficient or effective is an administrative system X in comparison to system Y? Obviously, there is no uniformity in cultures and political orientation thereby making comparison problematic in terms of finding a standard. Still, much like comparative politics, researchers must grapple with the intellectual difficulty of the investigator making comparisons of his or her country to a different geographical area. Intellectually, the same questions are raised for the derivative subfield – "comparative management." Nonetheless, the difficulties have to be overcome to maximize on the positive elements of the enterprise.

At first glance, observers might be inclined to ignore the study of administrative processes in countries that do not share the same levels of development. There is the temptation to de-emphasize administrative forms in areas that we know little about. This is because the study of pubic administration in its academic form has been until recently essentially a Western endeavor. However, scholars since the emergence of new nations in the 1950s and 1960s paid considerable attention to administrative processes in nonwestern settings. Still, others have preferred to examine in greater details the practice of administration, especially policy implementation, in countries that have similar economic and social developmental experiences. For years, the tendency of the leading comparative scholars and practitioners has been to emphasize different values, different organizational capacities, and different legal and political settings in which public administration occurs.

The roots of a more focused attention to comparative public administration trace back to the 1950s when pundits saw limitations in studying public administration narrowly (Dunsire, 1973). Specifically, the world was experiencing a new order in which the number of emerging nations surpassed that of the older more studied societies. Indeed, seminal works in the larger field including the Wilsonian attempt at distinguishing between administrative and political processes was considered worth testing in nonwestern settings.

The idea that administrative behavior was a function of the political condition of a state is not new. It was implicit in Max Weber's (1947) *The Theory of Social and Economic Organization*. Similarly, as John Gaus posited, the political environment was a key variable in determination of bureaucratic conduct (Gaus, 1947). Gaus triggered the entire gamut of studies on the ecology of public administration. According to Gaus, the people, place, physical and social technology, and culture determined the ebb and flow of the functions of government. The theme of the ecology of administration provided the basic framework for most of the early literature in comparative administration. Basically, work in the discipline tested the theory of environmental impacts on administrative practices. Riggs and others refined and perfected Gaus' work and applied it in nonwestern environments.

Briefly, environments include relationships between administrators and political leaders, negotiations and transactions with other political units, and links with public groups (Montgomery, 1990, p. 511; Riggs, 1961). Understanding the levels of political development in a specific country was a reasonable starting point in any search for meanings of bureaucratic behavior. Elaborate field studies are excellent testimony to this assertion and we include Joseph La Palombara's (1967, p. 6) "An Overview of Bureaucracy and Political Development," as exemplary exploration of the connections between the bureaucracy and political environment. La Palombara probably made the first charge that "comparative public administration" would not mature before laying out a conceptual framework for understanding the role of bureaucracy. For him, bureaucracy all over the world must be a part of the policy-making process and indeed inexperience on the part of administrators limits the path to development. Amazingly, some of the observations made about training of administrators in countries such as Nigeria and Pakistan are still valid today.[1]

Surely, in the 1950s as well as today, there are differences in bureaucracies under different political dispensations. There were attempts at providing a typology of the different bureaucratic types and power relations as they applied in different political settings (Beetham, 1996; Raadschelders, 1998). While we need not delve into these typologies, arguably, the East–West divide had the greatest impact on shaping bureaucratic behavior in the last century. True, the Cold War and its attendant ideological dispensations divided political systems that shaped administrative processes and institutions. Still, there were societies with strong agrarian and traditional tendencies. The result of these peculiar situations provided the basis for venturing into the comparative administration enterprise.

Hence, scholars in the 1950s and 1960s produced creative models and explanatory middle range theories to account for the obvious differences in bureaucratic responses to human organization. In fact, no work speaks to this effort better than Fred Riggs's (1964) book *The Theory of Prismatic Society, the Prismatic Model.* This attempt at theory building is reproduced in this volume.

In the "prismatic model," Riggs argued that the classical characteristics of a bureaucracy, the differentiation among layers of operatives, the hierarchies, and the qualification criteria were not the norm in all societies. According to the classical model, bureaucracy is a form of organization dedicated to the concept of rationality, and to the conduct of administration on the basis of relevant knowledge. In Riggs's formulation, administrative roles are highly specialized and differentiated. In addition, roles are well defined and hierarchical relationships are clearly understood. Riggs' model posited that some assumptions are made between the number of functions performed and the structures. He argued that a structure is functionally diffuse when it performs numerous functions. It is functionally specific if these are limited. Using language from physics, Riggs observed that the fused hypothetical model is characteristic of a society in which all component structures are highly diffuse; in the detracted model, component structures are highly specific. The model as originally presented is of the same hypothetical type as the fused and diffracted type. It was designed to represent a situation intermediate between the fused and the diffracted ends of a continuum, it combined relatively fused traits with relatively diffracted ones (Heady, 1984, p. 69). Accordingly, the diffracted systems tended to demonstrate more administrative efficiency and less corruption, and less nepotism.

Much like Weber's "ideal type," the model described no single society. However, it served as a useful heuristic device and sparked important debates in the field. For example, Kasfir Nelson's (1969) "Prismatic Theory and African Administration" in *World Politics* attempted to review Riggs' work and analyzed the extent to which the theory of prismatic society and the sala model of bureaucracy was applicable to Africa. It had its first test in Asia. For Kasfir, the model did not apply to Africa but offered an inventory of potentially important factors. Likewise, others argued that the proposition was biased against developing countries. This was because Riggs implied that Western societies were closer to the diffracted model.

Although a proliferation of scholarship arose to debate the relevance of Riggs' formulations, the core question regarding the focus of the field of comparative administration remained a source of concern. Riggs and a number of leading scholars of American public administration were enthused by the potential for a comparative approach. These scholars including Fred Riggs, Ferrel Heady, Richard Gable, Edwin A. Bock, Milton J. Esman, John D. Montgomery, Edward Weidner, Dwight Waldo, Alfred Diamant, John Dorsey Jr., and others organized into a Comparative Administration Group (CAG) of the American Society for Public Administration, to provide leadership in the emerging enterprise. CAG is the forerunner to today's Section for Comparative and International Administration (SICA).

Through their aegis, the CAG movement churned out voluminous publications. These included Dwight Waldo (1963), *Comparative Public Administration: Prologue, Problems, and Promise*, and Ferrel Heady, *Comparative Public Administration: Concerns and Priorities*; also in this genre was Ferrel Heady and Sybil Stokes (1962), *Papers in Comparative Administration* among others. Since this is not the central issue of the essay, our attention is directed to *Comparative Public Administration: An Annotated Bibliography* by Mark Huddleston (1984). This, together with Heady (1984) provide sufficient bibliographic summaries of the history of the comparative administration field. We have reproduced Heady's (1995) work, derived from his influential textbook.

Heady (1984, p. 11) considered literature in this field under four distinct categories. First, the modified traditional; second, the development oriented; third, the general system modified traditional and fourth, the middle range theory formulation. The modified traditional category showed the greatest continuity with more narrowly focused literature. Among the topics covered were administrative organization, personnel management, fiscal administration, and program fields such as health, education, and agriculture.

Dwight Waldo, an established leader in American public administration, while supporting the effort at taking the comparative approach seriously, took issue with the emergent chaos in the larger field of administration. Perhaps, to him, the parent field of public administration was itself in a state of disarray and therefore could not provide an adequate basis for the growth in comparative administration. Waldo's work raised questions about the place of comparative administration within the wider discipline.

Numerous other scholarly authorities spent considerable efforts describing this early evolution of the field. But in spite of the large array of literature in the field, the field lost its sparkle (Sigelman, 1976). We include Jreisat's (2006)[2] and Sigelman's work as presenting a more focused summary of the field's growth and predicaments. Later, in the 1980s, there was a great amount of skepticism about the entire comparative administration approach (Honadle, 1982). Scholars began to deride the apparent lack of staying power of comparative administration scholarship. As evident from the demise of its major journal outlets, comparative administration was clearly a less than vibrant endeavor. Scholars expressed disappointments and concerns in numerous volumes.

Later, in the 1990s, the comparative administration scholarship fatigue seemed to be a source of concern for the broader public administration field.

The field continued to search for binding theories with little success (Freid, 1990). Two accomplished scholars, Van Wart and Cayer (1990), published a most reflective self-diagnostic article in *Public Administration Review* (1990). In spite of self-doubt, key pundits felt the discipline would survive. By the mid-1990s, contemporary senior scholars were convinced that the field had indeed survived but required greater attention from mainstream American public administration (Riggs, 1991; Heady, 2001). Heady and Riggs' passionate charge to bring comparative administration back did not resonate strongly as evident from the paucity of scholarship in American journals. Instead, works describing administration in developing countries appeared as components of state theory and institutions in comparative politics.

NOTES

1. See, Joseph G. La Palombara's comments on the need to train administrative cadres at all levels in developing countries, pp. 18–19.
2. J. Jreisat (2006). "The Field of Comparative Administration through the Years." Paper written exclusively for this volume.

REFERENCES

Beetham, D. (1996). Theories of bureaucratic power. In: *Bureaucracy* (2nd ed.). Minneapolis: University of Minnesota Press.

Dunsire, A. (1973). The rise of comparative administration. *Administration: The word and the science* (pp. 134–153). New York: Wiley.

Fried, R. C. (1990). Comparative public administration: The search for theories. In: B. L. Naomi & W. Aaron (Eds), *Public administration: The state of the discipline.* Chatham, NJ: Chatham House Publishers, Inc.

Gaus, J. (1947). *Reflections on public administration.* Montgomery, Ala: University of Alabama Press.

Heady, F. (1984). *Public administration: A comparative perspective.* New York: Marcel Dekker.

Heady, F. (1995). Comparison in the study of public administration. *Public administration: A comparative perspective* (pp. 1–70). New York: Marcel Dekker.

Heady, F. (2001). Donald C. Stone lecture. *Public Administration Review, 61*(4), 390–395.

Heady, F., & Stokes, S. L. (Eds) (1962). *Papers in comparative public administration.* Ann Arbor: University of Michigan.

Honadle, G. (1982). Development administration in the eighties: New agendas or old perspectives. *Public Administration Review, 42*(2), 174–179.

Huddleston, W. M. (1984). *Comparative public administration: An annotated bibliography.* New York: Garland.

La Palombara, J. G. (Ed). (1967). An overview of bureaucracy and political development. *Bureaucracy and political development* (2nd ed., pp. 1–33). Princeton: Princeton University Press.

Montgomery, J. D. (1990). The strategic environment of public managers in developing countries. In: A. Farazmand (Ed.), *Handbook of comparative and development administration* (pp. 511–526). New York: Marcel Dekker.

Nelson, K. (1969). Prismatic theory and African administration. *World Politics, 21,* 295–314.

Raadschelders, J. (1998). The structure and functions of government: Organizational differentiation and bureaucratization. *Handbook of administrative history* (pp. 3–15, 109–137). New Brunswick: Transaction Publishers.

Riggs, F. W. (1961). *The ecology of public administration.* Published under the auspices of the Indian Institute of Public Administration, New Delhi. Bombay, Asia Publishing House.

Riggs, F. W. (1964). *The theory of prismatic society: The prismatic model.* Boston: Houghton.

Riggs, F. W. (1991). Public administration: A comparative framework. *Public Administration Review, 51*(6), 473–477.

Rockman, B., & Aberbach, J. D. (1998). Problems of cross national comparison. In: D. E. Rowat (Ed.), *Public administration in developed democracies: A comparative study,* Chapter 24 (pp. 419–440). New York: Marcel Dekker.

Rowatt, D. C. (1988). Comparisons and trends. In: D. C. Rowatt (Ed.), *Public administration in developed countries* (pp. 441–458). New York: Marcel Dekker, Inc.

Sigelman, L. (1976). In search of comparative administration. *Public Administration Review, 36*(6), 621–625.

Van Wart, M., & Cayer, J. N. (1990). Comparative public administration: Defunct, dispersed or redefined? *Public Administration Review, 50*(2), 238–248.

Waldo, D. (1963). *Comparative public administration: Prologue, problems and promise.* Sybil Stokes Papers Special Series, No. 2 (1964).

Weber, M. (1947). Introduction and Part III: The types of authority and imperative coordination. In: *The theory of social and economic organization* (pp. 8–55). New York: Oxford University Press.

FURTHER READING

Merriman, J. G. (1948/1947). The ecology of government. In: R. J. Stillman (Ed.), *Public administration: Concepts and cases* (7th ed.). Boston: Mifflin Company.

IN SEARCH OF COMPARATIVE ADMINISTRATION

Lee Sigelman

This article focuses on some methodological problems facing comparative public administration. I assume that the goal of the field is to build and test propositions about administration – an assumption that is not universally shared with the public administration fraternity. Many, practicing either the "old" or the "new" public administration, are less concerned with theory-building and testing, which they castigate as sterile academic exercises, than with advising political decision makers or reforming the political process. The problem with this view is that without a well-developed theoretical and empirical foundation, prescriptions can be rooted only in folk wisdom or personal prejudice. Ironically, a public administration which rejects theorizing and empirical research at its core activities denies its adherents any legitimate claim to political influence.

PROBLEMS OF THEORY AND RESEARCH IN COMPARATIVE PUBLIC ADMINISTRATION

How far has comparative public administration come in the relatively brief span of its existence? Let me first propose three criteria by which the status of the field can be judged. First, scholars in a relatively established field of study ought to be focusing their studies on a fairly small set of common

Comparative Public Administration: The Essential Readings
Research in Public Policy Analysis and Management, Volume 15, 9–16
ISSN: 0732-1317/doi:10.1016/S0732-1317(06)15001-0

issues. Second, if a field has reached even minimal theoretical–conceptual accord, a large proportion of its work should be "normal science" (empirical research designed to test existing theories) and a substantial percentage of this empirical should rely on systematic modes of analysis. Third, a field explicitly designated as "comparative" should lean toward work, which is cross-national in character.

In order to characterize the progress made by the field, I undertook a content analysis of full-length articles appearing in the *Journal of Comparative Administration* (JCA), the primary vehicle for scholarly publication in the field, between May 1969 and February 1974. Table 1 categorizes each article according to substantive focus and mode of analysis. According to Table 1, the highest percentage of articles in any substantive category was 14.6 percent in "policy administration," a figure, which suggests that no single topic or set of questions came close to dominating the field. But even this figure conceals a broad diversity of topics, including studies of both

Table 1. Substantive Focus and Analytic Mode of JCA Articles.

Type of Article	% of Articles
I. Substantive focus	
Policy administration	14.6 (12)
Concepts	9.8 (8)
Structural descriptions	9.8 (8)
Bureaucrats' values and behavior	9.8 (8)
Philosophy of science	8.5 (7)
Social background	6.1 (5)
Military government	6.1 (5)
Local politics	4.9 (4)
State of the field	3.7 (3)
Popular participation	2.4 (2)
Management theory	2.4 (2)
Other (single mentions)	22.0 (18)
	100.1 (82)
II. Mode of analysis	
Essay	46.3 (38)
Empirical non-quantitative	35.4 (29)
Empirical quantitative	
Low-level	12.2 (10)
More powerful	6.1 (5)
	100.0 (82)

policy-making processes and substantive policy areas in such divergent fields as public finance, welfare, technical assistance, rural development, and family planning. Another high frequency is, "concepts," also subsumes a broad range of topics, including analyses of the concepts of bureaucracy, differentiation, centralization, and institution-building. Also relatively prominent have been the descriptions or organizational structures in various national settings, general treatments of the philosophy of science, and the studies of bureaucratic values and behavior. Perhaps more revealing is the fact that the category into which the highest percentage of work falls is actually "Other," a classification embracing an astounding array of topics, e.g., communications models in social science, time, the ombudsman, law, problems of causal analysis, the nature of the political process, party coalitions, and anti-bureaucratic utopias. Surely, students of administration have not narrowed their interests to a manageable set of questions and topics. Substantial effort continues to be spent in "getting ready to get ready" – exploring epistemological matters, debating the boundaries of the field, and surveying the manner in which concepts have been used. Unfortunately, a great deal of work that is not pre-theoretical is non-theoretical, an appellation that applies with a vengeance to the still common generic descriptions of administration in a particular setting.

Each of the 82 JCA articles was also placed in one of the three methodological categories: (1) essay, including broad theoretical and conceptual pieces, summary-like critiques of the "state of the art," and the like, (2) empirical non-quantitative, including more narrowly gauged empirically oriented studies – most of them case studies – which do not employ quantitative techniques; and (3) empirical quantitative, including (a) studies which employ only simple counting or percentizing techniques (designated "low-level") and (b) studies which employ techniques assuming more than nominal measurement or utilizing tests of significance with nominal data (designated "more powerful"). Almost half of all the work published in the JCA has consisted of broad, discursive essays. Fewer than two of ten have been at all quantitative, and only one third of these have met even my minimal definition of "more powerful." These percentages indicate that a great deal of effort – far too much, in my estimation – is being devoted either to puzzling out border arguments on the scope of the field and the definitions of certain concepts, or to studying administrative questions far less rigorously than might be the case. By way of comparison, fully three-fourths of the articles printed by *Comparative Political Studies* have been empirical in character, and most of these have fallen into the "more powerful" category. Even more strikingly, the figures presented by Somit and Tannenhaus reveal a marked similarity between the modes of analysis evident in the JCA during the early 1970s and the *American Political Science Review* during the early 1950s.[1] Clearly, comparative administration lags far behind the fields to which it is most closely related in its application of systematic research techniques.

Finally, of the 41 studies, which focused on national or subnational units fully, 29 of them (70.7 percent) examined administration in only one national setting; and 6 (14.6 percent) undertook large-scale comparisons.

In sum, comparative public administration is far less developed than would have been anticipated a decade ago. Most of the work forming the field's slim theoretical–conceptual core is now quite dated. Nor has the field produced much in the way of a cumulative research literature. The essence of the problem is that research becomes meaningful only when reliable data are brought to bear on theoretically significant propositions. Because the field has not reaped the benefits that accrue from the interaction of theory and data, the underdevelopment of comparative administration, like the socioeconomic underdevelopment of the third world nations, has taken on aspects of a vicious circle. The strategic problem for students of adminis-tration is to break out of the circle.

SOME METHODOLOGICAL PERSPECTIVES FOR THE FUTURE

Some would carry on with the seemingly never-ending quest for an all-inclusive analytic framework. But it seems to me that we have spent so much time and energy debating issues of comparison, putting forth general an-alytic frameworks, and sketching out the environment of administration that we have been diverted from the study of administration itself. If ever there were a field to which Jorgen Rasmussen's supplication "O Lord deliver us from further conceptualization and lead us not into new approaches" could be applied, that field must be comparative administration.[2] At this point, continuing the search for new approaches and frameworks seems positively perverse.

A much more fruitful line of attack would involve initiating new strategies of data collection and maintenance. What is immediately needed is not a new vocabulary or conceptual lens, but the availability of data series that would facilitate the testing of a myriad of previously untested speculations and the building of theory.

AT THE MACRO LEVEL

There is little hope, even in the long run, for the emergence of reliable macro-level data on bureaucracy in any historical depth for even a handful of nations. If by no other logic than the process of elimination, then, students of bureaucracy must generate judgmental data if they are to test macro-level theories.

Although the use of judgmental data presents numerous difficulties,[3] these problems are not insuperable. To overcome many of them, the Delphi technique, a method of soliciting and aggregating the forecasts of experts, might be employed.[4] Most frequently, Delphis have been used to obtain an unbiased consensus of expert predictions of future events, in the form of dates (e.g., the year in which zero population growth would obtain) or amounts (e.g., the size of the gross national product in 1990). But there is no reason that the technique cannot be used to postdict as well as it can predict. Indeed, one recent application of Delphi technology, which focused on public administration, just contained such an element of retro-activity.[5]

A Delphi exercise aimed at generating macro-level data on bureaucracies might proceed as follows: (1) Based on a survey of the literature, researchers would specify the bureaucratic dimensions of interest. (2) The Delphi instrument would be submitted to a panel of judges. Such a panel should include both academicians and non-academicians and should be inter-disciplinary and international in makeup. (3) Judges would assign scores to each nation on which they had sufficient expertise for the specified dimensions. (4) Consensus among judges would be enhanced by the technique – standard in Delphi exercises – of instituting second (and if necessary, subsequent) rounds, in which scores would be validated by replicating the Delphi exercise with extant data sets which assess certain aspects of bureaucracy cross-nationally.

By means of Delphi technology, then, many of the problems, which typically beset judgmental data collections could be avoided, and at the cost which would be offset by the theoretical benefits of such an approach. Even if it accomplished nothing else, such an exercise would probably force students of administration to concretize their thinking about the dimensions of bureaucracy in which they are interested. More optimistically, such an approach could produce a badly needed body of macro-level longitudinal data on several aspects of bureaucracy – data that would facilitate theory-building and testing in comparative public administration.

AT THE MICRO LEVEL

I am convinced that the future of comparative public administration lies in
micro-level studies – in examinations of the backgrounds, attitudes, and
behaviors of bureaucrats and those with whom they interact. In fact, many
potentially significant micro-level studies have already been undertaken.
Unfortunately, many of these studies (particularly doctoral dissertations)
are never published, so their very existence remains largely unknown. Other
micro-level studies are often published in journals devoted to specific geographical areas, and pass unnoticed by a large portion of their potential
constituency in comparative administration. Ironically, too, much of the
best micro-level work on bureaucracy is being done by scholars who would
probably not identify themselves as students of public administration, but
rather approach their analyses from the perspective of mainstream political
science or sociology.

Despite the fact that some fascinating micro-level research is being done,
two problems have become acute. First, only the exceptional research
projects are cross-national in scope. But if comparative administration is
to build and test theories, which are generalizable across national borders, then a truly cross-national base must be maintained. Second, the
existing research literature in scattered and diffuse. Different scholars with
different research perspectives use different instruments to interview different types of bureaucrats in different nations. In order to overcome these
difficulties, some have advocated the establishment of a comparative
administration research center devoted to hammering out a common research program to be pursed by scholars in number of nations. My own
feeling is that such grand cross-national research projects are doomed to
failure. Not only are such ventures almost unconscionably expensive, but
I confess to extreme skepticism about the ability of any group of social
scientists to produce meaningful research results by adhering to a common set of ideas and measures. Despite the lack of cumulative research,
then, I do not think that a large-scale comparative data collection project is
the answer.

This is not a counsel of doom. I simply believe that a large-scale data
collection project would be both more costly and less beneficial than would
a large-scale data maintenance project. Because comparative research is
both essential and prohibitively resource-consuming, the most fruitful approach seems to me to involve the dissemination of data collected by various
independent researchers, each (inevitably) pursuing his own specific research

interests. Even if this falls short of the ideal, it realistically seems to be the best we can hope for, in the short run at least.

What I have in mind is the establishment of an archive for comparative administration research, the central purpose of which would be to facilitate a cumulative research tradition by disseminating information on existing data sets and making the data sets themselves available for secondary analysis. Operationally, this would involve, first, maintaining an updated listing of micro-level studies of administration. For each study, the archive would contact the primary investigator and attempt to obtain cooperation. For many reasons – some wholly selfish, others entirely laudable – some of those contacted would not be willing to lend their cooperation. I suspect that most would, however, be willing to go at least part of the way.[6] If nothing else, researchers could contribute copies of their research instruments, so that others could build comparable questions into their own instruments. More cooperative researchers might contribute copies of their codebooks, containing the instrument, coding categories, marginal responses, and the like. Finally, researchers might under specified conditions be willing to contribute copies of their actual data files. The archive would maintain a current catalogue of its holdings, which could be consulted while research was still in the design stage. This might present many of us with an unusual opportunity to broaden our horizons; Africanists, for example, might discover that Latin Americans have been studying some common problems, opening up exciting prospects for comparison. As for costs, such an archive could be maintained at minimal expense once a systematic search on literature has been undertaken and initial contacts with researchers established; the primary ongoing costs would involve periodic updates of the literature survey and archive holdings and normal administrative expenses, with consumers expected to help defray costs of the services rendered to them.

This proposal will strike some as hopelessly grandiose, while others will think it unduly modest. My own feeling is that such an archive could go far toward bringing some order to the chaos of micro-level administrative studies. As matters now stand, standard operating procedure seems to call for a researcher to design a survey instrument largely in ignorance of what others, interested in the same substantive topic but in different nations have been doing. This procedure essentially guarantees the noncumulative nature of research findings. This is a luxury that comparative administration can ill afford, but lacking an institutionalized mechanism for data maintenance is a problem that is not likely to be overcome.

CONCLUSIONS

Comparative public administration is floundering at a time when other social scientists have finally come to appreciate the centrality of bureaucracy
and bureaucrats in the political process. Unless specialists in comparative administration move quickly toward fostering a tradition of systematic
theory-building and testing, their movement will pass them by. The proposals outlined above are intended to represent a meaningful middle ground
between the present state of affairs and unrealistically optimistic schemes for
improving it. Unless something like these proposals is soon enacted, I see
little chance for comparative administration to fulfill its early promise.

NOTES

1. Albert Somit and Joseph Tannenhaus, *The Development of American Political
Science* (Boston: Allyn and Bacon, 1964).

2. Jorgen S. Rasmussen, "Comparative Politics: 'Once You've Made a Revolution, Everything's The Same'" in George Graham, Jr. and George Carey (eds.), *The
Post Behavioral Era* (New York: L. David McKay, 1972), pp. 73–74.

3. See Ted Robert Gurr, *Politimetrics* (Engelwood Cliffs, NJ: Prentice-Hall,
1972), pp. 83–84.

4. For an overview of the Delphi Technique, see Juri Pill, "The Delphi Method:
Substance, Context, a Critique and an Annotated Bibliography," *Socioeconomic
Planning Sciences*, Vol. 5 (February 1971), pp. 57–71.

5. Richard A. Chapman and Frederic N. Cleaveland, "The Changing Character
of the Public Service and the Administrator of the 1980s," *Public Administration
Review*, Vol. 33 (July/August 1973), pp. 358–366.

6. For evidence on this point, see Robert Charlick et al. (eds.), *An African Data
Bank?* (Columbia: SC: University of South Carolina, Institute of International
Studies, 1973).

THE PRISMATIC MODEL: CONCEPTUALIZING TRANSITIONAL SOCIETIES

Fred W. Riggs

In recent years, much effort, both practical and scholarly, has been devoted to examining the processes and problems of economic development in non-industrialized societies. Concurrently, there has been some – though much less – study of "administrative development" in these countries. We still lack a clear understanding of the forces that lead to administrative transformations, to changes from traditional, status-oriented bureaucracies to "modern" patterns of governmental organization in which the ideals of "efficiency" and "effectiveness" can become operating principles.

We lack, indeed, any consensus on what is characteristic of the administrative situation in transitional societies, on possible stages or sequences in the process of administrative transformation, on relationships between administrative change and corresponding processes of economic, political, social, and cultural development. There is even disagreement on the relation between administration and culture – whether administrative behavior is uniquely determined by particular cultures or corresponds to general levels of sociopolitical integration.

Clearly, if we are to progress in our understanding of this subject, to say nothing of our efforts to help governments modernize their administrative systems, we must devote more attention to the conceptual and theoretical

Comparative Public Administration: The Essential Readings
Research in Public Policy Analysis and Management, Volume 15, 17–60
Copyright © 2006 by Elsevier Ltd.
All rights of reproduction in any form reserved
ISSN: 0732-1317/doi:10.1016/S0732-1317(06)15002-2

basis of our work. This book inquires into some of these underlying assumptions.

What, to start with, do we mean by "development?" Why has there been so much disputes about the significance and use of the term "underdeveloped country?" Do alternative phrases, such as "less developed" or even "developing" areas, give us more conceptual clarity, or are they merely euphemistic phrases for what was once, more brutally, spoken of as "backwardness?"

It is becoming popular to refer to the countries seeking to speed up their own industrialization as "transitional societies." Is this phrase also a euphemism, or does it add conceptual clarity? It has been argued that all countries are in the process of transition, including, surely, the United States and the U.S.S.R. Moreover, the word "transition" suggests a temporary stage between a particular past and predictable future state. May not some "transitional" conditions turn out to be relatively permanent? Can we be certain, for example, that the present stage of public administration in Haiti or Bolivia or Afghanistan is temporary and transitional rather than permanent and final? Or if these societies are undergoing change, cannot the same be said of England, France, and Canada?[1]

In other words, to talk intelligently about conditions in a "transitional" society, we need concepts for the particular characteristics thought to prevail there, In theory of economic development, we can use such indices as levels of per capita income or, perhaps more precisely, in terms of Rostow's theory of *Stages of Economic Growth*, of "preconditions" or "take-off," in which particular combinations of crucial variables are said to occur. Whether or not Rostow's theory is empirically sound, it does give the economist a set of models, which can direct his research to significant variables in economic development.

Can we discover or create any comparable tools to identify key variables in "administrative development" to suggest, at least for preliminary examination, what some crucial relationships among these variables might be? Let us make such an effort, beginning with a few general remarks about models and conceptual frameworks.

THE INESCAPABLE MODEL

A distinguished authority on methodology in the social sciences has written: "We are using models, willingly or not, whenever we are trying to think systematically about anything at all."[2] As used here, a model refers to any "structure of symbols and operating rules" which we think has a counter-part in the real world. A circle, for example, may be used as a model to characterize the shape of a bowl or a crown. Governments are often de-scribed in terms of a model of the family, the ruler being likened to a father, the people to children. In one sense, a model is simply an elaborated simile or paradigm.

If the model is well chosen, it helps us understand the phenomena to which it is applied; if poorly chosen, it leads to misunderstanding. Hence, the degree to which our studies of public administration in transitional societies can lead to confusion or clarity may depend, in large measure, upon the appropriateness of the models that we employ.

\Some readers will protest that it is better to go directly to the subject matter concerned without reference to any model – especially if there is danger that the models chosen may be inappropriate and lead to confusion. The answer is that we have no way of thinking about unfamiliar things except in terms of models. Suppose, for example, that you try to describe the circular shape of a bowl without using the concept of a circle! When as-tronomers began to think of the earth as going around the sun, they had to think of its path as describing some pattern, and the circle seemed the most natural pattern to imagine. Later, more exact measurements led Kepler to see that the pattern could be better characterized as an ellipse. There was no getting away from models, but it was possible to substitute a model that corresponded more closely to reality for one which corresponded less closely.

In this sense, a model is never true or false. Obviously a circle, which does not exactly describe the path if the earth is going around the sun, may accurately characterize the shape of the earth at its equatorial midsection. Similarly, we shall not find administrative models to be inherently valid or invalid; a model that illuminates administrative realities in one setting may simply obscure the facts in another.

AN INDIAN EXAMPLE

This proposition may be illustrated from recent Indian history. I have read discussions of the question whether land revenues in India should be clas-sified as "rent" or "taxes." A controversy over this question was waged for many years by the British administration. In the latter part of the nineteenth century, Sir Henry Maine showed, rather convincingly, why the question could not be answered. A more recent discussion of this problem by Walter C. Neale (1957)[3] clearly reveals the fallacy in the question.

The dichotomy between taxes and rent assumes the existence of a market system. Only when land is regarded as a commodity, subject to sale in a market, does the concept of economic rent become quantifiable. "Rents" can be determined by the income received from the sale of produce and by the price received from land sales. Although "taxes" may be collected in kind where no market system prevails, tax assessments, as imagined by the British rulers, could only be calculated in terms of an assumed value of income from the land.

The traditional system of land revenues in India, according to Neale, could be called "reciprocative" and "redistributive," as suggested in his title. Under this system, every occupational group – barbers, washermen, carpenters – performed traditional duties for other members of the village without direct compensation. The cultivators, for their part, at harvest time distributed shares of the crop to the various groups in the village, as well as to the Raja who, in turn, distributed shares to officials in his court and to his own overlord. Hence a highly complex system of specialization and mutual assistance developed without reliance on money and price-making markets.

If the picture drawn by Neale is accurate, then the answer to the question whether land revenues were, properly speaking, "rents" or "taxes" is that they were neither, since they were something else. But because the model in the administrators' minds was that "All land revenue must be either rent or tax," it was inconceivable that the true answer could be "neither."

Had they grasped this point, they would no doubt have inquired whether they could rule through a redistributive system, or whether, in their developmental and trade interests, the economy ought to be marketized. If the latter alternative were chosen, the discussion would have turned to the best means of transforming the structure of Indian society and economy. In fact, of course, the society was subjected to fundamental transforming pressures, but many of these results came inadvertently as a result of new market and legal forces introduced without a full understanding of their implications for Indian traditional society.

IMAGES OF PUBLIC ADMINISTRATION

Similarly, we cannot speak of public administration without having in mind certain models or a priori conceptions of how an administrative system works, just as we have ideas about how a market system works – how prices are adjusted to equalize supply and demand. In the case of administration, this basic model assumes the existence of a structurally distinct government subject to control by a political organization, such as political parties, parliament, public opinion, popular suffrage, and interest groups. This political organization, established according to a formula called the "constitution," lays down a set of goals and policies known as "laws" and "regulations."

Under the control of this organization there is an administrative apparatus or bureaucracy charged with the task of implementing the laws. The bureaucracy is supposed to be politically "neutral": it does not participate in policy determination, it has no specific interests of its own, and it does not exercise any important power. It is, in other words, the obedient servant of the government, hence of the public whom the regime serves.

The chief questions in public administration arise under this set of assumptions. If the laws are to be carried out and if, at the same time, the resources in public funds, skilled personnel, buildings, and equipment are limited, then what is the most "efficient" way in which these scarce means can be mobilized to achieve the desired goals to the maximum extent?

When phrased this way, it will be seen that the basic model of public administration is analogous to the market model. In both instances the resources to be dispersed are considered as scarce, and the goals to be accomplished as given – to maximize profits, to implement policies and hence the objective to be the "rational' allocation of human and material means. Both administration and economics, in other words, assume a situation in which choices can and must be made because of insufficient means.

Karl Polanyi, in the book referred to above,[4] distinguishes between "formal" economics, which deals with the assumed market model just described, and "substantive" economics, which deals with the ways in which human beings interact with their natural and social environments so as to satisfy their material wants. From this viewpoint, substantive economics may include situations of insufficiency in which nevertheless no choices are made, or choices are made where no insufficiency exists. In other words, there may be no market for exchanges, but people may still find ways to satisfy their material needs, quite unconscious of the fact that in so doing they are behaving "economically."

Similarly, we may have administrative behavior without, in any sense, having the rational administrative model set forth above. Let us assume that there is no political organization to formulate policies. Imagine a king who may be regarded as a divinity with religious functions, as a judge who makes choices in individual cases, and as a war-leader, but not as a "policy-maker." Under these conditions, a set of officials may exist each of whom repeats, on a smaller scale, the same kind of activities as the king – judging cases, mobilizing war bands, and symbolizing divine harmonies. No policies are made or implemented. There is no separate administrative apparatus and no distinguishable political machine. Yet one cannot say that there is no "government." Somehow, public order is maintained, minimal public services are provided, the people sense that they live in a social order, not a chaos. Surely here some kind of substantive "administrative" process is at work, but not in the formal sense described above.

SUBSTANTIVE VERSUS FORMAL ADMINISTRATIVE MODELS

May we not, therefore, apply to administration the same distinction that Polanyi applies to economics, namely, the difference between "formal" and "substantive" administration? Just as formal economics assumes a price-making market, formal administration assumes a policy-implementing "bureau." The bureaucrat is to the formal administrative bureau what the entrepreneur is to the formal economic market.

But substantive administration can take place without a bureau, just as substantive economics need not presuppose a market. Without policies and bureaucrats, the work of government can nevertheless be done. No doubt, traditional government cannot build railways, operate airlines, and maintain agricultural experiment stations and public hospitals, but neither does traditional economics provide automobiles, radio stations, sewing machines, and mass-produced textiles. Human society is quite possible without these things, but it is not possible without substantive administration and economics – that is, the provision of minimal social order, of food and shelter.

The purpose of my argument is not, of course, to discredit the study of formal administration, any more than one would wish to abandon the study of formal economics. Indeed, the existence of modern, highly industrialized and productive societies may be possible only if bureaucratic and market systems of the type indicated are established. But it is one thing to talk about the creation of such systems and how they might work, and quite a different thing to assume that they do exist in actual societies. It is dangerous to act as though their existence had been established. But that was precisely the British experience in setting up a revenue scheme as though the Indian traditional economy were already marketized. Mark Twain shows the humor of such anachronistic perceptions when he projects a gadgeteering Yankee into King Arthur's court.

Where the "model bureau" does not exist, it is obviously futile to ask questions about what does exist as though it were a "model bureau." The first task is not to make this assumption, but to ask: "What does in fact exist?" One may discover, of course, that what exists is not at all a bad thing. I am sure many Indians think the traditional redistributive system superior to a market system, that many prefer handloomed *khaddar* to factory-manufactured textiles, not because the material product is superior but because the traditional way of life is more gracious, humane, or orderly than the hurly-burly of the factory and the higgling-haggling of the market. Similarly one may discover to his surprise that the traditional way of substantive administration has much to recommend it, even though it does not contain a policy-implementing bureau.

At least one English administrator and scholar came to admire the traditional administrative system and prefer it to the modern bureau. Explaining the old Fijian system which he had personally seen, Hocart observed that the peoples' "offering to the chief is even better than a charity bazaar; it combines a trip to town with glimpses of royalty, a display of food and manufactured articles, dances, a hearty meal, flirtations. Added to all this is the expression of loyalty to the father of the people, hero-worship."[5] From the offerings received, of course, the king not only maintained a sumptuous establishment in which everyone could take pride, but also distributed gifts and rewards to those who needed help or who served him. The traditional Fijian redistributive system – it seems– performed both administrative and economic functions.

Under foreign rule, however, the traditional system of tribute offerings to the king was replaced by the idea of tax payments to government, to finance public services. The result, according to Hocart, was to dampen the enthusiasm that had formerly sustained the people in their efforts. "They were left without an aim in life beyond eating and drinking; they reduced their output of work to fit the contracted aim; fields, ships, houses, everything dwindled with the dwindling pomp." In India, too, there are surely those who look on the ancient durbar as a glorious focus of social and religious as well as political life.

The crucial question at issue today, however, is not the traditional versus the bureaucratized way of government. In the contemporary world, transitional societies seek ways to survive and to protect their most precious values. To do that, they can no longer rely on traditional economic and administrative methods. But neither can we assume the effective existence in these societies of the formal market and bureau, however much we might regard them as necessary or desirable, despite the apparent willingness of modernizing elites to adopt such institutions by fiat. We must first find out what kind of administrative practices actually prevail. Polanyi and Neale

found that the traditional economic system could best be described as reciprocative and redistributive. Can we identify the kind of transitional administrative system that exists today in reality? I think we can, but to do so
we shall have to employ some new words and concepts, which cannot be
found in the standard literature on public administration.

PRESCRIPTIVE VERSUS DESCRIPTIVE MODELS

Before taking up this task, however, let us first note another characteristic of
the conventional model of public administration. Just as formal economics
presupposes a rationalizing market goal, formal administrative theory presupposes "efficiency" in policy implementation as a normative goal. In other
words, administrative theory is not only asked to tell us what now exists, or
has existed, but also what *should* exist. Indeed, the emphasis in much administrative literature is rather more on the prescriptive than on the descriptive side. The so-called "principles" of public administration take the
following form: "Authority should be commensurate with responsibility";
"Staff functions should be clearly separated from line functions"; "The span
of control should be ..."; "Communications should flow upwards as well as
downwards"; and "Equal pay for equal work."

We need not question the usefulness of such maxims. I wish only to point
out that prescriptions that are valid in one context and may be harmful in
another. Penicillin may cure one patient but it may kill another. Hence the
first question we must ask ourselves when confronted with one of these
maxims is not, "Is it true?" but rather, "Does it apply to this case?"

We cannot answer the question of applicability unless we know a good
deal about "this case." In other words, we need a pretty complete descriptive and analytical understanding of what now exists before we can make
useful judgments about what we ought to do, what changes should be made.
The model of administrative behavior, as of economic, was inspired by the
experience of Western Societies in which markets and bureaus existed
and corresponded, at least approximately, to the image conveyed by the
model. We are not to assume, however, that the situation in "transitional"
societies can be properly described in these terms, although we may be
tempted to do so.

The tendency to accept these models uncritically arises in part, at least,
from the lack of alternative models. The British administrators who puzzled
over the land revenue question would surely have taken a different view had
it occurred to them that there was an alternative to the rent–tax dichotomy.

When the redistributive model is offered, the possibility of this alternative becomes apparent.

Similarly, the possibility of describing administrative reality in terms other than the formal administrative bureau and the criterion of efficiency arises only when alternative models become available. These alternatives then give us a convenient way to analyze the conditions under which a particular administrative maxim or "principle" becomes relevant and useful.

The need for these alternative models may nevertheless be contested by those who point out that in "transitional" societies today, new specialized structures of government devoted to the tasks of public administration have already been established, so that the same prescriptions which work well in the "developed" countries ought to work equally well in the "less developed" ones. Certainly, we shall find in virtually every government of Asia, Africa, and Latin America today formal agencies of administration, which resemble those of Europe and the United States. Yet somehow, closer inspection of these institutions convinces us that they do not work in the same way, or that they perform unusual social and political functions.

Perhaps the explanation may be found if we note that the new market and administrative systems have *displaced* but not *replaced* the traditional systems. In other words, even though the market has invaded the village, it may not have fully eliminated the old redistributive system. At least, recent village studies by anthropologists show that the old system retains a firm grip. If the administrative bureau model holds at the level of the national administrative service, does it hold with equal force at the level of the village council or *panchayat?* Even at the central or national level, one suspects that some residual practices held over from earlier days still affect in fundamental, if often subtle, ways the actual operation of new governmental institutions. Indeed, this mixture of old and new practices, of modem ideas superimposed upon traditional ones, may be one of the distinguishing characteristics of "transitional" societies. If so, it may help to explain the frequent failure of reforms carried out in accordance with the best doctrines of public administration to achieve the desired results. Let us now try, as a first approximation, to suggest some characteristics of a "transitional" society, which may decisively mark its substantive administration.

THE EARMARKS OF TRANSITION

We may start by assuming that transitional governments typically involve a mixture of the traditional and the modern, the village elder or tribal chief combined with the urban, sophisticated secretariat official. This mixture can take place along several dimensions – for example, the urban–rural dimension extending from Bombay–New Delhi–Calcutta to the remote bill tribes, with "village India" lying stretched out in between; or the class and community dimension extending from the university graduate and administrative officer to the illiterate and the mystic. Korea, Cambodia, the Congo, and Colombia would all offer counterparts to this Indian example. Let us call such a broad mixture of attitudes, practices, and situations *heterogeneous*. To the extent that heterogeneity prevails, a model that characterizes only one element in the mix, however important that element, cannot be regarded as an adequate image for the whole.

May we assume that substantive administration in any transitional society is quite heterogeneous, and hence draw the conclusion that, however applicable the formal model may be to part of the governmental scene, it cannot comprehend the total scene? By the same reasoning, of course, the model of a traditional society – whether in its economic or administrative aspects – cannot be taken as a reliable guide to contemporary conditions, however much the traditional practices may survive in various segments of the transitional society.

OVERLAPPING AND HETEROGENEITY

In some ways the conventional administrative model is like a clock. Whatever the size or shape of a clock, it has a single function to perform, namely, to signalize the passage of the hours and minutes with precision. If a clock stops, or runs too slowly or too fast, we consider the mechanism defective. It may need to be wound, to have a spring repaired, or the timing adjusted.

In the same way the administrative bureau is considered to have a single function: to implement laws. If the laws are poorly enforced, if corruption creeps in, if the public is abused, we examine the "pathology" as we would a defective clock. The apparatus needs to be "set right."

Just as we employ a clock repairman to fix the clock, we hunt for an administrative specialist to tell us what needs to be done to make the administrative apparatus work properly. Do the examinations for recruitment to the service need to be improved? Perhaps the system of budgeting needs revamping, a position classification scheme might be installed, salaries readjusted, public relations offices set up, better bookkeeping or filing equipment acquired, and communications bottlenecks eliminated.

To some extent, this clocklike viewpoint is justified in industrialized countries where the bureau model was developed. For example, insofar as the political demand for services is well organized and policies are clear cut, where positions outside government are more remunerative and prestigious than posts inside, it is possible to recruit for specialized positions at various levels of the public service through technical examinations. One can treat problems of recruitment and promotion as largely autonomous, as technical and managerial, as matters that can and should be resolved solely by administrative criteria, and by means that are value neutral.

Where these conditions do not exist, however, other questions must be raised. If opportunities for employment outside the bureaucracy are limited, great demand for public posts may arise. Powerful family influences can be brought to bear. The number of posts may exceed the capacity of the public budget to pay adequate salaries to all. The incumbents may become powerful enough to influence policy formation as much as the politicians to whom they are nominally responsible. Here recruitment raises as many "political" as "administrative" questions. A change in one aspect of such a system has unpredictable consequences in other parts.

To revert to the clock model, let us suppose the existence of strong electric vibrations between the clock, the radio, and the refrigerator in a room. The clock begins to lose time. We call in a clock repairman who sets it right. We then discover that the change in the clock has affected the radio. When the radio is adjusted, it has a bad effect on the refrigerator, which no longer keeps food cold enough. When the refrigerator is fixed, we discover that this has caused the clock to gain. Every subsequent manipulation of one apparatus seems to disorganize another.

If this seems far-fetched, it helps to explain why the clock model misleads us as a way of thinking about the administrative system in a transitional society. Even in the most developed countries, public administration is not as self-contained or autonomous an "apparatus" as a clock. And in traditional agricultural societies, it is virtually impossible to detach administration as a "system" from other aspects of the society. It is only possible to view administration as an "aspect," although an important one.

In societies, which are in the process of industrialization and modernization, where the new and the old exist side by side in a heterogeneous mixture, one sometimes gets the impression that administration can be viewed as having a clocklike separateness, but this impression is surely misleading. Indeed, one of the characteristics we might add to our model of a country in the process of modernization is *overlapping*. By this I mean that the new formal apparatus, like the administrative bureau, gives an illusory impression of autonomousness, whereas in fact it is deeply enmeshed in, and cross-influenced by, remnants of older traditional social, economic, religious, and political systems. Hence, tinkering with administrative regulations and establishments is bound to affect these non-administrative systems, and reciprocally, economic and social changes will also affect the administrative system. Any attempt to understand public administration in a heterogeneous social system must therefore be based on a study of the "overlapping" interrelationships, as well as the internal mechanisms of the administrative structure viewed as an autonomous entity.

FORMALISM

This phenomenon of overlapping and heterogeneity is related to another element, which we may add to our model. If you set out to go to a strange house, you may try to follow a city map that tells you what streets to take. But if the map is poorly drawn, you find that the streets you have chosen lead you to unexpected places, while the house you seek cannot be found. Such a map is misleading because the shape or direction of the real streets does not correspond to the form of these shown on the map. Hence we may call such a map formalistic. Its forms do not represent reality.

Similarly, a timetable for trains, which is "formalistic," might mislead you into taking the wrong train, or missing your connection. A law, which is formalistic, sets forth a policy or goal that is not, administratively, put into practice. Social behaviors do not conform to the prescribed norm. Thus, legalistic administration is a particular kind of formalistic system. If you find an organization chart which purports to describe the structures of a government department, with elaborate statements of the duties of each unit and post in the department, you will hold this chart formalistic – if you find the real people and units in the department doing different things from those mentioned in the chart.

When a high degree of overlapping in administrative organization occurs, considerable formalism may be expected. Legislators adopt a particular law, for example, only to find that it cannot be enforced by the administrators. To insist on enforcement sets in motion secondary effects contrary to the declared intent of other laws. A legislative change in inheritance, marriage rights, or contractual obligations, for example, may disturb, if enforced, prospects for maintaining the peace, implementing the economic development plan, or gaining support for community development.

Again, because of heterogeneity, changes, which may work quite satis-factorily in the cities prove disruptive in the villages; reforms that are wel-comed in the North may be strongly opposed in the South; and a reorganization acceptable to one part of the public service proves unac-ceptable to another part.

Formalism adversely affects our ability to deal with administrative reality by means of the clock image, just as overlapping does. Some farmers make fun of "daylight saving time," saying we cannot increase the number of hours of daylight by changing the clock. Of course, the intention is merely to induce habit-bound city dwellers, who always rise at 7:30 and arrive at the office at 9:00, to start the day an hour earlier during the summer. It is easier to do this by manipulating the clock than by ordering everyone to start work at 8:00.

We can imagine the fate of an individual who, upon oversleeping, decides merely to set his watch back an hour and then go to work on his own new "double daylight saving time." He claims to arrive at the office at "9:00" by *his* clock, but his supervisor nevertheless reduces his wage for coming an hour late. Such a maneuver might be called formalistic, because it would set up an appearance contrary to reality. Reality, in this case, is obviously determined, not by the position of the sun, but by the simultaneous position of every clock, which has become an instrument for synchronization rather than for demarcating astronomical rhythms.

This example may help us understand the dilemma of the administrative reformer. Suppose he tries to set the administrative apparatus right, but discovers later that he has merely re-arranged the organization chart with-out affecting the behavior of people in the department. The more formalistic an administrative situation is to start with, the less effect on behavior a change in the prescribed norms will have. By contrast, if a system is highly realistic, this realism can be achieved only by a continuous effort to main-tain the correspondence officials to strive to achieve fully the set policy and goals, and the policy-makers limit their decisions to objectives for which the necessary resources are available and sufficient support already exists. Moreover, continuous pressure from interested parties – through the courts, by the voters and the press – serves to keep both lawmakers and admin-istrators in touch with reality. Consequently, a change in the rule system is followed by corresponding changes in behavior. People become accustomed to following prescribed rules and policy-makers learn not to set up imprac-ticable laws and regulations.

These two conditions do not prevail when a legal or administrative system becomes formalistic. The people subject to regulation become indifferent to the prevalence of non-conformity with policy. Policy-makers, exasperated with an intractable situation, try to correct it by drawing up more rules and passing more laws, which remain as formalistic as their predecessors.

An example of formalistic reform may help to clarify this point. Suppose we find a chaotic filing system in a central government bureau. We decide that what is needed is new equipment, an improved classification scheme, trained file clerks, and revised regulations. After these changes have been made, we discover that little improvement results, although our model leads us to think that these reforms would solve the problem.

We then push the matter further and discover that the reports that are filed are badly out of date, compiled in response to an antiquated questionnaire, and prepared by unqualified clerks who give inaccurate information. Consequently, the higher officials find them useless and do not bother to read them. Since the offices that prepare the reports know they would be read, they see no need to invest effort in improving the design of the questionnaire or providing better replies to old questions.

This means, of course, that there is little or no demand for reports from the filing section and, therefore, no incentive for the clerks to keep the reports in good order. Moreover, since the higher officials do not read the reports, they cannot set up criteria for throwing away unneeded materials, hence the clerks dare not discard anything, since they are personally liable for any losses. The files, then, become the repository of vast accumulations of unused reports, a situation that can scarcely be corrected by new filing procedures and equipment.

The existence of such a situation might seem paradoxical because, surely, the central office must want to know what its subordinate units are doing. We may learn that significant communication takes place largely through oral interviews rather than through the mountainous accumulation of paper. The reasons for, and consequences, of this situation would take us far afield, into the nature of the personal relationships between these officials and the content of their communications. It might be found that what they have to say to each other cannot be put on paper because it concerns office "politics," loyalty and disloyalty to cliques, and the disposition of extralegal perquisites. Perhaps, also, the policies to be implemented by the bureau are not clearly defined so that forms with significant questions cannot, with the best will in the world, be properly framed.

The example chosen may be extreme, but it should illustrate the dilemma of the administrative technician – the records management specialist, let us say – when called upon to correct the evils of a chaotic filing system in a formalistic bureau. His technology takes for granted the existence of an effective demand for good written communications. The most modern and scientific procedures and equipment will not remedy the situation if such a demand does not exist.

In societies where formal economic and administrative models provide relatively accurate images of reality, it is practical to study the models, including, on the administrative side, laws and regulations, since these provide good evidence of practice, and changes in them are followed by corresponding changes in practice.

But where the formal models are far removed from reality, such study of legal and administrative models becomes increasingly "legalistic"; that is, it provides a less and less accurate picture of reality and an increasingly ineffective technique for changing it. Unfortunately, the more formalistic a system, the greater is the pressure for scholars to limit themselves to "legalistic" studies. It is easier to read books or maps which purport to describe the world in simplified terms than to look directly at the highly confusing and heterogeneous facts themselves. It is simpler to test for knowledge of the formally prescribed than for an understanding of the more complex existentially real. What people actually do is often unpleasant, embarrassing, and even dangerous to know, hence carefully concealed, whereas what is prescribed is usually what people in authority approve and everyone is exhorted to learn.

Thus the problem which can perplex an administrative reformer in a transitional society is not only his inability to see the facts of a situation and to understand what ought, technically, to be done to remedy it, but also his inability to figure out a way to make any real impact on the situation. As in the fairy tale, he may elaborately create a suit of clothes for the emperor, which leaves him as naked as before – while everyone joins the conspiracy of illusion to declare how resplendently the emperor has been dressed.

A STRUCTURAL–FUNCTIONAL APPROACH

The preceding discussion has given us, perhaps somewhat impressionistically, an image of some salient characteristics, which we want to build into our model of the administrative situation in transitional societies. Let us now try a different and more formal method of approaching our subject. Hopefully, the two approaches will converge, giving us a more systematic framework in which to build our model of public administration in transitional societies.

This second method proceeds more abstractly than the one employed up to this point. We have hitherto spoken of the administrative process as a system, having an environment with which it interacts, and in which it operates. But we can also think of the larger society as a system containing administrative institutions as a subsystem. There is no reason why one or the other of these perspectives is the "right" one to choose. Each has its particular advantages, and may be more useful for some purposes than for others. By using the two in succession, we may benefit from their juxtaposition.

The administrative system was defined in terms of an "input" of goals, resources, and demands resulting in an "output" of related goods, services, and regulative acts. If we consider administration as a subsystem, as part of a larger social system, then its "outputs" may be viewed as "inputs" for the bigger system. Thus, maintaining the peace or building roads or defending the country may be outcomes of administrative action (outputs) which serve the survival needs (inputs) of a social order. When so viewed, we may try to understand the administrative subsystem, not in terms of its internal arrangements and relationships, but in terms of its interaction with the external, non-administrative subsystems of the same society. Instead of trying to characterize an administrative system by *outlining* its component structures, let us try to discern its salient features by *miming* the environment that gives it form. The outline and the inline should be identical, but they are discovered by contrasting approaches.

In order to do this, we shall use the distinction between "structure" and "function."[6] A *structure* is defined as any pattern of behavior that has become a standard feature of a social system. Thus a government bureau is a structure, or rather, a whole set of structures consisting of the many things the officials in the bureau do regularly: the decisions that make, the people they see, the papers they sign. The structure is not composed of the people and things themselves, but of their actions. It does not include all their actions, but only those actions that relate to the goals and work of the bureau. The bureau also includes the relevant actions of "outsiders" with whom it interacts in the normal course of business, its *clientele* or "audience." They may be served or regulated by it; they may be the subjects as well as the objects of its activity.

By *function* we mean any consequences of a structure insofar as they affect other structures or other total system of which they are a part. For example, the "function of a bureau concerned with the marketing of corn may be to facilitate corn sales, to regulate the prices for different grades of corn to set quality standards, to store surplus corn." These outcomes of the bureau's activity may affect the income of farmers, consumer costs, government revenues, political stability, the price of hogs, and many other related structures or activities going on in the larger society of which the bureau forms a small part. Thus a function is a pattern of interdependence between two or more structures, a relationship between variables.

The traditional study of government and public administration has been primarily concerned with structures. It has devoted itself to the analysis of behavior in legislatures, political parties, government departments, personnel offices, planning agencies, and field stations. Such concepts as "line and staff," "headquarters field," "span of control," "position classification," and "performance budgeting" relate chiefly to institutionalized patterns of behavior and to structures. Structural analysis, of course, leads to an examination of the functions performed by the structures examined, their impact upon related structures. In relatively homogeneous societies, the same structures perform uniform functions wherever they may be found. Hence generalizations about the functions of particular institutions hold up so long as they are not extended to areas where environmental conditions differ strikingly. Moreover, insofar as formal in situations – practices prescribed by law, public authority, or general consensus – are realistic, one may safely infer actual practice from examination of formation prescriptions. Another way of putting this is to say that the value of institutional analysis is greater whenever there is a high degree of congruence or mutual reinforcement of "formal" and "informal" patterns of organizational behavior, and when structures are functionally specific.

As we have seen, however, in transitional societies a high degree of formalism, resulting from overlapping of institutions and great social heterogeneity, results in striking incongruence between formally prescribed institutions and actual, informal behavior. Under these circumstances, institutional or structural analysis is likely to produce disappointing results. What might normally be expected to result from a particular administrative system or organizational pattern fails to appear.

Moreover, we find that particular institutions of government or administration with which we have become familiar have a limited distribution; they do not occur in many societies. We know, of course, that the presidential-congressional pattern of government is not to be found in parliamentary England, but we assume, perhaps unconsciously, that every system of government must have its "legislative" organs. If we made this assumption, we would have to conclude that a traditional monarchy or tribal chieftaincy is not truly a "government," insofar as it lacks any legislature. We come back to our earlier argument that the lack of a "formal" administrative system should not be taken as evidence for the lack of a "substantive" system of administration.

These difficulties may be overcome by starting our analysis with functions rather than structures. We know, of course, that not all functions are performed everywhere. Prior to the air age, the function of transporting people through the atmosphere could not be performed. But in every society there has been some physical movement of persons. Hence we can say that transportation or mobility has been a universal human function. Thus, although we cannot argue that all functions are performed in every society, we can start from the assumption that certain basic functions can be found in all societies.

More than that, we can argue that certain functions *must* be performed in every society if those societies are to survive as going concerns.[7]

An analysis of requisite functions for the survival gives us categories to identify structures that, though different, are analytically comparable. This procedure also enables us to study relationships or interdependencies between these institutions, hence to examine the way in which administrative practices affect and are affected by their social setting.[8]

I wish to draw attention to a general characteristic of the relationship between structures and functions, which will help us identify a crucial difference between traditional, transitional, and modern administrative systems. Structures vary in the number of functions they perform. Thus a family, especially the joint family in a traditional society, may perform a wide range of functions, including not only the biological role of reproduction, but also educational, economic, political, social, and religious functions. By contrast, a bureau of labor statistics has a much more limited and exclusive function, such as collecting and disseminating figures on employment and wage rates.

Whenever a structure performs a large number of functions, we may say it is "functionally diffuse"; when it performs a limited number, it is "functionally specific."[9] (In this work, the words "diffuse" and "specific" will be used as synonyms for the more cumbersome phrases "functionally diffuse" and "functionally specific.") We can now create two models for social systems of a purely hypothetical type: in the first, all structures are highly diffuse; in the second, very specific. We will call the first model *fused*, and the second, *diffracted*. The terminology is taken from physics and the analysis of light. (In earlier writings I have used the word "refracted," which refers to the changes in direction of light occurring as it passes through different substances, as from air through water. Technically, however, the more relevant – if less familiar – word is "diffracted," which points to a process whereby white light is broken by wavelength into the many colors of a rainbow spectrum. Readers familiar with my earlier essays may substitute "refracted" for "diffracted" since I have employed them as synonyms in this metaphoric usage.)

Fused light is a composite of all frequencies, as in white light, whereas diffracted light isolates the component frequencies, as in a spectrum. The component structures of a fused society, therefore, are highly diffuse; those of a diffracted society, highly specified.

Clearly our fused and diffracted models cannot be found in the real world. But these "ideal" or "constructed" types can serve a heuristic purpose by helping us to describe real-world situations. We may find some societies, for example, which resemble the fused model, and others the diffracted model. In the same way in mathematics, we may have a very small number, which approaches but does not equal zero, and a very large number which seems to approach but never reaches infinity. Some time ago, I tried to indicate some of the characteristics of traditional agricultural societies and modern industrial societies, in order to sketch in their corresponding administrative structures.[10] The procedure followed was impressionistic or inductive. I attempted to abstract from the concrete variety of the real world what seemed like salient characteristics of the models or "images" which were created. The first image was called "Agraria" and the second "Industria." Hereafter I shall use the word *image* to refer only to such simplified pictures of multifaceted concrete realities, reserving the word *model* for constructions composed, by definition, of a set of specified variables.

It should now be clear that although the "image" of Agraria resembles the "model" of a fused society, the two constructions are by no means identical. Indeed, one can create an image of a "folk society" which is much more fused than the relatively complex traditional agricultural civilizations reflected in the image of Agraria. Similarly, one can postulate that Industria resembles the diffracted model, leaving open the question of whether or not "postmodern" society will be more or less diffracted than Industria[11] (Fig. 1).

The different structural characteristics of folk and industrial societies – that is, the relatively fused character of the former and the diffracted nature of the latter – have deeply affected the way in which we think about these social orders. The extent to which the major structures of industrial societies are specific and relatively autonomous makes it possible for separate academic disciplines to arise, each concerned primarily with the study of one set of these institutions. Indeed, the process of diffraction goes so far that each discipline tends to become further subdivided as corresponding substructures within the society appear. Thus "public administration" is partitioned

DISCIPLINES

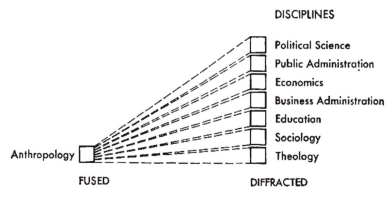

Fig. 1. Disciplines Represented by Fusion and Diffraction.

off from government to permit the specialized examination of institutions for the execution of public policy; and correspondingly, "business administration" is demarcated from the more general subject of economics.

Public administration, for its part, is further differentiated into "personnel administration," "budget administration," "planning," "public relations," and "forms management," while business administration gets subdivided into an even larger number of specialties. Fig. 1 is an attempt to symbolize these relationships.

When one looks for corresponding structures in traditional societies – which are relatively fused – one naturally fails to find them. Only one or a few basic institutions fulfill all the requisite functions for these societies. Consequently those social sciences, which took their origin from the analysis of conditions in relatively diffracted modern societies can only with difficulty be adapted to the study of folk orders. The result has been the emergence of a new discipline, social and cultural anthropology, which takes for its province the "whole" of a society. In order to view a society "holistically" it is only natural that members of this discipline should have begun their work among primitive tribal peoples where the fused character of social structure is strongest.

After analyzing folk societies, some anthropologists began to turn their attention to more complex agricultural civilizations, seeking to use there the models and techniques they had already developed. They naturally chose peasant "village" for particular study, because here the approach used to understand primitive tribes seemed relatively applicable. It could not serve so well as a model for understanding traditional cities, to say nothing of modern urban conditions.

It became apparent, therefore, that more complex models would be necessary in studying agricultural civilizations because the village turned out not to be really self-contained, reflecting significant influences from the larger society and the urban centers. Hence it became necessary to include in the anthropological model the "great community," the elite and city culture, as well as the "little communities," the village culture. Despite its important contributions, the anthropological approach leaves many gaps. It requires drastic expansion if it is to prove useful for the study of modern semi-industrialized countries (or transitional societies) such as Thailand, Turkey, or Tunisia.

Meanwhile the other social sciences also began to turn their attention to the "underdeveloped" countries. Students of economics, government, and sociology began to pay serious attention to "transitional societies." Just as the anthropologists used their holistic model of the self-contained, relatively fused folk community for the analysis of agricultural villages, so economists, political scientists, and sociologists looked for the equivalent of their specific diffracted structures in the emergent economic, political, and social institutions of these societies. They selected political parties, banking and currency, the family and juvenile delinquency, civil service, and the merit system for scrutiny, as they might have done at home. In each of these spheres, scholars found something roughly approximating what they were accustomed to dealing with, but yet something which behaved in unpredictable and, to them, "perverse" ways. Their inability to fit the facts of experience into the Procrustean bed of their intellectual models tended to confirm such stereotypes as the "inscrutable Orient," or reinforced their conviction that "backwardness," as a delayed stage of social evolution, could explain their difficulties.

THE PRISMATIC MODEL

The differentiating process cannot happen suddenly, and at equal rates of speed, throughout a society. How, indeed, does diffraction take place? What are the intermediate stages between the extremes? Using the original context from which our metaphor comes, let us imagine a prism through which fused white light passes to emerge diffracted upon a screen, as a rainbow spectrum. Can we imagine a situation within the prism where the diffraction process starts but remains incomplete? The separate colors, though differentiated, are captive, "imprismed." Let us, for lack of a better word, refer to such a stage as *prismatic.* Fig. 2 may illustrate.

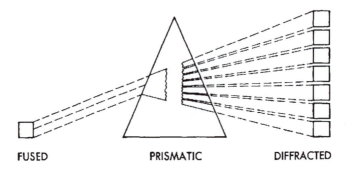

FUSED   PRISMATIC   DIFFRACTED

Fig. 2. The Prismatic Model: Conceptualizing Transitional Societies.

The "prismatic" concept helps us see why the models devised to study both ends of this continuum are inadequate for intermediate situations. The social sciences that study specialized structures are inadequate because, although differentiated structures arise in embryonic or prismatic form, they scarcely function autonomously. One cannot, therefore, comprehend any one of these structures without taking into account the related structures that continually and drastically modify its behavior. Our analysis here converges with the earlier discussion of the clock model and overlapping systems.

The family, for example, may impinge fundamentally on the political party, civil service recruitment, market behavior, and religious sects, whereas in a diffracted society, family influence would be secondary or negligible in these other spheres. Economic behavior in a prismatic society is also unintelligible without noting its interaction with politics and administration. Agricultural and medical practices are linked with supernatural beliefs and rituals. Educational policies are deeply implicated in social status, politics, and productivity. Hence any approach that tries to comprehend one of these sectors autonomously is doomed to failure.

On the other hand, the emphasis on diffuse structures that characterizes anthropology has its own limitations in the study of an intermediate, prismatic society. The holistic concept is not too difficult to apply so long as social structures remain largely undifferentiated. Indeed, any other approach would prove meaningless for a largely fused society. But in the prismatic situation the subsystems, in all their complexity, are already emergent, especially in the most industrialized parts of the society, the urban centers. This explains the tendency of anthropologists to restrict themselves to the village, whose structures remain nearest the fused end of the continuum, while eschewing consideration of the urban end, with its diffracted institutions. But in so doing their results remain as fragmentary and partial as those of their colleagues from the other disciplines, who concentrate on the cities where counterparts to familiar specialized structures can be found. The result, of course, is a curiously dissociated or schizoid image of the transitional society.

One is often told that to see the "real" Thailand one must get away from Bangkok to the rural hinterland. One must leave Caracas, Colombo, or Cairo to be with the true "people." Yet in what sense is Bangkok unreal as a part of Siamese society, or Lahore as a slice of Pakistani life? It is true that great differences exist between the city and the hinterland, but one cannot say that either is more or less "real" or representative. Of course, the hinterland is closer to traditional social structure, the city more characteristic of recent trends and a focus for external influences – but these influences are themselves among the important forces in the transitional society, especially as they affect its patterns of life. One can say that neither city nor countryside can be understood in isolation, just as the head or arms cannot be understood separated from the body of which they are parts.

If we could classify all individuals, or traits, in a given society on a scale extending between the fused and diffracted poles, we would be able to construct a "frequency distribution" curve of a standard type.[12] In both agricultural and industrial societies, we would expect to find a fairly high degree of concentration around points near the fused and diffracted poles, respectively. We would call such distribution patterns relatively *homogeneous*, as in Fig. 3.

By contrast a distribution curve for transitional society would show a wide range of variation between its still predominantly traditional hinterland, and its "modernized" urban centers. A *heterogeneous* curve of this type, as in Fig. 3, suggests the logical distribution pattern for our prismatic model. Approaching the matter from a different vantage point, we have rediscovered the heterogeneity of transitional society. Our prismatic model combines quite traditional, relatively fused traits, as symbolized by the area ABC in Fig. 3, as well as relatively diffracted traits, as suggested by the area DEF. These extreme rural and urban patterns are, naturally, the ones most easily explained by anthropology, and the other social sciences, respectively.

The most characteristic features of the model, however, are clearly those symbolized by the area BCDE. These would, presumably, be found in both rural and urban settings, and perhaps especially in small towns and secondary cities. Yet it is for this most "prismatic" type of situation that

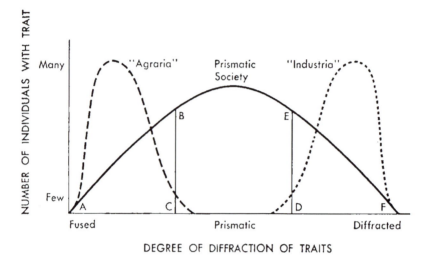

Fig. 3.   Degree of Diffraction of Traits.

available models offer us the least help. In this book, I shall emphasize those characteristics that seem to be logically prismatic, according to this deductive scheme. We may subsequently ask whether or not they help us understand actual administrative phenomena in transitional societies.

Fig. 4 may also help us see how a particular society might be classified at a particular point on the scale of diffraction even though its traits are widely distributed over the full length of the scale. Obviously, the point refers only to a central characteristic of the model, as represented by A and B.

As the technique becomes refined, it may be possible to locate individual countries – Thailand, Egypt, the Philippines, Mexico, Japan, Spain, Brazil, New Zealand, Ethiopia, the United States, China, Italy – on such a scale. We would imagine a central tendency for each country, which could be located at a unique point on the scale of diffraction. But an important part of the description of each system would also be the range of variation between its most fused and diffracted traits.

RELATED VARIABLES

It is important to remember that this scale is intended to refer to only one crucial variable – the degree of functional specificity of structures – of many,, which might be brought into our analysis. Considering the other

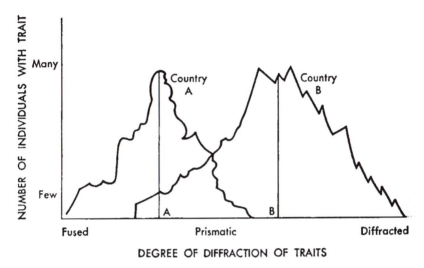

Fig. 4. Hypothetical Cases.

Parsonian pattern variables (mentioned in note 9), we might hypothesize that a diffracted system would rank high in terms of universalism and achievement orientations, a fused model high in particularism and ascription, with the prismatic model intermediate on these scales. However, such a correlation would be a matter of *hypothesis*, not of *definition.* Whether or not the correlation occurs in reality would be tested by observation. The definition of a diffracted model asserts only that the system is composed predominantly of functionally specific structures. The extent to which it is also universalistic and achievement-oriented is a matter for investigation.

The point may perhaps be made clearer by using some variables that cannot be assumed to have any natural correlation with degree of diffraction. For example, population density is an important demographic variable, yet one would certainly not suggest that population density tends to be either higher or lower in a diffracted system than in a prismatic or fused one. On the other hand, it seems plausible to suggest a rough correlation between population size and diffraction. Diffracted political systems can probably maintain effective control over larger areas than fused ones, and the need for a substantial domain would be greater to sustain the complex organization of a diffracted society than to maintain a simple fused order. Nevertheless, one can readily imagine that some fused societies may include large populations, and a diffracted society may have a small population. Typical cases might be the United States and the U.S.S.R. as relatively diffracted and quite large; African and American Indian tribal societies as rather fused and relatively small. However, Imperial China might be considered a somewhat fused, but large, exception to our generalization; and New Zealand, a quite diffracted, but small, exception at the other extreme on the scale.

One of the most crucial variables for our purposes will be the way in which power is distributed in a society. We may, for the moment, imagine a scale of power distribution ranging from highly consolidated to highly fragmented systems. I shall assume that great variation on this scale is possible for all degrees of diffraction. Thus a fused system may be more or less consolidated (centralized or concentrated) in its power distribution, as may a prismatic or a diffracted system. To illustrate, Imperial China and Medieval Europe were somewhat fused systems, but the difference between power centralization in bureaucratic China and power localization in feudal Europe was striking. Similarly, America and Russia today are both quite diffracted, but the United States has a rather dispersed power structure compared with the high degree of power concentration in the Soviet Union. Similar, though perhaps somewhat less striking, differences in power distribution may be found in transitional societies – contemporary China, India, Egypt, Nigeria, Colombia – countries which could be classified as somewhat prismatic, although in different degrees.

As we add more and more variables to this scheme of analysis, we realize that the approach proposed is by no means a simple, unidirectional evolutionary scheme. To say that two countries at a given point in time are equally prismatic need not imply any greater similarity between them than to say that they have the same size population or the same rate of infant mortality, the same per capita income, or rate of calorie consumption. All these variables might change independently of one another. Two equally prismatic societies might be quite different from one another in many other respects.

Societies are, of course, not homogeneous blends. We have already seen that great heterogeneity may be a distinctive quality of any prismatic system. But the extent of heterogeneity may itself vary between two societies, both of which are equally prismatic as a central tendency. One may expect, for example, that a country as large and complex as India will exhibit greater heterogeneity than will, for example, Thailand. We might choose sub-regions for analysis, seeking to rate, in terms of degree of diffraction, the situations in Assam, Uttar Pradesh, Kerala, and Andhra Pradesh. Clearly some parts of India may be more or less diffracted or prismatic than other parts. Northeastern Brazil is probably more prismatic than the region around São Paolo, southern Italy less diffracted than northern Italy, the American South more prismatic than the American North. The more prismatic – and heterogeneous – a society, the greater will be the social gap between its rural and urban sectors. In both fused and diffracted societies the urban–rural discontinuity will not, presumably, be so great.

If we can characterize particular sub-regions of a country in terms of the scale of diffraction, we can do something similar for the structures to be found within a society. Thinking of public administration as a function, we may remark that a diffracted society would necessarily have a set of concrete structures or institutions specialized for the performance of administrative functions. Although this condition may be only approximated in the Western "developed" countries, it is approximated to such a degree that it has made possible the emergence of "public administration" as a subject of specialized study and teaching.

By contrast, in a fused society, we would not expect to find any concrete structures specifically oriented toward administrative functions. This does not mean that the administrative functions would not be performed, but rather that they would result incidentally from the operation of non-specialized structures.

It is more difficult to characterize the structures of administration in the prismatic model, but we can say several things about them. Administrative functions may be performed both by concrete structures oriented primarily toward this function and also by other structures lacking this primary orientation. Because of the heterogeneity of the society, one may find certain administrative structures operating quite specifically and effectively, while in other fields or parts of the society, no such structures are found. To illustrate, in some transitional societies we may find some efficient administrative institutions in the central government devoted to telecommunications or aviation, whereas in the villages and remote tribal areas no specialized agencies for administration appear.

Perhaps a more significant characterization can be made if we distinguish clearly between the *manifest* and *latent* functions of a structure. The former are the stated objectives of an institution, contained in its charter or "formula." The latter are unacknowledged consequences of the given pattern of behavior. Once we observe that a given concrete structure may have manifest functions quite at variance with its latent functions, we can look for two types of quasi-administrative structures: those with manifest but not latent administrative functions, and those with latent but not manifest administrative functions. Both types may be found in prismatic systems. However, I should expect to find more of the latent but not manifestly administrative structures in a pre-modern Western country; more of the manifest but not latently administrative institutions in contemporary transitional societies.

The reasons will become apparent upon reflection. The transitional countries are influenced by external models or standards. It is easier to adopt by fiat or law a formal organizational structure with a manifest administrative function than it is to institutionalize corresponding social behavior. Hence many formally administrative structures in transitional societies turn out to be mere façades, while the effective administrative work remains a latent function of older, more diffuse institutions. By contrast, in Western history, new, specialized administrative functions often emerged as latent consequences of changes in the operation of older institutions whose charters still retained traditional formulas of a fused type. Only at a later stage of diffraction would the increasingly specialized character of new institutions be recognized and legitimated by the adoption of new formulas. Such statements about the qualitative characteristics of institutions in the prismatic model help to clarify the point that in calling one area or period more prismatic than another, we are not just using different words to say that it is more or less "developed." Rather, we are ascribing a particular kind of structural configuration to the area rather than, for example, attributing to it a particular level of per capita income, or specifying the degree to which it has utilized its resource endowment.

Similarly, to call a society prismatic is not equivalent to saying that it is "transitional." The idea of "transition" has a particularly strong connotation of movement and direction, which is not implied by the word "prismatic." Thus the American South today is perhaps more "transitional," because more dynamic, than it was a generation ago, but it was doubtless more prismatic then, and somewhat more diffracted now. Such statements must, at this point, strike the reader as pretty abstract, and I make them merely to illustrate ways in which the terminology will be used, and to point out differences between the concepts involved. "Transitional" and "underdeveloped" countries may turn out to have strongly prismatic characteristics, but this is not a matter of definition. The words are not synonyms. Thus the "prismatic model" is not merely another euphemism chosen to avoid invidious comparisons. Rather, it is used in an effort to identify and analyze a particular kind of social order of wide prevalence and importance.

TIME AND THE SCALE OF DIFFRACTION

What has been said should also clarify the non-teleological character of the framework offered here. The point may be illustrated by the analogy of population size. We know that population growth is taking place today. We

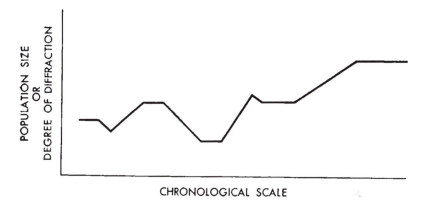

Fig. 5.　Changes over Time.

can explain this growth by changes in birth and death rates, such that death rates fall more rapidly than birth rates. There is nothing necessary or pre-determined about this course of events. We know that death rates can rise and birth rates fall. We are familiar with static and even declining population curves. A scale of population growth rates tells us little about the future course of events. We need to know much more to predict how population size will vary. The graph in Fig. 5 illustrates a possible population curve for a particular society.

The same graph may be used to symbolize possible changes in degree of diffraction over a period of time for a particular society. The kinds of changes which have taken place or are likely to occur can only be determined by examination of the relevant factors: they cannot be assumed on the basis of the mere concept of diffraction itself. This, again, is a reason for insisting on the utility of a term like "prismatic" which carries no inherent teleological connotation. Words like "transitional" and "modern" suggest such meanings. To be modern is to be up-to-date, contemporary. Normatively speaking, it is "better" to be modern than out-of-date. Hence "modernization" conveys the notion of moving toward a preferred condition. It often carries the idea of becoming "more like us."

The term also suggests something as inevitable and inexorable as time. No one living today can avoid being "contemporary" in the sense of living chronologically in this century, decade, and year. But the quality of living at this point in time can surely vary within wide limits. Hence, while everyone is "modern" chronologically, everyone is not necessarily "modern" substantively. The concept of "transition" carries an implicit connotation of moving toward the "modern," that is, of "modernization."

Can we clarify our analysis by restricting the way in which these words are used? I shall employ the word "contemporary" in a purely temporal sense. Thus the Tibetans and Americans, Russians and Mexicans, Samoans and Congolese, are all equally contemporary on the same date, in 1860 or 1960 or 2060. The words "transitional" and "modern" will then be reserved for more qualitative, composite images abstracted from real life. Thus a typically "modern" society is relatively industrialized, productive, and socially mobilized, with an effective government and system of public administration.

It need not be "democratic." This may be a point of controversy, but I am assuming that we can ascribe the typically modern quality of life to a Communist dictatorship as well as to a pluralistic democracy. I shall suggest that the structures of a modern society are typically functionally specific, and hence that they are also differentiated or diffracted, whether democratic or dictatorial.

A *transitional* society, however contemporary, is one whose leaders have an image of themselves as molders of a new destiny for their people, as promoters of modernization, and therefore as initiators of industrialization, as builders of effective governmental machines and national "power," as creators, indeed, of "progress." They may or may not be successful in this endeavor. Their perceptions of their own roles may or may not be accurate. But it is this sense of self-propelled change that gives a distinctive quality to transitional societies. The elites of *traditional* societies lack this sense of progress. Their outlook is retrospective and they seek, therefore, to preserve, or even to restore, the norms and way of life of their ancestors, to perpetuate the familiar, to avoid the novel.

We may expect to find among contemporary societies examples of the modern, transitional, and traditional. But there is no reason why transitional societies should succeed in their efforts to become modern, nor is it inevitable that the remaining traditional systems should become transitional or modern.

It will be seen that the defining characteristics of the traditional, transitional, and modern are different from those of the fused, prismatic, and diffracted. However, I believe there is a correlation between these scales, which is not merely a matter of definition. In other words, I believe that it can be shown empirically that modern societies – those which are industrially developed and administratively effective – are also relatively diffracted (differentiated), that is, their institutions are functionally quite specific. Conversely, those societies that retain substantial traditional orientations tend to be quite fused (undifferentiated), and transitional societies, similarly, are likely to have prismatic structural arrangements.

These statements are intended to be non-normative. I see nothing necessarily praiseworthy or desirable about the diffracted condition. Indeed, it imposes great strains upon the human personality. The typically diffracted person is the "organization man." He must fit into a multiplicity of socially defined roles, often incompatible with one another. Thus, social adjustment poses great tensions and creates fierce anxieties for members of a diffracted social order. By contrast, the way of life in a fused society may seem quite balanced, full, and whole, lacking in conflict or psychic tensions.

The prismatic society can offer its members a sense of excitement, challenge, "progress," and variety, which may not be given to members of either a fused or diffracted system. Who is to judge the moral worth or aesthetic value of these diverse social orders? I shall make no effort in this book to claim that one is "better" or "worse" than another, that the "good life" is to be found more surely in one than in another. Indeed, I suspect that the "good life" can be found by the gifted – perhaps by those who are "graced" in a Calvinist sense – in any kind of society, and that no social order assures its members "salvation" or "happiness."

Quite apart from the concepts of prismatic and diffracted, I believe we can construct a telling argument to the effect that, like it or not, there are forces in the world which tend to increase the degree of diffraction. Hence, although prismatic societies need not become diffracted, many will do so. Similarly, many transitional societies may not succeed in their efforts to modernize, but some will. The argument is similar to that for population growth. Growth emerges from extraneous considerations. There is a widespread desire to avoid death, and modern techniques of public health and medicine make it possible, at low cost, to reduce the death rate. There is no corresponding demand for reduction in birth rates. The syllogism leads to an inference about rising population curves. They may later decline if the demand for population control becomes as powerful as the present demand for death control.

The same forces led toward diffraction. Death control is spread by modern medicine, a typical result of specialization. Its carriers therefore also carry diffraction with them, institutionalizing hospitals, clinics, medical and nursing services, immunization programs. Rising population curves intensify demands for increasing productivity, merely to sustain existing standards of living. But productivity can only be raised by utilizing scientific knowledge and industrial techniques, creating capital, training technicians, professionals, specialists. Hence an overwhelming pressure is being exercised on every contemporary society in the direction of further diffraction. The results may be good or bad. This evaluation I leave to the reader. But the forces are due to historic developments over which we now have little control.

They are not given, however, by the concept of diffraction. A prismatic social order might remain prismatic indefinitely. Indeed, as I shall attempt to show, it has its own equilibrating mechanisms. Moreover, there are many possible types of prismatic society, depending on the extent to which other variables are present or absent. Thus, some prismatic societies may be more or less consolidated in their power distribution – as has already been noted. Changes in power distribution might take place while a society remains at a given position on the scale of diffraction. Such changes, indeed, might be considered more significant than changes in extent of differentiation.

ENDOGENOUS VERSUS EXOGENOUS CHANGE

Meanwhile it is important to say something about the relation of societies at different stages of diffraction to each other. It is convenient to make a rough distinction between the processes of *innovation* and *adaptation.* Although these words have been given more exact meanings, I will use them here in a general sense. By "innovation" I refer to the process by which, for the first time, a society discovers or invents and subsequently incorporates as a part of its regular practice some new structure or pattern of behavior. When the innovation has already been made by one society, it may subsequently be borrowed and put to use in another society. Since such borrowing usually involves modification of the imported institutions, it may be referred to as "adaptation."

We may, then, say that a society in which the process of becoming dif-fracted is primarily innovative has been motivated largely from endogenous forces. The pressures for change are largely from within. By contrast, other societies, experiencing the impact of a more diffracted system, and subse-quently transforming themselves through adaptive processes, may be said to change through *exogenous* pressures. We might, then, extend our terminol-ogy to speak of a prismatic society experiencing diffraction through en-dogenous forces as an *endo-prismatic* system, and one changing in response to external pressures as *exo-prismatic.*

These formal models can readily be associated with more concrete images. I have already suggested that transitional societies can be identified by the presence of elites who are determined to industrialize their economies and strengthen their government machinery. Whenever elites are found, who give the primary stimulus for basic social transformation within their own society, we may infer that they are probably subject to compelling external pressures which force them to take the lead in launching risky and even potentially suicidal processes of change. Elites not subject to such pressures would, presumably, have fewer incentives to lead the way on such a dangerous journey into the unknown future. Hence, we may conclude that the transitional societies are, at least for the most part, "exo-prismatic" systems. Common sense identifies with them the contemporary non-Western societies that are responding to the impact of the industrialized West.

To complete our set of images, we need a term for the "endo-prismatic" systems in which our innovations leading to diffraction have taken place. These, clearly, can be found only in the *pre-modern* societies of Europe – England, France, Holland, and so on – where the scientific and industrial revolution took place. Here the excitement of change and progress, which we identified with transitional societies, was clearly present. But for the most part, the dynamic element was provided not by the elite, but by an aggressive "middle class" which challenged the power of the older, aristocratic elites, subjecting them to constitutional restraints, and imposing on them changes which they themselves did not seek. It seems convenient, therefore, to make a distinction between the image of a pre-modern society, which can be seen only through historical records, and contemporary transitional societies whose elites are seeking their transformation along modern lines. No doubt the "modernity" that may eventually be achieved by the transitional societies will differ in many respects from what has already emerged from the pre-modern societies.

The frame of reference just presented is no more teleological or deterministic than the scale of diffraction. Nor do the polar concepts of endo-genesis and exogenesis imply a rigid dichotomy any more than the polar concepts of fused and diffracted. We can well construct a scale between the two extremes, involving various mixtures of innovation and adaptation. Indeed, most processes of change will probably be found to result from such mixtures. We might invent a term for sequences of change in which internal and external pressures – innovation and borrowing – are equally mixed. Following the logic of suffixes, this would have to be a *meso-genous* process. However, we shall not have much occasion to use the concept, and so let us conveniently forget this strange-sounding word!

Nevertheless, it may be useful to construct a graph, such as Fig. 6. The horizontal axis measures the strength of endogenous forces favorable to diffraction; the vertical axis, the strength of exogenous forces. Curve I represents a high degree of diffraction, III a low degree, and II an intermediate degree (the prismatic model).

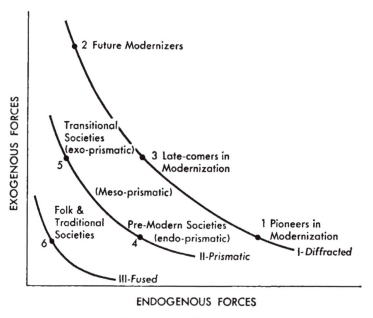

Fig. 6.   Exogenous vs. Endogenous Forces.

A society located at Point 1 would be the first to attain a highly diffracted status, by virtue of its strong endogenous forces. England is perhaps the best illustration. Society 2 lacks an endogenous basis for diffraction, but by virtue of the compelling strength of the exogenous forces imposed upon it, might become highly diffracted. There is no contemporary illustration, but if Communist China were to succeed in its industrialization drive, it might meet these conditions. In Society 3, a combination of moderate endogenous and exogenous factors produces a high degree of diffraction. Japan might be an example.

At the opposite extreme, Society 6 remains relatively fused, because both the endogenous forces for change are weak and the external influences for diffraction are negligible. So long as the rest of the world remains fused, and the endogenous forces for diffraction are weak, we could expect most societies to remain near Point 6 in the graph. Any folk or traditional society is illustrative.

Societies can become prismatic either under the influence of predominantly endogenous forces, as at Point 4, or under the influence of predominantly exogenous forces, as at Point 5. From these considerations, it appears that the configuration of forces impelling change in 4 would be different from those in 5. The former are endo-prismatic or pre-modern; the latter exo-prismatic or transitional.

The study of development in Western societies is, then, primarily the study of endo-prismatic change, whereas development in non-Western societies is predominantly exo-prismatic in character. In the following discussion, I shall usually refer to exo-prismatic conditions, rather than to endo-prismatic ones, to transitional rather than pre-modern societies. Consequently, the term "prismatic" may be taken to mean "exo-prismatic" unless otherwise stated. In ambiguous contexts, the term "exo-prismatic" will be used.

The concept of an exo-prismatic model gives us a useful starting point for analyzing changes in public administration in transitional societies. Change in this model is viewed as a response to the stimulus, threat, or challenge of an external world, especially from its diffracted societies. If the endogenous forces are sufficiently strong, the society responds to the threat by transforming (diffracting) its own structures enough to enable it to maintain its political independence – that is, to permit its own elite to guide the processes of change. But if the endogenous forces are weak, the society is subjected to the rule of a foreign elite (colonialism), which proceeds to impose structural changes upon the conquered people.

The pattern and sequence of events in the transformation vary widely, but they always result in economic development, so that the costs of government are bound to rise, usually more rapidly than national income. Such transformations also have major political, social, cultural, intellectual, and technical consequences.

To say that the results always involve economic development does not imply that they are necessarily desirable from any or all points of view. Here "development" is defined in terms of increasing interdependence marketization and extension of the money and price system. But productivity security, and the distribution of wealth among the members of a society are different and independent economic variables. Hence a society may develop, but per capita wealth may decline at the same time, while inequity and insecurity increase. Similarly, non-economic values – social welfare, morality, the sense of purpose and meaning in life, and the like – may be undermined or strengthened.

These variables probably always tend to change as development occurs, but the changes may be negative as well as positive, undesired as well as desired. When such correlative changes are for the most part desired, we may speak of *positive development*; when not desired, of *negative development*.

DYNAMICS OF CHANGE IN
TRANSITIONAL SOCIETIES

Before launching upon further theoretical discussions, couched abstractly in terms of the prismatic model, let us try to visualize more concretely some of the changes that occur as traditional societies confront the threat of industrial power.

At the simplest level, the external impact of an industrialized country on a traditional society may be viewed in purely military terms. The external world arrives with superior organization and weapons, which cannot be effectively resisted by bows and arrows, spears and shields. Hence a threatened country feels it necessary to adopt modern weapons and military organization. This response is expensive, however, for it entails the purchase and/or manufacture of new weapons and creation of new forms of social organization.

It is easier to purchase weapons than to manufacture them, but either alternative requires social and economic changes. To purchase them, the society must earn foreign exchange, and this in turn means that exports must be promoted. But a traditional subsistence economy inherently has little to export, since it produces only for its own immediate consumption needs and has little surplus.

If it is able to find foreign market for something it already produces for domestic use and whose production can be readily increased – rice, for example, or luxury goods – it may be able to buy defense material with minimal internal social change. The organization of export however, usually requires the establishment of credit and transportation facilities, the opening of new land, procedures for grading and standardization, improved processing, milling, and so on. Ultimately even basic changes in the family and social system became necessary.

If the threatened society determines to manufacture its own weapons, it must launch an even more far-reaching social transformation, since it must initiate the processes of industrialization. It is not enough, however, for the society to develop an export base for the purchase for manufacture of new weapons. It must also solve the problem of transferring part of the wealth thereby created to the government treasury so that it may be spent for the purchase of new weapons. Hence, revenue, budgeting, and accounting systems must be established. Whether the regime decides to monopolize exports and finance itself from the profits, or depend on private exporters and finance itself through taxation, is irrelevant to our present analysis; both methods, or any combination of them, are simply alternative solutions to a problem faced by a traditional society confronted by the military threat of industrialized countries.

The defense problem involves more than its military aspects. The internal organization of the traditional state must be restructured, including a profound reshaping of the public bureaucracy. The military threat usually rises, not as a frontal attack on the central regime, but as a peripheral attack on a frontier zone.

Such a zone is likely to be poorly organized for defense, and its ruler or administrator engaged in his own struggle for power with the central government whether feudal or bureaucratic, or with rival tribes and states. Hence he may at first welcome the foreign traders and officials since they provide a means for the enrichment or strengthening of his own office vis-à-vis the central government or rival chiefs and rulers who demand more tribute than he is willing or able to pay, or force him to spend more for self-defense than he can readily afford.

Ultimately, however, his own conflicts of interest with the foreigners led to disputes in which the aliens, now entrenched, demand extension or protection of their factories, concessions, personal rights, and so forth. The local official or ruler is caught between the aliens and his own central government or the rival rulers. Structural changes follow: he may submit to the aliens and let his territory become a protectorate or colony; he may declare his independence and try to "go it alone" – rarely a successful strategy; or he may submit to more control by his central government or form alliances with his rivals, a process which leads to the centralization and bureaucratization of administration.

This process in time causes a transformation of the bureaucracy from one with a patrimonial or prebendary basis to one based on salary and professionalization. The patrimonial basis, characteristic of a feudalistic system, or independent small-scale rulers, clans, and the like, permits hereditary succession of office and the greatest degree of power for local officials or chiefs. The prebendary basis, characteristic of traditional bureaucracies, permits substantially greater central control but still requires each official to procure a large part of his income for himself, as from fees, gifts, rents, tributes, or other payments not directly allocated or distributed to him by a central treasury.[13]

In the process of consolidation of bureaucratic power, two simultaneous and interdependent transformations are necessary. The first involves a change in the source of the bureaucrat's income from the patrimonial or prebendary basis to salary; that is, the central treasury must compensate officials at a level sufficiently high to enable them to live on their earnings without seeking external income. This requires the establishment of a large treasury; otherwise the bureaucrat's habit and need for prebendary income will not be overcome. Moreover, the general public, long accustomed to paying officials directly for services rendered, cannot be expected to abandon this practice suddenly. Thus the opportunities and temptations for officials to augment their incomes on a prebendary basis remain overwhelming, unless very sharply curtailed by the ruler or by new political and judicial control systems.

The second major transformation involves the differentiation of structurally specialized departments and bureaus, each staffed with specialists and limited in scope of activity. The reasons for this change are many, but include the need to increase the efficiency of tax collection and funds expenditures in order to consolidate control over the bureaucracy itself.

In the traditional system, funds tend to be accumulated by what may be called the "trickle up" system; that is, every level and department of government accumulates money and goods from those below, retains part, and transmits part to the next higher level. The amount, which ultimately reaches the central treasury is only a small fraction of the total amount collected from the public. The expenditure system relies on the reverse procedure, which may be called "trickle down." Heads of agencies or departments are paid, and they in turn pay their subordinates, after deducting a portion for themselves. Only a minute portion reaches the bottom levels of the bureaucracy.

Specialization in organization makes it possible to assign to one agency, or a few agencies, the tasks of revenue collection, to consolidate funds in a central treasury, and to assign to yet other agencies the distribution of funds and the application of control measures so that funds are actually allocated, according to procedures agreed upon, to the persons and in the amounts specified.

Such financial specialization makes possible centralized control over fund collection and disbursement. It makes possible also, the transformation of bureaucracy from a prebendary to a salaried basis. It also extends central government control to frontier zones, hence provides an effective way of defending a society from external aggression. If the traditional society was a fragmented collection of petty states, tribes, or villages, then defense could only be accomplished by unification and the establishment of a bureaucracy. More probably however, such a society could not prevent conquest; but then the same bureaucratic transformation would be carried out by alien rulers to consolidate and defend their own rule.

Indeed, in the long run, the same changes result with or without conquest, for a conqueror must make the same structural changes and must establish a bureaucracy no less than the defenders. The chief differences between a self-defending society and one under colonial rule concern the speed of transformation, which varies with the character of both the conquered and the conquering society and with the identity of the chief beneficiaries – a native elite in the first instance, an alien elite in the second.

A society which reasserts its independence by throwing off colonial rule faces the same problems of defense that confront a society never subject to alien conquest. It can only maintain its independence by utilizing and further extending the basic bureaucratic structure established by the imperial regime. Even where former alien administrators are replaced wholesale by native officers, the alien administrative system tends to be retained.

What has been said about administrative transformations applies to the military as well as the civil bureaucracy. Indeed, because the transformation typically originates in response to a military threat, it is probable that the changes tend to begin in the military sector more frequently than in the civilian sector of the bureaucracy.

A less direct, but in the long run perhaps more basic, response to the foreign threat takes the form of efforts to prevent disputes with the aliens from becoming pretexts for armed intervention. Foreign powers, and especially the more industrialized ones, are interested primarily in extending the trade network, which supports the expansion and development of their economies. Such expansion is not necessarily in conflict with the interest of their trading partners – indeed, their economic interests may be complementary.

However, in making and enforcing *contracts* – a requisite for any industrial system – some disputes are always bound to arise. These disputes may be settled in an organized way through the rule of law, with an impartial government acting as umpire. In a traditional society, however, interpersonal relationships are governed predominantly by *status*, not contract, and existing rules of conduct tend to be either of the local, customary type, varying from place to place, or designed as commands of rulers to maintain the viability of their regime.[14]

Foreign traders who seek to promote enterprises in such a setting inevitably become involved in sharp differences of opinion and interest with members of the local population. If they enjoy the political backing of a powerful foreign government, military intervention may follow. Hence a wise ruler in a traditional society, knowing that he cannot prevent the intrusion of industrialism, seeks to avoid the threat of conquest by minimizing this danger.

A way of temporizing and hence reducing the possibility of conflict is to grant concessions and extraterritoriality by creating foreign islands, geographically and functionally, in which the alien business interests can operate under their own system of law, contracts, and property rights. Such a policy also delays the necessity for basic transformations in the legal and social structure of the threatened society, but in the long run it too does not succeed, since developmental forces begin to infiltrate from the concessions throughout the body of the society. Ultimately, therefore, the self-transformation of the traditional society cannot be avoided.

The most effective approach to the threat posed by the industrial society is self-imposed reform through the adoption of a contract system, and a new legal and juridical regime. Such a regime may, of course, be applied selectively, but it gradually extends its scope as more and more people begin to take advantage of rights established by legislation, and as lawyers (specialists in this new system) begin to be produced. Natives begin to demand as "rights" what were initially designed as techniques for keeping aliens in order.

While a painful transition period ensues – involving incompatible demands made in terms of effective status rights clashing with formal contract rights – the introduction of contract procedures and safeguards begins to transform the whole social and economic structure, all the way from the nature of the marriage vows to the emergence of associations and the reorganization of the bureaucracy. Gradually the governmental structure is reoriented in terms of constitutional ideas, the rights and obligations of citizens and public servants, the roles of offices and official positions, of legislatures, politicians, and cabinets, all tending to displace former ideas of divine right to rule and traditional obligations to rulers.

The concomitants to these basic social transformations are innumerable and lead inexorably to an increase in public services. From its largely ceremonial defensive role in the traditional society, the government begins to provide and regulate a wide range of activities calculated to support the public welfare, defend the society against foreign attack, and promote further economic development.[15] A system of "development administration" arises out of a regime of "security administration."

The process of development creates problems which can only be solved through public organization and hence through an increase in governmental activities and a rising budget. The extent to which a viable ratio exists between the production of goods and services by private entrepreneurship and the output of regulatory and other services by government may be referred to in Galbraith's phrase as the *social balance*. The evolution of the problem of social balance may be clearly traced in the prismatic society.

Public health facilities, for example, first introduced into the army to prevent diseases that undermine morale and fighting power, gradually spread as more and more levels of the population demand modern medical services or become exposed to new diseases resulting from foreign contact. The standardization and improvement of commodities for export require the development of research laboratories, imposition of grading standards, and agreement on weights and measures. Improved monetary systems, banking and credit facilities, and regulation of foreign exchange accompany the extension of transportation and communication networks. Railroads, highways, airlines, post offices, and telephone, telegraph, and radio services are established with all their corresponding construction, maintenance, and regulatory activities, in which economic and defense objectives are inextricably mingled.

The establishment and operation of these specialized activities require the training of technical and professional personnel, both abroad and in new schools patterned after foreign models. This new education also begins to create new demands. The foreign cultural and economic systems begin to appear intrinsically attractive to the foreign-educated elite of the developing society. Hence, to the pressures generated by the desire to defend traditional culture, new forces are added based on a positive demand for selected characteristics of the alien culture.

Inevitably all these changes are costly. One cannot build hospitals, railroads, schools, radio stations, airports, laboratories, power stations, dams, and so on without large expenditures. If productivity could keep pace with the expanding costs of government, it might be possible for a transitional society to finance its new public activities without too great difficulty. Unfortunately, however, in transitional societies, production does not keep pace with the growing cost of government and per capita productivity may even decline, so that enormous tensions arise between expenditures needs and revenues.

It is unnecessary to go further in this introductory chapter in characterizing the particular features of transitional societies ... Perhaps enough has been said to justify our assumptions that there are uniformities in the transitional process which transcend either the cultural particularities of traditional societies, or the idiosyncratic patterns of colonial rule and self-directed transformations. If such uniformities can be discerned among the welter of contradictory tendencies to be discovered in the historical data, we may be justified in trying to create a formal model, by deductive methods, as a tool of analysis to help us discern the basic interwoven patterns on which the unique features of each cultural design are superimposed.[16]

NOTES

1. See, in this connection, Frank N. Trager, "Transitional societies in Asia," *American Behavioral Scientist*, Vol. 5 (June 1962), pp. 5–8.

2. Karl W. Deutsch, "On communications models in the social sciences," *Public Opinion Quarterly, Vol. 16* (Fall 1952), p. 356. Deutsch offers an expanded treatment of the nature and use of alternative models in political science in his more recent work, *The Nerves of Government: Models of Political Communication and Control* (New York: The Free Press of Glencoe, 1963).

3. Walter C. Neale, "Reciprocity and redistribution in the Indian village," in: Karl Polanyi, Conrad Arensberg, and Harry Pearson (eds), *Trade and Market in the Early Empires* (New York: The Free Press of Glencoe, 1957), pp. 218–235.

4. *Op. cit.*, p. 246.

5. A. M. Hocart, *Kings and Councillors* (London: Luzac, 1936), p. 203.

6. In the explanation that follows, I have drawn freely upon some of the basic concepts presented by Marion J. Levy, Jr. in *The Structure of Society* (Princeton, NJ: Princeton University Press, 1952).

7. Marion. J. Levy., Jr., *op. cit.*, pp. 111–197.

8. These interdependencies by analogy with biological and sociological theories may be referred to as "ecology." See my book, *The Ecology of Public Administration* (Bombay and New York: Asia Publishing Company, 1961).

9. The distinction between functional specificity and diffuseness is one of five "pattern variables" credited to Talcott Parsons. He writes that a pattern variable "is a dichotomy, one side of which must be chosen by an actor before the meaning of a situation is determinate for him, and thus before he can act with respect to that situation." Talcott Parsons and Edward A. Shils (eds), *Toward a General Theory of Action* (Cambridge, MA: Harvard University Press, 1959), p. 77. Parsons suggests that there are five and only five basic pattern variables in this sense, and that they involve (pp. 80–84) the dilemma of

(1) gratification of impulse versus discipline: affectivity – affective neutrality;
(2) private versus collective interests: self-orientation – collectivity-orientation;
(3) transcendence versus immanence: universalism – particularism;
(4) object modalities: ascription – achievement; and
(5) the scope of significance of the object: diffuseness – specificity.

Parsons does not consider the "rational–traditional" dichotomy a pattern variable in the same sense. He states that this dilemma refers to a mode of making choices. Thus a traditionally oriented person might consistently follow the same choice pattern, involving any possible combination of the foregoing dichotomies, whereas a rationally oriented person would adapt his pattern of each situation (p. 90). Parsons, of course, is referring to alternative patterns of action in any one society, not to characteristic differences between typical modes of behavior in diverse cultural settings.

The viewpoint adopted in this book is that a significant tendency exists for action in traditional societies to be predominantly ascriptive, particularistic, and diffuse; whereas choices in modem societies are more likely to be achievement-oriented, universalistic, and specific. Moreover, the model of a "fused" society is defined as one whose structures are highly diffuse and a "diffracted" society as one whose structures are highly specific. It is then hypothesized that action in a fused society will tend to be highly ascriptive and particularistic; in a diffracted society, highly achievement-oriented and universalistic. However, this is a matter of hypothesis, not definition: it would not be illogical to find ascriptive and particularistic choices in a diffracted society, achievement-oriented and universalistic decisions in a fused society.

No correlation with the first two variables is hypothesized. That is to say, no hypothesis is presented to the effect that affectivity and self-orientations are more or less prevalent in fused than in diffracted societies. It is also hypothesized that patterns of choice in a fused society tend to be traditional, to be highly repetitive, but it is not clear that in a diffracted society decisions would always tend to be rational, although certain kinds of choices in a diffracted society may be typically rational.

In this book, therefore, three of Parsons' pattern variables will be used extensively, but not the first two. Their meaning will be explained as the terms are used, and it seems unnecessary, therefore, to give further definitions here. The word "traditional" will be used primarily in references to "traditional society," and the "traditional–rational" dichotomy will not be employed to any extent.

An earlier formulation of the pattern-variable scheme may be found in Talcott Parsons, *The Social System* (Glencoe, IL: The Free Press, 1951).

10. See my "Agraria and Industria" in William J. Siffin (ed.), *Toward the Comparative Study of Public Administration* (Bloomington, IN: Indiana University Press, 1977), pp. 23–110.

11. The word "differentiated" has been extensively used to indicate a condition similar to what is meant by "diffracted" here. We may well consider it a synonym, and I shall often use it in this sense. However, the word also has disadvantages that should be faced. Most important, the word "differentiated" has a wider range of meanings than is intended here. For example, the emergence of mobilized but non-assimilated communities, leading to what has been called a "plural society," has also been referred to, by Karl Deutsch, as a "differentiated" society in *Nationalism and Social Communication* (New York: Wiley, 1953). Yet this meaning is clearly quite different from what I intend to signify by "diffracted." In common usage "differentiate" often means to "distinguish" between two or more objects, to identify differences. The word "diffracted" thus covers only one of the concepts referred to by the more general word "differentiated."

There is also a practical limitation on the word "differentiated" since it lacks an antonym except for the negative form "undifferentiated," whereas the choice of "diffracted" enables us to make a contrast with the different word "fused." When it comes to designating intermediate conditions on a scale between "fused" and "diffracted," it will be seen that these words enable us to introduce appropriate terminology more readily than were we to choose the word "differentiated."

12. For example, using Daniel Lemer's criteria, one might classify all members of a society on a five-point scale from "traditional" to "modern" with a three-stage intermediate scale. See his book, *The Passing of Traditional Society* (New York: The Free Press of Glencoe, 1958).

13. See Max Weber, *From Max Weber: Essays in Sociology*, trans. Hans Gerth and C. Wright Mills (New York: Oxford University Press, 1946), pp. 207, 296–298,

for a fuller definition of "prebendary" and "patrimonial" power. See also Weber's *The Theory of Social and Economic Organization* (New York: Oxford University Press, 1947), p. 351.

14. Henry Maine, *Ancient Law* (London: John Murray, 1861), gives a classical analysis of the transition from "status to contract."

15. Kenneth J. Galbraith, in *The Affluent Society* (Boston: Houghton Mifflin Company, 1958), has argued very persuasively that even in the highly industrialized United States, the increase in public programs and expenditures – which has astounded and alarmed many observers – has by no means equaled the increase which would be necessary to provide an adequate "social balance" for the tremendous increase in production of private enterprise. See "The theory of social balance," pp. 251–270. The growth in government services and regulation appears to be an inherent and necessary counterpart to industrialization, no matter how much stress is placed on the role of privately owned capital in production.

16. Further exploration of conceptual problems which arise in thinking about the administrative problems of transitional societies may be found in my essay, "Models in the comparative study of public administration" (Chicago, IL: American Society for Public Administration, 1963), pp. 6–43.

COMPARISON IN THE STUDY OF PUBLIC ADMINISTRATION

Ferrel Heady

PUBLIC ADMINISTRATION AS A FIELD OF STUDY

Public administration as an aspect of governmental activity has existed as long as political systems have been functioning and trying to achieve program objectives set by the political decision-makers. Public administration as a field of systematic study is much more recent. Advisers to rulers and commentators on the workings of government have recorded their observations from time to time in sources as varied as Kautilya's *Arthasastra* in ancient India, the *Bible*, Aristotle's *Politics*, and Machiavelli's *The Prince*, but it was not until the eighteenth century that cameralism, concerned with the systematic management of governmental affairs, became a specialty of German scholars in Western Europe. In the United States, such a development did not take place until the latter part of the nineteenth century, with the publication in 1887 of Woodrow Wilson's famous essay, "The Study of Administration," generally considered the starting point. Since that time, public administration has become a well-recognized area of specialized interest, either as a subfield of political science or as an academic discipline in its own right.

Despite several decades of development, consensus about the scope of public administration is still lacking, and the field has been described as featuring heterodoxy rather than orthodoxy. A current text reviews the

Comparative Public Administration: The Essential Readings
Research in Public Policy Analysis and Management, Volume 15, 61–127
Copyright © 2006 by Elsevier Ltd.
ISSN: 0732-1317/doi:10.1016/S0732-1317(06)15003-4

intellectual development of the field under the heading of public administration's "century in a quandary,"[1] and a recent survey describes trends in
the study of public administration as moving "from order to chaos?"[2] Such
features may be strengths rather than weaknesses, but they do rule out a
short, precise, and generally acceptable definition of the field. The identification of tendencies and of shared subjects of concern is more feasible, and
is all that is necessary for our purposes.

Public administration is presumably an aspect of a more generic concept –
administration – the essence of which has been described as "determined
action taken in pursuit of conscious purpose."[3] Most efforts to define administration in general add the element of cooperation among two or more
individuals and view it as cooperative human effort toward reaching some
goal or goals accepted by those engaged in the endeavor. Administration is
concerned with means for the achievement of prescribed ends. Administrative activity can take place in a variety of settings, provided the crucial
elements are present: the cooperation of human beings to perform tasks that
have been mutually accepted as worthy of the joint effort. The institutional
framework in which administration occurs may be as diverse as a business
firm, labor union, church, educational institution, or governmental unit.

Public administration is the sector of administration found in a political
setting. Concerned primarily with the carrying out of public policy decisions
made by the authoritative decision-makers in the political system, public
administration can be roughly distinguished from private, or nonpublic,
administration. Of course, the range of governmental concern may vary
widely from one political jurisdiction to another, so that the dividing line is
wavy rather than clear-cut. In the United States, actual usage in the past
somewhat narrowed the range of administrative action dealt with in most
writings on public administration, with the result that the term came to
signify primarily "the organization, personnel, practices, and procedures
essential to effective performance of the civilian functions assigned to the
executive branch of government."[4] This was acceptable for purposes of
emphasis but was unduly restrictive as a definition of the scope of public
administration. Consequently, in recent years the tendency has been to
move away from such a restricted range of concerns, even though no consensus has emerged as to the exact boundaries of the field. One indication is
the gradual abandonment of the sharp dichotomy between politics and
administration made by earlier writers such as Frank J. Goodnow and
Leonard D. White. Paul H. Appleby, whose career combined varied experiences both as a practitioner and an academic, was one of the first to stress
the interrelationships rather than the differences between the policy-making

and policy-execution aspects of governing, in his influential book *Policy and Administration*, published in 1949.[5] Since then, the dominant view has come to be that students of administration cannot confine themselves to the implementation phase of public policy. Indeed, one of the basic textbooks states that "the core of public administration is politics and public policy," and that "public administration can be defined as the formulation, implementation, evaluation, and modification of public policy."[6] One way of stressing this linkage has been the widespread use of case studies in the teaching of public administration. These case studies are narratives of the events constituting or leading to decisions by public administrators, taking into account "the personal, legal, institutional, political, economic, and other factors that surrounded the process of decision," and trying to give the reader "a feeling of actual participation in the action."[7]

A second line of questioning of earlier assumptions appeared as a by-product of the unrest centering on university campuses during the late 1960s and early 1970s, and found expression in the teaching, writing, and professional activities of younger public administrators both on the campus and in government. Generally, labeled the "new" public administration, this movement not only reaffirmed the breakdown of the politics–administration dichotomy but also challenged the traditional emphasis on techniques of administration, and stressed the obligations of public administrators to be concerned with values, ethics, and morals, and to pursue a strategy of activism in coping with the problems of society.[8]

Finally, the inadequacies of a narrow culture-bound definition of public administration became apparent early to those who were interested in the comparative study of administration across national boundaries. As we shall see, the comparative administration movement inevitably had to turn to a more comprehensive view concerning the scope of public administration than had been generally accepted in the United States before World War II.

These summary statements about the focus of public administration hide a host of knotty problems – conceptual, definitive, semantic – that do not have to be explored here. Sharp differences of opinion do indeed exist among students of public administration on important issues of approach and emphasis, but should not obscure basic agreement on the central concerns in administrative studies. These concerns include: (1) the characteristics and behavior of public administrators – the motivations and conduct of the participants in the administrative process, particularly those who are career officials in the public service; (2) the institutional arrangements for the conduct of large-scale administration in government – organizing for administrative action; and (3) the environment or ecology of administration

– the relationship of the administrative subsystem to the political system of which it is a part and to society in general. This combination of concerns, proceeding from the more circumscribed to the more comprehensive, provides a basic framework both for the analysis of particular national systems of public administration and for comparisons among them.

SIGNIFICANCE OF COMPARISON

The purpose of this study is to offer an introduction to the comparative analysis of systems of public administration in the nation-states of today.[9] This is not entirely a new venture, of course. European scholars have been comparativists for at least 200 years, as shown by the work of Prussian cameralists during the eighteenth century and by French students of public administration during the nineteenth. These studies tended to emphasize issues related to the continental system of administrative law, but the French literature particularly anticipated many of the concepts dealt with later by American public administration theorists.[10] In the United States, there has been a recurring interest by American statesmen and scholars in experience elsewhere. Among the founders of the American constitutional system and government leaders during its first century, this was mainly for purposes of adapting foreign experience to American needs. Pioneers in the study of public administration such as Woodrow Wilson, Frank Goodnow, and Ernst Freund drew upon European experience in their efforts to understand and improve American administration, but most subsequent writers concentrated on the local scene, with only incidental references to other systems of administration. Comparison and historical perspective were certainly not the main thrusts in most of the literature on public administration produced in the United States before the decade of the 1940s.[11] The limitations and hazards of such parochialism have now been recognized, and we have entered a new era in administrative studies that stresses comparative analysis.

Persuasive reasons lie behind this reorientation. Those attempting to construct a science of administration have recognized that this depends, among other things, on success in establishing propositions about administrative behavior which transcend national boundaries. This requirement was pointed out by Robert Dahl in an influential 1947 essay, when he said

the comparative aspects of public administration have largely been ignored; and as long as the study of public administration is not comparative, claims for "a science of public administration" sound rather hollow. Conceivably there might be a science of American public administration and a science of British public administration and a science of

French public administration; but can there be a "science of public administration" in the sense of a body of generalized principles independent of their peculiar national setting?[12]

Formulating general principles concerning public administration in the United States, Great Britain, and France may be difficult enough, but this would be quite inadequate in a world having the great number and diversity of national administrative systems that must now be included in our field of interest. Administration in current and former Communist countries and in the multitude of recently independent nations scattered around the globe must also be taken into account. Even cursory observation brings home the complexities involved in describing and analyzing the administrative variations and innovations that have developed in these settings. Aside from the demands of scientific inquiry, there are other advantages to be gained from a better understanding of public administration across national boundaries. The increasing interdependence of nations and regions of the world makes comprehension of the conduct of administration of much more importance than in the past. The degree of success shown by Zaire, Bolivia, and Indonesia in organizing for administrative action is no longer just a matter of intellectual curiosity; it is of immense practical significance in Washington, Moscow, and London, not to mention Manila, Cairo, and Beijing.

Various administrative devices developed abroad may also prove worthy of consideration for adoption or adaptation at home. The influence of Western patterns of administration in the newly independent countries is well known and easily understandable. Less obvious is the growing interest in larger countries concerning administrative machinery originated in smaller nations. An example is the Scandinavian office of Ombudsman, designed for protection of the public against administrative abuse or inadequacy, which has been widely studied and in numerous instances transplanted in Western Europe, the United States, countries of the British Commonwealth, Japan, and some of the new states.[13] Another example is the establishment in the Indonesian president's cabinet of several "junior ministers," with boundary-spanning functions designed to achieve better coordination on a government wide basis in the implementation of crucial development programs (such as food crops, transmigration, and community housing) involving two or more national departments as well as provincial government agencies.[14] On a broader front, some of the most extensive and crucial use of government corporations has been occurring in the developing nations, and they have joined more developed countries in worldwide experiments with privatization.[15] The laboratories for administrative experimentation provided by the emergence of many new nations should in the future continue to offer numerous instances of innovations in administration worthy of attention in the more established countries.

PROBLEMS OF COMPARISON

Recognizing the need for comparison is much easier than coping with some of the problems posed by efforts to compare on a systematic basis.

The basic dilemma is that any attempt to compare national administrative systems must acknowledge the fact that administration is only one aspect of the operation of the political system. This means inevitably that comparative public administration is linked closely to the study of comparative politics, and must start from the base provided by recent and current developments in the comparative study of whole political systems.[16]

During the last half century, comparative politics has been through transitions that deserve to be called revolutionary.[17] This has resulted from a combination of dramatic expansion of the range of coverage of the subject and a decisive rejection of approaches to comparison common before World War II. A field that was largely confined to consideration of the political institutions of a handful of countries in Western Europe and North America, plus at most a scattering of other countries, such as selected members of the British Commonwealth and Japan, suddenly confronted the urgent need to account in its comparisons for a welter of additional nations which had emerged on the world scene, with the resulting problem of numbers and diversity. The United Nations now has over 180 member states, and there are others waiting to get in, excluded from membership, or not wanting to be included. Moreover, their diversity is more of a complication than their number, since they range so widely in area, population, stability, ideological orientation, economic development, historical background, governmental institutions, future prospects, and a host of other relevant factors. Students of comparative politics must somehow undertake to provide a framework for comparison that can cope with such complexity.

The insistence on inclusion of the nations of Asia, Latin America, and Africa signifies recognition of the fact that these countries occupy approximately 63 percent of the land area of the earth and contain over 75 percent of the world's population. These statistics are particularly significant in view of the waning age of imperialism and colonialism, the "revolution of rising expectations" among the peoples of these countries, and the battleground they furnish for rivalry among competing world powers and political ideologies. As expressed by Ward and Macridis, it became essential that "the discipline of comparative politics keep abreast of such developments and expand its frames of reference and concern so as to include the political systems of these emergent non-Western areas. This is easy to say, but hard in practice to do."[18]

Nevertheless, the response to these needs has been impressive, with substantial, although not complete, agreement on means of fulfilling them. The common objectives have been that the purview of comparative studies must be capable of including all existing nation-states, that comparison to be significant must be based on the collection and evaluation of political data in terms of definite hypotheses or theories, and that some alternative to a simple institutional basis for comparison must be found.[19]

Heroic efforts have been made to define key concepts and formulate hypotheses for systematic testing. Attempts to define "political system" had first priority, with the result that a political system is now generally described as that system of interactions in a society which produces authoritative decisions (or allocates values) that are binding on the society as a whole and are enforced by legitimate physical compulsion if necessary. The political system, in the words of Gabriel Almond, is "the legitimate, order-maintaining or transforming system in the society."[20] According to Ward and Macridis, government is the official machinery by which these decisions are "legally identified, posed, made, and administered."[21] In a recent contribution, Herbert Kitschelt prefers the more inclusive term "political regime," defined as "the rules and basic political resource allocations according to which actors exercise authority by imposing and enforcing collective decisions on a bounded constituency."[22] Such formulations are intended to include a variety of states-developed and developing, totalitarian and democratic, and Western and non-Western. They also embrace types of primitive political organizations that do not qualify as states in the sense used by Max Weber, that they monopolize the legitimate use of physical force within a given territory. Other key concepts that have received much attention but are the subject of more disagreement are political modernization, development, and change.

The basic analytical framework that has been most generally accepted is a form of systems theory known as *structural functionalism*, originated and elaborated by sociologists such as Talcott Parsons, Marion Levy, and Robert Merton for the study of whole societies, and later adapted by political scientists for the analysis of political systems. In the terminology of structural–functional analysis, structures are roughly synonymous with institutions and functions with activities. Structures or institutions perform functions or activities. The linkage between structures and functions cannot be broken, but priority can be given in analysis either to the structural or functional aspects of the total system. Whether the preferred approach is through structure or function, the central question, as Martin Landau has pointed out,[23] is always some form of "What functions are performed by a given institution, and how?"

A simplified summary of the literature of comparative politics during recent decades is that a functional emphasis gained the upper hand and became accepted in what is often termed "mainline" comparative politics, but that currently there is a growing tendency toward reversing this preference and focusing primarily on political structures. This sequence will be explored under the labels of "functionalism" and "neo-institutionalism."

Functionalism

The most influential of the comprehensive efforts to substitute a functional approach for the earlier more traditional institutional approach to comparative politics was led by Gabriel A. Almond.[24] As to the advantage of this approach, his basic claim was that it attempted "to construct a theoretical framework that makes possible, for the first time, a comparative method of analysis for political systems of all kinds."[25] The indictment against comparisons on the basis of specialized political structures such as legislatures, political parties, chief executives, and interest groups was that such comparisons are of only limited utility because similar structural features may not be found in different political systems, or they may be performing significantly different functions. Almond conceded that all political systems have specialized political structures, and that the systems may be compared with one another structurally. He saw little to be gained from this, however, and a serious danger of being misled. Instead, he argued that the correct functional questions should be asked, asserting that "the same functions are performed in all political systems, even though these functions may be performed with different frequencies, and by different kinds of structures."[26]

What are these functional categories? Let us begin by saying they are derived from consideration of the political activities that take place in the most complex Western political systems. Thus, the activities of associational interest groups led to derivation of the function of interest articulation, and the activities of political parties, to the function of interest aggregation. In its revised form, this scheme of analysis suggests a sixfold functional breakdown for the internal conversion processes through which political systems transform inputs into outputs. These functions are: (1) interest articulation (formulation of demands); (2) interest aggregation (combination of demands in the form of alternative courses of action); (3) rule-making (formulation of authoritative rules); (4) rule application (application and enforcement of these rules); (5) rule adjudication (adjudication in individual cases of applications of these rules); and (6) communication (both within the political system and between the political system and its environment). The innovation in this list is clearly in the functions that have been traditionally related to policy-making rather than policy execution, which detracts considerably from the usefulness of this analytical framework to those principally interested in the administrative aspects of comparative study.

Despite the generally favorable reception given to the Almond functional approach, it did not escape sharp criticism. Leonard Binder acknowledged that it was an advance over institutional description, but dismissed it with the curt observation that it "may be praised as interesting or perceptive, without compelling further attention." He conceded that the categories, being broad and ambiguous, could be universally applied. The scheme claimed to facilitate the analysis of whole political systems, but Binder felt that it would be accepted "only if it lends itself to the analysis of specific systems as well as to problems of comparison, and only if the implicit assumptions of the scheme accord with the theoretical assumptions of individual researchers." The root defect that Binder saw was that these functions, having been located by "the device of generalizing what appeared to the theorist to be the broad classes of political activity found in Western political systems," were "derived neither logically nor empirically." He asked why these functions should be selected and not others, and he challenged the supposition that "a limited number of functions ... comprise the political system." Further, he argued that the weakness of the scheme was evidenced by the fact that the authors who attempted to apply the Almond scheme in the volume it introduced "judiciously avoided remaining within its limiting framework or, in the case of the 'governmental functions,' made it clear how insignificant has been the effort to apply the traditional categories of Western political science."[27]

Another critic of Almond's input–output model was Fred W. Riggs, who admitted that it was useful for the study of developed political systems, but found it inadequate for the analysis of transitional systems, such as that of India, which was, of course, precisely the kind of system to which Almond thought it would be most applicable. Riggs felt that a different model was needed for such a polity, which has "inputs which do not lead to rule-making, and rules which are often not implemented." The requirement was for "a two-tiered model, a system which distinguishes between 'formal' and 'effective' structures, between what is prescribed ideally and what actually happens."[28] Riggs suggested as more appropriate for such political systems his own "prismatic model."

An additional attack on the functional approach came from critics who associated this school of thought with a basic philosophical bias favoring the political systems which had evolved in liberal Western capitalist societies, and who argued that analytical schemes such as Almond's operate in practice to justify and perpetuate the status quo in developing countries to the benefit of the advanced industrialized societies and to the detriment of the countries subjected to study by social scientists using this methodology. This judgment has been made particularly by the dependency development theorists.

Finally, and more recently, functionalism has been questioned by a variety of "neo-institutionalists" who differ in important respects but are in agreement that the primacy of emphasis on functions should be replaced by increasing attention to structures.

Neo-Institutionalism

The phrase "return to the state" conveys the thrust of this proposed re-orientation toward a new emphasis in comparative politics on institutional comparisons. In addition to a burgeoning literature,[29] this trend is evidenced by organizational developments such as creation of the International Institute of Comparative Government, based in Switzerland, "to coordinate studies of government structures, activities, and policies on a genuinely cross-national basis,"[30] and the establishment by the International Political Science Association of a Research Committee on the Structure and Organization of Government, which in 1988 initiated publication of a new quarterly, *Governance: An International Journal of Policy and Administration.*

Revival of the concept of the "state" in some form is a common theme, with variations in detail as to definition but concurrence that "state" needs to be distinguished from both "society" and "government." The state and the society are viewed as distinct, despite being inevitably linked together. Likewise, the state is more inclusive than the government of the day and the institutional apparatus through which it operates. Basically, the emphasis is placed on the state and its institutions, composed, as Fesler says, "of a multitude of large and small parts," but sharing five interrelated characteristics: taking actions, holding distinctive values, having a history, sharing organization cultures, and maintaining power structures.[31] As both its advocates and its critics agree, this concept of the state differs from those of "mainstream" political scientists (based on behavioralism, pluralism, and/or structural functionalism) and of neo-Marxists. Even Almond, who generally is unimpressed by the statist movement, agrees that it "has drawn attention to institutional and particularly administrative history," and that this is "all to the good."[32]

Another aspect of neo-institutionalism is that it has generated a revival of concern with normative issues associated with such traditional concepts as "the public interest" and "civil science." Fesler, for example, welcomes re-examination of what has often been referred to in a derogatory way as the myth of the public interest. "The simple fact," he says, "is that the public interest is an ideal. It is for administrators what objectivity is for scholars – something to be strived for, even if imperfectly achieved, something not to be spurned because performance falls short of the goal."[33] Robert H. Jackson has argued for the benefits of a renewed interest in civil science, defined as "the study of rules which constitute and govern political life within and between sovereign states."[34] He maintains that there is a need "to resurrect and renew civil science in the comparative analysis of all countries today including those of Africa, Asia, Oceania, the Middle East, Latin America, and – not least – Eastern Europe."[35] He distinguishes between "civil science" and "social science," which in his terminology is essentially what I have called "mainstream" political science. He is not advocating replacement of the approach of "social science" with that of "civil science," but rather views them as equally important and related to one another in a complementary rather than a competitive way.

One facet of the neo-institutional literature of particular interest to us is the notion of "stateness" for use in making cross-societal comparisons. As early as 1968, J. P. Nettl argued that "more or less stateness is a useful variable for comparing Western societies," and that "the absence or presence of a well-developed concept of state relates to and identifies important empirical differences in these societies."[36] More recently, this idea of degree of stateness (referring to the relative scope and extent of govern-mental power and authority) has been applied more globally by *Metin Heper, who* has undertaken to distinguish four types of polity based on their degrees of stateness and to identify corresponding types of bureaucracy.[37] We will examine this application of neo-institutionalism more fully in Chapter 2.

The neo-institutionalist thrust has now been around long enough to gen-erate a critical reaction, mostly centered on the clarity and utility of the "state" as a focus. For instance, Pye deplores trying to bring back into vogue "the hoary, 18th–19th century concept of the 'state' as a unitary phe-nomenon," and suggests that culture is the concept "which makes it possible to merge many differences in attitudes and behavior into categories while still preserving an appreciation for the diversity that characterizes most of human life."[38] Mitchell advocates an approach that can account "for both the salience of the state and its elusiveness."[39] Jackman argues that it would be most fruitful to concentrate on the study of "political capacity" among contemporary nation-states.[40]

Although this summary has touched on only selected aspects of neo-institutionalism in comparative politics, it should be enough to demonstrate the impact already made and still being made on the more dominant functionalist school of thought.

Keeping in mind the centrality of the linkage between comparative politics and comparative public administration, it ought now to be evident that the problems of comparing national systems of administration are formidable. The primary requirement is that some way must be found for singling out the administrative segment of the political system as a basis for specialized comparison. This cannot be done without involvement in issues related to the comparison of whole political systems, where there is ferment and progress but no consensus. The dominant tendency has been to substitute a functional approach to comparison for one emphasizing political structures and institutions. Insofar as the functional approach receives exclusive or even preferred recognition as the proper basis for comparisons of less than whole political systems, a problem is created for the comparative study of administration, because the full range of concerns of public administration as a field of academic inquiry is less easily identified with one or more functions in a framework such as Almond's than with particular familiar institutions in Western political systems. The movement toward a new institutionalism has made a structural emphasis less difficult to justify, but does not make the choice either easy or obvious.

POSTWAR EVOLUTION OF
COMPARATIVE STUDIES

A sustained effort to undertake comparative analysis in public administration has taken place during the last five decades.[41] Beginning at the end of World War II, a comparative administration "movement" gained momentum that has continued to the present, with enthusiastic and industrious devotees whose efforts have evoked enthusiastic praise from some quarters for impressive accomplishments and criticism from others for what are regarded as pretentious claims.

The timing and vigor of this movement resulted from a combination of factors: the rather obvious need for this extension of range in public administration as a discipline; the exposure of large numbers of scholars and practitioners of administration to experience with administration abroad during wartime, postwar occupation, and subsequent technical assistance assignments; the stimulation of the largely contemporary revisionist movement in comparative politics, which has already been summarized; and the rather remarkable expansion of opportunities during the 1950s and 1960s for those interested in devoting themselves to research at home or field experience abroad on problems of comparative public administration.

Manifestations of these developments were numerous during the first two decades after the end of World War II. A growing number of colleges and universities offered courses in comparative public administration, and some of them made it a field of specialization for graduate study. Professional associations extended recognition, first through the appointment in 1953 of an ad hoc committee on comparative administration by the American Political Science Association, and later by the establishment in 1960 of the Comparative Administration Group affiliated with the American Society for Public Administration. The latter group, usually abbreviated as CAG, grew vigorously with the help of generous support from the Ford Foundation. The CAG, under Fred W. Riggs as chairman and leading spokesman, mapped out and entered into a comprehensive program of research seminars, experimental teaching projects, discussions at professional meetings, special conferences, and exploration of other ways of strengthening available resources, such as through the expansion of facilities for field research.

The most tangible product of these early endeavors was an output of published writings on comparative public administration which soon reached voluminous proportions and led, despite the short span of time, to several attempts to review and analyze the literature produced by the early 1960s.[42] Classification of this literature is best done by subject matter or focus of emphasis rather than chronological order, since it appeared in a variety of forms more or less simultaneously. I have suggested as a useful scheme of classification one that divides this literature as follows: (1) modified traditional, (2) development-oriented, (3) general system model-building, and (4) middle-range theory formulation.

The modified traditional category showed the greatest continuity with earlier more parochially oriented literature. The subject matter was not markedly different, as the focus shifted from individual administrative systems to comparisons among them, although there was often a serious effort to utilize more advanced research tools and to incorporate findings from a variety of social science disciplines. This literature may be further subdivided into studies made from a comparative perspective of standard administrative subtopics, and those that undertook comparisons of entire systems of administration. Topics in the first subcategory included administrative organization, personnel management, fiscal administration, headquarters–field relations, administration of public enterprises, regulatory administration, administrative responsibility and control, and program fields such as health, education, welfare, and agriculture.

The second subcategory included a number of studies that were basically descriptive institutional comparisons of administration in Western developed countries, with special emphasis on administrative organization and civil service systems.[43] Also worthy of mention is an outline for comparative field research formulated by Wallace S. Sayre and Herbert Kaufman in 1952, and later revised by a working group of the American Political Science Association subcommittee on comparative public administration. This research design suggested a three-point model for comparison, focusing on the organization of the administrative system, the control of the administrative system, and the securing of consent and compliance by the administrative hierarchy.[44]

Advocates of a focus on "development administration" sought to concentrate attention on the administrative requisites for achieving public policy goals, particularly in countries in which these goals involved dramatic political, economic, and social transformations.[45] "Development," according to Weidner, "is a state of mind, a tendency, a direction. Rather than a fixed goal, it is a rate of change in a particular direction. ... The study of development administration can help to identify the conditions under which a maximum rate of development is sought and the conditions under which it has been obtained."[46] He contended that existing models for comparison were of limited use because "they make inadequate provision for social change; characterize modern bureaucracy in very inaccurate ways; are unduly comprehensive, all-inclusive and abstract; and fail to take account of the differences in administration that may be related to the goals that are being sought." Hence, he urged the adoption of development administration as a separate focus for research, with the end object being "to relate different administrative roles, practices, organizational arrangements, and procedures to the maximizing of development objectives ... In research terms, the ultimate dependent variable would be the development goals themselves."[47] Although work with a development administration emphasis need not be normative, in the sense of a choice among development goals by the researcher, much of it has had a prescriptive coloration.

Dwight Waldo, among others, was intrigued by this approach and argued that a concentration on the theme of development might "help to bring into useful association various clusters of ideas and types of activity that are now more or less separate and help clarify some methodological problems," even though he admitted that he found it impossible to define development, as used in this connection, with precision,[48] Although the term did raise serious questions about what it meant and what was included and excluded, development administration continued as a focus of attention because it had the virtue of consciously relating administrative means to administrative ends, and of deliberately spotlighting the problems of administrative adjustment faced by emerging countries seeking to achieve developmental goals. As Swerdlow remarked, "poor countries have special characteristics that tend to create a different role for government. These characteristics and this expanded or emphasized role of government, particularly as it affects economic growth, tend to make the operations of the public administrator significantly different. Where such differences exist, public administration can be usefully called development administration."[49]

The remaining two groups were more typical of the dominant mood among students of comparative public administration during this period, and indeed of comparative politics as well. In contrast to the first two categories, the emphasis here was much more self-consciously on the construction of typologies or models for comparative purposes, and there was a strong concern to keep these value-free or value-neutral. The word "model" was used here, as by Waldo, to mean "simply the conscious attempt to develop and define concepts, or clusters of related concepts, useful in classifying data, describing reality and (or) hypothesizing about it."[50] Interdisciplinary borrowing was extensive, primarily from sociology, but to a considerable extent also from economics, psychology, and other fields. This emphasis on theory and methodology was repeatedly noted, often praised as indicative of sound preparation for future progress, as well as frequently disparaged as a preoccupation diverting energies that might better have been devoted to the conduct of actual field studies of administrative systems in operation. Any attempt to classify this plethora of models must be somewhat arbitrary, but the most useful distinction was made by Presthus, who distinguished between theorists attempting broad, cross-cultural, all-encompassing formulations and those advancing more modest and restricted "middle-range" theories.[51] Diamant likewise discerned "general system" models and "political culture" models among contributions in comparative politics.[52]

Among those who preferred the general system approach to comparative public administration, Fred W. Riggs was clearly the dominant figure. As I have said elsewhere, "mere acquaintance with all of his writings on comparative theory is in itself not an insignificant accomplishment."[53] Drawing essentially upon concepts of structural–functional analysis developed by sociologists, such as Talcott Parsons, Marion Levy, and F. X. Sutton, Riggs, in a series of published and unpublished writings, over a period of years formulated and reformulated a cluster of models or "ideal types" for so-cieties, designed to contribute to a better understanding of actual societies, particularly those undergoing rapid social, economic, political, and admin-istrative change. This work culminated in his book, *Administration in De-veloping Countries: The Theory of Prismatic Society*,[54] which continues to be probably the most notable single contribution in comparative public ad-ministration.

Another prominent source of comprehensive model-building was equi-librium theory, postulating a system of inputs and outputs as a basis of analysis. John T. Dorsey outlined an approach to theory of this type in his "information-energy model," which he believed that it might be useful in the analysis of social and political systems in general as well as for a better understanding of administrative systems.[55] Dorsey later used this scheme in an analysis of political development in Vietnam.[56] The model was later tested by William M. Berenson, who used aggregate data from a universe of 56 nations to examine the validity of propositions drawn from the infor-mation-energy model linking three ecological variables (energy, informa-tion, and energy conversion) to bureaucratic development in the Third World. His conclusion was that the model failed to offer an adequate ex-planation for bureaucratic changes in the countries studied.[57] Interest in this model has since waned.

As Waldo observed, the central problem of model construction in the study of comparative public administration is "to select a model that is 'large' enough to embrace all the phenomena that should be embraced without being, by virtue of its large dimensions, too coarse-textured and clumsy to grasp and manipulate administration."[58] The alleged gap between such "large" models and the empirical data to be examined led Presthus and others to stress the need for middle-range theory rather than theory of "cosmic dimension," to use his phrase. He advised social scientists working on comparative administration to "bite off smaller chunks of reality and ... research these intensively."[59] Similar expressions of preference for middle-range theories were made at about the same time in the field of comparative politics.[60]

By the early 1960s, the most prominent and promising middle-range model available for comparative studies in administration had already been established as the "bureaucratic" one, based on the ideal-type model of bureaucracy formulated by Max Weber but with substantial subsequent modification, alteration, and revision. Waldo found the bureaucratic model useful, stimulating, and provocative, its advantage and appeal being that this model "is set in a large framework that spans history and cultures and relates bureaucracy to important social variables, yet it focuses attention upon the chief structural and functional characteristics of bureaucracy."[61] He correctly pointed out that not much empirical research had actually been done using the bureaucratic model. However, this deficiency applied to other models as well, and there was at least a base of such studies upon which to build, with others on the way. The most notable such research, despite substantial flaws in execution, was Berger's *Bureaucracy and Society in Modern Egypt*,[62] but there were a number of other partial treatments of bureaucracy in particular countries, either in separate essays or as parts of analyses of individual political systems. The entire subject of the role of bureaucracy in political development had been explored in depth in papers prepared for a conference sponsored in 1962 by the Committee on Comparative Politics of the Social Science Research Council and published the following year in a volume edited by Joseph LaPalombara.[63] The bureaucratic perspective for comparison was thus already well rooted during the formative period of the comparative public administration movement.

This review of the literature during the emergence of comparative studies in public administration provides a base for describing the flowering of the movement during the decade beginning in the early 1960s. Trends, which continued into this period of expansion, had already been identified and encouraged by Fred Riggs in an essay published in 1962.[64] He discerned three trends that have been generally accepted as important and relevant. The first was a shift from normative toward more empirical approaches – a movement away from efforts to prescribe ideal or better patterns of administration toward "a growing interest in descriptive and analytic information for its own sake."[65] This consideration has already been mentioned, but it should be noted that the popular development administration theme often had a strong prescriptive motivation. The second trend was a movement from what Riggs called idiographic toward nomothetic approaches. Essentially this distinguished between studies "which concentrate on the unique case" and those seeking "generalizations, 'laws,' hypotheses that assert regularities of behavior, correlations between variables."[66] Model-building, particularly of the general system type, showed this nomothetic inclination. The third trend was a shift from a predominantly nonecological to an ecological basis for comparative study. Riggs described the first trend as being fairly clear by the time he wrote, but considered the other two as "perhaps only just emerging."[67] Obviously, he approved of these trends and was trying to encourage them. Indeed, he stated that his personal preference would be "to consider as 'truly' comparative only those studies that are empirical, nomothetic, and ecological."[68]

THE HEYDAY OF THE COMPARATIVE
ADMINISTRATION MOVEMENT

"The time of greatest vitality, vigor, influence, etc." is the dictionary definition of heyday, describing accurately the comparative administrative
movement during the period of about a decade beginning in 1962, the year in
which the CAG received initial funding from the Ford Foundation through a
grant to the American Society for Public Administration, CAG's parent
organization. During these years, students of comparative public administration demonstrated an amazing productivity, and their field of interest
grew rapidly in glamor and reputation.[69]

CAG Programs

At the core of all this activity was the CAG, with a membership composed
of academics and practitioners, including a considerable number of "corresponding members" from countries other than the United States, reaching
a total in 1968 of over 500. The principal source of financial support was the
Ford Foundation, which made grants to CAG of about half a million dollars in all, beginning in 1962 with a three-year grant that was extended for a
year and then renewed in 1966 for five additional years. In 1971 this support
was not renewed again, and after that CAG resources were much reduced,
with a corresponding curtailment of programs. The primary focus of interest
of the Ford Foundation was on the administrative problems of developing
countries, and the CAG was expected to analyze these problems in the
context of societal environmental factors found in these countries. The
foundation had a strong development administration orientation and was
eager to see a transfer of knowledge from CAG programs to practical applications through technical assistance projects and domestic developmental
undertakings within the target countries.

The CAG spun an elaborate network for carrying out its obligation to
stimulate interest in comparative administration, with special reference to
development administration problems. The primary device chosen initially
was a series of summer seminars, held two per year over a three-year period
at different universities, involving in each instance about a half dozen senior
scholars who prepared papers on a common theme, plus graduate assistants
and visiting consultants. Later, special conferences and seminars were
scheduled on various topics both in the United States and abroad. In addition, a number of small sub-grants were made for experimental teaching
programs.

A committee structure evolved under CAG auspices as areas of interest became identified. Several had a geographical orientation, relating to Asia, Europe, Latin America, and Africa. Others had a subject matter focus, including committees on comparative urban studies, national economic planning, comparative educational administration, comparative legislative studies, international administration, organization theory, and systems theory. These committees were not equally active or productive.

The work of CAG was reflected principally in publications, which it spawned, either directly or indirectly. A newsletter was issued regularly as a means of internal communication. More than 100 occasional papers were distributed in mimeographed form. After editing and revision, many of these were later published under various auspices. The primary outlet was provided by the Duke University Press, which published seven volumes in cooperation with CAG from 1969 through 1973, including general collections on political and administrative development and "frontiers" of development administration, volumes on development administration in Asia and in Latin America, studies of temporal dimensions and spatial dimensions of development administration, and a comparative analysis of legislatures. For a five-year period, from 1969 to 1974, the quarterly *Journal of Comparative Administration* was issued by Sage Publications in cooperation with CAG. There were also, of course, numerous articles published in other scholarly journals in the United States and abroad, which were written by CAG members.

Paralleling these research efforts, a corresponding growth was taking place in the teaching of courses in comparative and development administration in the United States, as evidenced by a 1970 report of a CAG survey which enumerated a proliferation of offerings beginning in 1945 at one institution and growing to over thirty by the time of the survey, but it also revealed very little uniformity as to approach, emphasis, or level of presentation. This interest in comparative aspects of administration was also reflected in the curricula and publications of numerous schools and institutes of public administration scattered around the world, usually as products of technical assistance projects, although the record was uneven as to the quantity and quality of these efforts.

CHARACTERISTIC FEATURES

The record of this "golden era" in comparative public administration is basically a continuation and expansion of what had already begun during the postwar period. The sheer bulk and great diversity of the output makes generalizations hazardous. Nevertheless, it is possible to identify some characteristic features, which not only show what was accomplished but also foreshadow some of the predicaments faced later by the comparative administration movement.

One obvious enduring influence can be traced to the large-scale postwar effort to export administrative know-how through unilateral and multilateral technical assistance programs. The CAG inherited the then favorable reputation and shared many of the attitudes associated with the public administration technical assistance efforts of the 1950s. Experts in public administration, not only from the United States but from numerous European countries as well, were scattered around the world, engaged in similar projects to export administrative technology, largely drawn from American experience, to a multitude of developing countries. Looking back, one of these experts describes the scene as follows:

> The 1950s was a wonderful period. The "American Dream" was the "World Dream" – and the best and quickest way to bring that dream into reality was through the mechanism of public administration. ... The net result of all this enthusiastic action was that in the 1950s public administration was a magic term and public administration experts were magicians, of a sort. They were eagerly recruited by the United States' aid-giving agencies and readily accepted most of the new nations, along with a lot of other experts as well.[70]

Another well-informed participant observer takes 1955 as the baseline year, and describes it as "a vintage year in a time of faith – faith in the developmental power of administrative tools devised in the West. It was a sanguine year in a time of hope – hope that public administration could lead countries toward modernization. It was a busy year in a brief age of charity – the not-unmixed charity of foreign assistance."[71]

Members of the CAG, many of whom had been or still were active participants in such programs, shared as a group most of the assumptions of the public administration experts, at least initially. Siffin has provided an accurate and perceptive analysis of the orientations, which marked this era, noting several major features. The first was a tool or technology orientation. The best developed and most widely exported of these processes were in the fields of personnel administration and budgeting and financial administration, but the list included administrative planning, records management, work simplification, tax and revenue administration, and at least the beginnings of computer technology. Part of the tool orientation was a belief that use of the tools could be essentially divorced from the substance of the governmental policies, which they would be serving. Second, there was a structural orientation that placed great emphasis on the importance of appropriate organizational arrangements, and assumed that organizational decisions could and should be based on rational considerations. For the most part, organizational forms then popular in the West were thought of as the most fitting, and organizations recommended for the developing countries usually emulated some model familiar to the expert at home.

Underlying these administrative manifestations were certain value and contextual orientations that helped explain the specifics of technical assistance recommendations. The instrumental nature of administration was the core value, with related supportive concepts of efficiency, rationality, responsibility, effectiveness, and professionalism. Education and training projects, including the sending of thousands of individuals to developed countries and the establishment of about seventy institutes in developing countries, were designed to inculcate these values as well as transmit technical know-how in specific subjects. Probably most important of all, these normative elements, particularly the commitment to responsibility as a basic value, were in Siffin's words "predicated upon a certain kind of sociopolitical context – the kind of context which is distinguished in its absence from nearly every developing country in the world." This context included economic, social, political, and intellectual aspects drawn mainly from U.S. experience and to some extent from other Western democratic systems. Politically, for example, these systems operated "within reasonably stable political frameworks, with limited competition for resources and mandates. In this milieu, administrative technologies provided *order* more than *integration*. The political context of administration was generally predictable, supportive, and incrementally expansive." In this and other respects, Siffin concluded that "the radical differences between the U.S. administrative context and various overseas situations were substantially ignored."[72]

It would be unfair to infer that misconceptions prevalent in the technical assistance efforts of the 1950s were accepted without question by students of comparative public administration during the 1960s. As a matter of fact, many of them voiced doubt and skepticism about approaches being used and opposed particular reform measures in countries with which they were familiar. Nevertheless, the comparative administration movement at its height can accurately be described as imbued with a pervasive overall mood of optimism about the practicality of utilizing administrative means to bring about desirable change. Commentators who disagreed on other assessments agreed on this. In a review of several of the major books produced by the CAG, Garth N. Jones remarked that they "make a case for positive intervention into the affairs of men. Men can take destiny in their hands, control, and mold it." Noting that many of the papers under review systematically eviscerated "past approaches and efforts in planned development in public administration," Jones pointed out that even so "scarcely a word is mentioned that questions the approach of positive intervention. The main task is to find a better way by which to do this."[73]

Peter Savage, who served as editor of the *Journal of Comparative Administration*, observed that the study of administration from a comparative perspective "possesses a peculiar quality; a concern for the management of action in the real world, for creating organizational and procedural arrangements that handle specified and identifiable problems in the public realm." Indigenous to the comparative administration movement, in his opinion, had been "a belief in the possibility of managing change by purposive intervention by administrative institutions."[74]

Even more than before, during the 1960s development administration became a term often used in the titles of books and articles with a comparative thrust. No doubt this reflected in part the faith in positive results just discussed and behind that the desire to assist developing countries in meeting their overwhelming problems. It was also responsive to the core interest of the Ford Foundation as chief financial benefactor in directing CAG programs toward developmental topics. Furthermore, it proved attractive to leaders in the developing countries themselves by highlighting an intent to assist in reaching domestic goals. From a more strictly scholarly point of view, strong arguments were made as to the benefits to comparative studies of a developmental focus. Whatever the motivations, development administration largely displaced comparative administration in the labeling of CAG output. This was shown most significantly in the Duke University Press series of books, each of which had in its title either the word "development" or "developmental," and none of which had "comparative."

Despite the trend toward greater usage, little progress appeared in defining more precisely what development administration meant. Riggs, in his introduction to *Frontiers of Development Administration*,[75] said that no clear answer could be given as to how the study of development administration differed from the study of comparative administration or the study of public administration generally. He did identify two foci of attention – the administration of development and the development of administration. In the first sense, development administration referred "to the administration of development programs, to the methods used by large-scale organizations, notably governments, to implement policies and plans designed to meet their developmental objectives."[76] The second meaning involved the strengthening of administrative capabilities, both as a means to enhance the prospects for success in carrying out current development programs, and as a by-product of prior programs such as in education.[77]

Writings under the heading of development administration did indeed explore both of these facets, but were not by any means confined to one or the other of these subjects of inquiry. As a matter of actual practice, development administration came in the 1960s to be synonymous with, or at least not clearly distinguishable from, comparative public administration. The two terms became virtually interchangeable. This usage was in part an affirmation of the faith in positive intervention for societal reform held by most of those identified with the comparative administration movement.

Among the middle-range models for comparative studies, bureaucracy continued to be widely preferred. Ramesh K. Arora identified the construct of bureaucracy drawn from the work of Max Weber as "the single most dominant conceptual framework in the study of comparative administration."[78] A large proportion of the literature dealt in one way or another with bureaucracies – refining what was meant by the term "bureaucracy," describing particular national or subnational bureaucratic systems, classifying bureaucracies as to type on the basis of dominant characteristics, debating the problem of relationships between bureaucracies and other groups in the political system, and so forth. Lacking, however, was any outpouring of field studies on the current operations of developing bureaucracies, in part because of the scarcity of financial support for the substantial costs involved.

The most conspicuous trait of the comparative administration literature during this period, nevertheless, was an extension of the search for comprehensive theory, with contributions from a wide range of social scientists, not just from students of public administration and political science. Savage noted the production of much "grand theory," and commented that if one envisioned a high and a low road to science, then certainly comparative administration "tended to travel loftily,"[79] and undervalued the approach of systematic inquiry directed toward reducing indeterminacy. James Heaphey found "academic analysis" to be the foremost among a few "dominant visions" in his analysis of characteristics of comparative literature.[80] Jamil E. Jreisat also concluded that the research orientation leading in influence had been macro-analysis of national administrative systems, with emphasis tending to be at "the level of grand theory in the sociological tradition."[81] All those who surveyed the output of the comparative administration movement during its peak agreed on this pervasive, but not dominant, characteristic.

When all of these partially overlapping and partially competing forces had been taken into account, the overwhelming impression was that diversity had been the hallmark of the movement, recognized as such by both its enthusiasts and its detractors. Fred Riggs, acknowledging that "dissensus prevails," with no agreement on "approach, methodology, concept, theory, or doctrine," considered this a "virtue, a cause for excitement," normal in a pre-paradigmatic field.[82] As Peter Savage put it, comparative administration "started with no paradigm of its own and developed none." No orthodoxy was established or even attempted. "The net result has been paradigmatic confusion, as much a part of Comparative Administration as it is held to be of its parent field, Public Administration."[83] This failure to draw the boundaries and set the rules of comparative administration as a field of study became, as we shall see, a main complaint of those disenchanted with accomplishments made by the CAG.

RETRENCHMENT, REAPPRAISALS, AND RECOMMENDATIONS

The years from about 1970 through the early 1980s became for comparative public administration a period of lessened support and lowered expectations. The exuberance of CAG's heyday was replaced by a mood of introspection. Individuals long identified with CAG joined earlier detractors and younger scholars in reappraising the past record and making recommendations for the future of comparative administration as a focus of study and action.

Retrenchment

Foreshadowing these trends in the comparative administration movement itself came a downshift in the attention devoted to public administration as a category for technical assistance efforts. Emphasis on these programs continued into the mid-1960s, but declined rapidly and sharply, beginning about 1967. By the early 1970s the annual rate of support from the United States for public administration aid was less than half what it had been during the decade from the mid-1950s to the mid-1960s. International as well as U.S. technical assistance agencies shifted their attention from administrative reform efforts to complex programs with an economic orientation designed to foster indigenous economic growth through policies jointly worked out by domestic and international agencies. As Jones dramatically put it, the public administration technicians, the POSDCORB types of the 1950s, were exterminated by a new animal "as fearsome and aggressive as the ancient Norsemen – the new development economists."[84] Projects high on the priority list of the experts in development economics largely displaced the administrative know-how export projects favored earlier. This transition not only reduced the number of practitioners in technical assistance agencies affiliated with the CAG, but also sharply curtailed even the theoretical possibilities of bringing the work of CAG to bear directly on technical assistance programs.

The 1970s also brought several direct alterations and reductions in the scope of activities of the comparative administration movement itself. The end of Ford Foundation support has already been mentioned. No substitute financial sponsor materialized with help approaching the level provided during the 1960s. Even during those years, the CAG was turned down in its search for funds to support field research in developing countries on any substantial, systematic, and planned basis. The *Journal of Comparative Administration*, after only five years of existence as the primary vehicle for scholarly research in the field, ceased publication in 1974. Although this move involved merger into a new journal, *Administration and Society*, rather than outright extinction, it clearly meant a more diffused focus with no assurance that the broader scope would assure success either. Publications in the Duke University Press series continued to appear as late as 1973, but these were products of work done several years earlier. Reports from university campuses indicated a falling off of student interest in comparative administration courses, and there was evidence that fewer doctoral dissertations were being written in the field.

Perhaps most symbolically if not substantively important, the Comparative Administration Group itself went out of existence in 1973, when it merged with the International Committee of the American Society for Public Administration to form a new Section on international and Comparative Administration (SICA). SICA continued with much the same membership, and engaged in many of the same activities as CAG, such as participation in professional meetings, issuance of a newsletter, and distribution of occasional papers, but all at a somewhat reduced level.

Reappraisals

These indications of decline were accompanied, and probably stimulated, by a series of critiques of the comparative administration movement, usually in the form of papers presented at professional meetings, several of which were subsequently published. These deserve our attention, not only for what they had to say about shortcomings and disappointments, but also about prescriptions and predictions.

The usual takeoff point was that the comparative administration movement, after over a quarter of a century in which to prove itself, including a decade of rather lavish support, needed now to be scrutinized for results.

Peter Savage took as his point of reference the propositions that any "fresh ideas, theories, and perspectives in Political Science have about a decade to 'make it' before they are dropped and replaced by even fresher ones," and that the first few years are the easiest. During this time, the "honey-pot syndrome" emerges, with money and professional rewards accorded the progenitors of the new movement. After that, "orthodoxy begins and the crucial test is then upon the innovation, namely to produce some results. If this does not happen, the pot is assumed not to contain honey, or not the right kind of honey, and it is quietly and sometimes abruptly abandoned in favor of an even newer one."[85] He thought comparative administration was no exception, and that the time for testing the honey in the pot had come.

Whatever the worth of this notion, comparative public administration certainly was well enough established to become one target of the general tendency to question older orthodoxies which surfaced dramatically at the turn of the decade of the 1970s. No doubt linked to campus unrest, in turn stemming from reaction to the unpopular war in Vietnam, this revolt against the establishment appeared in one form or another in all the social sciences and in some of the natural sciences. In the form of what was usually called the "new" public administration movement, this combination of attack and reform proposals reached its peak about 1970, just as comparative public administration was facing straitened circumstances and completing its period of scholarly probation. Comparative administration turned out to be attractive to some of the leaders of the "new" public administration because of its own relative newness, and also the subject of their skeptical questioning.

However stimulated, the tone of the appraisers was essentially negative, and they expressed generally unfavorable judgments. A few sample quotations will suffice to illustrate: "The auguries for Comparative Administration are not good."[86] Described as a declining and troubled field which had made only minimal progress, it was charged with lagging "far behind the fields to which it is most closely related in its application of systematic research technologies."[87] Comparative public administration was "floundering at a time when other social scientists have finally come to appreciate the central role bureaucracy and bureaucrats play in the political process."[88] Development administration as an academic enterprise appeared ill-prepared to meet the challenge it faced at a critical juncture. "Need and opportunity beckon: performance falls short."[89]

Like the writers in comparative public administration whose work they were analyzing, the evaluators did not by any means fully agree with one another as to what was wrong and what ought to be done about it, but there were some readily identifiable common themes.

The most frequent complaint was that comparative public administration had by then had time enough but had failed to establish itself as a field of study with a generally accepted range of topics to be addressed, and that despite the inclination to theorize no consensus had been achieved permitting primary attention to be given to empirical studies designed to test existing theories about cross-national public administration.

Keith Henderson, writing in 1969 about the "identity crisis" in the field, asked what was not within the scope of comparative public administration. Calling attention to the diversity of titles in CAG publications, he observed that although "there are certain dominant themes (the developing countries, the political system, etc.) it is hard to know what the central thrust might be and equally hard to find anything distinctly 'administrative' in that thrust. Seemingly, the full range of political science, economic, sociological, historical, and other concerns is relevant."[90] Lee Sigelman made a content analysis of the entire output of the *Journal of Comparative Administration* as the primary vehicle for scholarly publication in the field, and found that in comparative public administration "no single topic or set of questions came close to dominating." Among substantive categories, he placed the highest percentage of articles (14.6 percent) under the heading "policy administration," followed by categories such as concepts (of bureaucracy, institution-building, etc.), structural descriptions of organizations in various national settings, and studies of bureaucratic values and behavior. His residual category of "other" had the most entries (22 percent), "embracing an astounding array of topics, e.g., communication models for social science, time, the ombudsman, law, problems of causal analysis, the nature of the political process, party coalitions, and anti-bureaucratic utopias." To Sigelman, this suggested that "students of administration have not narrowed their interest to a manageable set of questions and topics. A substantial amount of their effort continues to be spent in activity that can best be characterized as 'getting ready to get ready' – exploring epistemological matters, debating the boundaries of the field, and surveying the manner in which concepts have been used."[91] Jones remarked even more acidly that the CAG movement "never got much beyond the researching of the definition stage of the subject. Some would say it did not even reach that stage."[92]

Similar concerns were reiterated elsewhere, often by commentators who observed that the prospects for integration had seemed promising only a few years earlier but had not materialized. For example, Jreisat believed that

"the absence of integrative concepts and central foci in comparative research and analysis" was a critical problem, manifested in recent CAG
literature indicating a "wide range of seemingly independent concerns." He
explored the reasons for the "kaleidoscopic development" of comparative
research, such as the movement from culture-bound to cross-cultural studies, the diverse backgrounds and interests of social scientists from a variety
of disciplines, the absence of cumulativeness in acquiring administrative
knowledge, and particularly the lack of an identifiable core that would enable scholars "to distinguish an administrative phenomenon when they see
one and to sift out its critical aspects from the uncritical ones." Recognizing
that there were reasons initially for sacrificing conceptual rigor for substantive breadth and methodological experimentation, Jreisat asserted that
such justification "is less convincing after more than two decades of research
in the comparative field and because prospective evolution toward consolidation and synthesis is not emerging."[93]

The indictment basically was that students of comparative administration
had simultaneously shown an unseemly addiction to theorizing and a lack of
ability to offer theories that could win acceptance and be tested empirically.
Savage said that the literature displayed "a melange of idiosyncratic theoretical formulations and organizing perspectives, many of which have more
to do with academic or personal fancy than with any generally acceptable
cumulative purpose." Using an illustration from Riggs, he suspected that
the proposals "were often not so much theories, in any scientific sense of the
word, as they were fantasies."[94] J. Fred Springer claimed that development
administration was "starved for theories which will guide the pooling of
empirical knowledge, orient new research, and recommend administrative
policy."[95] Sigelman likened the plight of comparative public administration
to that of the Third World nations being studied, in the sense that like them
the field was caught in a vicious circle. Reliable data must be brought to
bear on theoretically significant propositions for research to be meaningful,
but Sigelman believed that comparative administration had been sorely
lacking in both reliable data and testable propositions, resulting in theoretical and empirical underdevelopment, and presenting the strategic problem to students in the field of how to break out of the circle of stagnation.[96]

Explanations for this plight were not obvious, but one suggestion offered
was that students of comparative administration had not kept pace with
progress in closely related fields, and that this helped account for the lag in
accomplishment. Sigelman made an unfavorable contrast of the analytic
techniques employed in the comparative administration literature against
those used in research in comparative politics. According to his content

analysis of the *Journal of Comparative Administration*, less than one-fifth of the articles published were at all quantitative in their techniques, and only half of these used what he defined as "more powerful" measurement techniques. Most of the works published consisted of essay-type theoretical or conceptual pieces, or were empirical but nonquantitative, such as case studies. On the other hand, three out of every four articles published in *Comparative Political Studies*, representing comparative politics research, had been empirical in character, with the preponderance of these falling into the "more powerful" quantitative category. Linked to this fault, Sigelman also found that cross-national studies were the exception rather than the norm, with 70 percent of the studies which focused on national or subnational units examining administration in only one national setting, 15 percent comparing a pair of national settings, and only 15 percent undertaking comparisons on a larger scale.

Taking a different tack, Jong S. Jun faulted comparative public administration for not keeping pace with its own parent field of public administration, and suggested that revival in comparative studies must incorporate recent developments in the broader discipline, particularly with regard to organization theory.[97]

Turning to another theme, the term "development administration" became a frequent target, but from different angles of attack. Garth Jones bluntly scolded the CAG for appropriating and obfuscating this concept. He viewed development administration as "a polite way to talk about administrative reform, and this in all cases means political reform." After commending the CAG writers for recognizing that political reform must precede administrative reform and that the two cannot be separated, he found little else to say by way of approval of how the CAG had dealt with development administration. To start with, he accounted for the shift in the CAG usage from comparative public administration to development administration in a very simple fashion, calling it a device to secure money for research. By changing the name of the "game" to development administration, the CAG seized upon a term more marketable to the Ford Foundation. Besides being more exciting, the term was also more difficult to define, but not as difficult as the CAG tried to make it. Moreover, he thought that the work of CAG scholars fell more properly in the area of development politics than in development administration, and that they had very little to offer of practical utility to those who wanted to know how to "reform an archaic accounting system, integrate new national planning methodology within a dynamic administrative program, organize and administer a new national family planning effort, or design management operations for a new irrigation system." In sum, he accused the CAG of adopting the term development administration for its own advantage, without actually contributing much to the solution of development administration problems. The CAG stayed in its ivory tower and away from the field of action.[98]

A quite different complaint came from Brian Loveman, who raised questions about assumptions in the development administration literature concerning the ability of governments to strengthen administrative capabilities and carry out plans for meeting developmental objectives.[99] He grouped CAG members with others labeled liberal democratic theorists who were alleged to share these assumptions, similar to ideas about development and development administration held by Marxist–Leninist theorists as well. His summary of conclusion was that both the liberal democratic and socialist models of development cost more than they were worth to developing societies. These models, in his judgment, called for an "administered society" antagonistic to the important value of expanded human choice as an alternative to the extension of intervention by government administrators. In short, development cannot, or at least should not, be administered.

Loveman's criticism thus contrasted with the one made by Jones. He accused the CAG of overidentification with the aims of development administrators, and over-involvement in development administration programs. He quoted Milton Esman, a CAG spokesman, as writing that much of the change desired must be induced, and therefore managed. He identified the CAG as sharing the assumption that development can be administered and that it requires administration by a politico-administrative elite. The quest for such an elite had led often to the military as a stabilizing or modernizing force. "By the 1970s," according to Loveman, "administrative development and development administration had become euphemisms for autocratic, frequently military, rule that, admittedly, sometimes induced industrialization, modernization, and even economic growth. But this occurred at a great cost in the welfare of the rural and urban poor and substantial erosion if not deletion of the political freedoms associated with liberal democracy."[100] He mentioned Brazil, Iran (before the fall of the shah), and South Korea as "showcases." The CAG role, in his interpretation, had been both to elaborate an academic ideology of development and to encourage participation by its members in programs to induce development.

Ambivalence also showed up in related evaluations of the "relevance" of the comparative administration movement. CAG documents had frequently expressed the desire to have the work of CAG prove useful to technical assistance experts and to officials in developing countries, and this was one of the explicit expectations from the Ford Foundation grants. However, except for agreement on somewhat peripheral matters such as the establishment of links among scholars from various countries, the usual judgment was negative as to the success of CAG in achieving relevancy.

Disappointment on this score was conceded by Fred Riggs in a 1970 newsletter when he noted that CAG had an ivory tower image and had failed to form a bridge between academic life and practice. Others agreed, and some tried to explain why Jones found little in CAG writings "that will contribute to social technologies related to the burning issues of the day such as population control, environmental protection, and food production. These authors undoubtedly have something to say here, but it is best that they start all over again."[101] Savage concurred that CAG did not produce much in the way of socially useful knowledge. It was not a matter of producing "bad medicine," but "no medicine." These judgments may have been overly severe in what was expected of CAG, but whatever the worth of CAG efforts, there was another problem of getting attention and acceptance. Jones, speaking as a former practitioner, had this comment which he no doubt intended not to be restricted to one individual:

"As much as I admire Fred Riggs, and I do, his thinking had little relevance for my kind of problems. Certainly the AID [U.S. Agency for International Development] bureaucracy was not willing to accept it."[102] B. B. Schaffer wrote that CAG members "had their conferences and wrote their papers, but the practitioners did not seem to take much notice and changes in developing countries did not seem to be directly affected."[103]

These were typical common assessments, focused on the question of relevance to developing countries. Jreisat added an unusual fillip by pointing out that comparative studies had so concentrated on emerging countries and their problems that little was offered of theoretical or practical utility in Western, particularly American, contexts.

Some critics, on the other hand, seemed to view the comparative administration movement as all too relevant. In opposing the outcomes of technical assistance and development administration programs in recipient countries, they directly or implicitly chastised the CAG for participation by some of its members, and for its desire to be supportive to practitioners. Loveman, as part of his argument that development cannot be administered, repeatedly spoke of "United States–AID–CAG" models, doctrines, or programs of development administration. He credited the CAG with providing "an intellectual grounding for American foreign policy in the 1960s." According to his version, the failure of liberal democratic regimes to "develop" gradually made it clear that "United States policy and the CAG would have to make ever more explicit the relationship between growth, liberal democracy, anti-Marxism, and a strategy giving first priority to political stability." For this to occur, the problem of administrative development had to be resolved. "Administrative development had to precede effective development administration; any concern for constraints on bureaucratic authority had to be subordinated to the need to create effective administrative instruments." Hence the CAG and United States policy-makers turned to programs intended to build up administrative elites, often military elites. Recommendations of CAG spokesmen such as Esman "to be less concerned with control of the development administrators and more concerned with the capabilities of these elites to carry out developmental objectives" were heeded by officials making U.S. government policy, with the unfortunate consequences, as seen by Loveman, already mentioned. The point in connection with the relevancy issue is that Loveman, far from viewing the CAG as detached from and ignored by governmental technical assistance policy-makers, evidently pictured CAG members as closely allied with these officials and highly influential in crucial policy decision-making.[104]

The relevancy issue, then, received plenty of attention, with quite a spread of opinion on it. Few regarded the CAG as achieving the degree of relevancy desired by its members or its sponsors, but the explanations for the deficiency varied. As Jreisat put it, "although the cry of non-relevance is common, it comes to us from different sources for different reasons and, consequently, the remedial suggestions are not always consistent."[105] With measures of relevancy uncertain, and with such inconsistency in assessing the situation and what ought to be done about it, probably the only certain conclusion is that not all the commentators could have been right, but those who reported a close working collaboration between the CAG as a group entity and official policy-makers produced little evidence to support this interpretation.

Balancing somewhat the negative thrust of this review of the retrenchment evidence and the critical reappraisals, it should be noted that even the more severe critics of the CAG and its record (such as Jones, Jreisat, and Jun) acknowledged the impressive productivity of the 1960s and the vast accumulation of knowledge in comparative public administration which resulted. Others who had been more closely identified personally with the CAG (such as Savage and Siffin) were even more apt to temper their criticism with reference to specific accomplishments.

Savage emphasized that the intentions were commendable, despite flaws in priorities and methods, and that overall the legacy of the CAG could be viewed with considerable satisfaction. He mentioned, for example, that comparative studies had "shed a bright light on the existence and importance.

In many settings, of the public bureaucracy," and had called attention insistently to the importance of the administrative factor in political analysis. At the same time, he believed that the comparative administration movement had made a dent in "the myth of managerial omnipotence" by its increasing recognition and exploration of the cultural shaping of administrative techniques, and by identifying factors that must be taken into account when making prescriptions for administrative reform. More generally, he credited the movement with building bridges with comparative politics and other subfields in the discipline of political science, and providing a kind of "demonstration effect" of the attractions of venturing into unfamiliar territory. He thought that a lot of brush had been cleared out by the pursuit of false leads, which other scholars need no longer pursue. He also made the point, often overlooked, that the failure of the movement to achieve some of the early promises had "more to do with the complexities and intractabilities in its chosen domain than with faulty purpose."[106] Siffin, more directly concerned with efforts to export administrative technology, gave credit to students of comparative administration for inquiring into the reasons for technology transfer failures, and commended their attention to environmental factors as inhibitors in attaining development administration objectives.

Recommendations

Simultaneously, and as a part of the reassessment efforts, came analyses as to causes of past problems and recommendations for the future. The most often recurring complaint, as already indicated, had been that comparative public administration had never been able to reach paradigmatic consensus. As might be anticipated from this, the most common recommendation was that this deficiency had to be remedied if this field of study was to achieve intellectual standing and academic maturity. Repeatedly, the point was stressed that an adequate paradigm must be sought to bring coherence, purpose, and progress.

Given the urgency of the need expressed, one naturally looks hopefully for suggestions as to what the basis for consensus should be. On this score, most critics were embarrassingly silent or vague. Some immediately qualified the call for an accepted paradigm by disavowal of any intention to establish a paradigmatic orthodoxy in comparative public administration. "The search for common ground," according to Jreisat, was "not necessarily a call for the establishment of precise and rigid boundaries."[107] The main disappointment, however, was that when it came to specifics, the suggestions made were strongly reminiscent of those voiced much earlier, near the beginning of the movement's heyday. We find the repeated caution expressed in 1959 by Robert Presthus against "cosmic" theory and the advice to seek instead "middle-range" theory. Jreisat asserted, for instance, that "a higher degree of synthesis and relevance of comparative analysis may be attained through conceptualization of critical administrative problems at the 'middle range' level and involving institutions rather than entire national administrative systems."[108] Lee Sigelman described his views as representing "a meaningful middle ground between the present state of affairs and unrealistically optimistic schemes for improving it." Also in line with a preference already established by the early 1960s, Sigelman stated as his conviction that the future of comparative public administration lay in studies of bureaucracies, in "examinations of the backgrounds, attitudes, and behaviors of bureaucrats and those with whom they interact."[109]

Even though these commentators presented no drastically new directions to improve comparative studies, they did provide a number of thoughtful, useful, and helpful suggestions, some of which have since been acted upon. Most of these had to do with methodologies to be used, data to be gathered, or subjects to be studied – all rather persistent concerns of comparative administration students.

An exception was the contention by Jong S. Jun that methodological considerations had received too much attention, and that the problem was essentially one of epistemology rather than methodology. Jun raised questions as to the limits and validity of human knowledge as it is brought to bear on the comparative study of systems of administration. He presented what was essentially an epistemological critique of the structural–functional and bureaucratic models, which he regarded as the dominant ones, arguing that both models failed "to explore the subjective meaning of social action, to provide a mechanism for organizational change, and to consider the renewal effects of conflict-induced disequilibrium." He detected a common tendency for the researcher to superimpose "his perspective and method onto a culture not his own." Tending to imitate natural science methodologies, social scientists have had in his view inadequate tools to cope with the incredible variety of data from the world's political and administrative systems and have been unable to generate a suitable comparative perspective. His suggestion for a different conceptual framework, which he did not elaborate, was that scholars should adopt a phenomenological approach to comparative study to provide a new perspective for analyzing other cultures. He maintained that with this approach "the need becomes apparent to bracket one's own feelings and separate them from one's perceptions," and that this perspective would be "a useful way of standing aside from our presuppositions and cultural biases, and looking at someone else a good deal more in their own terms," but he did not give illustrations as to how this perspective would be applied. Richard Ryan has also stressed the importance of a contextual approach to reduce perceptual biases of development administrators, and he has provided several specific examples.[110]

On the themes of scope and method rather than psychological approach, several related points were made. Sigelman deplored the loss of focus on administration in comparative public administration, and believed that advice that students of administration should study unrelated or loosely related substantive fields was equivalent to institutionalizing that loss of focus. Continuing "the seemingly never ending quest for an all-inclusive analytic framework" seemed to him "positively perverse." He quoted as applicable to comparative public administration Jorgen Rasmussen's supplication "O Lord, deliver us from further conceptualization and lead us not into new approaches." In his view, scholars in the past had "spent so much time and energy debating issues of comparison, putting forth general analytic frameworks, and sketching out the environment of administration that we have been diverted from the study of administration itself."[111]

Both Peter Savage and J. Fred Springer called attention to choices in comparative studies among different levels of analysis. Although their terminology differed somewhat, they both were referring to a range of options running from whole social systems through descending levels of inclusiveness to units such as institutions, organizations, and even individuals. Springer argued that reliance on one level of analysis decreased the prospects for understanding complex systems. He stressed the use of concepts, such as those from role theory, which might have utility "in relating phenomena at different levels of analysis, and in sensitizing the analyst to contextually specific patterns of interaction and behavior." He cited a number of studies which had penetrated "into the structure of national bureaucracies to identify important contextual effects within the organization," including role analyses of public officials in Indonesia and Thailand, and a cross-national multilevel study of the administration of rice production projects in Indonesia, the Philippines, and Thailand.[112]

The problem of data for research was another serious matter addressed. The growth of availability of data from a multitude of countries was evident, but this did not equate with comparability and reliability of data. Sigelman stressed the importance of new strategies of data collection and maintenance, examining the matter at both the macro or system level of research, and at the micro level. In both instances, he concentrated on comparative studies involving bureaucracies, which he considered should be the core of future research endeavors. He was quite pessimistic about the availability of data for systematic testing of hypotheses in system level studies, leaving the testing of macro-level theory to be done primarily with judgmental data derived from experts considered to be knowledgeable, using methods such as the Delphi technique, which Sigelman recommended as promising. With regard to micro-level research, Sigelman believed that many potentially significant studies on bureaucracy had already been undertaken, but that many had never been published or had appeared in journals devoted to specific geographical areas that were not noticed by comparative administration students.

Besides the problem of inaccessibility, he identified two other acute deficiencies. Only occasionally had the research been cross-national in scope, and the literature was scattered and diffuse. "Different scholars with different research perspectives use different instruments to interview different types of bureaucrats in examinations of different problems in different nations." In short, micro-level research was noncumulative. Sigelman proposed an institutionalized mechanism for data maintenance through establishment of an archive of comparative administration research, arguing that this "could go far toward bringing some order to the chaos of micro-level administrative studies."[113]

As to the subject matter focus for research, certainly there was no consensus beyond the dominant view that the choice of substantive topic should be designed to test middle-range theory. Indeed, if anything, the range of suggestions broadened rather than narrowed. Bureaucracy as a common institution in political systems continued to be most frequently recommended as the target with the greatest promise for research efforts, although as we will discover in the following chapter, different people had different ideas even as to the meaning of bureaucracy, not to mention how it ought to be studied on a comparative basis.

A persistent strain in the recommendations of the commentators was that new advances in the area of organization theory could be brought to bear fruitfully in the analysis of organizational units of interest to comparative administration researchers, whether these might be whole national bureaucracies or bureaucratic subunits. Springer called for supplementing earlier work aimed at individual or systemic levels with increasing attention to conceptual and empirical work at the organization level. Jun advocated the introduction of concepts from modern organization theory that would focus attention on organizational change and development in a cross-cultural context. He referred particularly to experiments in industrial democracy or self-management attempted in several countries, and commented that comparisons among such experiments would "provide a new avenue for learning about the effectiveness of different organizations in different cultural settings."[114] Jreisat concurred that cross-cultural comparisons at the organizational level had rarely been attempted, even though studies of formal organizations within one cultural setting such as the United States, with stable environmental influences, were advanced and sophisticated. He regarded the few ventures that had been made toward comparative organizational theory as not representing genuine cross-cultural comparisons and as "not seriously concerned with the various possible patterns of human interaction which may be prevalent outside the limits of customary Western styles of behavior."[115] Jorge I. Tapia-Videla also asserted that research and writing in comparative public administration had not been much influenced by theoretical progress in the area of organization theory.[116] With a few exceptions, such as *Bureaucratic politics and Administration in Chile* by Peter Cleaves,[117] Tapia-Videla found that the potential benefits of blending organization theory into the comparative study of administration had not been realized. He himself then examined the characteristics of public bureaucracies in Latin America, and the relationships between these bureaucracies and the "corporate-technocratic" state, which had emerged in several Latin American countries as well as elsewhere in the Third World.[118]

Public policy-making was another subject receiving much attention during the 1970s. Attempts were being made on one hand to analyze the process of policy-making in a descriptive way, and on the other to analyze outputs and effects of policy in a fashion which was more prescriptive and aimed to improve both the process and the content of public policy.[119] With few exceptions, however, policy-making studies had not been comparative across countries, leading Jun in 1976 to urge comparative policy analysis as an additional field for pioneering work that might serve both scientific and practical purposes.[120]

This survey of recommendations made in connection with the reassessment efforts of the decade of the 1970s paves the way for consideration of what has been happening during recent years in comparative public administration, an appraisal of the current state of the field, and prognostication about future developments.

PROSPECTS AND OPTIONS

By 1980 the prospects for the comparative public administration movement were obviously not as bright as they had once seemed to be. The period of massive technical assistance in public administration, which had helped launch the movement, was over. The CAG, which had been the organizing force during the years of greatest activity, had lost its separate identity, and the programs it initiated had been ended or cut back. As a source of action-oriented plans for dealing with problems of development administration, the movement had generally been judged disappointing. At any rate, whatever the impact, it had lessened. Moreover, earlier optimistic expectations about the possibilities of transferring or inducing change in developing societies had come into question, as many of these nations were suffering from increasing rather than decreasing problems of economic growth and political stability. As an academic or intellectual enterprise, comparative administration had moved from a position of innovation and vitality to a more defensive posture, reacting to charges that the promises of its youth had not been fulfilled and to advice from various quarters as to remedial measures.

During the decades of the 1980s and 1990s, however, there has been a reassuring revival of activity in comparative public administration. The exuberance of the movement's youth has not been regained, but the field may have attained maturity – a stage of development bringing fewer drastic changes but presenting a new set of challenges and problems.

One obvious trend has been toward a proliferation of comparative studies concerned with public administration broadly conceived, and a branching off into subspecialties by many comparativists. Our interest focuses on what I will call "core" comparative public administration, but supplemental attention needs to be given to at least two of these branching but closely related subjects – development administration and comparative public policy. Some treatment has already been given to each of these foci of interest, particularly the former. They share the characteristic that they concentrate on something less than the comprehensive study of national administrative systems as the entities or subjects being compared. They also have in each instance demonstrated a tendency to assert and to seek recognition of their separateness.

For these reasons, we will review in sequence rather than together the prospects and options first of development administration, then comparative public policy, and finally "core" comparative public administration.

Development Administration

Since the early days of the comparative administration movement, development administration has been continuously studied. A great deal of effort has gone into setting boundaries as to what is and what is not included, improving strategies for implementation of development projects, and evaluating the results of what has continued to be a massive network of activity. Unfortunately, the results in each instance have been either disappointing or inconclusive.[121] As a result, development administration has been a subject of perennial controversy, and has presented issues that seem to be intractable to resolution. At best, as Siffin observes, it is "the indicative but imprecise label for a set, or at least a potential batch, of problems."[122]

Although widely used for about four decades, why has this term "development administration" never been given an agreed-upon definition, despite extended discussion and arguments on the matter? As we have seen, the original intent in coining and popularizing the phrase is not in doubt. It was to concentrate attention on the administrative requisites for achieving public policy goals, particularly in the less developed countries. This purpose was linked to an assumption that more developed countries could assist in this effort through a process of diffusion or transfer of administrative capabilities already possessed. As a phenomenon, development administration appeared to be confined to certain countries under certain circumstances, existing in some nation-states but not in others. This was the most common understanding during the heyday of the comparative administration movement, when the CAG was concentrating its attention on comparative studies with a developmental focus, leading to the terms development administration and comparative administration being regarded almost as synonyms.

As time passed, critics properly pointed out that even the so-called developed countries have difficulties in reaching their public policy goals, and hence should be viewed as sharing problems of development administration. The implication was that since all systems of public administration have goals and objectives to be achieved, development administration could best be used simply as a designator having to do with the degree of success achieved in movement toward the chosen purposes. Under such a definition, however, the Hitler regime in Nazi Germany could be considered as a model example of development administration, because of its proven ability to eliminate six million Jews in its campaign of extermination. Surely no user of the term had this application in mind, so some meaning needed to be sought which would specify more satisfactorily what public policy goals are appropriate as development administration targets.

My preferred choice for doing this is to accept the suggestion of George Gant in his book *Development Administration: Concepts, Goals, Methods*, published in 1979.[123] Gant himself is generally credited with having coined the term "development administration" in the mid-1950s when he was on the staff of the Ford Foundation, so his book represented a quarter century of thinking and writing on the subject.

Gant's approach is to avoid definitions that limit the general applicability of concepts such as "development" and "development administration." As he sees it, development is not an absolute but is a relative condition, with no country ever qualifying as fully developed.[124] Development administration is defined in a similar way. Originally it referred to the focusing of administration "on the support and management of development as distinguished from the administration of law and order." According to Gant, the term now denotes "the complex of agencies, management systems, and processes a government establishes to achieve its development goals. ... Development administration is the administration of policies, programs, and projects to serve development purposes." It is characterized by its purposes, which are "to stimulate and facilitate defined programs of social and economic progress," by its loyalties, which are to the public rather than to vested interests, and by its attitudes, which are "positive rather than negative, persuasive rather than restrictive."[125]

Such concepts and definitions mean that every country is concerned with and has its own problems of development administration, centered in what Gant calls "nation-building departments or ministries," in fields such as agriculture, industry, education, and health. These agencies, in comparison to more traditional ones, have special requirements with regard to structure, planning capabilities, staff analysis services, and a variety of professionally trained personnel. The original emphasis is also retained on the newly independent nations, which can be expected to have particularly acute problems in these areas, and the expectation is continued that at least to some extent less developed countries can benefit from the accumulated experience of those more developed.

Most later commentators seem to be in essential agreement with Gant. Nasir Islam and Georges M. Henault suggest that the label "development administration" can best be applied "to designing, implementing and evaluating policies and programmes leading to socioeconomic change."[126] Asmeron and Jam say that development administration "refers to an aspect of public administration in which the focus of attention is on organizing and managing public agencies and government departments at both the national and sub-national levels in such a way as to stimulate and facilitate well-defined programmes of social, economic and political progress."[127] Huque concurs that the term development administration indicates that "the administrative activities in developing countries are not concerned merely with the maintenance of law and order and the execution of public policies, but also with modernization, economic development and the extension of social services," and that these functions are of "overwhelming importance" in developing countries,[128] but he is skeptical as to the existence of a "science of development administration" that can be of much assistance.[129]

It is crucial to recognize that development administration, viewed this way, is not synonymous with either public administration or comparative public administration. As Gant explains, development administration is "distinguished from, although not independent of, other aspects and concerns of public administration. Certainly the maintenance of law and order is a prime function of government and is basic to development, although it precedes and is not usually encompassed within the definition of development administration." Similarly, the provision of essential communications and educational facilities, and the maintenance of judicial and diplomatic systems, would have an impact on but not be an integral part of development administration.[130]

Without insisting on any particular definitive meaning for development administration, it seems to me that at least we should abandon earlier tendencies to use it interchangeably with comparative public administration, and that we should reject any implication that the domain of comparative public administration is confined to issues of development administration, however defined.

This divergence does not mean, however, that significant shifts involving development administration are no longer relevant for comparative public administration. Strategies of management for technical assistance programs aimed at developmental objectives are of central concern to specialists in development administration, and continue to be of interest to those focusing on the overall comparison of national systems of administration.[131] Recent years have in fact produced a major reassessment and reorientation of technical assistance goals and strategies, resulting from mounting evidence that efforts to transfer administrative technologies have turned out often to have little discernible impact or else to have produced unanticipated negative consequences.

In simplest terms, what has occurred is a shift from one to another mode of thinking about development and development administration. Islam and Henault have labeled them model I and model II. The first model was associated with the technical assistance programs of the first two decades after World War II. The second is identified with the restructuring which has taken place since the late 1960s in the aid-giving projects of the World Bank and other multilateral development agencies, as well as of the U.S. Agency for International Development and other bilateral agencies. Both models can be thought of as appropriate under certain circumstances, rather than as competing alternatives or substitutes, one of which must always be chosen as preferred over the other, but the presumption is that the second is currently more suited to the requirements of developing countries.

The earlier Western model of development administration emphasized administrative reform in organizational structural arrangements, personnel management, budgeting, and other technical fields, and assumed that transference of administrative technology from one culture to another was feasible, without any necessary concurrent reformation in political, social, or economic conditions. It implied the separability of policy-making and policy execution, but its critics have argued that in fact it had an underlying ethnocentric bias based on Western values such as stress on economic growth as measured by gross national product (GNP), organizational and professional specialization, and an achievement orientation for determining social status – all of which were misrepresented as neutral indicators of development. The tendency was to concentrate on advances in administrative technology and isolate these from the activities really important for development, leading Islam and Henault to comment that "the hallmark of the Model I era was planning without implementation."[132]

The second and currently more acceptable model makes a more direct connection between public policy and administrative technology. It begins with policy choices and necessary institutional infrastructure and then moves to appropriate administrative technology. An early recognition of this tendency was shown in the work of Milton Esman and his associates, who focused on the process of "institution-building" through an interuniversity research program intended to systematize the cross-cultural analysis of institutions as appropriate units for comparison. During the 1960s empirical data were collected and analyzed for a number of countries, including Yugoslavia, Venezuela, Nigeria, Jordan, and Ecuador.[133] Jreisat described this model and suggested modifications of it intended to focus less exclusively on developing societies, to place more emphasis on cross-cultural comparison, and to draw more heavily on research in organization theory.[134] Siffin concurred as to the need for more knowledge to be marshaled about organizational design and the effects of alternative organizational arrangements, with special attention to environmental factors not intrinsic to the organizations themselves. He noted that traditional administrative technology efforts aimed more at maintenance needs than developmental needs, whereas the essence of development is not to maintain, but to effectively create. Typically, "the need for ability to design and implement arrangements involving technologies is greater than the need for the technologies," calling for a "developmental design strategy" focusing on the process of institution-building.[135]

More recently, increasing attention has been directed to the fundamental impact of cultural factors on development administration.[136] For example, as part of a symposium on cultural differences and development, Bjur and Zomorrodian presented what they described as "a conceptual framework for developing context-based, indigenous theories of administration." They assumed that "any administrative theory which pretends to describe existing reality, to guide administrative practice and clarify legitimate administrative objectives must necessarily spring from the cultural values which govern social interactions and dominate intra- and inter-organizational relationships," implying that different cultures have different value mixes, and that usually these differ from the mix in secular Western societies that have produced the most commonly accepted theories of administration. Hence when it comes to borrowing administrative techniques from outside a culture, they advised that unqualified adoption is never appropriate, but that the right approach is "self-conscious adaptation or, if the value mismatch is too marked, the invention of suitable tools and techniques consonant with the regnant value system."[137] Staudt, Huque, and I have all called attention to cultural factors at various levels of analysis (societal, bureaucratic, organizational, work group, etc.), and Staudt has pointed out both the importance of and the current limited knowledge about cultural influences at all levels.[138]

With this reorientation in approach has come a shift in emphasis for technical assistance projects to the concept of "basic needs," which is how Islam and Henault labeled their model II pattern of development. The policy objective is to make a direct attack on "absolute poverty," in World Bank terminology. The content of GNP becomes more important than its rate of growth, and the rural sector of the economy becomes the major focus for development. The aim is to bring about agricultural transformation through a decentralized system of small locally controlled organizations rather than through large-scale governmental organizations, requiring strengthening of local governments, increased local participation, creation of new intermediary organizations, and other major changes in sociopolitical conditions. The inference is that appropriate administrative technology will be much different under a model II approach. This requirement is stressed by Islam and Henault, who insist that a "new management strategy" must be formulated as developing countries focus on planned agricultural rural development as their primary policy goal.

Resultant current issues are whether such a new management strategy has been or can be devised, and to what extent and in what manner more developed countries should continue their efforts to transfer administrative technologies to those less developed. On the latter point, disillusionment with the record of experience is evident. Numerous technical assistance projects have admittedly failed, even when judged by the least demanding criteria as to their success.

Skeptics point out that supposedly policy-neutral assistance programs have often in fact bolstered and preserved, or protected beyond their time, repressive political regimes,[139] leading to the implication that administrative technology assistance activities are inevitably part and parcel of undesirable overall intervention in the affairs of other nations. Others, such as Esman, who is a knowledgeable and respected longtime student and practitioner of development assistance in public administration, react in more of an upbeat mood.[140] He sees the disillusionment among developmentalists in all fields as being replaced by a recognition of opportunities available within a more limited and realistic assessment of what is possible. Along with acknowledgment of the absence of general consensus on development strategies has come realization that modernization is not unilinear or inevitable, that technical assistance is a high-risk enterprise, "beset with daunting problems,"[141] and that public administration, in his words, "is a profoundly plural, not a universal phenomenon."[142] Consequently, he foresees demand for technical cooperation in public administration as likely to follow two parallel tracks. The first will be responses to requests for help in building basic governmental functions, which can be done basically in what he refers to as the well-established "Point IV mode," corresponding to model I of Islam and Henault. The second track, along the lines of their model II, will be the area of creative growth but also of problems, because it is characterized by high levels of uncertainty, severe resource limitations, and a need for creative administrative responses. Esman foresees a fresh orientation, with emphasis on innovation and experimentation rather than the transfer of known technologies.

In recent development administration literature, much attention is being devoted to devising management strategies for model IT-type projects.[143] A pronounced tendency is to formulate and lay out a suggested sequence of activities designed to avoid pitfalls and enhance prospects for success. One such effort, by Marc Lindenburg and Benjamin Crosby, focuses on the political dimension in managing development, and offers a model for political analysis designed to be useful for development administrators, supplemented by a number of case studies for use as teaching devices in applying the model.[144] Another, by Gregory D. Foster, presents an "administrative development intervention methodology," calling first for a demanding list of activities to clarify environmental and policy matters, followed by a strategy for implementation comprising two major stages – a *preparatory* stage and an *operational* stage – each with specified steps to be taken.[145] Dennis A. Rondinelli and Marcus D. Ingle, although they are concerned with and try to identify recurrent pervasive obstacles created by broad environmental or cultural factors, focus more directly on effective implementation of development plans and programs. They formulate a strategic approach to implementation consisting of six elements or steps to be taken: broad reconnaissance; strategic analysis and intervention; identification of the sequence for incremental interventions; engaged planning to protect and promote new programs; reliance on uncomplicated management procedures and use of indigenous institutions; and a facilitative style of management with less dependence on hierarchical controls and more reliance on local initiative and discretion.[146] Kathleen Staudt has pointed to the persistent dearth of participation by women in development activities, citing numerous specific case examples.[147] David C. Korten has stressed what he calls a "learning process approach" to replace the more usual "blueprint approach," and has attached great importance to voluntary action and the role of nongovernmental organizations (NGOs).[148] His emphasis is on leadership and teamwork at the local level, with reliance on help from knowledgeable outsiders. He perceives this process as ordinarily proceeding through time over three stages: learning to be *effective*, learning to be *efficient*, and learning to *expand*. Successful programs and their sustaining organizations were not "designed and implemented," but "evolved and grew." Instead of careful pre-planning of projects as the basic unit of development action, he has advocated a switch to "action-based capacity building" as an alternative to recurring failures in rural development activities crucial to progress in development administration.[149] In updating and elaborating on his people-centered approach after reviewing events through the 1980s, Korten has now reached the pessimistic conclusion that the "development industry" has become a "big business, preoccupied more with its own growth and imperatives than with the people it was originally created to serve. Dominated by professional financiers and technocrats, the development industry seeks to maintain an apolitical and value-free stance in dealing with what are, more than anything else, problems of power and values." The only hope he sees for dealing with the development crisis "rests with people who are driven by a strong social commitment rather than by the budgetary imperatives of huge global bureaucracies."[150] Hence, he stresses the potential role of voluntary NGOs, particularly those operating in the southern part of the globe, and presents an agenda for action during the 1990s.[151]

This sampling indicates common concerns but differences in response. This diversity is matched by the range of opinion as to how much progress has been made or can be expected in identifying appropriate strategies for managing development activities. Marcus Ingle is one of the most optimistic believers in the existence of a science of management from which such management technology can be derived. He advocates "a more generic and less contextual approach to development administration," claiming that its appropriateness "stems primarily from the fact that it is consistent with first principles, and only secondarily with the fact that it is situationally adapted. In fact, by definition the substantive core of appropriate management technology does not need to be adapted, it is universally applicable in any context."[152] He thinks that a preliminary technology based on such an approach has already evolved, and that prospects for future advances are excellent. Korten represents a much more cautious point of view. He faults the "blueprint approach" of models stressing definite goals, a definite time frame, and carefully specified resource requirements, because it is usually not well suited to the unpredictabilities of rural development activities. The implementing organizations in his preferred "learning process approach" are not valued for their ability to adhere to detailed prepared plans, but for having "a well-developed capacity for responsive and anticipatory adaptation."[153] He shows little confidence in the workability of universal or widely applicable management technology strategies. Esman also favors a pluralistic strategy of development that encourages the exploration of alternative channels for providing services through the use of "multiorganizational service networks,"[154] including contracting out to private enterprise and reliance on NGOs.

It is still much too early to pass judgment on the success or failure of the various proposed systematic approaches to the implementation of model II or second track development administration programs, but past experience would suggest that the better part of wisdom is to be modest rather than overconfident in predicting success.

Development administration thus is a topic exhibiting continual ferment and debate, with increasing tendencies to move toward greater autonomy as these issues are pursued. Nevertheless, the interests and concerns of development administration and core comparative public administration will continue to be intermingled.

Comparative Public Policy

Beginning in the mid-1970s, interest in comparative public policy has expanded enormously, paralleling in many ways the earlier history of the comparative public administration movement, both in achievements and uncertainties. The proliferation of studies in comparative public policy has resulted in numerous books, a large volume of journal articles (many in journals devoted exclusively to policy matters), graduate and undergraduate course offerings, and specialized panels and conferences sponsored by professional associations and other organizations.[155]

As had occurred previously in comparative public administration, this rapid growth has resulted in a diversity of approaches, leading to suggestions as to how the burgeoning output should be classified, intellectual debate as to whether consensus on a paradigm should be sought and if so what it should be, and proposals as to future research priorities. We can only highlight some of these issues, without treating them in detail.

The central focus is not in dispute. Comparative public policy, according to pioneers in the field, "is the cross-national study of how, why, and to what effect government policies are developed."[156] Although the research undertaken can be – and has – varied in emphasis, clearly the subject is more restricted than the coverage of either comparative politics viewed as the study of whole political systems, or comparative public administration viewed as concerned with their administrative subsystems.

Four substantive fields are emphasized in one major contribution to comparative policy research,[157] indicating major thrusts in the literature. These are environmental policy, education policy, economic policy, and social policy. In addition to examining the state of the art in each of these areas, the authors address issues of strategy, methodology, and application, and they comment on past results and future directions.

Although it has rapidly established its own divergent identity, comparative public policy is of great significance for us.[158] In the first place, it is the most impressive success story to date in applying on a comparative basis a major reorientation which has taken place in the United States, thus responding to the criticism that comparative studies have not kept pace with recent domestic trends. Second, comparative public policy research is also trying to cope with the dilemmas of dealing with cross-cultural factors, although in this case the sequence has been to move from more familiar American and European settings to the developing world, rather than the reverse order which was taken by the comparative administration movement.[159] Third, this subfield also confronts the familiar criticism that "the very existence of sharply different conceptualizations and research foci has severely inhibited cumulative scholarship,"[160] and that more unity of approach would be desirable.[161] Fourth, researchers are charged with producing studies that lack relevance for policy-makers and are chided for being overly fond of theorizing and speculating.[162] Finally, there is a similar ambiguity as to whether comparative public policy refers to comparisons among nation-states or more generally to use of a comparative methodology in public policy analysis.[163]

Efforts to tie together comparative studies in public policy and in public administration have been rare. Guy Peters has addressed the need he sees for more adequate conceptualization of the policy-making role of organizations in his contribution to the Ashford volume,[164] pointing out that a powerful policy-making role for the bureaucracy is probably a prerequisite for effective government in contemporary society, despite political pressure to minimize it, and that the crucial question is how to blend professional competence with mandates for policy change coming from elected politicians. Randall Baker has recently edited a volume intended to spearhead a major effort to introduce more comparative materials, including public policy components, into the curricula of public administration programs in the United States.[165] He deliberately uses the word "management" in the title instead of "administration" to stress the "applied and practical nature" of the undertaking, and because it connotes dynamism and change, but he explicitly says that this does not imply that government is a business.[166] The modules in this collection combine in about equal proportions what would usually be considered "administrative" (bureaucratic reform, public finance and budgeting, planning, intergovernmental relations) and "policy" (international trade, criminal justice, environmental protection, industrial competitiveness) matters. This may become a vehicle both for curricular reform to enhance comparative content and for bringing about closer ties between comparative public policy and other foci for comparison.

Core Comparative Public Administration

At the center of comparative studies in public administration during the past two decades have been several developments, which characterize the present situation and set the stage for the future as we near the end of the century.

One tendency has been to reappraise objectives for comparative administrative studies by scaling down somewhat claims for the attainment of scientific status and predictability of results from research efforts. Jonathan Bendor touched on these issues perceptively in a discussion of developmental versus evolutionary theories, in which he admits that evolutionary theory does have lower predictive power, but notes that this is not the only criterion of theoretical merit. Predictions from inadequate hypotheses may be precise but inaccurate. Explanatory power and predictive power are not the same; adequate explanation is not dependent on the capacity to predict correctly.

He mentions that biologists consider evolutionary theory adequate for the explanation of evolutionary processes, despite the fact that the theory generates only weak predictions, and suggests that social scientists might also settle for understanding rather than foresight.[167]

Related to this is recognition that comparative public administration not only has been and is in a pre-paradigmatic state, but is also likely to remain so for some time to come. No consensus has appeared bringing the coherence, purpose, and progress sought earlier by some. Diversity continues to be more descriptive of comparative studies in administration than does uniformity or orthodoxy. Those whose aim is the scientific testing of precisely stated hypotheses as a basis for prediction remain frustrated and unhappy about the rate of progress. I have argued earlier that escape from the kind of paradigmatic uncertainties long characteristic of the parent discipline of public administration is not required for comparative study and research, and that coercive superimposition of a feigned consensus would be futile and stifling.[168] There now seems to be more acceptance of the view that a real consensus will emerge if and when work done in the field leads to it in a cumulative fashion, but that premature urging of it as the top priority would be counterproductive.

During these same years, there is no question in my mind that there has been an increasing recognition of the bureaucratic model within middle-range theory as the dominant conceptual framework for comparative public administration. This emphasis on comparative studies of bureaucratic systems does not meet Kuhn's requirements for a scientific paradigm, but it does provide a focus that has proved its utility. No substitute has been suggested or advocated recently, to my knowledge. Meanwhile, most of the current output is based on this foundation in theory.

The growing volume of work in comparative public administration, much of it already published and some of it still in progress, is a notable feature of the current situation which contrasts with the lull of activity that was a cause of concern during the reappraisals made in the mid-1970s. Included in this output is periodical literature, which has continued to appear in a wide variety of professional journals.[169] In addition, numerous basic texts and several recent publications covering public administration generally include chapters or passages dealing with comparative administration.[170]

Some examples of this activity, more comprehensive in scope, are summarized at this point. Others, dealing with specific topics, regions,[171] or countries are referred to in subsequent chapters.

The most significant of these contributions in terms of its intent to assess the present state of affairs and prescribe for the future has been offered by

B. Guy Peters.[172] It should be pointed out immediately that Peters differs markedly from the rather rosy statement that I have just made concerning prospects in comparative public administration. Indeed, he says that his 1988 book is "about the apparent decline in the study of comparative public administration," which he describes as a field of inquiry in political science that "once displayed great promise and for some time made great strides," but "is now the concern of relatively few scholars ... and has become mired in endless descriptive studies of rather minute aspects of administrative structure or behavior in single countries, with little theoretical and conceptual development."[173] The validity of these judgments will be examined as we proceed. At this point, I want to concentrate on what I regard as more positive aspects of his analysis. First, he accepts, as his title indicates, that the comparison of public bureaucracies should be the principal objective; he is attempting "middle-range or institutional theories" while disclaiming any intent to "articulate an overarching paradigm for public administration." Second, he identifies "perhaps the first and most fundamental problem facing the comparative study of public administration" as being "the absence of any agreement as to what we are studying – as to what, in the language of the social sciences, constitutes the dependent variable." He points out that other institutions in government have readily available dependent variables, such as voting in legislatures and decisions in courts, but that such dependent variables have not been identified for public bureaucracies so as to permit use of "modern" social science techniques. Third, he selects four dependent variables, which he thinks will be useful in the process of cross-national comparison. These are (1) people who are public employees, (2) public sector organizations, (3) behavior within public organizations, and (4) the power of the civil service in making public policy. A chapter is devoted to each variable, and the purpose of the book is described by the author as "only to illustrate the ways in which each of them can be used."[174]

Other recent impressive additions to the literature are wide-ranging comparative surveys of public administration from a variety of perspectives. Donald C. Rowat and V. Subramaniam have edited similar volumes – one focusing on developed democracies and the other on developing countries.[175] Each contains contributions on specific countries by informed experts, plus chapters providing overviews of regions or related national systems and analyses of problems and emerging trends. Another valuable study is *Public Administration in World Perspective*, containing an essay on the state of the art in comparative administration by the editors, O. P. Dwivedi and Keith Henderson, a series of country or regional studies including both developed and developing areas, and an appraisal of future prospects by Gerald and

Naomi Caiden which is basically optimistic that a revitalization of comparative administration is occurring and which includes a list of suggestions as to areas "ripe for comparative treatment."[176] Ali Farazmand is the editor of two even more ambitious projects. One is a *Handbook of Comparative and Development Public Administration*,[177] with chapters on historical administrative systems, public administration in developed capitalist and socialist nations and in developing nations (on a regional basis), and analyses of administrative performance and political responsibility in a variety of social settings. The second, a *Handbook of Bureaucracy*,[178] is a compendium that includes historical and conceptual perspectives on bureaucracy and bureaucratic politics, chapters on a diversity of bureaucratic-societal relationships, and sections dealing with bureaucracy and bureaucratic politics organized by region. Two final examples are Baker's *Comparative Public Management*, already mentioned, and *Public Administration in the Global Village*,[179] edited by Jean-Claude Garcia-Zamor and Renu Khator, which combines several theoretical and conceptual chapters with case studies concerning development administration in different settings.

This wave of contributions is not without its share of criticisms, but the focus has shifted primarily to the issue of methodological sophistication from the broader array of shortcomings noted in earlier critiques.

Peters offers the most comprehensive brief as to this deficiency, its causes, its consequences, and its cure. The alleged deficiency, in short, is that comparative public administration has lagged far behind other areas in political science in progress toward meeting tests of scientific rigor as measured by the canons of normal social science. Some causes for this are examined, such as the absence of a useful theoretical language, the shortage of indicators, and the importance of "minute and subtle differences" in comparative administration.[180] The consequences are that comparative public administration does not conform "to the usual standards of scholarship in the contemporary social sciences,"[181] and must strive to "be made more a component of 'mainstream' political science."[182] Peters repeatedly contrasts progress in comparative public policy with this retardation in comparative public administration, accounting for it in part by "the presumed greater ease of measurement and hence the appearance of greater 'scientific rigor' in the comparative study of public policy."[183] The remedy proposed is to identify dependent variables such as those already mentioned, and to study them in ways that are both empirical and comparative, using quantitative information or systematic reasoning in conformity with modern social science requirements. Peters expresses the hope in his conclusion that the contents of his book "have advanced us at least a few yards down that long and difficult road."[184]

Without presenting a detailed analysis, I can summarize my reaction by saying that although Peters contends that the low status of comparative public administration is traceable to its failure to be sufficiently *both* empirical and comparative, and he seeks to remedy this, he seldom succeeds in accomplishing what he recommends. Being empirical is not the problem, but being comparative is. The comparisons that are made (this is acknowledged by the author and attributed to data constraints and his own knowledge) are almost completely limited to the United States and a few European countries – all Western industrialized democracies. Some models that he uses (such as those dealing with interactions between politicians and bureaucrats) seem to be applicable only to parliamentary or presidential democracies, and not to the much larger number of contemporary political entities which have regimes dominated by single parties or by professional bureaucrats. I have no doubt that he is to be commended and encouraged for what he has already done and proposes to do. However, his criteria for progress – that research must be empirical and quantitative, and hence limited to situations in which the database available for analysis is fully adequate – are not the same as mine, and they should not in my judgment be accepted as necessary requirements for legitimate efforts in comparative public administration. In my view, the best available approaches for the comparative study of public administration over the whole range of existing national political systems should be pursued, even though empirical and quantitative measurements are not always possible. If this means some loss of status or prestige in relation to comparative public policy or other fields of inquiry where such measurements are more readily available, so be it.[185]

These comments reflect the persistence of differences of opinion as to past accomplishments and future priorities in comparative studies of public administration. Nevertheless, my perception is that these differences are not as great as they once were, because of general acceptance (including by Peters and myself) of a primary focus on comparing public bureaucracies. In doing this, some may prefer comparisons that are more limited but more sophisticated methodologically, others may prefer comparisons that are more comprehensive even though less sophisticated. Both approaches may lead to worthwhile contributions.[186]

Another topic, which continues to be discussed, is the relationship between comparative public administration and the larger fields of public administration and political science. As long ago as 1976 Savage, Jun, and Riggs all questioned the virtue and feasibility of trying in the future to emphasize the separate identity of comparative public administration as a field of study. Savage, drawing a parallel with the effect of the behavioral movement on political science, argued that the impact of the comparative movement had been significant and lasting enough that a "movement" was no longer needed, because its concerns and perspectives had become a part of the broader disciplines. As he put it: "The movement's ten years are up and it passes. I judge that while it did not produce in sufficient ways to forestall its decline as a movement, its legacies are being absorbed into the larger Political Science and Public Administration. ... The problems, which spawned the movement, have not gone away. If anything, they have become exacerbated."[187] Jun expressed the view that comparative administration as an isolated field had served its purpose and should become an integral part of the larger field of public administration, which could be enriched by placing it in a world context.[188] Riggs also has foreseen convergence, but in the sense that comparative administration would become the master field within which American public administration would be only a subfield.[189] Peters agrees that the direction pointed out by Riggs "would certainly be the one offering the opportunity for the greatest theoretical development," and emphasizes how crucial it is "to foster more and better comparative studies."[190]

However expressed, I concur with the cardinal point that it is neither necessary nor feasible to strive for restoration of the degree of autonomy and separatism once characteristic of the burgeoning comparative public administration movement. The time has come to blend the comparative perspective with the traditionally parochial national emphasis of study and research in public administration. This promises to remedy some of the deficiencies in depth of analysis attributed to comparative efforts, but it also will enrich general public administration by widening the horizon of interest in such a way that understanding of one's own national system of administration will be enhanced by placing it in a cross-cultural setting.

Meanwhile, an overview of public administration from a comparative perspective cannot be undertaken without deciding upon a framework for presentation. It should be clear from this historical review of the evolution of comparative studies that systems of public administration in existing nation-states can only be treated comparatively after a choice of focus has been made among numerous and partially conflicting alternatives.

NOTES

1. Nicholas Henry, *Public Administration and Public Affairs*, 5th ed. (Englewood Cliffs, NJ: Prentice-Hall, 1992), Chapter 2, pp. 20–48.

2. Lennart Lundquist, "From Order to Chaos: Recent Trends in the Study of Public Administration," in Jan-Erik Lane, ed., *State and Market: The Politics of the Public and the Private* (London: Sage, 1985), Chapter 9, pp. 201–230. An excellent recent short summary is Donald F. Kettl, "Public Administration: The State of the Field," in Ada W. Finifter, ed., *Political Science: The State of the Discipline II* (Washington, DC: American Political Science Association, 1993), Chapter 16, pp. 407–428.

3. Fritz Morstein Marx, ed., *Elements of Public Administration*, 2nd ed. (Englewood Cliffs, NJ: Prentice-Hall, 1963), p. 4.

4. *Ibid.*, p. 6.

5. Paul H. Appleby, *Policy and Administration* (University, AL: University of Alabama Press, 1949).

6. James W. Davis Jr., *An Introduction to Public Administration: Politics, Policy, and Bureaucracy* (New York: Free Press, 1974), p. 4.

7. Harold Stein, ed., *Public Administration and Policy Development* (New York: Harcourt, Brace, and Company, 1952), p. xxvii. This case book, supplemented by other cases published by the Inter-University Case Program, has been *the primary* source of public administration cases used in the United States.

8. The main source book, containing papers presented at a conference in 1968, is Frank Marini, ed., *Toward a New Public Administration: The Minnowbrook Perspective* (Scranton, PA: Chandler Publishing Company, 1971). For a later presentation by a leading spokesman for this point of view, refer to H. George Frederickson, *New Public Administration* (University, AL: University of Alabama Press. 1980). A twentieth anniversary Minnowbrook conference was held in 1988, surveying trends during the intervening years. "Minnowbrook II: Changing Epochs of Public Administration," a symposium edited by Frederickson and Richard L. Mayer, based on papers presented at this conference, is in *Public Administration Review* 49, No. 2 (March/April 1989): 95–227.

9. Charles T. Goodsell, in his convenor's introduction to a panel on "The New Comparative Administration Applied to Service Delivery" at the 1980 Annual Conference of the American Society for Public Administration, and in "The New Comparative Administration: A Proposal," *International Journal of Public Administration* 3, No. 2 (1981): 143–155, has suggested that the scope of the term comparative administration should be enlarged to include comparisons at supranational and subnational levels of analysis, embracing "all studies of administrative phenomena where the comparative method – in some guise – is explicitly employed." This proposed extension of scope in defining comparative administration seems to me more confusing than helpful; therefore, I have retained the more accepted usage that focuses on cross-national comparisons. International administration, concerned with the administrative operations of agencies created by sovereign nation-states as instrumentalities for international or regional cooperation, is also outside the scope of this study, although comparative and international administration share many attributes and face numerous similar issues. For a discussion of connections between these two fields, see Ferrel Heady, "Issues in Comparative and International Administration," in Jack Rabin, W. Bartley Hildreth, and Gerald J. Miller, eds., *Handbook of Public Administration* (New York: Marcel Dekker, 1989), Chapter 15, pp. 499–521.

10. Daniel W. Martin, "Deja Vu: French Antecedents of American Public Administration," *Public Administration Review* 47, No. 4 (1987): 297–303.

11. For a fuller historical survey, see Ferrel Heady, "Comparative Public Administration in the United States," in Ralph C. Chandler, ed., *A Centennial History of the American Administrative State* (New York: Free Press, 1987), Chapter 15, pp. 477–508. Refer also to Fred W. Riggs, "The American Tradition in Comparative Administration," prepared for the 1976 National Conference of the American Society for Public Administration, mimeographed, 28 pp. For a recent critique of the "culture of modernity," see Guy B. Adams, "Enthralled with Modernity: The Historical Context of Knowledge and Theory Development in Public Administration," *Public Administration Review* 52, No. 4 (July/August 1992): 363–373.

12. Robert A. Dahi, "The Science of Public Administration: Three Problems," *Public Administration Review* 7, No. 1 (1947): 1–11, at p. 8.

13. Donald C. Rowat, ed., *The Ombudsman Plan: The Worldwide Spread of an Idea*, 2nd rev. ed. (Lanham, MD: University Press of America, 1985).

14. For descriptions and evaluations of this innovation, see Garth N. Jones, "Bureaucratic Structure and National Development Programs: The Indonesian Office of Junior Minister," in Krishna K. Tummala, ed., *Administrative Systems Abroad*, rev. ed. (Lanham, MD: University Press of America, 1982), Chapter 13, pp. 335–358; and "Boundary Spanning and Organizational Structure in National Development Programs: Indonesian Office of Junior Minister," *Chinese Journal of Administration* No. 33 (May 1982): 75–116.

15. For an overview, see Ezra N. Suleiman and John Waterbury, eds., *The Political Economy of Public Sector Reform and Privatization* (Boulder, CO: Westview Press, 1990). The pros and cons are analyzed perceptively in Donald F. Kettl, *Sharing Power: Public Governance and Private Markets* (Washington, DC: The Brookings Institution, 1993).

16. See Alfred Diamant, "The Relevance of Comparative Politics to the Study of Comparative Administration," *Administrative Science Quarterly* 5, No. 1 (1960): 87–112.

17. For recent overviews of comparative politics as a field of study, refer to Ronald H. Chilcote, *Theories of Comparative Politics: The Search for a Paradigm* (Boulder, CO: Westview Press, 1981); Howard J. Wiarda, ed., *New Directions in Comparative Politics* (Boulder, CO: Westview Press, 1985); Louis J. Canton and Andrew H. Ziegler Jr., eds., *Comparative Politics in the Post-Behavioral Era* (Boulder, CO: Lynne Rienner Publishers, 1988); Mattei Dogan and Dominique Pelassy, *How to Compare Nations*, 2nd ed. (Chatham, NJ: Chatham House Publishers, 1990); Martin C. Needler, *The Concepts of Comparative Politics* (New York: Praeger, 1991); John D. Nagle, *Introduction to Comparative Politics: Political System Performance in Three Worlds*, 3rd ed. (Chicago, IL: Nelson-Hall Publishers, 1992); Gabriel A. Almond, G. Bingham Powell Jr., and Robert J. Mundt, *Comparative Politics: A Theoretical Framework* (New York: HarperCollins, 1993); and Mattei Dogan and Ali Kazancigil, eds., *Comparing Nations: Concepts, Strategies, Substance* (Oxford: Basil Blackwell, 1994).

18. Robert E. Ward and Roy C. Macridis, eds., *Modern Political Systems: Asia* (Englewood Cliffs, NJ: Prentice-Hall, 1963), pp. 3–4.

19. "Comparison is significant only if it seeks to interpret political data in terms of hypotheses or theories. Interpretation must deal with institutions as they really function – which sometimes differs radically from the way in which they are supposed to function. It is also desirable that agreement be reached on the frame within which research is to be pursued. The comparative method thus requires an insistence on the scientific nature of inquiry, a focus on political behavior, and orientation of research within a broad analytic scheme." Bernard E. Brown, *New Directions in Comparative Politics* (New York: Asia Publishing House, 1962), pp. 3–4.

20. Gabriel A. Almond and James S. Coleman, eds., *The Politics of the Developing Areas* (Princeton, NJ: Princeton University Press, 1960), p. 7.

21. Ward and Macridis, *Modern Political Systems*, p. 8.

22. Herbert Kitschelt, "Political Regime Change: Structure and Process-Driven Explanations?" *American Political Science Review* 86, No. 4 (1992): 1028–1034, at p. 1028.

23. Martin Landau, "On the Use of Functional Analysis in American Political Science," *Social Research* 35, No. 1 (1968): 48–75, at p. 74.

24. Almond and Coleman, "Introduction: A Functional Approach to Comparative Politics," *The Politics of the Developing Areas*, pp. 3–64. For later reformulations and applications of this approach, see Gabriel Almond, "A Developmental Approach to Political Systems," *World Politics* 17, No. 2 (1965): 183–214; Gabriel A. Almond and G. Bingham Powell Jr., *Comparative Politics: System, Process, and Policy*, 2nd ed. (Glenview, IL: Scott, Foresman and Company, 1978); and Gabriel A. Almond and G. Bingham Powell, Jr., *Comparative Politics Today*, 5th ed. (New York: HarperCollins, 1992).

25. Almond and Coleman, *The Politics of the Developing Areas*, p. v.

26. *Ibid.*, p. 11.

27. Leonard Binder, *Iran. Political Development in a Changing Society* (Berkeley, CA: University of California Press, 1962), pp. 7–10.

28. Fred W. Riggs, *Administration in Developing Countries: The Theory of Prismatic Society* (Boston: Houghton Mifflin, 1964), pp. 456–457.

29. Major sources include: J. P. Nettl, "The State as a Conceptual Variable," *World Politics* 20 (1968): 559–592; Alfred Stepan, *State and Society: Peru in Comparative Perspective* (Princeton, NJ: Princeton University Press, 1978): Eric Nordlinger, *On the Autonomy of the Democratic State* (Cambridge, MA: Harvard University Press, 1981); Stephen Krasner, "Approaches to the State: Alternative Conceptions and Historical Dynamics," *Comparative Politics* 16 (1984): 223–246; James G. March and Johan P. Olsen. "The New Institutionalism: Organizational Factors in Political Life," *American Political Science Review* 78, No. 3 (1984); Peter Evans, Dietrich Rueschemeyer, and Theda Skocpoi, eds., *Bringing the State Back in* (Cambridge, MA: Harvard University Press, 1985); Metin Heper, ed., *The State and Public Bureaucracies: A Comparative Perspective* (Westport, CT: Greenwood Press, 1987); Rogers M. Smith, "Political Jurisprudence, the 'New Institutionalism,' and the Future of Public Law," *American Political Science Review* 82, No. 1 (1988): 89–106; Gabriel A. Almond, "The Return to the State," *American Political Science Review* 82, No. 3 (1988): 853–874; Eric A. Nordlinger, Theodore J. Lowi, and Sergio Fabbrini, "The Return to the State: Critiques," *American Political Science Review* 82, No. 3 (1988): 875–901; Robert H. Jackson, "Civil Science: Comparative

Jurisprudence and Third World Government," *Governance* 1, No. 4 (1988): 380–414; James W. Fesler, "The State and its Study," *PS: Political Science & Politics* 21, No. 4 (1988): 891–901; James A. Caporaso, ed., *The Elusive State: International and Comparative Perspectives* (Newbury Park, CA: Sage, 1989); James G. March and Johan P. Olsen, *Rediscovering Institutions: The Organizational Basis of Politics* (New York: Free Press, 1989); Szymon Chodak, *The New State. Etatization of Western Societies* (Boulder, CO: Lynne Rienner, 1989); Milton J. Esman, "The State, Government Bureaucracies, and Their Alternatives," in Ali Farazmand, ed., *Handbook of Comparative and Development Public Administration* (New York: Marcel Dekker, 1991), Chapter 33, pp. 457–465; Lucian W. Pye, "The Myth of the State: The Reality of Authority," in Ramesh K. Arora, ed., *Politics and Administration in Changing Societies: Essays in Honour of Professor Fred W. Riggs* (New Delhi: Associated Publishing House, 1991), Chapter 2, pp. 35–49; Timothy Mitchell, "The Limits of the State: Beyond Statist Approaches and Their Critics," *American Political Science Review* 85, No. 1 (1991): 77–96; John Bendix, Bertell Oilman, Bartholomew H. Sparrow, and Timothy P. Mitchell, "Going Beyond the State?" *American Political Science Review* 86, No. 4 (1992): 1007–1021; and Robert W. Jackman, *Power without Force: The Political Capacity Nation-States* (Ann Arbor, MI: The University of Michigan Press, 1993).

30. Proposal for an International Institute of Comparative Government (Lausanne: IICG, 1986).

31. Fesler, "The State and its Study," p. 894.

32. Almond, "The Return to the State," p. 872.

33. Fesler, "The State and its Study," p. 897.

34. Jackson, "Civil Science: Comparative Jurisprudence and Third World Governance," p. 380. Refer also to Jackson's earlier paper, "Civil Science: A Rule-Based Paradigm for Comparative Government," prepared for the 1987 Annual Conference of the American Political Science Association, mimeographed, 25 pp. A similar perspective, applauding more attention to the role of normative ideas in law, is taken by Rogers M. Smith in "Political Jurisprudence, the 'New Institutionalism,' and the Future of Public Law."

35. Jackson, "Civil Science: Comparative Jurisprudence and Third World Governance," p. 408.

36. Nettl, "The State as a Conceptual Variable," p. 592.

37. Heper, *The State and Public Bureaucracies.*

38. Pye, "The Myth of the State: The Reality of Authority," pp. 35, 46.

39. Mitchell, "The Limits of the State," p. 77.

40. Jackman, *Power without Force.*

41. The best comprehensive bibliographical sources are Ferrel Heady and Sybil L. Stokes, *Comparative Public Administration: A Selective Annotated Bibliography,* 2nd ed. (Ann Arbor, MI: Institute of Public Administration, The University of Michigan, 1960) for the earlier period; and Mark W. Huddleston, *Comparative Public Administration: An Annotated Bibliography* (New York: Garland Publishing, 1983) for the years 1962–1981. More specialized sources on important segments of the comparative administration literature are Allan A. Spitz and Edward W. Weidner, *Development Administration. An Annotated Bibliography* (Honolulu: East-West Center Press, 1963); and Manindra K. Mohapatra and David R. Hager, *Studies of Public*

Bureaucracy: A Select Cross-National Bibliography (Monticello, IL: Council of Planning Librarians, Exchange Bibliography #13851387, 1977).

42. These included Ferret Heady, "Comparative Public Administration: Concerns and Priorities," in Ferrel Heady and Sybil L. Stokes, eds., *Papers in Comparative Public Administration* (Ann Arbor, MI: Institute of Public Administration, The University of Michigan, 1962); and Dwight Waldo, *Comparative Public Administration: Prologue, Problems, and Promise* (Chicago: Comparative Administration Group, American Society for Public Administration, 1964). Earlier treatments *are* cited in these essays.

43. Paul Meyer, *Administrative Organization: A Comparative Study of the Organization of Public Administration* (London: Stevens & Sons, 1957); Brian Chapman, *The Profession of Government* (London: George Allen & Unwin, 1959); the parts dealing with administration in Herman Finer, *Theory and Practice of Modern Government*, rev. ed. (New York: Holt, Rinehart & Winston, 1949); Fritz Morstein Marx, *The Administrative State* (Chicago: University of Chicago Press, 1957).

44. This research design is discussed in Fred W. Riggs, "Relearning an Old Lesson: The Political Context of Development Administration," *Public Administration Review* 25, No. 1 (1965): 72–75.

45. Leading early expositions of this view are found in Edward W. Weidner, "Development Administration: A New Focus for Research," in Heady and Stokes, eds., *Papers*, pp. 97–115; Irving Swerdlow, ed., *Development Administration Concepts and Problems* (Syracuse, NY: Syracuse University Press, 1963); and Milton J. Esman, "The Politics of Development Administration," in John D. Montgomery and William J. Siffin, eds., *Approaches to Development: Politics, Administration and Change* (New York: McGraw-Hill, 1966), pp. 59–112. A later valuable contribution, focusing on the developmental role of the civil service in India, was V. A. Pai Panandiker and S. S. Kshirsagar, *Bureaucracy and Development Administration* (New Delhi: Centre for Policy Research, 1978).

46. In Heady and Stokes, *Papers*, p. 99.

47. *Ibid.*, pp. 103, 107.

48. Waldo, *Comparative Public Administration*, p. 27.

49. Swerdlow, *Development Administration*, p. xiv.

50. Waldo, *Comparative Public Administration*, p. 15.

51. Robert V. Presthus, "Behavior and Bureaucracy in Many Cultures," *Public Administration Review* 19, No. 1 (1959): 25–35.

52. Diamant, "The Relevance of Comparative Politics," pp. 87–112.

53. In Heady and Stokes, *Papers*, p. 4.

54. See Note 28.

55. "An Information-Energy Model," in Heady and Stokes, eds., *Papers*, pp. 37–57.

56. Dorsey, "The Bureaucracy and Political Development in Vietnam," in Joseph LaPalombara, ed., *Bureaucracy and Political Development* (Princeton, NJ: Princeton University Press, 1964), pp. 318–359.

57. William M. Berenson, "Testing the Information-Energy Model," *Administration and Society* 9, No. 2 (August 1977): 139–158. For a commentary raising questions both as to the model itself and the adequacy of Berenson's test of it, see

Charles T. Goodsell, "The Information-Energy Model and Comparative Administration," *Administration and Society* 9, No. 2 (August 1977): 159–168.

58. Waldo, *Comparative Public Administration*, p. 22.

59. Presthus, "Behavior and Bureaucracy in Many Cultures," p. 26.

60. See, for example, Brown, *New Directions*, pp. 10–11.

61. Waldo, *Comparative Public Administration*, p. 24.

62. Morroe Berger, *Bureaucracy and Society in Modern Egypt* (Princeton, NJ: Princeton University Press, 1957).

63. LaPalombara, *Bureaucracy and Political Development.*

64. Fred W. Riggs, "Trends in the Comparative Study of Public Administration," *International Review of Administrative Sciences* 28, No. 1 (1962): 9–15.

65. *Ibid.*, p. 10.

66. *Ibid.*, p. II.

67. *Ibid.*, p. 9.

68. *Ibid.*, p. 15.

69. An informative general treatment of the evolution of comparative administration up to 1970 is available in Ramesh K. Arora, *Comparative Public Administration* (New Delhi: Associated Publishing House, 1972), Chapter 1, pp. 5–29.

70. Garth N. Jones, "Frontiersmen in Search for the 'Lost Horizon': The State of Development Administration in the 1960s," *Public Administration Review* 36, No. I (1976): 99–110, at pp. 99–100.

71. William J. Siffin, "Two Decades of Public Administration in Developing Countries," *Public Administration Review* 36, No. I (1976): 61–71, at p. 61.

72. *Ibid.*, pp. 64–66.

73. Jones, "Frontiersmen in Search," pp. 105–106.

74. Peter Savage, "Optimism and Pessimism in Comparative Administration," *Public Administration Review* 36, No. 4 (1976): 415–423, at pp. 419–420.

75. Fred W. Riggs, *Frontiers of Development Administration* (Durham, NC: Duke University Press, 1970), Copyright 1971 by Duke University Press.

76. *Ibid.*, p. 6.

77. *Ibid.*, pp. 3, 6, 7.

78. Arora, *Comparative Public Administration*, p. 37.

79. Savage, "Optimism and Pessimism," p. 419.

80. James Heaphey, "Comparative Public Administration: Comments on Current Characteristics," *Public Administration Review* 29, No. 3 (1968): 242–249, at pp. 242–243.

81. Jamil E. Jreisat, "Synthesis and Relevance in Comparative Public Administration," *Public Administration Review* 35, No. 6 (1975): 663–671, at p. 667.

82. Riggs, *Frontiers of Development Administration*, p. 7. Paradigm is used here in the meaning suggested by Thomas S. Kuhn in *The Structure of Scientific Revolution*, 2nd ed. (Chicago: University of Chicago Press, 1970). He says (pp. 10, 11) that "the study of paradigms prepares the student for membership in the particular scientific community with which he will later practice. ... Men whose research is based on shared paradigms are committed to the same rules and standards for scientific practice. That commitment and the apparent consensus it produces are prerequisite for normal science." He regards social sciences generally as in a preparadigmatic stage, as compared to the physical sciences.

83. Savage, "Optimism and Pessimism," p. 417.

84. Jones, "Frontiersmen in Search," p. 101. POSDCORB was a word coined by Luther Gulick as an abbreviation for Planning, Organizing, Staffing, Directing, Coordinating, Reporting, and Budgeting.

85. Savage, "Optimism and Pessimism," p. 417.

86. *Ibid.*

87. Lee Sigelman, "In Search of Comparative Administration," *Public Administration Review* 36, No. 6 (1976): 621–625, at p. 623.

88. *Ibid.*, p. 625.

89. J. Fred Springer, "Empirical Theory and Development Administration: Prologues and Promise," *Public Administration Review* 36, No. 6 (1976): 636–641, at p. 636.

90. Keith Henderson, "Comparative Public Administration: The Identity Crisis," *Journal of Comparative Administration* 1, No. I (May 1969): 65–84, at p. 75.

91. Sigelman, "In Search of Comparative Administration," p. 622.

92. Jones, "Frontiersmen in Search," p. 102.

93. Jreisat, "Synthesis and Relevance," p. 655.

94. Savage, "Optimism and Pessimism," p. 417.

95. Springer, "Empirical Theory and Development Administration," p. 636.

96. Sigclman, "In Search of Comparative Administration," p. 623.

97. Jong S. Jun, "Renewing the Study of Comparative Administration: Some Reflections on the Current Possibilities," *Public Administration Review* 36, No. 6 (1976): 641–647, at p. 645.

98. Jones, "Frontiersmen in Search," p. 103.

99. Brian Loveman, "The Comparative Administration Group: Development Administration, and Antidevelopment," *Public Administration Review* 36, No. 6 (1976): 616–621.

100. *Ibid.*, p. 619.

101. Jones, "Frontiersmen in Search," p. 103.

102. *Ibid.*, p. 102.

103. B. B. Schaffer, "Comparisons, Administration, and Development," *Political Studies* 19, No. 3 (September 1971): 327–337, at p. 330.

104. Loveman, "The Comparative Administration Group," pp. 618–619.

105. Jreisat, "Synthesis and Relevance," pp. 666–667.

106. Savage, "Optimism and Pessimism," pp. 420–422.

107. Jreisat, "Synthesis and Relevance," p. 665.

108. *Ibid.*, p. 663.

109. Sigelman, "In Search of Comparative Administration," p. 624.

110. Sec Jun, "Renewing the Study of Comparative Administration," pp. 643–644; Richard Ryan, "Comparative-Development Administration," *Southern Review of Public Administration* 6, No. 2 (1982): 188–203.

111. Sigelman, "In Search of Comparative Administration," p. 623.

112. Springer, "Empirical Theory and Development Administration," pp. 639–640. For a published version of the latter study, see Richard W. Gable and J. Fred Springer, "Administrative Implications of Development Policy: A Comparative Analysis of Agricultural Programs in Asia," *Economic Development and Cultural Change* 27, No. 4 (July 1979): 687–704.

113. Sigelman, "In Search of Comparative Administration," pp. 623–625.
114. Jun, "Renewing the Study of Comparative Administration," pp. 645–646. A later example was the interest shown in other countries, including the United States, concerning Japanese practices in achieving worker satisfaction, setting up quality circles, conducting research and development activities, and contributing in other ways to Japan's success in competing in the world market. See, for example, William Ouchi, *Theory Z: How American Business Can Meet the Japanese Challenge* (New York: Addison-Wesley, 1981).
115. Jreisat, "Synthesis and Relevance," p. 668.
116. Jorge I. Tapia-Videla, "Understanding Organizations and Environments: A Comparative Perspective," *Public Administration Review* 36, No. 6 (1976): 631–636.
117. Peter Cleaves, *Bureaucratic Politics and Administration in Chile* (Berkeley, CA: University of California Press, 1975).
118. As Joel S. Migdal has observed, this term was later transformed "from one concerned parochially with traditional Iberian and Latin American societies to one dealing with the dynamics of change in a number of regions." See "Studying the Politics of Development and Change: The State of the Art," in Ada W. Finifter, ed., *Political Science: The State of the Discipline* (Washington, DC: The American Political Science Association, 1983), pp. 309–338, at p. 319. Hence it will be useful to us later in the classification of political regime types in developing countries.
119. For important examples of this literature, see Yehezkel Dror, *Public Policymaking Reexamined* (San Francisco: Chandler Publishing Company, 1968); Thomas R. Dye, *Understanding Public Policy*, 3rd ed. (Englewood Cliffs, NJ: Prentice-Hall, 1978); and Aaron Wildavsky, *Speaking Truth to Power, The Art and Craft of Policy Analysis* (Boston: Little, Brown and Company, 1979).
120. Jun, "Renewing the Study of Comparative Administration," p. 646.
121. These matters are discussed in my unpublished paper, "American Public Administration in Cultural Perspective: Lessons for and Lessons from Other Cultures," in more detail than is possible here. Recent published summaries of various views about development administration include: Ahmed Shafiqul Huque, *Paradoxes in Public Administration: Dimensions of Development* (Dhaka, Bangladesh: University Press Limited, 1990), pp. 112–114, 150–151; William J. Siffin, "The Problem of Development Administration," in Ali Farazmand, ed., *Handbook of Comparative and Development Public Administration* (New York: Marcel Dekker, 1991), Chapter 1, pp. 5–13; and H. K. Asmeron and R. B. Jam, "Politics and Administration: Some Conceptual Issues," in Asmeron and Jam, eds., *Politics, Administration and Public Policy in Developing Countries: Examples from Africa, Asia and Latin America* (Amsterdam: VU University Press, 1993), Chapter 1, pp. 1–15.
122. Siffin, "The Problem of Development Administration," p. 9.
123. George Gant, *Development Administration: Concepts, Goals, Methods* (Madison, WI: The University of Wisconsin Press, 1979).
124. "There is not a fixed point at which a people, region, or country passes from a state of underdevelopment to a state of development. The relative condition of development, rather, is comparative and ever changing – it fluctuates according to what is needed, what is possible, and what is desired. Development is relative also in terms of the possible; it fluctuates according to what is feasible at any particular time. A country which utilizes its resources effectively is considered to be more developed

than a country which does not." *Ibid.*, p. 7. Presumably a country, which utilizes its resources with 100 percent efficiency, could be considered fully developed. Obviously no country qualifies or is likely to qualify. More recent commentators concur. Milton Esman concedes that "the concept of development has been and remains imprecise," but says that "it connotes steady progress toward improvement in the human condition; reduction and eventual elimination of poverty, ignorance, and disease; and expansion of well-being and opportunity for all. It entails rapid change, but change alone is insufficient; it must be directed *to specific* ends. Development involves societal transformation – political, social, and cultural as well as economic; it implies modernization – secularization, industrialization, and urbanization – but not necessarily Westernization. It is multi-dimensional, with scholars and practitioners disagreeing, however, on relative emphasis, priority, and timing." *Management Dimensions of Development. Perspectives and Strategies* (West Hartford, CT: Kumarian Press, 1991), p. 5. H. K. Asmeron and R. B. Jam state that the concept of development "refers to the changes and improvements that have to be made in the socio-economic and political aspirations of society as integral components of the nation-building process. In particular, development is closely associated with nationally and locally initiated concrete socio-economic programmes and projects and with the creation of national and grassroots organizations in which the people can meaningfully participate in the formulation and implementation of policies." "Politics and Administration," p. 5.

125. Gant, *Development Administration*, pp. 19–21.

126. Nasir Islam and Georges M. Henault, "From GNP to Basic Needs: A Critical Review of Development Administration," *International Review of Administrative Sciences* 45, No. 3 (1979): 253–267, at p. 258.

127. Asmeron and Jam, "Politics and Administration," p. 5.

128. Huque, *Paradoxes in Public Administration*, pp. 113–114.

129. "Principles of administration developed in the West are seldom relevant to the needs and circumstances prevailing in the developing world. The two types of societies vary, often to a considerable degree, in almost all respects. ... Principles and procedures aimed at efficiency and economy may turn out to be counterproductive when applied to different circumstances. This represents the principal paradox of administration viewed in terms of development." *Ibid.*, pp. 150–151.

130. Gant, *Development Administration*, p. 21.

131. For a detailed chronological review of the links between comparative public administration and U.S. programs of foreign aid, see George Guess, "Comparative and International Administration," in Rabin, Hildreth, and Miller, eds., *Handbook of Public Administration*, Chapter 14, pp. 477–497.

132. Islam and Henault, "From GNP to Basic Needs," p. 257.

133. W. Blase, *Institution Building: A Source Book* (Beverly Hills, CA: Sage, 1973).

134. Jreisat, "Synthesis and Relevance," pp. 668–670.

135. Siffin, "Two Decades of Public Administration," pp. 68–70.

136. Wesley E. Bjur and Asghar Zomorrodian, "Towards Indigenous Theories of Administration: An International Perspective," *International Review of Administrative Sciences* 52, No. 4 (1986): 397–420; A. S. Huque, *Paradoxes in Public Administration*, "Administrative Behaviour Across Cultures," Chapter 3, pp. 65–70; Ferrel Heady, "The Cultural Dimension in Comparative Administration," in Arora, ed.,

Politics and Administration in Changing Societies, Chapter 5, pp. 89–100; Kathleen Staudt, *Managing Development: State, Society, and International Contexts* (Newbury Park, CA: Sage, 1991). Part I, Chapter 3, "The Cultural Context," pp. 35–61.

137. Bjur and Zomorrodian, "Toward Indigenous Theories of Administration," pp. 397, 400, 412.

138. "Attention to culture is fundamental to development work. Many levels of culture are part of that work, from the national level, to ethnic and class levels, to gender, organization, and disciplinary. Each cultural level has its insights and applications, but caveats about each level exist as well." Staudt, *Managing Development,* p. 56.

139. South Korea, Chile, Argentina, and Iran were cited as showcase examples before the political reforms that since have occurred in each case. For an example of soul-searching by Americans concerning Iranian public administration assistance projects during the regime of the Shah, see the following articles in *Public Administration Review* 40, No. 5 (1980); John L. Seitz, "The Failure of U.S. Technical Assistance in Public Administration: The Iranian Case," pp. 407–413; Frank P. Sherwood, "Learning from the Iranian Experience," pp. 413–418; William J. Siffin, "The Sultan, the Wise Men, and the Fretful Mastodon: A Persian Fable," pp. 418–421; and John L. Seitz, "Iran and the Future of U.S. Technical Assistance: Some Afterthoughts," pp. 432–433.

140. See Esman's earlier article, "Development Assistance in Public Administration: Requiem or Renewal," *Public Administration Review* 40, No. 5 (1980): 426–431; and his more recent book, *Management Dimensions of Development.*

141. Esman, *Management Dimensions of Development,* p. 160.

142. Esman, "Development Assistance in Public Administration," p. 427.

143. For a brief review, see George Honadle, "Development Administration in the Eighties: New Agendas or Old Perspectives?" *Public Administration Review* 42, No. 2 (1982): 174–179. For fuller treatments, refer to Coralie Bryant and Louise O. White, *Management Development in the Third World* (Boulder, CO: Westview Press, 1982); John E. Kerrigan and Jeff S. Luke, *Management Training Strategies for Developing Countries* (Boulder, CO: Lynne Rienner Publishers, 1987); Dennis A. Rondinelli, *Development Administration and U.S. Aid Policy* (Boulder, CO: Lynne Rienner Publishers, 1987); Louise O. White, *Implementing Policy Reforms in LDCs: A Strategy for Designing and Effecting Change* (Boulder, CO: Lynne Rienner Publishers, 1990); Esman, *Management Dimensions of Development;* and Staudt, *Managing Development.*

144. *Managing Development: The Political Dimension* (West Hartford, CT: Kumarian Press, 1981).

145. "A Methodological Approach to Administrative Development Intervention," *International Review of Administrative Sciences* 46, No. 3 (1980): 237–243.

146. *Improving the implementation of Development Programs: Beyond Administrative Reform,* SICA Occasional Papers Series, No. 10 (Washington, DC: American Society for Public Administration, 1981, mimeographed), 25 pp.

147. Staudt, see the index heading "Women in administration" in her book, *Managing Development.*

148. Korten, see his influential article, "Community Organization and Rural Development: A Learning Process Approach," *Public Administration Review* 40, No. 5

(1980): 480–511; and his most recent book, *Getting to the 21st Century: Voluntary Action and the Global Agenda* (West Hartford, CT: Kumarian Press, 1990).

149. Korten, "Community Organization and Rural Development," p. 502.

150. Korten, *Getting to the 21st Century*, p. ix.

151. For another work devoted to the contributions of NGOs, refer to Thomas F. Carroll, *Intermediary NGOs. The Supporting Link in Grassroots Development* (West Hartford, CT: Kumarian Press, 1992).

152. "Appropriate Management Technology: A Development Management Perspective," prepared for the 1981 National Conference of the American Society for Public Administration, mimeographed, 23 pp. at p. 17.

153. "Community Organization and Rural Development," p. 498.

154. Esman, refer to his *Management Dimensions of Development*, especially Chapters 5 and 6.

155. For valuable surveys of these accomplishments and problems during the formative stage, see Keith M. Henderson, "From Comparative Public Administration to Comparative Public Policy," *International Review of Administrative Sciences* 47, No. 4 (1981): 356–364; and M. Donald Hancock, "Comparative Public Policy: An Assessment," pp. 283–308, in Finifter, ed., *Political Science* (includes a select bibliography). For more recent comprehensive surveys of the field, refer to Douglas E. Ashford, ed., *History and Context in Comparative Public Policy* (Pittsburgh, PA: University of Pittsburgh Press, 1992); and Stuart S. Nagel, ed., *Encyclopedia of Policy Studies*, 2nd ed., revised and expanded (New York, NY: Marcel Dekker, 1994).

156. Arnold J. Heidenheimer, Hugh Heclo, and Carolyn Teich Adams, *Comparative Public Policy: The Politics of Social Choice in Europe and America* (New York: St. Martin's Press, 1975), p. i.

157. Meinolf Dierkes, Hans N. Weiler, and Ariane Berthoin Antal, eds., *Comparative Policy Research: Learning from Experience* (New York: St. Martin's Press, 1987).

158. This mutuality of concerns is not always acknowledged by writers in comparative public policy. As Naomi Caiden points out in her review of *Comparative Policy Research* (in *Public Administration Review* 48, No. 5 (1988): 932–933), this book makes no reference to the work of the Comparative Administration Group or its successors, and dismisses public administration as "ethnocenuic and parochial," p. 18.

159. Hancock estimated that approximately 70 percent of policy analysis work had dealt with advanced industrial democracies of Western Europe and North America, as contrasted with about 10 percent in either Latin America or Asia, and almost none in the Middle East and Africa ("Comparative Public Policy: An Assessment," p. 299). Hugh Heclo, in another review of *Comparative Policy Research* (in *American Political Science Review* 82, No. 2 (1988): 652–653), makes this relevant comment: "We should worry more about the parochialism in our choice of countries and the true equivalency of issues in different national settings."

160. Hancock, "Comparative Public Policy," p. 293.

161. "The aspirations for comparative policy research have been set high, and understandably results have fallen short. There are plenty of data, and even some theorizing, but the approach has not been systematic. It has been difficult to control

variables in comparative context, and differences come to overwhelm similarities. Theoretical assumptions diverge. Countries for study are chosen accidentally. Studies are often descriptive and lack theoretical interest. American methods and concepts are uncritically transferred to other contexts. Complexity and uncertainty defeat reliable prediction. Values and preferences pervade and influence analysis. Lack of a general theoretical framework hinders cumulation of research results." This is Naomi Caiden's summary of the situation in her review of *Comparative Policy Research* in *Public Administration Review*, previously cited. She goes on to observe: "All of this no doubt sounds familiar. The literature of comparative public administration is permeated with discussions of precisely these problems."

162. Heclo's review of *Comparative Policy Research* in *American Political Science Review*, previously cited, includes this tart observation: "Students of comparative public policy have enough theories, hypotheses, methodological tools, and conferencing opportunities to keep them going into the next century. What they do not have are decent data."

163. This was reflected, for example, in the scope statements of program sections for the 1983 annual meeting of the American Political Science Association, with one on public policy analysis and another on comparative politics: public policy. The issue is also mentioned by Henderson, "From Comparative Public Administration to Comparative Public Policy," p. 364.

164. Guy Peters, "Public Policy and Public Bureaucracy," in Ashford, ed., *History and Context in Comparative Public Policy*, Part III, Chapter 13, pp. 283–315.

165. Randall Baker, ed., *Comparative Public Management. Putting U.S. Public Policy and Implementation in Context* (Westport, CT: Praeger, 1994).

166. *Ibid.*, p. 7.

167. Jonathan Bendor, "A Theoretical Problem in Comparative Administration," *Public Administration Review* 36, No. 6 (1976): 626–630.

168. See my article, "Comparative Administration: A Sojourner's View," *Public Administration Review* 38, No. 4 (1978): 358–365, at p. 364.

169. The most comprehensive survey of this periodical literature is a content analysis of 253 articles published in 20 journals during the years 1982–1986. The investigators concluded that the literature is indeed substantial, and that it demonstrates the continued vitality of comparative public administration but also its lack of a clear identity. Important characteristics noted are "a significant practitioner component, substantial orientation towards policy recommendations, a relative paucity of theory-testing studies, wide and mature coverage of a range of topics, and methodological practices that seem slightly better than in the past but still far from ideal." See Montgomery Van Wart and N. Joseph Cayer, "Comparative Public Administration: Defunct, Dispersed, or Redefined?" *Public Administration Review* 50, No. 2 (March/April 1990): 238–248.

170. Examples include Chandler, *A Centennial History of the American Administrative State*; Rabin, Hildreth, and Miller, *Handbook of Public Administration*; Naomi B. Lynn and Aaron Wildavsky, eds., *Public Administration: The State of the Discipline* (Chatham, NJ: Chatham House Publishers, 1990); and Richard J. Stillman II, *Preface to Public Administration. A Search for Themes and Direction* (New York: St. Martin's Press, 1991).

171. A survey of administrative research in Europe since 1980, by Hans-Ulrich Derlien, concludes that secondary analysis of comparable national studies in subfields such as organizational structure and personnel policies is quite common, but that there has been a scarcity in research that is *"comparative by design* involving data collection in two or more countries." See Derlien, "Observations on the State of Comparative Administration Research in Europe – Rather Comparable than Comparative," *Governance* 5, No. 3 (July 1992): 279–311 (Based on Ferrel Heady revised 6th edition of *Public Administration: A Comparative Perspectives*, New York: Marcel Dekker, 2001).

172. His views are presented most fully in *Comparing Public Bureaucracies: Problems of Theory and Method* (Tuscaloosa, AL: The University of Alabama Press, 1988); and more briefly and recently in "Theory and Methodology in the Study of Comparative Public Administration," in Baker, ed., *Comparative Public Management*, Chapter 6, pp. 67–91.

173. Peters, *Comparing Public Bureaucracies*, p. xiii.

174. *Ibid.*, pp. 2, 13, 24.

175. Donald C. Rowat, ed., *Public Administration in Developed Democracies. A Camparatil'e Study* (New York: Marcel Dekker, 1988); and V. Subramaniam, ed., *Public Administration in the Third World: An international Handbook* (Westport, CT: Greenwood Press, 1990).

176. O. P. Dwivedi and Keith Henderson, eds., *Public Administration in World Perspective* (Iowa City: Iowa State University Press, 1990).

177. Ali Farazmand, ed., *Handbook of Comparative and Development Public Administration* (New York: Marcel Dekker, 1991).

178. Ali Farazmand, ed., *Handbook of Bureaucracy* (New York: Marcel Dekker, 1994).

179. Baker, *Comparative Public Management*.

180. Peters, *Comparing Public Bureaucracies*, pp. 22–24.

181. *Ibid.*, p. xiv.

182. *Ibid.*, p. 13.

183. *Ibid.*, p. 12. Peters does not cite specific examples of successful comparative public policy research, however. As has already been noted, this field has also been the target for a barrage of criticism.

184. *Ibid.*, p. 189.

185. My reading of the most current discussion of these issues by Peters is that he has considerably softened his earlier barrage of criticisms about the methodological deficiencies in comparative public administration relative to comparative public policy and comparative politics. He acknowledges that "there is now substantially more skepticism about the progress of comparative policy studies," and concedes that "rather than being peculiar to comparative public administration, the malaise of comparative studies may be a very widespread phenomenon." As to methodology, he says that in the complex world of administration, "identifying independent and dependent variables may require as much faith as science, so that somewhat less precise methods and language may be useful." He suggests some such alternative approaches that might be tried, and even acknowledges that efforts to be more sophisticated might turn out to be counterproductive. "Theory and Methodology," pp. 71, 82–85. I am in full agreement with his concluding statement that "most of the

issues that confound students of comparative public administration in 1994 are the same issues that have plagued us for decades and that have plagued students of comparative politics in general for the same length of time," and that "there is no quick technological fix for most of our research questions, nor any methodological medicine that will cure all our ills." *Ibid.*, p. 86.

186. Charles C. Ragin, *The Comparative Method: Moving Beyond Qualitative and Quantitative Strategies* (Berkeley, CA: University of California Press, 1987), addresses this problem perceptively. "I was trained," he states, "as are most American social scientists today, to use multivariate statistical techniques whenever possible. I often found, however, that these techniques were not well suited for answering some of the questions that interest me. ... This book represents an effort to step back from traditional statistical techniques, in comparative social science especially, and to explore alternatives. ... The problem is not to show which methodology is best hut to explore alternative ways of establishing a meaningful dialogue between ideas and evidence" (pp. vii, viii).

187. Savage, "Optimism and Pessimism," p. 422.

188. Jun, "Renewing the Study of Comparative Administration," p. 647.

189. Riggs has expressed this view more than once, using different words. See, for example, "The Group and the Movement," p. 652; and "Epilogue: The Politics of Bureaucratic Administration," in Tummala, ed., *Administrative Systems Abroad*, rev. ed., Chapter 15, p. 407.

190. Peters, *Comparing Public Bureaucracies*, p. 3.

COMPARATIVE PUBLIC ADMINISTRATION: PROLOGUE, PERFORMANCE, PROBLEMS, AND PROMISE

Dwight Waldo

My object is to review and analyze the comparative public administration "movement." I seek to understand it in terms of its origins, its present activities, its products and its aspirations. I wish also to probe into some of the crucial problems of methodology and philosophy that are posed.

As these crucial problems are crucial ones for the whole enterprise of Social Science, probed and argued again and again, it is quite unlikely that I shall be making a significant contribution to their resolution. However, the setting in which the issues will be posed may at least help in dramatizing their importance and throwing them into clearer relief. For the setting is the contemporary whole world and the issues, while in the most profound sense "academic," relate in a most profound way also to the present and future of this world. At least – if this sounds too pompous and pretentious – it is true if what objectives we seek and the techniques we use in their pursuit in so-called technical assistance programs are of consequence. Nor are the matters that concern me related only to technical assistance in any strict sense. Certainly, they relate to the varied ends and the appropriate means of "business" in differing national and cultural settings.

Comparative Public Administration: The Essential Readings
Research in Public Policy Analysis and Management, Volume 15, 129–170
Copyright © 2006 by Elsevier Ltd.
ISSN: 0732-1317/doi:10.1016/S0732-1317(06)15004-6

THE DEVELOPMENT OF PUBLIC ADMINISTRATION

It is appropriate to begin with some observations on the development of Public Administration, for the development of Comparative Public Administration and its present problems are most clearly viewed in historical perspective: The logical problems are related to a chronological development.

By Public Administration I refer to the discipline – or perhaps one should say the course of study or curriculum, as it is not very "disciplined" – not to the activity of administrators or civil servants. That is to say, there was public administration before there was a self-conscious study and teaching of Public Administration, just as business preceded a self-conscious study and teaching of Business Administration. The first textbooks and curricula of Public Administration in this country came in the 1920s. The authors of these textbooks and the organizers of these curricula were for the most part professors of Political Science. The discipline (or course or curriculum) consisted of information from several different sources, held together in the minds of the believers by certain beliefs about science, about government, about the nature and purpose of administration in general and public administration in particular.

The beliefs about government and public administration that were most important are perhaps these: that the proper ends of government are found in the ends at the people it serves; that the entire process of government can be divided into two phases, to decide on policy and then to execute or carry out the policy; that the values and processes of democracy apply to the first of these phases and that it is here (in voting, legislating, etc.) that the congruence of the ends of government with the ends of the people is brought about; that the values and processes of democracy have no (or at least little) direct relevancy to the second phase. The execution of decisions, but rather are secured through the first phase. That is to say, democracy under conditions of the twentieth century means not direct popular participation in government or even direct "meddling," but control through political parties and by the electoral and legislative processes of agents (officials) who would both pose meaningful alternatives for choice, and direct and be responsible for the actions of civil servants. Much of this is epitomized in the transition from the nineteenth century "spoilsman" to the twentieth century civil servant or career employee.

The substantial separation of democracy from that part of government concerned with executing or administering policy permitted – in the view of the founders of the discipline – the application to this part of government of very important values and processes. It permitted, for example, the application to governmental administration of the growing emphasis on specialization and professionalism in American life; in general, of bureaucracy in it sociological sense as against amateurism or democratic chaos. Most importantly, it permitted a definition of a discipline of Public Administration as a science (or at least subject to scientific methodology[1]), a science focused upon one end, efficiency. This science was conceived as value-free or, alternatively, single-valued, depending on whether efficiency was viewed as a value to be pursued or art end which, by definition, eliminated values when pursued. In any case, the choice of ends was posited as a pre-administrative act, and both the process of administration and the scientific study of administration had as their purpose the most efficient pursuit of these ends.

The central objectives of the scientific study of administration were presumed to be scientific "principles." These principles were conceived as being analogous to those of physics – or perhaps engineering, for they were conceived both as descriptive and prescriptive, as statements of cause and effect and as having an imperative quality, given the acceptance of efficiency as the goal of administration. In a manner that succeeds in appearing quaint to all shades of contemporary social science thinking, W. F. Willoughby put it thus: "There are fundamental principles of general application, analogous to those characterizing any science, which must be observed if the end of administration, efficiency in operation, is to be secured; and ... these principles are to be determined and their significance made known, only by the rigid application of scientific methods."[2] L. D. White, the author of the first textbook on Public Administration, stated his conception of "principle" in a way highly relevant to the present purpose of probing the significance of comparative study for science and action: "A principle, considered as a tested hypothesis and applied in the light of its appropriate frame of reference, is as useful a guide to action in the public administration of Russia as of Great Britain, of Iraq as of the United States." Holding in view that we are trying to teach Business Administration to the Pakistanis and Public Administration to the Koreans, is it "principles" we are trying to convey? Or what?

You are perhaps ahead of me – but I call your attention to the similarity of the mode of thinking of Willoughby and White to that of Frederick W. Taylor and his followers in the Scientific Management movement. Taylor's object was "the development of a true science," a "one best way," by what he conceived to be the tested scientific means of careful observation, measurement, and generalization. He and his followers had no doubt that their truths were universals, and in fact Scientific Management had become an international movement and organization by the 1930s. The similarity in thinking between early Public Administration and Scientific Management is not accidental; Public Administration was heavily in debt to the Scientific Management movement. In the opening sentence of the first textbook (in 1926), White explicitly states that his base is management, not law. Public Administration and Business Administration were not only born in the same period, but had many common ancestors.

Perhaps, in consideration of the later discussion, I should be explicit as to the nature of the "principles" of public administration, as conceived in the 1930s. These principles for the most part concerned theory of organization as represented at that time for Business Administration by Mooney and Reiley's *Onward Industry!* (or the later *Principles of Organization* by Mooney) and for Public Administration by the collection of essays edited by Luther Gulick and Lyndall Urwick, *Papers on the Science of Administration* (1937). More specifically, they concerned such matters as hierarchy or the "scalar principle," specialization and the "functional principle," the distinction between staff and line and their proper interrelation, executive functions and coordinating processes. They purported to tell one how he *ought* or *must* organize and operate *if* he wished to achieve ends sought by organizations *efficiently.* It is characteristic of the literature that while the existence and importance and indeed the inviolability of the principles are asserted confidently, there is nevertheless much "looseness" to a later generation highly self-conscious about methodological problems and scientific criteria of exactness. The principles were broad, imprecise and unqualified, generalizations (Graicunas' precision on the span of control is the only exception that comes to mind) as to how one ought to act if lie wishes to be efficient.

The 1940s were a traumatic and crucial period for Public Administration. One important phenomenon was that the majority of active and potential academic teachers and writers in the discipline held positions or at least had "administrative experience" of some kind – in the military or in some war-related civilian agency. The result was naturally a simultaneous broadening and sharpening of vision. Negatively, the existing textbooks seemed inadequate, inaccurate, dull; positively, reports on new experiences and new perspectives swelled to a large volume.

A second phenomenon was that critical dissatisfaction with the older literature, signaled in the 1930s, delayed or restrained by the War[3] burst forth in the late 1940s. Three items that I think were especially important in this critical attack were Robert A. Dahl's 'The Science of Public Administration: Three Problems,'[4] Herbert A. Simon's *Administrative Behavior, a*

Study of Decision-Making Processes in Administrative Organizations,[5] and
my own *The Administrative State; A Study of the Political Theory of American Public Administration.*[6] In general, the charges made and argued were
that the early writers bad proceeded on premises they had not examined
critically (if indeed they had been aware of them), that they had often
confused and unwarrantedly mixed fact and value categories, that the claim
to a knowledge of scientifically respectable principles was premature and
presumptuous, that the understanding of scientific philosophy and methodology was very inadequate if not indeed quite erroneous.

It would be inappropriate to comment on my own book, and it is unnecessary to comment on Simon's: It has probably been better known and
more influential in Business Administration than in Public Administration.
But Dahl's essay is worth a brief look, because it puts the question of the
significance of comparativeness for the development of theory. Actually,
only one of the "three problems" he saw as posed in an attempt to make
Public Administration a science is concerned explicitly with comparative
studies; but in fact the other two problems are involved, indeed magnified in
a serious attempt to use comparison in the development of theory.

The first problem "of constructing a science of public administration
stems from the frequent impossibility of excluding normative considerations
from the problems of public administration." The discussion charges that
the traditional theory of organization and administration had confused and
unjustifiably conflated fact and value categories, as seen by its treatment of
efficiency and by its response to such "public" matters as responsibility. The
conclusion is that while the distinction between fact and value is important,
nay crucial, "the student of public administration cannot avoid a concern
with ends, to refuse to recognize that the study of public administration
must be founded on some clarification of ends is to perpetuate the gobbledygook of science in the area of moral purpose."

The second problem "stems from the inescapable fact that a science of
public administration must be a study of certain aspects of human behavior." The discussion here concerns, in part, familiar methodological
problems arising from the diversity, complexity, and non-repeatability of the
phenomena, but centers upon a tendency of writers (the shaft is directed
toward the inviting target Urwick presents) to build a theory on a vastly
over-simplified view of human nature. The writers, he charges, ask us to
accept a ludicrously over-simplified administrative man rather like – in fact
related to – eighteenth century rational man. Administrative theory must
comprehend or at least allow for the emotional and non-rational; it must be

sensitive to biases deriving from its historical and geographical matrix: from capitalism, industrialism, rationalism, and so forth.[7]

The third problem Dahl presents is at the center of my later concerns: the relationship of "principles" to comparative study. Public Administration, he charges, has been all but oblivious to the significance of the social setting of administration. It has assumed that there are organizational and administrative universals rather than proving that there are; building on a parochial base, it pretends to universality. He concludes:

1. Generalizations derived from the operation of public administration in the environment of one nation-state cannot be universalized and applied to public administration in a different environment.
2. There can be no truly universal generalizations about public administration without a profound study of varying national and social characteristics impinging on public administration, to determine what aspects of public administration, if any, are truly independent of the national and social setting.
3. It follows that the study of public administration must become a much more broadly based discipline, resting not on a narrowly defined knowledge of techniques and processes, but rather extending to the varying historical, sociological, economic, and other conditioning factors.

THE RISE OF COMPARATIVE PUBLIC ADMINISTRATION

In referring to my files of *Public Administration Review* to re-examine Dahl's essay, I am reminded of its relationship to the course of events as well as to intellectual developments. For, in the post-War years, *Public Administration Review* was sprinkled with accounts of foreign administration, or at least of administration of some unusual type in an unfamiliar setting. Students of Public Administration were scattered about the world during the War and were deeply involved in two areas by the post-War occupations. What they were moved to write out of their experiences was of course largely reportorial, but some essays moved beyond simple description and into contextual and comparative analysis of some depth.[8]

As history had it, war and occupation were the beginning and not the end of overseas interests and operations. The Marshall Plan for economic recovery in Europe grew into, or was succeeded by, the Point Four program for the so-called underdeveloped areas. The idea of aid to the distressed was expanded into the idea of "technical assistance" in economic, social, and political development. The various programs of the U.S. government, and those of the United Nations and private foundations, have engaged scores, probably hundreds, of teachers and writers identified with the field of Public Administration in overseas assignments. These assignments have generally been in exotic cultures and for periods of residence of at least a year. In fact, a new professional specialization may be developing, for some persons have been abroad for more than a decade, moving from one assignment to another.

In light of these facts perhaps we should be surprised, not that a literature of and self-conscious interest in Comparative Public Administration has developed, but that the development has been so slow and halting. If the latter needs explanation I think it can be in these terms: First, that it tended to be presumed year to year that the programs of assistance were "temporary." Second, that we tended to presume (albeit with varying levels of sophistication and self-awareness) that we knew that Public Administration as a discipline *is* and what public administration as a practice ought to be – otherwise why should we be going out to teach it or install it? The present interest perhaps stems from our failures rather than from our successes, from bitter experiences and rueful reflections. On the basis of my own experience, my annual "foreign aid" worry that four billion dollars is not proportionate to the need is simultaneously increased and tempered by my reflection that we have not the clarity of objectives, trained manpower and know-how to spend that much money on overseas assistance without serious risk of more harm than good to both receiver and giver.

In any event, Comparative Public Administration grew from tentative beginnings in the early post-War years into a contemporary "movement" of considerable size, complexity, and intensity. For present purposes it suffices to note that courses (mostly graduate) in the subject began to appear (introduced one at the University of California in 1948) and are now offered in perhaps a score of institutions; that in the early 1950s, the American Political Science Association established a committee on comparative administration and that this was followed by a special committee – now the Comparative Administration Group – of the American Society for Public Administration; that the foundations became interested and began to give support; that beginning in 1952, several special conferences have concerned themselves with the subject. The Comparative Administration Group is the present focus of interest, and is in the early stages of a three-year program (financed by The Ford Foundation) of research and other activity.

RELATIONSHIPS WITH OTHER DEVELOPMENTS

Of more importance for our purpose than the mere history of the move-ment[9] are its relationships with certain developments – and perhaps lack of developments – in Public Administration and Political Science. We face here a tangled skein of ideas and interrelations of which it is hard to speak accurately and briefly. But the attempt must be made. I shall limit my observations to three themes. First, certain general tendencies and problems in Public Administration and Political Science; second, the significance of Herbert Simon's work; and third, the significance of the Comparative Politics movement.

I noted above that the matrix of ideas that gave meaning and force to Public Administration during the 1920s and 1930s collapsed in the 1940s under the combined impact of new experience and critical analysis. During the past 15 years, Public Administration as a focus of research and reaching, as a course of study or curriculum, has not only survived but also in many ways it has grown. In many respects, certainly the growth has been "healthy." Certainly there has been, in reaction to the older self-confident parochialism, a general willingness to incorporate new data, new ideas, new influences. There has been considerable experimentation with new ap-proaches,[10] there has been a strenuous attempt to relate Public Adminis-tration to other "fields," especially the various social science as the recent textbooks witness.

But while the discipline has greatly expanded, it has remained "undis-ciplined." That is to say, there has not developed any core of unifying and organizing ideas to replace those discredited in the 1940s. I appreciate that no social science lacks its deep schisms, but we are so amorphous as to make schisms difficult. We unite in paying dues to the society; and possibly in paying respect to some colleague's ability – but not to his ideas. Perhaps, there is no reason in the logic of things why we *should* be a discipline in the sense of having a common philosophical–methodological outlook. Perhaps, the proper analogy is to a profession – medicine or law, for example – not to a scientific discipline. However, the present lack of a sense of unity and direction relates to the hopes some entertain for Comparative Public Ad-ministration. I believe it is correct to say that there is a hope that *through mastering diversity we shall achieve unity.*

As noted above, Public Administration was created by professors of Po-litical Science, and the two fields of study continue to have close and im-portant relationships. For more than 20 years, there has been a separate professional society and in some instances Public Administration stands as a separate school or curriculum or is combined with Business Administration. But more customarily, Public Administration is taught as a course or branch of Political Science, and the parent discipline shows no disposition to exclude its offspring from its journals and meetings. By definition, Public Administration is a part of the governmental process, after all, even though it draws ideas and techniques from many fields of knowledge and relates to a multiplicity of functional areas such as welfare, agriculture, and education. What has happened in Political Science is therefore, also relevant to the development of Comparative Public Administration.

"Behavioralism" is the one word that best signifies and summarizes the development of Political Science during the past 15 years. Behavioralism is a controversial word even in its definition, but in general it refers to a desire and an attempt to make Political Science genuinely *scientific*. In general, it describes or implies an attempt to move from the philosophical to the positive, the empirical, the existential; to separate questions of fact from questions of value and to make the former the proper concern of Political Science; to learn and make use of proper scientific methodology; to draw inspiration, knowledge, and concepts from and to join in more closely with related fields of study that are deemed "behavioral science"; to seek more, and more unified, empirical theory.[11]

The behavioral movement has substantially altered Political Science without, however, thoroughly transforming it. Some new areas of study have been developed or else have been transformed – for example, the study of voting behavior. Shifts in emphasis, in the relative proportions of manpower and money, and in fashionable modes of study have occurred. No significant segment of Political Science remains unaffected by the new currents; but some segments have changed remarkably little. For all the tumult and change there has been no thorough conversion of a discipline; uneasiness, uncertainty and controversy remain.

That Political Science has been so "old fashioned," lagging behind its sister disciplines in the movement toward science, strikes me as easily explicable. I find the explanation in differences in disciplinary role and function. Political Science by historical development, institutional involvement, and public expectation is deeply rooted in the normative – more so than psychology, sociology, and anthropology, probably more so than economics, though here comparison becomes very complex. My point is that Political Science is deeply involved both in the processes of defining and inculcating civic loyalty and of shaping and executing public policy. Obviously, any request to be value-neutral about the moral imperatives of patriotism, of constitutionalism, of democracy, of traditional values associated with liberty and equality; any drive to abandon the *ought* in favor of the *is*; any push to make Political Science a value-free, descriptive enterprise, is bound to create confusion, raise tension, cause controversy.

In general, the impact of behavioralism on the Public Administration band of the Political Science spectrum has been slow and halting. The reasons relate, certainly, to the matters I have just indicated. But here is posed a special question. Herbert Simon's *Administrative Behavior* was not only a critique of the old Public Administration, it offered in its place a strongly argued reconstruction of the study of administration along behavioral lines. This work, it is agreed, has been influential in social science generally. But I think it is correct to say that it was received with deep reservations and often with hostility by students of Public Administration, and that while its influence long run and indirectly has been fairly large this influence has been just that: long run and indirectly. Since *Administrative Behavior* was directly focused on Public Administration, it would have been a reasonable presumption that its influence would have been immediate and great on the study of Public Administration. How does one explain this contrary?

I offer the following explanation. A central tenet of the old Public Administration, you will recall, was the separation of "politics" and "administration." As against Jacksonian direct democracy was posed a scheme deemed appropriate for a complex industrial society, restricting the citizen's role to the political (deciding) and permitting administration (carrying out decisions) to become an area of professionalism, expertise, and science. The critical attack of the 1940s was centered upon this attempt rigidly to separate the political and the administrative, and by 1950 the idea that separation was either possible or desirable was quite discredited. It seemed obvious from a wealth of personal experience and scholarly study that the political and the administrative were intimately joined over the major area of public administration, that policy-making of various important kinds and high levels cannot be kept free from bureaucratic participation. Some went further and argued that it is *desirable* that interest groups and perhaps political parties seek to influence administrators directly; or that administrators should be active in policy-making and perhaps even in partisan politics.

Now the reformulation offered by Simon was certainly in some respects novel and radical, but it was, curiously, in some respects much like the schema of the old Public Administration. To be precise, in three crucial ways: First, basing himself on logical positivism, Simon proposed a rigid distinction between questions of value and questions of fact. This is certainly a different distinction from that between politics and administration, but it is, like the latter, a sweeping twofold division of the "universe." Second,

having rigidly separated value and fact, Simon argued that the latter –
including the facts of public administration – are subject to scientific study
in exactly the same way that facts in the realms of the natural sciences are
subject to scientific study. He thus "rescues" and places on new and higher
grounds the belief and argument of the Fathers that Public Administration
is subject to science, potentially if not presently. Third, Simon took the
discredited concept of efficiency as the goal of the scientific study and practice of public administration, carefully defined and refined it, and placed it
again at the center as the criterion by which an administrator must be
guided in the factual aspects of decision-making.

The argument of *Administrative Behavior is* powerful, complex, and subtle.
No student in Public Administration could "refute" it.[12] Yet, an overwhelming number of these students refused to believe it, to be persuaded and
converted. They may have been – and increasingly they were – interested in
and knowledgeable about some of the matters discussed by Simon, in *Administrative Behavior* and his later works – for example, the role of authority
and communication: but on the central tenets they remained unconvinced.
The reason is, I think, that the conceptual scheme did not accurately reflect
the "real world" of public administration as they experienced or observed it.
All the points about fact and value may be true as a matter of logical
analysis, they thought, but in the real world of administrative action fact and
value are always joined, and "organically" joined. The abstractions do not
describe the essential facts of this real world or enable us "better" to deal
with it.

You may recall that Chester Barnard wrote a Foreword to *Administrative
Behavior*, in which he says in praise of the book, "It has the right 'feel'." I
present for your reflection an interesting paradox. Barnard was an experienced administrator as well as a major writer on administration and he
found the book "right." But students of administration generally, including
– especially including – the more experienced ones, found it "wrong." Simon
did his doctorate in Political Science, and *Administrative Behavior* is oriented
toward Public Administration: but students of Public Administration were
not persuaded. Students of Business Administration, on the other hand,
tended to be admiring, and in this they were joined by an impressive array of
behaviorally oriented students from a variety of disciplines. Simon's career
turned more and more toward Business Administration, his relations with
Public Administration became more and more attenuated.

How is one to account for these facts? I do not – understandably – think
they are accounted for simply by attributing intelligence to those who found
Simon right and ignorance and error to those who found Simon wrong. I

suggest, rather, that the explanation lies in differences in professional experience, outlook, and objectives, and in what broadly is indicated by the
phrase, sociology of knowledge. I think that the matters involved relate to
the study of Comparative Administration, to motivation in studying it, to
the approach taken, to the results achieved. Before speculating on this subject, however, 1 wish to review briefly the development of the study of
Comparative Politics for, complementary to and interrelated with the development of Comparative Public Administration, it is a necessary part of
the "story."

Comparative Politics as a focus of inquiry and as an accepted term has
developed in the same period – roughly the past 15 years – as Comparative
Public Administration. In general, it is a response to the same stimuli and
motivations: essentially to the emergence of new non-Western nations and
America's worldwide involvement, and to the complex of objectives, conceptions, and methods designated by the term behavioralism.

For decades, there has been a field of Political Science designated by the
term Comparative Government. It was concerned rather directly with the
comparison of constitutions and constitutional system, legislatures, executives, party systems, and so forth. It was not necessarily naive, certainly, the
better students knew that government did not exist in a vacuum and some
made a strenuous effort to relate governmental systems to their total physical and socio-economic contexts, Also, there was considerable innovation
or experimentation before World War II as the names Lowell, Michels, and
Lasswell suggest.

Be that as it may, the post-War years have witnessed a wave of protest
against Comparative Government and an attempt to replace it with Comparative Politics.[13] The charges against the old Comparative Government
ran as follows: that it was limited in its interests and its concepts to Western
countries; that it was too normative because of its commitment to the values
of constitutionalism and Western liberal–democracy (and perhaps too naive
in a belief that there is a natural evolution in this direction); that it concerned itself too much with studying words and too little with studying
action; that it concentrated on institutions to the neglect of processes; that it
was too descriptive and naively empirical, too little analytical and sophisti-
cately theoretical; that government was studied without properly relating it
either to the motivation of the actors on the one hand or to its socio-
economic context on the other; that the other social and (or) behavioral
sciences were in many ways more advanced than Political Science and that
they should be combed for concepts and techniques valuable in studying
Comparative Government; that more attention needs to be given to the

study of scientific method and to the crucial role of theory in the scientific enterprise.

"Movements" such as the Comparative Politics movement do not of course have abrupt beginnings, but 1953 was a significant date. In that category, the Social Science Research Council sponsored a Summer Seminar on Comparative Politics that enabled the young Turks to compare notes, reinforce convictions, and to prepare for scholarly and polemical action. Since then there has been a continuing stream of the "new" literature, and the creation by the Social Science Research Council of a Continuing Committee on Comparative Politics has afforded a central base of material and moral support.

As indicated, the Comparative Politics and the Comparative Public Administration movements have had much in common in outlook and aspiration. Since both have taken the entire world as their scientific universe, both have been engaged in a heroic attempt to find or create theoretical constructs adequate for the task of worldwide comparison. Since "to compare is to examine similarities and differences simultaneously," the effort is bent toward two main ends: (1) to discover, define, and differentiate the "stuff" (politics or administration) to be compared, wherever in the world it may be and (2) to develop criteria of differentiation that are useful in ordering and analyzing the "stuff" once it has been identified. In this task, the contemporary stock of proved or fashionable concepts in the social sciences (as well as those "indigenous" to Political Science) has been drawn upon extensively. The works of Weber and Parsons, structural-functionalism as conceived in various sources, the concept of culture, the decision-making schema, communications theory and cybernetics, systems theory – all these and several more sources have been drawn upon by both movements. If the results sometimes seem elaborately irrelevant or somewhat bizarre, this judgment should be tempered by the reflection that the task is, as I said above, heroic.

Not only is there similarity between the two movements in objectives, outlook, and core concepts, there is an overlapping of research interests and professional activities. In the spring of 1962, for example – perhaps I should say notably – the Committee on Comparative Politics sponsored a Conference on Bureaucracy and Political Development at the Center for Advanced Study in the Behavioral Sciences. Certainly, students of Public Administration perceive politics as part of or at least affecting administration, and students of Politics perceive that what takes place in public administration is a part of or at least affects politics.

But to speak of Comparative Politics as only revising or replacing Comparative Government as one part of Political Science, or to speak of

Comparative Politics as a Siamese twin of Comparative Public Administration, does not do justice to the facts. For Comparative Politics has been
not simply an effort to redefine and transform Comparative Government, it
has also been (or been involved with) an effort to redefine and transform
Political Science.[14] The students concerned, that is, have been deeply involved in the behaviorally inspired effort to define the "political" which is
the proper subject of the "science," to delineate "the political system" as an
entity conceptually if not empirically distinct from the total social system
and its other sub-systems. Public Administration is then a part of politics in
this use of the term, in these sweeping conceptualizations of the universe of
Political Science. Politics is used in its classic or generic sense, not in its more
limited sense to designate only the actions of voters, pressure groups, politicians, and political parties.

It will be useful to review briefly a prestigious recent essay, Gabriel Almond's "A Functional Approach to Comparative Politics."[15] as illustrative
of what it has just been said and to prepare the way for a closer look at
Comparative Public Administration. This essay is centrally concerned with a
definition of "the political system": this is viewed as a necessary preface to
the study of Political Science in general and to the enterprise of comparison
in particular. He defines a political system as "... that system of interactions
to be found in all independent societies which performs the functions of
integration and adaptation (both internally and vis-a-vis other societies) by
means of the employment, or threat of employment, of more or less legitimate compulsion."[16] This political system he distinguishes from other social systems by three "properties"

(1) comprehensiveness,
(2) interdependence, and
(3) the existence of boundaries.

By comprehensiveness is meant all interactions, which affect the use or the
threat of use of physical creation. By interdependence is meant that one
subset of interactions produces changes in all other subsets. By the existence
of boundaries is meant that there are points where other systems end and the
political system begins.

In developing the characteristics of the political system as he views it,
Almond adopts but expands upon some categories previously set forth by
David Easton; and he adapts the language of input–output analysis, which
is fashionable both in Comparative Politics and in Comparative Public
Administration. The political system is fed inputs that are processed
through the output functions into policy decisions. The input functions

include: (1) political socialization and recruitment, (2) interest articulation, (3) interest aggregation, and (4) political communication. The output functions include: (1) rule-making, (2) rule-application, and (3) rule-adjudication. These last are the "functional equivalents" of the legislative, the executive, and the judicial. Political structures or institutions exist or are constructed to fulfill each of these functions. The "modernity" of a system is a function of the extent to which structural differentiation and role differentiation have taken place.

I will note two things at this point. The first is that, as this schema putatively embraces the entire area of the "political," including the phenomena ordinarily deemed to be designated by the term "public administration," so some of the schemata proposed for the study of Comparative Public Administration go far beyond the "administrative." Some of them, in fact, embrace not only the "political" but the entire socio-physical context. The second point is that, while most students of Comparative Public Administration would find something of value for their enterprise in Almond's schema, they would argue that it provides no clear differentia and directions. The activities and functions of public administration are by no means all "output"; for example, public schools perform an important "input" function under the category of "political socialization and recruitment" and a great deal of "interest aggregation" may take place within the administrative process.

OF TRENDS, METHODS AND MODELS

In a recent essay on "Trends in the Comparative Study of Public Administration," Fred Riggs – who by most criteria would be adjudged the leading student of Comparative Public Administration – says that three trends may be discerned during the past half-century. Of these he judges the first to be "fairly clear," but the second and third to be "just emerging."

The first is a shift from normative toward empirical approaches. By the normative is meant "one in which the chief aim is to prescribe 'ideal,' *or* at least 'better,' patterns of administrative structure and action,"[17] in terms of such criteria as efficiency or "public interest." Empirical approaches, on the contrary, are identified with "a growing awareness of more and more relevant phenomena," with "a growing interest in descriptive and analytic information for its own sake."[18]

The second is a shift from idiographic toward nomothetic approaches. An idiographic study is defined as "one which concentrates on the unique case – the historical episode or 'case study', the single agency or country, the biography or the 'culture area'..."[19] A nomothetic study by contrast, is one "which seeks generalizations, 'laws', hypotheses that assert regularities of behavior, correlations between variables..."[20]

The third trend is from non-ecological toward ecological approaches. These terms are not defined, presumably because definition is deemed unnecessary. But we are informed that mere recitation of the facts of geography, history, social structure, and so forth is not enough, "for ecology implies not just a characterization of environments, but rather an analysis of the patterns of interaction between the subject of study and its environment."[21]

In general, my own perception of trends is in agreement with that of Riggs. This, presumably, has been indicated in various ways. However, there are differing emphases and varying perspectives. The period of time he reviews is much longer – the past 50 years or more; and his field of vision is wider, as he includes in his review various materials (e.g., some European materials) that I omit. We are both interested in trends, but he is not interested, as I am, in accounting for and analyzing the burgeoning of interest, the development of a self-conscious "movement" (which lie pre-eminently represents), during the past decade.

As the next step in understanding and assessing the Comparative Public Administration movement, let me indicate some of the trends and qualities of the recent literature and try to characterize the movement in terms of disciplinary connections and borrowings, of key concepts, and techniques.

First of all it should be observed that, while there is a revolution under way, there is considerable continuity of previous interests and methods. These interests become more sophisticated and the methods more refined, but the continuity is unmistakable and important. Ferrel Heady has recently used the term "modified traditional" to designate this part of the literature.[22] In terms of the subject to which it is addressed, what is meant by "traditional" is that attention continues to be addressed to the traditional categories of administrative anatomy and physiology; to chain of command, staff services, personnel classification, co-ordination, departmentalization, and so forth; and to common or "universal"[23] functions or problems of government; to military administration, planning, welfare services, regulatory activities, and so forth.

There is the further implication that the studies so described have a "practical" bias or intent, that they are "normative" in the sense that they are addressed (at various levels of intent and consciousness) to improvement, reform, or at least increased efficiency. As indicated, there is increasing sophistication. There is increasing awareness of national and cultural differences, less disposition to presume that American or Western experience is directly relevant to problems elsewhere. In what struck me as the most intriguing feature of his essay on Trends, Riggs specifies a threefold evolution in the normative literature. There is first the "mirror for America" period of two or more generations ago, in which Americans (such as Woodrow Wilson) studied European administration and held it up as a model for us to emulate. This was followed by the "mirror for others" style, in which our own experience was held up as a guide for the "underdeveloped" areas. We have now entered the "mirror for all" period in which there is much comparison of institutions and practices in all "advanced" countries and the student tries to identify "good" features wherever he finds them and to specify what, in a general way, should be done *if* development or progress is desired.[24]

Another development should be noted, one that is not "traditional" nor yet "behavioral," one that is certainly a part of what I have characterized as a "burgeoning" of interest and activity but not yet a part of the "movement" in the sense that it shares in the dominant methodological beliefs and aims. I refer to the extension of the case method to the study of comparative public administration. More particularly, I refer to the use of the case method as developed for the study of public administration during the past two decades.[25] Some six or seven years ago, the Inter-University Case Program began to promote the writing of "cases" abroad, and this has become a vigorous and successful enterprise in a number of countries. While the I.C.P. group has shared the dissatisfaction with the "old" Public Administration – indeed, the case method was motivated by such dissatisfaction, was an attempt to sweep away preconceptions and approach "reality" afresh – it has by definition remained the case method, the essence of which is an investigation and probing in depth of particular situations or events. That is, in the terminology employed by Riggs above, it is intensely idiographic, whereas the methodological commitment of behavioralism, on which the current movement feeds, is strongly toward the nomothetic. To be sure, there is no strict separation: Some students (James Fesler and Herbert Kaufman come to mind) are identified both with the case program and with a commitment to a more "scientific" study of comparative administration. Some argue that the two methods are mutually reinforcing, not exclusive or antagonistic. But of differing perspectives and expectation, and of some personal and intellectual tension, there is no doubt.

Turning to the self-conscious movement, I try now to characterize it by indicating disciplinary orientations and conceptual foci. There is strong attraction toward, interaction with, and borrowing from Sociology. There is some attraction toward, but no really substantial borrowing from or reliance on Social Psychology and Anthropology. There is very little attraction toward, borrowing from, or interrelation with Economics, Business Administration, Psychology, or History.[26] Of some of these fields I shall, by implication, have considerable to say below. Of others, a few remarks here: As to Economics, there is perforce a close contiguity of a sort. After all, "development," which in some sense is both cause and object of the study of comparative public administration, is usually conceived as economic development, in whole or part; and some of the "comparative" literature, such as that on national planning, is primarily the product of economists. However, certain professional blindness, intellectual habits, and disciplinary jealousies have kept the close relationship from becoming a partnership, much less a marriage. As to Psychology, there has been no serious attempt (with which I am familiar), to apply in comparative study any of the apparatus of "academic" psychology pertaining to such things as learning, personality development, adjustment, and motivation. For that matter – and this is more remarkable in view of the large "domestic" literature – there is no employment of the concepts and methodology of the Small Group. As to History, while "in principle" past behavior is as legitimate an object of behavioral research as present behavior, the methodological difficulties (observation, measurement, etc.) are multiplied in an effort to combine the two. For non-Western and especially primitive areas the problems are multiplied again; the present is very present, the future presses hard.

To advance to methodological concerns and conceptual foci: There has been a great preoccupation with "models." There has been much activity centered upon the construction of typologies of political regimes and institutions and the delineation of geographic–cultural areas – an activity prominent also in and shared with Comparative Politics. So-called action theory and the concepts and language of structural-functionalism have been often employed. The range of concepts associated with the term bureaucracy has been extensively used. The concept of culture has often been invoked; and the related and overlapping but different and broader concept of ecology is also frequently set forth as important. Equilibrium theory, and particularly the idea of a "system" with "inputs" and "outputs," is prominent.[27] One encounters somewhere most of the popular concepts and phrases of contemporary behavioral science; there is reference, for example, to such matters as communications theory and multivariate analysis. There are "gaps," however, such as the absence of small group theory, noted above. Surprisingly, and perhaps significantly, the term decision-making and the words closely associated with this schema are seldom encountered. (This relates to the problem posed above: the differential impact of the work of Herbert Simon in Business Administration and Public Administration.)

I turn now explicitly to the use of "models," by which I mean simply the conscious attempt to develop and define concepts, or clusters of related concepts, useful in classifying data, describing reality and (or) hypothesizing about it. As indicated, this has become a popular activity in the past few years, and it is impossible to do more than indicate the nature of some of the more prominent models. It should be emphasized that the situation is one of rapid change, and that the models are not necessarily discrete, logically mutually exclusive entities, but rather can be "joined" to different or larger models or "telescoped" one within another (at least in the mind and intent of the theorist).[28]

The bureaucratic model is one of the most widely used. By bureaucratic model is meant the ideal-typical model of bureaucracy as developed by Max Weber and since further developed, "applied," criticized, and altered. This model is so well known that to sketch it is unnecessary; and the complexities of a serious treatment far beyond present possibilities and purposes. I limit myself to some observations and to directing your attention to a first-class treatment of the subject not in your normal field of vision.

The first observation is purely personal: that I have found the bureaucratic model so useful, so stimulating and provocative, that 15 years after "discovering" it, I feel I have still much to learn through the avenues to exploration it opens. It came to my attention just at the point at which, dissatisfied with the old Public Administration as culture-bound and pretentious, I sought a "universal framework," a grammar and syntax to enable one to deal with "administration" wherever and whenever he encountered it. Whether it is in fact such a proper and useful universal framework, what kind of a universal framework it purports to be or can be made, these matters are of course complicated and controversial.

The second observation is that only in connection with this present review did I appreciate that not much empirical research has been done by students of Public Administration (as against Sociologists and others) in which the bureaucratic model is formally and seriously used.[29] In part, no doubt I was misled by my own preoccupations and enthusiasms. However, there is, I conclude, much more than this purely personal factor involved. The point is, perhaps, that the Weberian construct has become so well known among us, so much a part of our intellectual orientation toward the study of Comparative Public Administration, that, though we have little used it ourselves in careful research, it has generally been present in the form of (perhaps unexpressed) premises and (perhaps unarticulated) hypotheses in our teaching and our own explicit model building.

The essay to which I direct your attention is "The Bureaucratic Model: Max Weber Rejected, Rediscovered, Reformed," by Alfred Diamant.[30] In this essay, Diamant reviews the vast array of "bureaucratic" scholarship; carefully and penetratingly examines what Weber *wrote* on and relating to bureaucracy; evaluates, relates, and classifies; and ends by setting forth proposals "for the comparative analysis of bureaucracies; using the Weberian ideal-type, as we have modified it." I "incorporate by reference" this essay as expressing my own point of view – but better than I could express it!

Among students of Comparative Public Administration proper, the most prominent "model builder" is Fred W. Riggs. In fact, Riggs has developed not just a model, but a series of overlapping and interrelated models as his thinking has developed.[31] I can only outline some of the main ideas of a few essays.

In 1957, Riggs set forth his first major model, in a lengthy essay titled *Agraria and Industria Towards a Typology of Comparative Administration.*[32] This is an attempt to find and define what I called above a "universal framework." The search has turned toward Sociology and Anthropology, and especially to the language of structural-functionalism.[33] The object is to find the critical range of administrative variables within the entire range of the social, economic, and political. As the terms suggest, Agraria is a model of a pure traditional agricultural society, Industria of a pure modern industrial society. "Transitia" is the model of a society in transition from Agraria to Industria.[34] There are sub-models of the models; the analysis of the interrelations of the social, economic, governmental and, more strictly, administrative, are traced out in some detail. There is physiology as well as anatomy: especially there is an attempt to specify the dynamics of transition.

This model has been further "developed." Specifically, Riggs has changed the key terms from Agraria–Transitia–Industria to fused society–prismatic society–refracted society. This model is, in his hope and intent, "inductive" instead of "deductive" as was the earlier. It sets up "ideal types, not to be found in any actual society, but perhaps approximated in some, and useful for heuristic purposes and as an aid in the organization of the data."[35] In any event there are various changes and refinements, though the basic schema remains.

As Riggs' writings are voluminous, I shall not attempt further elaboration or summary. Suffice it to say that various essays develop various aspects of the basic models; that Riggs' emphasis upon ecology, noted above, is often prominent; and that his entire effort must be viewed in the binocular perspective provided, on the one hand, by his long residence and considerable experience in southeast Asia and, on the other, his above-noted methodological commitment to the "empirical, nomothetic and ecological."[36]

An example now of an input–output model: John T. Dorsey's "information-energy model."[37] This model has three conceptual sources, as seen by the author. One is his (long-standing) interest in communications theory and cybernetics as applied to organization. Another is some theories of energy and energy conversion. Another is the work of the "general systems" theorists.

In brief, Dorsey proposes that societies be conceived as highly complex information-processing and energy-converting systems (composed of subsystems, including human individuals, who may be similarly viewed). In general, high information input, storage, and processing permits high energy output. The "underdeveloped" societies are those in which information input, storage and processing, and hence the energy output, are comparatively low. Dorsey feels that such a conceptualization "should be useful in the analysis of social and political system in general," and that, in particular, it should have utility in understanding the problems of administration and development in underdeveloped societies. Several pages of hypotheses about such underdeveloped societies are suggested.[38]

I have dealt briefly and perhaps crudely with Dorsey's model and should in fairness add that his modesty is proportionate to the grandeur of his model: "What follows is at most only a beginning. It is crude and incomplete." His model is not, however, simply an armchair construction; it is related in his thought and research to significant field experience in East Asia.

As now has been often suggested, "development" is a concern of the model-builders, sometimes only peripherally or ultimately, as with Riggs, but sometimes centrally. One might, then, speak of a development model, or development models, as some have very explicitly. However, I reserve consideration of this matter.

PROBLEMS AND PROMISE

A year ago, speaking at the Institute of Social Science in The Hague, I made the statement that because of the Comparative Public Administration movement we should know within a decade a great deal more than we do now about whether a "science of administration" is possible or more likely, in what sense it is possible. I had in mind a wide range and variety of problems, but centrally the problem whether administrative means can be divorced from the ends of administrative action or, probably more precisely, the ways in which and the levels at which this is possible. This statement was made with easy optimism, for it had been a long time since I had taken a close look at the problems, and I presumed that my colleagues had advanced along the road farther than has proved to be the case.

I now find myself faced with what seems to me a welter of interrelated problems that I can hardly state, much less clarify and resolve. I will fail in stating them so that they strike you as clear and important I do not, nevertheless, retreat from my opening statement that the expansion of our enterprise, yours as well as mine, beyond the national and even the Western to the world-wide stage, presents not only new and pressing practical problems but poses old theoretical problems anew and urgently. But – perhaps again with too much optimism – I hope I can indicate how our two enterprises, yours of Business Administration and mine of Public Administration, each casts a light upon the other, and perhaps can find some meeting ground and partial solution to their respective and common problems in the concept and activity of development.

Two years ago, in reviewing several books devoted to organization theory or theory of organization, I observed that while the old *Encyclopedia of the Social Sciences* had no entry under either of these headings it was "wholly predictable" that the new encyclopedia then being planned would devote space to this subject.[39] So it will, I have since learned, and indeed it was obvious that it must, for this subject has become a fashionable one, as evidenced by the many symposia and "readers" recently off the presses. For this popularity, I conclude from obvious evidence that the schools of Business Administration are largely responsible, not only in the sense that they provide the market incentive for the publishers, but in the sense that the interests of students of business are served in the research undertaken and reported. The research and writing is done, actually, by persons with a variety of disciplinary bases; and located in a variety of institutional homes – and perhaps most of the writers are not in departments or schools of Business Administration; but business provides orientation, themes, support.

Now I have not read all the books in the recent spate, but speaking of those that I have, I observe what appears to be a curious gap between two types of empirical bases and two meanings assigned to "organization," as well as a certain presumptuousness or wishful thinking. Regarding empirical bases there is, on the one hand, a heavy concentration on the American factory, and, on the other, a scattering of pieces concerning a variety of institutions and settings – government agencies, labor unions, Indian villages, and so forth. Regarding the connotations of "organization," predominately it refers to a structure that is bureaucratic, or to the personal, informal, or "dysfunctional" aspects thereof; but it *may* mean the association of people in any regular and persistent pattern whatsoever – families, castes, etc. Regarding the presumptuousness or wishful thinking, my point is that, though there is a presumption that the "principles" of organization and administration that are the object of the research are universal, this is presumed not proved, assumed not demonstrated. In fact, some of the language suggests that of Public Administration a generation ago, before "comparativeness."[40]

I am far from being an expert on the literature of Business Administration, but I have made an effort to assess its interests and accomplishments in conscious comparative studies. Subject to correction, the following are my impressions. Generally speaking, those teaching Business Administration and those doing research on business organizations have not been and are not now interested in conscious, careful comparative study. There are, of course, exceptions: I recall, for example, a careful study of authority patterns in steel production in the Ruhr. And at the present time, some of my colleagues at the University of California are involved in an extensive field study of cultural patterns as they affect the role of the manager; 11 countries (Western or Western-influenced) are being studied, by means of questionnaire and interview techniques. Certainly, I do not perceive any literature or "movement" comparable to that in Public Administration in which there is an attempt to define "what" is being compared and "how" to compare. On the other hand, as my language has suggested, in those cases in which there is comparison in the business area, there is the appearance of a methodological confidence, and at least a fairly close fit between the hypotheses and the data; whereas in Comparative Public Administration the gap between the "models" and full and accurate data is broad indeed – though well recognized and lamented. On the evidence available to me, I conclude that though students of business organization and administration have highly developed research tools – there is probably more careful "behavioral" research on American businesses than on American governments – these tools have not been much employed in comparative research. (Whether these particular tools are the proper ones for comparative study I leave here a moot question.)

On the face of things, this seems queer. It is difficult to compare the overseas involvement of American business and government up to this point, but this is not necessary. It is enough to know that American business has for a long time been deeply involved in foreign operations, The "know-how" that the successful ones have developed is formidable indeed – oil companies operating in the Middle East, for example; they sometimes can and do instruct our diplomatic representatives on how to "do business" abroad. But the know-how remains largely private and uncodified, a combination of knowledge of the particular, lore, and skill developed from experience. It is not public, scientific knowledge. (Sometimes no doubt it is not "knowledge," but misinformation.)

Perhaps, I puzzle over which occasion should be without puzzlement. From one perspective it would seem surprising – almost a contradiction in terms – if American business (and American Business Administration) had developed an interest in comparative business administration. If it is assumed that the particular technical processes involved have their own imperatives, that in management there is One Best Way (or at least that American management technology in general supplies the best ways) that the object of a business enterprise is the comparatively limited one of profitable operation measured in financial terms, that the overseas enterprise shall be staffed by Americans or by foreigners trained (if possible) to act like Americans, then one might expect at very most some interest in what "social science" has to say of value about How to Win Friends and Influence People When Operating Abroad.[41]

However – if my reading of the contemporary world is reasonably correct, there is cause for American business to become interested in some of the problems that presently engage the attention of the students of Comparative Public Administration. I perceive an increasing "politicization" of what have been areas of business and the market, resulting from the operations of the twin – often Siamese twin – forces of nationalism and socialism (perhaps also from the twin forces of industrialization and urbanization, but here the lines of interrelationship are not so clear). If American business is to continue to operate abroad it must inevitably become more deeply engaged with government, that of the country concerned certainly, that of the United States perhaps; its objectives will inevitably be broadened and its operating style more and more "engaged" with the local social milieu. I am not suggesting, you understand, that it must learn how to become more cleverer at "manipulation," but rather that in many areas it can only survive and continue to serve its proper business ends by a flexibility and adaptability that would have been inconceivable a generation ago, and is now only dimly imagined.[42]

But perhaps my crystal ball is clouded. So let me present as directly and succinctly as I can the relationship – and lack of relationship – between the orienting concepts and objectives of the scientific and theoretical study of organization and management associated more or less with Business Administration and Comparative Public Administration. What I think I discern and what interests me very much is symbolized by, if it does not actually turn upon the question that I posed earlier: Why has *Administrative Behavior* and Simon's work generally been more influential and prestigious in Business Administration than in Public Administration?

The answer to this question is not a simple one. With regard to the leaders in the study of Comparative Public Administration, certainly the answer is not that Simon and his work is "behavioral," whereas they and their work are not. The predominant mood of the movement is strongly behavioral (i.e., scientific, theoretical, interdisciplinary, etc.). Yet there has been no disposition to rely on Simon, whose work is probably the most notable of any in "their" field in the past two decades. Apparently, they have not found the philosophic base, the theoretical formulations, suitable to their purposes. Why? More generally, why is there so little "interaction" between those interested in "theory of organization" and those interested in Comparative Public Administration?

Let me propose an answer which, I am aware, will be over-simple but may contain the essential points. At bottom, the assumption and the aim of Business Administration (as of the old Public Administration) has been *uniformity*, whereas the assumption and to some extent the aim of Comparative Public Administration is *diversity*.

As to Business Administration, by assumption of uniformity I mean that, while there is a record of increasing sophistication about the organizational environment, an increasing recognition of its heterogeneity and importance, it has been assumed that, after all, the important variables are within the organization.[43] Certainly, there has been little explicit recognition in the literature of Business *Administration*[44] of the existence and possible significance of cultural differences; what there is has been introduced gradually and peripherally.[45] By goal of uniformity I refer to the root biases given by a commitment to efficiency, lawfulness, rationality. The initial goal is a One Best Way or "principle." While, in Simon's terms, maximizing becomes satisfying, the search for the best ways of "satisfying" continues. With regard to Comparative Public Administration, it is not only concerned by definition with diversity, there is at this point a widespread "value commitment" to diversity – i.e. there is something of a conscious attempt not to presume that the American or Western "ways of doing things" are "better."

The respective concerns of Business Administration and Comparative Public Administration lead to perspectives that are very different if not in fact quite opposite.[46] Reflecting on the nature of theory of organization, Simon in 1952 wrote as follows:

> Organization theory has been largely culture-bound through failure to attack this problem [of the relevance of the mores of society]. The theory of bureaucracy as developed by Max Weber and his followers represents the furthest progress in dealing with it. The historical data appealed to by the Weberians need supplementation by analysis of contemporary societies, advanced and primitive. A comparison of intra-cultural uniformity and variation in organization patterns with inter-cultural uniformity and variation would provide the evidence we need to determine to what extent the cooperative patterns in organizations are independent of the mores of cooperation of the society.[47]

This would seem to be a fair enough recognition of the possible significance of the cultural factor, a clear warning of "relativity." But attention is directed to the last sentence and particularly to the word *independent.* I read this as a presumption, at least a hope, that comparative study, if pursued, will find or permit a universal–rational core of organizational behavior.

Be that as it may, I direct attention again to Robert Dahl's seminal essay of 1947, and to his assertion: "There should be no reason for supposing, then, that a principle of public administration has equal validity in every nation-state, or that successful public administration practices in one country will necessarily prove successful in a different social, economic and political environment." Obviously, administrative behavior here is viewed as inextricably enmeshed in the social–cultural context. To this outlook is later added, as we have seen, the formal terms and concepts of the Anthropologists' and Sociologists' "culture" and "structural-functionalism," and the result would seem to be the denial that administrative behavior can be treated as a universal independent variable.

OF STRATEGIES, DILEMMAS AND PUZZLES

I turn now to review some of the problems that confront the enterprise of Comparative Public Administration. Though all of these problems may be properly designated as methodological, I hesitate to use the term because it often suggests a question of technique to achieve and end, which is already clear and agreed upon. For some of these questions, certainly, the essential point is that they are not questions of technique in a narrow sense but raise questions about what kind of knowledge we seek and for what purpose. As I said in beginning, some of these questions are likely to seem old ones, raising as they do questions as to the nature of the whole enterprise of Social Science. But at least the world-wide setting poses them urgently and, perhaps, more clearly.

A cluster of questions concerns models – whether to use them, which are most appropriate and productive, and for what purposes. Intimately related are questions of research strategy and tactics; of the level of approach (macro or micro); of the geographical, cultural or functional range; of ecological depth, and so forth. Indeed, the question is which model, raised by implication of all of the key methodological–philosophical questions.

As I view it, the question of *whether* to use a model in research can be answered summarily: We have no choice. In the often-quoted words of Karl Deutsch, "We are using models, willingly or not, whenever we are trying to think systematically about anything at all."[48] One can, of course, raise the question whether there is not a fascination with model building as such among the students of Comparative Public Administration – a form of a pseudo-scientific "play" that postpones the serious business of research. But in general, I should argue that our error in Social Science has been the opposite: data gathering, description and prescription, without enough conscious reflection on conceptual framework.

Let me say further that I do not think that our problem is that of choosing or constructing "the" proper model. To be sure, models are better or worse, more useful and less useful. But models are better or worse, more or less useful for different purposes. Deutsch's "systematic thought" can take place in Fred Riggs' study as he contemplates the world or in the office of a technical assistance officer in Ghana as he contemplates the day's assignment. Models serve pedagogical and "action" purposes as well as research needs.

The central problem of model-selection (or model-construction) in the study of Comparative Public Administration is to select a model that is "large" enough to embrace all the phenomena that should be embraced without being, by virtue of its large dimensions, too coarse textured and clumsy to grasp and manipulate administration. Or so it seemed to me in my own early attempt to come to grips with the subject matter. Technical and normative considerations combine to push one toward breadth: By definition, one needs a model that will enable him to compare different countries, and then probably different (and ultimately all) cultures. And why risk the sins of ethnocentrism? Why presume that "our" ways are better? For that matter, why presume that our organization and administration are somehow "normal." Does not even a primitive tribe – and much more an ancient, non-Western civilization – has organization and administration: systematic, goal-oriented, cooperative? It is this path that led me to the door of Parsons and Levy, Malinowski and Benedict. In structural-functionalism, pattern-variable analysis, in the anthropologists' concept of culture I hoped to find a universal language of organization and administration.

Following this path I gained in insight and understanding – I felt – but I felt also that I had lost clarity and precision. Part of this feeling is attributable to a phenomenon noted earlier, the gap between "large" models and the empirical data. But there is another factor, namely, that the concepts and categories of these modes of thinking are different from those of the study of organization and administration, shaped as they are by ideas of rationality and efficiency, from which the student of modern administration takes his leave. Using the expanded scale one could in some sense compare Texaco's oil production and distribution with Dobuan yam culture, but was he comparing administration? Riggs has struggled mightily to retain worldwide breadth while yet adding precision. But I shall not try here to evaluate his results.

Let me, rather, note a related problem (or a different aspect of the same problem). This is the problem of relating the universal and the unique in one system. The idea of "universals" runs through administrative study from the assertions of the Founding Fathers to the most sophisticated of our contemporaries. But to compare implies not only an identification of the universals, but also criteria of differentiation. Perhaps, structural-functionalism helps identify the universals, while culture accounts for differences. But are these not two different, and not necessarily complementary, ways of viewing things? In any event, I submit there is in our literature some tension "between inherent uniqueness and enforced comparability."

The choice of models is of course ultimately related to the choice of a research strategy, to the most effective employment of limited resources. Here, I have in mind primarily the question of the relative utility of low-level and narrow-range theorizing and data collection as against high-level and broad-range theorizing and data collection, in institutional, cultural, and geographical terms. Much of our study, it has been charged, is culture-bound, taking into view too little of the administrative universe; but the opposite charge is made against contemporary Comparative Public Administration – losing the utility of operationally manageable research because of the grandeur and vagueness of its categories. Do we start at the "bottom" or at the "top"? Can we, perhaps, avoid the dilemma by striking at the "middle"?

Some have argued that we really have no choice: that science proceeds slowly and grows from a central core of what can be observed and tested, introducing into the model no more variables than can be handled; that we only deceive ourselves and invite pseudo-science if we think there is any alternative to the slow hard work of proceeding cautiously from where we are; that "where we are" is really only at the beginnings of an administrative science in one culture and that it will be a long time indeed before we can know much about the matters in which Comparative Public Administration is interested. The alternative view is that scientific theory does not necessarily grow in the manner of a coral island, slowly and around the circumference, but rather that spectacular advances are often made by imaginative new approaches (indeed, even by "accidents"); and one does not achieve macro theory by the gradual expansion of (or working out from) micro theory, but rather that these are separate and simultaneous though – hopefully – ultimately related approaches.

Of course, one can argue that the strategic way forward in general and especially for the study of Comparative Public Administration is neither to start at the bottom with, say, the Small Group and work upward, nor to start with Culture or Society and to work downward, but to move in the area of "theory of the middle range." Indeed, the arguments advanced by Merton on behalf of choosing for attention a range of variables important yet manageable are very compelling in this case. This is, I take it, the appeal and the advantage of the bureaucratic model: It is set in a large framework that spans history and cultures and relates bureaucracy to important societal variables, yet it focuses attention upon the chief structural and functional characteristics of bureaucracy.

No review of the status and problems of the study of Comparative Administration should avoid notice of the schema presented by James D. Thompson and his associates in the introductory chapter of *Comparative Studies in Administration*. This is "middle range" theory and has various interesting aspects.

This essay, though introducing *Comparative Studies in Administration*, is titled, simply and significantly, "On the Study Administration," its essential quality is given by a blend of the old and the new. It starts from the "orthodox" belief that beneath the superficial variety of administrative phenomena there is a substructure of regularity, and that "administrative science" can and will reveal its lawful regularity and "ultimately facilitate the prediction of administrative events in unknown but conceivable circumstances."[49] The authors note the variety of schools and departments teaching administration, the historic dispute whether administration of various functions is essentially different or "basically the same phenomena," and introduce the "comparative approach" as "the most promising way of settling the issue."[50] While it might be argued that there is nothing new *in* the idea that there is lawful regularity in organization and administration and that this is discovered by comparison – Mooney does much "comparing," you recall – this essay brings the argument up to date, so to speak, stating the case in the language of contemporary behavioral science. The intracultural dimension is introduced as a natural next step in the development of administrative science, not with fanfare and as a radical departure; as an extra dimension but not one requiring new elaborate or esoteric methodologies.[51] Whether this is sophistication or its lack only time will tell.

The schema is as follows. The problem is to define administration so that empirical referents permitting scientific theory building are identified. Collectivities – organizations – exhibiting "administration" are distinguished from those that do not, and these "administered organizations" arc found to have four characteristics: They "exhibit sustained collective action," "are integral parts of a larger system," "have specialized, delimited goals," and "are dependent upon interchange with the larger system."[52] These "organizational requirements" of administered organizations "provide the basis for hypothesizing the following functions of administration," namely, "Structuring of the organization as an administrative function," "Definition of purpose as an administrative function," and "Management of the organization-environment exchange system as a function of administration."[53]

These three functions "are appropriate subjects for comparison. Each of these is subject to variation or difference and thus is amenable to comparative research and conceptualization. If organizations differ in structure, we must seek to understand why this occurs and how it affects the contexts of administration. If organizations differ in purposes, we must examine the effects of purposes in other aspects of administration. If organizations operate in different environments, we must learn how environments impinge on and shape organizations, administrative functions and administrative processes."[54]

These, I believe, are the essentials, but it should be added that the authors envisage the development of a large amount of varied and sophisticated theory clustered around each and all of these functions, and that they hope for and expect interchange with and borrowing from a wide range of disciplines or sciences.

The essay by Thompson and associates serves as an appropriate bridge to another methodological puzzle, that of the role of "values" in or their relationship to the study of Comparative Public Administration. The problems presented are, to be sure, but other varieties of the hardy perennials of Social Science, and I risk a boring superficiality in giving some attention to them. However, they *are* centrally involved in the study, not to mention the practice, of comparative administration. For my part, I am repelled by the intellectual rigidity and moral smugness of both ends of the fact – value spectrum, yet I'am unable to find or create a wholly satisfactory "middle" position. Surely – I tell myself – there must be better answers.

Thompson and associates present in sophisticated, clear, and straight-forward manner the "orthodox" position of behavioralism, which is but a more careful statement of what has been the position of "administrative science" from its beginnings: "We firmly believe that there is in the making a rigorous science of administration, which can account for events in partic-ular times and places and for the ethical or normative content of those events without itself incorporating the particular conditions and values of those events." In a more extended or refined version of this position, there is customarily a distinction made between theoretical and practical, or pure and applied, science, which in general is conceived as the distinction between the student or researcher and the practitioner.

Certainly, I find this a useful and from certain perspectives "correct" formulation. Also, however, for certain purposes this formulation seems to me to lack utility or relevance, to be "incorrect." This may only reveal that I am confused. But let me indicate briefly and bluntly what, in relation to the subject of comparative administration (in business as well as government), I have in mind.

First, I affirm that in important ways fact and value cannot be separated, even in the area of "pure" science, as long at least as the science is social.[55] To be sure, they can be separated in logical analysis. But this does not dispose of the matter, for there are at least two other problems. One con-cerns the role of values in the selection of areas and problems for research. I think that there is rather general understanding and agreement on this matter by now: that, as we try to erase preconceptions and preferences from the mind, these inevitably might shape research choices, and that, since this is true, the best we can do is to be self-aware and self-critical. The other problem concerns the shaping of research problems, the conduct of research, and the interpretation of the research findings. Here there is less under-standing and agreement. But my own conclusion is that values inevitably infiltrate and suffuse, color if they do not distort, the "purest" of our social science. There is the least of this, probably when the social science is the most rigorous, especially when it is cast in mathematical form; but in such cases there is also less social science. That is, the rigor is achieved at the cost of relevance *in terms of theory important for social science*, even defining social science in behavioral terms.

The work of Herbert Simon is an important exhibit in this connection. This is because he is an important figure in the terrain we share, and because here, clearly, is a mind of extraordinary power that has been applied both to the separation of fact and value categories and to research putatively following his own methodological imperatives. My own assessment is that much of the coherence and force that *Administrative Behavior* possesses depends upon his definition of efficiency as a factual rather than a valuational matter. I should argue that, while one can speak meaningfully of whether alternative decisions are more or less efficient for given ends under specified conditions, and that this may be regarded as a "factual" matter, this by no means disposes of the matter. Other relevant questions concern why efficiency is "valued" as a means or ratio and whether it makes sense to speak of a science of efficient means for any ends whatsoever. When these matters are explored it is clear – to me – that the "hardness" of the scheme is achieved at the cost of narrowing its relevance to a certain area of concerns and values of our own culture.[56] I conclude, in short, that one can meaningfully pursue a science of efficient means if these means are properly related to certain ends. These "certain ends" in this case are the customary ends of administrative–bureaucratic action in our own culture. Since they have been so deeply imbedded in our culture, and because a student of administration has been almost by definition committed to them and the administrative–bureaucratic means they imply, we have little appreciated the "objective" qualities of our scientific–professional posture (i.e., its subjective qualities as viewed from outside, objectively).

I refer back here to the earlier discussion of Simon and his different reception by and impact upon Business Administration and Public Administration. If my analysis is correct, then I think it indicates one of the important clues to this puzzle: Business Administration, by virtue of its greater commitment to efficiency and its narrower range of – what shall I call it? – value-concern, found Simon more meaningful and acceptable than did Public Administration, which just at this moment in its history was breaking down the barrier between "politics" and "administration," admitting and emphasizing the relevance of administrative means to social, economic, and political ends.[57]

To me a more acceptable methodological response to the fact–value problem (though one with some other difficulties) is that exemplified in Robert Dahl and Charles Lindblom's *Politics, Economics and Welfare*. The approach there offered was signaled earlier by Dahl's statement, quoted above, that "to refuse to recognize that the study of public administration must be founded on some clarification of ends is to perpetuate the gobbledygook of science in the area of moral purposes." The utility and validity of separating a discussion of means from ends and of limiting "scientific" treatment to the former is accepted; but only if the latter are made explicit, so that the relationship between the two is visible for appraisal. Inquiry and its results, that is to say, follow the pattern: If A is desired, then B is a possible (and more or less efficient) means, taking into account as best one can a complex of related factors and the intricate interplay between what is valued and the means of achievement.

"DEVELOPMENT" AS A FOCUS

In conclusion, I wish to argue that a concentration on the theme of development may help to bring into useful association various clusters of ideas and types of activity that are now more or less separate and help clarify some methodological problems; more specifically, that your discipline and mine have something to gain by this both separately and by way of mutual understanding and reinforcement.

This essay is already unconscionably lengthy, and I begin by setting forth some "global" propositions that I shall not defend here.[58] These propositions have been argued, at least suggested, in the foregoing; but I shall not pretend that the case I have made for them is clear and indisputable.

1. The enterprise of Comparative Public Administration would benefit from a "lowering of its sights," a narrowing of its perspective, a closing of the gap between its models and field research, whereas the enterprise of Business Administration would benefit from the "raising of its sights," the broadening of its perspective, which would come from a conscious and careful facing of the problems of comparability. In terms of the above discussion, the former is at present too obsessed with "diversity"; the latter too fixed on the historic theme of "uniformity."

2. A science of administrative means is a meaningful and fruitful enterprise only if the ends it is to serve are posited, consciously or unconsciously. Historically, scholarship in both our disciplines obscured or denied this fact. Presently, because of its more limited objectives and perspectives, yours obscures or denies it more than mine. The obscuring or denying is understandable; but being now understood, is no longer justifiable. The main keys to the understanding of what happened are the interpretation given to *science* as a "value-free" inquiry, and the special "neutrality" presumed for *efficiency*. In fact, to confine attention to *organization* is already to limit attention to goals to be achieved by and through *organization*; and to further concentrate on *administration* or *administered organization* is to introduce by reference, even if unconsciously, the goals of people in societies at a high level of complexity and culture. In fact, our

"science" has been directed toward achieving the goals of modern, industrial Western society, depending on the physical and social technology thereof for its means.

3. Our level of achievement in administrative science is actually, high, in terms of the values of Western urban–industrial society. It is impossible to measure "height," obviously; but I rest the case on the fact that we do have an administrative accomplishment without historical rival, evidenced by the fact that present society exists. The organization and administration involved are not "instinctive" or "normal," and only a purist definition of science would prevent one from attributing our accomplishment to scientific achievement on the social as well as the physical side. At the same time, our scientific achievement is hampered by our systematic obscuring of the fact that our administrative means are related to values of a general type, even if not necessarily to particular goals. Morally, such behavior on our part is a curious form of prudery; psychologically, it is repression.

4. While there is a case for seeking universal, "principled" answers to the central problems of Social Science methodology just as there is a ease for attacking directly such grand concepts as justice and beauty, there is probably no more case for the former than the latter – though those addicted to the former tend to decry the latter. In particular, with regard to the recurring fundamental question of the relation of fact and value, it is sensible and fruitful to solve this problem in particular cases by asking: What is the subject matter? What are the objectives? What is the present level of knowledge and accomplishment? – and so forth.

So much prefaced – dogmatically asserted, if you like – I proceed to the case for focusing on development.

A reasonable first step would be to define development as used in the present connection. However, I find this impossible; and my approach rather is to try to make a virtue of my difficulty. I argue that one of the reasons for focusing on development is that, though there is a large literature and much activity concerned with development, there is much confusion and controversy over what it means and what it implies in terms of goals and means to goals. But the issues that are involved are important ones to our respective and mutual professional–scientific endeavors; and important in world politics if we concede only that American technical assistance and overseas business has some role on that stage. It is highly desirable that the issues and problems involved in trying to define development be posed as sharply and urgently as possible, to achieve as much clarity of ends and effectiveness of means as we can.

The essence of my argument for focusing on development is that, in the above terms, it "lowers" Comparative Public Administration and "raises" Business Administration. It gives both enterprises a programmatic goal or value orientation, which is an essential element in solving their respective methodological problems. It enables both of them to offer the considerable amount of science and technology they do have to offer, for the objectives for which it is efficient (or at least sufficient), but to do it with sophistication, that is, with knowledge of the interrelations of ends, means, and ecology where we have such knowledge and with awareness of ignorance where we do not. At the same time, it will bring these two enterprises into closer interrelation, so that complementarity and reinforcement may result.

The case goes beyond our two enterprises, and relates to the problem of definition. Many parts and aspects of Social Science are now concerned with development in an expanding, self-conscious way. Development economics now has an extensive literature. "Community development" may not be a respectable part of Sociology or Social Psychology, but certainly it is a perspective and an active movement with a now-considerable literature. There is a growing interest in development politics, and development administration is becoming a focus of interest among students of Comparative Public Administration.[59] I also note that development education is becoming a focus of interest among the Educationists. There is an obvious need for these various enterprises to be knowledgeable about each other, both intellectually and "in the field"; and for them to be as sharp and clear as possible on what they mean, respectively and collectively, by development. There will be much confusion, wasted effort, and conflict at best. But with much effort we might hope to avoid chaos. With luck, we might even advance a bit in Social Science and strengthen national and foreign policies in ways we would agree are desirable.

There are, some think, serious difficulties and strategic risks in the course I advocate. Centrally, it may be thought, by abandoning a commitment to value-neutrality we open the way to ethnocentrism, to cultural, ethical and ideological bias: to easy optimism about an evolutionary force or trend or to an obnoxious doctrinairism about "advance" from "traditional" to "modern" society, as the latter is pictured and suggested, say, in the pages of *Better Homes and Gardens.* Or to give this appearance or to be so accused. But as against these dangers, real or imagined (I think both) are posed the greater ones I have at least suggested.

Some of the dangers suggested *are* imaginary, as some acquaintance with the attempts to clarify the concept of development indicates. Indeed, one of the merits of focusing upon development as a process in relation to certain types of goals is that it avoids an excessive ethnocentrism as our own country is very "underdeveloped" in some parts and ways, and "development" is at the center of our national problems.[60] That is, all countries are placed on one plane, even if at different points along some scale or scales. Likewise, a defense is developed against the charge of cultural (or other) imperialism: if you wish – but only if you wish – certain types of development, here is the science and technology, and here is how it relates to your goals. Our own moral position is clarified: we know that a civilization with running water, airplanes, and aseptic surgery has also disadvantages and risks, and our question is, "Do you, on balance, prefer the combination to your present situation?"

To focus consciously on the theme of development in the study and practice of administration would mean of course a considerable shift in activities and in ways of viewing things. But, first, I do not propose that everyone should stop what he is doing and start doing something else; much would remain unaffected, in the short run at least, though some shift in the allocation of our professional resources might be indicated. The area of Operations Research and other highly refined techniques for achieving rationality are not immediately concerned, as I view it. They are highly efficient where they are "relevant," but they are relevant only in a relatively narrow range of administration in highly developed socio-administrative complexes. The focus on development would, hopefully, help in making rational decisions on the type and level of rationality that is possible in differing situations. If the study of Comparative Public Administration has done nothing else, it has fully demonstrated the relativity of administrative means to administrative ends.[61] Posing in one system of thought customary administrative ideas and techniques, different types of cultures, different levels of culture, different objectives, and borrowing concepts from Sociology and Anthropology – all this is to introduce "relativity." Its introduction does not "invalidate" what has preceded any more than relativity invalidates classical physics, but it does indicate limitation and, open new worlds.

Second, to focus on development does not mean that all other "models" are invalidated and should be abandoned. Of course, they continue to serve whatever purposes they now serve. It does mean that their purposes and their effectiveness be re-evaluated from time to time, and that their relationship to developmental goals be a matter of conscious thought rather than of accident. A special attention is needed to the charge that equilibrium models (of whatever discipline or type) are "static" and (or) "conservative" in their consequences for research and action.[62] More generally, the question is posed, do we need more "dynamic" and fewer "static" models?

The proposal to focus attention on development has risks. One possibility is that I am confusing fashionability with feasability, desirability, potentiality. Am I?

NOTES

1. The founders were not very clear on this point. Thus, W. F. Willoughby, the author of the second textbook, wrote in 1919 that administration "if not a science, a subject to the study of which the scientific method should be rigidly applied." Introduction to G. A. Weber's *Organized Efforts for rite Improvement of Methods of Administration in the United States* (New York: 1919), p. 30. Later writers have had available a literature on scientific method and philosophy presenting sharp distinctions between pure and applied science, science and technology, and so forth. The *validity* of such distinctions is another matter.

2. "The Science of Public Administration," in *Essays in Political Science* (Baltimore: 1937), J. M. Mathews and J. Hart, eds., Vol. 39, pp. 39–73.

3. Not entirely: See Schuyler C. Wallace, Federal Departmentalization: A Critique of Theories of Organization (New York: 1941).

4. *Public Administration Review* (Winter, 1947), 1–11.

5. (New York: 1947).

6. (New York: 1948).

7. And "If there is ever to be a science of public administration it must derive from an understanding of man's behavior in the area marked off by the boundaries of public administration." (p. 7), emphasis added.

8. Milton J. Esman's "Japanese Administration – A Comparative View," 7 *Public Administration Review* (Spring, 1947), 100–112, remains today a sophisticated and useful essay.

9. On the history of the movement see especially: W.J. Siffin, "Toward the Comparative Study of Public Administration," in *Toward the Comparative Study of Public Administration,* Siffin, ed. (Indiana University, 1957). Fred W. Riggs, "Trends in the Comparative Study of Public Administration," 28 *International Review of Administrative Sciences* (No. 1, 1962), 9–15. Ferrel Heady, "Comparative Public Administration Concerns and Priorities," in *Papers in Comparative Public Administration,* Heady, ed. (Institute of Public Administration, Ann Arbor, 1962) and R. S. Milne, "Comparisons and Models in Public Administration," 10 *Politico/Studies* (February, 1962), 1–14. The Siffin and Heady essays introduce collections of essays; all are excellent for summary, perspective, and introduction to other sources. The June 1960 issue of *Administrative Science Quarterly* is "Special Issue on Comparative Public Administration" containing essays both specialized and general. *Comparative Studies in Administration* (Pittsburgh: 1959), edited by James D. Thompson, Peter B. Hammond, Robert W. Hawkes, Buford H. Junker, and Arthur Tuden, is an interesting volume that seeks to bridge the gap between "public" and "business" administration to comparative administration. *See* especially Chapter 1,

"On the Study of Administration." For further exploration, see *Comparative Public Administration A Selective Annotated Bibliography*, by Ferrel Heady and Sybil L. Stokes, 2nd ed. (Institute of Public Administration, Ann Arbor: 1960).

10. Perhaps the most notable of these is the "case" approach. Under the Committee on Public Administration Cases and its successor, the Inter-University Case program, some 80 cases have been published and as many more are "in preparation." This is the most notable, but not the only, case series in Public Administration. See *Essays on the Case Method in Public Administration*, Edwin A. Bock, ed., published jointly by the Inter-University Case Program and the International Institute of Administrative Sciences (Brussels and New York: 1962).

11. See my *Political Science in the United States of America: A Trend Report* (UNESCO: 1956), especially Chapter II, for a fuller account of the nature and impact of behavioralism. A supplement and a more recent view is contained in the symposium *Tue Limits of Behavioralism in Political Science*, J.C. Charlesworth, ed., sponsored by the American Academy of Political and Social Science (October 1962).

12. The most effective critical attack to date is, I think Herbert J. Storing, "The Science of Administration," in *Essays on the Scientific Study of Politics* Storing, ed. (New York: 1962). In general, I find his criticism persuasive, I think he has found critical weaknesses in Simon's formulations. I add, however, that I do not wish to associate myself with the "positive" as against the "critical" part of the Philosophy and methodology represented in general by the authors of the book "Straussism." I add this because to many of my professional colleagues Straussism is evil equivalent to several of the capital sins.

13. On the Comparative Politics movement see: "Research in Comparative Politics," a report on a Summer Seminar on Comparative Politics sponsored by SSRC, with comments by six non-participants, p. 42. *American Political Science Review* September 1953, 641–675. Roy Macridis, *The Study of Comparative Government* (New York: 1955). David Eastoti, "Approach to The Analysis of Political Systems," 9 *World Politics* April 1957, 333–400. Gabriel Almond and James S. Coleman, eds., *The Politics of the Developing Areas* (Princeton: 1960); David Apter, "A Comparative Method for the Study of Politics," 14 *American Journal of Sociology* (November 1958), 221–237.

14. David Easton's, *The Political System: An Inquiry into the State of Political Science* (New York: 1953) is important in this connection. His definition of the political as "the authoritative allocation of values" has been widely influential.

15. The Introduction in the Almond and Coleman volume cited above. 3–58. Alfred Diamant's "The Relevance of Comparative Politics to the Study of Comparative Administration,' 5, *Administrative Science Quarterly* (June 1960), 87–112, is an excellent discussion of various methodological questions. Centrally, it is a comparison of "General Systems" models and "Political Cultures" models.

16. p. 7.

17. *Loc. cit.*, p. 9.

18. *Ibid.*, p. 10.

19. *Ibid.*, p. 11.

20. *Ibid.* Nomothetic studies are further divided between homological and analogical studies, the former focuses upon "structures in different systems which have parallel characteristics," the latter upon functions, which "often can be characterized

in terms of variables" (p. 13). His own interests and the most promising path of researches are identified with the latter.

21. *Ibid.*, p. 15. Riggs here backs up a step and says of the ecological approach, "My point, then, is not to claim a trend, but rather to indicate a necessity for the future." He concludes: "My own preference would be to consider as 'truly' comparative only those studies which are empirical, nomothetic, and ecological."

22. *Loc. cit.*, p. 4.

23. Of course, we little appreciated that this was what we were doing since, however parochial our interests and our empirical base, the language and the presumption was in terms of "universals."

24. The *Handbook of Public Administration*, issued by the Technical Assistance Programme of the United Nations is the outstanding exhibit here. For a highly perceptive review of this document, see Edgar L. Shor, "Comparative Administration: Static Study Versus Dynamic Reform," 22 *Public Administration Review* (September 1962), 158–164.

25. See footnote 10.

26. One cannot, of course, describe what takes place solely in terms of disciplines or fields. There is constant change of "lines," new "interests" form and reform, within and without older disciplines. Much of contemporary organizational research can be characterized more clearly by the institutional location (e.g., the "plant") or by the methodological focus (e.g., decision-making theory) than by identifying it with an academic discipline.

27. As Economics is much concerned with these matters, this would seem to question the above assertion that the relationship with Economics is not close. But the borrowing or inspiration, as I understand it, is from Systems Theory, not Economics.

28. Surveying the present situation, Heady concludes that "major tendencies among the more comprehensive theory building efforts" can presently be designated as (1) "modified traditional" (While I have discussed above this "traditional" literature, it does of course represent or follow a *"mode!"* in a general sense, whether this is recognized or not.); (2) "equilibrium or input–output"; (3) "bureaucratic orientation"; and (4) "ecologically oriented." *Loc. cit.*, p. 4.

29. Robert V. Presthus is a conspicuous exception. *See* "The Social Bases of Bureaucratic Organization," 38 *Social Forces* (December 1959) 103–108, and "Weberian v. Welfare Bureaucracy in Traditional Society," 6 *Administrative Science Quarterly* (June 1961) 1–24; "Behavior and Bureaucracy in Many Cultures," 19 *Public Administration Review* (Winter 1959) 2535 "The Sociology of Economic Development," *International Journal of Comparative Sociology* (September 1960) 195–201. These essays discuss various methodological problems in addition to presenting (and applying, in "Weberian v. Welfare Bureaucracy") the bureaucratic model. For a "Public Administrationist" approach *see* also, Edgar L. Shor, "The Thai Bureaucracy," 5 *Administrative Science Quarterly* (June 1960) 66–86.

30. In the *Papers* edited by Ferrel Heady and Sybil L. Stokes, cited above, 59–96. *See* also, Ferrel Heady, "Bureaucratic Theory and Comparative Administration," 3 *Administrative Science Quarterly* (March 1959) 509–525.

31. The volume of Riggs' writings, both published and unpublished, is so great that, as Ferrel Heady notes (both seriously and humorously), "mere acquaintance

with all his writings on comparative theory is in itself not an insignificant achievement." In most respects, Riggs is the central figure in the Comparative Public Administration movement. He is the Chairman of the so-called Comparative Administration Group of the American Society for Public Administration. The Ford Foundation recently made a sizable grant to the Society for a three-year program of activity, chiefly research, in the area of comparative public administration, focused especially upon problems of development and assistance; the Comparative Administration Group is the "agent" for the program.

32. In the volume edited by Siffin, cited above, 32.116.

33. For this, Riggs in his introduction credits my *Study of Public Administration* (New York: 1955), in which I had argued the probable value of the concept of culture, and of structural-functionalism, in the *attempt* to find a *framework* broad enough to be free of parochial bias and containing conceptual tools enabling us to discriminate between *types* of administration. Talcott Parsons and Marion Levy are drawn upon and, especially, F. X. Sutton.

34. Presumably, what in general these terms "imply" is known to this group. *See* especially footnote 29.

35. The new terminology has been set forth in a number of essays. I have before me "Models in the Comparative Study of Public Administration," mimeo, 1959. Quotation from footnote 22.

36. See "An Ecological Approach The Sala Model," in volume edited by Heady and Stokes, pp. 19–36 and The Ecology of Public Administration (New Delhi: 1961).

37. "An Information-Energy Model," in the Heady–Stokes volume, 37–57.

38. An example: "The relative scarcity of information inputs to control and maintenance systems results in adaptations of such subsystems and of the system as a whole to its environment under relatively high degrees of uncertainty. Hypothesis Administrative decision-making occurs under conditions of relatively high uncertainty" (p. 51).

39. In "Organization Theory An Elephantine Problem," 21 *Public Administration Review* (Autumn 1961) 210–225.

40. Although the dominant emphasis is on commercial and industrial organizations, the reader will appreciate that the principles discussed apply to any type of organization, including governmental, philanthropic, military, educational, voluntary or political. Albert H. Rubenstein and Chadwick J. Haberstroh, eds., *Some Theories of Organization* (Homewood: 1960), Preface.

41. Refer to Mason Haire, Edwin Ghiselli and L. W. Porter, *Management in the Industrial World: An International Analysis* (New York: 1959). The work by Frederick H. Harbison and Charles A. Myers, is of course a comparative study, and a good one. Reinhard Bendix' *Work and Authority in industry* (New York: 1956), is in comparison with historical depth and cultural breadth – but there is a question whether it can be identified with Business Administration.

42. Presthus, commenting, presumably, on American business personnel in the Middle East where he spent considerable time, says "It is most revealing to observe a group of skilled technicians and businessmen, who may have lived in a given foreign country a decade or more but are unable to define the existing problems and requirements of social change simply because they have not had the training which would permit a sociological or psychological conceptualization of the issue." "The Sociology of Economic Developrnent," cited above, p. 196.

43. Put in other terms, while there is a large literature viewing organizations as "adaptive" social systems set in larger social systems, into which actors carry the varied values of the larger system, the predominate view has been of organizations as "co-operative" systems, largely self-contained. Sometimes, of course, the two views are embraced in a single work. But even when cultural diversity within the enviroment has been an important element in the schema, these diversities have been generally "subcultural" or "intra-cultural" differences within the American environment.

44. It should be understood that I am using this expression as indicated above to include those writings having business as their focus and orientation, whatever the academic label or department of the writer.

45. I do not recall any explicit reference to culture in Administrative Behavior: It turns toward Economics, not toward Sociology or Anthropology. In March and in Simon's Organizations, the possible significance of the cultural factor is recognized 25 times (by my count), explicitly or implicitly. There is no direct confrontation of the issue, so to speak, but there is the recognition that evidence bearing on the generalization, or the generalization, may be culture-related. For example, "Second, the greater the cultural centrality of the organization, the greater the similarity of its norms to those professed by other groups in the same culture" (p. 78), which seems a safe-enough generalization.

46. I am indebted to the students in my seminar for much of what value this analysis may have. At this point I acknowledge a special indebtedness to Philippe O. Schmitter, who writes of the matter I am now discussing: "Because the comparative study of public administration and organization theory depart from different viewpoints on the matter of administrative behavior and operate at different levels of analysis, the two have not met, but only coexist competitively."

47. "Comments on the Theory of Organizations," 46 *American Political Science Review* (December 1952) 1130–1139, 1935–1936. It is interesting that, though Simon did not choose this road himself, he clearly marked its importance.

48. "On Communications Models in the Social Sciences," 16 *Public Opinion Quarterly* (Fall 1952) 356–380, 356. Deutsch defines a model as "a structure of symbols and operating rules which is supposed to match a set of relevant points in an existing structure or process" (p. 357). In this essay, I use "model" interchangeably with "schema" and "theory" meaning in all cases a conceptual framework to organize and manipulate data. I am aware of distinctions sometimes made in the use of these terms, but these distinctions do not seem useful or necessary here.

49. *Op. cit.*, p. 3. "Administrative science is establishing an identity and is gaining momentum. We firmly believe that there is in the making a rigorous science of administration, which can account for events in particular times and places and for the ethical or normative content of those events without itself incorporating the particular conditions and values of those events. The necessary theory must take such factors into account as variables. These variables must be broad enough to include the conditions and ethics found in all fields of administration and in all cultural contexts" (p. 4).

50. *Ibid.*, p. 9.

51. In fact, some of my students reported that Thompson and associates were interested only in intra-cultural comparison. The point is that all comparison,

intra- and inter-cultural, function or field as against function or field, and so forth, are placed on one plane.

52. *Ibid.*, pp. 5–6. Considerable emphasis is placed upon "process" and on defining administration in terms of what it *does* rather than what it *is*. As social science, this is both "correct" and fashionable, and I agree. However – I have never seen and cannot imagine a definition of administration other than in terms of what it *does*; for action, process, is the central idea of the word. A definition may begin "Administration is but the *is* is defined by what it *does*.

53. *Ibid.*, p. 7.

54. *Ibid.*, p. 9.

55. Some have argued that they cannot be disentangled even in the realm of physical science, but my affirmation does not extend to this area.

56. Rather paradoxically, I reach this conclusion by the route of behaviorally respectable Sociology of Knowledge. Incidentally, I should not like to be interpreted as "against Social Science."

57. My "criticism" of Simon here does not run to the vast range of his writing, some of which I cannot even understand and which it would be presumptuous of me even to praise. My argument is that, whatever the size of his "contribution," nevertheless he was wrong and misled others on some central methodological issues. As to whether he followed his own methodological prescriptions and on the subject of whether and how "values" entered or affected his work – exploration can at least begin with the essay by Storing, cited above, and Sherman Krupp's *Pattern in Organization Analysis: A Critical Examination* (Philadelphia and New York: 1953), Ch. 6.

58. Or qualify, which pains me more, as I realize that qualification is necessary to do justice to truth.

59. I am especially indebted to Edward W. Weidner's "Development Administration A New Focus for Research," in Heady and Stokes, pp. 97–115. If my argument has any appeal, then the Weidner essay is Recommended Reading. See also: Edgar L. Shor, "Comparative Administration Static Study Versus Dynamic Reform," 22 *Public Administration Review* (September, 1962), 1958–1964, the concluding sections of which is "Needed: A Model of the Process of Change."

60. "Development is ... never complete; it is relative, more or less of it being possible. Development is a state of mind, a tendency, a direction. Rather than a fixed goal *it* is a rate of change in a particular direction." Weidner, *loc. cit.*, p. 99. This skates quickly over thin ice covering deep and treacherous waters. My proposal raises the severest problems in definition and value clarification. But I repeat these problems are small when placed beside the costs of ignoring them.

61. The recent literature is interesting on the subject of "corruption": bribery of officials is now viewed as "functional" rather than "dysfunctional" in certain contexts.

62. "This is a general, and now rather old, question. But it is being asked sharply in the recent literature. The article by Shor, cited above, points out that our administrative norms do not necessarily "fit" *our* culture. It is now a frequently expressed opinion that development – by definition – involves disequilibrium and implies disequilibrium models.

COMPARATIVE PUBLIC ADMINISTRATION: THE SEARCH FOR THEORIES

Monty van Wart and Joseph N. Cayer

It is sometimes forgotten that while comparative public administration only developed a self-conscious identity as a field of inquiry in the late 1950s, comparative pieces were nonetheless being produced, before then. For example, from its inception *Public Administration Review (PAR)* has published articles with comparative and development concerns. In its "heyday" comparative public administration was a field of wide interest and prestige, and understandably comparative pieces increased, in *PAR*[1] and other journals. However, in the 1970s, many of the social sciences were criticized as in need of more relevance and, ironically, less ethnocentrism; comparative public administration was particularly hard hit. Symptomatic of the malaise that occurred in the field, the leading journal in the United States, the *Journal of Comparative Administration,*[2] was reconstituted in 1973 with a distinctly less comparative focus in 1976, the November/December issue of the *Public Administration Review*[3] featured a series of articles about the field which sounded like impressive eulogies at best,[4] and, at worst, sounded like the pre-sentence comments from a hanging judge.[5] The major criticisms were that the field was too involved in the quest for a comprehensive paradigm or meta-theory, that it was not empirical enough, and that it was too self-absorbed in academic concerns and insufficiently relevant. After that *PAR* issue of 14 years ago, most people in public

Comparative Public Administration: The Essential Readings
Research in Public Policy Analysis and Management, Volume 15, 171–192
Copyright © 2006 by Elsevier Ltd.
All rights of reproduction in any form reserved
ISSN: 0732-1317/doi:10.1016/S0732-1317(06)15005-8

administration and in other comparative areas seemed to think that the field had either merged with the field at large or simply ceased to exist altogether.

The demise of the field is clearly overstated. Nicholas Henry aptly notes, "Comparative public administration has been productive and active as a subfield; reports of its death are premature ... ."[6] in his authoritative text on the field, Ferrel Heady expresses the opinion "that it is neither necessary nor feasible to strive for restoration of the degree of autonomy and separatism once characteristic of the, burgeoning comparative public administration movement."[7] While these comments clearly dispute the field's demise per se, they give no indication of the extent or nature of the inquiry into comparative administration in the 1980s. While some scholarly works in the 1980s have reviewed limited aspects of contemporary comparative public administration literature, none 'has sought a comprehensive review of the journal literature nor dealt with it in an empirically systematic fashion.[8]

This study assesses comparative public administration by employing a content analysis of a wide variety of journals. The questions investigated are directed at defining characteristics of inquiry in the field. How substantial a literature is being produced? Who is active in research in the field and why? What are the topics that are stimulating the most interest? How is research being carried out? Answering these questions will allow more realistic appraisals of the current role of comparative public administration.

Briefly, this study reviews 20 journals for 5 years, from 1982 to 1986. These journals include six that are published outside the United States, six from political science, two that deal with development studies, and two from related fields. From these journals, 253 items were selected as having a comparative component, and they were analyzed for 59 variables.[9]

This article is divided into four sections. The first section provides a brief discussion of the history and issues of the field. The second section describes the study and the results of the investigation. The third section provides an analysis and interpretation and relates the results to major paradigmatic debates. Concluding remarks briefly speculate on the prospects for comparative public administration as an area of scholarly interest.

BACKGROUND

A Brief History

The 1950s and 1960s were times of haphazard and yet vigorous growth in many academic and policy disciplines. The end of the World War II left the

United States at the economic center of the world with commensurate technological, political, and cultural might. For many products, much of the higher technology, free-market leadership, and new social and administrative models, the world looked inordinately 'to the United States.' American leadership as a countervailing force to communism was particularly evident. However, foreign aid during the time, impressive though the Four Point and the Marshall Plan might have been, was as much an answer to an emergency as a strategic plan. Precursors 'to the U.S. Agency for International Development' (USAID) were little more than continuing resolutions. During this time comparative and development administration were coming into importance as academic domains of discourse with an inchoate sense of identity.[10]

The academic momentum in the 1960s accelerated rapidly. In the decade from 1962 to 1971, which Ferrel Heady dubs the heyday of comparative public administration, the field grew in numbers, funding, and academic attention.[11] Over 500 members had joined the Comparative Administration Group (CAG) of the American Society for Public Administration (ASPA) by 1968. Also during this period the Ford Foundation funded the CAG for two 5-year periods. While the funding itself was not massive, the stimulus was considerable. Even university curricula were not immune to the enthusiasm, and courses in comparative and development administration became far more common and in some cases were required.[12] External events also tended to propel American academicians and technicians abroad: the new thrust in Latin American affairs stimulated by the Cuban Revolution and the subsequent Alliance for Progress, the rapid decolonization of Africa, the Vietnam War in Asia, and the formalization of a standing foreign aid agency.

Yet the early promises of a better world in the Kennedy and early Johnson years were quickly to give way to questions, then statements, and finally condemnations about ethnocentrism and imperialism. Critics probed the modernization literature of political science and economics and the realism literature of international relations and found them doubly blinded by the "narrowness" of the Western liberal perspective and by the positivist "illusion" of a fact-value dichotomy. Comparative public administration was left peculiarly vulnerable; it was neither an established field of its own, nor did it have an institutional sponsor. The bubble burst as rapidly as it had formed.

In the 1980s comparative and development administration courses became fewer and chapters in basic textbooks shrank into sections in chapters.While the results of this study indicate that the journal literature continued to be substantial, some of the types of work that give a field identity and zest were largely missing. Gone were the heated debates, grand theorizing,[13] state-of-the-field critiques, and self-conscious discussions. Finally, it is only in the last few years that several major new works have been published, bringing together consolidated insights[14] which may begin to rekindle a genuine excitement that has long been lacking in comparative administration. Yet despite the lack of verve in the field as a whole, individual topics have continued to develop more comprehensive approaches and mature literature.

PARADIGMATIC DEBATES

Four debates have continued through the field's history. Is the study of comparative and development administration a "true" field? What is the "correct" or best methodology to use? Should comparative public administration be more theoretically or practitioner oriented? And where should comparative public and development administration look for inspiration and focus?

After 1976, many scholars with comparative interests in public administration seemed willing to accept a lesser status than a field or subfield, such as "perspective," but were unwilling to accede to a complete loss of identity. At least three factors argue for the need for its separate and distinct identity within public administration. First, all comparative studies face special challenges, and those of comparative public administration are especially acute.[15] Second, parochialism and ethnocentrism have many subtle manifestations that pervade areas that are not kept honest by the comparative perspective.[16] Third, a special need exists for the study of public administration in "developing" countries, and special problems are present in conducting such studies.[17] In a recent article on the problems confronting comparative study in public administration, Aberbach and Rockman point out that, "comparative study pushes ... and propels us to a level of conceptual methodological self consciousness and clarity rarely found in noncomparative studies of public administration."[18]

The two major methodological debates have to do with definition and quantification. What constitutes a comparative study has, at times, been very much an issue of contention. One loose definition is to classify as comparative all materials that are useful to scholars who are interested in polities other than their own. Thus articles on Australia in American journals and articles on the United States in Australian journals would qualify, even if only a single country were examined. This broad definition was used for inclusion in this study. A second, more restricted definition is offered by Sigelman and Gadbois[19] who suggest that a more stringent test is to require single-case studies (which make up the bulk) to be more readily theoretically comparable either by comparing intra-national governments, by being theoretically oriented, or by testing' hypotheses. The strictest definition requires that two or more countries be overtly compared. While the rigor of this last definition is admirable, it tends to produce narrow-gauged studies that are insensitive to environments in which administrations operate. Journals have occasionally overcome the single-case problem by having a single type of administrative structure or issue[20] explored in terms of different countries by different authors in a special issue. Taken individually the articles might be considered non-comparative, but taken as a whole the articles have a distinctly comparative quality. Also, editors of texts have subordinated country specialists to parallel presentations, that also increases the comparability of the whole, especially if augmented by summary chapters.[21]

Another methodological debate is the qualitative versus quantitative issue. Social scientists of the behavioralist tradition have been sharply critical of what they perceive to be the insufficient use of quantitative techniques.[22] The theoretical orientation versus an applied orientation has also been a shrill issue. The theoretical orientation of Fred Riggs and the CAG generally was seen as excessive by many. In fact, the grand theorizing of the ecological school coupled with the "pure research" attitude of the behavioralist school led some in development administration to complain that both approaches were too academic and lacking in relevance and ethical involvement. Some even talked of secession.[23] While most of the abstract end of the spectrum represented by grand theorizing has long since lost vogue, much question remains as to who the audience is or should be. Although there seems to be a continuing decline in the number of practitioners writing for and receiving scholarly public administration journals, the journal editors seem to resist the "academicians writing for academicians" syndrome, which long has been the fate of political science.[24]

Finally, one of the knottiest debates for comparative public administration has been the issue of where to look for inspiration and focus. Indeed, the parent discipline of public administration has also been plagued by this difficulty. One recent commentator acknowledged that "American public administration lacks a coherent theoretical foundation" and that it "is an eclectic field that lacks a clearly theoretical foundation, thus borrowing theories and analytic approaches from many disciplines."[25] The problems for comparative public administration are 'only amplified by cross-cultural factors demanding that sociological, political, and economic aspects be factored into administrative analyses.

THE STUDY AND THE RESULTS

To answer in part the question about how much is being published, who is publishing and why, what topics are being investigated, and how topics are being researched, a content analysis of 20 English-language journals was conducted for 1982 through 1986 inclusive. Books and other nonperiodical publications were not examined, limiting this study.

The journals were inspected by hand and articles were generally selected if they referred to the administration of a country other than the country of the publication or if the administrations of two or more countries were compared. Articles had to be 'a minimum of five pages' in length to be included. In a few cases the rules of selection varied because of the special nature of the journal. In the *International Review of Administrative Sciences* all articles in English were included because of its explicitly comparative focus and origin (Brussels) and its devotion to administrative science. Similarly, *Planning and Administration* has an explicitly, international focus, being underwritten by the International K Union of Local Authorities and the International Federation for Housing and Planning, but many of the articles were more oriented to policy than to administration and were not included. The range extended from 113 items for the *International Review of Administrative Sciences* to zero items from *Human Relations*.

ACTIVE OR DORMANT: THE JOURNALS

In order to rank journal selection, Mark W. Huddleston's 624-item bibliography (*Comparative Public Administration: An Annotated Bibliography*) was tabulated. The 74 journals that he identifies were ranked according to number of items cited. Some of the most highly cited are the *International Journal of Administrative Sciences* (116), *Public Administration* (58), *Administration & Society* (37), *Public Administration Review* (30), and *Administrative Science Quarterly* (20). In general, the 20 journals with the most citations in Huddleston were examined. Several substitutions were made. The *Philippine Journal of Public Administration* and the *Indian Journal of Public Administration* were deleted from consideration because their articles tend to be short and of mixed quality. In their places the *Australian Journal of Public Administration* and the *International Journal of Public Adminis-tration* were substituted. The former, older than *PAR*, has substantial, high-quality pieces, and the latter, while a relatively new journal,[26] does partially focus on comparative public administration, even if not as much as its title, would seem to indicate. *Planning and Administration* was substituted for the *Journal of Administration Overseas* because of availability. See Table 1 for a listing of the journals and their frequencies.

To get a sense of the significance of the 253 items coded, it is useful to think in terms of journal output. The range varies. A small journal with longer pieces such as the *Journal of Comparative Administration* produced only 82 articles in its 5-year tenure, or about 20 a year. The *International Review of Administrative Sciences* produced 113 in the 5 years studied, but some non-English articles were excluded prior to the journal's change in 1986 to both an exclusively English and a duplicate French publication.

Table 1. Comparative/Development Administration Articles in Journals by Frequency and Rank.

Journal	Frequency	Rank	Rank in Huddleston
International Review of Administrative Science	113	1	1
Public Administration (London)	22	2	2
International Journal of Public Administration	18	3	a
Public Administration Review	16	4	4
Planning and Administration	15	5	a
Administration & Society[b]	11	6–7	3
Asian Survey	11	6.7	10
Canadian Public Administration	6	8–10	9
Public Personnel Management	6	8–10	13
Australian Journal of Public Administration	6	8–10	a
Political Studies	5	11	6
Journal of Developing Areas	4	12–15	14
Comparative Political Studies	4	12–15	7
Comparative Studies in Society and History	4	12–15	17
Development and Change	4	12–15	18
American Political Science Review	3	16	12
Administrative Science Quarterly	2	17–18	5
Comparative Politics	2	17–18	11
American Journal of Political Science	1	19	16
Human Relations	0	20	19

[a]Not ranked in Huddleston.
[b]Formerly the *Journal of Comparative Administration*.

PAR, publishing six times a year with shorter pieces, produced about 40 standard articles a year during the period studied, or 200 in this 5-year time frame. On average it could be said that 253 items represent approximately the output of two journals.

As would be expected, journals with an international interest and a public administration focus were among the higher frequencies. Those journals (and their ranking in, this study) were the *International Review of Administrative Sciences,* ranked first; the *International Journal of Public Administration,* ranked third; and *Planning and Administration,* ranked' fifth. Not surprisingly, journals with an international interest but without a concomitant focus on public administration did not rank high.

Not expected was the high performance of the "flagship" public, administration journals for, the United Kingdom, the United States, and to a lesser extent, Canada and Australia. Twenty-two items were coded for *Public Administration,* ranked second; 16 items for *PAR,* ranked fourth; and 6 each for *Canadian Public Administration* and the *Australian Journal of Public Administration,* tied for ranks 8 and 10. As interesting is the fact that when using Huddleston's bibliography as a basis of comparison, the rankings of three of these journals, (the *Australian Journal of Public Administration* was not cited in the Huddleston bibliography) are virtually identical, that is 2, 4, and 9, respectively. This would seem to indicate that *Public Administration* and *PAR* have consciously and consistently tried to extend their perspectives beyond national borders under various editors.

WHO AND WHY: PRACTITIONERS AND ACADEMICIANS, POLICY RECOMMENDATIONS, AND THEORY TESTING

Who is practicing and teaching in comparative and development administration and why they work in this field are complex questions. One way to answer these questions is to look at the numbers of practitioners and non-practitioners. Another way is to look at the degree to which policy recommendations are featured in articles. Still a third way is to look at the degree to which theory testing is the mode of analysis used. Thus, the first question focuses on the occupations or affiliations of the authors. The second question focuses on the degree to which the result is practical or applied. The third question focuses on the degree to which the result is scientifically rigorous.

All articles were coded as having nongovernmental authors or government practitioners. Government practitioners were defined as either having titled government positions or specific jobs being performed (by academicians or others) for the government related to the topic of the journal publication. Academicians on government grants such as National Science Foundation Grants were not included in this category. Also, academicians in national public administration academies were not coded as in government. If any of multiple authors was government related, the, article was coded as "government practitioner." More common was the problem of poor or no indication of the author's affiliation. Unless there was clear indication of government affiliation, the item was coded as nongovernment.[27] Thus the number of items, recorded as government practitioner is undoubtedly a conservative figure. It was found that authors of 42 articles (16.6%) were government practitioners. This is in line with or slightly below other reports of practitioners as journal authors in public administration.[28] The *International Review of Administrative Sciences* was most predisposed to practitioner authors, whereas there was only a solitary case in the political science journals.[29] See Table 2 for the results.

To assess the degree to which the author seemed to want the article to have applied utility, each item was coded for practical advice in the form of

Table 2. Government Practitioners versus Nongovernmental Practitioners as Authors of Articles.

	Overall Frequency (N = 253)		IRAS[a] (N = 112)	P.A. Flagship[b] (N = 50)	Political Science[c] (N = 26)
	#	%	%	%	%
Government practitioners	42	16.6	24.1	14	3.8
Nongovernment practitioners	211	83.4	75.9	86	96.2
Total	253		100.0	100.0	100.0

[a]*International Review of Administrative Sciences.*

[b]Public administration "flagship" journals included here are *Public Administration Review, Public Administration (London), Canadian Public Administration,* and *Australian Journal of Public Administration.*

[c]The political science journals included here are *Asian Survey, Political Studies, Comparative Political Studies, American Political Science Review, Comparative Politics,* and *American Journal of Political Science.*

policy recommendations or prescriptions. Four levels of policy recommendations were used: none, low, moderate, and high. Briefly described, "none" means that there are no policy recommendations. "Low" means that policy recommendations are not the thrust of the piece and either appear only in the conclusion or are vaguely stated or implied throughout. "Moderate" means that the policy recommendations are a stated objective of the article. However, to be rated as "high," the policy recommendations must be the primary objective of the article and must also be clearly stated and specific. The categories "none," "low," and "moderate" were fairly well balanced with 77 items (30.4%), 74 items (29.2%), and 65 items (25.7%) respectively. The category "high" trailed significantly with 37 items (14.6%). While the items in the *International Review of Administrative Sciences* and the flagship journals were more likely to have stronger policy recommendations, the items in the political science journals were far more likely to retain a neutral scientific tone. See Table 3 for the results.

Just as the author's purpose can be indirectly assessed by examining the degree or strength of policy recommendations, the author's purpose can also be assessed by determining if a rigorous theory-testing mode was used. In other words, a rigorous theory-testing mode can be used as an indicator of the scientific (as opposed to the applied) purpose of the article. To measure this, all empirical studies were coded as having one of three "styles." The first category, "descriptive," is self-explanatory. The second category, "thesis assertion," refers to a fairly well-articulated statement or proposition around which data and arguments are structured. This was the predominant style for theory building prior to the behavioral revolution. The third category, "hypothesis or model testing," requires hypotheses or relationships to

Table 3. Policy Recommendations in Articles.

	Overall Frequency (N = 253)		IRAS (N = 112)	P.A. Flagship (N = 50)	Political Science (N = 26)
	#	%	%	%	%
None	77	30.4	19.6	30	61.5
Low	74	29.2	33.0	34	19.2
Moderate	65	25.7	28.6	20	15.4
High	37	14.6	18.8	16	3.8
Total	253	99.9[a]	100.0	100	99.9[a]

[a]Due to rounding.

Table 4. Empirical Mode of Analysis Used in Articles.

	Overall Frequency ($N = 236$) (%)	IRAS ($N = 105$) (%)	P.A. Flagship ($N = 49$) (%)	Political Science ($N = 26$) (%)
Descriptive	$N = 95$ 40.20	48.60	36.70	23.10
Thesis assertion	$N = 112$ 47.50	43.80	59.20	34.60
Theory testing	$N = 29$ 12.30	7.60	4.10	42.30
Total	$N = 236$	100	100	100

be spelled out prior to data gathering in an effort to test theoretical assertions rigorously. The most common mode was "thesis assertion" with 112 items (47.5%), followed closely by "descriptive" with 95 items (40.2%), and distantly trailed by "hypothesis-testing" with 29 items (12.3%). The subpopulations of the study show predictable patterns. Journals with a political science focus were far more likely to use a "hypothesis-testing mode" while flagship journals were the least likely. The *International Review of Administrative Sciences* was most likely to use the descriptive mode, and the flagship public administration journals were the most likely to use the thesis-assertion mode. The political science journals were the least likely to use either of these two modes. See Table 4 for the results.

WHAT: THE TOPICS

Unlike most other fields, comparative public administration tends to mirror rather than narrow the field. Thus the perspective is very broad. This can and has been faulted, especially in the 1970s when the field seemed to be making little or no progress,[30] but this breadth of perspective can also be seen as a strength. Whatever the assessment on this score, it is important to have an idea of the relative interests 'of the field.' Huddleston used nine fairly workable categories in his bibliography. This study also categorized all coded items into one (and only one) of the same nine categories. Thus, a fairly good idea of the concerns of the contemporary journal literature was obtained[31] and a rather rough comparison with, the pre-1980 interest also was obtained. However, since the Huddleston bibliography was neither comprehensive nor random, the comparison should only be seen as indicative rather than conclusive. Also, there is no inter-rater verification that the nine categories were operationally defined in identical ways.

Huddleston's first category is "concepts and paradigms." "The emphasis here is on methodology, and on the controversies and debates that have defined the conduct of scholarship in the field."[32] Eleven items (4.3%) were coded in this category compared to 5.4% in the Huddleston bibliography. Closer examination of this particular category is necessary to get a more accurate picture of the self-awareness of the field. Ten of the eleven items coded in this category in the current study were comparative concepts (e.g., "Policy-making and the Relationship between Politics and Bureaucracy") and were thus only marginally selected to this category. No studies focused primarily (or even secondarily) on methodological issues, and only two were broad state-of-the-art pieces.[33] Only 8 items (3.2%) were coded in "administrative history." Thirty-three items (13.0%) were coded in the category of "bureaucracy and politics," which was almost an identical percentage as in Huddleston.[34] "Personnel administration" (42 items, 16.6%) and "organization theory and behavior" (40 items, 15.8%) continued to be the largest categories, although the former was a far smaller share than was, reflected in Huddleston. "Public budgeting" had 25 items (9.9%), which was roughly the same percentage as in Huddleston. Interestingly, this topic figured far more largely in the flagship journals than elsewhere.

"Development administration" maintained about the same level as well, with 36 items (14.2%). "Local and field administration" experienced a small increase with 31 items (12.3%), in this category. "Citizens and administration," which pertains to "the relationships between bureaucrats and their clients or the public at large" (including ombudsmen), recorded a considerable increase, from 4.0% in Huddleston to 10.3% (26 items) in the current study. See Table 5 for the results.

HOW: QUANTIFICATION AND COMPARISON

Measuring the quantification of items is a deceptively complex issue. Does quantification mean the use of concrete statistics or does it mean the use of statistics in prescribed ways? In his content analysis of the *Journal of Comparative Administration,* Sigelman[35] defines quantification in the second, more restricted fashion. That is, he only considers items to have significant levels of quantification when measurement tests a hypothesis (ex ante), not when it supports an assertion (ex post). For example, Gross National

Table 5. Subject Categories of Articles.

Categories	In Huddleston Percentage	Number of Articles	Frequency Percentage
Concepts and Paradigms	5.40	11	4.30
Administrative History	5.10	8	3.20
Bureaucracy and Politics	12.60	33	13
Personnel Administration	30.10	42	16.60
Organizational Theory and Behavior	10	40	15.80
Public Budgeting	11.60	25	9.90
Development Administration	13.20	36	14.20
Local and Field Administration	8	32	12.60
Citizens and Administration	4	26	10.30
Total	100	253	99.9[a]

Source: Comparative Public Administration: An Annotated Bibliography.
[a]Due to rounding.

Product (GNP) growth (or decline) figures indicate significant quantification only if the trends are theoretically predicted by specified independent variables defined and related in advance of examination of the dependent variable. By this definition, all descriptive studies and most thesis- assertion studies are essays or nonquantitative.[36] This study uses Sigelman's (1976) general categories which define "essays" as "broad theoretical and conceptual pieces," "empirical nonquantitative" as "amore narrowly gauged empirically oriented studies," and low and more powerful "empirical quantitative" studies as those using percentages or more powerful statistical techniques.

Sigelman found that 46.3% of all the studies he examined were essays, 35.4% were nonquantitative, 12.2% were low-level quantitative, and 6.1% were high-level quantitative (adjusting figures for comparison). In contrast, this study found that 6.7% (17 items) were essays, 79.1% (200 items) were nonquantitative, 8.7% (22 items) were low-level quantitative, and 5.5% (14 items) were high-level quantitative. These data would indicate a large decline in the percentage of highly conceptual pieces[37] as well as a small decline in quantitative pieces using a testing methodology. It also indicates a large increase in the percentage of empirical, nonquantitative work. However, these indications must be qualified by keeping in mind that the Sigelman study was based on a lone journal that was not entirely representative of the field at large. This issue is discussed further in the analysis and interpretation section.

Intuitively one might suppose that studies in comparative public admin- istration by definition would involve the direct comparison of two or more countries. However, this is usually not the case. Most of the studies are comparative only indirectly. Single case studies of foreign or international administrations or administrative issues described in journals often invite the reader to make the comparisons. For example, while an article in a U.S. journal on the envelope system of budgeting in Canada, might never men- tion the United States, the reader would implicitly be invited to do so on his or her own. Also, it has been argued that single-case studies that have subnational comparisons, a significant theoretical or conceptual component, or involve hypothesis tasting might be argued to be more genuinely related to comparative public administration, at least in theoretical terms.[38] In the coding, then, studies were categorized as being nonempirical conceptual pieces (essays), single-case studies, and multiple-country studies (with ex- tended comparisons and nonextended comparisons); single-case studies were further examined for enhanced comparability.

Eighteen studies (7.1%) were coded as being conceptual pieces that lacked a significant empirical component, 167 single-case studies (66.0%) were coded, 49 (19.4%) were coded as involving extended comparisons between two or more countries, and 19 (7.5%) were coded as studies using multiple comparative examples in nonextended ways. Of the 167 single-case studies, 99 (56.3%) were coded as involving subnational comparisons, significant theoretical comparability, or hypothesis testing. Thus, from the strictest point of view, only 19.4% of all the coded studies involved extended com- parisons of two or more countries. This percentage increases to 26.9 if nonextended comparisons are included. If highly comparable studies are included, the percentage increases to 66.0. Comparison with the content analysis of the *Journal of Comparative Administration* indicates increased explicit comparison. On the other hand, comparison with a content analy- sis of comparative politics indicates that comparative public adminis- tration does not use explicit comparisons as much. Yet, ironically, in the present study the political science journals were least likely to use multi- country comparison, with 84.6% being single-case studies. See Table 6 for the results.

ANALYSIS AND INTERPRETATION

It is interesting to know how people look at the same data and come to completely different conclusions. While it seems possible; if difficult, to

Table 6. Explicit Comparison and Comparability Used in Articles.

	Overall Frequency (N = 253)		IRAS (N = 112)	P.A. Flagship (N = 50)	Political Science (N = 26)
	#	%	%	%	%
Number of countries	18	7.1	6.3	2	0
	167	66.0	66.1	60	84.6
	20	7.9	4.5	20	0
	7	2.8	1.8	4	7.7
	6	2.4	2.7	4	0
	1	0.4	0.9	0	0
None (Non-empirical)	3	1.2	2.7	0	0
	2	0.8	1.8	0	0
	1	0.4	0.9	0	0
	3	1.2	0.9	2	0
	6	2.4	4.5	2	0
	19	7.5	7.1	6	7.7
Total	253	100.1	100.2	100.0	100.0
Theoretical comparability of single-case studies					
Subnational comparison	–	3.2	5.4	4	0
Theoretical comparability	–	29.2	26.8	40	19.2
Hypothesis testing	17	6.7	3.6	2	23.1
Total	99	39.1[a]	35.8[a]	46.0[a]	42.3[a]

[a]Percentages based on entire 253 cases in study.

argue that facts are neutral,[39] it seems quite untenable to argue that the relationships between them are. In this line of thinking, the previous section included facts about which the investigators tried to be as objective in collecting and reporting as possible. This section presents the authors' interpretation; yet others may impose different standards and values, and therefore, reach different conclusions.

THE JOURNALS

It seems clear that the 253 items collected represent a considerable literature. That quantity represents approximately the annual output of two journals. While the *International Review of Administrative Sciences* continues to be the focal point, a diverse group of journals, tries to represent the comparative perspective, in particular the flagship journals. However, in many of the journals, one sometimes gets the feeling that comparative articles are sprinkled, about as potpourri rather than as distinct-field contributions. Development administration articles have a clearer sense of identity. The first research question was, how substantial a literature is being produced? The answer would seem to be, quite substantial; as Nick Henry observed, comparative administration is productive and active, and certainly not dead. Its status, however, seems somewhat indeterminate, neither fish nor fowl, more than a perspective but less than a field although it continues as a field of inquiry. Even if comparative public administration becomes more prominent again, as it seems likely to do in the latter 1980s, its status seems as likely to remain ambiguous.

PRACTITIONERS, POLICY RECOMMENDATIONS, AND THEORY TESTING

The answers to research questions asking about who is in the field and why indicate that varied types of people are in the field for different reasons. Practitioners are a significant proportion of authors of the literature, and they seem to be welcomed and encouraged. Judging from the fact that over 40% of the articles had moderate to strong policy recommendations, it would also seem that many authors have a substantial commitment to policy, dialogue, and applied issues.[40] On the other hand, nearly a third of the articles lacked even an implied policy recommendation. Articles in the "none" and "low" policy recommendation categories were largely by descriptivists or theory testers. Rigorous theory-testing pieces represent a little over 10% of the literature.

For those who would like to see public administration primarily as a science, the results are clearly disappointing. However, since the general consensus in public administration seems to be that it is simultaneously an art and a science and an academic field and a practicing profession, and since there is a commitment to applied research as well as to relatively pure research, no matter how messy and confusing these meldings at times seem to be, the results here do not seem out of line. The question becomes not which conceptualization to endorse but how to encourage a healthy balance, if indeed it is possible to decide what such a balance is. Questions of content and methodology need to be added to the discussion to tackle this issue.

THE TOPICS

Coverage of topics seems more evenly balanced in the 1982–1986 period than indicated in the Huddleston bibliography. Personnel administration does not seem so over-represented, and local and field administration as well as citizens and administration seem to be better represented. Traditions in the various topics have evolved that were largely lacking in the *Journal of Comparative Administration,* so that there is a clearer sense of maturity. Lee Sigelman complained in 1976 that occasionally he could not even determine the main point of articles written in that earlier journal.[41] That particular criticism would be very difficult to maintain with the current literature under consideration. While all of the topics seem more mature, some do seem livelier and more stimulating – for example, the political role of the bureaucracy, administrative corruption, administrative reform, budget systems, privatization, local administration, and ombudsmen. The vigor of discussion seems as much conditioned by academic spurts of interest, as by external events. The topics that do seem critically lacking for the literature under consideration are those that address the field as a whole. A total absence of methodological pieces seems unfortunate. The lack of work refining models at the broader, middle range was also striking.[42] While the field was heavily criticized in the 1970s for excessive theorizing coupled with insufficient empirical data, especially at the grand level, now it seems there is excessive data collection with insufficient theorizing, at least at the more ambitious theoretical levels.

QUANTIFICATION AND COMPARISON

While the results are mixed, comparative public administration continues to have some substantial weaknesses in these areas. In terms of quantification, several aspects must be examined separately. On one hand the use of statistics and limited quantification in descriptive and thesis-assertion articles is far superior overall to earlier work. Nor does it appear that the quality of the quantification in theory-testing articles is weaker. A strong argument can be made that there simply are not enough theory-testing articles; therefore, there is not enough of that type of quantification. This in turn seems partially to stem from a lack of new, broader, middle-range theorizing to test. It may also stem partly from the relatively weaker influence that the behavioral revolution had on public administration than on political science. While not ascribing to the school of thought that the only,

or even the most, important work is theory testing, such inquiry is an indispensable component, even in a field that professes to include art and
practical applications.

In terms of comparison, comparative public administration seems to
have ameliorated the excessive tendency toward nonempirical studies (50%
in the Sigelman study). If anything, the field may have gone too far in
reducing a category that often includes methodological pieces, state-
of-the-art critiques, broader normative investigations, and nonempirical
but theoretically inclined thought pieces. Also, the field seems to have improved somewhat in terms of comparison and comparability, sat least to the
degree that the *Journal of Comparative Administration* was indicative of the
field as a whole. Yet the bare fact that two-thirds of the studies examined
here were single-case studies still seems inverted from the natural order of
things in a field that labels itself comparative. Perhaps the critics function
in this regard is to serve as a constant reminder that while rigorous cross-
national comparison is methodologically challenging, sometimes daunting,
and theoretically complex, these hurdles are the very essence of comparative
administration.

CONCLUSIONS

While it has been relatively easy to argue that comparative public administration is not defunct, it has been far more difficult to delineate its current
identity. While some dispersion has undoubtedly occurred, in and of itself
this does not seem to have been a significant problem. Much more problematic has been redefinition or, perhaps more to the point, lack of definition. The distinct lack of methodological pieces; broader middle-range
theorizing (and perhaps even the near total absence of grand theorizing),
and overall state-of-the-art assessments or critiques leaves one without a
clear sense of purpose or identity. Book-length treatments, not part of this
investigation, did not compensate for this inadequacy for the period under
consideration. However, very recent full-length studies may stimulate interest in and awareness of comparative inquiry. Similarly, new criticism of
the ongoing work of the field, no matter whether it is seen as well-placed
methodological criticism or excessive purism, is likely to have a beneficial effect in kindling new interest and in challenging the lassitude: that
has typified comparative administration for over a decade. Since other
comparative areas also seem to be undergoing renewed interest, hopefully
there will be some spin-off for comparative public administration. Yet

whether this field of inquiry rises out of its languorous state and resumes a more vibrant role in the larger field of public administration still remains to be seen.

NOTES

1. By looking at the *Public Administrative Review Cumulative Index 1940.1979*, edited by Louis C. Gawthrop and Virginia L. Gawthrop (ASPA), the following number of articles categorized under comparative and development topics can be identified: 1940s (23), 1950s (30), 1960s (39), 1970s (36), (11 in 1976). The 1980s will probably exceed 30 items.

2. In 1973, *The Journal of Comparative Administration* became *Administration & Society*.

3. *Public Administration Review*, vol. 36 (November/December 1976). See also the July/August issue of *PAR*, pp. 415–423, for retrospective comments of Peter Savage, the former editor of the *Journal of Comparative Administration*.

4. Fred Riggs concluding comments in his article (*Public Administration Review*, vol. 36 (November/December 1976), pp. 648–654) are perhaps the best example. He notes: "As our consciousness expands, we shall no longer need to speak of 'comparative administration,' but only of the study of 'public administration,' and of its subfield, the study of 'American public administration'" (p. 652).

5. Brian Loveman, "The Comparative Administration Group, Development Administration and Anti-development," *Public Administration Review*, vol. 36 (November/December 1976), pp. 616–621, offers the best example from the critical.

6. Nicholas Henry, *Public Administration and Public Affairs* (Englewood Cliffs, NJ: Prentice Hall, 1986), p. 48.

7. Ferrell Heady, *Public Administration: A Comparative Perspective*, 3rd ed. (New York: Marcel Dekker, 1984), p. 48.

8. Some of the more recent comprehensive assessments of the field in the early 1980s include Keith M. Henderson, "From Comparative Public Administration to Comparative Public Policy," *International Review of Administrative Sciences*, vol. 48, no. 4 (1981), pp. 356–364; and Charles T. Goodsell, "The New Comparative Administration: A Proposal," *International Journal of Public Administration*, vol. 3, no. 2 (1981), pp. 143–155. For an excellent review of comparative public administration in the First World War, see Donald C. Rowat, ed., *Public Administration in Developed Democracies* (New York: Marcel Dekker, 1988), especially chapters au, 25, and the bibliography; and also B. Guy Peters' recent work, *Comparing Public Bureaucracies: Problems of Theory and Method* (Tuscaloosa: The University of Alabama Press, 1988). For a quasi-empirical analysis and critique of development administration, see Moses Kiggundu, Jan 1. Jorgensen, and Taieb Hafri, "Administrative Theory and Practice in Developing Countries," *Administrative Science Quarterly*, vol. 28 (March 1983), pp. 66–84.

9. Due to space limitations, not all variables investigated are discussed here.

10. An excellent work of the period is Paul Meyer's *Administrative Organization: A Comparative Study of the Organization of Public Administration* (Copenhagen, Denmark: NYT Nordisk Forlag Arnold Busek, 1957); for a bibliography of the

period see Ferrell Heady and Sybil L. Stokes. *Comparative Public Administration:*
A Selected Annotated Bibliography, 2nd ed. (Ann Arbor: Institute of Public
Administration, University of Michigan, 1960).

11. An excellent contemporary review is 8.8. Shaffer, "Comparisons," "Administration and Development," *Political Studies,* vol. 19 (September 1971), pp. 327–337.
For a recent and comprehensive review, Heady's text is best (note 7).

12. For a recent assessment of university curricula, see Richard W. Ryan, *Teach-*
ing Comparative-Development Administration at U.S. Universities: A Collection and
Analyses of Syllabi (West Hartford, CT: Kumarian Press, 1986).

13. Grant theorizing here refers to theories that focus on the interaction of social
structures and processes as a whole and thus are difficult to test without breaking
them into their constituent components, which destroys the theoretical *gestalt.*
This is the tradition of Telcoti Parsons, of which Fred W. Riggs's classic text
Administration in Developing Countries: The Theory of Prismatic Society (Boston:
Houghton Mifflin, 1964) is the best known example in comparative public administration. The new, largely political, school of thought that seeks to "bring the
state back in" is a more recent example. Two instances of this school of thought are
represented in the current study from the same journal. See Martin Heper, "The
State and Public Bureaucracies: A Comparative and Historical Perspective," *Com-*
parative Studies in Society and History, vol. 27 (January 1985), pp. 86–110, Richard
Kraus and Reeve D. Vanneman, "Bureaucrats Versus the State in Capitalist and
Socialist Regimes," *Comparative Studies in Society and History,* vol. 27 (January
1985), pp. 111–122.

14. See especially the Rowat and Peters texts (note 8). A new Journal worthy of
note in this regard is *Governance* ("*An International Journal of Policy and Admini-*
stration") that is advertised as filling "a gap in the current literature because it is
explicitly comparative and international in its approach."

15. The best review of the difficulties for comparative public administration is Joel
B. Aberbach and Bert A. Rockman, "Problems of Cross-National Comparison," in
Rowat (note 7), pp. 419–437.

16. For a perspective of this subtle point, see Wesley B. Bjur and Asghar
Zomorrodian, "Towards Indigenous Theories of Administration: An International
Perspective," *International Review of Administrative Sciences,* vol. 52 (December
1986), pp. 397–420.

17. For a case study that illustrates the real and theoretical comparative public
administration needs of a developing country, see Jong S. Jun. "Korean Public
Administration: Education and Research." *International Review of Administrative*
Sciences, vol. 49, no. 4 (1983), pp. 413–442 & for a general review, see Moses
Kiggundu et al. (note 8).

18. In Rowat, p. 437 (note 8).

19. Lee Sigelman and George H. Gadbois Jr., "Contemporary Comparative Politics: An Inventory and Assessment," *Comparative Political Studies,* vol. 16 (October
1983), pp. 275–305, especially pp. 284–285.

20. The *Indian Journal of Public Administration* frequently does this on an extensive basis, and the *International Review of Administrative Sciences* does this less
frequently. In his final editorial, G.R. Curnow ("Journals of Public Administration:
Conflicting Constituencies," *Australian Journal of Public Administration,* vol. 63

(December 1984), p. 315) noted as one of his self-criticisms that "surveys of public administration overseas have not been as systematic as they should have been."

21. For example, Krishna K. Tummala, ed., *Administration Systems Abroad* (Lanham, MD: University Press of America, 1984), 2nd ed.; and Rowat (note 8).

22. The best examples are Lee Sigelman, "In Search of Comparative Administration," *Public Administration Review*, vol. 36 (November/December 1976), pp. 621–625; and Peters (note 8).

23. George Honadle, "Development Administration in the Eighties: New Agendas or Old Perspectives?" *Public Administration Review*, vol. 42 (March/April 1982), pp. 174–179, for example, that not *only* is a distinction between comparative public administration and development administration necessary, but that "Comparative administration has largely fallen by the wayside" (p. 174).

24. Academicians Merrill R. Goodall, James Barry, and Marilyn B. Westing, "*Public Administration Review*: 1940–1969," *Public Administration Review*, vol. 32 (January/February 1972), pp. 52–57, note the decline of practitioners with some approval. Others note the practitioner decline but are not so sanguine about it. Thomas Vocino, Bald Beaumount, and Robert H. Elliott, "ASPA Membership Perceptions of the *Public Administration Review*," *Public Administration Review*, vol. 42 (March/April 1982), pp. 163–168, note the overwhelming general interest for more practitioner input and emphasis in the journal. Two editors noted the practitioner/academic distinction prominently in their valedictory editorials. Nevil Johnson. "Editoral: Writing about Public Administration – The Search for Common Ground," *Public Administration*, vol. 59 (Summer 1981), pp. 127–138, notes that the "real challenge then is to find ways of eliciting a more effective contribution to public discussion of administration from the practitioners than we presently have." (p. 135). Writing for the *Australian Journal of Public Administration*, Curnow (note 20) largely agrees.

25. Curtis Ventriss, "Two Critical Issues of American Public Administration: Reflections of a Sympathetic Participant," *Administration & Society*, vol. 19 (May 1987), pp. 25–26.

26. Begun in 1979.

27. As Dwight Waldo noted in an editorial in *Public Administration Review*, vol. 34 (March/April 1974) p. 95, it is increasingly difficult "to classify most manuscripts as 'academics' or 'practitioners.'"

28. Curnow (note 20, p. 316) estimates that the practitioner ratio has, declined to approximately one-quarter of the published articles in *Australian Journal of Public Administration* in the 1980s; and Goodall et al. only identify 17% as having federal, state, and local affiliations in the 1960–1969 period for *Public Administration Review* (note 24, p. 54). James S. Bowman and Sarni O. Hajjar, "English-Language Journals in Public Administration: An Analysis," *Public Administration*, vol. 56 (1978), p. 222, found authors of 28% of all articles to be government practitioners when surveying a wide variety of journals front 1970–1976.

29. It should be noted that the subpopulation sample for articles from political science was only $N = 26$.

30. Sigelman, note 22.

31. Two aspects of the journals selected should be mentioned because of the impact on content focus. First, English-language journals with a Second and Third

World focus are underrepresented. Also, journals with a focused topic (i.e., management) are underrepresented because of the low quotient of comparative pieces.

32. Mark W. Huddleston, *Comparative Public Administration: An Annotated Bibliography* (New York: Garland Publishing, Inc., 1984), p. 17.

33. The two broader pieces were Leonard Binder, "The Natural History of Development Theory," *Comparative Studies in Society and History*, vol. 28 (January 1986), pp. 3–33; and Bjur and Zomorrodian, note 16.

34. Naomi Caiden's critique and assessment of "Comparative Public Budgeting" (*International Journal of Public Administration*, vol. 7 (January 1985), pp. 375–401) deserves special mention as an interesting blend of the old comparative public administration style with the newer policy orientation.

35. Sigelman, note 22.

36. Some studies on the borderline of these two categories blend the thesis-assertion and hypothesis modes, thus blurring a sharp distinction. Thus a small number of studies were coded as being primarily in the thesis-assertion mode but nonetheless used quantitative techniques to support assertions, often with corollary information.

37. This is somewhat mitigated by the different operational definitions used for the "empirical nonquantitative" categories in the two studies. Sigelman appears to include in the empirical nonquantitative category only studies that are clearly country specifically data laden. All studies not clearly related to a country (or countries) or containing some critical mass of data are deemed "mere" essays. Thus he uses the term in a somewhat more restricted fashion than the current study. Even with this caveat in mind, the decline in essay-style pieces is still impressive.

38. See Sigelman and Gadbois (note 19, pp. 280–285) for an extended discussion of this point.

39. Facts can only be neutral when operational definitions are so clear that researchers in different schools of thought would come to nearly identical findings. In practice, this is rarely the case. As one set of researchers (in a different field) complained about interstudy comparability and replicability. The problems that arose, and choices made among alternative strategies at various points in the research enterprise, pass unremarked, as do the reasons these particular choices were made and their consequences. Charles Y. Glock and Randy Stark, *Christian Beliefs and Anti-Semitism* (New York: Harperbooks, 1966), p. 25. While a few of the problems and choices have been discussed or noted in this study, due to space limits-lions molt of them remain unremarked here as well.

40. Because this question has not been raised in either content analyses or survey of public administration, there is no indication as to how these proportions relate to the field at large.

41. Sigelman, note 22.

42. Middle-range theorizing in comparative public administration usually centers administration in the political context. Much excellent work at organizing possible frameworks was done in the 1960s and 1970s. Ferrell Heady's structuralist typology of political systems vis-a-vis the bureaucracy is a prime example (note 7, pp. 276ff.). A rare but noteworthy example in the current study is by Kyosti-Pekonen. "Policy making and the Relationship between Politics and Bureaucracy." *International Review of Administration Sciences* vol. 51 no. 3 (1985) pp. 207–220. He uses cycle theory to relate the degree of convergence and divergence of political/administrative interactions.

AN OVERVIEW OF BUREAUCRACY AND POLITICAL DEVELOPMENT

Joseph La Palombara

INTRODUCTION

It is now commonplace to depict the contemporary world as one of rapid, increasing, and frequently cataclysmic change. Such forces as disappearing colonialism, revolution in communications and technology, international technical assistance, and spreading ideology cancel out centuries of relative stability, replacing it with conditions of economic upheaval, social disorientation, and political instability. While the so-called developed nations prepare to harness at least a portion of space, most of the rest of the world – spurred along by the West and by the revolution of rising expectations – struggles to cross the threshold of social and economic modernity.

Indications of this mutation could be endlessly multiplied: political maps of the world become obsolete almost as soon as they are published; school children must add continually to the number of nation-state names they commit to memory; debater and voter in the United Nations dramatically announce the presence of new sovereignties and the shifting balance of power they portend; newspapers flash the names of exotic countries that may or may not have existed a few years ago, where conditions of economic distress, physical violence, or political maneuvering somehow seem to have a direct bearing on the peace and tranquility of the entire globe. The utterances of new leaders of small African states are as carefully pondered by the

Comparative Public Administration: The Essential Readings
Research in Public Policy Analysis and Management, Volume 15, 193–220
Copyright © 2006 by Elsevier Ltd.
ISSN: 0732-1317/doi:10.1016/S0732-1317(06)15006-X

statesmen of the West as the pronouncements of a major power. Coalition government in Laos, agricultural reform in China, India's Five-Year Plan, jungle warfare in Viet Nam, industrial development in Ghana, village change in Pakistan, a campaign to wipe out illiteracy in Nigeria, military coups in Turkey or Korea, civil war in Indonesia, spectacular economic changes in Brazil – all of these are symptoms of a tempo of development and change that the Western world simply cannot ignore. Perhaps because the changes now experienced are unprecedented in both tempo and scale, they have attracted the attention of a great many scholars, as well as those whose immediate concern is international politics and diplomacy. Some of these scholars are strongly motivated by an urge to provide useful counsel concerning governmental policy; others see in rapid processes of transformation an unparalleled opportunity both to apply and to test theories and methods of the social sciences, thus adding to our storehouse of theoretical and empirical knowledge. Whatever the motivation, the urge to sharpen our understanding of the propellants, processes, and consequences of change is clearly overwhelming, as the outpouring of professional literature in recent years attests.

For many reasons that do not require elaboration here, the professional literature concentrates largely on social and economic changes. We now have a fairly vast bibliography of studies dealing with both of these phenomena, particularly with the conditions – social and economic variables – that accompany and to some extent govern the evolution and the probable direction or modification in the social system and in the production and allocation of economic goods and services. By way of sharp contrast, relatively little systematic attention has been accorded the phenomenon of political development, i.e., the transformation of a political system from one type into another. Even more curious is the lack of attention accorded the public sector – particularly the bureaucracy – as an important independent variable that greatly influences any kind of transformation in the developing countries, be it social, economic, or political.

It scarcely requires exhaustive documentation to demonstrate that major changes in both the developed and the developing nations are inconceivable today without the massive intervention of government. The time is evidently past when public officials are expected to sit on the developmental sidelines, limiting their roles to the fixing of general rules and to providing certain basic services and incentives for those private entrepreneurs who are the major players in the complicated and exciting game of fashioning profound changes in economic and social systems. Whether it is the encouragement of electronic industries in the industrialized West, or the improvement of rice production in Pakistan or Viet Nam, or an increase in medical care in the United States, or the exploitation of petroleum resources in Latin America or the Middle East, the direct participation of government is immediate and intimate if not to say exclusive. When our focus shifts from the economic to other areas of activity, the presence of government is revealed in even sharper relief. Systematic campaigns to eradicate illiteracy, create or revitalize village-level government, remove ancient social barriers, or to replace atomistic parochialism with a sense of nationhood, are unthinkable without the participation of government. The same may be said for any effort to forge major transformations in the political institutions that characterize any particular society.

The reasons for heavy public or governmental involvement in the phenomena of economic, social, and political changes are as myriad as the kinds of development actually under way. In many places, government is the only significant social sector willing to assume the responsibility for transformation. In others, the bureaucracy husbands the vast majority of whatever necessary professional, technical, and entrepreneurial resources may be available to a society committed to change. In still other areas, the primary – even monopolistic –involvement of the public sector in programs of social and economic development may be a manifestation of fierce ideological commitment. Moreover, in every type of situation, both historic and contemporary, the creation of social overhead capital is a matter that requires the application of the full resources of political and bureaucratic capacity. Without such public participation, very few other plans for basic changes in the economic or social structure are meaningful or feasible. The chapter by Fritz Morstein Marx in this volume clearly demonstrates how unreal it would be to think of any type of national development in which the bureaucracy, even if its role is limited to the provision of data, advice, and management expertise, is excluded.

This book (as well as the conference out of which it emanates) is an effort to direct attention to the vital role that bureaucracies can and do play in the various kinds of transformations that the developing nations are experiencing. While some attention is accorded to certain problems and phenomena of social and economic change, the majority goes without saying that we need to know more than we do about the forces that mold one configuration of political institutions rather than another. If, as we assume, the bureaucratic sector in most of the developing nations is to be heavily involved in the general processes of transformation, we must be able to suggest with greater confidence than is presently possible what alternative roles are open to the bureaucracy – and with what probable consequences for the emerging political systems. If, as many of us hope, political development is to move in a generally democratic rather than anti-democratic direction, it is essential that we know in greater precision what patterns of bureaucratic organization and behavior aid or handicap the achievement of this goal. If, finally, we ever expect to be able to deal comparatively and scientifically with the process of political development as a generalized phenomenon, we simply must accord greater attention than in the past to the bureaucracy as a critical variable that both affects and is conditioned by the process itself.

DEFINITIONS AND MODELS

At first blush, bureaucracy does not appear to offer any difficulties of definition. On closer inspection, however, it is apparent that the meaning of this concept is far from self-evident. Does it refer to all persons, at whatever level, who are on the public payroll? Does it make much sense to cluster under the same generic category a postal clerk and a national planner, a local policeman and an undersecretary in a Home Office or Ministry of the Interior? When we speculate about the consequences of bureaucratic organization and behavior for political development, we are interested in the relationship of the "administrative class" to the legislature, as well as that of a field representative of a Ministry of Health or Agriculture to the rural village?

There is no single or simple answer to these queries. For some purposes, as for instance when one is concerned with the kind of public attitudes toward government that bureaucrats help to inculcate or fortify, it is reasonable to think of bureaucracy as encompassing all public servants. When such public attitudes are the paramount concern, the village aid worker may be a much more significant bureaucrat than the remote top-level officials of the ministry he represents. For the great mass of people in most countries, government is scarcely much more than the specific public officials with whom they come in direct contact. The upper reaches of a public administrative hierarchy may constitute a paragon of skill, rationality, and humaneness, but all of this will go relatively unnoticed if those who deal directly with the public are arrogant, aloof, arbitrary, and corrupt in their behavior. Those, the center of administration, may spin out beautiful and extremely insightful national plans, but these will appear as not very meaningful – or even bizarre – to the population if field administrators do not have the talent for translating what exists on paper to meet the requirements of human situations.

On the other hand, where one is concerned with the relative roles of bureaucrats and legislators in the formulation of public policy, a more restricted conceptualization of the bureaucracy is required. The same is true when the problem at hand is that of discovering what major internal characteristics evolve for any bureaucratic apparatus. In short, there are some occasions on which only those public servants at a relatively high level in the hierarchy constitute the relevant bureaucracy.

Problems regarding the development of effective administration in Viet Nam bring us to a relatively low level in the public administrative hierarchy, as do observations regarding the use of the extraordinary writs to protect both citizens and public servants against arbitrary and excessive bureaucratic behavior in Pakistan. When comments are made regarding venality and corruption in the public service, every level of the bureaucracy is involved. By and large, however, the bureaucrats of major interest to us are generally those who occupy managerial roles, who are in some directive capacity either in central agencies or in the field, who are generally described in the language of public administration as "middle" or "top" management. The reason for this more restrictive use is self-evident: the managerial group in the bureaucracy is more likely to have a direct bearing on political and other kinds of national development. It is those public servants at the upper administrative levels who will be called upon to provide policy counsel, to assist in the formulation of programs, and to engage in the management and direction of the people in the interest of translating policy hopes into realities.

Given this somewhat restricted view of the bureaucracy, is there any particular framework within which bureaucracies may be viewed? The several models of bureaucratic systems provided by the authors suggest that no obvious single approach is available. If, as John Dorsey suggests, change is essentially the outcome of modifications in the amount of information available to a society and the way that information is converted into energy, we may want to look at bureaucracies as they relate to that important process. It is obvious, for example, that the Vietnamese bureaucracy enjoys a near monopoly of certain crucial categories of information available to that country and that, for this and other reasons, it exercises a quantum of power that has had to be harnessed politically. It is equally obvious that, if power centers other than the bureaucracy are to be created in the developing nations, information that is essential to development will have to be more widely shared. Methods whereby such a situation might be brought into existence must certainly be suggested before we can solve the problem of creating the democratic pluralism, which underlies many of the contributions to this volume.

Bert F. Hoselitz offers a structural-functional model of bureaucracy, and would presumably classify public administrative systems according to how they relate to the critical sectors of cultural maintenance and transmission, national integration, systemic goal gratification, and environmental transformation. Where a reasonable amount of national integration has occurred and the basic concern of a system is economic development, the role of the bureaucracy in the goal gratification and allocative sectors is of critical interest and importance. All of these sectors are closely related and, although the bureaucracy will always be concerned with all of them to some degree, major involvement in the integrative sector will clearly limit the amount of involvement in sectors that are more intimately related to economic development.

A somewhat similar structural-functional model is suggested by S. N. Eisenstadt, wherein the major perspective in viewing a bureaucracy is the manner in which it handles the flow of demands and organizations that interact with the political system. What the bureaucracy does in this sense will have an immediate and direct bearing on the kind of development that occurs and on how rapidly change will proceed. Merle Fainsod develops a typology based on the relationship of bureaucracies to the flow of political power and suggests that others might be constructed that reflect the bureaucracy's range of functions, its internal characteristics, or its role as a carrier or inhibitor of modernizing values. Other treatments of bureaucracy reflect exactly some of these latter orientations.

It would certainly be premature at this time to attempt to make a final choice among various conceivable models or taxonomies. Each of them offers a particular window, perhaps a magnifying glass, through which to view an important aspect of the political process. What one glass may obscure, another may illuminate. Until we have seen more varied detail than we have thus far, no single vantage point is likely to serve our needs adequately. Moreover, it is apparent from what is said about bureaucracies, and the concerns that are expressed with regard to them, that the central focus of all of the suggested models is far less diverse than might appear at first glance.

THE PROBLEM OF "MODERNITY"

Somewhat more perplexing are problems of conceptualization and theory that confront us when we approach the subject of "modernization." This concept is often used in a shifting and imprecise way. When it is equated with "development," it can mean everything from increases in the amount of information and energy that societies use, to increased ability to absorb new demands and organization, to structural differentiation for the performance of systemic functions. For some, a modern system is essentially a society that has become urban and industrial. For others, a system cannot be modern, which has not achieved a high degree of political pluralism. Some would stress gross or net national product as an index of modernization; others would look for the degree of popular participation in politics and government as the most meaningful measure. Often several meanings can be detected in the same piece of writing.

The confusion induced by the shifting content of concepts like modernization and development is compounded by what appears to be an underlying culture-bound and deterministic unilinear theory of change. If modernization or development simply means industrialization and the mechanization of agriculture, the concept is reasonably neutral and does not necessarily imply a unilinear theory of evolution or a particular institutional framework within which this kind of economic change must take place. But as soon as either of these concepts takes on social and political content, it is apparent that what many scholars have in mind when they speak of a modern or developed system is one that approximates the institutional and structural configuration that we associate with the Anglo-American (in any event, the Western) democratic systems. When, in addition to such culture-bound conceptualization, it is implied that the evolution of political and social systems is moving in this direction and that any other line of development is an aberration, all sorts of difficulties arise concerning the matter of dealing empirically with existing social and political systems.

It is apparent, for example, that rapid economic change leading to industrialization can be effected without conformance to the social and institutional patterns that we might ascribe to the Anglo-American model. Indeed, it may very well be that rapid change in the economic sector is much more meaningfully related to what we might call an undemocratic pattern of social and political organization. This is certainly one of the principal – even if depressing – hypotheses that emerges from the contributions of Merle Fainsod and Carl Beck. In any event, if any kind of clarity is to emerge from our use of such concepts as modernization and development, it will be vitally necessary to specify what we mean by the concepts and to indicate explicitly when a shift in meaning occurs. Failure to do this is certain to encumber our discussions of political change with confusion and with culturally limited and deterministic baggage.

The limitation of our conceptualization is equally apparent when we shift our attention to public administration. Regardless of what Max Weber himself may have intended, it is apparent that his classical formulation of bureaucracy has come to be inextricably associated by some with the highly industrialized and democratically pluralistic society. Thus, the role of bureaucracy in effecting socioeconomic-political change is said to require, as central tendencies, such Weberian attributes in public administration as hierarchy, responsibility, rationality, achievement orientation, specialization and differentiation, discipline, professionalization. Insofar as public administrative systems fall short of this Weberian legal–rational model, they are said not to be modern. Moreover, it is often either claimed or implied that a public administrative sector that does not manifest these attributes cannot be an effective instrument for bringing about the kind of economic, social, and political changes that one associates with modernity.

Our ability to understand the process of change, and the role of the public sector in bringing it about, is considerably damaged by any association of the classical conceptualization of bureaucracy with a particular configuration of institutional or structural arrangements in economic, social, or political sectors. To assume, as have some of the public administration technical assistance advisors who have ventured abroad, that such an association is necessary is to neglect the nature of change in the West and in other countries. We know, for example, that at the time that Britain and the United States experienced their most rapid economic change, the respective bureaucracies, to considerable degrees involved in the facilitation of change, were conforming much less to the Weberian model than they are today. A striking degree of particularism and corruption in public administration can be associated with economic development in both of these countries.

Recognizing this, several of our authors come close to stating that corruption or its functional equivalent may be critically important to the developing nations. Fred Riggs, for example, suggests that a developing political party system may require spoils and that a bureaucratic system based on "merit" may aggrandize bureaucratic power at the expense of political institutional development in the early stages of growth of a party system. Hoselitz, who argues that economic development requires a shift from corruption to rationality in the bureaucracy, concedes that venality in the bureaucracy is acceptable when the primary need of a society is integration rather than goal attainment. Morstein Marx argues cogently that a merit bureaucracy makes constitutionalism more viable and helps to legitimize government, but his hypothesis need not be viewed as being at odds with the others mentioned if it is conceded that the particular *stage* of political development may call for different kinds of bureaucratic structure. The point seems to be that classical bureaucracy is not necessarily a precondition of development.

This last observation is made even more apparent when we analyze the Fainsod discussion of the Soviet Union and the Beck examination of development in Eastern Europe. The former makes the central point that economic modernization and democracy do not necessarily travel hand in hand. Moreover, it is apparent that the economic development that preceded the advent of the Bolsheviks evolved largely at state behest and under the guidance of a venal, corrupt, autocratic, inefficient, and particularistic bureaucracy that the efforts of neither Peter nor Alexander succeeded in reforming. One of Fainsod's important conclusions, which deserves more treatment as an interesting hypothesis, is that a bureaucracy can instill and implement economic modernity without itself absorbing any of the changes it seeks to disseminate.

That industrialization does not necessarily carry the seeds of democracy nor require the development of a Weberian bureaucracy is also suggested by Carl Beck. He shows that the countries of Eastern Europe have been able to absorb changes in their economies, administrative systems, and elites without creating classical administrative systems. While some flexibility in the Communist doctrine of development is evident, it cannot be traced to bureaucratization. Indeed, recent patterns of administrative devolution make the achievement of classical bureaucracy even more unlikely, but it may nevertheless play an important role in the future development of these societies. As Beck puts it, the classical theory seriously underestimates the role of political power and ideology in national development. His chapter, as well as that of Fainsod, should be sobering for those who associate a particular configuration of public administration with economic and social development.

To attempt to remake the bureaucracies of the developing states to conform to any abstraction derived from a Weberian model involves more than an effort of herculean proportions. The effort itself, insofar as it may succeed, is of dubious value in that a bureaucracy heavily encumbered by Weberian-derived norms may for that reason be a less efficacious instrument of economic change. To put the matter succinctly: one might simply observe that, in a place like India, public administrators steeped in the tradition of the Indian Civil Service may be less useful as developmental entrepreneurs than those who are not so rigidly tied to notions of bureaucratic status, hierarchy, and impartiality. The economic development of a society, particularly if it is to be implemented by massive intervention of the public sector, requires a breed of bureaucrats different (e.g., more free-wheeling, less adhering to administrative forms, less attached to the importance of hierarchy and seniority) from the type of man who is useful when the primary concern of the bureaucracy is the maintenance of law and order. On the other hand, as Ralph Braibanti notes for Pakistan, bureaucrats deeply rooted in the traditions of the Indian Civil Service, which are essentially British, may be much more effective as guardians of law and justice than the more impatient types for whom the single and essentially exclusive goal is economic development.

Hoselitz states that, as a practical matter, all of the bureaucracies of the developing areas are likely to be dual in character, reflecting the transitional nature and the conflicting needs of the societies themselves. In such a setting, the "primitive" will be juxtaposed with the "modern," the traditional with the legal-rational. If, as Hoselitz hypothesizes, economic development requires a streamlined and highly rationalized bureaucracy, many of the structures of a dual society will tend to undercut this goal. Whether, in order to push ahead economically, the political elite should seek to eradicate the traditional structure or seek somehow to harness it to developmental plans is not as easy a problem to resolve as we might assume. Westernized elites in the developing areas, imbued with notions of Western technology and organization, are prone to ride roughshod over the traditional elements in their society. Yet, as Morroe Berger discovered for the Egyptian bureaucracy,[1] traditional ways have amazing survival power; they are capable of adapting to even the most radical changes in formal organizational structure. And, as national bureaucratic planners in India are learning, the implementation of developmental schemes will have to occur as modified by traditional and parochial influences or it may not take place at all.

We need to know more than we do about how and why traditional patterns survive formal modifications in administrative structure, how and with what consequences they manage to exist side by side with the so-called modern bureaucratic patterns, and what implications such patterns have for national plans to effect social, political, and economic changes. For this reason we must take as merely tentative or limited the suggestion of Eisenstadt that a developed political system requires the centralization of the polity. This need may be greatest when the primary goal is integrative, that is, when the central effort is that of creating a sense of nationhood or national identification. Certainly the histories of Japan after the Meiji Restoration, of Prussia in the eighteenth century, and of Germany and Italy in the nineteenth century clearly demonstrate that a centralized bureaucracy can be a vital factor in the molding of a national entity out of disparate ethnic, regional, feudal, or otherwise atomistic groupings. Indeed, whether we are thinking of nation-states or empires, both their historical evolution and their maintenance reveal a central, perhaps critical, role played by the public administrative apparatus.

It is not obvious, however, that a centralized bureaucracy is required when the basic concern shifts from the integrative to the goal gratification sector, or when the end in view is the development of a pluralistic society. Such goals may very well require considerable administrative decentralization as well as efforts to encourage at the local level the kinds of political institutions that can serve both as supports for and as watchdogs over administrative officials. The revival of the panchayats in India is having exactly this kind of impact. Fred Riggs argues with great cogency that, from the standpoint of political development, it may be essential to create a fairly high degree of local political and administrative autonomy. To do so would presumably limit the centralized bureaucracy's tendency to displace its service orientation with that of aggrandizing its own power – a danger which Eisenstadt recognizes as clear and present in most of the new states.

We must, then, look with greater care to traditional structures before concluding that they are incompatible with social, political, or economic change. The vital question to pose is what the national goals of a society are, what role in accomplishing them the public sector is expected to play, and, given these aspirations, what patterns of public administration seem to be the most efficaciously related to goal achievement.

THE NEUTRALITY OF THE BUREAUCRACY

What we have said thus far has certain implications for the role of the bureaucracy in encouraging the evolution of democratic, constitutional systems. If, as seems essential, we must concede that the Weberian conception of the bureaucracy is nothing more than an ideal formulation not subject to empirical verification, and that the classical democratic formulation of a strictly neutral and instrumental bureaucracy is an equally idealized and probably unattainable standard, it is necessary to modify somewhat the general frame of reference within which the role and function of the bureaucracy is evaluated.

We may begin by noting – as several of our authors do – that the bureaucracy, particularly in its upper reaches, will always be deeply involved in the political process. Indeed, it is impossible even in the most structurally differentiated political systems to conceive of the complete separation of function that would be required were there to be an attempt to restrict the bureaucracy strictly to an instrumental role. Those who have looked closely at the public administrative systems of the Western world have long since abandoned the misleading fiction that assumed a neat, dichotomous separation between policy and administration. Among other things, we know that some policy implications are implicit in all significant administrative behaviors and that the power and influence-seeking groups of a society, sensing this, will cluster about administration decision points, hoping in this way to exert some leverage over the quite clearly political decisions that emanate from the bureaucracy. What is true of the more advanced countries is probably accentuated in developing nations, where the bureaucracy may be the most coherent power center and where, in addition, the major decisions regarding national development are likely to involve authoritative making and rule application by governmental structures.

In order to sharpen our understanding of the political role of the bureaucracy, it is also necessary to note that the bureaucratic arena will almost invariably reproduce in microcosm many of the basic political conflicts that characterize the developing system itself. If the "traditional" and the "modern" are in conflict, this tension will surely be reflected among bureaucrats. The bureaucrats in the field may ally themselves with local elites and politicians and to some extent oppose well-made developmental schemes that emanate from national planners at the center. If, as is invariably the case, capital and other developmental resources are in short supply, those who populate the bureaucracy's infrastructure will to some extent be at war with each other over the definition of goals and the allocation of resources. Whether a developing society is characterized by several competing political parties or is dominated by a single party, we can assume, first, that views concerning the setting of developmental goals will differ and, second, that the competing members of the political elite will search for and find allies in the bureaucracy. Not only will shifts in political power be reflected in the balance of power within the bureaucracy; the bureaucrats themselves, through the myriad policy-related functions they perform, will have much to do with the major shifts – even the slight nuances of change – that occur from time to time.

Tension between the political leaders and the bureaucrats of the developing nations grows in large measure out of the recognition that bureaucrats are never passive instruments to be manipulated at will, like inert pawns. Where the indigenous bureaucracy is deeply steeped in colonial traditions of law and order, or in the use of the bureaucratic apparatus for control rather than development, politicians bent on change, as well as intellectuals impatient with the rate of progress, will find themselves at odds with more conservative bureaucrats. When, in the interest of staffing administrative positions vacated by colonial administrators, or of filling new positions directly relating to economic change, a new group of ambitious and often badly trained bureaucrats is added to what had existed previously, a considerable amount of turmoil, with definite consequences for the political system, is predictable.

SCARCITY OF BUREAUCRATIC TALENT

It is also apparent that few if any of the developing nations possess the reservoir of bureaucratic skills that their often-grandiose developmental schemes would require. Some new nations, such as India, are reasonably well endowed with first-class administrative talent, particularly at the highest levels. In Africa, where the Congo would be an extreme but not untypical example, the situation is much more desperate. Colonial administration, which emphasized the services of police and law and which did not recruit large numbers of Africans to positions of policy responsibility, has been replaced by public administration that is closely tied to goals of national development. African administrators whose responsibilities until recently were characterized by routine are catapulted to the top of the hierarchy, where they are expected to advise ministers and politicians regarding major programs of economic and social developments. As J. Donald Kingsley aptly observes, the inexperience and other limitations of unseasoned public administrators necessarily set limits to the dreams of politicians. How much the state can accomplish in a setting that manages to steer clear of administrative chaos, to say nothing of just plain inefficiency, is clearly circumscribed by the nature of the bureaucratic talent available.

This is not to say that a few high-level administrators are of little use to a new nation. Kingsley shows us that in Nigeria top-level officers with a common education and tradition constitute a vital factor in the national integration of that country. Equally impressive are the related data that Braibanti adduces for Pakistan, which was compelled to create a state de novo with extremely limited administrative talent at its disposal and against great odds. A handful of men, some indigenous, some foreign, utilized extraordinary skills and creative leadership to hold the national house together during critical formative years. One is tempted to say that a central operating proposition can be extrapolated from the experiences of Nigeria and Pakistan, but doing so raises the frustrating question of how other new nations can get their hands on a reasonable quotient of bureaucratic leaders who display the Anglo-Saxon traits of respect for law and order, intellectuality, pragmatism, objectivity, and rationality in the organization and management of public administrative machinery. These traditions somehow enable the bureaucrats to survive the tensions that grow up between themselves and the politicians, as well as the tendency of the politicians, abetted by intellectuals and the citizenry, to lay the failures of development at the doorstep of the bureaucracy.

Even in places like Pakistan and Nigeria, it is abundantly apparent that much must be done to train the desperately needed administrative cadres at all levels. To some extent, revolutionary changes in secondary education will eventually fill the needs of the public sector. Yet changes in the opportunity for advanced education do not automatically take care of the matter of providing specific training for those who will enter the public service. What kind of training should lower-level administrators receive to assure, not merely that they can handle the technicalities of a particular position, but also that they will manifest the kind of behavior toward superiors and toward the public that is consistent with the particular kind of political system that may be the end in view? If field administrators in colonial areas have been aloof from and disdainful toward the public, how can such an orientation be changed. If higher-level bureaucrats have been primarily concerned with the maintenance of law and order and the rigid application of colonial regulations (often designed to inhibit economic development), what must be done to make them better attuned to the problems of development and change in the future?

One of the generalizations that emerges from Merle Fainsod's analysis of the Soviet Union is that there is probably no obvious substitute for a massive program of education maintained for at least a full generation. Those who are sanguine about the benefits to be derived from the use of international technical assistants in the field of administration should read with care what Fainsod reports of efforts to reform the Russian bureaucracy under Peter the Great. Hoping to borrow liberally from the Swedes, Peter the Great put into motion a striking program to bring about bureaucratic change. Fainsod concludes that, for all of his efforts, he left Russia pretty much as he found it. It required the single-minded campaign inaugurated by the Bolsheviks, and knowingly calculated to have its impact in the long run, to effect the profound modifications in the Soviet bureaucracy that have evolved over the last four decades. I might add that the same thing is true of Japan. Statements regarding bureaucratic change there after the Meiji Restoration often obscure the fact that many of the modifications we associate with the period since 1868 were evidently already very much in motion for at least a century during the Tokugawa Shogunate. It seems reasonable to suppose, then, that even those new nations, which begin the process of nation building and political development with few deeply rooted structures at the national level will have to develop a more reasonable expectation concerning the tempo with which political and administrative institutions can be built.

Regardless of the rate at which the training of new public administrators may proceed, the question must be posed concerning what kinds of top-level personnel are desirable. Braibanti, in his discussion of Pakistan, points out something that is typical of indigenous bureaucrats in countries where the British and French enjoyed relatively long periods of colonial control, namely, that the upper-level administrators are generally hostile to the scientific, mechanistic, egalitarian, and anti-intellectual bias of American public administration. It should be pointed out that efforts of Americans to export scientific public administration have met with negative responses not only in such widely dispersed places as Pakistan, Viet Nam, Turkey, and Brazil, but in West European countries like Italy as well. American public administration, like the Taylorism, which influenced the shaping of its traditional principles, is not very palatable in societies where science is less than a god, where traditional forces are still at work, even among the Westernized elites, and where the administrative legacy the new nations possess comes from older European countries that continue to have greater prestige among the political and administrative elite than does the United States. That the ability of these countries to resist American efforts to "modernize" public administration is formidable is clearly discernible in the reports of federal administrators and academicians – many of them experts in "O and M," personnel, classification systems, budgeting, and planning, etc. – who ventured abroad with great expectations, only to have their hopes shattered by the discovery that, even where institutional transfer is achieved, the consequences are often unanticipated. Thus, even where some evidence of the American institutional impact can be detected, it is hazardous to conclude that the heavy investments of money and men pay the anticipated dividends.

Moreover, it is far from obvious that the bureaucracies of the new states should uncritically adopt American principles of scientific management. Braibanti concludes that the British influence on Pakistan's bureaucracy has been anything but detrimental to the nation. He suggests that a bureaucracy less tied to the British tradition – i.e., less generalist in its orientation – would not have been as stable in an unstable situation. One of his generalizations that deserves further investigation is that the introduction of an egalitarian system of recruitment in a highly status-conscious society would serve to reduce the status of public servants. If this is true, the role of the bureaucracy as a politically stabilizing influence would be seriously undermined. He also hypothesizes that, in a setting where voluntary associations are unavailable to the political system, almost every act of government involves bureaucratic behavior. In this type of setting, he remarks that the isolation and aloofness of the bureaucrat from the public may be his only protection against an avalanche of demands for particularistic considerations. In other words, if Braibanti is correct, as he certainly seems to me to be, in asserting that the bureaucracy is necessarily a reflection of the larger social environment of which it is a part, it would appear somewhat irrational to superimpose on any of the developing nations the principles and organizational characteristics of public administration that have evolved in the United States. Indeed, the irony in much of this is that the principles we try to export do not even operate in the United States. Many scholars and professional administrators who went abroad on technical assistance missions in recent years are the first to attest *to* this axiom.

In thinking about what kinds of training programs should be instituted for top public administrative management, we must come to grips with what Morstein Marx has to say about the administrative specialist – the functional expert whose British generalist is so often lauded in the textbooks. His central proposition is that the growth of functional expertise in the bureaucracy seriously weakens the integrative function of status officialdom. The specialist is insular, narrow in his vision as well as his desires; he tends to turn the bureaucracy into a house divided against itself. This insularity and concern with limited interests blurs the bureaucrat's vision of the broader national problems and reduces his capacity to fulfill his vital role as a policy advisor. In Morstein Marx's terms, metaphysics yields to technology. In Braibanti's formulation, the loss of a strong intellectual orientation in the leading bureaucrats makes it less likely that they will play a creative and stabilizing role in the economic and political developments of society. In short, the implied proposition here is that, particularly in the new states where the need for national integration is paramount, the proliferation of functional specialists in administration will add to the many centrifugal forces that already exist. When a society is rent by all sorts of social and political forces pulling in conflicting, disintegrative directions, the administrative generalist may be a vital cement, holding the system together. It may well be that programs of economic development require a certain amount of functional expertise in administration; indeed it is difficult to imagine how the many technical activities implied by economic modernization could evolve without them. But there must be accorded equal attention to the critical political role that the administrative generalist can perform, as well as to the need for preventing these generalists from impeding the development of countervailing centers of political power.

I might add here that the literature of political science in the West raises a number of problems regarding the functional specialist that are also worthy of consideration. The most critical of these involves the general problems treated below regarding the exercise of effective political control over the bureaucracy. If it is true that legislative rule-makers find it increasingly arduous, if not impossible, to maintain meaningful control over the bureaucratic experts, proliferating these bureaucrats early in the histories of the developing new states may very well serve to tip the political balance permanently in favor of a bureaucratic elite. It is fairly obvious, for example, that the specialists in destruction, the military, often enjoy a position of superior power precisely because they are technologically the most "modern" element in the developing areas. To be sure, their power is often also owing to their control of troops and weapons, but they remain, nevertheless, among those groups that are more readily willing to accept change. In any event, if the new states are going to emphasize functional expertise in public administration, they should be clear regarding the possible political price that such a program may imply.

Finally, on the subject of finding adequate personnel for the developing nations, Walter R. Sharp's chapter is very suggestive. He notes, for example, value that may be derived from integrating technical assistants directly into the bureaucratic systems of the new states. Presumably, persons so placed will have a greater impact than those who function as advisors to host country counterparts. In addition, Sharp offers a number of generalizations of considerable importance. For example, he notes that most efforts to reform public services have tended toward too much centralization of administrative agencies. His axiom would be that where there is little decentralization there is very little creativity and innovation forthcoming from the bureaucracy. Riggs, who spends much time discussing the need for local politics, would certainly concur. So would John Dorsey, who recognizes that the need for greater administrative decentralization in Viet Nam is seriously impeded by the security situation in that unfortunate country. Presumably, Eisenstadt may be of the same view, if his comments regarding the need for administrative centralization are applied to the early activities of the bureaucracy in the integrative sector.

Another of Sharp's propositions is that the impact of United Nations (and presumably other) technical assistance programs depends on people and not on money. Plans for bureaucratic reform or economic and social change will be seriously inhibited if they run counter to powerful interest groups, if aid is sought to mask human failures in politics and administration, and if changes in political leadership cause, as they usually do, upheavals in public administrative leadership. For these as well as other reasons that we have already discussed, it is critical to understand – and for the developing nations to accept – that the short-run impact of strategies of bureaucratic reform, capital investment, social change, and the like will be very slight indeed. As Sharp notes, how the impact can be increased is a matter concerning which our information will remain limited until further research is undertaken.

BUREAUCRACY AND OTHER POLITICAL INSTITUTIONS

As several of our authors indicate, the bureaucracy is often called on to play a critical role when the major need of a society is that of creating a sense of nationhood. Bureaucratic behavior that relates to this function takes place in what Hoselitz calls the integrative sector. When, in addition to national integration, economic development also becomes an overriding goal, the bureaucracy, or "public sector," may also be asked to participate in the goal gratification and allocative sectors. When this happens, the probability of the bureaucracy becoming deeply enmeshed in the function of rule making (as well as rule application) is enormously increased. Such an increase in bureaucratic power in the developing areas may clearly inhibit, perhaps preclude, the development of a democratic polity.

As Riggs notes, the presence of a strong bureaucracy in many of the new states tends to inhibit growth of strong executives, political parties, legislatures, voluntary associations, and other political institutions essential to viable democratic government. Indeed, a significant problem in many of the ex-colonial areas is not that bureaucracy is too weak but that, as a result of the colonial experience itself, the bureaucracy in the post-independence period is the only sector of the political system that is reasonably cohesive and coherent – and able to exercise leadership and power. Where this is true, political parties tend to be ineffective, and voluntary associations, rather than serving as checks on the bureaucracy, tend to become passive instrumentalities of the public administrators.

The problem of how much control should be exercised over the bureaucracy is very perplexing. As John Dorsey illustrates for Viet Nam, President Diem's strategy has involved a combination of bureaucratic centralization, a network of tight political controls, the inculcation of attitudes of political reliability, and the use of a combination of kinship and personal charisma to assure the preponderance of the executive over the bureaucracy. Diem seems very much to have satisfied the Riggs stricture that in order to keep the bureaucracy in check, the executive needs a power base outside the bureaucracy itself. However, the general price of this control in Viet Nam has meant a political regime that is anything but democratic in its total configuration. In Pakistan, the civil bureaucracy has to some extent be checked by the military and martial law, but the situation there appears somewhat healthier from a democratic standpoint in the sense that the judiciary is functioning to check the excesses of both the military and the civil bureaucracy. It is apparent that finding the kind of balance that increases the chances of democratic development is extremely arduous and that it must be a task adapted to the particular set of circumstances that each developing area manifests.

Where economic development as a national goal is paramount, and its attainment is expected to take place largely at public hands, public administrators are in the political limelight because they tend to be injected into policy-making activities. Some feel that there is little alternative available to this pattern in the developing new states and that the question of how to relate bureaucrats to other political authorities is appropriately raised at a later stage. It is also asserted that what is political or non-political, partisan or non-partisan, varies from culture to culture and that in transitional societies the distinction is never neat. Yet, both the long-range development of a democratic system and the short-range goal of achieving a sense of the economy of the polity as a whole requires that some distinction between political and administrative roles be made, understood, and adhered to. To cite one of the least negative consequences of a failure in this area, one risks the consequence that few if any standards of professional competence will ever permeate the bureaucracy. This type of politicization can in turn weaken the capacity of the bureaucracy to perform its long-range developmental tasks.

I am arguing here that democratic development requires some separation of political and administrative roles. Joseph J. Spengler adds that economic development in turn cannot proceed with maximum efficiency unless it is managed by a combination of both the private and the public sector. Spengler suggests that the public sector is less rational in the recruitment of the manpower needed for economic development and less efficient in the management of the important economic input transformation function. He would, therefore, limit the economically relevant role of bureaucracy to the selection of the ends or objectives of development, the provision of objective conditions that aid the growth of an entrepreneurial middle class, and the addition of certain input transformation activities where the private sector is inadequate.

Spengler's is strictly an economic argument for limiting the role of the bureaucracy in economic development. He, like others, warns against having the public sector become an omnivorous and unproductive consumer of a nation's limited resources. Yet his position clearly has important political implications. Riggs, for example, sees the development of a middle class as a vital means of limiting bureaucratic power in favor of democratic development. The data, however, are discouraging. Kingsley tells us that in Africa the economic involvement of the bureaucracy is essential if the "leap to modernization" is to take place where a private entrepreneurial class is simply non-existent. Dorsey stresses that the public sector is often empha-sized precisely because little or no economic development would otherwise occur. The problem for the developing countries seems to be that of finding entrepreneurial skills and motivation wherever they may exist. That the bureaucracy usually harbors the vast concentration of this talent is the consequence of a particular pattern of historical and colonial evolution.

However, it is also apparent that, for ideological or other reasons, the bureaucracies of the developing areas will often hamper the growth of a private entrepreneurial class. Merchants and others who might work to transform the economy are incessantly harassed; what appear on the surface to be rational tax systems amount, in fact, to tribute. The price of com-mercial survival becomes a systematic campaign to corrupt the bureaucracy itself. Often whatever indigenous entrepreneurial talent there may be is concentrated in pariah classes, of foreign origin, and therefore not polit-ically available to the society at large. Thus, forces that might be harnessed to the tasks of nation building are dissipated in the most unproductive kind of petty political maneuvering, which enshrines corruption as the means of commercial and fiscal survival. Neither meaningful economic development nor political democracy are likely to emerge unless, as Spengler suggests, the bureaucracies of the new states make quite deliberate efforts to encourage the flourishing of the private sector. Spengler's general warning has a ring of authenticity: when the bureaucracy is once mobilized for the achievement of systemic goals, it is not likely to withdraw willingly when the pressure of systemic goals diminishes.

From a democratic standpoint, the general picture is not completely discouraging. Even where the bureaucracy is deeply involved in goal setting, the extent of its power may be checked by such factors as increased literacy, strong traditional institutions, and strong social elites of which the bureaucracy is not a part or into which it has not yet been absorbed. We know, for example, that even after a century of Prussian bureaucratic centralization, encompassing developments from the Great Elector to Frederick William I, the bureaucracy was limited in its powers by the necessity of having to effect all sorts of compromises with the Junkers. In Meiji Japan, at least until the upper-level bureaucrats began to be absorbed into the nobility, the dominant social class served as a check on bureaucratic excesses. In contemporary India, the Congress Party, the traditions of the Indian Civil. Service, and the growth of strong and articulate local centers of political power appear as partial checks on the central bureaucracy. In many of the developing areas – as witness abortive efforts to ride roughshod over village-level forces – a kind of *de facto* federal structure tends to circumscribe the amount of power the bureaucracy can exercise.

By and large, however, we are witnessing in many places the emergence of overpowering bureaucracies. Some feel that there is little alternative to a cautious acceptance of this development. It is pointed out that rapid economic change is the overriding need and that little can be done to moderate the revolution of rising expectations. In these circumstances one must accept an increasingly powerful bureaucracy and hope that, in the long run, other political institutions will catch up. Moreover, it is not always certain that attempts to limit bureaucratic power will have the desired results. For example, the encouragement of stronger political institutions, say, a two- or multiparty system, might be counter-productive as far as economic development is concerned. On this reasoning, one should prefer a one-party-dominant system and hope that the party itself might serve as a check on the bureaucracy, as it does in the Soviet Union or as it may do in Ghana. As another example, it is far from clear that encouraging the growth of local governmental institutions will give anticipated results. Where this was attempted by Alexander II in Russia, those who went into the zemstvos were, indeed at war with the central bureaucracy, but so much so that many of them became Cadets and made their appearance in the 1905 Revolution. It is also noteworthy that in many places in Africa strong bureaucracies are needed in order to hold together new countries that would otherwise fall apart under the impact of the many centrifugal forces that beset them. In places such as these, a powerful bureaucracy is said to be essential if one is to override the disintegrating influences of artificial political boundaries, the

competitive force of familial and tribal structures, the difficulty of organizing and financing political parties, the low energy output of the population,
and the tendency of the population to want to expend funds on consumer
gadgets rather than on a capital formation. In sum, there are those who hold
that, in the developing states, powerful bureaucracies are simply necessary
evils that one must learn to tolerate, hoping for the best from a democratic
standpoint.

For those such as Fred Riggs who are not sanguine about the probable
political outcome of trends now in motion, it is necessary to take certain
positive steps. Riggs' chapter contains a number of concrete suggestions. He
would encourage the long ballot at the local level as well as greater local
autonomy of taxing power. He rightly notes, as do others, that central
planning aggrandizes bureaucratic power aid that local participation in
developmental plans is not meaningful unless local citizens are asked and
empowered to pay for economic change through taxation, if they want to
and can. It may sound like a tired cliche, but there is apparently more
than blind faith in the generalization that political democracy begins at the
grass roots. The need for national integration, which calls for centralized
administration, must give way to greater decentralization if the need for
democratic development is to be met.

To summarize, there appears to be some incompatibility between rapid
economic development, on the one hand, and democratic political development, on the other. Riggs flatly states that the price of democratic development may have to be slower development in the economic sphere.
Certainly it is anything but apparent that a planned increase in the material
well being of a society will automatically bring about democratic institutions. Planned economic development, in which the public sector is dominant, tends to imply centralized control, the curtailment of public wants to
increase surplus value for investment, the weakening of traditional institutions of a society, particularly when they manifest values antagonistic to
economic development, and an intolerance of institutional arrangements,
such as many political parties or strong interest groups, that might divert
the society from its central purpose.

Bringing about democratic political development must be a consciously
sought goal. If it cannot be encouraged through a de-emphasis of economic
goals, it might be possible to experiment with such mechanisms as local
governmental autonomy, the integration of traditional structures into developmental plans, the use of democratic ideological indoctrination as a
means of controlling bureaucracies. Equally vital to democracy, it would
seem, is the development of the private sector economy. The bureaucracy

might limit the role to that of setting systemic goals and providing the objective conditions without which economic development is seriously hamstrung. Beyond this, the bureaucracy might exercise self-restraint, relying as much as possible on the private sector for the performance of the function of input transformation. To be sure, in most of the developing societies input transformation would require the dual participation of both the bureaucracy and whatever business community exists. But only if the latter is encouraged substantively to participate can one expect to witness the growth of the kind of social and economic milieu in which eventual democratic development amounts to more than a pious hope.

DEMANDS AND THE BUREAUCRACY

Eisenstadt tells us that all political systems are subjected to a pattern of demands and that all of them have some capacity to deal with increases in demands and organization that may develop. In reaction to demands, alternatives are available to the authoritative structures in the sense that the development of demands may be minimized, controlled, or manipulated, or absorbed by responding to them with governmental policies. The particular combination of these three patterns of response will divulge the degree to which a political system approximates democracy or totalitarianism. A modern democratic system would be one in which there exists both a high degree of structural differentiation for dealing with demands as well as a reasonable correspondence between the level of demands and their substantive satisfaction. In the satisfaction of demands in any system, the bureaucracy inevitably plays a very vital role. The point to note is that there are functional requisites for any given political system and that, if a democratic industrial society is desired, requisites such as the above, in which the bureaucracy is intimately involved, must be met.

In the developing areas, the bureaucracies are normally confronted with a level of demand that the system is simply not able to satisfy. Kingsley points out that colonialism itself leaves a legacy of greatly increased demands for the symbols of a well-endowed materialistic society. Dorsey phrases this problem as resulting from the permeation of low-information-energy societies with the information and values of high-energy societies. Morstein Marx, looking into the consequences of this, notes that the bureaucrats in developing societies are often squeezed by the excessive demands of politicians who tend to reflect and to generate what the masses seek from the political system. Whatever the formulation, it is obvious that bureaucrats often find themselves confronted by requests that they cannot meet. The situation is particularly difficult in those political systems where there are no well-developed political parties and voluntary associations that might serve to temper and aggregate demands and to provide an orderly means of communicating demands to the bureaucracy.

One bureaucratic response to this situation is what Riggs calls "formalism," involving the creation of the formal structures of high-energy societies but not their content. Another related response involves the encouragement, even the creation by the bureaucracy, of seemingly voluntary associations that are nothing more than the bureaucracy's instrumentalities. Such associations afford some structural means whereby demands can be transmitted in a reasonably orderly way. They help the bureaucracy, to some degree, to control the flow of demands and to implement policies that emanate from the bureaucracy itself. Needless to add, such a pattern of response is not consistent with the development of a pluralistic democracy.

Nevertheless, in any political system, something has to be done about the growth of political demands that occur as a social system moves from a traditional into a transitional situation. In the development of Western systems the situation was different in an important respect. There, the capacity of political systems for enforcement of decisions and the allocation of values increased along with the capacity of the society to generate demands. Where, as in the new nations, demands clearly outstrip any capacity of the system to meet them institutionally, one witnesses the evolution of symbolic and demagogic politics – an inflation of the language of politics as an effort to soak up those demands that cannot be met by concrete output. This is merely another mode of responding to the general problem – a mode in which the bureaucracy itself may play a central role. The fact is that, when confronted with this set of circumstances, the bureaucracy, by various devices, is forced to (1) limit the creation of demand, as in Salazar's Portugal, (2) control those demands not emanating from the government itself, as in the Soviet Union, and (3) absorb as many of the demands as possible through the utilization of existing institutions and the creation of new ones. While all political systems will exhibit some combination of these three responses to demand, the developing nations tend to focus primarily on the first two. This tends to institutionalize an unstable situation and to bring into operation patterns of political and bureaucratic behavior that are incompatible with democracy.

The management of demands is a deeply perplexing problem and in the developing nations the bureaucracy is certain to be heavily involved in the process. Unfortunately, the widest possible range of demands is directed against the government. The demands for independence against colonial powers accustomed the masses to convert most of their grievances into demands against the government of the central state. Additionally, in the post-independence situations, the existence of a bi-polar world helps to generate additional demands, which are still directed against *the* central government. In any case, the capacity of the government to meet demands will be limited by the capacity of the economic system. Here lies the pressure for rapid economic change, which leads the bureaucracy to push hard in this direction. That demands are not always spontaneous, that they may be manipulated and generated by elements of the articulate, educated elite, is not immediately relevant. The fact is that the demands are there and the bureaucracy is compelled to respond to them in some meaningful way. For, unless some way of institutionalizing and otherwise coping with demands is devised, the system itself is certain to disintegrate into violence and chaos. Certainly the nature, flow, and magnitude of demands will make any kind of development, political or economic, easier or more difficult. Difficulties are certain to increase in the degree to which the bureaucracy fails to manage demands in some systematic way.

This leads me to speculate whether it would not be possible to manipulate demands so that goals of democratic political development enjoy a status equal to that of economic change. Less emphasis might be given to grand schemes of economic development, more to local-level development that might bring forces of local political participation into play. This might also be a means of encouraging the evolution of the kind of private economic sector that would constitute an embryonic middle class and an eventual counterpoise to the power of the centralized bureaucracy. I might say that I strongly believe that it is more than historical coincidence that economic liberalism preceded the emergence of political liberalism in the West. A similar, even if not exactly duplicate, type of evolution might be encouraged in the developing nations. Some political benefits would surely derive from encouraging the kind of economic enterprise that is individually rather than collectively oriented, that exalts the place of the private entrepreneur rather than that of an all-embracing collectivity symbolized by large-scale, un-wieldily, and unbending public bureaucracies. While I do not expect the intellectuals, bureaucrats, and politicians to accept a Spencerian definition of the role of the public sector, it does seem possible that greater acceptance might be accorded the model assigning a more significant role to the private sector of the economy.

I am aware that it will be difficult to implement what is suggested here. Progressive limitations on the powers of bureaucracy are not easy to come by; de-emphasizing economic development goals will meet with a great deal of opposition everywhere in the new states. Yet, without some conscious effort in this direction, the pattern of political development in the new states will probably follow the Soviet – or Chinese – rather than the Anglo-American model. It is this possibility that compels us to give even greater attention to the role of the bureaucracy in political development.

SOME UNANSWERED QUESTIONS

Much more needs to be done in the field of comparative research – both historical and contemporary – before we can speak with confidence about the variables that push a nation in one political direction rather than another. How, for example, does a society go about inculcating the set of attitudes toward government and voluntary associations that are compatible with a pluralist democracy? What role can the bureaucracy play in this important function? What instruments of political socialization are most efficaciously related to this process? What kinds of training and statuses does the bureaucracy require if it is to exercise the quantum of self-restraint that will make of it a bulwark of democratic rather than totalitarian development? If economic and political developments are to move ahead simultaneously, what kind of balance of objectives and tempo of movement is to be prescribed for each sector? If, in the developing areas, the public sector is to achieve a position of great prominence from the very beginning of nation-statehood, what can be done to guarantee that healthy centers of countervailing power will come into existence? Questions such as these will surely suggest themselves to the reader. They deserve continuous attention from the practitioners of social science.

It will doubtless be noted that one important topic not treated in this volume is the role of the military in economic and political developments. It is apparent, for example, that in many of the new states, what development does occur will be managed by the military bureaucracy, either working largely alone, as the military has tried to do in places like Burma and Thailand, or in some kind of collaboration with the civil bureaucracy, as has been true of countries like Egypt, Turkey, and Pakistan.

From the standpoint of nation building and economic development, the military can often work as a very effective instrument. The role of the centralized military in breaking the power of feudal nobles, warlords, and caudillos is well known. The military was effectively used in this sense in Prussia after the Great Elector and in Japan following the Meiji Restoration, to cite only two of the obvious examples. The military can very quickly acquire a sense of the nation and develop hostilities toward vested interests and parochial enclaves. The military organization itself, by recruiting from disparate groups throughout the society, can be an important socializing instrument, inculcating values that are nation oriented.

By its very nature, the military will also tend to be the most modern group (in the technological sense) that one encounters in a transitional society. Defense needs more military leaders to accept new technologies and to train recruits in skills that one associates with an industrial society. These skills can be put to use when recruits are released from military service. Moreover, in situations where the military becomes directly involved in the creation of social overhead capital, it can be quite effective in the construction of roads, bridges, dams, and other projects essential to rapid economic change.

The list of positive characteristics does not terminate here. Armies can be important transitional experiences for those who leave the villages and wind up in urban centers. As officers are recruited from other than the dominant aristocratic strata of societies, armies can become a means of strengthening the middle class. The military, through its formal and practical educational opportunities, can be a most significant means of providing a reservoir of future administrative and technological leadership. In short, the military can be a very important impetus for change.

Yet, where the military has assumed control, it is often apparent that democratic development is impeded. The case of Japan following the American military occupation seems to be an exception, and, until recently, so was Turkey. Pakistan may offer another interesting exception, but it is yet too early to draw firm conclusions there. By and large, when the military assumes control it does not tend to encourage democratic institutions and practices; it is suspicious and disdainful of politicians; it is apt to short-circuit and to delay constitutionalism; and it is inclined either toward becoming a part of the existing aristocratic strata or toward developing a vested-interest status of its own. The history of Latin America clearly illustrates one pattern of political development that can emerge when the military bureaucracy gets into the driver's seat.

Nor should one exaggerate the utility of the military bureaucracy in economic development. For one thing, military leaders infrequently understand the myriad and subtle problems involved in the business of giving rational and coherent fiscal and financial leadership to the community. As national political policy makers, they tend to be less able than their civil bureaucratic counterparts. For another thing, military regimes invariably divert to the military area limited resources that might be better used for economic development. Perhaps the point to make here is that, whereas the military can be very useful as a limited instrument of economic development, its utility and effectiveness greatly diminishes as it moves toward complete control of the social system. In any event, it is reasonably clear that, where the goal-setting and goal-implementing bureaucracy is military rather than civil, the prospects for democratic political development are even more dismal than I have suggested above.

We have embarked on only the beginning of an intellectual journey that is fraught with all sorts of conceptual and theoretical difficulties. Some of these are empirically visible only above the surface, and we shall have to probe to greater depths before moving ahead with confidence. Unhappily, time does not stand still for the new states, and forces already in motion will probably lead to destinations that were set long before these pages were written.

NOTES

1. *Bureaucracy and Society in Modern Egypt: A Study of the Higher Civil Service*, Princeton University Press, 1957.

PART II

ADMINISTRATIVE DEVELOPMENT AND DEVELOPMENT ADMINISTRATION

Eric E. Otenyo and Nancy S. Lind

The concept of administrative development is closely associated with development administration. In its raw form, administrative development encompasses acts of forming new institutions – especially government agencies. In many parts of the world where this term was widely used, administrative development was about reengineering or simply establishing institutions that served colonial administrations to meet new objectives and goals in emerging countries. Among the first attempts at describing administrative development was Riggs (1964). Early forms of administrative development were basically analyses of institutional development in developing areas.

Riggs expanded our understanding of administrative development by observing that societies that sought to promote rapid development often had centrally controlled political systems that hampered progress. Such societies often lacked greater application of rational systems of managing bureaucracy. Thus, to undo, some of the excesses related to unnecessary bureaucratic formalities enhanced prospects for development. Accordingly, the greater the application differentiated rational bureaucracies, the more likely those systems would meet the goals for development. Moreover, "if a bureaucracy became increasingly more responsible," as an agent for the implementation of public policies, then chances for development would be

Comparative Public Administration: The Essential Readings
Research in Public Policy Analysis and Management, Volume 15, 221–230
Copyright © 2006 by Elsevier Ltd.
ISSN: 0732-1317/doi:10.1016/S0732-1317(06)15050-2

enhanced. That by itself was an important dynamic of administrative development (Riggs, 1966, p. 253). In a nutshell, expanding bureaucratic
outreach and sectoral and structural differentiation was a key element in
administrative development.

Unfortunately, conceptual writing on the phenomenon grappled with
operational definitions of development. However, there were numerous
country-level reports accounting for various levels of bureaucratic expansion. Significantly, most of the country-specific studies tended to be thick
descriptions of bureaucratic responses to political realities or more accurately, political responses to bureaucratic governance. Essentially these were
bureaucratic adjustments to changing political circumstances – especially
the changing of the guard from colonial administration to newly independent countries. Many of these adjustments had to do with orienting bureaucracies away from law and order to newer forms of administration and
perhaps more importantly, nation building (see for example, Tilman, 1964;
Adamolekun, 1976; Esman, 1972; Morgan, 1974; Hyden, 1970; Honey,
1968). Importantly, these were area studies, which gave deeper meaning to
our understanding of bureaucratic politics and the applicability of the politics – administration dichotomy from a global multicultural perspective.
The formation of new institutions attracted other studies, especially those
that tested the relevance of Western organization theories to non-Western
cultures. Obviously, such studies number in the thousands. The important
point is that there was widespread resentment of aping western style bureaucratic forms in the developing areas. This, in part, is Deva's (1979) discontent with the emerging discourses.

DEVELOPMENT ADMINISTRATION,
THEN AND NOW

Nearly three decades have passed since the "heyday" of development
administration. Huddleston (1984, p. 177) among others distinguished development administration from mainstream public administration at the practitioner level. He considered it as an area of comparative administration that
focuses on the special problems and possibilities of countries of the Third
World. Accordingly, it was an attempt to upgrade or develop administration
in these countries. It also entailed the creation of unique administrative
systems where none existed. The field was a product of its distinctive
zietgeist and reflected the age of pronounced confidence in big government

(Esman, 1988; Fried, 1990). Then, development theory scholars assumed incorrectly that progress would be linear with societies aiming toward a "take-off" stage. From there, development processes would be self-sustaining. Public administration was considered a vital tool for managing the economic growth and development process. Successive U.S. administrations from Harry Truman, Dwight Eisenhower, and John Kennedy promoted the doctrine of development assistance (aid) to the developing areas. Aid provided the academy with opportunities to study such issues as development economics, community development, development education, and finally, development administration (Weidner, 1962, p. 97).

Victor Thompson (1964) provided the most lucid statement of objectives for the emerging subfield of development administration. His work reproduced here specifies that development administration required objectives such as the ability to change and innovate. Besides, there is need for administrators to establish clear goals that must be shared among the implementing individuals. Development administration also requires a careful look at decentralization and centralization strategies as well as adopting a cosmopolitan-professional outlook. The later is considered a better orientation than parochialism.

At the conceptual level, several scholars grappled with providing working definitions and a locus for the field. The most widely read statements in the formative years were probably written by Riggs (1966, 1967, 1970, 1971, 1976a, 1976b), Gant (1979) and Waldo (1980). Weidner attempted to describe the emerging area of interest in a holistic sense. He wrote, "development administration in government refers to the processes of guiding an organization toward the achievement of progressive political, economic, and social objectives that are authoritatively determined in one manner or another" (1962, p. 98). Riggs, on the other hand, pointed out that development administration typically referred to the "administrative means to achieve developmental goals" (1966, p. 225).

Like all literature, works on development administration were value biased. The writings served a specific ideological purpose. To a large extent, the writings were a product of the "decades of development." Development then was the fashion. It stemmed from the desire by richer countries to provide aid to the poor and disadvantaged countries. These countries were in turn expected to conform ideologically. Brian Loveman (1976) in "The Comparative Administration Group, Development Administration, and Antidevelopment" makes a similar point, albeit with a different perspective.

A similar opinion is expressed by Deva (1979) in "Western Conceptualization of Administrative Development: A Critique and an Alternative" originally published in the *International Review of Administrative Sciences*. His central thesis is that development administration, as conventionally understood in the West, had its roots in the anti-communism movement of the 1950s. It therefore provides an inappropriate framework for administration in the Third World. He offers an alternative scheme built around values of decentralization, anti-corruption, economic equality, and political participation.

Regardless of the ideological frameworks, there were also local elite interests seeking to respond to the massive challenges of poverty, illiteracy, and disease. Previous administrative systems were tailored to provide basic security and law and order. On the other hand, development administration focused on establishing administrative systems for achieving these human development goals (Jones, 1976; Gant, 1979; Riggs, 1970).

In the 1960s, government was relied upon for the administration of development projects. Development occurred in several Asian countries but the African scene was less than admirable. Latin America had mixed experiences, but for the most part remained underdeveloped. Generally, development assistance or aid triggered some progress in a number of areas but not others. Countries without absorptive capacity failed to achieve sustainable economic growth (Dresang, 1973, pp. 76–85; Curtis, 1988, pp. 47–59). While development administration was dependent on the availability of development assistance, it showed promise, but project failures weakened its metamorphosis into a subfield of note. Numerous case studies spoke volumes about the negative attributes of employing western bureaucratic models on developing countries and other cultures (Adamolekun, 1976; Sigleman, 1976; Moris, 1977; Deva, 1979; Rondinelli, 1987). Scholars noted that analyzing bureaucracies in developing countries, with analytical tools not suitable for these cultures, was inappropriate (Moris, 1977, p. 75). As Dwivedi and Henderson (1990) observed, for most of the developing areas, a value-free bureaucracy was not a reality but a myth.

Briefly, in most developing countries, the most visible forms of development were through projects funded by western donor agencies. Arguably, the Cold War environment offered the best opportunities for development assistance. Then, funds were available to win over allies in the global ideological competition. There was also an element of compassion in the 1950s and 1960s when the more developed countries moved substantial amounts of resources into the Third World – especially through the expansion of education and health care. In the Cold War framework, the administration of development aid or technical assistance proved to be a challenge for both local and expatriate administrators.

Perhaps the most interesting debate in the larger public administration literature on the efficacy of aid was in *Public Administration Review's* 1980 reproduction of a debate among the field's most eminent development administration scholars and administrators. The debates capture the most salient features of transfer of bureaucratic styles from the developed countries to developing areas. Although there are several books (for example, Rondinelli, 1987) and articles written on transfer of managerial skills through technical assistance, none capture the nuances as well as the articles reproduced in this present work.

The failure of Western experts to understand political and cultural dynamics in foreign areas receiving aid was a key variable in many of the instances where aid failed to achieve sustainable development. This seems to have been the conceptual framework adopted by John Seitz (1980, p. 407). In his *"The failure of U.S. Technical Assistance in Public Administration: The Iranian Case"* he argued that the U.S. Technical assistance projects to ministries and police in Iran in 1953–1968 failed because American project implementers were ignorant of Iranian objectives. American technical assistance failed to recognize the existence of massive maladministration including overcentralization, lack of sufficient open debate, corruption, inefficiency, arrogance, and structural problems within the bureaucracy. Seitz placed blame on USAID for the success of the revolution in Iran that gave the Ayatollah political power. The article sparked a lively debate on the role of technical assistance in development administration and project management as a whole.

In the debate, Sherwood (1980) disagreed with Seitz and instead pointed out that public administration was a small component of the Shah's troubles, and it did not play a major role in the regime's fall. Other factors included class "struggles," and the rich versus poor dichotomy – especially because the educated were alienated. Moreover, there was attrition from the civil service to the private sector, when oil revenues rose as a result of the 1973 increases. Salaries were low and therefore civil servants were not motivated to perform optimally. Foreign aid to SAVAK (secret police) was also an impediment in the sense that it exacerbated ill feelings against the regime. The advisors could not understand the political implications of their work and could not forestall the revolutionary process.

For his part, William Siffin (1980) agreed that lessons were learned in the Iranian case. But, he thought it was not a failure of a well-intended solution. It was a failure to define the problems wisely. According to Siffin, the fact that developing countries did not initiate projects was their undoing. An assumption that developing countries could use Western Public Administration tools for development was also reason for failure.

A third rejoinder was John Montgomery's (1980) argument that neither capital aid nor technical assistance is an unmixed blessing to the receiving society. To him, the decision to prop up unsavory regimes was more responsible for the outcomes. He suggested that the greatest success in foreign aid occurred when two conditions maintain: (1) a political context of mutual purpose and (2) the existence of a sophisticated calculus of the benefits that could be appropriately expected from each partner. Consequently he concluded that, in Iran, aid did work for at least ten years and the fact that a revolution took place should not be blamed on aid. He opined that aid would have worked better with greater decentralization of authority and decision making. In tandem with this initiative, an increase of resources to the "field," use of informal organizations and improved project design were essential components for a successful strategy. Finally, Milton Esman (1980, pp. 426–431) argued that technical assistance personnel made false assumptions that development administration was a process that combined economic growth and modernization, and would also trigger development in the developing areas. Experiences such as in Iran proved the contrary; technical assistance and development administration did not seem to help much. Esman rejected the practice of employing the western style administrative model with its strong dosage of values such as political neutrality, efficiency, economy, and effectiveness. These values, he contended, were not necessarily appreciated overseas. Much of what is contained in the debates applies to contemporary situations and is worth our attention especially post-September 11, 2001 when the global war against Al Qaida and other terrorist groups has necessitated provision of western technologies to law enforcement forces in several countries.

RUNNING OUT OF STEAM

As a subfield of public administration, development administration matured and "ran out of interesting ideas," but retained a weak presence in the broader public administration discipline (Esman, 1988, p. 133; Van Wart & Cayer, 1990; Heady, 2001, pp. 390–395). More profoundly, Jreisat (2002) in a recent title declared that "plainly, development administration thinking at present seems to be at a crossroads." If development administration has lost its luster then a lot has to do with the phenomenon of failed states. This essay will not address the reasons for state failure, but accounts for the lull in the development administration enterprise. The very existence of war ravaged, failed, and collapsed states is in itself an antithesis for development. The failed states come in different shapes and forms and include "anarchic states, phantom or mirage states, anemic states, captured states and aborted states" (Collier & Hoeffler, 2002).

Recently, states that required considerable infusion of development assistance include Bosnia-Herzegovina, Angola, Congo, Nicaragua, East Timor, Somalia, Rwanda, Afghanistan, Iraq, Liberia, Sri Lanka, Indonesia, and parts of India devastated by a Tsunami in December 2004. More than 20 countries have, since the 1980s, experienced decline in economic productivity and growth from a host of causes including civil and internal wars, devastating natural disasters, and outright mismanagement or policy failures due to poor administrative practices including tardiness, incompetence, misconduct, inefficiency, discontent, and absenteeism.

Of course, there are cases of failed development arising from maladministration. Maladministration encompasses abuse of power, resistance to change, rigid adherence to rules, sycophancy, insistence on status symbols, xenophobia, paperasserie, account padding, and so on (Caiden, 1991, p. 486; Haruna, 2003, p. 347; Widner, 1995, p. 147). Arguably, maladministration and especially corruption was a key cause of poor performance in economic development in many countries of the south. In fact, several accounts attributed the negative growth rates to massive corruption and incompetent public administration systems (Sims & Voglemann, 2002).

There are several theories that attempt to explain state failure. Among these are conditions resulting from the newly emerging global realignments. The failure of several states to hold together at the end of the Cold War was in part a consequence of declining resources resulting from competition of resources widely unavailable in the post-Cold War developing areas – especially of Africa. The new global environment is the subject of Jean-Claude Garcia-Zamor's (1994) work reproduced in this volume. Garcia-Zamor's work continued the trend to contend that development is still a subject of interest in the Third World. He explored the subject of the implication of the "New World Order" at the end of the Cold War. According to Garcia-Zamor, the dramatic dismantling of ideological communism affected the disbursement of aid. If aid was one of the primary engines of development administration, then the changing aid environment required some new analysis. Garcia-Zamor proceeds to outline the major directions of aid in the post-Cold War era, especially the reduced flow of aid to Africa, Asia, and Latin America and its implications for development administrators.

REFERENCES

Adamolekun, L. (1976). Towards development oriented bureaucracies in Africa. *International Review of Administrative Sciences, 42*(3), 257–265.

Caiden, N. J. (1991). Unanswered questions: Planning and budgeting in poor countries revisited. In: A. Farazmand (Ed.), *Handbook of comparative and development administration.* New York: Marcel Dekker, Inc.

Collier, P., & Hoeffler, A. (2002). *Aid, policy, and growth in post conflict societies. Development research group.* Working Paper 2902. Washington, DC: World Bank.

Curtis, D. (1988). Development administration in the context of world economic recession: Some ideas on service provision in Southern Sudan. *Public Administration and Development, 8*(1), 47–59.

Deva, S. (1979). Western conceptualization of administrative development: A critique and an alternative. *International Review of Administrative Sciences, 45*(1), 59–63.

Dresang, D. (1973). Entrepreneurialism and development administration. *Administrative Science Quarterly, 18*(1), 76–85.

Dwivedi, O. P., & Henderson, K. (1990). *Public administration in world perspective.* Ames: Iowa State University Press 15.

Esman, M. (1972). *Administration and development in Malaysia: Institutions and reform in a plural society.* Ithaca: Cornell University Press.

Esman, M. (1980). Development assistance in public administration: Requiem or renewal. *Public Administration Review, 40*(4), 426–431.

Esman, M. (1988). The maturing of development administration. *Public Administration and Development, 8*(2), 125–134.

Fried, R. C. (1990). Comparative public administration: The search for theories. In: B. Naomi, N. B. Lynn & A. Wildavsky (Eds), *Public administration: The state of the discipline.* Chatham, NJ: Chatham House Publishers, Inc.

Gant, G. F. (1979). *Development administration: Concepts, goals, methods,* Chapter 1. Madison: University of Wisconsin Press.

Garcia-Zamor, J. C. (1994). Neoteric theories for development administration in the new world order. In: J.-C. Garcia-Zamor & R. Khator (Eds), *Public administration in the global village* (pp. 101–120). Westport, CT: Praeger.

Haruna, F. P. (2003). Reforming Ghana's public service: Issues and experiences in comparative perspective. *Public Administration Review, 63*(3), 347–357.

Heady, F. (2001). Donald C. Stone lecture. *Public Administration Review, 61*(4), 390–395.

Honey, J. (1968). *Toward strategies for administration in Latin America.* Syracuse: Syracuse University Press.

Huddleston, W. M. (1984). *Comparative public administration: An annotated bibliography.* New York: Garland.

Hyden, G. (1970). *Development administration: The Kenyan experience.* London: Oxford University Press.

Jones, N. G. (1976). Frontiersmen in search for the lost horizon: The state of development administration in the 1960s. *Public Administration Review, 36*(1), 99–109.

Jreisat, J. E. (2002). *Comparative public administration and policy.* Boulder: Westview.

Loveman, B. (1976). The comparative administration group, development administration, and antidevelopment. *Public Administration Review, 36*(6), 616–621.

Montgomery, J. (1980). Administering the poor if we can't help rich dictators, what do we do for the poor? *Public Administration Review, 40*(5), 421–425.

Morgan, P. (Ed.) (1974). *The administration of change in Africa*. New York: Dunellen Publishing Co.

Moris, R. J. (1977). The transferability of western management concepts and programs: An East African perspective. In: L. Stifel (Ed.), *Education and training for public sector management in developing countries*. New York: The Rockefeller Foundation 75.

Riggs, F. W. (1964). Administrative development: An elusive concept. In: J. D. Montgomery & W. J. Siffin (Eds), *Approaches to development politics, administration and change* (pp. 225–255). New York: McGraw-Hill.

Riggs, F. W. (1966). Modernization and developmental administration. CAG Occasional Paper. Reprinted in Philippine *Journal of Public Administration, 11*(1), 41–57. Bloomington, Ind.

Riggs, F. W. (1967). *The idea of development administration: A theoretical essay*. Bloomington, ID: CAG Occasional Paper.

Riggs, F. W. (Ed.) (1971). *Frontiers of development administration*. Durham, NC: Duke University Press (Includes three chapters by Riggs: "Introduction," pp. 3–37; "The context of development administration," pp. 72–108; "Bureaucratic politics in comparative perspective" (reprinted from 1969), pp. 375–414).

Riggs, F. W. (1976a). The group and the movement: Notes on comparative and development administration. *Public Administration Review, 36*(6), 1–20.

Riggs, F. W. (1976b). Introductory concepts on bureaucracy and development administration in Africa. *African Administration Review, 36*(6), 648–654.

Rondinelli, A. D. (1987). *Development administration and US foreign policy: Studies in development management*. Boulder: Lynne Rienne.

Seitz, L. J. (1980). The failure of US technical assistance in public administration: The Iranian case. *Public Administration Review, 40*(5), 407–409.

Sherwood, P. F. (1980). Learning from the Iranian experience. *Public Administration Review, 40*(5), 407–409.

Sigleman, L. (1976). In search of comparative administration. *Public Administration Review, 36*(6), 621–625.

Sims, H., & Voglemann, K. (2002). Popular mobilization and disaster management in Cuba. *Public Administration and Development, 22*(5), 389–400.

Thompson, V. A. (1964). Administrative objectives for development administration. *Administrative Science Quarterly, 9*(June), 91–108.

Tilman, R. O. (1964). *Bureaucratic transition in Malaya*. Durham, NC: Duke University Press.

Van Wart, M., & Cayer, J. N. (1990). Comparative public administration: Defunct, dispersed or redefined? *Public Administration Review, 50*(2), 238–248.

Waldo, D. (1980). Public administration and development: What is the answer? What is the question? In: D. Waldo (Ed.), *The enterprise of public administrative*. Novato, CA: Chandler and Sharp.

Weidner, E. W. (1962). Development administration: A new focus for research. In: F. Heady & S. L. Stokes (Eds), *Papers in comparative public administration*. Ann Arbor: University of Michigan.

Widner, A. J. (1995). States and statelessness in late twentieth-century Africa. *Daedalus* (XXIV), 147–150.

William, S. J. (1980). Decades of public administration in developing countries. *Public Administration Review*, *36*(1976), 61–71.

FURTHER READING

Riggs, F. W. (1961). *The ecology of public administration.* New York: Taplinger Publishing Co.
Riggs, F. W. (1970a). The concept of development administration. In: W. F. Riggs (Ed.), *Frontiers of development administration* (pp. 72–108). Durham, NC: Duke University Press.
Riggs, F. W. (1970b). The idea of development administration. In: E. Weidner (Ed.), *Development administration in Asia* (pp. 25–72). Durham, NC: Duke University Press.
Riggs, F. W. (1991). Public administration: A comparative framework. *Public Administration Review*, *51*(6), 473–477.

WESTERN CONCEPTUALIZATION OF ADMINISTRATIVE DEVELOPMENT: A CRITIQUE AND AN ALTERNATIVE

Satya Deva

The problems of conceptualization in comparative public administration are significant because they are related to the Third World's quest for a better future. Most of these countries have recently gained freedom from colonial rule. However, their people still remain poor, unhealthy, and uneducated. Other common maladies are rise in population, unemployment, corruption, and authoritarianism. Their people naturally want to get rid of these problems and are forced to visualize the possible alternative models. Each model has its own interrelated economic, social, cultural, political, and administrative aspects. Hence a choice related to public administration may really be dependent upon the choice of a worldview.

DEVELOPMENT: THE WESTERN MODEL

The chief model of modernization is that of Western Europe and North America, as these have developed since the seventeenth century. Its main elements may be described as the development of science and technology,

Comparative Public Administration: The Essential Readings
Research in Public Policy Analysis and Management, Volume 15, 231–240
Copyright © 2006 by Elsevier Ltd.
All rights of reproduction in any form reserved
ISSN: 0732-1317/doi:10.1016/S0732-1317(06)15007-1

the national state, democracy, and capitalism. The professed political ideals of this model were put forward by John Locke, John Stuart Mill, and T. H. Green among others. However, in practice, countries in the West have been imperial, warring powers, thus showing that they had little regard for democratic ideals. Internally also, a fascist tendency has often been present. Their economy has been beset with the ills of capitalism: inflation, unemployment, monopolies, and slums. Industrialization has resulted in dehumanization, social disorganization, misutilization of natural resources, and environmental pollution. Science and technology have been used more for private profit and war than for the betterment of human life. The civil administration in this model is expected to function like a large-scale industrial or business undertaking.

DEVELOPMENT: THE EAST EUROPEAN MODEL

The second model is that of the USSR and other Eastern European countries. Its professed ideals come from Marx, Engels, and Lenin. These are the elimination of class distinctions, increased production so as to provide for all, an end to the social divisions of labor and, ultimately, the withering away of the state. In practice, however, a ruling class and a social division of labor seem to be very much in existence. The state shows no signs of withering away. Under Stalin it became very powerful and authoritarian. The means of production in these countries are not privately owned; it is therefore said that capitalism has been abolished. However, the state itself has apparently come to function as a capitalist. Workers have been made to work for low wages under the slogan of saving for the posterity. The benefits of the system seem to go disproportionately to the ruling class. Science and technology grow, but in an atmosphere lacking in freedom. Preparation for war goes on; a new kind of imperialism takes shape. The bureaucratic machine is different from the West mainly in (i) the lack of opportunity to withdraw from the system and (ii) its duplication in, and control by, the party.

THE RISE OF COMPARATIVE PUBLIC ADMINISTRATION

The rise of comparative public administration has developed in the context of these models. In the United States, it grew largely from the effort to "save" Third World countries from communism; the Comparative Administration Group consisted largely of scholars who had served on US AID missions.[1] These scholars wanted to understand underdeveloped societies better so as to identify the forces working for and against communism. Also, the Western Capitalist Society was constantly put forward as the ideal. However its model was often presented in a "neutral" form as discussed below. At the same time fascist, often military, regimes were erected and supported in underdeveloped countries by the Western powers using the most dubious means in the name of protecting freedom. The USSR also tried to foment communist revolutions and to erect and support regimes favorable to it in a manner comparable to that of Western powers.

We, the poor of the world, should try to make a rational choice without being daunted by imperialism of either kind. While Western and Eastern Europe are antagonistic to each other, we may discern various similarities in their social behavior and may, on examination, reject both models partly in quest of a third alternative more suited to our own ethos. The Chinese experiment is attractive and interesting chiefly from this point of view: while it accepted Marxian ideals, it broke away from the Soviet system in quest of its own identity. In India, Mahatma Gandhi, Vinoba Bhave, and Jayaprakash Narayan have warned against a blind acceptance of Western culture and have made some positive contributions to the thought on the subject. In the following, we shall first examine what the West has to offer us and then explore other possibilities.

WESTERN CONCEPTS OF
ADMINISTRATIVE DEVELOPMENT

Western thinkers have been trying to conceptualize and operationalize administrative development. The effort is, ultimately, to discover "neutral" or culture-free concepts and variables. Joseph La Palombara tries to explore "dimensions along which basic changes in political systems – in any political system – might be usefully measured."[2] Lucian W. Pye expresses the hope that "we can surmount the difficulty" of the "clash between evolutionary theory and cultural relativism."[3] Fred Riggs tries to identify "key variables" in administrative development.[4] However, when we examine these concepts and variables resulting from these efforts, we find to our dismay that the hopes have been belied: the characteristics of bureaucracy as existent in the Western society are being acclaimed as neutral indicators of development. Unless we are willing to accept the Western society as the desired model, how can we accept the characteristics of its bureaucracy as the variables for measuring administrative development?

MAGNITUDE

One of the supposedly neutral measures of political and administrative development is magnitude. La Palombara says that by it he means essentially the ratio of political activity to all of the other activity that takes place in society.[5] Lucian Pye is more explicit and says clearly that according to one view, "political development consists of the organization of political life and the performance of political functions in accordance with the standards expected of a modern nation state."[6] The national state has a large size and its activities naturally have greater magnitude than, say, those of city-states. The Western World has had the national state together with the attendant centralization since the sixteenth century and must live with it. The question before the Third World is whether it accepts it as an ideal without question or modification. Mahatma Gandhi favored instead a decentralized political system: this would avoid the concentration of political power in a small group at the top, and do away with vast standing armies and civil bureaucracies. The national state is hardly an ideal to be striven for. It is idle to build it up all the time and talk of its withering away. One of the ways to make it wither away is to start building what Narayan calls the communitarian policy.[7]

SPECIALIZATION

Another of the commonly mentioned indicators of development is specialization. Adam Smith and Weber referred to it long ago; it is the key concept of Riggs' prismatic model. It is worth examining as to how it comes about. One of its causes is simply greater magnitude. As all students of organizations know, an increase in size results in greater specialization of roles. Thus a small business may have only one manager; as it expands, separate managers for finance, personnel, production, and marketing may be needed. Their roles result merely from the differentiation of the single manager's role. If we reject magnitude as an indicator of development, specialization resulting from it gets rejected by implication.

Specialization also results from the growth of science and technology. Thus specialists in the various branches of medicine take the place of the earlier medicine man. Such differentiation may certainly be treated as an

indicator of development, provided the specialized experts use their expertise with a sense of social responsibility, or at least with mechanical objectivity. If, however, they use their expertise to make private gains at the cost
of the common good, it must be said to lead to negative development. It is
the combination of expertise with formal authority that does the damage; it
is idle to consider the role of expertise in isolation. Thus if bad seed is
certified as good by experts for a consideration, their expertise may do more
harm than good. It is worth noting that this power may be given to them by
a new law requiring the certification of new varieties for sale. Before the
passage of such a law, the farmer could go and buy the seed that he thought
as best; the law puts him at the mercy of the expert, who in the situation of
underdevelopment often has little incentive to remain honest. He may be
unable to maintain honesty precisely because of being party of a corrupt
system. One honest official in a corrupt cadre may cause "problems" for
other officials. Hence the interaction of expertise with a bureaucratic setting,
in an underdeveloped society, may be compared to a chemical reaction
where after particular elements no longer function as before. Potassium may
be useful for the human body but not as potassium cyanide.

This also indicates how rationality in the garb of science and technology
may not have the same role in the underdeveloped setting. Having a large
number of "barefoot" doctors may lead to better health for millions suffering from malaria, cholera, rickets, and scabies, than a small number of
highly specialized ones who are often trying to emigrate to an affluent society. Similarly, small-scale industries using a middle-level technology may
have advantages over highly advanced large-scale industry: low capital and
energy consumption, provision of more employment, reduction in the pull
of the city through better dispersal of industries, better liaison with agriculture, better utilization of locally available raw materials due to transport
economies, less disturbance of the environment, and reduction in alienation.

ACHIEVEMENT ORIENTATION

Another commonly mentioned indicator of administrative modernization is
the extent to which recruitment is on the basis of achievement rather than
ascription. It is one of the "pattern variables" of role definition according to
Talcott Parsons. This variable also, if considered in isolation, may seem to
be valid. However it interacts with others. In underdeveloped societies, the
opportunity for education is not equal for members of different social strata.
The result is that those with an ascribed high status come to have the most

achievement also to their credit. The association between property and education was noted by Max Weber:

> When we hear from all sides the demand for an introduction of regular criteria and special examinations, the reason behind it is, of course, not a sudden awakened 'thirst for education' but the desire for restricting the supply for these positions and their monopolization by the owners of educational certificates. Today, the 'examination' is the universal means of this monopolization, and therefore examinations irresistibly advance. As the education prerequisite to the acquisition of the educational certificate requires considerable expense and a period of waiting for full remuneration, this striving means a setback for talent (charisma) in favour of property.[8]

This is much more true of underdeveloped societies than of Weber's own milieu. Hence the inadequacy of this variable as a measure of administrative modernization.

AN ALTERNATIVE MODEL OF
ADMINISTRATIVE DEVELOPMENT

Perhaps a good way of building a theory relating to administration in underdeveloped societies is to start with micro studies. With this end in view some case studies of Indian administration were made. One related to a program intended to help the growth of small industries in towns and villages,[9] another to the transfer of seed technology for promoting the growth of agriculture,[10] and a third one to the distribution of essential consumer goods.[11]

Significant findings in the first one were about the self-centered role of politicians: powerful political leaders were concerned solely with appeasing the people in their states and electoral districts by locating the projects there: the relative economic merits of the various possible locations were not considered. Many of the projects failed disastrously. Thus there was an obvious conflict between economic and political considerations. In the study related to agriculture, it was found that members of the upper classes were willing to sabotage developmental efforts for small private gains. Thus scientists who were producing the breeder seed were apparently wiling to pass off defective breeds as good ones for winning promotions and acclaim. Seed-growing farmers were willing to bribe government inspectors for getting bad seed certified as good and vice versa. The big farmers and government inspectors were thus conspiring to earn small private benefits at the cost of a possible green revolution. Seed dealers were willing to deprive the small farmer of the benefits of governmentally subsidized seed by selling it outside the State at higher prices. In the study of the public distribution agency it appeared that little more was being achieved through public investment than providing employment to those who could manage to get patronage.

The following hypotheses appear to emerge from these studies:

1. There is a concentration of wealth, social status, education, and power in the thin upper crust of society.
2. The upper classes in society care more for petty personal gains than for development in general if the two conflict with each other.
3. Large-scale government organizations provide foci of power, which are controlled by members of the upper class.
4. Corruption is a mechanism, which reconciles privilege with equality before the law.
5. One of the functions that large-scale government organizations perform is to provide employment, particularly to those who enjoy the patronage of the powerful.
6. The salaries and prerequisites, constituting the overheads, of developmental programs are disproportionately high in relation to the benefits flowing from them.

DECENTRALIZATION

If these hypotheses have any general validity, the way to development will not lie through large-scale government organizations. It will lie through a decentralized system having smaller organizations under the direct control of the people. They may take the shape of local government agencies such as *panchayats*, cooperative societies, or communes. Such agencies have hardly been given a trial in underdeveloped countries so far. Local government agencies are often set up by, and are part and parcel in law, central governments. In India, municipalities and *Zila parishads* may be superseded by State Governments: the focus of power is controlled by the top politicians. All benefits, be they subsidized seeds or fertilizers or loans for agriculture or industry, or employment, tend to be siphoned off to the thin upper crust; such allocation of resources cannot lead to development.

REDUCTION IN CORRUPTION

Western writers often refer to the benefits of corruption in underdeveloped societies.[12] They rightly perceive that corruption has a role in maintaining political stability. In an unjust society the semblance of justice is maintained and legitimacy is retained through the mechanism of corruption. All constitutional and legal formalities are ostensibly observed; at the same time the powerful elements gain benefits by underhand "informal" methods. In India, investigations relating to the nineteen-month Emergency Rule (1975–1977) have brought out how top politicians, bureaucrats, and the rich have been conspiring to get even richer and more powerful at the cost of the society. Party bosses minted money out of contributions to party funds by industrialists, who were granted special privileges at the cost of the society, by the bureaucracy. The bureaucrats in turn were rewarded by politicians. It is obvious that the stability of such a system is in the interest only of the upper class; reduction in corruption is a prerequisite of growth or development. Changes in the law, setting up of ombudsman-like authorities, avoidance of conspicuous consumption and citizen vigilance committees can be some of the mechanisms for combating it. These would however still be palliative measures in the absence of a change in the power structure. If a revolution be the only way to such change, then development would be measured by the degree of protest, not by that of persistence.

ECONOMIC EQUALITY

In this perspective, economic equality is not so much an end in itself as another prerequisite of development. In so far as riches, education, and power go together, the great gulf between the ruling and the ruled classes is the greatest obstacle to development. Hence one of the first concrete steps must be the reduction of glaring economic inequalities. These need to be reduced within governmental organizations as well as outside. The wages of lower level government employees often are very meager as compared to the salaries and perquisites of the high-ups. Millions of people, particularly in rural areas, get employment only in part of the year when operations like sowing and harvesting are in progress. This vast human resource is not participating fully in the development process. A policy aiming at employment for all must be the beginning of development.

POLITICAL PARTICIPATION

Western writers often show ambivalence with regard to the role of political participation. It is true that if elite manipulation can produce a mass response, and political demagoguery is the order of the day, political participation may not help immediately in the development process. However, in the long run, the way to political modernization must lie in the politicization of the apathetic masses. India's recent history provides a good example of this. During the Emergency, demagoguery reigned supreme as indicated by the ostensibly spontaneous mass congregations that cheered the leaders. However, it was the people's vote which ultimately threw off the authoritarian yolk. Credit for this must go to political mass movements started by Mahatma Gandhi, Jawaharlal Nehru, and others. During the Emergency, there was no opportunity to organize the people or even to approach them. However, the effort at rousing them had been going on for decades. But for it the restoration of democracy might have been impossible.

People's participation in underdeveloped societies need not take the same shape as it has done in the West. There the interest groups compete for the resources; political parties and the bureaucracy arbitrate among them. In underdeveloped societies, the situation is different: semi-feudalism or landlordism, money lending by rich usurers, domination by the high castes, settlement of disputes by strong arm methods, centralized police systems, utilization of the police and similar organs by powerful people for personal ends – these and such others are its characteristics. The aim of political activity here must be mainly a more even distribution of power. One mechanism for this could be people's committees as suggested by Jayaprakash Narayan.[13]

Development must be seen as a holistic process. The effort to develop the bureaucratic mechanism, while the rest of the society remains backward, leads to negative development as rightly pointed out by Riggs.[14] Hence, administrative development must be part of the process of beneficial social change encompassing economic, social, political, and cultural aspects.

NOTES

1. Fred W. Riggs (ed.), *Frontiers of Development Administration.* "Introduction" (Durham, NC: Duke University Press, 1971), p. 5.

2. Joseph La Palombara "Bureaucracy and Political Development: Notes, Queries, and Dilemmas," in: Joseph La Palombara (ed.) *Bureaucracy and Political Development* (Princeton University Press, 1963), p. 39.

3. Lucian W. Pye, *Aspects of Political Development* (New Delhi: Amerind Publishing Co., 1966), p. 55.

4. Fred Riggs, *Administration in Developing Countries* (Boston: Houghton Mifflin, 1964), p. 4.

5. Joseph La Palombara, *loc. cit.*, p. 42.

6. Lucian W. Pye, *op. cit.*, p. 37.

7. Jayaprakash Narayan, *Meri Vichar Yatra* (Varansai: Sarva Seva Sangh, 1974), 9. 56.

8. H. H. Gerth and C. Wright Mills (eds) *From Max Weber: Essays in Sociology* (London: Routledge and Kegan Paul, 1957), pp. 241–242.

9. Satya Deva, "Establishment of Industrial Estates in India: Two Case Studies," *Journal of Administration Overseas*, Vol. XV, No. 3 (1976), pp. 150–159.

10. Satya Deva, "The National Seed Project in India" to be published in the *Journal of Administration Overseas.*

11. Satya Deva, "Distribution of Essential Commodities through the Public Sector: A Case Study of the Punjab Civil Supplies Corporation" (mimeographed), presented at the 36th Indian Political Science Conference, Jodhpur, December 1976.

12. David H. Bayley, "The Effects of Corruption in a Developing Nation," in: Amitai Etzioni (ed.) *A Sociological Reader on Complex Organizations* (New York: Holt, Rinehart and Winston, 1969), p. 473.

13. Jayaprakash Narayan, *Toward Total Revolution* (Bombay: Popular Prakashan, 1978), Vol. 4, p. 91.

14. Fred Riggs, *Administration in Developing Countries*, p. 117.

ADMINISTRATIVE OBJECTIVES FOR DEVELOPMENT ADMINISTRATION

Victor A. Thompson

Administrative practices and principles of the West have derived from pre-occupation with control and therefore have little value for development administration in underdeveloped countries where the need is for an adaptive administration, one that can incorporate constant change. However, adaptive administrative principles can be derived from the researches and theories of the behavioral sciences, and these should become the administrative objectives of development administrators. Illustrative of such objectives are the following: an innovative atmosphere; the operationalizing and sharing of goals; the combining of planning (thinking) and acting (doing); the minimization of parochialism; the diffusion, of influence; the increasing of toleration of interdependence; and the avoidance of bureaucracy. These propositions are illustrated by the analysis of some concrete administrative problems, such as the centralization–decentralization issue.

Today, with so many nonindustrial, low-income countries trying desperately to raise their living standards, the question what contribution the discipline of public administration can make to economic development naturally arises. On the face of it the answer would seem to be "not very much" Economics, engineering, education, medicine, and so on, all are more important. In fact, a reader of the literature in the field of public

Comparative Public Administration: The Essential Readings
Research in Public Policy Analysis and Management, Volume 15, 241–256
Copyright © 2006 by Elsevier Ltd.
ISSN: 0732-1317/doi:10.1016/S0732-1317(06)15008-3

administration might reasonably fear that public administration, as it is commonly interpreted, and often practiced, would be a handicap to economic development. One shudders at the prospect of eager learners in Nairobi, Lagos, Karachi, or Saigon attempting to put into practice new learning about the proper roles of staff and line, the overriding importance of a position classification system, the need to organize by purpose or process, the importance of note overextending the span of control, the absolute centrality of clear, unambiguous lines of authority and responsibility, the indispensability of clearly defined jurisdictions and offices, the importance of a centralized planning agency, and so on.[1]

At a somewhat more sophisticated level, we are becoming conscious of the fact that administration in modern countries is permeated with behavioral norms, which are products of a modern culture. Such norms as rationality, the use of universalistic criteria, achievement, specificity, and impersonality are not adopted by management; they are not administrative objectives. They result from social and cultural conditions. Attempts to impose such behavioral norms upon an administrative system could only fail and would probably produce disintegrative effects upon a society. Surely it could not result in more than formalism, leaving a wide gap between administrative forms and administrative behavior. La Palombara must be correct when he says: "Once a reasonable differentiation of administrative roles has occurred, once these roles are filled with a minimum attention to achievement criteria, once the bureaucrats themselves are persuaded to approach the tasks in hand on the basis of secular attitudes, the minimum conditions of a developmental bureaucracy are met and it can proceed with its responsibilities."[2]

Is there then no contribution at all that the discipline of public administration can make to economic development? I believe such a contribution can be made, but it most definitely will not come from the doctrines of management or administration most widely prevalent in the West. As La Palombara says, these doctrines do not work well even here. The rituals and teaching of public administration have been fixated on control – almost neurotically fixated it would seem. Control is an ideal, of a static world. Economic development, however, takes place within a milieu of constant change. The rituals and principles of public administration developed in a time of relative stability of environment and incorporated within themselves, the ideal of perpetual stability – hence the morbid preoccupation with control.

In a situation of rapid change, control is much less relevant. The ideal must be *adaptation*, and this involves creativity and a looseness of definition and structure. Until now, a remarkably small proportion of time and effort within the administrative profession has been spent in trying to devise criteria and principles relevant to an adaptive administration as opposed to a controlled one. Consequently, a remarkably small amount either of our administrative practice or of our administrative principle is relevant to problems of development administration.

In this paper I suggest some administrative criteria, which seem to have some relevance to economic development. I realize that this is the merest beginning. These criteria stem from the growing, body of theory and research on organizations and human relations within the field of the behavioral sciences. In presenting them I would not be so foolish as to argue that economic development cannot take place under any other set of administrative conditions, but only that an administration that lives up to these criteria will achieve more development more quickly, with less human cost, with more imagination, with more attention to more values, and therefore with greater benefits. I believe this claim to be true whether the development administration is to take place in Kuala Lumpur, Ouagadougou, or Upstate New York.

What are the administrative conditions necessary for the most effective development administration? To answer this question is to establish a set of purely administrative objectives for development administrators. The list of administrative objectives, which I propose to discuss, is undoubtedly incomplete, but it provides a beginning. It suggests the link along with the discipline of administration can be of some small assistance in economic development. Among the purely administrative objectives of the development administrator should be the following: an innovative atmosphere, the operationalizing and wide sharing of planning goals, the combining of planning (thinking) with action (doing), a cosmopolitan atmosphere, the diffusion of influence, the increasing of toleration of interdependence, and the avoidance, of bureaupathology. These conditions are all interdependent, but it is helpful to consider them one at a time.

AN INNOVATIVE ATMOSPHERE

It seems reasonable to assume that the ability to change and create is a necessity for development administrative machinery. Innovative behavior seems to require certain prerequisite conditions, among which the following are most important: variety and richness of experience with the subject, psychological freedom, and psychological security.[3] Control-centered management, with its monocratic organization structure, denies or endangers all of these conditions. The analysis, which underlies this statement will be revealed as we progress through the other administrative conditions or objectives to be discussed, and so it will not be repeated here. However, it will be worthwhile at this point to list some very likely propositions about innovativeness in organizations.

1. Innovation or "creativity" is facilitated by a group administrative effort dominated by a professional outlook.[4]
2. Innovation is facilitated by program or subject matter uncertainty accompanied by personal security (by uncertainty without fear).[5]
3. Innovation is facilitated by a nonhierarchical climate, especially a nonhierarchical communication structure, and by "loose" organization in general.[6]
4. Innovative responsiveness is a function of both personality factors and cognitive or ability factors and can be influenced by appropriate training programs.[7]

OPERATIONAL AND SHARED PLANNING GOALS

Human beings need a cognitive structuring of their activities – need to know what they are doing – if regressive (childish) behaviors are to be avoided.[8] Clear goals can help to provide this cognitive structuring if they are "operational," meaning that the impact of a proposed action on the goal must be demonstrated with sufficient credulity so that a reasonable person can accept the demonstration without denying his own rational nature.

If the operational goals are also shared, planners' scan move toward them by using rational, analytic decisional processes. Otherwise, bargaining, political, or power processes are necessary to resolve planning disputes.[9]

By shared and operational goals I do not mean the fixing of overall goals or the complete specification of planning goals, for this practice kills creativity, as Braybrooke and Lindblom convincingly argue.[10] I mean the kind of sharing that free communication can promote and the kind of concreteness and practicality promoted by deep knowledge of the subject. Shared operational goals are products of a community of experts. Given certain other conditions mentioned below, shared operational planning goals, in addition to satisfying the need for a cognitive structuring of action, convert the problem of coordination into a procedural one.

COMBINATION OF PLANNING (THINKING) AND ACTION (DOING)

The separation of planning from action, of thinking from doing, is a special form of the mind–body error in earlier psychological theories. It is based on a mechanistic conception of human behavior, which assumes oversimplified human motivations when it does not indeed neglect the problem of motivation entirely. Unlike machines, people do not just act when the button is pushed; they both think and act at the same time. In fact, thinking is a kind of action, and action is a kind of thinking. What people do is a result of their own decisional thinking processes, including their definition of the situation.

The more administrative arrangements are based upon the mechanistic dichotomy of thinking and doing – some to think, others to do – the more enforcement activities (with associated intelligence activities) must be engaged in, and the more unsolicited, unplanned, unwanted consequences accumulate. At some point, the process is largely out of central control and the central planning becomes illusory.

It is sometimes argued that planning (thinking) must be separated from operations (doing) or planning will be pushed out by operations. However, this occasionally observed phenomenon has been misunderstood. The need for a cognitive structuring of activities leads people into those pursuits in which they can at least vaguely measure the consequences; it leads them into operational pursuits.[11] Thus, if planning goals are operationally defined, cognitive needs will not result in operations pushing out planning. In fact, other needs, such as the need for rewards or for seeing decisions eventuates as expected, can result in excited attention to planning and operations as a unity; for they are a unity; together they constitute action.

The attempt to separate thinking from doing tends to create classes: the thinkers, upper class; the doers, lower class. A gentleman does not do things: he does not dirty his hands; he tells others what to do. Within an administrative structure, self-protective reactions of the ascribed doers are likely to take the form of blocking responses to the thinker's overtures, most likely by cutting off communication with them. The thinkers are quite likely to become frustrated, ineffectual, isolates, unless they can employ unusual administrative or political power in their behalf. But even power cannot convert nonoperational thinking (planning) into effective action, and even operational planning, if organizationally segregated and hence dependent upon power tends to become illusory, as described above.

A COSMOPOLITAN ATMOSPHERE

Development administration requires the ability to respond to feedback information in an adaptive fashion. Particularly important is the ability to perceive, understand, and respond to information about unsolicited effects of actions upon a great variety of programs regardless of whether or not they are one's own. If the actions of bureau A react adversely upon the programs of bureau B, bureau A needs to be able to perceive, understand, and adapt positively to this fact. Such an ability requires a cosmopolitan point of view, and so we need to know what promotes such a point of view. A few hypotheses are suggested.

1. If the hierarchical institution is stressed, parochialism results. The rights of superiors include the right to control communication with the rest of the organization (going through channels) and the right to loyalty.[12] Groupings formed around authority roles result in differentiation of goals and perceptions of reality, in short, in a narrow parochialism. Conversely, free communication beyond the authority unit or grouping result in a broader sharing of goals and perceptions of reality, that is, in a more cosmopolitan outlook.
2. Professionalism tends toward the cosmopolitan viewpoint because of a professional or occupational identification rather than an authority group identification and because professional interdependence facilitates cross-channel communication.[13] Conversely, organizationally defined occupational roles – roles created out of specific program procedure – tend toward parochialism for a number of reasons: (1) occupational status or recognition is to be found only within the program unit; (2) interunit mobility and especially interorganizational mobility is low; (3) vested interests in specific procedures and programs arise; (4) program identifications restrict perceptions of, understanding of, and responsiveness to feedback information involving action effects on other programs and low evaluations of the worth of other program goals. This point will be more fully discussed below.
3. Extraorganizational associations of professionals or specialists encourage cosmopolitanism, or at least a nonprogram parochialism, and reduce the power of authority roles, further weakening the forces toward parochialism (i.e., the authoritative demand for loyalty and control of outgroup communication).[14]

THE DIFFUSION OF INFLUENCE

Development planning is a highly technical and scientific process involving a relatively large number of professionally and scientifically trained personnel. If such planning is to be undertaken seriously, such personnel must acquire positions of influence within the organization. This involves a de-emphasis on the line of command and a rather thorough rejection of a literal unity of command. Persons occupying authority roles are likely to experience a rather large gap between their expected authority and their actual authority. If primitive responsibility patterns continue to be followed under these circumstances, the performance of authority roles may become intolerable and the situation itself a source of debilitating and useless conflict.[15]

The acquisition and use of a large number of professionally, scientifically, and technically trained employees requires a rationalized reward system. The almost universal use of hierarchical authority roles as success roles forces the professionally trained out of the field of their greatest competence and into management; it also depresses the supply of these people below needs, depresses their morale within the organization, and exaggerates the friction between them and persons in authority roles as the latter lose power to the former.[16] A suggested remedy is to have two separate salary scales, related to real needs rather than the spurious need to maintain a single-status hierarchy, so that specially trained persons might achieve "success" without leaving their specialty, so that more people would undertake the special training, and so that tire dignity of those in authority roles would be adjusted to reality.[17]

THE TOLERATION OF INTERDEPENDENCE

Development administration is a highly interdependent activity, not only because it must use a large number of interdependent specialties, but also because it implies a concerted effort toward a national goal (or perhaps a few national goals). Interdependence creates the need for coordination, which, in turn, implies cooperation – an attitude of willingness to be coordinated.[18] The administrative problem here is to ease the pains of interdependence. What are the conditions that increase the toleration of interdependence? Some answers are suggested.

1. The cohesiveness of a group increases the toleration of interdependence.[19]
   This proposition has much more relevance when applied to small

face-to-face groups, but it does suggest that a free or permissive atmosphere with regard to communication within an organization should work in the right direction.

2. Acceptance of the reality or need for interdependence makes interdependence more tolerable. It is hypothesized that this acceptance is more likely to be forthcoming if real functions are involved rather than authoritatively created dependencies; for example, my dependence upon a doctor as opposed to my dependence upon a control-clearance point. The difference is that of dependence upon a person because of orders versus dependence upon him because of a service he can perform better than others – or dependence because of fear versus dependence because of need – or influence because of office authority versus influence because of technical skill.[20]

3. Interdependence between persons is more tolerable when communication between them is adequate. This fact helps to explain the increasing number of informal communication channels (nonhierarchical channels) to be found in modern organizations.[21] It, too, counsels an indulgent or permissive rather than a hierarchical pattern of communication within the organization.

AVOIDANCE OF BUREAUPATHOLOGY

All of the administrative conditions of development administration outlined above will be absent (or weak) in an organization dominated by personal insecurity. Personal insecurity in an authority position is likely to create personal needs of such magnitude as to dominate over organizational needs resulting behavior, then, will be pathological from the standpoint of the organization and so has been called "bureaupathic" (also "red tape," "bureaucratic," and so on). Bureaupathic behavior stems from needs that can be generalized as the need to control it manifested in such things as close supervision, failure to delegate, heavy emphasis on regulations, quantitative norms, precedents, and the accumulation of paper to prove compliance; cold aloofness; insistence on office protocol; fear of innovation; or restriction of communication.[22] It is characterized by a typical circularity in that such behavior by a superior tends to call forth responses from subordinates, which seem to call for more of the same behavior. Subordinates "cannot be trusted," "will not take responsibility," and "have to be told everything."[23] In an extreme bureaupathic situation, it is difficult to see how development planning can take place.

Such an atmosphere of insecurity can result from the existence of an arbitrary, nonrational, and unpredictable authority at the very top, as in the case of an authoritarian, single-party, political system;[24] or from the unfortunate impact of personality in a high-authority role; or from the adoption of an official incentive system, which heavily emphasizes individual competition for a few great status prizes and hence overlooks and tends to destroy the informal group structure with its group controls, loyalties, and rewards. It can result from impatience and inability of high-authority figures to wait for rewards – to wait for results of development planning. Impatience for results on the part of political leaders in underdeveloped countries is all too humanly understandable, but it is very likely to be self-defeating.

Above, I have discussed a list of purely administrative conditions as prerequisites for an adaptive as opposed to a controlled administrative organization. As I said before, these conditions are all intimately interrelated. This interrelatedness, and the cruciality of these conditions for producing an adaptive administrative structure, can be more forcefully demonstrated by applying the foregoing analysis to a few recurrent administrative problems. I have chosen three such problems: the problem of centralization versus decentralization; the problem of securing innovative responsiveness to feedback communication, and the problem of participation in planning.

CENTRALIZATION AND DECENTRALIZATION

The existing state of a technology decrees a technical level of centralization in decision-making. This is the level where the skills and equipment provided by the technology can be fully utilized – where the "market" is large enough so that the need for the highest skills can absorb the supply. However, centralization is frequently carried much further because of different nontechnical needs surrounding higher authority positions. These needs may be personal needs for power and prestige; they may arise from an unstable political situation; they may arise from the pressures of powerful organized interests. Whatever the cause, overcentralization (beyond what is technically decreed) creates poorly accepted interdependencies and hence conflict, tensions, low morale, sabotage.

Under conditions of overcentralization, the rational control of events is illusory to a greater or lesser degree. There are a number of reasons for this. In the first place, there is no necessary or even predictable relation between authority, as such, and rationality. Because persons or groups have the right or the power to make decisions, do not mean that they have the ability to make rational decisions. In the second place, as was indicated above, over-centralization based as it is on a machine model, rests on a partly false assumption about the behavior of subordinates. To be realistic, the plan or decision should be regarded as the actual behavior or action, which eventuates, and there are many slips between the decision recorded on paper and the final ensuing behavior. There is nothing impelling about a plan on paper unless it represents the results of one's own analysis and decision. The paper plan is only an additional source of information about planning behavior, and not the best by any means. In the third place, communication processes do strange and often unpredictable things to plans handed down from above. Usually, there is no time to read all the relevant documents and so to that extent the central planning might as well not have occurred. Often the documents are filed too well and are not available when needed. The only sure way of communicating planning is to incorporate it into the neural passages and memories of those to whom it must be communicated for purposes of execution. This implies participation in planning, or decentralization. Finally, motivation to act in the planned way is the absolutely crucial and controlling aspect of the whole process. Here, again central offices may depend upon administrative authority and power, but, as was said before, the more that power is used, the more unsolicited response consequences accumulate until at some point the process is largely out of central planning control, which then becomes illusory. Solution of the motivation problem probably implies participation in the planning process, namely, decentralization. In the final analysis, thinking cannot be separated from doing.

To apply the above analysis somewhat more concretely, compare planning by a large central planning department, divided inevitably into subject matter units, where bureaucratic patterns have been allowed to accumulate for various reasons (including frustration and isolation with resulting insecurities), with planning by divisions in several ministries backed up by thoroughly interested and committed ministers integrated into a politically homogeneous cabinet under a development-conscious chief executive. Would not the latter arrangement make quicker and more politically viable decisions with regard to plan priorities than the former? Arid, would not those decisions be more executable, more real than those of the large central planning department? Here we see the very secondary nature of formal legal structure. The important considerations concern the existence or nonexistence of shared, operational, national planning goals and an atmosphere that encourages creativity and cosmopolitanism.

The separation of thinking (planning) in a central planning department from the doing (executing) located elsewhere has a further administrative flaw, which contributes to the illusory nature of this separation. This flaw involves a misconception about the role of authority in planning for others. Within the planning structure, disagreements not susceptible to rational processes for resolution are referred to administrative authority for settlement. When a group is planning for its own behavior (i.e., when thinking and doing are not separated), such authoritative decisions may aid momentarily, but they never finally settle anything, because they can always be reopened and are only settled finally by action. But when a group is planning for the behavior of others (i.e., when thinking and doing are separated), such decisions or settlements are largely meaningless. The issue still exists and will be up for resolution in the action group, under a different system of authority, and might as well be resolved this second time in the contrary way. Consequently, a central planning body will have more influence on events the more bland (issueless) its plans are. A corollary is that a bureaucratic, authoritarian hierarchy-emphasized central planning body is administratively quixotic.

Attempts to justify overcentralization intellectually often rest on the illusion of elitism, or managerial determinism, perhaps a psychological offshoot of hero worship or father dependence. Involved is a confusion between right (authority) and ability. The former can be conferred; the latter is subject to limitations, which are amenable to human desires to only a very limited extent.

COMMUNICATION AND FEEDBACK

An administrative communications system is an attempt to assure at all relevant points in an organization the ability to detect, understand, and respond appropriately to appropriate data. Today, a new technology of decision-making greatly facilitates the gathering, storage, recall, and utilization of data and the determination of what data is appropriate. However, major communication problems arc still administrative or organizational rather than technological. Put in another way, technology at the present time is far in advance of administration.

A planning activity needs original data out of which to fashion plans and needs, also, feedback data on their effects. It should be concerned both with effects regarding primary goals and also with secondary effects – the effects on other goals, both those of other governmental units and those of non-governmental units.

Specialized detector roles are required, roles involving various specialized and technical qualifications. If the organization is able to respond to new data, these specialized detector roles become new power roles within the organization, further exaggerating the latent conflict between the general line and the cross-line occupational specialties. Resistance to this new diminution of authority, and hence to communication, will be especially pronounced in the insecure atmosphere of the bureaupathic hierarchy-emphasized organization. In that atmosphere, particularly, attempts will be made to restrict communication to channels (an exercise of the superior's right to monopolize communication), to the line of command, or to .the hierarchy – a channel technically inadequate for specialized communication, increasingly overloaded, and notoriously unreliable because of opportunities and motivations for censorship at each communication station. Development planning, on the other hand, calls for increasing specialization and hence increasing interdependence, the toleration of which depends in part upon the adequacy of communication. Growing pressure for new, nonhierarchical, specialized communication channels is likely to generate further resistance to the diminution of authority, especially in the bureaupathic or insecurity-dominated organization.

To detect and transmit data is only part of the problem. The organization must also be able to respond to it in an appropriate fashion. As was pointed out above, insecurity generates a need to control, which greatly restricts innovative responses (innovation or creativity is by definition uncontrolled behavior). Thus, in a bureaupathic, hierarchy-emphasized atmosphere, one of the basic ingredients of development administration – innovative responsiveness – is either absent or very weak.

Furthermore, the authority system (the system of boss-man roles) reinforced by the practice of single-subgoal assignment, stresses parochialism, a narrow loyalty to one's program unit, its boss and its personnel, and to one's own program goal to the exclusion of interest in all others. The effects of action on other goals tend to be ignored; in fact, they are usually not even perceived.

All of these phenomena are especially related to an emphasis on the hierarchical institution. They are also related, it is hypothesized, to the extent to which jobs or occupations within the organization are organizationally defined rather than socially defined, or to the extent to which they are skilled in operating specific procedures of specific programs of specific organizations rather than social functions relevant to a broad range, of human goals and programs. Persons whose skills are purely organizational, who were trained largely on the job, who had no relevant pre-entry training, who started as amateurs, have orientations and attitudes that differ from those of the professional, scientific and technical specialist, the person who did have relevant pre-entry training. The amateurs in organizations have been referred to conveniently as the "desk classes."[25] They have less interunit (or organization) mobility than others. They owe their function and status to the organization and thus tend to become organization, men. They are perhaps more responsive to organizational authority, thereby encouraging a hierarchical emphasis. They are apt to be conservative with regard to their programs and procedures, since their personal status and function are so tied up with their programs. There may even be a tendency for them to hypostatize their programs and procedures into natural laws and to forget their purely instrumental origin. All of this adds up to a greater loyalty to program goals, units, and authority – in short, to parochialism. Parochialism can make detection of and response to second-order consequences of action, second-order feedback, much less, likely to happen, thereby lessening the administrative structure's ability to carry on an integrated development-planning activity over a broad spectrum of social and economic life.

Real communication is two ways and is a form of mutual influence. Hence, if communication occurs, some decentralization or loss of central power occurs. These facts are equally true with regard to communication with the public, as we shall see below. The interpretation of communication with the public as restricted to "selling the plan" is based on some rather universal myths, such as "the stupidity of the masses" and "the indispensability of leadership." As would be expected, therefore, it results in considerable self-delusion in that actual public behavior is likely to deviate in unpredictable ways from planned behavior, making the planning illusory. It would seem that no political, let alone administrative, system could operate for long without some devices for articulating and aggregating public needs and interests and communicating the results to government for incorporation in the planning process.[26] If this interest articulation and aggregation is done administratively, it is almost sure to be either highly erroneous or downright spurious, a fact which stands behind the inevitable, periodic, colonial riot. Thus, central control, or the illusion of it, is going to be diluted in some way, either by real communication with the public (or any other group importantly affected by planning), or by peaceful or nonpeaceful nullification – the dilution of the desirable by the possible.

PARTICIPATION IN PLANNING

It has been stated recently that the participation hypothesis (the reduction in resistance to plans through participation in planning) should be taken as empirically established. This statement may be too strong in a strict sense, but from what has been stated thus far, it would appear to be good advice for the development planner to follow.

The participation in planning by those to be importantly affected by a plan (or their representatives) has two broad general functions: providing information and moving toward consensus.[27] In both cases, the participation will affect the final outcome of the plans and hence it involves decentralization or loss of power (control) by central planning authority. The information to be secured is of two kinds: that about current conditions and practice and that about possible future reactions to various planning devices or procedures. For the latter type of information, a representative advisory group is indicated. Both kinds of information, by influencing the plan in the direction of reality, make the final predicted behavior response come closer to the actual behavior response – the real plan, the plan in action. (The paper plan can usefully be regarded as a prediction of future behavior, and the actual resulting behavior as the test of the prediction.)

Participation, or consultation, moves toward consensus both by providing information to the planners, thereby making the plan more realistic, and by providing information to those to be affected (through their representatives) about problems of the planners, thereby promoting understanding. It also involves the consultees in commitment to or identification with the results, to the extent that they actually do affect the results. For this function a representative advisory group is indicated.

It should be clear that real participation of the type described, since it involves some loss of control by the administrative authorities, is more likely to take place in a secure administrative atmosphere, one relatively free from the need to control, one in which the hierarchical institution is not unduly emphasized. This kind of participation also implies an innovative responsiveness to communication and a minimum of parochialism.

An insecure, authoritarian, planning administration is more likely to engage in ritualistic consultative processes, if any, and to try to use consultative devices to increase control rather than to share it. Appearance deviates from reality in that consultation is more form than reality. Appearance is also likely to deviate from reality in another way, however, in that the actual behavioral responses are more likely to deviate from planned, behavioral, responses, and the "rational central planning" to be illusory to that extent.

Above I have suggested the lines along which the discipline of public administration could make some small contribution to economic development. Theorists and practitioners interested in making such a contribution must reorient themselves to the needs of adaptive, innovative administration rather than controlled administration. Although most of the doctrines and practices in the field of management are derived from the need to control, there is a growing body of knowledge and theory, which is applicable to an adaptive, innovative administration. It is precisely within the contributions of the behavioral sciences that this applicable knowledge and theory will be found. It will not be found within the fields of mathematics and decision-making, which have become servants of control-oriented administration.

Control-oriented administration assumes stability – fixed conditions, goals, and resources. The administrative problem appears as the maximal allocation of these fixed resources. This model is a poor analogue for development administration. If principles or lessons are to be drawn from our administrative experiences, which are applicable to development administration in underdeveloped countries, they should be drawn from crisis situations. Administration in a crisis is characterized by authority, status, and jurisdictional ambiguity; indefiniteness of assignment; uncontrolled communication; group decision; problem orientation; and a high level of excitement and morale. In crises, good ideas are likely to be regarded as the most valuable output, regardless of source, because they are needed most. Control, or public administration as usual, comes later, after the crisis has passed. Our doctrines and ideals of administration come from this later period. Development administration is in the crisis period; it desperately needs ideas. Ideas do not come from control. As John Stuart Mill said more than a 100 years ago, ideas come from freedom.

NOTES

1. As Joseph La Palombara says, "The irony of much of this that the principles we try to export do not even operate in the United States" (*Bureaucracy and Political Development* (Princeton, NJ, 1963, p. 20)). We export our management mythology.

2. *Ibid.*, p. 54.

3. Morris I. Stein and Shirley J. Heinze, *Creativity and the Individual* (Glencoe, IL, 1960).

4. Kurt W. Back, Decisions under Uncertainty, *The American Behavioral Scientist*, 4 (1961), 14–19.

5. See Morris I. Stein, Creativity and Culture, *Journal of Psychology*, 36 (1953), 311–322; also Erik H. Erikson, The Problem of Ego Identity, *Journal of the American Psychoanalytic Association*, 4 (1956), 56–121.

6. Tom Burns and G. M. Stalker, *The Management of Innovation* (London, 1961).

7. Center for Programs in Government Administration of the University of Wisconsin, *Education for Innovative Behavior in Executives* (Cooperative research project no. 975; US Office of Education).

8. Kurt Lewin, *Resolving Social Conflicts* (New York, 1948).

9. James G. March and Henry Simon, *Organizations* (New York, 1958).

10. David Braybrooke and Lindblom, *A Strategy of Decision* (New York).

11. March and Simon, *op. cit.*

12. Victor A. Thompson, *Modern Organizations* (New York, 1961).

13. Alvin W. Gouldner, Cosmopolitans and Locals, *Administrative Science Quarterly*, 2 (1957 and 1958); Harold L. Wilensky, *Intellectuals in Labor Unions* (Glencoe, IL, 1958); and William J. Goode, Community within a Community; the Professions, *American Sociological Review*, 22 (1957), 194–200.

14. Thompson, *op. cit.*

15. *Ibid.*

16. *Ibid.* See also Nigel Walker, *Morale in the Civil Service; A Study of the Desk Worker* (Edinburgh, Scotland, 1960).

17. Thompson, *op. cit.*

18. *Ibid.* See also Emile Durkheim, *The Division of Labor in Society* (Glencoe, IL, 1933).

19. Morton Deutsch, An Experimental Study of the Effects of Cooperation and Competition upon Group Processes, *Human Relations*, 2 (1949), 199–231; and Edwin J. Thomas, Effects of Facilitative Role Interdependence on Group Functioning, *Human Relations*, 10 (1957), 347–366.

20. Thompson, *op. cit.* Peter M. Blau and W. Richard Scott, *Formal Organizations* (San Francisco, 1962).

21. March and Simon, *op. cit.*

22. Thompson, *op. cit.* Burns and Stalker, *op. cit.*

23. Alvin W. Gouldner, *Patterns of Industrial Bureaucracy* (Glencoe, IL, 1954).

24. Reinhard Bendis, *Work and Authority in Industry* (New York, 1956).

25. Walker, *op. cit.*

26. Gabriel Almond and James S. Coleman, eds., *The Politics of Developing Areas* (Princeton, NJ, 1960).

27. Victor A. Thompson, *The Regulatory Process in OPA Rationing* (New York, 1950).

THE CONCEPT OF DEVELOPMENT ADMINISTRATION

George F. Gant

THE DEMANDS OF INDEPENDENCE UPON PUBLIC ADMINISTRATION

The term "development administration" came into use in the 1950s to represent those aspects of public administration and those changes in public administration, which are needed to carry out policies, projects, and programs to improve social and economic conditions. During a period of 15 years following the end of World War II, in 1945, colony after colony threw off the imperial yoke. Country after country achieved independence and political autonomy. This new status gave promise of freedom and liberty and self-determination in political systems of representative democracy. It gave hope of greater individual freedom and equality of treatment in the society. And independence created hopes of higher national and per capita income, a rapid rise in standards of living, and an increase in individual opportunity. Even in countries which had not been colonies but had been administered by some other form of authoritarian government, this was a generation of rising and insistent expectations pressing for rapid political, social, and economic change. New governments and their bureaucracies, their administrative agencies and processes, were expected to give reality to these anticipated fruits of independence and liberty. These new functions, these demands upon the administration system, were not only enormous in size and weight, they were novel and complex in character.

Comparative Public Administration: The Essential Readings
Research in Public Policy Analysis and Management, Volume 15, 257–285
Copyright © 2006 by Elsevier Ltd.
All rights of reproduction in any form reserved
ISSN: 0732-1317/doi:10.1016/S0732-1317(06)15009-5

An urgent and perhaps the first task of a new country was to establish its identity as a unified and integrated nation-state and to create a new system for deciding policy and for making decisions. This political development involved building a valid and recognized hegemony internally and achieving recognition externally by establishing effective communications and relationships with other countries and the international community. The task of building a national polity required the accommodation of diverse and even disparate social, tribal, and ethnic groups in the population. A foreign policy to achieve international recognition and amity involved the creation of a foreign service. At the same time, numerous and demanding specific needs had to be met by each new country at independence and by its new, inexperienced government and ill-equipped bureaucracy. Taxes had to be assessed and arrangements made for their collection. Courts and the continuity of justice had to be assured.

Perhaps even more important and more difficult than establishing its identity was the task of a new country to devise a system to translate the aspirations and demands of its population into viable policies and programs, a responsive process for making decisions on major matters. Most new countries have set up, or tried to set up, some system of representative democracy, with its accompanying institutions and processes including legislatures and assemblies, elected executives, political parties, the conduct of elections, and the control of the public bureaucracy. Perhaps there was no higher priority among the aspirations and expectations of the peoples of new and recently liberalized countries than an effective process of self-determination and self-government. Such new concepts and methods of decision-making are a governmental perplexity; in their execution they represent a new and pressing demand on the administrative system.

Another immediate though less tangible demand upon the governments of new countries, and recently democratized ones, is the correction of inequalities and injustices in the society. Such inequities are sometimes found in caste systems such as those in India, which subjugate certain members and limit their freedom of choice and opportunity. Other inequities are illustrated by land tenure systems such as those in Pakistan and the Philippines, by which a small and favored segment of the population is assured of prosperity at the expense of the opportunities of other, larger segments. An even more aggravated problem of justice and comparative equality of treatment is sometimes found in the status and relationships of different racial groups, as in Malaysia. The status of women is often a major and pressing issue. The pressures upon government to solve these problems are usually very heavy. The solutions are usually not readily apparent, however, and in terms of administration the application of solutions is often the most difficult and burdensome aspect of the situation.

High in the expectations of the peoples of newly independent countries, if not first in the priorities of self-determination, is the increase in their standards of living and the widening of their individual opportunities for personal expression and advancement. The additional burdens upon government and its administrative apparatus to bring about this social and economic development are enormous. The components of development – natural resources, capital, technology, and manpower – must be brought into focus for the purpose. The government must provide an environment of safety and stability which at least permits and even encourages development. To put all of these elements together in a productive process which provides benefits equitably and rapidly enough to be acceptable is an enormous and a complex burden on any system of administration. It is a burden which was of unaccustomed and difficult dimensions and characteristics.

These problems of economic policy and development with which governments and their bureaucracies must cope are even more staggering when considered in their specificity. Many new countries, such as Korea, have natural resources which are inadequate in quantity or quality or accessibility to yield satisfying products even with advanced technology. Or the technology is not available, or the capital. In countries like Pakistan and Ethiopia the resources are, or were, controlled by a few powerful families. Professional and skilled manpower does not exist in sufficient number, nor do the institutions to produce it. Savings in significant amounts have not been accumulated for capital investment. The orientation of colonial economies to the production of raw materials and their export was not usually the best basis or starting point for the most promising economic growth of the new country. The shift of the focus of economic systems and the institutions which support and depend upon them from the imperial orbit to the national interest is slow and hard, even when the targets and methods become known.

Another factor in the economic condition of a recently freed colony, and also in a recently democratized country, is the weakness of the private sector. If private enterprise were strong in a new country, with a generous endowment of entrepreneurship and adequate funds for investment, the administrative burdens on the government would be less severe and not so urgent. In most countries, however, such private enterprise as existed was oriented toward and had vested interests in the older extractive economy and was not necessarily interested in new economic ventures. Such enterprise, also, was usually foreign owned and controlled. Under such circumstances it is inevitably incumbent upon a new country which wishes to accomplish the aspirations of its people to give governmental attention and support to economic development.

Even when a private enterprise sector of respectable proportions is active or capable of becoming active in the economic life of a country, there may be reasons why a government feels obliged to intrude its administrative presence. One such reason is to assure that the nation's resources are developed in the interest of the people as a whole and not only of a select group. Another is to assure that an underprivileged region of the country or class in the population has a fair opportunity to share in the country's growing economic prosperity. Or it might be desirable for the government to undertake an economic enterprise in a field neglected by the private sector though necessary to the growth of the economy as a whole. One or more of these considerations has led many countries to extend their administrative apparatus to economic endeavors of a number of kinds. Governments and their administrative agencies become involved in economic development by encouraging and controlling the private sector, or by engaging in business directly or through new public enterprises, or both. Under any of these alternatives, however, new and enlarged and more complex administrative agencies, systems, and processes are required. The functions of public administration are increased by these undertakings and the demands of development upon the administrative apparatus are enlarged.

Administration in newly independent countries was sadly wanting in its capacity to meet these demands of independence. Bureaucracies, faced with new, staggering, and unfamiliar tasks they were not set up to perform, were further weakened by the overly rapid replacement of experienced expatriate personnel with inexperienced recruits and by inexperienced and often inept leadership. In almost every such country the immediate consequence of independence was the lessening of administrative efficiency and bureaucratic effectiveness. Administration for development was required to evolve from that point.

THE MEANING OF DEVELOPMENT

The words "developed," "undeveloped," "underdeveloped," and "less developed" are often used to denote the social and economic condition of the people in a given country or region. The concept of development is elusive; it is perceived not only as a condition of life but also as a goal to be attained, and as the capacity to grow and change and develop. These three ideas of development are bound together in efforts to understand and deal with the phenomenon of development. The evidences of the condition of underdevelopment are frequently given in terms of poverty. The starkest evidence of underdeveloped populations is found and expressed in terms of hunger and starvation, the scantiest of housing, the barest of clothing, and the poorest of health. According to the World Bank, "About 40 percent of the population of developing countries, 800 million people, are still living in absolute poverty."[1] They are hungry and are not sheltered adequately from hostile weather. They suffer ill health and those who survive childhood die early. These people are illiterate, insecure, and experience only unhappy leisure. Words such as "destitution," "privation," "want," and even "suffering" are used to describe their condition, certainly a condition of underdevelopment.

The comparative size of the national per capita income is frequently used to distinguish the developed from the underdeveloped countries. Low per capita income conceals even greater poverty in regions or classes because of an unequal distribution of the national product. The eradication of this poverty – that is, the achievement of a sustenance level of survival – is the first target of development. Increases in incomes as shown in per capita income statistics can be used thereafter as evidence of progress and of relative well being, at least in gross terms, in comparison with other countries. Such data also help to identify the relatively underdeveloped and relatively developed countries.

It is not possible, however, to state when the essential needs of a poverty-stricken people have been met nor when their basic wants have been satisfied. Definitions of "essential" and "basic" are fluid; they change, and the measures of minimum standards of sustenance fluctuate as knowledge of adequacy grows and as feasibilities and expectations expand. Scientific findings reveal new nutritional requirements for good health, productive lives, and longevity, so that what was previously considered adequate diet is no longer believed to be sufficient. As sanitary toilets, clean water, screens, electricity, and other contributions to better housing become more available and more desired, to that extent they come to be expected and included within the categories of "essential needs" and "basic wants." Development, then, is not an absolute condition. There is not a fixed point at which a people, region, or country passes from a state of un-development to a state of development. The relative condition of development, rather, is comparative and ever changing – it fluctuates according to what is needed, what is possible, and what is desired. Development is relative also in terms of the possible; it fluctuates according to what is feasible at any particular time. A country which utilizes its resources effectively is considered to be more developed than a country which does not. This utilization potential increases with the growth and application of scientific knowledge and technology.

A country which is not satisfying the expectations of its population is to that extent not developed; the goal of development has not been reached. Development is relative to the aspirations of the people – how the aspirations are defined and how firmly they are expressed. These expectations increase as the information about feasibilities becomes known. Because development is comparative in terms of scientific knowledge, feasibilities, and desires, it is also comparative in terms of time because what is known, possible, and desired all change as time goes on. People's desires and expectations are heavily influenced by comparisons of their own conditions with conditions in other regions, or countries or classes. There are examples of economically depressed regions in countries whose populations, aware of their less affluent condition, press for ameliorative development programs – such as the Appalachian region of the United States or the northeastern region of Thailand. There are examples of depressed racial or caste populations in countries whose members demand special measures of relief, such as the rural Malay population in Malaysia or the untouchables of India. Most such comparisons, however, are made between countries. The categorization of nations into developed and underdeveloped countries in accordance with per capita incomes of 500 dollars more or less, or other arbitrary measures, is useful for purposes of analysis and treatment, perhaps, but it does not describe a state of "development" beyond which no improvement of the human condition can be achieved or will be sought.

To define development as the goal of a people or a country is thus as elusive as to define it as a condition, and for many of the same reasons of feasibility and aspiration. There are two levels at which development as an objective can be considered. The first is the eradication of poverty. Destitution need no longer be the fate of most human beings. The world's knowledge and processes for development, if applied, should make it possible to meet essential needs and satisfy basic wants, even under changing conditions and ever higher standards of what the minimum requirements are. Even though droughts still bring crop failures and starvation, and even though swollen populations make the task greater, the job can be done. Certainly the first and highest goal of any legitimate development program is to accomplish this purpose – the elimination of poverty.

The potentials of development are not limited by the world's resources or by man's ingenuity to the elimination of poverty. Nor has man proved to be satisfied with a subsistence level of existence. It is not enough, therefore, to fix the target of development at this level, though it might be the first priority in many situations. Nor is it sufficient to state the purpose of development merely in terms of physical standards, or even income, because these increase with new opportunities and desires and hence are not static, to be achieved for once and for all. Certainly a concern of development is the quality of life beyond mere sustenance as assured by respect for the rights of human dignity and liberty. This is the second, higher purpose of development.

One way of stating the purpose of development at the higher level is that it is to increase progressively the choices, the opportunities, that individuals have in planning and leading their lives according to their personal ideas of happiness and fulfillment. This purpose extends to all of the individuals in a population or a country, and not merely to some of them. Such choices depend upon the freedom of people to move about, their mobility, and upon their voice in the social, political, and economic decisions which affect them. It is assumed that if they are given the choice and the opportunity, human beings are likely to make their optimum contribution to society and to express their individual geniuses most readily. The purpose of development is to advance that happy condition.

The capacity for development is the third conceptualization of development, along with development as a condition and development as a goal. This capacity, in the private and the public sector, consists of the methods and systems and activities by which development policies, projects, and programs are carried out to accomplish the specific goals of development, goals which are articulated for a particular period of time and place. The capacity for development involves the organizations and agencies and institutions, both private and public, to sustain and support the several processes of development. The capacity for development also includes the will of the people, and their preparedness as individuals – through or in spite of their social institutions – to engage in risk-taking and other adventures which promise change for the better while threatening change for the worse. Development, then, and the promise thereof, can be measured in terms of the comparative excellence of the relevant processes – that is, the delivery systems – and the capacity that exists in the social, economic, and political institutions. Processes and capacity which are effective and responsive should take people where they choose to go. The people of a country are the center of the development interest.

THE ROLE OF PEOPLE IN DEVELOPMENT

Development can be considered as the interaction of people with the natural resources available to them – that is, people's utilization of their resources. The involvement of people in this interaction has many interrelated and seemingly contradictory aspects, all of which must be taken into account and accommodated in a fully effective process of development. It is instructive to examine the several roles of people in the development process.

First of all, people are the target of the development process; their well-being is the purpose of development. Political units such as nations and states may also gain strength from systematic development, and it is desirable that they do so, but such strength is legitimately used to improve the welfare of the population as a whole, rather than to aggrandize some elite portion of the population, whether military, political, religious, or caste – or the state itself. It has been argued by some that a strong state is necessary to and will assure a happier and more prosperous population. This is true if the state is considered to be an instrument of that felicitous process and not its goal. In the latter case portions of the population will benefit at the cost of other portions, or the population as a whole will suffer lesser benefits from development than otherwise possible in terms of food or housing or social security, for example, because of the diversions of resources to the military or outer space or other excursions considered by the state to be important if not necessary to its own status.

At the same time that people are the target of development they are the instruments of development. In this respect people are a human resource and, from that point of view, in a category not unlike other resources such as soil and water. It is not particularly appealing to be thought of as a resource, to be managed and used, but the concept is useful as an aid to understanding the development process. Techniques and programs of manpower analysis and planning are based on this concept of people as resources, resources necessary in relevant numbers and skills to an effective program of development. These human resources are physical labor and they are also technical and professional skills of a variety of kinds and levels. Considered in this perspective, people are labor in the classical categorization of "labor and capital" as the prime factors in economic development. Their number and skills are of significance, in this context, only in terms of what is required for the optimum utilization of physical resources and efficient and effective planning and implementation of development policies and programs.

Fortunately or unfortunately, the number of people required as human resources to serve the development programs of a country is seldom the same as the population. The people are usually too few or too many – usually too many. They are too old or too young and possibly living in the wrong places to be efficient human resources. Therefore, while legitimate targets and beneficiaries of the development program and instruments of its conduct, populations are often a problem and a burden. Populations must therefore be dealt with, planned for, not only as people to benefit from development and as human resources to contribute to development but as a major complication both in fixing development targets and development methods. Populations, human resources, unhappily from this point of view, do not lie dormant like coal, not eating or talking. Their demands are vocal and insistent.

Hence, like manpower planning for human resources, there is population planning for the consuming and articulate public. Many countries are striving to find the biologically and philosophically correct population policy – without too much success. India clearly has too many people to feed and encourages family planning and birth control. Israel wants a larger Jewish population and encourages both immigration and larger families. Other countries, with less dramatically extreme population situations, are less clear on the appropriate course. The questions are practical – can the population be fed, can families give satisfactory upbringing to numerous children? And the questions are philosophical – is it necessary, or even desirable, that every adult have gainful employment? If every adult must work and development needs and opportunities do not require so much in human resources, how long should he work and at what? Should all adult members of the family be required to work? Only some? And if adults do not work, or cannot work, will the economy support them? How? Very few, if any, nations have resolved these and many other questions about their populations, considered from this point of view. Studies and policies on employment and public works and welfare and social security are in this area, and clearly related, but they do not encompass population policy as a whole.

People, then, are to be considered as populations to be supported, human resources to be utilized, and the public to be cherished as the beneficiaries of the development process. There are additional roles which people play, not the least of which is that of manager–entrepreneur in development agencies and undertakings. It is not enough to have the ingredients for development. Those ingredients have to be related to one another and made productive in a myriad of ways at local, national, and intermediate levels and in public, semi-public, and private sectors. It is the function of this manager–entrepreneur class to see and act upon the development opportunities in any particular environment or framework.

It is not enough for development and change to be merely possible. Development must also be attractive, powerfully attractive, to the participants and desired by them. The availability of resources and even of the knowledge and technology to utilize those resources will not assure their utilization if the people do not choose to change their ways. Even a literate population, and a healthy one, will not, merely because of its literacy and health, undertake development activities. It is true that resources and technology and literacy and health are also factors in development, but in themselves they are not sufficient. Development must also be attractive if people are to be motivated to make the changes in their lives, often drastic, to bring it about.

A major, perhaps the major, motivation to engagement in development activity is improved material well-being. More money and goods are, of course, interpreted in terms of better standards of living and wider opportunities of choice in work and leisure for present and especially future generations. If interest in material well-being or at least the improvement of material well-being is lacking, interest in development will also be lacking. The first requisite is that the concerned people know what the alternative feasibilities and choices for change and development may be. As long as they remain ignorant of the possibilities they cannot judge the desirabilities.

To the extent to which the benefits of growth are not shared with the people or are shared unevenly and unjustly by the population, to that extent does the environment discourage investment and participation in the process. Injustice, in this perspective, can take several different forms. One form of perceived social injustice which is not only theoretical but also real occurs when the state, the government, insists that the earnings of increased growth be reinvested in development so fully and for so many years that the population not only does not enjoy current fruits but cannot foresee future benefits. There is a real dilemma here, because so much of a country's current earnings and even capital could be distributed for consumption or social welfare that the whole development process would grind to a halt and become stagnant. Difficult judgments must be made, and accepted by the participating public, on the optimum balance between consumption and investment with consideration for both present enjoyment and future development. Some countries such as Singapore have found that investments in higher wage rates and pension systems and investments in education facilities commensurate with increased productivity are ways of sharing the benefits of development with the people while contributing further to the development process.

These are chiefly matters of choice which developing countries and their populations face all of the time. There are starker kinds of situations involving the comparative attractiveness of development to the people as a whole. One such situation is that characterized by economic domination by a small group or number of families to such an extent that the profits and benefits of development accrue to them rather than to the people, though the people may be providing much of the labor and professional and even managerial skill. Such vested and controlling interests might even oppose and resist and prevent change if it threatens their position. It is unlikely, however, as demonstrated even in China, that people will be attracted to new and risky economic activities and will work harder if they do not share in the profits sufficiently to be so motivated. This problem is illustrated by slow progress in extending multiple cropping systems under which the farmers grow two or three crops where one grew before, but when the landlords and not the farmers reap the rewards. The problem is illustrated more classically by land tenure systems which seem to limit the farm worker to a low level of sustenance, even when improved technology permits much higher yields and returns. The development process fails unless the people are motivated by shares in the fruits.

In almost all countries the target of development is the people. The purpose of development is to improve their lot, first by assuring a level of sustenance acceptable to them and second by increasing the choices they have for living their own lives up to their optimum expression. Only the people can decide as individuals and communities what standards of living and choices in life are acceptable. The people, one way or another, must be involved in setting the goals of any development program for any particular place and for any particular time. Beyond the general goals of development, this participation should extend for its effectiveness to the policies and the methods of development, to the several projects and perhaps above all to the timing. Many of the issues of present well-being and pleasure versus future security and benefits arise over questions of the speed and sequence with which development projects and programs are undertaken. The decisions depend upon the choice of the people.

THE ROLE OF INSTITUTIONS

Institutions are the forms in which people organize their affairs in relationship with each other. An institution is a system of action. Systems of action comprehend the structures and mechanisms which provide the capacity and support for action in the form of agencies or organization. Bureaus or departments are institutions of this kind, as are schools, prisons, hospitals, and banks. Systems of action also comprehend processes and delivery instruments by which specified tasks are executed or by which categories of functions are supported or controlled. Accounting and budgeting systems are institutions in this sense, as are arrangements to deliver credit to entrepreneurs and fertilizer or seed or water to farmers. Accepted patterns of economic and social behavior are also embraced by the term "institution."

An institution as a system of action possesses certain indispensable qualities. First of all the institution, the system, must have the capability to produce or deliver the product or perform the function for which it was created; the institution must be effective in accomplishing its purpose. Second, the institution, whether as agency or process or convention, must be accepted in the society and environment of its location. The institution must represent the way in which people, as individuals and in groups, wish to be served and to work with or relate to one another. The institution must therefore have value and meaning for those people if it is to serve in a fully effective and productive way. And in the third place the institution must be able to survive because *it is* adequately supported with the necessary financial, personnel, and political capacity and because it has the capability to adapt itself and its program to changing and evolving conditions and situations, including the ability to learn from its own experience and to correct its mistakes. If the institution is lacking with respect to any one of these three qualities of capability, public acceptance, and survival capacity, it fails as an institution.

Institutionalization thus is the process by which systems of action acquire capability and competence, public acceptance, operating resources and the stability of a standard way of doing things. The term should also embody the concept of expendability if and as relevance and competence and acceptability decline. Unfortunately the term "institutional behavior" has come to mean tenacity in the adherence to routinized ways of doing things which, although perhaps good ways when introduced, become outmoded. This tenacity may result from the creation of vested interests in the institution itself, or in some of its processes, or in the establishment of vested interests in minority portions of the clientele public served by the institution. The tendency to rigid adherence to the policies and procedures initially adopted to serve competence and achieve stability thus threatens to produce a condition of routinization and even ossification and stultification of the institution's operation. The problem is to find ways to establish effective institutions which are responsive and to keep them viable in terms both of function and of public purpose and acceptability.

Institutions are created and grow in a number of ways. Most institutions, and especially the traditional ones, are born out of custom or habit and evolve slowly and gradually. Revolution can bring about the need for new institutions, or make it possible to establish the kinds of institutions desired by the revolutionaries, but revolutions do not in themselves create institutions. Institutions can be established or changed by a central authority. Reform movements are an important and continuing influence in institution building and in the institutionalization process, an influence which seeks to correct those aspects of the institutionalization process which tend to ossification, or regimentation, or abuse by agency officeholders.

Still another way in which institutions are created or renovated is by plan, by a calculated program to produce agency capability and the capacity and effectiveness of relevant systems to implement designated parts of a development program. This method of creating new agencies and systems or of modernizing old ones has come to be known as "institution building." The logic of including institution building in a country's system of development planning and implementation is clear, considering the importance of planning and arranging for the ways of accomplishing the purposes and projects of the plan, as well as merely specifying its targets and activities. Fortunately, although tardily, planning agencies are giving increasing attention to the institution-building aspects of their responsibility. Their attention, to be most effective, requires knowledge of the nature of institutions – that is, their components, the environment needed to support and sustain them, and the processes involved in producing them.

Certain of the component parts of an institution are obvious and readily apparent. To take as illustration an institution in the form of an agency, it must have a capital plant fully adequate to the effective performance of its assigned functions. Such plant would include buildings and sometimes special facilities such as laboratories, libraries, a computer center – and even on occasion staff housing and cafeteria and other service facilities. The physical plant should be located in the place or places most appropriate to its work and it should be designed to meet the unique requirements and characteristics of the agency to be accommodated.

The competent agency must be well staffed with adequately trained personnel. The assurance of such staff depends of course upon the quality of personnel administration, including the adequacy of supporting educational agencies, provisions for compensation and security, and consideration for status and public esteem. The staff of the new institution must have the specialized qualifications to perform the work of the organization competently and with understanding and enthusiasm. It is unlikely that such staff is readily available in sufficient numbers in many developing countries to undertake novel and unfamiliar programs of social and economic and technological development. At the same time the institution is often expected and even required to go into operation before it has time to arrange for the technical and professional training of staff. Under such circumstances a less than fully qualified and committed staff is obliged to begin operations in a traditional way and tends to establish job rights in the patterns of an older system.

When men and women trained abroad return – and usually they are young people with little seniority in the older system – they have great difficulty in practicing their newly acquired skills in the older system which persists. Many give up and quit under such circumstances. The remedy, short of correcting outmoded personnel systems which do not adapt readily to the requirements of merit and specialized qualification, and short of postponing the operational aspects of new institutional programs until fully trained staff is available, is to train enough able persons, large numbers of them, so that when employed they can have the weight and influence of mass on program and management decisions. The availability and full utilization of highly trained and motivated staff is the crucial factor of success in a new institution and the first point of concern in the institution-building process.

Of prime importance to the institution is the quality of the administrative leadership and direction of the agency. The administrative qualities of this leadership should include those of outstanding competence in administration. The leadership of an institution in the process of its creation can fail if it does not have status and influence in the controlling power structure, if it does not have the respect and confidence of staff, or if it does not have sympathetic understanding of the novel purposes and functions and methods of the program or service to be accomplished. To find an administrator who possesses all three of these sterling qualities is difficult indeed. A senior official who has status and influence in the bureaucracy would not naturally, in the course of things, have great enthusiasm for a new development program of uncertain status and future, nor would he have compatible familiarity with the new technology involved. He and his staff would not be in easy accord, either, unless the staff also were on easy terms with the work of the new institutions.

The components of an institution also include a clear definition of purpose, policy, program activity, and method. They include the legal authority and the requisite delegation of administrative powers to be able to operate effectively as desired. An unambiguous assignment of agency purpose and program is important to the government and the development plan and the bureaucracy so that the agency's relative place in development administration is understood and so that there is an objective and fair basis for its reporting and for the evaluation of its performance. This component of purpose and program extends to policy and method, also, because the effects of program activity as governed by policy and the impact of projects as facilitated and cushioned by work methodology can be as significant in impeding or advancing the cause of development as the work program itself. The understanding and acceptance of purpose, program, policy, and methodology by agency staff is directly important to agency effectiveness. Ignorance of purpose and policy and program method or, if not ignorance, disagreement with these on the part of the responsible personnel could result in less than full agency effectiveness and even lead to program failure.

The institution of course needs the authority to act upon its designated purposes and to carry out its assigned program functions according to the policies and methods most appropriate to them. This authority and these powers are of both a legal and an administrative nature. A clear status in law, with foresighted statement of purpose and policy and function, contributes not only to clarity and understanding of program. Such legal status also provides the basis of stability and the assurance of continuity that most institutions need for their growth to maturity, a process which takes much time. Legal authority alone is not usually sufficient in itself to empower the agency to go ahead with its work. Required in addition are delegations of such administrative authority as will vest in the agency the capacity to operate efficiently and responsibly – delegations for personnel actions, for example, and for reasonable financial discretion and for procurement.

There are two remaining and essential components of an institution. One of these is assurance of financial resources for continuing operation, either from appropriations or from revenues or from borrowings or from combinations of these as are appropriate. The last component on the list is that of agency administration itself, not only the division of labor as represented in an organization chart and the erection of a work structure suitable to the job, but also a system of decision-making in happy consonance with agency staff on the one hand and concerned external agencies and communities on the other. This process of decision-making is not only for the purpose of agreeing on what projects and activities should be undertaken but also, and equally, on the policies and the methods of doing that work.

Agreement on policy and method, especially, as well as agreement on projects, is involved in the concept of coordination, which has the function of synthesizing all of the component parts of the institution into an effective instrument for program accomplishment – the components of physical plant, staff and leadership, assigned purpose and program, financial resources for continuing operation, and sound organization structure. All of these components must be present in an institution if it is to be viable and, more than that, the components must be synthesized into an efficient instrument for the prosecution of the assigned development task.

It is not only the adequacy of an institution's component parts and their articulation in a successful synthesis that determines its capability and its effectiveness. The environment in which the institution is expected to work is also important. Individual institutions do not exist in isolation; rather, they function in a complex of relationships and a network of interactions which, if friendly and supportive, enhance their effective performance and which, if hostile and uncooperative, can impede the intended operations and thwart the accomplishment of institutional purpose. The key elements in this environment include the enabling and controlling authorities, the agencies and systems of supply and service, the related sister or complementary institutions, the competing and potentially hostile institutions, the institutional and public consumers of the subject institution's product or the intended beneficiaries of its work, and the overall public and institutional perception of the role of the agency or the system in the bureaucratic and social environment.

Institutions, agencies, and systems have an essential and a complementary relationship with other institutions in a larger system which embraces them all. An institution is invariably responsible for providing a product or a service upon which another institution or other institutions are dependent. In turn, an institution is invariably dependent upon the work of other institutions for its own program success. Thus a series of complementary and interacting institutions in an effective association of relationships, a kind of network, is involved in the accomplishment of a program. The agency charged with the construction of an irrigation system and the agency charged with the engagement of farmers in the use of the system complement one another in an inseparable way. Too often this complementary is not recognized adequately in program coordination or expressed effectively in project timing and execution so that program objectives are not met or are delayed or are not achieved to their full expectation. Complete institutional success depends on an environment of well-coordinated and thus effective relationships among sister institutions, complementing each other to their mutual advantage as they progress toward a common program purpose.

THE MEANING OF DEVELOPMENT ADMINISTRATION

Traditional systems and institutions of public administration were not designed to respond to demands for social and economic development, whether in colonies such as Indonesia and Nigeria or in kingdoms such as Thailand and Ethiopia. They were not expected to be responsive to legislatures or other representatives of the people. They did not recognize the function of rectifying inequities in the social system. They were not as much concerned with the encouragement or support of economic growth or the distribution of the benefits of that growth as with the allocation of resources to assure continuing profits and revenues to government or, rather, to those who controlled the government. These traditional administrative systems were established to perform other functions. Those functions included the maintenance of law and order so as to assure a reasonable degree of security and of stability in the community. They included the provision of certain public services considered to be essential at the time, such as roads, and they included mechanisms for settling disputes.

Traditional governments and their bureaucracies were highly centralized. Authority was focused in the capital city and comparatively few decisions could be made by officials in outlying districts. Even at the center, authority was not well dispersed for expeditious and well-informed expression. The top officials could not or did not share the power of office with colleagues or with subordinates or even with other officials in the same office. They were not supported by specialist staffs which could give informed advice based upon sound analysis. They were not supplied with an adequate number of middle-level personnel trained to handle the routines and details of office management. This personnel situation and the limited and narrow concept of the exercise of authority were aggravated by ponderous procedures of administration. The failure to delegate decision-making powers to field officers in the outlying districts and the dilatory pace of action at the center had the effect of impeding and not expediting action.

The major supportive systems of these traditional bureaucracies, notably the fiscal and the personnel systems, also represented barriers to development processes no matter how relevant they seemed to be to the processes of security and stability and status quo which they had been designed to support. Budgets in this environment tended to be more restrictive than energizing both in their form and in the limited authority they granted for expenditure. The personnel, the civil servants who manned these systems, were the instruments of throne and empire and not of nations and particularly not of the people of nations. These civil servants were on the whole honest and efficient and effective in preserving order and maintaining stability and in assuring the revenues. They were governors, in that sense, and were not involved in the realization of popular aspirations.

The term "development administration" was coined in 1955 or 1956. It seemed to be a simple and clarifying way to distinguish the focus of administration on the support and management of development as distinguished from the administration of law and order. In some respects it is the counterpart of the term "development economics," which came into renewed and heightened usage with the growing impact of economic planning in newly independent countries after World War II. The term and concept of development administration is now found in the titles and programs of many agencies and institutions, such as the Institute of Development Administration in Thailand and the Development Administration Unit in the prime minister's office in Malaysia. The U.S. Agency for International Development changed the name of its public administration unit to development administration in the mid-1960s. The United Nations' regional center for training and research in administration in Asia has the title Asian and Pacific Development Administration Center. Many universities have introduced courses in development administration.

The five-year plans and the reports of the administrative reform commissions of many countries in Africa and Asia as well as Latin America call for the strengthening of administration to assure acceptable levels of implementation of national plans of social and economic development. These include, for example, India and Pakistan, Indonesia and Malaysia, Nigeria and Ghana, Kenya and Tanzania. There are many others, reflecting the fact that administration for development is the concern and the responsibility of each of the developing countries.

"Development administration" is the term used to denote the complex of agencies, management systems, and processes a government establishes to achieve its development goals. It is the public mechanism set up to relate the several components of development in order to articulate and accomplish national social and economic objectives. It is the adjustment of the bureaucracy to the vastly increased number, variety, and complexity of governmental functions required to respond to public demands for development. Development administration is the administration of policies, programs, and projects to serve developmental purposes.

Development administration is characterized by its purposes, its loyalties, and its attitudes. The purposes of development administration are to stimulate and facilitate defined programs of social and economic progress. They are purposes of change and innovation and movement as contrasted with purposes of maintaining the status quo. They are 10 make change attractive and possible. These purposes are to apply policies and to conduct programs of development specified by the people as a; whole through evolving political systems of democratic decision-making This definition of purpose makes the bureaucracy for development, administration accountable to the public, through its representatives. Bureaucratic loyalty in development administration must thus be to the people and not to its own vested institutional interests nor to a nonpublic sovereign such as king or empire. The attitudes of development administration are positive rather than negative, persuasive rather than restrictive. Development administration encourages innovation and change where desirable or necessary to accomplish development purposes and discourages adherence to traditional norms and forms for their own sake. The attitude of development administration is outward reaching and not inward looking.

Development administration is distinguished from, although not independent of, other aspects and concerns of public administration. Certainly the maintenance of law and order is a prime function of government and is basic to development, although it precedes and is not usually encompassed within the definition of development administration. Similarly the provision of such essential services as roads and other communication systems and health and school facilities, as well as water supply and other utility systems and the organization for tax collection, are distinguished from development administration because they have been a responsibility of government traditionally. The comprehensiveness and effectiveness of these services support and strengthen the environment for development, however, and their provision in adequate measure is necessary to development.

Distinctions should also be made between administration for development and other systems of administration such as those for the police and the military, the judicial, and for foreign representation. Each of these other systems has its own unique requirements, attitudes, and methods. Again, each system, depending upon its operation, has an impact upon development administration, and therefore development administration and the government as a whole must be aware of and accommodating of the consequences of these impacts and interrelationships. The police and military systems could be repressive toward the people, for example, and inhibit the kinds of freedom of movement concomitant with the development process. Or they could be so intertwined with district administration as to inhibit the conduct of development activities. On the other hand, enlightened police and military systems can, through their own or the regularly constituted agencies, encourage and support educational, health, social welfare, and even public works programs so as to enhance markedly the overall programs of development. These separate systems thus become a concern of development administration.

The quality of the administration of justice, similarly, is related to attitudes toward development administration by giving evidence to the people of the government's intentions of achieving equality of treatment and opportunity regardless of wealth, class, or race. The administration of foreign representation can have a direct bearing on development, not only by facilitating the good general relationships conducive to business associations but even more by providing for economic experts in the embassies who can work directly to realize fruitful trade and investment connections.

The methods of administration in these diverse systems vary, and vary quite appropriately, because of the distinctive purposes of the several systems. The methods of law and order, for example, are those of restraint and punishment. Law and order administrators, and also those who collect the taxes, must by nature be objective, aloof, and even distant in their relationships with the public. The primary interest of public administrators who provide public services is efficiency in the performance of their specified functions. Efficiency – that is, the achievement of economies in time, personnel, and materials in the accomplishment of purpose – is an important aspect of public administration. These aspects of administration might be called "internal administration" as distinguished from the primary methodological concerns of development administrators, which might be called "external administration." Internal administration is defined here to mean the management of an organization, an agency. It involves the systems and processes and methods by which needed resources of personnel, materials, and technology are used to perform prescribed functions.

External administration, on the other hand, refers to the activities and processes of administration which are needed to establish and to activate relationships with agencies and groups outside the administrative control of an agency, relationships which are essential to the achievement of that agency's purposes. These relationships are required to implement a policy or program or to carry out a project because such implementation would be impossible without the participation and contribution of these external entities. External administration thus involves patterns of interagency collaboration and of client participation above and beyond the regular patterns and systems of coordination and supervision.

Forms of interagency collaboration range from informal, unstructured relationships expressed in meetings, conferences, and the exchange of information to more formal associations expressed in contracts or agreements calling for systematic methods of cooperation. Patterns of client participation are needed to involve the people served by and also those engaged in the execution of a collaborative effort-people in their private capacity either as individuals or, more usually, through their autonomous private organizations. Such groups include agency sponsored or encouraged committees or councils for advisory purposes; cooperatives and farmers' organizations; special districts for conservation, education, and sanitation; trade associations; unions; and professional organizations. Patterns of client participation also range from the informal to the formal, the unstructured to the structured. A program which illustrates external administration is a major irrigation project involving the collaboration of a central agency such as the public works department, a state or local agency such as the department of agricultural extension, and the farmers as individuals and through their private organizations. Development administration is outward looking; it is basically external.

Efficiency is by no means inconsistent with development administration, or out of place in its conduct. Quite the contrary; the application of technology to the performance of management functions and the improvement of management skills, particularly at the middle levels of management service, have their own important contribution to make to the effectiveness of administration for development. In spite of this dependency on competent administration, however, the term "development administration" is usually not employed to refer to scientific management or administrative efficiency as such. For the purposes of understanding development administration, and discussing it, emphasis is placed upon its distinctive features. If all of its interdependencies were included in the definition, "development administration" would be but another term for public administration and too broad therefore to permit the particularized consideration it deserves and requires as a phenomenon in the development process.

Another aspect of this consideration of efficiency in public administration calls for attention in this context. A part of the concept of development administration is that its function is to achieve specifically defined development purposes; its effectiveness should be measured and judged in these terms. If the purposes of administration are accomplished, it is considered good; if the purposes are poorly or inadequately accomplished, administration from this development point of view is considered bad. This approach to the design of administrative systems is quite different from approaches based on some generalized concept of what is considered to be "good administration." Development administration is designed to achieve specified results and is good or bad in terms of its delivery of results. This approach to administration does not exclude efficiency or considerations of time and money and honesty, but it begins with a definition of the target and proceeds with the formulation of administrative methodology suited to its achievement, rather than with an abstract conception of efficient administration as such. Merely efficient administration could in fact thwart development if it were its purpose to do so.

To use the development approach to administration, sometimes called "sectoral administration," is to design management systems needed to carry out defined and agreed-upon policies, programs, or projects. This approach is quite different from that usually expressed in the term "administrative reform." The targets of administrative reform are typically the central management system and, predominantly, the civil service. The function of development administration is to assure that an appropriately congenial environment and effective administration support are provided for delivery of capital, materials, and services where needed in the productive process – whether in public, private, or mixed economies.

THE APPLICATIONS OF DEVELOPMENT ADMINISTRATION

The manifestations of development administration, its unique purposes, loyalties, and attitudes, are found in new and reoriented agencies and in new management systems and processes. These agencies include planning boards to facilitate decisions about development policies and the allocation of resources toward the accomplishment of those policies, and reconstituted "nation-building" departments such as those for agriculture, industry, education, and health. An essential aspect of the competence of these agencies is their ability to judge the management as well as the technical and financial and economic feasibilities of development projects and programs and, when such feasibilities are suspect, to take the leadership in assuring the adequacy of such programs and projects from the management point of view. The essence of development administration is its concern with the "how" of accomplishing the "what" of the development plan and its constituent programs and projects. New kinds of agencies are often needed for development. Public enterprises and also stronger private enterprise management systems are called for. In the field, cooperative organizations, community development programs and a variety of farmers' organizations are evidence of requirements for new agencies to support development.

The major expression of development administration in the field is decentralization, the unclogging of business at the center by delegating authority to a larger number of agencies and to a larger number of places in the countryside. New management systems, as well as management agencies, must be devised to make such decentralization possible – new budget and fiscal as well as planning systems, information and reporting systems, personnel systems, and systems of coordination. Development administration, therefore, is not only the administration of development; it is the development of administration. Development administration encompasses the innovations which strengthen the capacity of the bureaucracy to stimulate and facilitate development. For these purposes development administration needs its own supporting institutions, chiefly in the form of training, research, and consulting agencies, but also in the form of an articulate and informed public expectation of good administrative behavior and performance.

The reorientation and strengthening of each of the nation-building departments or ministries to accommodate the development dimension of its responsibility requires first of all an overhaul of its organization to assure a structure suitable to the ministry's function. This reorganization should concern itself with the adequacy of the subdivisions of departments and bureaus in terms of the specializations needed to do the work and the need to share the work load. It should concern itself with the clarification of delegations and lines of communication so that both the powers for acting and the accountability for actions are assigned sufficiently to permit effective and expeditious decision and performance. The distinctive capacities needed by nation-building departments to discharge their development responsibilities are planning competence, staff analysis capability, expert specialized personnel, management skill, field organization, and effective coordination.

The introduction of competent planning in the central ministries and departments is a key factor in reorienting and strengthening the nation-building departments upon whom the heavy and diverse burdens of development fall most heavily. With the assignment of development duties, these central departments and ministries can no longer satisfy the requirement of their existence by merely presiding over mechanisms to manage comparatively modest operations. They are now obliged to arrange for and to carry out urgent and much larger programs of road building and other construction of utilities and infrastructure, a much larger system of schools and training institutions, nationwide systems of family health clinics, and, most prominently, complex programs to increase agricultural productivity and investment in industry and trade. These programs and projects must be formulated, their several feasibilities tested, and they must be integrated in the national as well as in the appropriate sectoral plan. For these purposes a planning capability and process is needed in each nation-building department.

These central ministries in their traditional form did not have the capacity for staff analysis, for setting up and operating or monitoring delivery and support systems, or effective mechanisms in the provinces and districts to express their program and project interests throughout the country. Staff analysis involves the application of objective and scientific skills to the data and the problem. At an earlier time, in the days of traditional administration, the public establishment was on the whole small and the functions comparatively simple rather than complex in nature. The conduct of the public business did not seem to require much specialized professional analysis. The burdens and complexities of development, however, and the larger and unfamiliar programs to be carried out compel the utilization of expert and specialized staff services. Staff services of this kind depend upon information and data systems, including systematic appraisal of project and program progress, which provide material accurate and complete enough to permit operable conclusions. These staff services include personnel, budget, and operations and management research as well as planning analysis.

A nation-building department needs professionally trained personnel in the field or several fields of its substantive interest, and it needs the services of staff analysts. The applications of technology to development opportunities depend upon the capability of the relevant ministry to give the specialized support and leadership which only such experts can provide. This personnel requirement means the introduction of specialists into the civil service not only in much larger numbers, but also at higher levels of influence and decision-making in relation to the generalists in the administrative services. The dedication of these specialists to the application of their professional skills and their sympathy with the problems and opportunities of the public community are additional attributes of the personnel complement of the effective nation-building department.

Ministries reconstituted for development administration must have the management skill and capacity to establish or to arrange for the establishment and competent operation through private or other public agencies of management systems to carry out or support development programs. To use a familiar example, the increase of any consequence in grain production usually involves the introduction of a new variety of seed, which is fruitful only if it is supported with adequate amounts of fertilizer, water, insecticides, herbicides, and cultivating implements available at the right times and places. The introduction of the new seed depends upon systems which will assure the production of the support items and their delivery to the farmers. These are in addition to, but related to and interdependent with, price policies which will motivate the farmer, credit facilities which will finance the farmer, and extension services which will advise the farmer. A plan that contemplates the increase of grain production with the use of new seeds is obviously not viable unless it also contemplates and provides for the essential support systems. Those systems could be in the private sector, or could be provided by cooperatives or other public or semi-public enterprises, or could be undertaken by the regular government departments.

Nation-building departments need to be retooled in their capacity to apply their plans, programs, and projects for development throughout the country. This capacity depends in part upon the evolution of competent agencies and mechanisms in the field and in part upon the devising of methods by which the central ministry can relate its guidance and support to the field agencies. In traditional administration the bureaucracy in the field was preoccupied with keeping the peace and collecting the taxes. Central ministries sometimes had their own agents there also, agents who performed somewhat vague, desultory, and procedural duties. A very few countries at independence, such as India and Nigeria, set up state governments and bureaucracies with their own authority for planning and carrying out development programs. Most did not, however, but sought to strengthen their field organizations by assigning more comprehensive duties, including those of development, to the district commissioner or other head civil servant in the district or province. In some countries the specialists of the central ministries were made a part of a newly integrated field bureaucracy, but in most cases these specialists continued to report back to the center with only uncertain coordinating relationships in the district. There is movement now to increase the size and competence and also the powers of the administrative establishment in the field. This process of decentralization is necessary to speed up decisions relating to program and project matters peculiar to the field or to a particular location in the field, and to make the decisions more realistically and accurately because of the likelihood of fuller knowledge and understanding of the requirements of the local situation.

Thus development administration involves the establishment of new agencies and the reorientation of existing agencies in order to discharge the enormous responsibilities and to perform the multifarious and complex functions of social and economic development. Institutions involved in the development process are not limited to those of government but include also the agencies and systems of the private sector. They include the relationships of individuals and private and public agencies and programs in such evolving and complex social economic systems as those for agricultural production.

NOTE ON SOURCES

The conceptualization of development administration owes a great debt to: Comparative Administration Group (CAG). Organized in 1960–1961 under the aegis of the American Society for Public Administration, it focused its efforts in the development administration. The CAG was put together by a small group of political scientists and students of public administration who had been frustrated and disappointed with efforts at technical assistance for public administration – developing countries. The CAG, with financial support from the Ford Foundation, sponsored fruitful research and seminars and issued, in mimeograph form, the CAG "Occasional Papers." These were widely distributed. Many of them have been revised, related to one another, and published in book form. The most prominent of them are the following:

Ralph Braibanti, ed., *Political and Administrative Development* (Durham, NC: Duke University Press, 1969). Ralph Braibanti was also general editor of the whole CAG series.

Bertram M. Gross, ed., *Action under Planning: The Guidance of Economic Development* (New York: McGraw-Hill, 1967).

James P. Heaphey, ed., *Spatial Dimensions of Development Administration* (Durham, NC: Duke University Press, 1970).

Allan Kornberg and Lloyd D. Musolf, eds., *Legislatures in Development Perspective* (Durham, NC: Duke University Press, 1970).

J.D. Montgomery and W.L. Siffin, eds., *Approaches to Development: Politics, Administration and Change* (New York: McGraw-Hill, 1966).

Fred W. Riggs, ed., *Frontiers of Development Administration* (Durham, NC: Duke University Press, 1970).

Clarence F. Thurber and Lawrence S. Graham, eds., *Development Administration in Latin America* (Durham, NC: Duke University Press, 1973).

Dwight Waldo, ed., *Temporal Dimensions of Development Administration* (Durham, NC: Duke University Press, 1970).

Edward W. Weidner, ed., *Development Administration in Asia* (Durham, NC: Duke University Press, 1970). Edward Weidner also wrote the interesting article "Development Administration: Origin, Concept, and Diffusion," *Korean Journal of Public Administration 6*, no. 1 (1968): 237–243.

Fred W. Riggs was the prime mover of CAG's interest in and devotion to the new field of development administration, and he was the long-time chairman of the group. His own earlier books, still of great value in development administration, set much of the tone, the framework, for CAG's subsequent studies. Among them are two pioneering works: *The Ecology of Public Administration* (London: Asia Publishing House, 1961), and *Administration in Developing Countries: The Theory of the Prismatic Society* (Boston: Houghton Mifflin, 1964).

Other books contributed to the understanding of development administration: although not sponsored by CAG, several were written or edited by scholars active in CAC:

Joseph La Palombara, ed., *Bureaucracy and Political Development* (Princeton: Princeton University Press, 1963).

Irving Swerdlow, ed., *Development Administration: Concepts and Problems* (Syracuse, NY: Syracuse University Press, 1963).

Edward W. Weidner, *Technical Assistance in Public Administration Overseas: The Case for Development Administration* (Chicago: Public Administration Service, 1964).

C.Y. Wu, *Development Administration: Current Approaches and Trends in Public Administration for National Development*, Sales No. E. 76. 11. H. I (New York: United Nations, 1976).

Bibliographies have been published from time to time. These are three of the most recent:

Milton J. Esman and John D. Montgomery, "Systems Approaches to Technical Cooperation: The Role of Development Administration," *Public Administration Review* 29, no. 5 (Sept./Oct. 1969): 507–539.

Richard W. Gable, Development Administration: Background, Terms, Concepts, Theories and a New Approach, American Society for Public Administration, Section on International and Comparative Administration, Occasional Papers, Series No. 7 (Washington, DC: American Society for Public Administration, 1976).

Garth N. Jones, *Planning, Development, and Change: A Bibliography in Development Administration* (Honolulu: East-West Center Press, 1970).

An effort closely allied to that of the Comparative Administration Group and involving many of the same people was the Inter-University Research Program on institution Building composed by Indiana and Michigan State universities and by the University of Pittsburgh under the leadership of Milton J. Esman. The productive and stimulating work of this group was used by the U.S. Agency for International Development (AID) and some of its cooperating land grant universities as an aid to planning and evaluating technical assistance projects in agriculture. The emphasis is continued in the AID-financed activities of PASITAM – the Program of Advanced Studies in Institution Building and Technical Assistance Methodology. PASITAM is a program of MUCIA – the Midwest Universities Consortium for International Activities, whose members are the universities of Illinois, Iowa, Minnesota, and Wisconsin, and Indiana, Michigan State, and Ohio State universities. The sections in this chapter on institution building rest heavily upon the literature produced by this group, especially:

Melvin G. Blase, *Institution Building: A Source Book* (Beverly Hills, CA: Sage Publications, 1972).

Milton J. Esman, "The Institution Building Concepts – An Interim Appraisal," mimeographed, produced as part of the Inter-University Program in Institution Building (Pittsburgh: University of Pittsburgh, 1967).

Milton J. Esman, "Building Institutions for Management Development," *Interregional Seminar on the Use of Modern Management Techniques in the Public Administration of Developing Countries*, Vol. 2, Add. 3, Sales No. E/F/S. 71. II. H. 8 (New York: United Nations, 1971).

George F. Gant, "The Institution Building Project," *International Review of Administrative Science* 32, no. 3 (1966): 1–8.

Hiram S. Phillips, *Guide for Development: Institution Building and Reform* (New York: Praeger, 1969).

Donald Woods, *Institution Building: A Model for Applied Social Change* (Cambridge, MA: General Learning Press, 1972).

There is a wealth of literature relevant to the economic and social components of the development process. The World Bank's *World Development Report, 1978* (New York: Oxford University Press, 1978) is a review of the progress and current status of developing countries with a very useful annex of "World Development Indicators." Everett E. Hagen's studies are among the best. They include *On the Theory of Social Change: How Economic Growth Begins* (Homewood, IL: Dorsey, 1962) and *The Economics of Development* (Homewood, IL: Richard D. Irwin, 1975). On the importance of human factors, reference may be made to Irma Adelman and Cynthia Taft Morris. *Economic Growth and Social Equity in Developing Countries* (Stanford, CA: Stanford University Press, 1973) and Gunnar Myrdal's monumental *Asian Drama: An Inquiry into the Poverty of Nations*, 3 vols. (New York: Pantheon, 1968); see also his *Challenge of World Poverty* (New York: Vintage Books, 1970).

With respect to traditional administrative systems, and political systems as well, the following are particularly helpful:

A.L. Adu, *The Civil Service in New African States* (New York: Praeger, 1965).

Harold Alderfer, *Public Administration in Newer Nations* (New York: Praeger, 1967).

Gabriel A. Almond and James S. Coleman, eds., *The Politics of Developing Areas* (Princeton: Princeton University Press, 1962).

Ralph J. Braibanti, ed., *Asian Bureaucratic Systems Emergent from the British Imperial Tradition* (Durham, NC: Duke University Press, 1966).

Ferrel Heady, *Publics Administration: A Comparative Perspective* (Englewood Cliffs, NJ: Prentice-Hall, 1966).

Popular Participation in Decision Making for Development, Sales No. E. 75. IV. 10 (New York: United Nations, 1975).

Lucian W. Pye, *Aspects of Political Development* (Boston: Little, Brown, 1966).

The requirements of nation-building departments in order to meet the obligations of administration for development are referred to in the works listed below:

Appraising Administrative Capability for Development, Sales No. E. 69. II. H. 2 (New York: United Nations, 1969).

George F. Gant, "A Note on Applications of Development Administration," *Public Policy* 15 (1966): 199–211.

Kenneth J. Rothwell, *Administrative Issues in Developing Economies* (Lexington, MA: Heath, 1972).

Albert Waterston, *Development Planning: Lessons of Experience* (Baltimore: Johns Hopkins University Press, 1969).

NOTES

1. World Bank, *World Development Report, 1978* (New York: Oxford University Press, 1978), p. 7.

THE COMPARATIVE ADMINISTRATION GROUP, DEVELOPMENT ADMINISTRATION, AND ANTIDEVELOPMENT

Brian Loveman

In the years after World War II, the idea of 'development' replaced progress and utopia as a synonym for the good life. This change in nomenclature brought human beings no closer to agreement concerning the process and character of development than they had been in defining progress or utopia in the past.[1] Even the more generally shared values associated with development – adequate nutritional levels, health care, shelter, and life expectancy – are challenged, at least in the short run, by those who claim that feeding and providing health care for the world proletariat creates further problems for human-kind.

Further, the efforts to define and then bring about development have been complicated by the confrontation between proponents of seemingly incompatible ideological prescriptions offering alternative visions of the good life. On the one hand, Marxist Leninists offer a teleological process that culminates, theoretically, in a society in which poverty, exploitation, alienation, and the nation state apparatus itself disappear. Human beings "become accustomed to the observance of the elementary rules of social life that have

Comparative Public Administration: The Essential Readings
Research in Public Policy Analysis and Management, Volume 15, 287–296
Copyright © 2006 by Elsevier Ltd.
All rights of reproduction in any form reserved
ISSN: 0732-1317/doi:10.1016/S0732-1317(06)15010-1

been known for centuries and repeated for thousands of years in all school books; they will become accustomed to observing them without force, without compulsion, without subordination, without the *special apparatus* for compulsion which is called the state."[2]

Variations in the Marxist–Leninist model of development incorporate national idiosyncrasies and theoretical refinements but share the basic objectives spelled out by Marx and Lenin: an end to class society through the development of productive forces; raising of political consciousness; an end to the social division of labor; and, ultimately, the withering away of the state. For, while the state exists there is no freedom; when there is freedom, there will be no state. To achieve these objectives, however, requires an indeterminate period of transition during which the means of production become the common property of all and the socialists "demand the *strictest* control *by society and by the state,* of the quantity of labor and the quantity of consumption ..."[3] In short, development toward the higher stages of communism must be administered – that is ordered through decrees, administrative regulations, and implementation. Human behavior must be controlled by reference to hierarchically imposed rules of conduct enforced by "society and the state."

In contrast to the Marxist–Leninist vision of the good life, Western liberal democracy and social democracy offer the material progress and pluralism of the variants of modified capitalist economies (i.e., regulated markets and some government policies for redistribution, including social security, public health services, public education, unemployment insurance, and so on). While rejecting the Marxist assumption that private ownership of the means of production is necessarily incompatible with development, the contemporary liberal vision of the good life also recognizes a need for an expanded role of administrative institutions to regulate "market imperfections" in countries seeking to achieve economic and political development.

In the United States, in particular, a concern to find a non-Marxist definition of development gave rise to collaboration between those making and implementing foreign policy, private foundations, and academic specialists in economics, political science, and public administration. From this concern emerged in 1960 the Comparative Administration Group (CAG), which focused attention upon "administrative development" and "development administration." In the words of Fred Riggs:

> The CAG consisted largely of scholars who had served on technical cooperation missions in many parts of the third world, under conditions which showed the accepted administrative doctrines of American practice to be severely limited in their applicability to different cultural situations. It was natural, consequently, that the members of the CAG

would be keenly interested in the revision of these doctrines on the basis of an improved understanding of the forces affecting administrative behavior in these countries.[4]

Over the next decade, the CAG elaborated a conceptualization of administrative development and development administration that has been reviewed, critiqued, and attacked on a variety of grounds.[5] In fairness, it must be noted that the individual scholars associated with the CAG did *not* represent a unified intellectual or organizational whole. Thus, no effort to synthesize "the" CAG literature can avoid neglecting the differences of approach and emphases within the CAG. Recognizing this problem, it is still possible to identify the major themes of "administrative development" and "development administration" that were set out by certain members of the CAG and further elaborated by other American scholars who came to share the basic theoretical and doctrinal assumptions of "administrative development" and "development administration."

According to Fred Riggs, the focus of the development administration literature was the methods used by large-scale organization, notably governments, to implement policies and plans to meet their developmental objectives and the strengthening of administrative capabilities. Since inadequate administrative capabilities inhibited development administration, administrative development was a necessary condition for effective development administration. Most of the scholars within the CAG assumed that intentional instrumental action by officials of the nation state, i.e., administrators, could induce development and, even more, that the degree to winch societies, through political and administrative action, could change their own environments was a measure of the extent to which development had occurred. Thus development meant the expansion of a government's capabilities "to reshape its physical, human, and cultural environment."[6]

All this further assumed that administrative development and development administration were compatible with United States foreign policy; that since development would lessen the chance of interest demanded development in the Third World. Thus John T. Dorsey, Jr., described United States efforts to promote "political development" in South Vietnam and David S. Brown pointed to the accomplishments of American technical assistance in public administration (administrative development) as represented in "the placing of public administration advisers in more than fifty countries, the undertaking of several hundred projects in administrative improvement, and the training of several thousand officials in the United States ... ."[7]

These orientations led, as we will see, to a United States foreign policy and an academic literature (including some authored by CAG members) that supported highly authoritarian and military regimes as the "only" or "best" administrators of development in the Third World. Despite the explicit commitment of most CAG members to Western liberal democracy, the generally shared conception of administrative development and development administration led logically to the conclusions of Milton Esman: "Much of the change desired today must be induced, and therefore managed."[8] In short, development must be administered.

While the CAG largely ignored basic questions posed by the Marxist–Leninist model of development, including the deliberate, administered reshaping of human values in order to make a particular vision of the good life widely shared and desired,[9] the assumption that development can and must be administered was no different than the assumptions of the Marxist–Leninists.[10] Thus, Esman's contention that "far-reaching and purposeful social change usually requires the sustained initiative of relatively small energetic and cohesive groups," comes quite close to Lenin's call in "What Is to Be Done?" for a revolutionary elite to act as the vanguard of the proletariat in bringing about socialist development.[11] As Alfred Diamant neatly summed up: "A great many students of the politics of the new states have identified the primary need of these states to be acquiring the capacity to marshal men and resources for the development tasks by any means at their disposal ... we have obviously identified a process of marshalling resources by an elite."[12] As Diamant accurately foresaw, "administrative development" and "development administration" came more and more to mean expanded state control and manipulation of human beings. Indeed, development administration meant "mobilizing human resources" (that is, human beings) and the expanded capability of the state to "reshape its physical, human, and cultural environment."

These euphemisms contained implicit authoritarian (if not totalitarian) assumptions, which were no more consistent with the liberal democratic values of most of those participating in the CAG than with Lenin's *State and Revolution*. Yet, in practice, administrative development and development administration have meant progressively increased state and bureaucratic control over individual human beings.

THE ADMINISTRATION OF DEVELOPMENT: THE PARADOX OF CAG-AID AND LIBERAL DEMOCRACY

For most members of the CAG, development administration involved no (explicit) teleological vision, but rather "organized efforts to carry out programs or projects thought by those involved to serve developmental objectives." The better human societies were able to carry out "developmental objectives" through development administration; "... the essential idea of development lies in this increased ability of human societies [as collectivities] to shape their physical, human, and cultural environment." Thus, "development administration refers not only to a government's efforts to carry out programs designed to reshape its physical human and cultural environment, but also to the struggle to enlarge a government's capacity to engage in such programs."[13]

This sort of formulation by an intellectual who in other writings made clear his own democratic values led to both theoretical and practical dilemmas – as Riggs himself had earlier recognized.[14] For despite disclaimers by some, limited government and constitutional rule, or what John Montgomery referred to as "political democracy" *did* provide an underlying political morality for most of the members of the CAG although they were not so forthright about it as Montgomery: "Western contributions may be as important for their moral and teleological components as for their capital and technical infrastructure."[15]

If development administration required increasing government control over resources and human beings, how could development in the Third World be made compatible with liberal democracy or "Western political morality?" Riggs attempted to wrestle with this problem, suggesting that a strong "constitutive system" might exercise substantial power and impose effective control over the bureaucracy.[16] But the fragile distinction between politics and administration, or "constitutive system" and "bureaucracy" did nothing to reconcile the underlying incompatibility between a government ever more capable of shaping the physical, human, and cultural environments, and the fundamental values of individual liberty and limits upon state authority and power – the cornerstone of liberal democracy. It became evident, then, as Carl Friedrich pointed out, that the dilemmas of development were both quite like those of modern government in general and also another way of referring to a set of issues with which classical political philosophy had wrestled since "the beginning."[17]

Just as the Marxist–Leninist theorists sought to administer the development of productive forces in order to create a society of abundance, so the CAG and other social scientists interested in development and development administration were concerned with economic growth. This concern was founded upon the three interrelated assumptions: (1) economic growth (increasing per capita product or income) would reduce poverty and provide a larger array of goods and services to Third World peoples; (2) economic growth with rising average incomes would, ultimately, be compatible with, and even provide support for, liberal democracy, "economic autonomy," and a situation in which "more of the representative individual's time and income become discretionary ..."[18] and (3) that these processes of development (economic growth and liberal democracy) would "contain communism." Thus development administration and administrative development were linked to the strategy of containment.

The CAG – both through the members' own participation in United States international programs to induce "development" and by elaborating an academic ideology of development – provided an intellectual grounding for American foreign policy in the 1960s. With the failure of liberal democratic regimes to develop, it gradually became clear that United States policy and the CAG would have to make ever more explicit the relationship between growth, liberal democracy, anti-Marxism, and a strategy giving first priority to political stability – which would, when achieved, be the foundation for economic growth and democracy. For this to occur, however, an intermediate or parallel problem of "administrative development" had to be resolved.

Administrative development had to precede effective development administration; any concern for constraints on bureaucratic authority had to be subordinated to the need to create effective administrative instruments. As Esman stated:

> To a number of scholars, including this writer, the emphasis on control of bureaucracy in the context of most of the developing countries is a misplaced priority, one that might seriously retard their rate of progress. We ought to be much more concerned with increasing the capacity of the bureaucracy to perform, and this we see as a function of greatly enhanced professional capabilities and operational autonomy rather than further controls.[19]

The implications of Esman's analysis for American foreign policy and for development administration became evident only gradually over the course of the 1960s. But the course of future "development" was foreshadowed in a set of papers published in 1962 concerning the role of the military in "underdeveloped" countries. In this volume Lucian Pye noted that in large measure the story of the third world "is one of countless efforts to create organizations by which resources can be effectively mobilized for achieving new objectives" (i.e., administrative development), and that "the acculturative process in the army tends to be focused on acquiring skills that are of particular value for economic development." Pye concluded that "the military stand out because in a disrupted society they represent the only effectively organized element capable of ... formulating public policy." Pye also argued that we should not be biased by our Western values and see the military, necessarily, as a "foe of liberal values." While Pye emphasized the need to pay attention to it the "growth of responsible and representative politicians," he concluded that "the military in the underdeveloped countries can make a major contribution to strengthening essentially administrative functions."[20]

There was the answer to the CAG's (and United States policymakers') quest for an administrative elite to carry out development administration: the military. This answer emerged despite the warning of certain other academic specialists in "development" that "where the goal-setting and goal-implementing bureaucracy is military rather than civil, the prospects for democratic political development are ... dismal ..."[21] Thus, a revisionist view of military regimes came to dominate much American and Third World thinking about development administration the military represented a "stabilizing force;" a 'modernizing force," and a reservoir of the administrative and technological skills needed for development administration.[22]

By the 1970s administrative development and development administration had become euphemisms for autocratic, frequently military, rule that, admittedly, sometimes induced industrialization, modernization, and even economic growth. But this occurred at a great cost in the welfare of the rural and urban poor and substantial erosion if not deletion of the political freedoms associated with liberal democracy. The substance of Esman's recommendations – to be less concerned with control of the development administrators and more concerned with the capabilities of these elites to carry out developmental objectives – was heeded by United States policymakers.

Brazil, Iran, and South Korea became the showcases of development administration. These nations achieved very high economic growth rates, rapid industrialization, and modernization – accompanied by expansion of the capabilities of the state apparatus to "reshape" the human environment, especially through terror, institutionalized torture and repression of the opposition in a style (if not on a magnitude) to leave Stalin no room for envy. Economic growth, instead of bringing increased welfare and democratization, intensified inequalities, made the poorest even poorer, and concentrated power in the hands of the administrative elites that "administrative development" and "development administration" sought to establish.[23]

ACHIEVEMENTS AND CONSTRAINTS

Like the administrators of socialist development administration, authoritarian civilian regimes and, more frequently, military regimes that have come to dominate almost all the "beneficiary nations" of the United States-AID-CAG programs of administrative development and development administration, have beers able to stimulate industrial growth, although in a much less consistent manner than in the socialist nations. The progressively more authoritarian rule of these regimes is also similar to the coercion of induced modernization in Eastern Europe and China. Moreover, in general, the rural labor force (and to a lesser extent, the urban workers) have paid the costs of capital accumulation, while military and civilian administrative elites and industrialists concentrate the benefits of economic growth. But while socialist development administration at least provides more equal access to public services (health care, education, and so on) and the basic nutritional needs of human beings, the development administration inspired by the United States-AID-CAG doctrines reinforced or increased income disparities and inequality of access to life-chance opportunities, and actually made the poorest even poorer in absolute terms.

If the inefficiency of the socialist development model leads to repressed consumer demand and uneconomic utilization of resources and labor, the CAG model of development and modernization has led to extreme unemployment problems and increased impoverishment of the worst off among the working classes of the Third World. If we return to Dudley Seers' criteria of development cited earlier (eliminating or reducing poverty, unemployment, and inequality), we are forced to conclude that the development administration which the United States-AID-CAG inspired has *often* led to antidevelopment, supporting the thesis of many dependency theorists that "underdevelopment" is caused by particular patterns of capitalist development."[24] By the criteria widely shared within the CAG itself, the focus upon administrative development and development administration has *nowhere* led to the liberal democracy or even to liberalization. Instead, it has led to progressively more authoritarian (and generally no more efficient) regimes.

It would appear from the evidence so far accumulated that the CAG-posited linkage between administrative development and development administration has produced little more than physical facilities (dams, roads, bridges, hospitals etc.) accompanied by restrictions upon human liberty and freedom. It has increased the capabilities of nation-states to reshape the physical, human, and cultural environment – but most of the human beings whose environment or bodies, in the case of regimes with systematic torture of political prisoners, are reshaped in these "free-world" nations have very little discretion over the way in which the state does its "reshaping." Administrative development has led to further control of state institutions over human beings; to further coercion of human beings; but not to development in any meaningful human sense. Beyond certain superficial material achievements, development administration *a la* CAG has merely demonstrated on a lesser scale than in the Soviet Union, Germany, or Eastern Europe that factories, public works, and labor camps can be administered – but not the good life.

While this is clearly not the place to propose alternative strategies for attaining the good life, the discussion in this article at least calls into question the results we can expect from "development administration." Though administration is a necessary condition for development, development cannot be administered. For development to occur, not only must subsistence needs to be met, but the initiative of individual human beings must be encouraged. Human beings must be able to rethink and redefine their own values and the conditions of their daily lives. Human choice must be expanded. This cannot take place to great extent when government administrators continually increase their capabilities to "reshape" the physical, human, and cultural environment – at their discretion.

NOTES

1. In a special issue on "Development Indicators" of the *Journal of Development Studies* (April 1972), 11 authors compile well over 100 measures of "development." Dudley Seers ("What Are We Trying to Measure?") remarks that development is almost a synonym for improvement; lie goes on to define development, at a minimum, as reducing poverty, unemployment, and inequality. Seers' normative focus on distribution of life chance opportunities is a refreshing break with the too common focus upon "objective" indicators such as gross national product, energy consumption, newspapers per capita, and so on. Still, it remains exceedingly difficult to specify abstract criteria of development independent of a knowledge of the values, living conditions, and dreams of the human beings whom elite policy makers and academics hope to mobilize for "developmental objectives."

2. V.I. Lenin, *State and Revolution* (International Publishers, 1971), p. 74.

3. *Ibid.*, pp. 79–80.

4. Fred W. Riggs (ed), *Frontiers of Development Administration*, "Introduction" (Durham, NC: Duke University Press, 1971), p. 5.

5. See, for example, Abdo Baakiini, "Comparative Administration, the Persistence of an Ideology," *Journal of Comparative Administration* (May 1973); J.G. Gunnell, "Development, Social Change, and Time," in D. Waldo (ed.), *Temporal Dimensions of Development Administration* (Durham, NC: Duke University Press, 1970), pp. 47–89; W.F. Ilchman, "Comparative Public Administration and Conventional Wisdom," *Sage Professional Papers in Comparative Politics* (1971); (ed.), *Politics and Change in Developing Countries* (Cambridge: Cambridge University Press, 1969), pp. 177–211; Joseph La Palombara, "Political Science and the Engineering of National Development," in Monte Palmer and Larry Stern (eds.), *Political Development in Changing Societies* (Lexington, Mass: Heath Lexington, 1971), pp. 27–65; and William J. Siffin, "Two Decades of Public Administration in

Developing Countries An American's View," International Development Research Center (Indiana University, 1974).

6. Fred W. Riggs, "The Context of Development Administration, in Riggs (ed.), pp. 74–75.

7. John T. Dorsey, "The Bureaucracy and Political Development in Vietnam," in Joseph La Palombara (ed.), *Bureaucracy and Political Development* (Princeton, NJ: Princeton University Press, 1963), pp. 318–359; David S. Brown, "Strategies and Tactics of Public Administration Assistance: 1945–1963," in J.D. Montgomery and W.J. Siffin (eds), *Approaches to Development* (New York: McGraw-Hill, 1966), p. 219.

8. Milton J. Esman, "CAG and the Study of Public Administration, in Riggs, (ed.), p. 71.

9. An important exception to this was Gideon Sjoberg "Ideology and Social Organization in Rapidly Developing Societies," in Fred Riggs (ed.), pp. 274–301.

10. Of course the Marxist–Leninist emphasis upon a strong centralized party and party auxiliaries trade union leaders, intellectuals, women, youth leaders, and so on), differs somewhat from the CAG emphasis on administrative elites.

11. Milton J. Esman, "The Politics of Development Administration," in John D. Montgomery and William J. Siffin (eds.), p. 72.

12. Alfred Diamant, "The Temporal Dimension in Models of Administration and Organization," in Dwight Waldo (ed.), pp. 131–132.

13. Riggs, "The Context Development Administration," pp. 73–75.

14. Fred W. Riggs, "Bureaucrats and Political Development, a Paradoxial View," in Joseph La Palombara (ed.), pp. 120–167.

15. John D. Montgomery, "A Royal Invitation: Variations on Three Classic Themes," in Montgomery and Siffin (eds.), pp. 292, 294.

16. Fred W. Riggs, "The Structures of Government and Administrative Reform," in Ralph Braibanti (ed.), *Political and Administrative Development* (Durham, NC: Duke University Press, 1969), p. 244.

17. Carl J. Friedrich, "Political Development and the Objectives of Modern Government," in Braibanti (ed.), pp. 107–135.

18. See Joseph J. Spengler, "Allocation and Development, Economic and Political," in Braibanti (ed.), pp. 588, 611–612.

19. Esman, "CAG and the Study of the Public Administration," p. 62.

20. Lucian W. Pye, "Armies in the Process of Political Modernization," in John J. Johnson (ed.), *The Role of the Military in Underdeveloped Countries* (Princeton, NJ: Princeton University Press, 1962), pp. 80–89.

21. Joseph La Palombara, "An Overview of Bureaucracy and Political Development," in La Palombara (ed.), p. 33.

22. See John P. Lovell, "Military Dominated Regimes and Political Development: A Critique of Some Revisionist Views," in M. Palmer and L. Stern (eds), pp. 159–179; Eric Nordlinger, "Soldiers in Mufti: The Impact of Military Rule upon Economic and Social Change in the Non-Western States," *American Political Science Review,* Vol. 64 (December 1970), pp. 1131–1148.

23. See, for example, Alfred Stephan (ed.), *Authoritarian Brazil* (New Haven: Yale University Press, 1973); Marvin Zonis, *The political Elite of Iran* (Princeton, NJ: Princeton University Press, 1971).

24. See, for example, the collection of essays in James D. Cockcroft, et al., *Dependence and Underdevelopment* (Anchor, 1972).

NEOTERIC THEORIES FOR DEVELOPMENT ADMINISTRATION IN THE NEW WORLD ORDER

Jean-Claude Garcia-Zamor

The problems of public administration in developing countries are so vastly different from those of the developed world that a new discipline, development administration, has emerged since the 1960s to study them. Although a large number of books and articles have been written on the subject, questions still persist as to whether such a discipline exists or is necessary.[1] Nevertheless, development has become a major focus of administrative activity in the countries of the Third World.[2] The industrialized societies have recognized the need for these countries to gear their administrative machinery to new developmental tasks and responsibilities. The mounting external debts of the Latin American, African, and Asian countries have lent a new urgency to the problems of administrative reorganization and reform.

In 1976, the Section on International and Comparative Administration (SICA) of the American Society for Public Administration (ASPA) published a paper entitled "Development Administration: Background, Terms, Concepts, Theories, and a New Approach." Its author, Richard W. Gable of the University of California at Davis, reviewed the basic literature in the field and traced the development of the concepts and practice from the U.S. experience with technical assistance and scholarly interest in comparative administration (Gable, 1976). Gable's excellent paper presented a strategy

Comparative Public Administration: The Essential Readings
Research in Public Policy Analysis and Management, Volume 15, 297–320
Copyright © 2006 by Elsevier Ltd.
ISSN: 0732-1317/doi:10.1016/S0732-1317(06)15011-3

for administrative change toward a "new" development administration. That new strategy was a tacit recognition that external assistance is indispensable for public organizations and institutions of the Third World. The earlier theories, most of them reviewed by Gable, were written by American scholars who had started or pursued their interests in the working of developing countries' administrative structures while bringing assistance sponsored by the United States or United Nations to these countries. These earlier theorists, all members of the Comparative Administration Group (CAG) led by Fred Riggs and operating within ASPA, were so convinced of the indispensability of foreign aid for the functioning of the Third World bureaucracies that they responded in a fashion consistent with that conviction when their own "external" funding from the Ford Foundation was terminated: CAG simply ceased to exist; fortunately, it was replaced by SICA. Although the termination of the Ford grant was the main reason for CAG's demise, many of the early theorists blame it on the lack of a clear definition of the parameters of the emerging field. Keith Henderson, Lee Sigelman, Garth N. Jones, Jamil E. Jreisat, and several others made that point in their writings (Heady, 1984, pp. 25–26). As that early period was one of searching for definition and identity, a variety of CAG writers, among them Jong S. Jun and Milton J. Esman, contributed enormously to the establishment of comparative and development administration as a distinct discipline. However, Fred Riggs and others were already questioning the relevance of the field in 1970. Garth N. Jones went even further. He criticized the U.S. Agency for International Development (AID) for its lack of viable doctrine and policy of expediency. He viewed AID as overbureaucratized and lacking in imagination and risk-taking capability (Jones, 1970).

Interestingly enough, the bureaucrats of the developing countries were the most vocal supporters of the dependency approach.[3] They questioned why capitalist development, which had occurred in the United States and Western Europe, had not taken place in the Third World. In their efforts to obtain more and more foreign aid, they deliberately presented an image of being unable to cope by themselves with the tasks of development. Lacking in funding and strategies for responding to this challenge, international donors have limited their actions to timid innovations such as expounding the virtues of public participation in the planning and executing of projects (Garcia-Zamor, 1985). However, a recent work by Derick W. Brinkerhoff, focusing on program management, draws some systematic lessons for improving the sustainability of development program performance (Brinkerhoff, 1991).

Another factor that inhibited the development of the discipline was the inability of some American scholars to see the relevance of foreign aid to U.S. domestic programs. As early as 1969, John D. Montgomery compared the U.S. foreign aid program to its domestic aid program. He concluded that poverty and the promise of development are the common elements in programs of foreign and domestic aid. He also concluded that the foreign aid program had operational advantages over the fragmented domestic aid program and that the procedures developed by AID employed a higher level of programming skill than that available to other government agencies (Montgomery, 1971, pp. 469-470).

However, students at American universities have been reluctant to enroll in development administration seminars, viewing them as irrelevant to the core concerns of public administration. This attitude has prompted some scholars to emphasize similarities between the tasks of the developing countries' bureaucracies and those of poor municipal and county governments in the industrialized countries (Goodsell, 1981). In both situations, the struggling bureaucracy finds itself dependent on external technical assistance and financing to develop projects and programs and to deliver services. While in the developing countries such external assistance is provided by international institutions such as the World Bank and the International Monetary Fund, as well as "donor countries," in the municipal and county governments of the United States, the dependency is on state and federal assistance. In both cases, the recipient governments are subjected to an array of restrictions that often limit the capability of their bureaucracies to give priority to the urgent needs of their communities. However, one thing is quite clear: the tasks of these bureaucracies to promote development would not be possible without outside assistance.

This decade has started with a dramatic change in the geopolitical alignment of the world, and this chapter will examine whether the existing approach to development administration should be revised to be more relevant to this New World Order.

THE NEW WORLD ORDER

After President George Bush coined the phrase "New World Order," he tried to articulate it in terms that would infuse a new sense of mission to America. He seemed to regard instability abroad as a danger for America.[4] Although President Bush wanted to continue the U.S. internationalist policies of the last forty-five years, Americans and the Congress tended to lurch between isolationism and idealism. But as the Cold War has wound down, there can be little doubt that a New World Order is emerging that creates challenges for the United States and other Western nations that might be equal to those that existed when world politics turned on the confrontation between East and West. Unfortunately, most of the attention has been focused on the major events that created the New World Order: the dramatic dismantling of the Berlin Wall, the fall of communism in Eastern Europe and in the former Soviet Union, and the resurgence from their remains of independent republics. It appears that the 1990s will see foreign aid both from the United States and from the other Western countries going primarily to help establish free-market economies in the former communist countries.

An underlying concern in the West is the control of the Soviet nuclear arsenal. At the present time 80 percent of the Soviet strategic nuclear weapons are located in the Russian Republic, and the remainder are deployed in Ukraine, Byelorussia, and Kazakhstan. Tactical nuclear weapons are distributed more evenly across the republics. In 1991, the U.S. government provided $400 million for the dismantling of nuclear weapons deployed in Ukraine and Kazakhstan.

Although the bulk of U.S. foreign assistance has been provided only to five countries over the past decade,[5] many of the countries of Latin America, Africa, and Asia were receiving substantial U.S. assistance before the rise of the New World Order. These countries stand to lose a sizable portion of that aid. Other political developments are contributing to the diminishing interest being shown to these nations (Berg & Gordon, 1989; Hellinger, Hellinger, & O'Regan, 1988; Schraeder, 1992).

In the New World Order, the former Soviet Union has become primarily a recipient of foreign aid rather than a donor (to Cuba, the Warsaw Pact countries, and African states leaning toward communism). Among the major donors, the individual Western European states might soon coordinate their strategies to operate within the new European Community. Thus, in the New World Order, this chapter identifies five major groups of recipients: (1) Latin America, (2) Africa, (3) Asia, (4) Eastern Europe, and (5) the former Soviet Union. Among the international donors, this chapter identifies three: (1) the United States, (2) the European Community, and (3) the World Bank. This new grouping of recipients and donors reflects the fact that, while the pool of recipients has grown considerably, the pool of donors has shrunk. More importantly, the new geopolitical alignment of some countries has shifted the interests and motivation of donors, who might want to relocate their grants to maximize the "return on their investments."

Needless to say, in the face of this new reality, the bureaucracies of Latin America, Africa, and Asia – the traditional recipients of foreign aid – will need to design new approaches to development administration. Following is a brief review of recipients and donors in the New World Order.

THE MAJOR RECIPIENTS

Latin America

In 1980, 12 of the 18 countries of Latin America were governed by military regimes. The United States often supported these regimes because of their fierce anticommunist stands. The free market system even flourished under some of them (e.g., Chile). However, with these countries now governed by democratically elected presidents and with the disappearance of the Soviet threat, U.S. economic assistance has shifted. The fear of communism has been superseded by the fear of drugs. The meager aid that was previously provided in the form of military assistance is now going to fight the perceived new regional threats to the vital interests of the United States: drug trafficking, massive immigration, and environmental degradation.[6] However, the bureaucracies of these countries continue to lack the resources needed to develop the projects that could counteract these new threats and improve social and economic conditions. In Brazil, one-third of the population lives in poverty while 1 percent controls 60 percent of the country's wealth. In Venezuela, currently about 43 percent of the population, compared with 18 percent in 1987, makes less than $130 a month. Considering the fact that an increase in oil revenue helped the Venezuelan economy to grow at an estimated rate of 9.2 percent in 1991, those statistics dramatize the polarization between the wealthy and the poor in Third World countries at a time when their economies seemed to be growing. The deteriorating economy prompted the Venezuelan military to attempt a coup in early 1993. Costa Rica has a foreign debt of $3.5 billion, in a country of only 3 million citizens, and is dependent on foreign credit to service that debt. Thus, the largest country of the region and two of the most stable ones have joined the others in increasing the uncertainty of the future of the poor in Latin America. With Castro's ability to pose a threat severely diminished by the events in Russia, the Sandinistas out of power, peace in Central America, and democracy prevailing in the region, Latin America stands to lose the priority for foreign developmental aid. Except for token gestures to Nicaragua and Panama, toward which the United States justly feels some responsibility, any aid going to the region will be targeted to curbing drug production and export.

Africa

Faced with the specter of pouring money into a bottomless pit, Western aid donors, together with the World Bank and the International Monetary Fund, have used the threat of a cutoff in financial support to encourage domestic disenchantment with state control of economic activity. Strengthened by the wave of democracy that swept through Eastern Europe and the end of the Cold War, Africans have been demanding changes in their political systems. A half-dozen leaders have been forced out of office during the past four years, and at least sixteen others have grudgingly legalized opposition parties. Unfortunately, unlike the people of the former Soviet Union, Africans do not have Western industrialized nations enthralled with their struggle, eager to pour billions of dollars into an effort to avert hunger that could threaten freedom in its infancy. The United Nations recently reported that Western efforts to help Africa shake off disease, debt, hunger, and endemic crises during the past five years have been a failure (*Miami Herald*, January 5, 1992, p. 23A). Africa might end up being the big loser in the New World Order. This is most unfortunate, especially as newly published data showed that their trade has worsened by almost 25 percentage points over the past decade (United Nations Development Program, 1991, p. 4).

The countries of Latin America and Africa, except for a few exceptions, have too little to offer and lack too much economic infrastructure to be able to use the New World Order to their advantage. For them, the New World Order will go the way the "New World Economic Order" went after it was promulgated in 1974.

Asia

Several of the countries of the region are emerging from their underdevelopment. Four of them – Taiwan, Hong Kong, Singapore, and South Korea – have benefited from their cheap labor and some value-added export strategies to dominate exports to other Asian countries as well as the rest of the world. South Korea is probably the first country to be successful in reversing its brain drain. Several of its citizens who have succeeded abroad have been enticed back to take top managerial positions in the private sector. These four countries have a disciplined workforce, but the key factor in their growth has been entrepreneurship. Their success has inspired other countries of the region to follow their path. A new foursome is already emerging to compete for a share in the export trade: Indonesia, Malaysia, Thailand, and, to a somewhat lesser extent, the Philippines. Some people believe that, as its political system has now stabilized, Vietnam may soon join them. The leader of the new pack is Thailand, which has the fastest-growing economy in the world – at about 10 percent a year. These nations' success, based on deeply ingrained cultural values, will be difficult to duplicate in the rest of the Third World. Nevertheless, lessons can be learned from it.

Japan is in a class by itself. It has a $41 billion trade surplus with the United States. It has established tariffs and marketing obstacles that make most American products extremely difficult to sell in Japan. In addition to their manufacturing excellence, the Japanese have utilized basic education as a source of economic power. As in the cases of South Korea and Singapore, domestic and external competition has very often spurred innovation, the diffusion of technology, and an efficient use of resources. These countries have established a global competitive advantage through the rigors of competition (World Bank, 1991, p. 7).

Asia will be better off in the New World Order since it may acquire new markets for its exports. Although the countries of the Pacific Rim are not yet significantly involved in foreign assistance, except for Japan,[7] they will probably end up dominating the world economy in the next decade. These Asian countries stand to benefit from the new geopolitical alignment in the world.

Eastern Europe

In 1989, the U.S. Congress passed the East European Democracy Act to help the emerging democracies of Eastern Europe. In the fiscal year 1990–1991, the United States provided assistance of $2.1–12 billion to Central and Eastern Europe. That assistance was primarily through grants, rather than debt forgiveness, long-term credits and the like, which some other nations use, largely because the United States believed that the grants better protected the fragile economies of the region. This policy was based on what former U.S. secretary of state James Baker called the "new democratic differentiation." In 1991 and 1992, American programs were designed to support democratic and free-market reforms and were tailored to meet the needs of the countries as they moved toward the following four objectives:

(1) political pluralism, including free and fair elections;
(2) economic reforms through the development of a market economy, with a dynamic private sector;
(3) respect for internationally recognized human rights; and
(4) the desire of the country to enter into a friendly relationship with the United States.

The United States is presently providing assistance in three broad areas, with a major priority in each to improve trade vital to the region's economic development.

Democratic Initiatives
This area accounted for 7–9 percent of assistance provided. Aid is granted to encourage the development of institutions and practices of democratic pluralistic societies, based on Western values of human rights and individual freedoms.

Economic Restructuring
About 70 percent of assistance went for the transformation of centrally planned economies into market-based economies that are led by the private sector and integrated into the world economy.

Quality of Life
Roughly 17–19 percent of assistance was for improving the basic quality of life through medical and food assistance (ACIPA, 1991).[8] The massive U.S. assistance toward consolidating democracy in Eastern Europe has had mixed immediate results. In the case of Poland, the privatization of small businesses has been a success. Seventy-five percent of shops and 43 percent of the construction industry are now in private hands. Private enterprise currently accounts for 30 percent of all economic activity, compared to 3 percent under communism. Eighty to 85 percent of industrial output, however, remains in the hands of some 7,000 state-owned factories. Almost all of these factories are money-losers, and at least 100 of them have gone completely bankrupt. Poland's gross domestic product, the main indicator of a nation's economic health, was expected to drop by 3.7 percent in 1991 (*Miami Herald*, December 1, 1991, p. 3L).

In Bulgaria, the situation is the same. It was the first former Warsaw Pact country to adopt a new constitution modeled on Western democratic principles, and it is the first to hold a second round of open, free elections. Bulgaria has also adopted one of the strictest economic reform packages in Eastern Europe. However, the nation is in serious economic trouble. Inflation in 1990 reached 400 percent, and many goods are in short supply. Unemployment has skyrocketed, as inefficient state enterprises have shut their doors and laid off thousands of workers (*Miami Herald*, November 10, 1991, p. 6C).

The situation is similar in most of the Central and Eastern European countries. But U.S. officials are nevertheless optimistic. For one thing, despite these countries' economic woes, their populations have far stronger educational backgrounds than those of prior aid recipients. Therefore, results should come more quickly and be longer lasting. Officials are hoping that aid to the region might no longer be necessary by the end of the 1990s. That would be a welcome change for the donors, who have seen the past forty years of foreign assistance bearing very little fruit.

The Former Soviet Union

The demise of the Soviet Union and the emergence of the independent republics present a challenge to the Western world. A few statistics, gathered before the breakup of the central economy, hint at the depth of the crisis facing these new nations of 286 million people spread across 11 time zones. In the first six months of 1991, gross national product (GNP) fell 10 percent compared with the same period in 1990, hard-currency earnings plummeted with the drop in Soviet oil exports, and inflation ran at about 100 percent. The Soviet economy was in such a shambles in early 1991 that it was exhibiting some characteristics of Fred Riggs's prismatic model (Riggs, 1964, pp. 27–31), a mixture of raw superpower and Third World standards. In fact, it was only the massive nuclear arsenal of the Soviet Union that qualified it as a superpower. Those nuclear warheads became the focus of attention after the breakup of the country. The United States and the Western powers soon demanded their destruction as a condition for foreign aid. Indeed, most of the aid went to disabling and dismantling the former empire's nuclear arsenal. The former superpower was pushed by its former archenemy to accept such targeted aid to qualify for other urgent aid for medical and food supplies.

In 1991, some $400 million was given by Congress to channel assistance to Russia. As usual, as soon as the money was allocated, several government agencies were competing for a piece of the action. In early 1992, President

Bush pledged to ask Congress to provide another $650 million in new tech-
nical assistance and humanitarian aid for the new republics. This new pledge
raised total U.S. aid – in food credits and grants, medical and technical
help, and nuclear disarmament assistance – to over $5 billion.[9] This is an
extraordinary amount of money to stabilize a former enemy's system when
one considers that the Marshall Plan, initiated to help former allies in war,
cost just over $100 million dollars in 1991. Also, in 1947 the United States
was the richest nation in the world. Today it feels comparatively broke. This
broad aid, however, will not necessarily endear the United States to the
Soviet people. After a recent visit there, former secretary of state Henry
Kissinger responded that he experienced an anti-American side of Russian
nationalism when he met in Moscow with a group of "up-and-coming
young Russians. They argue that the United States was taking advantage
of the current situation, and that the term 'New World Order' was highly
presumptuous because it assumed that Russia would no longer be a significant factor in world affairs" (Kissinger, 1992).

THE MAJOR DONORS

The United States

Historically, U.S. foreign aid has always been motivated by national security concerns. When the Berlin Wall tumbled in the autumn of 1989, experts
noted that the end of East–West conflict rendered the main regional threats
to the vital interest of the United States not communism, but rather drug
trafficking, massive immigration, and environmental degradation. Although
the argument was advanced that the best was to counteract these threats
was to improve social and economic conditions in donor countries, the sheer
cost of doing so and the uncertainty of effective results have prompted the
U.S. government to adopt alternative policies. Although it is obvious that
the new massive aid to the Soviets will require the United States to prioritize
anew its entire foreign aid program, no open initiative do so has been aired
by cautious bureaucrats. They fully understand that the name of the game is
politics and they would rather leave it to the politicians (Congress). This is
unfortunate because Congress's yearly brawl over the passage of the foreign
aid bill has clearly demonstrated its incapacity to deal with such a topic in
a dispassionate manner, with only the long-range best interests of the United
States as the sole objective.

Some countries have argued recently that the United States should make more significant cuts in its defense budget to allocate much-needed funds to other domestic and foreign programs. In September 1991, the Brookings Institution recommended in a report that with the end of the Cold War, the United States should slash its military budget by up to 50 percent annually over the coming decade, well beyond the cuts planned by the Defense Department. The report called on the Defense Department to retool its defense investments in light of the nation's new "one superpower status." According to calculations by the privately financed Center for Defense Information, however, after a slight election-year dip to $281 billion (from $284 billion), military funding will increase steadily in current dollars each year until 1997.

In 1991–1992, other urgent economic problems prevented the United States from focusing in any significant way on foreign assistance except for that to the Soviet republics and Eastern Europe. The U.S. economy was in shambles. The country was pinned down by a recession. Unemployment lines were getting longer. In desperation, President Bush was embracing a once-shunned notion, "industrial policy," to stem the nation's shrinking technological edge.[10] In the meantime, new figures released by the U.S. Commerce Department in July 1991 did nothing to change the underlying shift of the United States from its standing as the world's largest creditor country as recently as 1983 to that of the world's largest debtor nation. To complicate even further the bleak economic outlook, a U.S. State Department conference in 1991 predicted that the United States will continue to depend heavily on Middle East oil through the 1990s. A Bush administration eighteen-month study for a new American energy strategy concluded that no feasible combination of domestic or foreign energy policy options can fully relieve the United States of the risks of oil dependency in the next two decades.

The European Community

In December 1991, the twelve nations of the European Community took their boldest step toward creating a united Europe. They approved two wide-ranging treaties that will create a single European currency and move the member countries toward common defense, foreign, and economic policies. It is too early to tell how that will affect the individual countries' present foreign assistance programs. But a logical assumption is that a portion of that external aid will need to be diverted to level off the economies of the less-affluent members of the community. At the present time, Germany is the biggest donor. It has been generous toward the remnants of the former Soviet empire. As in the case of the United States, however, it has acted in its own interests as well by paying Moscow to remove Soviet troops from German soil. Also, Germany, like the United States, faces a financial slump. Germany's five leading economic think tanks produced their grimmest forecasts in years, warning of prolonged budget deficits and rising unemployment, growing government debts, and shrinking trade surplus (*Miami Herald*, November 4, 1991, p. 11A).

The European Community has become a trading bloc richer than the United States, with 350 million people and an estimated gross national product of $6 trillion, compared with a population of roughly 250 million and a GNP of about $5.7 trillion for the United States. Nevertheless, future admission of other small and poor nations into the community will lessen its ability to help Third World countries. Eventually, even the Eastern European countries are expected to join. The attitude of the new Europe to the outside world will be deeply affected, as the countries start turning their backs on the Third World to develop instead a European destiny.

The World Bank

There is little doubt that no other institutions, or countries, possess the combination of money and expertise possessed by the World Bank and its sister institution the International Monetary Fund. The two institutions were created to help restore the economies of Western Europe after World War II. They later funneled more and more of their resources into the development and growth of Latin America, Africa, and Asia and, later, into an international war on poverty. However, with both institutions girding for the massive job of helping Eastern Europe and the former Soviet Union, the Third World countries rightly fear that those nations will draw funds and staff away from traditional recipients.

In its 1991 World Development report, the bank suggests three approaches by which the industrial countries and multilateral agencies, including the bank itself, can strengthen development prospects in developing countries: (1) increase financial support, (2) support policy reform, and (3) encourage sustainable growth. However, no solid figures accompanied the prescribed enhancement in the quantity and quality of external financial assistance. Furthermore, the report clearly states that the developing countries' prospects are principally in their own hands. To assure the benefits of better external conditions, the bank recommends that developing countries undertake domestic reforms in these areas: (1) invest in people, (2) improve the climate for enterprise, (3) open economies to international trade and investment, and (4) get macroeconomic policy right (World Bank, 1991, p. 11). These approaches alone will not succeed, because in the New World Order the developing countries' funding is not being withheld only because of their lack of compliance with structural adjustment programs. The situation is a shifting of the interest of donors from traditional recipients to new ones who offer prospects of a better "political and economic return on their investments."

NEW DECADE, NEW GOALS, NEW APPROACHES

Despite all the talk about a New World Order, those who look for very radical changes in the international strategy for the 1990s will be disappointed. The New World Order strategy does emphasize programs and funding that will consolidate the emerging democracies. As in the past, the solidification of the status quo has always been more appealing than the creation of new conditions. None of the strategic players in the technical assistance area played a role in the events that brought down communism. Those events came about as a result of internal changes provoked by new domestic policies of the countries involved. Therefore, the Third World bureaucracies should learn from that new experience and deemphasize their dependence on foreign technical assistance to create real changes in the Third World. Despite new goals and approaches that regularly have been announced at the beginning of each decade since 1940, the only dramatic change that occurred in Africa and Asia that was provoked by external policies has been the geographical repartition of the two continents into a series of independent states.

The creation of new international forums where meaningful North–South dialogues could take place has not narrowed the gap between the First and the Third Worlds. The World Bank, the International Monetary Fund, and to a certain extent even the regional financial institutions have not allowed the Third World countries to escape the domination of the West. The voting power of the Western nations in these institutions gives them an absolute majority to rule them. At the United Nations, the one-nation/one-vote system in the General Assembly has allowed the emerging countries to have some impact in the programs and strategies of the United Nations Development Programme (UNDP), even though the money still comes from

the West. In addition, it is a matter of legal dispute to what extent any U.N.
or UNDP plan is binding on the member countries.[11]

What then is the solution to the problem of underdevelopment? What
kind of policies can realistically be made at the bureaucratic level?
This chapter suggests a series of new approaches. Not all of them can be
initiated in the bureaucracies. Some vital approaches must come from the
political leadership of the Third World countries. Then, and only then, will
the bureaucracies be able to play a meaningful role in facilitating their
implementation. If and when these new approaches are initiated, international donor aid might become crucial in their successful completion.
Therefore, the approaches prescribed in this chapter are deemphasizing the
present total reliance on external initiatives and replacing it with new strategies conceived by the political leadership of the Third World countries.

Again and again the structural adjustment programs strongly encour
aged by the International Monetary Fund (IMF) and supported by the
World Bank have proven politically and socially disastrous for many Third
World countries. These outside prescriptions conceived at headquarters in
Washington, DC, often fail to recognize the marked differences that exist
among Third World countries. Domestic conditions vary so much from one
country to another that the economic recipes for development conceived
abroad will always risk failure unless they are flexible enough to allow broad
fixes.[12] Nothing illustrates better the contrast between UNDP on one hand,
and the IMF and the World Bank on the other in their approaches to
development strategies than a quick comparison between their 1991 annual
reports. Although the president of the World Bank stated in the foreword of
its report that "markets alone generally do not ensure that people, especially
the poorest, receive adequate education, health care, nutrition, and access to
family planning" (World Bank, 1991, p. iii), an overview of the report failed
to reveal any strategy to address that issue. By contrast, the UNDP report
clearly stated that "the lack of political commitment, not of financial resources, is often the real cause of human neglect" (United Nations Development Program 1991, p. 1). The UNDP report primarily addresses
financing human development through a restriction of national budgets
and international aid. The report concludes that much current spending is
misdirected and inefficiently used.

The concept of human development was first introduced in the 1990
UNDP report. For years, economists, politicians, and development planners
have measured per capita income to chart year-to-year progress within
a country. As a result, a great deal of national development activity was
focused on economic growth, often neglecting the human dimension of

development. As a new way to measure human development, a team of leading scholars created a new Human Development Index (HDI) for UNDP. It revealed that even countries of a low per capita GNP may rank higher on the HDI. In comparison, countries with high per capita GNP may still have low rates of human development. The difference lies in the way national leaders set their priorities and allocate government funds and in the degree of freedom that citizens enjoy to act on their choices and influence their own lives. The triple-component HDI considers life expectancy as one component not only for its own value but also because it speaks to health care delivery and the ability of people to live long enough to achieve goals. The second component, literacy, not only helps people to get and keep jobs but also assists them in understanding their surroundings and culture. The third one, purchasing power (per capita income adjusted to account for national differences in exchange rates, tariffs, and tradable goods), demonstrates the relative ability to buy commodities and meet basic needs (World Bank, 1991, pp. 5–6).

This chapter suggests four new approaches to guide the task of development administration practitioners: (1) population control, (2) indigenous democratization, (3) regional alliances, and (4) reversal of the brain drain flow.

POPULATION CONTROL: THE MISSING STRATEGY

Although global population growth still strains natural resources and exceeds the world's ability to provide jobs and decent living standards, the U.S. government, owing to its fear of antiabortion forces, refuses to contribute to the United Nations Population Fund or to support domestic or foreign family planning programs. In Latin America and the Caribbean, 44 percent of the labor force is unemployed or underemployed. In many countries of Africa and Asia, the situation is similar or worse. It is almost tragic how curtly and vaguely some Western countries deal with the most serious human problem of all, the population increase. Even the North–South program for survival, better known as the Brandt Report, managed to skip the issue entirely despite devoting long sections to hunger and food and suggesting a program of priorities (Brandt, 1981). Prior to the Brandt Report's publication, the much-heralded "New International Economic Order" failed to address the subject (United Nations, 1974).[13] One reason for such omissions was probably the assumption that the world population would grow at a much slower rate than it actually did. Advances in public health and medical care have in fact led to a rate of population growth twice or three times as great as the one predicted in the 1960s.

Only the Pearson Commission, at the behest of the World Bank, has presented a well-reasoned document on overall development strategy. The commission recommended as early as 1969 that the World Bank in consultation with the World Health Organization should sponsor a broad international program for channeling, coordinating, and financing research in the field of contraception and control of human fertility (Esman, 1991; Jackson, 1969; Martin, 1969; Pearson, 1969; Peterson, 1970).

The focus of development administrators on this problem is imperative in the New World Order when development assistance resources are becoming more restricted and scarcer.[14] Furthermore, effects of rapid population growth in the developing countries include potentially irreversible stresses on the land and other natural resources and increasing inadequacies in human services. The problem of rampant population growth in the Third World is exacerbated because it is occurring in areas where available resources are inadequate to accommodate this increase. Tropical rain forest countries are particularly vulnerable to obstacles to sustainable development, according to one expert. This is due in part to the conduciveness of moderate climates to high population, coupled with the unique characteristics of tropical rain forests – fragile and complex ecosystems developed over millions of years that, once destroyed, cannot be returned to their original diversity and complexity (Baldi, 1989).

Population growth has to be carefully controlled so that growth will be slow enough to allow for the adjustment of land use practices, human services, and economic development. Rapid and uncontrolled growth is occurring in many developing countries because of declining death rates due to improved living conditions and health care, combined with high birth rates and lower infant mortality. Population control is still the missing strategy in the planning of development administrators. With the formidable reduction in the dollar amount of foreign aid in the New World Order, population control should be one of the priorities when development administrators reconsider their strategies.

INDIGENOUS DEMOCRATIZATION

The Western powers have been constantly pressuring the Third World countries to hold free elections. In the late 1970s, President Carter's democracy activism paved the way for the two succeeding Republican presidents. At the present time, all the governments of South America have been elected; and twenty-five African nations, about one-half of the total, are either democratic or committed to democratic changes. However, these democracies have not been indigenous, and often the poor have not profited from them. Somehow, the elites of these countries have managed again to fool the Western countries into continuing their financial assistance to them by staging democratic "coups." In Peru, for example, there is a copy of the constitution in every telephone book. But the middle and upper classes effectively circumvent the law, and the judges are corrupt, ill-educated, and inept. *Habeas corpus* is ignored. The poor are marginalized and disdained (*Miami Herald*, January 29, 1992, p. 11A). In February 1992, another South American country, Venezuela, with thirty-four years of two-party democracy and the highest rate of economic growth, was threatened by an unsuccessful coup. Instead of celebrating, the majority of the Venezuelans in the slum areas of the capital were sad because of the failure of the coup and the consolidation of democracy. The democratic system had fomented generalized corruption that has helped a few well-connected Venezuelans make fabulous fortunes in recent years (*Miami Herald*, February 6, 1992, p. 19A). Other countries of Latin America and the rest of the Third World are exhibiting the same phenomenon. The advance of democracy in Africa also has occurred because Western donors have been requiring it as a condition for their loans. Although in some cases democracy breeds prosperity and produces stability, it has not brought social progress. Only if the poor are as well protected as the rich, and share in the progress that the rich usually monopolize, will they care about the virtues of democracy.

An indigenous democracy should

- encourage public participation in development planning and management;
- view local initiatives as something positive for development;
- have a national bureaucracy that accepts participatory methods as an avenue to the economies of scale that are sought;
- have coordination at the national level to allow the government to formulate coherent development strategies;
- have coordination at the local level to allow development agents to discuss among themselves the technical and physical inputs required by their programs, the implications their programs have for each other's activities, or any sequencing of activities that could make everyone's task easier;
- hold public servants and other government officials accountable. "Accountability is the foundation of any governing process. At the very

roots of democracy lie the requirements for public responsibility and accountability of ministers and public servants" (Jabbra & Dwivedi, 1989, p. 8); and

- close the gap that usually exists between the national and local governments. In developing countries, most government resources are concentrated in the capital. There is a total lack of administrative manpower, even poorly trained manpower, in other areas of the country. This gap between the national and local governments is constantly widening. An indigenous democracy should work at reversing it.

The world is presently on a democracy binge. But the triumph of democracy will not affect the poor if it is not indigenous and limited to free elections. The Western nations have developed their democracies over centuries in the framework of popular participation and prosperity. But democracy by itself does not necessarily bring prosperity if the democratically elected government does not choose the right policies. In Asia, for example, the pattern seems to be the reverse: South Korea, Taiwan, and Singapore all built up booming economies under regimes that tolerate little opposition (Auchincloss, 1992, p. 28). As another writer said appropriately, "Democracy means more than not killing voters on election day" (Matthews, 1991).

REGIONAL ALLIANCES

Latin America has taken the lead in forging regional alliances to further economic integration. The trend has been recognized by the developed nations (the European Community). The Andean group became a reality in January 1992 after twenty-three years of false starts, when the free-trade zone agreement among Venezuela, Colombia, Ecuador, Bolivia, and Peru became effective. The five countries established common tariffs and unitary customs and also agreed to ban weapons of mass destruction. The formation of the Andean group was propelled by progress in negotiations among Mexico, Canada, and the United States to sign a free-trade agreement. At the signing of the Andean agreement, one of the five presidents invoked the Bolivarian vision by saying, "After 1993, we'll practically become a single country" (*Miami Herald*, December 11, 1991, p. 20A). The Rio group of Latin American countries is a reincarnation of the defunct Contadora group, formed in 1982 by Colombia, Mexico, Panama, and Venezuela to mediate Central American conflicts. A support group of Argentina, Peru, Brazil, and Uruguay was organized a year later. In 1986, the countries came together as the Group of Eight, emulating the international trend of forming economic blocs. Since then Chile, Bolivia, Ecuador, and Paraguay have joined the group, which is not a formal trading bloc.

President Bush's "Initiative for the Americas," announced in June 1990 and expected to open U.S. markets to Latin products, gave further impetus to the revived Latin American interest in regional integration. Indeed, Rio member nations agreed in 1991 to designate the existing Association for Latin American Integration (ALADI) as the major institution for efforts that could lead to the establishment of a Latin American common market. The backbone of the Rio group's efforts is two fledgling subregional blocs: the Group of Three, consisting of Mexico, Venezuela, and Colombia; and the Southern Cone Common Market (MERCOSUR), which includes Argentina, Brazil, Paraguay, and Uruguay. The Rio group is appealing for the European community to consider major investments in the region and for the participation of the European Investment Bank in development plans. Europe is more attractive to the group because, unlike the United States, it does not demand that the countries establish a particular economic program in exchange for economic cooperation (*Miami Herald*, April 11, 1991, p. 16A).

In Asia, there is an alliance among Singapore, Malaysia, Indonesia, Thailand, Brunei, and the Philippines – the Association of South East Asian Nations (ASEAN) – but it was established primarily because of political and security concerns. However, ASEAN has increased trading among its members and coordinated trading outside the group.

Africa has been the continent with the most regional alliances, perhaps in recognition of the idea that the states are too small and not viable. Most of these alliances are not very effective. The pre-independence East African Community was a solid economic union, but it deteriorated and finally disappeared after the British left. Present regional alliances include a customs union between the six central African states of Gabon, Chad, Cameroon, Central African Republic, Equatorial Guinea, and Congo-Brazzaville; another customs union between the four southern African states of Botswana, Lesotho, Swaziland, and southern Africa; an association between the four Indian Ocean states of Madagascar, Reunion, Mauritius, and the Seychelles; and a North African Association with Morocco, Tunisia, and Algeria. Most of these alliances are not real trade or economic pacts. In fact, they have very specific and sectoral objectives. For example, the South African Coordination Conference, with more than ten members, is primarily concerned in developing alternative communications for avoiding linkage with South Africa. Only the West African Community ... has the kind of broad economic objectives of ASEAN and the Andean group. However, it has never really functioned effectively.

The proliferation of regional alliances will not aid development if it does not lead the way to reduced dependency. In the area of research and development, where most small poor countries are not doing well, individual countries' efforts should be coordinated and linked. Some of these small countries cannot pay their researchers, cover minimum maintenance cost, or buy equipment. The most advanced developing countries in the area of science and technology (e.g., Barbados, Costa Rica, Botswana, and Zimbabwe, in the group of small nations) should take a leading role with the countries in their regions to reduce their dependency on Western nations' technology (Segal, 1990, p. 224).

The donors should initiate more regional projects instead of extending their country-level activities. These regional programs, when multiplied, will help the developing countries develop economic linkages and diminish their dependency on the developed nations.[15]

REVERSAL OF THE BRAIN DRAIN FLOW

Brain drain has always been one of the biggest obstacles to development in the Third World. Recently, however, several countries have been recruiting their own nationals who have been successful abroad. The Asian countries, especially South Korea, have been quite active in doing so. Unfortunately, most developing countries do not have the capacity to attract their expatriates back. The new strategy suggested here is only for countries with solid economic prospects.

Several Latin American countries are now trying to get skilled workers from the former Soviet bloc. Five southern Latin American countries are involved in the program: Argentina, Venezuela, Uruguay, Paraguay, and Bolivia. These countries know that Russia and Eastern Europe have a surplus of hospital equipment maintenance technicians, electrical engineers, construction foremen, and plumbers, and they happen to have a shortage of such experts. After studies showed that between 2.5 and 10 million Russians and Eastern Europeans could flood Western Europe in coming years because of growing economic trouble at home, Argentina's government made a formal request to the European community to help finance the resettlement of a hundred thousand such experts in Argentina. Venezuela has already approved a project to bring in ten thousand of them (*Miami Herald*, February 12, 1992, p. 1A).

The four approaches suggested in this chapter may not be entirely new, and the list is definitely not exhaustive. The four approaches, however, if jointly executed, could be a good strategy to enable Third World development administrators to succeed despite the inevitable neglect they will experience from donors in the New World Order. These macro approaches should be reinforced by sectoral strategies (especially in the sectors of health, education, and agriculture) and "realistic" structural adjustment of the economies. In all cases the commitment for reform from the political leaders and the management capacity of the public sector as a whole will be major and crucial factors in the success or failure of development efforts.

NOTES

1. Some of the earlier theories developed by the author of this chapter dealt with the inner work of development administration (Garcia-Zamor, 1968, 1973, 1990).

2. It is a commonplace to refer to the underdeveloped countries of Asia, Africa, and Latin America as the "Third World." The "Second World" used to be the communist countries. It is not certain whether this term will still apply to the few remaining communist nations. The "First World" comprises the United States, Canada, and Western Europe.

3. The attitude of these bureaucrats was in sharp contrast with that of leftist nationalists, who viewed dependency as an obstacle to political development. The debate over dependency theory has been rich in content and relevant in application (Chilcote, 1982).

4. UNESCO Director General Frederico Mayor Zaragoza remarked in early 1992 that the term "New World Order" is being abused and is meaningless. He reminded an interviewer that Benito Mussolini was the *first* leader to use it. He also stated that the world had a "New World Order" since 1948 when the Universal Declaration of Human Rights was promulgated, and supposedly a "New World Economic Order" since 1974, but rich countries just ignore them (*Miami Herald*, January 31, 1992, p. 17A).

5. However, an increasingly large fraction of the program has been in the form of military assistance, which provides weapons and defense services to friendly foreign countries on a grant basis. At the beginning of the Reagan administration, this form of assistance totaled $110 million. By 1987 it totaled $950 million. For example, the military assistance to Spain, Turkey, and Portugal increased by 200 percent between 1980 and 1985. Comparing the 1978 foreign assistance program with the 1987 program, military assistance increased from 26 to 36 percent of the entire program while resources devoted to development assistance declined from 21 percent of the total to 15 percent, and food assistance declined from 14 to 10 percent (Hamilton, 1988).

6. Even in the case of environmental degradation in which the industrialized societies' interests are at stake, the United States has been slow to play a leading role. An important United Nations-sponsored meeting, the Earth Summit, took place in June 1992 in Rio de Janeiro, Brazil, to debate how to resolve environmental crises

such as global warming, forest destruction, and ocean contamination. Although more than 100 heads of state had committed themselves to attend, President Bush reluctantly decided only at the last minute to accept the invitation. A main reason for his coyness was the concern that developing countries, led by China and India, would press the United States and other wealthy nations for large and unrealistic funding transfers to the Third World to pay for environmental programs (*Miami Herald*, February 2, 1992, p. 7A).

7. Japan is already a leading source of foreign assistance, which comprises about 1 percent of its gross national product, approximately the same percentage that Japan spends on defense. By comparison, the United States devotes about 8 percent of its GNP to its world role, unfortunately almost all of it going to the far-flung military effort. If Japan could be persuaded to spend more on global leadership – say, 5 percent of its GNP – the result would be a vast increase in assistance to poorer countries (Newsweek, November 25, 1991, p. 47).

8. For the fiscal year 1991–1992, U.S. assistance to Eastern Europe was focusing on national public administration. Previous efforts were centered on ways of improving local or regional administration. The American Consortium of Public Administration (ACIPA) has developed an unsolicited proposal to establish and operate an International Public Service Executive Corps (IPSEC) to provide public administration technical assistance services to Central and Eastern European governments.

9. The U.S. pledge was made at the conclusion of a two-day international conference called by President Bush to coordinate worldwide aid to the former Soviet Union. The conference was held in Washington, DC, in early January 1992. Representatives of 47 nations and seven international organizations reported at the meeting the formation of "action plans," to ensure orderly shipments and distribution of food and medicine and to ensure the coordination of help to solve housing and energy shortages. The wealthy Arab nations of Saudi Arabia, Kuwait, and the United Arab Emirates have pledged an additional $4 billion in Soviet relief. Such an extraordinary amount of foreign assistance had never been contemplated to lift the Third World nations out of their misery.

10. The High Performance Computing Act was signed by President Bush in December 1991. It authorizes eight federal agencies to spend $638 million to develop hardware and software for a teraflop computer capable of performing one trillion computations a second. At the same time, Energy Secretary James Watkins announced that the government's 726 national laboratories – facilities that spend more than $20 billion annually, mostly on weapons research – will now be available for joint research projects with private businesses.

11. When national governments felt that a U.N. plan made a negative impact on them, they had always distanced themselves from it. In the early 1960s, when the Soviet Union and France disapproved of U.N. Secretary General Dag Hammarskjold's Congo Operation, they simply ceased to pay their annual dues to prevent any part of their money from going toward the financing of that operation.

12. A policy and scholarly consensus is emerging on reducing the role of the state in the economy, but with relatively little consideration of its meaning and potential consequences. Thomas J. Biersteker (1990) of the University of Southern California published an article distinguishing six different forms of state economic intervention. He combined them to characterize different national economic regimes. IMF and

World Bank recommendations for policy reform are then identified, and the consequences of those recommendations are assessed for different forms of economic intervention.

13. The "New International Economic Order" was adopted by the United Nations in 1974 to encourage the transfer of resources from the poor to the rich. It had numerous supporters in the Third World and some of the specialized agencies of the United Nations. In the more developed countries, however, it was popular only among nongovernmental organizations. Two American scholars, William Loehr and John Powelson, have published an interesting book on the pitfalls of the New International Economic Order (Loehr & Powelson, 1983).

14. Colombia has been an exception and one of the Third World's greatest success stories in family planning, driving down its birth rate from an average of six children per woman in 1970 to 2.2 children at present.

15. Interregional projects will not, however, meet these objectives, because they take place in countries that have totally different kinds of economies and are geographically too remote from each other. Of course, these projects were not initiated for that purpose. For example, one of UNDP's interregional projects is in the field of public administration. It covers Africa, Asia and the Pacific, Latin America and the Caribbean, and Arab states and Europe. Its overall goal is to assist countries in these regions in improving their public sectors by enhancing the management capabilities of their governments.

REFERENCES

ACIPA (American Consortium for International Public Administration) (1991). *Minutes of governing board meeting*, December 9.

Auchincloss, K. (1992). Limits of democracy. *Newsweek*, January 21, pp. 25–30.

Baldi, P. (1989). Address to the 1989 society for international development (Washington Chapter), Annual Conference, May 10.

Berg, R. J., & Gordon, D. F. (1989). *Cooperation for international development: The United States and the Third World in the 1990s.* Boulder, Colo: Lynne Rienner Publishers.

Brandt, W. (1981). *North-South: A program for survival.* Cambridge, Mass: MIT Press.

Brinkerhoff, D. W. (1991). *Improving development program performance: Guidelines for managers.* Boulder, Colo: Westview Press.

Chilcote, R. H. (1982). *Dependency and Marxism: Toward a resolution of the debate.* Boulder, Colo: Westview Press.

Gable, R. W. (1976). *Development administration: Background, terms, concepts, theories and a new approach* (June 7). Washington, DC: American Society for Public Administration (SICA).

Garcia-Zamor, J.-C. (1968). A Typology of creole bureaucracies. *International Review of Administrative Science*, 38(1), 49–60.

Garcia-Zamor, J.-C. (1973). Micro-bureaucracies and development administration. *International Review of Administrative Science*, 39(4), 417–423.

Garcia-Zamor, J.-C. (1985). *Public participation in development planning and management: Cases from Africa, Asia and Asia.* Boulder, Colo: Westview Press.

Garcia-Zamor, J.-C. (1990). Risks and conflicts in centralized state intervention in development organizations. In: M. J. Pelaez (Ed.), *Studies in economics* (pp. 215–219). Barcelona, Spain: University of Malaga Press.

Goodsell, C. T. (1981). The new comparative administration: A proposal, International. *Journal of Public Administration*, *3*(2), 143–155.

Hamilton, L. (1988). Remarks on activity of the Foreign Affairs Committee Task Force on Foreign Assistance (September 14). Washington, DC: U.S. Congress.

Heady, F. (1984). *Public administration: A Comparative perspective*. New York: Marcel Dekker.

Hellinger, S., Hellinger, D., & O'Regan, F. M. (1988). *Aid for just development: Report on the future of foreign assistance*. Boulder, Colo: Lynne Rienner.

Loehr, W., & Powelson, J. P. (1983). *Threat to development: Pitfalls of the NIEO*. Boulder, Colo: Westview Press.

Matthews, J. T. (Ed.) (1991). *Preserving the global environment*. New York: Norton.

Montgomery, J. D. (1971). Transferability of what? The relevance of foreign aid to the domestic poverty program. *Journal of Comparative Administration*, *2*(4), 455–470.

Newsweek (1991). *Newsweek*, November 25, p. 47.

Peterson, R. (1970). *U.S. foreign assistance in the 1970s: A new approach*. Report to the President from the Task Force on International Development. U.S. Government Printing Office, Washington, DC.

Schraeder, P. J. (1992). *Intervention into the 1990s: U.S. Foreign policy in the Third World* (2nd edn.). Boulder, Colo: Lynne Rienner.

United Nations. (1974). *Declaration of the establishment of a new international economic order*. New York: U.N. Resolution 3201 (S–V1), May 1.

United Nations Development Program. (1991). *Human Development Report 1991*. New York: Oxford University Press.

World Bank. (1991). *World development Report 1991: The Challenge of Development*. New York: Oxford University Press.

THE FAILURE OF U.S. TECHNICAL ASSISTANCE IN PUBLIC ADMINISTRATION: THE IRANIAN CASE

John L. Seitz

INTRODUCTION

One of the causes of the Iranian revolution of 1978–1979 was that the Iranian government had serious administrative deficiencies. Amir Taheri, a well-known Iranian journalist, wrote in the mid-1978 that public disturbances were "due to an accumulation of discontent with tight control, over-centralization, lack of sufficient open debate and a general feeling that corruption and inefficiency together with arrogance have struck the bureaucracy."[1] These administrative problems were not new. An important scholarly examination of the Iranian political system in the early 1970s concluded that the "problems of governance in Iran are profound. Inefficiency is their hallmark ... ."[2]

It is likely that the Iranian revolution will force some Americans involved in providing technical assistance to Third World nations to confront the fact that one of their largest technical assistance efforts in Iran had failed. For fifteen years – from 1953 to 1968, when AID,[3] the American foreign aid agency, ended its activities in Iran – the U.S. government had provided technical assistance to the Iranian government in public administration.[4]

Comparative Public Administration: The Essential Readings
Research in Public Policy Analysis and Management, Volume 15, 321–334
Copyright © 2006 by Elsevier Ltd.
ISSN: 0732-1317/doi:10.1016/S0732-1317(06)15012-5

TWO PUBLIC ADMINISTRATION PROJECTS

Aid to Iranian Ministries

The largest public administration project in Iran (in terms of the number of Americans working in it) lasted from 1956 to 1961, cost approximately $2.3 million, and involved about 26 American advisers. The project provided one general public administration adviser to each of the Iranian ministries except foreign affairs and war, and advisers in budgeting, accounting, taxation, auditing, customs, personnel administration, statistics, and organization and methods (O&M). The principal accomplishment of the project was considered to be, for many years, the establishment in the Iranian government of a High Council of Administrative Undersecretaries, a body which was to concern itself with administrative reform on a continuing basis. But 5 years after the end of the project the High Council no longer existed, "nor [were] the remaining administrative undersecretaries," as an AID case history of the project admitted, "the force for reform that was planned." The AID report goes on to say that "Ministries have O&M offices, but the offices are not staffed with vigorous trained personnel and many produce little results. Accounting is still archaic and slow. The volume of tax delinquencies in the Ministry of Finance is again substantial."[5]

Even with these admitted failures, the AID mission rated the project as successful. Its judgment in 1967 was that although "an evaluation of Iranian public administration would uncover many deficiencies and the need for major reform, the general level of performance is unquestionably much better today than it was in 1956. That change has been this rapid can be attributed in part to this project."[6] But the AID mission did not give any evidence about improvements in the government's "general level of performance" nor did it offer any evidence of why improvements in Iranian performance, if they did exist, were the result of this project.

Aid to the Iranian National Police

In 1953 a project was begun to assist the Iranian police. The long-range object of the project was "to produce a suitable climate of internal security and public stability conducive to economic and social development."[7] American advisers provided assistance to the National Police Administration in developing an improved organization and procedures, training facilities, a national communications system, narcotics control, motor vehicle traffic control, and improved criminal investigative techniques. The project was also designed to advise the National Police Administration on "anti-subversive methods, civil disturbance control, and other matters pertaining to internal security."[8] It was this last-mentioned function that led to the creation of SAVAK, the feared Iranian secret police. In 1957 a report on accomplishments in public administration assistance in Iran, under a section on civil police administration, mentions that "Responsibility for all civilian counter-intelligence activities has been concentrated in a new internal security agency (SAVAK) which is attached to the Prime Minister's Office."[9] By 1963 the work of SAVAK and assistance to it appeared to be so sensitive that there was no mention of the agency in the case history of the internal security project administered by AID's Public Safety Division.[10]

From 1955 through 1963 the U.S. spent about $3 million on this project. Included in this total was $500,000 which was approved for civil disturbance control equipment in fiscal year 1963. The supplying of riot control equipment to Iran was eventually criticized by some members of the U.S. Congress and AID became more sensitive about giving such assistance.

During most of the 1950s the assistance to the Iranian police was managed by the Public Safety Branch of the Public Administration Division of AID. In 1959 public safety became a separate division in the AID mission in Iran, partly because of the connection of the public safety program with the CIA. One of the chief supervisors of the public administration program in the AID headquarters in Washington, DC, in the 1950s has stated that he worked to get the public safety program removed from the public administration division because public safety was too involved with the CIA.[11] At least one CIA agent, who was undoubtedly working with SAVAK, had a "cover" in the Iranian police project when it was a part of the public administration program.

POLITICAL SUPPORT FOR
ADMINISTRATIVE REFORM

The two public administration projects described in the previous section received different levels of support from the Iranian government. Strong political support went to the project to assist the police as the Shah recognized the need for an effective police in order to safeguard his throne. The project to improve the administrative structures of the Iranian ministries did not receive strong support from the Iranian government. It is this lack of support, which will be examined in detail in this section.

A former public administration adviser to one of the Iranian ministries in the late 1950s described the lack of political support:

> They rushed us over there and then there was nothing to do. The Iranians were very willing to accept the American advisers as well as the dollars which they wanted to get in other areas. They especially wanted to get military aid. The Iranians weren't geared to reorganize their government. There were many people on the government's payroll who did no work, but the Shah had no intention of reducing the government's payroll because he didn't want to disenchant any large group. ... Once I realized that the host government was only going to go so far and had accepted the advisers because they were part of a bigger package, this realization diminished my horizons. I was able to eliminate sonic duplication of activities in the Iranian ministry in which I worked, but my accomplishments were limited.[12]

During the period of the major American effort to aid the Iranian ministries, political pressures forced the government to hire freely and to ignore the regular retirement laws. According to Binder, the "consequences of these arrangements and pressures have been a great over-staffing of the service."[13] The practice of filling the bureaucracy with personnel for political reasons continued into the 1970s. The Shah used co-optation as one of the means to silence his critics and this "cooptative means of recruitment," according to Zonis, bred cynicism among the political elite. The "qualities of cynicism, mistrust, insecurity, and interpersonal exploitation are the central character variables that explicate that which is peculiar to Iranian politics."[14] What effect did this situation have on the administrative performance of the government? Zonis believed that such a system could not lead to administrative reform: The system is highly conducive to the avoidance of assuming responsibility for any bureaucratic act. Conflicts are pushed ever higher in the bureaucracy for resolution. Still more committees and groups are created for decision making. This was caused in large part, according to Zonis, because of the "fear of coming to the attention of the monarch."[15]

The Shah often spoke about the need for administrative reform in Iran. In 1963 he announced a six-point program for the country, the so-called White Revolution. One of these points was an "educational and administrative revolution." According to Bill, all "indications are ... that this revolution is to exist on paper only."[16] In the 1960s, the United Nations sent public administration advisers to Iran. In 1975, the Shah again spoke of the need for administrative reform in his country and selected an American company headed by David E. Lilienthal, former chairman of the Tennessee Valley Authority, to study this subject.[17]

One of the main reasons why the American-sponsored administrative reforms did not win high-level political support in Iran was that, as will be shown below, the American public administration advisers were generally ignorant of the political implications of their work. As an analysis of administrative problems in Pakistan states, "Administrative reform ... is ordinarily fraught with political implications. ... It is doomed to failure when undertaken for its own sake, for the traditional rationale of efficiency or economy."[18]

If high-level political support for administrative reform did not exist in Iran at the time of the large American effort in the Iranian ministries, why did the Americans undertake this assistance? I think the basic reason was given by a former supervisor of the public administration assistance program who worked in *the AID* headquarters in Washington for about 10 years from the mid-1950s to the mid-1960s. He said that this was something we felt they needed and something we wanted to do. Nowhere around the world did the foreign aid agency make a serious attempt to answer the question, Would they support such assistance? We talked with people who told us what we wanted to hear, he said, and not with those elements in the country, such as the political opposition, who might have given us different answers to the question of support. This was, in part, because it would have been politically difficult to talk with the opposition.[19] But, in the author's opinion, this is only a partial answer. Not uncommon in the foreign aid agency, especially in the 1950s, was a belief that the Americans could introduce reforms in spite of the indifference of political leaders to these reforms. The belief was that these reforms would eventually be accepted.

AMERICAN LEVERAGE

If political support for certain administrative reforms did not exist in the Iranian government in the late 1950s and early 1960s, could the U.S. have applied pressure on Iran to obtain this support? The answer is, probably not. In countries, which receive large amounts of U.S. aid, such as Iran, one cannot be sure whether the donor or the recipient has greater leverage. A large aid program may mean that the U.S. is totally committed to the regime in power. This fact can be as important as the fact that the country needs the American aid. Such a situation existed in Iran; the U.S. was committed to the Shah. As a former foreign aid official who held high administrative positions in the foreign aid mission to Iran in the late 1950s and early 1960s put it, the aid mission's objective was "to secure the Shah on his throne" and "to broaden his support."[20] In 1967, Cottam wrote that "American capabilities for persuading the regime to alter its course are at best limited. As long as American policy calls for a stable and noncommunist Iran and American policy makers are convinced that only the Shah can provide such an Iran, the American leverage position will remain a weak one."[21]

Another important facet of the subject of "leverage" concerns the following question: Can the foreign aid adviser be certain that the reform he or she is proposing is suitable for the foreign country? The question is not only whether the reform is needed and is efficacious, but also whether it could have unintended harmful consequences. The adviser might not be able to answer these questions or he or she might feel certain of the answers but actually be mistaken. If either situation exists, there is no justification for trying to apply leverage on the foreign government in order to get it to support the proposed reforms. In the Iranian case the Americans thought they could answer the above questions pertaining to suitability but actually could not, because nearly all advisers in the public administration program arrived in Iran with no knowledge of the language and with a very superficial knowledge of Iranian culture, its history, and its social, economic, and political systems.

ASSUMPTIONS ABOUT TECHNICAL ASSISTANCE

It was recognized by AID that political support by the foreign government was essential if administrative reforms were to be carried out and that the U.S. did not have the leverage to persuade the foreign government to support such reforms.[22] Given this, why were the Americans so ignorant of the lack of political support by the Iranian government? Part of the reason for the ignorance of foreign aid personnel on this subject was the explicit AID assumption that technical assistance was nonpolitical.[23] Potentially sensitive assistance such as public administration, which could be attacked by critics of the U.S. as being interference by the U.S. in the internal operations of the foreign government, was defended as being totally unconcerned with local politics of the aid-receiving country. As Cleveland, et al. have written: "If the overseas Americans have been slow in developing political awareness, it is in part because the organizations for which they work do not want their field people to be accused of 'interfering,' and therefore do not encourage them to talk or even think in political terms."[24] The active involvement in the internal political affairs of the aid-receiving countries by other agencies of the U.S. government, such as the CIA, was another matter. For most AID personnel the standing instruction was to stay out of internal politics.

One way the organization could make sure that its personnel would keep out of the politics of the foreign country was to give no encouragement to the acquiring of political information. Evidence that AID's socialization was fairly effective is indicated by the authors of *The Overseas Americans.* This study of Americans, both governmental and private, abroad in the late 1950s, rated foreign aid personnel "fairly low on a sense for politics."[25] AID did not have difficulty, especially in the 1950s, in including the value of being nonpolitical in the advisers' socialization. The conclusion of the study was that "To attune an American to the internal politics of a strange country requires radical shifting of his habits and attitudes. Most Americans are not deeply immersed even in [U.S.] politics."[26]

Also pertinent was the assumption of AID public administration officials at this time that policy and administration were separate spheres.[27] Public administration advisers were instructed to stay away form policy matters, and this instruction contributed to their tendency to be ignorant of the political systems in which they worked. For public administration advisers the lack of political knowledge of the foreign countries was especially detrimental. This lack caused the advisers to be ignorant of the political implications of their work, implications, which made it inevitable that many of the reforms they recommended would not be implemented by the foreign governments. In Iran during the late 1950s proposed administrative reform, such as tax reform and the reduction of surplus government employees, threatened the interests of various groups upon whose support the Iranian government depended.

ADAPT NOT ADOPT

Public administration advisers were instructed to adapt and not adopt American administrative procedures and principles for use in the developing countries. The difficulty was that most public administration advisers did not have enough knowledge of the local environment to develop solutions, which might be appropriate for the country. A majority of foreign aid advisers surveyed in the late 1960s recognized that there was a need to adapt American practices to the local culture, but they believed AID advisers "often try to change local practices without really understanding why they exist."[28] There was one exception to the generally recognized need to adapt American practices. Interestingly, and perhaps ominously, foreign aid police advisers found that their techniques could be easily transferred across cultural boundaries.[29]

Major American public administration activities in Iran did not indicate knowledge of the political and administrative situations which existed in that country at the time. The idea of setting up "permanent"[30] administrative undersecretaries in Iran came from an American who had worked in a U.S. federal government department, which had an assistant secretary of administration, a relatively permanent official. The American thought that the Iranian ministries would benefit from having similar officials since there was a frequent turnover of the heads of the ministries.[31] As had been shown above, the attempt to make these officials the locus of administrative reform and "permanent" was not successful. This was because, as Binder shows,[32] the effort did not indicate an understanding of how power was actually exercised in the Iranian bureaucracy at that time.

The idea of appointing permanent administrative undersecretaries runs counter to the entire [bureaucratic] system, in which all positions are fluid and only grades and pay rates fixed. Fixing personnel in positions of relatively high authority is not to rationalize the administration but to legitimize for long periods the influence of power structures built upon nonrational hierarchical bases, the systemic function of which depends upon their exercising only temporary authority.

The instruction "adapt not adopt" was often not followed and, in fact, could not be followed, given the low level of the Americans' knowledge of the aid-receiving countries. The conclusion of Esman and Montgomery is that "'adapt not adopt' is more a slogan than a set of tested practices" in AID.[33]

THE "SUCCESSFUL" PROJECT

Most of what I have written so far concerns the project to promote administrative reform in the Iranian ministries. But what about the project which provided aid to the Iranian police? For many years this assistance was considered to be a success.[34] The project's objective of internal security and "public stability" (which meant political stability) had obviously been accomplished. Until the Iranian revolution of 1978–1979 the Shah seemed secure on this throne, and SAVAK had a world-wide reputation for "efficiency." What went wrong with this assistance?

American assistance to the police in developing nations in the 1950s and 1960s had been based on the assumption that political stability was a necessary prerequisite for economic development. A former police advisor who worked in the Iranian project, expressed this reasoning:

> Development is an unsettling experience. It creates sonic harm and the process of development is irrational. For example, one pump can put a lot of people out of work, as

can a tractor or a road. Iran was in an upheaval caused by development during part of the 1950s and 1960s. Our health programs led to a big population increase and there was a large movement into the cities. Tehran grew very fast. Many of these people who came to Tehran were without education or skills needed to get work. So there was potential discontent growing. Law enforcement was needed to help the country get through this time. Thus, it was a necessary part of development. Iraq is an example of a country which has moved backward and forward and is now way behind Iran in development. But the question of how the police would be used was a key one. We couldn't do anything about this.[35]

Some of the reasons for this "successful" project turning into a failure were the same reasons as the project to aid the Iranian ministries failed. The two main features of the police project which were not shared with the Iranian ministries project – strong Iranian political support and no cultural barriers which prevented the transfer of technology – were offset by two features which were common to both projects – the mistaken assumption that policy and administration can be kept separate and the ignorance of Iran by the American advisers. While it is true that the U.S. could not control how the police would be used in a country to which the U.S. gave public safety assistance, not much knowledge of Iran is needed to know that throughout Iranian history the police have been used by the rulers to suppress dissent. And while it seems reasonable that assistance to the Iranian police, as the adviser said above, was buying time for the country so it could get through the transitional period between underdevelopment and development, why should the U.S. have assumed this was only a temporary period and that the police would not become a repressive instrument for the ruler?

No matter how "efficient" police control had become in Iran, the police could not assure the stability of a government that had grown to be out of touch with its own people. And, as Cottam states, "Any regime considered by its attentive public to be an American creation, or at least dependency, will be fundamentally fragile."[36]

American foreign aid policy makers in the 1950s and 1960s believed that all good things go together, that economic development, social reforms, political stability, and democracy were interrelated.[37] The experience of many developing countries such as South Korea, Brazil, and Iran have shown that this assumption was incorrect.

CONCLUSIONS

Why study failure? The answer, of course, is to prevent repeating in the future the mistakes one made in the past.

Although one must be cautious about generalizing from a single case, or a few cases, there is a strong suggestion from the Iranian case – and others[38] – that we do not know how to help developing nations reform their administrative structures. The large American effort in Iran to help the Iranian ministries become effective so they would aid the development effort instead of hindering it was not successful. The American effort to aid the Iranian police so that public order could be maintained led to the creation of a secret police force known for its brutality.

With hindsight it is now clear that the Americans' general ignorance of Iran when they initiated major assistance in public administration, made it most likely that the assistance would not be successful. Also, there was a strong political motive behind the American aid program – to strengthen a pro-American and anti-communist government in Iran. This political objective undermined other objectives of American foreign aid. The value of the technical assistance advisers as visible evidence of U.S. support for the anti-communist Shah conflicted with their value as agents to help Iran achieve economic development, The anti-communist task was best served by getting the advisers to Iran as quickly as possible, while the economic development task would have been best served if the public administration advisers had been able to receive adequate training in Iranian culture, language, history, economics, and politics before coming to Iran. In fact, however, it is doubtful that the American public administration advisers could have obtained enough knowledge about Iran to make the advisers effective. The U.S. knew very little about Iran in the 1950s when the American assistance began and, 30 years later, it still knows very little about the country.[39]

Even if adequate knowledge about Iran had been available to make the advisers effective, is it realistic to assume that economic development objectives could take precedence over political objectives? Is it realistic to expect a nation which gives foreign aid to another not to be dominated by political objectives which reflect its fears and needs, however narrowly and short-sighted? Undoubtedly not.

What can be learned from the Iranian case and other failures of foreign aid? One lesson could be that the time is here to substitute technical cooperation (something the U.S. foreign aid program said it was doing but never actually did) for technical assistance. The industrial and non-industrial nations of the world should focus on developing training programs for foreign nationals. A nation which has a desire to learn how something is done in another country could send people to the other country to study that activity.

There would be obvious advantages accruing to nations participating in this exchange. On the one hand, the nation providing the training opportunity (on-the-job, observational, or academic) would find this a natural way to show off its best features and maybe even to influence foreign opinion leaders (a common foreign policy goal). On the other hand, the nation requesting training in a foreign country would obtain information and skills which could help it accomplish its own objectives. Some non-industrial nations will want to learn ways to become industrialized and to raise living standards. Some industrial nations will want to learn how non-industrial nations have dealt with some crucial problems, problems which threaten the industrialized nations' very survival – such as energy use, depletion of resources, destruction of the environment, and materialistic values.

One of the advantages of this approach over the present form of foreign aid is that a large part of the foreign aid bureaucracy could be dismantled and replaced by a relatively small training office. The U.S. would need a presidential directive prohibiting the CIA from using the American and foreign participants for its own purposes, a decree which would be similar to the present CIA directive which pertains to scholars, teachers, and students receiving Fulbright grants.[40]

Freed of the unjustifiable task of interfering in the internal affairs of another nation and of the impossible task of giving advice to a foreign country one does not understand, the technical cooperation participants would help promote the flow of ideas in the world.

NOTES

1. As quoted in James A. Bill, "Iran and the Crisis of '78," *Foreign Affairs*, v. 57, Winter 1978/79, p. 331.

2. Marvin Zonis, *The Political Elite of Iran* (Princeton: Princeton University Press, 1971), p. 337.

3. The Agency for International Development (AID) has only existed since 1961, but for the sake of simplicity the term "AID" is used throughout this article to refer to the present foreign aid organization as well as its predecessors: the Economic Cooperation Administration (1948–1951), the Mutual Security Agency (1951–1953), the Foreign Operations Administration (1953–1955), and the International Cooperation Administration (1955–1961).

4. Although public administration is a small part of AID's total technical assistance program – receiving about 7 percent or 8 percent of the funds approved for technical assistance in the past – it was one of the largest technical assistance activities in Iran. Only assistance in agriculture, health and sanitation, and education were larger. Public administration is out of favor in AID at present, both with regard to the amount of funds allocated to it and with regard to the term itself.

"Development administration" is the preferred phrase, although some of AID's reports and the foreign aid legislation continue to use the term "public administration." For a discussion of the differences between public and development administration as they apply to AID see Milton 3. Esman and John D. Montgomery, "Systems Approaches to Technical Cooperation: The Role of Development Administration," *Public Administration Review*, v. 29, no. 5 (Sept./Oct. 1969), pp. 507–539.

5. Agency for International Development-Tehran. "Technical Assistance Project History and Analysis Report, Project No. 265-11-790-110, GUI Public Administration," *Department of State AIRGRAM,* TOAID A-733, unclassified, date sent April 8, 1967, p. 23.

6. *Ibid.*

7. Agency for International Development-Tehran. "Development Grant Program Evaluation – Case History," Department of State AIRGRAM, TOAID A-1341, unclassified, date sent January 29, 1963, p. 2.

8. *Ibid.*, p. 3.

9. Robert W. Herder, "Report on Public Administration Assistance in Iran," mimeograph, March 1, 1957, p. 10. Herder was chief of the Public Administration Division in Iran.

10. AID-Tehran, 1963.

11. Personal interview by author on October 23, 1974. As part of a foreign aid research project, in-depth, confidential interviews were held with 54 present and former employees of AID who had been associated with the public administration technical assistance program. These interviews were conducted over three months in 1974 in Washington, DC and surrounding areas.

12. Personal interview by author on November 1, 1974. The remarks cited in this paragraph are paraphrased statements based on extensive notes taken during the interview. An Iranian study of the American technical assistance program agrees, in part, with the former adviser's analysis. In this study, which is fairly critical of the American effort, Amuzegar found that while "Point IV was braced to offer plenty of advice and not much money, the Iranians felt that they needed a considerable amount of the latter and a minimum of the former." Amuzegar's conclusion was that the "purpose, role, and limitations [of the U.S. technical assistance program] received little sympathetic understanding from the host country." Even to the end, the Mission was still expected to act as another dispenser of U.S. financial aid. Jahangir Amuzegar, *Technical Assistance in Theory and Practice: The Case of Iran* (New York: Praeger, 1966), pp. 124, 255.

13. Leonard Binder, *Iran: Political Development in a Changing Society* (Berkeley: University of California Press, 1962), p. 135.

14. Zonis, pp. 16, 333.

15. *Ibid.*, p. 334.

16. James A. Bill, *The Politics of Iran: Groups, Classes, and Modernization* (Columbus, OH: Charles E. Merrill, 1972) p. 141.

17. The failure of administrative reform efforts by Lilienthal's Development and Resources Corporation is described in *Public Administration Times*, May 15, 1979, pp. 1, 4–5, 7, and June 1, 1979, pp. 3, 7, by some American consultants who worked in Iran.

18. Albert Gorvine, "Administrative Reform: Function of Political and Economic Change," In: Guthrie S. Birkhead (Ed.), *Administrative Problems in Pakistan* (Syracuse: Syracuse University Press, 1966), p. 186.

19. Personal interview by author on October 29, 1974.

20. Personal interview by author on October 4, 1974.

21. Richard W. Cottam, *Competitive Interference and Twentieth Century Diplomacy* (Pittsburgh: University of Pittsburgh Press, 1967), pp. 176–177.

22. For a statement on the need of political support for administrative reform see International Cooperation Administration, *ICA Work in Public Administration* (Washington, DC: International Cooperation Administration, 1960), p. 4. For a statement by a high AID official on the limits of American leverage, see David S. Brown, "Strategies and Tactics of Public Administration Technical Assistance: 1945–1963," in: John D. Montgomery and William J. Siffin (Eds), *Approaches to Development: Politics, Administration and Change* (New York: McGraw-Hill, 1966), p. 218.

23. As Benveniste shows, experts and advisers to governments are involved in politics whether they like it or not. Guy Benveniste, *The Politics of Expertise* (Berkeley: Glendessary Press, 1972), p. 21.

24. Harlan Cleveland, Gerard J. Mangone, and John C. Adams, *The Overseas Americans* (New York: McGraw-Hill, 1960), p. 146.

25. *Ibid.*, p. 127.

26. *Ibid.*, p. 149.

27. Esman and Montgomery, p. 512.

28. James R. Brady, "Problems of Implementing American Foreign Assistance Projects: Perceptions of the US AID Advisor." Ph.D. dissertation (Ann Arbor: University of Michigan, 1971), p. 158.

29. *Ibid.*, p. 145.

30. The administrative undersecretaries were supposed to be "permanent," that is, to be appointed for five years and not subject to change by incoming ministers. But this also did not turn out as planned, as none of the permanent undersecretaries appointed in 1958 was in office by 1960. See Amuzegar, p. 25.

31. Personal interview by author on October 14, 1974.

32. Binder, p. 141.

33. Esman and Montgomery, p. 509.

34. Congress eventually came to have serious doubts about aiding police in developing nations; in 1973 it instructed AID to "phase out" all police assistance, that is, to give no new assistance in this area. See Public Law 93–189, 93rd Congress, Dec. 17, 1973.

35. Personal interview by author on October 3, 1974. The remarks cited in this paragraph are paraphrased statements based on extensive notes taken during the interview.

36. Richard Cottam, "Goodbye to America's Shah," *Foreign Policy*, No. 34 (Spring 1979), p. 14.

37. Robert A. Packenham, *Liberal America and the Third World: Political Development Ideas in Foreign Aid and Social Science* (Princeton: Princeton University Press, 1973), pp. 123–129.

38. Another very large public administration assistance program was set up in the late 1950s and early 1960s and also failed. This project, in Brazil, was to aid DASP,

the Brazilian central management agency. See John L. Seitz, "The Gap Between Expectations and Performance: An Exploration of American Foreign Aid to Brazil, Iran, and Pakistan, 1950–70." Ph.D. dissertation (Madison: University of Wisconsin, 1976), pp. 195–200.

39. See Bill, 1978/79, pp. 323–324.

40. Final Report of the Select Committee to Study Governmental Operations with Respect to Intelligence Activities. U.S. Senate, 94th Cong., 2nd Sess., April 26, 1976, Book I, p. 190.

ADMINISTERING TO THE POOR (OR, IF WE CAN'T HELP RICH DICTATORS, WHAT CAN WE DO FOR THE POOR?)

John D. Montgomery

Time does not always treat kindly the attempts of large, rich states to "help" small or poor ones. Even when they succeed, trouble may be in store. Neither capital aid nor technical assistance is an unmixed blessing to the receiving society. And because the purposes of both the giver and the receiver are too complex for easy appraisal, judgment on their experience should look to the future more than the past.

The benevolence of even the most charitable *individuals* is suspected today; how much more so is the good will of *governments,* whose obligations are to their own citizens and not to those of other states? If rich governments decide to aid other countries, not just to curry favor but in the hope of improving the international setting, they have to engage in collaborative activities that are either mutually beneficial or that provide a fair trade to each partner. Finding suitable benefits and tradeoffs is therefore a prime task of development diplomacy. The choice of ends often involves exchanging long-term, high benefits for immediate, but small gains. That is the first, though not the only, crucial decision. If the wrong programs are chosen, as in Iran and Vietnam, it is not necessarily beneficial even when they are well

Comparative Public Administration: The Essential Readings
Research in Public Policy Analysis and Management, Volume 15, 335–344
Copyright © 2006 by Elsevier Ltd.
ISSN: 0732-1317/doi:10.1016/S0732-1317(06)15013-7

executed. Failure there may be attributable in some measure to poor administration, but surely the decision to use development assistance to prop
up unsavory regimes was more responsible for the outcomes.

The greatest successes in foreign aid have occurred in the presence of two
features: a political context of mutual purpose, in which both parties could
think of long-term goals, and a sophisticated calculus of the benefits that
could be appropriately expected by each partner. The reconstruction activities after World War II were relatively easy because they did not require
interventions in an existing social or economic order, and they could take
place within a context of harmonious purposes among American and foreign political actors. Another collection of success stories could be written of
the Point 4 transfers of technology, which improved agriculture and industry in the less developed countries, brought both the benefits and costs of the
Green Revolution and of competitive, small-scale industry to Asia, and
increased the flow of international trade. It is true that these silver clouds
had dark linings: premature urbanization that accompanied industrial development; dissatisfaction with the pace of change and the inequities that
accompanied it; and declining terms of trade in international transactions.
But much worse results attended the extravagant and misguided efforts of
the Kennedy–Johnson–Nixon–Carter era to use foreign aid to foster "stability" directly by improving central administrative sub-systems and sacrificing developmental goals in the interests of national security. Thus, even
when successes came, as in the propping up of regimes in Vietnam and Iran
for a decade or so beyond their just merits, they looked so much like failures
when it was all over that they discredited the entire enterprise of international assistance.

Discredited or not, international assistance will continue to be a diplomatic option; the alternative of abandoning it no longer exists. Many world
problems transcend both the national boundaries and the national resources
of individual great powers. For the moment, policies and programs to deal
with planetary ecology and unclaimed global resources are opportunities for
which technology exists, but not the political will. And beyond these technological challenges lies, a more serious mutual concern for which even
when the political will exists, the technology is weak; the rising incidence of
poverty as an international concern, which has both immediate and long-
term consequences for modern statecraft. International poverty alleviation
is especially a challenging problem of technical assistance because governments have not served these needs very well even in the case of their own
citizens. Moreover, whatever techniques they have developed for this purpose have not yet begun to dominate programs of international assistance,

though recognition of their importance is rising. It is only recently that the United Nations, the U.S. Congress, the World Bank, and a cadre of national leaders have begun seriously looking for ways of relieving poverty without diminishing the prospects for the rest of society. They still need to develop for that purpose a set of principles of development administration that can serve those citizens who have remained beyond the reach of the market and of normal government operations.

Applying these principles will not be any more sensitive in an international context that our late unlamented efforts to build up secret police forces or strengthen the hands of tax collectors in developing countries. But, it will draw on experience not mearly as well established in the tradition of western public administration, and therefore it poses somewhat greater risks of failure to the governments involved. Still, at least those engaged in developing technical assistance programs to deliver benefits to the poor can be proud of their efforts if they succeed, as they never could have in Iran or Vietnam. And even if they fail, the situation is not likely to be worsened by their efforts. Thus, success in the atavistic objectives pursued in Iran is more to be dreaded than failure in efforts to alleviate the burdens of poverty. No one will demand an accounting before an international tribunal even if such interventions occasionally reach the wrong target.

I

Administering to the poor means superimposing a new set of problems upon the still imperfect administration of other government programs, for which conventional assistance in public administration may still be required. These special problems of human resource development may be grouped into six categories:

1. They involve new-styles of projects[1] design and management. Traditional development projects aim at providing a good or service to the general public; they succeed if they generate more revenue, or more income or wealth, than they absorb; they are designed to take advantage of state-of-the-art technologies, and they are best implemented when they are more or less self-operating; they involve standard governmental roles; and they are considered rational so long as they continue to produce a return on the investment. As the accompanying table suggests, none of these familiar characteristics applies to "new-style projects."
2. They must deal with the "cognitive distance"[2] that separates administrators from the public. One of the most intractable problems in administering

to the poor is the difficulty that administrators have in perceiving their needs, and the corresponding sense of remoteness that these isolated groups feel from the government. There are physical and geographical reasons for this cognitive distance; the very poor often live in parts of the cities where the government officials do not go, or on farms far from the road where their vehicles cannot travel. And there are social distances as well, springing from differences in education and culture, class interests, and personal life styles. These distances cannot be traversed by goodwill alone. The cognitive elements can be addressed through training and special job assignments: even the general bureaucratic reluctance to work on these difficult problems can be reduced through changed incentive structures in the administrative system. But there would still remain the sacrifices that these assignments impose on the families of the administrators involved – remote locations lacking in health and education and other amenities taken as the entitlement of members of the civil service, for example. On the part of the special public itself, the distance is not diminished by any of these policies. It is distrust of the government, a product of the generations as well as of personal experience, that is encountered even in countries whose regimes are rated liberal, democratic, arid concerned. Dealing with cognitive distance on both sides of the social gap will require time and conscious effort, and when neither are abundant, changes will be required in the whole administrative approach to poverty.

3. They are likely to require numerous small-scale projects as well as wholesale economic approaches to poverty. The current preference of planners and donors for large-scale activities is not capricious: they economize on scarce design and administrative resources by reducing the number of enterprises to be monitored. Even the initial costs of gaining project approval do not diminish much when the dimensions of a program are reduced (one version of Parkinson's law holds that decision-makers' attention to projects occurs in the inverse proportion to their dimensions). Apart from these administrative considerations, there is the inevitable fact that large projects are more impressive and therefore produce greater short-term benefits to politicians than do the activities of humbler proportions. But the experience in dealing with poverty has not encouraged the belief that a few large-scale interventions will suffice. When direct transfers are possible through social security programs or food stamp programs, a nationwide system based on uniform eligibility criteria may serve even special publics, but where resource constraints do not permit wholesale redistribution, efforts on behalf of the poor have to

be targeted to those most in need of specific government services. Such targeting requires, in addition to a diagnosis of needs, a large number of small projects capable of reaching isolated groups. Multiple projects require major changes in the procedures used to choose, design, implement, and evaluate public activities.

4. They depend on peripheral, as well as central, administrative resources. Centralized administrative systems cannot cope with the numerous small projects required to elicit response from hard-to-reach disadvantaged groups. But if governments are to rely instead on decentralized systems, they must apply new standards of performance in the field. Yet, changes in performance at peripheral posts are hard to achieve; they do not necessarily follow reforms at the center. Improvements like civil service reforms and centralized purchasing innovations among the new member states of the United Nations have probably improved efficiency in many central agencies, but in field offices their influence is negligible. "New-style" projects will require far-reaching changes in the behavior of local officials as well as Central bureaus. They are the ones who will have to identify special publics in need of the new services, manage small local efforts with whatever administrative resources are available, and design, implement, and evaluate programs using the new standards and procedures appropriate to 'Type II' projects.

5. They are slow acting remedies. It takes longer to train teachers than to build a school, and still longer to achieve full adult literacy or to eliminate pre-school malnutrition. Programs with such social objectives cannot be measured by their physical accomplishments alone; criterion of success requires analysis of community behavior. Relative to the funding involved, and the size of the public served, human resource development projects are administration-intensive and time-extensive. They call for styles of organization that conventional management theory applies to projects like a massive irrigation system.

The implications for international donors and development planners are disconcerting: a longer time frame for project support, more experimentation with sustained but unconventional operations, and a willingness to provide funding for recurrent costs as well as start-up investments to prevent premature cessation of activities in the event the political commitment of the host government erodes. These requirements are sufficiently different from those of most development projects that willingness to provide them may be considered in itself an early indicator of the commitment of a government to human resource development – as well as a predictor of the prospects for its success.

6. They require the use of unconventional administrative resources. The characteristics already described suggest the need to extend the reach of administrators to remote or otherwise isolated areas, and to special publics who are unlikely to seek them out for assistance. These kinds of human resource development services almost inevitably require intensive relationships with the public because they involve changing attitudes and behavior, which in turn calls for specially adapted educational activities, a supportive or reinforcing attitude, and a quick reactive posture that monitors and accommodates changing public responses. But hierarchic, formal bureaucracies are not well suited to playing that role; apart from the costs of enlarging them sufficiently to perform the needed services, their inclinations, established procedures, and comparative advantage lie in the directions of standard routines that can be applied to the public at large, not to the exceptions. Centralized bureaucratic systems do have a role to play in reaching special publics, but it lies in developing new, unconventional administrative resources rather than in direct service to the poor.

Perhaps, the greatest role bureaucracies can plan is to find ways of extending their own reach: to recruit, train, supervise, and deploy paraprofessionals; and to use their knowledge of legal requirements for the management of public resources to mobilize local self-help efforts in the urban and rural slums; to improve the efficiency and effectiveness of voluntary groups willing to work with the poor; and, most important of all, to help organizations that already exist among the poor, giving them guidance in their own internal management, arbitrating among rival claimants when necessary, and providing them with information about the resources that might be available for their own further development. They can also act as links between these informal organizations in the field and the political and administrative leadership at the center, to the benefit of both.

All of these extensions of the administrative system have been employed in poverty and human resource development programs, and when they succeed, they can provide services that could not come from traditional bureaucracies. But these administrative resources are hard to develop and harder to manage, and while they add to the effectiveness of development administrators, they do not simplify their lives.

II

No administrative system would find it easy to deal with all of these problems simultaneously. Individually, these six problems could be addressed by changes in public policy or administration without necessarily affecting government performance very much. Projects can be designed for more emphasis on citizen response; longer commitments to project funding can result from agreements between governments and international donors; small projects can be generated locally and supported under national plans; improving administration at the periphery is a slow process but a natural consequence of training and better procedures; even changing administrators' perceptions of the needs and capacities of the poor can be brought about as the bureaucratic system structures itself to respond to them. Each of these requirements is individually possible, though difficult. The real problem is that major improvements in human resource development efforts will not occur until all of them are addressed successfully. It is the combination of these problems that calls for radically different approaches in administering to the poor.

Yet, addressing each of these problems separately would introduce contradictions and incompatibilities that could not be reconciled by incremental or marginal improvements. For example, redesigning projects so that they enlist a positive response from each of many special publics is an administration-intensive operation in itself. In conventional systems, it would call for more expertise and wider uses of performance incentives than are usually available for public services; yet the larger a bureaucracy grew to redesign projects and administer personnel for these purposes, the more self-contained it would become, and the greater its cognitive distance from the poor. The more small projects there were in the system, as required by the mission of reaching special publics, the more difficult it would be to maintain long-term commitment to all of them and to control the quality and equity of their operations. The greater the extent to which the administration relied on local participation, the greater the strain would be on the periphery of the administrative system itself – which is the element least qualified to bear the weight of innovation. In short, trade-offs among the policies required to "administer to the poor" include the need for response-oriented investment, which calls for administration-intensive projects; the use of small-scale projects, which require administration-extensive approaches; the reliance on peripheral administrative resources, which threaten the professional standards of central management; the need for longer time frames, which requires the highest degree of professionalism and at the same time reduces the discretionary capacity of local administrators to respond creatively to changing project needs; the use of informal organizations as an aid to administration, which challenges the authority of both central and peripheral managers; the call to reduce the cognitive distances between government officials and the poor, which requires closer contact between these elements – a condition that becomes inoperable as projects multiply in number, the use of intermediaries increases.

The solution most likely to provide the flexibility necessary to weigh those trade-offs involves decentralization of decision-making. The purpose would be to make better use of locally chosen authorities supplemented by the field offices of the responsible national agencies. Such decentralization is politically difficult, and sometimes impossible, but it is also a pre-condition to most of the other remedies. Only when development planners are prepared to share decision-making authority over details of project design, sitting, and implementation, while retaining responsibility for program priorities and major funding allocations, is it possible to mount a large number of projects and engage field staffs and civic organizations in development activities. De-concentration also gives central authorities, a longer time perspective than their engagement in project minutiae would allow if they retained these functions for themselves. It does not, of course, reduce the cognitive distance between central authorities and special publics, but it provides an incentive for peripheral administrators to do so, since they would have to take responsibility for project outcomes.

Transferring major developmental policies to local jurisdiction also runs counter to the intuitions of national planners; and indeed, much of the experience with local government reinforces these perceptions. Certain (but not all) provincial and municipal affairs are inefficiently managed nearly everywhere, and it is only to be expected that a nation's best talent in politics and administration is drawn to the center. The trend toward centralization is centuries old, dating from the triumph of the nation-state over the feudal principality and the walled town. It is a necessary antidote to the conflicting local interests and priorities that impede national development. But the trend to centralization has to be merged with an outward flow of authority if the emergent problems of social development are to be addressed.

For there is no such incompatibility of purpose between central and local programs of human resource development as there is in other matters of intergovernmental relations like highway construction or the maintenance of standards in education or public employment, matters about which local and national leaders are often in conflict. Decentralization is a safer bet in Type II programs, where improvement benefits both levels of the polity, than in Type I activities.

Effective decentralization is not achieved by a single act. It requires a carefully planned sequence of authority-transferring decisions. These decisions can follow several alternative courses, beginning with either the elimination of review procedures for releasing funds for projects already agreed upon, or with assignment of responsibility for developing projects to be funded automatically within defined financial or substantive limits. A third course, to increase the resources available locally by enlarging the tax basis of municipal or rural governments so that they can carry out the desired programs on their own initiative, is not very often available in less developed countries. Either of the first alternatives involves central funding and therefore requires new procedures for control or audit: decentralization usually involves simplifying these procedures, making them less onerous administratively, or granting more discretion politically. Both involved risks, for both donor agency and host government.

III

The dimensions of these new programs call for equally drastic changes in international assistance policy. Perhaps the U.S., a declining superpower whose national leadership faces other urgent demands, can no longer provide the model for other donors to follow. The fact is that the potentialities of foreign aid have not interested American presidents very much in the past two decades. If the retrenchment in foreign aid continues, there are not likely to be in the 1980s the kinds of fully staffed, fully confident U.S. field missions that advised the Vietnamese and Iranian autocrats in the 1960s and 1970s: those particular mistakes will not be repeated.

On the other hand, the vision of using foreign aid to administer to the poor is developing a strong appeal in the international agencies.[3] Their directors, investors, donors, and national constituencies are somewhat more tolerant of long-term objectives than is the U.S. Congress or domestically oriented presidents. The World Bank and United Nations experiences have reconfirmed what the U.S. should have learned long ago about the vulnerability of prestige projects and elite-oriented development programs to subsequent political challenge. For their part, governments in the less developed countries, too, have been experimenting more than they get credit for with new organizational approaches like those described in this article: new ways of managing irrigation, urban land reform, and integrated rural development, for example, that permit at least some of the national investments to reach the poor. But these experiments are not yet systems. Their implications for national and international policies are only beginning to emerge.

Administering to the poor is a function that requires a powerful political commitment, even to the point of self-denial by both politicians and central administrators. The self-denial is, however, only apparent: what they relinquish are functions that they have never been able to discharge very effectively. The approach suggested here requires political and administrative leaders to take on a new role in building institutions capable of serving special publics that cannot be reached through conventional means. But the payoff is good: it is now generally agreed that when all members of a society can gain access to services that are required for the collective development of human resources, performance in both economic and political spheres improves. That fact should provide the dominant guidance to development administration in the 1980s.

NOTES

1. The term "new-style projects" is now used by the World Bank economists to describe poverty-oriented activities.

2. The phrase was coined by Robert Chambers.

3. The World Bank's third annual Development Report (August 1980) considers these dimensions in its review of human resource development programs.

DEVELOPMENT ASSISTANCE IN PUBLIC ADMINISTRATION: REQUIEM OR RENEWAL

Milton J. Esman

IN THE BEGINNING

The announcement of Point IV in 1949 heralded large-scale technical assistance. At that time, development was conceived as a process that combined economic growth with modernization. The mainstream consensus on the meaning of development, shared by academics and practitioners alike, was supported by the following propositions:[1]

(1) Modernization is the outcome of historical necessity. Economic growth occurs through a deterministic sequence of stages. All societies are destined to participate in this beneficial evolution, but it can be accelerated by wise policy.
(2) Development can be facilitated by the transfer of resources and technologies from advanced to underdeveloped countries. Imported capital speeds up growth, while technology increases efficiency and facilitates modernization.
(3) The state is a benevolent institution and the principal instrument of development. The Roosevelt reforms, the Stalinist transformation, the Keynesian prescriptions for economic management, all required a proactive state. Modernizers work primarily through the central government where

Comparative Public Administration: The Essential Readings
Research in Public Policy Analysis and Management, Volume 15, 345–358
Copyright © 2006 by Elsevier Ltd.
All rights of reproduction in any form reserved
ISSN: 0732-1317/doi:10.1016/S0732-1317(06)15014-9

they can manage and control the "macrosystem," often in opposition to conservatives and traditionalists whose power base is local. The center can determine what happens at regional and local levels.

(4) Balanced development requires the mastery of modern science, including the science of economics, and control of the main levers of public policy. Development decisions should be in the hands of benevolent, technocratic planners, protected by enlightened, modernizing political leaders.

(5) Bureaucracy is the main vehicle and exemplification of modern administration. When its members are adequately trained and equipped with the appropriate technologies, it can be a reliable and effective instrument of modernizing elites.

(6) Attentive publics and especially the leaders of developing countries are eager for growth and modernization, will sacrifice other values in order to achieve these goals, and welcome the material contributions and intellectual tutelage of westerners.

(7) The transformation from backwardness to progress will be rapid and benefits will be widely shared. Since economic growth produces full employment and increased labor productivity, there is little need for explicit concern with distributive issues.

(8) Development will yield enhanced well-being as well as the preconditions for political democracy, but these depend on the maintenance of political stability. Since premature democratic participation could overload and destabilize fragile political institutions, it should not be emphasized during the transition period.

This broad framework harbored many specific variations. Some emphasized private enterprise, others the entrepreneurial functions of the state. At times other themes surfaced, such as grassroots community development and, later, human resources development. But for a quarter century until the mid-1970s, this paradigm held together. It commanded the allegiance of enlightened publics in both developing and developed countries and furnished the rationale for the flow of most international development assistance that was not directly related to security goals.[2] It provided the curricula through which thousands of students of economic development were socialized into their roles as officials in developing countries or administrators of foreign-assistance programs.

What were the functions of public administration within this paradigm? Because of the expanding role of the state in promoting and guiding development and because of the increasing complexity of modern economies, good public management was obviously necessary. The capabilities of the state and of its administrative organs would have to be increased, and rapidly, in order to cope with new requirements both from the productive sectors and from the "nation building" and welfare services instituted by post-colonial governments to legitimatize new regimes. This explosive expansion of the state and its heavy dependency on public administration implied the need for rationalization of government services, in effect Weberianization of the structures and procedures of the burgeoning public bureaucracies.

There have been several streams in American public administration, but the dominant stream in the 1940s followed the tradition of Woodrow Wilson, F. W. Taylor, and Luther Gulick and was prominently represented in international technical assistance.[3] By its advocates it was described as a set of politically neutral techniques that could produce economy, efficiency, and effectiveness in implementing policies and programs sanctioned by responsible political leadership. It was not addressed to the controversial substance of policy, to politics, but to the most efficient processes for carrying them out. As codified in the POSDCORB framework, American public administration was a technocratic science (1) universally applicable to all cultures, all regimes, all sectors of the state and the economy; and (2) committed to rationalizing structures and procedures within the bureaucratic institutions of the state. The focus was on the agencies of the cultural government, primarily on such system-wide activities as budgeting and accounting, personnel management, supply systems, organization and methods activities and only secondarily on line management, which later came to be known as "delivery systems."[4] Administration at sub-national and local levels was neglected because this could be determined by decisions taken at the center of the system.

This conception of public administration fitted hand-in-glove with the macro-growth and modernization models previously discussed – centralizing, elitist, technocratic, optimistic about the inevitability of progress and confident of the capacity of modern science and the state, through social engineering, to transform societies from backwardness to modernity. Because they were generalizable and replicable techniques, American public administration would be a component of the diffusion of "Yankee know-how," which, through technical assistance, could rescue the new nations from their inherited but remediable backwardness and speed their participation in the material and spiritual benefits of modern scientific civilization.

THE END OF INNOCENCE

Three decades of experience since Point IV, and the influence of the behavioral social sciences have produced a disillusioned mood among developmentalists in all fields, including public administration.[5] This mood is far
better informed of differences among and within developing countries, of
the multiple goals of their regimes, and of the complexities and frustrations
of guided societal change than was the naive, ahistorical optimism of the
earlier period. It is now recognized that neither economic growth nor institutional modernization are unilinear or historically inevitable. Economies
may stagnate, institutions may decline in effectiveness, and societies may fail
to deal with their central needs. The benefits of rapid economic growth,
especially those derived from mainline urban-industrial investment models,
have been skewed toward a relatively small minority in the "modern" sector,
leaving rapidly increasing majorities especially in rural areas as impoverished, insecure, and powerless as they were three decades ago.[6] In the face of
exploding populations and increasing concentration of the ownership of
productive assets, the prediction that rapid economic growth, even where it
does occur, would automatically distribute benefits widely has not been
realized.

Confidence in the efficacy of planning, in science, and in the benevolent
role of the state, has also been shaken. Most of the states of the Third World
have taken on vast new functions in economic management and the provision of public services. The size of their bureaucracies has burgeoned and
so have their budgets, but many have proved to be incompetent or repressive
and sometimes both. State bureaucracies both in socialist and in mixed
regimes have demonstrated a tendency to become self-serving, even corrupt
centers, producing modest benefits often at high costs to the societies that
support them. Administrative techniques when transplanted or installed can
be bent to the interests of established elites or survive as formalisms without
producing new capabilities or substantive reforms. Even when new, rationalized capabilities are produced with the help of foreign technical assistance,
they can be used to enhance regime objectives, which few observers would
define as developmental.

Further complicating the picture is the convincing evidence from comparative studies of administration that, except at operationally unmanageable levels of generalization, public administration is a profoundly plural,
not a universal phenomenon. The management of a central bank, of a
research station, of a postal service, or of a small irrigation system confronts
the analyst with different administrative requirements even within the same

political system. Regulatory (e.g., police), promotional (e.g., cooperatives), service (e.g., health clinics), construction (e.g., road building) activities directed at the same rural publics produce distinctive sets of problems and require different treatment. To be useful, the universe of public administration must be disaggregated to facilitate both analysis and action, a need that the present state-of-the-art has yet to address systematically.

The expectation of the early developmentalists that the modern sectors of the economy would gradually incorporate or absorb the traditional peripheries has not been realized. This misplaced confidence contributed to the concentration of public administrationists on the central administrative systems and the central government ministries. The vital links of government agencies with their publics and the impacts of administrative action on these publics were accorded very low priority. The consequences have been urban bias and neglect of the periphery, especially of the rural areas where majorities continue to live in poverty.[7] It now appears that the standard vehicle of western public administration, the hierarchically organized and functionally specialized bureaucratic agency, may be ill-suited or insufficient to provide services for mass constituencies in many developing countries. The reasons are not only the excessive costs and the inappropriateness of highly specialized services for poor and scattered rural publics, but also the physical, social, and cognitive distance between officialdom and these publics. The new combinations of methods required to extend services oriented to the basic needs of these very large but diverse constituencies, as outlined in Montgomery's paper in this series, greatly expand the understanding of administrative resources, channels, and methods that informed the classical version of public administration.

As the concepts and methods of public administration were stretched and strained through confrontation with unfamiliar environments, so too were those of technical assistance. Few regime elites, including U.S.-trained career administrators, desire increased efficiency or program effectiveness, not to mention social equity, when these conflict with more salient personal or institutional objectives. Outsiders can influence but cannot determine the values even of client regimes. Since cultural differences can impede the transferability of technologies and of institutions, there is a growing consensus that building incrementally on familiar practices – assuming agreement on goals – is likely to be more effective than "installing" efficient methods and procedures from other cultures. Many societal needs, moreover, cannot be met by the transfer of known technologies. The prevailing consensus in the early days of technical assistance was that much knowledge was available (the "storehouse"), but too little was being used. Subsequently, the emphasis shifted to adaptation to unfamiliar social and natural environments. More recently has come the sober realization that for many of the most urgent needs in developing countries there are no known or reliable technologies to transfer, only ideas or hypotheses that need to be tried and tested.[8] One of the most important unanswered questions is how resource-poor governments can extend minimal services to physically dispersed and resource-poor publics.

Technical assistance has proved to be a high-risk enterprise. In no set of activities is this more evident than in public administration. Technical assistance in public administration involves all the uncertainties connected with working in unfamiliar environments with ambiguous goals and imperfect knowledge. But beyond that it means interventions that directly affect the distribution of power, power within and among bureaucratic groups, between bureaucrats and politicians, and among societal interest groups. Only the most trivial technical assistance in public administration can ever be considered apolitical. Administrative innovations not only convey the threatening behavioral changes that interest organizational sociologists, but also shifts in structures of power that concern political scientists. The risks of failure or malfunctioning can be reduced by greater knowledge of the institutional dynamics of the host society, but such knowledge is often speculative and the subject of disagreement among experts. Even when the technology is appropriate – and this can seldom be assumed – the political environment may turn sour. A minister who favors performance budgeting or land reform may be replaced without notice by one who does not; the formers' enthusiasm may be eroded by the skepticism and hostility of his staff, of other ministers or of important interest groups. Knowledge cannot supersede power. More Farsi-speaking American students of Iranian culture could not have blocked technical assistance to the Shah's police, nor guaranteed that their increased capabilities would be used humanely, for when the chips are down, technical assistance will be instrumental to the political objectives of the principal parties.

The discipline of public administration has shared in the prevailing disillusionment and this has been aggravated by its own crisis of identity and by the skepticism it has encountered from other developmentalists concerning the utility of its knowledge.[9] More compromising even than the failure of transferred technologies to work has been the discovery that some of the transplants had not been successful in their home environments. Public administration is impaled on a dilemma that continues to split its constituency: if it is conceived primarily as a set of apolitical technologies, these methods even when they work can be as instrumental to reactionary and repressive as to developmental goals. If it is implicated in policy and politics, it must be concerned with substantive and usually controversial issues and outcomes.[10] In the first case, it can aspire to the dignity of "public management science," but without moral responsibility for the use to which its knowledge and techniques are put.[11] In the second case, it becomes an amorphous version of policy studies with a soft core of standardized knowledge, compromising its professional credentials and raising questions about what distinctive skills, knowledge and practices it conveys. The World Bank, now the largest source of development assistance, has never developed a staff capacity in public administration, nor established links with the public administration profession even though its field reports emphasize that deficiencies in "management" are the main cause of shortfalls in the projects it sponsors.

The cumulative effect has been a sharp decline in enthusiasm and in morale, a sense that the tasks of development are too daunting, that the field of public administration has little to offer, and that technical assistance may be a morally impermissible intervention in weaker and dependent societies, producing more harm than good.[12] Combined with declining support for foreign aid and for technical assistance in conventional public administration, this has precipitated a notable withdrawal of interest and participation, especially among academics. The end of innocence has prompted no little retrospective professional self-flagellation, especially in the pages of this journal, the argument being that since technical assistance in public administration has usually been ineffective and when effective, exploitative, the time has come to bury it, without even the courtesy of an appropriate requiem.[13]

RECONSTRUCTION AND RENEWAL

The original Point IV consensus on the development process and on the function of technical assistance in public administration is in shambles, but no more so than the disarray in cognate disciplines and profession. In economics, for example, the elegant Harrod–Domar growth model, which guided so many ambitious planning exercises has proved to be simplistic and virtually useless. Keynesian "policy instruments" have been unable to produce stability or full employment, not to mention equitable distribution in the dual economies that characterize most developing countries. The panoply of agricultural services drawn from recent experience in North America and western Europe has by-passed the rural majority of small farmers, tenants, and landless labors; and expansion in standard programs of elementary education has been unable to stem the relentless increase in illiteracy or the production of ill-trained graduates alienated form the land, but unqualified for urban employment. This litany could be expanded to include nearly every sector and discipline. Developmentalists in all fields, including public administration, have been compelled by painful experience to eat humble pie, to unlearn much of the inherited wisdom of their professions, and to begin to reconstruct a body of knowledge and practices more relevant to the diversity and unanticipated realities they have confronted in developing countries.

Today there is no universal consensus on development strategies. Many of the elites and their intellectual spokesmen in developing countries remain committed to catching up with the advanced economies and thus to strategies in which heavy industry is the leading sector, with emphasis on high technology. This has been the dominant theme among advocates of a new international economic order (NIEO) – that the capitalist west must increase the flow of financial resources to developing countries and improve their access to the most advanced technologies.[14] This pattern of growth would involve the construction and operation, for example, of petrochemical plants, often in the public sector, nuclear generators, and satellite communications. For such capital and technology-intensive enterprises, the appropriate public administration is closely akin to the main body of western management concepts and practices, subject of course to indigenous adaptation. Technical assistance in the manner of the 1950s can deal with these requirements by assisting with management educational and training facilities, and by the installation and adaptation of standardized management technologies similar to the process by which airlines have been successfully established in developing countries. But the NIEO argument has no answers to the compelling problems of unemployment, the distribution of income, the persistence of mass poverty, and the neglect of large majorities, especially in rural areas. For high technology, enclave development and for the slow process by which a fortunate minority is incorporated into the "modern sector," conventional public administration practices and methods of transfer remain valid.

During the past decade, in response to the dilemma of increasing poverty even in countries that have experienced high and sustained overall growth rates and the manifest failure of conventional growth strategies to deal with this problem, a new set of priorities has emerged. These are variously designated as employment strategies, basic needs strategies, growth with redistribution strategies.[15] What they have in common is an emphasis on reducing the incidence and intensity of poverty, especially in rural areas, and achieving greater equity in the distribution of the benefits of development; some of them are also committed to enhancing participation by low-income publics in decisions that affect their economic productivity and social welfare. This view of the development process has become official doctrine in USAID and has made substantial headway in international agencies, notably the World Bank, FAO, and ILO. The implementation of equity-based rural development strategies requires far-reaching changes in investment priorities and in the direction of public services, it implies a fresh conceptualization of the priorities for public administration; an emphasis on reaching large mass publics often in remote areas, developing programs that are responsive to their very diverse needs, capabilities and preferences, and organizing these publics so that they may interact more effectively with the service-providing agencies of the state, while assuming greater collective responsibility for their own development.[16]

If public administration doctrine and practices are to be instrumental to these strategies of development, they must de-emphasize the internal machinery of the staff agencies and the central ministries in capital cities and focus on the publics that need greatly improved services within the constraints of resource-poor governments. This means experimentation both in the context of services – more productive mixed-farming practices for small farmers, village health services, feeder roads, rural small industry – and with methods of providing them, including much greater attention to field operations, the use of paraprofessionals to extend service delivery, devolution to constituency organizations, and the fostering of local action capabilities. Although the needs of local publics must be the point of departure, this shift in priorities will have important implications and will necessitate reforms in the organization and operation of the departments of government, especially those that provide services in support of the new strategy.

With such a menu of requirements, the major need is the innovation of appropriate services and practices required to reach these vast underserved publics in support of basic needs strategies, not the transfer of established and replicable techniques. This does not mean, however, that the cumulative wisdom of public administration is irrelevant to these requirements or has nothing to contribute. While no standard packages are on the shelf awaiting transfer, there is much useful experience that can be tapped in the design of rural development activities, not only from recent U.S. poverty programs, but also from earlier experience with public services when western societies were still relatively poor.[17] Much of the bread and butter of administrative practices, such as record keeping, monitoring and reporting methods, and public information procedures, which have always interested line managers, but have not been of concern to academic public administrationists are available to inform programs oriented to mass publics. The innovation of practices suited to concrete rural development activities requires the skills not only of public administration, but also of social anthropology and development sociology as well as the knowledge of such subject matter specialists as agronomists, animal scientists, and public health engineers. The environment today is more receptive than ever before to multi-disciplinary cooperation and to field experimentation. If public administrationists do not become involved in such experiments, other more alert professions will occupy the field of development administration under other names, just as economists preempted public policy analyses in the U.S. during and after the heyday of PPBS.

The new strategies for development produce a set of intellectual and operational challenges as demanding and sophisticated as those that precipitated previous periods of growth and excitement in the field of public administration – the New Deal state in the 1930s, the war mobilization in the 1940s, the Great Society in the 1960s. The predominant method, given the existing state of knowledge, must be hypothesis and experimentation; and indeed the rural areas of developing countries are rife today with experiments in all sectors ranging from paraprofessional health services and nutritional supplements to participatory agricultural research and rural works programs. Opportunities for technical cooperation are abundant, not the tutelage relationship of technology transfer, but applied research and learning that link researchers with practitioners and local with foreign specialists. The theme is the joint search for workable programs and methods, which draw on comparative experience, incorporate tested administrative practices, and adopt them by trial and error to specific local conditions. Such technical cooperation can take place and is taking place on the ground; there is frugal but adequate financing for these activities; and there is likely to be continuing demand for such cooperation. The methods and the skills required, however, are more akin to mutual learning than to the conventional transfer of known technology from donor to recipient.

I have noted that public administration at the level of action is a profoundly plural, not a universal phenomenon. Consequently, demand for technical cooperation in the 1980s is likely to follow two parallel tracks: central staff agencies, central government ministries, and parastatal enterprises will continue to request help in such established technologies as computerized data processing, job classification, accounting and supply management, public administration training, and occasionally overall administrative reform. Some countries will continue to ask for help in building some of their basic administrative institutions. In these activities, the transfer of technologies and even institutions will continue pretty much in the Point IV mode, modified by what has been learned in the interim about bureaucratic behavior and the need to build institutions with effective environmental linkages to house major technological innovations.[18] There will also be requests for assistance in the maintenance of order, e.g., urban terrorism, and for law enforcement, e.g., tax collection. When such assistance meets the mutual needs of two friendly governments, it is naive and wrong-headed to expect that technical assistance in one form or another will not or should not flow.

The second track, constituting the area of creative growth in development administration, will be instrumental to equity-based strategies of development. This priority addresses a set of compelling human needs that developmentalists have as yet been unable to deal with effectively. At its core is a series of problems in public administration characterized by high levels of uncertainty and severe resource limitations. The priority and emphasis shift from extracting greater efficiency and achieving tighter control in the internal machinery of central government structures to identifying and responding to some of the urgent, diverse, but ill-defined needs of desperately poor and hard to reach rural publics. As I have already noted, equity-oriented administration imposes demands for innovation in bureaucratic structures and methods of delivery. It expands the instruments of service provision and linkage to publics beyond bureaucratic structures to include and combine voluntary agencies, market mechanisms, local governments, associational groups, and even political parties. Instead of transferring known technologies, the emphasis in foreign assistance must be on innovation and experimentation, moving gradually from pragmatic, site-specific successes to tested practices that can be tried out, but not replicated or installed, where similar conditions prevail, in this effort public administrationists, academics and practitioners, indigenous and outsiders can enrich the art and science of public administration, while contributing to the productivity, welfare and self-esteem of those whom the original vision of Point IV was intended to serve.

This fresh orientation to the tasks of development and of international technical cooperation cannot be immune to the frustrations and defeats that accompany all social interventions. Nevertheless, a hardy and earnest cohort, many of them with Peace Corps experience, has been attracted by the intellectual, operational, and normative challenges of participating in the design and implementation of equity-based strategies of development. While

they retain much of the enthusiasm and optimism of the Point IV generation, they are much more accurately informed of the conditions they will
encounter, they have a much more realistic time perspective and set of
expectations, and they are far better equipped conceptually, technically,
linguistically, and attitudinally than their predecessors. They have no difficulty combining an interest in management with a commitment to substantive outcomes. They have absorbed much of the painful learning from the
experience of the past three decades, but without succumbing to cynicism,
withdrawal or revolutionary utopianism. While most of them are committed
to enhanced participation of low-income publics in what they are doing.
Enough of them identify enhanced participation of low-income publics in
their own development, they recognize that this requires linkages and exchanges between organized publics and reformed administrative agencies of
the state, and that neither can be effective without the other. Those who are
affiliated with cognate disciplines and professions do not identify directly
with public administration, though public administration is what they are
doing. Enough of them do so identify to ensure the vigorous participation of
public administrationists in international technical cooperation for the balance of the century.

The processes of rectification and renewal are well under way in an enterprise that should be stimulating and rewarding to the field of public
administration.

NOTES

1. Among the leading representatives of the mainstream consensus were
W. W. Rostow, *The Stages of Economic Growth* (Cambridge, England: Cambridge
University Press, 1960); Paul N. Rosenstein-Rodan, Notes on the Theory of the 'Big
Pash,' in Howard S. Ellis (ed.), *Economic Development for Latin America* (New York:
St. Martin's Press, 1961); and Benjamin H. Higgins, *Economic Development*
(New York: Norton, 1959). A good compendium of the leading writers can be
found in Gerald Meier (ed.), *Leading Issues in Economic Development*, second edition
(Oxford, England: Oxford University Press, 1970).

2. See, for example, Lester B. Pearson, Chairman, Report of the Commission on
International Development, *Partners in Development* (New York: Praeger, 1969).

3. The classic is Luther Gulick and Lyndall Urwick (eds.), *Papers on the Science of
Administration* (New York: Institute of Public Administration, Columbia University,
1937).

4. The best application of this doctrine to developing countries was the United
Nations, Department of Economics and Social Affairs, *A Handbook of Public Administration* (New York: United Nations, 1961).

5. Behavioral approaches to public administration in developing countries appear prominently in the work of the Committee on Comparative Politics of the SSRC, especially Joseph La Palombara (ed.), *Bureaucracy and Political Development* (Princeton: Princeton University Press, 1963); and in the publications of the Comparative Administration Group of the ASPA, including John D. Montgomery and William J. Siffin (eds.), *Approaches to Development; Politics, Administration, and Change* (New York: McGraw-Hill, 1966); and Fred W. Riggs (ed.), *Frontiers of Development Administration* (Durham, NC: Duke University Press, 1970).

6. This position was first popularized by Robert McNamara in his Nairobi speech to the Governors of the World Bank and IMF in 1973. See *The New York Times*, September 30, 1973, Section 4, p. 14.

7. On urban bias, see Michael Lipton, *Why Poor People Stay Poor* (Cambridge, MA: Harvard University Press, 1977).

8. For an early statement of this position, Milton I. Esman and John D. Montgomery, *Systems Approaches to Technical Cooperation: The Role of Developmental Administration*, in this Journal, September/October, 1969, pp. 507–539.

9. On the chronic crisis of identity in the field of public administration, see the Silver Anniversary of this journal, XXV(1), March 1965.

10. For examples of the large literature on the public policy approach to public administration, see Y. Dror, *Public Policy Making Reexamined* (San Francisco: Chandler, 1968); and Michael Reagan, *The Administration of Public Policy* (Glenview, IL: Scott-Foresman, 1969).

11. See, for example, Felix A. Nigro and Lloyd G. Nigro, *Modern Public Administration*, third edition (New York: Harper & Row, 1973).

12. For example, William and Elizabeth Paddock, *We Don't Know How* (Ames, Iowa: Iowa State University Press, 1973).

13. For example, the *Symposium on Comparative and Development Administration: Retrospect and Prospect*, in the November/December 1976 issue of this Journal, pp. 615–654. A lively critique of both classical and behavioral approaches to public administration, including their application to developing countries can be found in Frank Marini (ed.), *Toward a New Public Administration: The Minnowbrook Perspective* (Scranton: Chandler Publishing Company, 1971).

14. Three good sources on the NIEO are Jagdish N. Bhagwati (ed.), *The New International Economic Order: The North-South Debate* (Cambridge, MA: MIT Press, 1977); Karl P. Sauvant and Hajo Hasenpflug, *The New International Economic Order* (Boulder, Co.: Westview Press, 1977); and Robert L. Rothstein, *Global Bargaining* (Princeton: Princeton University Press, 1979).

15. See, for example, Hollis B. Chenery, *Redistribution with Growth* (Oxford, England: Oxford University Press, 1974); Edgar Owens and Robert Shaw, *Development Reconsidered* (Lexington, MA: Lexington Books, 1972); and a series of articles in *World Development*, Volume 7, Number 6, June 1979.

16. On the role of public administration in connection with equity based on strategies of development, see Norman T. Uphoff and Milton J. Esman, *Local Organization for Rural Development: Analysis of Asian Experience* (Ithaca, NY: Rural Development Committee, Center for International Studies, Cornell University); Milton Esman, Development Administration and Constituency Organization, *Public Administration Review*, Volume 38, Number 2, March/April 1978; John M. Cohen

and Norman T. Uphoff, *Rural Development Participation* (Ithaca, NY: Rural Development Committee, Center for International Studies, Cornell University); Milton J. Esman and John D. Montgomery, *The Administration of Human Resource Development*, World Bank Staff Paper (Forthcoming, July 1980).

17. The literature and state of knowledge on the administrative dimensions of the U.S. poverty programs of the 1960s are summarized in three *PAR* symposia: symposium on *Alienation, Decentralization and Participation*, January/February, 1969, pp. 3–64; symposium on *Neighborhoods and Citizen Involvement*, May/June, 1972, pp. 159–223; and *Citizen Action in Model Cities and CAP Programs*, special issue, September, 1972.

18. For a summary and clarification of the institution building literature, see Melvin Blase, *Institution Building: A Source Book* (Washington, DC: AID, U.S. Department of State, 1973), distributed by Sage Publications.

PART III

MANAGING INSTITUTIONS THROUGH PLANNING AND DECENTRALIZATION

Eric E. Otenyo and Nancy S. Lind

This part focuses on the operational aspects of development administration. Rather than muddling through conceptual definitions, this preview underscores the salience of planning and managerial techniques from a comparative perspective. Perhaps discussing the adoption of these approaches through a time frame might capture the field's core orientations. To do this, we choose an analytical lens developed by George Honadle (1984). Honadle observed that the field of development administration has experienced three shifts in the years between 1960 and 1980. Each of these three shifts served as the beacons within which important conceptual themes were situated. The first phase was referred to as the "decline of the grand theories." Rigg's prismatic model of administration is perhaps the most famous theory of this phase. Most of the work outlined in the previous two parts of this volume fall within this phase.

The second phase, termed "peasant recognition," saw a proliferation of important studies on rural areas. The final shift was in the area of "growth to capacity via equity." Perhaps these categories are not mutually exclusive. They provide a framework for understanding the growth and evolution of the broad field and interest in comparative administration. We turn our attention to the operational aspects of the field of interest and consider

Comparative Public Administration: The Essential Readings
Research in Public Policy Analysis and Management, Volume 15, 359–369
Copyright © 2006 by Elsevier Ltd.
ISSN: 0732-1317/doi:10.1016/S0732-1317(06)15051-4

management of institutions and capacity building. These topics continue to influence global administrative practices.

We start by noting some of the defining works in the area of institutional change and its impact on development. The underlying assumption is that development continues to be a primary concern of most societies, especially those in the global south. While no one can deny that development studies are a dynamic multidisciplinary endeavor, the place of governance and administration continues to be a central question in the larger field. Indeed, early comparativists including Fred Riggs in the 1960s posed the same question. Development scholars then and now debated on the meaning of development and the implications of weak institutions. In addition, scholars of political development including Lucien Pye, Samuel Huntington, Myron Weiner, and Amartya Sen added other dimensions such as freedom and ability of political systems to amicably handle challenges of political integration (Pye, 1963; Huntington, 1987; Weiner, 1987; Sen, 2000). Even though their formulations were important and endure, the economic angle of development continues to attract most interest (Brohman, 1996; Nussbaum, 2000; Stiglitz, 2000; World Bank, 2002). These contemporary writers focused on aspects of institutional development and capacity building for purposes of understanding development, in a comparative sense. As Norman Uphoff argues, in recent years, international donor agencies including the World Bank (WB) and United States Agency for International Development (USAID) have "come to recognize how crucial institutional development is for overall development success" (Uphoff, 1986, p. 1).

Perhaps the key question throughout the decades has been why some institutions propelled some parts of the world to development and others to poverty and despair. Organization and institutional theory scholars have long grappled with these issues. Ali Farazmand put it nicely when he stated that organizations are indispensable to human and civilization progress and in meeting societal needs (Farazmand, 1994, p. 1). Farazmand adds that organizations act as both political and spiritual institutions by the fact that they provide comfort and calm to people (Farazmand, 1994, p. xiv). Stated differently, the problems of development have everything to do with institutional growth and capacity building in the relevant organizations.

This collection traces antecedents to contemporary thinking in the larger field of development administration, especially the place of institutions and their attendant organizations. Theo Toonen sets the tone by laying out the framework for understanding institutional changes for administrative transformation.

To coincide with Hondale's (1982) "shift to the village" scheme, we highlight the importance of understanding administration in rural areas because administration in several countries is about reaching people outside the major cities. Indeed, administering rural communities occupies a central part of what comparative and development administration is all about. Current literature in this genre is vast, but continues to provide theoretical frameworks for understanding the place of administration in managing societal change. The works of Robert Chambers (1974, 1984), Jon Moris (1977), and David Leonard (1987) provide themes in "peasant recognition" as an important part of using administration to promote development. More recently, Jean Oi shows that economic growth in rural areas is premised on institutional changes. For example, she demonstrates that in China, which has a large rural population, a combination of resources, political leadership, and skillful local leadership were important variables in the push toward reform (Oi, 1999). Rural China attained a considerable degree of industrialization through institution of an active decollectivization and fiscal reform. These authors and others made the case that institutions are an important element in the bid to understand development.

We utilize Leonard's work to highlight the centrality of organizational linkages to the objective of promoting rural development. Leonard, an avid student of organizations, based most of his findings on the work done in Africa and perhaps more than any theorist articulated the view that many of the differences in organizational behavior between Africa and the USA/Western Europe are fundamentally not due to managerial failures, but to fundamental dissimilarities in the value of the societies that encapsulate them. What seems to be the case is that contrary to the belief and contention in the works of most development administrators, it is not the science of public administration that was exported that is a problem (Leonard, 1987; Leonard & Marshall, 1982, pp. 899–916). Much like the authors we read in Part 2, Leonard (1977), Uphoff (1986, p. 7), and Chambers (1984) all speak against transplanting institutions based on western cultures in foreign lands. Chambers' work expands this logic by noting that western advisors and technical assistant administrators have to appreciate the perspectives of rural beneficiaries (Chambers, 1984).

PLANNING AND DECENTRALIZATION

The collection includes work on planning and decentralization because these are all tied together in the broad attempt at enhancing rural and community administration theory. Planning is a decision-making activity. It is also a process of control because it involves gathering information and marshalling resources "in a sequential priority framework in order to maximize agreed-upon objectives" (Murray, 1975, p. 369). Although planning is an integral part of development administration, its origins are not hard to find in western administrative thought. In fact, American public administration students can easily trace planning to classical works of Frederick W. Taylor and Luther Gulick. The former articulated the process in his design for work practices in corporations. For his part, Gulick's principles included a statement to the effect that planning was a central managerial role. Arguably, the American planning variant had more to do with the business world as opposed to the public sector. It was also largely decentralized and not comprehensive. This is in sharp contrast with the vast majority of countries, especially in the 1960s and 1970s. The planning discourse then assumed ideological proportions. This was in part due to the association of planning with command-type Communist Soviet administrative styles. Ironically, centralized planning achieved some limited success and was considered a useful tool for promoting development and industrialization.

Although a great many countries claimed to employ development planning as an administrative tool in the immediate post World War 2 period, few actually realized substantial success (Meier, 1965, p. 31). In countries such as the then USSR, planning was seen as the road map to the establishment of an industrial establishment that was able to defend the country from its internal and external enemies. The Soviet system was transplanted to its former allies of Poland, Hungary, and other satellite states abroad. Similarly, the decentralized type of planning was promoted in Britain and the Scandinavian countries primarily for forestalling unemployment and eliminating depression. The decentralized type was transplanted to areas where Britain had strategic influence such as its colonies in Asia and Africa (Meier, 1965, p. 31). Since the literature on planning as an economic enterprise is vast, we cannot attempt to synthesize its main arguments.

While the literature agrees that planning is not an end in itself, this collection seeks to tease out the significance of planning as a process in administrative development. Waterston's (1965) work provides a starting point to provide a rational meaning of planning. For him, planning is an "organized, intelligent attempt to select the best available alternatives to achieve specific goals" (Waterston, 1965, p. 8). He also makes the important point that if planning did not deliver its promise, it was because of political rather than economic and administrative factors. Of course, he adds that comparative scholars continue to make certain that countries learn from the experiences of each other (Waterston, 1965, p. 3). This is as true of 1965 as it is now in 2006. More recent writings attest to this claim; for example, Frances Stewart (1985) in promoting a basic needs (BN) approach to planning explicitly recognized that certain types of political economy were conducive to the successful implementation of development plans (Stewart, 1985, p. 2).

The literature especially from the funding donor agencies promoted the idea that reaching remote areas lacking in developmental indicators such as health centers and transport and communication infrastructures would best be served if specific projects were decentralized. Most plans, therefore, associated progress with decentralization. The field continues to draw on the vast volume of literature pinpointing the efficacy of forms of decentralization in the attainment of development objectives. The 1980s, in particular, witnessed a proliferation of decentralization literature. The entire gamut of literature on project failure might be properly placed on Hondale's generalized "growth to capacity via equity" scheme. It might not be a perfect match, but offers a convenient lens with which to analyze the evolution of development-related literature.

Of interest was how different bureaucracies managed poverty reduction programs and redistributive roles. This equity focus reinforced participation by the disadvantaged as seen in bureaucratic decentralization, community participation, and empowerment literature. For better or worse, funds supporting most of the studies on project implementation and service delivery were channeled to writers associated with the World Bank and other interested donor agencies. Many of these writers included write-ups on capacity building – the efforts to strengthen the abilities of institutions in developing countries. Without question, the 1980s and 1990s were characterized by initiatives on capacity building, natural resource use, public and private sector interactions, and the politics of implementation and sustainability (see, for example, Lindenberg & Crosby, 1981; Grindle, 1980).

However, as the rate of project failure continued to worry donor agencies, more countries were urged to decentralize their administrative institutions. Perhaps Diana Conyers was right on the mark to refer to the emerging orientation as "the latest fashion in development administration" as seen in support from academics, donor groups, and national governments (Conyers, 1983). Her work is an important statement on this important era in the development discourse. Although her analysis was global in scope, it did not mean all countries decentralized for the same reasons. Importantly, though, she observed that decentralization was in part, "a means of improving the planning and implementation of national development – especially those concerned with rural development" (Conyers, 1983, p. 99).

Much work has been done since Conyers' charge about decentralization. Importantly, Richard Stren reiterated the salience of decentralization in modern administrative processes (Stren, 2003). Surprisingly, Stren argued that decentralization is still a "development buzzword." However, he dismissed the notion that the impetus for decentralization was derived from a single source. In the new millennium, it seems countries implemented decentralization as a response to neo-liberal agendas of powerful bilateral concerns and multilateral institutions (Stren, 2003; Rondinelli, 2005[1]). In explaining the neo-liberal aspects of decentralization, Rondinelli posits that the process was occasioned by the need in the 1990s for the movers of the world economy to provide structures that would ensure easy mobility of capital, human resources, and technology (Rondinelli, 2005).

Previously, in many instances, decentralization emerged as a natural consequence of a polity's desire to respond to systemic demands. Stren recognizes this fact as well and notes that decentralization in the new millennium is also entirely a local initiative (Stren, 2003). Decentralization could as well have been initiated as a response to enhance participation or as a cost-saving device, or merely as an administrative device to "delegate" responsibilities. In a sense, Lawrence Graham's synthesis of the debate between decentralization and centralization in public administration summarized the major points of contention in the debate (Graham, 1980). Graham sought to clarify the issues as played out in the wider state and international public administration literature (Graham, 1980, p. 220).

Importantly, donor agencies saw decentralization as a means to promote rural development. With its prominent role as a partner in development matters globally, the World Bank linked planning and institution building to decentralization. Implementation of plans often required decentralized institutions. We include Conyers' as an example of exemplary writing on the decentralization debate. We add Dennis Rondinelli's reformulation of his earlier collaborative work on providing a typology of the various types of decentralization (Rondinelli, Nellis, & Cheema, 1984; Rondinelli, 2005). Rondinelli's work, previously unpublished, was written as an overview of the decentralization process generally. He traces the evolution of the "decentralization movement" from the 1950s into the 1990s and provides key concepts and efficiency and equity motivations for decentralization. He argues that decentralization in Asia, Africa, and Latin America was also closely identified with democratization movements in these countries.

While planning oversight remained in the purview of national ministries, the lending institutions enjoyed overwhelming influence on the outcomes. At the macrolevel, enabling policies were tied to donor objectives. In some cases, donor agencies including the World Bank, USAID, and the United Nations Organizations (UN system, including UNDP) support[ed] national policies that were at odds with broad interests of a majority of people in developing countries. However, the agency's stated objective is to promote development starting with provision of aid for institutional development.

END OF CENTRALIZED PLANNING?

In particular, the World Bank's position is informed by its principal mission to promote sustainable development and improve the quality of life for all people (World Bank, 2000, p. 13). Remarkably, the failure of planning to reduce poverty in many of the countries of the South must, therefore, be in part attributed to poor formulation or implementation of the plans. Perhaps no one makes this statement better than Caiden (1994, p. 428) and Lempert, McCarthy, and Craig (1995). The latter mainly based their research on Latin American experiences to successfully make the case that development plans failed to work because "they were written by bankers and economists (World Bank and USAID personnel) or western technicians from developed countries and most privileged sectors of the developing countries"(Lempert et al., 1995, p. ix). Lempert and his collaborators provide an alternative framework for planning for development that includes using full potential of human resources and influencing the state of mind – attitudes in the institutions in which development occurs.

Perhaps it is important to note that frustration with the donor community is not a new idea in the planning literature. Don Lavoie articulated a similar position and offered suggestions to replace the abandoned planning strategies (Lavoie, 1985). Since the 1980s were a lost decade in most of the South, the implication was that planning had for the most part failed. The 1980s also saw the rise in public choice ideologies that promoted market-based "guided planning" practices. These, in essence, meant the abandonment of comprehensive planning that had been the norm in most of the developing areas.

While Lavoie recognized that planning in a modern economy was not an easy task, he wondered what was left if the market was to be the main allocator of resources. But he was right to posit that no society was based entirely on the market as its coordinating principle (Lavoie, 1985, p. 237). Indeed, the World Bank, the foremost articulator of the market-driven global political economy, shared similar views (World Bank, 2000, 2002, p. 4). According to the Bank, "markets allow people to use their skills and resources and engage in higher productivity if there are institutions to support those markets" (World Bank, 2002, p. 3). In its bid to attain the development goal, the place of government institutions assumed great prominence in scholarly and practitioner discourses. For example, the Bank's reports continue to emphasize institution building, especially those that provide multinational corporations (MNCs) with an enabling environment to invest.

MNCs cannot be studied in isolation because they were among the first "development partners" to numerous governments that lacked a strong private sector culture. Many of the planned economies promoted manufacturing and industry through joint investments with MNCs. Indeed, in the 1980s state-owned enterprises (SOE) added up to 10% of the world gross domestic product (GDP) and are therefore important. Through SOEs, many Eastern European, Asian, Latin American, and African governments sought to achieve development through SOE-driven industrialization. SOEs were also key players in the transfer of economic power to local elites. Likewise, SOEs or parastatals were the major providers of vital administrative services such as postal services, telecommunications, port authorities, banking, and manufacturing.

Since many SOEs failed to achieve their stated objectives and were a tremendous burden to the economies of several developing countries, reform pundits especially funded by the World Bank targeted them for reform and privatization.[2] However, for several countries in Africa, there are historical and economic reasons why full privatization of SOEs will not be acceptable even if the World Bank wants this to happen (World Bank, 1983). Similar arguments are posited for transition economies of eastern and central Europe (Nellis & Lee, 1990). There is also evidence that failure of a number of SOEs had nothing to do with false reasoning claiming the superiority of the private sector, but rather that factors such as undercapitalization and politics are at the heart of failed firms (Nellis, 1999; Nellis & Shirley, 1991; Grosh & Mukandala, 1994). While privatization by itself is considered as an aspect of decentralization (Kiggundu, 1989), it is also an element of institution building as much as is deregulation that seeks to create conditions for market-driven economies.

Institutional support in this direction also includes providing support to rural credit firms, small-scale industries, and governmental law enforcement agencies to enforce property rights, enhance land titling, and remove transaction costs arising from inadequate information systems. Through donor support, several governments have supported establishment of agencies and units within government to oversee these changes. These forms of institution and capacity building enrich dispositions on organization development.

Contemporary institution-building support continues to promote policies that reduce government regulation and to eliminate political and bureaucratic corruption, especially in the developing areas (World Bank, 2002, p. 12). Government deregulation therefore is an important component in understanding development administration. At the international level, perhaps one of the well-written overviews of deregulation processes is Gayle and Goodrich's piece on "Exploring the Implications of Privatization and Deregulation," reproduced in this volume (1990). They make the case that the debate on privatization must grapple with conceptual muddles and recognize that more often than not, public and private sectors are not mutually "exclusive, static, or unidimensional" (Gayle & Goodrich, 1990, p. 2). Citing economic and social rationale, they also provide numerous examples of areas in which privatization has been put to effective use. An equally nuanced comparative note highlighting examples of approaches to the attendant privatization regime is represented in Chang and Jones (1992). Many of these themes resurface in subsequent discussions on "new public management" considered in Part IV.

In conclusion, we present a collection of literature informing important subjects, mostly affecting developing areas. These topics continue to attract scholarly attention in both developed and developing areas. The former are concerned through dominating and controlling institutions that provide funding for international development. The latter have since the 1950s sought to enhance economic development within their jurisdictions. Among the strategies adopted for managing development, especially in rural communities, are institution and capacity building and planning, often through decentralization. In more recent times, donor-led deregulation and privatization strategies have been touted as a panacea for development.

NOTES

1. Rondinelli, D.A. (2005). *"Government Decentralization and Economic Development the Evolution of Concepts and Practices."* Previously unpublished and kindly provided for inclusion in the present volume.

2. Privatization means several different things to different authors. Perhaps, one common trend is the idea of withdrawal from the whole to the part engagement or involvement in the real public sphere. See P. Starr (1988). "The Meaning of Privatization," *Yale Law and Policy Review* 6(1): 6–41.

REFERENCES

Brohman, J. (1996). *Popular development: Rethinking the theory and practice of development.* Malden, MA: Blackwell.

Caiden, N. (1994). The management of public budgeting. In: R. Baker (Ed.), *Comparative public management* (pp. 135–152). Westport, CT: Praeger.

Chambers, R. (1974). *Managing rural development: Ideas and experience from East Africa.* Uppsala, Sweden: Scandinavian Institute of African Studies.

Chambers, R. (1984). *Rural development: Putting the last first.* New York: Longman.

Chang, S. Y., & Jones, R. A. (1992). Approaches to privatization: Established models and a U.S. innovation. *Government Finance Review, 8*(4), 17–22.

Conyers, D. (1983). Decentralization: The latest fashion in development administration. *Public Administration and Development, 3*(2), 97–109.

Farazmand, A. (1994). *Modern organizations administrative theory in contemporary society.* Westport, CT: Praeger.

Gayle, J. D., & Goodrich, J. N. (1990). Exploring the implications of privatization and deregulation. In: J. D. Gayle & J. N. Goodrich (Eds), *Privatization and deregulation in global perspective* (pp. 1–23). New York: Quorum Books.

Graham, L. S. (1980). Centralization versus decentralization in the administration of public service. *International Review of Administrative Sciences, 46*(3), 219–232.

Grindle, M. S. (Ed.) (1980). *Politics and policy implementation in the Third World.* Princeton, NJ: Princeton University Press.

Grosh, B., & Mukandala, R. S. (1994). Tying it all together: What do we know. In: B. Grosh & R. S. Mukandala (Eds), *Public enterprises in Africa.* Boulder: L. Rienner.

Hondale, G. (1982). Development administration in the eighties: New agendas or old perspectives. *Public Administration Review, 42*(2), 172–179.

Huntington, S. P. (1987). The goals of development. In: S. Huntington & M. Weiner (Eds), *Understanding political development* (pp. 3–32). New York: Little Brown.

Kiggundu, M. (1989). *Managing organizations in developing countries: An operational and strategic approach.* West Hartford, CT: Kumarian Press.

Lavoie, D. (1985). *National economic planning: What is left?* Cambridge, MA: Cambridge University Press.

Lempert, H. D., McCarthy, K., & Craig, M. (1995). *A model development plan: New strategies and prospectives.* Westport, CT: Praeger.

Leonard, D. (1987). The political realities of African management. *World Development, 15*(7), 899–916.

Leonard, D. K., & Marshall, D. R. (1982). *Institutions of rural development for the poor: Decentralization and organizational linkages.* Berkeley: Institute of International Studies, University of California.

Lindenberg, M., & Crosby, B. (1981). *Managing development: The political dimension.* West Hartford, CT: Kumarian Press.

Meier, R. L. (1965). *Developmental planning.* New York: McGraw-Hill.

Moris, R. J. (1977). The transferability of western management concepts and programs: An East African perspective. In: L. Stifel (Ed.), *Education and training for public sector management in developing countries* (p. 75). New York: The Rockefeller Foundation.

Murray, M. A. (1975). Comparing public and private management: An exploratory essay. *Public Administration Review, 35*(4), 364–371.

Nellis, J. R. (1999). *Time to rethink privatization in transition economies.* Washington, DC: World Bank.

Nellis, J. R., & Lee, B. W. (1990). *Enterprise reform in socialist economies.* Washington, DC: World Bank.

Nellis, J. R., & Shirley, M. M. (1991). *Public enterprise reform: The lessons of experience.* Washington, DC: World Bank.

Nussbaum, M. (2000). *Women and human development: The capabilities approach.* New York: Cambridge University Press.

Oi, J. C. (1999). *Rural China takes off institutional foundations of economic reform.* Berkeley, CA: University of California Press.

Pye, L. W. (Ed.). (1963). *Communications and political development.* Princeton, NJ: Princeton University Press.

Rondinelli, D. A. (2005). *Government decentralization and economic development: The evolution of concepts and practices.* Unpublished paper.

Rondinelli, D. A., Nellis, J. R., & Cheema, G. S. (1984). *Decentralization in developing countries: A review of recent experience.* World Bank Staff Working Paper no. 581. Washington, DC: World Bank.

Sen, A. (2000). *Development as freedom.* New York: Anchor Books.

Starr, P. (1988). The limits of privatization. Report of the economic policy Institute, Washington, D.C. Reprinted in Dennis J. Gayle and Jonathan N. Goodrich, *Privatization and Deregulation in Global Perspective* (Quorum, 1990).

Stewart, F. (1985). *Planning to meet basic needs.* London: Macmillan.

Stiglitz, J. (2000). *Globalization and its discontents.* New York: W.W. Norton.

Stren, R. (2003). Decentralization and developing countries: Rhetoric or reality? Paper presented at the Canadian Political Science Association meeting, Toronto, Canada. See http://www.cpsa.-acsp.ca/template_e.cfm?folder = conference = 2003

Uphoff, N. T. (1986). *Local institutional development: An analytical sourcebook with cases.* West Hartford, CT: Kumarian Press.

Waterston, A. (1965). Development planning: Lessons of experience (assisted by C. J. Martin, A. T. Schumacher & F. A. Steuber, pp. 1–23). Baltimore: Johns Hopkins Press.

Weiner, M. (1987). Political change: Asia, Africa, and the Middle East. In: S. Huntington & M. Weiner (Eds), *Understanding political development* (pp. 33–64). New York: Little Brown.

World Bank. (1983). *World development report.* New York: Oxford University Press.

World Bank. (2002). *World development report.* New York: Oxford University Press.

FURTHER READING

Caiden, N. J. (1991). Unanswered questions: Planning and budgeting in poor countries revisited. In: A. Farazmand (Ed.), *Handbook of comparative and development administration.* New York: Marcel Dekker.

Toonen, T. J. (1993). Analyzing institutional change and administrative transformation: A comparative view. In: J. Kooiman (Ed.), *Modern governance* (Chapter 19). Newbury Park: Sage.

World Bank. (1984). *World development report* (pp. 421–434). New York: Oxford University Press.

ANALYSING INSTITUTIONAL CHANGE AND ADMINISTRATIVE TRANSFORMATION: A COMPARATIVE VIEW

Theo A. J. Toonen

1. INTRODUCTION

This contribution presents an effort to develop a public administration perspective on the ongoing process of institutional reform and transformation in Central and Eastern Europe. It is organized around three rather straightforward questions. The first refers to analytical issues. How should we study the subject at hand? We are dealing with a multi-dimensional and multi-level reform and transformation process. The Central and Eastern European experience has not yet generated any models and theories of its own which might drive the administrative analysis. The question is how one could arrive at a theoretically orientated perspective to explore adequately the ongoing, multifarious and turbulent administrative reform processes, without being unduly biased by 'western' presuppositions and preoccupations (Section 2).

The next question is: what may we learn from the developments? Which aspects of the administrative reform efforts merit attention from a comparative point of view, given the fact that the analyses so far, have been

Comparative Public Administration: The Essential Readings
Research in Public Policy Analysis and Management, Volume 15, 371–392
Copyright © 2006 by Elsevier Ltd.
ISSN: 0732-1317/doi:10.1016/S0732-1317(06)15015-0

predominantly historical, economic and political in nature? What are striking features of the historical revolution in Central and Eastern Europe from the viewpoint of building a solid administrative system for guidance, evaluation and control in the public sector? Such a system, after all, is an indispensable cornerstone of the sustained development of the liberal market economies that serve as a guide for the ongoing reforms in Central and Eastern Europe (Section 3).

The observations in this paper refer predominantly to developments within the administrative systems of Poland, Hungary and the former Czechoslovakia as reflected in the country reports of the national experts represented in this volume. Empirical research and standardized data collection on the basis of an explicit public administration interest and a common theoretical framework are still rare. This analysis is part of an attempt to explore the topic of administrative reform in post-socialist countries and to formulate some issues and research questions from an administrative point of view. The third question is, therefore, whether we might be able to identify some needs, both in terms of research and of prescriptions for public sector reform that merit attention from a public administration perspective. Is there, on the basis of the material available, anything else that can be said other than the standard prescription that public sector management and training are still much needed in the aforesaid countries? (Section 4).

2. ASSESSING ADMINISTRATIVE REFORM IN POST-SOCIALIST COUNTRIES: ANALYTICAL PROBLEMS

Developments in Central and Eastern European countries are currently rather overwhelming and thus not easily categorized. The efforts to reform the administrative systems of the countries of the former Communist Bloc are dominated by an overall effort to 'privatize' state agencies, particularly in the industrial production sector. The current attention of scholars and researchers in the area of public administration is mainly focused on the question of how to 'reform' the respective administrative systems, which are mostly grouped together in one, undifferentiated category. A prescriptive bias dominates: how can we improve the system?

Rice (1992, p. 166) has presented an overview of what should be done to bring the public administrations of Eastern European countries into the post-socialist era. On the basis of several documents from Hungary, Poland, Romania and Bulgaria, he identifies five principles that are likely to guide

Central and Eastern European societies in building their governments:

- the retreat from the discredited central government in favour of decentralization and privatization;
- the improvement of channels of communication between governments and their citizens in response to a demand for participation;
- the creation of a hospitable business environment and an adequate institutional infrastructure for a market economy;
- a concern for public welfare and social justice in terms of services and human rights;
- an efficient government administration at all levels within a setting of public review and internal and external accountability.

With this 'model' as the yardstick, Rice (1992, pp. 117–122) identifies a number of administrative needs and problems for public administration reform. To improve policy making, he primarily emphasizes the need to strengthen the capacity for economic projections and the development of strategies. The former central planning system was merely a bureaucratic device and not a system of forecasting in a market situation. Most basic statistical and other types of policy information are lacking or entirely missing.

Rice observes that the devolution of significant powers and responsibilities to sub-central governments has already advanced considerably, but that this radical shift also complicates the reform process in a number of ways. Questions about the desired central–local relationship have not been resolved, although formal pieces of legislation and local government reform offices have been established – Hungary and Poland in particular display strong activities in this field – but actual performance capacities at the local level are still far from clear. One of the problems is that, since the state enterprises formerly served as the main source of government revenue, a tax management and effective revenue-raising system, in the broadest sense, is largely absent.

Much in the same way, the various countries according to Rice (1992, p. 121) have so far largely ignored the need for civil service reform '... even though it is their civil servants who must implement planned reforms ... . Governments have apparently not conceived of their employees as a bureaucracy-wide civil service.' They have yet to develop comprehensive reform strategies. He suggests that to this end central government change agents are necessary. Central government directorates should formulate and implement comprehensive action plans to overhaul the civil service by (1) transforming the bureaucratic culture and organizational structure,

(2) introducing mechanisms to assure accountability and (3) expanding training capacity.

Such prescriptions are not uncommon, but they also raise questions. In most Western European countries, the administrative modernization process over the past decade has taken the form of a rather incremental approach, but has seldom been a centrally steered innovation process (Hesse & Benz, 1990; Dente & Kjellberg, 1988). Available evidence seems to indicate that successful institutional development is usually best perceived as an evolutionary pragmatic political process using and blending the social and political forces and dynamics within the system.

Comprehensive plans have seldom resulted in the desired administrative reforms in Western administrations. Effective reform must largely come 'from within.' Former Eastern Germany is likely to remain the only example where the transition from 'socialist' to 'post-socialist' is being tried in a comprehensive, synoptical way on the basis of a complete 'management buy-out' and subsequent 'reorganization' of the system. All other countries will necessarily be required to make the transition in a more incremental, step-by-step way. It remains to be seen which societies, in the end, are or will feel themselves better off. But it is certainly true that, with massive help from elsewhere in the world, the starting point for Central and Eastern European countries will be to rebuild themselves with what they have.

Some will find this proposition difficult to accept. The primary task of an evolutionary-orientated approach to administrative reform is to provide a solid assessment of the actual existing situation, its deficiencies and its growth or development potential. The development in the former socialist countries is, however, primarily defined in terms of a process of getting away from the previous situation instead of arriving at a desired state of affairs. The label 'post-socialist,' as such, indicates a preoccupation with what has been, without a perception of what should or will be. The future is left open.

For all three countries under observation here, a tendency is reported towards a degree of 'over-transformation' in terms of decentralization and massive streams of newly enacted legislation; distrust of the old regime and the rejection of both the 'old' central planning system and the former *cadres*, whatever their precise role, are identified with it. The people have a better idea of where they are coming from than where they are going to. Sometimes 'administrative reform' has become a goal in itself. Few people within the system – so far, but times may quickly be changing – will take the risk of 'defending' the previous situation, or show an interest that might be perceived as being associated with the Communist *ancient régime.*

The positive aspects of what was or is might, under the prevailing conditions, easily remain unarticulated. For the outsider looking at the situation, it is still very difficult to assess the precise nature and accuracy of the criticism and cynicism abundantly available with regard to both the past situation as well as the ongoing reform processes. The historically distinct character of the ongoing developments might imply that analysts have to concentrate on the innate characteristics of a transformation process which, from established Western theoretical perspectives – and their former 'Eastern' antipodes, are 'unknown.' These observations might easily be considered to be 'too romantic,' 'too optimistic' or 'naive' for a strongly built and 'modern' public administration. As with developing non-western countries, however, one might envisage tendencies towards self-governance and self-administration of parts of the society outside the domains which we – i.e. 'western' analysts – would normally identify and recognize as government and administration 'proper.'

The ongoing reform processes can be studied from different administrative angles (cf. Toonen, 1983; Kiser & Ostrom, 1982; Hood, 1991). The economic orientation of both the reform efforts and the analysis stresses the need for building an efficient and responsive administrative system. With respect to the Polish case it is observed that the ultimate result of public administration reform is to achieve a pro-citizen mentality amongst the officials and a change for the better in society's attitude towards the administration. An interest in a more effective, responsive and responsible administration is the stated purpose of many western recommendations.

As time and developments progress, however, attention has shifted to complement a mere concern for economy and responsiveness with a concern for cooperation and rectitude in the public sector. Administrative scandals in Czechoslovakia as well as a growing critique of the Polish government have contributed to the awareness that the legitimation and acceptance of administrative systems rely not only on their effectiveness and efficiency in reaching goals, but also on the way in which goals are being reached and tasks are being accomplished. The achievement of a degree of joint decision making, fairness, reciprocity in public obligations and a proper discharge of duties in substantive and procedural terms, among the parties involved, are becoming increasingly important administrative concerns in the various reform processes.

The third angle which causes observers to worry and merits attention in an administrative analysis, is the robustness and sustainability of the reforms set in motion. Not enough attention is paid to the need to build administrative capacity to implement and follow through political and legislative initiatives. People are becoming frustrated by undelivered promises and are losing their faith in the process and the credibility of the operation in the longer term. Almost all observers, most explicitly in Poland and Czechoslovakia, express their anxiety about the danger of stagnation of the reform process and a resultant fundamental political instability. There is a clear concern about the 'constitution' of the reform processes, not only – in terms of its legal structure and containment, but more importantly in terms of the basic trust and feelings of reliability among the general population.

The different angles represent more or less distinct administrative value systems (Hood, 1991). They also seem to refer: to different worlds of action and administrative reform (Kiser & Ostrom, 1982). The values of responsiveness, goal-orientation and 'effectiveness' refer to the 'world of operational choice' and the management of day-to-day actions and decisions, within a given framework of rules and institutions. Issues of accountability, reciprocity, public obligation and procedural legitimation refer to the 'world of collective choice' and situations of joint decision making, policy formulation and implementation. The sustain-ability of the reforms, the question of reliability, trustworthiness and resilience of newly erected institutions refer to a concern about the soundness of the 'constitution' of the reform processes.

2.1. Multi-Dimensional and Multi-Level Problems

Every sound administrative system will have to satisfy the three different value complexes at more or less the same time. The different value systems and underlying questions apply not only to stable liberal democratic market economies, but to transitionary systems as well, as the various reports clearly indicate. The only difference is that in stable situations and institutionally well-developed and established administrative systems the different functions and corresponding core values are usually served by more or less separate institutions and procedures. They are conventionally studied and evaluated accordingly by different theories and disciplines. To simplify: constitutional courts deal with constitutional issues, policy makers and legislatures deal with questions of collective decision making, and public managers, executives and civil servants deal with operational issues. Each type of issue requires more or less its own consideration, logic and approach. Constitutional questions are different and are therefore separated from operational management decisions.

The analytics of the ongoing transition process in Central and Eastern Europe are much more complicated than in more stable environments. The complexity and turbulence of the reforms are caused partly by the fact that, with respect to any concrete decision or development, almost all dimensions have to be considered at the same time. This often causes the different value systems to be in conflict and to overload any specific situation with analytically rather different considerations. Decisions on privatization, for example, serve in the Central and Eastern European countries different value systems at the same time. Privatization is defended for reasons of efficiency and economy. But privatization is also aimed at bringing about 'constitutional' changes in, for example, the economic or property rights structure. In the case of 're-privatization' or the restitution of private property to former owners, the 'constitutional' and 'operational' considerations are further complicated by questions of equity, fairness and rectitude.

On the other hand, efficient privatization at the operational level presupposes the existence of a market-like infrastructure (property rights, banking systems, public enforcement agencies, etc.) at the 'constitutional' level. The difference in meaning of privatization within the various perspectives implies that western knowledge and expertise in the area are often not easily transferable. Where Western efforts to 'privatize' in say Britain are usually aimed at increasing the efficiency of the economy, privatization efforts in Central and Eastern Europe are largely aimed at constructing a market system. This strongly limits the lessons that British 'privatization' may hold for Central European countries. Other examples come easily to mind: many Western business firms and companies are interested in 'privatizing' firms or factories in one of the post-socialist countries precisely because these occupy a monopoly position. The 'hospitable' part of the business environment in the post-socialist countries, is 'constitutionally' just the opposite of what the privatization philosophy entails.

The confusion of the various dimensions and levels of analysis is also reflected in proposals to privatize public transport 'because the government can make no profit out of it.' Instrumental operational considerations often dominate constitutional questions. Constitutions, legal procedures and courts, on the other hand, are given a role in the operational management of the political process. This might be understandable in the short run, but the constitutional rule of written constitutions and independent courts might easily be evaded, if not threatened, when they are systematically drawn into solving policy and operational issues. Developments with respect to the role of the Revisional Chamber in the case of Hungary provide a case in point.

The reason that courts become easily involved in the world of operational action and collective choice has to do with their well-developed organizational and operational skills and capabilities. However, operational capacities within the system are sometimes easily overlooked because of veiling 'constitutional' contexts. The problem, for example, is not that people in the post-socialist countries do not know how to compete or how to deal with 'competitive and market-like situations.' They have always been competing: not for the favour of clients or citizens, but for suppliers of goods and services, their party bosses, government officials, etc. A desired capacity comes often in a different guise. Instead of writing off whole 'lost generations' in the respective countries, one may try to find ways to organize the institutional infrastructure and the relevant policy incentives away from hierarchy towards a responsiveness by which people can and will learn to apply their already existing competitive skills in the new (constitutional and policy) setting.

2.2. Framing and Reframing

Whether we like it or not, the existing situation in Central and Eastern European countries requires an analytical capacity in which, in principle, it is possible to 'think the unthinkable' and, potentially, recognize 'the efficiency of inefficient approaches.' We need a sufficiently broad theoretical view and analytical framework. The topical issue in western public administration and organization and management sciences, i.e. to be able to (theoretically) frame and reframe the administrative problem at hand from various perspectives, is particularly relevant in the present case. 'Foreign models' and experiences are valuable and inspiring for the various countries, but cannot be applied directly and without modifications.

In Taras's opinion, '... it is better to fight against the causes of existing evil, than to search for a hypothetical good.' Indeed, we do not need a model to guide us in 'the search for a hypothetical good,' but – apart from empirical evidence – an analytical and theoretical framework that allows us adequately to conceptualize the various dimensions of the complicated multi-level and multidimensional reform process at hand. The starting point of such a framework has to be that the market economy is only 'free' within a public and legal set of enforceable rights and constraints (Riker & Weimer, 1992). Privatization presupposes a very elaborate and collectively maintained and publicly enforced 'economic constitution.' The success of introducing the mixed-market economy critically hinges upon the development of a reliable public infrastructure in terms of legal systems, regulatory agencies to safeguard competition, promotional agencies for economic and regional development and for scientific arid technological development, as well as the exploration of potential markets for export and of the provision of some kind of basic welfare administration.

3. ADMINISTRATIVE REFORM IN CENTRAL AND EASTERN EUROPE: COMPARATIVE OBSERVATIONS

From a comparative point of *view*, there is at least one point that cannot but surprise any Western European administrative observer when he looks behind the curtains of the formerly 'centrally planned' administrative systems of Central and Eastern Europe. Employment rates in public administration and particularly the segment identified as 'the civil service' are extremely difficult to compare. But the reported figures of, for example, Poland, with a total of 1,58,000 civil servants of which 53,000 are employed at national level and out of which about 10,000 work for the central ministries, are somewhat surprising for an outside observer. Rice (1992, p. 121) equally observes that compared to western standards, the central government civil services in Eastern Europe are surprisingly small, with staffing levels in government ministries ranging from 8,000 in Hungary, to 25,000 in Romania.

Lack of accurately defined comparative data means that it is hard to draw firm conclusions. Many services are conducted outside the 'proper' civil service. A surprise reaction is unavoidable, however, if one recollects that a relatively small country like the Netherlands has over 1,50,000 national civil servants without ever having had the ambition to be a centrally planned economy. Indeed it gives rise to the counter-intuitive thought that '... rather than looking for ways to streamline these core civil services, the countries of Eastern Europe may need to consider strategies to expand and improve them' (Rice, 1992, p. 121).

Experiences like these underline the fact that it would be difficult but very necessary and profitable to probe into the comparative facts and figures and the 'nuts and bolts' of comparative administrative systems and civil service reforms in Eastern European countries. Obviously the required retrenchment policies have to mean something else than the 'downsizing' of the civil service which is the main definition of reducing government intervention in western countries. If the figures are at all comparable, then, also from a comparative 'western' point of view, the charge of excessive outlays on public administration in terms of money and personnel are part of a misconception. In some cases public administration will have to grow instead of diminish.

It also means that one has to rethink the 'off hand' initial prescription that administrative modernization in Eastern Europe would imply the mere decentralization of administrative systems and the handing over of power from the central to the local authorities. Looking more closely at the situation in the different countries, one sometimes gets the impression that the real problem was that not only were there no local authorities, but, even worse, initially there was hardly any effective central power to hand over to them.

In one of the initial comparative assessments of administrative developments in Central and Eastern Europe, Hesse presents a somewhat gloomy overall analysis. The shared characteristic of the transformation process of these administrative systems is the development from a one-party rule to pluralist, multi-party systems with democratically elected and accountable governments; the principle of 'democratic centralism' is being abandoned in favour of the deconcentration and decentralization of political power under the rule of law; and it is universally accepted that administrative effectiveness, efficiency and flexibility need to be increased. According to Hesse (1991, p. 199) the task of modernizing public administration goes much beyond ... responsibilities in the majority of the industrialized countries of the Western hemisphere. The challenge with which public administration is faced is to redefine its role in society, or, more concretely, its relations with politics, the economy and the civil community ... . Administrative restructuring arid reorganization must be pursued with the same vigour as political and economic reforms, and they require a similarly sustained effort.

The situation varies, however, from country to country. There are no standard solutions.

3.1. Czechoslovakia

Czechoslovakia witnessed the quickest 'velvet revolution' of all countries, but in a way the two Republics are now lagging behind in modernizing their state structures. Despite the fact that much energy has been absorbed by trying to concentrate on resolving fundamental constitutional problems, one should not overlook another important explanation. The Communist regime in Czechoslovakia was amongst the most strict and conservative, particularly since it suppressed the 1968 liberalization movement. They also stayed in power to the very last minute, until at the end of 1989, the regime gave way to a surprisingly swift take over.

Soon after the take over, several ministries were abolished in an effort to reduce central state control over the economy, but perhaps also to take away power from the federal government. New institutions were created for revitalizing the economy. Over the, following year the entire federal state system has come under consideration. Federalization, or rather efforts in favour of its realization, had already led to a transfer of powers and responsibilities from the federal level to the Republics. Local government had already ceased to be part of the state administration. Discussions and ongoing constitutional and administrative reforms became burdened if not entirely stalled by the long-standing historical distinctions among Czechs and Slovaks and inherent centripetal tendencies.

The breaking up of Czechoslovakia may be understood *as* a classic case of the struggle between autonomy and influence or co-determination of the component parts of the state, in this case the Czech and the Slovak people. The striving for 'autonomy' by the Czech and particularly the Slovak Republic goes back a long time in history and has more often been dealt with, but not resolved, under the Communist regime by mere repression. The division of the territory by the Czechs and the Slovaks originates in the 1970s and the changes of November 1989 merely serve to expose them. More than dissatisfaction with the old regime, the striving for autonomy, particularly by the Slovaks, seems to follow from a distrust of the centre over joint decision making; the central authority of the Federation has long been seen not as a centre of decision making but as being dominated by one of the two component parts, the Czechs. In addition, the Slovaks were more adversely affected, economically speaking, by the administrative transition. Their economy had faired relatively well under the Communist regime, being the regional centre of heavy steal (arms) industry.

The continued striving for 'autonomy' by both parties was caused less by a dislike of the *ancient regime*, than by the fact that the federal structures were invariably *not* perceived by at least one of the participants (the Slovaks), as just or fair with mutual administrative arrangements for joint decision making. This rift could be exploited by conservative forces aiming at strengthening their regionalized power bases.

The outside world might have tried to prevent the developments by giving selective and 'velvet' support to those symbols, institutions, projects and persons representing the remaining world of collective choice. Perhaps President Havel might have been more effective in building joint decision-making structures, if at the operational level he had something more to offer than a relatively widespread trust in his personality and charisma.

The striving for 'autonomy,' i.e. the separation of the Czech and Slovak Republics, might actually stabilize the situation and need not result in a total stagnation and conflict of the reform processes in the two Republics. Experiences in Spain and Belgium come to mind, where the granting of autonomy has stabilized the 'constitutional' situation, thus opening avenues for pragmatic joint policy making in the operational world of action, thus gradually contributing to efforts to talk from 'community to community' and to try to develop different and mutually acceptable forms of co-operation.

The process of (con)federalization, and eventually the breaking up of the Federation in January 1993, has complicated administrative reform efforts primarily because it absorbed most of the political energy. With all the attention concentrated on various constitutional issues at the federal and state level, the two Republics now both face the need to build their structures for joint decision making and effective operational management within their newly established states. Particular attention has to be paid to developing integrative institutional arrangements at the intermediary levels between the national and local levels of the two Republics. Operational administrative capacity to deal with the implementation of a stream of legislation seems required, with a view to enforcing agreed legislation, but also towards injecting realistic and feasibility considerations into an otherwise somewhat inflationary legislative process.

3.2. Poland

In Poland, the most notable developments are perhaps the (re)establishment of a system of democratic local government and the seemingly stagnating reform processes, due to institutionalized (should one say bureau-political?) rivalries and conflicts among the major institutional and political actors that comprise the national government. Both the functional and the territorial institutional differentiation entails a sharp break with the previous system of uniform, hierarchial and highly centralized state administration. This is true, despite the fact that, for example, centrally appointed governors of the (regional) *voivodships* still perform substantial supervisory functions.

At the national level, crumbling identification within the ranks of Solidarity has not been very favourable for designing and implementing a comprehensive plan for civil service reorganization. Nor has it been replaced by other integrative forces, although sometimes informal networks of civil servants are thought to be able to take over that role and act as an integrative force in a rather fragmented governmental system. It is questionable whether a strong presidency will be able to overcome the problems. From the outside, it sometimes seems as though the main problem is not so much the highly plural political game, which is being played, but the lack of appropriate rules for the game of pluralistic politics. The game has to be played with inadequate constitutional, political and cultural rules for the game of consociational politics and joint decision making which is based upon accommodation and mutual adjustment.

In Poland it is equally observed that the conflict between 'autonomy' and 'co-determination' among rival political factions is resulting in stagnating reforms. Some maintain that one might even have to await the return of political stability in order to be able to make some progress. The ongoing difficulties do not start from scratch either, and need to be understood in the light of the reforms of the years of Communist rule. The difference with Czechoslovakia, in terms of our comparative framework is that the difficulties originate at another level or institutional world of action. The inertia, paralysis, incompetence, bureaucratism, arrogance and corruption, as observed by country specialists, seem to originate less in the world of constitutional action and more in the world of collective choice. Although the problems may spill over into a constitutional crisis in terms of sustainability, trust and the break down of the system, the observed problems at the operational level of government seem to be particularly caused 'by problems at the level of joint decision making.' It is noticeable that the once-held-fundamental principles of legality, justice and equality of opportunity are more and more questioned. Letowski therefore prescribes a basic code of administrative conduct, rules of a moral nature such as that the agency does not lie, does not prevaricate, keeps its promises, behaves honestly and decently. The values of the world of collective choice and joint decision making deserve attention owing to the lack of effective institutional arrangements to that end.

The problems of the actual legislative process, and the civil service or local government reorganization and decentralization exemplify the problems of joint decision making surrounding contemporary Polish administration. Within the institutionally and politically fragmented system the historical development has led to a situation in which the administrative hierarchy is missing and – more importantly – one in which little or no constitutional provision for conflict resolution and will formation has yet been developed. The great speed of legislation, the problem of the binding nature of 'ministerial law,' the use of the legally wrong 'tools' for dealing with citizen affairs (instructions instead of statutes), the way in which 'emergency powers' are being demanded and the administrative battles between government, ministries, Parliament and President are all serious threats to the future development of the system.

At the same time the problems all sound familiar. The system of joint decision making in Poland displays in an extreme and enlarged form all the problems of ministerial collegial government which can also be found elsewhere. The Council of Ministers is obviously too weak to act as an integrating force, and the same is true for the President and Parliament which have not been able to tip the balance to either's advantage. Where a collegial ministerial and cabinet system already creates serious problems of interdepartmental co-ordination, this is a fortiori true for Polish government, where the informal culture and routines of consociational and consensual politics and administration have also had no time to develop. In such a system the 'hands-on manager' who is politically pressed to undertake activities and 'solve problems' is almost forced to use whatever means are available within the existing situation. The goal starts to justify the means. Achieving results becomes more important than the way in which these results are achieved, which often leads to counter-productive outcomes.

The abuse of legal 'instruments' by goal-directed politicians, keen to score, is, in such a context, a familiar phenomenon in other administrative systems as well. In the operational world of action, the law is a binding act and therefore a vehicle for resolving problems of administrative uncertainty and incoherence. In such a system emergency powers may also provide a temporary solution, but are likely to be used instrumentally for too narrow and ad hoc purposes since they do not rest on a broader constitution which ensures the use of the special mandate for a broader purpose, thus eroding the 'instrument.' The desire for interministerial co-ordination or even a ministry for home affairs or the civil service centrally to direct the required reforms is predictable from a comparative perspective. From the experiences of other systems with collegial administration it is to be expected, though, that these will not do the job, since 'co-ordinating' ministers very often acquire the responsibility but seldom the power to co-ordinate their colleagues. The reason is simple: such a provision would erode the principle of collegial ministerial government since one of them would become the superior.

Experience with hierarchical non-consensual reforms – as in for example Thatcher's UK – suggests that a strong commitment from the Prime Minister is necessary to implement radical administrative reforms. The question is, however, whether such a centralized and non-consensual reform would fit in the rather diverse Polish political structure and culture and would generate enough support to last in the long run. In this case, outside instigation of a sustained but incremental and more consensual reform process could take the form of exerting external pressure on some strategic operational goals so as to force opponents into joint action. For a while an outside community like the European Community (EC) could play the role of 'external coordinator,' by generating pressures that indirectly and directly require goal-driven opponents to co-operate and co-ordinate their activities vis a vis the common (external) challenge. In the process, one might be able to generate sustainable, reliable and robust 'constitutional' routines, procedures and techniques for mutual problem solving.

Offering a perspective on future economic co-operation with the ECs in exchange for the requirement to meet European financial and economic standards might provide such pressure and 'external co-ordination.' The promises of the European integration process have more often, and for several EC countries, turned out to be able to integrate and coordinate fragmented national decision making and foster effective informal co-ordination and mutual adjustment at administrative and political levels.

At the subnational level of the Polish administration, decisions are needed concerning proper relationships between various public and private actors. The regional government level has to be defined either as some kind of prefectorial system, which is responsible for the co-ordination of national executive functions in the region or as a territorial council which represents certain regional interests and may act as a partner in carrying out state functions as well. A mixed model – on the basis of comparative experience – would not be a bad solution for shaping complex Polish intergovernmental interests. But clarity about the role of regional government seems warranted.

The problems of local government seem to originate particularly in the operational world of action. Legislation has been issued. The problems re-ported indicate that a degree of politicization and 'confessionalization' of administration is frustrating its operations. From a comparative perspective it might be helpful to point to systems such as the Netherlands or Belgium and Italy where local-state–Catholic Church relationships were a prominent feature of the local government organization. Given the Catholic principle of 'subsidiarity,' local authority in these systems usually means more than simply 'local government.' In the Catholic administrative doctrine a net-work of non-profit 'privatized' subsidiary organs may play an important role in carrying out local state functions. In that case a different concept of 'local *governance*' instead of 'local government' is called for. It has not prevented the development of strong local administrative systems in coun-tries facing similar social features.

The politicization and party-political appointments in the local admin-istration, again, exemplify a lack of trust in joint decision-making institu-tions and will not easily evaporate. Rather than criticizing the practice, one might consider the creation of institutionalized opportunities for political appointments in the higher ranks of the local administration while basing the award of these positions strictly on the grounds of merit.

3.3. Hungary

The most stable progress, so far, seems to have been made in Hungary, which has the longest history of market-orientated reform experiences. The legal foundations for a pluralist liberal democracy seem to have been laid. The most basic arid also controversial change in Hungarian public administration concerns not so much the internal national government organization, but its relationship with the other levels of government. In 1990, the legal conditions for far-reaching regional and local autonomy and self-government were created as a reaction to the democratic centralism of Communist rule. Local and regional administration have been put under the control of elected councils. As elsewhere, the durability of reform of economy and public administration is threatened most by a stagnating economic development.

In Hungary, the administrative modernization and adaptation to a liberal market economy seem to be relatively well under way. The problems which are reported may be identified in terms of the 'operational world of action:' the goal-directedness, the economy and the frugality of the system. A flood of legislation is being observed, to the extent that one may wonder about its effectiveness, suitability and enforcement. This is true, despite the fact that an equally abundant number of deconcentrated state services for supervising the implementation of national legislation has emerged in the region.

The relative success of developments so far seems to be due to the fact that the Hungarians entered the modernization process at the end of the 1980s 'with their feet down running.' Again the roots of current developments are to be found in the past under the Communist regime. The 'Hungarian secret' seems to consist of three pre-existing conditions. First, already in the 1960s and 1970s, Hungarian government implemented a local government reform characterized by scale-enlargement and decentralization. A relatively strong local government system and the determined application of it is an important feature of the ongoing reform and modernization process. Secondly, even under the central planning of the *ancient regime*, Hungary used to be the regime most liberated from central planning, including as many liberal-economic elements as was politically possible. The Leninist-state and economic system was liberated to the utmost degree. Finally, Balázs observes that, just prior to the transformation, a new generation of bureaucratic 'mandarins' – technically well skilled and politically with a low profile – had risen to a position just below the top. When the established ministries were politically beheaded they were ready and able to take over, thus limiting the human resource problems which faced so many other administrative systems when faced with changes of regime. Thus a situation emerged, which is quite the opposite of Czechoslovakia, where leadership had to be brought in from the outside and was confronted with art administrative system which had not been reformed at all and needed to be fully 'reorganized.'

The 're-emergence of history' gives rise to all kinds of differential institutional logics and developments. It is this continuity, not the quick shift ('big bang') which has brought about what seems to be the relatively most stable ongoing reform process in the direction of a liberal market economy. The main problems in Hungary are being created by the decline of economic resources due to the economic stagnation following the transformations which revealed the gross inefficiencies – both economically, as well as in terms of human and environmental resources – of the previously 'centrally planned' economies. The trust of citizens in the transformation has been undermined by the fact that the reforms have not resulted in an immediate increase in welfare, but rather the contrary.

Also in other areas the arrangements for joint decision making and collective action among different administrative units are under pressure. Intergovernmental relations now seem to suffer from an initial tendency to move away and by-pass the county level which under the *ancient regime* performed many disputed intermediary tasks. This has left an institutional vacuum which is still not properly filled. In aspects of local government one may observe the tendency to feel the shortcomings of overstretched concepts of local 'autonomy' and a move back to stressing the need for developing adequate interrelationships among different planes of government.

The most fundamental problem the Hungarian administrative system seems to face, however, is the alienation of citizens and the lack of civic interest in participating in elections and other forms of collective choice procedures. Western nations may learn from the historical developments in Central and Eastern Europe that states do not easily lose the diffuse, general trust and confidence – regime legitimacy – of their citizens. Once it is lost, however, the impact is dramatic and it will be difficult to get it back. A regime shift is a necessary, but not sufficient measure. Regaining this trust primarily requires time.

4. ADMINISTRATIVE REFORM IN CENTRAL EUROPE: CONCLUSIONS

What conclusions may one draw from the previous analysis? One may want to take issue with the observation that '... all the same, public administration across these (post-socialist) countries is more notable for similarities than differences both in its shortcomings and the stages of reform' (Rice,

1992, p. 117). Administrative reform never starts from scratch. The analysis provided here suggests that there is no watershed or 'big bang' between the Communist and post-Communist era from the viewpoint of the recreation of an effective public administration system. The relative advantage (of Hungary) and disadvantage (of Czechoslovakia) in terms of the ongoing reform process, are clearly rooted in events, preconditions and decisions sometimes dating far back into the history of Communist rule.

Given the magnitude of the changes and transformations at the end of the last decade, the degree of continuity and influence of the past comes as somewhat of a surprise. The ease with which countries seem to adapt to a capitalist mode of production so far seems to be determined as much by the historical circumstances during the Communist era as the decisions of the post-socialist reformers.

The common challenges which the different countries face entail at least the disentanglement of public administration and the civil service from party bureaucracy and membership. Whole sections of the administrative systems, previously responsible for the 'democratic centralism' of the centrally planned and controlled economy, are being eliminated, while, at the same time, new administrative capacities for economic market development have to be created. Planning and monitoring procedures need to be reorientated from the imperial categories of the internal 'central plan' towards external performance and public service delivery. Effective mechanisms for the protection of citizens against arbitrary or unlawful actions by administrators need to be installed.

In coping with these challenges, the systems have to deal with various puzzles. Removing civil servants closely connected with the previous Communist regime (as in Poland and Czechoslovakia) is prone to the accusation of politicizing public administration under a different label. Neither will the ideal of liberal democracy, based on the rule of law, feel comfortable in the company of a requirement that civil servants are not allowed to be members of a given political party, even if this is a Communist party in name.

Perhaps some new talents may be drawn into the civil service. Resources for attracting new people are scarce, not only in terms of pay, but also in terms of all other kinds of incentives: prestige, image, infrastructure. This is not only because the private sector has so much more financial appeal. Just as important is that, again contrary to what one might have expected under Communist rule, the administration and its employees were treated as a necessary evil which would vanish when the state was transformed into Communist self-government. Quite different from what one might expect from a 'state-oriented system' of government, employees were already in low esteem before the changes, had the least protection by the state and were not respected by the citizens.

One has to find ways to restore pride and self-esteem in relation to working for and within the public sector. The existing rank and file members of the different civil service systems, which have been trained, recruited and socialized under a completely different set of bureaucratic and decision-making premises, will have to go through a time-consuming and difficult process of adaptation to the changing role of public administration in their societies.

In several cases, the danger sometimes seems to become more acute, that economic developments might not give the Central and Eastern European countries quite the time nor the incentives necessary for such infrastructural changes. There is little possibility of 'buying-off' frustrated interests. The redistribution issues which are inherent in any reform process have to be resolved in the present context of declining resources or, at best, in the short run, stabilizing resources. This often turns the reform efforts into a zero-sum or even negative-sum process. The call for strong political leadership to avoid chaos is, internally and externally, potentially dangerous. This is particularly true for the societies under consideration here. They have not yet had the time to develop a basic democratic, self-governing infrastructure. The same applies to a political culture and societal reflexes in which strong but checked and balanced leadership may develop.

The various countries sometimes seem to be half way through the reform, which results in situations in which the parties representing the conservative anti-reform interests may use the already introduced procedures and rules of democratic decision making to protect their interests and strengthen their vested positions. In one country – Hungary – an 'incomplete' constitutional structure seems to create fewer difficulties than in another country – Poland – where the 'flexibility' of the constitutional structure owing to lack of appropriate informal consociational devices contributes to stagnation and deterioration.

The retrenchment of state organization, i.e. denationalization, in favour of market organization has proceeded to a certain degree, but it is now generally considered to have slowed down considerably. Lack of (foreign) capital and investors is a frequently mentioned cause. Also, there is still much variation in the degree of state influence considered necessary or desirable. Furthermore, entrepreneurial skills to run complex, large-scale business organizations are almost completely lacking.

Stagnation of the reform processes and a corresponding destabilization of the political and social situation are explicitly expressed concerns particularly in the Polish and Czechoslovakian cases. The initial concern with respect to the developments behind the former 'iron curtain' was about the 'rationalization,' 'decentralization,' 'administrative modernization' and the 'upgrading' of system and personnel. This followed from an understandable, but in retrospect clear underestimation of the problems at hand. The main contemporary concern is, or rather, should be, that the current developments in the formerly socialist countries primarily ask for the capacity for stable and sustainable administrative development. Almost all country reports refer to, or reflect, a certain fear of social and political destabilization, stagnation of the reform efforts and a risk of escalating into potentially dramatic directions.

Instead of the design of a 'responsive and efficient system of governance and administration,' the situation in the respective countries seems primarily to call for the constitution of a reliable, stable and adaptable system of self-governance, joint decision making and the corresponding forms of public management and administration, Some progress has been made and political prerogatives for developing an effective administrative system have been installed. The situation is far from stable, however.

On the basis of their comparative study of politics and society in Western Europe, Lane and Ersson (1991, p. 321) conclude that the degree of political instability is a function of the perceived (im)balance within these societies, which depends on the different social groups and interests in terms of sub-group autonomy on the one hand and the influence on national government on the other: 'Political stability in the long run perspective is related on the one hand to social cleavages and their conflict implications and on the other to the decision making system, in particular to the distribution of influence and autonomy between major groups within a society' (p. 322).

Lane and Ersson also observe that people and organizations in western societies demand both increased institutional and increased individual autonomy and that this demand is related to the perceived distribution of influence within centres for joint decision making. Citizens and organizations demand more autonomy when they experience government as unresponsive, inefficient, unfair or unreliable. When channels for co-determination and joint decision making do not work or are mistrusted, citizens ask for more autonomy.

When citizens feels that their activities in a certain field are no longer 'autonomous' they will try to influence government or other institutions for joint decision making in which they trust. If such an option is not available, this will easily result in a striving for autonomy regardless of the repercussions. Others that adopt a slightly different perspective of joint decision making will easily perceive this as an unproductive 'over-transformation.' This is basically what, in different forms, has been happening in all the countries under consideration here.

In cases where resources decline and the trust in public and other institutions for collective action is low on the basis of past experience, as is the case in present day Central and Eastern Europe, the situation is unstable indeed. It is predictable that people will strive for individual and institutional autonomy, even if this autonomy is shrinking too. Granting a certain degree of institutional autonomy may contribute to the overall stability of the system. Stability does not require a 'strong centre.' The development of several viable, strong and trusted collective decision making centres with ample opportunity for co-governance by the respective social, political, economic and administrative interests might alleviate the pressure for 'autonomy' which is anxiously identified by the Polish, Hungarian and Czech researchers.

The collective distress and psychological stress of the individual citizens have been reported more than once as important constraints on possible reform measures. It is obviously something that needs to be taken very seriously. Indeed, there is much more to privatization than economics or legal instrumentality. More than to economics, political and administrative structures and processes, attention must be paid to the needs and fears of the citizens in the ongoing reform process. For more than one reason, if worries me, that as a western analyst I cannot easily get to grips with this problem.

REFERENCES

Dente, B., & Kjellberg, F. (Eds) (1988). *The dynamics of institutional change*. Beverly Hills: Sage.

Hesse, J. J. (1991). Administrative modernisation in Central and Eastern European countries. *Staatswissenschaft und Staatspraxis*, 2(2), 197–217.

Hesse, J. J., & Benz, A. (1990). *Die Modernisierung der Staatsorganisation*. Baden-Baden: Nomos.

Hood, C. (1991). Public management for all seasons? *Public Administration*, 69(1), 319.

Kiser, L. L., & Ostrom, E. (1982). Three worlds of action: A metatheoretical synthesis of institutional approaches. In: W. Ostrom (Ed.), *Strategies of political inquiry*. Beverly Hills: Sage.

Lane, J., & Ersson, S. O. (1991). *Politics and society in Western Europe*. London: Sage Publications.

Rice, M. (1992). Public administration in post-socialist Eastern Europe. *Public Administration Review*, 52(2), 116–125.

Riker, W. H., & Weimer, D. L. (1992). *The economic and political liberalisation of socialism: The fundamental problem of property rights*. Paper for the Social Philosophy and Policy Center, Bowling Green State University, OH, April.

Toonen, T. A. J. (1983). Administrative plurality in a unitary state. *Policy and Politics, 11*(3), 247–271.

ANALYZING THE ORGANIZATIONAL REQUIREMENTS FOR SERVING THE RURAL POOR

David K. Leonard

Rural development has never been easy. Like the agriculture to which it is tied, rural growth has always taken hard work and intelligent implementation in the face of local variability and an unpredictable environment. Now development is even more difficult. The current challenge is to provide services for the world's poor majority – the marginal farmers and the landless who make up the bulk of the developing countries' rural population. The farmer who begins to cultivate on rich bottomland must eventually extend operations to the rocky slopes if the enterprise is to reach its full productive potential. Even more so must development be brought to the world's poor majority, for not only production but also life itself depends on the expansion. Still, growth is harder to achieve with poor resources, whether it be the soil or the cultivator that is poor. The environment is harsher; the fragility is greater; the margins for error are narrower. President Julius Nyerere once remarked that while the United States was trying to reach the moon, Tanzania was striving to reach its villages. It appears that Tanzania had the harder and more critical task for development.

Growth in per capita income is no longer accepted as development. Dudley Seers, for example, argues that development is best indicated by

Comparative Public Administration: The Essential Readings
Research in Public Policy Analysis and Management, Volume 15, 393–425
ISSN: 0732-1317/doi:10.1016/S0732-1317(06)15016-2

reductions in (i) absolute poverty (most importantly, malnutrition); (ii) un-employment; and (iii) inequality. He readily agrees that in the long term, growth in gross national product (GNP) is necessary to such development, but insists that it is not sufficient (Seers, 1972, pp. 21–25). Even those who use productivity as a definition of development point out that it is different from economic growth and produce substantial evidence to indicate that it is more likely to occur in societies in which the "Basic Needs" of which Seers speaks have been met (Uphoff & Ilchman, 1972).

We presume that the achievement of development so defined will require public programs and interventions. Under free market conditions, the early stages of economic development produce a dramatic widening of socio-economic differentiation (Migdal, 1974). Because the welfare and productivity of the majority of the population is thereby neglected, national development is unnecessarily slowed (Johnston & Clark, 1982; Uphoff & Esman, 1974; Uphoff & Ilchman, 1972). Intervention by the state can make these inequalities still worse and therefore it is not always desirable. If de-velopment is to be broad-based, however, appropriate public programs are required. We need better knowledge about when and how those programs can be made effective in reaching the rural poor.

To provide development for the rural poor, then, implies a variety of programs: land reform; extension of agricultural technologies that are ap-propriate to the resource endowments of poor farmers; improved markets and input supply for the crops the poor grow; rural primary health care services; labor-intensive rural road construction; the building of sanitary water systems and other rural public works; etc. These sorts of rural service programs are not necessarily new. In the past they often have been struc-tured in such a way as to give special advantage to rural elites, however. Assistance has been given for crops, which only the well endowed could grow, for example, or subsidized inputs have been monopolized by the better off. Such programs left the condition of the poor majority unchanged or even worsened relative to their richer neighbors. What is needed now are programs that will set right this historic imbalance of services and devel-opment against the poor majority.

THE ORGANIZATIONAL REQUIREMENTS

Such rural development programs are quite demanding in their organiza-tional requirements. First, the implementing agency must have a special *commitment* to the delivery of program services to the rural poor. In social systems it is unnatural for benefits to be dispensed equally, much less redistributed toward the disadvantaged. Some inner or outer dynamic force must motivate the organization to overcome the momentum of inequality.

Second, the implementing agency must have or be able to find the *resources* and *technical skills* for the program. As the intended clientele is disadvantaged, it will not have these itself.

Third, the implementer needs *adaptability.* One component of the rural development problem is that our knowledge of how to achieve it is incomplete. Project implementation constantly produces unexpected consequences. Rural development requires major doses of incrementalism; one learns as one proceeds what works and what does not. Those managing the project must be able to adapt to the lessons of its experience (Johnston & Clark, 1982, Chapter 1).

Fourth, implementation of rural development programs usually entails the incorporation of community *participation.* A considerable body of literature stresses the advantages of closely involving local peoples (Uphoff, Cohen, & Goldsmith, 1979; Uphoff & Esman, 1974; Ralston, Anderson, & Colson, 1981). (i) It is necessary to mobilize local resources. (ii) It facilitates the collection of the information that is needed to adapt a program to local conditions. (iii) As rural development frequently involves the promotion of social change, active involvement of the community is generally necessary in order to bring about its transformation. (iv) Local participation may begin to build the public demand structure for a service which will lead to its continued funding.

THE STRUCTURAL IMPLICATIONS

The foregoing organizational requirements for the successful implementation of rural development have several structural implications. The importance of commitment to the delivery of program benefits to the poor requires that the allocation of implementation responsibilities be structured by the presence or absence of this attribute in different parts of the social system. The need for technical skills and resources in rural development most often implies some degree of centralization. The rural areas in general usually have a weak tax base and need an infusion of funds from national sources if anything significant is to be undertaken. The involvement of the center is also essential if there is to be any redistribution of resources from well-off regions to the poorer ones.

On the other hand, the adaptive and participatory requirements of rural development dictate decentralization. Even if participation means nothing more than consultation and negotiation, discretion is needed at the field level to institute the bargain that is appropriate to each locale (Heiby, Ness, & Pillsbury, 1979, p. 7). Problem solving and learning are inhibited by centralization as well. An organization operating in an environment characterized by change and incomplete knowledge must have decentralized management in order to cope (Thompson, 1967, pp. 72–73, 86–87); otherwise, adaptation will be too little, too late, or inappropriate.

The decentralization required for rural development is not necessarily incompatible with central government involvement. Decentralization is a difficult concept to define and we will come back to it later. For the moment it is sufficient to note that the important thing for rural development is to have the resources and authority for timely adaptation to locally specific conditions in the field, not in the capital. Such authority can be exercised in a variety of ways, including the involvement of national government. The operative agency could be, for example, a field office of a central ministry or a local organization with national financial assistance.

In most circumstances the organizational arrangements appropriate for rural development will not be based on a choice between either central or local involvement, but on a combination of the two. The problem will be to specify exactly what kind of combination, with what division of responsibilities, and with what relationships between them.

In their review of the rural development experience of 16 Asian states, Norman Uphoff and Milton Esman concluded that one of the prerequisites for rural development is a strong system of local organizations together with effective links to compatible national agencies that can support them (Uphof & Esman, 1974, pp. xi–xii). A few examples may help to illustrate the point. The preparation of coffee for the market requires a small processing and drying factory. Large estates will have their own factory, but the operation of one is impossible for a smallholder. The Kenyan experience suggests that the optimal "factory" serves about 2,000 small growers. Any economies of production that would come from a larger unit are more than offset by transport costs for the growers. Such factories have become the basic unit of cooperative organization in central Kenya and are managed independently of one another. Nonetheless, these primary societies have difficulty retaining competent accountants and so they turn to the district cooperative union for these services. Similarly, the international marketing of the coffee produced is far beyond the resources of even a district union. This function is performed by a national cooperative organization. Coffee smallholders thus are served by a three-tier cooperative system, each level with its distinctive competence and linked to the others in a complementary manner.

Another example concerns the interdependence of the community health worker and the M.D. in rural health care. There are a variety of economic and social reasons why paramedical personnel are generally more appropriate than doctors as the basic providers of health services and education in the developing world. Yet these community health workers will tend to be ineffective if they are not closely supported by M.D.s in the larger medical system. Each has an appropriate role and scale of operation.

Effective primary education systems also depend on at least three levels of organization. At the level of the classroom the participation of parents is a tremendous asset in motivating the children and assisting them with learning. The construction and maintenance of school facilities is also usually done better and more quickly when it is handled at a local or intermediate level. On the other hand, the development of curricula, the setting of qualifying examinations, and other functions closely related to the professional aspects of education are almost always best handled at the national level.

Finally, the construction and maintenance of rural roads involves links between community organizations and intermediate levels of subnational government. The local group is needed to organize voluntary labor for construction and to oversee and/or provide maintenance. It can also make extremely helpful contributions at the planning stage in order to ensure the optimal fit between local use and road layout (Tendler, 1979). On the other hand, the engineers to design the road and the earth-moving equipment to do the heavier construction work must be found in a supra-local organization. Rural work projects function best when each is in communication with and in support of the other (Garzon, 1981).

The preceding examples simply reemphasize the ideal of partnership of central and local organizations in rural development. Thus, we will focus both on the division of responsibility between them and *on* the nature of their inter-organizational linkages. We are concerned with the transactions between local participatory organizations, the national government, and the subnational governments and field offices, which mediate between them. *Linkages are the mechanisms by which one organization is tied to or attempts to influence another.* Note that as we use the term, linkages are synonymous with inter-organizational relationships. This definition is narrower than that of economists, for example. Thus, although we are concerned with organizations that mediate between the state and the poor, it is not they or their relationships with the poor that we refer to as linkages. Instead, we are concerned with the links these organizations have to the state – financial and technical assistance, regulatory controls, influence, etc. Our linkages are *organizational linkages,* and although we use the term "linkages" by itself for convenience, in this book it always has this restricted meaning.

Organizational linkage mechanisms cannot be explored adequately unless attention is also given to: (1) the organizations being linked and their commitment to rural development, and (2) the kinds of programs which will benefit the rural poor. Thus, our analysis of linkages includes a focus on program content and the types of local and national organizations most likely to be congenial to those programs. Our major concern is to give a more systematic treatment of the problems of linkage than is currently available in the development literature.

Why organizational linkages? Are they more important than appropriate national policies? No, they are shaped by those policies. Do they matter more than congenial national or local organizations? Again, no, these are the units they work with. Appropriate policies made in a national ministry have to be implemented, however, and congenial local organizations have to be provided with resources – or even to be created. Implementation entails linkages. As perplexing as the policy issues of development have been, those of implementation have been even more frustrating. At this very basic level, development practitioners have had very limited guidance in dealing with local organizations. They have created schemes of local technical assistance, training, financial aid, regulation, and representation with little more than instinct to guide them. The results have varied among dangerous dependence, throttling control, reckless discretion, and so on. It is time that we began to answer questions such as: "Just what is it that a national or international agency can *do* to create or sustain a cooperative which services the poor?" "What kinds of services and regulation should the outside agency provide for a community-based health care system?" "What kinds of representative structures do the rural poor need in order to obtain from the center the minimal resources they need to maintain their health or roads or agricultural production?" The issue is not just what the desirable end result is, but what actions should be taken toward that end. These are organizational linkage questions.

THE PARAMETERS FOR
ORGANIZATIONAL DESIGN

Once a policy or program objective has been conceived that requires work with local units, it has still to be implemented. This involves very important questions of design. The program must be given specificity; national agencies and local organizations must be selected as the implementers; and linkages must be created between them. It is important to give careful and wide consideration to the available alternatives, for the success or failure of the program will depend on the choices made. Occasionally, the analyst will be in a local organization and be looking for assistance from the optimal national agency. More often, he or she will be in a government bureau trying to find the best type of local group to work through. Both of these analysts have to take as given one of the implementing organizations – their own. Policy analysts also look out from the offices of presidents, planning ministries, and international donors, however, and these have a much greater degree of choice in designing the structure of implementation. It is vital that they use the choice fully and wisely. The selection of the wrong type of agency or organization spells failure for a project. Frequently, the analyst takes a narrow, short-term view and considers the performance of the agency or organization only so long as it is closely linked to and monitored by a donor or the president's office. The project functions well for a time and then begins to malfunction in ways that should have been foreseeable. Our analysis is directed at averting such failures.

The choice of an organizational strategy for the implementation of a program depends both on the nature of the program and on the social character of the task environment in which it is to be placed. The distribution of benefits to the rural, poor majority is difficult to achieve, in the normal working of social structures, the poor rarely receive even an equal portion of the benefits society creates. The most effective strategy for overcoming this handicap and providing the poor with needed services depends on the interaction of the program and social structure. Some types of programs are harder to administer or lend themselves more readily than others to the appropriation of benefits by a minority. Similarly, some social structures are more likely than others to permit local elites to take advantage of programs for themselves.

The success of program implementation depends on the following parameters or contextual variables: (i) the program's vulnerability to inequality; (ii) the nature of local elites and their interests; (iii) the nature and variability of interests among national agencies; and (iv) the distribution between national and local organizations of the capacity to meet the program's technical and administrative requirements. We will analyze each of these factors in turn. They are not determinative by themselves, however. Each variable creates certain propensities that may or may not be realized depending on the effect of the others. The presentation of these factors sets the analytic framework for this book, and it will be used frequently in the chapters that follow. In the conclusion we will pull together the ways in which they interact with one another and suggest the decentralization strategy and the type of inter-organizational linkages that tend to be more appropriate for programs for the poor majority in a particular context.

Program Vulnerability to Inequality

The first step to take in devising an implementation strategy for a program is to analyze its vulnerability to inequality.[1] A wide distribution of benefits is inherent in some types of programs, while elite advantage is extremely easy in others. Inequality is an endemic social condition and develops readily in most settings. Perfect equality is unobtainable, if the experience of the existing social systems – socialist as well as capitalist – is any guide. Nonetheless, there are significant differences among programs in the likelihood with which inequity will develop ... . Whether or not a program that is vulnerable to inequity will in fact produce it in any particular setting will depend on the operation of the other three contextual variables. The importance of identifying vulnerable programs is not to avoid them, but to know when they can be undertaken only with the support of other favorable conditions.

As a rule, programs are more vulnerable to inequality to the degree that they have one or more of the following attributes:

(i)   The individual or family, rather than the community, is the unit of consumption. For example, it is much easier for local elites to gain disproportionate benefit from a water system piped to individual dwellings than from one piped to communal-use points. Most services are consumed on a non-communal basis, however. Individual consumption units take on their greatest significance when combined with one of the other following attributes.

(ii) The demand far exceeds the supply. For example, the numbers wanting to attend highly selective educational institutions or to receive subsidized credit will always exceed supply. It is possible to assure equal or even preferential access for the disadvantaged to such goods, but it is always difficult. Elite efforts to obtain such scarce services make them perennially vulnerable to inequality.

(iii) Service quality can be improved at the expense of quantity. Because elites are the ones most likely to obtain scarce services they have no motive to lower service standards in order to assure wide access to them. Instead, their interests are best served by pressing for higher quality and letting the clientele reached shrink. Curative veterinary and human medicine illustrate this type of vulnerability to inequality particularly well. It is common to find expensive treatments being available for a few, while funds run out for inexpensive, basic treatments for the many.

(iv) Other scarce inputs are necessary to utilize the service effectively. Roads or agricultural extension in an area in which the available market crops require inputs beyond the means of the majority of farmers will serve to benefit and strengthen the better off. Another example of high vulnerability to inequality is free university education accompanied by fee-paying primary and secondary systems.

(v) The service provider passively awaits client demand in distributing benefits. In most circumstances, the most advantaged members of society possess considerable advantages in information as well. Thus, passive suppliers of services are almost certain to have disproportionate numbers of the well-to-do among their clients. An organization with benefits to offer the poor, therefore, most often needs to be active in promoting its services for them.

(vi) The service involves coercion or the creation of monopolies. When the state creates a monopoly in a service area or when it uses coercion to achieve its objectives, those who have political power (either local or national) are most likely to benefit. In most instances, these will be the advantaged members of the society, who will then gain unearned benefits beyond those whose wealth is already buying them. Of course, when state power is used on behalf of the poor and is effective, coercion and monopoly may have a beneficial, redistributive effect. It takes much greater effort on the part of the state to use these tools to help the poor than it does for elites to turn them to their own advantage, however.

Programs which are less vulnerable to inequality in the distribution of benefits have one or more of the following characteristics:

(i) Indivisible, widespread benefits. Many services are public goods – once they are provided in a community, all who reside there can utilize them. Some of these public goods will improve the welfare of all segments of the community. The best example of such a public good is village sanitation. Everyone in a village is vulnerable to disease until all have and use proper sanitation facilities. Once they are in place, the rich and the poor alike will experience less disease. Another example of this type of public good is a road to a community in which all residents can or already do participate significantly in the external market economy. All will then spend less time getting to the market and/or will receive higher profits for their goods from middlemen who find it easier to reach them. On the other hand, if most families are engaged in subsistence agriculture only and cannot shift to cash crops easily, the few who are engaged in the market will reap a disproportionate benefit which might even have a negative impact on the village's poor. This would occur if the increased profits of the better off enabled them to put pressure on the less advantaged to sell off their land. It is important to remember that many public goods offered in the development process are *not* inherently beneficial to the poor.

(ii) Benefits are linked to the use of a resource the poor have in abundance. When a program makes heavy demands on capital or education and provides high returns to those with these resources, the gap between the rich and the poor is likely to widen. Conversely, activities that increase the demand for labor will provide direct benefits to the poor in the form of jobs and quite possibly the indirect benefit of higher wages as a result of the increased demand. Labor-intensive public works projects therefore will have widespread benefits for the working poor – at least for their duration. (If a crash works program were to create a temporary labor shortage and induce employers to purchase labor-saving equipment, workers might have difficulty getting jobs when it ended. Thus, the most beneficial works projects create an extended demand for labor.) Similarly, technical innovations in agriculture that make the increased use of labor profitable are almost certain to benefit the poor, even if it is the wealthy who are the first to adopt the change. Thus, Bruce Johnston has argued with us that research investments in more labor-intensive agricultural technologies and machinery are indirectly highly beneficial to the poor. Programs that promote economic growth and productivity through the increased use of labor are doubly desirable because they improve income distribution while increasing the society's investable surplus.

(iii) The service deals with problems or opportunities that are more common to the poor. Some diseases are more common among the poor and interventions aimed specifically at their prevention or cure are not so likely to be diverted to the rich. For example, efforts to prevent cholera will disproportionately benefit the poor, for they are the ones who lack the needed sanitation facilities and uncontaminated water. In a different vein, some foods are more commonly consumed and grown by the poor. Efforts to improve the productivity of these crops will probably be targeted on the poorer producers with little extra effort. In East Africa, for example, wheat is a capital-intensive, luxury crop, while sorghum and cassava are consumed by poorer subsistence farmers. Programs to assist with the latter crops are almost inevitably redistributive.

(iv) The supply exceeds the demand. If the market is flooded with a commodity, the poor then will be able to get it. This effect can be achieved in two, complementary ways. The first is if there is a natural, upward limit on demand. A woman needs only one contraceptive at a time; a child must be provided with primary education only once; smallpox vaccinations are required but once in three years; etc. The second method of creating surplus supply is for a non-profit organization (usually a government) to subsidize the production and distribution of the goods or service to the point of saturation. The two methods intereact. The saturation point usually is not reached without subsidy and it cannot be reached unless there is some kind of natural point at which demand drops off sharply.

(v) Units of service provision significantly exceed the demands of local elites. The earliest units of service to a community are usually "lumpy." If the service is to be provided to one person then it can be provided to a goodly number for very little additional cost. A primary school teacher for 10 elite children will be able to instruct 20 non-elites as well. A clinic for the half-dozen well-off families can easily provide care for large numbers of poor ones. Especially in the early stages of development, local elites may be instrumental in acquiring services that can accommodate the demands of many more than themselves. These service increments will benefit at least some of the poor. Elite demand, however, will be concentrated on the first unit of service … .

These guidelines on the vulnerability of a program to inequality indicate the kind of analysis which a program designer must make to increase the likelihood of reaching the rural poor.

Nonetheless, just because a program is vulnerable to monopolization of benefits by local elites does not mean that inequality will inevitably result. The character of the local social structure, of the national, local and intermediate organizations involved, and of the linkages between them will determine the outcome. Vulnerability is a sign of danger; as it increases, the other elements of implementation design must be more carefully crafted. Conversely, as vulnerability declines, weaknesses can be tolerated elsewhere in the implementation structure.

The Responsiveness of Local Leaders

Will the leaders of local organizations press for the distribution of benefits to their rural poor or will they seek to divert them to local elites? Just how responsive are local leaders to the needs of the poor? If local leaders have a weak commitment to the poor, programs that are vulnerable to inequality will tend to become welfare for the better off. If there is a high degree of responsiveness to the less advantaged, those same programs will provide widespread benefits with few outside controls. Such a congenial local leadership structure can be achieved in three different ways: (1) the leaders share the interests of the poor themselves; (2) there is significant competition for leadership positions from those who seek to represent non-elite interests; or (3) alternative organizations are used which limit their membership to non-elites.

The responsiveness of leaders to the interests of the poor is assured most easily (but all too infrequently) when they share those interests. This need not mean that they are identical to their constituents. Leaders are atypical. All organizations are led by individuals who differ in significant ways from their followers. Leaders generally are more educated, wealthier, and so on, than the average member of their organizations (Almond & Verba, 1963, pp. 380–381; Migdal, 1974, p. 232; Ralston et al., 1981, pp. 24–28). If the most advantaged members of a community are excluded from leadership, then the next most advantaged group will be disproportionately represented among those who run things (Hank, 1974, pp. 76–77; Schurmann, 1966, pp. 445–451). Those guiding the affairs of a community's organizations thus most frequently are local elites in some degree – and not just because they are leaders. This inequality is a near universal and as such need not concern us. The issue is not necessarily whether organizations are run by local elites, but whether those leaders share the interests of their followers.

An elite may differ from others only in degree, rather than in kind. The existence of stratification in a community or group does not establish that there necessarily are class differences. The greater the extent to which the members of a community share a common mode of existence, the greater the similarity in elite and non-elite interests.

The distinction between differences in degree and differences in kind is most clearly demonstrated by the interests surrounding agricultural production. Bruce Johnston (Johnston & Kilby, 1974; Johnston & Clark, 1982) is one of the many who argue over the crucial advantages of unimodal over bimodal patterns of agricultural development. In a unimodal system, farmers have broadly similar amounts of land, produce much the same crops, and are equal in their integration into the market. A bimodal pattern, on the other hand, is characterized by two distinct modes of agricultural production. A minority of farms are large and geared toward the production of market crops, generally for export. Meanwhile, the great majority of farmers is small; they produce different, subsistence-oriented crops and frequently provide labor for the export producers.

The local elites in a bimodal agricultural system have quite dissimilar agricultural interests from the landless, near-landless, and small farmers in their communities. They have a qualitatively different resource base, produce different crops, are involved in a different market, and have an employer relationship with the rest of the community. Although these local elites most often lead their communities (either openly or indirectly), they do not share the agricultural interests of their poor majority.

A local elite is most likely to have common interests with the poor when they have a broadly similar set of circumstances in common. On agricultural matters Uphoff and Esman have suggested that this occurs when the richest 20% of the rural population have no more than six times the income of the poorest 20% (Uphoff & Esman, 1974, p. xvii). Within this range of difference, producers are able to profit from similar cropping patterns, marketing arrangements, production technologies, and so forth. Uphoff and Esman developed the 6:1 ratio by analyzing 16 national systems in Asia. It seems to us to be possible that an even smaller ratio – but certainly not perfect equality – would be needed to produce commonality of interest in some cropping systems if we calculated the ratio at the community level. It is very unlikely, however, that richer and poorer farmers would be operating under similar production conditions at any ratio larger than 6:1.

It is hard to overestimate the importance for development of commonality of interest among rural dwellers. Where it exists, the general, communitywide (or inclusive) local leadership structures can be used relatively easily and supported fairly freely. Where it does not exist, there will always be the danger that the direction of benefits toward the poor will be subverted and that their lot may be made even worse with development.

Nonetheless, it does not follow that local elites who differ in interests from the majority of their communities in one area will differ in all the other areas as well. A local landlord might have deeply conflictual interests with the area's poor majority on many agricultural matters and yet share with them a need for a health clinic (Uphoff et al., 1979, p. 68). An agency oriented toward the poor would eschew his leadership in the first area, but welcome it for the second.

The degree of inequality in a community's social structure interacts with the character of a program to indicate the compatibility of local elite and poor interests. Where either local inequality or the vulnerability of a program to inequality is low, local elite leadership is suitable for poverty-alleviating projects. Where both are high, programs oriented toward the poor majority are probably best carried out without local participatory structures or with organizations that confine their membership to the poor (alternative organizations).

The second and third strategies for achieving congenial local leadership apply to those arenas where the interests of the local elite conflict with those of the poor majority. In such situations, the former's dominance generally must be challenged if significant benefits are to reach the latter. There are two, frequently complementary, ways in which this can be done. One (i.e., the second strategy) is the existence of significant competition for leadership positions from those who seek to represent non-elite interests (Uphoff et al., 1979, p. 68). Then, even if local elites continue to be over-represented among the community's influential, they will have to be more responsive to the interests of the poor majority in order to maintain their positions. For responsiveness to the poor to be achieved in elite-run systems three conditions must be met: (a) there is competition for leadership; (b) the support of the poor is a necessary component of most strategies for achieving leadership; (c) at least one serious candidate for leadership appeals directly to the distinctive interests of the poor. The last condition is more likely to be met if the less advantaged are organized, and that leads us to the third strategy.

The national government usually has to link its efforts to those of local organizations if it is to promote development effectively. The links need not be to community-wide groups like local governments; however, because they tend to be elite dominated. Instead, the government can link with (and perhaps assist in forming) alternative groups which are more homogeneous in their membership and which exclude those elites and others who have dissimilar interests (Uphoff et al., 1979, pp. 116, 193, 208). The leaders who emerge in these groups may be among the more advantaged of their members – and thus different in degree. If relative homogeneity is attained, however, the interests of these leaders will not differ in kind from those of their followers.

Alternative organizations representing the interests of disadvantaged groups are generally necessary if local elite dominance of inclusive local governments and organizations is to be challenged effectively. Thus, the third method of dealing with local elites with distinct interests generally is a prerequisite to the second, competitive option.[2]

Alternative organizations need not directly enter the wider local arena as competitors, however. They can and very often should exist solely to service the needs of their own members and constituents. They then will be seen as "non-political" and less threatening by local elites.

Still, alternative organizations of the poor and powerless are likely to come under indirect dominance by local elites if they do. The less advantaged are far more difficult to organize as a separate group in a rural environment than workers are in an urban one. They live farther apart from one another, work alone or in small groups, reside closer to the elite, and have much more social interaction with them. The ties of the less advantaged to rural elites are more personal. Furthermore, the rural poor can aspire to upward mobility through land ownership, a condition similar to, if smaller than, that of the local elite. Urban workers, on the other hand, rarely find upward mobility through businesses that even remotely resemble those of the elite. For all these reasons, solidarity and organization of the less advantaged are more difficult to achieve in the countryside.[3]

Because of the difficulties they face, local alternative organizations of the rural poor generally need outside support if they are to survive. The sustenance to survive under pressure might come from a trade union, a church, a political party, or a government agency. In many cases central linkages with alternative organizations are not just a convenient channel for the distribution of national services; they are essential to the protection of the groups from local elite dominance.

Of course, income is not the only basis of division within rural communities. In many societies other forms of differentiation are far more significant. Conflicts of interest can be found along the lines of ethnicity, religion, caste, kinship, sex, and mode of production (e.g., pastoralists vs. agriculturalists) as well. Whenever such differences become a significant basis for the distribution of benefits, they deprive a community of homogeneity of interest. To the extent that these differences coincide with income, they have the same effect as income inequalities. Their presence often makes it easier to organize the disadvantaged separately from their elite leaders, as there are additional sociological reasons for the separation.

When ascriptive differences crosscut the income differences and are a basis for benefit distribution, however, they pose a special problem for local organizations. Whether there are differences in interest between the poor and the elites or not, the ascriptive conflicts over distribution will disrupt local organizations – both inclusive and alternative – and tend to keep them weak. In Kenya, for example, kinship politics has seriously disrupted the functioning of many cooperatives in the small-farm areas. Although rich and poor belong to all the factions, the ability of these cooperatives to operate effectively and to serve the interests of small producers has been hurt by the resulting distributional conflicts (Hyden, 1973).

A lack of homogeneity of interest in a community that crosscuts income and is based on ascriptive divisions is not a cause for promoting new local organizations. The ensuing conflicts are likely to be largely neutral with respect to the special interests of the poor. The consequence of their existence will be an inherent weakness in the community's organizations – a weakness that is a factor in deciding how to use them for rural development. The state generally will be unable to devolve as much responsibility to such local organizations or will have to maintain tighter controls over them than would otherwise be the case.

We have found the interaction between program content and local elite interests to be very important. The nature of the interaction is one of the major influences on what types of decentralization are to be preferred and what types of organizational linkage are to be developed with them. Where local leaders are responsive to the interests of the poor, inclusive, relatively autonomous forms of local organization and government are to be preferred. Where such responsiveness is missing, alternative local organizations of the rural poor generally are needed together with strong external support.

Support from the Center

The needs of the rural poor usually will not be met if local organizations are left to their own, separate devices. Development strives to be catalytic – to produce forces that are more than the sum of the combined parts. Still, development is not alchemy – it cannot create something out of nothing. If the pace of change is to be at all adequate, linkages must be forged between base-level organizations and supra-local entities that have resources and power. Such support for progressive action by localities might be found in a state or national government agency, an international donor, or a non-governmental organization (e.g., a union or a foundation). Obviously, the greater the resources and power of the organization, the larger the potential support. For this reason, we focus on linkages to the nation-state; typically it controls the largest quantity of resources and has the greatest power to alter the conditions that stifle progressive change. This is the "center" which most often structures decentralization. Even the nation-state offers a plurality of agencies with which a local government or organization might be linked, however.

These "centers" can vary in their resources and commitment to the rural poor. Obviously, the greater the resources committed to their cause the better for the poor majority. Still, commitment is the most important and problematic variable. We focus our analysis on this dimension of national government agencies.

The national political system provides the basic context which shapes the behavior of individual politicians and civil servants and within which rural development policies are formulated. Nonetheless, there probably will be differences in the progressiveness of agencies within that framework. For any particular proposed program activity it is important to ask, "Can a national agency be found to administer the program which has a positive commitment to these particular benefits' reaching the rural poor?" If not, can such an agency or subordinate unit be created in this political context? Simple willingness that the poor benefit is not enough; a firm purpose is needed. Problems or resistance are almost always encountered in attempts to improve the lot of the poor, and these obstacles will not be overcome without the resolution to spend energy and resources on them.

Whether and where one will find an agency with a positive commitment to the poor in a program area depends very much on the particularities of national politics and institutional development in the country concerned. An analysis of the commitment of national systems to their poor would require a major discourse on political economy. Such an effort is beyond the scope of what we can attempt here. It is a general theme of political science and is treated in numerous general (e.g., Uphoff, 1980) and country-specific studies. Most program designers will have a reasonable idea of the general status of their country on this question.

Nonetheless, within the context of a political system, whether supportive of the poor or not, particular national agencies may be more or less progressive. This source of variation is much less widely analyzed. The major factors determining agency stance are its external alliances and its professional and institutional patterns of socialization. Over time, agencies acquire customary clienteles, upon which they rely in the ubiquitous battles for budgetary resources and for assistance in doing their work. If a particular program evokes opposition among an agency's historical clientele, its administrators are unlikely to pursue it vigorously, even if the activity has support in the larger political system. Thus, when the Ministry of Health in Guatemala first encountered opposition from the national medical association to its plan for paraprofessional rural health care, it simply dropped the idea (Long & Viau, 1974). Similarly, agricultural extension services which have developed strong symbiotic relations with well-to-do progressive

farmers in the promotion of export agriculture have real difficulty in creating new networks oriented toward less-advantaged, subsistence production (Thoden van Veizen, 1977).

Equally powerful are the internal patterns of recruitment and institutionalization that determine the professional orientation of an agency's decision
makers. Professional training and organizational experience tend to instill a
commitment to the value of certain types of activities, methods of doing
them, and ways of analyzing when and where to do them. These technologies, methodologies, and decision-making modes often have significant implications for benefit distribution. For example, most contemporary Western
medical practice is oriented toward and attaches high prestige to high technology, hospital-based, curative medicine. Agencies dominated by these
types of doctors will find it difficult to give priority to the types of promotive,
preventive, and paramedical medicine that mean the most to the health of the
rural poor. This is the case with ministries of health in many developing
countries, where agencies have been deeply involved with hospital and medical school administration. On the other hand, health practitioners trained in
public health have a different orientation from the rest of the medical profession and value precisely the types of service that the disadvantaged most
need. Where an agency has traditionally had its dominant functions in public
health and has had relatively little to do with mainstream medical practice,
its recruitment patterns and organizational socialization are likely to produce
an orientation that effectively helps the poor. This is what has occurred *with*
the Public Health Service in the United States.

A similar illustration is provided by the engineering profession. A civil
engineer's training is best used and his prestige is most enhanced by large,
capital-intensive projects. The labor-intensive road building projects which
best benefit the poor are technically undemanding, are professionally un-
rewarding, and may even involve specifications that are "substandard" in
the industrialized countries toward which engineering education is oriented.
Agencies dominated by engineers who have not been resocialized will tend
to upgrade and recapitalize labor-intensive public works projects (Tendler,
1979, pp. 42–44; Garzon, 1981).

These examples demonstrate that the national political context, although
very influential, is an insufficient predictor of the extent to which an agency
will give real energy to getting program benefits to the rural poor. Depending on the way in which a program fits into the professional and institutional
orientation of an agency, the response may be more or less progressive than
the national "average." The particular character of the program in question,
the way in which it relates to the national political framework, and the

institutional character of the agency all come together to determine whether or not a national organization can be found with the necessary commitment to deliver benefits to the rural poor in this program instance.

The foregoing discussion has focused on agencies of a national government. In principle other "centers" might be subjected to a similar form of analysis. We wish to call attention at this point, however, to the danger of treating international aid agencies as interchangeable with domestic organizations for the purposes of providing supporting linkages to local governments and organizations. A major attribute of the donors is that their commitments to a program area are usually relatively brief (5–10 years). To the extent that local organizations and governments develop strong links to and dependency on an international donor, the continuity of the program is highly vulnerable. A link to a domestic "center" is needed as well if the program and its benefits are to be institutionalized. We argue that the types of links that should be constructed depend on the characteristics of the central and local organizations being linked. If the eventual domestic agency at the center and the international aid agency have different linkage attributes and if those that fit the donor prevail, an inappropriate set of links will have been institutionalized. The local organization may have become dependent on a set of financial or technical supporting links that cannot be sustained by the domestic "central" organization when the donor leaves. Or the local unit may have been forced to accept a set of well-intentioned controls from the international agency that becomes destructive when an unsympathetic national agency takes them over. Precisely, because the linkage to the donor will be temporary, it may easily be inappropriate for the long run. Hence our insistence on focusing analysis on national agencies in the linkage relationship. Eventually their character, not that of the donor, will determine the nature of the working relationship with local governments and organizations.

The nature of the implementing agency at the national center thus is another critical variable in determining the type of decentralization and the nature of the linkages to be favored for a program. Where a supportive "central" organization exists, the structure of implementation should build on it. Where it is missing, local autonomy is necessary.

Technical and Administrative Requirements and the Distribution of Capacity

To implement a program effectively an organization must be more than well intentioned; it must also have the capacity to translate those intentions into reality. Administrative capacity, be it at the center or in a local organization, is an elusive concept, for it involves more than the presence of skilled personnel. True, the organization has to be able to recognize the existence of problems and opportunities that affect it and to identify the solutions that will be appropriate to them. It also must have the ability to manage the personnel and materials required for implementing the solutions. These abilities involve technical and managerial skills.

In addition, however, the organization has to produce a decision to act, to sustain the legitimacy of that decision against internal and external challenges, and to mobilize the human and material resources needed to execute the program decided upon. These attributes are "political." As we noted in our discussion of support from the center, they derive from the interaction of leadership and institutional history. Leadership is the art of using and manipulating the organization's institutional heritage to make decisions, legitimate them, and mobilize resources for their execution (Ilchman & Uphoff, 1969). Poor leadership may have difficulty acting even within the confines of its institution's history; good leadership is able to expand on it creatively. In either case, an organization will lack the capacity for certain types of actions and have adequate capacity for others.

Programs or program components have a number of critical features that must be matched with the capacities of an organization if effective implementation is to be achieved. The first is technical. If a program is based on a particular technology the organization will need to have personnel with that technical skill, be able to obtain them, or be assured of access to them through technical assistance. This attribute is important and obvious. Consequently, it frequently dominates consideration of appropriate organizations for program implementation. Sometimes this emphasis is unfortunate, for if the skill is generally available in the society it is one of the easier capacities to add to an organization. The attention given to it then may preclude attention to other attributes that are harder to provide.

The second attribute is that of scale. For reasons of efficiency or technology a program may need to be operated with a certain size of unit. An irrigation system built around a hydro-electric dam has a vast scale of operation compared to the one using a tube well and pump. A hospital requires a much larger clientele to be efficient than does a clinic. The organizations constructing macadam arterial roads must be much larger than those providing maintenance or building dirt feeder roads. The implementing organization must be able to operate effectively at the particular levels of scale required, be they large or small. Many organizations are simply too small or limited in geographical scope to undertake projects with large-scale requirements; others lack the capacity to operate at the village level required by some technologies. Frequently, a program has some components that have large economies of scale and others that are best managed by small or local units. Then one needs either to find a single organization with both capacities or to share the components between small organizations and a large one, with linkages between them.

The third attribute is the complexity of the administrative process required. Programs that call for a single set of tasks to be executed by a group of workers under the immediate supervision of a single superior are simple from the point of view of administration. Those that involve several work units that are independent and uncoordinated with one another are somewhat more difficult, but still fairly simple. Those that require the closely coordinated action of several different operations, either in sequence or simultaneously, are administratively complex. A much higher level of managerial expertise and experience is needed for the latter than for the former types of programs ... .

The fourth program attribute is the contributions that it requires from extra-organizational actors. A smallholder tea program will need to have feeder roads built and maintained in order to get the leaf to the factories promptly. If the implementing organization is an agricultural one, will it obtain the necessary services from a public works department? A promotive health program would need the cooperation of villagers to have latrines built and used. Note that the tea program depends on the use of influence over a government agency, while the second relies upon standing with the village community. The ability of the organization to elicit the appropriate forms of cooperation is a part of its administrative capacity.

The fifth attribute is related to the preceding one and might even be seen as an extension of it. This is the magnitude of resources, largely financial, needed for the program. The more money needed to run a program, the greater must be the ability of the organization to raise uncommitted funds. If the program is managed by a national agency with international donor financing, will that agency successfully fight for an increased share of the national budget when the overseas aid ends? If the program is a pilot one, does the organization have potential access to funds, not just for the first stage but for the expansion as well? If the program is to be run by a local organization but financed by a central agency of some kind, is there the possibility of a meaningful local matching contribution? As will be argued later in this book, either local commitment or independence tends to be lost if there are no matching funds.

There are further attributes of specific programs that draw upon administrative capacity. The preceding list covers the most important ones, however, and is sufficient to illustrate the kind of analysis that is needed in assessing administrative requirements.

Administrative capacity virtually always falls below the ideal – in all parts of the world and at all levels of the political system. The issue therefore must be the capacity as measured by minimal and relative standards, not the absolute ones. If an organization cannot be found or created with the minimal capacity to administer the program acceptably or to absorb the technical assistance necessary for it to do so, then the program should simply not be implemented and another less-demanding one should be found.

If two or more minimally adequate organizations exist, the question then will be which one to use. Since, as we will argue later, administrative weakness is easier (but not necessarily easy) to repair than commitment, the decision will usually be made on the basis of the other criteria advanced in this chapter. Once the decision about the local recipient has been made, the issue of the distribution of responsibilities between the central and local organizations will arise. Relative administrative capacity for the various specific facets of the program would then play a major role in determining the allocation of tasks. (Just because a local organization or government has administrative problems does not prove that a central one is any better, although national governments tend to behave as if it were so.) The relative administrative strength of the central and local organizations will also influence the kinds of linkages that should be built between them.

When an administratively weak local organization is attractive by other criteria as a program implementer and where a supportive "central" organization is administratively strong, the deficiency might be overcome with supportive linkages. If even these requisites are missing or if the local organization is too weak to absorb such technical assistance, another less-demanding program must be found or governmental action abandoned in this area.

MODES OF DECENTRALIZATION

In the preceding pages several factors have been analyzed which have implications both for the structures of decentralization adopted and the types of inter-organizational linkages that are developed to serve them. Prior to discussing these implications in the following chapters, we need to lay out the major structural alternatives.

First, we require a more precise explanation of what is meant by centralization and decentralization. The Oxford English Dictionary defines centralization as a concentration of administrative powers in a single head or center. The concept has been used in this way for almost two centuries and its meaning is quite stable. Decentralization is the opposite of centralization – the undoing of centralization (Landau & Eagle, 1981, p. 1). Unfortunately, this antonym lacks the clarity of "centralization." Martin Landau and Eva Eagle suggest: "A perfectly decentralized system is one in which each member is authorized to make decisions on the basis of information which comes to him alone" (Landau & Eagle, 1981, p. 17). In practice, such a condition never obtains. Even in a market economy of small enterprises, most members would lack the authority or resources to make many of the decisions suggested by the information they receive. For example, they cannot respond to a profitable, but expensive investment opportunity they perceive without a loan – and thus must transmit their information to those with capital and defer to their ultimate authority on this matter. In the real world perfect decision autonomy and hence pure decentralization do not exist.

As Stephen Cohen and his associates observe, "to decentralize" is not to reach an end state but is the process of moving toward it. The term loses clarity because there is more than one path along which a system can move toward the unobtainable condition of pure decentralization. There are several non-comparable dimensions along which decentralization can take place. For example, "administratively France is more centralized than Britain; politically, through the party system, Britain is more centralized than France." Thus, "Decentralization is not one thing; nor is it even a series of degrees along a single spectrum or scale. For comprehensibility and utility in policy circles, the overarching abstraction 'decentralization' must be split into a host of separate, occasionally conflicting entities" (Cohen, Dyckinan, Schoenberger, & Downs, 1981, pp. 5–6).

The classical distinction between "devolution" and "deconcentration" is recognition of the futility of analyzing decentralization along a single dimension. The former refers to the process of empowering autonomous units of local government, the latter, to the granting of authority to field units of a central government hierarchy. These two forms of decentralization are conflicting. Devolution involves a weakening of the local authority of central government; deconcentration generally involves strengthening it through an increase in the discretion of its agents.

The Dimensions for Analyzing Decentralization

There are numerous dimensions along which grants of authority can be analyzed. Thus, the variety of forms of decentralization threatens to become unmanageable if we try to be comprehensive. To impose a limit one must specify the purpose for which the typology is being created and elaborate only those dimensions that are useful to it. Our purpose here is to analyze organizational forms that are helpful in bringing development to the rural poor. We therefore have devised a typology of decentralization that will serve that end. It will not have universal utility, although we have used terms that have an already established meaning wherever possible. The typology is based on four dimensions.

First, we argued earlier that rural development programs depend on having the resources and authority for timely adaptation to locally specific conditions present in the field, not the capital. We also expressed our interest in local participatory organizations. "The field" and "local organizations" are not the same thing, however. With the growth in the size and developmental responsibility of the modern state the structure of local governance now usually involves at least three actors – the central government, intermediate structures, and local participatory organizations. The last include village councils, neighborhood self-help groups, and local action organizations. These units serve up to 1,000 families, usually in the range of 100. The intermediate structures are the town and county councils and the field offices of the national administration, which used to be thought of as the base of the structure of government. The decline of traditional face-to-face groups, their replacement with more flexible and formalized participatory organizations, and our awareness of their importance for development have all contributed to a new interest in the way these truly base-level units interact with the rest of the system. Thus, our typology includes local-level as well as intermediate organizations.

Second, to do justice to poverty-oriented programs we must differentiate between structures of local participation and governance which are inclusive (and thus potentially open to the whole population in an area) and those which are exclusive and serving the poor part of it. Following the American convention, we call these latter structures alternative organizations. (For present purposes we are interested in only those organizations limited to the poor; a comprehensive typology would include, for example, ones limited to doctors, to farmers of a particular type, etc.)

Third, a distinction between those governmental organizations that are generalist (multi-functional) and those that are specialized (restricted range of related functions) is needed. When the political system as a whole is more committed to the interests of the poor than are the specialized agencies or professionals working in a program area, then a structure that subordinates the latter to generalists at the local level is more likely to be progressive. When the converse is true, a specialist autonomy will be preferable. On a different issue, multi-functionality generally increases complexity; so when administrative capacity is weak, specialist organizations with a limited range of functions will be attractive.

Finally, the option of minimizing the involvement of all forms of collective organization and relying upon the market or philanthropies – privatization – must be considered. We presume that if the historic imbalance in the delivery of services to the poor is to be righted, action will be necessary by progressive governmental or representative organizations. There are circumstances, however, in which redistribution is not the relevant issue; instead the challenge is to minimize governmentally caused inequality or incompetence in the delivery of services. Privatization is relevant to such situations.

A Typology of Decentralization Oriented to the Poor

Thus, we see four dimensions of decentralization that are relevant to rural development: (1) What type of organization is involved at both the intermediate and the local level? (2) Are the mediating organizations representative, private, or agencies of the central government? (3) Are the governmental bodies generalist or specialist? (4) Are the representative entities inclusive or alternative organizations limited to the poor? The answers to these four questions lead to the identification of eight major types and a total of twenty-four sub-types of decentralization. The full range of possibilities is presented in Table 1.

The traditional typologies of decentralization refer to the character of the intermediate organizations. We will follow that convention and not attempt to invent names for the forms as they relate to the varieties of local participation.

The inclusive, generalist, intermediate representative bodies are the classic form of local government with a full electorate and a wide range of functions. When they are promoted, it is called *devolution.* Beneath them and relating to them may be inclusive groups such as neighborhood organizations or alternative community groups such as those of minorities or perhaps an unorganized citizenry.

Table 1. Examples of Forms of Decentralization Serving the Poor.

Intermediate Representative Organizations		General Type of Decentralization	Local Participatory Organizations		
			Inclusive	Exclusive (Alternative)	None
Inclusive	Generalist	Devolution	(a) Local government w/neighborhood groups	(b) Local government w/pressure groups of poor or minorities	(c) Local government w/an unorganized citizenry
	Specialist	Functional devolution	(d) Cooperative unions w/primary societies	(e) U.S. school district boards w/school site advisory committees (SAC) of poor parents	(f) Local utility authority w/an unorganized citizenry
Exclusive (alternative)		Interest organization	(g) Caste or ethnic associations	(h) India's Organization of the Rural Poor	(i) Trade unions without shop committees
(None by center itself cont.)	Generalist	Prefectorial deconcentration	(j) Prefects w/village councils	(k) Chinese commune party secretaries w/party cells	(l) Kenyan district commissioners w/appointed chiefs

	Specialists		
Ministerial deconcentration	(m) Rural health agency w/village committees	(n) Nutrition education w/groups of poor women	(o) Agricultural extension to individual farmers
Delegation to autonomous agencies	(p) National irrigation board w/water-course committees	(q) Kenya Tea Development Authority w/smallholder advisory committees	(r) Regional development authority hiring for labor-intensive public works projects
None, privatization			
Philanthropy	(s) CARE w/village community development committees	(t) Ford Foundation w/alternative local organizations	(u) Catholic Relief direct to individuals
Marketization	(v) Private wholesalers w/primary cooperative societies	(w) Commercial loans to groups of poor peasants	(x) Full privatization, i.e., private wholesalers and retailers

Note: w/ = with.

Decentralization to inclusive, specialized, intermediate representative organizations can be called *functional devolution*. In the United States, school boards are such units. Beneath them have grown alternative, poverty-oriented participatory groups working in the schools and pressuring the elected boards. They now supplement the traditional, inclusive parent–teacher associations. An example of functional devolution with inclusive local organization is the cooperative union. In many developing countries such unions service the more face-to-face primary societies and are governed by indirectly elected committees.

Intermediate bodies that limit their services to the poor are a form of *interest organization*. An example of such a body relating to alternative local organizations is India's new Organization of the Rural Poor (International Confederation of Free Trade Unions, 1977). An example of an alternative organization without local face-to-face groups would be a trade union of agricultural laborers. Intermediate organizations limited to the poor would serve whole communities only in quite poor, undeveloped areas, so cases in the intermediate alternative – local/inclusive boxes are infrequent empirically. One example would be an organization of a geographically concentrated, poor ethnic group. The village branches of such an association would include all those living there.

If the center is to reach the villages and if it does not use other bodies, it must serve as its own intermediary, relating to the various types of village organizations or to the poor themselves directly. When this is done at all effectively, some degree of decentralization is involved. The variability of the conditions in the rural areas and the need for flexible response to them makes centralization, with no discretion for field staff, impracticable if any positive impact is to be achieved.

When authority is retained by the national government, but is decentralized to one of its field agents we speak of *deconcentration*. This delegation of authority is an administrative action and does not alter the ultimate structure of control, for the center retains the power to appoint its field agents. Thus, deconcentration is quite different from devolution, in which a shift in the locus of final command is involved (Cohen et al., 1981, p. 19).

Decentralization of authority to a functionally specialized field agent of the national government can be called *ministerial deconcentration*. When villagers or their organizations are reached by generalist national government machinery, we use the term *prefectorial deconcentration*. A prefectorial system is the most common form of such multifunctional organization. In it a *prefect* or district commissioner heads a team of ministerial field officers and exercises general control and coordination of government operations in his area. A variant of the prefectorial system is found in disciplined one-party states where the party secretary serves as the de jure or de facto head of government in his jurisdiction.

Parastatals represent a special form of decentralization. These specialized, legally distinct corporations vary in their character depending on the method of constituting their boards of directors. A regional development corporation with a board appointed by autonomous local governments is a form of functional devolution. When the board of a state corporation is centrally appointed, however, the parastatal becomes much like a national government department. It differs from the latter in being free of detailed supervision by the standard, generalist agencies of national control – the Treasury and the Civil Service Commission. Such parastatals are grouped under the heading of *delegation to autonomous agencies* (Ronclinelli, 1979; Cohen et al., 1981; United Nations Centre for Regional Development, 1981, pp. 10–12).

Where neither the national government nor the intermediate representative bodies extends its reach into the villages, the role may be played by business or voluntary organizations. The resulting coverage provided often is uneven, but the results actually achieved are frequently superior to those of governments. The generic name for this form of decentralization *is privatization*. When services are provided directly to villagers by businesses (with their own networks of intermediary supply, wholesale, and service firms), the term *marketization* is used. *Philanthropy* provides the alternate non-governmental linkage organization for inclusive and alternative local groups – and sometimes for the villagers themselves. Churches, foundations, and secular private voluntary organizations all operate to provide services to the poor. These many forms of decentralization provide a significant range of alternatives for the program designer. The appropriate choice depends on the program and its context.

THE ARRAY OF LINKAGES

The preceding typology of decentralization provides the framework for specifying the organizations involved in a particular rural development program and for identifying which of those bodies has the lead responsibility for it. It does not tell us what the relationships are between the organizations, however. The character of such linkages has almost as much of an impact on program implementation as does the structural allocation of responsibilities embodied in a form of decentralization.

Center–local linkages can take a number of forms and be conceptualized in various ways. The simplest would be a purely descriptive classification, based on the mechanism used, and might distinguish five types of linkages:

1. *Finance*: provision of credit, savings bank facilities, direct grants of various types, material transfers, etc.
2. *Regulation and monitoring*: audits, administered market prices, required ratios of credit to savings, registration or certification of local organizations, recruitment and program standards, inspections, evaluations, etc.
3. *Technical and personnel assistance*: in-service and entry-level training, temporary and perpetual acceptance of staff, technical, management and program advice, etc.
4. *Services*: provision of inputs, performance of selected tasks, etc.
5. *Representation*: various forms of formal and informal local participation in planning and implementing programs, community consulting groups, political parties, patron–client networks, etc.

A central government can utilize any of these mechanisms singly or in combination to attempt to influence local units. Representational linkages also may involve influence going "upward" from the local unit toward the central unit.

The descriptive classification just given is helpful in providing a concrete image of the actual linkage mechanisms used. Its utility for the program designer is limited, however, for it has little prescriptive significance. Additional methods of categorizing linkages are needed that will help to identify them according to the purposes they serve and the consequences they are likely to have. All five descriptive types of linkages can be distinguished as well by their underlying purposes.

Control Linkages

Inter-organizational linkages perform two major functions – control and assistance.[4] The purpose of control linkages is to enable one organization to determine some aspect of another's performance. Their very existence indicates that one organization is concerned that the other may perform in an unacceptable manner. A wide variety of control mechanisms can be used. All regulation and most monitoring devices are control linkages. Technical and personnel assistance ... may also be designed to gain influence over the aided organization. All of these linkages are used by central organizations to control intermediate and local ones. The latter units may have their links for control of the center too, through various forms of representation. Some of these may be formal, as when a legislature of locally elected representatives sanctions and regulates the programs of central agencies. Others are informal, as in the wide variety of ways in which localities may seek to influence agency decisions – ranging from patron–client ties to interest groups.

Control linkages need not be simple dyadic relations between two organizations. Frequently, different central agencies will regulate different aspects of a local organization's performance. Similarly, a central agency may be subjected to conflicting influence attempts from a variety of local bodies.

Assistance Linkages

The other purpose of linkage is to provide assistance. Finance, service, and most technical and personnel assistance have this facilitative function. It develops when a local or intermediate organization has certain advantages for implementing a program, but is lacking in others. A central organization then facilitates the program by filling the gap.

In principle, assistance can be provided without control; in practice, this rarely is the case. Inter-governmental assistance virtually always has some degree of control attached to it – facilitative linkages with regulation. Nonetheless, the mix between them does vary. Furthermore, controls by the center are sometimes counter-balanced with representative ones by intermediate and local organizations. The nature of the linkage amalgam is important to performance.

CONCLUSIONS

Linkages are not a minor theme in development administration; they are one of its most important issues. Linkages can be extremely powerful and can have at least as much effect on implementation as the designation of the formal structures to be involved. In the United States, for example, state and federal "grants" have transformed local school boards from autonomous to dependent organizations without any change in formal structure. Linkages are a central component of all international aid. The expectations for their performance are frequently exceedingly high; they are often expected to turn inegalitarian organizations into progressive ones. Yet the development literature has very little to tell us about how effective various linkage devices are and why. Without this knowledge, effective institutional development and program implementation for the rural poor are impossible. Thus, we turn in the following chapters to concrete experiences with different forms of decentralization and with inter-organizational linkages. In our concluding chapter we will then draw these experiences together into a number of generalizations and lessons for program design.

NOTES

1. Our thinking in this section has been influenced by a manuscript draft by Judith Tendler and by correspondence with Bruce Johnston.

2. These and our other points on alternative organizations draw heavily on Marshall's analysis of the U.S. War on Poverty in Chapter II, as well as on Schurmann's (1966) discussion of land reform and collectivization in China.

3. Several of these points are drawn from a draft manuscript by Judith Tendler.

4. This distinction parallels and is derived from that made by Inayatullah (1972, pp. 253–255) in his study of cooperatives between regulative and facilitative linkages.

REFERENCES

Almond, G., & Verba, S. (1963). *The civic culture*. Princeton: Princeton University Press.

Cohen, S. S., Dyckinan, J. W., Schoenberger, E., & Downs, C. B. (1981). *Decentralization: A framework for policy analysis*. Berkeley: Project on Managing Decentralization, Institute of International Studies, University of California.

Garzon, J. M. (1981). Small-scale public works, decentralization, and linkages. In: D. Leonard & D. Marshall (Eds), *Linkages to decentralized units*. Berkeley: Project on Managing Decentralization, Institute of International Studies, University of California.

Hank, F. (1974). *The political mobilization of peasants: A study of an Egyptian community*. Bloomington: Indiana University Press.

Heiby, J. B., Ness, G. D., & Pillsbury, B. L. K. (1979). *AID'S role in Indonesian family planning: A case study with general lessons for foreign assistance*. Washington, DC: U.S. Agency for International Development Program Evaluation Report no. 2.

Hyden, G. (1973). Government and cooperatives. In: R. Jackson, G. Hyden & J. Okumu (Eds), *Development administration: The Kenyan experience*. Nairobi: Oxford University Press.

Ilchman, W., & Uphoff, N. (1969). *The political economy of change*. Berkeley: University of California Press.

Inayatullah, B. (Ed.) (1972). *Cooperatives and development in Asia: A study of cooperatives in fourteen rural communities of Iran, Pakistan and Ceylon, Vol. VII of Rural institutions and planned change*. Geneva: United Nations Research Institute for Social Development.

International Confederation of Free Trade Unions. (1977). *Organization of the rural poor: Progress report, April 1975–March 1977*. New Delhi: ICFTU Asian Regional Organization.

Johnston, B. F., & Clark, W. C. (1982). *Redesigning rural development: A strategic perspective*. Baltimore: Johns Hopkins University Press.

Johnston, B. F., & Kilby, P. (1974). The design and implementation of strategies for agricultural development. *Agricultural Administration, 1*(3), 165–197.

Landau, M., & Eagle, E. (1981). *On the concept of decentralization.* Berkeley: Project on Managing Decentralization, Institute of International Studies University of California.

Long, E. C., & Viau, A. D. (1974). Health care extension: Using auxiliaries in Guatemala. *Lancet, 7848*(26), 127–130.

Migdal, J. S. (1974). *Peasants, politics and revolution: Pressures toward political and social change in the Third World.* Princeton: Princeton University Press.

Ralston, L., Anderson, J., & Colson, E. (1981). *Voluntary efforts and decentralized management.* Berkeley: Project on Managing Decentralization, Institute of International Studies, University of California.

Ronclinelli, D. (1979). *Administrative decentralization and area development planning in East Africa: Implications for United States aid policy.* Madison: Regional Planning and Area Development Project, International Studies and Programs, University of Wisconsin.

Schurmann, F. (1966). *Ideology and organization in Communist China.* Berkeley: University of California Press.

Seers, D. (1972). What are we trying to measure? *Journal of Development Studies, 8*(3), 21–36.

Tendler, J. (1979). *New directions for rural roads.* Washington, DC: Office of Evaluation, U.S. Agency for International Development.

Thoden van Veizen, H. U. E. (1977). Staff, kulaks and peasants: A study of a political field. In: L. Cliffe, J. S. Coleman & M. R. Doornbos (Eds), *Government and rural development in East Africa: Essays on political penetration.* The Hague: Martinus Nijhoff.

Thompson, J. D. (1967). *Organizations in action.* New York: McGraw-Hill.

United Nations Centre for Regional Development. (1981). *Implementing decentralization policies and programmes: Report of UNCRD workshop held at Nagoya, Japan from 21 to 27 July, 1981.* Nagoya.

Uphoff, N. (1980). Political considerations in human development. In: P. T. Knight (Ed.), *Implementing programs of human development.* Working Paper no. 403. Washington, DC, The World Bank.

Uphoff, N., Cohen, J. M., & Goldsmith, A. A. (1979). *Feasibility and application of rural development participation: A state-of-the-art paper.* Ithaca: Rural Development Committee, Center for International Studies, Cornell University.

Uphoff, N., & Esman, M. J. (1974). *Local organization for rural development: Analysis of Asian experience.* Ithaca, Rural Development Committee, Center for International Studies, Cornell University. Rural Local Government Monograph no. 19, November.

Uphoff, N., & Ilchman, W. (1972). *The political economy of development.* Berkeley: University of California Press.

FURTHER READING

Adams, R. H. (1981). *Growth without development in rural Egypt: A local-level study of institutional and social change.* Ph.D. dissertation, Department of Political Science, University of California, Berkeley.

DEVELOPMENT PLANNING: LESSONS OF EXPERIENCE

Albert Waterston

Since the end of the World War II, a considerable literature on development planning has accumulated. Most of it is concerned with how planning ought to be practiced, or more explicitly, how planning would work if it worked as originally conceived or as the writer might wish. While examples from experience have been used to illustrate principles, most authors have chosen to concentrate on theory rather than practice. These writers have generally been as aware as anyone that there was always a gap – often a great one – between the theories they espoused and planning as it is practiced, especially in less developed countries. But mostly they have considered discrepancies between the two as short-run aberrations, which would tend to disappear as more planners were trained and acquired experience.

The formal training of planners has reflected these attitudes. In universities of the industrialized countries, as well as in universities and institutes of the less developed countries themselves, to which would-be planners from less developed countries have come to learn the art or, as some may aver, the science of developmental planning, courses have largely concentrated on techniques for getting the highest possible returns from the allocation of economic resources. These techniques have in the main included such subjects as econometric model-building based on linear or curvilinear programming, the construction of input-output matrices, shadow-pricing methodology, simulation technique, operations research, and the theory

Comparative Public Administration: The Essential Readings
Research in Public Policy Analysis and Management, Volume 15, 427–431
Copyright © 2006 by Elsevier Ltd.
All rights of reproduction in any form reserved
ISSN: 0732-1317/doi:10.1016/S0732-1317(06)15017-4

of games. While this training may be valuable to some, it has thus proved to be of little practical use to planners in most less developed countries.

This is only partly because of a dearth of reliable statistics without which refined technique cannot work, an absence of technicians capable of joining in the formulation of an econometrically based comprehensive plan, or a failure of government leaders to understand what planning is all about. Of far greater importance is the fact that in most less developed countries the major unresolved planning problems are primarily political and administrative instead of economic. Against these problems, econometric techniques, which constitute the main stock in trade of the modern planner, have thus far made almost no headway.

Even a casual examination of the results achieved from development planning in most less developed countries indicates that they are falling short of what is reasonable to expect. The record is so poor – it has been worsening in fact – that it has sometimes led to disillusionment with planning and the abandonment of plans. Even in India, a citadel of planning, planning has been under unprecedented attack. Indeed, participants in the United Nations Meeting of Experts on Administrative Aspects of National Development Planning, held in Paris in June 1964, went so far as to suggest that national development planning was in crisis.

Perhaps this goes too far. Nevertheless, the record is not one in which planners can take pride. It can hardly be a source of complacency for planners when they reflect how few are the less developed countries, which succeeded in achieving even modest plan targets. It behooves planners to re-examine their approach to planning in the light of actual experience.

Although national development planning is very young – it has been practiced on a continuing basis for little more than 35 years in the USSR, for less than 20 years in countries which started planning soon after the end of World War II, and for much less than a decade in most of the rest of the world – development planning has already acquired its orthodoxies and high priests.

In the socialized countries, the official doctrine has been that rapid and balanced development could be carried out only through centralized plan formulation and execution. Amidst increasing indications over the last decade that centralization decision-making was seriously interfering with the ability of socialized enterprises to fulfill their plan targets, and clear evidence in Yugoslavia had decentralized implementation that was producing far better results than centralized controls, the accepted tenets and ways were retained and expanded in the most socialized countries. While these tenets were questioned, at first hesitantly and then more boldly and insistently, they were vigorously defended by the most respected savants. What was needed, they replied, were more, not fewer controls. The theory was good, but practice was bad. Practice had to be brought into line with theory.

But events proved more persuasive than words. Despite valiant efforts to reform the system within the limits laid down by theory, planning problems multiplied. And, as will be seen later, eventually theory gave way. New forms are coming into use. Rigid adherence to precept hallowed by use is being followed by flexible experimentation. What form of planning will take is uncertain, except that it will be different from the past.

In the mixed-economy countries, also, a basic credo took root early. It holds that comprehensive development planning, based on econometric techniques, is so superior to any other type that all countries, at all stages of development, would be well advised to use it in preference to any other. The rationale for this belief is discussed in detail in Chapter IV. There is little question that from the theoretical point of view, comprehensive development planning excels. It may also be granted that it works effectively in some countries, especially in the more advanced nations or in those less developed countries that are so firmly committed to development planning that the usual problems seem to be more manageable. It may even be granted that some countries, which plan only partially could benefit from the introduction of comprehensive planning. But it must also be said that comprehensive development planning does not work in most less developed countries where it has been tried.

Here, as before, those who believe in the established doctrine argue that what is wrong is practice- not theory. Here, too, those who consider comprehensive planning the "be all and end all" of planning, contend that the many failures only prove the need for more – not less – comprehensive planning. But here, also, the pressures or circumstances are convincing many countries to abandon an "idealized outlook" and adjust practice to needs dictated by realities.

Forced from the chrysalis of theory by the imperative of events, national development planning has emerged as a diverse phenomenon, which almost invariably differs in some important respects from one country to another. To an even greater extent, diversity arises because not only the aims of planning but the methods used to formulate and implement plans are closely conditioned by a country's political, economic, and social values and institutions, and its stage of development. Since in these respects every country is unique in some way, the results in one country usually differ markedly from those in another even when both have adopted the same planning methods.[1]

Yet, every country has qualities and planning problems, which are common to all. It is, therefore, a mistake to believe that the planning experience of one country has no relevance to others – as much a mistake as it is to think that one type of planning is the answer to development in all countries at all times. Indeed, the material in the chapters which follow provides much evidence to support the view that, although methodology and approach may vary greatly from one country to another, certain principles have emerged in the planning experience of socialized and mixed economies, and in the industrially developed and less developed nations, which are valid in any country. One need to cite only one example: Experience demonstrates that when a country's leaders in a stable government are strongly devoted to development, inadequacies of a particular form of planning used – or even the lack of any formal planning – will not impede the country's development. Conversely, in the absence of political commitment or stability, the most advanced form of planning will not make a significant contribution toward a country's development.

It is therefore a mistake to imagine that a certain system of planning or a certain kind of plan is the key to national development. Those planners who insist that it is, when most countries do not in practice accept this view, only succeed in separating their activities and their plans from the planning process as it operates in most less developed countries. While planners may be shifting resources about on paper and proving to their own satisfaction that a country's national income can be doubled within a decade, the country may be having great difficulty in maintaining much lower rates of growth.

When planners look up from their plans, they cannot fail to become aware that their theoretical formulations have greatly outstripped practical capabilities. They can then appreciate the advice of one planner to survey things as they are, observe what needs to be done, study the means you have to do it with, and then work out practical ways of going about it.[2]

When this sequence is followed, the forms of planning are likely to be quite different from those set by reference to abstract concepts. Thus, it may be found that improvements in budgetary practice should precede the formulation of a comprehensive development plan in some countries; or that the establishment of machinery to improve the preparation and execution of projects, and the formulation of sectoral programs may be more important in some countries at some times in their history than the establishment of a central planning office.

The shortage of good, well-prepared projects which is a well-nigh universal feature of the planning experience of less developed countries is now widely recognized as a major impediment to the execution of plans for development. Planners are also beginning to realize that the absence of appropriate policies and measures, more often than the absence of additional investment funds, accounts for shortfalls in plan targets. But the implications of these truths are not yet fully understood by most planners. Thus, they do not comprehend that they must mold their plans to "things as they are." Planners must, of course, try to improve the planning milieu in which they work. But to accomplish this, it is of little use to start with a set of theoretical abstractions of planning as it might be and seek to force them upon an inhospitable environment. Theory is important – nay, vital. But an important lesson of experience is that a priori abstractions from theory, no matter how penetrating, are only a beginning; to complete the story, there is need for a posteriori abstractions from history. The problems of planning are not likely to be settled by the continuing elaboration and refinement of purely logical and mathematical analysis. This is because much of the empirical basis of current theorizing appears to consist of a priori 'common sense' assumptions of fragmentary or obsolete data. If theoreticians avoid the discipline of empirical verification for too long, they run the risk that their work will attenuate into a different kind of sterile scholasticism. Elegance is not a substitute for evidence ... it is never enough to judge theories, decisions, models, etc., only by their logical validity; they must always also be submitted to such empirical verification as may be possible.[3]

NOTES

1. U.N. TAA. *Introduction to Public Administration in Development Policy, Preliminary survey of the experience of several Latin American countries.* p. 3. (See list of works cited at end of book for full citation for this and succeeding footnotes).

2. Ionides, Michael G. "The Objects and Implications of Economic Development," p. 15.

3. Colm Gerhard and Geiger, Theodore. "Country Programming as a Guide to Development." p. 66.

GOVERNMENT DECENTRALIZATION AND ECONOMIC DEVELOPMENT: THE EVOLUTION OF CONCEPTS AND PRACTICES

Dennis A. Rondinelli

Governments around the world are initiating or expanding administrative and fiscal decentralization to give subordinate administrative units more responsibility for providing a wider range of functions and services. Many governments are also decentralizing their economic and political institutions and privatizing state-owned enterprises (SOEs) to strengthen market systems. Decentralization – the transfer of responsibilities and authority to lower levels within the central government (deconcentration), or from the center to local government units (devolution) and nongovernmental organizations (delegation), or from government to the private sector (deregulation and privatization) – has a long history. Many industrialized nations began to decentralize in the late 1960s after their governments consolidated power and responsibility for nearly two decades.

A review of the evolution of theories and practices of decentralization over the past half century can provide a better understanding of governments' successes and failures with an idea whose popularity has surged and waned several times and that is now being seriously re-examined. This

Comparative Public Administration: The Essential Readings
Research in Public Policy Analysis and Management, Volume 15, 433–445
Copyright © 2006 by Elsevier Ltd.
ISSN: 0732-1317/doi:10.1016/S0732-1317(06)15018-6

article traces the evolution of decentralization since the 1950s, examines the reasons why governments have pursued decentralization, and summarizes lessons from experience about conditions for implementing decentralization policies in the 21st century.

The centralization of financing and management of public services and infrastructure and of economic development activities took place in both industrialized and developing countries during the 1950s and 1960s. In the post-colonial period after World War II, many indigenous political leaders in developing countries sought to build their new nations through central government control of the economy. During the 1970s and 1980s, some governments and most international assistance organizations began to recognize the limitations and constraints of central economic planning and management. The demise of authoritarian regimes first in Latin America and then in Central and Eastern Europe, along with the spread of market economies and democratic principles in East Asia, during the 1980s and 1990s led to the current widespread interest in decentralization.

CENTRALIZATION IN THE 1950s AND 1960s

National governments took responsibility for expanding their economies and providing public services during the 1950s and 1960s for many reasons. In North America and Western Europe the strength of central government bureaucracies grew from their crucial roles in mobilizing resources during World War II and, afterward, they took on expanded responsibilities for economic and social reconstruction. Strong central management in industrialized nations offered convenient models for new governments in developing countries. In the post-colonial period, many newly independent governments in Africa and Asia saw local jurisdictions as colonial institutions or as strongholds of ethnic or religious minorities that could be sources of political opposition. Weakening their powers and concentrating resources and authority in the central government was a crucial instrument for nation building.

The dominant development theories of the 1950s and 1960s called for a strong central government control over industrial and agricultural sectors as well as the public services and infrastructure needed to accelerate economic growth. As in many other developing countries, the government in Thailand established more than 50 state-owned industries during the 1950s and 1960s because of the lack of domestic and foreign investment capital and the private sector's weaknesses in mobilizing resources for expansion. The state, by default, emerged as the strongest institution for providing services and promoting economic growth. State enterprises – ranging from national tobacco and distillery industries to electricity generating and public transportation corporations – were kept in government ownership for more than 35 years ostensibly to guarantee supplies of strategic commodities and to stabilize the prices of politically sensitive goods and services. They were to standardize the quality of products for export, provide jobs, and generate public revenues.

The central government became the primary public service provider in many countries because local administrative units were weak and because complex networks of infrastructure had to be created quickly as a foundation for economic growth. Central management and provision of public services grew stronger in developing countries during the 1960s as more governments faced the difficult tasks of nation-building. In Indonesia, for example, public services were provided to local communities largely by the central government's Ministries of Public Works, Home Affairs, and Health. The Ministry of Communications was responsible for urban traffic control and local public transport and the National Electricity Corporation for street lighting in towns and cities. In many Latin American countries, where the constitution gave municipalities and local governments some autonomy, most public services and much of the investment in physical infrastructure came from central government ministries, public corporations, and centrally funded public foundations. Where the private sector was allowed to play a role in economic development, as in South Korea, industrial development took place largely under the supervision of the military or sectoral ministries. Central ministries strengthened their authority during the 1950s and 1960s, in part, because international assistance organizations required governments in developing countries to formulate comprehensive national development plans for investment. International financial institutions such as the World Bank and regional development banks could only lend to sovereign national governments. Although national planning was not necessarily incompatible with decentralization, few national governments seeking to control investment budgets effectively included localities in decision-making. They gave central ministries and agencies primary responsibility for setting investment priorities, for allocating financial resources for infrastructure development and, later, for delivering a wide range of public services from education and health care to electricity and telecommunications.

Moreover, in the post-colonial period national governments in many developing countries gave high priority to the reconstruction of their capital cities as symbols of political independence and modernization. Central ministries invested heavily in constructing modern buildings and utilities to make their national capitals "showcases." Indeed, only central governments had the ability to generate sufficient public revenues or to borrow internationally to finance these capital facilities, and many governments had easy access to loans and grants from international aid and development organizations. Municipal and local governments, even in metropolitan areas, usually lacked the legal authority or the financial, technical, and managerial resources to provide services and facilities needed for their rapidly growing populations. In Caracas, Venezuela, for example, observers point out that during the 1970s "the provision and maintenance of acceptable levels of public services for Greater Caracas has required major efforts. In education, as with many services, high costs rendered a purely municipal approach unrealistic. ... Aqueducts and sewers while less costly than education, also were beyond the financial and technical capabilities of local government."

As the number of central government agencies in both industrialized and developing countries proliferated, many took on commercial functions and assumed control over expenditures and revenues that had previously been under local control. In countries with unitary fiscal systems, like Peru, the central government collected all revenues and reallocated them to local administrative units. The nationalistic and paternalistic attitudes of some African and Asian leaders provided a political rationale for strengthening the central government's control of the economy. Central economic planning and management was practiced, to one degree or another, in all Central and Eastern European countries under communist control.

DECENTRALIZATION FOR EFFICIENCY AND EQUITY IN THE 1970s AND 1980s

Interest in decentralization and privatization emerged in the 1970s and spread during the 1980s. Growing dissatisfaction with central government planning focused public attention on the inefficiencies of SOEs. Critics argued that central government ministries and state enterprises in most developing countries, for a variety of reasons, were poorly organized to extend services to local communities efficiently or equitably. Most central governments were primarily concerned with management of macro-economic policies and with maintaining national political stability. They paid less attention to public service delivery or to maintenance of services and infrastructure. One economist noted the problems with centrally planned projects in both urban and rural areas:

In Colombia, new tarmac roads have suffered rapid and premature deterioration for lack of maintenance. Throughout West Africa, many new schools have opened without qualified teachers or equipment. Agricultural projects are often starved for extension workers, fertilizer, or seeds. In the Sahel, pastoral wells constructed for livestock projects have fallen into disrepair. In Bolivia, doctors are often stranded at health centers for the lack of gasoline for their vehicles ...

Many ministries saw their political power and budgets grow from control over the planning and implementation of large-scale, capital-intensive investments and were reluctant to allow private or non-government organizations to participate or compete in many of the service sectors. Service delivery suffered because few central government ministries rewarded civil servants for dealing with citizens as customers and government bureaucracies grew more unresponsive to the needs of their constituents.

Despite their strong control and authority, weak administrative capacity in central government agencies in many developing countries limited their ability to extend services or to improve delivery. Among the most serious administrative problems were weaknesses in planning and managerial capability at all levels of central government administration, difficulties in coordinating service delivery among national ministries and with local governments, ineffective managerial and supervisory practices in the field, and severe shortages of trained professionals. Dissatisfaction with central government control of public services and infrastructure was reflected, for example, in assessments of the results of Indonesia's national development plans, which prescribed standard urban investment priorities for all cities in the country. Government officials themselves later pointed out that "this sectoral and centralized approach did not meet local needs in a balanced way." In South Korea, as in the Philippines, Malaysia, Indonesia, and Thailand, the central government investments in infrastructure had a strong influence on the pattern of urbanization. Korean observers argued that although central government agencies and public corporations had been efficient in providing housing and some types of physical infrastructure, "they lack sensitivity to local needs and priorities since they operate on standard procedures formulated for the whole country.

Other problems arose from the way in which centrally provided services were perceived by users as "free" public goods for which they should not have to pay. Thus, user charges and other forms of beneficiary payment were unpopular, hard to collect, and easy to relax when the central government treasury could subsidize the cost. No price rationing systems existed to relate supply and demand. In Central America, water authorities resisted the principle of economic pricing, a necessary condition for raising the capital to extend services to poor neighborhoods. They viewed water services as a "right" that households should enjoy without having to pay for capital costs. As a result, some services were provided at levels that exceeded

real demand as measured by willingness to pay. Or governments underes-
timated the willingness of people to pay for services that previously had been
provided either free or at highly subsidized rates. In either case, scarce
central government resources were drained off from other uses to support
local services that could, in most cases, be paid for locally.

A shift in development theories and strategies in international aid agencies during the 1970s away from macro-economic planning and toward
meeting basic human needs, community development, growth-with-equity,
and participatory planning led to increasing calls for decentralizing resources, responsibilities, and control over development activities to local
levels. International assistance organizations promoted decentralization as
an essential part of a "process approach" to economic and social development that depended primarily on self-help by local communities.

Heavy borrowing during the 1970s, and the economic recessions of the
early 1980s left central governments in most countries with little capital for
investing in new infrastructure or for expanding public services. From the
mid-1970s to the mid-1980s the indebtedness of developing countries increased from $140 billion to almost $700 billion. The ratio of interest payments and amortization to exports (debt-service ratio) for developing
countries doubled during the period. The world economic recession of the
late 1970s and early 1980s also played an important role in increasing the
interest of governments in both economically advanced and developing
countries in decentralizing the finance and management of services and infrastructure. The recession led many governments in Africa and Latin
America to restrict the provision of "free goods" and services and to shift
responsibilities to local levels of administration.

The dominance of central governments, however, had greatly weakened
the capacity of local governments to raise revenues. National governments in
most countries appropriated to themselves the most lucrative sources of
public revenue, leaving localities with low-yielding taxes and fees. Moreover,
the legal status of local governments – as agents of the central government
with little authority or taxing ability of their own – left them dependent on
financial transfers and grants-in-aid. In countries like Korea, the Philippines,
and India, where local governments accounted for a substantial percentage
of general government expenditures, much of the money went for administration rather than service delivery.

Both international assistance organizations and government agencies began to recognize the limitations of central economic management in the late
1970s and early 1980s. For example, The National Economic and Social
Development Board (NESDB) in Thailand pointed out in the National

Economic and Social Development Plan for 1977–1981, that "most of the existing state enterprises are inefficient and are not capable of achieving the objectives for which they have been set up." The NESDB assessment concluded that the SOEs were slow to grow, that their value-added in the industrial and public service sectors had been quite low, many were loss-making and required subsidies from the government rather than generating revenues, most had high per-unit costs of production and low rates of return. All of the revenue-generating SOEs were strongly protected monopolies. The overall low rates of return made SOEs unreliable instruments for price stabilization or public revenue generation.

The NESDB attributed the inefficiencies in SOEs providing public services to their lack of operating flexibility and slow decisions on investment and expenditure resulting from "too much supervision by too many government agencies, including the Ministry of Finance, the budget Bureau, and the National Economic and Social Development Board." In addition, the executives and managers of many of the SOEs were political appointees or government bureaucrats with little experience in business. Political intervention resulted in overstaffing and high costs. Ideological changes in governments of western industrial countries – notably, the Reagan Administration in the United States and the Thatcher government in Great Britain – during the early 1980s reinforced pressures on other countries to downsize bureaucracies, rely more heavily on markets for economic growth, privatize state enterprises, and devolve powers and responsibilities to local governments.

DECENTRALIZATION AND DEMOCRATIC MARKET DEVELOPMENT DURING THE 1990s

By the end of the 1980s governments in Latin America, Central and Eastern Europe, and Asia that had long relied on central planning and management were being replaced by more democratic, market-oriented regimes. In Central Europe, for example, policies for promoting transition from socialist to market economies focused on strengthening the private sector, privatizing or liquidating state enterprises, and downsizing and decentralizing large central government bureaucracies. After years of socialist central planning, the private sector and local governments had been weakened almost fatally.

In the late 1980s, private enterprises contributed only 3 percent to gross domestic product in the former Czechoslovakia, for example, and only 15 percent each in Poland and Hungary. Large SOEs produced more than 90 percent of national output in the Czechoslovakia's economy. Nearly

89 percent of employment was in the state-owned industrial and service sectors, with an additional 10 percent in state-dominated agricultural cooperatives. Less than 1 percent of the population was self-employed. The state sector in Poland accounted for more than 80 percent of national output and 88 percent of employment in the nonagricultural sectors. Only 300 SOEs accounted for 59 percent of the net income of Poland's 3,177 state industrial enterprises. Although production in Hungary and the former Yugoslavia was somewhat more decentralized, much of the manufacturing in all four countries took place in huge, inefficient, and unproductive SOEs that rapidly lost their markets in the former Soviet bloc after political independence. Demands for economic, political, and fiscal decentralization spread rapidly within Central and Eastern Europe, Latin America, and Asia.

Decentralization of fiscal responsibilities, administrative structure, and governance was strongly advocated during the 1980s and 1990s by groups seeking stronger political representation or autonomy. Calls for devolution or autonomous rule came from ethnic, religious, and political minority groups in Belgium, Quebec, Wales, Scotland, Malaysia, the Baltics, Mexico, the Philippines, India, Yugoslavia, and the former Soviet Union that were dissatisfied with their political representation or the allocation of political power. In other countries, including the United States, Great Britain, and Canada, calls for fiscal and administrative devolution were driven largely by conservative political leaders opposed to the increasing political power and fiscal dominance of the central government and who were committed to returning more control and responsibilities to local communities.

In many poor countries, decentralization was prescribed by international financial institutions such as the World Bank and the International Monetary Fund as part of the structural adjustments needed to restore markets, create or strengthen democracy, and promote good governance. The Canadian International Development Agency (CIDA), for example, sought to improve governance in developing countries by assisting projects aimed at strengthening organizations of civil society, democratic political institutions, and human rights groups. Similarly, the Swedish International Development Agency (SIDA) focused its assistance on "making government work" at both central and local levels. It supported public administration development projects "enabling governments to reform, improve, and perfect their existing systems, instruments, and structures of government in order to execute their policies and programs more democratically and effectively." Decentralization was closely identified with democratization movements in some Asian countries such as the Philippines, Nepal, and Bangladesh after long periods of authoritarian rule. With the passing of authoritarian military rule in Latin American countries such as Brazil and Argentina, many elected state and local officials and opposition groups embraced decentralization as a form of democratic institution-building. In many African countries, calls for decentralization emanated from politically and economically peripheral ethnic groups. Growing discontent with the inability of central government bureaucracies to deliver effectively almost any types of services to local areas fueled the decentralization movement in Africa.

Moreover, continued economic globalization through international trade and investment gave cities and metropolitan regions important new economic roles in the 1990s. The world economy was being restructured by technological changes and by the geographic movement of all factors of production – capital, human resources, and technology. This mobility changed the location of production as well as the direction and volume of trade and investment flows among nations and cities. The continuing integration of the world economy also created new opportunities for trade and investment in cities in the formerly socialist countries and in developing nations, requiring municipalities and metropolitan areas to provide new infrastructure and services quickly and effectively. In countries like China, where growth took place rapidly in coastal cities such as Shanghai and Guangzhou, provincial and metropolitan governments assumed powerful new functions, often *de facto* rather than *de jure*. The opening of the world economy and the expansion of cross-border transactions made cities around the world more interdependent, and sometimes more financially independent of their own central governments. To meet the challenges of an open world economy, new initiatives had to be taken in cities to form internationally oriented communities centered around "agile" public and private organizations promoting innovation and creativity – not only in manufacturing, trade, and services, but also in the physical sciences, technology, education, and the arts. To remain economically vital, cities had to adapt their economies, physical infrastructure, and institutions to the requirements of expanding international trade and investment.

LESSONS OF EXPERIENCE: CONDITIONS FOR POLICY IMPLEMENTATION

At the threshold of the 21st century decentralization is widely perceived as an instrument for promoting democratization, market development, and administrative and fiscal efficiency. Advocates argue that when applied appropriately decentralization can help break the bottlenecks in decision-making that are often caused by central government planning and management. Decentralization can be a means of cutting through complex central bureaucratic procedures in getting decisions made and implemented. It can also increase government officials' sensitivity to local conditions and needs. Moreover, decentralization can help government and the private sector to extend services; allow greater political representation for diverse political, ethnic, religious, and cultural groups in decision-making; and relieve top managers in central ministries of "routine" tasks to concentrate on policy. In some countries, decentralization may create local administrative mechanisms for coordinating national, state, provincial, district, and local programs more effectively and can provide better opportunities for local residents to participate in decision making. More creative, innovative, and responsive programs and more local "experimentation" often accompany decentralization. And it can be an effective means of increasing political stability and national unity by allowing citizens to control more effectively public programs at the local level.

But decentralization is not a panacea, a universal prescription for all of government's administrative, fiscal, or political problems. Decentralizing, in some circumstances, may have potential disadvantages. Decentralization may not always be efficient, especially for standardized, routine, network-based services. It can result in the loss of economies of scale and control over scarce financial resources by the central government. Weak administrative or technical capacity at local levels may result in services being delivered less efficiently and effectively in some areas of the country. Administrative responsibilities may be transferred to local levels without adequate financial resources and make equitable distribution of services more difficult. Decentralization can sometimes make coordination of national policies more complex and may allow important functions to be captured by a local political elite, deepening the distrust between public and private sectors and undermining local cooperation.

Experience suggests that in order for decentralization to be effective, national leaders must provide strong political commitment and support for transfer planning, decision-making, and managerial authority to field agencies, to lower levels of administration or government, or to the private sector. Political leaders must be willing to accept the participation in planning and management of local organizations that are outside of the direct control of the central government or the dominant political party. Support of and commitment to decentralization must also come from line agencies of the central bureaucracy and ministry officials must be willing to transfer those functions that they traditionally performed to local organizations. Ironically, decentralization usually requires strengthening administrative and technical capacity within central government agencies and ministries to carry out national functions and to support – with adequate planning, programming, logistical, personnel, and budgetary resources – their field agencies and lower levels of government. Effective channels of political participation and representation must be developed that reinforce and support decentralized planning and administration, and that allow people to express their needs and demands and to press claims for national and local resources.

The organizational factors most conducive to decentralization include the appropriate allocation of planning, administrative, and fiscal functions among levels of government and local organizations with each set of functions suited to their existing or potential management capabilities. Decentralization requires laws, regulations, and directives that clearly define the relationships among different levels of administration, the allocation of functions among organizational units, the roles and duties of officials at each level of government, and their limitations and constraints. Decentralization, must be supported by flexible legal arrangements, based on performance criteria, for reallocating functions as the resources and capabilities of local governments change over time. Clearly defined and relatively uncomplicated planning and management procedures for eliciting participation of local leaders and citizens and for obtaining the cooperation or consent of beneficiaries of services are also needed.

Above all, the success of decentralization depends on increasing the managerial and technical capacities of local administrators and officials and on granting localities appropriate authority to raise and expend financial resources needed to support decentralized functions. Financial and organizational arrangements for decentralization must be tailored to local conditions and needs. Ultimately, decentralization – especially delegation, devolution, and privatization – requires extensive institutional development and managerial capacity building at local levels in both the public and private sectors. The success of decentralization is inextricably tied to strengthening the managerial and political capacity of those organizations to which responsibility and authority are transferred.

FURTHER READING

Ascher, W., & Rondinelli, D. A. (1999). Restructuring the administration of service delivery in Vietnam: Decentralization as institution-building. In: J. I. Litvack & D. A. Rondinelli (Eds), *Market reform in Vietnam* (pp. 132–152). Westport, CT: Quorum Books.
Aziz, A., & Arnold, D. D. (1996). Introduction. In: A. Aziz & D. Arnold (Eds), *Decentralized governance in Asian countries* (pp. 13–33). New Delhi: Sage Publications.

Behrman, J. N., & Rondinelli, D. A. (1995). *Urban development policies in a globalizing economy: Creating competitive advantage in the post-cold war era.* In: W. Crotty (Ed.), *Post cold war policy, the social and domestic context* (Vol. I, pp. 209–230). Chicago: Nelson-Hall.

Bird, R., Carolina, F., & Wallich, C. (1994). Decentralization of intergovernmental finance in transition economies. *Comparative Economic Studies*, 36(4) 149–160.

Cheema, G. S., & Rondinelli, D. A. (Eds) (1983). *Decentralization and development: Policy implementation in developing countries.* Beverly Hills, CA: Sage Publications.

Choi, J. H. (1987). Republic of Korea country paper. In: C. E. Lindbloom & D. Braybrooke (Eds), *Asian Development Bank* (pp. 477–528). Manila: ADB; quote at p. 512.

Dennis, A. R. (1993). *Development projects as policy experiments: An adaptive approach to development administration* (2nd ed.). London: Routledge.

Government of Thailand. (1976). *The fourth national economic and social development plan (1977–1981).* Bangkok: National Economic and Social Development Board, Office of the Prime Minister pp. 201–202.

Heller, P. (1979). The under financing of recurrent development costs. *Finance and Development*, 16(1), 38–41; quote at p. 38.

Korten, D., & Alfonso, F. (Eds) (1981). *Bureaucracy and the poor: Closing the gap.* Singapore: McGraw-Hill.

Mason, E. S., & Asher, R. E. (1973). *The world bank since Bretton Woods.* Washington, DC: The Brookings Institution.

Mawhood, P. (Ed.) (1983). *Local government in the Third World: The experience of tropical Africa.* Chichester, England: Wiley.

Mawhood, P. (Ed.). (1993). *Local government in the third world: The experience of decentralization in tropical Africa* (2nd ed.). Johannesburg, SA: Africa Institute of South Africa.

McDermott, G. A., & Mejstrik, M. (1991). *The role of small firms in industrial development and transformation in Czechoslovakia.* Prague: Charles University Center for Economic Research and Graduate Education, Working Paper.

Myers, D. J. (1978). Caracas: The politics of intensifying primacy. In: W. A. Cornelius & R. V. Kemper (Eds), *Metropolitan Latin America* (pp. 227–258). Beverly Hills, CA: Sage Publications; quotes at pp. 247–248.

Nicholas, P. (1995). The policy of fiscal decentralization in Brazil. In: L. S. Graham & R. H. Wilson (Eds), *State and local policymaking in Brazil, policy research project 1994–1995.* Austin: University of Texas at Austin, Chapter 5.

Organization for Economic Cooperation and Development. (1992). *Reforming the economies of central and eastern Europe.* Paris: OECD.

Padmopranoto, S. (1987). Indonesia country paper. In: C. E. Lindbloom & D. Braybrooke (Eds), *Asian Development Bank, Urban Policy Issues* (pp. 431–476). Manila: ADB; quote at p. 445.

Peterson, G., Kingsley, G. T., & Wines, S. (1986). *Urban infrastructure pilot studies and development strategy.* Washington, DC: U.S. Agency for International Development.

Rondinelli, D. A. (1990). *Decentralizing urban development programs: A framework for analyzing policy.* Washington, DC: U.S. Agency for International Development.

Rondinelli, D. A. (1994). Privatization and economic reform in central Europe: Experience of the early transition period. In: D. A. Rondinelli (Ed.), *Privatization and economic reform in central Europe: The changing business climate* (pp. 1–40). Westport, CT: Quorum Books.

Rondinelli, D. A., Nellis, J. R., & Shabbir Cheema, G. (1983). *Decentralization in developing countries: A review of recent experience.* World bank staff working paper no. 581. Washington, DC: World Bank.

Rondinelli, D. A., & Priebrijvat, V. (1999). The dynamics of privatization during economic adjustment: State enterprise restructuring in Thailand. *Chulalongkorn Review, 42*(11), 96–117.

Rondinelli, D. A., & Vastag, G. (1998). Urban economic growth in the 21st century: Assessing the international competitiveness of metropolitan areas. In: R. Billsborrow (Ed.), *Migration, urbanization and development: New directions and issues* (pp. 469–514). Norwell, MA: Kluwer.

Rondinelli, D. A., & Wilson, P. A. (1987). Linking decentralization and regional development planning: The IRD project in Peru. *Journal of the American Planning Association, 53*(3), 348–357.

Smoke, P. J. (1994). *Local government finance in developing countries: The case of Kenya.* Nairobi: Oxford University Press.

Sundquist, J. L., & Davis, D. W. (1969). *Making federalism work.* Washington, DC: The Brookings Institution.

Swedish International Development Agency. (1991). *A making government work: Guidelines and framework for SIDA support to the development of public administration.* Stockholm: SIDA, p. 11.

United Nations Centre for Human Settlements. (1987). *Global report on human settlements 1986.* New York: Oxford University Press.

Waterston, A. (1965). *Development planning: Lessons of experience.* Baltimore, MD: Johns Hopkins Press.

DECENTRALIZATION: THE LATEST FASHION IN DEVELOPMENT ADMINISTRATION?

Diana Conyers

There has been a resurgence of interest in decentralization, but decentralization is now somewhat differently conceived from the way it was in the 1960s. With somewhat different objectives, decentralization also takes different forms and this calls into question the value of the well established categories of devolution and deconcentration.

THE RECENT INTEREST IN DECENTRALIZATION

During the last decade, there has been a growing interest in decentralization among the governments of a number of Third World countries, especially, but not only, in Africa. Countries that have introduced significant organizational reforms described as, or having elements of, 'decentralization' – or are in the process of doing so – include Tanzania, Zambia, the Sudan, Nigeria and Ghana in Africa (Adamolckun & Rowlands, 1979; Conyers, 1981a; Mawhood & Davcy, 1980; Rondinelli, 1981; Tordoff, 1980), Sri Lanka (Craig, 1981) and a number of countries in the South Pacific, including Papua New Guinea (Conyers, 1981a, 1981b; Ghai, 1981; Tordoff, 1981). Several other countries in Africa and Asia are attempting to achieve

Comparative Public Administration: The Essential Readings
Research in Public Policy Analysis and Management, Volume 15, 447–462
Copyright © 2006 by Elsevier Ltd.
All rights of reproduction in any form reserved
ISSN: 0732-1317/doi:10.1016/S0732-1317(06)15019-8

some degree of decentralization within the existing organizational structure. In Latin America, government structures have generally remained more centralized and there appears to be little prospect of any major change in the near future; nevertheless, calls for decentralization recur periodically and there have been a few attempts, albeit generally of limited duration and success, to introduce some measure of decentralization (Graham, 1980).

The interest in decentralization in Third World countries has been paralleled by an even greater interest on the part of international development agencies, bilateral aid donors and academic circles in Europe, North America and Australia. The more obvious current examples of this interest include the decentralization research programme of the United Nations' Development Administration Division, which included an international seminar in Khartoum in September 1981 (United Nations, 1981), a research programme launched by the United Nations Centre for Regional Development (UNCRD, 1981a) in Nagoya, Japan, at a seminar in July 1981 (UNCRD, 1981b), a study of decentralized planning by the International Labour Organization (ILO, 1981) and a variety of activities funded by the United States Agency for International Development (USAID), including a major research programme (the Project of Managing Decentralization) now drawing to conclusion at the Institute of International Studies in the University of California at Berkeley (Institute of International Studies, 1981).

On a more modest scale, the Commonwealth Secretariat's Division of Applied Studies in Government has supported technical assistance and workshops in the field of decentralization, including a workshop in Arusha, Tanzania, in April 1982, and it has commissioned the preparation of a bibliography on the subject, while the International Center for Law in Development (based in New York) has also supported dialogue on decentralization, including a small workshop in Nottingham in May 1981 (Institute of Planning Studies, University of Nottingham, and International Center for Law in Development, 1981). Finally, the Development Studies Association (DSA) of the United Kingdom and Ireland held a meeting of its Regional Development and Planning study group on the topic of Decentralization and Planning in March 1982 (DSA, 1982).

This is not the first time that decentralization has been advocated by those concerned with the theory and practice of development administration. A somewhat similar interest in the late 1950s and early 1960s was manifested in the expansion and development of local government systems in many countries and in publications such as the classic works by Maddick (1963) and Hicks (1961) and handbooks produced by the United Nations (1962).

The current resurgence of interest could be interpreted in two ways. On the one hand, it could be seen as just another temporary phase, likely to be followed sooner or later by a swing in the other direction towards increasing centralization. This would be understandable, since the relationship between centralization and decentralization is, to some extent, similar to the movement of a pendulum, in the sense that a strong movement in one direction may well result in an opposite move as a reaction. On the other, it could be interpreted as a more fundamental change, stimulated by different factors and involving different forms of decentralization and, therefore, not necessarily likely to be followed by a reversion to relative centralization.

In reality, both interpretations probably have some validity. The present interest in decentralization is in part a reaction against an earlier period of relative centralization but, at the same time, it has certain characteristics that distinguish it from previous decentralization efforts and, therefore, warrant special study. This paper examines the current decentralization 'fashion' in this context, with the aim, first, of identifying the extent and form, of the differences between current and earlier approaches and, second, of examining the implications of this for future trends in development administration. With these intentions in mind, the next two sections of the paper examine the objectives and the characteristics of recent decentralization programmes, and the last section considers their achievements to date and the possible future implications.

OBJECTIVES OF DECENTRALIZATION

The decentralization programmes of the 1950s and 1960s were closely associated, especially in Anglophone Africa, with the transition from colonial status to political independence. Local-level government, was seen as a necessary part of the structure of an independent democratic government and, more specifically, as a means of removing some of the burden of providing local services from the central government while, at the same time, encouraging political education and involvement at the local level. These objectives were not so very different in many respects from those of the colonial powers when first establishing local-level governments (Hicks, 1961) and the continuing colonial influence was reflected in the characteristics of the decentralization programmes, which tended to be modelled on western systems of field administration and local government – a point to which we shall return in the next section. However, the concern with decentralization was also influenced by the desire of the newly independent governments to demonstrate that they were more concerned with achieving democracy and meeting local needs than their colonial predecessors.

In examining the reasons for the current interest in decentralization, it is useful to recognize that there are some differences between the objectives of the various governments actually involved in decentralization and those of the international agencies, academics and others whose interest is somewhat more detached. The objectives of the two groups are obviously very closely related, but their different perspectives and forms of involvement inevitably result in some differences in objectives and priorities. Moreover, it is also important to recognize that, within each group, the reasons for encouraging decentralization are usually complex and they are likely to include both reasons that are clearly stated and openly debated and implicit reasons, which are more difficult to identify and discuss.

The difference between the two groups – the governments of the countries concerned on the one hand and international agencies and other more detached parties on the other – is less in the case of the explicit objectives. One of the most significant aspects of the current interest in decentralization is that although decentralization is, as in the past, still seen as a way of encouraging local involvement in the provision of government services, it is now considered by both groups to have a much wider role. Decentralization is in particular seen as a means of, first, improving the planning and implementation of national development – especially those concerned with rural development – and, second, facilitating effective popular participation in the process of development in a more profound way than envisaged in the earlier decentralization programmes.

The role of decentralization in improving the planning and management of rural development programmes, is part of a general concern, with rural development which has characterized the policies of individual countries and international agencies during the last decade or so, as a result of the failure of earlier policies that focused more on industrial and urban development. In recent years, this concern has been manifested not only in efforts to increase the amount of resources devoted to rural development programmes but also in increasing dissatisfaction at the limited achievements of such programmes. In this context, decentralization has been seen as a way of increasing the effectiveness of rural development programmes by making them more relevant and responsive to local needs and conditions, allowing greater flexibility in their implementation and providing a means of coordinating the various agencies involved at the regional or local level (Rondinelli, 1981; Cohen et al., 1981; Conyers, 1981a). This rationale is most clearly stated by international agencies, academics and others less directly involved in de-centralization programmes, but it also features in the stated objectives of most of the programmes themselves, even though there may also be other explicit and implicit motives.

The desire to increase popular participation in the planning and implementation of development programmes is sought partly as a means of making plans more relevant to local needs and, in some cases, enlisting local support in their implementation, thereby also helping to improve the quality of rural development efforts. However, it is also seen as an end in itself. This is, as such, nothing new, since it is a characteristic of all democratic states and, as already noted, was particularly emphasized by the governments of Third World nations during the period immediately following independence. What is significant about the current interest in popular participation is a concern for more direct participation in decision making, particularly on the part of the mass of the rural poor who have received little or no benefits as a result of earlier approaches to development. This concern is reflected in international agencies in policies such as those associated with the 'basic needs' approach to development, which regards the right to such participation as a basic human need (Ghai, 1977). And in developing countries themselves it is reflected in official policy statements justifying decentralization and other related programmes, which emphasize the need for 'participatory democracy' (Kaunda, 1974), rather than democracy that merely gives people the right to vote in elections. Whether or not the programmes concerned actually meet this objective is, of course, another question – and one that will be addressed below – but it is at least present in the rhetoric, which accompanies the introduction of most decentralization programmes.

The implicit objectives of decentralization are more complex and it is more difficult to identify them and assess their relative importance in any particular situation. Discussion of the implicit motives of international agencies, bilateral aid donors and academics involved in development studies is beyond the scope of this paper. Two brief comments may, however, be made. First, there is no doubt that such motives exist, particularly on the part of bilateral aid donors and academics. Second, there is a tendency for such organizations and individuals to concentrate their attention at any particular time on a few specific policies or approaches that, for one reason or another, happen to be popular at the time, thereby creating what can only be described as 'fashions' in development administration. It must, therefore, be accepted that the current widespread interest in decentralization is at least partially due to the fact that it has been promoted in this way.

The implicit motives of the individual governments of the countries actually involved in decentralization warrant more detailed discussion. At this point, it is perhaps useful to distinguish between those decentralization programmes initiated by the central government with little or no pressure exerted from below, as in the cases of Tanzania, Zambia and Ghana, and those resulting to a large extent from pressure from regional or local groups, as in Papua New Guinea and the Sudan and, to a lesser extent, Nigeria, Sri Lanka and the Solomon Islands. This distinction is particularly important in terms of the extent and form of popular participation that is likely to occur as a result of the decentralization programmes.

In both cases the governments concerned usually state that popular participation is a major objective of their decentralization programmes, but there is considerable variation in the degree and form of commitment underlying such statements. In those cases where decentralization is initiated from above, the commitment to participation is unlikely to go so far as to threaten national interests and solidarity and decentralization programmes may actually be seen – at least in part or by certain interested groups – as a way of strengthening the role of the national government or ruling party at the local level, as appears to be the case in Zambia. In those countries where decentralization is initiated from below, the situation tends to be more complex, since the regional or local groups which are pressing for decentralization have very high expectations about the degree of participation while the central government – or at least some interest groups within the central government – may not really want to encourage any significant participation at all. In such cases, the degree and form of decentralization – and therefore participation – that results will depend on the relative bargaining powers of the various central and local-interest groups.

There are, however, points of similarity between decentralization programmes initiated 'from above' and those initiated 'from below.' In both cases there is – at least in intent – a genuine desire to achieve a relatively high degree of popular participation, in the belief that such participation is not inconsistent with national unity and development. This view has, for example, been expressed both in Zambia, where the initiative for decentralization has come from the centre, and in Papua New Guinea, where there was strong pressure from below. Thus, President Kaunda has advocated decentralization in Zambia as a means of achieving 'unity based on a frank and positive acceptance of the diversity of our peoples' (Kaunda, 1974, p. 40); while in Papua New Guinea Leo Hannett, a well-known local leader who was instrumental in bringing about decentralization, has declared that he sees decentralization as a positive step 'towards building genuine unity and nationalism based on the recognition and acceptance of our regional cultural and ethnic diversities' (Hannett, 1974).

This concept of 'decentralization within centralization' – or decentralization as a means of 'recentralization' (Apthorpe & Conyers, 1982) – is one of the important features of the current interest in decentralization, particularly as seen by the countries concerned. Decentralization is regarded, at least in part, as a means of harmonizing the interests of both national and local development, through both the improved management of rural development – which is essential for the well-being of the nation as a whole as well as the inhabitants of individual rural areas – and the achievement of popular participation combined with national unity. The extent to which it is actually possible to reconcile these apparently conflicting objectives of decentralization is examined in the last section of the paper. Meanwhile, however, it is necessary to consider what effect these objectives have had on the characteristics of the decentralization programmes.

CHARACTERISTICS OF THE DECENTRALIZATION PROGRAMMES

The term 'decentralization' is used in this paper in a broad sense to refer to any transfer of the 'authority to plan, make decisions and manage public functions' (Rondinelli, 1981, p. 137) from the national level to any organization or agency at the sub-national level. This is consistent with the way in which the term is used by those governments involved in the decentralization programmes examined here that cover a very wide range of organizational reform. Because the range is so great, some attempt to classify the different types of decentralization programme is required.

It is not the intention of this chapter to enter into a lengthy debate on alternative methods of classifying decentralized systems of government. However, a brief discussion will be useful at this point, partly as a basis for identifying the different types of decentralization programme currently being introduced, but also in order to highlight some of the differences between the 'old' and the 'new' decentralization efforts. One of the arguments in this chapter is that conventional methods of classification have some limitations in the present context and that these limitations can best be explained in the light of the objectives of the new decentralization programmes. This is why any attempt at classification has been left, until this point, in the discussion level.

Conventional methods of classifying decentralized systems of government have adopted a legal perspective. In countries influenced by the British system of government – and therefore in much of the literature on decentralization written in the English language – it has been usual to distinguish between two main types of decentralization: *devolution* to legally established, locally elected political authorities and *deconcentration* of administrative authority to representatives of central government agencies (United Nations, 1962; Maddick, 1963; Wraith, 1972). In the former case, the activities of central and local government authorities are clearly differentiated, each having its own legal powers and responsibilities. The ideal concept of local government in the British tradition involved semi-autonomous bodies, employing their own staff and (as far as possible) controlling their own financial affairs, although (except in a federal system) the activities of the local-level authorities are subject to control and regulation by the central government. Deconcentration, on the other hand, is regarded as a much more limited form of decentralization, in which effective control – particularly over what Faltas (1982) has called 'allocative' decisions – remains at the centre, while only control over 'decisions of implementation' is decentralized. It should, however, be noted that this distinction has never been universally applicable. Thus in the French tradition, for example, local authorities are not intended to be autonomous bodies, a point which will be taken up at a later stage. The distinction between devolution and deconcentration provided a useful framework for analysing the decentralization programmes, which were introduced in English-speaking parts of the developing world in the 1950s and 1960s. This does not mean either that all such programmes could be neatly classified into one category or the other or that there was no variation in the degree and form of decentralization within each category. Moreover, it should also be noted that earlier attempts at decentralization introduced by the British during the colonial period, involving the establishment of 'native authorities', bore more resemblance to the French than the British local-government model (Wraith, 1972, p. 18). However, decisions about the degree and form of decentralization in the 1950s and 1960s were frequently seen, at least in part, as a choice between the establishment of semi-autonomous local-level governments, modelled more or less on the British local government system, and a much more limited deconcentration of the central government machinery.

When considering the recent decentralization programmes, however, a slightly different approach is required. Legal questions about the nature of the authority to which decision-making powers are decentralized are as important as ever, but it is often difficult to distinguish between the two conventional models, devolution and deconcentration, not only in the way in which the decentralization programmes are actually operating but also in the intentions behind them. The main reason for this seems to be an increasing tendency to see significant decentralization in terms not of the establishment of semi-autonomous local governments but of the decentralization of the central government machinery. This results in considerably more decentralization than is conventionally associated with deconcentration models, since powers are frequently devolved to local-level bodies with a separate legal identity, and particular emphasis tends to be placed on the decentralization of functions that play a central role in rural regional development. However, the local-level bodies are frequently seen as arms of the central government rather than semi-autonomous entities and so they often differ significantly from conventional local governments modelled on the British system.

It thus appears that, instead of trying to classify the new decentralization programmes into broad categories such as devolution and deconcentration, it is necessary to ask more detailed questions about the degree and form of decentralization in each programme to make useful generalizations and comparisons. It is, in particular, important to recognize that a number of different criteria can be used to measure the degree of decentralization – including the number and significance of the powers or functions decentralized, the level in the political or administrative hierarchy to, which they are decentralized and the type of individual or organization that exercises power at this level – and that a system which is 'more decentralized' according to one criterion may be 'less decentralized' according to another. This approach is reflected in some of the more recent literature on decentralization (Kochem & Deutsch, 1980; Landau & Eagle, 1981; Cohen et al., 1981). A more detailed examination of some of the recent decentralization programmes will demonstrate the need for this approach more clearly.

Three main types of decentralization programme will be described briefly here. It should, however, be noted that these three types are intended merely to illustrate the range of decentralization programmes currently being introduced, not to provide a comprehensive classification of all such programmes. There are, for example, some programmes, such as the 1976 local government reforms in Nigeria, which are still based on the conventional British local government model. Moreover, it should also be recognized that within each of the three types there is considerable variation from one country to another, particularly in terms of the nature and extent of the powers that are decentralized.

One of the most significant types of decentralization programme that has emerged in recent years is that where powers are devolved to legal bodies composed of a mixture of locally elected and centrally appointed representatives, the latter sometimes including both political appointees and administrative officials; This sort of programme was introduced in Ghana in 1971 (Tordoff, 1980), Tanzania in 1972 (Rondinelli, 1981; Conyers, 1981a) and Sri Lanka in 1980, and the same sort of system is currently being introduced in Zambia (Conyers, 1981a). This approach differs from the conventional British local government model in that the local authorities to which powers are devolved cannot be described as, and are not intended to be, autonomous bodies. They are composed only partially of locally elected representatives, they usually use central government administrative personnel rather than employing their own staff and they tend to be heavily dependent on the central government in financial matters. However, the fact that they are legal entities to which wide-ranging formal powers are decentralized suggests rather more decentralization than in conventional deconcentration models, especially since these powers generally relate to developmental functions and include allocative as well as implementation powers. This form of decentralization is in many ways similar to the French system of local government.

The second type of decentralization resembles the first in that powers are decentralized to local-level bodies with a mixture of central and local representatives. However, these bodies seldom have proper legal status, the powers decentralized to them tend to be less significant and, in some cases, they exist alongside conventional local governments and function as a means of co-ordination between central and local government. These local-level bodies are usually known as development committees or coordinating committees, rather than local governments.

This form of decentralization, found in many countries, especially in Africa, is not in itself new and its existence is of no special significance, since this sort of local coordinating committee was first introduced in most of these countries towards the end of the colonial period. What is significant is that in a number of countries the current trend is to decentralize 'increasing powers to these committees, rather than to more autonomous local governments, even where such governments already exist. The most obvious example of this trend is perhaps Kenya (Rondinelli, 1981). It is also significant that this sort of decentralization tends to precede the introduction of the more radical reforms, characteristic of the first type of decentralization.

The third form of decentralization is in many ways very different from the first two, since it has many of the characteristics of the conventional devolution model. It involves the establishment of fully elected local governments with full legal rights and the decentralization of significant powers to these bodies. This is the case in the decentralization programmes in some

South Pacific countries, such as Papua New Guinea, where the provincial government system established in the latter part of the 1970s bears some resemblance to a federal system (Ghai, 1978).

However, closer examination of systems such as that in Papua New Guinea reveals that they also differ from the conventional British local government model in some significant ways. Thus, although Papua New Guinea's provincial governments are semi-autonomous bodies, with clearly defined legal powers, in many respects they function – and are regarded – as arms of the central government rather than as separate entities, This is reflected particularly in the administrative arrangements; the provincial governments are serviced by decentralized departments of the central government in the same sort of way as the much less autonomous local authorities in countries like Ghana, Tanzania, Zambia and Sri Lanka (Conyers, 1981a, 1981b). In fact, it is particularly significant that Tanzania is now moving towards this model of decentralization, since it is replacing the district development councils, which were composed of a mixture of central and local representatives, with fully elected local authorities.

What factors have led to the emergence of these various types of decentralization and, in particular, to the common characteristics that can be identified in all three types despite the existence of significant differences? The fact that there seems to be a movement towards the French rather than the British concept of local government cannot apparently be explained by any conscious attempt to adopt the French model as such. Part of the explanation probably lies in the political systems of the countries concerned. Thus, the most obvious examples of the first type of decentralization are the products of one-party or (in the case of Ghana) military governments, where the conventional division between political and administrative systems tends to become blurred, and this is reflected in the composition of the local decision-making bodies. Even in those countries with a multi-party system, such as Sri Lanka and the countries of the South Pacific, there is – as in most developing nations – a tendency for the political and administrative systems to be less clearly differentiated than in conventional 'western' systems of government. However, this does not by itself provide adequate explanation.

To fully explain the characteristics of the recent decentralization programmes, it is necessary to look back at the objectives of the programmes, which were discussed in the previous section. In the first place, it must be remembered that decentralization is frequently seen as a tool for improving the management of rural development. 'This means that, in designing the decentralization programmes, the desire to rationalize the overall structure

of government in the rural areas has been at least as important as the desire
to divide responsibilities between different levels of government.' There
has, in particular, been a concern to improve co-ordination and eliminate
duplication between the various agencies involved in rural development
within an area, including both central and local government agencies, and
this is reflected in the establishment of councils or committees with mixed
central and local government representation and the tendency to amalga-
mate central and local government personnel. This aim is explicitly stated
in Zambia's decentralization, which involves the amalgamation of local
governments and the field administration of the central government in
order to reduce duplication and make better use of scarce financial and
manpower resources (Zambia, 1978), and it is implicit in many of the other
programmes.

Equally significant is the more general feeling that 'decentralization need
not be inconsistent with the achievement of national unity and can,' in fact,
enhance it – the belief in 'decentralization within centralism.' This characteristic, present to varying degrees in the objectives of most of the decentralization programmes, helps to explain the tendency for the distinction
between central and local government to be blurred – and, therefore, the
difficulty of classifying the programmes into conventional categories. The
majority of the decentralization programmes are seen as attempts to *decentralize the national government*, rather than to establish a second tier of
government – a subtle but significant distinction.

Finally, it is interesting to note that the recent decentralization programmes have attracted the attention of a much wider range of disciplinary
interests than their predecessors of the 1950s and 1960s. In the past, interest
in the decentralization of government structures was generally confined to
those in the fields of political science and public administration (including
lawyers concerned with these fields); but today it has been extended to
include a variety of other specialists, including regional planners (whose
main interest is in the co-ordination of activities within an area or region), a
much wider range of lawyers (who are increasingly concerned with the role
of law in development and, therefore, the role of decentralization in meeting
basic human needs), organization and management specialists (who are interested in decentralization as a way of improving organizational efficiency)
and many people from a variety of disciplines who share a general concern
with either rural development or popular participation – or both. This
increase in the disciplinary scope of interest in decentralization can be
explained in terms of the objectives of the current decentralization programmes. It reflects the fact that, in short, such programmes are part of a

wider concern to improve the allocation of functions within the whole system of government in order to meet the developmental needs of the majority of a country's population. Moreover, this multi-disciplinary interest can itself help to explain not only the rather loose way in which the term decentralization is now used but also the greater variety of decentralized systems of government which is emerging.

DECENTRALIZATION: ACHIEVEMENTS AND PROSPECTS

In comment on the decentralization efforts of the last decade there does seem to be an increasing feeling – both, within the countries concerned and among international agencies, academic's and other interested 'outsiders' – that many of the programmes are not living up to the initial expectations (Rondinelli, 1981; United Nations, 1981; UNCRD, 1981b). The problems vary, but they can be divided into three broad categories. First, in many cases the actual degree of decentralization seems to have been very limited, either because the proposed reforms have not been implemented as intended or because the initial proposals did not provide for significant decentralization. Second, there are claims that decentralization has done little to improve the planning and implementation of local development programmes and, therefore, to contribute to rural – and national – development. Third, there are complaints that powers have been decentralized to the 'wrong' people – either central government appointees or a local elite – and so there has been no meaningful increase in the participation of the mass of the people (Rondinelli, 1981).

Recognition of these problems is resulting in some scepticism about the sincerity of the governments of the countries concerned and about the value of 'decentralization' as a means of either improving rural development management or encouraging popular participation. This is, perhaps, an overreaction, based on inadequate understanding of the nature of the decentralization programmes. It is necessary to recognize the complexity of the motives behind the decentralization programmes and, in particular, the fact that in many cases they are trying to achieve both 'centralization' and 'decentralization.' Added to this is the complexity of the reforms themselves, which generally involve a major restructuring of the whole political and administrative system – literally the decentralization of the national government. This requires a great deal of organizational ability, which is not always readily available, and it inevitably arouses considerable opposition, frustration and confusion (Iglesias, 1981). And finally, even if a decentralization programme is introduced successfully with relatively few problems or undesirable side-effects, it cannot be expected to solve all a country's problems. A significant improvement either in the management of rural development or in effective popular participation will not be achieved easily or quickly – and certainly not only by a decentralization of government.

This does suggest the need for a more realistic view of both the potential and the limitations of decentralization but it does not suggest, at least so far, that it should be totally abandoned as a strategy for development. This paper has suggested that, although current decentralization programmes are in many ways similar to their predecessors in the 1950s and 1960s, there are some significant differences in both their objectives and their characteristics. In particular, decentralization appears to be receiving widespread attention at present because it is seen as a means of achieving certain objectives – rural development and popular participation – which occupy a focal position in mainstream thinking at this time. In view of this concern, there is a need for more information on appropriate legal systems, the design and management of a decentralized national public service, alternative forms of, financial decentralization and methods of achieving meaningful popular participation through representative local institutions (Institute of Planning Studies, University of Nottingham, and International Center for Law in Development 1981). It is encouraging that a number of international agencies – including the ILO, the Development Administration Division of the UN and the UNCRD – are currently engaged in much studies, although, there is perhaps a need for closer communication and a more systematic division of labour between them, in order to make maximum use of the information and resources available. In the *International Handbook on Local Government Reorganization* (Rowat, 1980), Subramaniam concludes his summary of the experiences of developing countries as follows:

> Local government in developing countries has been judged too long by the artificial standards derived from exceptional developments in nineteenth and twentieth century Britain, Puritan New England, the expanding United States, and the free cities of Europe. It is time 'that its "limited" development in the new nations is set against the similar history of Western Europe, particularly France, and against the historical compulsions of colonialism, nationalism, and economic development (Subramanian, 1980, p. 591).

The nature of the decentralization programmes described in this paper supports the need for such an approach – and the widespread interest in decentralization now being shown by international agencies, academics and others concerned with development studies suggests that it is, in fact, already emerging.

REFERENCES

Adamolckun, L., & Rowlands, L. (Eds). (1979). *The new local government system in Nigeria: Problems and prospects for implementation.* Ibadan: Heinemann.

Apthorpe. R., & Conyers, D. (1982). Decentralization, recentralization and popular participation towards a framework for analysis. Paper presented to programme in Communication Policy and Planning, for Development. Institute of Social Studies. The Hague. June 1982.

Conyers, D. (1981a). Decentralization for regional development: A comparative study of Tanzania, Zambia and Papua New Guinea. *Public Administration and Development, 1,* 107–120.

Conyers, D. (1981b). Papua New Guinea: Decentralization and development from the middle. In: W. B. Stöhr & D. R. Fraser Taylor (Eds), *Development from above or below? The dialectics of regional planning in developing countries.* Chichester: Wiley.

Craig, J. (1981). Continuity and change in Sri Lanka's district administration: A political perspective. *Studies in decentralization: Manchester papers on development* (No. 3). University of Manchester, Manchester.

DSA (Development Studies Association). (1982). Report of regional development and planning study group. *DSA Newsletter,* 13.

Faltas, M. (1982). Decentralization and the design of planning systems. *Meeting of DSA regional development and planning study group on decentralization and planning.* University of Nottingham, March.

Ghai, D. P. (Ed.). (1977). *The basic needs approach to development.* Geneva: International Labour Organization.

Ghai, Y. (1978). *Classification of the Papua New Guinea system of government.* Mimeo. Workshop on Constitutional and Legal Aspects of Decentralization, Department of Decentralization. Papua New Guinea.

Ghai, Y. (1981). *Decentralization in the Pacific.* (draft, unpublished).

Graham, L. S. (1980). Latin America. In: D. C. Rowat (Ed.), *International handbook on local government reorganization.* London: Aldwych, Chapter 40.

Hannett, L. (1974). *Getting closer to the people.* Post-Courier (Papua New Guinea). Arawa House Feature, 5 December. p. 2.

Hicks, U. (1961). *Development from below: Local government and finance in developing countries of the commonwealth.* Oxford: Clarendon Press.

Iglesias, G. U. (1981). Local and regional development in Southeast Asia. Focus on ASEAN: Experience, main issues and perspectives, *International conference on local and regional development in the 1980s, UNCRD,* Nagoya. Japan, November.

ILO (International Labour Organization). (1981). *Series of reports on decentralized planning published as part of World Employment Programme Research.* Working Paper series. (The first such report was WP 99 published in 1981.)

Institute of International Studies. (1981). *The Project on Managing Decentralization: Proposed Plan of Work 1981–1982 (University of California, Berkeley).* (The Project also produced a newsletter entitled Decentralization and Development Review, The project is, however, now being terminated earlier than expected.)

Institute of Planning Studies. University of Nottingham and International Center for Law in Development. (1981). *Report of Workshop on Decentralization.* Mimeo. Institute of Planning Studies. Nottingham.

Kaunda, K. (1974). *Humanism in Zambia and a guide to its implementation. Part II.* Lusaka: Government Printer.

Kochem, M., & Deutsch, K. W. (1980). *Decentralization: Sketches toward a rational theory.* Cambridge, Mass: Oelgeschlager, Gunn and Hain.

Landau, M., & Eagle (1981). *On the Concept of Decentralization.* Project on Managing Decentralization, Institute of International Affairs. University of California, Berkeley.

Maddick, H. (1963). *Democracy, decentralization and development.* Bombay: Asia Publishing House.

Mawhood, P., & Davcy, K. (1980). Anglophone Africa. In: D. C. Rowat (Ed.), *International handbook on local government reorganization.* London: Aldwych, Chapter 34.

Project on Managing Decentralization. Cohen, S. S., Dyckman, J., Schoenberger, E., & Downs, C. R. (1981). *Decentralization: A framework for policy analysis.* Institute of International Studies. University of California, Berkeley.

Rondinelli, D. A. (1981). Government decentralization in comparative perspective: Theory and practice in developing countries. *International Review of Administrative Sciences, 67,* 133–145.

Rowat, D. C. (Ed.). (1980). *International handbook on local government reorganization.* London: Aldwych.

Subramanian, V. (1980). Developing countries. In: D. C. Rowat (Ed.), *International handbook on local government reorganization.* London: Aldwych.

Tordoff, W. (1980). Ghana. In: D. C. Rowat (Ed.), *International handbook on local government reorganization.* London: Aldwych, Chapter 32.

Tordoff, W. (1981). *Decentralization in Papua New Guinea in Studies in Decentralization.* Manchester Papers in Development (University of Manchester, Department of Administrative Studies), no. 3.

UNCRD (United Nations Centre for Regional Development). (1981a). *Implementing Decentralization Policies and Programmes.* Report of UNCRD Workshop. Nagoya, Japan, July.

UNCRD (United Nations Centre for Regional Development). (1981b). *Implementing Decentralization Policies and Programmes.* Report of UNCRD Seminar. Nagoya, Japan, August 24–30.

United Nations. (1962). *Decentralization for national and local development.* New York: United Nations.

United Nations. (1981). *Report of the interregional seminar on Decentralization for Development.* Mimeo. Khartoum, September 1981, United Nations, New York.

Wraith, R. (1972). *Local administration in West Africa.* London: George Allen and Urwin.

Zambia. (1978). *Decentralized government.* Lusaka: Government Printer.

EXPLORING THE IMPLICATIONS OF PRIVATIZATION AND DEREGULATION

Dennis J. Gayle and Jonathan N. Goodrich

At least since 1978, privatization and deregulation have continued to provoke intense controversy as to the acceptable applications and inherent implications of such public policies. This is reflected in an extensive and rapidly expanding literature. This chapter explores some of the fundamental and interactive questions that remain incompletely resolved and examines the emergent responses that have been advanced, applying a fairly broad cross-national perspective.

The basic questions addressed ... are as follows:

- How are the central concepts of "privatization," "deregulation," "liberalization," "public," and "private" best unpackaged so as to facilitate understanding?
- To what extent do privatization and deregulation represent complementary policy choices?
- What are the most broadly sustainable economic arguments for privatization and deregulation?
- To what degree are the political, social, and economic consequences of such policies mutually supportive in terms of direction and velocity?
- Are there benefits of privatization and deregulation that remain independent of variation in the policy environment?
- What second- or third-order solutions to excessive public-sector expansion can be identified where optimal policy is impractical?

Comparative Public Administration: The Essential Readings
Research in Public Policy Analysis and Management, Volume 15, 463–488
Copyright © 2006 by Elsevier Ltd.
ISSN: 0732-1317/doi:10.1016/S0732-1317(06)15020-4

Some forms of privatization may imply sharply increased regulation, and there is abundant evidence that regulated private property can be quite inefficient. As the 1978 U.S. Airline Deregulation Act demonstrates, deregulation in some areas (routes and fares) might demand more effective regulation in others (aircraft maintenance and pilot training).[1] At the same time, standard ownership controls – such as maximum shareholding provisions and "golden" shares, or the right of a government to veto-specific ownership changes – can make hostile takeovers impossible and thus limit the potential for improved cost efficiencies.[2] In turn, deregulation can yield decreased competition as well as declining factor productivity, when accompanied by reduced public infrastructure growth. Neither bureaucratic nor market and corporate policy failure represents an attractive policy outcome, although it may be ideologically convenient to emphasize one set of deficiencies rather than another.

Given that all modern political systems contain distinctive mixtures of authoritarianism, populism, and liberalism, in every current economy the public and private sectors represent a continuum characterized by multiple hybrid forms. Similarly, social systems range from individualistic societies, where strong government is illegitimate, to communitarian (hierarchical or egalitarian) societies, where government plays a central role in creating consensus. Whereas, individualism tends to produce a regulatory state, as in Britain and the United States, communitarianism is characterized by intensive interaction between strong executive and corporate bureaucracies, as in Japan, Germany, Sweden, and France.[3]

Within most systems, hybrid institutions have emerged, exemplified by "public television" (supported by private contributions) and the Federal National Mortgage Association (privately owned but government sponsored) in the United States, "private day care centers" in Sweden (dependent on public grants), and "private urban housing" in contemporary China, where all land remains the property of the state. Both privatization and deregulation can be desirable policy mechanisms to the extent that they advance the public interest.

Such an interest is probably best defined by adopting a rather utilitarian orientation, operationalized by changing the balance of political advantage within pluralistic democracies. In the course of introducing privatization and deregulation, the sections that follow successively explore the related conceptual and definitional problems, major supporting economic arguments, sociopolitical costs and benefits, and some of the practical policy options for consideration.

CONCEPTUAL AND DEFINITIONAL PROBLEMS

As both concept and process, privatization possesses ambiguous connotations and multiple meanings. *Webster's Dictionary* (1981) defines one related noun, *privatism*, as "an attitude of uncommitment or uninvolvement in anything beyond one's immediate interests," while another associated noun, *privacy*, denotes a state of "withdrawal from society or the public interest" (Oxford English Dictionary, 1972). If government is a means of providing a wide range of collective goods, which do not necessarily lend themselves to market exchange, the public sector is naturally a highly visible target.[4] At the same time, unrestrained public-sector expansion inevitably leads to public policy failure, as problems of communication, coordination, effective cost–benefit control, and revenue satiation accumulate.[5] Privatization represents a logical reaction.

As a process, privatization denotes reducing the roles of government, while increasing those of the private sector, in activities or asset ownership.[6] In practice, privatization may include "load shedding" or divestiture, the replacement of budgeted public activity by private market mechanisms such as consumer cooperatives, coproduction, variously structured public/private-sector partnerships, state management contracts such as monopoly franchises for the private supply of public services, user charges, lease-purchase arrangements, and even tax reduction, intended to stimulate private-sector investment.

Privatization has become an increasingly important public policy phenomenon: for instance, some 80 percent of U.S. cities and counties presently use or plan to use private companies to produce such services as building, vehicle, and street maintenance, and 69 percent of U.S. cities increased user fees in fiscal year 1989.[7] When the small city of Ecorse, Michigan, was placed under the control of a court-appointed receiver, every city facility, except for the police force and firefighters, was privatized or closed.[8] In Britain, nearly 2,000 municipal contracts, with a total value of £2.7 billion, were subjected in stages to compulsory competitive tendering, as of August 1, 1989. At the same time, local council workers have been restructured into semi-autonomous contractors, labeled "direct service organizations," lacking employment guarantees of any kind.[9] At another level of government, Canada intends to sell its remaining 57 percent stake in Air Canada by mid-1989, with the expectation that a private owner will achieve reduced unit labor costs (which increased by 19.3 percent during 1983–1988) and replace the airline's aging fleet.[10] In a different country category, immediately after the government of President Carlos Menem took office in Argentina in July 1989, Economy Minister Miguel Roig announced privatization plans for all SOEs not involved in security and national defense.[11]

Electricity is transmitted on the basis of private-sector franchises in Barbados and Ecuador; telephone equipment is subject to supply contracts in Chile, India, and Malaysia, where 22 state enterprises, such as the Malaysian Airline System, have been sold since 1983, and Prime Minister Mahathir Mohamad plans to dispose of 434 public entities, including the National Electricity Board, with gross assets of over US$3.9 billion.[12] British post office counters as well as parcel delivery services, were placed on the auction block by April 1989. In Sweden, where state spending remains the most extensive within the OECD (some 60 percent of GDP in 1987), the state is searching for market mechanisms that might enhance public-sector efficiency (see Chapter 24). Meanwhile, Finance Minister Kjell-Olof Feldt has announced plans to eliminate central government income tax for 90 percent of the wage-earning population by 1991.[13]

However, the concepts of the public and private sectors are not mutually exclusive, static, or unidimensional. First, some aspects of government may grow as others remain static, or even decline.[14] Britain offers several examples. Subsequent to passage of the 1988 Education Reform Act, which encouraged schools to opt out of local authority control and linked incomes to the number of students served, the secretary of state for education acquired 415 entirely new powers.[15] Again, under current proposals for privatizing the 10 English and Welsh water authorities, a new National Rivers Authority is projected, along with a director general of water services and customer service committees.[16]

British Transport Secretary Paul Channon has indicated that if British Rail is privatized (probably in the form of five regional companies), extensive new regulation would be required.[17] If the changes projected by a January 1989 White Paper on *Reform of the National Health Service* take effect in April 1991, general practitioners (GPs) will compete for patients; hospitals will become self-governing trusts, selling their services to district health authorities and GPs as well as to private patients; and the Department of Health together with the Audit Commission, will have extensive new regulatory duties.[18] Similarly, the Home Office envisages that should prisons be privatized, a public monitor would be required at each remand center to protect prisoners' rights as well as a Board of Visitors. As a consequence, private prison governors would be subjected to a degree of scrutiny that their public counterparts never had to face.[19]

Across the Atlantic, the Corrections Corporation of America, the nation's largest for-profit prison management company, increased its revenues from $2.5 million in 1984 to $25 million in 1988, but lost money every year. An industry-sponsored evaluation by the American Correctional Association has been unable to identify any instances where prison operating costs have been reduced significantly under private management.[20] At the same time, in 1988 the federal prison budget grew by 23 percent to $933.7 million.[21]

Second, private-sector productivity growth depends significantly on public capital investment in basic infrastructure, such as airports, highways, and waterworks. For example, total U.S. factor productivity declined from a 1950–1970 annual rate of 1.8 percent to only 0.8 percent in 1970–1985, partly because public infrastructure growth decreased from 4.3 percent to 1.5 percent during the same periods reviewed.[22] That public-sector expenditures can contribute to economic stabilization and growth is easily forgotten (see Chapter 8). At the same time, since 1978 significant disparities between federal and private-sector salaries have generated substantial difficulties in government recruitment and retention.[23] Yet private-sector executives usually find that effective coalitions, including government as well as corporate allies, are essential to their success, as exemplified by most U.S. semiconductor companies.[24]

Third, the private sector is highly differentiated along several dimensions. To the notion of the formal profit-making private sector (with wide variation in ownership and scale) must be added the informal for-profit and non-profit private sectors, as well as private professional associations and the private household economy sector.[25]

Fourth, the principal–agent problem persists in both the private and the public sectors: Management does not necessarily act in the best interests of either widely diffused shareholders or taxpayers, so that effective performance monitoring remains problematic.[26]

If privatization means withdrawal from public to private provision and/or production of goods or services, the explicit determination to *provide* (or make available) must be distinguished from the decision to *produce*, whether in the public or private sector. In turn, to deregulate is to reduce or eliminate specific governmental rules and regulations that apply to private business. Regulation may be either industry specific, where costs and benefits can usually be estimated, or economy-wide, with virtually unlimited scope for expansion.[27] Regulation may provide significant competitive advantages for specific firms (by chance or design) through certification, permit, and licensing systems that raise entry barriers.[28] Consequently, many companies have strongly supported at least some of the socioeconomic regulations to which they are subject.[29] Within regulated markets subject to rapid technological change, corporate interest groups frequently seek continued regulation and selective deregulation simultaneously.[30]

Deregulation is often accompanied by efforts to encourage corporate self-regulation by means of company codes, social audits, and industry codes. Competition is seen as the ultimate guarantor of corporate performance. However, insufficient (or ineffective) industry-specific regulation may facilitate corporate fraud. After the administration of former U.S. president, Reagan sharply reduced the regulation of the drug industry, the Food and Drug Administration eventually found it necessary to confront a widespread scandal involving its approval process for generic drugs, leading to at least 128 product recalls and suspensions in 1989.[31]

In the case of U.S. savings and loan industry, which was deregulated in 1982, thrifts were no longer held to deposit or interest rate limits, and the requirement to have 80 percent of available funds invested in mortgages was eliminated. The regulatory capabilities of the Home Loan Bank Board were also sharply reduced in effect because no additional staff was provided, and widespread insolvency resulted during 1988.[32] The gradual deregulation of Korea's money markets since 1980 proved a more viable approach. Similarly, the French government has found extensive intervention necessary in order to encourage the emergence of a substantially deregulated and competitive banking sector.

China's post-1978 drive toward market liberalization and privatization has largely stagnated since 1988 because of high inflation, rampant corruption, and urban unrest.[33] Even so, the persistence of serious socioeconomic problems in such critical sectors as urban housing implies that the development of China's private sector will probably continue (see Chapter 21). Indeed, more than 6,000 state enterprises have raised US$1.6 billion by selling shares. Before the violently terminated student protests of June 1989 in Beijing's Tianamen Square, influential economists, such as Hua Sheng, Zhang Xuejun, and Luo Xiaopeng, proposed that stock be sold to factory workers, managers, local authorities, and even foreigners.[34]

As public policies, both privatization and deregulation imply expanded private-sector activity, with complementary contraction in public-sector size, in the interests of productive efficiency. In turn, liberalization maximizes efficiency gains by sweeping away bureaucratic barriers to competition. However, as Cento Veljanovski explains, privatization in practice may actually be antithetical to market liberalization. Moreover, regulatory decisions are ideally characterized by concern for the protection of "merit goods," such as employee health and community safety as well as individual constitutional rights. Such decisions should also address market failures, as discussed below.[35] Additionally, deregulation may release resources from inefficient activities without necessarily directing them toward their most competitive uses. For instance, following New Zealand's financial market deregulation in 1985, capital inflows, rather than the nation's trade balance, dominated the direction of the kiwi dollar's float.

To recapitulate, particular forms of privatization such as state contracting, are usually accompanied by new regulatory systems designed to provide accountability, consumer protection, and quality assurance. Even so, conflicts between the goals of equal access to publicly provided products and economic efficiency remain inescapable.[36] For example, the British government was embarrassed when the 29 existing private water companies in England announced 30–50 percent increases in their charges, effective April 1, 1989, given prior official assurances that privatization would not lead to "excessive" price increases.[37]

All domestic interest groups do not benefit in the same measure from policies of privatization and deregulation. Accordingly, democratic pluralist states usually provide some protection for existing income distribution patterns, even where such a policy limits competition and potential efficiency gains.[38] The Canadian telecommunications sector offers a case in point.

In any case, regulated natural monopolies can be difficult to privatize in a responsible manner. Rate regulation typically involves pricing criteria, which allow cost recovery together with a "normal" return on capital. Regulators may find themselves either managing privatized utilities, in effect, or serving producer rather than consumer interests.[39] Even antitrust action, undertaken in the interests of market liberalization, may produce perverse results: In the United States, since the divestiture of AT&T on January 1, 1984, the seven regional holding companies that resulted have found themselves grappling with the sometimes inconsistent requirements of 50 state regulatory bodies, as well as those of the U.S. Justice Department and Judge Harold Greene who oversees the divestiture decree.[40]

AT&T remained the only regulated long-distance telephone company. Regulatory efforts to hold AT&T's profit to a "fair" rate of return on capital were replaced by price caps on July 1, 1989, allowing annual price increases 3 percent less than the rate of inflation. At the same time, the Federal Communications Commission provoked harsh criticism when it responded to consumer group complaints that the five new alternative operator companies were imposing charges 250 percent higher than AT&T rates by merely requiring that all rates be disclosed on request.[41] Fuat Andic

(Chapter 3) provides a methodology, based on detailed project evaluation, intended to indicate whether a given privatization process will yield net socioeconomic benefits.

Thus, in the case of either privatization or deregulation, a recurrent problem is that wider competition and consumer benefits do not automatically follow. A further prototypical problem is that freshly privatized firms may be driven to increase prices in response to prospective factors, such as inflation or investment requirements, thus fueling popular demands for price controls. Should such controls be imposed, product or service quality might decline as managers seek to maintain profit margins. In turn, such actions could well generate eventually irresistible public pressures for renewed or additional regulation. The U.S. air transport sector may become a prime example, as both passenger flight miles and public complaints of poor aircraft maintenance and of delayed, canceled, or "cattle-class" flights mount, while competition declines with industry reconcentration.[42] Additionally, U.S. efforts to liberalize international air transport may eventually yield perverse political and commercial results.

THE MAJOR ECONOMIC ARGUMENTS

A private firm is a corporation in which prices and output are guided by the product market, while the capital market constrains costs. Such a firm can trade, transfer partial ownership rights by the sale of shares, and be acquired by investors who perceive unexploited profit opportunities.

The expected economic benefits of privatization include increased production quantity, improved output quality, reduced unit costs, expanded employment as well as growth opportunities over the longer term, and the generation of new technologies. When accompanied by liberalization, privatization encourages the emergence of managers who are willing to champion an entrepreneurial, risk-taking culture.[43] Corporations then become more results oriented, displaying such new attributes as aggressive marketing styles, improved management information systems, and reduced overhead costs.

In principle, the empirical evidence for the relative economic efficiency of private, as opposed to public, production is overwhelming. To cite just a few more cases, a 1982 World Bank study of road maintenance in Brazil determined that contracted-out upkeep costs were 37 percent less, on average, than those incurred by the Brazilian National Highway Department.[44] Similarly, during the early 1980s in Abidjan, Ivory Coast, public buses covered only one-third the vehicle/miles per employee of private buses, while in New York City, private buses cost 10 percent less per hour operated than their public counterparts cost.[45] Additionally, London Regional Transport, which put almost a quarter of its network out to competitive tender during 1986–1989, has found such bus services more reliable and about 15 percent cheaper than the public units replaced.[46]

In the American states of Arizona, Florida, New Mexico, Tennessee, and Texas, Rural Metro Services, a private firefighting and paramedic concern, has generated cost savings approximating 25 percent of the comparable public-sector services for its 95,000 fire and 30,000 ambulance subscription customers.[47] During the first quarter, following the privatization of the Mexican government airline, Aeromexico, in October 1988, 97 percent of its flights arrived on time, compared with the earlier established average of 75 percent, and complaints concerning customer service declined dramatically.[48]

Privatization can assist in balancing the national budget, reducing government expenditure, financing capital investment programs, decreasing foreign debt, lowering consumer prices, broadening share ownership across a society, and altering public attitudes toward business.[49] Employee stockholding can improve motivation and productivity. Decentralized decision making can empower local governments and create new opportunities for small-scale regional firms.[50] Even when proposals for private contracting are not implemented, the associated analysis and scrutiny can result in improved public-sector performance.[51] Most goods and services produced by government might more economically originate in the private sector.

Indeed, Friedrich Hayek and others have even contended that money should be competitively provided by private-sector banks: efficiency would then dictate that just a few kinds of money (perhaps only one) would become universally accepted.[52] The underlying premise is that government should concentrate on monitoring the quality of private-sector output, providing only agreed public goods and services, including a legal framework for production and trade.[53] Within highly pluralistic societies, where there is little social agreement on key values, so that definition of the public interest is often moot, significant reduction in the scope of national government may be essential.

On the other hand, a recent study of Britain's experience with privatization indicates that privatized firms did not perform substantially better than public-sector firms did between 1983 and 1988. For instance, British Telecom (privatized in 1984) demonstrated a total annual factor productivity growth of only 2.5 percent, compared to British Steel's 12.4 percent in the public sector.[54] Moreover, by 1987 some customers saw British Telecom as a byword for inefficiency, over-manning, high charges, and complacency.[55] In West Germany, although the federal government reduced the state share of the VEBA industrial and service conglomerate to only 25.7 percent in 1985, and sold its remaining holdings in Volkswagen in March 1988, there are no notable differences between modal perceptions of public- and private-sector economic performance.[56] Similarly, Tomislav Mandakovic and Marcos Lima (Chapter 12) and Melvin Burke (Chapter 14), who examine the cases of Chile and Honduras, respectively, find no necessary distinction between the efficiency of public- and private-sector delivery systems.

In retrospect, public or state-owned enterprises (SOEs) were widely promoted during the 1960s and 1970s on the basis of eight principal premises:

- Such enterprises encouraged broad social responsibility and responsiveness to the public interest.
- SOEs helped to create stable investment and employment patterns.[57]
- SOEs provided models for improved industrial relations.
- SOEs were essential for production in sectors characterized by extended time horizons and great perceived risk, as in nuclear power generation.
- SOEs could beneficially replace private natural monopolies, producing higher output at lower prices, with the utilities as a favorite example.
- SOEs provided irreplaceable means of direction and control in defense-related industry.[58]
- SOEs could successfully stimulate sectoral competition, as shown by the cases of Renault and Credit Lyonnais in France and Volkswagen (initially) and Westdeutsche Landesbank in Germany. As in the case of Singapore, free information flows between SOE managers and senior political decision makers also encouraged efficiency (see Chapter 19).
- SOEs were potent instruments of decolonization, given the desire of nationalist political elites to radically reduce foreign corporate ownership within the private sector, as in the early post-independence periods in Algeria, Indonesia, and Ghana.[59]

In summation, public enterprises were seen as effective means of dealing with six interactive sources and consequences of market failure: (1) imperfectly distributed information; (2) notable negative externalities, such as substantial oil spillages within sensitive ecosystems in the case of the petroleum industry; (3) inadequately safeguarded merit and public goods, such as national defense and clean air and water; (4) involuntary unemployment; (5) real demand deficiencies, arising from sharply skewed patterns of income and wealth distribution; and (6) natural monopolies, where it is clearly more cost effective for one firm rather than two or more companies, to supply a given market.[60]

However, in many cases, SOEs created new problems of bureaucratic failure. Inadequate planning led to massive, yet ill-conceived investments. Political interference in routine operations guaranteed inefficiencies, particularly in staffing and finance.[61] SOE managers frequently found themselves contending with unclear, multiple, or even conflicting objectives.[62] Progressively increasing government intervention in national economies paradoxically diminished the degree of state control.[63] At the same time, such economists as James Buchanan and Ronald Coase had long contended that negative externalities could be eliminated by the respecification of property rights and that competition was multifaceted, so that monopoly was often either illusory or merely a matter of degree.[64]

Meanwhile, the essence of the argument for deregulation is that government restrictions on corporate activities, products, and location decrease the range of options available to consumers and artificially increase prices by limiting competition.[65] Such protection reduces the incentive for regulated firms to minimize current costs. It also reduces their need and desire to adopt innovations that might lower costs in the future. Some of the costs added by regulation are visible: Regulated companies bear compliance costs, while regulatory institutions incur monitoring expenses. Other such costs may be much more extensive, but less visible: Restrictions on permissible activities can prevent the realization of economies of scale and scope.

As a result of such arguments, proposals for privatization and deregulation gradually gained a measure of political acceptance in many countries. Governments presiding over diverse political systems increasingly agreed that collectivist state policies, which discouraged private investors and entrepreneurial initiative, inevitably contributed to economic stagnation. For example, since the Soviet Union opened its economy to joint ventures with Western companies by means of a January 1, 1987 decree, more than 1,000 such agreements have been registered, although only 10 percent have been implemented. In November 1989, Soviet Prime Minister Nikolai Ryzhkov declared that his country's public sector, which accounted for some 85 percent of gross social product, should be drastically reduced.[66] Similarly, Vietnam eliminated subsidies as well as most restrictions on private enterprise, granted autonomy to state enterprises as part of the continuing process of economic restructuring, or *doi muoi,* between 1986 and 1989.[67] Similarly, the Iranian Cabinet proposed that scores of state-owned factories be sold to the private sector, in the course of a five-year plan, which was presented to the Iranian *Majlis*, or parliament, in October 1989.[68]

In the meantime, private production expanded dramatically in Hungary's agricultural, construction, and retail trade sectors during 1980–1987.[69] On October 19, 1989, the Hungarian parliament voted to radically amend the nation's 1949 constitution, so as to create a multi-party democratic republic. To be sure, such state agencies as the Ministry of Finance and the Planning Board have continued to allow special subsidies for large enterprises and cooperatives, even at the expense of more profitable, but smaller firms.[70] However, the process of systematic, if slow, state shrinkage persists ... .

Similarly, Kalman Mizsei explains ... that agricultural deregulation has become a recurrent theme in Poland, despite limited support from both the People's Party and the Catholic Church. Meanwhile, Poland's Parliament approved legislation in late 1988 intended to encourage foreign investment, removing all limits on the size of private business, as inflation increased to almost 90 percent and external debt mounted to US$39 billion.[71] Within a year, the nation's new Solidarity-led government was planning to abolish price controls and privatize SOEs. On the other hand, during 1987–1988, the U.S. Federal Bureau of Investigation's probe into trading practices within the Chicago Board of Trade and the Chicago Mercantile Exchange dramatically demonstrated the continuing potential for private-sector corruption as well as for ineffective market self-regulation.[72] In early 1988, the Brady Report on market mechanisms also contended that substantially expanded government intervention was required in order to correct serious flaws in the stock, futures, and options markets.[73] Such concerns were supported by KPMG International's 1989 survey of 50 major international financial institutions, which cited evidence that fraud and insider abuse had contributed to about one-third of U.S. bank failures, and found that ethical failures within the industry increasingly generated justified critiques.[74]

SOCIOPOLITICAL COSTS AND BENEFITS

Economic analysts associated with the New Classical school assume that markets work efficiently when allowed to function. Rational traders learn from their mistakes and develop increasingly accurate expectations. Empirical work dealing with privatization and deregulation in this tradition tends to describe movement toward the adoption of free market mechanisms within particular policy environments, omitting detailed assessment of the results, which may be assumed to be self-evident. Yet action to increase the relative range of private-sector activity and/or asset ownership is inescapably political. For example, where significant market failures are evident, a small population cohort within any given economy may possess far greater economic opportunities than do other social groups. In such cases, much of the economy can eventually consist of *planning* rather than *market* sectors.[75] Socioeconomic life may be extensively politicized, and distributional coalitions become pervasive.[76] Within such highly distorted economies, market losses are not necessarily social losses.[77]

To be sure, programs of privatization can be successfully implemented, even when primarily driven by ideology or electoral considerations. However, once a decision to deregulate or to privatize is made, the balance of political advantage does not necessarily remain static. For instance, in Costa Rica, as Neal Zank reports, long after the incremental implementation of a 1984 government policy decision to privatize the commercial banking sector and limit credit subsidies, an agricultural coalition succeeded in having delinquent farm loans rescheduled at subsidized rates. Similarly, the May 1989 decision of the California Supreme Court to uphold Proposition 103, heralded a new wave of regulation in America's largest property and casualty insurance market.[78]

In the case of Japan, the 1987 Maekawa Report had advocated only limited regulatory reform, intended to address foreign charges of protectionism – proposals that were set aside by the ruling Liberal Democratic party. By 1988, a panel of government advisors had recommended deregulation in seven areas: retail distribution, trucking, telecommunications, finance, energy, agriculture, and business incorporation. The declared purpose was to increase domestic consumer satisfaction. Even so, these proposals avoided such controversial areas as the government's ban on rice imports and restrictions affecting the opening of large retail stores.[79] Furthermore, Nippon Telephone and Telegraph (NTT), which was partially divested (35 percent) in 1987, resisted an AT&T-style breakup by effective lobbying on the part of the 276,000 – strong Japanese Telecommunications Workers Union, as well as by public proposals to reduce labor costs and telephone-call prices. NTT's president, Haruo Yamaguchi, also argued that divestiture costs could total Y300 billion, and that telephone charges to noncorporate customers in the United States had risen since the dismantling of AT&T. In November 1989, the Keidanren business group suggested that no changes be made in the structure of NTT for the next three to five years.[80]

Privatization remains essentially an advanced industrial country phenomenon. With the exceptions of Bangladesh and Chile, there has been little developing-country activity to mirror the major programs of asset sales that have taken place in such nations as Britain and France.[81] Most of the 94 structural adjustment programs supported in developing countries by International Monetary Fund (IMF) during 1980–1984 required that state subsidies to SOEs be reduced and that prices charged cover operating costs, while making a reasonable contribution to capital maintenance and new investment.[82] Similarly, 73 percent of the 40 structural adjustment loans made by the World Bank to 21 developing countries during 1980–1986 demanded deregulation and a reorientation of public enterprises toward greater competitiveness.[83]

In the case of sub-Saharan Africa, a 1986 World Bank report estimated that up to 1985 no more than 5 percent of all public enterprises had been privatized or closed down.[84] To be sure, the emergent results of the 1984 Ivory Coast decision to privatize the health care sector encourage caution because the poorest population cohorts have been largely excluded from access to both preventive and curative medical assistance. Since 1982, President Hasting Banda's Malawi has undertaken the most extensive rivatization program of any African country, divesting almost all the 25 agricultural estates formerly owned by the Agricultural Development and Marketing Corporation. However, British-based Commonwealth Development Corporation purchased the world's largest macadamia nut plantation as well as one of the most modem tea factories, while the U.S.-based Cargill assumed control of the National Seed Company, given the lack of a ready local market. Meanwhile, Lonhro, the British multinational, continues to monopolize the sugar industry, and maintains a major presence in several other sectors of the economy.[85] Additionally, a 1980–1986 survey found that partial or total sale of SOEs had occurred in only 15 developing countries and had included fewer than 100 enterprises.[86] However, the U.S. Agency for International Development has encountered some success in facilitating financial sector deregulation and privatization within recipient developing countries.

Intractable problems persist. In Bolivia, the concept of privatization remains so controversial that a Commission on Industrial Transition was instituted almost covertly to develop related options, including leveraged buyouts, debt for equity swaps, lease contracts, and employee stock option purchases. One immediate irony was the realization that public-sector loans would be required in order for the domestic private sector to purchase state assets.[87] There is still no consensus as to the merits of privatization within the governing Bolivian coalition, led by President Paz Estenssoro. Similarly, the Philippine Committee on Privatization has been unable to proceed rapidly in part because many members also sit on the boards of corporate candidates, which remain important vehicles for political patronage. At the same time, after the Jamaican government replaced the public transport system in the Kingston Metropolitan Region with a system of private franchises in 1982, the efforts of operators to increase earnings at all costs-generated caustic and persistent, but largely ignored customer complaints.

Some countries such as Nigeria might be characterized by a fragmented indigenous private sector, lacking both the incentives and the managerial capacities necessary (if not sufficient) for the success of privatization. For many developing countries a prerequisite may be to privatize only nominally private sectors, which remain based on government franchises, licenses, and subsidies. To the extent that asset sales might mean increased unemployment and reduced real wages in the short run, workers typically resist bitterly. SOE managers frequently conclude that their salaries and benefits may be at risk as well. For example, when Thailand's Finance Minister Pramaul Sabhavasu sought to list the country's 61 SOEs on the Bangkok stock exchange, both labor and management opposed him.[88]

Similarly, the government of former Mexican President Miguel de la Madrid divested some 510 "non-strategic" SOEs between 1982 and 1988 without substantial impact on public-sector revenues or deficits.[89] However, these privatizations pleased Mexican businessmen, partly because some sales were made at bargain prices, but more because the program demonstrated that the government seriously wanted to restructure the economy in response to the country's $104 billion foreign debt. At the same time, the governing party suffered significant erosion of its working class support, and the current president, Carlos Salinas de Gortari, assumed office in December 1988 with the weakest mandate of any Mexican leader in decades.[90]

In partial response, President Salinas increased the minimum wage by 8 percent in January 1989 and froze the prices of some basic foods as well as of cooking gas and petrol, thus expanding the range of market regulation.[91] In an effort to achieve greater legitimacy, the Mexican government also filed criminal charges against two leading brokerage houses, citing widespread abuses that ranged from dealing in expired treasury certificates to buying on margin without the permission of their clients.[92]

When a nation's bureaucratic and entrepreneurial groups overlap insufficiently in ethnic composition, as in Trinidad and Tobago, privatization may be perceived as an intergroup transfer of income and assets. Additionally, privatizing governments often offer new flotations as well as service contracts, to political allies, in either prospect or actuality. There is some evidence that privatization and deregulation can increase income inequality over time as share ownership becomes concentrated, even where asset sales are initially widely dispersed.[93] Indeed, stock ownership remains limited in Britain: Fewer than 16 percent of all Britons own shares (56 percent in only one company), compared with some 25 percent of all Americans.[94]

The association of privatization with such concentration may be intentional: In France, the socialist government of Prime Minister Michel Rocard contended that most of the 10 large companies privatized in 1987 by former Prime Minister Chirac were placed in the hands of conservative core shareholders. By the late fall of 1988, Finance Minister Pierre Berengovoy proposed a law that would annul secret pacts in which such core shareholders committed themselves to sell shares only to one another, and in any case not before 1992.[95] A related point is that the elimination of domestic cross-subsidies forces higher-cost users such as consumers in isolated rural areas to pay higher prices unless other compensating transfers are introduced. In most of the country cases discussed in this volume, the sociopolitical and economic consequences of privatization and deregulation explicitly diverge or become apparent at different rates so that mutual support is infrequent.

PRACTICAL POLICY OPTIONS

Policies of privatization and deregulation can only be implemented within supportive domestic policy environments. A common denominator of successful privatization programs consists of greatly broadened capital ownership by individuals rather than institutions. In such situations, the concentrated interests of potential new shareholders or owners can outweigh the calculations of public-sector managers and SOE employees, as well as those of others dependent on subsidized public-sector benefits. For example, the 51 percent divestiture of Jamaica's National Commercial Bank in December 1986 was structured so as to mobilize unprecedented broad-based support.

If the domestic policy environment is not immediately conducive to the required degree of privatization, second- or third-order policy options may include limited management contracts or leases, trade sales, and debt-equity swaps in which public-sector external debt is exchanged for SOE shares. Chile reduced its commercial bank debt from US$14 billion in 1985 to only US$6.4 billion in 1989, mainly by means of aggressive equity conversion arrangements, and the central bank is considering additional proposals valued at some US$1.0 billion.[96] Such options may need to be underpinned by financial sector deregulation, revised legal codes that adequately address such issues as asset ownership and property rights, and effective public education programs intended to explain the potential socioeconomic benefits of properly executed privatization programs. These benefits could range from substantial worker ownership, increased job stability, and expanded employment opportunities to the generation of significant new capital investment funds, product or service enhancement, and rising per capita national income. New privatization programs might include substantially expanded and responsible regulation in such sectors as banking and finance.

In the case of major state assets, it may be necessary to reserve the majority of a planned share issue for domestic investors so as to counter potential nationalist charges of handing critical economic sectors over to foreign control.[97] Alternatively, multinational tenders might be encouraged where regionalization and diversification would result. Time-payment plans for share purchase may help to widen the shareholding base significantly, as exemplified by Austria's 49 percent sale of the Verbund electrical utility in November 1988.[98] In many developing countries, a privatizing government might also find it absolutely necessary to encourage substantial foreign direct investment, given the existence of only a thin domestic capital market. For instance, as a consequence of fewer than 700,000 Pakistani investors out of a population of over 100 million, and only 424 listed companies on the Karachi Stock Exchange, the government of Prime Minister Benazir Bhutto is exploring the possibilities of setting up a $50 million Pakistan Fund, with the Asian Development Bank and Merrill Lynch.[99] (Foreign investors can assuredly make welcome contributions for other reasons.) Each policy environment requires a distinctive mix of initiatives.

One solution to the problem of a limited domestic capital market in relation to privatizable asset values is to offer each registered voter a loan to be repaid from future asset earnings. As a variant, shares in selected SOEs might simply be distributed free of charge, thus creating an "ownership shock," which could significantly stimulate capital market growth. Where the main constraint on privatization is posed by established social and bureaucratic tradition, an interim approach is to corporatize SOEs, or mandate that such enterprises respond to a degree of competition, under public limited company law.

In 1988, for instance, New Zealand's Labour government split Electricorp (the state electric utility) into four separate divisions, relating to each other on a commercial basis: production, transmission, marketing, and design and construction. Electricity production and wholesale supply were also deregulated. In the United States, however, electric utility executives have expressed increasing concern that should independent power producers continue to build lines that tie into the nation's long-distance transmission system, given the industry's de facto deregulation, the technical reliability of the entire system could be impaired.[100]

During the process of deregulating such utilities, an optimal approach may be to arrange for franchise bidding, with specific bids invited as to the prices to be charged and the services to be offered to consumers, as in the cases of some French municipality water suppliers. Yet such bidding may not be truly competitive, particularly where new firms are invited to bid against an existing supplier. Although contract enforcement itself might be privatized on the basis of appropriate audit incentives, the procedures for determining an ideal price structure and product mix, as well as adequate environmental safety measures, may require the kind of expertise associated with a full-fledged regulatory commission. In fact, utility privatization has typically been accompanied by a proliferation of single-industry regulatory agencies, as is the case in Britain. However, where several such commissions exist, it may be possible to structure active competition between related agencies in such sectors as finance and telecommunications. Such competition could provide valuable information as to the deficiencies of each.[101]

At the same time, it is evident that government initiatives intended to implement programs of privatization and deregulation, with insufficient regard for the longer-term implications in each case, invite new charges of policy failure. Management contracts may result in ultimately higher costs due to "low-balling," poorer service, fraud, and the lack of genuine accountability.[102] Government held golden shares, as well as legislation such as the Exxon-Florio amendment to the U.S. Omnibus Trade and Competitiveness Act, can arbitrarily entrench incumbent management at the expense of shareholders.[103] In some British sectors such as television, deregulation could mean that financial imperatives rather than program quality, will completely dominate management decision making. In others such as energy production, the operating environment may remain subject to economic nationalism, as evidenced by the results of the Kuwait Investment Office's (KIO) late 1987 purchase of a 21.6 percent stake in British Petroleum.[104] Indeed, the British government's decision that KIO had to reduce its holdings in British Petroleum sharply was approvingly cited by Spain's Minister of Industry and Energy, Claudio Aranzadi, who made it clear that foreign investors would not be allowed to purchase Spanish utilities.[105]

In conclusion, the political, social, and economic consequences of either privatization or deregulation do not necessarily converge or become evident within identical time frames. Neither privatization nor deregulation inevitably implies increased competition. The net socioeconomic benefits of such policies depend directly on environment and timing. As with "public" and "private" sector, "privatization" and "deregulation" are composite concepts that must be unpackaged for effective policy formulation and choice in the course of attempted solutions to excessive government expansion.

NOTES

1. Nancy L. Rose, *Profitability and Product Quality: Economic Determinants of Airline Safety Performance*, Sloan Working Paper #2032-88 (Cambridge, MA: MIT, June 1988).

2. Catherine Eckel and Theo Vermaelen, "Internal Regulation: The Effects of Government Ownership on the Value of the Firm," *Journal of Law and Economics* 381, no. 29 (October 1986), 381–403.

3. For further discussion, see George C. Lodge and Ezra F. Vogel, *Ideology and National Competitiveness* (Boston: Harvard Business School Press, 1987).

4. Karl Frieden, "Public Needs and Private Wants: Making Choices," *Dissent* (Summer 1987), 324.

5. Richard Rose, "What If Anything Is Wrong with Big Government?" *Journal of Public Policy* 1 (1981), 5–36.

6. E. S. Savas, *Privatization: The Key to Better Government* (Chatham, NJ: Chatham House, 1987), pp. 1–2.

7. In the United States, the President's Commission on Privatization, chaired by David F. Linowes, also offered 78 recommendations for the privatization of a wide range of services, including low-income housing, housing finance, federal loan programs, air traffic control, education, the postal service, Medicare, international development programs, and urban mass transit. The commission also proposed that Amtrak and the Naval Petroleum Reserves be sold and that military commissaries as well as prisons, be contracted out of the public sector. See David F. Linowes et al., *Privatization: Towards More Effective Government* (Washington, DC: President's Commission on Privatization, 1988), pp. xx–xxi.

8. John A. Barnes, "The City That Privatized Everything," *Wall Street Journal*, 17 May 1989. Ecorse has a population of 13,000 and an area of 2.2 square miles.

9. "Competitive Tendering: Small Earthquakes in Town Halls," *Economist*, 9 September 1989, pp. 71–72.

10. Nicholas C. Kernstock, "Government to Sell 41.1 Million Shares of Air Canada Stock, Finish Privatization," *Aviation Week & Space Technology*, 19 June 1989, pp. 71–72.

11. Tim Golden, "Argentine Prescribes Painful Economic Cure," *Miami Herald*, 10 July 1989.

12. Lim Siong Hoon, "Malaysia's Masterplan Sets the Pace for Privatisation," *Financial Times*, 21 September 1989.

13. "Second Thoughts in Sweden," *Economist*, 10 December 1988, p. 73.

14. Richard Rose, "Disaggregating the Concept of Government," in *Why Governments Grow: Measuring Public Sector Size*, ed. Charles Taylor (Beverly Hills, CA: Sage, 1983), pp. 157–176.

15. "Government: Still Too Much," *Economist*, 20 August 1988, p. 52. The Education Reform Act also created four new quasi-governmental organizations,

dealing with the national curriculum, school examinations, and the financing of universities as well as polytechnics.

16. "Water Privatisation: Down the River," *Economist*, 8 October 1988, p. 57.

17. "Trains of Thought," *Economist*, 4 March 1989, pp. 54–55.

18. "No Stopping Her," *Economist*, 4 February 1989, pp. 49–50; Alan Pike and John Mason, "Tories 'May Lose 12% of Vote' Over NHS Policy," *Financial Times*, 10 October 1989. A 1989 opinion survey commissioned by the British Labour Party found that 62 percent of all respondents thought the planned reforms would lead to poorer standards of health care, and that up to 12 percent of Conservative supporters might switch their votes.

19. "Private Prisons: Slowly Does It," *Economist*, 4 March 1989, pp. 55–56.

20. Michael Selz, "Wackenhut Goes to the Slammer," *Florida Trend* (July 1989): 32–43.

21. Scott Ticer, "The Search for Ways to Break Out of the Prison Crisis," *Business Week*, 8 May 1989, pp. 80–81.

22. Alan S. Blinder, "Are Crumbling Highways Giving Productivity a Flat?" *Business Week*, 29 August 1988, p. 16. International comparisons corroborate this relationship. For example, the United States displayed both the slowest productivity growth rate and the lowest public investment/GNP ratio for 1973–1985 among the seven most advanced industrial economies.

23. "Beltway Brain Drain: Why Civil Servants Are Making Tracks," *Business Week*, 23 January 1989, pp. 60–61.

24. David B. Yoffie, "How an Industry Builds Political Advantage," *Harvard Business Review* (May–June 1988), 82–89. Also see Michael E. Porter, *Competition in Global Industries* (Boston: Harvard Business School Press, 1986).

25. Thomas J. Biersteker, "Appropriating the Concept of Privatization for Development" Paper presented at the annual convention of the International Studies Association, London, 28 March–1 April 1989, pp. 3–4.

26. D. R. Steel and D. A. Heald, eds, *Privatising Public Enterprises: Options and Dilemmas* (London: Royal Institute of Public Administration, 1984); J. Pratt and R. Zeckhauser, *Principals and Agents: The Structure of Business* (Cambridge, MA: Harvard Business School Press, 1985); J. Heald, "Will Privatization of Public Enterprises Solve the Problem of Control?" *Journal of Public Administration* 63, no. 7 (1985). Since 1985, when the Delaware Supreme Court found that Trans Union Corporation's directors had not acted in the best interests of the stockholders in accepting a takeover bid. shareholder lawsuits charging directors with dereliction of duty have multiplied in the United States.

27. George Wilson, "Regulating and Deregulating Business," *Business Horizons*, July–August 1982, pp. 45–52.

28. Mary Livingstone (Center for Public Interest Law), "Justifications for Government Regulation," *National Public Accountant* 33 (June 1988), 16.

29. Barry M. Mitnick, "The Strategic Uses of Regulation and Deregulation," *Business Horizons*, March–April 1981, pp. 71–83.

30. Douglas A. Houston, "The Mixed Interest in Regulation and Deregulation," *Land Economics* 63 (November 1987), 404.

31. Bruce Ingersoll and Gregory Stricharchuk, "Generic Drug scandal at the FDA is Linked to Deregulation Drive," *Wall Street Journal*, 13 September 1989.

32. See comments by Daniel Wall, chairman of the Federal Home Loan Bank Board in *The Miami Herald* of 28 January 1989. There are 3,000 savings and loan associations (S&Ls) in the United States. During the third quarter of 1988, 404 S&Ls with assets totaling $289 billion accumulated net losses of $239 million. One hundred and fifty such institutions had a tangible net worth of −$1.3 billion. It will cost some $100 billion to compensate the depositors of insolvent S&Ls. A recent report by the U.S. House Committee on Government Operations concluded that lack of successful prosecution and tough punishment constituted the greatest single impediment to deterring criminal behavior in the banking and thrift industry ("Flashy Federal Posse Pursuing S&L Abuses Bungles Effort in Texas," *Wall Street Journal*, 10 February 1989).

33. Adi Ignatius, "Beijing, Faced with Economic Crisis, Draws Back from Liberalization Drive," *Wall Street Journal*, 26 September 1988.

34. Julia Leung, "China Faces Huge Ideological Hurdles in Plan to Sell Shares in State Concerns," *Wall Street Journal*, 2 March 1989; "China: Next Round," *Economist*, 21 January 1989, p. 36.

35. A July 1988 survey of almost 200 members of the National Federation of Independent Business indicated a strong majority view that interest rates for small businesses with annual sales of less than $150,000 were five percentage points higher than they would probably have been without banking deregulation.

36. Arthur M. Okun, *Equality and Economic Efficiency: The Big Trade Off* (Washington, DC: Brookings Institution, 1975).

37. "Out of Their Depth," *Economist*, 11 February 1989, p. 53; Larry M. Greenberg, "Britain's Political Misfortunes Threaten Confidence in Plan for Water Industry," *Wall Street Journal*, 13 February 1989. The private water companies contended that a combination of heavy new investment costs and high debt–equity ratios implied a compelling need to raise prices substantially.

38. W. M. Corden, *Trade Policy and Economic Welfare* (Oxford: Oxford University Press, 1974).

39. Steve H. Hanke and Stephen J. K. Walters, "Privatization and Natural Monopoly: The Case of Waterworks," *Privatization Review* 3, no. 1 (Spring 1987), 24–31.

40. Mary Lu Camevale, "Slow Progress: Phone Service Shows Only Minor Advances 5 Years after Breakup," *Wall Street Journal*, 6 January 1989.

41. Mary Lu Carnevale, "FCC Imposes Mild Curbs on 5 Providers of Telephone Services to Big Institutions," *Wall Street Journal*, 5 February 1989.

42. "Deregulating America's Airlines: Happiness is a Cheap Seat," *Economist*, 4 February 1989, pp. 68–71; Paul W. Bauer, "Airline Deregulation: Boon or Bust?" *Economic Commentary*, Federal Reserve Bank of Cleveland, 1 May 1989; "Flying against the Rules," *Economist*, 24 June 1989, pp. 14–15. The eight largest American airlines now carry some 90 percent of all U.S. passengers. However, between 1978 and 1989 the number of workers in the airline industry grew by only 48 percent, compared to an 86 percent expansion in the number of passengers and a 109 percent increase in the number of miles flown. At the same time, inflation-adjusted airfares declined by 20 percent. By summer 1989, Congress was considering proposals to reduce congestion at hub airports by charging higher takeoff and landing fees during peak hours, capping the number of flights that dominant carriers were able to

schedule out of particular airports, and forcing the sale of widely used computer reservations systems owned by United and American Airlines.

43. Robert W. Bailey, "Uses and Misuses of Privatization," in *Prospects for Privatization*, ed. Steve H. Hanke (New York: Academy of Political Science, 1987).

44. C. Harrol, E. Henriod, and P. Graziano, *An Appraisal of Highway Maintenance by Contract in Developing Countries* (Washington, DC: World Bank, 1982).

45. Gabriel Roth, *Competitive Urban Transportation Services* (Washington, DC: World Bank, 1984).

46. Kevin Brown, "London Bus Routes Put Up For Sale," *Financial Times*, 25 October 1989.

47. David Lyons, "For Rent: Public Jobs," *Miami Herald Business Monday*, 17 October 1986, pp. 1, 13, 15.

48. Matt Moffett, "Service on Mexican Airline Soars after Deregulation," *Wall Street Journal*, 17 April 1989.

49. Raymond Vernon, "Introduction: The Promise and the Challenge," in *The Promise of Privatization*, ed. Raymond Vernon (New York: Council on Foreign Relations, 1988), pp. 5, 17; Yair Aharoni, "The United Kingdom: Transforming Attitudes," in Vernon, *The Promise*, pp. 27, 36.

50. Stuart M. Butler, "Changing the Political Dynamics of Government," in *Prospects for Privatization*, ed. Steve H. Hanke (New York: Academy of Political Science, 1987), pp. 87–101; L. Gray Cowan, "Divestment, Privatization and Development," *Washington Quarterly* (1985), 47–56.

51. Ed Doherty, "Alternative Delivery of Services in Rochester, New York," in *Public Sector Privatization: Alternative Approaches to Service Delivery*, ed. Lawrence K. Finley (Westport, CT: Quorum Books, 1989), pp. 32–33.

52. Peter Brimelow, "Do You Want to Be Paid in Rockefellers? In Wristons? Or How about a Hayek?" *Forbes*, 30 May 1989, pp. 243–250.

53. Gabriel Roth, The Private Provision of Public Services in Developing Countries (New York: Oxford University Press, 1987), p. 5.

54. Matthew Bishop and John Kay, *Does Privatization Work? Lessons from the United Kingdom* (London: London Business School, 1988). It is, however, worth noting that British Steel continued to receive significant government subsidies during the period reviewed.

55. Paul Johnson, "When Terms Are Politics," *Spectator*, 18 July 1987, p. 1.

56. Jan Pieter Van Oudenhoven, "Privatization in Europe," in *Public Sector Privatization: Alternative Approaches to Service Delivery*, ed. Lawrence K. Finley (Westport, CT: Quorum Books, 1989), pp. 172–174.

57. David R. Cameron, "The Expansion of the Public Economy: A Comparative Analysis," *American Political Science Review* 72, no. 4 (December 1978), 1243–1261.

58. For example, following the Second World War, which increased security concerns as to the integrity of international cable systems, the 1945 Commonwealth Telecommunications Conference agreed that overseas cable links should be managed by SOEs. More recently, the prospective 1985 sale of Britain's Westland helicopter company to an American buyer sharply split the British Cabinet. In turn, the Reagan administration prevented the planned 1987 sale of Fairchild (a semiconductor company with defense contracts) to a Japanese corporation.

59. Paul Streeten, "Twenty-One Arguments for Public Enterprise." in *Global Development: Issues and Choices*, ed. Khadija Haq (Washington, DC: North South Round-table of the Society for International Development, 1983), pp. 124–136.

60. M. Waterson, *Regulation of the Firm and Natural Monopoly* (Oxford, England: Basil Blackwell, 1988). Francis M. Bator provides a seminal discussion of market failure in "Anatomy of Market Failure," *Quarterly Journal of Economics* (August 1958).

61. Ray Rees, "Inefficiency, Public Enterprise and Privatization," *European Economic Review* 32, no. 2 (1988), 422–441.

62. Mehdi Haririan, *State-Owned Enterprises: The Conflict between Micro and Macro Objectives* (Boulder, CO: Westview Press, 1989).

63. D. Lall, "The Political Economy of Economic Liberalization," *World Bank Economic Review* 1, no. 2 (1987), 273–299.

64. Ronald Coase, "The Problem of Social Cost," *Journal of Law and Economics* 3 (1960); James Buchanan and W. Craig Subblebine, "Externality," *Economica* (November 1962).

65. W. Lee Hoskins, "Rethinking the Regulatory Response to Risk-Taking in Banking," *Economic Commentary*, Federal Reserve Bank of Cleveland, 1 June 1989, pp. 2–3.

66. "Soviet Union: Leader Backs Cut in State Ownership," *The Miami Herald*, 19 November 1989; Peter Gumbel, "Soviets Have Taken Many Wrong Turns on the Road to Economic Restructuring," *Wall Street Journal*, 21 November 1989.

67. Barry Wain, "Vietnam's Economic Reform Is Still a Delicate Planting," *Wall Street Journal*, 24 May 1989; Alysoun Coles, "Vietnam Puts Its House *In* Order – and Awaits First Visitors," *Financial Times*, 2 November 1989. In 1979, the Vietnamese government floated the dong, and made the black market exchange rate official, thus sharply reducing the level of inflation. Vietnam's 1988 Law on Trade and Foreign Investment is the most liberal in Asia. By November 1989, there were 26 private enterprises in Hanoi and 50 foreign investment projects.

68. Kamran Fazel, "Rafsanjani Proposes Sale of State-Owned Factories," *Financial Times*, 10 October 1989.

69. *Statistical Yearbook 1987* (Budapest: Hungarian Central Statistical Office, 1988).

70. Andras Nagy, "Why Doesn't the Hungarian Economy Work?" *Business in the Contemporary World* 1, no. 2 (Winter 1989), 71–83.

71. *Miami Herald*, 24 December 1988. The Anglo-Polish economist Jacek Rostowski estimated that private economic activity accounted for between 38 and 45 percent of personal money incomes in Poland, while most agriculture remained private and 40 percent of all the new housing was constructed by private-sector firms (Timothy Garton Ash, "Trying for Thatcherism in Poland," *Wall Street Journal*, 31 October 1988).

72. "Life in the Pits Will Never Be the Same," *Business Week*, 6 February 1989, pp. 32–34.

73. Nicholas F. Brady (chairman), *Report of the Presidential Task Force on Market Mechanisms* (Washington, DC: GPO, 8 January 1988). This report argued that a single powerful regulatory agency was required for adequate oversight of the effectively integrated stock, futures, and options markets. It also proposed a unified clearing system to ensure the financial integrity of these markets, a single standard

for margins so as to control speculation, better information systems to monitor market activity, and the installation of "circuit breakers" to give the markets time to cool down, should overheating occur.

74. Stephen Fidler, "Financial Sector Worried Over Questions of Principle," *Financial Times*, 31 October 1989.

75. See John Kenneth Galbraith, *Economics and the Public Purpose* (New York: New American Library, 1973), pp. 53–89. Where the planning sector consists of large-scale corporations that benefit from special relationships with the public sector, market-sector firms include unstandardized and geographically dispersed enterprises, the expansion of which may be precluded by legal licensing requirements.

76. See Mancur Olson, *The Rise and Decline of Nations: Economic Growth, Stagflation and Social Rigidities* (New Haven and London: Yale University Press, 1982), p. 74. Distributional coalitions are exclusive special interest groups that retard a society's capacity to adapt new technologies and to reallocate resources in response to changing economic conditions, thereby reducing the rate of economic growth.

77. Jagdish Bhagwati and T. N. Srinavasan, "Revenue Seeking: A Generalization of the Theory of Tariffs," *Journal of Political Economy* 88 (December 1980), 1069–1087. The main argument – that the shadow (or social) cost of productive factors withdrawn from productive use into directly unproductive activities may be negative – is made in the context of trade policy, but has obvious implications for privatization and regulatory policy choice.

78. Richard B. Schmitt and Ken Wells, "California High Court Upholds Prop 103: Across the U.S. Insurers Brace for the Effects," *Wall Street Journal*, 5 May 1989.

79. "Japanese Committee Steps Cautiously in Recommending Economic Reforms," *Wall Street Journal*, 15 November 1988. In *The Enigma of Japanese Power* (New York: Knopf, 1988), Karel van Wolferen argues that factional disputes so permeate Japanese organizational life that no single individual or group can be decisive.

80. Stefan Wagstyl, "NTT Under Fire as Critics Seek to Ring the Changes," *Financial Times*, 24 October 1989; "Nippon Telegraph and Telephone: The Empire Strikes Back," *Economist*, 4 November 1989, p. 88. NTT has annual sales in excess of 5.9 trillion yen, and purchases 1.2 trillion yen worth of equipment each year from suppliers such as Fujitsu and NEC, which, in turn, strongly support NTT's management.

81. J. Aylen, "Privatization in Developing Countries," *Lloyds Bank Review* no. 163 (January 1987), 15–30.

82. International Monetary Fund, *Fund-Supported Programs, Fiscal Policy and Income Distribution*, Occasional Paper #46 (Washington, DC: IMF, 1985). In January 1989, structural adjustment arrangements totaling SDR 1.4 billion were in place in 24 developing countries, accompanied by enhanced structural adjustment arrangements in an additional six such nations, totaling SDR77S.69 million. See International Monetary Fund, *International Financial Statistics* (Washington, DC: IMF, 1989), p. 23.

83. Paul Mosley, "Privatization, Policy-Based Lending and World Bank Behaviour," in *Privatization in Less Developed Countries*, eds Paul Cook and Cohn Kirkpatrick (New York: St. Martin's Press, 1988), pp. 135–138.

84. World Bank, *Financing Adjustment with Growth in Sub-Saharan Africa, 1986–1990* (Washington, DC: IBRD, 1986).

85. Mike Hall, "Political Premium on the Price of Selling the Malawian State," *Financial Times*, 30 August 1989.

86. E. Berg, "Privatization: Developing a Pragmatic Approach," *Economic Impact*no. 57 (1987), 6–11. Bangladesh and Chile were not included in this survey.

87. In a related 1988 U.S. case, EOSAT, a joint venture between the General Motors subsidiary Hughes Aircraft and the General Electric subsidiary RCA, was afforded an opportunity to purchase the Landsat remote sensing satellite program, along with a subsidy of $250 million, after a competitive bidding procedure. Laurie Clements, "Privatization: Confronting the New Leviathan," *Labor Studies Forum* 1, no. 4 (Winter 1989), 1, 5.

88. Helen White, "Thai Finance Minister Defies Doubters in Moves to Liberalize Booming Economy," *Wall Street Journal*, 21 March 1989.

89. Ben Ross Schneider, "Partly for Sale: Privatization and State Strength in Brazil and Mexico," *Journal of InterAmerican Studies and World Affairs* 30, no. 4 (Winter 1988–1989), 100–105. Article 28 of the Mexican Constitution defines the following sectors as strategic: national mint, post office, telecommunications, central banking, petroleum, basic petrochemicals, radioactive minerals and nuclear energy, electricity, railroads, and "the public service of banking and credit."

90. Mark Moffat, "Mexico Is Pressing Divisive Privatizations," *Wall Street Journal*, 19 October 1988.

91. "Mexico, After the Elections," *Economist*, 24 December 1988, p. 53.

92. "Global Wrapup," *Business Week*, 27 February 1989, p. 61.

93. Thomas M. Callaghy and Ernest James Wilson III, "Africa: Policy, Reality or Ritual?" in Vernon, *The Promise*; Yair Aharoni, "The United Kingdom," p. 49; Alejandro Foxley, *Latin American Experiments in Neo-Conservative Economics* (Berkeley: University of California Press, 1983); Thomas J. Biersteker, *Multinationals, the State, and Control of the Nigerian Economy* (Princeton, NJ: Princeton University Press, 1987), Chapters 3 and 6.

94. "Who Needs Privatization Now?" *Economist*, 19 December 1987, pp. 49–50.

95. "French Banking: Affairs of State," *Economist*, 19 November 1988, p. 88; E. S. Browning, "Paris to Propose Removal of Restrictions on Sale of Privatized Companies' Shares," *Wall Street Journal*, 9 December 1988.

96. Barbara Durr, "Election Lays Siege to Chile's Swaps Program," *Financial Times*, 31 August 1989; Barbara Durr, "Brady Plan Proposal for Chile's Debt Buy-Back," *Financial Times*, 13 September 1989.

97. Such charges are effectively advanced not only at the national, but also at the regional level. For instance, in the Canadian province of Saskatchewan, Premier Grant Devine found it necessary to stress that his planned divestment of the province's Potash Corporation would allow potential foreign purchasers, such as India and China, not more than 10 percent of any equity.

98. "Austria's Sale of Verbund Stake May Be Breakthrough for Privatization Market," *Wall Street Journal*, 21 November 1988.

99. Christina Lamb, "Pakistan Strives After the Big Time," *Financial Times*, 26 October 1989. One declared goal in establishing a Pakistan country fund is to attract back some of the estimated $1.7 billion that Pakistanis themselves have invested abroad.

100. Bill Paul, "As Independent Producers Send Energy, Utilities Worry about Load on System," *Wall Street Journal*, 1 November 1988.

101. See Cento Veljanovski, "Privatization in Britain: The Institutional Constitutional Issues," *Marquette Law Review* 71 (1988), 576–577.

102. Gerald W. McEntee, "City Services: Can Free Enterprise Outperform the Public Sector?" *Business and Society Review* no. 55 (Fall 1985), 43–47.

103. The Exxon-Flono amendment authorized the President to suspend or prohibit any acquisition, merger, or takeover of a U.S. firm by a foreign citizen or firm if the President determines that the acquisition would threaten U.S. national security, and that other laws would not provide adequate protection.

104. "Thatcher Gives Kuwait a Rap on the Knuckles," *Business Week*, 17 October 1988, p. 48. The British Monopolies Commission ruled that the Kuwait Investment Office should reduce its holdings in British Petroleum to a maximum of 9.9 percent in the public interest, given the potential for declining oil industry competition.

105. Peter Bruce and Tom Burns, "Sparks Fly Over Spanish Utilities," *Financial Times*, 6 October 1989.

APPROACHES TO PRIVATIZATION: ESTABLISHED MODELS AND A U.S. INNOVATION

Stanley Y. Chang and Roberta Ann Jones

The pros and cons of four privatization models are charted, comparing approaches that have been used in Great Britain and New Zealand with the old standby – contracting out – and a United States innovation.

Governmental units today are often confronted with a major dilemma: there are growing demands from their constituents for more and better services along with an increasing inclination for tax limitation, if not tax reduction. Limitations on the property taxing authority of state and local governments, compounded with the simultaneous dwindling of federal shared revenues and other subsidies, puts these governments in a constant search for alternative financing sources. Among those alternatives, privatization is an option receiving growing attention. Indeed, President Bush signed an Executive Order on April 30, 1992, to remove regulatory impediments and encourage state and local governments to sell or lease their infrastructure assets obtained with federal assistance to private investors.

Privatization enables private enterprises to perform what has been an exclusively public task or a government dominant function. While gaining popularity, privatization is still a somewhat sporadic event rather than a growing trend in the United States. There has been, however, a systematic effort in the United Kingdom and a national campaign in New Zealand to privatize government operations. Governments have found privatization,

Comparative Public Administration: The Essential Readings
Research in Public Policy Analysis and Management, Volume 15, 489–499
Copyright © 2006 by Elsevier Ltd.
ISSN: 0732-1317/doi:10.1016/S0732-1317(06)15021-6

when properly implemented, useful in reducing public expenditures, increasing efficiency, raising capital, and/or providing improved services.

Because of the diverse goals and endemic needs of governments, the privatization process varies greatly. Two outwardly similar situations may call for different procedures implemented in different stages, over different time spans. Government finance officers and accountants in both the public and private sectors have been heavily involved in the privatization process. Their potential responsibilities span all of the stages of the transition, and the manner in which they discharge these responsibilities impacts everything from early planning to completion. In addition to various levels of planning, they are involved in such activities as asset valuation, service, pricing, and contract negotiation.

Government officials involved in privatization must thoroughly understand the various approaches and processes if they are to ensure a smooth transition that achieves the goals of all concerned. Because the privatization of a governmental function is not commonly part of a finance officer's/accountant's career training or experience, the necessary level of understanding is seldom present when the need first arises. Lessons can be gleaned from the experience of others, however. While the individual process may need to be tailor-made, commonality of methodologies can generally be observed.

This chapter summarizes three general privatization models used in the United Kingdom, New Zealand and the United States. The authors have recently experienced a fourth alternative, which incorporates some of the elements of the other three but remains unique in many respects. This new privatization approach is contrasted with the other models. The authors do not suggest that any one method is superior to another, for clearly, the goals of the government and other relevant constraints should dictate which privatization methodology may be most appropriate in any given situation.

Based on their roots and history, the four approaches introduced in this paper are referred to as (1) the British Model (2) the New Zealand Experience (3) the Old Standby and (4) a United States Innovation. Each of these approaches is separately described, with a discussion of some relevant advantages, disadvantages, and examples. Exhibit 1 summarizes the major features of the four methods.

THE BRITISH MODEL

The outright sale of government assets is probably the most common form of privatization in the United Kingdom.[1] Two primary pricing conventions have been used. Fixed-price stock offerings make single-priced shares available to the public. Tender stock offers, however, do not fix stock prices in advance; thus the price is determined by market forces.

In a sale of assets, the entity to be sold follows typical private sector procedures. These include, among others, developing a prospectus, identifying underwriters and issuing houses, and selecting the stockbrokers. Since the market values of assets to be sold often are unknown in a governmental environment, determining the fair market value to use in a fixed-price offer or establishing the minimum bid in a tender offer can be difficult and expensive.

In England, it has been found that fixed-price offers tend to undervalue the assets, despite governmental efforts to establish a fair price.[2] A major reason for this phenomenon is that the underwriters also are often the prime bidders, and any shares not sold can be purchased by the underwriters at bargain prices. Thus, there is a built-in incentive for the underwriters to refrain from bidding, which leads to underpricing of assets.

Advantages. The advantage of this public offering method is that there are many accountants, bankers, underwriters, and issuing houses which are familiar with the process. It should thus be relatively easy for a governmental entity to find the necessary specialists to assist with a privatization. The proceeds of the sale may provide additional revenues if depreciated assets have higher market values. Therefore, this often is the method of choice when capital generation is one of the goals of government. Further, should the government desire that a wide ownership of assets be a major result of the privatization process, this method can achieve that goal.

Disadvantages. This approach can be very expensive. There may be no market for the assets to be sold. There may be no guarantee that the assets will be fairly valued in order to avoid a loss of net worth to the community. It has been suggested that the British model for wide ownership of assets prevails only in the short-term for many sales and that revenue gains may only be an accounting illusion.[3]

Examples. Mexico, aggressively privatizing its governmental enterprises, sold its national telephone agency, Telemex, using this approach. Southwestern Bell of the U.S. was part of a bidding group that acquired 20.4 percent of the stock for $1.76 billion.[4] Also, Bancomer, the second largest Mexican bank, was put on the auction block for bids in the $5 billion range.[5]

In the U.S., stocks have not been a common vehicle for government assets sales – most transactions have been consummated in dollars. In 1986, the Navy auctioned off its Truman Annex, located on Key West, to a private developer for $17.5 million. Other recent examples include the $2 million cash sale of a former school to a nonprofit corporation by Stamford, Connecticut, and the sale of the Conrail system.

THE NEW ZEALAND EXPERIENCE

Corporatization is a term coined in New Zealand, where privatization of most governmental services is an all-out effort.[6] Using the corporatization approach, the government creates a for-profit corporation having a governing board typically composed of members from the government as well as from the local business community. The government owns all the stock in the new corporation. The net assets of the spin-off entity are transferred to the new corporation at book value in exchange for the stock.

This process enables the newly created corporation to operate free of most of the constraints of government while allowing the government to maintain control and ownership. Entities that have previously obtained their funding from the public budget are required to earn their own revenues after incorporation. Once the corporation has established itself and generated a credit history, the stock is sold on the open market.

There are some who argue that the final sale of the stock – the actual privatization – is an unnecessary step. Proponents of this method, however, insist that privatization is essential to keep the corporation free of unnecessary government constraints in the long-term.[7]

Advantages. Corporatization, in and of itself, provides no additional revenues, but it presumably enables the government to correct inefficiencies and bypass bureaucratic red tape. The sale of stock could generate revenues if the assets have appreciated.

There is generally no shortage of expert assistance in establishing the corporation and effecting the asset transfer. The corporatization process need not be expensive, although the privatization itself would entail expenses similar to those involved in any other sale of assets. This method also allows the government to retain control for as long as it deems necessary while enabling the spin-off entity time to adjust to the corporate environment. From an accounting perspective, this may be relatively unimportant for functions already accounted for in proprietary or enterprise funds, but crucial for activities in governmental funds. Buyers may be reluctant to invest in a governmental entity that has never shown the capacity to be self-supporting, much less the ability to generate profits. Corporatization enables the entity to prove itself to potential investors before an offer of sale is made.

Disadvantages. The disadvantages of a sale of assets also apply to the privatization phase of corporatization. The two-step process of first incorporating and then privatizing is usually much more time consuming and expensive than a direct asset sale. Also, there may still be no willing buyers when the stock is offered for sale. The legislative and political barriers may be greater for this method, as well. The process may even require two trips to the appropriating legislature which can be time consuming and politically risky.

Examples. Using this approach, New Zealand has incorporated its post office, energy services, forest services, airways system, and land and survey trading activities. Recently, it also privatized its government computing services. This South Pacific approach has no known counterparts in the U.S. yet, probably due to the fact that most of such privatized functions always have been privately owned in the United States. Similar privatization formats, however, have been used in developing countries such as Taiwan.

THE OLD STANDBY

Contracting out, an old standby approach in most western societies, is perhaps the simplest method available to accomplish privatization. Contracting for services has historical roots in governmental circles and has been used in the U.S. by federal, state, and local governmental agencies. The governments establish contractual relationships with outside businesses to provide necessary services. The private businesses supply the personnel and perform the needed service for an agreed upon fee. Assets required to perform the contracted task may be provided by the government or by the private business.

Advantages. The advantages of contracting services are numerous. Governments would normally have the procedures in place for contracting routine services, and legislative involvement may then not be necessary. Because contracts can be rescinded or revised, there is less risk to the government. Suppliers can be changed or the government can resume providing the service if contracting proves ineffective or more costly. Contracting can be accomplished in a relatively shorter-time period than an asset sale, thus allowing the government to quickly expand services, if necessary (Table 1).

In the U.S., the use of tax-exempt financing for the physical facilities may be an important factor in some contracting-out arrangements. Using what were in the past referred to as Industrial Development Bonds (IDBs), state or local governmental units could issue bonds whose interest was exempt

Table 1. Advantages and Disadvantages of Four Privatization Approaches.

Approach	Advantages	Disadvantages
The British Model	• Available specialists • Raise capital • Provide wide ownership of assets • Reduce public expenditures • Correct inefficiencies • Enhance services	• Expensive • No market • Revenue gains an accounting illusion • Wide ownership short-term only
The New Zealand Experience	• Same as above • Allows adjustment time • Allows profit generation time	• Same as above • Requires more legislative effort • Time consuming
The Old Standby (Contracting out)	• Procedures in place • Enhances services • Legislative involvement not necessary • Short-time frame • Ease of change • Correct inefficiencies	• Suppliers not available/acceptable • Some not cost effective • No capital generation
The United States Innovation	• Less costly than asset sale • Nonprofit • Allows service continuity • Reduce public expenditures • Correct inefficiencies • Interstate involvement easily possible • Enhance services	• Lacks arm's-length independence • Special legislative effort required • No capital generation

from federal income tax and use the proceeds to acquire, construct or re-habilitate industrial facilities, which they then might contractually lease to a private company. The lessee would pay the rent sufficient to cover interest and amortization of the bonds, an attractive arrangement for the private sector since the interest on the bond would be lower than on a comparable taxable bond. However, various federal laws passed in recent decades, and the Tax Reform Act of 1986 (TRA) in particular, have significantly re-stricted the uses of tax-exempt financing for private activities. To qualify for tax-exempt status under the TRA, a private-activity bond must meet several strict tests concerning the extent of private sector use of the bond proceeds. IDBs have been limited to $10 million per individual issue and restricted primarily to manufacturing purposes. The tax-exempt financing issue also is raised in the case of the sale to a for-profit entity of a public asset that has been financed with tax-exempt bonds.

Disadvantages. There may not be any willing suppliers of the service, or the available suppliers may not be acceptable to the government. Moreover, contracting some governmental services may not be cost effective. The li-ability for providing contracted services may remain with the government, thereby requiring the government to monitor contractors, which can be costly and difficult. Also, contracting will not raise capital and may not reduce public expenditures. When the contract-awarding decision becomes political, as in the case of clean-up activities in the wake of Hurricane Alicia in Houston, service performance may be sub-par or never completed.[8]

Examples. In recent years, governments have broadened their scope in selecting possible functions to contract out. In 1988, municipalities were reported to have contracted out, on the average, about 27 percent of their services to private companies.[9] Almost all major cities have their public park maintenance done, in part or in whole, by private contractors, who also do garbage collections in Houston, Indianapolis, Los Angeles, Miami and New York, to name a few.[10] Mass transit, motor pool maintenance, enter-tainment facility (e.g., sports arena, golf course), management, and property tax collection are other popular functions that are outsourced. In a 1992 report on state privatization, all states reported contract-out services. Areas where such activities were found most frequently were corrections, health, higher education and mental health. More than 67 percent of the reporting agencies have more than $80 million of external contracts.[11] At the national level, weaponry always has been a big outsourcing item, and the Depart-ment of Defense has gone so far as to let a civilian firm operate a small Army airfield on its behalf.[12]

A UNITED STATES INNOVATION

A somewhat different approach to privatization has been observed recently in the U.S. Much like corporatization in the initial stages, this technique has a key difference: A nonprofit organization, instead of a for-profit entity, is formed and the government does not retain full control of the new institution. Through this mechanism, a previously governmental function is transferred to a new entity.

The government is actively involved in all phases of the transfer; however, the new nonprofit entity is overseen by its targeted citizen/customer group rather than by the government. The oversight group provides initial start-up capital and shares representation with the government on the governing board of the new entity. Once established, the government and the newly formed entity enter into a contract to provide the required services.

Unlike the British and New Zealand models, in this approach governmental assets are not sold to the entity. Rather, a transfer of asset ownership and performance obligation from the government to a responsible citizen/customer group is the goal.

Transfer rationale. If the governmental function has been accounted for as a proprietary or enterprise fund and supported primarily by user fees – rather than tax revenues – that specific operation might have been viewed as self-sufficient. However, regular subsidies and hidden overhead for supposedly self-sustaining programs can become burdensome to the government.

During times of shrinking budgets and dwindling resources, concern over hidden costs can often prompt the spin-off of these functions to a separate entity. This allows a more accountable cost allocation and recovery – so that actual users of specific services pay the full costs of those services. More resources can then be made available for functions benefiting the general citizenry. On the other hand, a spin-off may allow the new organization to avoid the absorption of unnecessary overhead allocation and be more responsive to personnel and facility upgrade needs without bureaucratic constraints.

There can be a perception that no real change has occurred if the current staff is maintained and the same task performed by the new entity. It also may be difficult for the various parties to distinguish the legal differences between the previous governmental entity and the new nonprofit operator. This may lead to the view, held by some, that to require the new entity to purchase the governmental assets will cause possible double charging of the customers. The government's perspective, however, will probably be that the transferred assets were originally acquired with governmental resources and, therefore, are governmental assets.

Federal, state or county laws generally may not allow governmental assets to be given away. As a consequence, a transition mechanism may be needed to facilitate the transition of a governmental function to the user group.

A transition mechanism. One transfer mechanism that can be used is cost-plus billing. Government personnels who are to become employees of the new entity, perhaps because of their expertize, are hired by the new entity at the beginning of the contract period. This enables the new entity to competently perform the necessary services. The government's assets are utilized by the nonprofit entity to perform those services. The nonprofit entity bills the government for the contracted services on a cost-plus basis.

The cost-plus or the "mark-up" on the services is designed to exhaust the possibility of actual cash settlements on the government's side, thus eventually requiring that the government pay for the contracted services by signing over title to the net fixed assets. The agreed-upon fair market value of the net fixed assets is used as the exchange basis.

The process of transferring assets to the new entity can be timed rather closely with this procedure. If the privatization is to take three months, the new entity bills of the government in sufficient amounts to completely exhaust the privatizing entity's net assets after three months. Some adjustments in the cost-plus ratio in the final period may be needed to completely transfer the assets.

The "plus" in the cost-plus ratio may need to be quite large to accomplish the asset transfer within a relatively short-time period. This may endanger the nonprofit status of the new entity and be a cause of concern for uninformed parties. Therefore, tax experts and involved groups should be regularly consulted when this approach is utilized.

Advantages. This method can be less costly than the British approach, but more expensive than contracting out, at least in the short-run. Because there is no need to deal with underwriters or stockholders, the actual cash-related costs under this approach usually are considerably smaller.

This may be the approach of choice when the government is discontinuing a service that a group of citizen/customers desires to continue. This method may also be appropriate when a sale of assets is desired and there are no willing or acceptable buyers available. When a governmental service has evolved to have its primary customers from other governmental entities, perhaps even crossing state lines, this also may be the appropriate choice. If the government wants the service to be performed by a nonprofit entity, this may be the best method to use.

Disadvantages. This type of privatization most likely will not be consummated as an arm's length transaction and therefore may require special legislative efforts. Further, since the government usually will not realize a profit with such a transfer of assets, this would not be an appropriate approach if capital generation is the goal.

Example. A Western state governmental agency providing statewide network database services to other public entities was recently privatized with this approach. The database, which utilized specially designed software, was established with government seed money. Its customers are billed monthly for the use, maintenance, and update of the services.

Under the operation of the state agency, the subscriber base grew, and total revenues peaked and stayed at around $5 million for several years. Then the agency started to decline, mainly because the software and technology – which were state-of-the-art at the agency's inception – were becoming outdated.

Out-of-state subscribers attributed the lack of development to the bureaucratic budgeting and management processes of the founding state. Fearing technological decline, these customers were willing to incur the costs of switching to a private enterprise competitor if control remained with the single government. Losing the out-of-state subscribers – who had increased to the point that they contributed the majority of the revenue – would mean the death of the agency and the end of services.

Because of the high quality of the database, it was in everyone's interest to keep the agency alive. The founding state had an additional incentive: switching its instate departments to a competitor would mean excessive hook-up and communication costs, as all alternative providers were outside the state. Consequently, the privatization decision was reached and the transition took place.

The first-year operation of this newly formed nonprofit organization, which has just ended, includes a savings of $600,000 in staff costs and state service cost allocations – a 12 percent savings compared to the previous year. The reduced budget level, approximately $4.4 million, is expected to be maintained for several years until a stable, self-sufficient operation of the new entity is assured.

CONCLUSIONS

Privatization is a viable option when the government is seeking methods to reduce public expenditures, increase efficiency or enhance services. As privatization activity increases among state and local government entities in the U.S., more and more finance officers and accountants will become involved in the planning and implementation stages of the process. To aid in approaching these tasks, this paper summarizes the pros and cons of three proven approaches to privatization and an emerging hybrid type now seen in the United States.

Privatization is not a panacea for governmental woes: some governmental services are usually excluded – those of the "public goods" nature, such as police protection. Proprietary activities, on the other hand, where a clear customer–vendor relationship can be identified, tend to be more feasible candidates for privatization.

When considering privatizing a governmental function, the government needs clearly specified objectives in order to ascertain whether such a transformation will produce the desired results. The cost-effectiveness of the chosen method of privatization is an important consideration. To ensure ultimate success, a privatization approach must be carefully weighed and carefully implemented, with attention given to applicable laws, the financial condition of the government, and the needs of the citizens.

NOTES

1. Mayer, C. P. and Meadowcroft, S. A. "Selling Public Assets: Techniques and Financial Implication," *Fiscal Studies,* Vol. 6, No. 4, 1985, pp. 42–56.

2. *ibid.*

3. *ibid.*

4. *Pension & Investments,* January 7, 1991, p. 19.

5. *Houston Chronicle,* October 24, 1991, p. 3E.

6. Clark Margaret and Sinclair, Elizabeth (Eds), *Purpose Performance and Profit: Redefining the Public Sector,* Studies in Public Administration No. 32, Wellington: Government Printing Office, 1986.

7. Bowman, R. J. and Buchanan, J. "Corporatization and Asset Valuation for a Government Corporation," *Financial Accountability & Management,* Vol. 6, No. 2, 1990, pp. 79–81.

8. Goodrich, Jonathan, "Privatization in America," *Business Horizons,* January–February 1988, pp. 11–17.

9. Lierbag, Bill, "Privatizing America," *Journal of Accountancy,* April 1988, pp. 48–51.

10. Goodrich, Jonathan, "Privatization of America."

11. Apogee Research, Inc., *State Government Privatization* 1992 (Maryland: *Apogee Research,* Inc.), 1992, p. 13.

12. *Wall Street Journal,* "Privatization Lets Small Firms Manage Everything from Libraries to Golf Courses," April 2, 1991, pp. 81–82.

PART IV

NEW PUBLIC MANAGEMENT AND REFORMS

Eric E. Otenyo and Nancy S. Lind

Reforms in public organizations have been a key feature of public administration. We cannot trace a specific date for reform movements in any part
of the world. In the USA, although 1883 was a landmark year in the transformation from patronage to merit personnel administration systems, the
passage of the enabling Pendleton Act was not the seminal reform action.
Reforms had already been initiated at several micro levels. Although not
usually described, public managers have always sought to improve on how
public services are delivered. Reforms range from mundane revisions in
administrative procedures to large-scale transformations of critical and
strategic operational tasks. Most reforms reflect fundamental tensions in the
political ecology in which public administration occurs. To put it mildly,
governments institute reforms to "obtain or broaden their legitimacy,"
"improve administrative performance, become more responsive to their citizens," and for the Third World, satisfy donor conditionality (Braibanti,
1966, p. 137; Farazmand, 1994, p. 76). Reforms come in different forms and
labels including rightsizing, downsizing, reengineering, performance management, and reinvention. These are some of the code words used around
the world.

Globally, efforts at improving administrative processes and enhancing
competency are at every level of public bureaucracies (Hood & Lodge,
2004). Perhaps, leading public administration scholars Donald Kettl and

Comparative Public Administration: The Essential Readings
Research in Public Policy Analysis and Management, Volume 15, 501–514
Copyright © 2006 by Elsevier Ltd.
ISSN: 0732-1317/doi:10.1016/S0732-1317(06)15052-6

James Fesler captured this phenomenon best by asserting that "administrative reform is a fixture of government everywhere – indeed, it may well
be the feature that governments share more than any other" (Kettl & Fesler,
2005, p. 100). Even though the reform impulse is universal, motivations are
specific to each country or administrative unit. In the developing world,
pressure for reform is occasioned by the desire for public service managers
and their political leaders to correct problems brought about by old bureaucratic orthodoxy, maladministration, and dysfunctional systems. Indeed,
maladministration and bureaupathology have for decades been part
and parcel of several administrative systems. As Caiden states, "as long as
government is run by human beings and human beings are imperfect, then
mistakes are bound to occur," and these mistakes call for reforms (improvements) (Caiden, 1994, p. 109). For example, in the last decade, Mohan
Kaul (1996) of India edited an entire volume titled "Civil Service Reforms:
Learning from Commonwealth Experiences," Public Administration and
Development, Vol. 16, February 1996.[1] Similarly, numerous World Bank
Annual Development Reports address the constant need for administrative
reforms, especially combating bureaucratic corruption (World Bank, 2002).
However, the vitality of reforms is best described in Caiden's contribution
reproduced here. Bureaupathologies were not the only triggering factors
providing an impetus for reforms. There were significant forces as well.

Notably, reforms were also a consequence of changing global economic
order. Specifically, former socialist economic systems sought to tailor both
their economic and administrative systems to suit the emerging market
driven global dispensation. As Guy Peters observes, "market based reforms
began with the basic steps of privatization and economic liberalization."
(Peters, 2001, p. 169) One common thread in the reform movement was the
need to cut down the size of government and revamp bureaucracies all over
the world. Essentially these forms entailed "rolling back the state." An
important finding in Caiden's work is that "panaceas for government ills"
were not to be found in copying foreign administrative practices (Caiden,
1988, p. 351; see also Peters, 2001, p. 169). This echoes the sentiments of
previous comparative administration scholars considered in Part 1 of this
book who emphasized pragmatic experimental approaches. Perhaps Part
Four is one of the remarkable features of this book because it is most recent.
Recency might mean some of the articles selected have yet to make a full
impact on the disciplines' development. Yet we must begin to assess the
literature with a keen eye to recognize significant contributions. Divided
into three distinct mutually exclusive sections, we capture current reforms in
international administration. The first section deals with the emergence of

New Public Management (NPM) as a global administrative enterprise. The second section concerns the growing expansion of e-government in public administration. Granted the literature in this area is still unfocused and theoretical, but tentative threads can be discerned. In large measure, the benefits of information technology have spread to all corners of the world. However, how this ensuing environment impacts administrative practices is the focus of our attention.

Furthermore, new technologies have changed the way public administration is conducted and comparative administrators have begun to present empirical studies on differences and similarities between nations. The third section of this part is a statement on the contemporary ecology of public administration. Though different countries are at different stages of globalization, all administrative systems have reacted to these changing environments. The literature selected concerns these adaptations.

Against the aforementioned, let us briefly recapitulate these scholarly contributions. We must begin by observing that NPM is an administrative approach in which there are attempts to slow down government growth, shift services toward privatization, enhance automation – especially information and communication technologies (ICT) or simply information technologies (ITs) in service provision, and development of a more international and globally oriented public workforce (Hood, 1991; Gray & Jenkins, 1995; Lynn, 2002). Savas (2005) called it "the latest manifestation of the never ending process of government reform." (p. 4) Savas and other leading American scholars emphasized NPM's goal to place citizens or customers at the core of public service delivery systems (Savas, 2005; Rosenbloom & Kravchuk, 2005, p. 21; Osborne & Gaebler, 1992; Page, 2005). Perhaps there is some consensus that Hood's work on the practice of NPM was first among equals; however, Gray and Jenkins' work included here captures the intellectual essence of the movement. NPM also sought to deregulate government and empower employees to use creativity in serving customers. In this regard, NPM sought to promote decentralized control through inculcating competition in service delivery as well as accountability for results. Overall, its advocates, much like the reinvention of government pundits, sought to get government activities done better.

Although its origins were in Great Britain, New Zealand, Australia, and many OECD countries where reformers sought to split policy oversight of public services work into smaller manageable bureaus, NPM found worldwide appeal and was vigorously embraced in Africa, Asia, Transitional European countries, and Latin America in the 1990s. One must, however, recognize that for several developing areas, NPM is only one of the many reform currents and is more rhetorical than substantive (Polidano, 1999). No question therefore, the results of NPM are mixed.

The results of NPM reforms have been extensively discussed in the wider literature (Lynn, 2001; James & Manning, 1996; Deleon, 1998; Maesschalck, 2004; Peters, 1996; Polidano, 1999; Jones & Kettl, 2003). Lynn's work, reproduced in this volume, for example, contends that there is no agreed-upon body of facts concerning the nature, extent, and consequences of the changes brought about by NPM. He adds that the entire movement does not constitute a new paradigm (Lynn, 2002). The claim of a paradigm shift abounds in the wider literature, for example, Kevin Yuk -fai Au, Illan Vertinsky, and Denis Yu-long Wang (2001) consider the NPM reform in-itiatives to have transferred social legitimacy among stakeholders in several Asian countries. For them, shifts have occurred from reengineering admini-strative systems from the earlier colonially derived systems to new formu-lations dictated by market imperatives. A third view presented by Jones and Kettl (2003) is that it is "simply too early to tell whether NPM is or is not a new "paradigm," in the Kuhnian sense." In brief, undoubtedly, NPM has left an indelible mark all over the world. Measured against its self-proclaimed objectives, NPM fared poorly in developing areas where bureau-cratic systems still resemble much of the forms described in the early comparative administration literature. Polidano contends that successful implementation of NPM reforms is dependent on contingency factors. In developing countries, factors such as corruption and low administrative capacity continue to frustrate reform efforts (1999). Although there have been some successful reforms, these remain in a limited number of sectors such as in Health and Human Services (Polidano, 1999; Batley, 1999). Be-cause some of the actual reports on individual lessons from the two decades of NPM reforms are written in languages other than English, perhaps the best attempt at synthesizing and reviewing specific transformations is in Jones and Kettl (2003) reproduced in this volume. The two suggest a series of propositions including the following:

Public management reform is not complete as no reform can ever solve the problems that led to its creation.

NPM is truly something new and there is a convergence of reforms around general themes. Political reality rather than managerial concerns drives reforms. However, the political clout is negligible.

While NPM reforms problems are different in developed as well as deve-loping countries, the central question of the role of national government continues to occupy the minds of the reformers.

Assessments of lessons learned from NPM must include administrative and policy management changes spurred by the spread of ITs. In areas of automation and increased usage of ITs, NPM-driven reforms also achieved limited sectoral success (Castaneda, 1997). However, failure rates were higher in parts of Asia, Africa, and Eastern Europe (Allen, 1999; Manning, Mukherjee, & Gokcekus, 2000; Nickel, 1998). We shall return to this topic shortly.

In the important area of deregulation, Peters notes that transitional and poor developing areas required more regulation than NPM stated. This is because more rules were required to create conditions for institution building including elimination of nepotism and misuse of public office (Peters, 2001, p. 176). Clearly, the difference between regulatory environments varies across nation states. A country such as the U.S. might be concerned with limiting access to certain goods available to the public generally, such as what is morally correct to be aired in the broadcast media, or issues of consumer and workplace safety. In other cultures, priorities are different. For example, several developing countries might not even have the resources to police regulatory rules prohibiting smoking in public areas, let alone consider workplace safety standards. Significantly, a country with a large economic base such as China does not fare well in instituting regulatory reforms. Under certain conditions, regulation challenges state power and might not be conceptualized in a universalistic sense as is implied by some in the NPM logic.

Closely linked to reform trends and the need for better government is the management of public finance. Globally, budgeting, as an administrative practice, seeks to curtail government expenditures and was viewed by reformers as an aspect of good government (Schick, 1987, pp. 2–3). Budgeting reforms in the developing areas are an integral part of the reform movement, in part because NPM is premised on the notion of reducing the size of government. As the main provider of employment in several poor countries, the administrative state has been forced to review its budgetary procedures to conform with new initiatives emphasizing deregulation and privatization. Partly an effort in response to donor pressures, reformers endorsed systems that promote accountability and transparency in financial transactions. In her analysis printed in this volume, for instance, Naomi Caiden (2006) appraises the importance of budgetary reforms in administrative processes in developing countries.[2]

Finally, Donald Savoie's attempt to answer the question "What is wrong with the New Public Management?" goes further than other detractors of the NPM movement to claim that it is different from traditional public administration (Savoie, 1995, p. 113). We include his contestation in this section to demonstrate the discomfort caused by the movement, especially its conversion of citizens into "clients" and emphasis on doing and not policy thinking. Savoie notes, "there is a world of difference between citizens and clients." He adds, clients are sovereign, but citizens have common purposes and hold politicians accountable – the NPM movement would therefore require we fix our political institutions to suit this changed ecology of administration (Savoie, 1995, pp. 115–116).

ITS AND PUBLIC ADMINISTRATION

Perhaps the increased use of technologies is the hallmark of the new global managerial dispensation. Worldwide, the tendency to use especially information technologies is legend. By far the most widespread use of ITs has been for governments to post information about themselves on the internet. Literally all governments have web sites with information about government structures, foreign embassies, and tourism and investment opportunities.

New forms of IT's include two-way capabilities whereby governments communicate with citizens and business partners via the internet. For example, it is not unusual for governments to advertise positions and bids for contracts online. Still, governments – mostly in the advanced countries now allow citizens to conduct business through the internet. Among the most popular services provided online are renewal of licenses, paying fines, checking the status of applications, and enrollment into state sponsored education centers. The use of ITs is not limited to these functions – additional services include filing tax returns and viewing personal data. The potential use of these technologies has grown tremendously with some state and national governments "building" single portals in which a "customer" can be led to a host of different government sites.

Regarding applicability of ITs, we know that the "e-fever"[3] is basically a function of how rich a country is, and it will continue to be the trend of the future, even in countries where the overwhelming majority is offline. We also know that this subject was explored as early as 1986. Then, Danziger contended that automation was attractive because it enhanced efficiency and reduced the number of staff working in some public service areas including record keeping, printing, and calculations-electronic data processing (Danziger, 1986, p. 219). ITs were also touted to improve decision-making capabilities in various public service organizations. Anderson (1999) articulates the connections between the proliferation of ITs and the enabling reform ethic.

Beyond the ensuing technological environment, Bellamy and Taylor (1994) explore the possibilities of ITs in public administration in the contexts of differing value systems. They make it clear that new ICTs have created new relationships among participants in any given polity. More specifically, they argue that as governments adopt new technologies, new governance systems emerge in which the relationships between different levels of government, customers, suppliers, and politicians have been irreversibly altered. This has important implications for academic public administration communities all over the world. They must now understand the relationships of these stakeholders in the larger polity.

As we begin to think about the impact of technologies applied to public administration, the political implications of these changes come next. According to Donk and Tops, the proliferation of ITs changed our understanding of representation in democratic governance (Donk & Tops, 1992). Since there is more awareness of public policy over the internet, informatization expanded democratic frontiers. While e-governments have transformed public bureaucracies world-wide, they also raise profound questions about control and democracy. It is quite obvious that keys to computer applications are not in the hands of the citizenry. These are issues that must be addressed if the full extent of their usage is to be well managed and understood. Bidhya Bowornwathana (2003) and Donk and Tops (1992) help us return to the issues we raised in the first part of this book, the ecology of public administration.

Democracy is a component of the political environment in which public administration occurs. Advancements in technology are also an unfolding ecological issue. The 21st century will see more technological advances and the expansion of a new democratic governance paradigm. Bowornwathana (2003) reviews the ensuing contemporary pressures. Newer forms of ITs now mean we require new assumptions and new sets of strategies to conduct political recruitment, articulation, and aggregation. Students of public administration always know that these processes inevitably challenge bureaucratic forms and forms of power. Donk and Tops present research that affirms that informatization is at once an opportunity and threat to democratic administration. The task, therefore, is for public administrators to continue to study the applications of the new forms of technology in a comparative perspective and to draw out lessons on ideas that work and those that do not.

If ITs have contributed to changes in the way public administration is conducted, we also must learn about other dimensions of an increasingly globalizing world. To summarize, there is a correlation between ITs and

global connectivity. ITs more than travel and trade have made it possible
to share information and create a truly global world. "Managing Public
Bureaucracies under a Globalizing Environment," is the subtitle of the final
section of this collection. In this set of literature, we will consider the more
recent works, especially those that are concerned with the changing global
political environment.

THE INTERNATIONAL NEO-LIBERAL CAPITALISM AND DEMOCRATIZATION CONTEXT

If most of the literature churned out at the peak of the development administration movement was ideologically linked to promoting capitalism in
opposition to socialism, the new reform literature is situated in a public
choice neo-liberal paradigm. The triumph of global capitalism strengthened
the impetus toward more market centered administrative enterprises. Trends
in reform must be situated in the context of the enabling international political environments. If contemporary international settings necessitate new
public administrative orientations, then they must be carefully studied.

The selected sets of articles present a sample of the emergent nexus between globalization and international public administration. While the
1980s was a decade of decentralization, the 1990s of privatization and
deregulation, the first decade in the new millennium appears to be an age of
increased internationalization of administrative machineries. With an ongoing "global war against terrorism," and increased international cooperation in matters such as immigration crises,[4] and relief support for victims of
disasters such as the Tsunami in Asia (November 2004) and Hurricane
Katrina in Louisiana, Mississippi, and Alabama (September 2005), the role
of state actors seems to have halted the stride toward absolute marketism.
Besides, globalization through greater state cooperation in regional bodies
such as the European Union (EU)[5] and the North American Free Trade
Area (NAFTA) demand that responses be based on a solid understanding of
administrative processes from a comparative point of view.

Globally, we are in the midst of fundamental rethinking about the scope
of government activity. Much of the discussion centers on the role of local,
state, and national governments in meeting challenges that are local but
have international dimensions or those that are international but have local
implications. The section examines these dimensions beginning with
Ali Farazmand's critical essay (1994), Caiden's (2004) presentation of the

trends and challenges brought about by globalization, and Fred Rigg's (2000) intellectual articulation of the problematic for the new century and millennium. While Riggs acknowledges that global connectivity has grown with the internet, he has issues with aspects of isolationism within the administrative fabric of the U.S., the world's richest nation. Riggs derides the lack of seriousness on the part of the American Congress and other governance structures to pay attention to issues that affect the universe that have direct implications on public administration such as floods of refugees, environmental challenges, and regional wars and conflicts.

Farazmand predicts an increase in the visibility of a "global bureaucracy" that include departments such as U.S. Department of State, Homeland Security, World Bank, USAID, UN Organizations, Universities and Colleges among other organizations tied in a global communication web (Farazmand, 1994, p. 78). Besides, he predicts the consequences of the emerging world order to include the emergence of a "global public administration model" which would inevitably trigger a variety of reforms. Caiden's contention is that increasing global interdependence has dissolved jurisdictional boundaries and weakened the capacity of traditional self-governance structures. Accordingly, public administrators globally must pay attention to the external dynamics of the new administrative ecology.[6] The connection between state structures, globalization, and democracy is then well developed in Fred Riggs' conclusions written for this volume (2006).

If the changes outlined have implications for administrative reform in the poor countries, then they must be understood. The literature is replete with elaborate exposes on these dynamics. From a practical standpoint, the administrative environments in these countries must continue to adapt to changes described (Werlin, 2003). Moreover, when changes are regional, substantial structural reforms become necessary. In many areas, changes are transnational and involve wider federal and constitutional questions. Significantly, Walter Kickert and Stillman (1996) and his collaborators provide an example of how regional bodies transform administrative processes and are therefore an important aspect of the changing ecology of international administration. Further, the literature does not ignore those dimensions of international cooperation that speak to managing for developmental purposes. The selected article, written by Derrick and Jennifer Brinkerhoff (1999) provides this nuanced perspective. In the end, the quality of reforms depends on a government's broad resourcefulness and quite profoundly inclinations toward democratic and accountability of bureaucratic systems. Reforms all over the world that sacrifice those core governance values limit the possibility of attaining the very goals they intended to solve.

The restating of public administrative reforms as a matter of improved governance is reiterated in Nicholas Henry's remarkable exposition of the concept of "good government" written for this volume. He discusses the resurgence of the term and its significance as an encompassing frame of reference in improving administrative processes and procedures universally. He argues that, although "good government" is a discarded phrase in the U.S. (and, to some degree, a discarded concept), the values that it represents have never been more salient in the developing world. Those values are democracy, honesty, and competency. Globally, a large array of prescriptive scholarship on bureaucratic reforms is indeed premised on promoting those important values and must continue to be part of our discourse, now and in the near future.

Finally, the return of cross-cultural public administration to the mainstream literature as articulated by Jreisat (2006), in the preface to this volume is best reinforced in Fred Rigg's concluding chapter (2006), also written exclusively for this volume.[7] Prior abandonment of cultural and comparative administrative factors from mainstream public administration is no longer acceptable. As Riggs' observes, the renaissance of comparative administration has arrived because it must face challenges brought about by an emerging world system. He observes correctly that globalization and the reduced role of the state as an actor in international affairs offers new opportunities for comparative studies. Since the state is no longer the unit of analysis, scholars must rethink their research tools. No doubt, recent catastrophic events such as war on terrorism, Tsunami in Asia, hurricane Katrina in Louisiana and Mississippi, earthquake in Pakistan provided scholars opportunities to examine international public administrative systems in a globalizing world. Riggs also describes the role of the internet – especially blogs in providing comparative administration new avenues for discussing administrative issues. Arguably, he offers what might be considered the agenda for the future of comparative administration. Riggs' optimistic outlook is reflected elsewhere. As testimony for future studies, articles of a comparative nature are increasingly occupying front positions in reputable public administration and management journals. Significantly, the proliferation of online journals has increased outlets for scholars in this field. Perhaps the more we overcome American and European ethnocentrism, the better the prospects for mainstreaming comparative administration.

NOTES

1. The reform movement is well documented and represented in a vast array of literature. See for example: Guy Peters (2001), Kettl (2000), Lindenberg and Bryant (2001), and Rondinelli and Cheema (2003).

2. Although Caiden's article was written for this volume, she builds on her previous classical work on budgeting in the developing countries. See, Caiden (1994, 1996).

3. Term borrowed from Elder (2000).

4. See, Adolino and Blake (2001).

5. See, for example, Peters (2002), Pollit and Bouckaert (2000), Kassim (2003), and Palombara (1976).

6. See also, Luke and Caiden (1992).

7. Riggs (2006) and Jreisat (2006).

REFERENCES

Adolino, J. R., Blake, C. H. (2001). *Comparing public policies issues and choices in six industrialized countries* (pp. 99–143). Washington, DC: Congressional Quarterly Press.

Allen, R. (1999). New public management: Pitfalls for Central and Eastern Europe. *Public Management Forum, 1*(1).

Anderson, K. V. (1999). Reengineering public sector organizations using information technology. In: R. Heeks (Ed.), *Reinventing government in the information age international practice in IT-enabled public sector reform* (pp. 312–330). New York: Routledge.

Batley, R. (1999). *The role of government in adjusting economies: An overview of findings.* Birmingham, AL: International Development Department, University of Birmingham.

Bellamy, C., & Taylor, J. A. (1994). Introduction, exploiting IT in public administration: Towards the information polity. *Public Administration, 72*(1), 1–12.

Braibanti, R. (1966). Transnational inducement of administration reform: A survey of scope of issues. In: J. D. Montgomery & W. J. Siffin (Eds), *Approaches to development politics, administration and change* (pp. 133–185). New York: McGraw-Hill.

Brinkerhoff, D. (1999). International development management in a globalized world. *Public Administration Review, 59*(4), 473–506.

Caiden, G. E. (1988). The vitality of administrative reform. *International Review of Administrative Sciences, 54*(3), 331–357.

Caiden, G. E. (1994). Administrative reform. In: R. Baker (Ed.), *Comparative public management putting U.S. public policy and implementation in context* (pp. 107–117). Westport, CT: Praeger.

Caiden, G. E. (2004). *The administrative state in a globalizing world: Some trends and challenges.* New York: ECOSOC, United Nations Organization.

Caiden, N. (1994). The management of public budgeting. In: R. Baker (Ed.), *Comparative public management* (pp. 135–152). Westport, CT: Praeger.

Caiden, N. (1996). From here to there and beyond: Concepts and applications of public budgeting in developing countries. In: N. Caiden (Ed.), *Public budgeting and financial administration in developing countries* (pp. 3–17). Greenwich, CT: JAI Press.

Caiden, N. (2006). *Budget issues in developing countries.* Unpublished paper.

Danziger, J. N. (1986). Computers, local governments, and the litany to EDP. In: F. S. Lane (Ed.), *Current issues in public administration* (3rd ed., pp. 215–227). New York: St. Martin's Press.

Deleon, L. (1998). Accountability in a reinvented government. *Public Administration: An International Quarterly, 76*(3), 539–558.

Donk, W. B. H. J. Van de., & Tops, P. W. (1992). Informatization and democracy: Orwell in Athens, a review of the literature. *Informatization and the Public Sector, 2,* 169–196.

Elder, R. Jr. (2000). State agencies see going online as alternative to waiting in line. *Wall Street Journal,* January 5, pp. T1, T3.

Farazmand, A. (1994). The new world order and global public administration: A critical essay. In: J. C. Garcia-Zamor & R. Khator (Eds), *Public administration in the global village* (pp. 61–82). Westport, CT: Praeger.

Gray, A., & Jenkins, B. (1995). From public administration to public management: Reassessing a revolution. *Public Administration, 73*(1), 75–99.

Hood, C. (1991). A public management for all seasons? The rise of new public management (NPM). *Public Administration, 69*(1), 3–19.

Hood, C., & Lodge, M. (2004). Competency, bureaucracy, and public management reform: A comparative analysis. *Governance An International Journal of Policy Administration and Institutions, 17*(3), 313–333.

James, O., & Manning, N. (1996). Public management reform: A global perspective. *Politics, 16*(3), 143–149.

Jones, L. R., & Kettl, D. F. (2003). Assessing public management reform in an international context. *International Public Management Review, 4*(1). Electronic Journal available at < http://www.ipmr.net >

Jreisat, J. (2006). The field of comparative administration through the years, Papers written exclusively for this volume. Riggs work available at: http://webdata.soc.hawaii.edu/fredr/conclusion.opening.htm

Kassim, H. (2003). The European administration: Between Europeanalization and domestication. In: J. Hayward & A. Menon (Eds), *Governing Europe.* Oxford University Press.

Kaul, M. (1996). Civil service reforms: Learning from commonwealth experiences. In: M. Kaul (Ed.), *Public administration and development* (Vol. 16, Issue 2, pp. 131–150).

Kettl, D. (2000). *The global public management revolution: A report on the transformation of governance.* Washington, DC: Brookings.

Kettl, D. F., & Fesler, J. W. (2005). *The politics of the administrative process.* Washington, DC: Congressional Quarterly Press.

Kickert, W. J. M., & Stillman, R. J. (1996). Introduction: Changing European states: Changing public administration. *Public Administration Review, 56*(1), 65–68.

Lindenberg, M., & Bryant, C (2001). *Going global: Transforming relief and development NGOS.* Bloomfield, CT: Kumarian.

Luke, J. S., & Caiden, G. A. (1992). Coping with global interdependence. In: F. S. Lane (Ed.), *Current issues in public administration* (6th ed., pp. 376–385). New York: St. Martin's.

Lynn, L., Jr. (2001). Big questions for public administration the myth of the bureaucratic paradigm: What traditional public administration really stood for. *Public Administration Review, 61*(2), 144–160.

Lynn, L. Jr. (2002). The new public management as an international phenomenon: A skeptical view. *Presentation at the conference on the new public management in international perspective.* St. Gallen, Switzerland, 11–13 July.

Maesschalck, J. (2004). The impact of new public management reforms on public servants ethics: Toward a theory. *Public Administration: An International Quarterly, 82*(2), 465–489.

Manning, N., Mukherjee, R., & Gokcekus, O. (2000). *Public officials and their institutional environment: An analytical model for assessing the impact of institutional change on public sector performance.* Policy Research Working Paper No. 2427. Washington, DC: World Bank.

Nickel, J. L. (1998). *Institutional reform of public research organizations: autonomy, legal status and governance.* Working paper prepared for Rural Week, World Bank, Washington, DC, March.

Osborne, D., & Gaebler, T. (1992). *Reinventing government.* Reading, MA: Addison-Wesley.

Page, S. (2005). What's new about the new public management? Administrative change in the human services. *Public Administration Review, 65*(6), 713–727.

Palombara, J. L. (1976). An overview of bureaucracy and political development. In: G. Joseph & L. Palombara (Eds), *Bureaucracy and political development* (2nd ed., pp. 1–33). Princeton: Princeton University Press.

Peters, G. (1996). *The future of governing: Four emerging models.* Lawrence, KS: University of Kansas Press.

Peters, G. (2001). *The future of overning.* Lawrence: University Press of Kansas.

Peters, G. (2002). *Government and politics of the European Union.* Durham, NC: Duke University Press.

Polidano, C. (1999). *The new public management in developing countries.* Institute for Development Policy and Management. IDPM Public Policy and Management Working Paper no. 31, Manchester: University of Manchester. Available <http://unpan1.un.org/intradoc/groups/public/documents/APCITY/UNPAN014322.pdf>

Pollit, C., & Bouckaert, G. (2000). *Public management reforms: A comparative analysis.* Oxford: Clarendon Press.

Riggs, F. (2000). *Global perspective on comparative and international administration.* Unpublished. Available at <http://www.webdata.soc.hawaii.edu/Fredr/>

Riggs, F. (2006). Conclusion: Impact of the study and practice of public administration. In: E. E. Otenyo & N. S. Lind.

Rondinelli, D. A., & Cheema, S. (Eds) (2003). *Reinventing government for the twenty first century: State capacity in a globalizing society.* Bloomfield, CT: Kumarian Press.

Rosenbloom, D. H., & Kravchuk, R. S. (2005). *Public administration understanding management, politics, and law in the public sector.* Boston: McGraw-Hill.

Savas, E. (2005). *Privatization in the city success, failures, lessons.* Washington, DC: Congressional Quarterly Press.

Savoie, D. J. (1995). What is wrong with the new public management. *Canadian Public Administration, 38*(1), 112–121.

Schick, A. (1987). Budgeting as an administrative process. In: A. Schick (Ed.), *Perspectives on budgeting* (2nd ed). Washington, DC: ASPA.

Werlin, H. H. (2003). Poor nations, rich nations: A theory of governance. *Public Administration Review, 63*(3), 329–342.

World Bank. (2002). *World development report, 2001.* Washington, DC: World Bank.

Yuk-fai Au, K., Vertinsky, I., & Yu-long Wang, D. (2001). New public management in Hong Kong: The long march toward reform. In: L. R. Jones, J. Guthrie & P. Steane (Eds), *Learning from international public management reform* (Vol. 11B, pp. 311–336). Oxford: JAI – Elsevier Science.

FURTHER READING

Bowornwathana, B. (1997). Transforming bureaucracies for the 21st century: The new democratic governance paradigm. *Public Administration Quarterly*, *21*(21), 294–308.

Dunleavy, P., & Hood, C. (1994). From old public administration to new public management. *Public Money and Management*, *14*(3), 9–16.

Hood, C., & Peters, G. (2004). The middle aging of new public management: Into the age of paradox? *Journal of Public Administration Research and Theory*, *14*(3), 267–282.

Minogue, M. (1998). Changing the state: Concepts and practice in the reform of the public sector. In: C. Polidano, M. Minogue & D. Hulme (Eds), *Beyond the new public management: Changing ideas and practices in governance*. Cheltenham, UK: Edward Elgar.

Mukherjee, R., & Wilkins, J. K. (1999). Unbundling bureaucracy through agency creation. Adjudicated paper presented at the IPAC national conference, August 30, New Brunswick, Canada.

Peters, G. (1998). Governance without government: Rethinking public administration. *Journal of Public Administration Research and Theory*, *8*(2), 223–243.

Peters, G., & Savoie, D. (1994). Civil service reform: Misdiagnosing the patient. *Public Administration Review*, *54*(5), 418–426.

Redding, C. (1994). Comparative management theory: Jungle, zoo or fossil bed. *Organization Studies*, *15*(3), 323–359.

Wollmann, H. (2003). Public sector reforms and evaluation. Patterns and trends in an international perspective. In: H. Wollmann (Ed.), *Evaluation in public sector reforms*. Aldershot: Edward Elgar.

THE ADMINISTRATIVE STATE IN A GLOBALIZING WORLD: SOME TRENDS AND CHALLENGES

Gerald Caiden

Possibly as never before in human history has public administration wit- nessed such turbulent times. There have been periods in the past when it has undergone considerable upheavals in scope, reach, impact, organization, technology, and process, but rarely at one and the same time, rarely at so fast and furious a pace, rarely so radical if not revolutionary, and rarely so varied, contradictory and confusing on a global scale. Within living memory, it used to be fairly simple and straightforward to define the administrative state, to delineate the public sector, to differentiate and distinguish public adminis- tration, and to identify the profession of government as consisting of trained and experienced public administrators who devoted their working lives to running governmental organizations. This tradition could be traced back to the Napoleonic concept of the nation-state and the 18th century European study of the cameral sciences and public law, and further back to the grand bureaucratic empires of yesteryear, if not to the very dawn of civilization when people in different parts of the globe first settled down in river valleys, built elaborate public works, invented writing, records and accounting, and separated the private and personal from the public and the communal.

Given the speed and scope of change, public administration cannot re- main the same. It has to adjust and innovate just to keep pace with events or

Comparative Public Administration: The Essential Readings
Research in Public Policy Analysis and Management, Volume 15, 515–542
Copyright © 2006 by Elsevier Ltd.
ISSN: 0732-1317/doi:10.1016/S0732-1317(06)15022-8

else it finds itself falling further and further behind expectations and its performance deemed more and more disappointing. But even when it does reinvent itself, vestiges of every stage of the past still exist or something very similar wherever inertia prevails and public administrators stick to the true and tried rather than risk adopting something new, no matter how promising and attractive. Administrative traditions and administrative cultures seem to endure even amidst transformations in almost every other aspect of everyday life. Administrative habits appear to be difficult to develop and just as difficult to abandon. So there is much continuity in running societies, giving the superficial appearance that things remain unchanged when in fact behind the scenes they are being fundamentally transformed. Such may now be the case with the traditional view of public administration considered as being predominantly an instrument of the (administrative) state, which is currently fast being overtaken by an emerging international public arena that is superseding the sovereign nation-state and the replacement of the concept of government with that of the wider notion of governance.

While the state as such continues to be important, and in many parts of the world government and public administration need to be strengthened to cope with their challenging tasks, state sovereignty is being weakened by the evolution of vast networks of international and global organizations, public and private, which may exceed the power and influence of any state or combination of individual states. These networks play an increasingly important role in the life of peoples all over the planet whether they are aware of this fact or not. They now determine public policies, deliver public goods and services, enforce their own rules and regulations, and employ growing numbers of public administrators, professionals, and employees. All states, big and small, have to acknowledge their subordination to such world authorities, to international treaties and conventions, to embryonic global public policies that attempt to deal with global objectives, issues and challenges, to the counsel of international leaders and public servants, and to the decisions of international regulatory agencies and world courts. All acknowledge the potential and real benefits from such global intervention in the conduct of public affairs and welcome any international assistance not just in improving the quantity and quality of public goods and services worldwide, but also in advancing the major goals of civilization of which governance, government, and public administration are only a part, if not a crucial and indispensable part in improving the human lot minimally in warding off pending global disasters and relieving desperate local situations.

This means that public administration is becoming an instrument of an emerging global community and now shares many of its activities with a host of other instrumentalities in a societal partnership in delivering public goods and services from a global to a very local reach in a very convoluted system of interrelationships. This in turn requires a different style of public service leadership, a different style of public management, and a different approach to human resources development. In turn, this reappraisal of public administration has been compounded by the emergence of new tasks and activities for government, the transformation of many of its traditional functions, and the recent revolution in information technology that alone requires a radical change in work, management, and decision making in all organizations, but especially in traditional style bureaucracies that dominate public administration because of its size, legalism, and inherent public service values.

Domestically, public administration had for some time begun to realize that it could no longer be wedded to its traditional bureaucratic style of operation. Indeed, it had to rethink its whole place in the scheme of things. If it did not, it would fall increasingly out of favor and if it did not change fundamentally it might well be superseded altogether in much of its domain. Basically, the conclusion reached was that it was not desirable that it be the sole source of public goods and services. Not that it ever had been, not even in the most totalitarian of states. True, in certain areas such as the maintenance of armed forces and the manufacture and distribution of weapons of mass destruction, the administrative state should never relinquish its monopoly of public control to preserve public safety and security and avoid their private deployment. Otherwise, there were advantages to multiple suppliers, redundancy, competition, and the availability of alternative suppliers when necessary, even where the administrative state was more economic, efficient, effective, and labor intensive (thereby expanding employment opportunities for the general populace). There seemed no compelling reason why the administrative state had to do everything for itself, why it should discourage other institutions from meeting public needs, why it should continue to provide inferior public goods and services when its clients clearly preferred some other institution to do the same job, and why it should avoid the stimulus and challenge of competition when that was clearly in the public interest.

So the administrative state in some parts of the world, particularly in the more-developed countries, has been abandoning some of its traditional activities and functions where other alternative institutions have been available and superior. In them, it has been privatizing, contracting out, farming out, sharing, engaging in joint ventures, and subsidizing other suppliers in both traditional and new state activities until the whole of government has been or is being transformed into complicated networks of service providers described under the rubric of governance. Less-developed countries have not been able to follow their suit while they still struggle to build up their instrumentalities, government and public administration included, to the point where they finally can join in this transformed organizational society. Even in these countries, so much is happening all at once that in this new world of service delivery within the public sector, new terms, new definitions, new approaches, and new criteria for appraisal are required. Nonetheless, certain challenges stand out as needing immediate attention lest all other efforts fail to realize their potential. Among these for public administrators everywhere, in both more-and less-developed countries , are coping with globalization, restoring the capacity to govern, furthering democratization, adapting to the knowledge society, and attracting talent into public service.

COPING WITH GLOBALIZATION

For centuries, dreamers have looked forward to the day when people would overlook their differences and recognize all as brothers, that under their skin they were very much alike and aspired to much the same future. Then, they would see the advantages of cooperating together, burying their disagreements, and working toward common objectives. Barriers between people would be removed. People and goods would move freely across the globe. Every human being would be accorded the same rights and be treated with the same consideration. And people would lay down their arms and make peace, not war. The world would unite and all human beings would realize that they shared a common fate. In time, the advancement of technology has indeed reduced distance and increased mobility, thereby bringing people closer and closer together and uniting the planet. But the experience of global warfare in increasingly horrifying form has made imperative an end to the madness of continued internecine conflict and a need to create universal bonds. Slowly, in fits and starts, the world's statesmen began to devise a new international order that would better suit humanity until in the last quarter of the 20th century, the world awoke to the fact that the future had at last arrived at thanks to globalization.

Globalization describes a world of increasing international interactions and accelerating international flows, particularly of trade, capital, and information, and of the diffusion of global norms and values and the proliferation of treaties. It incorporates the idea of one world, a united planet, a common future for all humankind, inclusiveness, everybody being in the same boat, everybody deserving the same respect and treatment, everybody working for the same goals, everybody sharing much the same ethical standards, every state trying to be on the same page, embracing universal objectives, eliminating unnecessary barriers, contributing to the common welfare, helping the less fortunate, and generally reducing fear. The spirit of globalization is best seen in the Charter of the United Nations Organization (UNO) and the founding principles of the family of UNO together with those of global business, trade, humanitarian, charitable, religious, cultural, and sporting associations. The administrative state is being put in its place, subordinate to this fast growing international superstructure.

In response to this new global context, the administrative state has to learn to adjust and to realize that it has to assume additional duties and obligations. The first obligation on the administrative state is to actively participate, that is, to join and contribute, not to stand aloof, boycott, contract out, and ignore what is happening in the rest of the world. Global problems and challenges require global solutions and inputs. Almost all global institutions worthy of the term are only too pleased to embrace any active participant and they are all too willing to bend their own rules to encourage meaningful contribution. But more is expected than just showing up. Providing officers and staff when called upon prevents such institutions from being monopolized or dominated by the same people as does willingness to provide space, accommodation, hospitality, and scarce resources.

A second obligation is to provide information when requested. As international institutions are notoriously secretive, insufficiently transparent, and too closed and inaccessible to outside stakeholders, there is little danger as things now stand that confidentiality is likely to be breached. What is more common is that members fail to provide needed information because they just do not have the means to obtain it or knowingly provide inaccurate or false information either for the same reason or because they intend to mislead or deceive. Member administrative states that lack the expertise should request aid and assistance from those who can spare the missing elements. None should feel guilty either for asking for or giving help in providing crucial accurate information to guide more realistic global policies and keener analysis of global predicaments.

A third and perhaps more difficult obligation to fulfill is to follow the spirit as well as the letter of what the international institution intends. This is where the most serious challenges to member sovereignty arise and where globalization is most likely to disappoint. When compliance fails, international institutions are reluctant to impose sanctions because as members well know that sanctions are very difficult to apply and enforce. Often, sanctions do not exist so members ignore international institutions with impunity and expose all to ridicule. Almost every state takes advantage of this lack of discipline when it suits them and when the stronger states set a bad example or when a state believes it will be supported in its defiance unofficially by friendly states. When this occurs, the whole credibility of globalization is undermined and the world citizenry becomes cynical. What it means to the latter is that there may be no redress for anybody, no overriding authority, nothing to stop the unscrupulous, immoral, defiant from exploiting the international system and taking advantage of other members' willingness to comply.

Right now, because this globalization process has taken place so suddenly, so selectively, so experimentally, so inconclusively, every administrative state is feeling its way in this new global environment. Some have adjusted quickly and learned how to manipulate the new system of international and super national relations. Others have not yet realized its possibilities and have failed to take advantage of the new opportunities presented to them to better themselves. In some areas, it has been amazingly successful, almost unnoticed and unheralded, as for example has been the case with postal communications and civil air navigation, where all states cooperate and abide by international authority. In other areas, it has been so far a virtual failure or quite disappointing by anyone's standards, such as in peacekeeping and arms reduction. As might be expected, globalization in technology, scientific research, meteorology, and geology, has been more successful than in its application to human and social sciences. It has proved to be much more successful in economics than in politics. These imbalances are disturbing and present many an administrative state with challenges that it cannot as yet even prepare to meet.

Economic liberalization has greatly benefited international business simply because states which wanted to attract more global business as most of them did (and have) to be more business friendly. New markets were opened up. Tariffs and taxes on business were universally reduced. As a consequence, international multilateral corporations have aggrandized, along with their propensity to monopolize, their capacity to drive out smaller local competitors, their ability to influence regulators, governments, and international agencies, their avidity to richly reward themselves regardless of the social costs, and their inventiveness in exploiting public relations. Business did so well that for several years at the end of the 20th century, it persuaded many world leaders that what prevented its further success was government itself, including all those restrictions placed on it by unimaginative government officials, all those activities monopolized by public enterprises, all those heavy public expenditures caused by low performing, incompetent, unduly protected public organizations, all those taxes that handicapped entrepreneurship and private enterprise, all those outdated bureaucratic procedures (red tape) that handicapped resourceful management, and all that state paternalism favoring the weak at the expense of the strong. The case was simple and the arguments were well rehearsed and so overwhelming that many sympathetic leaders weakened the state, reducing its capacity to perform, releasing public service talent, and relying on business to perform functions and activities in which it (business) was once inexperienced and discriminatory.

In the rush to appear modern and enjoy the benefits of greater global wealth, the lessons of history were overlooked. The transfer of huge public investments to private hands at some times nominal cost constituted public fraud and deception on a large-scale and hid naked self-interest. The intrusion of big international business not only drove out small local businesses but undercut trade union protection of their employees. The conversion of public monopolies to private monopolies rarely benefited their clients with lower prices and better service as promised. The emphasis on materialism changed the social climate for the worse. Legal and regulatory codes were unable to cope with business evasions and exemptions and tax avoidance. Since business seemed so unconcerned, the social and environmental costs of business mounted. The gap between rich and poor widened. The wealth of a few rich outmatched the combined wealth of billions of neglected and powerless poor. Public policy was distorted to favor the already privileged and public laws were altered to exempt them from public obligations and duties. The application of business philosophy to the public sector has damaged cherished principles and values of public administration and made public service less attractive as a vocation.

In brief, economic globalization and the weakening of government and public administration have been accompanied by an upsurge of a variety of harmful activities including an upsurge international organized crime, money laundering, environmental damage, worsening working conditions, and the exploitation of vulnerable folk such as children and women. Even business, despite its success, found itself more vulnerable than it suspected. To do better and do well, it required political and social stability. Investors needed some guarantee of security. Consumers needed some guarantee of product reliability, safety and quality. Good business practices and private property needed legal assurances beyond mere mutual trust and good faith. Even business could not ignore numerous conflicts around the globe, international terrorism (which involved the kidnapping of business people and the destruction of private property), the growing number of refugees and stateless persons, the inability of tens of millions of children and elderly to survive, the tolerated trade in illegal and harmful products, ubiquitous corruption, and the deteriorating situation in the poorest areas of the world, conditions that business had left much to government and public administration. In short, there were more important values and more important objectives for globalization that only government, the administrative state, and the public sector could ensure. The globalization pendulum that had swung so strongly in favor of business had to once again shift back more in favor of the administrative state and to restore the capacity to govern.

RESTORING THE CAPACITY TO GOVERN

Despite the successes of globalization, the world does not seem to be that much better off than it was a quarter of a century ago. Some places are definitely better off but others are much worse and conditions in them are fast deteriorating. There is more wealth in the world but it is still quite unevenly distributed. There are more gadgets and devices that ease the burden of labor but again access to them is highly skewed. There are more medical and health devices but the major killers still persist and if anything have worsened. The cold war has gone but has been replaced by different ideological splits and the spread of fearsome weapons of mass destruction has hardly abated and instead has been joined by global terrorism. Too many of the world's population have little chance to live long lives in reasonable comfort and too few feel that they have any say in their fate. People everywhere express disappointment in their government, complain about its inability to make that much of a difference, and wish for a better quality of life free from age old human fears.

Government performance has not lived up to people's expectations, probably because they have been too high, partly as a result of extravagant promises made by public leaders, promises beyond humankind's capacity to fulfill, partly because people who live mainly for the present have been too impatient, and partly because government has been insufficiently strengthened to keep pace with the demands placed on it. Governments no longer show the same ability to cope as they once did admittedly in less turbulent times when life was so much easier or so it now seem to have been. The gap between promise and performance has widened and widened until it cannot be hidden and no excuses suffice. Public leaders seem to be of lesser caliber, i.e., not up to the task and so many are damaged by a ruthless international mass media that shows little self-discipline in knocking individuals off their perch and exposing all their frailties. They in turn blame insufficient support and bad advice from incompetent public professionals and lackadaisical employees. The general public blame the distance between all these and themselves, with all elites and the all powerful organizations they run being far too remote, unrepresentative, impersonal, manipulative, inward looking, insensitive if not uncaring and selfish.

At the very height of globalization in the 1990s, concern about the apparent decline in the capacity to govern was shown by the Club of Rome, a self-styled "undisputed moral authority of global recognition and the voice of consciousness," which commissioned an investigation of "the root causes of the incapacities of governments to fulfill their responsibilities" and suggest "how governance might be improved and enabled to cope with the global transformations now under way." Its daunting conclusion was that all forms of governance were failing to perform not just government. But shortcomings in government were the most serious as it would remain the dominant form of governance for the foreseeable future although other forms were assuming larger roles. Conventional reforms of government and public administration, while useful for improving traditional activities, were inadequate for handling future building tasks. Only a radical remodeling of governance would do, principally "politics must be revitalized, democracy must be refocused, and governance must be radically redesigned" (Dror, 2001, p. 3), simply because "no overall progress can be discerned in the range of statecraft qualities." In short, the core features of critical decision-making had stayed much the same, including "its persistent serious weaknesses" (p. 4). Unless the capacity to govern was strengthened and government decision-making improved, human society might not be able to avoid catastrophe.

This analysis questioned the very philosophical basis of governance, namely, government for what? It pointed out how contemporary governance had become obsolete, how it could not deal with global predicaments, and how it was obstructed by political culture. Then it jumped to the "higher-order tasks" of governance as contrasted with its "ordinary tasks" and outlined major requirements for its redesign ranging from a redirection of political will to improving the central minds of government, from refashioning elites to empowering an educated democracy, from governing private power to augmenting oversight. A key was to restore the credibility and authority of central government and another was to stress the importance of fulfilling the ordinary tasks of governance because until they were properly performed governance could not engage in its higher-order tasks

and failures in their performance could "undermine the very fabric of society and governance" (p. 63). But once a minimum level of success in these
tasks was attained, more attention and priority should be given to the
higher-order tasks.

While this analysis addressed administrative states that had already
achieved an agreeable level of performance in the traditional, routine, and
everyday activities of government and could begin to think about reorganizing for a future that would concentrate more on their higher-order tasks,
the great majority was still grappling with how to get even to an acceptable
level of performance in their ordinary tasks. A few countries still have no
government at all to speak of but remain in the hands of rival local warlords. Other countries are so poor that they can only supply public goods
and services within reach of their capital city, and within that city only to the
wealthier parts of it. Elsewhere, corruption is so rife that only those who can
pay or are well connected receive any decent public services at all. And a
goodly number of poor states blame international authorities for making
their plight worse. For instance, they fault the International Monetary Fund
for imposing its structural adjustment programs that penalized their public
sectors, favored private enterprise, ransomed their public finance, and promoted brain drain, the World Bank for favoring the pet investment schemes
of their (former) corrupt elites at the expense of everything else but especially human development, and the World Health Organization for protecting the health of rich countries at the expense of ill health in poor
countries. They resent the elaborate and sophisticated universal schemes
being fostered on them by the richer countries and by the international
organizations, which they claim the richer countries dominate. They want
simple, cheap, basic schemes that would bring them greater social stability,
law and order, economic investment, more equitable public administration,
professionalism, and competent officials. Belatedly, the United Nations
Development Program (UNDP) and some other international aid agencies
now realize that emphasis on the basics of statecraft is crucial to the development of poor countries and that one pet solution does not fit all.
Instead, the specifics of each country have to be considered and appropriate
programs tailored to meet the local contexts.

Poor countries are poor for many different reasons and being poor they
cannot soon attain what richer countries may consider even a minimum
level of public services, certainly not without considerable injections of
outside assistance. A start has to be made with preserving what already
exists and preventing any further deterioration. Just holding the line will be
difficult enough in many parts of the world. Globalization continues to pull

away many talented local people who can find employment and a better quality of life elsewhere. All the expensive investment in their education and training and initial local experience is lost when they move away to richer countries eager to employ them and eventually grant them permanent residence and citizenship. This brain drain undermines the capacity of the less-developed countries to govern themselves while the developed countries add to their talent pool and increase their development capacity. The task of administrative states suffering from such brain drain is to try to halt the outflow and reverse it by attracting qualified people from elsewhere willing to lend their assistance temporarily just to gain experience in working in a different country or find competent retirees willing to give a helping hand and to train local prospects.

What all administrative states but especially the poor need to do is to raise more public finance as the sheer lack of money prevents governments from embarking on new ventures and investing more in human resources. Inadequate funding generally lowers their ability to act and thereby their capacity to govern. True, everyone complains that they never have enough money to do what needs to be done but for some time the public sector has been starved of funds and while administrative reform programs have done much to make the same resources stretch ("doing more with less"), budget cuts have caused reductions in public services, postponement of needed maintenance and repairs, and the cancellation of plans for new projects. Governments just do not have the money anymore (or so they claim), principally because they are reluctant to add to their debts or raise taxes, they turn a blind eye to seepage, and they still throw too much money after bad.

Not all governments that borrow live high on the hog. Just because they cannot live within their means does not necessitate that their people should suffer unduly. That is what borrowing is for – to improve current conditions as long as there is some guarantee that the loans will be paid off without extra sacrifice. Unfortunately, in the past, there was too little financial discipline. That on the whole has now been remedied around the globe although administrative states and the international monetary authorities that regulate such matters still have to remain vigilant. The fault lies more with the political reluctance to impose and collect taxes. Taxation is undoubtedly an unpopular business but it has to be done and governments may have no other alternative. People do not resent taxes as such but their concern is that they do not get value for money, that too much public expenditure is unjustified, and that they could do better for themselves with that money. And they may be right when they know that others are unfairly exempt or get away with evasion or that the tax collectors are too lax. The whole area of taxation has long been ripe for overhaul and reexamination by the administrative state.

The overhaul of taxation systems goes hand in hand with seepage. Money that is collected mysteriously disappears and cannot be accounted for. Some seepage is unavoidable and the cost of tracking it down is just too expensive. But there are governments where significant portions of the budget disappear for years in a row. The officials responsible do not even hide their rapaciousness of the treasury; they treat public money as if it were their private desserts. One can readily tell just by looking at the sudden acquisitions made and the exhibit of private wealth from the proceeds of public money obviously siphoned off undeservedly (and one might add unashamedly). Financial management systems and budget processes have also to be overhauled and vigilance maintained at all times to see that the minimum seepage occurs, all public monies are accounted for, and the financial books open all the time to inspection and auditing by independent public watchdogs. Strangely, governments that most complain about financial scarcity always seem to afford to do what they want to do and find the money from somewhere, which says much about their real priorities. Clearly, immorality and corruption have to be tackled if the capacity to govern is to be strengthened.

Throwing good money after bad is a different matter. Here, all involved are not pigging at the public trough as if it were their rite of office. Rather, they sincerely believe that they are doing right, acting responsibly, achieving public good, although they may be unconscious of their self-interest in perpetuating what they do although what they do is no longer worthwhile or necessary. But in their heart of hearts they know or they suspect that their day is over. For example, the disease they cure has been virtually eradicated. The poor they assist actually no longer need their assistance and would be better off if they fended more for themselves. The programs they subsidize should have long been discontinued or made to be self-supporting. The products they purchase are obsolete or never ever worked or are simply inferior. The work they do is pretense or fraud or a total waste of time and resources. All these continue because of sheer systemic inertia, that is, nobody wants to change anything and all get away with it because nobody else cares enough or they are being generously protected by powerful patrons who want the money flow to continue just as it is (and has been). Governments are so big that some areas evade proper supervision or the self-perpetuators can always justify their continued existence and too few are willing and able to challenge them. Again, the administrative state could improve the capacity to govern by rooting out such poor returns when so much else is wanting.

While the higher-order tasks of the administrative state may be too demanding and even out of reach of less-developed countries, there is no longer any excuse why proper surveillance of the traditional tasks continues to be so neglected. There is nothing new or novel about them. All countries publicly maintain that they already have in place all the necessary machinery even if privately they admit that the machinery barely functions for much the same reason why the whole machinery of government also fails to perform properly. And the major reason why government does not perform as it should and could is because too few in government want it to perform that way. Government serves them very well and they have few complaints. It is the great mass of their people who are losing out and see government as their enemy and themselves as its victim. Government is unrepresentative and irresponsible, a law to itself, abusing collective power, penalizing the poor and powerless for the benefit of the rich and powerful, and enabling elites to further enrich themselves at public expense. Ever since the French Revolution, if not before that, greater democratization has been the obvious answer.

FURTHERING DEMOCRATIZATION

Ever since the gloomy days of the Second World War, the spread of democracy has been remarkable, from a dozen or so of countries in the early 1940s until 60 years later over half of the independent states now consider themselves to be democratic. Many more are hopeful that once circumstances permit, they too will transform themselves into democracies. In this, they are being aided by the world's long-established democracies and by the international aid community, which is now threatening to withdraw assistance to countries that are thwarting the democratization process. Nor is any of this a matter of mere semantics. The leading democracies have in mind a model of what they consider constitutes democracy, which is more than just elections to political office but includes such features as an open society, universal human rights, rule of law, responsible, accountable and transparent government, a higher degree of economic and social equity, and progress to a more just society. It is not enough for any country just to profess that it is now democratized. International agencies and the leading democracies have increasingly reliable measures by which they can rank countries and really justify reputations.

Given that government matters more than ever, attention turns to what is meant by good government in less-developed countries and good governance in more-developed countries, terms that denote institutionalized systems that presumably benefit the most people, that most work in the public interest and in which most people identify or see themselves as genuine stake holders. In them government should minimally include the following conditions:

1. Public policy is constitutionally vested in elected public officials.
2. Elected officials are chosen in frequent and fairly conducted elections free from coercion.
3. All adult citizens have the right to vote in elections.
4. All adult citizens have the right to run for office.
5. All citizens have the right to express themselves.
6. All citizens have the right to seek information.
7. All citizens have the right to form independent associations, including political parties and interest groups.
8. Popularly elected officials can exercise their constitutional power without being subject to over-ride from unelected officials.
9. The self-governing polity can act independently (Schmitter & Karl, 1993, p. 45).

These clearly point to a self-governing democracy over any other form of government, even the most paternalistic autocracy. People in a genuine democracy are able to realize more of their potential. They can be more enterprising, creative and original. They can contribute more to the collectivity and therefore their societies are assumedly more productive because in them human resources development can overcome deficiencies in natural resources and capital, and their institutions encourage economic utility and the redistribution of wealth.

Presumably, in fully fledged democracies, governments advance the general welfare and share out communal wealth, whereas other polities exploit the masses and expropriate whatever wealth is around. Democracies are more pacific: they do not rush into war; they are more stable and cohesive domestically. They relish law and order, provide more just systems of social regulation, encourage sounder investments, promote inventiveness, permit both more choice and greater dissent, and altogether enjoy a cultural climate that makes for better if not good governance. No wonder that it is argued that the world is reaching "the end point of mankind's ideological evolution and the universalization of Western liberal democracy as the final form of human government." (Fukuyama, 1989, p. 3).

But even within the prescribed conditions, democracy comes in all kinds of shapes and sizes. It remains premature to conclude that whatever form is selected is inevitable or will manage to stick. Democracies have a strange habit of collapsing and being superseded by other polities. Democratic institutions get manipulated and twisted out of shape. Initially installed, democracies sometimes find that they can go little further because their contexts prove too unpromising. In any event, the quantity of democracies does not ensure their quality. Besides, if half or so of the world's states consider themselves democracies, the other half never has been. It still contains dictatorships, theocracies, absolute monarchies, aristocracies, borderline totalitarian, even one or two states without any central government, and their rulers, national and local, have no intention of relinquishing their hold and sharing power with anybody else. In countries that have only recently adopted democracy or had democracy thrust upon them, the new polity is insecure and the masses continue to look back when things felt more secure and when they believe, rightly or wrongly, they were economically better off. Newfound liberalization has revived old divisions, old rivalries, and old hatreds that have sparked fragmentation, civil war, and genocide way beyond the new polity's capacity to control, govern and even to survive. But even in well-established democracies, the people have become less enchanted with government which has been losing credibility, raising the question among the most disillusioned whether any government can be truly democratic.

If liberal democracy is to be globalized, the administrative state faces taxing tasks ahead. First, the ground has to be properly prepared for democratization. Democracy cannot be imposed from the outside. The masses have to be educated not just about their rights but also about their duties and obligations. Elected officials have to be educated as to what office in a democracy demands, what code of conduct is expected of them, what personal–private sacrifices they may have to make, and what skills and knowledge they will have to acquire. Non-elected officials have to be educated about their subordinate role in the new state of things, how they have to allow credit for official performance to go to others even if they get unfairly stuck with the blame for unsatisfactory performance, and how they have a professional obligation to soldier on regardless. This educative role is not a one-time event that can be assumed once it has been initially performed. It is a continuous socializing function and necessitates much formal instruction. Just because bright, articulate, presentable candidates have been elected, does not mean that that they know by instinct what has to be done or what is expected of them. Just because people register to vote, does not mean that they know how to vote or care to vote. Too often, it is assumed that people will do the right thing automatically or that they will pick up the required skills by osmosis or because one person knows what to do, everybody else can be assumed to know. Some things are simpler to do than others, and some democratic processes are quite complicated, as for instance in ensuring open meetings or following fair administrative practices.

Second, democratization is a process of trial and error. It is experimental. Nobody can predict with certainty whether this or that instrument will work out exactly as anticipated. What may be suitable one day may be outdated on another. What may work here may not work there. What satisfies one set of people may not satisfy another, despite every expectation to the contrary. For this reason, every set principle, every universal formula, every general directive, has to be questioned, examined, and monitored to see whether it is appropriate and works satisfactorily or not, and in whose opinion it does or does not. No situation is exactly identical and no group is the same as another. It is convenient when the differences are so minor and insignificant that they can be discounted and when people collectively do seem to fit a consistent and fairly predictable pattern, but democracy does bring out if not exaggerate the differences, so the administrative state has to be nimble at making adjustments and even improvisations when nothing seems to fit. Just because a selection has once been well made is no reason for sticking with it through thick and thin. The administrative state takes on the task of chopping and changing arrangements whenever they no longer fit, of evaluating performance as best as it can, and continuously seeking better alternatives whenever people in a democracy start complaining.

Third, besides adapting the array of democratic instruments which exist somewhere in the world, there are some imperatives that all administrative states should heed as follows:

(a) *Devolution.* Governments appear to most people to be too distant from them and in practice too much power does tend to amass at the center. After all, it is tempting to interfere wherever one can whether invited or not and to resist yielding up the powers one has. What activities can better be devoluted to regional and local governments or to other social institutions? If there is no need for uniformity to ensure equity or equal treatment, why not let the people solely concerned deal with such matters directly instead of having to refer everything to some higher authority that could not care less? As long as nobody else is affected, why not trust them to do the right thing by themselves? This applies particularly to huge geographical areas separated by physical barriers and to large multicultural populations with specific local concerns.

(b) *Deconcentration.* Just as power tends to amass, so does the whole flow of public business to one location, that of a capital city that grows and grows and grows to the detriment of both the speed with which public business can be completed and the existence of employment and cultural opportunities outside the capital city. The capital city becomes increasingly choked and overcrowded as it draws more and more people to itself while other cities and other regions fall further and further behind and from a national perspective lose ground. With the advent of the new information technology, there is no essential reason why all large public employers have to be located in the same place and why they cannot be redistributed and spread more evenly across a country to open up other regions, to create alternative employment opportunities, and to prevent or at least reduce urban sprawl.

(c) *Decentralization.* Within individual public sector agencies, too much flows to the apex that could be confined further down the organization by judicious delegation and greater trust further down the chain of command. Distrust is the hallmark of non-democratic polities just as is the inculcation of fear and suspicion. The spirit of democratic government has to be translated into democratic (public) administration, as several contemporary democracies now at last are attempting on a grand scale, humanizing the administrative state, and bringing more citizens as stake holders into the administrative process. The old style public management was probably far too bureaucratic but the new style as epitomized by the current New Public Management movement seems to have paid insufficient attention to democratizing the administrative state, to bringing government much closer to the people for whom it is supposed to work, and to stressing public values other than economy and efficiency.

(d) *Complaint Channels.* Most people do not understand the way public administration (and possibly any large-scale organization) operates, and it is not for the want of trying. Government remains much of a mystery for them. They do not know which organization is responsible for what, what the limits of responsibility are, and what rights (if any) they have against any organization with which they deal. So they complain but they do not always know who or where to complain to or how to use the complaint channels available to them. When complaints to the office of ombudsman are examined, most are found unjustified because the public are too ill-informed. Their complaints show this desperate need for more public education and better public relations by public authorities. The complaints that are justified reveal how even the best-administered public organizations make mistakes and how aggrieved the public feels when obvious shortcomings fail to be remedied. Competent accessible complaint channels do bring public administration and the public it serves closer together, do point to remedial administrative failures, and do indicate where public organizations need to work more on public education and public relations.

(e) *Human Rights.* Probably, no other social institution safeguards human rights more than government in action, i.e. public administration. The right to complain is just one such right but there are many more important rights that have to cherished and protected by public officials, elected and appointed, at all levels of government. Unless human rights are enforced, they might as well not exist. People know this. They see some privileged folks acting above the law or a law to themselves because that is exactly what happens. They know that when it comes to implementation, some have full rights and others have none. They experience daily the inequities and the discrimination that occurs without redress of any kind. Minorities feel the sting whenever the tyranny of the majority exploits democratic machinery but every so often the majority has cause to question how it is being abused by well-placed insiders.

(f) *The Powerless.* In every democracy, there are people who cannot exercise the rights accorded to others. Many actually fall under the direct care of the administrative state. These include children below voting age, the elderly placed in the full-time care of public welfare, prisoners deprived of their liberty, aliens excluded from citizenship and citizen rights, patients and the mentally ill unable to exercise their rights, the dependent poor who are officially precluded from normal activities or subject to special requirements and conditions, orphans in public care, handicapped persons, and the like. They are underrepresented in the political system and on the whole, the adage "out of sight, out of mind" applies. Too often, they slip between the cracks and they need a voice to speak for them. That voice has to be the administrative state itself and all the officials who come into contact with them to see that they are accorded equal protection, decent treatment, and a presence in decision making that directly concerns them.

(g) *Civic Culture.* The danger in state paternalism and citizen dependency is that people forget to act for themselves and do things for themselves that they are perfectly capable of doing and should do. But inexperienced people do not know where to start. That is where the administrative state comes in. It is a much quieter life for officials when the citizenry is passive and accepts whatever is dished out to it. For citizens to organize and bring pressure to bear on officialdom which is their fundamental right in a democracy is bothersome and can become too much of a nuisance. But the wellspring of democracy is precisely this active participation and agitation of ordinary people, their willingness to assume responsibility, their keenness to contribute, participate, and volunteer, their propensity to cooperate and share, their accumulation of social capital, their stock of appreciation and admiration for public amenities; and their support and advocacy of public service. If the task of the administrative state is to construct democracy on a global scale, the least one expects is its active encouragement of civic culture, the mobilization of citizens into constructive social channels, provision within public administration for the direct participation of the general public, and efforts to prevent people from feeling powerless and vulnerable.

(h) *Open Mind*. Given the hectic pace of contemporary life, people tend on the whole to close up, to become self-absorbed, to restrict their view only to their immediate surroundings, to deal only with things that they have to attend to, and to restrict their company to folks like themselves. They do not exercise the opportunities that the contemporary world offers them. They follow fashion and hate to stick out. The administrative state has to keep providing amenities that offset these predispositions to concentrate only on what people prefer in their closed or narrow minds and to appreciate the value of diversity. This also applies within the public sector too where officials used to doing much the same routines year in and year out tend to filter out what they do not want to hear and stick to what they know rather than try something different. They develop a closed mind and prefer to deal with the customary rather than explore the strange and the unknown. Again, ensuring that people do not close their minds is an educative function of the administrative state certainly in a democracy.

Fostering global democracy is a new challenge, one that has not been undertaken before in a practical way as opposed to paying the idea lip service. Never, it seems, have the prospects been brighter. Alternatives have been discredited. International opinion is solidly behind the idea and any country seeking help to move toward greater democratization gains ready cooperation and support. And one major difference today is that the unequal balance that has always existed in the past between experts and others is fast being readjusted because knowledge has never before been so easily accessible, so available and so digestible. Governments have lost or are about to lose their control of information and their ability to keep things to themselves and consequently are being challenged by other social instruments, by

outsiders willing to devote time to match officialdom, and by the general
public with access to new advances in information technology.

ADAPTING TO THE KNOWLEDGE SOCIETY

If human progress depended solely on knowledge, then this current era
should be the most progressive in history. Thanks to international multi-
media, airwaves, computers, fax machines, mobile telephones; never before
has information been so abundant, accessible, and cheap. For people with
access and means, it has become impossible to keep up with the overwhelming daily flow of information and its retrieval. They have to skim
through masses of documents to find the few gems they seek, hastily select
what appears to be relevant, and discard every thing else. They have to
ignore the criticism that they pay insufficient attention to advances being
made elsewhere and for not immediately adopting the latest discoveries in
the state of whatever art they happen to be engaged on. This knowledge
society has emerged so suddenly that the administrative state like much else
has been taken by surprise and found wanting in many respects, which is not
surprising given that so many changes have appeared so close together that
no sooner has one system been installed when it has had to be discarded for
another at appreciable expense.

The impact on contemporary society has been overwhelming. For a start,
peoples everywhere have had their eyes opened up, discovered new vistas,
and invariably begun to compare their lot with others. Their expectations
have risen. They want what others take for granted even though that may be
way beyond humanity's ability to provide. Whatever is provided no longer
seems good enough. As their sense of unjustified deprivation builds, they
seek scapegoats, and unfortunately the most convenient at hand appears to
be the administrative state because it probably is the most impersonal institution and has the hardest time proving it performs well or to the best of
its ability. These days, any wrongdoing, any mistake, any error can no
longer be hidden or brushed aside as inconsequential. Public administration
works within a glass bowl where any faults are easily exaggerated, taken out
of context, and generalized by its many ill-wishers. In short, whatever the
administrative state does is never going to satisfy its critics or match their
rising expectations.

Although the administrative state has grown to live with malice, it is
beginning to realize that it has to answer its unjustified critics and to exploit
the potential that the new knowledge society gives to restoring much of its

lost credibility. It now has the capacity to demonstrate its improved performance, better delivery of higher-quality public goods and services, less waste, speedier attention, greater effectiveness, and a greater ability to reshape the future. The information revolution enables public authorities to supply more accurate measures of their performance and to discover where their clients and other stakeholders are least satisfied. It is not true that mass media concentrate on the newsworthy bad than the humdrum good. They may be biased and slanted in what is presented but they allow space for success stories, offer opportunities to respond, maintain respect for public authority, give praise to exceptional public service, answer appeals for support and cooperation, open channels of access, and generally provide many chances to improve the image of public administration if done professionally. The knowledge society dictates a closer relationship between the governors and the governed than previously, and the administrative state has been too slow on the uptake.

The distance between officialdom and citizens is greatly reduced and can even be eliminated altogether through e-government. Intermediaries can be cut down and cut out altogether if street-level bureaucrats are given more responsibility and decision-making power and trusted to use their own judgment when things do not quite fit standard procedure. Imperious bureaucracy is thereby humanized, softened, sensitized, and made less severe, unbending, and self-righteous. Processes are transformed, time is saved, record keeping is simplified, and working relations are less stressful and strained. But all this requires a rethinking of all official activities, a redesign of work, reinvention and reengineering wherein the status of citizen receives higher respect and better service is the highest priority. This is not a one-time transformation of conducting public business, but a continuous review and overhaul from what is being done to how it could be done better. In this, the clients are directly consulted, given opportunities to suggest changes, and brought into administrative procedures as volunteers, interns and the like.

The information revolution has been and continues to alter internal arrangements. Where once there were hordes of clerks, typists, and other categories of white-collar workers, there are fewer middle-level staff as machines replace people and the machines need servicing by skilled technicians. Career paths are changing constantly and employees understand that somewhere during their work life they will need to be retrained as their skills become obsolete and they have to acquire different skills. Traditional male dominated occupations are opening up to females and many government jobs have become feminized. The new knowledge society seems to demand greater sophistication and flexibility with the implication that literacy counts more than ever before and everyone is expected to know where to find information and how to use it. Thus, any administrative state that does not invest in education and fails to utilize the potential of its educated citizens is likely to be left further and further behind.

That was the conclusion of the Arab Human Development 2003. Report published under the auspices of the UNDP, which attributed much of the backwardness of Arab societies to their failure to understand the knowledge society. Besides the lack of political freedom and organizational account-ability, Arab countries lagged behind the rest of the world (other than the poorest of non-Arab countries) in terms of knowledge. The report cited numerous indicators to show the Arab knowledge gap, how access to the internet was so confined, how scarce were computers, how many scientists and engineers in research and development emigrated (brain drain), and how illiteracy limited newspaper readership. To remedy the situation, the report advocated legally guaranteeing freedom of expression, higher quality universal education, greater investment in research and development, en-hanced knowledge-based production in the economy, linguistic reform, and the promotion of cultural diversity. Obviously, the report's recommenda-tions had wider application outside the Arab world but its message was clear, namely, that all these recommendations were one package that should not be separated and adopted piecemeal.

In the Arab world, as elsewhere, the knowledge society already exists within cafes where teenagers flock to surf on the Internet and watch giant television screens. Here is illustrated the heavy hand of the administrative state which employs skilled technicians to manipulate the working of the computers while the television stations are quite selective about what can be received by viewers. Thus, instead of empowering people, as first thought, the new information technology further strengthens the hold of the regime over its people. Much more than a knowledge society is required to improve civic consciousness, literacy, interest in public affairs, and political partic-ipation. In theory, democratization should be quickened, but in practice authoritarian regimes have been able to tighten their grip and influence huge audiences through their control of the new information technology, which they use to censor, spy, silence, and inculcate a culture of fear. They merely have to engage extra security agents, use government-linked servers to track on-line information flows, trap potential dissenters, and use e-government services and chat rooms to brain wash their users.

Thus, adapting to the knowledge society is not as straightforward as it might appear. It promises to boost global liberalization, democratization, universal literacy, more economic, efficient, and effective government, more widespread, accessible, cheaper public goods and services, better governance, friendlier relations between governors and the governed, less arduous work, and so forth, but it may do nothing of the kind by making government even more distant, sinister, off-putting, mistake-prone, and manipulative and widening the gap between the haves and the have-nots. Not everybody is going to possess a computer or know how to operate the latest advance in information technology or have access to e-government. The old, outdated systems of conducting public business will still have to be retained to serve all those who for no fault of their own will still be excluded from the knowledge society. What may benefit the administrative state may not be such a blessing for society and may turn out to be more of a curse for the disadvantaged, poor, and anyone left behind or left out altogether. For these unfortunates, new safeguards, such as free local training sites for the uninitiated and global encryption sites that prevent interference, are going to have to be devised and enforced by the administrative state.

Already, the nature of management, public and private, has been changed by the knowledge society. Managers need to master the latest information technologies, for that gives them instant access virtually to anything they need to know. Computers make life so much easier to plan, coordinate, file, budget, report, correspond, share, and decide. But they can also be very time consuming, sitting before a screen, sifting out all the unwanted and unsolicited communications, and waiting for technical assistance when programs fail to work and technical glitches occur unexpectedly. But they can save unnecessary travel, repeated telephone calls, office help, storage space, and the like. Altogether, managers need to be more personally talented than the old style administrators who could depend on costly back up staff to look after routine details. But then all public business needs much more talented, competent, and devoted people at all levels to deal with all the new policy issues, all the new problems, all the daily crises, and all adjustment and accommodating processes that occupy contemporary governance, government, and public administration.

ATTRACTING TALENT INTO PUBLIC SERVICE

Progressive public organizations are acutely aware of the many challenges confronting them that arise from their increasingly turbulent contexts, policy predicaments, technological transformations, and possibly most important of all severe scarcity of means, both financial and human resources. As they look ahead and try to predict what shape they need to be in to cope with the conditions they anticipate they will have to operate in, they are becoming more and more conscious that they are going to have to attract and retain a greater share of talent than they have been able to do over the past few decades. They need to bring into public service people not just capable and competent but also willing to devote themselves through thick and thin to finding creative solutions to make their organizations more effective and to face up to shifting societal pressures worldwide that want different outcomes than currently being offered. This change in outlook was echoed in the United Nations Millennium Declaration (A/56/26, dated September 6, 2001) that set targets for the international community, especially global public administration, to be met by the year 2015. Public leaders the world over expressed the dire need to change direction and called particularly upon public organizations to reach higher in their efforts to make the planet a better place to live in for all humanity but especially for the world's poorest dwellers.

If human aspirations are to be met, the administrative state has to reverse the unfortunate outflow of talent that has been experienced virtually worldwide over the past quarter of a century. The public sector has rarely been able to compete in the labor market. It has been deliberately held back and unable to match the surge in business glamour accompanied at middle and higher levels with conditions of employment far outdistancing anything that could be offered in the public sector handicapped by financial and staffing cutbacks. In their haste to replace the public sector with business (and nongovernmental organizations) as the engine of development, public leaders have joined others in a spate of public service bashing that has discouraged young people from working for government organizations and participating in public service. The assumption long held by public service organizations that they could always attract and retain their fair share of society's talent has not been borne out by reality. The more-developed countries have been unable to fill many vacancies at entry levels in the public professions, have experienced higher turnovers at all levels, and have lost key experienced and seasoned employees lured away to the private sector. The less-developed countries, already strapped for talent, have witnessed brain drain of key public sector staff to the more-developed countries trying to make up gaps in their own public sector establishments and to international and other organizations seeking to be more representative of the world community and also offering conditions of employment superior to those found locally in the public sector.

The emphasis on private as opposed to public development has had the unfortunate effect of diminishing the call to public service, with its appeal to promoting the common weal, advancing the public good, and putting self interest secondary to communal needs, while promoting self-interest, narrow concerns, individualism, and personal fortune, irrespective of social dysfunction whereby people even become deaf to communal appeals and the fortunate few become blind to others and think only of themselves when trouble looms. Fading has been the notion that youth put aside its personal comforts and interests, volunteered to serve good causes, devoted itself to helping strangers less fortunate than themselves, actively engaged in improving public service performance, and tried to emulate the public service model presented by its elders. This trend has probably been best documented for the United States where Americans where people have become increasingly disconnected from one another in a process of shrinking access to social capital (Putnam, 2000) but it applies much further afield.

Yet never before in human history has there been the need to bolster public service. Governance, government, and public administration have never been more demanding, more complex, more challenging. They demand more talent, not less, at least their fair and fairer share of a society's talent. Without sufficient talented people in public service, much else being proposed to improve public sector performance will have little real impact. Throwing good money at problems probably wastes it. Only competent, capable and devoted people can make all else matter more and bring about better outcomes. Selflessness and integrity count. Genuine commitment to the concept of the public interest and the ability to recognize and avoid corrupt practices are crucial elements to restoring public faith and credibility in governance, government and the public sector. This has always been known. There is nothing new in any of this.

What is new is that these traditional ideas have been overlooked in the past few decades and almost eclipsed by the fads and fancies of the administrative reformers. So enthused by their own pet remedies and their reformulations and their adoption of a host of new vocabularies (such as cutback management, downsizing, reinvention, reengineering, renovating, outsourcing, performance budgeting) that they have almost forgotten who exactly is going to implement their proposals. They call for public leaders to be granted the authority to act which they already have, to be put in charge of lean, responsive organizations which they already are, to hire and nurture knowledgeable, motivated employees which they already can do, and give them the freedom to innovate which they already assure them they have. But where are such employees to be found? Where are these being educated, trained, and developed? Where are they being hired, supported, and given sufficient resources to make a difference? How are they being attracted, enthused, rewarded, and prevented from leaving to greener pastures? The fact is that such potential employees if they exist at all are not willing to enter public service in the public sector in the first place because these selfsame public leaders discourage them with their criticisms of public organizations or when they do the stress and strain they experience along with other negative aspects of their work (rather than the attractions of their options) push them out again.

What emerges from this relative neglect of human resource development in the public sector is a series of challenges that can no longer be ignored with impunity. Where is the public sector to find dedicated leaders, managers, professionals, and employees and associated creative problem-solvers working in the public interest, who elevate purpose over process and democratic values over the bottom line? Where is it to find a solid core of honest, trustworthy administrators who form part of a new *thinking* higher-order government receptive to bold new ideas? Where is it to find its visionaries, change agents, flexible broadminded public-spirited staff to humanize bureaucracy and inspire constructive team workers? What would make more insiders overcome their disillusionment and recommend careers in the public sector to others? How is the public sector to recapture some of its former appeal, idealism and benevolence? How is it to attract and retain administrators who are patient enough to stay the course and see through policy changes and administrative reforms? Who is willing to support serious research on public sector concerns and invest more not less in public administration?

If only a fraction of the answers now being offered were adopted, immediate progress would be made with beneficial outcomes in public sector performance. The question is one of selectivity. No public sector is identical. Some are sufficiently similar to assume that common solutions are available. Others are so idiosyncratic that specific solutions have to be tailored very carefully to fit their unique circumstances. Inevitably, administrative reforms in the public sector are highly complicated and emotional. They deal not just with techniques and processes but they are also bound up with ideology and values. They deal not with mere details but with key societal issues. What should be considered public and how far should public intervention go? How should public goods and services be provided and delivered and to whom? How should public organizations be run and by whom? What should be the social standing of public servants and what should their duties and obligations cover? Where are key public personnel to be found and how are they to be educated and developed? To whom and how should they be accountable and for what? Who should be denied public office or removed from office for which offenses? How is performance, capacity, competence, and talent to be measured, by whom and for what purpose? How are any of these questions to be enlarged to include the whole emerging scene of world governance and to be reduced to the level of individual organizations operating at purely local community level?

Whatever answers and solutions are eventually adopted, cognizance has to be taken of two emerging trends that will only make the task of overhauling the administrative state even more difficult. One is that of fragmentation. Contemporary government has become increasingly specialized. The traditional idea that there should be one unified public service governed by uniform rules, and conditions centrally administered and presenting a common front is fast disappearing. Instead, public sectors are devolving power, deconcentrating responsibilities, decentralizing administration and delegating authority. Consequently, there are many different and distinct public services at different levels of governance, many different and distinct specializations with separate career paths, and each public organization is developing its own administrative culture if not several sub-cultures. In short, there is a distinct move toward corporatization on the business model with each making its own staffing arrangements and free to operate in the labor market as it deems fit. This fragmentation is susceptible to all the old diseases of former decentralized systems such as excessive politicization, cronyism, corruption, capture by special interests, disobliging parochialism, managerial imperialism, and weakened public accountability.

Offsetting fragmentation, but possibly more likely to add to it, is the trend toward more diversity and more representativeness in the public sector. Obviously, diversity is a way of opening up public service to formerly excluded peoples and clearly a way of attracting newcomers into public service. Diversity means greater opportunities for all social groups to be hired, to advance up the organization, and their differences to be valued. Diversity promises to integrate individuals from different racial, religious, and ethnic backgrounds and also men and women, the elderly and disabled, and those with different sexual orientation. Previously excluded or under-represented groups will now be able to challenge narrow power over policy making, bureaucratic isolation, secrecy, hierarchy, over reliance on rigid rules, insensitivity to those excluded, and lack of responsiveness. Yet, safeguards will be necessary to prevent the cornering of public service privileges by these newcomers to public office, as if the administrative state had no other challenges to ponder over the coming decade or so.

THE BOTTOM LINE

Will the administrative state be able to cope with all these new challenges selected from a whole host of other problems flooding in on it from so many different directions? It has little choice. Looking back, it has done remarkably well in the circumstances, not as well as the world situation demands, but far better than commonly supposed. There have been many failures but these can be attributed as much to ideological division, lack of political will, still sheer economic scarcity, maybe the lack of individual genius and charisma, and alas lasting human weaknesses as they can be to institutional failure, public sector defects, and bureaucratism. These will continue to plague humanity's quest for betterment just as the imperfections of the administrative state. At least, the shortcomings of the latter can be identified, diagnosed, if not completely cured by the range of nostrums and medicines accumulating in the arsenal of public administration.

REFERENCES

Dror, Y. (2001). *Capacity to govern: A report to the club of Rome*. London: Frank Cass.

Fukuyama, F. (1989). The end of history? *The National Interest, 16*(Summer), 3.

Putnam, R. D. (2000). *Bowling alone: The collapse and revival of American community.* New York: Simon & Schuster.

Schmitter, P. C., & Karl, T. L. (1993). What democracy is ... and is not. In: L. Diamond & M. F. Plattner (Eds), *The global resurgence of democracy* (p. 45). Baltimore: Johns Hopkins University Press.

FURTHER READING

Abramson, M. A., Breul, J. D., & Kamensky, J. M. (2004). *Four trends transforming government*. Washington, DC: IBM Center for the Business of Government.

Argyriades, D. (2004). Institutional reinforcement for human resources development: How to implement the goals of the millennium summit. In: A. Benz, H. Siedentopf & K.-P. Sommermann (Eds), *Institutionenwandel in regierung und verwaltung* (pp. 661–684). Berlin: Duncker & Humblot.

Caiden, G. E. (2004). The erosion of public service in the United States. In: P. L. S. Reddy, J. Singh & R. K. Tiwari (Eds), *Democracy, governance and globalization* (pp. 37–70). New Delhi: Indian Institute of Public Administration.

Kamarck, E. C., & Nye, J. S. (Eds) (2002). *Visions of governance in the 21st century*. Washington, DC: Brookings Institution Press.

Kurlantzick, J. (2004). Dictatorship.com: The web won't topple tyranny. *The New3 Republic*, April 5, pp. 21–25.

FROM PUBLIC ADMINISTRATION TO PUBLIC MANAGEMENT: REASSESSING A REVOLUTION?

Andrew Gray and Bill Jenkins

Changes to the study of public administration tend to follow those in the practice of the administration of government. The recent shift to public management is characterized and assessed both as a practice and a field of study. The result has been less a revolution in paradigm than the emergence of a vision of government, which competes with but does not supplant traditional public administration.

In March 1994, Vice President Gore of the United States presented a report to President Clinton entitled *From Red Tape to Results Creating a government that Works Better and Costs Less.* On reading its 800 recommendations to improve the US Federal Government, President Clinton is reported to have observed 'government is broken' (Moe, 1994, p. 111). A few months later, the US government published a White Paper on the Civil Service (Cm 2627, 1994). Stressing continuity and change, the document set out the key principles on which the Civil Service was seen to be based and to which the government claimed to be committed integrity, political impartiality, objectivity, selection and promotion on merit and accountability through ministers to Parliament (Cm 2627, 1994, p. 1). However, against this framework of continuity it also stressed the need for the service to adapt to a

Comparative Public Administration: The Essential Readings
Research in Public Policy Analysis and Management, Volume 15, 543–572
ISSN: 0732-1317/doi:10.1016/S0732-1317(06)15023-X

changing world characterized by a sharper focus on management and performance, new staffing procedures and an overall cut in total civil service size.

These two initiatives are separate and distinct. Yet, drawing on common
ideologies, they represent the practical face of the new public management
and a critique of traditional public administration. Further, as a commentator
on the Gore report noted, they also reflect the shifting theoretical focus in the
study of public administration as 'all reports on government organization and
management have as their basis some theory about the nature of government
and about the management of that government' (Moe, 1994, p. 111).

This last point is significant both for its explicit emphasis on theories of
government and governance and for its implicit underlining of the *values*
that underpin the study and practice of both public administration and
public management. Thus, it is important to recognize that neither the study
nor practice of public administration or public management can be divorced
from politics. As Caiden (1994) has argued, 'all public administration
is political it is an instrument of politics and political values dominate'
(p. 126). Such an argument also highlights the question of values and the
importance of identifying them in any study of what 'public management' or
indeed 'traditional public administration' is or might be. Although, the focus of this article is on developments in the United Kingdom, it would be
wrong to neglect the worldwide debate embracing the theory and practice of
public administration in contexts that include at least Australia, Canada,
New Zealand and the United States. In each of these countries the traditional theories and practices of public administration are under attack from
reform agendas and appear driven by what, on the surface at least, seem to
be common ideologies and strategies. Further, in each there has been much
talk of administrative revolutions and paradigm shifts.

The idea of a paradigm is, of course, borrowed from the work of the
philosopher of science, Thomas Kuhn (1970). It relates to the evolution of
scientific disciplines and in particular when the commonly held value consensus breaks down and is replaced by a new and generally externally constructed set of values and assumptions. The revolution therefore brings new
values, new agendas and often new personnel redefining the area, which is
driven by the new paradigm. How far this analysis can fairly be transferred
to the study and practice of public administration is another matter. Nevertheless, numerous claims of a paradigm shift have been made for example,
the move to a 'post-bureaucratic' paradigm (Aucoin, 1990; Kernaghan,
1993) or from bureaucratic to entrepreneurial government (Osborne &
Gaebler, 1993). There has also been extensive discussion of the shifting set of
values that underlies the transition from traditional or 'progressive' public

administration to the new public management (Hood, 1991; Dunleavy & Hood, 1994).

It is against this background that this article seeks to explore the evolution of public management and public administration in the UK in terms of *both* theory *and* practice. Such breadth of coverage cannot be comprehensive but is necessary since it is the relationship (and often separation) between ideas and practice that is important. To establish whether a revolution in a Kuhman sense has taken place may not be all that fruitful but it may help to discern what value shifts have taken place and their consequences.

The article will therefore consider the development of traditional public administration and the subsequent emergence of public management as a field by charting its links to and possible divorce from public administration. We then discuss in greater detail the way public management offers structural solutions to administrative problems, the rise of financial management as a major influence on public management theory and practice and the emphasis on quality and entrepreneurship. Finally, the conclusion attempts to portray the strengths and weaknesses of public management as an approach to the study and practice of public administration and government. This will hopefully facilitate the identification of core problems and assist in establishing an agenda for what is to be done.

THE EMERGENCE OF PUBLIC MANAGEMENT: REDEFINING A FIELD?

It is a point of continuing debate whether the study of public administration can in any circumstances be graced by a disciplinary label. Rhodes (1996), for example, has argued that the study of British public administration was traditionally insular, dominated for a long period by an institutionalist tradition characterized by an interest in administrative engineering, but a distaste for theory. As Rhodes also observes, this position emphasized, albeit in a traditional sense, the political and ethical context of administration public administration existed within a wider framework of accountability relationships and political and moral responsibilities. We might add to this the way government and public administration was seen as linked within a framework of administrative law, which, while not formalized in the sense of continental Europe, was important.

It is within such a framework that the values attributed to the UK civil service and recently rearticulated by the government (Cm 2627, 1994) can be analysed in that they represent an ideal and perhaps an idealized world where the administrative practice is set in a traditional structure of parliamentary accountability. This almost Weberian model of administrative structures – hierarchical, neutral, technocratic, salaried, pensioned and rule bound – was perhaps not often analyzed as such but was seen as an adequate and necessary model for the UK political system. Hence, while there might be calls for structural and procedural reforms, there was generally consensus both on the relationship between the polity and the administrative world and the values that public administration should promulgate and represent. Traditionally, then, British public administration as an academic subject was seen as an adjunct of the study of politics and its practice was dominated by generations of politicians and administrators, who operated within a consensus on the political context of administration and the structures required to service such a combination of political and administrative values.

It may be argued that such a portrayal is too broad-brush, neglecting the historical sweep of political and administrative developments including the wartime experience, the post-Second World War welfare expansion and the administrative reforms that sought to reshape traditional assumptions and analysis (Hennessy, 1989, 1993; Rhodes, 1996). However, for a substantial period, reform of both the study and practice of public administration took place within a consensus regarding both the context of the political–administrative relationship and the basic values underlying administrative behaviour. In the last decade or so, with the rise of what is now termed the new public management, this is no longer the case.

This shift in focus in the study of public administration may be illustrated from its literature. One of the standard texts for students of public administration in the 1970s, for example, was *The Administrative Process in Britain* by Brown (1970) (with a second edition co-authored by Steel, 1979). This text focused on central government, especially the history of civil service reform, theories of decision-making and organizational behaviour, and a set of problem areas, including planning, the machinery of government and 'management'. The discussion of management in the second edition is brief (25 pages), but includes sections on accountable management and hiving off central government activities. As such this text represents the study of public administration in transition with the traditional under pressure from a desire to inject a theoretical dimension and a shift in focus. By and large, however, the text reflects the consensus outlined above.

Less than two decades later we find *Public Sector Management* by Flynn (1993) as a standard text. The contrast with Brown and Steel could not be more striking. The first three chapters address the perceived crisis in the British public sector and the remainder deal with aspects of public management in practice including markets and prices, performance measurement and 'a user-oriented service'. The first reference in Flynn's bibliography is to the Adam Smith Institute, the second the Audit Commission and the last to Williamson's (1975) *Markets and Hierarchies.*

One should hesitate from drawing easy conclusions from such a comparison. However, this simple exercise indicates how public management has, to a considerable extent, redefined the focus, language and theoretical basis of study of the public sector, drawing on literatures and ideas often external to traditional public administration. As noted above, the reasons for this include the insularity and fragmented focus, organization and theoretical underpinning of the subject. As a consequence it has been reactive rather than proactive, open to colonization by marauding theoretical hordes and changing agendas, often driven by outside forces. This situation has also been compounded by the fact that the links between theory and practice have also been weak. Rarely has the traditional academic community of UK public administration or the ideas it developed been sought out by practitioners as offering useful guides to practice or reform. This state of affairs, charted by Hogwood (1995) elsewhere in this volume, has also been commented on recently by the current head of the UK Home Civil Service (Butler, 1992).

It can be argued that the rise of public management as a threat to the study of public administration can be traced to the late 1960s and early 1970s, a period charted by Rhodes (1996) as an age of 'eclecticism'. This period undoubtedly was characterized by the efforts of many academics to strengthen the analysis of UK central and local administration through the application of decision making and organization theory anid the development of policy analysis and policy studies (Hogwood, 1995). These efforts went hand in hand with reforms in the practitioner community that focused on corporate or strategic planning in local government and the National Health Service, rational techniques of budgetary reform and an increased emphasis on the strategic management of the public services. Such reforms were championed on both the left of the political spectrum (the Fabians) and the right (Conservative Research Department). Although their objectives differed (better service delivery vs. a smaller state), the argument that the state was badly managed was common. Moreover, the arguments were often found in official reports such as that by the Fulton Committee on the Civil Service (Cmnd 3638, 1968) and others on local government and the welfare services. Yet, these reform efforts rarely questioned the fundamental links between political and administrative structures, the role of government and the value basis of the public service. Structural reform efforts remained within the accepted consensus while debates in the academic community as to the place of organization theory in public administration and the relationship between public administration and management studies, while at times acrimonious, were generally accommodated within current structures and values (Rhodes, 1996).

Generally, then, this period was characterized by a confidence shared by practitioners and academics that the practice of public administration could be reformed effectively by a combination of strategic management, structural reorganization to create more responsive and accountable units, and the development of better personnel management systems. In embracing these beliefs, the study of public administration widened to accommodate not only political scientists but also organization theorists and other management specialists, all seeking to contribute to the field. In the early 1970s at least, there were also attempts to place the study of administration on a firmer theoretical footing (Dunsire, 1973; Keeling, 1972; Self, 1972). These were followed by efforts to develop policy analysis (Jenkins, 1978, Hogwood & Gunn, 1984) and provide a clearer understanding of the internal politics of administrative organizations, an interest stimulated by the pathbreaking study of Heclo and Wildavsky (1974) on the operations of the UK Treasury.

However, the political agenda was even at this time changing and with it the framework both of politics and public administration. In particular, the failure to control the economy led to the rejection of old solutions for the management of the state and a search for new methods of control (Smith, 1994). This in turn was accompanied by a changing political ideology, particularly on the right, that broke with the old consensus (Kavanagh, 1987). Thus, even in the mid-1970s (and before the dawn of the Thatcher era) policy analysis and its related prescriptions had been rejected in the political world in favour of a focus on management and control, particularly of resources.

From these small beginnings, the erosion of traditional administration and the development of public management have developed at a remarkable pace and by the 1990s have emerged as a worldwide movement (Hood, 1990, 1991; Governance, 1990; Pollitt, 1990; Schick, 1990). Its foundations lie in redefining the role of government for example as a 'steerer' rather than a 'rower' (Osborne & Gaebler, 1993) and approaching macro-economic policy via control of public spending.

The emergence of public management as a supplement to or even replacement of traditional public administration therefore begins with a political theory of the role of the state in modern life (Dunleavy & O'Leary, 1987). The debate engendered is complex and detailed but for the sake of simplicity can be seen to range from the conservative call for a smaller state through the socialist demand for a more responsive state to more radical demands for a more empowering state where real power is devolved to lower-level organizations and citizens (Hambleton, 1992). The importance of distinguishing between such visions (and they appear in other shades and combinations) is that they represent different ideological positions and sets of values (Hood, 1991). Thus, while reform strategies appear similar they may represent different *political* stances, i.e., such strategies are *not* neutral (see below).

Linked with this ideological analysis is a theoretical onslaught on traditional public administration, led principally by economists and management scientists, aided and abetted by practitioners of personnel management (now termed human resource management) and by those who argue more generally that the arts of private sector management should be transposed to the public sector in the name of improving efficiency. If none of this is new (Rhodes, 1996), it is now an integrated and sustained attack on what is perceived as the 'failure' of traditional government and public administration. Moreover, this intellectual baggage (or selected elements of it) has been harnessed by many political actors as a means to promulgate and fashion their ideological vision of the state (Pollitt, 1990).

As a consequence of the latter, the new public management is often used to redefine politics rather than simply improve state management within current structures. This approach is illustrated by the work of think tanks such as the Institute of Economic Affairs (IEA) and the Adam Smith Institute. In contrast, economic analysis that has focused on the nature of the state as a mechanism for service provision and delivery may simply and less radically seek to improve the relative efficiency of its operations. Hence, as venous writers have pointed out (Taylor-Gooby & Lawson, 1993a; Le Grand, 1990, 1993; Levacic, 1993), questions can be raised on failings arising from the monopolistic nature of state provision and co-ordination of activities. Solutions to such problems include creating markets, charging for services, liberalizing administrative regimes and even privatizing (Heald, 1983; Vickers & Yarrow, 1988). In separate but related critiques, management accountants have characterized traditional systems as lacking accountability for resource use and contributing to inefficiency. They have proposed delegated financial management to remedy this and re-organize institutional budgeting (Hopwood & Tompkins, 1984). Meanwhile, the motivation and incentive systems of traditional public organizations (incremental pay scales, career systems, job security) have also been attacked and reforms advocated which focus on performance-related reward systems and management against targets (even in the British Higher Civil Service, Cm 2627, 1994, pp. 44–45).

Hence, for its advocates, public management represents less an addition to the traditional practice of public administration in the UK than the intellectual and practical means to achieve true 'cultural change' by which the old internal order is swept away (Dunsire, 1995). This coming together of political ideology, economic theory and perspectives from private sector management lie behind the last decade of change in the UK public sector and include the mission to eliminate waste (Hennessy, 1989; Metcalfe & Richards, 1990), introduce delegated financial management (Gray & Jenkins, 1991, 1993a), develop performance measurement (Carter, 1991) and create executive agencies (Davies & Willman, 1991), citizens' charters and regimes of market testing (Connolly, McKeown, & Milligan-Byrne, 1994; Doern, 1993). Thus, the Head of the UK Civil Service, Sir Robin Butler (1992, 1993) and the former Civil Service Minster (Waldegrave, 1993) can talk of an administrative revolution involving the federalization of central government administrative structures.

Yet does this emergence of public management represent the development of a new paradigm in either theory or practice? Undoubtedly its rhetoric suggests so and its advocates champion change over stability. However, as a commentator on recent US reforms points out

> To say that we are living in a rapidly changing world is simply to recite a truism under the guise of intellectual insight. Change is an instrumental value and like efficiency, another instrumental value, has no normative content until linked with another concept or objective. What we need today therefore is to think what we really expect from our government (Moe, 1994, p. 119).

This political dimension of the new public management, however, is often swept away in the UK by the language of its reforms and those who claim to contribute to its theories. In particular, the reform agenda is often predicated on the basis of a distinction between politics and administration that resuscitates in a novel way what some earlier reformers thought to be misplaced and outdated dichotomy (Dunsire, 1973; Self, 1972; Ham & Hill, 1993). From this perspective, public management is offered as neutral or transferable technology to improve the public sector without offending traditional values. Hence it offers a return to the classical view of public administration in which administrative structures are simply 'providers' of services and activities determined in the political sphere (Efficiency Unit,

1988). The validity of this position can and should be questioned (see below).

The new public management has brought with it a new epistemology, a redefinition of accountability and a fresh batch of seers. The issue of epistemology is dealt with by Dunsire (1995) elsewhere in this volume. It is worth emphasizing, however, that a focus on cost, price, market, customer and similar terms constitutes not simply a relabelling as an introduction of different (and often dominant) values into the dialogue of public administration. This is often at the expense of professional groups (and their own languages) who in the past controlled particular areas of administrative life (for example, education, health, housing) (Richards, 1992). Indeed, the thrust of the reform agenda is almost unhesitatingly hostile to the values of traditional public sector professionals. Yet the outcome of such changes has often not been so much the de-professionalization of administrative life as the superimposition of a new 'management' cadre over established professional groups, thus redefining the internal and external politics of administrative organizations.

The reconceptualization of accountability is based on this epistemology as well as on the dictates of what has been termed the new managerialism (Pollitt, 1990). Thus, in a decentralized, target-driven world of public management, responsibility and performance are often redefined in individualistic ways driven by particular conceptions of terms such as efficiency, effectiveness and quality that reflect the beliefs and values of the new faith (Jackson, 1993; Likierman, 1993). Moreover, faith is not too strong a word to describe public management and its growth. Many of its advocates are dearly true believers in the power and sanctity of markets or the ability of other nostrums to rescue what they perceive as the theoretically weak and misconceived field of public administration. They would replace the traditional emphasis on *public* administration by commitments to excellence, quality, flexibility, responsiveness and mission.

The consequences of these developments for the study of British public administration have included the redefining, isolating or relocating the study of public administration as public management, the drawing of a number of new actors into the area and the restructuring of the relevant literature. The location of public management studies is increasingly, therefore, not traditional university departments of political science but business schools (e.g., London, Aston, Warwick), dedicated research institutes (e.g., Institute of Local Government Studies, School of Advanced Urban Studies), various professional bodies that attempt to link the world of theory, practice and consultancy (The Public Management Foundation and Public Finance

Foundation) and even various polemical 'think tanks' (Adam Smith Institute, European Policy Forum, institute for Economic Affairs, Institute for Public Policy Studies). These organizations vary widely but they often share an approach and perspective that differ radically from organizations that supported public administration in a more traditional sense (e.g., the former Royal Institute of Public Administration). Many also promote a literature that has its own distinctive signature and focus while traditional journals have grafted on public management sections to stimulate practitioner interest (e.g., *Public Administration*), or adjusted their content to reflect changing concerns in specific professional areas (*Local Government Studies, Policy and Politics*). Practitioner journals have, of necessity, followed management trends if selectively (*The Health Services Journal, Local Government Chronicle* and *Public Finance* (formerly *Public Finance and Accountancy*).

But how far do all these developments represent the development of a unique area different from traditional public administration? Has the context and content of the field of study simply changed or is public management an area with distinct characteristics from public administration? Such questions are less academic quibbles as prerequisite enquiries in understanding the logic of recent developments and assessing the current study and practice of public management. Public administration is based on an acceptance of a political model of parliamentary government and a professional and essentially bureaucratic model of state structures and operations. Neither its alleged failures nor the superiority of alternative administrative arrangements should be taken for granted, especially when arguments are expressed in apolitical terms. What is important about the theory and practice of traditional public administration is the value system embraced and served. What we need to know of public management and its new agenda are its values and basic assumptions. With this in mind we proceed to an examination of some of the developments in both the theory and practice of public management.

STRUCTURES FOR PUBLIC MANAGEMENT

There is a growing literature on public management in the UK. The more generalist has a distinct flavour from what has gone before in public administration (e.g., Flynn, 1993; Pollitt & Harrison, 1992) even if other texts take a more traditional approach discussing developments in specific areas (e.g., civil service, local government, education) under a public management guise (e.g., Taylor & Popham, 1989). Moreover, much of the literature is

more specialistic, dealing with recent reforms in areas such as health care (Harrison, Hunter, & Pollitt, 1990), the welfare services (Taylor-Cooby & Lawson, 1993b) or local government (Walsh, 1989). Much of this offers incisive analysis of recent public sector reforms and changes many of which, if not all, have been driven by a mission to change the structures of public sector organizations and reshape relationships with the political world on the one hand and the public on the other.

Within all the above has been a common concern with organizational structures. This has been a traditional issue for the study of public administration for decades (Self, 1972; Dunsire, 1973, 1995) although, as Rhodes (1996) illustrates, theoretical concerns with structural reform (e.g., as in classical management theory) initially had limited impact. However, in the 1960s and 1970s an interest in organization theory, policy analysis and management attempted to refocus the study of public administration on such issues as structures for strategic planning, policy implementation and policy co-ordination. In addition, the concern with strategic financial management (as reflected in such innovations as planning programming budgeting (PPB)) also had a structural emphasis in its attempts to refocus and integrate hierarchical organizational structures (e.g., via corporate planning). The practical expression of these concerns in this period were giant merged Whitehall departments, mechanisms of corporate review (e.g., the Central Policy Review Staff), local government reorganization, social service departments and the restructuring of the National Health Service. Undoubtedly, many of these reforms were driven by a technocratic agenda, based on ideas of rational decision making and the perceived inefficiencies of political structures (e.g., failures to define goals, or to evaluate options, etc.). Nevertheless, within the conventional study and practice of public administration the role of the state was rarely questioned, a minority task undertaken only by those of more radical (usually left wing) persuasion (Ham & Hill, 1993).

In the late 1970s and throughout the 1980s, however, these consensus approaches were ferociously attacked for their theoretical weakness and practical failures. In their place came an emphasis on markets, flexible and responsive organizations and decentralization. In the lexicon of public sector studies the word 'management' began to usurp 'administration'.

Even if the evidence for discrediting the ideas of traditional administration and the values underpinning the so-called 'bureaucratic' paradigm (Kernaghan, 1993; Osborne & Gaebler, 1993) seems often more assumed than demonstrated (Jordan, 1994), the attack which emerged from the Chicago School of Political economy (e.g., Friedman), the Austrian School of Political Economy (e.g., Von Hayek), public choice (Buchanan, Tullock, Niskanen) and neo-classical economic was fierce (Dunleavy, 1991; Flynn, 1993; Le Grand, 1990, 1993; Levacic, 1993; Taylor-Gooby & Lawson, 1993a). This set of ideas (or perhaps selective interpretations of them) became powerful influences on British politicians and public sector reformers, while also shaping the new agenda of public management studies. Hence, while public management theory is not the exclusive preserve of public choice or economic theory, it frequently draws on these disciplines for its structural diagnosis and prescription. In essence, this analysis identifies state involvement as encouraging monopolies, suppressing entrepreneurial behaviour, limiting choice, overproducing unwanted services and encouraging waste and inefficiency. In contrast, markets encourage competition, maximize choice and freedom, increase efficiency (in its various forms), co-ordinate fragmented activities via the price mechanism and create conditions for entrepreneurial behaviour to flourish. Such solutions are not necessarily seen as unproblematic and some role for state and administration is acknowledged, but only as a 'facilitator' and minimalist regulator for market systems.

The practice of public management is seen, therefore, to need structures which encourage the creation of external and internal markets whenever possible This means investigating a range of options ranging from privatization and market testing to the purchaser–provider split, the concept of the 'enabling' authority and the contracting state (further see Hardin, 1992; Stewart, 1993). That such strategies have captured the political agenda is immediately clear. Whether there exists empirical evidence to support the claims made on their behalf is another matter. Perhaps, as Goodsell (1993) notes (p. 86), 'A good sales pitch does not go into the messy details or carefully weighed pros and cons'. Nevertheless, there has been no formal effort, for example, to evaluate the introduction of the internal market in health care in the UK nor any assessment of the adequacy of its theoretical assumptions (Butler, 1992; Hunter, 1994). Further, in areas of public life such as contracting-out or market testing, the supporting evidence for the universal success of such innovations is far from overwhelming (Audit Commission, 1993b).

In these and other areas there is considerable controversy over the conceptual basis on which any assessment can be made, a fact that illustrates the conflicting value positions underlining the public management debate. This is compounded by a tendency to blur or eliminate the distinctions between the public and private sectors (government as a business) and perhaps, as importantly, often to treat the public sector as homogenous in organizational terms rather than a differentiated system of organizations with different tasks, values and relationships often linked into complex policy networks (Prior, 1993). Thus, the mission to impose a new 'culture' on public sector organizations via structural solutions based on market theory often fails to analyse the old culture or the underlying value structures and administrative politics or, if it does recognize it, seeks to depoliticize it by fragmenting the organizational world into quasi-markets and a contract culture (Dunleavy & Hood, 1994).

Market-based theory often pays little attention to the internal structures of organizations. As an antidote, or perhaps in sheer need for a defense against the more extreme ideas thrust upon them, practitioners in the UK public sector have turned for salvation to contemporary literatures emerging from organizational management consultants especially in the United States. Based mainly but not exclusively on the experience of private companies, this literature has also shaped the structural doctrines of public management through the works of Peters and Waterman (1982), Peters (1988, 1992), Waterman (1994), Kanter (1983, 1989) and, most significantly in the public sector itself, Osborne and Gaebler (1993). An almost exclusively North American product (see Kay, 1993), this literature focuses on how organizations can survive in an increasingly hostile environment (political, economic and social), adjust to change or, in the title of one of Peters' later works, 'thrive on chaos'. The authors' answer is that the old command and control structures (reminiscent of Weberian organizations) have become redundant with the need for organizations that are more flexible and adaptable. This in turn is achieved by the flatter and more focused structures which encourage entrepreneurial rather than bureaucratic management and more flexible personnel regimes.

Although criticized for exaggeration, simplification and selective use of anecdotal evidence, Peters and Waterman (1982) were hugely influential. In the early 1980s, for example, it was easy to gain the impression that this was the only management text that UK senior civil servants had read, so common was their reference to it. Similarly, the Audit Commission used the 7S framework (which identifies organizational success with the seven elements of strategy, structure, staff, management style, systems and procedures, shared values, and skills) to promote 'excellence' in local government.

In the 1990s, however, the cult of Peters and Waterman appears to have been replaced by that of Osborne and Gaebler, the major literary influence behind Vice President Gore's report discussed at the start of this article. For Osborne and Gaebler, the reinvention of government requires structures, which are 'mission rather than rule-driven', 'decentralized' and 'entrepreneurial'. This analysis has much in common with that of Peters' (1988) later work and also that of another US management guru Rosabeth Moss Kanter. Indeed, the Kanter model (Kanter, 1989) of successful organizations designed around a small central core overseeing a flatter-fragmented structure has recently become fashionable in British central government and local authorities. Kanter claims that these structures are more responsive to external forces and changes, facilitate closer personnel identification (the creation of an organizational culture), and encourage entrepreneurship (albeit in a limited sense). The fact that they are often seen to be cheaper ('restructuring' as a euphemism for cutting staff) is also probably significant, especially at a time when shedding numbers from the public sector has become a matter of high political priority.

The new theories of public management therefore appear to unite in attacking the traditional bureaucratic model of administrative structure and advocating efficiency and responsiveness through some form of decentralization. Such ideas, in theoretical terms at least, often prescribe greater 'freedom' for administrative organizations and their members. They attack the restrictive nature of central controls and rule-bound systems that are considered to restrict prized values such as entrepreneurship, staff empowerment and client sensitivity. However, as Hambleton (1992) notes, while different analysts may agree on this diagnosis and advocate decentralization as a solution to such problems, the form and nature of 'decentralization' favoured may vary. Decentralization via markets liberates both organizations and customers, the latter expressing their freedom through choice in the market place (e.g., parents and schools). In contrast, administrative decentralization does not reject state delivery of services but seeks to create organizations more consumer (or citizen) responsive while retaining control over political strategy and service distribution. Thus, its structures follow the Kanter model with a small core that has strategic responsibilities and co-ordinates the highly differentiated and sharply focused organizational units of service delivery. Political decentralization goes further in promoting 'empowerment' by providing structures where financial and decision-making control is pushed down the organization and sometimes outwards to clients involving them in the operation of services. Hambleton notes, not surprisingly, that while administrative decentralization is often a fashionable strategy (e.g., amongst UK local authorities) political decentralization may often be discussed but is rarely practiced.

This analysis is clearly not definitive but it demonstrates the differing ideologies that can underlie public management theory and from here filter into practice. Thus a seemingly common reform strategy, decentralization, may emerge from different ideological positions and value sets, each leading to different frameworks of analysis and offering differing structural solutions. Public management theory is therefore neither coherent nor neutral, rather, it represents a different political perspective not only on the structure and functioning of public organizations but also on the political basis of the pubic sector itself.

In its most radical form the difference between the public management agenda for the structuring of public sector organizations and that of traditional public administration begins with the assumption that the current political system is inefficient. Further, what has previously been positively valued (e.g., bureaucratic routines and professional codes of conduct) are assessed as costs rather than as benefits. This analysis is also transposed to networks of organizations (better fragmented) as well as to internal structures (better individualized and destabilized). Thus, efficiency is valued over accountability and responsiveness over due process.

This perspective undoubtedly has it strengths but it is also based on a universal and neo-managerial view of government and its processes. We now turn to discuss some of these, notably the recent emphasis on finance and performance management as well as the focus on quality and entrepreneurship.

FINANCIAL AND PERFORMANCE MANAGEMENT

A survey of the traditional literature on public administration in the UK (e.g., Brown & Steel, 1979; Greenwood & Wilson, 1989) reveals little on the *internal* financial and informational workings of public sector organizations and even less on systems of personnel management. Even a concern with the public as consumers and customers was rare indeed. Such matters were seen either as dull and distant from policy concerns or as the bailiwick of specialist literatures. This is even true of the more theoretical public administration literature of the 1970s (Dunsire, 1973; Keeling, 1972; Self, 1972) and, notwithstanding the work of Heclo and Wildavsky (1974), it was not until the 1980s that finance and expenditure (mainly in terms of public expenditure management) became a subject deemed worthy of detailed consideration and even then only by a select group of specialist economists and political scientists (Heald, 1983; Hood & Wright, 1981).

Meanwhile at the more micro-level there was intensive but perhaps transient interest in organizational budgetary reform (e.g., planning programming and budgeting (PPB)) and, in the wake of the Fulton

Committee's Report into the Civil Service, some support for improved accounting and management techniques promulgated by enthusiasts such as Garrett (1972). Some, but not all of this, appeared on the political agenda as experiments in programme budgeting and evaluation but few of these reforms were long lived. Instead, as 'big governments faced hard times' (Hood & Wright, 1981) from the early 1970s, the prevailing economic voices that gained political attention in the UK were writers such as Bacon and Eltis (1976), US public choice economists such as Buchanan, Downs and Niskanan, and emerging think tanks such as the Adam Smith Institute and the Centre for Policy Studies. These were to change the political agenda and focus, aided by populist voices which claimed that financial management in the public sector was characterized by waste and inefficiency (Chapman, 1978).

Faced with deepening crises of public expenditure the prime policy goal of government in the UK and elsewhere became the control of public finances. The importance of this cannot be over-estimated both in terms of the internal management techniques called upon to serve this objective and of the regimes of personnel management that accompanied it. In brief, between the late 1970s and early 1980s there was a conscious shift of political emphasis from the management of policy to financial control and a search for mechanisms to serve this end. Practical developments such as delegated financial management and individualized personnel management systems therefore represent strategies developed to support a particular set of political values and agenda. Further, the theories deemed necessary to service this agenda were those of management accounting and finance rather than any identifiable sub-discipline of traditional public administration.

In the practice of public management, the 1980s and 1990s have become the age of the financial manager. Accounting, budgeting and auditing have dominated the discourse about the delivery of public services and changed the language and rules of resource allocation in areas as diverse as education, health, and policing both in the UK and overseas (Cothran, 1993; Gray Jenkins, & Segsworth, 1993b; Schick, 1990). The theoretical literature used to legitimize this transformation has been drawn frequently from the fields of academic accounting and, to a lesser extent, the work of economists interested in the public sector and public management processes (Jackson, 1982; Hopwood & Tomkins, 1984). This has also been aided by the emergence and development of bodies such as the National Audit Office in central government and the Audit Commission in local government (and now the National Health Service), bodies who in their staffing and focus have reached beyond the traditional role of audit to value for money studies.

The period has also seen the publication of new journals such as *Financial Accountability and Management, Accounting, Auditing and Accountability* and *Public Finance,* a publication of the CIPFA, which is also involved with *Public Money and Management* and, through its research arm the Public Finance Foundation (PFF).

The most significant practical impact of these changes has been the emergence of accountable management and regimes of performance measurement. Even if defining accountable management precisely has its difficulties, it is clearly based on a management accounting theory that commends the decentralizing of responsibility for resource use within organizations by identifying individuals and holding them responsible for budgets and performance (Gray, Jenkins, Flynn, & Rutherford, 1991). Backed up by the development of information systems to enhance top management control, accountable management is therefore concerned with 'the economics of public sector delivery' (Humphrey, Miller, & Scapens, 1993, pp. 14–15) and aims to change the nature of public sector management processes. It is also, in the view of some of its academic advocates, a way of liberating managers from over rigorous central controls. Hence 'entrepreneurial' budgeting (Cothran, 1993) is seen as a device where budget holders can use resources in a creative and innovative way to serve their needs within accepted limits of accountability.

Such logic lies behind a host of recent reforms (e.g., local financial management of schools, general practitioner fund holders) and links with some of the centralization initiatives discussed above and which have been subject to critical debate, including in the accounting community (Andrew & Bill, 1993). Moreover, it also underpins the conception of a results – driven organization that can measure its performance. Two different issues are involved here, the nature of performance measurement and its related reward systems. The issue of performance measurement is far from new in either the theory or practice of public administration, having been central to earlier discussions of policy evaluation (Hogwood & Gunn, 1984), as well as featuring in debates on successive innovations such as cost–benefit analysis (CBA), planning programming budgeting (PPB), zero-based budgeting (ZBB) and management by objectives (MBO). In terms of current fashions, the last of these is of greatest interest. Once rejected, MBO now appears to have gained a new lease of life on the coat-tails of accountable management. Thus, systems of budgets managed against negotiated targets appear to be an MBO in all but name. However, in this current guise, more grandiose ideas of effectiveness measures (a feature of reform movements such as PPB) appear to have been abandoned in favour of target systems that assume the sanctity of higher level values and goals (i.e., fundamental questions are rarely asked of goals).

In a similar way, the growing literature on performance measurement appears to play out old debates in a new arena. How can effectiveness be measured and performance assessed in a world of ambiguous or conflicting objectives'. Does the easy to measure drive out the more difficult'. Indeed, the emphasis on measurement, performance and cost has been one of the prime causes of the labeling of this financial focus of public management theory and practice as 'managerialism' and 'neo-Taylorism' and criticized accordingly (Pollitt, 1990). However, as Flynn (1993, Chapter 8) also points out, performance cannot be ignored and, if any organization is to learn and progress, mechanisms for assessing performance at different levels and different ways are necessary. This is clearly the position of writers such as Jackson (1993) and Carter (1989, 1991, 1992) who make a strong case for the development of performance measures and indicators while noting the difficulties in developing such systems in the public sector (recognized also by Pollitt, 1986, 1988 and Likierman, 1993).

Meanwhile, in government itself, more robust systems of performance measurement have been promoted by the Treasury (1992) and by the Audit Commission (1988). In the eyes of current gurus such as Osborne and Gaebler (1993), this focus on performance is crucial if one is to develop a 'results-driven' government that learns from its mistakes (Chapter 5). They also argue that such a perspective is absent from bureaucratic government that focuses on inputs rather than outputs. Yet reforms such as programme analysis and review (PAR) and PPB were all output orientated, they failed not because of the weaknesses of bureaucratic government but because they did not gel with the political values that shaped administrative structures and behaviour.

Similar problems also arise in terms of the development of new personnel regimes to match the new delegated and resource-driven culture. Personnel management in local government and the National Health Service, for example, has traditionally drawn on an institutional literature that focuses on the development of professional groups and service conditions dominated by central pay bargaining mechanisms and professional career and reward structures (Poole, 1978). However, both these professionally based systems in local government and the career structures of central government have been neglected areas in the literature of traditional public administration. Nor has the latter drawn extensively on the literatures of disciplines such as organizational sociology and psychology.

This picture, however, has now dramatically changed not least since the achievement of a political vision of a public sector based on fragmented financial structures and a contract culture is deemed to require the dismantling and federalizing of professional and occupational groups. Hence, the practical agenda of public management includes a vision of personnel management dominated by contracts and performance-related reward schemes and the 'opening-up' of appointment systems to both public and private sector candidates. The practical face of this agenda can be seen, for example, in recent reform proposals for the UK police service (Cm 2280, 1993), the Higher Civil Service (Cm 2627, 1994) and more generally for the public sector (Cm 1730, 1991).

Given its current fashionable status, one might have expected a substantial empirically based literature on the merits or otherwise of performance-related reward systems. Such evidence, however, appears at best limited both at home and abroad. In a recent review, for example, Ingraham (1993) notes that 'the diffusion of pay-for-performance has been based less on careful analysis and evaluation than on a perception of success in other settings, informal communication among bureaucratic and elected decision makers and perhaps wishful thinking' (p. 348). Ingraham (1993) goes on to note the fact that reviews of the effects of performance-related pay in the US (commissioned by the Office of Personnel Management) and by bodies such as the Organization for Economic Co-operation and Development (OECD) demonstrate that many of the assumptions held about the effectiveness of performance-related reward systems appear to have little empirical foundation. The author then concludes that what is required is an assessment of what systems *public* organizations need rather than what *private* organizations do. This should involve integrating such innovations closely into other reforms and into the reality of public sector work (pp. 354–355).

Such reservations, echoed by inquiries in the UK by research bodies such as The Institute of Manpower Studies, indicate the tenuous theoretical basis on which some of the practice of the new public management is based or, in a different way, the selective use of particular literatures to sustain a practical political agenda. This, in turn, is characterized by paradoxes in which liberated 'managers' (a feature of theory of accountable management) find themselves facing new constraints (e.g., chief executives in Next Steps agencies (Dopson, 1993)), a feature commented on by an astonished David Osborne (of Osborne and Gaebler fame) in a recent visit to the UK (Local Government Chronicle, 1993).

QUALITY, EMPOWERMENT AND ENTREPRENEURSHIP

Over and above financial and performance management, both the theory and (sometimes) practice of public management identifies a commitment to quality and clients within organizational systems that empower managers and offer scope for entrepreneurial activity. The advocacy of such characteristics emerges seamlessly from the models of 'excellent' organizations discussed above and to a lesser extent on from the management accounting literature of delegated budgeting. In the UK, such exhortations have in different ways been given political impetus by initiatives such as the Citizen's Charter (Cm 1599,1991) and efforts by bodies such as the Audit Commission (1993a) to raise the quality of local authority services. Yet, while the language of such theories and theorists has often been pilfered by political and administrative reformers, difficulties abound in determining what these concepts actually mean in public services. What is the distinction between citizen, customer, client and consumer? What does quality actually mean in the context of different circumstances of government? When should the emphasis appropriately be placed on entrepreneurial risk? How far can quality and entrepreneurship be accounted for and to whom (back to citizens and customers)?

These provide clear examples of the epistemological problems discussed above where language is deemed to be value free and infinitely transferable first, an assumption that the values embedded in these concepts are compatible with the major values in administrative systems that reformers might wish to retain and, second, that the cultures of public sector organizations are homogeneous. Here public management mirrors traditional public administration with its failure to provide an anthropology of public organizations that gives due weight to cultural diversity of organizations (Morgan, 1986, 1993). This weakness has substantial implications for both the design and implementation of administrative reform programmes.

The discovery of quality is a by-product of a developing strand of general management thinking that links organizational *success* with a concern for quality. Beginning with questions on the reasons for the dominance of Japanese industry, this has moved from a focus on product quality through a flirtation with techniques such as quality circles to the rediscovery of the works of Edwards Deming (1986) and his concept of Total Quality Management (TQM). This approach, first offered as a way forward for private industry in the USA, has been transferred to the government (Carr & Littman, 1990). It is now the subject of a fast growing literature on public management (Morgan & Murgatyrod, 1994). Yet, as in performance-related pay, questions have been raised concerning its appropriateness to public sector organizations unless redesigned to take account of the government's unique circumstances (Swiss, 1992).

The underlying problem with an emphasis on quality is that no one is against it but definitions depend on values and circumstances (e.g., what is a quality health service?) (Walsh, 1991a). Similar problems characterize other aspects of the new public management lexicon such as 'empower-ment' and 'entrepreneurship'. The literature of the new management, both public and private, extols the virtue of systems where rules are relaxed and opportunities given for organizational members to take the initiative in the interests of providing a quality service. But who is to determine what quality means? It is clear from any study of the established literature on organizational behaviour and psychology, especially in the areas of moti-vation and organizational design, that there exists a firm theoretical basis for some aspects of these prescriptions. What is less clear, however, is how far the general and often anecdotal arguments of writers such as Osborne and Gaebler can be applied *generally* to public sector organizations and more particularly to their *political* context. Thus, for example, the com-plaint of advocates of the agency initiative in UK central government is that 'freedoms' granted are in fact severely constrained to the extent that such new systems may be characterized less by the 'empowerment' of public managers as by the centralizing of control and the displacing of blame (Dopson, 1993; Mellon, 1993).

This last point is of importance but not the least since it indicates the potential of public management or at least the *use* of some of its ideas to depoliticize the operations of the governmental process and to redefine ac-countability relationships. In this there is a sharp difference between the ideas that sustain theory and practice in traditional public administration and those of public management. As was outlined earlier, traditional visions of public service place this within a system of accountability relationships that while sometimes ill defined (e.g., the firm line between politics and administration) do place administrators as accountable to the public through the political system. In the new world, however, it appears pos-sible not only for politics and administration to be 'separate' but 'separated' with the former actors entering a 'blame free' zone, leaving administrative actors in the front line. It would be unwarranted and unwise to blame public management for this situation but it is as unwise to see traditional public administration structurally and theoretically to have failed or to regard the development of public management simply as a linear progression from an old to a new world. The central point of interest of the Kuhnian vision of a paradigm shift is that it represents a discontinuity rather than a continuity in value systems. Our contention is less that a paradigm shift has taken place but rather that competing visions exist that in many ways remain separate and distinct. Whether they can be drawn together is an issue we now address in the conclusion.

CONCLUSIONS

Over two decades ago, Ridley (1972) wrote that there was cause for discontent in the subject public administration. 'It is reasonable to ask', he observed

> whether progress in the field of public administration is more likely to come in response to a demand from administrators or whether demand itself depends on the existence of a recognized *subject*. If administrators are to ask for more than instruction in a miscellaneous bag of techniques, if they are to ask for something actually called public administration, they must surely first see the existence of an integrated discipline clearly different from other disciplines which between them offer the miscellaneous techniques they currently study (p. 68, emphasis in original).

At the time of Ridley's comments, public administration was still the preserve largely of political science and constitutional law. It had enjoyed an opportunity to use these disciplines to forge a clearly defined and at least interdisciplinary subject with its own territories and conceptual and methodological framework. Yet neither before nor since have those in the positions of academic leadership sought to seize this opportunity. It will not return. Yet in some ways this may not matter as both traditional public administration and public management may never be more than a foci for study in which a variety of disciplines make a contribution. It may thus be more important to seek ways in which these fields can be integrated rather than remain as mutually exclusive areas occupied by different academic communities with differing theoretical values and prescriptions.

The need for such a move may be urgent since in terms of practice, the advance of public management may be unstoppable. As Prior (1993) has observed

> It is arguable that the fundamental change that has occurred in the public sector is not the replacement of one broadly uniform set of arrangements with another uniform set, but the fracturing of the public sector into a plethora of different sets of arrangements with few common features. It is then questionable whether the term 'public sector' is any longer useful as a generic analytical concept (p. 459).

These remarks, mainly directed at changes in UK local government, could with equal validity be applied to changes in central government and the National Health Service. Thus, in practical terms, the 1990s has seen the UK public sector not only structurally transformed but also projected into a situation characterized by uncertainty and ambiguity. This may be a consequence of what Smith (1994) has termed post-modern politics or government by exhaustion 'a political system disorientated, deficient and out of sorts with itself' (p. 137) or what others have termed the 'hollowing' of the state in which central functions have either been removed or redistributed to a complex and fragmented organizational system with little attention to the corresponding need to design new systems of governance to manage this situation (Moe, 1994; Rhodes, 1994).

Given this reality, there is little to be gained by harking back for a return to some lost world of public administration or of simply offering a blanket critique of the new public management which would in no way be deserved. Rather, it is necessary to examine the strengths and weakness of the public management approach and to assess whether there are aspects of traditional public administration that need to be 'rediscovered' and incorporated into its framework (Goodsell, 1993).

As outlined above and clearly articulated by other commentators, public management differs from traditional public administration. It has developed an analytical agenda based heavily on the concepts and theories of public choice economics (and associated fellow travelers such as Osborne and Gaebler) and strands of corporate management thinking that attempt to define the structures and processes of 'excellent' or 'well-performing' organizations in rapidly changing and complex economic and social environments. Although, as Aucoin (1990) points out, such perspectives are not necessarily complimentary, such a theoretical approach has identifiable strengths. It meets the need for a variety of alternative organizational structures and delivery systems to be recognized (contingency theory is alive and well – even Burns and Stalker (1961) are to be reprinted) and for the motivation of staff and relations between organizations and the clients they serve to be given high priority. Further, the exploration of alternative financial/budgetary arrangements may clarify and redefine the politics of the budgetary process, while a focus on goals and results, together with an interest in institutionalized systems of evaluation, have the potential of at least creating the 'learning' organizations sought for so long by advocates of strategic management. The progressive and attractive aspects of public management theory therefore stress decentralization, deregulation and delegation within a framework of executive models of centralization, co-ordination and control (Aucoin, 1990, pp. 119–125).

Theories of public management also have identifiable weaknesses both individually and in terms of their ability to be drawn together into some conceptual 'gestalt' that might qualify for the term paradigm. In particular their often apolitical perspective may lead to a downgrading of values considered important in both theorizing about and reforming systems of public administration. Examples of such difficulties include the championing of results over administrative processes, the imposition or substitution of economic values for legal values and a conception of accountability that replaces or redefines traditional mechanisms by quasi-markets and producer/consumer relationships (Caiden, 1994; Kernaghan, 1993; Moe, 1994). A fundamental basis of government and traditional public administration in most states is the role of law and its attendant regulations. However, commenting on US experience, Moe (1994) argues that in the entrepreneurial paradigm results come first, processes second or never. He adds that this represents a fundamental misunderstanding of government where 'if certain laws, and implementing regulations, hinder effective and responsible management, we should amend those laws and regulations' (p. 115).

When discussing management changes in British government *in* the early 1980s, Metcalfe and Richards (1990) argued that the application of reform techniques represented 'an impoverished conception of management'. This may still be true for public management theory since its approaches often avoid any discussion of mechanisms of governance. On this point Hood (1991) has called for an assessment of public management in terms of what he terms administrative values since this one will allow judgment on 'good administration' separate from political values that deal with the role of state in society. That such a distinction must remain artificial has been stressed in different contexts by Ranson and Stewart (1988, 1989), Walsh (1991b) and Moe (1994). The agendas of these writers differ but their case for the distinctiveness of the public sector and the values it represents rests on such features as collective choice in the polity, equity, citizenship and collective action as a policy instrument. In different ways these are features of the agenda of traditional public administration. Their presence in the lexicon of public management is somewhat less predictable.

As Aucoin (1990) has pointed out, the changing political agenda of the last decade and the emergence of public management has led to tensions and even contradictions in models of governance and administration. Thus, theoretical divergence within public management itself (i.e., between public choice and the managerialist perspective) may result in principles of organizational design and management that push in opposite directions (centralization and decentralization, co-ordination and deregulation, control and delegation). He also notes that these perspectives may have 'radically different understandings of the "politics" which underlie the exercise of management functions' (p. 127).

This issue of resolving the political dimension of public management is one of the core problems in both the theory and practice of public management. So too is the development of a capacity to deal with the values particular to the public sector outlined above. In this, public management may need the stimulus of traditional public administration just as much as the latter doubtless required that of many of the concepts and theories of public management.

So what of a future agenda? First, the theoretical approaches of public management have to be recognized and studied for what some (although not all) of them are – distinctive contributions to economic and political thought. Dunleavy (1991) was exemplary in recognizing this about public choice theory and provides a model for others to follow. Second, and as outlined above, we can employ the tenets of traditional public administration to add a necessary constitutional dimension to the theories and prescriptions of public management. There are signs too that this is underway. For example, the democratic deficit argument used against the proliferation of unaccountable organizations in the UK public sector (Bogdanor, 1993; Stewart, 1993) has been telling enough to warrant a public response by ministers (Waldegrave, 1993), not least since it is based on a clear political theory and also exposes the claimed neutrality of recent initiatives in this area (see Goodsell, 1993). Third, there must be a willingness to examine, test and, if appropriate, adopt the conceptual and methodological frameworks which the new approaches held are bringing with them and to employ them more rigorously to help forge an empirically based range of theories that bring together both public administration and public management. This seems to apply especially to the practical and political implications of basing the management of public service on some form of separation of policy and execution and the resulting organizational fragmentation. Unless both public management and public administration seek to do this the consequence will be a government sector and, more widely, a public sector, which continues to be ill informed, where the implementation of reform changes may lead to perverse results and where public disillusionment with government and administration will continue to increase.

REFERENCES

Andrew, G., & Bill, J. (1993). Special edition on 'Accounting, accountability and the "New" UK public sector'. *Journal of Accounting, Auditing and Accountability, 6*(3), 52–67.

Aucoin, P. (1990). Administrative reform in public management paradigms, principles, paradoxes and pendulums. *Governance, 3*(2), 114–117.

Audit Commission. (1988). *Performance review in local government a handbook for auditors and local authorities.* London: HMSO.

Audit Commission. (1993a). *Putting quality on the map measuring and appraising quality in the public sector.* Occasional Paper no. 18, March.

Audit Commission. (1993b). *Realising the benefits of competition.* London: HMSO.

Bacon, R. W., & Eltis, w. A. (1976). *Britain's economic problem too few producers* (2nd ed.). London: Macmillan.

Bogdanor, V. (1993). The democratic deficit, *The Guardian,* 14 June.

Brown, R. G. S., & Steel, D. (1979). *The administrative process in Britain* (2nd ed.). London: Methuen.

Bums, T., & Stalker, G. M. (1961). *The management of innovation.* London: Tavistock.

Butler, J. (1992). *Patients, policies and politics.* Buckingham: Open University Press.

Butler, Sir R. (1992). The new public management the contribution of Whitehall and academia. *Public Policy and Administration, 7*(3), 1–14.

Butler, Sir R. (1993). The evolution of the civil service a progress report. *Public Administration, 71*(3), 395–406.

Caiden, G. S. (1994). Administrative reform American style. *Public Administration Review, 54*(2), 123–128.

Carr, D. K., & Littman, J. D. (1990). *Excellence in government total quality management into the 1990s.* Arlington, VA: Coopers and Lybrand.

Carter, N. (1989). Performance indicators "backseat driving" or "hands-off" control. *Policy and Politics, 17,* 131–138.

Carter, N. (1991). Learning to measure performance the use of indicators in organizations. *Public Administration, 69*(1), 85–101.

Chapman, L. (1978). *Your disobedient servant.* Harmondsworth: Penguin.

Cm 1599. (1991). *Raising the standard the Citizen's charter.* London: HMSO.

Cm 1730. (1991). *Competing for quality.* London: HMSO.

Cm 2280. (1993). *Inquiry into police responsibilities and rewards* (The Sheehy Report). London: HMSO.

Cm 2627. (1994). *The civil service continuity and change.* London: HMSO.

Cmnd 3638. (1968). *The civil service* (The Fulton Report). London: HMSO.

Connolly, M., McKeown, P., & Milligan-Byrne, G. (1994). Making the public sector user friendly a critical examination of the Citizen's Charter. *Parliamentary Affair, 47*(1), 23–37.

Cothran, D. A. (1993). Entrepreneurial budgeting an emerging reform. *Public Administration Review, 53*(5), 445–454.

Davies, A., & Willman, J. (1991). *What next? Agencies, departments and the civil service.* London: Institute of Public Policy Research.

Deming, W. E. (1986). *Out of the crisis.* Cambridge: MIT Press.

Doern, C. B. (1993). The UK Citizen a Charter origins and implementation in three agencies. *Policy and Politics, 21*(1), 17–30.

Dopson, S. (1993). Are agencies an act of faith. The experience of HMSO. *Public Money and Management, 13*(2), 17–23.

Dunleavy, P. (1991). *Democracy, bureaucracy and public choice.* London: Harvester Wheatsheaf.

Dunleavy, P., & Hood, C. (1994). From old public administration to new public management. *Public Money and Management, 14*(3), 9–16.

Dunleavy, P., & O'Leary, B. (1987). *Theories of the state the problems of liberal democracy.* London: Macmillan.

Dunsire, A. (1973). *Administration the wont and the science.* Oxford: Martin Robertson.

Dunsire, A. (1995). The state of the discipline administrative theory. In: K. A. W. Rhodes (Ed.), British Public Administration the state of the discipline. *Public Administration, 73*(1) 1–15.

Efficiency Unit. (1988). Improving management in government the next steps (The Ibba Report). London: HMSO.

Flynn, N. (1993). *Public sector management* (2nd ed.). London: Harvester Wheatsheaf.

Garrett, J. (1972). *The management of government.* Harmondsworth: Penguin.

Goodsell, C. T. (1993). Reinvent government or rediscover it? *Public Administration Review, 53*(1), 85–87.

Governance. (1990). Special edition on Managerial reform. *3*(2), 115–218.

Gray, A. G., & Jenkins, W. I. (1993a). Markets, managers and the public service. In: P. Taylor-Gooby, & R. Lawson (Eds), *Markets and managers* (Chapter 1). Buckingham: Open University Press.

Gray, A. G., & Jenkins, W. I. with Flynn, A. C., & Rutherford, B. A. (1991). The management of change in Whitehall the experience of the FMI, *Public Administration,* 69(1), 41–59.

Gray, A. C., Jenkins, W. I., & Segsworth, K. V. (Eds). (1993b). *Budgeting, auditing and evaluation.* New Brunswick: Transaction Publishers.

Greenwood, J., & Wilson, D. J. (1989). *Public administration in Britain today* (2nd ed.). London: Unwin Hyman.

Ham, C., & Hill, M. J. (1993). *The policy process in the modern capitalist state* (2nd ed.). London: Harvester Wheatsheaf.

Hambleton, R. (1992). Decentralisation and democracy in UK local government. *Public Money and Management, 12*(3), 9–20.

Hardin, I. (1992). *The contracting state.* Buckingham: Open University Press.

Harrison, S., Hunter, D., & Pollitt, C. (1990). *The dynamics of British health policy.* London: Unwin Hyman.

Heald, D. (1983). *Public expenditure.* Oxford: Martin Robertson.

Heclo, H., & Wildavsky, A. (1974). *The private government of public money.* London: Macmillan.

Hennessy, P. (1989). *Whitehall.* London: Sacker and Warburg.

Hennessy, P. (1993). *Never again.* London: Vintage Books.

Hogwood, B. (1995). Public policy. In: R. A. W. Rhodes (Ed.), British Public Administration the state of the discipline. *Public Administration, 73*(1), 59–73.

Hogwood, B., & Gunn, L. (1984). *Policy analysis in the real world.* Oxford: Oxford University Press.

Hood, C. (1990). De Sir Humphrying the Westminster model of bureaucracy a new style of governance. *Governance, 3*(2), 204–214.

Hood, C. (1991). A public management for all seasons? *Public Administration,* 69(1), 3–19.

Hood, C., & Wright, M. (Eds). (1981). *Big government in hard times*. Oxford: Martin Robertson.

Hopwood, A., & Tompkins, C. (Eds). (1984). *Issues in public sector accounting*. London: Philip Allan.

Humphrey, C., Miller, P., & Scapens, R. W. (1993). Accountability and accountable management in the UK public sector. *Accounting, Auditing and Accountability*, 6(3), 7–29.

Hunter, D. (1994). Why the world should be wary. *The Guardian*, 9 March.

Ingraham, P. W. (1993). Of pigs in pokes and policy diffusion another look at pay-for-performance. *Public Administration Review*, 53(4), 348–356.

Jackson, P. M. (1982). *The political economy of bureaucracy*. Oxford: Philip Allen.

Jackson, P. M. (1993). Public service performance evaluation a strategic perspective. *Public Money and Management*, 13(4), 9–14.

Jenkins, W. I. (1978). *Policy Analysis*. Oxford: Martin Robertson.

Jordan, G. (1994). Reinventing government but how will it work. *Public Administration*, 72(2), 271–279.

Kanter, R. M. (1983). *The change masters*. New York: Simon and Schuster.

Kanter, R. M. (1989). *When giants learn to dance*. London: Unwin Hyman.

Kavanagh, D. (1987). *Thatcherism and British politics the end of consensus?* Oxford: Oxford University Press.

Kay, J. (1993). *The foundations of corporate success*. Oxford: Oxford University Press.

Keeling, D. (1972). *Management in government*. London: George Allen and Unwin.

Kernaghan, K. (1993). Reshaping government the post-bureaucratic paradigm. *Canadian Public Administration*, 36(4), 636–644.

Kuhn, T. (1970). *The structure of scientific revolutions*. Chicago: Chicago University of Chicago Press.

Le Grand, J. (1990). *Quasi-markets and social policy*. Bristol: School of Advanced Urban Studies.

Le Grand, J. (1993). *Quasi-markets and community care*. Bristol: School of Advanced Urban Studies.

Levscic, R. (1993). Markets as co-ordinative devices. In: R. Maidment, & G. Thompson (Eds), *Managing the United Kingdom* (Chapter 2). London: Sage.

Likierman, A. (1993). Performance indicators twenty early lessons from managerial use. *Public money and management*, 13(4), 15–22.

Local Government Chronicle. (1993). Gore's own guru, 4 July.

Mellon, E. (1993). Executive agencies leading change from the outside in. *Public Money mid Management*, 13(2), 25–31.

Metcalfe, L., & Richards, S. (1990). *Improving public management* (2nd ed.). London: Sage.

Moe, R. C. (1994). The reinventing government exercise misinterpreting the problem, misjudging the consequences. *Public Administration Review*, 54(2), 111–122.

Morgan, C., & Murgatroyd, S. (1994). *Total quality management in the public sector*. Buckingham: Open University Press.

Morgan, G. (1986). *Images of organizations*. Newbury Park, CA: Sage.

Morgan, G. (1993). *Imaginization*. Newbury Park, CA: Sage.

Osborne, D., & Gaeblar, T. (1993). *Reinventing government*. New York: Plume Books.

Peters, T. J., & Waterman, R. H. (1982). *In search of excellence*. New York: Harper and Row.

Peters, T. J., & Waterman, R. H. (1988). *Thriving on chaos*. London: Pan Books.

Peters, T. J., & Waterman, R. H. (1992). *Liberate-in management*. London: Macmillan.

Pollitt, C. (1986). Beyond the managerial model the case for broadening performance assessment in government and the public services. *Financial Accountability and Management*, *2*(3), 155–170.

Pollitt, C. (1988). Bringing consumers into performance measurement. *Policy and politics*, *16*(2), 77–87.

Pollitt, C. (1990). *Managerialism and the public services*. Oxford: Blackwell.

Pollitt, C., & Harrison, S. (Eds). (1992). *Handbook of public services management*. Oxford: Blackwell.

Poole, K. P. (1978). *The local government service*. London: George Allen and Unwin.

Prior, D. (1993). In search of the new public management. *Local Government Studies*, *19*(3), 447–460.

Ranson, S., & Stewart, J. D. (1988). Management in the public domain. *Public Money and Management*, *2*, 13–19.

Ranson, S., & Stewart, J. D. (1989). Citizenship and government the challenge for management in the public domain. *Political Studies*, *37*, 5–24.

Rhodes, R. (1996). Rhodes rod, from institutions to Dogma: Tradition, eclecticism, and ideology in the study of British Public Administration. *Public Administration Review*, *56*(6), 307–516.

Rhodes, R. A. W. (1994). The hollowing out of the state the changing nature of public service in Britain. *Political Quarterly*, *65*(2), 138–151.

Richards, S. (1992). Changing patterns of legitimation in public management. *Public Policy and Administration*, *7*(3), 15–28.

Ridley, F. F. (1972). Public administration cause for discontent. *Public Administration*, *50*(1), 65–77.

Schick, A. (1990). Budgeting for results recent developments in five industrialized countries. *Public Administration Review*, *50*, 26–34.

Self, P. (1972). *Administrative theories and politics*. London: Unwim Hyman.

Smith, T. (1994). Post-modern politics and the case for constitutional renewal. *Political Quarterly*, *65*(2), 128–137.

Stewart, J. D. (1993). The limitations of government by contract. *Public Money and Management*, *13*(3), 7–17.

Swiss, J. F. (1992). Adapting total quality management (TQM) to government. *Public Administration Review*, *52*(4), 356–362.

Taylor, I., & Popham, G. (Eds). (1989). *An introduction to public sector management*. London: Unwin Hyman.

Taylor-Gooby, P., & Lawson, R. (1993a). Where we go from here the new order in welfare. In: *Markets and Managers* (Chapter 9). Buckingham Open: University Press.

Taylor-Gooby, P., & Lawson, R. (Eds). (1993b). *Markets and managers*. Buckingham: Open University Press.

Treasury, H. M. (1992). *Executive agencies: A guide to setting targets and measuring performance*. HMSO, London: HM Treasury. Archive, archive.cabinetoffice.gov.uk/eeg/1998/gui_areps.pdf

Vickers, J., & Yarrow, G. (1988). *Privatization an economic analysis*. London: MIT Press.

Waldegrave, W. (1993). The myth of the democratic deficit. *Public Finance and Accountancy*, *16*(July), 6–7.

Walsh, K. (1989). *Marketing in local government*. Harlow: Longman.

Walsh, K. (1991a). Quality and public services. *Public Administration*, *69*(4), 503–514.

Walsh, K. (1991b). Citizens and consumers marketing and public sector management. *Public Money and Management, 11*(2), 9–16.

Waterman, R. H. (1994). *The frontiers of excellence.* London: Nicholas Brealey.

Williamson, O. (1975). *Markets and hierarchies.* New York: Free Press.

FURTHER READING

Audit Commission. (1989). *Loosing an empire, finding a role.* London: HMSO.

Carter, N., Klein, R., & Day, P. (1992). *How organisations measure success the use of performance indicators in government.* London: Routledge.

Stewart, J. D. (1986). *The new management of local government.* London: George Allen and Unwin.

Stewart, J. D. (1992). *Accountability to the public.* London: European Policy Forum.

Stewart, J. D., & Walsh, K. (1992). Change in the management of public services. *Public Administration, 70*(4), 499–518.

THE NEW PUBLIC MANAGEMENT AS AN INTERNATIONAL PHENOMENON: A SKEPTICAL VIEW

Laurence E. Lynn Jr.

In the field of public administration, the talk throughout the world is of change, of the transformation of governments: new forms of governance, new relationships between citizens and their governments and between the public, private, and nongovernmental sectors, new processes of policy making.

It is now widely believed that the 1980s represented a watershed in administrative reform around the world. According to Gerald Caiden (1991, p. 1), "... inherited administrative systems were proving to be sluggish, inflexible and insensitive to changing human needs and novel circumstances."[1] These inherited systems included those of the East Bloc, which had embraced statism, bureaucratic centralism, central planning, and scientific or technocratic management. The West in the meantime had developed the apparatus of the welfare state, the idea of representative bureaucracy, command and control regulation, and, in many countries, state enterprise. The Third World was saddled with what Caiden calls "law and order administrations" which lacked the experience, resources, and trained personnel to perform competently, much less to switch directions suddenly; rule was autocratic and personal, backed by force.

Comparative Public Administration: The Essential Readings
Research in Public Policy Analysis and Management, Volume 15, 573–591
Copyright © 2006 by Elsevier Ltd.
ISSN: 0732-1317/doi:10.1016/S0732-1317(06)15024-1

In this view, administrative states of every type were visibly falling short of adapting to the changes in politics, markets, and public attitudes clearly gaining momentum everywhere. Today, the Organization for Economic Co-operation and Development (OECD) calls reform "a burning issue," based on official member country reports, and, even if there is no crisis, there are insistent, strong pressures for further change (OECD, 1996).

OECD cites as sources of these pressures, factors such as, the development of a global market place; national perceptions that member country public sectors are not performing well, yet are growing steadily larger and, in the process, creating mounting budget deficits and public debt burdens; citizen dissatisfaction with services and with political administrations that are seemingly impotent to improve matters; and restive public employees who are becoming increasingly insecure, beleaguered, and defiant of criticism (OECD, 1996, p. 19). Even in Japan, whose bureaucrats are perhaps the most secure, competent, and powerful in the developed world, and where the best and brightest university students aspire to careers in the bureaucracy, "the national trust in the bureaucracy has collapsed," according to recent press accounts. A series of missteps and cover-ups has aroused public concern that the Japanese bureaucracy is unable to respond to the wishes of the people, and the language of change is transforming politics there, too. Mexico and other Latin American nations have been facing similar pressures from an increasingly critical public to improve the quality and responsiveness of public administration.

Moreover, there is a strong suggestion of convergence. In a recent paper, Patricia Ingraham (1996, p. 4) insists that, despite obvious differences in national experiences, "the commonalities are more important than the differences." In their best-selling *Reinventing Government*, David Osborne and Ted Gaebler (1992) say of change in American government that "the reforms represent a paradigm shift" (p. 19). The OECD, along with many other students of government such as Peter Aucoin (1990) and Michael Barzelay (1992), among others, concur. If these students of administration are right, we are moving inexorably into a world of post-bureaucratic, post-modern, post-industrial government.

What is being celebrated – and that is the right way to characterize this literature – is expressed in various ways in various places: a withering away of "direct bureaucracy" in favor of a "hollow state," "virtual organizations," and networked organizations, a shift of power from bureaucrats to citizens, a rebirth of community and of democratic accountability, the realization that incentives and competition are the guarantors of growth and efficiency when public resources are scarce. In his National Performance

Review conducted for the newly elected Clinton Administration, U.S. Vice-President Al Gore urges that Americans view themselves as customers of government rather than as citizens (Gore, 1993). The role of citizen, says Gore, is inherently weak – the individual voter cannot determine the outcome of an election – whereas customers can compel response to their wishes by insisting on receiving value for what they pay or shopping elsewhere. Firms survive in markets. Bureaucrats should similarly endure the discipline of competition.

The new paradigm itself has been variously denominated. In addition to the popular "post-bureaucratic" label, other terms include "managerialism," "the new public management," "market-based public administration," and "entrepreneurial government." According to OECD, the key reform thrusts are:

> a greater focus on results and increased value for money, devolution of authority and enhanced flexibility, strengthened accountability and control, a client- and service-orientation, strengthened capacity for developing strategy and policy, introducing competition and other market elements, and changed relationships with other levels of government.

As Andrew Dunsire (1995) depicts it for the United Kingdom, the goal is to replace the "administrative, hierarchical and professional cultures" by a "private, commercial, market culture."[2]

It seems incontrovertible, then, that, at the very least, the role of government is under rather intense scrutiny in a great many if not most countries and is, in many places, yielding to parliamentary and public demands for change. By the logic of the argument that commonalities dominate, moreover, administrative states worldwide must be becoming more alike.

This particular proposition raises an issue of far deeper significance than mere isomorphism in managerial practice. This significance can be grasped if we reformulate the argument.

BUREAUCRACY AND THE NATION STATE

Bureaucracy, the structural form of the modern administrative state, is, by any credible theory of social development, endogenous to social and political transformation. Bureaucracy is not imposed, not exogenous. It is created by polities; it solves problems.

More specifically, the contemporary administrative state is widely held to be a product of modernization. This, of course, was Weber's view, and there is wide scholarly concurrence. In his book *Surveillance, Power and Modernity: Bureaucracy and Discipline from 1700 to the Present Day*, Christopher Dandeker (1990) associates the growth of what he terms "bureaucratic surveillance" in modern societies – by this he means processes of information gathering, storage, processing, retrieval and their application to administrative decision-making (p. 202) – with the emergence of the modern nation state. "Both the nation state and business enterprise," he argues, "depend upon the 'visible hand' of bureaucratic surveillance for their survival." Bureaucratization of the modern state involves four distinct processes: formal-legal rationalization of social relations; non-proprietary administration of the means of administration, and especially, of discipline and enforcement; the increasing knowledgeability of organizations; and specialization as a source of advantage in competing for scarce resources (pp. 196–197). "The outcome of these four linked processes of change has been that modern societies are now in large part under fairly dense networks of surveillance" (p. 197).

Among the sources of bureaucratic growth, Dandeker argues, are both strategies of control by central authorities and also popular demands for citizenship rights (p. 202). "Bureaucratic co-ordination of organizations is understood in terms of the performance of tasks for collective interests rather than [merely] as an exercise of power over subject populations" (p. 203).

Though modernization is paradigmatic, it by no means leads to a homogeneous configuration of the administrations of all modern states. Mediated by national differences, modernization produces differentiated bureaucracies. In *Cages of Reason: The Rise of the Rational State in France, Japan, the United States, and Great Britain*, for example, Bernard Silberman (1993) identifies two contributors to the dynamics and resulting structures of state building: the level of uncertainty concerning political succession, and the nature of political leadership structure, and, in particular, whether leadership is a question of social or party identification. This leads to four cases: (1) high uncertainty combined with a social basis for leadership produces high levels of bureaucratic autonomy; (2) high uncertainty coupled with party-oriented political leadership produces single-party dominated, organizationally oriented bureaucracies; (3) low uncertainty and social-network organized leadership produces a party-dominated professional bureaucracy; (4) low uncertainty and a party system produces an American-style professional bureaucracy accountable to party-dominated politics (pp. 82–83).

As an historical matter, political strategies, then, reflect choices of ways of resolving tensions and problems existing between the state and civil society, solutions to problems of conflicting values. Silberman concludes:

> The rationalization of the administrative role – the creation of the norms of bureaucratic role in modern society – was the consequence of political struggles. These were struggles to redefine the structures of power and the criteria for access to them by groups of putative leaders who sought to reduce the uncertainty over their status and power and, as a consequence, their material well-being (p. 425).

Ferrel Heady puts the matter succinctly: "what has become more and more obvious is the extreme importance of variation among political regimes as a major explanatory factor for variation among public bureaucracies" (Heady, 1996, p. 472).

A related proposition is evident in the recent work of Robert Putnam (1993). Putnam's logic suggests that state building and the performance of administrative structures are a reflection of underlying, historically determined civic culture; a strong civic culture produces effective administrative performance. But, argues Sidney Tarrow (1996), the causal arrow may go the other way: from politics as the mobilization of bias to civic culture and association based on trust as a premise for the conduct of civic affairs. If civic capacity is the by-product of politics, as Tarrow argues, then one must understand the historical bases of these politics in order to understand the character and performance of modern states, and, as Putnam's work illustrates, regions within states. The dynamics of state building are complex and differentiated. Struggles for political power are mediated by national institutions.[3]

If one accepts the foregoing logic, then the proposition that we are witnessing a fundamental transformation in modern bureaucracies, as opposed to incremental modifications, must be based on a belief that we are witnessing a fundamental transformation in the historic role of the nation state and of the force of nationalism, in the generative forces of public administration, socio-political and economic transformation of a character that "predicts" the new paradigm as a resultant. If the bureaucratic paradigm is rational/legal in the Weberian sense, then a post-bureaucratic paradigm must be founded on a different basis of legitimacy: perhaps different forms of rationality, different jurisprudential principles, a different allocation of property rights.

CONVERGENCE CONTESTED

The proposition that the new paradigm is producing convergence in administrative states is an even more dramatic claim. It must be true that postmodernization, unlike modernization, is more powerful than the mediating characteristics of nationalism. The isomorphism of the post-modern administrative state, then, represents a historical discontinuity, the internationalization of administrative elites, of administrative forms, of praxis, indeed, of politics.

Can such an Argument Withstand Scrutiny?

As already conceded, there can be little doubt that we are experiencing some kind of ferment on an international scale. For the moment, let us concede further that what we are witnessing is quite possibly a fundamental change in governance. What accounts for this change?

Viewed from one perspective, the sea change in public administration worldwide reflects the triumph of capitalism and market-based social allocation, indeed, of the global marketplace, over socialism and state-directed social allocation.

Viewed from another, not necessarily inconsistent, perspective, this change reflects the triumph of democracy and of the rule of law over authoritarianism and statism within the framework of heightened, not diminished, nationalism. Habermas notes that "even in established democracies, the existing institutions of freedom are no longer above challenge, although here the populations seem to press for more democracy rather than less" (Habermas, 1996, p. xlii). The recent OECD Ministerial Symposium on the Future of Public Services produced the observation that organized interest groups, long a major factor in American politics, are multiplying in many countries, as long-standing benefit structures are threatened by the demand for public administrative and fiscal reform. In cases where such groups as the elderly or those with vested interests in public pensions become sufficiently mobilized, the opportunities for long-term reform may be severely constrained. This is especially true when a political leader or his challengers finds large political advantage in playing to such groups (Allen, 1996).

Further, the opportunities for the public to confront the politician have vastly expanded because of new communication technologies. One participant in the OECD ministerial symposium observed that "it is a great deal easier to talk about the need for long-range reform in the abstract than it is to sustain public support for the particulars when those are made clear" (Allen, 1996).

A choice of perspective is crucial to one's views about the character of the transformation taking place in the administrative state for the simple reason that the two perspectives produce opposite predictions concerning administrative transformations.

Global capitalism requires the dismantling or substantial weakening of command and control bureaucracy and statist enterprise, of all distortions in prices and interference in capital and labor mobility. If nationalism required a strong bureaucratic state, internationalism requires the unrestricted movement of factors of production within and across borders. One would expect to see, as we indeed appear to be seeing, a considerable weakening of political support for redistributive policies. Bureaucracy should dissolve into a series of successor institutions whose shape we may not yet fully grasp but which yield property rights and control of scarcity rents to private entities.

Nationalism and democracy, however, require the rule of law, legally sanctioned regulation of markets, and competent bureaucracies subject to control by statute and by judicial institutions. Carl J. Friedrich (1940) argued that democracy would have no chance to survive without bureaucracy because it would not be able to carry out the programmatic promises of its elected leaders. Weber viewed a system of bureaucratic rule in the modern state as inescapable; he could discover no known example of a bureaucracy being destroyed except in the course of a general cultural decline (Bendix, 1960, p. 458). Bureaucratic power, says B. Guy Peters, "may simply be a prerequisite of effective government in contemporary society" (Peters, 1992).

Weber precisely identified what the rule of law means for bureaucracy (Bendix, 1960): official business is conducted on a continuous basis in accordance with stipulated rules by an administrative agency in which personnel have defined duties, authority to carry them out, strictly defined powers, and appropriate supervision. They have no property rights in the resources at their disposal or in their offices. Official business is conducted in writing. Without these features, "there cannot be a system of legal domination in which the exercise of authority consists in the implementation of enacted norms" (p. 424). I repeat this familiar list of criteria not because they define bureaucracy – the usual function of such a listing – but because they define the rule of law and the means for assuring the constraint of authority by enacted norms.

Belief in the equivalence of bureaucracy and the rule of law explains why many public administration theorists have reacted to claims that "traditional" bureaucracy is being overthrown by reasserting neglected principles of public and administrative law.

If it is spread of democracy, and not of capitalism, that is the story of the late twentieth century, then we should not expect to see bureaucracy shrivel and weaken so much as we should expect to see it come into its own as an indispensable adjunct to competitive nationalism. Fred Riggs (1996) characterizes the current period not as post-modernism but as "para-modernism," i.e., a necessary confronting of the negative consequences of modernization and of bureaucracy as its instrument.

In the modern (or para-modern) state, bureaucracy has turned out to be both solution and problem, an apparatus that provides structure and continuity to modern states but, at the same time, poses a threat to democratic and party control. Our age is characterized, according to Henry Jacoby (1973), by "the forceful transformation of rational administration into the irrational exercise of power, the lack of clearly defined limits to coercion [or corruption], and the increasing competence of a state, which arrogates independence to itself" (p. 2). The self-aggrandizing tendencies of bureaucratic elites have, according to Heady, heightened the issue of political control of public administration around the world. It is this suspicion of bureaucratic power that began to intensify in the 1980s, producing the changes documented by public administration scholars and inspiring discoveries of "new paradigms." This intensification is occurring, however, in the context of heightened concern for national identities, the legitimacy of authority, and long-term political viability of governments, and it is this linkage that is of significance.

THE NEW PUBLIC MANAGEMENT DECONSTRUCTED

We can see the primacy of national political requirements if we begin with the metaproblem that appears to be inspiring administrative reform: political control of public administration, or the responsiveness of bureaucracy to citizens and their representatives. This is, of course, a generic, structural problem of modern democratic government. If we consider more specific kinds of solutions being pursued by different national governments, we will discover the great variety of forms that administrative restructuring is taking.

In Australia and the United Kingdom, for example, the favored term for reform appears to be "managerialism," a term that has distinctly pejorative implications in the United States. A recent Australian textbook (Hughes, 1994), replete with bows toward Osborne and Gaebler, says that the managerialist agenda is, in essence, quite simple. Governments would like to know that public ends are being served in an efficient and effective manner.

Corporate planning techniques can specify what departments are to do; program budgeting means that scarce funds can be better targeted; performance indicators allow some measure of how well targets are being achieved; and the personnel changes increase flexibility so that the most able are rewarded and the inadequate can be removed.

To an American, such an agenda summarizes largely discredited American administrative reforms of the 1960s and 1970s. Even the language, featuring cost-effectiveness and program budgeting, is the same as that of Planning-Programming-Budgeting (PPB).

A decade of administrative reform in New Zealand has a distinctly different cast. "The reform of the system of government," says one experienced observer, has these elements: moving purely commercial activities from departments to corporations owned by the government; privatization of those corporations in commercially competitive markets; structural reorganization of government administration to promote efficiency through competition ...; a management framework for central government service delivery which centers on the achievement of detailed performance objectives; shrinking budgets.

In short, in New Zealand reform has meant "thinking about the public sector in private sector terms." This formulation, too, has echoes in American experience, this time of the later studies and report of the Grace Commission created by President Ronald Reagan. You fix big government not by planning and analysis but by having a lot less of it.

The most arresting development in New Zealand is the decision to draw a sharp distinction between "outputs" and "outcomes" of governmental activity and to manage both commercial and core activities strictly in accordance with "outputs," not "outcomes" (in this respect, it resembles the UK's Next Steps reform). From this single decision, much else follows. Chief executives are now held accountable for producing outputs; appropriations and accounting are for outputs, not programs. In effect, Ministers and Parliament now must decide to acquire services/outputs from executive agencies based on their reported efficiency ("return on capital") in output production. Governmental activity is now managed in accordance with principles and structures appropriate to profit-making enterprise. Parliament and the government are assessing performance in the same transparent, measurable terms.

This is the precise opposite of the approach adopted in the U.S. in the Government Performance and Results Act (although it echoes the performance budgeting orientation of America's post-war Hoover Commissions). Through this Act, Congress intends to promote a fundamental shift of administration and accountability away from a preoccupation with staffing and activity levels toward a focus on *outcomes* of federal programs expressed in terms of the real difference federal programs make in people's lives (U.S. Government Accountability Office (GAO), 1996, pp. 1–2).

If our test of the new public management is transforming change in the core functions of government around the world, then the verdict must be not only "not proven," but "not yet" and very probably "not ever." The OECD (1995, p. 19) correctly observes that "there is no single model of reform, there are no off-the-shelf solutions" to the problems of the bureaucratic state. Indeed, the variations in the models of reform being tried around the world strongly suggest that *there is no new paradigm*, if by paradigm we use Thomas Kuhn's (1970) original definition: achievements that for a time provide model problems and solutions to a community of practitioners. A community's paradigms are "a set of recurrent and quasi-standard illustrations of various theories in their conceptual, observational, and instrumental applications" (p. 43). Can a community (assuming for the moment that public administration scholars and practitioners constitute a community – many doubt this) without an accepted theoretical canon (or with one so inclusive of behavioral and social science as to be unhelpful as a source of guidance) and without accepted methods of application (not within a single country's public administration community and not across national communities) be said to possess paradigms?[4]

Indeed, the foregoing argument calls into question not only the notion of a "post-bureaucratic" paradigm but of a "bureaucratic" paradigm as well. Though one can artfully create a tale of convergence around model problems and bureaucratic solutions from America's administrative history, such tales are not entirely persuasive. "Solutions" from the time of the Progressive era, the New Deal, the Great Society, and the Reagan era to the present have been sharply contested among citizens, practitioners, and scholars. Is public management unique or generic? Can the logic of business enterprise be adapted to the needs of government's core functions? Does bureau-based "managerialism" threaten liberty? Is legislative oversight of administration essential or inimical to effective management?[5]

The features that these formulations have in common are, first, the extent to which they reflect the political preoccupations of individual national governments rather than implementation of model solutions, and, second, the extent to which the promises of the reforms remain almost wholly unfulfilled, as if the symbolism of adoption was the point, not results. There is little evidence of convergence on anything remotely approaching a new paradigm.

Dunleavy and Hood (1994) explicitly reject Osborne and Gaebler's assertion of the inevitability of a new paradigm. They describe alternative, multiple futures for public management based on constitutional issues arrayed on two dimensions: the degree to which there are general, system-wide rules of procedure, and the degree to which the public sector is separated from the private sector (pp. 13–14). The future, they suggest, may hold gridlock and "headless chicken" administration, "virtual proximity systems," conventional bureaucracy, or any of a wide variety of administrative states that represent political solutions to problems of national politics.

JUST THE FACTS

Champions of a post-bureaucratic paradigm, of managerialism, or of the new public management, might reasonably respond by insisting that facts should be brought forward to quiet the skeptics and reassure the doubtful. The facts strongly suggest, many seem to insist, that we are witnessing in the acts of governments and their emerging consequences not just "outlier" developments of only random interest (and not just heterodoxy expressed in a meta-language) but significant, convergent movement toward a successor to bureaucracy. At the very least, proponents might argue, we are witnessing "structuration of the international administrative field," as sociologists might put it, under the spreading influence of public choice doctrines or of a revived business-based managerialism. Even if such a world-wide transformation is, to at least some degree, mimetic, it is nonetheless consequential for administrative practice.

Will "the facts" vindicate the new public management? I want to make five points in response. Though those concerned with administrative reforms are increasingly conversing in a common meta-language,[6] I am not convinced that we have an agreed-upon body of facts concerning the nature, extent, and consequences of change worldwide. For one thing, we lack the conceptual foundations for designing appropriate measurements. "There are no general theoretical frameworks," Page (1987) argues, "which allow one to distinguish between salient and marginal differences of bureaucracies," differences which must include "differences in institutional structures and relationships" that constitute the environment of administration. (Heady's (1996) *Public Administration: A Comparative Perspective* may be an exception.) For another, many of the most acclaimed features of the new public management – an emphasis on quality and continuous improvement, devolution and expansion of managerial autonomy, a commitment to customer satisfaction – are virtually unmeasurable. Further, and a consequence of the first two, evaluative claims are plagued by selection bias, ex post rationalizations, irrefutable or unverifiable arguments, and the absence of either empirical or conceptual context. A typical sentence from obviously sympathetic evaluations includes expressions such as "widely held impressions are," "informed observers believe," "there has been substantial impact," and "there is a real difference."[7]

Scholarly "customers" of such vague, subjective, and unproven claims are justified in expressing dissatisfaction with the product. A "new public manager" would never accept them.

The evidence suggests that the extent of change is modest at best and that many documentable changes may be transitory, awaiting the verdict of political succession. Of the impact of managerialism so far, one Australian scholar observes that "in most senses, the new approach is simply untested." Evidence to demonstrate the gains from the New Zealand reforms is said to be "somewhat limited." The OECD reports that "the rate of take-up of reforms is uneven and the pace of implementation is slow."

Reform may be slow, but is it nonetheless inevitable? A skeptic might wonder if New Zealanders, discussed with their pre-fiscal crisis regime, have really repealed the principles of political economy and public choice (well explicated, for example, in Murray Horn's (1995) recent book). Are New Zealand's public choices no longer tainted by self-interest or idiosyncracy? Or is it, rather, that the governing party has such a powerful majority (or the opposition is so fragmented) that issues and controversies, conceptual and political, have for the time being been suppressed? I don't believe for a minute that theorists, technocrats, and accountants have taken over New Zealand's public sector.

A recent report by the US GAO on one of the centerpieces of the Clinton Administration' s administrative reform, agency "reinvention labs," characterizes their purpose as testing ways that agencies could improve their performance and customer service by reengineering work processes and eliminating unnecessary regulations. The GAO observed, however, that there was very little evidence of change beyond the lab sites; change remained highly specific and localized. Other Clinton Administration initiatives include "downsizing of the federal workforce," the possible elimination of entire agencies, the establishment of strategic goals and plans to measure their results, and the consolidation of the functions of several agencies. For these changes, too, one is hard-pressed to identify anything approaching a dramatic, long-lasting outcome, and interest in them has noticeably waned.

Third, to the extent that the facts are suggestive, they suggest that basic transformations are occurring primarily in the state-owned enterprise sectors and that a substantial amount of privatization is probably taking place. This is not an insignificant achievement, of course. As for those governmental sectors producing collective goods, including the regulation of markets, I suspect that the story is substantially different and that, if anything, the rule of law is and has been growing in importance. Partial documentation of the efficiency gains of privatization should not be allowed by scholars to obscure the extraordinary difficulties of appraising changes in those functions producing collective goods.

Fourth, the evidence strongly suggests that political origins of reform differ from country to country and, therefore, that administrative reform is, indeed, the reflection of the ongoing processes of nation-building. The uniting of a fiscal crisis with public choice doctrines in New Zealand, Thatcherite animus toward the administrative/professional mandarinate in the Great Britain, and the Reagan/Bush/Clinton preference for deregulating business and shifting policy and financial responsibilities to the American states are distinctly different brands of national politics. All, moreover, are subject to reversal at the polls.

In a recent paper, Richard Stillman (1996) observes that "... much of the recent scholarship in Germany in the 1990s is directed at the challenges of imposing 'state' reunification; in the Netherlands, new forms of governance with or through complex 'steering' networks; or in England, the application of business models to force 'efficiency and economy' on government as symbolized in recent government reports like *Citizen's Charter* or *Next Steps*. In the post-socialist East European nations, policy planning, judicial oversight, economic control, and effective program implementation are major themes reflected in administrative training and education" (p. 15). This suggests considerable heterodoxy, a variance that should serve as a useful stimulus to comparative study linking politics and administration.

Fifth and finally, whatever one concludes as to the extent and direction of bureaucratic transformation as a worldwide phenomenon, very little transformation is occurring in the United States, where many of the boldest claims of change originated. The United States has had relatively little state-owned enterprise, and the sell-off, devolution, and deregulation have been gradual for some time, so privatization has limited impact on U.S. government operations.

Osborne and Gaebler (1992) argue that education is the public system in America "that has moved farthest toward a paradigm shift" (p. 325). Yet just in recent weeks, stories have appeared in the American popular press reporting documented failure of one of the principle hopes of the reformers: using private management companies to direct the affairs of schools and school systems toward greater efficiency and accountability. Earlier hopes for the rapid emergence of a national chain of private, proprietary schools delivering results for a reasonable price, in sharp contrast to American public schools, have only a handful of experimental sites to show for it.

Much of the evidence suggesting widespread rapid change in the United States is unreliable and often self-serving. If one resorts to dispassionate sources, such as GAO assessments and some academic evaluations, one cannot find evidence to support a claim of widespread transformation, much less a claim that a new paradigm has emerged.

THE NEW PUBLIC LAW DEMOCRACY?

For public administration, then, a more appropriate focus of inquiry might be the nature of transformations taking place around the world in democratic institutions and practices and in their indispensable concomitant, the rule of law and the approaches to and practices of lawmaking by legislative bodies. These are, after all, the independent variables in the study of bureaucracy. Walter Kickert and Richard Stillman (1996) put the question correctly in their recent symposium on public administration in Europe in *PAR:* "At the close of the 20th century, will the redefinition and redirection of basic tasks, responsibilities, and purposes of the nation-state once again influence a fundamental reform of European administrative systems and administrative sciences?" (p. 66). What is of interest is the changes in tasks, in the primary work, or core technologies, of government as they are viewed in an appropriately specified national contexts.

This should produce a rich picture of lawmaking and administration in international perspective. In a recent paper, Stillman (1996) observes, for example, that the European positive law tradition, unlike the American common law tradition, decisively influences the content, logic, and the institutional autonomy of its public administration, particularly on the European Continent. If the Anglo-American common law tradition 'builds-up' precedents based upon an accumulation of discrete cases, the positive law tradition works in reverse: i.e., deducing from general 'state' legal principles to decide rulings in discrete cases. The former looks to cases for finding precedents, the latter, to higher legal principles to impose on specific cases. That of course gives courts, lawyers and the law in Europe critical influence and autonomy in defining the study of public administration (pp. 11–12). Extending and enriching these kinds of insights across a wider spectrum of national experiences justifies a high priority for public administration scholars.

This is not an argument for a return to earlier notions of public administration as a derivative of public law or for a normative view of public administration as jurisprudentially legitimated. It is, instead, an argument for viewing public administration in a democratic context of law-creating and law enforcing. Inspired by nationalism, an historic number of peoples around the world are selecting their governments by ballot. There are growing, albeit controversial, pressures for genuine party competition, for more transparent administration, and for a freer press. Citizens have their most direct recourse to public administration through law creation and law enforcement, however imperfectly they main constrain administration.

To the extent that the problem of modern public administration is democratic accountability (and not all scholars agree that it is), then we must once again focus attention on politics and the role of public law. For it is through public law that the citizens of democratic states collectively express their specific wishes for the role, government is to fulfill. "The most fundamental distinction between public and private organizations is the rule of law," argue James Fesler and Donald Ketti (1991). "Public organizations exist to administer the law, and every element of their being – their structure, staffing, budget, and purpose – is the product of legal authority" (p. 9).

The meaning of "rule of law" is spelled out by Martin Shapiro. "In most English-speaking nations administrative decisions are subject to judicial review for abuse of discretion, which is commonly measured by whether officials have (1) considered something they should not have considered, (2) not considered something they should have considered, (3) given improper weight to something they should have considered, or (4) decided without sufficient evidence" (Shapiro, 1994, p. 503). Abuse of discretion is an appropriate term to use in summarizing widespread public dissatisfaction with bureaucracy and politics.

Perhaps the most important aspect of regimes built on the rule of law for purposes of assessing the prospects for a new public management is that there is a general tendency, as governance institutions mature, for legislative bodies and courts to narrow the boundaries of discretion over time, partly by substituting rules for discretion and partly by introducing various devices that permit at least post-auditing of the prudence of the decisions reached. A participant in the OECD Ministerial Symposium on the Future of Public Services insisted that "Whatever the textbooks might say about decentralization, about taking risks, and better public management, the fact was that most of the pressures on politicians worked in the opposite direction – pushing towards centralization of decision-making and risk aversion" (Waterford, 1996).

Many administrative reformers, including those that inspired the Clinton Administration's National Performance Review, fail to notice that what they pejoratively deride as bureaucracy run amok is in fact the institutional manifestation of the continuous effort to create responsive, accountable government, to prevent abuse of discretion. The government that fails to "serve the customer" is in reality the government that attempts to insure that discretion is not abused, that due process is the rule rather than the exception, and that undue risks are not taken in the peoples' name.

Ultimately, in democratic regimes, elections are the central pre- and post audit of administrative, and sometimes of judicial discretion. Especially in nations moving from one-party socialist systems to party competition and mixed economies, however, establishing the rule of law and transparency are of particular concern (Shapiro, 1994, p. 507). "Enormous revivals of administrative law, usually based on European models, are now underway in such countries designed to increase administrative obedience to law, transparency, and review of discretionary action."

Creating models and solutions to this problem involves reconciling two central tensions that shape the practice of public administration: between national legal and political traditions, on the one hand, and universalistic principles of management, on the other; and between models of governance built on the premise that self-interest governs the public behavior of citizens and their representatives, on the one hand, and models built on the premise that a preference for trust and voluntary cooperation motivates public behavior.

The post-bureaucratic paradigm presupposes that universal principles of management and the premise of gemeinschaft are ascendant and already transcending national rational/legal traditions and the premise of gesellschaft in countries around the world. I doubt it. The important task facing public administration is to discover better approaches to creating rational/legal order, approaches which address popular dissatisfactions in practical, contextually prescient ways using the structural tools that are the stock in trade of the legislator.

NOTES

1. It is worth quoting Habermas on these novel circumstances: "In contemporary Western societies governed by the rule of law, politics has lost its orientation and

self-confidence before a terrifying background: before the conspicuous challenges posed by ecological limits on economic growth and by increasing disparities in the living conditions in the Northern and Southern Hemispheres; before the historically unique task of converting state socialism over to the mechanisms of a differentiated economic system; under the pressure of immigration from impoverished southern regions – and now eastern regions as well; in the face of the risks of renewed ethnic, national, religious wars, nuclear blackmail, and international conflicts over the distribution of global resources" (Habermas, 1996, p. xlii).

2. See Hood (1995, p. 96) for a convenient summary of the doctrinal components of new public management.

3. For example, Andrew Dunsire (1995) cites Christopher Pollitt to the effect that "Whitehall macro-reorganizations [under Margaret Thatcher] were better put down to the political requirements of the Prime Minister than to any administrative reform doctrines" (p. 24).

4. I may be wrong about this. My list of "model problems" includes services integration, choice, contracting, accountability, targeting, comprehensiveness, cultural change, and efficiency. My applications emphasize heuristics from public choice, political economy and institutional sociology, and cognitive psychology. How widely do these lists resonate?

5. Useful histories of American administrative reforms include Downs and Larkey (1986) and Knott and Miller (1987).

6. "The term NPM [new public management] was coined ... to cut across the particular language of individual projects or countries ... " (Hood, 1995, p. 94).

7. Research purporting to show that reforms produce results seldom consider whether "non-reforms," i.e., orthodox managerial initiatives such as enforcing dormant rules, also produce results. Can anyone contest the claim that orthodox reform is more effective than post-bureaucratic reform in producing documentable improvements in performance?

REFERENCES

Allen, J. T. (1996). Summary of session three: Managing for the future: Seeking solutions to long-range problems in a world that demands immediate action. *Ministerial symposium on the future of public services*, March 5–6. Paris: OECD.

Aucoin, P. (1990). Administrative reform in public management: Paradigms, principles, paradoxes and pendulums. *Governance*, 3(2), 115–137.

Barzelay, M. (1992). *Breaking through bureaucracy: A new vision for managing in government*. Berkeley, CA: University of California.

Bendix, R. (1960). *Max Weber: An intellectual portrait*. Berkeley, CA: University of California Press.

Caiden, G. E. (1991). *Administrative reform comes of age*. New York: Walter de Gruyter.

Dandeker, C. (1990). *Surveillance, power and modernity: Bureaucracy and discipline from 1700 to the present day*. Cambridge, UK: Polity Press.

Downs, G. W., & Larkey, P. D. (1986). *The search for government efficiency: From hubris to helplessness*. New York: Random House.

Dunleavy, P., & Hood, C. (1994). From old public administration to new public management. *Public Money and Management, 14*(3), 9–16.

Dunsire, A. (1995). Administrative theory in the 1980s: A viewpoint. *Public Administration, 73*(Spring), 17–40.

Fesler, J. W., & Ketti, D. F. (1991). *The politics of the administrative process*. Chatham, NJ: Chatham House.

Friedrich, C. J. (1940). Public policy and the nature of administrative responsibility. *Public Policy, 1*, 3–24.

Gore, A. (1993). *Creating a government that works better and costs less: Report of the national performance review*. Washington, DC: U.S. Government Printing Office.

Habermas, J. (1996). *Between facts and norms: Contributions to a discourse theory of law and democracy*. Cambridge, MA: The MIT Press.

Heady, F. (1996). *Public administration: A comparative perspective* (5th ed.). New York: Marcel Dekker.

Hood, C. (1995). The 'new public management' in the 1980s: Variations on a theme. *Accounting, Organizations and Society, 20*(2/3), 93–109.

Horn, M. J. (1995). *The political economy of public administration: Institutional choice in the public sector*. New York: Cambridge University Press.

Hughes, O. E. (1994). *Public management and administration: An introduction*. New York: St. Martin's Press.

Ingraham, P. W. (1996). Play it again, Sam, it's still not right: Searching for the right notes in administrative reform. Paper prepared for delivery at the Waldo symposium, The Maxwell School, Syracuse University, June 27–29.

Jacoby, H. (1973). *The bureaucratization of the world*. Berkeley, CA: University of California Press.

Kickert, W. J. M., & Stillman, R. J., II. (1996). Changing European states; Changing public administration: introduction. *Public Administration Review, 56*(1), 65–87.

Knott, J. H., & Miller, G. J. (1987). *Reforming bureaucracy: The politics of institutional choice*. Englewood Cliffs, NJ: Prentice-Hall.

Kuhn, T. S. (1970). *The structure of scientific revolutions* (2nd ed., Enlarged). Chicago, IL: The University of Chicago Press.

Organization for Economic Co-operation and Development. (1995). *Governance in transition: Public management reforms in OECD countries*. Paris: OECD.

Organization for Economic Co-operation and Development. (1996). *Responsive government: Service quality initiatives*. Paris: OECD.

Osborne, D., & Gaebler, T. (1992). *Reinventing government: How the entrepreneurial spirit is transforming the public sector*. Reading, MA: Addison-Wesley.

Page, E. C. (1987). Comparing bureaucracies. In: J.-E. Lane (Ed.), *Bureaucracy and public choice* (pp. 231–255). London: Sage Publications.

Peters, B. G. (1992). Public policy and public bureaucracy. In: D. E. Ashford (Ed.), *History and context in comparative public policy* (pp. 283–316). Pittsburgh, PA: University of Pittsburgh Press Part III, Chapter 13.

Putnam, R. D. (with Robert Leonardi & Raffaella Y. Nanetti). (1993). *Making democracy work: Civic traditions in modern Italy*. Princeton, NJ: Princeton University Press.

Riggs, F. W. (1996). "Para-modernism and bureau power," An essay honoring Dwight Waldo, April 3. Paper prepared for delivery at the Waldo symposium, The Maxwell School, Syracuse University, June 27–29.

Shapiro, M. (1994). Discretion. In: D. H. Rosenbloom & R. D. Schwartz (Eds), *Handbook of administrative law* (pp. 501–517). New York: Marcel Dekker.

Silberman, B. S. (1993). *Cages of reason: The rise of the rational state in France, Japan, the United States, and Great Britain.* Chicago, IL: The University of Chicago Press.

Stillman R. J., II. (1996). American vs. European public administration: Does public administration make the modern state or the state make public administration? An essay in honor of Dwight Waldo, prepared for the Waldo symposium, The Maxwell School, Syracuse University, June 27–29.

Tarrow, S. (1996). Making social science work across space and time: A critical reflection on Robert Putnam's making democracy work. *American Political Science Review, 90*(2), 389–397.

U.S. General Accounting Office (GAO). (1996). *Managing for results: Achieving GPRA's objectives requires strong congressional role GAO/T-GGD-96-79.* Washington, DC: US General Accounting Office.

Waterford, J. (1996). Summary of session one: The setting: Changing the scope, role and structure of government. *Ministerial symposium on the future of public services*, March 5–6. Paris: OECD.

WHAT IS WRONG WITH THE NEW PUBLIC MANAGEMENT?

Donald J. Savoie

The new public management or, as the jargon has it, the "entrepreneurial management paradigm," has been in fashion in many countries, especially in the Anglo-American democracies, for about fifteen years.[1] One can trace its origin to the political leadership which came into office in these countries in the late 1970s and 1980s. It arose from the conviction that bureaucracy was broken and needed fixing, and that private sector solutions were the key. The enthusiasm did not wane when a new political leadership assumed power. In the United States, President Clinton launched, with considerable fanfare, a National Performance Review (NPR) exercise designed to overhaul the civil service and asked his vice-president to lead the charge. It is hoped that the Review's 800 recommendations will "reinvent" government by borrowing the best management practices found in private business. As Ronald Moe points out, "virtually the entire thrust of the [NPR] report and its recommendations make sense only if this premise [i.e., the public and private sectors are alike] is actually the operative concept."[2]

In Britain, Prime Minister Major has vigorously pursued the various reforms introduced by Margaret Thatcher and has added some of his own, including the "Citizen's Charter."[3] Meanwhile, the Canadian civil service has over the past 10 years or so witnessed "a story of orgies of reform hardly punctuated by even brief periods of routine."[4] The Canadian reforms include the introduction of Increased Ministerial Authority and Accountability

Comparative Public Administration: The Essential Readings
Research in Public Policy Analysis and Management, Volume 15, 593–602
Copyright © 2006 by Elsevier Ltd.
ISSN: 0732-1317/doi:10.1016/S0732-1317(06)15025-3

(IMAA), special operating agencies, the make-or-buy concept and Public Service 2000 (PS 2000). Prime Minister Chrétien's new government appointed Marcel Massé, a former senior public servant, to a newly created position in the cabinet responsible for public service renewal. Massé lost no time in declaring his intention to "get government right." His agenda for action borrows heavily from the new public management movement and its literature. Indeed, his statements on public service renewal speak to the need for instilling an entrepreneurial spirit in government operations and for making organizations more "client-centred."[5]

WHAT IS THE NEW PUBLIC MANAGEMENT?

The new public management philosophy holds obvious appeal. It promises to provide the "Big Answer" to real and imagined shortcomings in public bureaucracy. How else does one explain such telling titles as "Reinventing Government" and "Getting Government Right"?

The philosophy is rooted in the conviction that private sector management is superior to public administration. The solution, therefore, is to transfer government activities to the private sector through privatization and contracting out. Given that all government activities can hardly be transferred to the private sector, the next best solution is to transfer business management practices to government operations. However, public *management* is different from public *administration*: the former is derived from commercial operations and is meant to bring about a new mindset, a new vocabulary and a proliferation of management techniques.[6] It is also meant to "debureaucratize" government operations and to reduce red tape substantially.

Unlike the traditional public administration language that conjures up images of rules, regulations and lethargic decision-making processes, the very word "management" implies decisiveness, a dynamic mindset and a bias for action. Indeed, the vocabulary of the new public management reveals that to what extent it borrows from the world of private sector management practices: "empowerment"; service to "clients" or "customers"; "responsiveness"; a shift from "process" to "performance"; and an emphasis on the need to "earn" rather than to "spend." David Osborne and Ted Gaebler summed up the essence of the new public management when they called for a cultural shift away from bureaucratic government towards an entrepreneurial government.[7] Entrepreneurial government is both competitive and customer driven.

The new public management is also attractive to politicians who are unwilling to make tough decisions in a very difficult fiscal environment, it is one thing to call for cutting government down to size while in opposition; it is another to discover that decisions to cut programs are not easily made once in office. Again, the next best solution is to insist that public servants run government operations like private concerns.

THE NEW PUBLIC MANAGEMENT:
A FLAWED CONCEPT

I argue that the new public management is basically flawed. By its very nature the public administration field does not lend itself to big answers because private sector management practices very rarely apply to government operations. As James Q. Wilson explains, public administration "is a world of settled institutions designed to allow imperfect people to use flawed procedures to cope with insoluble problems. ... Because constraints are usually easier to quantify than efficiency, we can often get a fat government even when we say we want a lean one."[8] To be sure, the manner in which programs are conceived and delivered can be improved. This, however, usually happens incrementally and on a program-by-program basis.

I am astounded that some 30 years after the Glassco Commissions' Report on Canadian government operation, we still hear the call for "letting the manager manage" as if it were a new concept. I am equally astounded that we still need to remind people that the public sector is not the private sector.

Perhaps because the two sectors are "fundamentally alike in all unimportant ways," changes proposed by the new public management movement have been strong on prescriptions, but weak on diagnosis. We are told that governments must steer rather than row; that managers, like their counter in business, must be empowered; that new emphasis must be placed on serving "clients"; and that, to measure success by customer satisfaction, we must replace regulations with incentives. Rather than spend time on diagnosing the problems, supporters of the new public management rely on "old time religion to sell their message."[9] However, "as with other types of evangelical messages the authors expect readers to take a leap of faith and act out the vision they describe."[10]

But, what were the problems that needed fixing? What is so wrong with the public administration that has evolved and taken shape over the past

130 years (in this country, at least) that warrants its replacement by an "entrepreneurial paradigm."[11] We hear that bureaucracy is lethargic, cau, bloated, expensive, unresponsive, a creature of routine and incapable of accepting new challenges. Assuming for a moment that some or even all of these charges are accurate, it only begs the question: why? I argue that it has more to do with parliament, politicians and Canadians themselves than with public servants.

Public administration operates in a political environment that is always on the lookout for "errors" and that exhibits an extremely low tolerance for mistakes. The attention of the national media, Question Period and the audi general's annual report are sufficient to explain why public servants are cautious and why they strive to operate in an error-free environment. One would have to let the imagination run wild to visualize a headline in the *Globe and Mail* or an opposition member of Parliament in Question Period applauding the fine work of the "empowered" manager of the local Reve Canada office in Saint John's. Imagine, if you will, an opposition members saying that the opposition accepts that the local manager made two – or even just one – high-profile mistake because that is the price to pay for empowerment. The point is that in business it does not much matter if you get it wrong 10 per cent of the time as long as you turn a profit at the end of the year. In government, it does not much matter if you get it right 90 per cent of the time because the focus will be on the 10 per cent of the time you get it wrong.

The new public management has yet to deal head on with accountability in government. In Canada, as in Britain, the principle of ministerial response still applies, though admittedly it has been battered about in recent years. The principle, however, still underpins the relations between senior officials and ministers and, in turn, relations between ministers and Parliament. The principle of ministerial responsibility makes the minister "blam" for both policy and administration, but he in turn can reach into the bureaucracy, organized as it is along clear hierarchical lines, and secure an explanation as to why things have gone wrong as well as how things can be made right. The civil service, meanwhile, has "no constitutional personality or responsibility separate from the duly elected Government of the day." As Herman Finer explained in his classic essay, the views and advice of civil servants are to be private and their actions anonymous: "Only the Minister has views and takes actions. If this convention is not obeyed, then civil ser may be publicly attacked by one party and praised by another and that must lead to a weakening of the principle of impartiality."[12]

Those who argue that the principle of ministerial responsibility is dated have a responsibility to outline a new regime and to detail how it is to work.

This has never been done. When Sir Robert Armstrong, then secretary of the British cabinet, was asked to deal with the issue in the 1980s, he tabled a memorandum in Parliament essentially restating the principle of ministerial responsibility and then proceeded to make the case for the status quo.[13] Yet, it is the centrally prescribed rules and regulations that so inhibit effective management, force governments not only to steer but also to row, and to con on inputs that underpin the principle of ministerial responsibility.

Lest we need to be reminded, there is also a world of difference between citizens and clients. Clients are sovereign. They can hold business account through their behaviour in a competitive market. In short, clients can turn to the market to defend their interests or walk away from an unsatisfactory firm and turn to one of its competitors. Citizens, on the other hand, have common purposes. They hold politicians accountable through the requirements of political institutions and through exposure via the media. Politicians, meanwhile, hold public servants accountable through the application of centrally prescribed rules and regulations. Albert Hirschman spoke to the issue when he wrote that in the business world "the customer who, dissatisfied with the product of one firm, shifts to that of another, uses the market to defend his welfare and to improve his position." This is neat, tidy, impersonal, effective and quiet. It easily lends itself to quantifying success and failure. With government, however, the customer uses "voice" to express dissatisfaction. Voice is, of course, much more messy than a quiet exit since it can range "all the way from faint grumbling to violent protest; it implies articulation of one's critical opinions rather than a private secret vote in the anonymity of a supermarket; and finally, it is direct and straight rather than roundabout."[14] Public opinion surveys now capture voice on a monthly basis, or even more frequently if political parties desire it and are prepared to pay. The great majority of politicians react to the voice expressed in public-opinion surveys, and government operations are often in their direct line of attack as they seek to introduce corrective measures.

Business executives are also accountable for their activities, but the success of a business executive is much easier to assess than that of a government manager. There is also much less fuss over due process in the private sector than in government, if only because of the difference involved in managing private and public money. It is rarely simple and straightforward in governing where goals are rarely clear.

The new public management gives short shrift to these considerations: it simply ignores them. Rather than tangle with these fundamental issues, the disciples of the new public management employ "a new highly value-laden lexicon to disarm would-be questioners. Thus the term 'customer' largely replaces 'citizen' and there is heavy reliance upon active verbs – reinventing, reengineering, empowering – to maximize the emotive content of what other has been largely a nonemotive subject matter."[15]

If the problem with bureaucracy is one of insensitivity or inflexibility in dealing with the specific concerns of individuals, of rigidity or of over-religious on red tape, rules and regulations, then it may well be that the problem itself is fundamentally an institutional and legal problem. We all too often forget that one person's red tape is another's due process. The solution lies in fixing our political institutions and the laws of Parliament rather than in "periodic preaching from the pulpit" that resorts merely to emotive words about the failings of bureaucrats and the public service.[16]

The new public management has been with us for over 10 years and it has very little to show for itself. To be sure, management consultants have profited extensively. The British government, for example, reported that it had spent over £500 million on consultants, but could only identify about £10 million in savings that could be directly attributed to their advice.[17] It may be that it is better to steer than to row, but if you are a management consult it is much more profitable to row.

What about the executive agencies in Great Britain? A recent study of the impact of these agencies, a number of which are now several years old, reveals that they have "failed to spark off a cultural revolution at the local operational level of the civil service."[18] Interviews with career officials in Washington over one year after the tabling of the NPR report suggests that if there is a consensus emerging about its impact it is that "this too shall pass."[19] Who in Ottawa still sings the praises of IMAA? The few who do insist that it is not dead, but that it has been replaced or overtaken by the PS 2000 exercise. What about PS 2000? Marcel Massé now reports that "PS 2000 put its tail between its legs. In many government departments, managers no longer refer to it, as it has lost credibility as a symbol of reform and renewal."[20] One ought not to be surprised by this turn of events. Jonathan Boston summed up the problems with the new public management in 1991 when he wrote: "It has been challenged on the grounds that it enjoys neither a secure philosophical base nor a solid empirical foundation. It has been crit for its constitutional illiteracy, its lack of attention to the need for pro and due process within government, its insensitivity to varying organizational cultures and its potential for reducing the capacity of govern to deal with catastrophes."[21]

There is a substantial price to pay, however, for the rise and likely disappointment of the new public management. For one thing, it contributes to the "disbelief culture" found in government. Les Metcalfe and Sue Richards argue that the culture acts as a psychological defense mechanism against proposals or initiatives from the outside designed to overhaul the way they go about their work.[22] One only needs to consider the alphabet soup of past efforts at reforms that have not lived up to expectations in order to appreciate why such a culture exists in government: among others, Pras (Planning, Reporting and Accountability), PEMS (Policy and Expenditure Management System), IMAA (Improved Ministerial Authority and Accountability), and zero-based budgeting. These efforts, like the new public manage, failed to live up to expectations. They too promised to deliver the Big Answer, but they too ignored the realities of work in the public service. The new public management is again offering the Big Answer, this time through simple palliatives that will remain simple palliatives as long as the prescriptions are not rooted in a proper understanding of the requirements of political institutions and public administration.

The new public management, perhaps unwittingly, is leaving in its wake problems of morale in the public services. Its basic premise is that private sector management practices are superior to those found in government and that they should be imposed on government. Moreover, because it also suggests that whenever possible its activities should be transferred to the private sector, the implication is that public service has no intrinsic value. It also belittles the noble side of the public-service profession: public servants became public servants because they wanted to serve their country. If they had wanted to become entrepreneurs, they would have joined the private sector or started their own businesses.

But the real damage inflicted by the new public management is that once again we have been diverted from confronting substantial issues of government and public administration.[23] I can hardly overstate the fact that public administration begins and ends with political institutions, notably Parliament and cabinet. Big answers – if they exist, and I am not suggesting that they do – are to be found by fixing these institutions. If the global economy now requires a well-honed capacity on the part of a national public service to innovate, to challenge the status quo, to take risks, to change course quickly, and to have the capacity to speak simultaneously to both the global and to subnational perspectives, then political leaders must begin to question the workings of their own institutions, what they do, and how they do it.

The new public management has also overlooked important problems that urgently require our attention. For instance, there was far more evidence in 1980 that the policy side of government and the ability of bureaucrats to be innovative and self-questioning needed more fixing than did the machine or production-like agencies.[24] The new public management has very little to offer on policy. Instead, with its emphasis on private sector management techniques, it speaks to the need for more "doers" and fewer "thinkers."

If nothing else, we need a fundamental review of the merits of advising on policy from a sectoral or departmental perspective. The current machinery of government tends to compartmentalize such advice. It was no doubt appropriate at the turn of the century to establish vertical sectoral lines and deal with problems in agriculture, transportation and industry at various levels, but in relative isolation from other departments. Issues and challenges confronting nation states; however, now increasingly cross-departmental lines. If key-policy issues are more and more lateral or horizontal in their implications, then the bureaucratic policy formulation and advisory structure must become horizontal as well. Public servants will have to bring a far broader and more informed perspective to bear on their work since issues are now much more complicated and interrelated.

The new public management is ignoring these new challenges. Indeed, it may well be making matters worse, given its call for a decentralized and empowered machinery of government. Empowerment and hiving off of activities into new executive or special operating agencies will make it more difficult to promote coherence in government policy and action. It will also make it more difficult for the political leadership to secure the necessary information to focus on the broad picture. With the lost of "sameness" in government departments and operations, one is left with the question: What kind of information will be necessary to gain a cross-cutting look at policy? How will one secure the information in a consistent fashion, given that governing bureaus are now being asked to look to clients for guidance and are being told that client satisfaction will measure their success?

ADMINISTRATION MATTERS TOO

The above is not to suggest that government should now concentrate solely on policy. Improvements in administration are also necessary. The solution, however, lies not in searching for the Big Answer: government will not be reinvented nor are we finally about to get it right.

Improvements in the administration of government will be made, as they have, for that matter, in recent years. One only needs to look to the participants in the INSTITUTE OF PUBLIC ADMINISTRATION'S Annual Innovative Management Award to see solid progress being made on many fronts in the administration of programs. Many made full use of new information technology to strengthen their capacity to provide services, while cutting back on costs; others looked to new partnerships with other government departments to coordinate services and resources; and still others decided to streamline their operations (e.g., cutting back on the number of government offices in one community delivering somewhat similar or overlapping services and programs). No one would take these achievements to task and the great majority of observers applaud the innovative thinking and the community of public servants behind the efforts. Government bureaus have always sought to improve their operations ever since they were first established. We must recognize that innovative thinking in government did not start with the new public management movement. Yet, one senses that any significant thinking taking place to strengthen the public sector tends to be attributed to the new public management by its advocates. Much more often than not, however, improvements are the results of new circumstances whether it is a tighter budget, new development in computer technology or old-fashioned common sense. The point to bear in mind is that the solutions that work are practical, rooted in the political and legal realities of government. They should not be expected to represent anything more than gradual and incremental improvements to public administration.

NOTES

1. See Donald J. Savoie, Thatcher, Reagan, Mulroney: In Search of a New Bureaucracy (Pittsburgh: University of Pittsburgh Press, 1994); Christopher Pollitt, Managerialism and the Public Ser: The Anglo-Americait Experience (Oxford: Basil Blackwell, 1988); and Ronald C. Moe, "The Reinventing Government Exercise: Misinterpreting the Problem, Misjudging the Conse," Public Administration Review 54, no. 2 (March/April 1994), pp. 111–122.

2. Moe, "The Reinventing Government Exercise," pp. 111–122.

3. "Citizen's Charter" (London: HMSO, July 1991), CM 1599.

4. Donald J. Savoie, "Reforming Civil Service Reforms," *Policy Options* 15, no. 3 (April 1994), p. 3.

5. "The Renewal Government: An Evolving Strategy." Notes for an address by Marcel Massé, minister of intergovernmental affairs and minister responsible for public service renewal to the APEX Symposium, 10 May 1994, p. 8.

6. Nevil Johnson, "Management in Government," in Michael J. Earl, ed., *Perspectives on Man: A Multidisciplinary Analysis* (Oxford: Oxford University Press, 1983), pp. 170–196.

7. David Osborne and Ted Gaebler, *Reinventing Government: How the Entrepreneurial Spirit is Transforming the Public Sector Prom Schoolhouse to State House, City Hall to Pentagon* (Reading, MA: Addison-Wesley, 1992).

8. James Q. Wilson, "Can the Bureaucracy Be Deregulated?: Lessons From Government Agen," in John J. Dilulio Jr., ed., *Deregulating the Public Service: Can Government Be Improved?* (Washington, DC: The Brookings Institution, 1954), p. 59.

9. See Paul Thomas, "Book Review," *Public Sector Management* 3, no. 2 (1993), p. 27.

10. *Ibid.*

11. See, for example, Moe, "The Reinventing Government Exercise," p. 112.

12. Herman Finer, *The British Civil Service* (London: Allen and Unwin, 1937), p. 196.

13. See Great Britain, Minutes of Evidence taken before the Treasury and Civil Service Sub-committees on the Armstrong Memorandum (London: HMSO, 1986).

14. Albert O. Hirschman, *Exit, Voice and Loyalty: Responses* to *Decline in Firms, Organizations and States* (Cambridge, MA: Harvard University Press, 1970), pp. 15–16.

15. Moe, "Reinventing Government Exercise," p. 114.

16. Christopher Pollitt coined the phrase "preaching from the pulpit" in his "Management Tech for the Public Sector – Pulpit and Practice," in B. Guy Peters and Donald J. Savoie, eds., *Governance in a New Environment* (Montreal: McGill-Queen's University Press, 1995).

17. *Ibid.*

18. Jan Brooks and Paul Bate, "The Problems of Effecting Change Within the British Civil Ser: A Cultural Perspective," *British Journal of Management* 5 (1994), p. 185.

19. See B. Guy Peters and Donald J. Savoie, "Managing Incoherence: The Co-ordination and Empowerment Conundrum" (Ottawa: Canadian Centre for Management Development, 1995).

20. Marcel Massé, "Getting Government Right," an address to the Public Service Alliance of Canada, Regional Quebec Conference, Longueuil, 12 September 1993, p. 7. See also Savoie, "Reforming Civil Service Reforms," p. 3.

21. Jonathan Boston, "The Theoretical Underpinnings of Public Sector Restructuring in New Zealand," in Jonathan Boston et al., eds., *Reshaping the State: New Zealand's Bureaucratic Rev* (Melbourne: Oxford University Press, 1991). p. 20.

22. Lea Metcalfe and Sue Richards, *Improving Public Management* (London: Sage Publications, 1987).

23. Ronald Moe makes a similar observation in his "Reinventing Government Exercise," p. 118.

24. Rourke and Schulman, for example, argued that "bureaucratic think tank comes close to being an oxymoron." See Rourke and Schulman, "Adhocracy in Policy Development," *The Social Science Journal* 26, no. 2 (1981), p. 133.

INTRODUCTION: EXPLOITING IT IN PUBLIC ADMINISTRATION: TOWARDS THE INFORMATION POLITY?

Christine Bellamy and John Taylor

This introduction to the theme ... *Towards the Information Polity? Public Administration in the information age* presents the case for the systematic academic investigation of the changing relationships that characterize the 'information polity.' This perspective on the information polity focuses on the significance of new kinds of informational resources and flows in government, and their interaction with broad directions of reform in contemporary public administration, including the new public 'management. It is argued that, whereas the literature of business strategy has emphasized the economic logic by which 'informatization' encourages organizational transformation, this article demonstrates the importance of wider cultural, organizational and political factors to understanding processes of informatization and the changing nature of the emergent 'information polity' ....

In particular, new information capabilities, and the information and communication technologies (ICTs) which make' them possible, are analysed as a core element in modernizing and 'reinventing' government. Systematic research on these matters is long overdue, for although the potential significance of IT for government has been widely recognized, the social

Comparative Public Administration: The Essential Readings
Research in Public Policy Analysis and Management, Volume 15, 603–613
ISSN: 0732-1317/doi:10.1016/S0732-1317(06)15026-5

scientific study of the 'information age' has been largely concentrated on the 'information economy' and the information society.' What has been signally missing from research agendas is systematic investigation using a parallel and overarching concept which embraces the informatization perspective[1] that of the 'information polity' (Taylor & Williams, 1990, 1991; Bellamy & Taylor, 1992). While the informatization perspective has as its primary focus on the development and use of information in public services, the concept of the information polity emphasizes the role of information in the changing system of relationships which is emerging in and around government in the' information age.

As governments adopt new ICTs, so, new capabilities for the mediation of relationships embodied in systems of governance present themselves. New information resources and new information flows are profoundly implicated in the changes which are beginning to give definition to the emergent 'information polity:' changing horizontal and vertical relationships within government; changing inter-governmental relationships; changing relationships between managements, suppliers and customers; and changing relationships between citizens, politicians and the state.

The information polity perspective provides a focus, therefore, for sustained inquiry that places ICTs and information flows at its centre, and which analyzes the changing nature and meaning of relationships as they form around, and are mediated by, the information systems associated with new technologies. Moreover, detailed, balanced research is all the more necessary because of the prevalence of stereotypical attitudes towards new technologies.

New technologies of all kinds have always excited controversy among those who see themselves to be practically affected by them, as well as among academics analyzing their development, application and social impact. IT is no exception. It has provoked fierce debates, many of them characterized by polarized opinions (Dunlop & Kling, 1991). For the pessimists, information technology poses threat; threat to employment, as human labour is substituted by machine, and threat to human dignities embodied in personal skills and competencies, as information systems 'robotize' the labour process, de-skilling and dehumanizing all in their way in a new wave of Taylorized workplace relationships inspired by the potential for stronger and mere intrusive forms of managerial control. Threat is seen too in the Orwellian sense, with the specter of IT as the instrument of political and bureaucratic control and the reduction of the citizen to fearful compliance and surveillance by the 'big-brother' state (Van de Donk & Tops, 1992). It is not surprising, in this context, to find computing 'disasters

celebrated as proof that the rush into computerization has been too head-
long, too ill-considered and perhaps too much dominated by hugely powerful commercial interests.

These views are countered at least as strongly by those who have taken
more optimistic positions. For the optimists, IT is an instrument for humanizing bureaucracy, as technologies create the conditions for flatter,
smaller, more decentralized and more egalitarian organizations in which
employees can achieve greater responsibility and fulfilment (Masuda, 1990).
Furthermore, IT is seen as a potential source of more flexible production,
enabling the customization, targeting and differentiation of goods and
services. New forms of service delivery enhance the role of the consumer,
transforming him or her from passive recipient to active choice-maker. In
contrast to older, 'Fordist' production technologies, IT is seen to be directly
applicable to the service sector, and thus to public administration: public
services can become much more similar in style and orientation to those
delivered by commercial enterprises. There are new opportunities not only
to reduce costs and to increase efficiency, but also to sensitize bureaucracy
to the needs of the customer. In these ways IT is identified as the key to
the reinvention and indeed to the reinvigoration of public administration
(Dutton, O'Connell, & Wyer, 1991; Muid, 1992; OECD, 1992).

While these views present contrasting interpretations of the application of
IT, they share a common technicist predisposition. That is to say, both
positions assume that it is the technology, qua technology, which is primarily
determining the outcomes which are observed and predicted (Scarborough &
Corbett, 1992). In contributing to the development of a more balanced
understanding of IT in public administration, this special issue draws out a
crucially important distinction between *technological impacts* on government,
on the one hand, and the significance of *new forms of information and communication* for government on the other.

New technologies provide innovative and highly sophisticated means for
the development, management and application of information in public
administration and in consequence are an important subject for study.
However, for the social scientist, it is the social *artifact* of communicated
information, which should be the primary academic focus. This perspective
does not deny the significance of the technology. On the contrary, technology (including new information systems) is itself seen as emerging from
a complex set of social influences which become embedded in it, thereby
both delineating the nature of systems and establishing biases in the
information carried on them. We provide insights into the emergent
information polity through our examination of the interaction between

technological change and new forms and flows of information in public administration.

NETWORKS AND RELATIONSHIPS:
FROM AUTOMATION TO INFORMATIZATION

... In this issue, information is analysed not as a static resource, housed and managed by computers, but as dynamic flows on computer networks, networks which permit information to be communicated, shared, distributed and integrated (Taylor, 1992). As we have seen, what is distinctive in the information polity is, therefore, the changing nature of relationships both in and around governmental organizations, and their electronic mediation.

A focus on information networks moves forward debates about new technologies in public administration from a sterile automation perspective, which focuses on the substitution of human labour by machine, towards perspectives utilizing the concepts of *informatization* and *transformation*, which focus on distributional issues and changing social relationships. *Automation* is usually undertaken to achieve gains in efficiency or economy and tends to be associated with a narrow preoccupation with the technological infrastructure of projects. Thus it occurs in isolation from wider informational agendas, and involves little reassessment of organizational structures or business strategies. It is a focus which leads to the ad hoc computerization of discrete tasks or functions, and hence to the creation of 'islands of automation.' In contrast to the automation perspective, the concept of *informatization* has been developed in the literature of business strategy to refer to wide-reaching qualitative changes in and around organizations stemming from enhanced capabilities which derive from new information flows (Zuboff, 1988; Scott Morton, 1991).

... Public service organizations have always collected, stored and processed many items of data, arid automation has considerably enhanced their capacity to do so. Informatization occurs, however, when data collected for a multitude of purposes, at different times and places, can be integrated and shared to become resources of vastly increased significance and application. Fresh analysis of operations, services, administration and markets is permitted, and information can thus be developed to enrich policy making, service delivery and monitoring. In these ways informatization can be interpreted as helping to overcome the bounds of organizational rationality (Frissen & Snellen, 1991; Frissen, 1992).

An important facet of the informatization perspective ... is the challenge to formal boundaries presented by new flows of information over electronic networks. These challenges are analysed at three levels.... first, to explore the challenges which new transnational information flows present both to the regulatory authorities of individual states but also, arid most significantly to the capacity of inter- and supra-national organizations to develop and co-ordinate appropriate responses to them.

Second, contemporary ideas for reinventing government at the level of national administrations also assume the feasibility of introducing and managing boundary-challenging information flows. For example, as public services become more customer-oriented, so information-dependent reforms are being introduced. Three major trends can be discerned, each of which is predicated on the availability of appropriate technical and organizational capabilities for distributing, accessing and integrating information man increasingly wide variety of institutional and geographical locations.

The first of these trends involves the relocation of the intelligence of public services to the point of contact with customers. The provision of information resources at the front office desk, or, on 'touch screens' in public libraries or shopping malls, supports advice giving and the exchange of information with the public (EIP) in ways that are both immediate and geographically independent of back office processing in public bureaucracy (Doulton, 1993). The second trend is towards the lateral integration of customer records across existing organizational structures so that customers become 'whole persons' in their relation with the state. Holistic approaches to patient care in the NHS or to claimants in DSS, as well as one-stop shopping facilities for local authority services, exemplify this trend (Benefits Agency, 1992; LGMB, 1993) .... Thirdly, and as yet least developed in practice, is the trend towards 'prosumption' (Toffler, 1980), whereby information networking is used to draw the consumer of a service simultaneously into its production, as in current proposals for electronically supported self-assessment for UK personal taxation and social security benefits.

The third level at which new information flows challenge the traditional boundaries of public administration is at the level of transaction and production cost structures of the businesses of government. As substantial space and time economies become available from real-time electronic transmission of information, so the relative costs of other factors of production – particularly those costs associated with geographically differentiated labour markets – are exposed. In turn this leads to important strategic questions being asked about traditional organizational designs, particularly geographical and functional configurations. New information flows are seen both as supporting, and requiring, the steering of loosely coupled, slimmed down organizations, which consequently enjoy reduced coordination costs. Customer-facing business processes, supported by information systems, have been identified as the key to realizing both efficiency and quality advantages (Davenport, 1993; Hammer & Clumpy, 1993).

The tenor of this argument is, therefore, that the economic and business logic of the information age gradually but inexorable drives service organizations, including those in the public sector, towards profound *transformations* in the design of their production processes and structures (Scott Morton, 1991). Typically in analyses of public administration, this transformation is captured in changes associated with the new public management (NPM) (Bellamy & Taylor, 1994).

INFORMATION AND NPM: THE POLITICAL DYNAMICS OF EXPLOITING INFORMATION TECHNOLOGY

Given this analysis, it seems paradoxical that the informational issues associated with NPM have been so under-analysed, and that discussions of IT in public administration have been largely conducted through those polarities of pessimism and optimism which characterize generic controversies about new technologies. What is needed is attention to the detail and subtleties of the relationships between new technologies, information flows and the complexities of management in government. The articles collected here offer insights into disjunctions in these relationships which inhibit the efficient and effective exploitation, of the new technologies and the new information flows which they convey. These disjunctions relate, firstly, to factors which arise from the cultural, organizational and political dynamics of government; and, secondly, to factors generated by the wider techno-political environment in which ICTs and information science (IS) are being developed and implemented. In short, while the informatization perspective is useful in providing a framework for the study of organizational development, its emphasis on the business and economic logic of the new informational agenda urgently needs to be augmented by analyses which are more sensitive to the wider political dynamics associated with the management of change (Coombs, 1992).

What these analyses underscore is that much of the thinking about, and appraisal of, new technology in government seems locked in an automation perspective. Information technology projects are still undertaken in ways that are not clearly related to strategic change, and efficiency improvements remain an overriding consideration. In 1988, a Cabinet Office paper stated that: technological improvements have generally been introduced to improve the efficiency of working procedures and to make resource savings. Improvements in service to the public have tended to be a welcome but indirect by-product' (OMCS, 1988). Five years later and this comment still holds. It reflects an attitude whose legacy is still found in Treasury rules which require technology projects to be self-financing in terms of jobs saved and efficiencies gained, regardless of the contribution they make to qualitative improvements or developments in public services. For example, should the computing systems needed to support one-stop shopping by claimants of social security benefits be authorized only if they can also be shown to reduce the costs of social security administration?

Why has a more strategic approach to the development of ICTs and IT in government not been more strongly developed? Different answers to this question, each relating to the culture of management in government, are suggested by Willcocks, Muid and Pratchett. What is clear from all these papers is that information agendas are usually perceived to lie in the technologists' domain, and this seems to be a product of the 'two-cultures' thinking which still afflicts public life in the UK. As we have noted elsewhere, the management of information systems in government has tended to remain the province of IT directorates, the responsibility in the civil service of 'operational' management at senior and middle management grades rather than of top management and ministers (Bellamy, 1994). The logic of this thinking, as Muid points out, is that the divorce of informational issues from strategic management has been strengthened rather than weakened by the creation of Next Steps agencies. An interesting question, implicitly raised by this article, is whether the relocation of CCIA (the Government Centre for Information Systems) from the Treasury to the Office of Public Service and Science will, however, align informational issues more strongly with other government-wide change agendas.

A paradox emerges from, these discussions of recent management reforms in central government. Muid illustrates the general argument we develop here: that the realization of NPM depends upon the strategic development of IS. He shows that the disaggregation of departments into agencies, and the more extensive contracting-out of IT under the market-testing programme, are creating new informational dependencies along with new managerial relationships. The increasing fragmentation of government is making the strategic development of government more difficult, while at the same time it highlights the new relationships and informational flows on which new management processes and organizational structures critically depend. Likewise, Willcocks argues that managerialism in government, the renewed emphasis on bottom line criteria and. in particular, the ill-considered rush to contract-out IT, together increase substantially the risks associated with large-scale new technology projects and inhibit the development of a strategic vision.

These important organizational and managerial issues are reinforced by the organizational politics of new information flows. Whereas traditional bureaucracies were built around command structures and reporting regimes which emphasized the vertical flow of information, and hence encouraged its compartmentalization, we have seen that the rhetoric of consumerism assumes that new electronic networks can facilitate new lateral flows of information which thereby challenge informational domains ...

In contrast, administrative change in the 1990s assumes that information can be made to flow across organizational boundaries, which have hitherto remained relatively impermeable. The ideologically driven assault on producer power in public services, which this assumption reflects, can be seen for example in political pressure for the development of open systems in public administration ...

Thus, the analysis of new information flows and of new technologies to support them, raises highly sensitive political issues at both the operational and policy levels. Herein lie many important barriers to exploiting new information technologies: encouraging information to flow in new directions is not simply a matter of organizing an 'electronic highway.' The real issues lie in the structure, meaning, ownership and regulation of the information flowing on the highway, and in its dissemination (Mulgan, 1991).

For information to be integrated and shared, it must carry agreed meanings and be organized according to agreed specifications. At one level this problem is a techno-bureaucratic one. For example, for customer records to be integrated, common identifiers and common data specifications must be employed so that, for instance, names and other pieces of data can be recognized arid used by different information systems. In some contexts, for example, the amalgamation of the computer systems and administrative codes by which the wide range of UK social security benefits are processed, integration presents problems of scale rather than of complexity. However, in other contexts, this requirement also presents significant political problems because it challenges the rights of professions, organizations and countries to define, control and customize their own data .... The difficulty is that information does not carry agreed values and interpretations. Rather, the meanings attached to information and to data derive from the discourses of the groups which generate and own them and hence the status, cultures and identities of these groups are frequently seen to be at stake. It is far from surprising, therefore, that most systems fail not because of technological problems per se but because the politics of systems implementation proves unmanageable.

THE TECHNO-POLITICAL ENVIRONMENT OF INFORMATION TECHNOLOGY

... By the 'techno-political environment' we mean the environment created by macro-decisions about the trajectory of technological development, and the broad social, economic, commercial and organizational factors that determine them. There are a number of interesting issues here. One concerns the extent to which the technologies, which are deployed possess inherent properties which determine their impact in specific organizational contexts, for example public administration.

CONCLUSIONS

What are the general conclusions, which can be drawn from the perspectives developed in the chapter presented here? It will be clear that we make equally unattractive both the optimists' view that the widespread deployment of new ICTs offers the golden route to reinventing government and the pessimists' view that it will inevitably result in 'disaster faster' or the big brother state. Ultimately, both are technicist positions, which ignore the socio-political complexities of the information and communication agenda in government.

This article dwells more on the details of the difficulties associated with exploiting IT in government than on the opportunities which, in some pure sense, are embodied in the technologies. An important question, therefore, is whether the technological capabilities for informatization are outstripping the organizational, political and managerial capabilities of constructing, controlling and regulating new information systems and new information flows. The organizational and political issues in managing IT are complex. The very process of informatization disturbs inter- and intra-organizational relationships in ways that are not easily controlled and reordered. Its outcomes emerge from the interaction of managerial, political, professional and commercial stakeholders around technological infrastructures and the design and distribution, of informational resources. As in all sectors of government, the results of new projects will often be compromised and the exploitation of new opportunities patchy.

What, however, gives the application of information and communications technologies special interest is their role in realizing the broad reform initiatives in public administration. If we are right in arguing that the modernization of public administration depends on the effective exploitation of new information flows in government, then those factors that inhibit this exploitation will also inevitably compromise the realizing of the NPM.

It has often been alleged that a specific cultural property of new ICTs is that they are inherently rational tools, and are thus intolerant of ambiguity and incoherence. By exposing much more clearly the information resources and flows which underpin public administration, the process of informatization throws into relief important and largely neglected dimensions of the political dynamics of change in government. As informational issues are increasingly recognized to be strategically central to reform of public administration, so the information dimension will also become more central to academic research in government. Then the study of the 'information polity' will begin in earnest.

NOTES

1. A seminar series on this subject was funded in 1992 and 1993 by the Economic and Social Research Council's Industry, Economy and Environment Group. The ESCR's Programme on Information and Communication Technology (PICT) also funded or partly funded events in 1992 and 1993. The support of ESRC LEE and their and their officers is gratefully acknowledged.

REFERENCES

Bellamy, C. (1994). Managing strategic resources in a next steps department: Information agendas and information systems in DSS. In: G. Jordan & B. O'Toole (Eds), *Next step: Improving management in government?* London: Dartmouth Publishing Co.

Bellamy, C., & Taylor, J. (1992). Informatization and new public management: An alternative agenda for public administration. *Public Policy and Administration, 7*, 29–41.

Bellamy, C., & Taylor, J. (1994). Reinventing government in the information age. *Public Money and Management, 14*(3), 59–62.

Benefits Agency. (1992). *One stop.* Leeds: Benefits Agency Publishing.

Coombs, R. (1992). *Organisational politics and the strategic use of IT, ESRC/PICT Policy Research Paper 20.* Newcastle: Centre for Urban and Regional Development Studies.

Davenport, T. (1993). *Process innovation: Re-engineering work through IT.* Boston: Harvard Business School Press.

Doulton, A. (Ed.) (1993). *EIP report 1992 and case studies.* Oxford: Dragonflair in Association with CDW and Associates.

Dunlop, C., & Kling, R. (Eds) (1991). *Computerisation and controversy.* Boston: Academic Press.

Dutton, W. H., O'Connell, J., & Wyer, J. (1991). *State and local government innovation in electronic services.* Report to the office of technology assessment, US congress. University of South California, Los Angeles.

Frissen, P. (1992). Informatization in public administration. *International Review of Administrative Sciences, 58,* 307–310.

Frissen, P., & Snellen, I. (1991). *Informatization strategies in public administration.* Amsterdam: Elsevier.

Hammer, M., & Clumpy, I. (1993). *Re-engineering the corporation.* New York: Harper Collins.

Local Government Management Board. (1993). *One stop shops.* London: LGMB.

Masuda, Y. (1990). *Managing in the information society: Releasing synergy Japanese style.* Oxford: Basil Blackwell.

Muid, C. (1992). The new public management and informatization: A natural combination? *Public Policy and Administration, 7,* 75–79.

Mulgan, C. (1991). *Communication and control networks and the new economics of communication.* Oxford: Polity Press.

OECD. (1992). *Information technology in government: Management challenges.* Pans: OECD Publications Service.

Office of the Minister for the Civil Service. (1988). *Service to the public.* London: HMSO.

Scarborough, H., & Corbett, M. (1992). *Technology and organisation.* London: Routledge.

Scott Morton, M. (Ed.) (1991). *The corporation of the future: Information technology and organisational transformation.* New York: Oxford University Press.

Taylor, J. (1992). Information networking in public administration. *International Review of Administrative Sciences, 58,* 375–389.

Taylor, J., & Williams, H. (1990). Themes arid issues in an information polity. *Journal of Information Technology, 5*(Sept), 151–160.

Taylor, J., & Williams, H. (1991). From public administration to the information polity. *Public Administration, 70,* 171–190.

Toffler, A. (1980). *The third wave.* London: Pan Books.

Van de Donk, W., & Tops, P. W. (1992). Informatization and democracy: Orwell or Athens? *Informatization and the Public Sector, 2,* 169–196.

Zuboff, S. (1988). *In the age of the smart machine: The future of work and power.* Oxford: Heinemann Professional.

REENGINEERING PUBLIC SECTOR ORGANISATIONS USING INFORMATION TECHNOLOGY

Kim Viborg Andersen

ABSTRACT

Business process reengineering, although initially developed for and within the private sector, is an approach that can form a valuable part of information age reform if it can transform the work processes of public sector organisations. Information technology (IT) has played a central role in reengineering. This chapter therefore describes many ways in which IT can be used to support public sector reengineering, including applications identified from analysis of the 'political value chain'. Nevertheless, IT-supported reengineering originated from technical/rational organisational models that do not necessarily reflect the realities of the public sector. The chapter therefore proposes the concept of public sector process rebuilding (PUPREB): an approach to reengineering that includes a special awareness of the public sector context.

BACKGROUND

With government expenditure on information technology (IT) growing annually, public sector stakeholders want some quantitative or qualitative return

Comparative Public Administration: The Essential Readings
Research in Public Policy Analysis and Management, Volume 15, 615–634
Copyright © 2006 by Elsevier Ltd.
All rights of reproduction in any form reserved
ISSN: 0732-1317/doi:10.1016/S0732-1317(06)15027-7

on this investment. This could involve cost savings through a reduction in staffing levels, improvements in the quality of service to internal and external clients, or an increase in the range of services offered. Unfortunately, new government information systems (IS) have often failed to produce these returns, creating a continual source of vexation for government officials.

How should governments deal with the criticism provoked by the burgeoning IT budgets and the inability of IT to fulfil expectations? One method has been to change – where appropriate – from an IT approach to an information systems approach. In other words, to expand the range of factors taken into account during the process of development and implementation from the solely technical to also encompass human, organisational and environmental issues. The rationale here is that these latter issues are fundamental to IT success and failure.

Another method, not mutually exclusive with the first, has been to change to a process approach. Recent studies have highlighted the importance of internal and external work processes at both macro and micro levels in the organisation. There has also been considerable interest in the relationships between IT, business process reengineering (BPR) and organisational transformation.

In this chapter, we focus on taking a closer look at the concepts underlying BPR and discussing whether and how they can be applied in the public sector by using IT. Two main points are emphasised.

First, the concepts of BPR need to be modified somewhat within the context of the public sector. Certainly, in line with Taylor, Snellen, and Zuurmond (1997), we note that the public sector is being transformed from a professionalised and functionally organised bureaucracy into new organisational patterns. However, this type of transformation prompts a broad range of questions about context and values. Such questions suggest that some of the underlying assumptions of BPR may not hold in the whole public sector, for example, those about the potential for true 'clean-slate' transformation.

As a modification of BPR, we therefore introduce the concept of public sector process rebuilding (PUPREB). Although based on BPR, this includes a special appreciation of public sector context and values. While BPR has been seen as a theoretical means for reinventing government and governance, for cutting red tape and for rightsizing or downsizing (Osborne & Gaebler, 1993), PUPREB is more modest in its promise to reform these areas through the use of IT.

This brings us to a second focus of this chapter. BPR and information systems have been closely associated with the concept of the 'value chain'. While the specifics of the private sector value chain as taught in business schools will not be entirely appropriate to the public sector, the overall concept can be applied. We therefore propose a 'political value chain' that can guide IT-supported reengineering in the public sector.

REENGINEERING THE PUBLIC SECTOR

Hammer and Champy (1993, p. 32), the fathers of the reengineering concept, define reengineering as 'the fundamental rethinking and radical re-design of business processes to achieve dramatic improvements in critical contemporary measures of performance such as cost, quality, service and speed'. The reengineered organisation also becomes process-oriented

- processes are recognised and named;
- everyone is aware of processes;
- process measurement is performed; and
- process management is the norm.

However, the origins of BPR lie firmly within the private sector. We are therefore prompted to ask three questions discussed below.

Can BPR be Applied in the Public Sector?

The BPR approach emphasises that changes in processes are to be dras-tic rather than incremental. Also, the approach points to broad, cross-functional processes and, if needed, a radical change in such processes. All of these mean that BPR is predicated on the idea of radical organisational transformation, with a high risk of failure. How does all these square with a public sector context?

Traditionally, the public sector has been characterised by stability and risk aversion. Not surprisingly, then, when ideas about BPR were first floated, the public administration community did not applaud them. Rather, they jeered that BPR applied in the public sector would, at worst, lead to serious misjudgements and to actions inconsistent with the 'spirit' of the public sector. Yet, as we stand at the turn of the 20th century, we can see this traditional model changing. We might no longer be so quick to say that radical transformation is uncharacteristic of the public sector. Table 1 sum-marises some of the key current trends in the public sector, all of which encompass some fairly radical changes in the way that government conducts its business.

Table 1.   Key Trends in the Public Sector.

Key Trend	Implications for the Public Sector
Reinventing democracy	Treating citizens as customers and including them in the process of governance
Information technology	Providing dramatically better ways of simplifying government and involving citizens via the rapid advances in IT
Alternative mechanisms for government	Increasing use of quasi-autonomous non-governmental organisations (quangos)
Outcomes and performance	Identifying and measuring desired outcomes, reporting results and holding government accountable for those results
Partnerships	Creating new intergovernmental, public–private and labour-management partnerships
Cutting red tape	Developing strategies for results requiring reform of human resource, budget, procurement and other rule-based systems by cutting red tape
Rightsizing/downsizing	Cutting the size of the public sector workforce in accordance with output needs or to increase efficiency
Community-based strategies	Implementing strategies to achieve better service outputs for resources expended, and including citizens and capitalising on their diversity within these strategies

Source: Adapted from NAPA (1996).

As we have known for some time from the work of writers such as Osborne and Gaebler (1993), these kinds of transformations are not just rhetoric but are really taking place. Taking the third table entry as an example, there has been increasing use of alternative mechanisms for government. Table 2 summarises the situation in the Netherlands and the UK, indicating the substantial proportion of public spending now being channelled through such alternative mechanisms.

Parts of the public sector therefore are changing radically and taking risks, so these issues present no overwhelming logical barrier to the idea of BPR in the public sector. As we shall see later, however, this should not blind us to the fact that the public sector is different from the private sector.

Should BPR be Applied in the Public Sector?

The very idea of reengineering processes originates from basic questions: Are we doing our business in the optimal way? Are we doing our job well enough? Are we giving it all we have got? These questions may not be so

Table 2.   Status of Semi-Public Organisations and Quangos in the
Netherlands and UK.

Variable	Netherlands	UK
Number of organisations defined as quangos and semi-public organisations	500	5,521
Number of employees in quangos and semi-public organisations	20,000	65,419
Total annual budget of quangos and semi-public organisations	US$18.5b	US$70b
Total budgets of quangos and semi-public organisations as a proportion of total public budget	18%	30%

Source: The Netherlands data from Leuw and Van Thiel (1996); UK data from Weir and Hall (1994).

clearly understood in the public sector as they are in the private sector, but they are just as relevant.

Reinvention may mean that governments should be as small as possible and contract out tasks as much as possible, but the core of the public sector still needs to be in optimal working order. On top of that, if all existing work procedures are merely outsourced without any reorganisation, little will be accomplished and counterproductive outcomes may emerge.

Not surprisingly, then, NAPA (1996) also lists BPR as a further key trend for public sector reform to add to those listed in Table 1. NAPA (1994a, p. 1) defines reengineering within the public sector as 'a radical improvement approach that critically examines rethinks, and redesigns mission-delivery processes and subprocesses, achieving dramatic mission performance gains from multiple customer and stakeholder perspectives'. It is seen as a key part of a process management approach for optimal performance that continually evaluates, adjusts or removes processes.

Is BPR being Applied in the Public Sector?

Yes it is. As part of their public sector reform efforts, almost all governments have been undertaking process reengineering, although not all have explicitly recognised this. Examples of BPR in the public sector include

- In Phoenix, Arizona, a new 20-story city hall towers over the city's downtown centre. City officials insisted that the building's layout emphasise citizen service. Now Phoenix bundles its city hall services at 'super counters' and eliminates the endless maze citizens once had to negotiate in going from door to door, floor to floor, to obtain service forms and signatures.

- The Social Security Administration now issues social security cards in three to five days instead of six weeks, processes retirement or survivor claims in 13–18 days instead of one month, does cost-of-living adjustments in one day instead of three weeks, and issues an emergency payment in three to five days instead of 15 days.
- In Minnesota, the Department of Revenue creates new processes for their sales tax system, paying attention to both the department's internal operational capability and to helping taxpayers willingly determine their tax liability, file accurate information, and pay on time. The reengineering has resulted in more accurate tax compliance by at least $50 million annually.
- In the United Kingdom, the Royal Mail revamps postal operations through strategic visioning and organisation-wide process management efforts, including a strong performance measurement piece, which cascades process goals from the top of the organisation to the individual level. The result is postal operations recognised as 'world class' (NAPA, 1994b, p. 2).

ANALYSIS: INFORMATION TECHNOLOGY AND REENGINEERING IN THE PUBLIC SECTOR

If BPR does have a place in the public sector, what does this mean for IT?

As a starting point, we can study the following list of practices recommended by the OECD (1995) for obtaining greatest organisational benefits from information systems:

- enhancing management, planning and control of IT functions;
- using technology to redesign and improve administrative processes;
- providing better access to quality information;
- harnessing the potential of new technologies;
- developing and applying standards;
- attracting and retaining high-caliber IT professionals;
- increasing research into the economic, social, legal and political implications of new IT opportunities; and
- assessing experiences.

The second list item – using technology to redesign and improve administrative processes – suggests a role for IT in promoting or supporting reengineering. Within the context of the private sector, this role has been investigated and commented upon by a number of writers from the technical/rational school of organisational literature.

Besides the initial articles and books (Davenport & Short, 1990; Hammer, 1990; Hammer & Champy, 1993), numerous other books have been published showing how IT has supported BPR to effect dramatic and radical organisational change (e.g. Caudle, 1995; Champy, 1995; Davenport, 1993). Davenport (1993, p. 12), for example, argues that IT 'should be viewed as more than an automatic or mechanizing force; it can fundamentally reshape the way business is done'. In other words, IT is seen as an all-powerful force changing the work that is done.

But what does this mean for the public sector? What transformational BPR-supporting role does IT have to play here? We shall provide two examples of the way in which private sector approaches to IT and BPR can be converted and applied in the public sector. First, Davenport's (1993) work, which groups the impact of IT on process innovation into nine categories:

- *Automational*: eliminating human labour from a process.
- *Informational*: capturing process information for purposes of understanding.
- *Sequential*: changing process sequence.
- *Tracking*: closely monitoring process status and objects.
- *Analytical*: improving analysis of information and decision making.
- *Geographical*: coordinating processes across distances.
- *Integrative*: coordinating between tasks and processes.
- *Intellectual*: capturing and distributing intellectual assets.
- *Disintermediating*: eliminating intermediaries from a process.

In Table 3, examples of each of these are given, showing their application in a public sector setting. Examples are provided of generic information systems and of more specific systems to support public sector service/product delivery and public sector internal logistical functions.

Of course, IT can be used to innovate processes across service delivery logistical divisions. Some social welfare systems, for example, can encompass the first four types of system in doing this. They provide a one-stop service point for clients by allowing access to different welfare information systems through a single workstation; they track the progress of individual client's cases and issue alerts at required points; they provide support for decision making about the client, such as the type of benefits they require; and they draw together the work of several separate public agencies. Not only do such systems create a much keener awareness of work processes,

Table 3.   IT-Supported Process Innovation in the Public Sector.

Generic Information System	Service/Product Delivery	Internal Logistical Functions
Automational, informational, and sequential systems	Integrated service delivery via one-stop shops	Management information systems for personnel management
Tracking systems	Automated workflow systems to monitor and control case status in delivery of welfare services	Public asset management systems
Decisional analysis systems	Systems for microanalysis and forecasting of welfare demand	Systems for microanalysis and forecasting of public finance
Interorganisational communication systems (integrative and geographical)	Government-wide electronic mail	Electronic data interchange systems linked to suppliers
Intellectual asset systems	Expert systems to advise on client assessment	Textual composition
Disintermediation	Direct delivery of public services via the internet	Automated ordering of stocks

Source: Based on Davenport (1993, pp. 50–63).

they also both drive and need the reengineering of those processes in order for the information system to work properly.

There are many real-world examples of IT-supported reengineering. For instance, all four cases of BPR provided above involved the use of new IT-based information systems. To take another example, Singapore has been at the forefront of IT application to reengineer the work of government

- More than 87 per cent of Singapore's population live in government-provided housing and the government's Housing Development Board manages more than one million properties. Starting in the early 1990s, the Board invested heavily to retool its IT in support of process reengineering. The result was a one-stop service for customers and a reduction in waiting time from several hours to less than five minutes (Turban, McLean, & Wetherbe, 1996).
- Cars passing through a tollbooth on a Singapore highway do not need to toss money into a receptacle or to an attendant. Instead, smart cards with bar codes are read rapidly by means of telemetry, thus replacing or automating a large number of previous work processes (Teo, Tan, & Wei, 1997).

- The Singapore government – has set up an extensive electronic data interchange system that communicates trade-related data among international trade bodies, traders, intermediaries, financial institutions and port and airport authorities. The implementation of this information system has thereby replaced or automated many work processes. This new information system and the concurrent reorganisation of other work processes in the Trade Development Board enabled the Board to handle more cases more quickly with a reduced complement of staff, thus significantly increasing efficiency (Teo et al., 1997).

A second private sector concept that can be adapted to public sector purposes is the value chain. Porter's (1985) description of the value chain allows a systematic analysis of the primary and secondary business processes in an organisation and of the way in which they do or do not add value to the organisation's outputs.

Several authors have argued that value chain analysis helps to identify application areas for IT that can transform the organisation (Laudon & Laudon, 1998; Moreton & Chester, 1996). Fig. 1 identifies such potential application areas in a public sector setting. It covers both primary activities that relate to production and delivery of public services and support activities that relate to the internal administrative and logistical functions of the public sector.

In the public sector, there is typically no financial margin of value to be added by innovation. Instead, the public sector can partly add value by shaping the business environment and helping companies be more efficient and effective. In part, too, the public sector is legitimised by its political actions in the democratic domain. So the margin of value in Fig. 1 is cast as some combination of the economic, the democratic and the technical. In recognition of this difference, the term 'political value chain' is used. Table 4 expands on this notion by identifying ways in which conventional reengineering challenges would be modified for the public sector by following a political value chain approach. In all of these, IT has a potential role to play.

The next section goes on to analyze IT-supported reengineering in the public sector in more detail. Before proceeding, however, it is worth reflecting a little more on the relationship between IT and BPR. On the one hand, BPR benefits are heavily dependent on IT: 'to suggest that process designs be developed independently of IS or other enablers is to ignore valuable tools for shaping processes' (Davenport, 1993, p. 50). Nonetheless, IT is only a tool; a means to an end. In achieving those ends, 'managers ... must begin to think of process change as a mediating factor between

	Automatic	Flexible	Links to	Front	Remote	
Primary **Activities**	warehousing	service delivery	suppliers, citizens, board members, politicians	office, one-stop shopping	online access points	The margin
Support **Activities**	Electronic data interchange/electronic commerce/electronic mail					(economic, democratic, technical)
	Staff selection and scheduling systems					
	Planning models (budgeting, economic, demographic)					
	Groupware					
	Computer-aided/multimedia					

Fig. 1. IT Opportunities with the Political Value Chain. *Source:* Constructed after Inspiration from Moreton and Chester (1996, p. 56).

the IT initiative and economic return' (*ibid.*, p. 46). Thus, on the other, IT benefits are heavily dependent on BPR. Process modifications or adjustments should therefore accompany IT changes within organisations.

RATIONALITY, POLITICS AND REENGINEERING IN THE PUBLIC SECTOR

One criticism of BPR is that it represents 'old wine in new bottles' since it derives from the traditional 'classical school' of organisational thought

> If we analyze the underlying philosophy of BPR, we can see immediately that it fits most closely with the classical school. Profit maximization is the key; little thought is given to more pluralistic outcomes; there is little concern for cultural, contextual issues other than to deal with them as obstacles to change; the process is a deliberate one – a rational

Table 4. Modifying Key Reengineering Challenges for the Public Sector.

Challenges for the Process Members, Owners, Coach and Leaders	Conventional BPR Definition	Political Value Chain Definition
Intensification	Improving processes to serve current customers better	Enriching processes with existing clients and partners
Extension	Using strong processes to enter new markets	Using strong processes to reach marginalised client groups
Augmentation	Expanding processes to provide additional services to current customers	Expanding processes to provide additional services to current clients and partners
Conversion	Taking a process that you perform well and performing it as a service for other companies	Extending and sharing process strength with client groups, other public sector organisations, and business partners
Innovation	Applying processes that you perform well to create and deliver different goods or services	Applying processes that you perform well to create and deliver different public services
Diversification	Creating new processes to deliver new goods or services	Creating new processes to deliver new public services

Source: First two columns adapted from Hammer (1996, p. 198).

analysis (undertaken by senior executives) of the key business processes in line … It seems, then, that our radical new departure from the staid approaches of yore is in fact more of a return of the classical approaches of the 1960s.

(Galliers, 1994, p. 54)

One thing that marks out the classical school, and at least some of the analysis so far in this chapter, is that it adheres quite strongly to very rational conceptions of organisations. These tend to focus on the formal, the quantitative and the technical aspects of organisations. However, there are very differing ways in which organisations may be conceived, and other schools of thought tend to focus on the informal, the qualitative and the human aspects of organisations. For example, the 'political game' perspective emphasises the importance of organisational politics, power games and informal groupings within organisational practice.

These two viewpoints – the rational/analytical and the political game – each have something very different to say about BPR. Table 5 summarises these differences in the context of six critical aspects of BPR. It is obvious from the table that organisations, which conform more closely to the political game perspective, will find BPR difficult. So what of the public sector?

Thaens, Bekkers, and van Duivenboden (1997) provide a sample indicator to test the perspective to which public sector organisations conform. They distinguish between sequential (rational–analytical) and interdependent (political game) models of the public policy cycle

Table 5.   Principles of BPR Compared from Rational–Analytical and Political Game Perspectives.

Principle of Reorganising the Processes	Rational–Analytical	Political Game
Productivity	*Non-problematic* • Stable implementation conditions • High degree of standardisation • Large number of transactions with a well-defined target group	*Problematic* • Productivity itself is controversial • No stable implementation conditions • Flexible procedures
Clean slate	*More or less possible* • Programme is self-contained • No discussion about goals	*Impossible* • Controversy about goals and means
Strong management	*Possible* • Top-down • Pyramid structure	*Problematic* • Bottom-up • Arena structure
Process orientation	*Rather easy* • Stable processes	*Very difficult* • Flexible processes
Role of IT	*IT is enabling* • Standardised information and transaction needs	*Problematic role of IT* • Changing information and transaction needs
Creativity	*Problematic* • Obstruction by organisational and legal procedures	*Possible* • Controversy stimulates creativity

Source: Adapted from Thaens et al. (1997, p. 32).

> The sequential perspective sees the policy process as a rational process which contains well defined and sequential stages: development, decision-making, implementation, and monitoring. ... [The interdependent perspective] sees the formulation and implementation not as a rational-analytical process of design, but as a product of a political game, in which many interdependent actors with different goals and power resources, strategically interact.
>
> (Thaens et al., 1997, p. 29)

Some public sector organisations do fall into the rational–analytical category. They enjoy stable conditions for the implementation of policy with little or no political controversy or disagreement over goals and means. Organisations that gather and process information for government, such as national census bureaus, could be seen as belonging in this camp. Their policy environment is stable, and they undertake standardised, formalised and massive transactions that are readily amenable to IT-supported BPR.

Other public sector organisations, however, fall into the political game category. Thaens et al. (1997) concluded of the Dutch Tax Department, for example, that

> Firstly, the specific law and policy in force and the general democratic principles applying to government organizations change the meaning of productivity as the main goal of BPR ... [since these have to respect] the (democratic) principles of legal security, legal equality, the rule of law and the system of checks and balances .... Secondly, it is problematic for government organizations to start redesign with a clean slate as well as to make use of creative strategies ... because of the regulatory connections with other government organizations, the strict budget regulations and the specific status of public servants.
>
> (Thaens et al., 1997, pp. 34–35)

Similarly, research by Bjørn-Andersen and Chatfield (1997) showed that initial reengineering initiatives in organisations including government departments progressed incrementally, not in a 'clean-slate' manner. This is, perhaps, to be expected, given the prevalence of 'politicking' within the public sector. A prominent example is the gap between vision and reality of Japan's information society (West, Dedrick, & Kraemer, 1996). There has been tremendous rhetoric about increasing the use of IT in the Japanese public sector, and in the society more generally. But institutional fights between different levels of government and between different ministries have created unwieldy implementation problems.

Where does this leave public sector reform? Given that reform does create instabilities and conflicts, it may be that there is a greater emergence of the political game model during reform. If so, we may be led to the conclusion that IT-supported reengineering is a necessary part of information age reform, and yet is made problematic by reform. To progress this potential dilemma, we propose the idea of PUPREB: an approach to reengineering that takes the specific context and conditions of the public sector into account. This can be seen as an approach in the tradition of 'soft BPR', which has emerged during the 1990s to emphasise human issues rather than just organisational shape (Coombs & Hull, 1996).

CONCLUSIONS AND RECOMMENDATIONS

Conclusions

Originally, IT-supported reengineering was principally seen as the preserve of the private sector. Today, this is no longer true. The use of IT in the public sector has taken a shift from routine automation to broader application areas, and it is seen as a vital device in transforming public organisations. Although it is often difficult to evaluate whether the transformation itself or the use of information systems has actually been successful, there are clearly cases in which they bring about new organisational forms, and new work/interaction patterns both within the organisations and in relation to the surrounding environment of citizens, politicians, companies and other public organisations.

However, IT-supported reengineering of the public sector can bring both benefits and woes

- Virtual organisations and teleworking can be a vehicle for rebuilding public organisations, but they can also be a threat to managerial control and to organisational culture.
- Use of the Internet in local government can be a powerful tool in rebuilding a relationship with citizens and companies by means of the World Wide Web and electronic data interchange, but it can also be a waste of taxpayers' money, serving only bureaucratic interests and fortifying gatekeeping rather than destroying it.
- Quangos, modernisation of budgeting methods and inter-/intraorganisational information systems can lead to clean-slate changes, but can also damage political decision-making processes.

Without steering and commitment, the adoption of new information and communication technologies is not likely to break down gatekeeping, organisational routines or interaction patterns, and it will do even less to reduce organisational costs or to deliver better services. Similarly, there are likely to be major problems if the specific context of the public sector is not taken into account.

IT-supported reengineering in the public sector must therefore be both defended and upheld, but this requires a public-sector-specific approach. Hence the idea of PUPREB, is a public-sector-specific approach to IT-supported reengineering that reflects the needs of public officials, citizens and politicians.

IT-Supported Reengineering in the Public Sector: Recommendations

Low-risk automation has been proceeding relatively smoothly in the public sector during recent decades. However, we believe that higher-risk reengineering and paradigm-shifting uses of IT will increasingly appear in future as the reinvention of government gathers pace. The PUPREB concept seeks routes to minimise the risks and maximise the gains from these initiatives in ways that meet public sector needs. It attempts to glean some useful parts of BPR and the ideas on process innovation while taking a critical look at the concept's application in the public sector.

In a generic sense, this approach will involve three components

- First, an explicit recognition of the public sector's political environment that coexists with any managerial rationalism. Some approaches to analysis and reengineering of processes in the public sector exclude the political dimension. Our message here, however, is as clear as day: leaving such considerations out of the analysis is at best a dead end. For better or for worse, politics does matter.
- Second, the PUPREB approach must strive for a balance between the individual and the collective level. In the public sector, affected individuals include a wide range of actors, such as elected officials, public employees, political activists, voters, taxpayers, members of interest groups and recipients of public goods and services. Collective political actors range from small groups (e.g. a local interest group) to mass organisations (e.g. a political party) to public organisations (e.g. a government department) to societal subsystems (e.g. the educational system) to international collectives (e.g. the United Nations) (Andersen & Danziger, 1997). When IT is used to enable the reengineering of public processes, then needs at both levels must be kept in mind. This is a difficult task but, if one level is left out, it is easy to be caught between conflicting interests.
- Third, there need to be continuous customer orientation. Apart from the obvious cases, where citizens fill out a complaint form or public quangos

are hammered by private entrepreneurs, it is often hard to know whether work processes in the public sector are organised in the most optimal manner. Who is to judge? According to one view, the answer is simple enough: the customer's perspective will judge whether rebuilding has been successful: 'Taking a process approach implies adopting the customer's point of view. Processes are the structure by which an organisation does what is necessary to produce value for its customers' (Davenport, 1993, p. 7). Does this approach mean that the public sector and government are to be steered strictly by opportunistic means? Should they ultimately operate in pursuit of what all taxpayers want: lower taxes and more and better public services? Certainly, there may be problems in this of preferences that conflict or vary over time. However, if anyone is to benefit and therefore drive the process of public sector rebuilding, it has to be the consumer of public services, not the employees, the politicians or the institutions.

Researchers at the US National Academy of Public Administration have formulated six basic points for starting to reengineer in public administration. We have adopted their results and adjusted their list of critical factors for successful IT-supported reengineering in the public sector to form the basis of PUPREB (see Table 6). The table reminds us that it is not IT in itself that is interesting. It is merely a tool to help the key activities: ongoing improvement of public sector services and processes, the actual fulfilment of the organisation's mission, and the overall steering of the organisation.

The point of departure is to understand what rebuilding is. There need to be valid reasons to rebuild the processes by using IT, because this requires organisational commitment and capacity to initiate and sustain. These first two points are extremely important since IT can be used for other purposes, such as quality improvement. In short, not all situations and organisations are ready or suitable for rebuilding.

Third, we believe in adopting a management approach, yet we do not want to lose the benefits that come from integrating workers into the design and decision process that relates to major technological changes in work activities. It is important to set specific goals, but it is equally important to rebuild the structures that support these goals in connection with implementing the new information system. This requires that we know the work processes. Although this is the case in a large part of the public sector, our knowledge is in fact quite limited when it comes to items such as the flow of information, the sharing of information and the manipulation of

Table 6. Critical Success Factors for Rebuilding the Public Sector Using Information Technology.

Factor	Characteristics
Understand process Reengineering	Understand political process fundamentals
	Know what reengineering/rebuilding is
	Differentiate and integrate process improvement approaches
Build a case	Have necessary and sufficient business (mission and political delivery) reasons for the rebuilding process
	Have organisational commitment and capacity to initiate and sustain the reorganisation
	Secure and sustain political support for the process
Adopt a process management approach	Understand the organisational mandate and set mission strategic directions and goals cascading to process-specific goals and decision making across and down the organisation
	Define, model and prioritise processes important for mission performance; do not start out with unimportant ones
	Practice 'hands on' senior management ownership of process improvement through personal responsibility, involvement and decision making
	Adjust organisational structures to improve support of process management initiatives
	Create an assessment programme to evaluate process management
Measure and track performance continuously	Create an organisational understanding of the value of measurement and how it will be used
	Tie performance management to customers' and stakeholders' current and future expectations
Practice change management and provide central support	Develop human resources management strategies and a technology framework to support process change
	Build information resources management strategies and a technology framework to support process change
	Create a central support group to assist and integrate rebuilding efforts and other improvement efforts across the organisation
	Create an overarching and project-specific internal and external communication and education programme
Manage projects for results	Apply clear criteria to determine what should be redesigned
	Place the project at the right level with a defined rebuilding team purpose and goals
	Use a well-trained, diversified, expert team and enable it to work well
	Follow a structured, disciplined approach

Source: Adapted from Candle (1995).

information, just to mention a few areas. However, if we do not know the work processes prior to rebuilding the structures, the outcome will depend more on luck than on professional responsibility, commitment and involvement.

Fourth, the keywords 'measurement' and 'expectations' should be considered carefully. Within the public sector, it is difficult, but not impossible, to measure the processes (including their inputs and outcomes). Likewise, the expectations from the stakeholders must be identified and tied to performance management. Naturally, this will be complicated by political instabilities such as elections and by the often rigid systems that customers must use to impose their influence on the content of the public service. Nevertheless, our message is that rebuilding public organisations is not successful if it is only able to increase the satisfaction of employees or provide information systems with a better user interface. The clue is that the expectations have to be known, and that the important ones are not the employees' expectations, regardless of whether they are short term or long term.

Fifth, rebuilding efforts are nevertheless dependent on support from the organisation's employees. Needless to say, incentives to change are more effective than threats. To that effect, management of the rebuilding process should include internal communication and educational programmes as well as external training. However, it is not a wise strategy to rely solely on external consultants in such matters.

Finally, the table emphasises that the results should be kept in mind, not lost in the process. Therefore, it is important to start out by applying clear criteria for what should be rebuilt and what should be left intact. The same persons or groups must be held responsible for their outcome and rewarded for their successes. To some degree, this is in conflict with the nature of process improvement, but it is imperative that whoever is successful (be it a person, a group or an entire organisation) should be rewarded to sustain the incentive to engage in further innovation of work processes.

Conception-Reality Gaps

Business process reengineering and its related use of IT have generally been conceived according to a technical, rational model of organisations. This emphasises the formal structures and disinterested behaviours within the organisation. Although BPR has much to offer the public sector, we have seen that some of its underlying conceptions do not match the realities found in some public sector organisations.

Gaps highlighted relate to the objectives and management and structure dimensions of the ITPOSMO model since traditional BPR conceptions do not match public sector realities of informal groupings, power games and self-interested behaviours. Within this conception,reality gap lie the seeds of potential failure in applying IT-supported reengineering to such organisations. We hope that the PUPREB approach is conceived in a way that closes this gap. Indeed, it is on this that its success or failure hinges: the extent to which it provides a match to the present realities of a significant part of the public sector.

REFERENCES

Andersen, K. V., & Danziger, J. N. (Eds). (1997). Impacts of IT on capabilities, interactions, orientations, and values. *Proceedings of the 3rd Pacific Asia conference on information systems.* Brisbane, Australia: Queensland University of Technology.

Bjørn-Andersen, N., & Chatfield, A. (1997). Reengineering with EDI. In: Ky. Andersen (Ed.), *EDI and datanetworking in the public sector.* Amsterdam: Kluwer.

Caudle, S. L. (1995). *Reengineering for results. Keys to success from government experience.* Washington, DC: National Academy of Public Administration.

Champy, J. (1995). *Reengineering management: The mandate for new leadership.* New York: HarperCollins.

Coombs, R., & Hull, R. (1996). The politics of IT strategy and development in organizations. In: W. H. Dutton (Ed.), *Information and communication technologies: Visions and realities.* Oxford: Oxford University Press.

Davenport, T. (1993). *Process innovation: Reengineering work through information technology.* Boston, MA: Harvard Business School Press.

Davenport, T., & Short, J. E. (1990). The new industrial engineering: Information technology and business process redesign. *Sloan Management Review, 31*(1), 11–27.

Galliers, R. D. (1994). IT and organisational change: Where does BPR fit in? Paper presented at conference on 'Information Technology and Organisational Change', 28–29 April, The Netherlands Business School, Nijenrode University, Netherlands.

Hammer, M. (1990). Reengineering work: Don't automate, obliterate. *Harvard Business Review, 90*(3), 104–112.

Hammer, M. (1996). *Beyond reengineering: How the process-centered organization is changing our work and our lives.* New York: Harper Business Press.

Hammer, M., & Champy, J. (1993). *Reengineering the corporation: A manifesto for business revolution.* New York: Harper Business Press.

Laudon, K. C., & Laudon, J. P. (1998). *Management Information Systems* (5th ed.). Upper Saddle River, NJ: Prentice-Hall.

Leuw, F. L., & Van Thiel, S. (1996). *Quango-cratization in the Netherlands.* PERC Occasional Paper no.13. Political Economy Research Centre, Sheffield.

Moreton, R., & Chester, M. (1996). *Transforming the business: The IT contribution.* London: McGraw-Hill.

NAPA. (1994a). *Business process reengineering: Glossary.* Washington, DC: National Academy of Public Administration (http://www.alliance.napawash.orglalliance/index.html).

NAPA. (1994b). *Business process reengineering: Overview.* Washington, DC: National Academy of Public Administration (http://www.alliance.napawash.org/alliance/index.html).

NAPA. (1996). *Reinventing Government.* Washington, DC: National Academy of Public Administration (http://www.aiiiancenapawash.orc/alliance/index.html).

OECD. (1995). *Governance in transition. Public management reforms in OECD countries.* Paris: OECD.

Osborne, D., & Gaebler, T. (1993). *Reinventing government: How the entrepreneurial spirit is transforming the public sector.* New York: Penguin Books, First Published Reading, MA: Addison-Wesley, 1992.

Porter, M. E. (1985). *Competitive advantage: Creating and sustaining superior performance.* New York: The Free Press.

Taylor, J., Snellen, I., & Zuurmond, A. (1997). *Beyond BPR in public administration.* Amsterdam: IOS Press.

Teo, H. H., Tan, B. C. Y., & Wei, K. K. (1997). Organizational transformation using electronic data interchange: The case of TradeNet in Singapore. *Journal of Management Information Systems, 13*(4), 139–165.

Thaens, M., Bekkers, V., & van Duivenboden, H. P. M. (1997). Business process redesign and public administration: A perfect match? In: J. A. Taylor, I. Snellen & A. Zuurmond (Eds), *Beyond BPR in public administration.* Amsterdam: IOS Press.

Turban, E., McLean, E., & Wetherbe, J. (1996). *Information technology for management.* New York: Wiley.

Weir, S., & Hall, W. (1994). *EGO – trip: Extra – government organisations in the United Kingdom and their accountability.* London: Charter 88.

West, J., Dedrick, J., & Kraemer, K. L. (1996). Reconciling vision and reality in Japan's NII policy. *Information Infrastructure and Policy, 5*(1), 15–39.

INFORMATIZATION AND DEMOCRACY: ORWELL OR ATHENS? A REVIEW OF THE LITERATURE

W. B. H. J. van de Donk and Pieter W. Tops

The authors present a review of the literature regarding the threats and opportunities modern information- and communication-technologies (ICT) bring about for several aspects of political democracy. They conclude that two "classic" scenario's, "Orwell" (surveillance bureaucracy and disappearing political freedom) and "Athens" (electronic forms of direct democracy) dominated the (often highly speculative) literature. Recent empirical research seems to confirm that the characteristics of ICT are relevant for democratic and political life. Id can support different views on political democracy. ICT can help to make representative democracy more responsive. Some forms of direct democracy can now be realized with help of ICT. New forms of political and societal participation can arise by introducing ICT in issue-groups and social movements. New media, like computer conferences and interactive cable-TV can enlarge the amount of people involved in public decision-making. On the other hand, however, there are some threats: alienation of "citizens" in a "push-button" democracy, in which political parties and traditional social institutions like unions

Comparative Public Administration: The Essential Readings
Research in Public Policy Analysis and Management, Volume 15, 635–666
Copyright © 2006 by Elsevier Ltd.
ISSN: 0732-1317/doi:10.1016/S0732-1317(06)15028-9

and private organizations will no longer be able to integrate different views and interests.

1. INTRODUCTION AND THEMATIZATION.
WHERE DID ORWELL GO WRONG?

Two extreme positions set the tone in learned literature on the feasibility of democracies in the information society. In the opinion of a number of authors, the widely proclaimed "electronic revolution" will inevitably take us to "direct democracy". The only question these *computopeans* hold different views on is to what extent active steering of the further introduction of technology is necessary to reach direct democracy. Some of them (like De Sola Pool, 1983) are of the opinion that *technologies of freedom* are involved, which will almost automatically result in a more democratic society, provided that the free market is left to its own devices. Other authors believe that the new technology enables a drastic renewal of political culture and structure, provided that it is used deliberately in a practical and sensible way (Etzioni, Laudon, & Lipson, 1975; Becker, 1981; Hollander, 1985; Barber, 1988; Abramson, Arterton, and Orren, 1988).

On the other hand, a lot of authors believe that the electronic revolution is primarily a technocratic revolution, which will result in Orwellian forms of surveillance and control of citizens (Rule, 1974; Burnham, 1983; Sterling, 1986; Morris-Suzuki, 1988). The perspective of surveillance and control is dominant and to a large extent technically induced (Laudon, 1986). "In a wired society, surveillance is (...) the logical extension of automating the tax system" (Martin, 1978, p. 256).

When we review literature, we must come to the conclusion that extremely much attention has been paid to the question *Orwell or Athens?* However, we must also conclude that this question has distracted attention from other important questions, which can be asked about the relation between *informatization and democracy*. Between the two extreme positions mentioned earlier are a large number of intermediate positions, often based on research on a more moderate scale or on research focused on one aspect of the functioning of democracy, such as the role of the parliament.

In this chapter, a survey of the literature on the subject of *democracy and information society* is given. This survey concentrates on literature that – in analysis or research – contains views on the relation between politics, democracy and computer- and communication technology. Literature that is principally focused on legal aspects of privacy and literature that deals with the use of mass media in a democratic society have not been taken into account. This also applies to literature primarily concerning the meaning of informatization for the relation between citizens-as-customers and the government (such as Gaoulledec-Genuys, 1980; Snellen et al., 1989; Scheepers, 1991).

We will start our review with a short exploration of some characteristics of new ICT. Some of these characteristics (like interactivity, decentralization and increased possibilities for controlling information flows for both senders and receivers) make ICT very relevant for several aspects of democracy and political decision-making. ICT creates new possibilities, which can be considered both as threat and opportunity for democracy. Much depends on what kind of conception of democracy one prefers.

In Sections 3–5, we will first concentrate on literature that links informatization to different views on democracy. First, we discuss the way new technologies are used to realize an old ideal: direct democracy. Some authors have suggested that ICT can finally help us to overcome traditional hindrances that kept us away from "real democracy". But many authors who have studied experimental projects in this field are not very optimistic, and point at several dangers "push-button-democracies" can bring about.

Some others claim that even in the information-age, direct democracy is not feasible. Instead of trying to realize "computopia" we should better try to resolve some traditional problems of representative democracy. In Section 4, we present some ways ICT can make traditional representative democracies more responsive. Some normative implications arise, however: where lies the border between a "responsive democracy" and forms of "instructed representation" that many authors see as a consequence of opinion-polling?

In some other cases, ICT is used to strengthen democracy along the lines of a "communitarian" conception of democracy. ICT is implemented in such a way that it enlarges and intensifies political participation and public debate. In Section 5, we will present some examples as well as some critical remarks that are made with regard to them.

In the following Sections 6–9, we will concentrate on the way ICT is influencing the positions of the most important actors in the democratic arena. First of all (Section 6), we will present some research-results, interesting hypotheses and provocative speculations about the significance of ICT for all kinds of intermediary organizations: pressure groups, political parties and the (new) media. Again, the literature suggests both threats and opportunities as far as those actors are concerned. Some say political parties are likely to disappear, others point at new possibilities, and believe parties as well as pressure groups can strengthen their position in the political arena. In Section 7, we zoom in on "Joe Citizen". As far as the individual citizen is concerned, a great deal of the literature is not very optimistic. Citizens of electronic democracies seem – at first sight – to have more influence on political decision-making. In the politics of the information-society, however, they may turn out to be transparent objects of intelligent political campaigning and bureaucratic surveillance.

In Section 8, we will discuss some trends concerning the way ICT is affecting the politician: in order to survive he will be forced to make use of "political marketing" and "geo-demographics", as it is called in the New-speak that accompanies the introduction of ICT in political life.

In Section 9, the significance of ICT for the functioning of parliament and other representative organs gets our attention. In the literature, several strategies are mentioned that have been successfully implemented to use ICT for strengthening the position of parliament. Furthermore, we will discuss some consequences of ICT for relations within parliament and political debates. Ultimately, in Section 10, a few concluding observations will be given. In Section References, the reader will find an elaborate bibliography, which also contains a number of titles that were not discussed here.

2. COMPUTER- INFORMATION- AND COMMUNICATION-TECHNOLOGY; WHAT IS NEW ABOUT IT?

This chapter highlights new forms of computer-, information- and communication-technology. This technology includes computers, satellites and cable networks, but also videocassette recorders and glass-fibre cables. Consequently, things like direct mail, electronic mail, video-, computer- and teleconferences, instant-polling, computer-assisted telephone interviewing, teletext, on-line databases and interactive television have become possible. A complete survey of the historical developments in the field of information- and communication-technology, which is also easily accessible for non-technicians, can be found in Van Dijk (1991a) (Westin, 1971; Forester, 1985, 1981; Barnouw, 1982; Dizard, 1982; Breton, 1987, are interesting in this respect as well).

Some authors call it *ICT*, information- and communication-technology (McLean, 1989). Others call it *com-com-technology*, computer- and communication-technology. Abramson et al. (1988) simply call it *new media*. In each case, these descriptions indicate new methods of gathering, processing,

conveying and storing information, which fundamentally affect communication processes between various actors. Van Dijk (1991, p. 243) defines a new medium as "(...) a medium that gives shape to the *integration* of infrastructure, transport, management, services and/or varieties of data in the fields of tele-, data- and mass-communication and moreover as a medium that to a certain extent is *interactive*". In this survey, we will no longer deal with precise definitions. The most concise description of the specific features of these new technologies can be read in Abramson et al. (1988, pp. 32–66). In the opinion of these authors, new media have at least six specific characteristics which make them of special value to politics and democracy.

In the *first* place, the new media enormously increase the amount as well as the accessibility of information for politicians as well as citizens. *Second*, the new media accelerate the processes of gathering, distributing and storing information. Time and place (distance) are hardly restrictive factors. Information about political events is virtually immediately available at large distances for everyone who has a need for it. Politicians have increasingly less time to react to events. The opinions and reactions of the general public are more and more readily available as well (e.g., by means of advanced forms of instant-polling, see McLean (1989) and Moore (1992)).

A *third* characteristic is that the new media (by means of a larger amount of possibilities of selection) enable the receivers of information to exert more control over the information.

A *fourth* characteristic is that new technologies make information-targeting by the sender of information possible; the information can be geared to ever more specifically defined target groups. Besides talking about broadcasting, we can now also increasingly talk about narrow-casting. Politicians may, for instance, use new media to compose very detailed profiles of groups of voters and subsequently approach each group in a specific way (direct mail, video tapes) and with a specific message. Opposed to possible advantages, such as a deepening of information and a better fulfillment of people's needs there are possible disadvantages, like a reinforcement of fragmentation and of opportunities for manipulation (see also Aisle, 1977, p. 9; McLean, 1985).

A *fifth* feature concerns the tendency to decentralization, which would be incorporated in new technologies. However, this feature is not completely unambiguous and according to Abramson et al. (1988), it would be sensible to make a distinction between ownership and use of new media. The ownership of new media becomes more and more concentrated in the hands of a few media giants (see also McLean, 1985). However, decisions about their use, that is about the question what is recorded and broadcasted by new media, are taken at a more and more decentralized level. Several technological developments contribute to this tendency to decentralization. The invention of microcameras has, for instance, drastically reduced the cost of the production of professional TV-programmes. Due to this, local TV-stations in the United States have become an increasingly stronger competitor for the national networks. Anyway, as far as the application of computer networks is concerned, this tendency to decentralization remains controversial. In these networks, decentralization always takes place within a framework of centralization: due to the transparency of such networks, central supervision on decentralized processes remain possible (see Sterling, 1986; Snellen & van de Donk, 1987).

The *sixth* and last feature of the new media is their capacity to bring about interaction between sender and receiver. It is by this interactivity that the old media (such as TV, radio and newspapers) are most sharply contrasted with the new media. It enables viewers and other receivers of information to react immediately to what is presented to them. They are no longer passive receivers of programmes made by others, but active participants who can also exert influence on the content of programmes. Abramson et al. (1988) state that interactivity is still the least developed feature of the new technologies. This can be explained by the costs that go with it, but also by the adaptations it requires to existing habits with regard to the use of media.

It is particularly this possibility of interactivity that has resulted in wild speculations about the possible impact of new media on the functioning of democracy. The central point is the idea that new life could be breathed into the long cherished ideal of direct democracy by means of interactive media. As will turn out later, very particular views on democracy appear to play an important role here.

3. OLD IDEALS AND NEW TECHNOLOGY; DIRECT DEMOCRACY

Many authors suppose that the ideal of direct democracy can finally be realized by means of new technologies. Particularly, futurologists like Naisbitt and Toffler have high expectations of the possibilities of self 'representation', which new media would make possible (Toffler, 1980; Naisbitt, 1982; see also Den Hollander, 1985; Masuda, 1985). These media would create the technical and organizational opportunities for individual citizens to participate directly in political decision-making. Because of this, the raison d'être of representative institutions – to make democracy possible in large-scale societies in an organizational way – expires, so they argue. Technology makes it possible to list the opinions of individual citizens in a short period of time and at a low cost. Due to this, intermediary organizations, such as political parties and pressure groups, will loose their function and representative institutions may disappear. Citizens can become self-governing and will no longer need to transfer decision-making power to political representatives. Thus a direct, plebiscitarian democracy will have become reality.

In reality, such a plebiscitarian democracy can be depicted as a system in which issues are presented to citizens, for instance via television, on which they subsequently can give their opinion by way of electronic voting. Such a voting can take place by telephone or by means of a special keyboard, which is connected to the television. In this manner, instant-referenda can be held as often as is considered desirable and at relatively low participation costs for citizens (Martin, 1978; McLean, 1989; Van Dijk, 1991).

As far as we have been able to gather, electronic plebiscites with formal decision-making power have not been carried out anywhere yet. In 1970s and 1980s some experimental projects, which have been inspired by this concept of democracy but without formal decision-making power, were started in the United States. Famous examples are the Hawaiian Televotes and the Columbus Cube Tube (Becker, 1981; Arterton, 1987b).

Experiences in the United States show that participation in these forms of opinion-polls is relatively low (Abramson et al., 1988, p. 169). Although the participation rate is still higher than in more traditional forms of partic-ipation via hearings and surveys, the assumption that new media will breathe new life into the ideal of direct democracy is by no means justified. Anyhow, the instant-referendum does not appear to be the practical and time-saving alternative to political participation in which Joe Citizen – "bored with baseball and too broke for video gambling" – would like to take part (see also Eulau, 1977; McLean, 1989).

Besides the instant-referendums just mentioned, the opinion-polls and the influence they exert on the behaviour of politicians are by some authors also called a form of electronic plebescitarian democracy. Abramson et al. (1988, p. 20), for instance, argue that at this moment the ideal of direct democracy finds its greatest triumph in American politics by the influence of opinion-polls on the behaviour of politicians (see also Roll, 1982; Moore, 1992). And McLean alleges that an inherent relation exists between direct democracy and random selection (selection determined by lot), as was understood in ancient Athens. Today, this form of random selection has been reintroduced by means of opinion-polls; after all, citizens' opinions are listed by way of random sampling. Due to the increase in quality and velocity of the polls, the impact of these opinion-polls on the behaviour of politicians is increased more and more, says McLean, who considers this an element of direct democracy in an otherwise indirect system of democratic decision-making. Following Burnheim, he talks about a system of demarchy, a combination of (statistical) democracy and anarchy (McLean, 1989, p. 130).

These concepts of electronic plebiscitarian democracy have been critically received in literature (Laudon, 1977, 1980; Eulau, 1977; Grewlich & Pederson, 1984; Burkert, 1985; Calhoun, 1986; Arterton, 1987a, 1987b; Abramson et al., 1988). They would, for instance, reduce the role of a political citizen to that of a passive person who pushes a button or fills out a questionnaire. This *push-button* democracy undermines active involvement of citizens with policy making and implementation. In the plebiscitarian version, democracy is reduced to the passive recording of points of view. Because of this, the risk of instant-decision-making arises, whereas one of the merits of the democratic system is that in a relatively long process the advantages and disadvantages are considered and that all interested parties can make a contribution to the discussion.

Moreover, electronic plebiscites (certainly when they are confined to simple consultation and are not organized within a framework of a broader social discussion) would have an atomizing effect on the political behaviour of citizens (Laudon, 1977). They assume that political opinions are formed in an isolated way in private situations (at home in front of the TV). However, research proves that political views are often formed in the context of organizations of which people are a part (work, neighbourhood, club). If the setting of the formation of political views shifts from group-settings to isolated citizens, the protective and stabilizing function of such groups would disappear, says Laudon. Subsequently, the mediating and informing role performed by these groups will disappear. This could, among other things, result in individual citizens becoming more accessible to and more mobilizable by political bureaucratic elites. The atomization of society and the elimination of intermediate organizations may make the masses into objects of manipulation by politicians and their advisors. It will be very difficult for citizens to effectively organize themselves if the responsible decision-makers disregard the results of the plebiscitarian polls. When used in this way, ICT will contribute little to the organizational and political competence of citizens.

The electronic plebiscites do not only enhance citizens' control over decision-makers, but also the decision-makers' control over citizens; it is the (political bureaucratic) elites that decide on the questions, determine the information channels and decide what will be done with the results. The information can be used in such a way that the elite manipulates the citizens until the majority of them agrees with its plans (Lenk, 1976).

4. MORE RESPONSIVE INDIRECT DEMOCRACY

For many authors representative democracy is not "a sorry substitute for the real thing", i.e., direct democracy, but an authentic and even superior form of democratic decision-making. Direct democracy, they state, does not come with merely practical objections. The most important objections are matters of principle and always have to do with the observation that in a system of direct democracy decisions are too easily made by applying the majority rule. Consequently, the functions that are also considered to be essential for a good democracy, such as the protection of minorities, the correcting effects of checks and balances, the restraining influence of deliberation and compromising and the arbitrating and informative effects of intermediate organizations, do not come out well enough in forms of direct democracy.

Of course, representative democracy has its problems as well. Many of these problems have to do with the question to what extend there is a congruity between the views of the representatives and the views of the voters. This question has a normative as well as a factual component. The normative component refers to the question to what extend there has to be congruity. Must the MP follow the views of the electorate in everything or does he have room for personal considerations? If so, how much room? (OTA, 1987, p. 7). The factual component concerns the question in what way congruity can be accomplished between the views of representatives and the people they represent. Which institutions, procedures and codes of behaviour can contribute to that? This is where modern information and communication technologies come in.

First of all, they enable the MP to be informed about the opinions and views of his electorate in a relatively simple and accurate way. By regularly conducted opinion polls, the MP can more easily be kept informed about the preferences of his electorate. These polls, carried out in any form whatsoever, can provide an important supplement to the relatively primitive information channels that are often dominated by party activists.

At the same time, a normative problem emerges here as well, as Roll observes (Roll, 1981; also see OTA, 1987). Does the introduction of all these forms of instant-polling not in a way undermine the MP's autonomous position (Williams, 1982)? What in fact remains of his constitutional obligation to make decisions without any assignments or instructions? The results of polls force themselves more and more emphatically on politicians. It becomes increasingly difficult to ignore the results of opinion polls with impunity. Will there be a point at which this technologically induced conception of democracy (the OTA study speaks of instructed representation) can no longer be brought into line with an MP's constitutional position? What is still a point scored from the point of view of direct democracy (see the previous section), seems to be a loss from the perspective of representative democracy, at least beyond a certain point.

A second contribution of the new media to a more responsive representative democracy lies in the fact that it makes more direct forms of contact possible between an MP and the people he represents. An example of this form are the telephone and television conferences, in which a parliamentarian can communicate with citizens, if need be spread over a large number of locations. In the United States, such forms of contact between voters and representatives are rather popular (Abramson et al., 1988, p. 141). Furthermore, direct mail and video facilities enable the MP to inform his electorate about his parliamentary activities and the positions he takes in them more frequently and livelier than in the past. In addition, direct communication lines arise between representatives and voters, with elimination of the filtering effect of the official media (Frantzich, 1982).

The use of new forms of information and communication technology in support of existing systems of representative democracy has up to now expanded enormously in the organization of election campaigns, which occupy an important place in a representative democracy. Abramson et al. (1988) give some fascinating examples of this. One of those refers to the way in which the Republican Party developed a database containing information about the opponent of the Democratic Party, Walter Mondale, in the campaign for the presidential elections of 1984. During the election campaign, a data file of about 75,000 items was built up containing 45,000 quotations of Mondale, which covered his entire political career. At the height of the campaign, the database was updated every 24 h. Each time when Mondale made a statement about a certain topic, his earlier statements about the subject were consulted, which allowed the Republican Campaigners to immediately confront the Democrats with any inconsistencies. The database was set up in such a way that users had easy access to the system by means of user-friendly software. Moreover, the database was also available on a decentralized level by using computer networks. Because of this database, among other things, the Republican Party managed to keep the initiative during the election campaign of 1984 and undermined the campaign of the

Democrats on numerous occasions (Abramson et al., 1988, pp. 92–93; see Broder, 1987b; McLean, 1989; for other examples).

5. DEMOCRACY AS ACTIVE CITIZENSHIP

In a number of discussions about the relation between new media and democracy a third conception of democracy plays a part, beside the plebiscite and representative variety. We are talking about what Abramson, Arterton, and Orren call the *communitarian democracy* and Barber refers to as *strong democracy*. In this approach, active citizenship and participation of citizens in the public debate are the key issues. It is consultation and persuasion that leads to a collective definition of general interest. Here democracy is not only a method of decision-making, but especially 'a course in civic education'. Whether the decisions are in the end made via a system of direct or indirect democracy is a matter of secondary importance. Essential in this conception is the active participation of citizens in discussions about affairs that are of general interest.

Information- and communication-technology can, according to some, contribute to the realization of this ideal of democracy (Becker, 1981; Barber, 1988). For instance, cable television, modern telephone networks and computer networks create several kinds of possibilities for active and interactive discussion among interested citizens. In this respect, electronic town meetings or *The Electronic Commonwealth* (which is the title of the book by Abramson et al.) are sometimes mentioned. The new media can see to it that information about political matters are accessible to everyone and that it is geared to the need for information of specific groups. At the same time, they can considerably increase the scale on which town meetings take place and so the number of participants. Consequently, the somewhat parochial character, sometimes attached to this idea of communitarian democracy, can be broken with (Abramson et al., 1988, p. 280).

Well-known examples of the use of new media in the United States are the Berks Community Television (BCTV) in Reading (Pennsylvania) and the Public Electronic Network in Santa Monica (California). In the Netherlands, we have the Amsterdam 'city talks' (Tops & Kommers, 1991).

A problem with the electronic town meetings is the supervision of the agenda. Who determines what will be discussed? Teleconferences are relatively easy to manipulate by lobby (groups) and interest groups. That is why it would be naive to suppose that the electronic town meetings automatically lead to a greater equality of and admission to participation possibilities (Abramson et al., 1988, pp. 1–84; see also McLean, 1989; Arterton, 1987a, 1987b). On the other hand, Barnouw (1982) and McLean (1989) point at increased possibilities some groups will have to place their '*burned issues and hidden agendas*' on the political agenda.

6. INTERMEDIARY ORGANIZATIONS

In the previous paragraph, it has been mentioned that information technology can also have various consequences for the different intermediary organizations between government and citizens. Among these organizations, both social connections (such as organized interest groups and social movements) and political parties are to be considered. Investigation into the application of new technologies in these organizations (which many authors think are invaluable for a stable democracy) is actually still in its infancy, and was somewhat pushed into the background by all the attention that has been given to the significance of informatization for political democracy.

6.1. Issue and Pressure-Groups

In an investigation into the sociological aspects of the discussion about abortion in the United States it turned out that modern technology enabled many volunteers to contribute to the activities of the (pro-life) movement, while simply staying at home (Luker, 1984). Via personal computers, in which address and telephone lists were kept up to date, a large number of letters could be sent in a relatively short time from a number of different homes to politicians. A switchboard system on the organization's telephone automatically put incoming calls through to the private telephone of one of the many volunteers who made themselves available at certain hours. Technology, in short, made it possible for many people to be active in the pro-life movement (with an average of 10 h a week), while attending merely four meetings a year. On top of that, the investigation proved that a relatively large number of pro-life activists came from groups with a low social status. That is why the use of the new technologies contributed to an 'external democratization' of the pro-life movement. As a result the nature of the participation changed greatly, say Abramson et al. (1988). Activities are after all developed by isolated and autonomous individuals, who seldom have direct contact with each other or exchange and test opinions and information. In order to (be able to) function, people are also strongly dependent on the information that is provided by the movement's leaders or administrations.

Electronic communication differs largely from face-to-face contacts: citizens are approached individually, they do not receive the political information in a social context, the opportunity to communicate directly with other members of the group is lacking, and the differences in status and power with political leaders are often rather great (Abramson et al., 1988). This causes a quite radical change in the bases of participation. The new technology mobilizes more or less isolated citizens instead of groups of citizens with a collective identity and a mutually shared system of meaning. As a result, rather loose and flexible organization patterns arise in which the quantitative size of the mobilized group is not infrequently the most important criterion. The membership of such an organization has a very transitory nature. Instead of activities meant to tie the members as much as possible to an organization, the leadership will more likely make use of marketing techniques from time to time in order to activate as many people as possible. The larger the amount of people they can bring together (in a "virtual" organization), the greater their political influence.

Laudon (1977, pp. 112 ff.) too, made some interesting remarks about the application of ICT in issue-groups and social movements (see also Neustadt, 1985; Montes, 1986). The often flexible "structures" of these movements may prevent a frequent application of ICT. But according to Laudon, real barriers are especially present in the tradition of acting collectively on the basis of ideological certainties. He assumes that particularly the symbolics of many activities of this type of political movements will not be easy to replace by electronic interaction with the action computer. He sees possibilities for umbrella organizations. But the use of ICT enforces some structuralization of connections and communications, which will make them more easily recognizable for authorities, which can also implicate a threat to their identity.

6.2. Political Parties

On the basis of developments in the United States, Abramson, Arterton, and Orren argue that the new media will further strengthen the already existing tendency towards a more and more direct relationship between political leaders and individual voters. "The politicians reach the people via television; the people reach the politicians via polls" (1988, p. 90). The influence and role of political parties and other intermediary organizations between government and citizen is pushed back more and more. Benjamin (1982) directly relates technological development with disintermediation, which he considers to be an important characteristic of informatized political systems. Just as the local shop disappears and is replaced by electronic shopping, the new technology can excavate other intermediary structures (Everson, 1982; Benjamin, 1982; Pederson, 1984). But naturally ICT can also work the other way round, and create new possibilities (Benjamin, 1982; Bogumil, 1987; Bogumil & Lange, 1991). However, Bogumil and Lange, who investigated the use of ICT in German political parties and trade unions, observe that the new possibilities (the use of modern telephone switchboards for a direct, intern democracy, opinion polls and the like) often still come to a standstill in existing structures and interests. The English political parties seem to be more creative (McLean, 1989).

In an electronic democracy, politicians chiefly have the role of popular leaders, and much less the role of a representative of a political movement. The voters are mostly addressed as atomized individual media-users, and hardly (ever) as citizens who are actively involved in the developments in their country or municipality. The media play an increasingly important part in activities, which used to be (part of) the exclusive domain of the political parties. For example, selection and spotting of 'high-potential' candidates is becoming an increasingly important, almost autonomous criterion, which can only partly be influenced and controlled by political parties. Information about the views of the electorate no longer reach the party leadership primarily via the reports from party channels, but via coverage in the media and polls of opinion-agencies. The (new) media are in a way becoming competitors of the political party organizations as connecting links between political parties and their voters. In the long term, this will undoubtedly have great consequences for organization and functioning of the political parties. For the national party organs, the necessity to maintain a extensive (and expensive) network of local departments can increasingly decline. A part of the functions which make these departments so interesting for the national party leadership (like obtaining information about the views of the electorate) is more and more taken over by the new media.

7. THE TRANSPARENT AND FRAGMENTED CITIZEN

Winner (1986) describes the romantic image that accompanies the introduction of the PC in households. Almost mythical qualities are attributed to the personal computer. The spread of the PC is compared to the weapons that were handed out to the people during the Commune of Paris and the Spanish Civil War. Winner warns for the misleading character of this metaphor: armed with a PC the citizen does not become any more powerful – in relation to the institutions of the government's bureaucracy than an individual hang-glider versus the air force. In his book, *The Dossier-Society* (1984) Laudon also warns for utopian fantasies about the relationship between informatization and democracy.

Through fine-grained registrations off all kinds, the citizen becomes more easily a victim of surveillance, as all forms of behaviour – even phoning to a certain government agency – can be registered. *Digital footprints* of social interactions make citizens and groups of citizens transparent, and expose them to commercial and political forms of *demographic stereotyping* (Meadow, 1985). Here too, technological development is to be considered a potential threat to public liberties (Winner, 1986). Sterling points out that two important landmarks have been passed on the way to a more important role of surveillance bureaucracy, namely the possibility to link extensive files by so-called universal identifiers and the established effectiveness of surveillance to trace fraud or, on the contrary, problem groups who need extra attention from government (Sterling, 1986, p. 31). There is a threat of a movement which will likely reinforce itself: information systems enable politicians to zoom in on problems of certain groups in society, and to urgently request the issuing of rules or financial aid. Groups which are largely dependent on government regulation and support will be far more extensively registrated than other groups, and are probably also more vulnerable to illegal invasions on their privacy (and public liberties) than others (see Eulau, 1977; OTA, 1987).

As a result of the extension of the supervision and of options for recipients of information and the reinforcement of the 'targeting' possibilities for senders of information, the public can be divided and defined into distinct groups. "Mr. Average" will get company, because he will turn out to represent too many rough categories for the purpose of an electoral strategy.

Especially in electoral systems in which they have a clear, territorial electorate, politicians increasingly possess of computer-based census profiles, which enable them to become acquainted with policy preferences and probable reactions to policy-initiatives which fit the characteristics of their electorate (Benjamin, 1982; Martin, 1978; McLean, 1989).

Moreover, these groups will get almost exclusively information (through forms of computer-based vote-targeting), which confirms their own world view. Some say this will lead to a further "balkanization" of the electorate. Taylor (1990) warns for the arising of *demographic ghettos*.

Abramson et al. (1988) observe in this connection that the general, national (old) media can be looked upon as an important source of general 'civic culture', in which a collective political vocabulary, a common political agenda and a homogenization of the public opinion are stimulated. The rise of the new media puts this function under pressure. In a *living-room democracy*, the voters' attention can be drawn to – what already has been defined as – their interests. Politicians can conveniently make use of this by showing, by means of *direct mail*, to a certain part of the electorate that they struggle for their interests, without having to inform other groups with opposite interests (Burnham, 1983). Sterling sees possibilities for political parties as well. He expects that better insight in policy preferences and opinions in various parts of the electorate will enable political parties to include "... more divergent positions into a party structure and of holding them together in a coalition" (Sterling, 1986, p. 28).

Politics is becoming a matter of intelligent direction rather than of ideology. Further, on we will see that this also becomes important on the level of the skills of the individual politician.

You only go duck-hunting where the ducks are.

Not only your own electorate, but also the electorate of the political rivals can be adequately shown by means of the new technology. Opinion polls and political marketing lead to a *transparent electorate* which can be intelligently manipulated (McLean, 1989). In the United *States political marketing, campaign management, geodemographics and lobbying* are subjects, which already have an important place on Graduate Schools for Political Management. The means (addresses, profiles and the like) for a digital election strategy are for that matter often provided by specialized companies and *direct-mail consultants* (Everson, 1982; McLean, 1989). This type of companies helped American politicians, but also trade unions, to win elections in a remarkable way (Burnham, 1983, pp. 92 ff.).

In the United States, direct mail is also used successfully to finance expensive election campaigns. Legislation (Federal Election Campaign Act) has imposed a limit to the contributions of individual sponsors. That is why campaign strategists needed *a* means that enabled them to reach larger groups. Direct mail proved to be an effective means with an unexpectedly high response (McLean, 1989, pp. 65 ff.). By means of a database with addresses and information about earlier contributions to campaigns, voters are humoured with 'personal letters', which are composed of well chosen *canned paragraphs*.

Admission to data files in the executive not only leads to a better "*oversight*" of the executive (see Section 9), but also creates new possibilities for political marketing for the members of the American Congress. When a certain subsidy is decided upon, partly owing to an initiative of a certain politician of a certain state, he is allowed to inform the interested parties in his constituency about it: the address files of the government bureaucracy make it possible to circumvent the politically not always easily passable road via the media (Burnham, 1983). The new technologies create *unmediated media* (Abramson et al., 1988). The arbitrating and filtering effect, which the established media, such as newspapers and the TV, have on the data transmission between government/politician and the citizens is under great strain. The new media enable politicians to have direct contact with their electorate on a large scale, and get round what they not infrequently experience as an annoying and negative influence of reporters. In the United States Congressmen make, for instance, their own news reports, which are transmitted to local TV stations in their own states via satellite.

8. THE BROKER IN MAJORITIES: THE ELECTRONIC POLITICIAN

Potentially, the new media also have great consequences for the characteristics of the political trade. In concise terms: data analysis would take the place of gut feeling, quantitative calculation would replace political intuition (Eulau, 1977; Pederson, 1984). Eulau exposes the concept of politics, which is – sometimes implicitly – held by "supporters" of electronic politics. They look upon politics as the search for truth and politicians as information recipients. Than ICT would make a form of rational administration and democracy possible, in which the 'irrational' element of political decision-making is eliminated. In this conception, the specific role and contribution of politics – making decisions on the basis of ideological meaning – is based on an 'information shortage'. ICT will assure that this information shortage is cancelled out, which causes rational decision-making to become 'perfect' and politics to become superfluous (see also Frissen, 1991). That the complex process of political decision-making on the contrary is more than rational decision-making and looking for truth, and that it is particularly the challenge and assignment to always consider and choose between different interests and opinions, is forgotten in this approach to politics. More information is often not desired at all, and it sooner causes more inconvenience instead of adding anything to the political process of wheeling and dealing (Eulau, 1977, p. 19).

The swiftness with which the media report on political events has reduced the time politicians have to react and to form a measured opinion. More and more often they have to give 'instant reactions'. The direct media coverage not infrequently turns small events into great incidents. A slip of the tongue can have great consequences. The time and space to negotiate, deliberate, form compromises and effective coalitions come under pressure. The polling-politics push political leadership and discussion and deliberation – two important components to come to consensus within the political community – to the background (McLean, 1989). In connection with that, the long-term perspective, which is already under a great strain, disappears as well (Roll, 1982). Partly under the influence of the new information technology, political decision-making is more dominated by more or less coincidental ad hoc-coalitions in which other changing political majorities occur. The role of the politician becomes the role of a "broker in majorities" (see also Albeda, 1992), Reagan, for example, did not accede to power by a majority based on consensus, but by a coalition – partly thought out by computer strategists – of many related "single issue-groups". Sailing on unstable coalitions is of course also possible without computers (Roosevelt, Mitterand), but the new media give a head start to politicians and parties that know how to use (and can afford) the new possibilities well. In itself, all this does not necessarily mean that the political process changes fundamentally, but the new media reinforce the already present tendencies to a staccato-like democracy, in which short-term decisions tumble on top of each other.

9. THE ELECTRONIC AGORA: INFORMATIZATION IN PARLIAMENT

In several publications the meaning of informatization for the functioning of parliament and other representative organs is more specifically investigated (Chartrand, 1968; Steinbuch, 1978; Gau, 1980; Rose, 1980; Frantzich, 1982a, 1982b; Breman, 1983; Kevenhörster, 1984; Kraemer & King, 1987; OTA, 1987; Snellen et al., 1989; Van de Donk, Frissen, & Snellen, 1990). There is much attention to the possibilities, which informatization offers to reinforce the position of power of the representative body in relation to the executive. We also find publications in which an account is given of empirical investigations into the consequences of parliamentary informatization for the internal functioning of the representative body. In this paragraph, we give an account of the most important views, results and conclusions with regard to the internal and external dimension of parliamentary informatization. We start off with a survey of the most important applications of this technology.

9.1. Applications of ICT in Parliament

From publications by Chartrand (1962), Saloma (1968), Chartrand and Borell (1981), Rose (1980) and Frantzich (1982) we can infer that the

American Congress started to apply several forms of information technology much earlier than the parliaments in Europe. Particularly the increasing growth of legislative work (size and complexity), the considerable growth of the members' contacts with their grass roots supporters and the growing informatization in the executive were reasons to invest in information systems. These are of a rather varied nature which can, according to Frantzich, be accounted for by Congress's heterogeneous need for information. There is a need for systematically accessible parliamentary documentation, which also in the Dutch (Breman, 1983), French (Gau, 1980) and German parliaments (Kevenhörster, 1984) was realized first. Systems, which provide insight into the progress of parliamentary activities can usually be linked to it. In Frantzich's *Computers in Congress* (1982, pp. 145 ff.), a large number of the parliamentary systems is extensively described (e.g., the "Geographic Reporting System" (GRS), which shows the distribution of federal funds over the various states and districts graphically and/or in accessible tables).

Decision-making procedures (legislation) in the American Congress could be followed electronically already in the 1970s (Rose, 1980; Frantzich, 1982). The increased possibilities for data-communication have especially been important to the opening up of bureaucracy, but are also used by members of the American Congress for internal communication (electronic mail) and for gaining access to data-files of various social groups, professional organizations and interest groups. For the preparation of opinion forming and decision-making, several (external) files can be consulted.

But also in parliamentary decision-making (voting), information technology plays an important part. In 1973, an operational electronic voting system was introduced (not without fierce resistance, see Frantzich, 1982, pp. 91 ff.) which can quickly register the votes given and – we will see this further on – make an instant-analysis as well. This instant-analysis already stimulates interventions during the voting procedures in order to put members who have not yet voted under maximum pressure to obey the leadership.

9.2. The External Dimension of Parliamentary Informatization

In surveys on parliamentary informatization, the parliament's relative position in the trias politica gets much attention (Gau, 1980). The informatization arrears, which Congress had in respect to the government bureaucracy was increasingly seen as an information arrears. In the U.S., they have chosen a triple-fold strategy to make up for the arrears.

First, Parliament can block the development of important informatization projects in the executive during the budget debates. When blocking is impossible there is still a whole series of delaying tactics available (Kraemer & King, 1987, p. 95).

The second strategy is more important. Many times members of parliament (or parliament committees) successfully attempted to gain access to data files of the executive (data on progress, statistical information on various fields of policy). Especially Frantzich (1982), and to a lesser extent also Gau (1980), Kevenhörster (1984) and Kraemer and King (1987) give a fascinating account of the *access wars* that accompanied it. Sometimes services and departments were unwilling and access could only be got by appealing to the Freedom of Information Act. Sometimes those parliamentary information requests received a warm welcome: the agencies saw a good chance to bring their programmes and policy projects to attention. Miewald and Muller (1987) warn for a possible blurring of the different positions which a representative body and an executive are supposed to have.

A third strategy concerns the construction and the extension of its own informatization-resources. The development of its own information systems, analysis and calculation models was a necessary step for the reinforcement of its position. A good example of this is the Congressional Budget Office (CBO), which was given authorization to develop its own fiscal calculation models after a collision between Congress and President Nixon (who, according to the Congress, fiddled with the calculation models of the American Tax Authorities). On top of that, these models were more geared to the needs of the Congressmen, who were henceforth able to "compute politically". The consequences of fiscal policy proposals could be visualized per (election-) district.

The balance of power between legislative and executive had been disturbed by the computers in the executive, but this third strategy made it possible to bring the development of the independent parliamentary automatization into balance again. The member budget information system (MBIS), which permanently enables a thorough analysis of the budget (and can also visualize exceedings and depletions) has given the American Congress – according to Frantzich – a considerably stronger position of power (see for comparable conclusions Ryan (1976) and Worthly (1984).

Other investigations give a mixed picture, however. Kreamer and King make mention of an investigation into informatization in a large number of states, from which it turns out that the increase of possibilities to check the executive is usually restricted only to some fields of policy and never becomes better on all points. Fear of incompatible databases keep many parliaments from developing their own information systems: apparently they are afraid that they will still lose the "data-wars" with the bureaucracy – which slowdown the decision-making processes – in the end. Moreover, they often have great confidence in the information that is delivered by the bureaucracy, which hinders the development of their own information systems. Another interesting outcome of this investigation – contrary to Frantzich's findings, which we mentioned earlier – is that when they invested in their own parliamentary information systems it rarely becomes visible in major changes of policy (Kraemer & King, 1987, p. 96).

When Congress or other representative organs succeed in adequately using informatization for better control ("oversight") over the executive, then this does not necessarily mean that parliament will win the battle with the executive. The complexity of the political arena in which the executive and the legislature make war makes it difficult to draw unambiguous conclusions about the influence of informatization on their mutual balance of power.

9.3. The Internal Dimension of Parliamentary Informatization: The Democratization of Parliaments

Greater transparency, which always seems to involve the application of automatized information systems, puts an end to the traditionally strong position of – usually elder members who had important positions in parliamentary committees in the American Congress. The (in)formal pecking order was both cause and effect of the poor accessibility and spread of important information before the arrival of these information systems. The elder members had a good appreciation of the situation, and for a long time led the resistance against further parliamentary automatization. In the end, the politically successful work of younger members using ICT made further resistance impossible (Frantzich, 1982; OTA, 1987).

Sometimes computer innovations were effectively blocked, as the staff of the informatization bureau of the American Congress discovered when they wanted to automatize the scheduling of committee meetings (Committee Information and Scheduling System). By doing so they would, however, take an important strategic weapon from the committee chairmen, namely their capacity to plan meetings at the most suitable times or places (in order to avoid publicity or, on the contrary, to seek it, or to make that certain persons would or would not be present at the meeting, etc.). The chairmen of the committees strongly resisted the automatization plan and managed to prevent it from being carried out (Frantzich, 1982, p. 147; Abramson et al., 1988).

The democratization of parliament, which was the result of digitalizing information networks has also caused an emancipation of the individual representative. New members can be settled in more quickly, because the accessibility of computer networks turned out to be larger than the previously used "Old Boys" networks. Formerly, only the chairmen of the committees were able to give the correct information about the progress of legislation projects. Now it appears fully automatically on the screen of every member who has asked the computer system (Bill Status System) to keep him or her posted about critical decision-points of legislation projects in certain fields of policy. For this type of information, the dependence on information from party specialists and chairmen of committees belongs for the greater part to the past. It seems reasonable to expect that the traditional structure of the parliamentary information network, which is characterized by, among others, hierarchy and solid anchorage in committees and procedures (see Van Schendelen, 1975, pp. 108 ff.), will be put under pressure by informatization. The parliamentary lion's den seems to have become more transparent.

Computer-based voting also contributes to this transparency, at least in the United States. An electronic voting system gives party leaders the opportunity to closely follow the course of a (15-minutes) ballot. "The system is more complicated than a simple tabulating system. It involves CRT's (terminals WD/PT) placed on the floor that are used by the leadership and those concerned with in-progress vote information to determine how subsets of the members are voting. For example, at ten minutes into the voting period the leadership could see how the Democrats from California are voting en masse. Or they could observe how Republican members of the Science and Technology Committee are voting. This is important, because there is a traditional need for revising strategies, while a vote is in progress". The system gave cause for strategic behaviour: votes were changed, under pressure, at the last moment, some Congressmen voted, in order to avoid this pressure, at the voting machine which had been installed at the exit of the hail, and so to be able to quickly leave the meeting hall after voting (Frantzich, 1982, p. 162; Ryan, 1976, p. 25). The objective to save time was not achieved, because considerably more votes were entered than before, as the voting takes place at a higher speed and more easily now.

A number of secondary functions of the system may be more important. For parties and members analyses of the voting behaviour of certain groups of members, which have been made by the system contain very important politically strategic information, but are also important externally.

First of all in election campaigns, where (the large and systematic amount of) information about representatives and senators is important political ammunition. But the executive also gains by it. At the time of the Carter administration, the White House was able to gain access to the system, because the Vice President of the United States is presiding officer of the presidium of the Senate. Especially post-vote analyses and progress information turned out to be interesting. The White House based very effective lobbying-strategies on it. Afterwards more detailed rules led to more restrictive agreements about the access of the White House to the data-files of the Senate (Kevenhdrster, 1984; Hager, 1978).

9.4. Electronic Politics

According to a number of authors, the increasing possibilities to provide and reveal the consequences of parliamentary decision-making for different parts of the electorate will result in a fierce battle (Frantzich, 1982a, 1982b; Kevenhörster, 1984). The political battle can increasingly be waged on the basis of a keen insight into who will be the winners and who will be the losers of a certain policy proposal. In connection with what has already been mentioned above about the transparent electorate and political computing, it is to be expected that particularly (the consequences of) *allocations* will be more highlighted in the political debate.

Consequences of decisions, even if they display themselves in other fields of policy, can be easier revealed by the opponents of these decisions. Frantzich expects that, due to this, reaching a consensus – certainly in cases in which one fights at daggers drawn – will become more difficult. When the luxury of "not knowing" no longer exists, political decision-making will become more difficult and compromises will sometimes not be able to persist. Fragile compromises and coalitions of mixed expectations thrive in low-information settings (Frantzich, 1982).

Not only winners and losers can be shown more clearly, but also the *presuppositions* and *points of departure* of the used models emerge more clearly. Frantzich elaborately sketches how President Reagan's proposals for the reform of taxes got bogged down in an unexpectedly heated debate in Congress, when the opposition – which calculated the consequences of the proposals by way of its own calculation models – could ascribe many of the expected effects of policy to the *supply side* propositions which lay at the bottom of the calculation models of *reaganomics* (Frantzich, 1982; see also W. Dutton, 1982).

10. FINAL CONCLUSIONS

The preceding sections make clear that the Orwellian and Athenian scenarios initially played a dominant part in the literature on the relations between democracy and information society. It was, among other things, this dominance – with all its ideological tension – that obstructed more empirical research.

By now, this situation seems to have changed somewhat. More and more studies see the light in which the relation between democracy and ICT is no longer studied from a primarily normative, but from an empirical point of view. This development has been strongly stimulated by the fact that there are more and more concrete applications of forms of information- and communication-technology in a context of political and democratic decision-making. The number of cases that could be studied has enormously increased in the past years; a number of projects could even be followed for a few years (Arterton, 1987a, 1987b). More empirical research has not resulted in a systematic development of theories, yet (Kling, 1986), but a number of temporary conclusions is worth mentioning.

In the first place, successful modernization of political decision-making by means of ICT often seems to take place by way of, what Laudon calls, an add-on-strategy. This is a strategy, which elaborates on existing procedures and institutions whose functioning may indeed be influenced by information technology, but seldom changes radically, certainly not in the short term. Information technology alone cannot remove the "democratic deficit" in our society. A non-existent political community cannot be created by way of information- and communication-technology. New media can be implemented into existing structures and consequently produce sometimes expected and even more often unexpected effects. However, in the short term do they rarely result in fundamental changes in existing views and conduct. Even the introduction of ICT seems to be subject to the old governmental pattern of incrementalism.

A second conclusion is that all kinds of images and expectations that are alive for the persons concerned exert a strong influence on the application and success of ICT. In this respect, technology is a social construct. From a research by Arterton, who studied a score of teledemocracy projects, it appeared for instance that there were large discrepancies between the presuppositions of the project leaders. These discrepancies were related to the character and intensity of democracy and participation and determined to a large extent the way in which technology was used in the different projects (Arterton, 1987a, 1987b).

However, research by Guthrie and Dutton shows that we cannot depart from simple voluntarism. In an analysis of informatization projects in four Californian cities they state that technology radiates its own power. In a certain way technology creates new technology, particularly because existing technology has a large influence on the way in which problems and solutions are defined (MacKenzie & Wajcman, 1985). Technology creates, what Guthrie and Dutton call, dominant paradigms (Guthrie & Dutton, 1991). These paradigms very much have a structuring influence on the design of new applications of ICT.

A third conclusion is that both a vertical and a horizontal perspective are present in dissertations on democracy and ICT. Authors, who consider the relation between informatization and democracy in the context of a vertical perspective, in the first place emphasize the power relation between citizens (as voters) and the elected. The second power relation, which is emphasized by this perspective is the relation between citizens and government, between the individual and the state. Dissertations on the consequences of ICT which are primarily orientated towards the vertical perspective (Schick, 1971; Lasswell, 1971; Mowshowitz, 1976; Rule, McAdam, Stearns, & Uglow, 1980; Vitalis, 1981; Burnham, 1983; Sterling, 1986) portray its meaning in the form of power shifts at the expense of one of the parties in this vertical relation. ICT, for instance, is said to restrict the liberties of citizens and increase the power of the government (threat to privacy) or, on the contrary, to increase the influence of the voters at the expense of the influence of the representatives (direct democracy).

The one-sidedness of this vertical literature is breached by a number of authors who consider democracy principally from a horizontal perspective. Within this perspective, other views on democracy are put forward. In these views, democracy is in the first place the process of deliberation among citizens (and their relations) themselves. Considering interests and reaching a consensus, involvement of minorities and participation are keywords in this view on democracy. A second line is that of checks and balances and pluralism. This perspective is certainly a reaction to and a critique of the literature of the first, vertical generation to which it is certainly a reaction. This horizontal perspective is characterized by a considerably more complex definition of democracy. Due to this definition, one-sided optimism (direct democracy) or pessimism (totalitarian state and populist democracy) about the consequences fade into the background. Abramson, Arterton, and Orren sketch the fundamental problem of selection that is connected with the emphasis on vertical or horizontal perspectives in the relation between democracy and ICT (Abramson et al., 1988, p. 295). They argue that the possibilities of technology can be used to expedite democracy and strengthen the grip of the public opinion on political decision-making. This is made possible by opinion-polling, electronic voting and instant feedback-mechanisms. Instead of this vertical perspective the horizontal perspective can also be highlighted, in this case the new media are, on the contrary, used to slow down the democratic process. The quality of democratic discussions, debates and dialogues are then highlighted. Both options, acceleration as well as deceleration, are conceivable. Which of these options will be dominant is hard to foresee. As we see it, it will depend largely upon current political and democratic cultures. Only a few authors still believe in a simple technological determinism (for better or for worse). There is, however, a consensus on the fact that ICT will go on to provoke democracy and democratic politics to renew and adapt themselves.

REFERENCES

Abramson, J. B., Arterton, F. C., & Orren, O. R. (1988). *The electronic commonwealth. The impact of new technologies upon democratic politics.* New York: Basic Books Inc.

Albeda, W. (1992). Mozaïek-democratie. *NRC Handelsblad,* 24 januari, p. 7.

Arterton, F. Ch. (1987a). *Representation, information technology and democratic values.* Report to the Office of Technology Assessment, Washington, DC, May.

Arterton, F. Ch. (1987b). *Teledemocracy: Can technology protect democracy?* Newbury Park, CA: Sage Publications.

Barber, B. R. (1988). Pangloss, Pandora or Jefferson? Three scenario's for the future of technology and democracy. In: R. Plant, F. Gregory, & A. Brier (Eds), *Information technology: The public issues* (Fullbright Papers, 5, pp. 177–190). Oxford: Alden Press.

Barnouw, E. (1982). Historical survey of communications breakthroughs. In: G. Benjamin (Ed.), *The communications revolution in politics* (pp. 13–23). New York: Academy of Political Science.

Becker, T. L. (1981). Teledemocracy: Bringing power back to the people. *The Futurist, 15*(6), 6–9.

Benjamin, G. (1982a). Innovations in telecommunications and politics. In: G. Benjamin (Ed.), *The communications revolution in politics* (pp. 1–12). New York: Academy of Political Science.

Benjamin,, G. (Ed.) (1982b). *The communications revolution in politics.* New York: Academy of Political Science.

Bogumil, J. (1987a). Chancen einer Gegenmacht? Computer in Umweltpolitischen Gruppen. *Wechselwirkung,* 35–39.

Bogumil, J., & Lange, H. J. (1991). *Computer in Parleien und Verbände.* Opladen: Westdeutscher Verlag.

Breman, I. W. (1983). De documentaire automatisering bij het parlement. *Informatie, 25*(4), 13–19.

Breton, P. (1987). *Histoire de l'informatique* (p. 239). Paris: Editions La Decouverte.

Broder, D. S. (1987). Electronic democracy. *The Washington Post,* 30 augustus, p. C7.

Burnham, D. (1983). *The rise of the computer state* (1st ed.). New York: Random House.

Calhoun, G. (1986). Comments on democracy in an information society. *The Information Society, 4*(1/2), 115–122.

Chartrand, R. L. (1968). Congress seeks a systems approach. *Datamation, 14,* 46–49.

Chartrand, R. L., & Borrel, J. (1981). *The legislator as a user of information technology.* Congressional Research Service Report (81-187 SPR).

Dijk, J. A. G. M. van (1991a). *De netwerktnaatschappij. Sociale aspecten van nieuwe media.* Houten: Bohn Stafleu Van Loghum.

Dizard, W. P. (1982). *The coming information age. An overview of technology, economics and politics.* New York: Longman.

Donk, W. B. H. J. van de, Frissen, P. H. A., & Snellen, en I. Th. M. (1990). Spanningen tussen wetgeving en systeemontwikkeling: De Wet Studiefinanciering. *Beleids wet enschap, 4,* 3–20.

Dutton, W. (1982). Technology and the federal system. In: G. Benjamin (Ed.), *The communications revolution in politics* (pp. 109–120). New York: Academy of Political Science.

Dutton, W. F. L., & Guthrie, K. (1991). An ecology of games: The political construction of Santa Monica's public electronic network. *Informatization and the Public Sector, 1,* 279–301.

Etzioni, A., Laudon, K. C., & Lipson, S. (1975). Participating technology: The minerva communications tree. *Journal of Communication, 25*(Spring), 64–74.

Eulau, H. (1977). *Technology and civility. The Skill Revolution in* Politics. Stanford. California: Stanford University. (Hoover Institution Publ. 167).

Everson, D. H. (1982). The decline of political parties. In: G. Benjamin (Ed.), *The Communications revolution in politics* (pp. 49–60). New York: Academy of Political Science.

Forester, T. (Ed.). (1985). *The information technology revolution.* Oxford: Basil Blackwell.

Frantzich, S. (1982a). Communications and congress. In: G. Benjamin (Ed.), *The communications revolution in politics* (pp. 88–101). New York: Academy of Political Science.

Frantzich, S. E. (1982b). *Computers in congress: The politics of information.* Beverly Hills: Sage Publications.

Frissen, P. H. A. (1991). *De versplinterde staat. Over informatisering, bureaucratie en technocralie voorbij depolitiek.* (Oratie Katholieke Universiteit Brabant). Aiphen aan den Rijn: Samsom H.D. Tjeenk-Willink.

Gallouedec-Genuys, F. (1980). *Une informatique pour les administrés?* Editions Paris: Cujas.

Gau, J. A. (1980). Le rôle de l'informatique parlementaired. *Actes du Colloque International Informatique et société* (Vol. V, pp. 109–113). Paris: Documentation Francaise.

Grewlich, K. W., & Pedersen, F. H. (Eds). (1984). Power and participation in an information society. Brussel: European Commission.

Hager, B. M. (1978). Computers help White House lobbying. *Congressional Quarterly Weekly Report,* (11 februari), 366.

Hollander, R. (1985). *Video democracy: The vote-from-home revolution.* Mt. Airy, MD: Lomond Press.

Kevenhdrster, P. (1984). *Politik im Elektronischen Zeitalter. Politische Wirkungen der Informationstechnik.* Baden-Baden: Nomos Verlagsgesellschaft.

Kling, R. (1986). The struggles for democracy in an information society. *The Information' Society, 4*(1/2), 1–7.

Kraemer, K. L., & King, J. L. (1987). Computers and the constitution: A helpful, harmful of harmless relationship? *Public Administration Review, 47*(1), 93–105.

Lasswell, H. D. (1971). Policy problems of a data-rich civilization. In: A. F. Westin (Ed.), *Information technology in a democracy* (pp. 187–197). Cambridge, MA: Harvard University Press.

Laudon, K. C. (1977). *Communications technology and democratic participation.* New York: Praeger Publishers.

Laudon, K. C. (1980). Informatique et democratie: l'expérience américaine. *Actes du Colloque International Informatique et Société*, *V*, 135–142.

Lenk, K. (1976). Partizipationsförderende Technologien? In: K. Lenk (Hrsg) (Ed.), *Informationsrechte und Kommunikationspolitik*. Darmstadt: Toeche/Mitler.

Luker, K. (1984). *Abortion and the politics of motherhood*. Berkely: University of California Press.

MacKenzie, D., & Wajcman, J. (1985). *The social control of technology. How the refrigerator got its hum*. Buckingham: Open University Press.

Martin, J. (1978). *The wired society*. Englewood Cliffs: Prentice-Hall.

Masuda, Y. (1985). Parameters of the post-industrial society. In: T. Forester (Ed.), *The information technology revolution*. Oxford: Basil Blackwell.

McLean, I. (1989). *Democracy and new technology*. Cambridge: Polity Press.

Meadow, R. G. (1985). Political communications research in the 1980s. *Journal of Communications*, *35*(5–6), 157–173.

Miewald, R., & Mueller, K. (1987). The use of information technology in oversight by state legislatures. *State and Local Government Review*, *13*, 17–24.

Montes, F. (1986). Prospects for the era of computing comments on democracy in an information society. *The Information Society*, *4*(1/2), 65–86.

Moore, D. W. (1992). *The super pollsters. How they measure and manipulate public opinion in America*. New York: Four Walls Eight Windows.

Morris-Suzuki, T. (1988). *Beyond computopia. Information, automation and democracy in Japan*. London: Kegan Paul International.

Mowshowitz, A. (1976). *The conquest of will: Information processing in human affairs*. Reading, MA: Addison-Wesley.

Naisbitt, J. (1982). *Megatrends: Ten new directions transforming our lives*. New York: Warner Books.

Neustadt, R. (1985). Electronic politics. In: T. Forester (Ed.), *The information technology revolution* (pp. 561–568). Oxford: Blackwell.

OTA, (1987). *Science, Technology and the Constitution (background paper)*. U.S. Congress, Office of Technology Assessment, September.

Pedersen, F. H. (1984). Power and participation in an information society. In: K. W. Grewlich & F. H. Pedersen (Eds), *Power and participation in an information society* (pp. 249–289). Brussel-Luxembourg: European Commission.

Roll, Ch. (1982). Private opinion polls. In: G. Benjamin (Ed.), *The Communications Revolutionin Politics* (pp. 61–74). New York: Academy of Political Science.

Rose, C. (1980). L'informatique et l'avenir de la démocratie. *Actes du Colloque international Informatique et société* (Vol. V, pp. 81–87). Paris: Documentation Française.

Rule, J. (1974). *Private lives and public surveillance: social control in the computer age*. New York: Schocken.

Rule, J. B., McAdam, D., Stearns, L., & Uglow, D. (1980). Preserving individual autonomy in an information-oriented society. In: L. J. Hoffmann (Ed.), *Computers and privacy in the next decade* (pp. 65–87). San Diego, CA: Academic Press.

Saloma, J. S. (1968). Systems politics: The presidency and congress in the future. *Technology Review*, *71*, 23–33.

Schendelen, M. P. Ch. M. van (1975). *Parlementaire informatie, besluitvorming en verlegenwoordiging*. Rotterdam: Universitaire Pers.

Schick, A. (1971). Toward the cybernetic state. In: D. Waldo (Ed.), *Public administration in a time of turbulence* (pp. 214–233). New York: Chandler Publishing Company.

Snellen, I. Th. M. en, & van de Donk, W. B. H. J. (1987). Some dialectical developments of informatization in public administration. Contribution to the conference on new technologies in public administration: Socio-economic aspects from an interdisciplinary viewpoint. Zagreb, 13 November.

Snellen, I. Th. M., Balfoort, C., van de Donk, W. B. H. J., Henkes, H., Stevens, J. J. M., & Westra, en R. L. N. (1989). *Informatisering in het openbaar bestuur. Indicaries voor politiek-inhoudelzjke sturing*'s-Gravenhage: SDU uitgeverij. (NOTA-studie V11)

Sola Pool, I. de. (1983). *Technologies of freedom. On free speech in an electronic age.* Cambridge, MA: Harvard University Press.

Steinbuch, K. (1978). Computer und politik. *Datascope, 28,* 3–10.

Sterling, Th. D. (1986). Democracy in an information society. *The Information Society, 4*(1/2), 9–47.

Taylor, P. (1990). Citizenship fades among disconnected Americans. *Washington Post, 6*(May), A1.

Toffler, A. (1980). *Third wave.* New York: HarperCollins Publishers.

Tops, P. W. en, & Kommers, C. M. B. (1991). Informatization and local democracy in the Netherlands: An exploration. Paper for the FOPA conference on informatization in public administration. The Hague, August 29–31.

Vitalis, A. (1981). *Informatique, Pouvoir et Libertés.* Paris: Economica.

Westin, A. F. (1971a). Prologue: Of technological visions and democratic politics. In: A. F. Westin (Ed.), *Information technology in a democracy* (pp. 1–11). Cambridge, MA: Harvard University Press.

Williams, F. (1982). *The communications revolution.* Beverly Hills: Sage Publications.

Winner, L. (1986). *The whale and the reactor. A search for limits in an age of high technology.* Chicago: University of Chicago Press.

FURTHER READING

Armstrong, R. (1988). *The next Hurrah: The communications revolution in American politics.* New York: Beech Tree Press.

Arterton, C. F. (1984a) *Media politics: Scenarios, standards and benchmarks* (Chapter 6, pp. 143–192). Lexington, MA: Lexington Books. (Heath: 0669075043).

Arterton, C. F. (1984b). *Media politics: The news strategies of presidential campaigns.* Lexington, MA: Lexington Books.

Arterton, F. Ch. (1988). Political participation and teledemocracy. *Political Science Quarterly, 21,* 620–627.

Arterton, F. Ch., Lazarus, E. H., Griffin, J. W., & Andres, M. C. (1984). *Telecommunication, technologies and political parties.* Washington, DC: Roosevelt Center for American Policy Studies.

Barber, B. R. (1984). *Strong democracy: Participatory politics for a new age.* Berkely: University of California Press.

Bennet, J. M. (1983). Computers and citizen participation in politics and government. In: A. Mowshowitz (Ed.), *Human choice and computers.* Amsterdam: North-Holland (2 parts).

Berkman, R., & Kitch, L. (1986). *Politics in the media age.* New York: McGraw-Hill.

Betts, M. (1989). Gerrymandering made easy in 1990. *Computerworld, 23*(28 augustus), 1–18.

Bjerknes, G., Ehn, P., & Kyng, M. (Eds). (1987). *Computers and democracy: A Scandinavian challenge.* Avebury: Aldershot.

Blakely, S. (1985). Computers alter the way congress does business. *Congressional Quarterly, 13,* 79–82.

Bogumil, J. (1987b). Computereinsata in den Gewerkschaften. Den erste Schritt zur politischen Modernisierung? *Gewerkschaftliche Monaishefte* (nummer 4), 35–39.

Broder, D. S. (1927). The amazing new high-speed dial-a-president machine. *The Washington Post,* 8 juli, p. A19.

Brurinstein, K. (1985). Representative democracy and information and communication technology: The Malady, the cure, its effect. In: L. Yngström, R. Sizer, J. Berleur & R. Laufer (Eds), *Can information technology result in benevolent bureaucracies?* (pp. 113–123). Amsterdam: North-Holland.

Conseil d'Etat. (1988). *Administration et nouvelles technologies de l'information. Une nécessaire adaptation du droir.* Paris: Documentation Francaise.

Danziger, J. N., Dutton, W. H., Kling, R., & Kraerner, K. L. (1982). *Computers and politics. High technology in American local governments.* New York: Colombia University Press.

Depla, P., & Tops, P. W. (1992). Technology and local democracy. Five experiments in the Netherlands. Paper presented at the ECPR-conference in Limerick.

Dijk, J. A. G. M. van (1991b). Teledemocraie: Mogelijkheden en Beperkingen van Nieuwe Media voor Burgerschap. *Beleid en Maaischappij, 3,* 142–149.

Donk, W. B. H. J. van de. (1990). De Opkomst van de Surveillance Bureaucratie? Kanttekeningen bij de toepassing van beslissingsondersteunende expert-systemen. *Bestuur. Maandblad voor Overheidskunde,* 144–147.

Donk, W. B. H. J. van de. (1990). Harmonjeuze coalities of weerspannige verhoudingen? Eenverkenning van de verhouding tussen politici, wetgevingsjuristen en informatici bij synchrone wetgeving en systeemontwikkeling. *Recht doen door wet geving. Opstellen over wetgevingsvraagstukken aangeboden atm mr. E.M.H. Hirsch Ba//in* (pp. 307–321). Zwolle: W.E.J. Tjeenk Willink.

Downs, A. (1967). A realistic look at the final payoffs from urban data systems. *Public Administration Review, 27*(September), 204–210.

Dutton, W. H. (1989). Looking beyond teledemocracy: The politics of communications and information technology. In: A. A. Berger (Ed.), *Political culture and public opinion* (pp. 79–96). New Brunswick: Transaction Publishers.

Dutton, W. H., Blumler, J. G., & Kraemer, K. (1987). *Wired cities.* Boston: G.H. Hall.

Dutton, W., Steckenrider, J., & Ross-Christensen, D. (1984). Electronic participation by citizens in U.S. local government. *Inforincztion Age, 6/2,* 78–97.

Dutton, W. H. (1982). Computer models in the decisionmaking process. *Information Age, 4,* 86–94.

Elstain, J. B. (1982). Democracy and the Qube tube. *The Nation,* (7–14), 108–110.

Everts, G. T. (1990). The electronic commonwealth. Book review. *Michigan Law Review, 87,* 1393–1400.

Faber, S. (1985). Parlementaire informatievoorziening. In: E. M. H. Hirsch Baum & J. A. Kamphuis (Eds), *Trias Autornatica. Automatisering in wetgeving, bestuur en rechtspraak* (pp. 51–54). Deventer: Kluwer.

Forester, T. (Ed.). (1980). *The microelectronics revolution.* Oxford: Basil Blackwell Publisher.

Friedland, E. I. (1971). Turbulence and technology: Public administration and the role of information-processing technology. In: D. Waldo (Ed.), *Public administration in a time of turbulence* (pp. 134–150). New York: Chandler Publishing Company.

Friedrichs, G., & Schaff, A. (Eds). (1982). *Microelectronics and society: For better of for worse. A report to the club of Rome.* Oxford: Pergamon Press.

Godwin, R. K. (1988). *One billion dollars of influence: The direct marketing of politics.* Chatham, NJ: Chatham House Publishers.

Grémion, P. (1980). Le technicisme détnocratisant. *Actes du Colloque International Informatique et société* (Vol. V, pp. 115–118). Paris: Documentation Française.

Gurwitt, R. (1988). The computer revolution: Microchipping away at the limits of government. *Governing, 1*(34–38), 40–42.

Guthrie, K. (1991). *The politics of citizen access technology: The development of public information utilities in four cities.* Unpublished dissertation. Annenberg School for Communication/University of Southern California.

Hattery, L. H. (1962). EDP: Implications for public administration. *Public Administration Review, 22,* 129–130.

Howell, D. (1985). IT and relations *between* government and the public. *Catalyst, 1,* 75–85.

Kamp, J., & Kerres, M. (1992). De huidige parlementen zijn museumstukken. (Interview met Alvin Toffler). *NRC-Handelsblad, 4 februari,* pp. 13, 14.

Keane, J. (1991). *The media and democracy.* Cambridge: Polity Press.

Kling, R. (1982). Social analyses of computing. *Information Age, 4,* 25–55.

Kraemer, K. L., & Dutton, W. H. (1979). The interests served by technological reform. The case of computing. *Administration and Society, 11*(1), 80–106.

Kraemer, K. L., & Kling, R. (1985). The political character of computerization in service organizations. *Computers and the Social Sciences, 1*(2), 77–90.

Kraft, M. E., & Vig, N. J. (Eds). (1988). *Technology and politics.* Durham: Duke University Press.

Lapham, L. H., et al. (1985). *High technology and human freedom.* Washington, DC: Smithsonian Institution Press.

Laudon, K. C. (1984). The possibilities for participation in the democratic process: Telecommunications, computers and democracy. In: K. W. Grewlich & F. H. Pedersen (Eds), *Power and participation in an information society* (pp. 153–168). Brussels: European Commission.

Laudon, K. C. (1986a). *Dossier Society: Value choices in the design of national information systems.* New York: Columbia University Press.

Laudon, K. C. (1986b). The Dossier Society (Comments on Democracy in an Information Society). *The Information Society, 4*(1/2), 87–90.

Lenk, K. (1982). Information technology and society. In: G. Friedrichs & A. Schaff (Eds), *Microelectronics and society: For better of for worse. A report to the club of Rome* (pp. 273–310). Oxford: Pergamon Press.

Licklider, J. C. R. (1983). Computers and government. In: L. Dertouzos & J. Moses (Eds), *The computer age: A twenty-year view* (pp. 87–126). Cambridge, MA: MIT Press.

Lowi, Th. J. (1980). The political impact of information technology. In: T. Forester (Ed.), *The microelectronics revolution* (pp. 453–472). Oxford: Basil Blackwell Publisher.

Lowi, Th. J., & Lytel, D. (1986). Making it a real revolution (Comments on Democracy in an information Society). *The Information Society, 4*(1/2), 91–99.

MacBride, R. (1967). *The automated state. Computer systems as a new force in society.* Philadelphia: Chilton Book Company.

Magleby, D. (1984). *Direct legislation: Voting on ballot propositions in the United States.* Baltimore, MD: John Hopkins University Press.

Malbin, M. (1982). Teledemocracy and its discontents. *Public Opinion, 5*(3), 55–59.

Marien, M. (1985). Some questions for the information society. In: T. Forester (Ed.), *The information technology revolution.* Oxford: Blackwell.

Moss, ML. (1978). Interactive television: Reading, PA; research on community uses. *Journal of Communication, 2,* 160–167.

Mowshowitz, A. (1977). *Inside information: Computers in fiction.* Reading, MA: Addison-Wesley Publishing Co.

Murchland, B. (1983). Citizenship in a technological society: Problems and possibilities. *Journal of Teacher Education, 34*(6), 21–24.

Orton, B. M. (n.d.). *Media-based issue balloting for regional planning* (177 pp.). Dissertation, New Brunswick, NJ: Rutgers University, University Microfilms 80-13.

OTA, (1988). Informing the Nation: Federal information Dissemination en an Electronic Age. U.S. Congress, Office of Technology Assessment, October.

Parry, G. (1989). Democracy and amateurism – the informed citizen. *Government and Opposition, 24*(4), 489–502.

Pitt, D. C. & Smith, B. C. (Eds). (1984). *The computer revolution.* Brighton, Sussex: Wheatsheaf Books Ltd.

Plant, R., Gregory, F., & Brier, A. (Eds). (1988). *Information technology: The public issues.* New York: Manchester University Press.

Price, D. G., & Mulvihill, D. E. (1965). The present and future use of computers in state government. *Public Administration Review, 25,* 142–150.

Rawley Saldich, A. (1979). *Electronic democracy. Television's impact on the American political process.* New York: Praeger Publishers.

Ryan, F. B. (1977). Computing as an aid to political effectiveness. In: T. Oden & Ch. Thompson (Eds), *Computers and public policy* (pp. 22–27). Hanover, NH: Dartmouth College.

Schneier, E. (1970). The intelligence of Congress: Information and public policy patterns. *Annals of the American Academy of Political and Social Science. 388*(March), 14–24.

Snellen, I. Th. M. (1988). Informatisering in en voor het openbaar bestuur. *Beleidswetenschappen, 2,* 18–32.

Sola Pool, I. de. (Ed.) (1973). *Talking back: Citizen feedback and cable technology.* Cambridge: MIT-Press.

Stoyles, R. L. (1989). The unfulfilled promise: Use of computers by and for legislatures. *Computer Law Journal, IX,* 74–102.

Street, J. (1988). Taking control? Some aspects of the relationship between information technology, government policy and democracy. In: R. Plant, F. Gregory & A. Brier (Eds), *Information technology: The public issues* (Fullbright Papers, Vol. 5, pp. 1–20). Oxford: Alden Press.

Vig, N. J. (1988). Technology, philosophy and the state: An overview. In: M. E. Kraft & N. J. Vig (Eds), *Technology and politics* (pp. 8–32). Durham: Duke University Press.

Wecramantry, C. (1983). *The slumbering sentinels.* London: Penguin.

Westin, A. (1971b). *Information technology in a democracy.* Cambridge, MA: Harvard University Press.

Westin, A. F. (1980). The long-term implications of computers for privacy and the protection of public order. In: L. Hoffman (Ed.), *Computers and privacy in the next decade* (pp. 167–182). NY: Academic Press.

Winner, L. (1988). Do artifacts have politics? In: M. E. Kraft & N. J. Vig (Eds), *Technology and politics* (pp. 33–53). Durham: Duke University Press.

Yngström, L., Sizer, R., Berleur, J., & Laufer,, R. (Eds) (1985). *Can information technology result in benevolent bureaucracies?* Amsterdam: North-Holland.

TRANSFORMING BUREAUCRACIES FOR THE 21ST CENTURY: THE NEW DEMOCRATIC GOVERNANCE PARADIGM

Bidhya Bowornwathana

INTRODUCTION

We enter the 21st century with our societies undergoing a radical transformation amidst an atmosphere of optimism that global economic prosperity and peace will prevail. At the same time, there is an increasing awareness of the important role government and public administration play in facilitating economic and social change together with a growing realization of the shortcomings of that role. The general belief holds that the far-reaching socioeconomic, political, and technological changes currently taking place will render 21st bureaucracies obsolete. Thus, transformation of our public bureaucracies becomes imperative to avoid the stigma of obsolescence. Major administrative reform undertaking must be launched in every country, western or eastern alike, "governance" matters more and more these days.

The necessity for reform arising in the practitioner's world has occurred contemporaneously with cumulative advances in the body of knowledge in

Comparative Public Administration: The Essential Readings
Research in Public Policy Analysis and Management, Volume 15, 667–679
Copyright © 2006 by Elsevier Ltd.
All rights of reproduction in any form reserved
ISSN: 0732-1317/doi:10.1016/S0732-1317(06)15029-0

the field of public administration. A new perspective or paradigm has emerged providing order to our thinking about administrative reform. This author calls this perspective the "new democratic governance" paradigm. The purpose of this article is to explain the guiding principles of the newly emerging paradigm and discuss its implications for the practitioner's world. The article is divided into two parts: one outlines the guiding principles of the new democratic governance and the other discusses implications for administrative reform.

THE NEW DEMOCRATIC GOVERNANCE PARADIGM

The new democratic governance paradigm advocates a multidimensional approach toward understanding administrative reform. We ask four critical questions: (1) What should government do? (2) How should government work? (3) Who should control government? and (4) Who benefits from government? These four questions form "the four pillars" for future paradigm construction in the comparative study of administrative reform. The author now explains the guiding principles with regard to the four fundamental questions.

Principle 1. *A Smaller Government that Does Less.* What should government do? The new democratic governance paradigm advocates a smaller government that does less. At present, it is common practice for governments to launch administrative reform policies that call for cutback management, downsizing, streamlining, privatization, contracting-out, and deregulation (Gore, 1995; Citizen's Charter Unit, 1995). The usual explanations given in support of this minimal role of the state revolve around the following arguments.

Argument 1. Governments in general, and public bureaucracies in particular, have grown too big and costly to maintain. Governments allocate such a large portion of their annual budgets to cover salary and maintenance costs of the bureaucracy that not enough is left for developmental purposes. According to popular belief, despite the enormous size of the public bureaucracy, its performance has fallen far short of public expectations. Besides being too large to be affordable, the bureaucracy has proven inefficient. Therefore, the logical thing to do is to transform bureaucracy so that it becomes smaller in size and more performance oriented.

Government officials are known to display a decided proclivity for domain expansion so retrenchment is of course easier said than done. Therefore, the first guiding principle has as its prerequisite a reorientation of government officials' values, in particular, those values supportive of domain expansion. The new motto is: "No domain expansion, please!" This leads to further questions such as: Are government officials capable of restraining themselves? or do we need external mechanisms to do the checking?

Argument 2. The private sector can do a better job than the state in providing quality services and products to the public. According to this argument, the private sector is more efficient because market mechanisms force competition to survive (Peters, 1995; Pierre, 1995). By contrast, the government sector has a tendency to monopolize public services delivery; it has no incentive to improve the quality of its services. Nationalized industries allowed by the state to monopolize have performed poorly. Furthermore, countries *that have adopted* the welfare-state *model are* finding *such a* policy *to* be financially overwhelming. State intervention, they believe, has proven to be a failure. Privatization seems to be the answer.

Thus, the second prerequisite of the small government thesis is that government officials stop thinking of themselves as the "saviors" of all problems in the society. Many problems can be better taken care of by non-governmental actors. This prerequisite, therefore, calls for government officials to trust and facilitate the non-government sector in solving the problems of communities.

Argument 3. Globalization of the world economy along free trade and market principles has put the business sector in the forefront of economic development (Naisbitt, 1994). There is now another belief that prosperity can best be gained by allowing the business sector to lead the economic development of a country. The new role of the state should be to create and support the operation of an unrestricted market economy. Government officials should play the role of a "facilitator" that supports the growth of global market economy. Bureaucracies are no longer either "masters or servants" of the people, they are instead "partners" and "referees." Administrative mechanisms have to be set up to foster this new partnership between government and the private sector. Government officials should see themselves as "partners" who facilitate, not as "masters" who regulate, the business sector.

The preceding arguments are usually invoked in support of the thesis for smaller government. Note should be taken that, when one talks about a small government, the word "government" here refers to the central government. By advocating a smaller central government, the implicit assumption is that the power of governance should be localized. By this logic, decentralization of power and responsibility from the central government to local government units constitutes a major reform policy of democratic regimes.

The more say and control communities have over the provision of public goods, the better off they will be. By streamlining the work of the central government, central officials and elected executives will suffer less from work overload and will be able to concentrate on their national responsibilities. The creation of various local government units will therefore benefit both the central officials and local communities.

Principle 2. *A Government with a Global Vision and Flexibility.* The second guiding principle of the new democratic governance paradigm calls for a government bureaucracy with a global vision and flexible organizations. This implies a reorientation in our thinking of how government should work. The phenomenon of globalization has led to task environments of government agencies transcending national boundaries. National governments are now more dependent on the global environment than ever before.

In this rather borderless world, to function well, government agencies and officials must have a global vision. They must understand their niche in the global community. A rapidly changing and more uncertain world requires new organizations characterized by flexibility. Government officials must respond to these global challenges creatively (Bowornwathana, 1995a). They must learn to think globally and be open-minded in their search for alternative organizational designs.

The second guiding principle requires that, to be able to think globally, government officials must understand the phenomenon of globalization. First, government officials must realize that the world economy is becoming more and more borderless. Trade barriers among nations are being dismantled. Global corporations are allowed to compete with domestic companies so that the "consumer" citizen can benefit from the best product offered. At the same time, domestic companies are trying to enter the global market in the near future.

Government officials must be alert to the new rules and regulations of the world trade system. They must participate actively in international meetings such as the WTO, GATT, the World Bank, UNCTAD, and special meetings such as the Europe–Asia Meeting. Trade blocs such as the EU, OPEC, NAFTA, and APEC are becoming more and more important. Government officials stationed abroad must also supply information about recent economic and trade policies of the country and region where they are stationed. To know what to look for they need a global vision with an understanding of their country's needs.

Second, government officials must understand the significance of the current revolution in information technology. We live in an era where people are increasingly able to receive instant information about events around the world. Distance no longer matters. For example, through cable television and satellite dishes people learn about one another's life styles. Government no longer monopolizes information.

With the revolution in information technology, not only are people better educated, they also tend to share a common understanding of right and wrong. People around the world support the United Nation's principles of sustainable development, environmental protection, and human rights. In this regard, government officials will unavoidably experience the "third wave civilization" (Toffler, 1994). They must utilize the overflow of global information intelligently.

Third, government officials must realize that the countries of the world have become more globalized politically. The triumph of democracy over communism in the last two decades had guided many nations to choose a more democratic form of government. Democracy is spreading around the world fast because, through the global telecommunications system, people learn that life is better under a democratic rule than a communist regime. Economics, not political ideology, now drives government leaders. Democracy brings into play a complex set of democratic values such as citizens' rights, elected government, openness of government, and local government. Therefore, government officials will have to adjust to the new requirements of democratic principles.

Uncertainties created by globalization mean that government must search for more flexible ways of organizing. Governments can no longer operate with a hierarchical Weberian-style bureaucracy (Golembiewski, 1995a, 1995b; Rhodes, 1996). Management scholars have proposed several alternative organizational designs such as innovative organization (Benveniste, 1994), the information-oriented organization (Drucker, 1989, 1994), the learning organizations (Senge, 1990), and the reengineered organization (Hammer & Champy, 1993).

The richness of ideas in the management literature about new ways to run organizations has tempted public administrators to import popular management ideas into the practice of government. A well-known example of the application of new management designs to the field of government is the concept of the entrepreneurial, customer-driven government (Osborne & Gaebler, 1992).

The second guiding principle proposes another way to run government by separating government from its output or operating units. Government officials still retain their policy functions. However, at the implementation level, it does not matter who does the performing, government officials or outsiders, as long as the job is accomplished. Whenever appropriate, government can contract-out the necessary operations (Kirkpatrick & Lucio, 1996). Hired on a contract basis, vested with considerable financial autonomy and authority over personnel matters, chief executives of operating units are not permanent civil servants in the Weberian sense. This new way of organizing government work is prevalent in the United Kingdom in the form of executive agencies (Bowornwathana, 1995b).

Principle 3. *Accountable Government.* The third guiding principle of the new democratic governance paradigm has to do with the increasing importance attached to the issue of accountability of government officials. Hierarchical accountability within government bureaucracy is no longer sufficient; government must be highly accountable to outsiders. The new trend calls for government officials to be accountable to the citizens and elected politicians, that is to MPs and cabinet members.

The future will generate even more demands for government accountability. Through the information super-highway, people, rich and poor, will learn about a better quality of life and better standards of living. They will exacerbate their demands upon their governments for a better life. Political pressures will multiply in high-growth economies where the growing middle-class becomes more and more empowered with knowledge and money. A new universal code of conduct for public officials of the 21st century has been proposed (Naisbitt, 1994). Citizens of the global community will show less tolerance for unethical conduct of public officials whose conduct will come under close scrutiny. In countries where the mass media enjoy freedom of the press, the demand for an accountable government will intensify. As public expectations grow, bureaucracy bashing will become more common.

With the globalization of democracy and economy, the monopoly of political and administrative power of government bureaucrats will be increasingly challenged by the new principles of democracy and by a growing middle class. Believing in the superiority of democracy, many countries will push for democratically oriented administrative reform, focusing on the accountability of government officials.

The reform vision advocates a reform design, which democratizes the public bureaucracy. Commonly proposed measures center on: introduction of openness, transparency, accountability, and accessibility to government, more say on the part of politicians over the affairs of the bureaucrats, transfer and promotion power, increasing efficiency of bureaucrats or better value for money, smaller government by downsizing, streamlining, privatizing, etc., better quality public services, customer-oriented services, and the establishment of the ombudsman office (Bowornwathana, 1999; Wong & Chan, 1999).

Many countries around the world are in the process of imitating and adopting accountability mechanisms that have proved successful in western democracies. Examples of these mechanisms include: the ombudsman office, administrative courts, freedom of information act, administrative procedures act, public hearings, private watchdogs, anti-corruption agencies, British executive agencies, and citizen charters, etc.

For a government bureaucracy to be accountable to its citizens, provision must exist for citizens to control and monitor the use of discretionary power by bureaucrats. Accountability, therefore, implies that citizens have certain democratic rights, for example, the right to a clean and honest government; the right to high-quality public services and products; the right to question and appeal bureaucratic decisions and rulings; the right to know what government officials are doing; the right to self-government especially at the local level; and the right to remove a bad government official. In other words, a government bureaucracy that is accountable is one that is less corrupt, more efficient, transparent and open, decentralized, and removable, therefore temporal.

How these five dimensions are interrelated is the subject of future empirical research. Perhaps they are connected in such a way as to allow identification of "stages" of reform targets. For example, talk about open and transparent government constitutes a logical inconsistency when corruption is prevalent. Nor can one speak about efficiency when the central government is overloaded.

To ensure that government officials are accountable to elected politicians, administrative reform programs must aim at increasing control by politicians over the bureaucracy. More power should be given to elected politicians over permanent bureaucrats so that the politicians can ensure that government officials are less corrupt, more efficient, open and transparent. The implicit assumption concerns the legitimacy of political oversight of government officials because politicians are elected by the people. Whether politicians are bad or good is not the point. We are here talking about administrative reform, not political reform.

Principle 4. *A Government That Is Fair.* The last guiding principle of the new governance paradigm centers on the belief that we should pay serious attention to the question of who benefits from government reform. Administrative reform programs and policies may have positive and negative consequences for particular groups of people.

For example, a new salary scale introduced by the government to solve the brain-drain problem and boost the morale of civil servants may widen the salary gap between senior and junior officials. Reform measures for which senior bureaucrats show enthusiasm and support may contain clauses that add to the long list of executive privileges. The creation of a new ministry such as a Ministry of Labor may result in greater central control over labor affairs instead of actually solving labor problems. Changes in rules and regulations may block or facilitate the entry and promotion of women in government jobs.

We should not forget that administrative reform is "politics" (Bowornwathana, 1996, forthcoming/a, forthcoming/b). How one would like to see the government bureaucracy changed depends where one sits. If administrative reform becomes the prerogative of permanent officials, then the most powerful bureaucratic groups will benefit the most. Central agencies such as the civil service agency and the budget bureau will push for more central control, meanwhile line departments will be more likely to advocate greater autonomy and wider domains. The diffusion of administrative reform experienced from abroad will be carried out selectively to the benefit of the group in power.

When the government introduces programs of reform, powerful groups and agencies will most likely be the first to experiment with the ideas. To understand administrative reform, one must therefore have a substantial knowledge about the unique political context of a country. Which groups in the government bureaucracy have what power? What is the power relationship between political executives and permanent bureaucrats? New reform policies can alter the power balance among the various interest groups in the bureaucracy. Policy stalemates may occur because agreement could not be reached on the issue of who should have authority over a particular reform policy.

This fourth guiding principle faces grave complications in determining whether an administrative reform program is fair or not. Generally speaking, there are four types of fairness. First, there is what one can call global fairness. Because of globalization, a new set of global values has emerged regarding the conduct of governments. Examples of these new international values are sustainable development, human rights, and environmental protection (Naisbitt, 1994; Commission on Global Governance, 1995). Though nations may disagree as to the extent that these values should constitute guidelines for the conduct of the state, there is no denial that they do exist. Second, constitutional fairness refers to the choice of administrative reform policies and measures congruent with the nation's constitution. Third, government fairness occurs when administrative reform follows the policy statements of the ruling government. For example, if decentralization is the policy of the government, then the government must not support policies, which enhance centralization of power by the central government. Finally, individual fairness happens when the citizens perceive that certain administrative reform measures are in general fair to everyone.

Complications arise owing to the plurality of opinions among citizens. Should majority rule prevail when citizens have different perceptions of fairness? Or should the state pay more attention to the needs of minorities? While the criterion of fairness remains contentious, the issue of who benefits from government reforms occupies a central place in the "new democratic governance" paradigm.

IMPLICATIONS OF THE NEW PARADIGM

The new democratic governance paradigm is not without opponents. To call for a government that is smaller and does less and is more accountable to outsiders is, this author believes, threatening to government officials because they stand to lose their domains and traditional power. Unless alternative solutions acceptable to bureaucrats can be worked out, government officials are likely to put up stiff resistance. For polities with politically powerful bureaucrats, such resistance may shake the stability of elected governments (Bowornwathana, 1994).

Government bureaucrats normally share a reform vision that runs counter to democratic principles. Bureaucrats favor reform that contains pro-bureaucrat clauses – usually at the expense of elected politicians and citizens. Pro-bureaucrat clauses refer to the reduction of transfer power of politicians, increased bureaucratic control, higher salary and benefits, and structural expansion of bureaucratic agencies (Bowornwathana, 1999). It comes as no surprise to find that in polities with strong bureaucracies, little progress has been made in transforming the government bureaucracy into a smaller and more accountable one. A recent World Bank (1995) report indicates that privatization of state enterprises around the world, especially in developing countries, has failed partly because bureaucrats want to continue running the business.

As for the belief in a global vision and flexible organizations, the reform experience of various countries has shown that government officials are quite enthusiastic about learning about globalization and experimenting with new ways of organizing. Reform blueprints issued by governments always contain both futuristic and globalization elements.

Two major concerns command attention. First, there is a good chance that government officials will overemphasize the global vision and flexible organization aspects of governance while ignoring other aspects, i.e., small government, accountability, and fairness. To have a global vision and flexible organizations makes government officials look good and modern. To ignore or postpone discussions about issues of small government, accountability, and fairness means that government officials can retain their bureaucratic power at least until their retirement.

Second, there is the danger of believing in the superiority and transferability of private sector management skills and techniques, such as reengineering, total quality management, and strategic management, to the public sector. Scholars, of course, have regularly pointed out that a country is not a company (Krugman, 1995; Lane, 1994). Peters and Savoie (1994) have shown that Anglo-American reform efforts of the 1980s, which relied heavily on management practices, overlooked the question of accountability and the morale of civil servants. Moe (1994, p. 119) has emphasized that the mission of government agencies is determined by the representatives of the people, not agency management.

By advocating a government that is fair, the new democratic governance paradigm puts government officials in an uneasy position. No longer can government officials ignore the consequences of their actions for society and particular groups of people. Government officials will increasingly be challenged by citizens as to the appropriateness of their actions. The emergence of universal and democratic codes of conduct and professionalism will become more and more important in the future.

From the point of view of the new democratic governance paradigm, there is a need to reorient public servants so that they can have a bureaucratic mentality that supports the principles of a small government that does less, a global vision and flexible organizations, greater accountability, and a fair government. For countries that are not used to these principles, the transformation will involve a major change in the organization culture and practices of the public bureaucracy. In countries where it is not practically feasible to reduce the size of the bureaucracy, government leaders will be contained by the nature of the existing human resources. They may find out that there are certain groups of public servants whose skills are no longer needed and whose educational backgrounds are not conducive toward developing new techniques and higher competencies.

Training programs in government must be aimed at introducing the guiding principles of the new democratic governance paradigm. Government officials must be made to understand the necessity of a small government and the dominant role of the private sector in national development. Central bureaucrats must support the growth of local governments. Education and training programs must be organized so the government officials can think globally and understand the dynamics of world economy and politics. New ideas about organizing the government bureaucracy must be exposed to government officials so that they can see that there are many alternative ways to run their agencies.

To understand the concept of accountability, government officials must learn administrative law and be introduced to the various accountability mechanisms that exist all over the world, such as the ombudsman in Sweden, the administrative courts of France and Germany, the freedom of information act of the United States, and the citizen's charters of the United Kingdom. For the principle of "a government that is fair" to be effective, government officials must be socialized to the emerging global values and standards. They must also adhere to the nation's constitution, the government's policies, and societal culture and values. Government training programs should be used as instruments for socializing government officials to these values.

REFERENCES

Al Gore (1995). Common sense government: Works better and costs less. New York: Random House.

Benveniste, G. (1994). *The twenty-first century organization: Analyzing current trends – imaging the future.* San Francisco: Jossey-Bass.

Bowornwathana, B. (1994). Administrative reform and regime shifts: Reflections on the Thai polity. *Asian Journal of Public Administration, 16*(December), 152–164.

Bowornwathana, B. (1995a). Response of public administration system of Thailand to global challenges. In: S. H. Salleh & L. Carino (Eds), *Globalization and the Asian public sector.* Kuala Lumpur: Asian and PacificDevelopment Centre.

Bowornwathana, B. (1995b). *Comparative administration reform: The United Kingdom, the United States, Japan, and Thailand.* Bangkok: Chulalongkorn University Printing Office (in Thai).

Bowornwathana, B. (1996). Political realities of local government reform in Thailand. In: S. Kurosawa, T. Fujiwara & M. Reforma (Eds), *New trends in public administration for the Asia-Pacific region: Decentralization.* Tokyo: Local Autonomy College, Ministry of Home Affairs.

Bowornwathana, B. (1999). Democratic reform visions and the reinvention of Thai public officials. *Asian Review of Public Administration, 8*(1), 40–49.

Bowornwathana, B. (forthcoming/a). The politics of reform of the secretariat of the prime minister in Thailand. *Australian Journal of Public Administration.*

Bowornwathana, B. (forthcoming/b). The phenomenon of new ministries and policitian bureaucrat perspective. *Asian Review of Public Administration.*

Citizen's Charter Unit. (1995). *The civil service: Continuity and change.* London: HMSO.

Commission on Global Governance. (1995). *Out global neighborhood.* New York: Oxford University Press.

Drucker, P. F. (1989). *The new realities.* Great Britain: Butterworth Heinemann Ltd.

Drucker, P. F. (1994). *Managing in a time of great change.* Great Britain: Butterworth-Heinemann Ltd.

Golembiewski, R. T. (1995a). *Managing diversity in organizations.* Tuscaloosa and London: University of Alabama Press.

Golembiewski, R. T. (1995b). *Practical public management.* New York: Dekker.

Hammer, M., & Champy, J. (1993). *Reengineering the corporation: A manifesto for business revolution.* New York: Harper Business Press.

Kirkpatrick, I., & Lucio, M. M. (1996). The contract state and the future of public management. *Public Administration: An International Quarterly, 74*(Spring).

Krugman, P. (1995). A country is not a company. *Harvard Business Review, 40–51*(January/February), 42–51.

Lane, J.-E. (1994). Will public management drive out public administration? *Asian Journal of Public Administration, 16*(December), 139–151.

Moe, R. C. (1994). The 'reinventing governmane' exercise: Misinterpreting the problem, misjudging the consequences. *Public Administration Review, 54*(2), 111–122.

Naisbitt, J. (1994). *Global paradox.* London: Nicholas Brealey Publishing.

Osborne, D., & Gaebler, T. (1992). *Reinventing government: How the entrepreneurial spirit is transforming the public sector.* Reading, MA: Addison-Wesley.

Peters, B. G. (1995). The public service, the changing state and governance. In: B. G. Peters & D. J. Savoie (Eds), *Governance in a changing environment.* Montreal and Kingston: McGill-Queen's University Press.

Peters, B. G., & Savoie, D. J. (1994). Civil service reform: Misdiagnosing the patient. *Public Administration Review, 5.4*(5), 418–425.

Pierre, J. (1995). The marketization of the state: Citizens, consumers, and the emergence of the public market. In: B. G. Peters & D. J. Savoie (Eds), *Governance in a changing environment.* Montreal and Kingston: McGill-Queen's University Press.

Rhodes, R. W. (1996). The new governance: Governing without government. *Political Studies, 44*(September).

Senge, P. M. (1990). *The fifth discipline: The art and practice of the learning organization.* New York: Doubleday.

Toffler, A., & Toffler, H. (1994). *Creating a new civilization: The politics of the third wave.* Atlanta: Turner Publishing.

Wong, H., & Chan, H. S. (1999). In: H. S. Chan (Ed.), *Handbook of comparative public administration in the Asian Pacific Basin.* New York: Marcel Dekker.

World Bank. (1995). *Bureaucrats in business: The economics and politics of government ownership.* New York: Oxford University Press.

FURTHER READING

Aberbach, J. D., Putnam, R. A., & Rockman, B. A. (1981). *Buraucrats and politicians in western democracies.* Cambridge: Harvard University Press.

Aucoin, P. (1990). Administrative reform in public management: Paradigms, principles, paradoxes, and pendulums. *Governance, 3*(April), 115–117.

Barzelay, M. (1992). *Breaking through bureaucracy.* Berkeley and Los Angeles: University of California Press.

Campbell, C. (1993a). Public service and democratic accountability. In: R. A. Chapman (Ed.), *Ethic in public service.* Edinburgh: Edinburgh University Press.

Campbell, C. (1993b). Political executives and their officials. In: A. W. Finifter (Ed.), *Political science: The state of the discipline II.* Washington, DC: American Political Science Association.

Campbell, C., & Wilson, G. K. (1995). *The end of whitehall: Death of a paradigm?* Oxford: Blackwell.

Cooper, P. J. (1995). Accountability and administrative reform: Toward convergence and beyond. In: G. B. Peters & D. J. Savoie (Eds), *Governance in a changing environment.* Montreal and Kingston: McGill-Queen's University Press.

Hood, C. (1995). Emerging issues in public administration. *Public Administration: An International Quarterly, 73*(Spring), 165–183.

Peters, B. G. (1994a). New visions of government and the public service. In: P. W. Ingraham & B. S. Romzek (Eds), *New paradigms for government: Issues for the changing public service.* San Francisco: Jossey Bass.

Peters, B. G. (1994b). Government reorganization: A theoretical analysis. In: A. Farazmand (Ed.), *Handbook of bureaucracy.* New York: Dekker.

Romzek, B. S. (1996). Enhancing accountability. In: J. L. Perry (Ed.), *Handbook of public administration.* San Francisco: Jossey-Bass.

Savoie, D. (1995). Globalization, nation–states, and the civil service. In: B. G. Peters & D. J. Savoie (Eds), *Governance in a changing environment.* Montreal and Kingston: McGill-Queen's University Press.

United Nations. (1995). *A vision of hope: The fiftieth anniversary of the United Nations.* London: The Regency Corporation.

AN EXPLORATION INTO THE FAMILIAR AND THE NEW: PUBLIC BUDGETING IN DEVELOPING COUNTRIES

Naomi Caiden

Public budgeting is important. Governments at all levels – local, national, regional, and international – have to manage their finances in a capable fashion: to raise resources equitably and efficiently, make deliberate and wise spending choices, maintain a good credit standing, and control and account for their transactions. Non-profit organizations often depend at least partially on government financing, and so share concerns about effective public budgeting; where they have an important role in carrying out public policies, their own standards for financial management are also the subject for public attention.

While every country or region faces its own budget predicament, it may probably be summarized in similar terms: public needs appear infinite, while public resources are only too finite (Caiden, 1981, p. 7). Even the budgets of rich industrialized countries are under strain, as they attempt to meet all the demands placed upon them. How much more difficult is the situation in the developing world, especially in the poorest countries, where the struggle to defeat poverty is undermined by poverty itself. Here, the budget problem is

Comparative Public Administration: The Essential Readings
Research in Public Policy Analysis and Management, Volume 15, 681–699
Copyright © 2006 by Elsevier Ltd.
ISSN: 0732-1317/doi:10.1016/S0732-1317(06)15030-7

defined by the enormity of the tasks and difficulty in mobilizing resources to meet them.

Budgeting in developing countries is thus characterized by its agenda to overcome poverty, the lack of resources to achieve it, and the way both affect the decision-making process. Other characteristics may or may not apply in some degree, such as a high proportion of international donor funds, conditions imposed by international organizations (such as the World Bank or International Monetary Fund), considerable indebtedness, dependence on single export commodities, the peculiar situation of countries with oil resources, or a large informal economy. Taken together, despite obvious variations among countries, these features justify treating budgeting in developing countries as a separate category for analysis.

Over a quarter of a century ago, Aaron Wildavsky and I undertook to explore the world of budgeting in developing countries through the voices of those actually involved in its day-to-day vicissitudes (Caiden & Wildavsky, 1980). A quick survey of the field, today, reveals much that is familiar from that early study. Many countries still suffer from poverty, stagnation, conflict, and isolation. Governments have difficulties in raising resources from poor societies. Budgets also frequently fall victim to uncertainties, and the combination of poverty and uncertainty results in repetitive budgeting i.e. budgets made throughout the year according to cash flow. Budgets are often fragmented into earmarked or special funds, and participants are forced into self-defeating strategies. Experts tout the latest fashions in budgeting reform, with little concern that such reforms have met with doubtful success in the much less adverse context of rich countries.

But, much has also changed. The developing world now presents a much more varied picture. While some countries have stagnated, or even regressed, others have moved forward, developing both economically and politically. The end of communism and the break up of the Soviet Union have changed the budgeting practices of the large group of countries that previously managed through command economies and centralized planning. While the persistence of poverty remains overwhelming for many countries, and a severe problem for others, there are also signs of improvement. In particular, globalization, for good or ill, has set in motion forces for change whose ultimate impact is still unclear. And, while experts continue to advocate the latest ideas in budgeting reform, irrespective of context, their solutions are different.

This chapter seeks to explore the current situation of budgeting in developing countries, from the perspective of both the familiar and the new. It begins with the familiar – how a context of poverty and uncertainty affects orderly budgeting – and moves on to the new – how that context has changed. The next section focuses on how globalization has affected the demand for public expenditures, on the one hand, and ability to raise revenues to meet them, on the other. The third section deals with proposals for budget reform, related to broader reform proposals in public administration. The final section takes a set of recent experiences with those reforms, and assesses their success.

THE FAMILIAR AND THE NEW: THE ENVIRONMENT OF PUBLIC BUDGETING

World poverty is well documented. It is estimated that 1.2 billion people live on less than a dollar a day (Bryant & Kappaz, 2005, p. 17). Another one and a half billion people, who are not among the "extreme poor", suffer "chronic financial hardship and a lack of basic amenities such as safe drinking water and functioning latrines". Together, these two groups make-up around 40 percent of humanity (Sachs, 2005, p. 18). Nor is the position improving: Joseph Stiglitz notes that "over the last decade of the twentieth century, the actual number of people living in poverty actually increased by almost 100 million", at a time when total world income was increasing by an average of 2.5 percent annually (Stiglitz, 2002, p. 5). The position of children – the generation of the future – is of particular concern.

A recent UNICEF report documents serious deterioration. In sub-Saharan African countries, not only has AIDS has killed a generation of parents, diminishing their sons' and daughters' chances for survival but also children are increasingly exposed to the dangers of untreated diseases, conscription into militias, trafficking, abuse and exploitation. It has been estimated that between one and three million children in Africa die of malaria every year (Sachs, 2005, p. 7), and hundreds of millions lack adequate shelter or access to sanitation, safe water, healthcare, education, and nutrition (Daniszewski, 2004, p. A13). In recent years, also, many areas have seen an increase in insecurity. Wars, civil wars, terrorism, rebellions, and persistent low-level conflicts have eroded many governments' capability to govern over much of their nominal territory. Violence has bred militias beyond government control, millions of refugees and displaced persons. In 2001, the World Refugee Survey estimated that there were nearly 35 million refugees and internally displaced people around the globe – the equivalent of a whole nation of refugees! (Bryant & Kappaz, 2005, p. 19). At the extreme, some governments are characterized as failed states, while others are undermined by rampant corruption and organized crime.

Finally, disasters have continued to play their part in increasing poverty and misery. In 2004, the tsunami in South East Asia and in 2005, the huge earthquake in Kashmir left thousands dead, injured, and homeless, while hurricanes and flooding in Central America had lesser, but still severe impacts. In sub-Sahara Africa, where the World Bank estimates that almost half of Africa's population already lives in extreme poverty (Sachs, 2005, p. 21), regional droughts recur with depressing regularity, and 2005–2006 brought the second hunger crisis in five months, affecting millions of people in Niger, Malawi, Zimbabwe, Zambia, Mozambique, Lesotho, and Swaziland (Wines, 2005). As an extreme example, the plight of Malawi has been described as "the perfect storm, a storm that brings together climatic disaster, impoverishment, the AIDS pandemic, and the long-standing burdens of malaria, schistosomiasis, and other diseases" (Sachs, 2005, p. 10).

Poverty represents more than a condition to be overcome or an obstacle to investment. As the lack of "functional redundancy", it impedes the smooth working of society, and may wreak havoc with orderly budgeting and planning (Caiden & Wildavsky, 1980, p. 49). Martin Landau defined redundancy as "an excess or superfluity of anything" (Landau, 1969). Redundancy is often condemned as waste, the opposite of efficiency. But, it may also work to help societies to cope with change and uncertainty, especially in budgeting, where forecasting is difficult in conditions of rapid change and volatility. Thus, existence of a reserve enables governments to absorb unforeseen contingencies without resorting to expedients or borrowing. Redundancy may provide a variety of options for getting things done, competition, reliability, and choice among revenue sources.

Governments have more "political capital", rather than competing against the loyalties of region, kinship, and tribe. Duplication and versatility – of data, talents, and skills – allow for better and more timely information and flexibility in the use of resources. Above all, complex, functional redundancy cushions change, allowing exploration of more than one option at a time, enabling easier recovery from mistakes, providing extra resources to put into new directions while maintaining continuity of the old. Without this kind of redundancy, budgeting in developing countries is vulnerable to any number of disruptions, contingencies are hard to forecast, new adversities are difficult to cope with, changes cannot be easily absorbed, and governments have to resort to borrowing and expedients.

So far, the familiar. But despite the persistence of widespread poverty, indicators in several countries are showing improvement. In Bangladesh, for example, it has been estimated that since 2002, life expectancy has risen from 44 to 62, infant mortality has declined from 145 to 48 per thousand, and economic growth has been about 5 percent a year (Sachs, 2005, p. 13). In China, per capita income is now estimated at about $4,000, and there has been sustained economic growth of about 8 percent a year. In India, the urban population has swelled to as much as 28 percent, more move in and out of cities for temporary work and improved roads and communications have transformed age-old ways of life in the villages (Waldman, 2005). According to a recent United Nations study, poverty in Latin America has fallen over the past two years by 13 million people, a record 5.5 million jobs were created in urban areas last year, and the Latin American economy registered 6 percent economic growth (*Los Angeles Times,* December 8, 2005, A9).

These improvements may easily be discounted – the number of people living in poverty is still immense, urbanization has created, in the words of one commentator, "the mass production of slums" (Davis, 2004, p. 18), industrialization has occurred only in specific areas at the cost of low wages and substandard conditions, and prosperity has touched only a few. But it is now possible to discern a difference – the notion that the persistence of extreme poverty is not inevitable. In September 2000, 189 governments agreed to Millennium Development Goals, targets to achieve measurable reductions in poverty over the next 15 years, followed by pledges of support from donor nations to increase official aid to developing countries (Bryant & Kappaz, 2005, pp. 135–137). Whatever the fate of this initiative, it represents an awareness that if the forces of globalization that have already wrought powerful changes in economies and societies are to fulfill their promise, the international community must take action to deal with their dysfunctions and spread their benefits.

GLOBALIZATION AND BUDGETING[1]

Globalization represents an acceleration of complex changes. It has been defined as "the closer integration of the countries and peoples of the world which has been brought about by the enormous reduction of costs of transportation and communication, and the breaking down of artificial barriers to the flows of goods, services, capital, knowledge, and (to a lesser extent) people across borders" (Stiglitz, 2002, p. 9). Globalization covers international trade and investment liberalization; international population movements; speeding up of communication and transactions; spread of scientific knowledge and technology; and the inter-connectness of markets. Globalization is also often blamed for worldwide financial crises; wide-spread ecological changes, including global warming; emergence of new diseases that are quickly spread across the globe; and pressures on resources, especially oil. Some people and nations have been able to take advantage of globalization to strengthen government organizations, corporations, and legitimate and illegitimate markets. Others seem overwhelmed and marginalized.

The effects of globalization may be especially marked in developing countries. Global problems are only global in concept – they are local problems to those who have to deal with them. Global problems turn into local problems, which are again transformed into global problems, as they spread from one part of the globe to others. Local responsibilities become global responsibilities as local resources and responses are insufficient to prevent potential grave worldwide disasters.

Globalization pushes up demands for government expenditures. Countries and regions are increasingly vulnerable to forces from outside their boundaries that require government response. A case in point is HIV/AIDS, which has spread from one part of the globe to another, infecting nearly 40 million people, over half of whom are concentrated in sub-Saharan Africa (Mestel, 2004, p. A3).

At the same time, the international community tries to hold governments responsible for the effects of their own actions or inaction on matters within their borders that can spread danger to others. Emerging diseases, such as SARS and avian flu, demand early measures by public health authorities to prevent epidemics. Industrial pollution of rivers quickly moves from its source to contaminate regions and countries downstream. Failed states provide havens for drug smuggling, people trafficking, illegal arms trade, and money laundering. The threat of international terrorism brings pressure for better policing.

International competitiveness drives a high-risk context, and governments are forced to deal with the consequences where the private sector fails or produces adverse consequences. Investment ebbs and flows, depending on the fickle currents of international trade. Pressures to produce crops at lower prices have often forced an urban migration, without commensurate job creation in the cities, as well as increased environmental risks in diminished biodiversity and ecological degradation. Global warming and climate disturbances lie beyond the ability of one government to counter.

Uneven economic changes create demands to deal with social dislocations. Borders are increasingly permeable, and conflicts and lawlessness often cannot be contained within them. The economic and social disruptions related to the exploitation of oil reserves may be wrenching, as local populations may reap few of the benefits while bearing consequent environmental and social costs. Prevailing economic and political insecurity drives migration of populations, both legal and illegal.

The pressures for government expenditures to meet these challenges have distinctive, and to some extent, new characteristics. They come on top of other commitments, and so squeeze budgets even further. In many developing countries, as many as half the population are under the age of eighteen, raising demands for education, nutrition, and health services. Much of the budget may be earmarked for debt payments, or locked up in donors' projects. Resources available for discretionary spending are therefore likely to be very small.

Expenditures associated with globalization are also often long-term in nature, requiring investment in physical infrastructure, human capital, or research. Benefits are not immediate, and they often do not accrue to a single area or even country. Solutions for global problems often require cooperation by numerous authorities, and there is rarely a single authority that can impose payments. Governments do not want to pay for benefits they do not think they will receive.

Many of the expenditures are problematic in nature. Since neither the causes nor solutions for many global problems are straightforward or even clearly understood, their alleviation depends on changes in the behavior and attitudes of populations that are difficult to achieve. The fast changing environment demands, on the one hand, immediate reaction to adverse events (natural or economic disasters), and on the other, planning for contingencies, that would require locking up and committing resources for eventualities that might never happen.

The upward pressure for public spending superimposed by the demands of globalization is not matched by an equivalent availability of revenues. But globalization, as its advocates point out, has opened up new opportunities and new sources of wealth. Even if the benefits are uneven, the world economy has evidenced increased economic growth. Global military spending has been estimated as at least one trillion dollars a year (not counting outsourcing) (*New York Times*, June 24, 2005). The amounts revealed by recent corruption scandals are enormous, and it is estimated that annual worldwide transactions tainted by corruption are close to $1 trillion (Kaufmann, 2005). But raising revenues for the needs of developing countries is still problematic. Few international organizations have their own taxing power, and although some governments do contribute to international causes, such aid is limited. Governments that try to raise taxes on major sources of wealth, particularly international investors, risk seeing those sources flee to other countries. Tax collections are disrupted by wars and internal conflicts. Where the "informal sector" makes up a large proportion of the economy, taxes are evaded altogether. Similarly, agriculture is notoriously difficult to tax, and some countries have given up the effort. Lack of transparency and accountability promote suspicion of corruption, and provide a facile justification for tax evasion and avoidance. Finally, most often the places where expenditures are most needed are those where resources are most lacking, and there is no certainty that even where resources are directed to them, they will be well spent.

Faced with the familiar constraints of poverty, the newer pressures for expenditures and uncertainties derived from globalization, and the difficulties of raising revenues (even though resources may be there), what are governments to do? Let us turn now to the ever-fertile field of budget reform.

THE NEW AND THE FAMILIAR: BUDGETING REFORM

Budgets and their implementation are critical to the success of economic policies, projects, and reforms. They do not stand apart from their context: they are as much part of the problem as the solution. And whatever philosophy infuses initiatives for progress, it also needs to permeate the processes and institutions, the practices and culture of budgeting.

The centrality of a well-working budget system may be appreciated by what happens in its absence. Where financial administration suffers from muddle, rigidity, ill-advised choices, inability to account for expenditures, oppressive and ineffective taxation, over-burdening debt, lack of control, poor execution, erratic funding, and corruption, and the consequences are severe. Projects fall behind and overrun cost estimates; priorities are distorted; money disappears into black holes; accounts are fiction; budget plans are meaningless; accumulating debt and debt service overwhelm capacity to pay; deficits are routine; societal needs go unanswered while illicit dealings flourish; infrastructure crumbles; and new initiatives are found in bureaucratic inertia sustained by budgetary inflexibility. To these may be added waste, mismanagement, over-staffing, useless or abandoned projects, lack of maintenance, inability to coordinate capital and recurrent expenditures, and lack of transparency.

For over a 100 years, reformers have looked for ways to improve budgeting and financial administration. These efforts share certain similarities:

they attempt to transform the way budget decisions are made; they are episodic, occurring in waves of activity followed by disillusion; they originate in Western industrialized countries; and their advocates believe they should be applied universally, irrespective of context.

In *Planning and Budgeting in Poor Countries*, Aaron Wildavsky and I addressed the mismatch between the experts' advocacy and the reality of public budgeting in poor countries (Caiden & Wildavsky, 1980). At that time, comprehensive economic planning and Programming, Planning, Budgeting (PPB) were all the rage. Countries that did not, or were not able, to put these nostrums into practice were castigated for their lack of will or their backwardness. Never mind that these reforms were either deemed unsuitable (comprehensive planning) or found unattainable (PPB) in rich countries either! Rather than joining the chorus of condemnation, we asked budgeters in poor countries about their budget practices, and why they behaved as they did. We found that their resort to such practices as repetitive budgeting (making the budget throughout the year), padding estimates, ear-marking revenues, and setting up special funds, were rooted in survival as reactions to general conditions of uncertainty and constraint. The proposals of the experts (plan ahead, coordinate with the economic plan, make choices rationally according to program effectiveness), however desirable, did not work well in these circumstances.

In due course, comprehensive economic planning was discredited, and PPB was abandoned. The 1980s and 1990s saw advocacy of a "neo-orthodox macroeconomic approach" (known as the Washington Consensus), comprising liberalization and reliance on private markets, rather than governments, to bring about development (Bryant & Kappaz, 2005, p. 85). Structural adjustment programs and conditionality demanded that developing countries cut government spending drastically. As the hardships accompanying structural adjustment became glaringly apparent, alternative prescriptions have been put forward, such as community participation, the sustenance of civil society, micro-lending, investment in social capital, and governmental reform.

By the 1990s, the need to reform government was widely acknowledged. Public bureaucracies were criticized as slow, rigid, wasteful, inflexible, and unresponsive. New conditions – rapid change, the global market place, an information society, an educated workforce – demanded a new kind of government, based on such values as flexibility and adaptability, provision of high-quality goods and services, efficiency, customer service, citizen empowerment, and public-private partnerships (Osborne & Gaebler, 1993, p. 15). In practical terms, government should be "reinvented" by flattening hierarchies, decentralizing authority, and privatizing services. In the new paradigm, input controls and a focus on rules and procedures would be substituted by management flexibility and accountability for results (Shah, 2005, p. 220). In terms of budgeting, management for (or by) results means a quite specific reform: performance-based budgeting. Performance-based budgeting seeks to tie the efficiency and effectiveness of programs to budget allocations. The aim is "to transform public budgeting systems from an input and output orientation to an output and outcome orientation, introducing a new results-oriented accountability into public organizations. It does this by changing the rules of budgeting – influencing both budgetary processes and budgetary roles" (Andrews, 2005, p. 33). Performance budgeting is not a new idea. In the somewhat tangled categorization of reforms, it preceded and was absorbed into the more sophisticated PPB, so that "program and performance budgeting" was adopted by many governments. The basic elements – emphasis on outputs rather than inputs, and basing budgetary decisions on performance indicators – are echoed (often with the addition of outcomes to outputs) in today's performance-based budgeting.

But there is an important difference. Earlier budget reforms assumed that programs would be carried out by government entities, even if (as in PPB), the ultimate aim might be their reshuffling and rationalization. So although the reforms were expected to improve decision making, they were not essential to the structure of accountability for expenditures. In contrast, performance-based budgets are critical to accountability, because, in the new scheme of governance, governments are only one of many players in carrying out programs. Where private organizations, and particularly non-governmental organizations (NGOs) are equally important, if not more important, in spending money, performance-based budgeting has to take the place of hierarchical, bureaucratic controls. Holding those who spend money responsible for results is the critical link between funding and accountability.

The link was made clear in the United Nations XIVth Meeting of Experts in 1998, which took performance monitoring and evaluation as one of its main agenda topic. It tied performance measurement specifically to resource allocation, performance improvement, value for money, and cost-effective pursuit of the public interest. It linked performance measurement, monitoring and evaluation to the pursuit of "subsidiarity" i.e. decentralization, deconcentration, devolution of responsibility, and offloading or outsourcing.

Many governments in industrialized countries have embraced performance-based budgeting. In its most extreme version, New Zealand implemented a private sector management approach to all government functions, treating public services as commodities subject to renewable contracts, and managers as autonomous within defined budgetary allocations and policy frameworks (Shah, 2005, p. 221; Schick, 1998, p. 2). In the United States, performance-based budgeting has been linked to a strategic planning model. Agencies are required to set out a mission and measurable goals and objectives. From these are derived indicators through which outputs and outcomes may be measured. Annual performance plans then are set out, and actual performance is compared to the target. This information should then be used to determine budgetary allocation for the agency (Government Performance and Results Act, 1993). In Canada, an "alternative service delivery" framework has been used to re-examine programs to determine whether they should be privatized altogether, be handled by federal or provincial governments, reorganized to make them more efficient, or not (Shah, 2005, p. 222).

There is an eerie familiarity to all this – a uniform prescription for budgeting everywhere; an impeccable logic (who would not want results from spending?); an emphasis on process to the exclusion of policy; an elevation of the reform to "best practice"; and a covey of experts busy spreading the gospel all over the globe. Perhaps, this time round, the reforms may work to cure dysfunctions of current budget systems, and stand the test of time to become standard practice. But even in industrialized countries, there is evidence that performance-based budgeting may be difficult to put into practice.

There are undoubtedly good reasons why governments should provide information about the results of the money they spend, and why their citizens should demand them (see Caiden & Caiden, 1998). But there have been a number of problems. First, there have been difficulties in designing appropriate, accurate, and measurable goals, output and outcome measures. Second, even where measures have been agreed, there are problems relating those measures to budget allocations: if a program or agency is not reaching its target, is it because it is inefficient, or is it because it needs more money? Third, the results represented by the indicators may be diffused i.e. they may not necessarily be attributed to the program concerned. Fourth, budgets are annual, but results of many programs do not show up in a single year, and in any case, the information from the current year is not available at the time of budget deliberations for the forthcoming budget. Fifth, if budget cutting is used as a sanction to punish those agencies not meeting their targets, there may be considerable "collateral damage" among the beneficiaries of the programs concerned. Finally, budget decision making is political, and according to James Swiss, "political concerns almost always trump managerial concerns for elected officials". On the basis of several studies, Swiss concludes that "state and federal legislatures in the United States have based almost no major decisions on the outcome information they receive" (Swiss, 2005, pp. 597–598; see also Lomas, 2005, p. 12).

If countries with well-organized budget systems, and relatively ample re-sources, are having difficulties in implementing performance-based budget-ing, what about developing countries? In a much quoted article on "Why Most Developing Countries Should Not Try New Zealand Reforms", Allen Schick argues that where there is lack of reliable, workable external con-trols, a wide gap exists between the formal budget and the real budget, governments are unable to control inputs and account for cash, and non-compliance with internal rules prevails, a system that relies on external control of results to maintain accountability is inappropriate, and informal norms (based on the reality of budgeting) will prevail over reforms (Schick, 1998, pp. 123–131). Yet disillusion with the dysfunctions of bureaucracies, and the failure of developing countries to attain sustainable development, have led their governments to look into new directions (Jreisat, 2005, p. 236; Umeh & Andranovich, 2005). How have they fared?

BUDGET REFORMS IN PRACTICE

To survey all the experience of budget reforms in recent years lies beyond the scope of this chapter. However, a special *Symposium on Budgeting and Financial Management Reform Implementation,* recently published in the *International Journal of Public Administration,* provides several insightful case studies of budget reform in developing countries. This section, with some additions, draws primarily on the selected experiences reported in that symposium.

Efforts toward budget reform in the majority of these countries are not new. Malaysia made a sustained effort to implement program budgeting in the 1980s (Caiden, 1985); Ghana had a legacy of unsuccessful reforms (Roberts, 2005, p. 291); and Thailand had a somewhat half-hearted effort at program budgeting during the 1980s (Caiden, 1985). Bolivia had a long experience in attempting to integrate its financial management system in the 1980s (Montes & Andrews, 2005, p. 274). These earlier reforms had foundered on such factors entrenched incremental budget processes, unwilling-ness of central budget agencies to give up control, disruptions leading to unscheduled cutbacks and freezes, weak financial management, lack of ca-pacity to produce information and lack of willingness to use it.

The initiative for the new wave of reform varied somewhat: in Thailand, budget crises and later a new regime provided the impetus; (Dixon, 2005, pp. 357, 363) in Ghana, South Africa, and Tanzania, the World Bank's requirement for a Medium Term Expenditure Framework was instrumental; (Roberts & Andrews, 2005, pp. 292–293; Andrews, 2005, p. 38; Ronsholt & Andrews, 2005, p. 315) in Bolivia, sectoral reform and the need to deal with corruption drove new efforts toward integrated financial management, of which performance budgeting was one aspect (Montes & Andrews, 2005, p. 274).

Malaysia represents the "poster child" for the reforms. According to Anwar Shah, Malaysia "has gradually and successfully put in place aspects of results-oriented management to create a responsive and accountable public sector governance structure". All public agencies are required to state their mission and values; a "clients' charter" requires specification of standards of services to form the basis of public accountability; an output-based budget system requires program agreements for delivery of outputs, while allowing managerial flexibility in achieving agreed upon results; performance indicators for government agencies and other service providers are maintained and widely disseminated; federal government functions have been decentralized and deconcentrated by strengthening local governments; a partnership approach, involving public–private collaboration, has been adopted for service delivery (Shah, 2005, p. 224).

Other countries have moved along similar lines. Bolivia's Institutional Reform Project, initiated in the late 1990s, incorporates results driven financial management systems and budgets. Institutional reform agreement are designed to tie organizations to their performance; financial management and decision making are devolved to line departments, which practice results oriented strategic budgeting and management; more resources are provided to local governments to accomplish decentralization (Montes & Andrews, 2005, p. 275). In Ghana a Public Financial Management Reform Programme (PUFMARP), initiated in 2001, required all ministries to produce a three year integrated budget, based on agreed objectives, outputs and activities, and linked to Ghana's Poverty Reduction Strategy (Roberts & Andrews, 2005, p. 295). In Tanzania, the Public Sector Reform Programme's first phase in the late 1990s required performance management systems in ministries, departments, and agencies, including performance-oriented budgets (mandated by the 2001 Public Finance Act). Individual agreements with public servants were to provide incentives and accountability. Performance-oriented budgets were intended as an important link to the Medium Term Expenditure Framework overall poverty reduction strategies (Ronsholt & Andrews, 2005, pp. 315–316). In South Africa, the 1999 Public Financial

Management Act mandated measurable objectives for the main spending programs to be submitted to Parliament, and from 2001–2002 departments were required to identify targets for delivery in the main out put areas. The budget format was changed to show programs and sub-programs, to conceptualize what each department does with its inputs (Andrews, 2005, p. 40). In Thailand, in 1999, in a "hurdle approach", the Bureau of the Budget gradually agreed to reduce rigid control of line items in six pilot agencies, if agencies met certain conditions, including budget planning and financial and performance reporting. In 2001, an initiative by a new prime minister hastened reforms by requiring output identification and costing for all agencies for the 2004 budget, and changing the whole basis of budget allocations to the cost of delivering the outputs in the agency's service level agreement (Dixon, 2005, p. 363).

Whatever the formal compliance with the reforms, the major problem remains that of actually using performance information in the budget. Even in Malaysia, a poor connection between allocations and performance targets has been reported (Andrews, 2005, p. 47). In Bolivia, Montes and Andrews comment that "Government is increasingly using the "language" of performance measurement, especially in target settings, but most public sector entities have not translated this language into practice" (Montes & Andrews, 2005, p. 277). Even in the ministry of education where performance measures have been set out, they do not directly affect budget allocations. The agreements are mostly legalistic documents that focus on processes, spending, and salaries rather than on performance; the system for monitoring performance has generally not been integrated into core government processes, and is carried out in a perfunctory ad hoc manner with little regard for quality or transparency; targets are not linked to budget allocations (Montes & Andrews, 2005, p. 278). In Ghana, by 2002, implementation of performance management mechanisms was limited, and only two pilots had used verifiable indicators to measure performance (Roberts & Andrews, 2005, p. 297). In Tanzania, "the adoption of performance-based budgeting has been questionable at best. Indeed there is very little evidence that performance targets, where developed, are in any way mainstreamed into the budget process or document" (Ronsholt & Andrews, 2005, p. 322). In South Africa, the performance part of the budget is kept separate from the money part, and so there is no connection between results of programs and budget allocations (Andrews, 2005, p. 46). In Thailand, in 2001, "transition to results focused budgeting ... was as far away as ever" (Dixon, 2005, p. 363). (It is too early to assess the later reforms.)

A second problem lies in the capability to produce useful performance measures and information. In Bolivia, implementation has been slow and variable, with few modules operating in central finance agencies and few in line agencies (Montes & Andrews, 2005, p. 277). In Tanzania, targets were unrealistically determined and poorly costed (Ronsholt & Andrews, 2005, p. 321). In South Africa, despite changes in budget format, there is no outcome data; output measures are questionable, often being really inputs into the production process; measures lack details that would make them measurable and evaluable; and "outputs, indicators and targets seem totally unrelated" (Andrews, 2005, p. 51).

A third problem has been the issue of the use of the performance-based system to change budgetary decision making, and to link resource allocation to broader plans. Unfortunately, it seems that in many cases, the opposite has happened. In Bolivia, it seems that informal norms have undermined the formal reforms, achieving "little budgeting and financial management change in most areas of government, falling short of introducing effective personnel management, binding financial control and budgets, accountability, and client responsiveness" (Montes & Andrews, 2005, p. 279). In Ghana, despite some progress in the first year of the reforms, they have made little impact on a situation where allocations rarely corresponded to actual releases of funds, there were few departmental audited accounts, and planning and budgeting were not related (Roberts & Andrews, 2005, p. 296). In Tanzania, uncertainty about funds has undermined reform, budgets continue to be unpredictable, actual expenditures differ markedly from budgeted expenditures, and linkage to the poverty programs has remained problematic (Ronsholt & Andrews, 2005, pp. 321–322). In South Africa, targets and measures are unrelated to responsibilities for achieving them (despite individual performance contracts with civil servants) (Andrews, 2005, p. 46). In Thailand, resistance to reform by the Bureau of the Budget has meant continued control through line items (Dixon, 2005, p. 363).

Given previous experience with budget reform, and difficulties experienced even in rich, industrialized countries, these problems are not unexpected. Observers have pointed to political will or lack of administrative capacity for disappointing progress: with more time, greater effort, and more understanding, it might be hoped that things will improve. With the wisdom of hindsight from past failures, and new conditions, such as information systems based on computers, persistence may bring better results. However, one may query, as Allen Schick has done, whether the whole direction of the reform is appropriate for budgeting in developing countries (Schick, 1998).

WHAT IS FAMILIAR AND WHAT IS NEW?

In much of the developing world, poverty and uncertainty still press hard on governments. But the picture is now more complex. Globalization has contributed to prosperity for some, and possible to greater impoverishment for others, while simply leaving some behind. Whatever its impact, though, it has created more demands for public action, generated internally in response to external threat or in support of economic change, or externally, as domestic dangers affect a wider environment. Economists would call this inter-connectedness or mutual vulnerability a case of multiple externalities – conditions for which responsibility lies beyond a single jurisdiction. The logic of externalities is to internalize them by pushing responsibility to a higher level or broader geographical constituency. Global problems thus would require action by the global community, since they affect us all: this is a justification for international assistance.

But in the real world, this simple solution runs into practical difficulties. Not only does it require the raising of large sums of money without the taxing authority of the nation state, but it also involves trust on the part of those who pay that their payments will be properly devoted to the purposes for which they are provided. Where the management of government revenues and expenditures is subject to corruption, mismanagement, and waste, there is no assurance that funds will not be diverted, spent inappropriately, or simply vanish into a black hole. Such is the case of many developing countries today.

The observer of budgeting in these countries still reads familiar accounts of weak systems in which planned budgets fail to coincide with actual spending, where ministries of finance are forced into repetitive budgeting according to cash flow, where departments and agencies attempt to evade the uncertainties of budget funding by various ploys and by finding (where possible) their own revenue sources. Meanwhile international agencies and consultants advocate still more planning, and place their confidence in performance-based budgeting to achieve accountability. The small sample of country experiences outlined above, and the continued reporting of the same deficiencies matched by the same proposed solutions, indicates that something is not right.

Time has not stood still. In part because of donors' mistrust of government budgeting, and in part because of the new ideology of New Public Management, governments of developing countries are no longer the only recipients and spenders of funds. NGOs have proliferated in the landscape of the developing world. Some, with their own sources of funding, bypass governments altogether; others are primarily financed by governments, or engage in public–private partnerships. Private companies too may contract with governments. All pose problems of accountability, and a challenge to cohesive public policy.

If the logic of shared global problems demands a global response, if government budget practices in developing countries are considered inadequate, and if the proliferation of NGOs and contracting further weakens budgetary accountability, what is to be done? One possibility is re-imposing and strengthening central controls, including NGOs, which may already be taking place. Without any change in underlying conditions, such controls may be counter-productive (see Premchand, 2005, p. 22). A second possibility is to persist in promoting performance measures to gain and maintain accountability over governmental bureaucracies and contractors alike, but the experience related above does not appear encouraging.

The similarity of budget institutions that we observe all over the world is the triumph of an early nineteenth century invention, a flash of insight that has stood the test of time. This superficial similarity has been responsible for a parallel development – the spawning of "one size fits all", "best practice" reforms to improve on the original model or make up for its shortcomings. But budget processes reflect their environments; they are complex; and they depend on a variety of institutional capabilities, including the political.

The path to reform of public financial management is therefore not a straightforward one, and its implementation depends on feasible strategy and realistic sequencing of reform, based on detailed specific knowledge and long-term commitment (see Peterson, 2004).

As the star of New Public Management begins to wane, and comparative public administration begins to revive, it may be hoped that initiatives will be based on solid research and patient analysis of specific situations, rather than quick fixes and current fashions. In budgeting in developing countries, the familiar and the unknown coexist in uneasy tandem. Can we build on the insights of the familiar to overcome its constraints, and to meet the challenges of the unknown to create a better world?

NOTES

1. This section of the paper is based on Naomi Caiden, *Public Budgeting in an Era of Globalization.* Paper presented at a conference on *The Repositioning of Public Governance – Global Experience and Challenges,* Civil Service Development Institute, Taipei, November 18–19, 2005.

REFERENCES

Andrews, M. (2005). Performance-based budgeting reform: Progress, problems, and pointers. In: A. Shah (Ed.), *Fiscal management* (pp. 31–70). Washington, DC: World Bank.

Bryant, C., & Kappaz, C. (2005). *Reducing poverty, building peace*. Bloomfield, Connecticut: Kumarian Press.

Caiden, N. (1981). Public budgeting amongst uncertainty and instability. *Public Budgeting and Finance, 1*(1), 6–19.

Caiden, N. (1985). Budgeting in ASEAN countries. *Budgeting and Finance, 5*(4), 23–38.

Caiden, N., & Caiden, G. (1998). Approaches and guidelines for monitoring, measuring and evaluating performance in public sector programs. Paper presented at United Nations Fourteenth Meeting of the Group of Experts on the United Nations Program on Public Administration and Finance, New York, May 4–14.

Caiden, N., & Wildavsky, A. (1980). *Planning and budgeting in poor countries*. New Brunswick, NJ: Transaction Books.

Daniszewski, J. (2004). U.N. details plight of children. *Los Angeles Times, 10*(December), A13.

Davis, M. (2004). Planet of Slums. *Harper's Magazine*, (June), 17–22.

Dixon, G. (2005). Thailand's quest for results-focused budgeting. *International Journal of Public Administration, 3 and 4*(28), 355–370.

Jreisat, J. (2005). Comparative public administration is back in, prudently. *Public Administration Review, 2*(65), 231–242.

Kaufmann, D. (2005). Back to basics – 10 myths about governance and corruption. *Finance and Development, 3*(42).

Landau, M. (1969). Redundancy, rationality and the problems of duplication and overlap. *Public Administration Review, 4*(29).

Lomas, A. (2005). What has been the impact of the program assessment rating tool. *PA Times*, December 12.

Mestel, R. (2004). HIV rates rise among women. *Los Angeles Times, 24*(October), A3.

Montes, C., & Andrews, M. (2005). Implementing reforms in Bolivia: Too much to handle? *International Journal of Public Administration, 3 and 4*(28), 273–290.

Osborne, D., & Gaebler, T. (1993). *Reinventing government: How the entrepreneurial spirit is transforming the public sector*. New York: Plume Books.

Peterson, S. (2004). *How to get there: Financial reform in a poor country*. Harvard University: Kennedy School of Government.

Premchand, A. (2005). *Controlling government spending: The ethos, ethics, and economics of expenditure management*. Oxford: Oxford University Press.

Roberts, J., & Andrew, M. (2005). Something funny happened on the way to reform success: The case of budget reform implementation in Ghana. *International Journal of Public Administration, 3 and 4*(28), 291–312.

Ronsholt, F., & Matthew, A. (2005). Getting It Together … or not. An analysis of the early period of Tanzania's move towards adopting performance management systems. *International Journal of Public Administration, 3&4*(28), 313–336.

Sachs, J. (2005). *The end of poverty*. Penguin: Penguin Books.

Schick, A. (1998). Why most developing countries should not try New Zealand reforms. *World Bank Research Observer, 13*, 123–131.

Shah, A. (2005). On getting the giant to kneel: Approaches to a change in the bureaucratic culture. In: A. Shah (Ed.), *Fiscal Management* (pp. 211–229). Washington, DC: World Bank.

Stiglitz, J. (2002). *Globalization and its discontents*. New York: W.W. Norton.

Umeh, O., & Andranovich, G. (2005). *Culture, development, and public administration in Africa*. Bloomfield, CT: Kumarian.

Waldman, A. (2005). All roads lead to cities, transforming India. *New York Times*, 7(December).

Wines, M. (2005). Drought deepens poverty, starving more Africans. *New York Times*, 2(November).

FURTHER READING

Daniszswski, J. (2005). U.N. report focuses on 'Invisible Children'. *Los Angeles Times*, 15(December), A3.

Swiss, J. (2003). A framework for assessing incentives in results-based management. *Public Administration Review*, 5(65, September/October), 592–602.

THE NEW WORLD ORDER
AND GLOBAL PUBLIC
ADMINISTRATION:
A CRITICAL ESSAY

Ali Farazmand

The history of world civilization has always been characterized by revolutionary upheavals and changes in human organization of governance and in
political, social, and economic structures of societies. Both quantitative and
qualitative changes have contributed to the evolutionary process of human
societies and to their social systems. The qualitative, transformational
changes from slavery and feudalism to capitalism have been a remarkable
human progress. If we accept the Marxist view of historical evolution, the
next transformational qualitative change would have to be to socialism and
communism. But the fall of the Soviet Union and most other socialist systems has led to a widespread belief in the death of socialism and communism. Whether this is a foregone conclusion or an illusion is not the concern
of this essay. Nonetheless, it is a relevant point, for the changes of the
twentieth century have been of a different nature with far different significance and with fundamental implications for public administration theory
and practice.

The rise and fall of empires from ancient times, the rise of the nation-states, and the revolutions in science and technology have brought

Comparative Public Administration: The Essential Readings
Research in Public Policy Analysis and Management, Volume 15, 701–728
Copyright © 2006 by Elsevier Ltd.
ISSN: 0732-1317/doi:10.1016/S0732-1317(06)15031-9

significant qualitative changes to human civilization. But the twentieth century has been a turning point in human history. Fundamental political, social, economic, cultural, and scientific changes in this century have been remarkable. The bourgeois transformation of feudal and absolute systems of empires, the reign of mercantilism–colonialism and its transformation to modern capitalism and imperialism, and the following revolutionary changes leading to decolonialization and the emergence of new nation-states are among the most outstanding transformational, qualitative changes that occurred during this century. Perhaps one of the most outstanding changes of this century was the emergence of the new sociopolitical system of world socialism as a result of the Russian Revolution of 1917.

The rise of world socialism led by the Soviet Union altered the nature of ideological, political, social, cultural, and military relations at global level for the next seventy years, until 1992. The global division into capitalist and socialist camps was not an illusion; it was a profound division with profound implications for politics, economics, and public administration. More than anything else, perhaps, it had tremendous implications for the Third World countries struggling for the numerous advantages the advanced industrialized nations of the West have taken for granted for a long time. The polarization of the world into two global camps was further reinforced after World War II; the victorious Allies, including the Soviet Union – with a human loss of twenty million of its population – defeated Nazi Germany and Japan, two warring nations claiming global superiority. Had they succeeded in defeating the Allies, what would have been the fate of the nations and their peoples today? But that is not the issue here. The relevant issue is that Hitler and Mussolini also claimed a new "world order." Hitler's vision was perhaps a global system of government under Germany; he definitely had a global design in mind.

In short, the Cold War era was a major change with great implications for humanity and the nations. The socialist system promoted a greater need for trained and professional public administrators to manage a huge, monopolized economy. The capitalist nations of the West invested tremendous amounts of resources every year in infrastructural programs and in economic projects domestically and internationally to outcompete the socialist system, which was always struggling to compete with the West but, less exploitative by nature, had little success in competing with the capitalist system.

Both systems devoted monumental amounts of resources and energy to military competition, and both engaged in a constant war of attrition through their client states or peoples. The Cold War was fought on many grounds, but it was also always fought as a "hot war" in developing countries. In the capitalist nations the governments were forced to take a more active role in resource allocation, in redistribution of wealth, in managing the disenchanted citizens, and in controlling the "explosive mix" of their populations. They spent more and more on "welfare" measures in order to prevent potential revolutions, to level off income distributions, and to save and enhance their systems. They faced many crises and responded to these crises in many ways.

The rise of the welfare state or administrative state has been a direct result of the inevitable responses the modern capitalist system has had to introduce. There has been an increasing expansion of the administrative state and a greater demand for professionalization of public administration in the capitalist nations, both developed and developing, ever since the turn of this century. An immediate implication of this global trend has been a greater demand for a theory of public administration as a self-conscious enterprise as well as for a continuous expansion of public administration. But the trend tended to take a different global swing in the 1980s, when neoconservative politicians and their economic allies were able to take leadership seats in Washington and London.

Privatization and the turning back of many state functions to the private sector were the ideological answer to the many deep problems of the economic crisis that the capitalist systems have been facing since the 1970s. The market was considered the only answer to economic and social problems. That ideological current for a decade had fundamental impacts on all aspects of politics and administration not only in the United States and Great Britain but also almost everywhere else on the globe. Such a trend is still in full motion, although it has somewhat slowed down recently. Change, therefore, has been a key denominator of twentieth-century history, as it has always been.

Unfortunately, not all these changes have been positive. The ability to destroy the environment and all humanity is a consequence that is also associated with the twentieth century. This is not the place to analyze the nature and significance of "change" in human history. However, it is important to note that change has been the norm of history, politically and socioeconomically. If change has been the norm, so has been continuity in the social system structure and process of societies. Hence, it seems that both change and continuity work together in a dialectical way, both reinforcing each other and bringing qualitative transformation to human society.

The significant revolutionary upheavals and changes that have taken place in governments and in their economic and political systems since the 1970s have had profound structural consequences economically, politically, and administratively for peoples in various societies. However, fundamental inconsistencies characterize these changes and the forces or ideologies – external or internal – that are behind them. Just as the formerly divided world had major implications for public administration, so the fall of the Soviet Union and socialist power and the new global era has important but contradictory implications for public administration and public management.

The only superpower leading and dominating the world is the United States, with its allies sharing the same ideology and goals. Almost the entire world, developing and developed, is forced to adjust to the new global conditions and reconfigurations dominated by the United States and other major Western nations. Undoubtedly, there are many positive and negative aspects of this new changing world order dominated by the United States. Social scientists have been less critical about the usage of this term. Some public administrationists have enthusiastically analyzed the emerging global order with implications for public administration. The concept of "globalism," not even mentioned in most textbooks of the field, has suddenly become a frequently cited term in public administration publications. Globalism and global interdependence are frequent subjects and topics of conferences and publications. Some theorists have even attempted to develop a universal, global theory of public administration (Caiden, 1991b), and others have envisioned a new world of public administration in a "global village" (Garcia-Zamor, 1992; Khator, 1992).

This chapter attempts to analyze some of the key changing patterns of public administration and politics under the New World Order, or "disorder," as some critics (Sedghi, 1992) have argued, and also to suggest an emerging global public administration. The focus is on the following five topics: (1) the nature of the New World Order and what it would mean for different countries; (2) the global slogan of democratization and its theoretical and practical paradoxes or inconsistencies around the world; (3) marketization and globalized privatization; (4) the issue of structural adjustments in political, economic, and administrative systems in various countries with uneven consequences in prospect for an emerging "global public administration model"; and (5) the challenges and opportunities that these changes and newly global public administration will likely create for public management education and practice around the globe. The chapter's conclusion pulls together the overall discussions.

THE NATURE OF THE NEW WORLD ORDER

The concept of a New World Order is a rhetorical device that is not new. In fact, it is as old as the notion of empire building in ancient times. When Cyrus the Great conquered virtually the entire known world and expanded his "World-State" Persian Achaemenid Empire, his vision was to create a synthesis of civilization and to unite all peoples of the world under the universal Persian rule with a global world order characterized by peace, stability, economic prosperity, and religious and cultural tolerance. For two centuries that world order was maintained by both military might and Persian gold: Whenever the military force was not applicable, the gold did the job; and in most cases both the military and the gold functioned together (Frye, 1963, 1975; Farazmand, 1991a). Similarly, Alexander the Great also established a New World Order. The Romans and the following mighty empires had the same concept in mind. The concept was also very fashionable after World Wars I and II. The world order of the twentieth century was until recently a shared one, dominated by the two superpowers of the United States and the USSR.

This world order was dual in nature, characterized by superpower competition, rivalry, suspicion, hostility, and wasteful consumption of human, natural, material, and technological resources in all spheres of life. Ideology played a key role in the two world systems. Consequently, players in the international arena – politicians, administrators, theorists, and the like – knew what the dividing lines were. The rules of the game were spelled out under this dual world order system, and events seemed predictable to a great extent. In an excellent book, *Turbulence in World Politics,* James Rosenau (1990) gave a clear picture of the New World Order to emerge from this new world system characterized by constant change and challenges. To Rosenau, the new world system would enjoy more stability and peace than ever before. He predicted that ideology would decay, governments would narrow in competence, people would demand more and that "an emergent global culture" would be characterized by global interdependence (Rosenau, 1990, p. 419). Somewhat similar arguments were made earlier in a collection of essays edited by Keohane and Nye (1977) in their book, *Power and Interdependence.*

With the emergence of Gorbachev as the reformist leader of the Soviet Union calling for restructuring, openness, a new way of global thinking, peace for all, superpower cooperation, and an end to the Cold War era, the concept of a New World Order emerged again. In fact, Gorbachev used the term in his speech addressed to the United Nations (U.N.). General Assembly in December 1988, at which then U.S. President Reagan and Vice

President Bush were present (Sedghi, 1992). After the Helsinki summit with Gorbachev in September 1990, Bush increasingly used the term. It should make no difference who borrowed the term from whom. What is important is its meaning and implications.

The New World Order denotes a system of collective world security where states and peoples can live in peace with each other, ideologies aside, and "observe each other's borders and maintain collective security interests" (Sedghi, 1992, p. 62). Policing others will not be required by powerful states; rather, a combination of several states will maintain stability in unstable areas. The Persian Gulf War was arguably fought in the service of the New World Order. In fact, during that international crisis, Bush announced that the war was to "stand up for what is right and condemn what is wrong" (Trudeau, 1992, p. 21).

Two schools of thought seem to have dominated the literature on world order and global power relationships: the "declinist" and the "anti-declinist." Analyzing the "longevity" of the U.S. ability to maintain the "number one" position in world affairs, the declinists, represented by Paul Kennedy (1989), make analogies with previous Great Powers and point to the risks they ran: Their imperial stretch went too far, and their deaths eventually did come. According to Kennedy, America will inevitably decline because of the imperative economic development at home, the imbalance in international military commitments, and the changing nature of the global power players. Rejecting this view, the anti-declinists, represented by Rostow (1988) and Brzezinski (1986), argue that the United States is more powerful than any other country in the world and will continue to occupy the leading position in international affairs.

Regardless of which school of thought is accepted, the fundamental underpinnings of this New World Order include the following: U.S. military might and its capability to destroy the world, an unprecedented phenomenon in world history; the globalized economic nature of the United States, with its performance crisis at home and its corporate opportunities and dominance abroad; her cultural penetration and dominance of the global environment; her self-declared guardianship of the marketplace and its ideology; her political ability to maneuver globally on economic and military grounds; her ability to manipulate the U.N. as a collective instrumentality for action legitimation; the young age of the nation and its people; the lack of another superpower as competition; and the economic system of capitalism with its global penetration and dominance.

The United States has achieved outstanding economic and military might in a relatively short period of time, and the nation still is full of youthful energy. Defending U.S. interests globally is the central aspect of the New World Order (Hamilton, 1989). Under the New World Order the United Nations and its vast number of affiliated organizations will likely play a more active role in various international affairs, primarily under the U.S. hegemonic banner. It will serve as a conduit for legitimating international actions or inactions. "National sovereignty" may be overridden by international community actions, and a "world government" with a "global management" will likely emerge (Wilson, 1994).

Whatever the argument, the United States will no doubt continue to play the leadership role in the New World Order based on such underpinnings. But what will this mean for other developed and developing nations? It is beyond the scope of this chapter to analyze this question fully, but suffice it to say that the implications are far greater for developing nations than for the advanced ones. Unlike the past, the new era will likely be characterized by North–South conflicts and struggles. The New World Order will have major consequences for developing nations and their public administration. It will have a complex web of dominant structures that will encompass the developing nations' economic, political, social, cultural, security, and military systems. There will be few, if any, nations capable of escaping such a penetrating and dominating structure. Exceptions will likely exist, however.

Governments in the developing world will likely adopt similar policies toward their domestic and international affairs. Washington will be the city that most roads will lead to. The developed countries of the world will probably resemble the United States to some extent, but internal competition and rivalry are also likely to drive advanced nations like Germany, France, and Japan in the race for global market supremacy. However, the military and science and technology and their selective application will likely keep the United States in the leading position for decades to come as long as it is willing to press for global submission, defend the capitalists and large landowners around the world, protect global trade routes, police the world, and provide an "insurance policy" for the free world (Klare, 1988, 1990).

Under the dual world order, the two superpowers and their allies provided support and protection to developing nations struggling for independence from the colonial rule or experiencing internal revolutions. The superpowers counterbalanced each other in the international community of nations. As under the New World Order there will be no such counterbalancing, the New World Order will have uneven consequences for developing versus developed nations, the former being subjected to pressures from every direction. As will be seen later, this fact has major implications, positive and negative, for developing nations and for some developed countries.

DEMOCRATIZATION

A key aspect of the New World Order is claimed to be democracy and democratization. Democracy and democratization as political processes are valued as basic foundations for human freedom and free society. It is argued that the socialist systems of the Soviet Union and Eastern Europe, as well as others in Africa and Asia, have not been democratic. Their totalitarian system has been centralized and controlled by a planned, command economy inhibiting individual freedom and incentives for growth. The only way to be free, then, is to get rid of this system and to join the free capitalist world in which the marketplace provides all opportunities for individual growth and economic development. Politically, individuals are free to choose their preferences, which is done through voting. Voting is therefore considered an exercise of individual freedom, a necessary condition for good citizenship.

The concept of democracy, however, is not clearly defined. There are confusions over the fundamentals of its meaning. Various theories attempt to explain it from various perspectives. The Marxists present several forms of democracy, including feudal democracy; capitalist or bourgeois democracy, in which the upper-class minority rules the middle class and the working class; socialist democracy, in which the majority of the working class and the middle class rule the minority through the state ownership of almost all properties; and communist democracy, a classless society, in which there is no class-based ruler (Lenin, 1971).

The pluralistic explanation of democracy rests primarily not on class-based society, but on the function of different groups, all striving for collective decisions through participation, compromises, and majority rule. Citizens get organized into interest groups in order to influence or to change the decision structures in pursuit of maximizing their interests. Participation through voting is an essential aspect of the democratic process leading to the election of representative officials and separation of powers regulated by constitutional laws. Money, however, is a key requirement for success in pluralism, for those with more resources are better organized and are better equipped to influence the public policy process and policy outcomes (Jones, 1984; Parenti, 1988; Zeigler, 1964). While conservatives favor a limited role of government in society and economy, liberals realize a more active governmental role. Both viewpoints stress the central role of elections for regime legitimation and agree on having private enterprise or the market as the economic basis in society (Dahl, 1971; DiPalma, 1990; Huntington, 1991; Luebert, 1991).

Diamond, Linz, and Lipset (1990, p. 6) define democracy to "signify a political system, separate and apart from the economic and social system to which it is joined." The proponents of the market-based elite theory of democracy (Dye & Zeigler, 1990) and the critical theorists (Parenti, 1988) argue for a democracy based on broad representation, but the latter is critical of the pluralistic system in which democracy works for the "few," those who have the "sword and the dollar" (Parenti, 1989).

Whatever the ideological underpinning, the term *democracy* is appealing to peoples around the world. A key problem, therefore, is the confusion over its meaning. As Waldo notes, the definitional problem is "severe." "Democracy of course means 'rule by the people.' But what does that mean?" asks Waldo (1990, p. 202). Obviously, the confusion arises when key questions are raised over who the people are, what the rule is to look like, who makes the rule, and what limitations exist to control the rulers. The problem seems to be solved by the strictly political meaning of democracy as a commonly accepted Western concept to denote "secret or at least uncoerced voting, broad suffrage, free expression, free association (including the right to form political parties), representation, legislative bodies, [and] a considerable respect for and guarantees of rights" (Waldo, 1990, pp. 202–204). Waldo soundly defines democracy as "a striving toward equality and freedom."

However, an immediate problem may arise from this sound definition: How long should people or a nation strive toward equality and freedom? Who should determine that period? Dictators around the world, from Somoza of Nicaragua to the shah of Iran, from General Pinochet of Chile to Marcos of the Philippines, and others elsewhere frequently argued that their peoples were not ready for democracy and freedom and that freedom is dangerous and that there should be a long waiting term! Are elections sufficient to ensure representation? Who usually is able to run and get elected to public office in a market-based society? Above all, can a democratic society or people or its government promote or support authoritarian regimes or help overthrow democratically elected representative governments abroad because they are not friendly to other democratic governments, say, the United States? Put differently, can the United States as a democratic form of government remain democratic when it continues to support nondemocratic, repressive regimes around the world? Is there a contradiction or inconsistency here? These are some of the key questions critics raise.

As the leader of the free world, the United States has claimed to promote democracy and democratization abroad. "Exporting democracy" has been an international role the United States has played for decades, with some qualifying positive results (Lowenthal, 1991). But the record does not seem to be very encouraging. In fact, great democracies of the West including the United States have a strong record of supporting "some of the most repressive and exploitative dictatorships" around the globe (Kitschell, 1992). Many revolutions of the twentieth century occurred as a result of such support of those repressive regimes by the United States and other Western nations (Farazrnand, 1991b; Schutz & Slater, 1990). Whether fighting communism in the Cold War era is a justifiable reason, as many argue, or simply serving the American national and business interests, as others have argued, is not the point here. The point is that there is an inconsistency in the way that the great democratic powers of the free world carry out the democratization slogan. Cases like Iran, Chile, Turkey, Egypt, Zaire, Argentina, Nicaragua, and the Philippines, to name a few, are good examples.

The slogan of democratization has been emphasized as a necessary condition for normalizing relations with governments that are not so friendly and with some with socialist orientations, such as Nicaragua under the Sandinistas, Angola, Vietnam, North Korea, and Cuba. During the gigantic wave of major changes taking place in the Soviet Union and the Eastern European nations, the United States and other major Western powers seem to have encouraged and supported democratization through political elections and representations. While democratization of the socialist "totalitarian" systems has been emphasized, repressive regimes around the world have continued to receive the full political, military, and economic support of the United States. Hence, there is a big inconsistency in raising the slogan of democratization in the free world.

It may be argued that the major source of this inconsistency would have to rest on the problem of equating democracy with market. Therefore, the global slogan of democratization is misleading and may have dangerous consequences. It is misleading because it is equated with market supremacy while market and democratic ideals have many reasons to clash and contradict on both individual and societal levels. As Heilbroner (1990, p. 105) notes, "It is of course, foolish to suggest that capitalism is the *sine qua non* of democracy, or to claim that democracy, with its commitment to political equality, does not conflict in many ways with the inequalities built into capitalism." But this equating concept has been repeatedly used by both politicians and social scientists, including public administrationists. Marketization of the socialist world is considered democratization, even without elections. And the nondemocratic regimes of Africa, Asia, the Middle East, and Latin America with market-based economic systems are considered already democratic and therefore part of the free world. No free political parties, no free associations, no free labor unions, no freedom of expression, and no representative governments exist in most of these nations; their elections, if any, are usually farcical and meaningless and are "demonstration elections" (Hermand & Broadhead, 1984). Nicaragua under Somoza had an election a few months before the popular revolution toppled the regime. Similar phenomena were observed in Iran under the shah and in the Middle East (Bill, 1984; Binder, 1962; Farazmand, 1989a).

Democratization as a slogan is also dangerous because it has been applied unevenly and inconsistently. While socialist and independent states are targeted for democratization, dictatorship in friendly states with market capitalism is often overlooked, to say the least, and justified, promoted, and protected for national and business/corporate interests' (Gibbs, 1991; Hamilton, 1989). The democratization slogan is further dangerous because it tends to raise expectations for freedom and democracy among peoples who may choose alternative democratic governments not too friendly to the West. An example is the Kurdish and Shia peoples in Iraq, who were highly encouraged by the U.S. slogan of democratization during and after the Persian Gulf War but were allowed to be slaughtered by Saddam Hussein's repressive regime.

The neoconservative democratic theory of the last two decades seems to have dominated the entire world. Based on the neoclassical conservative "public choice" theory, methodological individualism, and the decentralization of organizational and administrative arrangements for service delivery are the central characteristics of the market-based democratic model. The individual is seen as a self-interested, self-utility maximizer in the marketplace, searching freely with adequate information for political, economic, and administrative choices that maximize his or her interests. Therefore, the free, self-maximizing individual engages in collective actions that would benefit his or her self-interests both domestically and internationally.

Highly promoted under the Reagan administration in the United States and abroad in the 1980s and still dominating the world, this conservative theory has had profound implications for public administration and politics around the globe; it is a market theory of democracy, organization, and public administration. It has called for shrinking government, limiting its intervention in society and economy, market supremacy, and consumer sovereignty (Buchanan & Tullock, 1962; Downs, 1957; Ostrom, 1973). Despite its intellectual and theoretical utilities, the market-based public choice democratic theory has serious flaws and is criticized on many grounds (DeGregori, 1974; Golembiewski, 1977; Farazmand, 1994c).

The market-based conservative economic theory of democracy has been internationalized since the 1980s and has been an integral part of the New

World Order, as explained below. Equating democracy with market alone, therefore, has been a major pattern pervading public administration and will likely continue, despite the election of Democrats to office in the United States. Unfortunately, students and scholars of public administration have used the concept of democratization and marketization uncritically, which has set a distorted trend of explaining public administration in democracy.

MARKETIZATION AND PRIVATIZATION

Marketization and privatization are two key elements or requirements that have been emphasized by the United States and other Western nations. Both concepts have been elevated to an ideological level, particularly during the 1980s, in the United States and Britain. Conservative governments under Reagan and Thatcher pursued a rigorous policy of privatization in America and England, with serious consequences for public administration and for developing nations. Although privatization of public, government-owned enterprises has been pursued nonstop everywhere, it is more intense in the former socialist nations in Eastern Europe and in the nations of Asia and Africa. Marketization and the privatization of public sector functions have been major preconditions for democratic development and requirements for foreign aid to these and other nations. The newly independent nations of the former USSR and the Eastern European socialist countries have adopted the market system. The American and Western European experts have been consulting them on how fast to implement it. The countries resisting full-fledged marketization have not received important support – financial or political – from the capitalist powers. Investment in these nations has been withheld by multinational corporations. Under pressure many formerly so-cialist nations of Eastern Europe have already marketized their economies.

At the same time, the privatization of state-owned enterprises is also being pursued in capitalist nations, developed and developing, East and West. Research on privatization is growing every day and has already produced a significant body of literature, but the results are mixed. Privatization is not a new concept; in fact, most nations have experienced it over time. What is significant about it today is that it has become almost a theology in politics and administration. It has been considered a solution to most problems supposedly created by big government and by the welfare state. It is beyond the scope of this essay to analyze the theoretical, practical, and ideological aspects of this concept. What follows is a brief discussion of privatization and its forms and its implications for global public administration.

Elsewhere (Farazmand, 1989b), I have argued that two of the central characteristics of the American political system are its "consistent inconsistency" and its "reactive nature." For almost a century, the two ideological, political, and economic orientations of conservatism and liberalism represented by the Republican and Democratic parties have dominated the policy process and outcomes in the United States, creating a framework or mainstream arena for acceptable and unacceptable policy choices. The inconsistency has consistently appeared in society when one political party in power tried to undo what the other party administration had introduced and implemented. For example, the Berger Court tried to undo what the Warren Court had accomplished. Similarly, the Reagan administration tried, and succeeded to some extent, in undoing what had been accomplished by the Roosevelt administration during the New Deal era. The damages of the 1980s to the economy and society are now being repaired by the new administration. These inconsistencies have consistently produced damaging effects to the society, economy, and peoples. Certainly, they have had major implications for public administration.

The reactive nature of the government and political system may be explained by its tendency to act after damages that have been inflicted and problems or crises that have occurred. The history of the United States and many other capitalist nations is characterized by periodic crises in economic and political systems. The state and its public administration have also faced significant crises of legitimacy as a result of these (Arrow, 1963; Farazmand, 1989b; Habermass, 1975; Macpherson, 1987; O'Conner, 1973; Offe, 1985). The state must respond in a reactive way to the crises and problems that it faces. For several decades, the administrative state was allowed to grow. The 1980s was the turning point, and the 1990s were the years to repair the damages to the infrastructure and other aspects of society. This damage was done mainly by equating the concept of conservative democracy with marketization and privatization. But the monumental literature on market failure seems to have been overlooked or ignored, and the government has been advised to turn its functions over to the private sector for efficiency and economy. However, the purpose of democratic governments is not to produce efficiency, although it is a desirable objective. Rather, they must provide economic, social, and political justice for all citizens to preclude the exercise of tyranny and arbitrary power (Rosenbloom, 1989, p. 19).

Marketization and privatization, although valued for many purposes, are not the answers to the problems and crises faced by modern governments. The rising expectations of peoples around the globe, the environmental crises, the population explosion, the demand for better services, the technological revolutions, and many other issues have pressed nations and governments to find solutions. Privatization has been an ideological answer that the corporate sector and the conservative theorists of the West have tried to push on a global scale. The result has been a movement that has invaded almost all countries of the globe.

However, privatization can be misleading because state-owned functions and enterprises – generally established and operated for broad social, political, and economic purposes – may not be transferred to private individuals and businesses. Often, these enterprises end up in the hands of large, often multinational corporations, which are hardly private. As Dahl (1970, p. 102) notes, "Surely it is a delusion to consider it [the corporation] a private enterprise."

Privatization as an economic and political strategy has had mixed results in advanced democratic countries where more stringent laws and regulations exist. Its implementation in developing countries may have serious ramifications, where there is no self-regulating, strong market system and no strong representative governments capable of keeping corporations accountable. Full-fledged privatization, in which state enterprises and governmental functions are turned over to the marketplace, and semiprivatization, in which major functions of government are contracted out to the private sector providers, have both advantages and disadvantages. Admittedly, there are certain functions that the market could perform more efficiently, which have been recognized by almost all governments for millennia.

But privatization of the functions essential to society and people may be dangerous. In areas where there is an incentive for the market to perform, there could be, as has always been the case, enormous social costs that the market produces – costs that ultimately the government and its people must pay. Some costs are so heavy that they may never be compensated. Technological externalities and environmental pollution are but two examples (Ascher, 1987; Cook, 1988; Cowan, 1990; Farazmand, 1994b; Letwin, 1988; Savas, 1982; Vernon, 1988). Privatization also incurs significant costs on the part of governments in the form of monitoring the expanded functions of the marketplace and controlling abuse and fraud. Examples of market failure, fraud, and abuse of public funds are not few. Privatization of these functions in advanced capitalist nations like the United States where the market is well developed, albeit not necessarily free (Galbraith, 1974), has had major problems and therefore is not being recommended by the critics (Goodsell, 1990). Needless to say, it will produce far greater problems for governments of the Third World societies, where the market is neither well developed nor adequately regulated.

It is worth noting that the concept of privatization, as promoted by its proponents in the United States and Europe, does not include the nonso-cialist, cooperative systems organized and operated on the principles of capitalism. In fact, such a system, even if it is efficient and productive, has been denounced by U.S. foreign service advisers and American agricultural experts. For example, a U.S. Presidential Agricultural Task Force to Peru in 1981 argued that cooperative enterprise "decimated the basic structure of Peruvian agriculture," while, according to a U.N. Food and Agriculture Organization (UN-FAO) study, the country's "yields for sugar and rice (majorities of which [were] produced on the cooperatives) [were] among the highest in the world some ten years after the reform" (McClintock, 1987, p. 88). The underlying purpose of the privatization movement, the critics argue, is the transfer of the huge sector of the public enterprises, particularly the profitable ones, to large corporate private enterprises with direct ties to multinational corporations (Parenti, 1978, 1988).[1]

As mentioned earlier, privatization and marketization have been used by the major international donors to pressure the recipients of foreign aid. For example, the International Monetary Fund (IMF), the World Bank, and the United States, Germany, and other Western nations have made it clear that receiving foreign aid is contingent upon nations' efforts to privatize government enterprises and marketize their state-controlled economies[2] (Garcia-Zamor, 1992; Hayter, 1971). Consequently, many developing na-tions, highly dependent on international aid, have been forced to implement the measures of privatization and structural adjustments. Such structural adjustments, however, are reported to be global in nature. Privatization and structural adjustments have had significant implications and consequences for developing countries and for public administration theory and practice; there is an emerging global public administration with a fundamental shift of service focus toward private business interests rather than the general public interest.

STRUCTURAL ADJUSTMENTS AND GLOBAL PUBLIC ADMINISTRATION

The changes in the 1980s and the New World Order have led almost all nations, particularly developing countries, to reform and readjust to the new global conditions. The structural adjustments in developing countries to conform to the norms, rules, and values of the new global order have led to fundamental revisions in the public and private sectors' relationships, in the role of government in society and the economy, and in the extent to which the market can stretch its sphere of political and economic influence. The key terms under the new conditions are readjustment, reform, redefining, reconsideration, redevelopment, reintegration, reevaluation, and reinvention (Farazmand, 1994a). These structural adjustments or readjustments have, and will likely continue to have, major impacts on public administration in the United States and abroad.

The following section suggests some structural changes leading to the emergence of a global public administration.

READJUSTMENT IN PUBLIC AND
PRIVATE SECTOR RELATIONSHIPS

The global movements of marketization and privatization have significantly altered the scope and boundaries of public sector functions and activities in both developed and developing countries. Almost all nations around the world have undergone a significant process of redefining and restructuring their public and private sector relations in favor of the private market sector. The underlying rationale behind this conservative movement has been to attain greater efficiency in managing governmental functions and to improve economic productivity and performance. Privatization and contracting out, as discussed above, have been used as means of achieving greater efficiency and economy by governments.

Privatization has also affected the third, nonprofit sector as well as the cooperative sectors around the globe. Many governments in developing countries with successful and productive cooperative enterprise systems have been forced to cut financial and technical support to these enterprises and to abandon and sell them to large landowners and agribusinesses. The major international influential force behind this boundary readjustment has been the United States since the 1980s. This redefinition of the boundaries and scope of public administration and business enterprises has led to massive layoffs and displacements in many countries around the globe. Ironically, at the same time the private corporate sector has enjoyed all types of tax breaks and financial supports from these governments. Often, the corporate enterprises have even been bailed out by their governments.

The structural boundary readjustment toward marketization has had and will continue to have significant implications for public administration. Although the size of the workforce may have decreased, the governmental responsibilities and public administration functions have not. Unless governments vacate the field of given public policy areas totally, in favor of a complete privatization scheme of production and service provisions, "then the responsibilities of public organizations do not disappear" (Wise, 1994).

ORGANIZATIONAL RECONFIGURATION AND REDESIGN

The sectoral boundary restructuring has led to organizational reconfigurations and restructuring in order to meet the demands of the new era. The traditional organizational designs have been questioned for their inflexibility, while new alternative design structures have been proposed, adopted, and implemented in many countries, including the United States and Europe. A number of organizational design problems emerge as a result of these reconfigurations. These may include the key issues of organizational complexity, centralization and decentralization, the changing role of environment and its effects on organizational adaptiveness and flexibility, the tasks of coordinating multiorganizational efforts in service delivery, the problem of overlapping organizations, the problem of achieving accountability in both public and private sectors, the problem of national resource allocation, the task of coordinating and balancing public and private sectors, the problem of private sector regulation and enforcement of those regulations, and a host of other issues.

These and many other organizational design issues will likely present major problems in the reconfiguration of public organizations of governments around the globe. Already many old organizations have been dismantled in many former socialist nations without a clear idea of what to do with the functions that they had performed. Also, public organizations have been abolished because of popular sentiments against the bureaucracies of the old regimes. It is much easier to abolish an institution than to build one, and replacing the old bureaucracy has not been an easy challenge for the new regime leaders, revolutionary or otherwise (Carino, 1991; Farazmand, 1989a, 1991b; Lenin, 1971).

The new organizational reconfiguration around the globe will likely reflect the requirements for flexibility of decentralization and fragmentation, on the one hand, and adequate coordination and control through centralization of authority and power, on the other. The managerial, political, economic, and organizational dimensions of the new design configurations will have to be adaptive to the changing local and global environmental determinants. Developing countries have a formidable challenge to deal with, for it is the international capital and public administration experts of the leading global powers that will determine the key factors of the organizational reconfiguration structure. The economic and political dependence of many Third World countries on the West leaves them with little room to maneuver in the new global era.

Changes in the organizational structure and behavior will be directed more toward serving the private market sector than toward serving the general public. Decentralization will likely lead to chaos, while centralization will appeal as an imperative instrument of political and security control.

Consequently, more bureaucratization will likely characterize the organizational structure of developing countries. Their administrators and the bureaucratic cultures will have to internalize the exogenous, imported values and norms of administration and culture. Conversely, they will have to externalize their indigenous cultural and institutional values of their administrative systems. One manifestation of this externalization tendency is, and will be, the internalization of Western organizational values of rationality, impersonalization, formalization, and other bureaucratic values associated with the Weberian ideal-type bureaucracy. Such a system of organization has by nature proven to be alienating and at odds with the native cultures of the non-Western world. A result of this organizational and value transformation will likely broaden the gulf that already exists between the corrupt bureaucratic culture on the one hand and the popular, mass culture on the other. Eventually, this will have serious political consequences for political authorities and regimes around the globe.

ADMINISTRATIVE REFORM

Administrative reform has been a common feature of most governments around the world. It is beyond the scope and purpose of this essay to discuss the extensive literature on this important subject. Suffice it to say that, generally, governments reform their administrative system in order to obtain or broaden their legitimacy, improve their administrative performance, become more responsive and accountable to citizens, increase managerial efficiency, make the system more flexible, satisfy international donors' requirements, satisfy opposition groups' demands, restructure the governmental system, and often just for the sake of reform itself.

Unless seriously taken and genuinely followed and implemented, administrative reforms are nothing but ideas on paper. Comparative research shows that administrative reforms have often failed, although for varying reasons (Caiden, 1991a, 1991b; Farazmand, 1989a, 1994a; Peters, 1994).

The administrative reforms that have taken place or will take place around the globe have mainly corresponded with the objectives of marketization, privatization, and democratization. These reforms include centralization and decentralization of local administrative systems, changes in the personnel and budgeting systems, changes in the civil service systems, changes in administrative regulations and deregulation, and changes in a host of other sectoral administrations, namely, the rural, urban, commercial, industrial, and service areas of a country (Subramaniam, 1990; Dillman, 1994; United Nations-DESD, 1992; William, 1993).

The new administrative reforms in the developing and some of the developed nations appear to develop a fundamental structural integration linked to the leading Western nations, particularly the United States and Western European countries. This structural integration refers to the vertical and horizontal restructuring, bringing the administrative systems of other nations in line with the American and Western structures. Patterns of communication, decision-making, data analysis, strategic coordination, strategic planning, and other strategic managerial functions will likely be developed and integrated into a new hierarchical form along with a heterarchical structure denoting the multiple centers of command, decision coordination, and control[3] (Daft, 1992; Farazmand, 1994c; Hedlund, 1986). These multiple centers of the heterarchy will likely be located in key nations around the globe, but they will be linked together and controlled by the hierarchical command system located in the United States. Such a hierarchical–heterarchical structure of the new globally integrated administrative system will be facilitated by the advancement in new computer technologies in the United States and other leading capitalist nations.

The new global structure of the administrative system will increasingly socialize the bureaucrats of the international community into a global village-like culture in which values and norms of administrative behavior will originate from different sources, but eventually they will mainly be of the American ethnocentric nature. Of course, they may be influenced by other cultural perspectives. The critics and dependency theorists may label this cultural imperialism of the United States in the new era (New York Times, 1982; Parenti, 1989). Consequently, the dependency of developing countries on the West will likely be perpetuated, leading to a "neocolonization" of the developing nations of the South by the developed nations of the North.

Such a new global administrative system will no doubt have advantages as well as disadvantages for the developing countries of the global community.

One advantage would be the amount of administrative and managerial expertise that these countries will gain through this new structurally integrated system of administration. Second, their administrators will be exposed to the explosive knowledge constantly advancing in the multidisciplinary field of public administration and management. Third, their administrative system will likely be modernized along with the global administrative system, with its apex being in the United States. Fourth, their public administration will resemble the American and other Western administrative systems. Finally, this may shift the blame of their administrative failures externally to the Western/American system. No excuse, of course, but a practical possibility!

The disadvantages of such a globally integrated public administration system will be many, including the high dependency of these countries on Western technology, knowledge, expertise, and other resources. Not all information will be shared with the developing countries; strategic pieces will no doubt be withheld as special privileges. Also, administrative colonization will mean cultural transformation through the internalization of external values, norms, and procedures that are often at conflict with the native traditions.

THE GLOBAL BUREAUCRACY

The global coordination of this new global administrative system would also require a proliferation of the huge global bureaucracy characterized by diversity, extensive complexity, and significant interdependence. This global bureaucracy will probably be in two forms: an invisible one and a visible one.

The invisible bureaucracy is already in the making and will increasingly be developed into a full-fledged system around the complex web of economic, political, social, academic, cultural, and military relations between the United States and other nations, particularly the developing world. The U.S. Department of State, the C.I.A., the World Bank, IMF, U.S. AID, the multinational corporations and their subsidiaries, and other suprainternational organizations form such a global bureaucracy. Universities and colleges, sister cities, state governments, and other organizations have also been joining this bureaucracy. Their activities are generally coordinated and monitored by a complex system of communication, rules, laws, and regulations in the United States and other leading Western nations.

The second and visible global bureaucracy is the U.N. and its thousands of affiliated organizations and nonaffiliated associations created for a variety of purposes. Located in different parts of the globe, these U.N. organizations will likely continue to be expanded and more centralized to include more nations of the "global village" created and promoted by "the telecommunications and transport technologies" (Wilson, 1994). More and more international issues, global problems, and conflicts, and more global opportunities of diverse nature will likely be handled through these international organizations of the global bureaucracy. The United Nations at the apex of the visible global bureaucracy will be an important channel through which opportunities for research, development, and policy implementation will take place.

IMPLICATIONS FOR PUBLIC ADMINISTRATION THEORY AND PRACTICE

The New World Order and the global public administration with a global bureaucracy discussed above will have major implications for public administration theory, education, and practice. Students and scholars of public administration will be learning to think more globally rather than parochially. American public administration theory has been characterized by "ethnocentrism" (Caiden, 1991b; Farazmand, 1994d; Riggs, 1994; Thayer, 1981). As Caiden (1991b, p. 5) notes correctly, "even current attempts to reformulate American public administration theory despite their recognition of the global nature of the field still tend to be insular and myopic." American administrative theories and doctrines have often been "thwarted time and time again by aid recipients as being culturally imperialistic" (Caiden, 1991b, p. 5).

However, the ideal of a global public administration is increasingly finding its way in the frame of mind among American social scientists, including public administration theorists (Caiden, 1991b; Goodsell, 1990; Riggs, 1994). Citing the tradition of international business, finance, and the military, Goodsell argues that "a newly globalized civilian public administration can do the same, if equipped with equivalent resources and mandate" (Goodsell, 1990, p. 503). More and more textbooks in organization theory and management are treating sections on global aspects of business and public administration (Adler, 1991; Daft, 1992). Thinking globally enables public administration and organization theorists to understand better the field in general and American public administration in particular.

Another implication of this new global public administration will be the proliferation of research centers and other institutional arrangements in promoting research and development studies in a variety of public policy and public management subject areas. More universities are redirecting their focus of research activities on international and global aspects related to public policy and management. Experts on public administration, whether educators or private consultants, will be involved in research assignments and in a variety of training programs. This will likely broaden their understanding of and appreciation for other cultures and their administrative systems abroad.

As Heady (1991) notes, there is little known in the United States about the administrative features of small nations, such as the Scandinavian system of the Ombudsman. The new global administration will eventually make American theorists understand that there are historically rich traditions of excellent administrative theory development and practice of governance in other parts of the world, such as those found in the Middle East and Asia for millennia (Farazmand, 1994c; Whyte, 1957). Additionally, the former Soviet Union was managed by public administrators, and a great deal can be learned from them.

Still another implication of this new global public administration will be the vast opportunities that would be created by the global bureaucracies in the future. Training and development is one area in which numerous opportunities would be created. The global bureaucracy will be in need of expertise in a wide spectrum of fields and skills. The global bureaucracy will be an emerging organizational arrangement for the global public administration activity coordination in the future. Consequently, we might expect a new organizational person to emerge with a global I.D. for control purposes (Farazmand, 1994c).

A significant characteristic of the global public administration will be its high degree of professionalism, diversity, and demographic representation. However, it will not be representative in terms of public policy, organizational decision-making, and managerial and leadership structures. Still another implication will be the changed nature of elite orientation in the global public administration with the big multinational corporations and the governmental officials in the United States at the top level of the hierarchy, to be followed by significant professional managers in the middle, and the key bureaucrat and business leaders of the developing countries at the bottom. The last group in the hierarchy will be the professional administrators and bureaucrats – public and private – around the globe (Farazmand, 1994c).

The entire system of public administration around the globe will likely reflect the private, business/corporate interests and those of the dominant governments pursuing market-based policy interests. The elite orientation of the global public administration will be directly linked to the security and military–bureaucratic structure, as well as to the international corporate structure, which is highly concentrated and centralized. This would have serious implications for public administration in developed and developing nations, but it will be consistent with the New World Order. As corporations expand their global domains, so do their governments with larger and newer bureaucracies, civilian and military. They also require an expanding public administration to facilitate their operations and to protect their interests around the globe.

CONCLUSIONS

The New World Order has caused a restructuring and reshaping of the global power structure ever since the fall of the USSR and other socialist nations a few years ago. Under the two-world system of the Cold War era, superpower competition and rivalry had offered both advantages and disadvantages for peoples and nation-states around the globe. The entire world was divided between the two ideological, economic, military, political, and administrative orientations. Different nations sought alliance and protection from one superpower against the other.

Generally, the capitalists and landowners had strong allies in the West under U.S. leadership, while the less advantaged and the poor of the urban and rural areas found moral and political support in the East. Caught in the middle were the professional public administrators whose job was to implement public policy decisions. Public administration grew fast and became highly professionalized during the twentieth century.

With the fall of the Eastern superpower, the only superpower is the United States, determining the parameters and conditions of the New World Order that has significant political, military, economic, social, and administrative implications for developed and developing nations. The globalized slogans of democratization, marketization, and privatization have had and will continue to have significant consequences for public administration in the developed and developing worlds. While offering many advantages to peoples and their social systems around the globe, these slogans will also have significant negative and even dangerous consequences for many developing nations. In the developed world, the conservative ideology of the New World Order will promote the enterprise of public administration as a growing, sound field of study.

The emerging global public administration is based on a number of structural adjustments or readjustments that have been taking place around the globe. These readjustments have been in the forms of redefining the scope and boundaries of public and private sectors, of administrative reforms, of civil service reforms, of organizational reconfiguration and restructuring, and many more. The elite-oriented global bureaucracy will likely perform numerous functions and act as a conduit of international problem solving, policy development, and policy implementation toward achieving the goals of the New World Order. The emerging professionalized and elite-oriented global public administration will have significant implications for public administration theory and practice in developed and developing countries.

The implications of the New World Order and the emerging global public administration will likely be more negative than positive for developing nations. This is in part due to the aggravating economic and political situations that the conservative New World Order will likely produce for the majority of the population – the lower class and lower middle class of the urban and rural areas – in developing countries. Pushing marketization and privatization, with a globally dominant public administration model, will have a tendency to empower further the ruling elites – the big capitalists, large landowners, big corporate powers, and regimes that are too often corrupt, undemocratic, and repressive. Such a scenario will likely fuel a new wave of revolutionary upheavals, calling perhaps for another New World Order. A dialectical process of change and continuity will continue.

NOTES

1. An excellent analysis of this subject is presented by David Gibbs in his paper "Private Interests and Foreign Intervention: *Toward a* Business Conflict Model," presented at the 1991 Annual Conference of the American Political Science Association, Washington, DC, August 1991.

2. Evidence shows that "three-fourths of U.S. foreign-assistance money remains in the U.S." (Barry, 1984, p. 159*)*. According to AID administrator Peter Macpherson, "Two-thirds of what we give comes back in 18 months in the form of purchases" (*ibid.*).

3. For more information on the concept "heterarchy," see Hedlund (1986) and Daft (1992, pp. 238–243).

REFERENCES

Adler, N. (1991). *International dimensions of organizational behavior*. Boston: Kent Publishing Co.

Arrow, K. (1963). *Social choice and individual values*. New York: Wiley.

Ascher, K. (1987). *The politics of privatisation: Contracting out public services*. New York: St Martin's Press.

Bill, J. (1984). *Politics in the Middle East* (2nd ed.). Boston: Little, Brown and Co.

Binder, L. (1962). *Iran: Political development in a changing society*. Los Angeles: University of California Press.

Brzezinski, Z. (1986). *Game Plan: The geostrategic framework for the conduct of the U.S. Soviet contest*. Boston: Atlantic Monthly Press.

Buchanan, J., & Tullock, G. (1962). *The calculus of consent*. Ann Arbor: University of Michigan Press.

Caiden, G. (1991a). Administrative reform. In: A. Farazmand (Ed.), *Handbook of comparative and development public administration*. New York: Marcel Dekker, Chapter 27.

Caiden, G. (1991b). Getting at the essence of the administrative state. Paper presented at the 4th Annual Symposium of the Public Administration Theory Network. George Washington University, Washington, DC, March 21.

Carino, L. (1991). Regime change, the bureaucracy, and political development. In: A. Farazamand (Ed.), *Handbook of comparative and development public administration*. New York: Marcel Dekker, Chapter 54.

Cowan, L. G. (1990). *Privatization in the developing world*. New York: Praeger.

Daft, R. (1992). *Organizational theory and design* (4th ed.). New York: West Publishing Co.

Dahl, R. A. (1970). *After the revolution*. New Haven: Yale University Press.

Dahl, R. A. (1971). *Polyarchy: Participation and opposition*. New Haven: Yale University Press.

DeGregori, T. (1974). Caveat emptor: A critique of the emerging paradigm of public choice. *Administration and Society, 6*(2).

Diamond, L., Linz, J., & Lipset, S.M. (Eds). (1990). *Politics in developing countries: Comparing Experiences with Democracy*. Boulder, CO: Lynne Rienner Publishers.

Dillman, D. (1994). The Thatcher agenda, the civil service, and total efficiency. In: A. Farazmand (Ed.), *Handbook of bureaucracy*. New York: Marcel Dekker, Chapter 14.

DiPalma, G. (1990). *To craft democracies: An essay of democratic transitions*. Berkeley: University of California Press.

Downs, A. (1957). *An economic theory of democracy*. New York: Harper and Row.

Dye, T., & Zeigler, H. (1990). *The irony of democracy*. Pacific Grove, CA: Brooks/Cole.

Farazmand, A. (1989a). *The state, bureaucracy, and revolution in modern Iran: Agrarian reform and regime politics*. New York: Praeger.

Farazmand, A. (1989b). Crisis in the U.S. administrative state. *Administration and Society, 21*(2), 173–199.

Farazmand, A. (1991a). State tradition and public administration in Iran in ancient and contemporary perspectives. In: A. Farazmand (Ed.), *Handbook of comparative and development public administration*. New York: Marcel Dekker, Chapter 55.

Farazmand, A. (1991b). Bureaucracy and revolution: The case of Iran. In: A. Farazmand (Ed.), *Handbook of comparative and development public administration*. New York: Marcel Dekker, Chapter 55.

Farazmand, A. (1994a). Introduction: The multi-facet nature of organizations. In: A. Farazmand (Ed.), *Modern organizations: Administrative theory in contemporary society* (pp. xi–xxiii). Westport, CT: Praeger.

Farazmand, A. (1994b). Organization theory: An overview and appraisal. In: A. Farazmand (Ed.), *Modern organizations: Administrative theory in contemporary society* (pp. 3–54). Westport, CT: Praeger.

Farazmand, A. (1994c). Introduction. In: A. Farazmand (Ed.), *Handbook of bureaucracy*. New York: Marcel Dekker.

Farazmand, A. (1994d). *Administrative reform in developing countries*. Westport, CT: Green-
    wood (and JAI Press).
Frye, R. (1963). *The heritage of Persia*. New York: World Publishing Company.
Frye, R. (1975). *The golden age of Persia*. New York: Harper and Row.
Galbraith, J. K. (1974). The U.S. economy is not a free economy. *Forbes*, *113*(10), 99.
Garcia-Zamor, J.-C. (1992). Neoteric theories for development administration in the New
    World Order. Paper Presented at the 1992 Annual Conference of the American Society
    for Public Administration, Chicago, April 11–15.
Gibbs, D. (1991). Private interests and foreign intervention: Toward a business conflict model.
    Paper presented at the 1991 Annual Conference of the American Political Science As-
    sociation, Washington, DC, August.
Golembiewski, R. (1977). A critique of "democratic administration" and its supporting ide-
    ation. *American Political Science Review*, *17*(4), 1488–1507.
Goodsell, C. T. (1990). Emerging issues in public administration. In: N. Lynn & A. Wildavsky
    (Eds), *Public administration: The state of the discipline* (pp. 495–509). New York:
    Chattam House.
Habermass, J. (1975). *Legitimacy crisis*. Translated by Thomas McCarthy. Boston: Beacon.
Hamilton, E. (1989). *America's global interests: A new agenda*. New York: Norton.
Hayter, T. (1971). *Aid as imperialism*. London: Penguin Books.
Heady, F. (1991). *Public administration: A comparative perspective*. New York: Marcel Dekker.
Hedlund, G. (1986). The hypermodern MNC – a heterarchy. *Human Resource Management*,
    25(Spring), 9–36.
Heilbroner, R. (1990). *An inquiry into the human prospect*. New York: Norton.
Hermand, E., & Frank, B. (1984). *Demonstration elections*. Boston: South End Press.
Huntington, S. (1991). *The third wave: Democratization in the late twentieth century*. Norman:
    University of Oklahoma Press.
Jones, C. O. (1984). *An introduction to the study of public policy* (3rd ed.). Monterey, CA:
    Brooks/Cole.
Kennedy, P. (1989). *The rise and fall of the great powers: Economic change and military conflict*.
    New York: Vintage Books.
Keohane, R., & Ney, J. (1977). *Power and interdependence*. Boston: Little, Brown.
Khator, R. (1992). Administering the environment in an interdependent world. Paper presented
    at the 1992 Annual Meeting of the American Society for Public Administration, Chi-
    cago, April.
Kitschell, H. (1992). Political regime change: Structure and process-driven explanations. *Amer-
    ican Political Science Review*, *86*(4), 1028–1034.
Klare, M. (1988). *North–South vs. East–West: Shifting focus of U.S. military power*. Middle East
    Report, March/April.
Klare, M. (1990). *Policing the Gulf and the world*. The Nation, October 15.
Lenin, V. I. (1971). *State and revolution*. New York: International Publisher.
Letwin, O. (1988). *Privatizing the world: A study of international privatization in theory and
    practice*. London: Cassell.
Lowenthal, A. (Ed.) (1991). *Exploring democracy: The United States and Latin America*.
    Baltimore: Johns Hopkins University Press.
Luebert, G. (1991). *Liberalism, fascism, or social democracy: Social classes and the political
    origins of Regimes in interwar Europe*. New York: Oxford University Press.

Macpherson, C. B. (1987). *The rise and fall of economic justice*. New York: Oxford University Press.

McClintock, C. (1987). Agricultural policy and food security in Peru and Ecuador: Agrarian reform in reverse: The food crisis in the third world. Boulder, CO: Westview Press.

New York Times. (1982). January 13.

O'Connor, J. (1973). *The fiscal crisis of the state*. New York: St. Martin's Press.

Offe, C. (1985). *Contradictions of the welfare state*. Cambridge: MIT Press.

Ostrom, V., Jr., (1973). *The intellectual crisis of public administration in America*. Alabama: University of Alabama Press.

Parenti, M. (1978). *Power and the powerless*. New York: St. Martin's Press.

Parenti, M. (1988). *Democracy for the Few*. New York: St Martin's Press.

Parenti, M. (1989). *The sword and the dollar: Imperialism, revolution, and the arms race*. New York: St Martin's Press.

Peters, G. (1994). Government reorganization: A theoretical analysis. In: A. Farazamand (Ed.), *Modern organizations*. Westport, CT: Praeger, Chapter 4.

Riggs, F. W. (1994). Public administration: A futuristic vision. *International Journal of Public Administration, 12*(3), 355–384. (Also in J. Rabin, S. M. Bartell & R. F. Munzenrider (Eds). *E-book, principles and practices of public administration* (Part 2.2). New York: Marcel Dekker, 2003).

Rosenau, J. N. (1990). *Turbulence in world politics*. Princeton: Princeton University Press.

Rosenbloom, D. (1989). *Public administration: Understanding management, politics, and law in the public sector* (2nd ed.). New York: Random House.

Rostow, W. W. (1988). Beware of historians bearing false analogies. *Foreign Affairs, 66*(4), 863–868.

Savas, E. S. (1982). *Privatizing the public sector*. Chatham, NJ: Chatham House.

Schutz, B., & Slater, R. (Eds) (1990). *Revolution and political change in the third world*. Boulder, CO: Lynne Rienner.

Sedghi, H. (1992). The Persian gulf war: The new international order or disorder. *New Political Science, 21–22*, 41–60.

Subramaniam, V. (Ed.) (1990). *Public administration in the third world*. Westport, CT: Greenwood.

Thayer, F. (1981). *An end to hierarchy and competition* (2nd ed). New York: Watts.

Trudeau, E. (1992). The world order checklist. *New York Times*, February 19, p. 2.

United Nations-DESD. (1992). Size and cost of the civil service: Reform programmes in Africa. New York: DESD/ESM.92/1, INT-90-R78.

Vernon, R. (1988). *The promise of privatization: A challenge for US policy*. New York: Council on Foreign Relations.

Waldo, D. (1990). Bureaucracy and democracy: Reconciling the irreconcilable. In: F. Lane (Ed.), *Current issues in public administration* (pp. 455–568). New York: St Martin's Press.

Whyte, W. (1957). *The organization man*. New York: Anchor.

William, J. O. (1993). Inside Chinese bureaucracy: Civil service reform in the Ministry of Light Industry. *International Journal of Public Administration, 6*(7), 1035–1052.

Wilson, D. (1994). Bureaucracy in international organizations: Building capacity and credit-ability in a newly interdependent world. In: A. Farazmand (Ed.), *Handbook of bureaucracy*. New York: Marcel Dekker, Chapter 19.

Wise, C. (1994). The public service configuration problem: Designing public organizations in a
    pluralistic public service. In: A. Farazmand (Ed.), *Modern organizations: Administration
    in contemporary society*. Westport, CT: Praeger, Chapter 3.
Ziegler, H. (1964). *Interest Groups in American Society*. Englewood Cliffs, NJ: Prentice-Hall.

FURTHER READING

Cook, P., & Colin, K. (1988). *Privatization in less developed countries*. New York: St Martin's
    Press.

GLOBAL PERSPECTIVE ON COMPARATIVE AND INTERNATIONAL ADMINISTRATION

Fred W. Riggs

The year 2000 marks not only the start of a new century and millennium, but also a turning point in world history that has, in fact, already started. Its dominant forces are well captured by the word globalization, which symbolizes a fundamental transformation in the role of the post-Westphalian state. *Public Administration* as the study of governance in America, and *Comparative Administration* with its complementary focus on the administrative problems of new states, have both been state-centered, taking for granted the salience and sovereign role of independent states in a world-system of states. Regardless of how the political institutions of these states were formed, we have assumed that they all required public bureaucracies able to attend to the most important needs of their citizens in an increasingly complicated age of industrialization and interdependence. That assumption has informed our analysis of the American system as though it were a prototype that could serve as an exemplar for all the new states born out of the collapse of the modern empires that had first occupied the world and then shredded it by their great inter-imperial wars.

Comparative Public Administration: The Essential Readings
Research in Public Policy Analysis and Management, Volume 15, 729–733
Copyright © 2006 by Elsevier Ltd.
All rights of reproduction in any form reserved
ISSN: 0732-1317/doi:10.1016/S0732-1317(06)15032-0

The end of the "Cold War" actually brings this period in world history to a close. Although during the past half-century we learned to focus on the ideological aspects of the gigantic power struggles among the remaining super-powers, this focus blinded us to a more far-reaching transformation whose true character is only now beginning to become apparent. We have tended to assume that the collapse of the Soviet Union would launch a "new world order" in which democracy and capitalism would prevail and the United States would now, as the sole super power in the world, be enabled to play the role of peace maker and exemplar for the global development of a world system marked by continuously expanding prosperity, peace, and justice.

Unfortunately for Americans, this rosy illusion is scarcely shared by anyone in other countries of the world, and many Americans are themselves becoming disillusioned by the rise of transnational crime, ethnic protest movements, vast environmental challenges, floods of refugees and apparently insoluble nationalist conflicts and local wars. This disillusionment manifests itself in a new kind of isolationism well reflected in the unwillingness of Congress to pay its share of the costs of the United Nations even though we have come increasingly to depend on its umbrella to implement costly peace-keeping and humanitarian projects throughout the world. The technological revolution best exemplified by the INTERNET, the World Wide Web and the universal availability of person-to-person linkages for every imaginable purpose by means of instantaneous e-mail access to individuals located anywhere in the world. Increasingly states are side-lined as useful but not essential players in the games of world politics.

The INTERNET well symbolizes the trans-state networks that by-pass state authority and create new sodalities of interest and power most conspicuously manifested in the rise of gigantic multi-national corporations, often headquartered in tax havens and money laundering archipelagos of sub-visible power, thereby undermining the capacity of responsible states to fund the necessary services that we have learned to count on as prerequisites of a civil society. The MNCs are augmented by powerful ethnic nations whose diasporas create global structures of power that challenge the fragile authority of new authoritarian regimes whose inability to maintain order and provide basic public services merely intensifies the anarchy, crime, and protest movements that make many of the new "quasi-states" essentially non-viable. The patent inability of contemporary states to cope effectively with a host of gigantic problems created by the interdependence of a global industrializing world system heightens momentous trends that students and practitioners of public administration alike need to think about, analyze and try to deal with. To think that we can continue to rely on stale and out-moded ways of understanding our situation in the world is, indeed, to blind ourselves to the emerging realities of globalization as an overwhelming reality.

To be more concrete, can we not visualize the new problems and pos-sibilities that will confront us in the coming years, decades, century and millennium? Let me offer a few suggestions.

1. *The Decline of States.* The state as we have known it will scarcely wither away, but many of its functions and resources will be transformed and replaced. Increasingly, its powers will move to trans-state organizations created by governments and by non-governmental groups (both com-mercial and not-for profit in character). This makes the comparative study and administration of international organizations of all kinds in-creasingly fundamental to the survival of our global world system. Ferrel Heady in the recent SICA issue of PAR stressed the great importance for comparativists of paying serious attention to the organization design and functions of international organizations. I can only applaud and support his appeal: globalization now makes it even more urgent than it has been in the past. These trans-state organizations face huge problems that hinge on the activities of non-state actors of many kinds that states by them-selves can no longer manage. Useful as administrative reform may be, it no longer offers solutions for many of the most urgent problems con-fronting our world today.

   Consider that today's news includes a report of U.S. efforts to help Iran, despite our antipathy for this Islamic regime, to cope with drug trafficking across its frontiers with Afghanistan. Neither Iran nor the U.S. nor any established IGO is able to stop the growing flood of dan-gerous drugs reaching the world markets that are well organized globally by illegal syndicates whose power has become a growing threat to the health and good order of many states, including our own. Of course, this is not a new problem – we have simply become aware that it not only involves our familiar frontiers in the Western hemisphere but it is, indeed, a global problem.

2. *Sub-State Entities.* The authority of independent states will also, increas-ingly, devolve to sub-state authorities. This is already apparent in the United States in the insistent demands, both locally and in Congress, to devolve more functions to state, city, and local governments each of which, incidentally, has become increasingly active on its own authority in world affairs. The rising demand by indigenous peoples and other

non-state nations for autonomy or independence as "nations within a nation" is encouraged by the United Nations and by many of our own citizens who have come to recognize the gross injustices that were historically imposed on the peoples we conquered and abused.

The new knowledge of how to organize, to use the internet, to acquire weapons, and to coordinate global struggles in a rapidly evolving network of ethnonational movements will make their demands increasingly irresistible. Public administration needs, therefore, to take into account an increasingly complex network of cross-cutting jurisdictions that go far beyond traditional notions of federalism to create what I have begun to think of as a *"syntropic"* world system.

3. *Syntropy*. This is not the notion of a "world federation of states" which some of our idealists have long pressed for an antidote to the anarchy of increasingly violent world wars. Indeed, any such federation would probably collapse from its own internal contradictions, or generate some kind of global authoritarianism. By contrast, a syntropic system involves a host of autonomous and self-powered organizational structures that are able to take form, manage their own affairs, negotiate with each other, sometimes engage in violent confrontations but often evolve workable compromises and mutual adaptations. In a way, this is just the kind of world system (order? disorder?) that we already have. We will not, I think, have any more world wars, and major clashes between "civilizations" is a fantasy-based on the illusion that a new basis for gigantic power struggles is bound to emerge. We tend to remain preoccupied with conditions in a world that is already dead, but we are too close to the emergent new world system to discern its real shape.

I do not see any likelihood that any states in the world today will aggregate enough power and ambition to create new empires, no super states or mega-polities are likely to emerge. Instead, we are already living in a syntropic world (a world that links synthesis with entropy). Many of our colleagues have already started to recognize and talk about this phenomenon under the heading of "globalization."

My personal vision of the challenge facing comparative and international administration is to face up to the implications of such a system. How can the officers (military and civil) who are working in a host of trans-state, sub-state, and state organizations understand and master the tasks they need to perform? In the past, each of them has accepted a set of prescribed duties-based on the policies of whatever organization, at each of these levels, provides the context for their employment. Rarely, however, will it be possible during the coming years for these "glocal" bureaucrats (the office holders of a wide range of global and local organizations – including states, as residual if battered strongholds of power) to focus on the tasks prescribed for them by formal political authorities. Instead, we need to recognize that office holders (bureaucrats) are themselves the bearers of a kind of personal sovereignty that compels them to take stock of their own actions in terms of a higher morality anchored in global accountability, and at the same time to become increasingly aware of the competing sensitivities and obligations of the officers of other organizations with which they must interact.

In such a context, office holders are also power holders – their interests and capabilities interface with a wide range of overlapping and competing organizations and agencies, at all levels. Whether or not our syntropic world will survive and satisfy the basic needs of a rapidly growing world population, providing for the survival of a global environment that has become increasingly threatened by the mining of resources and pervasive pollution, is a question specialists on public administration, both in academia and government, now need to think about most seriously.

The SICA-sponsored mini-symposium in Seattle has been organized in response to a manifesto that points to "Sweeping global trends [that] are forcing public administrators here in the US to confront such new issues as transnational organizations and cultural differences." I applaud this initiative but urge participants to think even more broadly and fundamentally about the far-reaching transformations of states and the system of states that globalization is producing. We are, indeed, on the hinge of a major transition in world history. We need to think more profoundly about the fundamental changes this transition will necessitate in the way organizations at all levels, throughout the world, will have to manage their activities. Among these changes will be far-reaching transformations in the design and structure of the American system of government. This means that we can no longer take our own forms of governance for granted as a kind of safe haven for orthodoxy or a model for others to follow – instead, we need to examine ourselves as well as the rest of the world in a global framework that is rapidly replacing the fading world of Westphalia. We are, indeed, on the threshold of a new era that compels us to think and act with far more imaginative creativity than ever before.

CHANGING EUROPEAN STATES, CHANGING PUBLIC ADMINISTRATION:

INTRODUCTION

Walter Kickert and Richard Stillman

More than at any time during the half century since World War 11, Europe's roughly 320 million people and its state structures are experiencing decisive, far-reaching forces for change in the 1990s. These powerful forces include:

- Collapse of the Soviet Union and the end of the Cold War;
- Reunification of Germany;
- Creation of newly independent post-socialist East European nations;
- Growth of ethnic tensions and New Right politics;
- Outbreak of civil war and ethnic cleansing in the former Yugoslavia;
- Strengthening of overhead European Union authority;
- Trends toward regionalization below the European nation-state;
- Prolonged European unemployment above 11 percent;
- Reduction of American forces and redirection of NATO policies;
- Intense competition from Pacific Rim and American businesses;
- Increasingly wired society, governments, and businesses; and
- Redefined international responsibilities for immigration, population growth, health and environmental policies.

Comparative Public Administration: The Essential Readings
Research in Public Policy Analysis and Management, Volume 15, 735–740
Copyright © 2006 by Elsevier Ltd.
All rights of reproduction in any form reserved
ISSN: 0732-1317/doi:10.1016/S0732-1317(06)15033-2

How do these external and internal forces forge new tasks and responsibilities for European states? In the process, how do they serve to restructure
and redefine their administrative systems? Will these changes shift European
priorities and alter the content of activities that European public administrators perform? How well – or poorly – do they carry out their new roles?

What does this rapidly changing European state system mean for the
scope and substance of European administrative sciences – their values,
methods, and approaches to training and research?

In the past, the evolution of the European state and the development of
European public administration have been closely linked. The rise of the
absolutist European state in the 16th and 17th centuries in Germany and
France led to a significant expansion of state functions, increased the numbers
of state officials, and resulted in the growing complexity of responsibilities
especially in the fields of revenue collection, military professionalism, and
economic affairs. European universities responded by establishing the first
chairs of "cameralism" (1729) concerned with training public personnel as
well as the study of nation–state structures and their official management. By
the end of the 1700s, every German university had created a new chair in this
field, and France had developed the new *science de la polity*, although without
separate university chairs or curricula for public administration. The emerging concept of "state" played a central role during the 17th and 18th centuries
in developing both the German *polizey wissenshaft* and the French *science de
la polity*. By the end of the 18th century, administrative sciences, with texts,
journals, and schools, became well established throughout continental Europe. Americans had to wait neatly a century for Woodrow Wilson's "The
Study of Administration" (1887) to argue for this new field in America.

The changes in Europe after the French Revolution in the late 18th century did not leave European public administration unaffected. The abolition
of absolute monarchy and the transfer of power to a liberal constitutional
state meant that government's primary role became the protection *of* rights
and liberties: the right of property, basic for free-market capitalism, and
individual human rights, and liberties basic for a parliamentary *Rechtsstaat*
(i.e., law-based state). The state's *raison d'être* became making and enforcing
laws. Thus, the study of public administration shifted to the study of administrative law. Lawyers replaced managers as "the elite" in the upper and
middle ranks of government. So when the European absolutist state gave
way to the European constitutional state – in which parliament, not the
crown, largely directed national policies by the mid-19th century – a
new type *of* continental European public administration emerged. Cameralism was replaced almost entirely by a judicial approach to training public

officials. By the dawn of the 20th century, the "scientific," positive-law tradition came to dominate the education of bureaucrats throughout continental Europe. It emphasized such topics as the rights and duties of citizens *vis à vis* the state, integration of the nation–state, and definition of its welfare functions. However, England (and some small European nations) resisted these continental trends. In England, the liberal arts, Oxbridge tradition remained the preferred route of preparation for the public service throughout much of the 20th century.

Will the 1990s, given the decisive aforementioned transformations occurring in the European nation–state system, prove to be a historic watershed, a major turning point for the European state and its administrative sciences? At the close of the 20th century, will the redefinition and redirection of basic tasks, responsibilities, and purposes of the nation–state once again influence a fundamental reform of European administrative systems and administrative sciences? If so, what new, unforeseen directions will European public administration take in theory and in practice?

This Public Administration Review (*PAR*) symposium attempts to examine these important questions and explore the changing patterns of contemporary European public administration as it evolves in theory and practice in five countries or regions: France, Germany, the Netherlands, Scandinavia, and the United Kingdom. The editors selected these five to study because: (1) they play pivotal roles as "the leading edge" of European public administration reform; (2) each reflects an example of a major European state style – Napoleonic (France), Germanic (Germany), Anglo-Saxon (Britain), or a combination (Holland and Scandinavia); (3) they represent both large and small nations; and (4) they also symbolize the most interesting and influential changes in administrative sciences currently happening within Europe. Space limitations obviously precluded coverage of all European nations in this *PAR* symposium.

The authors chosen to write the following essays are among the most prominent and respected European administrative scholars: Professor Jacques Chevallier, Université Panthéon-Assas (Paris, France); Professor Wolfgang Seibel, the University of Konstanz (Germany); Professor Waiter Kickert, Erasmus University (Rotterdam, the Netherlands); Professor Christopher Pollitt, Dean of Social Sciences, Brunel University (Middlesex, England); and Professor Torben Beck Jørgensen, Institute of Political Science, University of Copenhagen (Denmark).

Each author was asked to:

1. Introduce to an American audience recent developments in contemporary European administrative sciences, including the major schools

of thought, scholars, texts, and intellectual trends in their respective countries or regions;

2. Relate these administrative theoretical developments to recent changes in the European nation–state system relative to their respective countries or regions;

3. Outline these new theoretical and practical developments in order to generalize about the present and future directions of European public administration for the 21st century; and

4. Raise the germane issues, dilemmas, and challenges for the future agenda of European public administration.

It may surprise American readers that the theme(s) addressed by the authors in this *PAR* symposium is "a first of its kind," not only for Americans, but Europeans as well. No systematic overview has been published to date by European – or American – scholarly journals on this topic. So perhaps this symposium can break new ground and stimulate further debate and research on both sides of the Atlantic.

However, it is reasonable to ask: why should an American audience care about this topic? In particular, why should busy American public administrators find this symposium worthwhile *or* helpful? Why should Americans bother to read about what is happening to European public administration?

This topic may seem remote to many in the United States, but is it? First, the United States, for better or worse, is increasingly interconnected globally with administrative systems throughout the world. International influences significantly shape the course of *both* private and public American administration. Therefore, simply learning about what occurs in Europe, one of the largest and most powerful regions on earth, is vital to the conduct and thinking about public administration in the United States.

Second, Europe, of course, is not just any region in the world but the founding source of American constitutionalism as well as its public administration. While the American founders rejected many European practices, they adopted many critically important ones. From the 18th century heritage of the U.S. Constitution to the late 19th century founding of American public administration, European thinkers and institutions were immensely influential role models. James Madison and the other Federalists drew on Locke, Hume, and Montesquieu, to name a few; Woodrow Wilson and other founders of American administrative science looked to Mill, Bagehot, and Von Stein, to name others. There has always been a brisk trade, back and forth, in terms of institutions and ideas. Today is no different. What happens to Europe, therefore, should be of no small interest to those

Americans concerned with acquiring a better perspective on their own past and present governmental system.

Third, this symposium can be invaluable to those Americans interested in gaining a deeper comprehension about their future. The U.S. administrative system and its administrative sciences, much like European public administration, are experiencing rapid changes because of a variety of complex environmental factors. Viewing the profound transformations of the European state and their influence on public administration may assist Americans to make some sense of what is happening to them. This is not to suggest that both Europeans and Americans are enduring the same transitions – nor are they necessarily converging in their cultural patterns of change. Indeed the patterns of change may well be dissimilar. However, a study of the comparisons can be an important way to see more clearly the unique aspects of these changes and their current directions.

Finally, this symposium may perhaps serve to stimulate further research in comparative public administration. Regrettably, comparative public administration research has been poorly funded in the United States in recent years. Whereas the 1950s and 1960s saw comparative studies as a fruitful and flowering subfield (mostly aimed at Asia, Latin America, India, Africa, *and not Europe*), the 1970s and 1980s proved to be a relatively dry spell in this valuable research arena. Thus, much of our comparative research is now badly dated and of little use for comprehending the administrative world of the 21st century. Possibly, the publication of this *PAR* symposium can encourage renewed academic interest in this sadly neglected subfield.

Planning for this symposium began in fall 1991, when the two editors first met at Leiden University in the Netherlands. Later in spring 1993, the symposium idea developed in more detail after a second meeting at Budapest University of Economic Sciences in Hungary. A proposal was formalized by that summer and submitted to *PAR*. The editors wish to thank Professor David Rosenbloom, the editor in chief of *PAR* and Professor Melvin Dubnick, the managing editor, for commissioning this symposium and for their sustained support of this project. We have benefited as well from the advice of Professor Geert Bouckaert, Public Management Training Center, Catholic University of Leuven, Belgium, who is the European correspondent for *PAR*. Support for a meeting of the authors and editors at the 10th anniversary of the founding of the Leiden–Erasmus Public Administration Programs on October 29, 1994, where draft essays were presented, was funded by Erasmus University, Rotterdam. The editors wish to thank Erasmus University for the generous funding that proved so helpful in preparing this symposium, as well as Professor Ferrel Heady, Professor

Emeritus, the University of New Mexico; Professor Louis Gawthrop, University of Baltimore; Professor Dwight Waldo, Professor Emeritus, the Maxwell School, Syracuse University; and Professors Jos C. N. Raadschelders and Mark R. Rutgers, both of Leiden University, the Netherlands, for their useful ideas and suggestions. Thanks must also go to Dean E. Driscoll Poole for support.

CHANGING EUROPEAN STATES, CHANGING PUBLIC ADMINISTRATION:

PUBLIC ADMINISTRATION IN STATIST FRANCE

Jacques Chevalier

ABSTRACT

The French strong stare tradition decisively shapes both its past and present development of public administration. France created some of the earliest continental administrative institutions and the first studies of public administration. The development of the French liberal stare in the 19th century led to the predominance of law and lawyers emphasizing the guarantee of citizens' rights and limits on state power. The shift to law eclipsed social science-based public administration. Since the 1960s, for various reasons, France has witnessed the reemergence of a broader administrative science, with law-based models competing with managerial and sociological-based models. Today several analytical approaches exist, reflecting a complex and rich pluralism, although legal dogma remains strong and poses dilemmas for the independence of French administrative sciences.

Comparative Public Administration: The Essential Readings
Research in Public Policy Analysis and Management, Volume 15, 741–758
Copyright © 2006 by Elsevier Ltd.
All rights of reproduction in any form reserved
ISSN: 0732-1317/doi:10.1016/S0732-1317(06)15034-4

The development of administrative science in France is inextricably linked
to a particular French model of the state. The uniqueness of the state in
France rests on the combination of two phenomena.

The first of these phenomena is the stare's social autonomy, which is
guaranteed by a series of protective arrangements. In France, this autonomy
is accentuated by its combination of three different dimensions: an organic
autonomy, which clearly defines the state's contours and ensures its unin-
terrupted functioning; a legal autonomy, which is expressed in the application to the state apparatus of distinct rules which form exceptions to
common law; and, finally, a symbolic autonomy, in which the state presents
itself as the incarnation of a general interest that transcends the particular
interests that dominate the private sphere. The foundations of bureaucratic
organization (only a few examples of which existed under the *Ancien Régime*
and only at the ministry level) were laid under the Empire, but it was not
until the end of the 19th century that the logic of professionalism was
imposed through the spread of recruitment by examination and the granting
to civil servants of guarantees against the arbitrary nature of politics. The
state's autonomy was reinforced by its legal emancipation from the common
law. Here again, even if some foreshadowing elements are to be found under
the *Ancien Régime*, the appearance of a body of administrative law dates
from the creation of the *Conseil d'Etat* in the eighth revolutionary year. The
state's special status was thus guaranteed by the powers of legal dogma,
contrary to the British notion of the rule of law. Finally, the ideology of the
general interest exists to maintain a belief, on the part of both public servants and private citizens, in the uniqueness of the public sphere: the state
is set up as the organizing and totalizing principle that permits society
to achieve integration, to make its unity real by overcoming individual
identifications and sectarian selfishness.

The second and closely related phenomenon is a social supremacy, illustrated by France's deeply rooted tradition of interventionism. Already
under the absolutist regime, the state had broad and diversified functions,
not only those associated with the monarchy but also social, cultural, and
economic functions. This interventionism did not weaken at any time during
the 19th century. Despite a liberal discourse, which advocated strict controls
on the state, justified by the primacy of the individual and by a belief in the
benefits of a "natural" order, the state continued to take on wider functions.
Although the nature of its social interventions changed at the end of the
century, the state remained active in the economic sphere, maintaining regulatory services, creating the basic infrastructure indispensable to the expansion of production, and taking the place of private enterprise in running

unprofitable services. Based on these traditions and nourished by a belief that state management was justifiable for the sake of the public interest, the welfare state gained acceptance easily in France. Even more than in other Western countries, the state then established a veritable protectorate over social life through the linked development of functions of economic regulation and of social redistribution.

This notion of the state was obviously propitious for the development of an administrative science. On the one hand, the sharp differentiation between the state and society implied the need to create a specific body of knowledge concerning public administration, with no question of diluting it in a more general science of organization. On the other, the state's preeminent status justified the study of the structures and functioning of the apparatus through which the state carried out its social interventions. All the conditions indispensable to the existence of an independent science of public administration were, therefore, present, a fact that explains the rapid emergence of such a science in France. The underlying political and ideological stakes, however, were also a cause of confusion and fuzzing of categories. More than elsewhere perhaps, administrative science in France has had great difficulty in fulfilling the epistemological conditions necessary to strengthen it as a science.

THE GENEALOGY OF ADMINISTRATIVE SCIENCE

The appearance of an applied administrative science in France coincided with, and was intended to contribute to, the setting up of modern state and administrative structures. Nevertheless, the advent of the liberal state was to modify the viewpoint and the agenda of this "science" and lead to its decline as it was supplanted by administrative law. Only the growth of state interventionism, in the second half of the 20th century, brought about the rebirth of a body of thought concerning administration that would attempt to throw off the ascendancy of the law.

THE CONSTRUCTION OF THE NATION-STATE AND THE BIRTH OF AN APPLIED SCIENCE OF PUBLIC ADMINISTRATION

Closely tied to the development of the monarchical state and the rise of administrative centralization was the emergence in France at the beginning of the 18th century of a science of organization that foreshadowed German

cameralistik theory. Codes of civil organization and administrative dictionaries were drawn up by jurists and civil service professionals (De la Mare's
Traité tie police, which was published between 1705 and 1710, is the best
known and the most representative of these). These works were presented *as*
empirical surveys of the field, Free from doctrinal pretensions, and intended
principally to inform readers about administrative practices and to find
ways of ensuring the effective management of public affairs.

This science of organization was continued during the 19th century by
more ambitious works, which set out to formulate the underlying principles
of administrative actions. Charles-Jean Bonnin was the first in France to
break away from the earlier tradition. Claiming to "treat administration as a
science," he insisted on the necessity for a systematic and descriptive study
of public administration, endeavoring to "determine, first of all, the general
principles covering this subject." This approach was adopted, during the
first half of the 19th century by those interested in administrative questions.

This model of administrative science appeared from then on to be a
"social science" in the strongest sense of the term, and a total science because it claimed to be able to master all the social data informing administrative action, with the help of the most varied investigative tools,
particularly statistics. It tended to incorporate what would later come under
the heading of political science, economic science, or sociology, but it had an
essentially pragmatic aim in seeking to improve the effectiveness of state
action, and thus social well being. Therefore it was thought indispensable to
teach this type of administrative science to future civil servants. Because not
enough administrative science was taught in the faculties of law, a debate
began under the July Monarchy about the appropriateness of creating
"faculties of administration," which led in 1849 to the creation of a short-
lived School of Administration. The opening in 1872 of the *Ecole Libre ties
Sciences Politiques* represented a continuation of this movement.

It might seem that the development of administrative science had taken a
decisive step forward, but the expansion of administrative law studies, the
result of the growth of liberal thought, blocked this development and led to
a long eclipse of a science that had not had time to assert itself.

THE DEVELOPMENT OF THE LIBERAL STATE AND
THE ECLIPSE OF ADMINISTRATIVE SCIENCE

With the advent of the liberal state at the end of the 19th century, the problem
of a legal framework for the state came to the fore. The need was no longer

to reinforce a feared state power but to give guarantees against it, and these guarantees were to be found in the law. The promotion of the legally legitimate state brought the expansion of administrative law studies in countries like France where there was a demand for a special body of law, but this administrative law underwent a veritable transformation. Its existence was no longer perceived as a privilege for the civil service, but as a means of reinforcing its subordination. During this period, the applied science of public administration was relegated to the background; not only was it useless but it was dangerous as well because it sought to reinforce the efficiency of the civil service and thus its ascendancy over society. From then on, the attention of theoreticians was concentrated on curbing administrative actions, especially control by the courts, while the organization and the internal functioning of the state apparatus were left to the empiricism of administrators. During nearly a century, jurists gained a virtual monopoly in the field of administrative studies.

This predominance of the law and of legal disputes was not absolute. The preoccupations of the first theoreticians of administrative science in the 19th century did not completely disappear. The creation of the *École Libre Des Sciences Politiques* ensured the persistence of a view of administration other than the legalistic one. Answering a specific need, the *École* managed to monopolize a type of training that the faculties of law did not provide, and its dominance over the recruitment of upper civil servants clearly showed that it was not enough for them simply to be good lawyers. Next, a body of thought that focused on problems of internal organization and the management of services, and that was open to the innovations of business management, developed on the fringe of the university, and foreshadowed the renaissance in administrative science (Chardon, 1911; Fayol, 1916). Finally, in the faculties of law themselves, the preeminence of administrative law did not exclude a wider interest in the political and administrative sciences. The monopoly enjoyed by legal knowledge in the field of administrative studies was thus far from complete. Administrative law coexisted with other disciplines; nevertheless, these disciplines remained marginal compared to a law anchored in its certainties, enjoying great prestige, and assured, because of its powerful structure, a place of honor at the center of public law.

THE ADVENT OF THE WELFARE STATE AND THE REBIRTH OF ADMINISTRATIVE SCIENCE

The political and administrative sciences suffered a long eclipse. Their rebirth was inseparable from the advent of the welfare state. Indeed, the growth of administrative regulatory functions was to reveal the limits of the law. On the one hand, the imperative of efficiency was now emphasized. Required to play the role of a driving force in social life, the civil service had to aim at constantly improving the appropriateness of its management policies and the quality of the results – conformity with the law no longer constituted a sufficient guarantee. On the other hand (the two developments were closely linked), the new tasks that the civil services had to confront implied a profound transformation of its structures and methods, whereas the law not only could not be of any help but also seemed rather to be a factor of rigidity and sclerosis. It was, therefore, elsewhere that the ways and means of change had to be found. So the renaissance in administrative science was closely tied to movements for administrative reform and motivated by a desire for "rationalization."

The claim of administrative law to be the privileged if not exclusive tool for understanding administrative realities was again questioned. Among the jurists themselves, it became progressively clearer that the adoption of an exclusively legal point of view had resulted in certain weaknesses and inadequacies in their approach to the study of public administration. The need was no longer simply to study legal texts and jurisprudence but also to envisage, through empirical research, the conditions for the application of these rules, by sticking as close as possible to administrative reality. In a parallel development, starting in the 1950s, sociologists invaded the field of administrative studies. A very different vision of administration now appeared, thanks to the formulation of new problems and approaches, often breaking with classic legal analysis.

All the conditions were now present to allow the constitution of a new field of knowledge concerning administration. The development of administrative science was, however, to be put in jeopardy by controversies and uncertainties about the epistemological status of the discipline.

THE CONSTRUCTION OF
ADMINISTRATIVE SCIENCE

The 1960s in France were marked by a spectacular growth of studies claiming to draw their inspiration from administrative science. This development was accompanied by powerful tensions; research on many different topics, informed by diverse points of view, was now classed under the heading of administrative science. Three essential models existed: a legal model, whose essential goal was to arrive at a better knowledge of the structures and functioning of public administration, while emphasizing the reference to legal texts; a managerial model that was geared toward finding and implementing the most efficient management techniques and intended to go beyond the public/private split; and a sociological model, which aimed to improve the understanding of administrative phenomena with the aid of sociological concepts and methods.

The Legal Model

According to the legal model, the purpose of administrative science was the study of public administration, considered a unique institution, which could not be lumped with any other organization. Most jurists, who were interested in going beyond the narrowly legal and litigious points of view, referred to this model. Its importance was due to the still considerable preeminence of the law faculties in the reaching of administrative science.

In theory, the adherents of this approach were careful to distinguish administrative science from administrative law. The former was a descriptive discipline, with the aim of showing administration as it was, whereas the second was a normative discipline, based on the methods of formal logic and deductive reasoning. Both remained, in fact, broadly dependent on the models of administrative law. On the one hand, the object to be studied by administrative science was constructed based on legal criteria; if administrative *science* was concerned with public administration alone, it was because the latter had a specific status and was subject to a legal regime, which lay completely outside the common law. In the same way, the distinction between the civil service and the political realm was based on legal texts (and especially after 1958, on Article 20 of the Constitution according to which "the *civil* service is at the disposal of the government"). On the other hand, the law was still perceived as a privileged means of knowing about and understanding administrative realities, and this conviction had as a corollary a certain mistrust, even hostility, toward the sociological approach which was believed to neglect the importance of legal rules in administrative law and in *the con*duct of civil servants. The effort made to approach problems in a more concrete manner was thus not accompanied by a break with the modes of reasoning and concepts associated with administrative law. Highly representative of this legal approach were the first manuals of administrative science published at the beginning of the 1970s (Debbasch, 1971; Drago, 1971–1972), which had an analogous inspiration; even though they attempted to broaden and to go beyond the legal analysis of the civil service, nevertheless they remained faithful to the analytical framework and concepts furnished by administrative law. These manuals simply continued down the trail blazed by the *Traité de science administrative* (Langrod, 1966). The desire to provide an overview of the subject could not conceal the overwhelming predominance of jurists.

The Managerial Model

The managerial model lumped administration together with management and pursued an essentially pragmatic goal, since it sought to discover and put into practice the most rational and effective methods of organization. According to this model, administrative science appeared to be purely and simply another name for management theory. Nevertheless, with the progressive refinement of managerial theories, certain characteristics of the civil service had to be taken into account. Administrative science, therefore, tended more and more to become the branch of management theory, which was applied to public management.

The application of management theory to public administration came up against strong resistance in France where public administration had been based on diametrically opposed theories. Beginning in the 1960s, however, a true revolution in attitudes took place with the conversion of upper-level civil servants to managerial principles. The old axiom that public management could not be assessed in terms of efficiency gradually gave way to the idea that the civil service, like private enterprise, was under an obligation to work toward increased productivity and to rationalize its work methods by calling on modern techniques of organization and decision making. The movement for rationalizing budgetary choices, launched in 1967, constituted the first systematic and coherent attempt to experiment with management theory in the French civil service. This was closely related to the endeavor to formulate the principles of a new public management (Massenet, 1975), which meant the construction of a management theory that would take account of the unique aspects of public administration (Delion, 1969), the effectiveness of which cannot be reduced to simple efficiency.

This ambition led gradually to the formation of a true school of public management theory tied to the great French business schools (the *HEC* and the *ESSEC*) and to management programs in higher education. The publication of surveys of the work in the field (Laufer & Burlaud, 1980; Santo & Verrier, 1993) and the creation in 1983 of a specialized journal (*Politiques et management public*, editor-in-chief P Gibert) signaled the birth of a discipline for which the *Institut du Management Public* (a private research institute) provided a center of gravity and institutional support. The goal of this public management theory was resolutely utilitarian and task-oriented. Its objective was to create tools and define styles of management that would be appropriate to the unique nature of public institutions and would allow them to attain their assigned goals with maximum efficiency. In the 1980s, public management theory took on a new dimension with its application to public policy. Going beyond the narrow frame of organization that was its original interest, it now took a larger view of political and administrative actions in general by studying their tangible effects.

The Sociological Model

The development in the 1960s of an administrative science influenced by sociology was the product of work by three groups. First were political scientists, such as Nizard, Sfez, and Quermonne, who became interested in the administrative actor as part of projects in political sociology. Second, sociologists who became interested in public administration, either as part of a sociology of the state continuing in the tradition of Weber or (as in the case of Crozier, Grémion, or Thoenig) in the context of a sociology of organizations which was destined to grow spectacularly. Third, the jurists who tried to break away from legal dogma by reappropriating sociological knowledge. Sociological methods and concepts penetrated the field during the 1960s because of the intersection of the interests of sociologists in public administration and of political scientists and jurists in sociology. This led to a profound revolution in administrative studies. Abandoning legal norms, this sociologically inspired administrative science turned its attention to real administrative functioning, based on the observation of concrete administrative situations. The principle used in the approach was organizational, influenced by the achievements of the sociology of organizations. This sociological approach went from strength to strength in the 1960s and 1970s, gradually consolidating its position by discrediting, competing points of view. After many concrete studies had been published, theoretical works signaled the birth of a true discipline.

Three major currents claimed to represent this sociological approach. First, the sociology of organizations was represented above all by the *Centre de Sociologie des Organisations* (*CSO*), which, following Crozier (1963), produced many empirical inquiries into the mechanisms of decision making and the central bureaucracy, how corporate strategies are interwoven with public policy, the links between administrative organizations and their social partners, and the relations between the central and local levels in the political and administrative system. From a quite different point of view,

Darbel and Schnapper (1969–1972) endeavored to point out the sociocultural characteristics of civil servants. Next, studies of political sociology took the form of monographs on local power, the links between the civil service and politics (Birnbaum, 1977), bureaucracy and technocracy. Third, the decision-making approach, which stood midway between the other two, was exemplified by a series of works aimed at shedding light on the way decisions are made, by designating the various participants in this process and evaluating their influence (Jamous, 1969; Sfez, 1992).

This sociologically inspired administrative science, however, went through a period of stagnation during the 1980s, which can be explained by several different factors. The sociopolitical context characterized by the crisis in the welfare state and the law's return to the fore clashed with an administrative science that put the civil service at the heart of social processes, following the example of the 19th century. Furthermore, the limitations of a kind of sociological imperialism were revealed. Many different analyses of the civil service existed and administrative science could be confused with a simple administrative sociology. Finally, the organizational paradigm that had been the basis for this administrative science seemed to have exhausted its capacity for innovation, and much of the research in this period contented itself with applying approaches that were by now very familiar. This period of doubts and desertion (Thoenig, 1990) now seems to be behind us, thanks especially to the emergence of a new paradigm, that of public policy, which has permitted the revival of administrative research.

Thus, the administrative science that emerged in the 1960s seemed to be torn between opposite models, to the point that its coherence sometimes appeared doubtful. These divergences did not have only negative effects. The dynamism of administrative science during this period can be explained, at least partly, by the interplay of these oppositions, these confrontations, which helped to enliven the field and mobilize researchers. Nevertheless, the absence of a real scientific community could only harm the development of the discipline over the long term. Today, this period is clearly over.

THE PRESENT STATE OF FRENCH
ADMINISTRATIVE SCIENCE

At the end of an indispensable period of clarification, administrative science in France has succeeded in solidifying its position in the field of the social sciences. The first thing that needed to be clarified was the relation between administrative science and administrative law. To be sure, administrative science cannot ignore the essential place held by the law in administrative life, as, entirely molded by the law, the civil service is characterized by the high degree of legalization. Nevertheless, one cannot study administration through the prism of legal texts without taking those texts for the expression of reality and falling into the trap of normativism.

The second issue to be clarified was the relation between administrative science and management theory. Knowledge of the achievements of administrative science is useful in attempting to improve the functioning of public organizations or to make sure that decision making is based on more accurate information. As a social science, however, the goal of administrative science cannot be to define the principles of improved administrative efficiency, if it is to avoid the trap of pragmatism.

Also to be clarified was the relation between administrative science and sociology. To be sure, sociology has made a decisive contribution to the renaissance in administrative science by bringing out certain latent or hidden aspects of administrative realities, but sociology cannot claim to hold the only key to the understanding of administrative phenomena.

French administrative science is enriched by a variety of approaches and a diversity of areas of investigation that result from the achievements of rapid institutionalization.

Rapid Institutionalization

Administrative science in France since the beginning of the 1960s has benefited from solid institutional ties, calculated to ensure its expansion. First, the *Institut Français des Sciences Administratives* (*IFSA*) plays an essential role as a place for academics and civil service professionals to meet and exchange ideas. Close ties exist between the *IFSA* and the upper civil service, especially the *Conseil d'État*; the *IFSA* has its offices in the building that houses the *Conseil d'Etat*, and the institute's president and secretary-general are members of the *conseil*. These ties have allowed the *IFSA* to carry on regular activities such as conferences and publications including the *Cahiers tie IFSA*. More recently, the creation of regional divisions has extended the Institute's geographic influence. The *IFSA* has important contacts on the international level; it participates very actively in the work of the *Institut International des Sciences Administratives* (*IISA*), based in Brussels, and is well represented in its governing bodies.

Administrative science in France can also count on the network of *écoles administratives*, whether general – such as the *Ecole nationale d'administration* (*ENA*) or more specialized – the several *Instituts régionaux d'administrations*

(*IRA*). The practical expertise taught to civil servants in these schools not only makes extensive use of the achievements of administrative science but also contributes new approaches to the science (for example, the new emphasis on quality circles and human resource management), while conferences and seminars ensure the spread of these innovations. The *Institute International d'Administration Publique*, which serves as a vehicle for all projects in administrative cooperation, especially with African countries, has no intention of abandoning its basic research in administrative science. Administrative science, as a branch of political science, has been made part of classes in the faculties of law (generally at the advanced undergraduate level or in graduate specializations), and in the schools of political science, but it occupies only a minor place in these schools. Elsewhere, and especially in the business schools and management programs, administrative science gives way to more practical courses in public management.

As far as research and publications are concerned, the position of administrative science is less solid. The *Revue française d'administration publique* (which replaced in 1977 the 10-year old *Bulletin tie l'Institut*) can be considered to be in the field, whereas *Politiques et management public*, lies rather in the field of management theory, even if many of the articles which appear in it touch on questions of administrative science. Research groups in the universities or associated with the *Centre tie La Recherche Scientifique* rarely specialize in administrative science, as their activities stand at the intersection of several disciplines. Finally, research projects are labeled according to academic discipline, and administrative science does not appear on the official list of these disciplines.

The institutional position of administrative science does not mean that its social and political impact in France is very great. Indeed, one should not be misled by the success of a few popularizing works intended for a wide readership and the occasional interest shown by those in power. The audience for research publications remains small and the opinions of experts on administrative questions receive very little attention. The achievements of administrative science do not constitute a real guide for action in France (Thoenig, 1987). Furthermore, the position of administrative science has deteriorated during the last few years. In the scientific arena, researchers have tended to reduce their involvement in administrative science. While sociologists have turned to the study of other areas, administrative science has tended to be squeezed between the growth of political science and the resurgence of legal studies. In addition, the disciplines failure to obtain a separate status in university programs, especially at the doctoral level, has had the effect of putting young researchers in a difficult position. At the same time, the place of administrative science in the training of civil servants has been reduced in favor of more technical knowledge. Administrative and political sciences have gone from being required subjects to optional ones in the entrance exam at the *ENA*, and the *Instituts Regionaux d'Administration* have dropped courses in administrative science.

This reduced visibility of administrative science has, however, been compensated for by the spread of the discipline's approaches and analyses outside their original scope. The success of administrative science can be measured as well by the fact that it is no longer possible to study the administrative phenomenon using traditional approaches. In any case, the ebb in the fortunes of administrative science, which was inseparable from more general developments, especially the crisis of the welfare state, now seems to have been stopped.

Pluralism in Approaches

Administrative science in France continues to be characterized by varied approaches and is enriched by contributions from various sources. In the 1960s, as we have seen, administrative studies in France were a favorite area for confrontation between jurists and sociologists, both of whom were trying to appropriate the field. In fact, all the social sciences came to be interested in the civil service, with very different preoccupations, goals, and methods. For example, given that the civil service is not an immutable institution but is, in the words of Legendre (1968–1992), the fruit of "successive sedimentation," the study of history is indispensable to the study of developments in the administrative phenomenon (Burdeau, 1989; Thuillier; and Tulard). The geographical dimension is more recent with interest being shown in the way that the civil service takes up space and takes over a piece of territory by covering it with networks that allow it to control the population. The economic approach is more traditional. Public economics studies the forms and effects of the civil service's interventions in the economy and economic analyses of bureaucracy relate to the interpretation of the phenomenon of bureaucracy. There is a quite logical progression from there to a philosophical inquiry into the goals of the civil service, the values that inspire it, and the effects of its increasing hold on society. The contribution of linguistics is indispensable to the analysis of the content, mechanisms, functioning, and effects of an administrative discourse, which constitutes not just a simple technical medium but also a privileged vehicle for the inculcation of group of representations. Finally, no study of administrative behavior can be carried out without referring to the teachings of psychology, which help to explain the attitudes of partners in administrative relationships (CURAPP, 1985), and even more profoundly still, the teachings of psychoanalysis. If we admit that administrative power, like all power, is related to desire, then psychoanalysis can contribute to explaining its motivating forces and the relation of individuals to the law, the state, and bureaucracy (Legendre, 1976). For a long time, these different analyses of public administration were perceived as divided, fragmented, and heterogeneous. They seemed to be the concern of specialists, incapable of going beyond the narrow boundaries of their discipline. Starting in the 1960s, an effort was made to break down these impenetrable and sterile barriers between disciplines, to produce a new analysis of the civil services (Chevallier & Loschak, 1978); administrative science has thus become an interdisciplinary science.

Now that this stage has been reached, several analytical approaches to the administrative phenomenon exist, which lead to a relatively complex map of French administrative science. First, the institutional point of view conceives of the civil service as a product of history and society but nonetheless with a specific identity. Second, the organizational point of view puts the emphasis on the complex processes that go on inside the administrative entity. Finally, those interested in administrative action aim to shed light on the mechanisms by which the civil service acts in relation to society as well as the social impact of administrative functioning. The study of organizations has merged progressively with the study of administrative action, and this change expresses a change in the paradigm, which is dominant inside French administrative science.

These angles include different methodological options taking as their starring point either particular administrative actors, or the civil service conceived as an entity, a system. The strategic analysis of Crozier is the typical illustration of the first approach, centered on the participants (Crozier & Friedberg, 1977). Underlying this analysis is the hypothesis that an organization is structured around power relations, resulting from the interactions between the interdependent individuals and groups, which make up the organization. Focusing on the behavior and the strategies at work inside the organization, this analysis can be extended by taking into account the influence exerted on the organization by outside actors. Grémion (1976), for example, has shown, based on a study of the French political and administrative system, that power relations inside an organization cannot be studied without taking into account the networks of exchange woven between the organization and the environment; systems of action form between internal actors and their social team-mates. The systemic analysis focuses on the organization itself by analyzing the processes by which it succeeds in becoming a unified and active entity. From there, the way is open for a mote general theory of administrative systems. So it is that in the view of Timsit (1986), the construction of an administrative science would involve the definition of administrative constants, the finite number of elements that are inherent to all administrative systems. This would mean creating an administrative grammar, which would be applicable to all administrative models, whether practical or theoretical, and would be constructed around two basic precepts: relation and transformation.

Explanatory models have emerged, based on systems of interpretation that differ from social reality. The culturalist analysis has exerted a profound influence on French administrative science. This approach was the center of the analysis put forward starting in 1963 by Crozier, according to whom public administration, like any other organization, is the product of certain cultural traditions, and national peculiarities must be taken into account in analyzing it (see Sainsaulieu's (1987) idea of "national cultural contingency"). Thus the French administrative system would reproduce a typically French cultural model characterized by the isolation of individuals and groups; the impersonal and absolutist model of authority; difficulties in communication, ritualism, centralization. This analysis has been severely criticized as promoting a vision of culture that is at once idealistic, normative, and conservative, but the emphasis on organizational cultures has recently given it new life. This means defining the wealth of traditions and values that are peculiar to public administration and constitute a privileged means of regulating its internal functioning. On the other hand, the Marxist analyses, which endeavored to explain the logic of organization and evolution observable in public administration in terms of production relations (and which had a definite impact in the 1960s on studies of urban sociology and local power), suffered a clear loss of influence.

These different approaches have been tested in various areas of research, which have created a corpus of new analyses of the civil service.

THE VARIETY OF SUBJECTS FOR RESEARCH

Although French administrative science has progressively enlarged the scope of its investigations, different lines of research remain unequally developed. Some notable achievements can be cited.

Research on local administration occupies a unique position. Through it, administrative science, which had been buried since the end of the

19th century under the accumulation of legal studies and especially studies of litigation, began to reassert itself. The work of the *Centre de Sociologie des Organizations* (Crozier, Worms, Grémion, and Thoenig) at this time contributed to a profound renewal of the view of local administration inherited from legal theory, and the traces of this reconstruction persist today because local administration has remained the domain of choice and the cutting edge of research. This *over-development* is no doubt explained by considerations of proximity and accessibility; it also results from the facts of a socio-political nature. In France, local institutions have been the site of very profound change in society (the urban explosion), in politics (the decline of the notables), and in bureaucracy (the redrawing of administrative territorial boundaries in 1982). So it was logical that researchers' attention should turn to one of the favored sites for administrative change, and that the 1982 reform should be favored for the analysis of the system of relations between the civil service and society. The 1982 reform opened up a vast area of study for researchers in administrative science through observation of the concrete conditions of its application.

The analysis of the relations between rise civil service and the interests of the larger society constitute the second favored domain of investigation of administrative science. Nizard (1974) and Grémion (1976) revealed the existence of an intersection between the civil service and society, of systems of integrated and interdependent relationships, based on the notion of mutual dependence. Administrative bodies responsible for individual sectors came to take on a representative function (Nizard, 1974). By becoming the defender of the milieu for which it is responsible, each of these bodies appears to be not just society's messenger to the political powers, but equally the instrument for political action affecting society. These analyses served as a support for interpretations of French-style neocorporatism that multiplied during the 1980s. In a parallel development, the questioning of administrative secrecy through the adoption at the end of the 1970s of three major laws concerning computer files, access to documents, and the motives of decision making brought about the flourishing of analyses of relations between civil service and citizens (CURAPP, 1983, 1985, 1988), which had until then received very little attention.

The studies of the top ranks of the civil service, starting with the pioneering work of Darbel and Schnapper (1969–1972), followed by the studies by Suleiman (1976) and Birnbaum (1977), moved from the periphery of the administrative system to penetrate the central core, focusing on the group which, not content with being in charge of the civil service, also tends to colonize all positions of social power. This posed the question of the relation between the civil service and politics (Quermonne & Baecque, 1982; CURAPP, 1986) and made it necessary, following the path indicated by Jamous (1969) and Sfez (1992), to assess the importance of upper civil servants in decision-making processes and, more generally, in the central decision-making milieu (Grémion, 1979). Writers on public policy have taken over since the end of the 1980s, as methodological instruments have been developed that match the requirements of specific case studies (Padioleau, 1982; Thoenig, 1985; Mény & Thoenig, 1989; Muller, 1990).

Finally, although comparative studies have long remained the weak point of French administrative science, the gap is beginning to be filled (Timsit, 1987; Ziller, 1992). This is no doubt the indirect effect of the recent opening up of borders and of European integration, both of which have necessitated a comparison between French and other administrative models.

The present state of French administrative science is thus mixed. The undeniable growth in research and the spread of the discipline's approach to problems do not exclude persisting signs of fragility. Caught between legal dogma (which has found new material in the reactivation of the theme of the state's legal legitimacy and the increased power of the constitutional judge), public management theory (which is responding to the challenge of efficiency which now confronts public management), and political science (which always takes a broader and more integrative view) administrative science is having difficulty in staking an exclusive claim to its field of interest. It is nevertheless through such confrontations that a scientific community can achieve recognition and institutional status.

REFERENCES

Birnbaum, P. (1977). *Les sommets de l'Etat.* Seuil.

Burdeau, F. (1989). *Histoire de l'administration francaise du 18e au 20e sècles.* Montchrestien.

Chardon, H. (1911). *Le pouvoir administrative.* Perrin.

Chevallier, J., & Loschak (1978). *Science administrative* (Vols. 1 & 2). Loschak (LGDJ).

Crozier, M. (1963). *Lephénornène bureaucratique.* Seuil.

Crozier, M., & Friedberg, E. (1977). *L'acteur erie système.* Seuil.

CURAPP (1983). *La communication administration – administrés.* PUF.

CURAPP (1985). *Psychologie et science administrative.* PUF.

CURAPP (1986). *La haute administration et lapolitique.* PUF.

CURAPP (1988). *Information et transparence administatives.* PUF.

Darbel, A., & Schnapper, D. (1969–1972). *Le système administrative* (Vols. 1 & 2). Mouton.

Debbasch, C. (1971). *Science administrative.* Dalloz. (4éme éd. 1980).

Delion, A. (1969). Administration publique et management. *Bull IIAP, 9*(15), p. 55.

Drago, R. (1971–1972). *Science administrative.* Les cours du droit (2ème éd.: 1976–1977).

Fayol, H. (1916). *Admimstration induscrielle et générale*. Reed: Dunod (1970).

Grémion, C. (1979). *Profession: décideurs*. Gauthier-Villars.

Grémion, P. (1976). *Le pouvoir péripherique*. Seuil.

Jamous, H. (1969). *Sociologic de la decision*. CNRS.

Langrod, G. (Ed.). (1966). *Traité de science administrative*. Mouton.

Laufer, R., & Burlaud, A. (1980). *Management public*. Dalloz.

Legendre, P. (1968). *Histoire de l'administration de 1750 à nos jours*. PUF, Coll. Thémis.

Legendre, P. (1976). Jouir du pouvoir. *Traité cit Ia bureaucratic patri ore*. Minuit.

Massenet, M. (1975). *La nouvelle gesrion publique*. Homrnes *et* techniques. Paris.

Mény, Y., & Thoenig, J. C. (1989). *Politiques publiques*. PUF, Coll. Thémis. Paris.

Muller, P. (1990). *Les politiques publiques*, PUG, Coll. Que sais-je no. 2534. Paris.

Nizard, L. (1974). *Planification et société*. PUG.

Padioleau, J. G. (1982). *L'.Etat au concret*. PUF.

Quermonne, J. L., & De Baecque, F. (Ed.). (1982). *Administration et politique sous la Verne République*. Presses FNSP.

Sainsaulieu, R. (1987). *Sociologic de l'organisation et de l'entreprise*. Presses FNSP–Dallz.

Santo, V. M., & Verrier, P. E. (1993). *Le management public* (No. 2724). PUF, Coll. Que saisje.

Sfez, L. (1992). *Critique tie La decision*. A. Cohn (1973, 4ème éd.). Presses FNSP, Coll. Références.

Suleiman, E. (1976). *Les hauts fonctionnaires et la politique*. Seuil.

Thoenig, J. C. (1987). *Pour une approche analytique de la modernisation administrative* (No. 4, p. 526). RFSP.

Thoenig, J. C. (1990). La science de l'administration. *La politia, Encyclopedic IAC-Jaca Book*.

Timsit, G. (1986). Théorie de l'adminisrration. *Economica*.

Timsit, G. (1987). *Administrations cc. Etats: étude comparee*. PUF, Coil. Politique d'aujourd'hui.

Ziller, J. (1992). *Administrations comparées: les syrèmes potico-administratifs de l'Europe des douze*. Montchrestien.

FURTHER READING

Bodiguel, J. L., & Quermonne, J. L. (1983). *La haute fonction publique sous la Verne Republique*. PUF, Coll. Politique d'aujourd'hui.

Bodiguel, J. L., & Rouban, L. (1991). *Le fonctionnaire détrôné?* Presses FNSP.

Chevailier, J. (1986). *Science administrative*. PUF, Coll. Thémis.

Crozier, M. (1987). Etat modeste. *Erat moderne*. Fayard.

Dupuy, F., & Thoenig, J. C. (1983). *Sociologie de l'administration française*. Paris: A. Colin.

Gournay, B. (1966). *Introduction à la science administrative*. A. Colin (3ème éd.: 1980).

Muller, P. (Ed.). (1992). *L'administration française est-elle en crise?* L'Harmattan, Coll. Logiques politiques.

Quermonne, J. L. (1991). *L'appareil administratif de l'Etat*. Seuil, Coll. Politique.

Rouban, L. (1990). *La modernisation de l'Etat et la fin de la specificité française* (No. 4, p. 52). RFSP.

Sadran, P. (1992). *Le système administrarif français*. Montrchrestien, Coll. Clefs.

Thoenig, J. C. (1973). *L'ère des technocrates* d'organisation.

CHANGING EUROPEAN STATES, CHANGING PUBLIC ADMINISTRATION:

ADMINISTRATIVE SCIENCE AS REFORM: GERMAN PUBLIC ADMINISTRATION

Wolfgang Seibel

ABSTRACT

What most characterizes German public administration since the 18th century is its early modernization relative to the political regime. The "rule of law" became the central mechanism of modernization when the "rule of man" – the nonconstitutional monarchy – was still intact. The "science" of administration was, until recently, dominated by jurisprudence, as were the institutions of public administration. A social science-oriented concept of administrative science only emerged with the reformist drive for accelerated modernization of public infrastructure and public planning in the 1960s. The article outlines the phases of development of this new administrative science from the 1960s to the 1990s and argues that today, as in the past, reform remains the central focus of German public administration, especially with its current emphasis upon the problems of German reunification.

Comparative Public Administration: The Essential Readings
Research in Public Policy Analysis and Management, Volume 15, 759–776
Copyright © 2006 by Elsevier Ltd.
ISSN: 0732-1317/doi:10.1016/S0732-1317(06)15035-6

What characterizes German public administration since the 18th century is its early modernization relative to the political regime. Germany is not a classic constitutional state. The identity, as well as the stability of German statehood, are based on administration and its organizing principle of public law. Even when the political regimes completely broke down, as was the case in 1918 and 1945, public administration never ceased to operate more or less regularly.

Regardless of the criticism against bureaucracy, the reliability of public administration has its place in German collective memory. Inclination to change basic modes of administrative operation is, therefore, limited. German public administration has a remarkable history of self-reform. Exam-pies are the integration of the nonruling "bourgeoisie into the administrative elite stratum during the 18th century, the reorganization of state bureaucracy as well as the partial democratization of municipal administration after Prussia's defeat by Napoleon Bonaparte in 1806, the several waves of readjustment of county and regional administration during the 19th century, the flexible adaptation to the new political regimes during the 20th century (a more than ambiguous flexibility during the Nazi regime, 1933–1945), and the territorial reform of county and regional administration in the 1970s." Those processes were mostly initiated by top-level bureaucrats (at least it was never enforced against them) and then smoothly organized by the rank-and-file professionals.

The prerequisite of this pattern of administrative behavior was a combination of rigidity and flexibility that was provided by public law and the people handling it. What the Germans call the *Rechtsstaat* evolved in the course of the 19th century as a compromise between the "rule of man" (i.e., the monarchy) and the requirements of a modern administration. Modern administration as a complex machinery demanded a reliable mechanism to keep it running. This mechanism was provided by the law and by those knowing the law and how to apply it (*Rechtsanwendung*). Germans are far less apt than Anglo-Americans to think in terms of enforcing law as the will of the constitutionally organized public.

What the Germans call public law or state law, by contrast to the civil law governing in civil society, became a nonpublic affair of professionals. In a decisive period that roughly covers the second half of the 19th century, the scholarly treatment of public administration changed from a common sense-based catalogue of what administration actually did (Stein, 1866–1884) to strictly formalized prescriptions of professional administrative procedures (Mayer, 1895).

Not surprisingly, these legalistic prescriptions shaped scholarly approaches to public administration directly and indirectly in several respects.

First, the science of administration became dominated by jurisprudence. The study of public administration was interpreted and developed by lawyers. Second, the influence of jurisprudence in shaping administrative behavior became relatively independent from parliamentary lawmaking. Instead, jurisprudence – under the label of state-law precept (*Staatsrechtslehre*) – *acquired* a crucial separate power in terms of how to apply the law.

The structural and the political conditions for sustaining this academic monopoly were particularly favorable. The relatively rigid legal structure that was the backbone of public administration turned out to be a desirable counterweight to the volatility of the political structure in 20th century Germany. By the same token, however, the German public law system was compelled to incorporate structural flexibility when adjusting the guidelines for public administration. Beneath the surface of parliamentary lawmaking, lawyers in academia, in the courts, and in public administration shared the role of defining and adjusting what was right and wrong, what was "appropriate" and what was not. This flexibility enabled German jurisprudence to preserve its hegemony *over* the academic discipline of public administration despite considerable practical and academic challenges.

THE RISE OF MODERN GERMAN ADMINISTRATIVE SCIENCE

Verwaltungswissenschafl (administrative science), thus, remained a vague term in the German language. The common sense understanding of the term associates it with *Verwaltungsrecht* (administrative law), but more sophisticated understanding would associate it with "something else" or "something more" than just *Verwaltungsrecht*. This something may be matters of personnel, finance, or organization. German jurisprudence tried to incorporate these operational aspects of administration into textbook and common sense levels (Peters, 1949; Thieme, 1967), linking it, at least in a sort of reminiscence, to the mid-19th century style of *Verwaltungslehre* according to Lorenz von Stein.

The relevance of administrative science, however, was characteristically shaped by factors external to academia and scholarly reasoning. In general, sensitivity for the limits of administrative law as the sole academic approach to public administration was stimulated by a turbulent political environment, which somewhat over stretched the well-developed structural flexibility of the public law system. Some historic indicators for such flexibility include both the period after 1933 – when the Nazis had to deal with an apolitical bureaucracy – and after 1945 – when the British and U.S. authorities had to deal with what they perceived as an obedient administrative tool of dictatorship. Some Nazi lawyers such as Otto Koellreutter (1941) stated that mere administrative law would be an inappropriate basis for the new regime (because in preserved niches of formal legality) and that administrative science would be an appropriate vehicle for training public administration in accordance with the Nazi ideology. After 1945, American occupation authorities insisted on the abolition of the German civil service system, which they perceived, with some reason, as the mechanism by which formal legality had been used for the purposes of state crimes (Eschenburg, 1972; Brecht, 1967).

Finally, the reform era in West Germany, which started with the Grand Coalition between the Christian Democrats and the Social Democrats in 1966, caused another wave of political and scholarly attempts to break the dominance of public law jurisprudence, which was perceived as a structural impediment to sustainable political innovation (Scharpf, 1970). This time, however, a scholarly reform movement was triggered and sustained primarily by sociologists and political scientists claiming to represent an administrative science, based not on law but the social sciences (Hesse, 1982; Seibel, 1983; for comprehensive accounts).

On the one hand, a social-science-based administrative science was perceived, again, as a more realistic approach to public administration than a public-law-oriented approach of jurisprudence. On the other hand, *the* motivations were clearly normative. Administrative science was seen as a reform science in the sense that reform-oriented public policy would require enhanced knowledge of public administration and its presumed structural conservatism (Ellwein, 1982; Fach, 1982). Moreover, administrative science was designed to replace public law jurisprudence as the dominant academic discipline in the training of civil servants (Scharpf, 1970). Along with the general discussion about the future of the West German civil service at that time, administrative science was supposed to become the academic backbone of a renewed civil service (Stutienkommission, 1973).

Both the practical and the academic ambitions of this *Neo-Verwaltungswissenschaft* were nonetheless doomed to fail: First, the then West German civil service was not subject to an all-encompassing reform. A radical form of the state apparatus as the core of German statehood and its civil service (the *Beruflbeamtentum*) could have threatened what was duly perceived as the symbol of continuity and stability in a country with such a rich background of political discontinuity and instability in its recent history.

Second, administrative science did not become a scholarly discipline, as was hoped, with homogeneity in terms of theory and methodology. What caused the failure to develop a strong social-science-oriented administrative science involved the complex dynamics of professionalization within the social sciences themselves. Sociology and political science especially were still hardly established as academic disciplines in Germany by the 1960s. This changed dramatically in the late 1960s and early 1970s when German public education witnessed quantitatively and qualitatively an extraordinary expansion. The new interest in public administration, especially among political scientists (Dammann, 1971; Hirsch, 1970; Scharpf, 1973; for an overview) had, at least, two sources. Not only did the growth of political science become perceived as part of the general movement toward reform, but institutional public administration with its intrinsic inertia was perceived as a particularly well-suited target for reform-oriented normative, political science. Last, but not for least, political science as a relatively new discipline was looking for targets of opportunity. Therefore, rather than growing as an independent variable in the scholarly landscape, administrative science became a dependent variable in the process of creating the social sciences as academic disciplines. The movement toward a social-science-based administrative science did not materialize into another autonomous discipline. This nonevent might have been expected: not only was the resistance of public law jurisprudence too strong but also the incentive among the social sciences was too weak, without creating a new, separate, and powerful discipline.

Although its full potential did not materialize, there were institutional outcomes of the administrative science movement in the late 1960s and the early 1970s in higher education. Administrative science was established as an academic curriculum at the University of Konstanz in 1973 and as a postgraduate curriculum in the Graduate School of Administrative Science in Speyer in 1976. These attempts to establish the discipline in higher education, however, were the only sustainable ones. What remained was the relative incompatibility of any non-jurisprudence training, on the one hand, and the regular institutional recruiting patterns of German public administration, on the other. Because general reform of the civil service had failed in the early 1970s, recruiting lawyers for higher civil service remained the standard pattern, thus seriously limiting career options for nonlawyers.

Public administration continues no be a persistent scholarly subject even though a social-science-based administrative science did not achieve the status of a scholarly discipline. As an object of research, however, public administration is subject to a variety of research interests and paradigms that vary according to a changing political environment and also according no the peculiar dynamics of scholarly activity. The remainder of this article will outline these various approaches since 1970.

THE DEVELOPMENT OF THE
NEW ADMINISTRATIVE SCIENCE

We can observe characteristic shifts of general hypotheses and focuses of attention during this period in the new administrative science (*Neo-Verwaltungswissenschaft*) in Germany. During these years, the linkage between public policy and scholarly activity loosened gradually and autonomous development of research agendas gained momentum. There were essentially four periods.

The first period, which lasted throughout the early 1970s, was characterized by a normative approach in perceiving public administration as a, if not *the*, constraint to reform-oriented public policy.

The second period, which covered the late 1970s and the early 1980s, reflected not only a take-off in politically independent research but also a remarkable shift in general hypotheses that pointed to the flexibility and intelligence of bureaucracy instead of its conservatism and inertia.

The third period, which covered the rest of the 1980s, was characterized by the relative backlash to specialized research on public administration.

The fourth period began with the reunification of West and East Germany in 1990. German scholars have started to investigate the dimensions and logic of institution building in the administrative sphere as it unfolds in East Germany.

THE EARLY 1970s: THE "BUREAUCRATIC
PHENOMENON" AS A CONSTRAINT TO
PUBLIC POLICY

The role of administration in political life became a broadly discussed scholarly issue in the late 1960s. German political science had treated administration either as negligible or as a static element of government (Ellwein, 1963). Political science as a tool of democratic re-education after 1945 had not focused intensively on what seemed to be the most controllable element of the new West German democracy – the government. Furthermore, public administration had proved its effectiveness not only during the immediate postwar period but also during the 1950s when West Germany had no cope with the economic and social consequences of World War II and the giant migration from the former German territories in the east.

The issue of government, including public administration, was raised during the 1960s from two different perspectives. Conservatives sought to establish a counterweight not the focus on democratic values and political participation (Almond & Verba, 1963). Government, considered as a critical governing element of the polity in its own right, therefore, deserved attention as an important subject of political science (Hennis, 1965).

A more liberal and pragmatic perspective focused on government as a tool of political reform. The proponents of this perspective were stimulated by a political climate in which "reform" was a viable label. The substance of this new political climate was the quest for modernization of government in terms of planning capacity and infrastructure. At stake was the adjustment of government and public infrastructure to the postwar era that was characterized in West Germany by a strong and prosperous economy and a stable democracy. Modernization and adjustment enhanced planning capacity in the federal ministries, the structure of fiscal redistribution among the different layers of government (federal, state, and municipal), the territorial reorganization of public administration at the county level, and the general improvement of infrastructure (especially transportation, education, and hospitals).

It was not modernization as such, but rather the culmination of several dimensions of modernization that presented a challenge to the knowledge and routine of German public administration. It is here that the roots of the *Neo-Verwaltungswissenschafi* and its linkage with public polity are located. The variety of dimensions of modernization caused a quest for control and coordination. "Planning" became an appropriate label for this kind *of government* activity. Planning tools such as the U.S. Planning Programming Budgeting *System* (PPBS) became popular among "enlightened" politicians, top-level bureaucrats, and their scholarly advisers (e.g., Böhret, 1970).

Sponsored mainly by the federal and state governments, empirical investigations into the nature of top-level bureaucracy as a tool of government were launched. These studies focused on presumed weaknesses of both the legal and the organizational structures of bureaucracy in terms of planning and coordination. Fritz W. Scharpf (1970) pointed out what he called the "political costs of the *Rechtsstaat.*" He portrayed public law as too rigid and inflexible to respond to a changing societal and political environment. Instead, independent government agencies along with an enhanced capacity of central coordination were supposed to be a more appropriate structure. While the criticism against public law remained ineffective, challenging the organizational structure of bureaucracy became an issue in both the academic and practical spheres.

Research into the organization of planning and coordination of public administration pointed not the fragmentation of oversight and the weakness in coordination of vested interests as the main constraints on coherent administrative action. Using the concept of selective perception (Dearborn & Simon, 1958), researchers described the negative impact of fragmented and poorly coordinated divisions of the federal ministries on comprehensive planning (Mayntz & Scharpf, 1973; Scharpf, 1973). Other research focused on the planning capacity of the state governments (König, 1975) and the potential of new planning methods (Böhret, 1975; Reinermann, 1975).

The weakness of planning research was its normative style and selective choice of variables. The normative approach was due to the political circumstances that called for the restructuring of bureaucracy for the sake of what was termed "active policy" (Mayntz & Scharpf, 1973, pp. 115–145; the connotation of Amitai Etzioni's (1968) *Active Society* was intended). The selection of the top segment of public administration and its organizational structure as variables was due to both the government sponsorship of most of the research and the academic development of research itself during that era. Not surprisingly, the agenda changed according to a changing political environment and the momentum of more self-conscious administrative research.

THE LATE 1970s: APPROACHES OF
IMPLEMENTATION AND THE
"INTELLIGENCE OF BUREAUCRACY"

The West German reform era of the early 1970s was ended by the oil-price shock of 1973 and the ensuing economic recession. Coping with the recession, which soon led to sustained unemployment, instead of active policy, became the general agenda of West German domestic policy. Under the circumstances, the funds for reform-oriented research dried up and the shortcomings of normative approaches to the study of public administration with a limited set of variables became apparent. What gradually emerged from this shift was a more empirically complex and politically less ambitious version of administrative science.

Empirically, the scope of research included more state and municipal level topics of public administration. The federal structure with the *Laender,* as both powerful political actors and the backbone of public administration, became the subject of scholarly attention (Lehmbruch, 1976; Scharpf, Reissert, & Schnabel, 1976/1978) as did the municipalities, which were an important political arena and basis of local infrastructure (Wollmann, 1975; Ellwein & Zoll, 1976; Haussermann, 1977). Methodologically, the normative approach still prevailed in some studies, depending on individual preferences and political inclinations. Scharpf's (1976/1977) analyses of interweaving politics *(Politikverflechtung)* were designed to explore the possibilities of structural reform of West German federalism. *Politikverflechtung,* in the form of negative coordination between the *Laender* and the state and the federal levels of government, was interpreted as the crucial impediment to coherent policy making. Similarly, the conditions of effective lawmaking, including their organizational constraints, were examined on an empirical basis (Böhret & Hugger, 1978; Hugger, 1983).

Mainstream research in the late 1970s refrained from normative considerations for either opportunistic or methodological reasons. The general assumption about bureaucracy as little more than a constraint upon public policy making was much less convincing as soon as the state and the municipal levels of public administration were taken into account. What makes German public administration complex and fragmented – its three main vertical layers of administration and a broad variety of horizontal specialization – at the same time makes it flexible and responsive. As soon as the formulation and especially the implementation of public policy were evaluated, it turned out that the lower levels of public administration represented a reservoir of adaptation to regional and local circumstances or to any changes that could never be entirely anticipated by top-level policy makers (Mayntz, 1979b; Mayntz & Hucke, 1978).

Adaptation and learning as a virtue of what is otherwise perceived as structural inertia was precisely what Charles Lindblom (1965) had termed the "intelligence of democracy." What was called implementation research (Pressman & Wildavsky, 1973; Mayntz, 1979a, 1980; Wollmann, 1980) resurfaced as a benevolent description of the intelligence of bureaucracy Environmental protection was a case in point (Mayntz, Derlien, & Mitarbeiter, 1978). The broad variety of regional and local administrative implementation patterns of federal law as well as the different degrees of enforcement efficiency were analyzed and appreciated for the first time.

Although there was still a hidden political agenda, much of this research was directly or indirectly stimulated by the relative failure of political and administrative reforms in previous years. The second half of the 1970s witnessed a remarkable enhancement of general knowledge about public administration. For the first time public administration was subject no more or less systematic empirical inquiry by many fields and from different dimensions (Grunow, Hegner, & Kaufmann, 1978; Grunow, 1978a, 1978b; Hegner, 1978, 1979; Kaufmann, 1979; Hesse, 1982; Seibel, 1983). In retrospect, the 1970s were the Golden Age of the West German *NeoVerwaltungswissenschaft.*

THE 1980s: DISILLUSIONMENT ABOUT *VERWALTUNGSWISSENSCHAFT* AS A SCHOLARLY DISCIPLINE

In the early 1980s, the further consolidation of *Verwaltungswissenschafi* as a scholarly discipline was subject to new external and internal constraints. Externally, there were no requests by federal, state, or local authorities for knowledge about public administration. Internally, the scholarly community of social-science-oriented administrative scientists was, on the one hand, too small to create a critical mass of people with a common identity in terms of research subject, method, and theory. On the other, it was questionable whether just such a common research subject would be attractive enough to forge a community of scholars when the institutionalization of administrative science as an academic curriculum took place so far only on a limited scale. Under these circumstances, those engaged in research on public administration, for the sake of their academic careers, had to remain loyal to their respective basic disciplines, be it political science, sociology, or economics.

Accordingly, the thrust of *Neo-Verwaltungswissenschafi* was fading in the 1980s. This decline caused the ironic effect that German administrative scientists, despite their considerable accumulation of knowledge about public administration, neither contributed to nor significantly participated in the new debates about the state and its institutional substructure that emerged internationally in the 1980s. Again, this debate had both its political and its scholarly side.

Politically, the legitimacy of the welfare state, "big government," and a huge bureaucracy was challenged. Privatization, deregulation, and de-bureaucratization became crucial political issues in most of the Western industrialized countries (Wright, 1994). In West Germany, the federal government parliamentary switched from the Social Democrats to the Christian Democrats in 1982, and the new coalition of Christian Democrats and Free Democrats emphasized the importance of divesting public administration of too many tasks and too much regulation (Seibel, 1992).

In the academic field, especially in the United States, the state and its administrative substructure were rediscovered as scholarly subjects (Evans, Rueschemeyer, & Skocpol, 1985; Nordlinger, 1981; Skowronek, 1982). What was acknowledged in this literature was that the structure of the state, in terms of organization, legal system, fiscal system, personnel, and the ideas and ideologies attached to them, was a strong set of independent variables shaping the political behavior of nations and their degree of political stability and dynamism. The medium institutional level, with public administration at its core, was increasingly perceived as much mote important than it had been before in concepts such as the political system (with an emphasis on macro-structures) or the political culture (with an emphasis on micro-structures).

None of these highly visible and influential developments had a significant and sustainable impact on West German *Verwaltungswissenschaft.* Amazingly enough, West German scholars did not use their remarkably broad empirical knowledge for advancing their own methodology and theory building. There were some exceptions (Ellwein & Hesse, 1985), but administrative science knowledge was generally not looked to for advice when the wave of debureaucratization came in the 1980s.

Although we can only speculate about the reasons for its methodological and theoretical weakness, the reasons for the peripheral role of administrative science in the context of administrative reform in the 1980s are more obvious. What happened in West Germany during the 1980s in terms of debureaucratization (Seibel, 1986; Hesse, 1987) was part of a routine pattern of administrative self-reform, which German public administration had been used to since its early beginnings. Debureaucratization, German style, was above all, a thinning out of law, which was periodically used to reduce the complexity of public law (Seibel, 1992). Here, no scholarly expertise was needed nor were substantial changes in terms of organization, personnel, or financing at stake. Thus, research on public administration in the 1980s was more or less incoherent although, in some cases, important contributions were made to the knowledge about the state and its institutional substructure.

Three major and especially innovative studies in this era might be mentioned. One was the investigation of Hans-Ulrich Derlien and Renate Mayntz (1988) into the behavioral patterns of top-level bureaucrats. Their study led to the conclusion that West German top-level bureaucrats represent a hybrid type of semi-politicized and fully professionalized decision maker. Another major contribution to the understanding of the peculiarities of German statehood was the investigation into the history of public administration (Buck-Heilig, 1989; Ellwein, 1983, 1987, 1989, 1994; Roth, 1995; Schmitt, 1994; Weingarten, 1989). Ellwein and others analyzed the compromises between private and public interests in the new field of technological risks at production plants in the 19th century. They found than public administration was remarkably successful in achieving durable institutional arrangements. Third, Gerhard Lehmbruch (1987) initiated and conducted research on what he called "administrative interest mediation."

The hypothesis was that public administration by virtue of its expertise and organizational complexity would have a capacity to integrate and coordinate societal interests relatively independent from legislative or governmental guidance. The findings, so far, support this hypothesis as they show that public authorities and private interests are subject to mutual dependence that forces them to cooperate (Czada, 1992; Baumheier, 1994).

THE 1990s: THE CHALLENGE OF INSTITUTION BUILDING IN A REUNIFIED GERMANY

After a short, but arduous debate in the spring of 1990 over whether the unified Germany should have a new constitution or should the East German Democratic Republic (GDR) just join the West German constitutional order (which provided for both of these options in articles 23 and 146 of the *Grundgesetz*), the strategic political decision was made than the *Grundgesetz*, as well as the political and administrative order based on it, would be extended to the eastern territories. Accordingly, the reunification of the Federal Republic of Germany and the GDR meant for East Germany that, for the first time in German history, the change of the political regime coincided with the change of the economic system and the administrative order alike. Public administration had to be reconstructed in East Germany literally from scratch.

The history of this unique, complicated, and highly accelerated process of institution building remains to be written. This process is based on a massive transfer of money and knowledge from west to east. The money was provided by the West German Federal Government, which transferred roughly 150 billion Deutschmark to the East German *Länder* and municipalities. The knowledge was provided by thousands of West German civil servants, who voluntarily served as counselors and consultants in East German state and municipal administrations. It soon turned out that within the general pattern of institutional isomorphism, which was imposed by the constitutional framework, there will be enduring East German peculiarities of administrative structures. In general, East German public administration will remain more centralized than its West German counterpart. The institutional successors of the central privatization authority, the *Treuhandanstalt* (Seibel, 1994b), as well as the much smaller base of municipal property, (König & Heimann, 1994) are the most notable cases in point.

Not surprisingly, the reconstruction of public administration in the East has become a major issue of research. Scholarly attention focuses primarily on the dimensions of organization and personnel, while financing and legal issues are relatively neglected (Seibel, Benz, & Maeding, 1993). Central research topics on organization are the reconstruction of the municipalities and their property and infrastructure (König & Heimann, 1994), the building of new administrative organizations such as an environmental protection administration (Eisen, 1993, 1995), the administrative reform of economic reconstruction across different industries (Lehmbruch, 1994, 1995), and the state-economy relationship (Seibel, 1994a, 1994b). Personnel issues are the replacement of administrative elites (Derlien, 1993), the integration of West and East German staffs in the unified city of Berlin (Reichard & Schröter, 1993), and the integration of East German workers into the institutions of organized labor.

In general, the reunification of Germany is the most important challenge since 1949 to the administrative institutional order of what was the West German Federal Republic. Indirectly, reunification has stimulated research on public administration issues, even where political and administrative institutions were not directly affected. This holds true especially for issues of redistribution and multi-level decision making, particularly the redistribution of monetary resources among the three layers of federal, state, and municipal administration as a core element of the German polity (to which even a section of the constitution is devoted, articles 104a to 115 of the *Grundgesetz*).

CONCLUSION

The vague notion of *Verwaltungswissenschaft* (administrative science) had existed since the days of Lorenz von Stein in the mid-19th century. But, only the *Verwaltungswissenschaft* movement begun in the late 1960s and early 1970s, ultimately forged a small community of social scientist supporters, mostly political scientists and sociologists. Given the long tradition of the scholarly treatment of public administration in Germany, this Renaissance can be called a *Neo-Verwaltungswissenschaft* movement. Even though its theoretical or methodological integration was not achieved over the last three decades or so, the identity of this movement evolved, based on the common subject of research emphasizing reform.

While German reunification presents new challenges for the study of public administration, the trends in the 1990s properly can be viewed as a continuation of the *Neo- Verwaltungswissenschaft* movement in which German administrative sciences are an important research focus as well as a force for change and innovation within the society. If the past is any guide to the future, these reformist themes will persist and present *both* opportunities and dilemmas for the future development of public administration as a field of study.

REFERENCES

Almond, G. A., & Verba, S. (1963). *The civic culture: Political attitudes and democracy in five nations*. Princeton: Princeton University Press.

Baumheier, U. (1994). *Staat und pharmaindustrie: Sicherheitskontrolle, preisregulierung and industrieforderung im internationalen vergleich*. Baden-Baden: Nomos.

Böhret, C. (1970). *Entscheidungshilfen für die regierung*. Instrumente, proleme. Modelle: Opladen.

Böhret, C. (1975). *Grundrifl'der Planungspr~zxis: Mirteifristige Programmplanung and Angewandte Planungsrechniken*. Opladen.

Böhret, C., & Hugger, W. (1978). Praxisrest etnes geserzentwurfes: Zur zusammenarbeit von wissenschafi, verwalrung, und verb nden. In: C. Böhret (Ed.), *Verwaltungsreform und politische wissenschafi: zur zusammenarbeit von praxis und wissenschafi bei d.er durchsetzung von evaluierung und neurungen* (pp. S185–S210). Baden-Baden.

Brecht, A. (1967). *Mit der kraft des geistes: Lebenserinnerungen. Zweite Halfie 1927–1967*. Stuttgart: Deutsche Verlags-Anstalt.

Buck-Heilig, L. (1989). *Die gewerbeaufiicht: Entstehung und entwicklung*. Opladen.

Czada, R. (1992). *Administrative interessenvermirtlung (am Beispiel der kerntechnischen sicherheitsregulierung in den vereinigten staaten und der bundesrepublik deutschland)*. Habilitanionssch rift. Konstanz.

Dammann, K. (1971). Vom 'arbeitenden Staat' zur 'Politischen Verwaltung'. *Neue Politische Literatur, I:* 188–204; *II:* 457–481.

Dearborn, D. W., & Simon, H. A. (1958). Selective perception: A note on the departmental identification of executives. *Sociometry*, 140–144.

Derlien, H.-U. (1993). Integration der staatsfunktion re der DDR in das berufsbeamtentum: Professionalisierung und suberung. In: W. Seibel, A. Benz & H. M. ding (Eds), *Verwalrungsreform and verwaltungspolitik im proze der deutschen einigung* (pp. S190–S206). BadenBaden: Nomos.

Derlien, H.-U., & Mayntz, R. (1988). *Comparative Elite Study II*. CES 11. Bamberg, Germany: Universitat.

Eisen, A. (1993). Zur entwicklung der umwelnverwaltung in den neuen bundesl ndern – Ein vergleich der bundesl nder sachsen und brandenburg. *Die offentliche verwaltung, 46*(heft 16, August), 677–688.

Eisen, A. (1995). *Wege tier verwaltungstransformation: Die bildung adminzstratzver Institutionen auf dem gebiet der umweltverwaltung in den neuen bundeslndern sachsen und brandenburg*. Doctoral thesis, Universitan Konstanz.

Ellwein, T. (1963). *Das regierungssystem der bundesrepublik deutschland: Leitfaden and quellenbuch, 1*. Aufi. Koln: Westdeutscher Verlag.

Ellwein, T. (1982). Verwaltungswissenschaft: Die herausbildung der disziplin. In: J. J. Hesse (Ed.), *Politikwissenschafi und verwalrungswissenschafi* (pp. S34–S54). Opladen: Westdeutscher Verlag.

Ellwein, T. (1983). Geschichte der Offentlichen Verwaltung. In: K. König, (Ed.), *Offentliche Verwalrung in der Bundesrepublik Deutschland* (p. S73ff). Baden-Baden.

Ellwein, T. (1987). Entwicklungstendenzen der deutschen verwaltung im 19. *Jahrhundert. jahrbuch zur staats- und verwaltungswissenschaft,, Bd. 1/1987,* S13ff.

Ellwein, T. (1989). Verwaltungsgeschichte und verwaltungstheorie. *Jahrbuch zur staats- and verwaltungswzssenschafi, Bd. 3,* S465ff.

Ellwein, T. (1994). *Beitr ge zur theorie der verwaltungsentwicklung – vorläufiger ergebnisbericht eines von Thomas Ellwein Geleiteten forschungsprojektes.* Konstanz.

Ellwein, T., & Hesse, J. J. (Eds). (1985). *Verwaltungspolitik und verwaltungsvereinfachung.* Baden-Baden: Nomos.

Ellwein, T., & Zoll, R. (1976). *Wertheim: Politik und machtsrtukrur einer deutschen stadt.* München: Juventa Verlag.

Eschenburg, T. (1972). Den bürokratische rückhalt. In: R. Löwenthal & H.-P. Schwarz (Eds), *Die zweite republik. 25 Jahre bundesrepublik Deutschland – eine bilanz* (pp. S64–S94). Stuttgart: Seewald Verlag.

Etzioni, A. (1968). *The active society: A theory of societal and political processes.* London: Macmillan.

Evans, P. B., Rueschemeyer, D., & Skocpol, T. (Eds). (1985). *Bringing the state back in.* Cambridge: Cambridge University Press.

Fach, W. (1982). Verwalnungswissenschaft – Ein paradigma und seine karriere. In: J. J. Hesse (Ed.), *Politikwissenschafi und verwisltungswisssenschaft* (pp. S55–S73). Opladen: Westdeutscher Verlag.

Grunow, D. (1978a). In: Bürger und verwaltung (Bd. 1). *Steuerzahler und finanzamt.* Frankfurt a.M.: Campus.

Grunow, D. (1978b). In: Bürger und verwaltung (Bd. 3). *Alltagskontakt mit der verwaltung.* Frankfurt a.M.: Campus.

Grunow, D., Hegner, F., & Kaufmann, F.-X. (1978). In: Bürger und verwaltung (Bd. 4). *Steuerzahler und finanzamt. Forschungsdesign und ergebnis.* Frankfurt a.M.: Campus.

Haussermann, H. (1977). *Die politik der bürokratie: Einführung in die soziologie tier staatlichen verwaltung.* Frankfurt a.M.: New York.

Hegner, F. (1978). *Das bürokratische dilemma: Zu einigen unauflöslichen widersprüchen in den bezienhungen zwischen organisation.* Frankfurt a.M., New York: Personal und Publikum.

Hegner, F. (1979). Bürgerhahe' von politik und verwaltung als anliegensund problemgerechnigkeit. In: *Die verwaltung* (pp. S187–S202). Frankfurt a.M., New York: Personal und Publikum.

Hennis, W. (1965). Aufgaben einer modernen regierungslehre. In: *Politische vierteljahresschrifi* (pp. S422–S441).

Hesse, J. J. (Ed.). (1982). *Politikwissenschaft und verwaltungswissenschaft.* Opladen: Westdeutscher Verlag.

Hesse, J. J. (1987). Zum stand der verwaltungsvereinfachung bei bund und ländern. In: *Die öffentliche verwaltung, 40 heft 11*(Juni), 474–485.

Hirsch, J. (1970). *Wissenschaftlich-technischer fortschritt und politisches system: organisation and grundlagen administrativer wissenschaftsförderung in der BRD.* Frankfurt

Hugger, W. (1983). *Gesetze – Ihre vorbereitung, abfassung und prüfung: Ein handbuch für praxis und stadium mit einer einführung von Carl Böhret.* Baden-Baden: Nomos.

Kaufmann, F.-X. (Ed.). (1979). *Bürgernahe sozialpoitik: Planung, organisation und vermittlung sozialer leistungen auf lokaler ebene.* New York: Frankfurt a.M.

Koellreutter, O. (1941). Die verwaltung als leistungstr ger: Ein beitrag zum problem der verwaltungslehre und verwaltungswissenschaft. *In Reichsverwalrungsblatt, 62*(46/47), 649–651.

König, K. (Ed.). (1975). *Koordination and integrierte planung in den staatskanzleien.* Berlin.

König, K., & Heimann, J. (1994). *Vermö genszuordnung im aufgabenzuschnitt des offentlichen sektors tier neuen bundesl nder: Ein zwischenbericht.* Speyer: Forschungsinstitut für Offentliche Verwaltung.

Lehmbruch, G. (1976). *Parteienwettbewerb im bundesstaat.* Stuttgart: Kohlhammer.

Lehmbruch, G. (1987). *Comparative political economy of neo-corporatism: Inter-organizational and institutional logics.* Konstanz.

Lehmbruch, G. (1994). Institutionen, interessen und sektorale variationen in der transformationsdynamik der politischen okonomie ostdeutschlands. *Journal für Sozialforschung, 34,* 21–44.

Lehmbruch, G. (1995). Institutionen, interessen und sektorale variationtn in der transformationsdynamik der politischen okonomie ostdeutschlands. In: W. Seibel, A. Benz & R. Klimecki (Eds), *Regierungssystem and verwaltungspolitik: Beitr ge zu einem symposium zu ehren von Thomas Ellwein anl zlich seines 65.* Geburtstags.

Lindblom, C. E. (1965). *The intelligence of democracy. Decision making through mutual adjustment.* New York: Free Press.

Mayer, O. (1895). *Deutsches verwaltungsrecht* (1. Aufl.). Munchen: Leipzig.

Mayntz, R. (Ed.). (1979a, 1980). *Implementation politischer programme and empirische forschungsberichte* (2 Bde). Kronberg: Ts.

Mayntz, R. (1979b). Regulative politik in der krise? In: J. Matthes (Ed.), *Sozialer wandel in westeuropa. Deutschen soziologentages in Berlin 1979* (pp. S55–S81). Frankfur a.M: New York.

Mayntz, R., Derlien, H. U., & Mitarbeiter, E. (1978). *Vollzugsprobleme der umweltpolitik. Empirische undsuchung der implementation von gesetzen in Bereich der Luftreinhaltung und des Gew sserschutzes.* Stuttgart.

Mayntz, R., & Hucke, J. (1978). Gesetzesvollzug im umweltschutz. Wirksamkeit und probleme. *Zeitschrift für Umweltpolitik* (pp. S217–S244).

Mayntz, R., & Scharpf, F. W. (Eds.). (1973). *Planungsorganisation. Die diskussion und die reform von regierung und verwaltzing des bundes münchen*: Piper.

Nordlinger, E. (1981). *On the autonomy of the democratic state.* Cambridge: Harvard University Press.

Peters, H. (1949). *Lehrbuch tier Verwaltung* (3 Bde.). Berlin/Götningen/Heidelberg.

Pressman, J. F., & Wildavsky, A. (1973). *Implementation. Expectations in Washington are dashed in oakland: or, why it's amazing that federal programs work at all, this being a saga of the economic development administration as told by two sympathetic observers who seek to build morals on a foundation of ruined hopes.* Berkeley/Los Angeles/London: University of California Press.

Reichard, C., & Schröter, E. (1993). Berliner verwaltungseliten. Rollenverhalten und einstellungen von führungskr ften in der (Ost- und West-) Berliner verwaltung. In: W. Seibel, A. Benz & H. M. Ding (Eds), *Verwaltungsreform und verwaltungspolitik im prozefs der deutschen einigung* (pp. S207–S217). Baden-Baden: Nomos.

Reinermann, H. (1975). *Programmbudgets für regierung and verwaltung: möglichkeiten and grenzen formaler entscheidungsysteme in regierung und verwaltung.* Baden-Baden.

Roth, G. (1995). *Die entwicklungder organisation kommunaler sozialverwaltung in ausgew hlten St dten zwischen 1925 and 1985: Aufgaben and organisation, doppelte kontingenz und institutionelle bestimmung.* Doctoral Thesis, Universität Konstanz.

Scharpf, F. W. (1970). *Die politischen kosten des rechtsstaats: Eine vergleichende untersuchung der deutschen und amerikanischen verwaltungskontrollen.* Tübingen.

Scharpf, F. W. (1973). Verwaltungswissenschaft als teil der politikwissenschaft. In: F. W. Scharpf (Ed.). *Planung als politischer prozep. Aufsätze zur theorie der planenden demokratie* (pp. S9–S32). Frankfurt a.M.

Scharpf, F. W., Reissert, B., & Schnabel, F. (Eds). (1976/1977). *Politikverflechtung. theorie und empirie des kooperativen föderalismus in der bundesrepublik Deutschland* (2 Bde). Kronberg.

Schmitt, R. (1994). *Kooperationsbeziehungen in der Sozialverwaltung – Geschichte und Gegenwart der institutionellen Zusammenarbeit von Offentlichen and Freien Trägern der Kommunalen Wohlfahrtspflege.* Doctoral Thesis, Universität Konstanz.

Seibel, W. (1983). *Regierbarkeit und verwaltungswissenschaft. Ideengeschichtliche untersunchung zur stabilit t des verwalteten rechtsstaates.* Frankfurt/New York: Campus.

Seibel, W. (1986). Entbürokratisierung in der bundesrepublik Deutschland. *Die Verwaltung, 2,* 137–162.

Seibel, W. (1992). *Task reform: Privatization, deregulation, debureaucratisation, third sector development.* Country Report West Germany, Project: Administrazione centrale e integrazione communitaria: Modelli organizzativi e gestione del p-ersonale. European University Institute, Florence, p. 62.

Seibel, W. (1994a). Stranegische fehler oder erfolgreiches scheitern? Zur entwicklungslogik der treuhandanstalt 1990–1993. *Politische Vierteljahresschrift, 35,* 1–35.

Seibel, W. (1994b). Das zentralistische erbe. Die institutionelle entwicklung der treuhandanstalt und die nachhaltigkeit ihrer auswirkungen auf die bundesstaanlichen verfassungsstruknuren. In: *Aus politik und zeitgeschichte, beilage zur wochenzeitung "Das Parlament"* (Vol. B43–44/94, pp. 3–13).

Seibel, W., Benz, A., & Maeding, H. (Eds). (1993). *Verwaltungsreform and verwaltungspolitik im prozef? der deutschen einigung.* Baden-Baden: Nomos.

Skowronek, S. (1982). *Building a new American state. The expansion of national administrative capacities, 1877–1920.* Cambridge: Cambridge University Press.

Stein, L. (1866–1884). *Die verwaltungslehre.* Aalen: Scientia Verlage.

Stutienkommission zur reform des offentlichen dienstrechts. (1973). (11 Bde.). Baden-Baden: Nomos.

Thieme, W. (1967). *Verwaltungslehre* (I. Aufl.). Köln/Berlin/Bonn/Munchen: Carl Heymanns Verlag KG.

Weingarten, J. (1989). *Staatliche wirtschafisaufiicht in Deutschland. Die eniwicklung der apothekenaufsicht preuf3ens and nordrhein-westfalens von ihrer grundung bis zur gegenwart.* Opladen.

Wollmann, H. (1975). Stadtbaurecht und privates grundeigentum. Zur politischen okonomie der gemeinde. In: W. Hans-Georg (Ed.), *Kommunalpolitik* (pp. S183–S253). Hamburg.

Wollmann, H. (Ed.). (1980). Politik im dickicht der bürokratie. *Beiträge zur implementationsforschung.* Leviathan Sonderheft 3/1979: Berlin.

Wright, V. (Ed.). (1994). *Privatization in western Europe: Pressures, problems, and paradoxes.* London: Pinter.

FURTHER READING

Bensel, R. F. (1990). *Yankee leviathan: The origins of central state authority in america, 1859–1877.* Cambridge: Cambridge University Press.

Benz, A. (1994). *Kooperative verwaltung: Funktionen, voraussetzungen, folgen.* Baden-Baden: Nomos.

Benz, A., Fritz, W. S., & Zintl, R.-h. (1992). *Horizontale politikverflechrung: Zur theorie von verhandlungssystemen.* Frankfurt a.M.: Campus.

Einstellungen der politisch – Administraniven elite des bundes (1988). Bamberg: Universität.

Ellwein, T. (1993). *Der staat als sufall und als notwendigkeit: Die jüngere verwalrungsentwicklung in Deutschland am beispiel Ostwestfalen-Lippe* (2 Bde). Opladen.

North, D. C. (1988). *Theorie des institutionellen wandels: Eine neue sicht der wirtschaftsgesrhichte.* Tübingen: Mohr.

North, D. C. (1990). *Institutions, institutional change, and economic performance.* Cambridge: Cambridge University Press.

Scharpf, F. W. (1971). *Das* konstanzer verwaltungsstudium nach drei jahren. *Die Offentliche Verwaltung, 24,* 771–773.

Williamson, O. E. (1975). *Markets and hierarchies: Analysis and antitrust implications: A study in the economics of internal organization.* New York: Free Press.

Williamson, O. E. (1985). *The economic institutions of capitalism: Firms, markets, relational contracting.* New York: Free Press.

CHANGING EUROPEAN STATES, CHANGING PUBLIC ADMINISTRATION:

ANTISTATIST REFORMS AND NEW ADMINISTRATIVE DIRECTIONS: PUBLIC ADMINISTRATION IN THE UNITED KINGDOM

Christopher Pollit

ABSTRACT

British public administration has endured radical antistate reforms since 1979. This essay outlines the three phases of these administrative reforms, their sources of support, underlying rationales, basic institutional elements as well as their limitations. As a result of profound administrative changes, UK academic administrative sciences have undergone a redefinition and relabelling. Yet, there is still not a distinctive British School of public administration, nor a pronounced shift to Continental European thinking. Indeed, the author concludes, "UK academic public administration is still more that of a North American satellite than a core European State."

Comparative Public Administration: The Essential Readings
Research in Public Policy Analysis and Management, Volume 15, 777–792
Copyright © 2006 by Elsevier Ltd.
All rights of reproduction in any form reserved
ISSN: 0732-1317/doi:10.1016/S0732-1317(06)15036-8

Compared with the United States, the United Kingdom is a strong unitary state. There are few constitutional constraints on the central executive; that executive is controlled by one, highly disciplined political party; and that same party is usually able to dominate the proceedings of the legislature. The government of the day is accustomed to being able to get more than 90 percent of its legislation through Parliament unscathed (Rose, 1989). It is also able to constrain the activities of local governments to a degree that would be regarded as extraordinary in many other liberal democracies. When, during the mid-1980s, Mrs. Thatcher fell out with Labour-controlled authorities in the largest metropolitan areas, including London, she simply abolished them (Mather, 1989). Such executive freedoms must have appeared luxurious indeed to most American presidents.

This is, therefore, a state in which the musculature of the central executive is well developed – some would say overdeveloped. During the period of one party (Conservative) rule since 1979, these muscles have been flexed to considerable effect. More than 60 percent of the civil service presently works in executive agencies of a kind that scarcely existed 5 years ago. Market-type-mechanisms (MTMs) have been introduced into the National Health Service (NHS) and in community care. Prime Minister Major's *Citizen's Charter* program for quality and standards has left few public services untouched. Local government is in the throes of restructuring. Large-scale privatization has taken place and extensive further market testing is underway.

Although the scale of these movements is unmistakable, their significance remains a matter for debate. Are they signs of the strong heartedness of the British state and of the Conservative government's willingness to modernize and adapt public sector institutions? Alternatively, is the government displaying a weak-hearted acceptance of continuing economic decline or (even) a deep doctrinal prejudice against the public sector? Are we witnessing bold modernization or an unsubtle mixture of demoralization and demolition? The last may sound far-fetched, yet there is persistent evidence that ministerial hearts are unsympathetic to the public sector (Pollit, 1993, pp. 35–48). Many commentators agree that Mrs. Thatcher "and her close circle of ideological confidants saw themselves as the prize crew of a hostile vessel" (James, 1993, pp. 504–505). Indeed, sometimes it has seemed that the public sector was guilty until proven innocent, while the private sector was innocent until proven guilty. Although such a stance has become familiar in American politics, it remains much less common in Europe, where the state is still widely seen as an indispensable force for integration and the promotion of social welfare.

RECENT CHANGES IN THE STATE AND PUBLIC ADMINISTRATION

With some oversimplification, the period since Mrs. Thatcher's coming to power in 1979 can be divided into three phases. First, from 1979 to about 1982 there was a fierce but relatively crude drive for economies. This corresponded with the government's macroeconomic policy objective of reducing public expenditure. Originally, this aim was formulated as one of making real cuts in total spending, but bitter experience obliged ministers to reformulate their objectives progressively in less draconian terms (Thain & Wright, 1992, p. 219). Even so, civil service numbers were cut by 14 percent (from the 1979 levels) and subsequently by a further 6 percent. Civil service pay was brought under tighter ministerial control, and the Civil Service Department was abolished. Some major departments of state suffered severe cuts in their programs, especially those concerned with housing, the environment, industry, and energy. Central government also embarked on a series of new legislative measures designed to tighten its grip *on* local authority expenditure.

The limitations of such a strategy were apparent from the beginning, and the government soon moved to emphasize efficiency rather than economy. Greater efficiency (doing more with less; improving input/output ratios) held out the politically attractive possibility that public expenditure could be cut without reductions in popular public services such as education or health care.

This second phase lasted through to the late 1980s. Although the government constantly referred to the "three Es" (economy, efficiency, and effectiveness), most of the new procedures and performance indicators put in place throughout the public sector actually concerned the first two, with effectiveness coming a poor third (Pollit, 1990). Huge efforts were put into improving the financial management skills of public officials (much less attention was given to human resource management). New national audit bodies were created with terms of reference that extended their activities well beyond traditional regularity audit and into questions of efficiency and value for money (VFM – the National Audit Office was set up in 1983, the Audit Commission in 1982). Renewed emphasis was accorded no evaluation, but it tended to be evaluation of a particular kind – summative assessment by the central departments or top management of peripheral agencies or lower level staff, usually against fairly instrumental criteria of economy and efficiency (Henkel, 1991, pp. 19–25).

During this second phase, an increasingly ambitious series of public utility privatizations assumed a central position in the government's political program. British Telecom was privatized in 1984, followed by British Gas (1986), the British Airports Authority (1987), water supply and sewerage (1989), electricity (England and Wales, 1990; Scotland, 1991; Northern Ireland, 1993), and British Rail (1994). The market capitalization of these industries exceeded £100 billion. In the decade from 1979 to 1990, 800,000 employees were transferred into the private sector, and the share of the gross domestic product accounted for by state-owned industries fell from 11 percent in 1979 to 5.5 percent in 1990.

The third phase was in many ways the most radical. After Mrs. Thatcher's victory in the 1987 general election, the Conservative government was riding high. The economy boomed, and the Labour opposition was demoralized by its third defeat in less than a decade. Encouraged by the prospect of long-term retention of power, the government launched a series of public-service-sector reforms which:

1. Made much bolder and larger scale use of MTMs (sometimes referred to as quasi- or internal markets) than ever before. The NHS was the most controversial example (see Robinson & Le Grand, 1994, for a detailed evaluation).
2. Intensified organizational and spatial decentralization of the management and production of services (but *not* necessarily their financing or policymaking).
3. Laid constant rhetorical emphasis on the need to improve service quality (Prime Minister, 1991, 1992).
4. Insisted that services should become more customer focused (Pollit, 1993, pp. 179–187).

This was a program for both cultural and structural change. It entailed a more profound transformation of the public services sector than anything that had happened between 1979 and 1987. It continued unabated when, in 1990, Mr. Major took over from Mrs. Thatcher as Prime Minister. During the first phase of Mrs. Thatcher's reforms, the public utilities and services had, by and large, been left in their existing organizational forms. They had been subjected to cuts and a general tightening of control, but not fundamentally restructured. In the second phase, the public utilities (gas, water, electricity, etc.) had been restructured by being sold off. The public services (health care, education, and personal social services), however, had generally retained their existing shape, although within the context of an increasingly intense drive for efficiency and VFM. From the late 1980s, however, the public services in turn were shaken out of their traditional bureaucratic forms. They were divided into, on the one hand, agencies set up to purchase services on behalf of communities and, on the other, a range of provider organizations (public, private nonprofit, and private for-profit) which competed within the MTMs to win contracts from the purchasers. Thus, for example, a District Health Authority now became a purchaser of health care services and shed its responsibilities for actually managing hospitals and other facilities. The latter task was entrusted to autonomous provider units, many of them taking the new form of corporately independent NHS trusts.

The purchaser/provider split, in its various guises, was accompanied by a rapid extension of the use of contracts or quasi-contracts to govern relationships between public authorities. Often a contractual relationship was substituted for what had previously been a hierarchical relationship (as between District Health Authorities and individual hospitals, for example). This development holds out the possibility for greater precision and transparency (and therefore greater accountability). However, there are dangers, too. The framework of public law governing contractual relations between public bodies has not yet caught up with management practice, so some significant ambiguities have been created. There are also concerns about services such as health care, personal social services, or education, where it may be difficult if not impossible to write a technically complete contract (i.e., one that covers all possible states of the world). Incentives may be created for service providers to exploit their informational advantages by covertly reducing service quality in order to be more competitive on price (Harden, 1992; Le Grand & Bartlett, 1993).

Following the *Next Steps* report, the central government also drew a firmer line between the executive work of service provision and the policy work of the most senior civil servants. The traditional departments shed their executive work to more than 90 new executive agencies (e.g., the Benefits Agency, the Driver and Vehicle Licensing Agency, the Patent Office). These bodies were to carry on their businesses within quasi-contracts called "framework agreements." The framework agreements specified their performance targets, budgets, and personnel freedoms (Chancellor of the Duchy of Lancaster, 1993). They were negotiated (and periodically renegotiated) with the parent department. Unlike NHS trusts, however, agencies did not become statutorily independent of their parent departments, and the government claimed that the constitutional principle of ministerial responsibility for their activities remained undiminished. Notwithstanding this claimed continuity, it was noted by many commentators that the agency form would make it much easier to pursue a policy of radical privatization, should any government subsequently wish to do so.

These far-reaching structural changes were supposed to be accompanied by both a continuing emphasis on efficiency gains and decisive shifts in public service organizational cultures. Cultural change became a favorite expression for describing the thrust toward a new, output-oriented, cost-conscious, decentralized, customer-focused public service. In practice, however, matters were more complicated. To begin with, it is not entirely clear that, despite all the management texts and exhortatory speeches, there is available either the knowledge or the will to redesign cultures (or, at least, not in the short term). Cultures are belief sets, complex mixtures of attitudes, expectations, stereotypes, and myths. They exist in the minds of members of the organization. A single organization may support several quite different cultures, each of them deep-rooted within a particular occupational group. To make all the members of an organization change their behavior in some particular way is difficult enough; to make them change their beliefs – and then replace them with another set, designed by top management – is a formidable task indeed (Harrison, Hunter, Marnoch, & Pollit, 1992, pp. 9–17, 65–66).

In addition to the inherent difficulties of purposeful cultural change, there is an ambiguity about the nature of the new culture that ministers and top managers say they are seeking to create. Little explanation has been forthcoming as to how the rhetoric of customer-focused and customer-driven services can be reconciled with the more traditional demands of the center for top-down control. The latter have, if anything, intensified during the 1980s and 1990s. Empowerment (another fashionable term) of public service users often seems to consist of little more than improved information brochures and the occasional survey of customer satisfaction. Where user wants and top-management objectives diverge (as they frequently and inevitably will), there is little sign yet that users will be put first, or will be admitted as partners in the decision process (Pollit, 1994; Harrison & Pollit, 1994, pp. 94–112).

Prime Minister Major's *Citizen's Charter* program illustrates these ambiguities well. Citizens are only infrequently mentioned after the title page – the main focus is on *customers* and *consumers* of services rather than on the broader, more explicitly political and collective concept of a citizen. Managers are to consult customers and then set standards for the service in question. Arrangements for any collective participation or representation for citizens are not discussed. The implication seems to be that the consumer the government has in mind is the individual, actively choosing shopper rather than the publicly concerned citizen. Certainly, there is little in the Charter to extend either citizens' legal rights or collective arrangements whereby they may demonstrate their empowerment by active participation (Pollit, 1994).

While the three-fold periodization outlined above captures much of the administrative change of the last 15 years or so, it is, of course, too neat to be remotely comprehensive. One particularly important set of developments that it does *not* capture is the process by which public authorities in the United Kingdom became steadily more bound up with, and influenced by, the institutions of the European Union (EU). Not only the central government, but also local authorities and other public bodies have found it necessary to develop direct links with Brussels and Strasbourg. This progressive entanglement with things where the European Union has been given very little prominence either by politicians or the media, with the unedifying exception of the occasional bout of "Eurocrat bashing" in the popular press. Politically, there has been a somewhat craven reluctance – across most of the domestic political spectrum – to appear publicly enthusiastic about Britain's membership in the European Union.

Yet, the significance of EU membership has been considerable and is growing. The UK state apparatus has, for example, had to implement European directives and regulations with respect to trading standards and consumer protection and has become subject to elaborate new rules governing public procurement. It has bid for loans and grants from the European Investment Bank and the European structural funds. It has fallen foul of various judgments of the European Court, and so on. Since the Maastricht Treaty of 1992, a new administrative principle, that of "subsidiarity," has begun to show up on the curricula of management seminars and academic courses in policymaking and administration. More and more, public officials are becoming familiar first hand with the consensual, multilateral style of negotiating and bargaining than usually characterizes decision making in EU institutions. The cultural effect of this widening experience (in sharp contrast to the centralized, directive character of British public administration) has yet to be adequately researched or assessed.

THE HISTORY AND INTELLECTUAL ROOTS OF THE CONTEMPORARY APPROACHES

The strongest political impulse for each of the three main phases of administrative reform came from the "new right." It would be a mistake, however, to suppose that successive waves of change could be satisfactorily attributed solely to a small number of ideologues, or, indeed, to the charismatic and determined leadership of Mrs. Thatcher. These were important influences, but it seems unlikely that change would have gone as far as it has if the new right had not been at least tacitly supported by a wider constituency and if the defenders of the old order had not themselves been weakened and divided.

The new right critique of the old order comprised at least seven elements:

1. Prevailing patterns of pluralism and (still more) corporanism were said to lead to deals between the state and powerful interest groups (especially the trade unions), which resulted in higher public spending than the median voter would have supported.
2. Public officials were characterized as being mainly concerned with the maximization of their own budgets and status. By extension, the whole of the public sector was regarded as relatively inefficient.
3. The professions were seen as self-interested monopolists, restricting the supply of their services, demanding high salaries/fees, and pursuing their own professional ends rather than responding to the wishes of those who used their services. Given the central role the caring professions play in the welfare state, this critique held harsh implications for the organization of health care, education, and a number of other public services.
4. The growth of government had reached the point where it was beginning to undermine the freedom of the individual.
5. "Big government" had also sapped the citizens' spirit of enterprise and sense of self-reliance.
6. Center-left governments had mistakenly pursued artificially egalitarian notions of social justice, thus undermining both individual freedom and the fiscal self-discipline of the state.
7. The relentless expansion of the state sector had crowded out private sector growth (Bacon & Eltis, 1978), for a particularly influential analysis along these lines.

The conservative governments of the 1980s and 1990s had repeated recourse to this relentlessly anti-state analysis (Pollit, 1993, pp. 28–49). In the glaring failures and discomfitures of the 1970s, they had plentiful ammunition with which to bombard their opponents. In academic terms, their main theoretical sources were monerarism (Jackson, 1985), Austrian school economics (Parsons, 1988), and public choice theory and libertarian philosophy (King, 1987). Hayek (1986) was made into something of a guru. In practice, these different theories were fed to ministers through a variety of right-wing think tanks (James, 1993), and, when it came to policy formulation, were often mixed together in a fairly inconsistent way (Aitken, 1988; Jackson, 1985, pp. 11–31, 36). Following Mrs. Thatcher's replacement by Mr. Major, there was some softening of the anti-public service line, but the new blend appears opportunistic and pragmatic rather than being based on any particular theorist or model.

Allies for a new-right program of administrative reform were not hard to find. Business people, especially from the world of finance, liked the sound of a government apparently devoted to reducing public expenditure, minimizing state regulation, and lowering taxation. The qualifier "apparently" is necessary because in practice the Conservative administrations since 1979 have presided over a substantial increase in the tax burden and continuing growth in public spending, though at a reduced rate. Top managers in industry, and senior civil servants and other high-level public officials, reacted positively to the restoration of the "right to manage" and the corresponding restrictions on trade unions. Private sector management consultants have done very well out of the business of reforming public administration without always having many tangible successes to show for their lucrative reports and advice (Jones & Hibbs, 1994). Other sectors of the commercial world have also profited extensively from Conservative policies of compulsory competitive tendering and contracting out of public services, especially cleaning, laundry, catering, refuse collection, and auditing and accountancy (Pollit, 1993, pp. 134–137).

The intellectual program of the new right has been noticeably enriched by the presence of these allies. In particular, the business world, especially management consultants, contributed important ideas about how to manage large, complex organizations. The traffic here has been largely one-way, reflecting ministerial beliefs that the public sector had much to learn from the virtuous private sector, but the latter would have little to gain from greater familiarity with civil service thinking. What is more, the flow has been geographically specific – it is American management ideas and American management gurus that have seized the attention of UK politicians and public officials.

Thus, in the mid-1980s, notions of excellence drawn from *In Search of Excellence* by Peters and Waterman (1982) became a very popular component of seminars and conferences for managers in the UK state sector. Subsequently, the public services served as test beds for a series of management techniques drawn from U.S. private sector practice, including performance-related pay (PRP), total quality management (TQM), benchmarking (BM), and most recently, reengineering. Many public service managers testify to the usefulness of such techniques, and it seems clear that often they have been successfully adapted to noncommercial environments.

On the other hand, there is also widespread evidence that sometimes politicians and top managers have failed to take sufficient account of the distinctive contexts of many public services. Techniques which really do not fit the political, organizational, and technological circumstances of the public service in question have been parachuted in, sometimes at considerable financial and opportunity cost, sometimes with a public relations' fanfare, only to disappoint.

An example of such inadequately thought-out transplants (by no means the most extreme) is TQM. One recent evaluation of the application of TQM to the NHS compared progress at a number of NHS sites with that in selected commercial companies. It concluded that the commercial companies made more progress than the NHS TQM sites on all TQM criteria, except customer empowerment. It was difficult to draw simple conclusions from these findings because the NHS was grappling with vastly more complex issues in relation to service delivery ... . However, the companies showed a level of commitment to TQM that was higher than in all but one or two NHS sites. More attention to preplanning, a greater willingness to make resources available, a higher level of senior management commitment and understanding, and a more obvious relationship between survival and customer satisfaction all contributed to the difference in progress (Center for the Evaluation of Public Policy and Practice, 1994, p. vii).

This list of issues may stand as an accurate *précis* of difficulties encountered in many parts of the public services when private sector management techniques are abruptly imported.

Two factors, in particular, limit the beneficial impact of such techniques. First, there is the volatile and short-term nature of politicians' attention span (when most of these techniques require 3 to 5 years of sustained effort if their full potential is to be realized). Second, is the fact that so many of these attempted improvements are implemented against a background of acute resource shortages, often coupled with the threat of job losses and/or privatization. In such circumstances, management's task of achieving a sustained focus on careful implementation of the new technique is made much more difficult.

Finally, it would be wrong to leave the impression that the ideas, which fueled the three phases of administrative reform identified above were the only ideas in circulation. The mixture of new right doctrine and generic managerialism was dominant, but there *were* alternatives (Pollit, 1993, Chapter 6). Perhaps, the most important of these was the Public Service

Orientation (PSO). This approach acknowledged the deficiencies of the old bureaucratic model and committed itself to the development of more user-responsive public services. However, its creators also claimed that

> concern for the citizen as well as the customer distinguishes the PSO from the concern for the customer that should mark any service organization. For this reason, issues such as participation and public accountability are raised (Stewart & Clark, 1987, p. 170).

Based primarily in the local government and the academic world, the PSO gained some support and publicity. This support did not extend to central government where the Thatcher administration was unwilling to countenance a set of ideas that seemed too closely associated with municipal labourism.

ADMINISTRATION AND ACADEME: TEACHING AND RESEARCH

Within UK universities, public administration as a taught subject has undergone serial redefinition and relabeling. In one sense, the old academic public administration community of the late 1960s and early 1970s has almost disappeared. What used to be taught as public administration became policy analysis or public policymaking or government and then, later, public management. The original title now survives mainly in courses run by the "new universities" (former polytechnics). During the 1970s, these institutions developed an array of undergraduate degrees in public administration which soon outstripped (at least in volume terms) the offerings of the "old" universities (Council for National Academic Awards, 1992). The old universities, however, continued to play a larger role in postgraduate degrees and research. Another significant difference was that the polytechnics/new universities grew up favoring a more vocational approach, whereas their older counterparts tended to a slightly more distant, or even snobbish attitude to the day-to-day problems of the practicing public administrator/manager. This concern with "applied" issues of management techniques and competencies deepened during the 1980s and early 1990s. Topics such as information technology in the public sector, employment law, or continental European languages were added to curricula. Also, many of the polytechnic degree courses included an internship period where the student gained work experience within public sector organizations – although securing good placements became increasingly difficult as state organizations laid off staff, and employment conditions generally worsened from the late 1980s onward.

It is symptomatic that, at the time of writing, the only reasonably up-to-date survey of public administration *teaching* has been written by a professor at a new university and (because of the nonavailability of systematic data) largely excludes developments at the old universities (Council for National Academic Awards, 1992). Meanwhile, the best-known recent essays on public administration *theory* are both authored by political science professors at old universities who display little interest in linking their theoretical preoccupations with either methods of teaching the subject or the needs of practicing administrators for specific training or advice (Dunleavy, 1982; Rhodes, 1991).

The academic locations in which public administration is taught have also shifted. Thirty years ago the subject was most commonly regarded as a subfield of politics and was to be found mainly in university departments of politics or government. Degrees of this kind still exist, but alongside them, the contributions of departments or schools of management or business studies have grown. At the Open University, for example, the 1970s saw courses in public administration being developed by the government and politics discipline, but in the late 1980s, it was the School of Management that created a master's course in public management, located within a broader MBA program. Also during the 1980s, the contribution of other academic disciplines has become more prominent – particularly accountancy and law. This trend can be explained partly by the increasing role of accountants and lawyers in facilitating the efficiency drives which characterized both the second and the third phases of central government's public sector reforms (Laughlin, 1992).

Academic research into the restructured state apparatus was somewhat inhibited by the Thatcher administrations' instinctive hostility toward the social sciences in general and political studies in particular (Pollit, Harrison, Hunter, & Marnoch, 1990). The "conviction politics" favored by Mrs. Thatcher did not sit easily with academic pretensions of independence and objectivity. Government departments have tightened their control over the dissemination of research that they fund themselves, and it appears that unfavorable evaluations of sensitive issues have sometimes been suppressed (e.g., on inner city policy, see Blackhurst, 1994).

Nevertheless, the main academic funding body, the Economic and Social Research Council, which has supported major programs of research into management in government, contracts and markets, local governance schemes have displayed the basically descriptive, atheoretical approach which has long characterized British public administration (half the articles appearing in the premier journal, *Public Administration* between 1980 and

1989 were case studies (Rhodes, 1991, p. 536). At the same time, however, highly theoretical work has begun to flourish. Overall, it could be said that the last 15 years have been a particularly fruitful period in British public administration theorizing as traditional institutional/descriptive approaches have been complemented and modified by infusions from public choice theory, organization theory, accounting theory, and public management theory.

Most notably, public choice theory has been detached from its politically rightward tendencies and fashioned into a powerful analytical tool. More and more scholars are now using the bureau-shaping model first developed by Dunleavy (1991). Others, working within the broad tradition of political economy, have elaborated our understanding of the conditions under which different forms of organizational coordination – markets, hierarchies, and networks – prosper or malfunction (a good example would be Thompson, Frances, Levacic, & Mitchell (1991); a seminal work in the "new institutional economics" was that of Williamson (1975)). Finally, others have developed sophisticated taxonomies of government tools and techniques, seeking to simplify and classify all possible modes of state intervention, as a first step to fitting types of intervention to types of problem or circumstance (Hood, 1983, 1985; Stewart, 1992). In much of this work, as in preceding attempts to establish a science of "bureaumetrics" (Hood & Dunire, 1981), British scholars have made original theoretical contributions that owe relatively little to the "big brother" of American public administration.

In sum, it cannot quite be claimed that there is a distinctive British school, but British scholars have nonetheless made a set of substantial, original contributions – both theoretical and more vocational/practical – to the field. However, it must also be acknowledged that the cultural bias in UK academic public administration remains profoundly anglophile. Only a handful of continental European scholars are cited more than occasionally in the UK literature, whereas the leading US scholars are well known to most of the British academic community. There are some tangible signs that among the younger generation of scholars, this bias may be lessening, but on the whole, the textual identity of UK academic public administration is still more that of a North American satellite than of a core European state. On the other hand, it is possible that this allegiance is now quite fragile, and that, as more research grants, consultancy contracts, and exchange students come from the European Union, the external focus of British scholars may shift eastward rather suddenly.

REFLECTIONS

The trajectory of promarket, antistate doctrines probably reached its apogee at the end of the 1980s during Mrs. Thatcher's third term of office. At that time, resort to market or market-like solutions to the problems of public administration had begun to seem automatic, almost ritualistic. The distinctiveness of the public sector was repeatedly minimized, its particular values ignored or downgraded.

During the 1990s, these same doctrines have begun to wane. No single critique or alternative has yet emerged to form a new orthodoxy, but the limitations of the Thatcher/Major brand of marketization and managerialism are being more and more widely acknowledged, both in the world of politics and in academe. The *Citizen's Charter,* with its contradictory mixture of propublic service rhetoric and firm commitments to market testing and privatization, neatly represents the shifting balance.

The unwillingness to acknowledge the distinctiveness of public services, so typical of the high Thatcher period, seems to have been replaced not by a sudden willingness, but by deepening uncertainty. If the great wave of privatization is approaching its end, if certain public services are henceforth to be acknowledged as distinctively *public,* if the need to retain and motivate public officials is once more to become a respectable objective, then what system of ideas and practices and education is appropriate to this new, smaller (but not small) state sector? If I am correct in my supposition that the *unwillingness* at the heart of government has diminished, to be replaced by *uncertainty,* then this is indeed an important opportunity for politicians, administrators, and academics alike. Those of us who teach and research in public administration may derive some encouragement from the thought that unwilling but confident leaders are unlikely to think they have anything to learn, whereas the uncertain may just be open to new (or even old) ideas.

REFERENCES

Aitken, I. (1988). Samizdat in search of a Gilmour. *Guardian,* 24th October, p. 2.

Bacon, R., & Eltis, W. (1978). *Britain's economic problems: Too few producers* (2nd ed.). London: Macmillan.

Blackhurst, C. (1994). l0bn wasted on failed inner city policy. *The Independent,* 17th June, p. 1.

Center for the Evaluation of Public Policy and Practice. (1994). *An evaluation of total quality management in the National Health Service: Synopsis of the final report to the Department of Health.* Uxbridge: CEPPP, Brunel University.

Chancellor of the Duchy of Lancaster. (1993). *Next steps review 1993 (Cm. 2430)*. London: HMSO.

Council for National Academic Awards. (1992). *Public policy and administration: Towards the year 2000*. London: CNAA.

Dunleavy, P. (1982). Is there a radical approach to public administration? *Public Administration, 60*(2), 215–233.

Dunleavy, P. (1991). *Democracy, bureaucracy and public choice*. London: Harvester-Wheatsheaf.

Harden, I. (1992). *The contracting state*. Buckingham: Open University Press.

Harrison, S., Hunter, D. J., Marnoch, G., & Pollit, C. (1992). *Just managing: Power and culture in the National Health Service*. Basingstoke: Macmillan.

Harrison, S., & Pollit, C. (1994). *Controlling health professionals: The future of work and organization in the NHS*. Buckingham: Open University Press.

Hayek, F. (1986). *The road to serfdom*. London: Ark Paperbacks (First published 1944).

Henkel, M. (1991). *Government, evaluation and change*. London: Jessica Kingsley.

Hood, C. (1983). *The tools of government*. Basingstoke: Macmillan.

Hood, C. (1985). *Administrative analysis: An introduction to rules, enforcement and organization*. Hemel Hempstead: Harvester-Wheatsheaf.

Hood, C., & Dunire, A. (1981). *Bureau-metrics*. Farnborough: Gower.

Jackson, P. (1985). *Implementing government policy initiatives: The Thatcher administration 1979–1983*. London: Royal Institute of Administration.

James, S. (1993). The idea brokers: The impact of think tanks on British Government. *Public Administration, 71*(4), 491–506.

Jones, G., & Hibbs, J. (1994). Labour attacks 500M fees to save 10M. *The Independent*, 27th April, p. 4.

King, D. (1987). *The new right*. London: Macmillan Education.

Laughlin, R. (1992). *Accounting control and controlling accounting: The battle for the public sector?* Sheffield: Sheffield University Management School Discussion Paper 92.29.

Le Grand, J., & Bartlett, W. (1993). *Quasi-markets and social policy*. Basingstoke: Macmillan.

Mather, G. (1989). Thatcherism and local government: An evaluation. In: J. Stewart & G. Stoker (Eds), *The future of local government*. Basingstoke: Macmillan.

Parsons, S. (1988). Economic principles in the public and private sectors. *Policy and Politics, 16*(1), 29–39.

Peters, T., & Waterman, R. (1982). *In search of excellence: Lessons from America's best-run companies*. New York: Harper and Row.

Pollit, C. (1990). Performance indicators. Root and branch. In: M. Cave, M. Kogan & R. Smith (Eds), *Output and performance measurement in government: The state of the art* (pp. 167–178). London: Jessica Kingsley.

Pollit, C. (1993). *Managerialism and the public service* (2nd ed.). Oxford: Blackwell.

Pollit, C. (1994). The citizen's charter: A preliminary analysis. *Public Money and Management, 14*(2), 9–14.

Pollit, C., Harrison, S., Hunter, D. J., & Marnoch, G. (1990). No hiding place: On the discomforts of researching the contemporary policy process. *Journal of Social Policy, 19*(2), 169–190.

Prime Minister. (1991). *The citizen's charter: Raising the standard (Cm. 1599)*. London: HMSO July.

Prime Minister. (1992). *The citizen's charter: First report, 1992 (Cm. 2101)*. London: HMSO November.

Rhodes, R. (1991). Theory and methods in British public administration: The view from political science. *Political Studies, 34*(3), 533–554.

Robinson, R., & Le Grand, J. (1994). *Evaluating the NHS reforms*. London: King's Fund Institute.

Rose, R. (1989). *Politics in England: Change and persistence* (5th ed.). Basingstoke: Macmillan.

Stewart, J. (1992). *Managing difference: The analysis of service characteristics*. Birmingham: Institute of Local Government Studies/Local Government Management Board.

Stewart, J., & Clarke, M. (1987). The public service orientation: Issues and dilemmas. *Public Administration, 65*(2), 161–178.

Thain, C., & Wright, M. (1992). Planning and controlling public expenditure in the UK, Part 2: The effects and effectiveness of the survey. *Public Administration, 70*(2), 193–224.

Thompson, G., Frances, J., Levacic, R., & Mitchell, J. (Eds) (1991). *Markets, hierarchies and networks: The co-ordination of social life*. London: Sage.

Williamson, O. (1975). *Markets and hierarchies: Analysis and anti-trust implications*. New York: Free Press.

FURTHER READING

Flynn, N. (Ed.) (1994). *Change in the civil service: A public finance foundation reader*. London: CIPFA.

Hood, C. (1991). A public management for all seasons? *Public Administration, 69*(1), 3–19.

CHANGING EUROPEAN STATES, CHANGING PUBLIC ADMINISTRATION:

EXPANSION AND DIVERSIFICATION OF PUBLIC ADMINISTRATION IN THE POSTWAR WELFARE STATE: THE CASE OF THE NETHERLANDS

Walter J. M. Kickert

ABSTRACT

Until the 1960s, the Dutch state was characterized and limited by "pillarization," "corporatism" and "consensus-democracy." Its public administration reflected the juridical perspective that dominated continental European administration during the 19th and 20th centuries. The rise of Dutch administrative science in the 1960s is related to the postwar expansion of its welfare state. The growing welfare state needed scientific support for policy making and planning. Legal expertise alone was no longer sufficient. The one-sided orientation in U.S. literature in the 1970s made way or a growing self-identity and self-confidence. Dutch

Comparative Public Administration: The Essential Readings
Research in Public Policy Analysis and Management, Volume 15, 793–810
Copyright © 2006 by Elsevier Ltd.
All rights of reproduction in any form reserved
ISSN: 0732-1317/doi:10.1016/S0732-1317(06)15037-X

administrative research today has reached a relatively high level of maturity, which might possibly contribute to the development of a new kind of European thinking about public administration.

Although public administration is now taught in The Netherlands at 10 of the existing 13 Dutch universities, Dutch public administration seems to be relatively unknown abroad, in the 1954 revision of the well-known German textbook on *Verwaltungslehre* by Theime, the international survey indicates that Dutch public administration is offered only at the Groningen faculty of Law and the Free University of Amsterdam. In the recent *gründliche* and comprehensive textbook on *Öffentliche Verwaltung* by Becker (1989), Dutch public administration is also said to be taught only at these two places.

Public policy and administration is, however, in reality, a separate, full-scale, regular degree program at Twente, Leiden, and Rotterdam Universities. In these three places, some 700 students enroll yearly making a total of over 2,000 students. The Twenne Department of Public Administration has some 60 staff members, and the combined Leiden–Rotterdam department, well over 100. Apart from that, public administration is a specialization at another seven universities. The Netherlands suffers from the tiny but crucial disadvantage that almost nobody in the world reads Dutch.

This article covers the history and state of affairs of the Dutch policy and administration sciences[1] – from the educational perspective and from the point of view of topics and trends in research – in relation to the development of the state and administration in The Netherlands.

POSTWAR WELFARE STATE AND ADMINISTRATIVE SCIENCE

The creation of Dutch administrative science in the mid-1960s and its subsequent rapid growth are related to the postwar rise and expansion of the Dutch welfare state. The enormous increase in public tasks and the role *of* the state in providing welfare arrangements in the various policy sectors called for government planning and policy making. The traditionally weak central state, with most public tasks performed by the "pillarized private initiative," now had to become actively involved in sectoral policy making and develop new policy instruments besides the usual legislation and regulation, such as budgeting and planning systems. Legal expertise alone was no longer sufficient for this type of government planning. The days of the legalistic state where law dominated the study of administration were over. The welfare state was in need of other scientific support for the rationalization of its sectoral policy design. This explains the growing popularity of the social sciences in general and the rise and growth of the Dutch policy sciences in particular.

DUTCH STATE AND ADMINISTRATION: PILLARIZATION, CORPORATISM, AND CONSENSUS

The three main characteristics of The Netherlands in the 20th century are the sociological characteristic of "pillarization," the socioeconomic characteristic of "corporatism," and the political characteristic of "consensus-democracy" (Hemerijck, 1993).

Although Catholics were almost 40 percent of the population in The Netherlands in the 19th century, the traditional Protestant conception that Catholics were second-rate citizens still dominated. This tradition originated in the successful 16th century struggle of the Protestant–Calvinist Dutch for separation from the Catholic Habsburg-Burgundy Empire. The consequent necessity for Catholics to establish a countervailing social and political power accounts for the "pillarization" of Dutch society (Kossmann, 1986), which divided society along ideological rather than class lines. Early 20th century Dutch society became divided along four "pillars" – Protestant, Catholic, Socialist, and Liberal–Neutral. The whole social organization of the Dutch state, ranging from political parties, trade unions, employer organizations, schools and universities, health and welfare institutions, media organizations, and even sports clubs, followed these four divisions.

Both the Protestants and the Catholics had clear ideological ideas about limitations on the power of the central state. In the Dutch state and society, therefore, many public tasks, such as education, health, and welfare, were performed by social organizations having the legal status of private foundations or associations belonging to one of the four pillars. The execution of public tasks was left to the so-called private initiative.

Dutch society was not split along the class division between capital and labor. The threat of labor revolt and rising socialism was countered lane in the 19th century by the creation of corporatism. The Netherlands forms an almost perfect and extreme example of the modern nonstatist concept of neocorporatism (Williamson, 1990). This European model of democracy emphasizes the interests represented by a small, fixed number of internally coherent and well-organized interest groups that are recognized by the state and have privileged or even monopolized access to the state. In The

Netherlands, in most policy fields, the major interest organizations are legally recognized and have formal access to policy as reflected in statutory rights of consultation, formal seats on advisory and regulatory bodies, and in a number of bi-, tri-, or multi-partite semi-state agencies. Neocorporatism is well established and highly institutionalized.

A third essential characteristic is consensus-democracy (Lijphart, 1984). In The Netherlands, all parties are minority parties and thus have to accommodate no share parliamentary power in broad coalition cabinets. Accommodation, deliberation, compromise, and consensus are the key words in the Dutch political culture. In his classic study of the politics of accommodation, Lijphart (1985) analyzed the paradox of a society that is deeply divided along strongly antagonistic ideological lines – the pillars – and at the same time could be such a politically stable state. His explanation was that the political leaders of the pillars were pragmatically oriented toward compromise and consensus, and the rank and file of the pillars were obedient followers of their leaders. In this sense, compromise and consensus form the very basis of the stable Dutch society.

DEPILLARIZATION AND INDIVIDUALIZATION

Since the late 1950s and early 1960s, the pillarization of society has decreased (Lijphart, 1982). Secularization and democratizaton were accompanied by a growing individualization of society. The behavior of individual citizens was being determined less and less by the traditional cohesive value patterns and the accompanying ordering social institutions of the pillars. The leadership role of church membership has decreased. The sociological concept of pillarization no longer characterizes Dutch society. Confessionalism in the sense of church going and active believing has also decreased. The remaining Protestant, Catholic, and other denominational institutions in The Netherlands have apparently lost their ideological groundings. As to the two other characteristics – corporatism and consensus – Dutch multi-parry politics of today are still characterized by compromise and consensus, and Dutch sectoral policy making still rests heavily on organized interest groups.

POSTWAR-CENTRALIZED WELFARE STATE

Well into the 19th century, Dutch state power was in the hands of the provinces and the merchant and aristocratic elites. The traditional absence of a strong, central, state authority has definitely changed with the postwar creation and expansion of the welfare state, which implies a growth of public tasks. Until the 1960s, those tasks continued to be carried out by predominantly private initiative as had been the custom since the early 20th century. With depillarization and individualization, the role of the state has increased, and state influence on public service delivery has grown. The fact that more and more state funds have been made available has contributed to that development. The influence of the state on the implementation of social services has steadily increased by means of legislation, planning, and budgeting systems. The ideology-based pillarized social institutions have become state-based, client-oriented, nonprofit, professional organizations. The constitutional balance between central and local government has shifted in favor of the central level, resulting at the end of the 1970s in a strongly centralized Dutch state.

SCIENTIFIC STUDY OF PUBLIC ADMINISTRATION

Apart from classical political thinkers like the lawyer Hugo de Groon (1583–1645) and the philosopher Spinoza (1632–1677), explicit attention on the functioning of public administration in The Netherlands dates from the end of the 18th century (Rutgers, 1993). The first Dutch administrative publication was Van den Spiegel's *Sketch of Administration* in 1786. The more elaborate French and German thinking about public administration only penetrated The Netherlands early in the 19th century, particularly in the work of the founding father of the Dutch constitution of 1848, the liberal member of parliament Thorbecke, a law professor at Leiden University. Like the rest of Europe in the 19th century, the juridical aspects of public administration were emphasized in The Netherlands (Raadschelders, 1994), and the field became dominated by lawyers. Thinkers about public administration paid only minimal attention no nonjuridical aspects, with few exceptions like the reformer of German administration, Lorenz Von Stein.

The first Dutch scientist to approach the study of administration from a mainly nonjuridical perspective was G.A. van Poelje, a municipal official who became the first professor of public (municipal) administration in Rotterdam in 1928 and published the first Dutch book on public administration, *General Introduction to Public Administration,* in 1942 (Rutgers, 1993; Twist & Schaap, 1992). Van Poelje knew of the German experiences and the writings of Von Stein, and he was interested in American public administration. In his book, he stressed the distinction between politics and administration. Van Poelje was the co-founder, in 1922, of a foundation for education in administrative sciences, which succeeded in getting the study of the field introduced as a separate academic specialization in the state and economics curriculum in Rotterdam in 1928. He was also the co-founder, in 1937, of the Institute for Administrative Sciences and in 1947 of the journal, *Administrative Sciences*, the joint journal of the Institute, the Association of Administrative Law, and the Association of Dutch Municipalities. His activities and initiatives formed the basis for the start of a separate administrative science in The Netherlands.

ADMINISTRATIVE LAW AND ADMINISTRATIVE SCIENCE

For a long time in many European states, administrative law was considered the main, if not the only, administrative science. In the 19th century, European *Rechtsstaten* capitalist economies were ideologically accompanied by liberalism, which called for a state that refrained from active interference in society and the economy. Because the state had to care for individual freedom and property rights, legislation and regulation were its main tasks. Such states were mainly in need of lawyers. With the transformation into welfare states, law gradually became considered only one of the administrative sciences. Administrative law creates a basis of authority for administrative discretion and sets the conditions but leaves administration discretionary freedom. Administration science is more broadly based on juridical, economic, social, and political sciences, and it analyzes the factual functioning of administration in various respects. The growing Dutch welfare state needed more than juridical scientific support for the rationalization and improvement of its planning and policy making. At the end of the 1950s, it became clear that administrative science deserved a proper place at universities. A committee for administrative studies was installed by the Ministry of Education, Arts and Sciences to examine how this should be realized. The 1963 report of this Wiarda-Committee opened the way for separate specialization programs and chairs.

PUBLIC ADMINISTRATION PROGRAMS

The marked acceleration of public administration in The Netherlands in the 1970s put an end to the predominant relationship with law and produced an increase in other disciplinary relationships. After the creation of a growing number of places where public administration could be studied as a specialization, the development of a separate science of public administration reached the next phase with the establishment of the first, full-scale public administration regular degree program at the Technological University of Twenne in 1976. This program was based on four separate disciplines. The Twente program centered around two themes: The contents of policy making and the structures and processes in which policy is made.

A second full-degree program was established in 1984 as a joint venture between the universities of Rotterdam and Leiden, which are located close to the political and administrative capital, The Hague, where parliament and government departments are located. The program aims at integrating the approaches of the basic disciplines of law, economics, sociology, and political science. Because the two universities possess faculties in all four disciplines, the staff of both public administration departments could concentrate and specialize on the integrative subject itself, different from the Twente situation where the distinct identities of the four disciplines prevail.

Besides these two full-degree programs, public administration is taught in another seven universities (Table 1). The number of students in public administration grew steadily in the mid-1980s by about 30 percent yearly, but has gradually declined since the end of the 1980s. During that period, social science as a whole underwent a remarkable dip in student popularity. The popularity of public administration is often compared to the popularity of business administration in the 1980s, a phenomenon not unknown in the United States.

Table 1. Establishment of Chairs in Public Administration, 1928–1976.

Year	University	Disciplinary Affiliation
1928	Economic Academy (Rotterdam)	Economics
1953	Institute for Social Studies	Social (developmental) sciences
1961	Free University (Amsterdam)	Political science
1966	Erasmus University (Rotterdam)	Sociology
1969	University of Utrecht	Law
1970	University of Amsterdam	Political science
1971	Technical University Delft	Law
1972	University of Leiden	Law and political science
1973	Catholic University Nijmegen	Political science
1976	Interuniversity Institute Delft	Business administration
1976	University of Groningen	Law

The disciplinary background of the study of public administration has shown a clear shift. Until the end of the 1950s, the study of public admin- istration was dominated by the juridical discipline. Since the 1960s, more and more chairs in public administration sciences have been created with various disciplinary backgrounds. At some places, the program was insti- tutionalized in law faculties; at some places, like Nijmegen, the sociological approach has become dominant, but in many other places, political science has become the main supporting discipline (Table 2).

CLOSE RELATIONS WITH ADMINISTRATIVE PRACTICE

A remarkable feature of Dutch administrative science, particularly in com- parison with other countries, is its close relationship with the practice of public administration. The early professors of public administration typi- cally came from administrative practice, and many professors today have dose relations with the public service, some leaving for or coming from top positions in government and administration. Many professors and staff members play an active role in local or national politics. Some professors have been director general or secretary general at ministries. A number of professors are members of major national government councils, such as the Social Economic Council, the Scientific Council for Government Policy (WRR), the Council for Home Administration (RBB), and the Council for Welfare Policy (HRWB), and many are members of various temporary ad- visory committees. Faculty members also do consultancy work and serve as advisers of different government organizations. However, a substantial number of contemporary professors have spent their entire careers inside a university, which indicates the scientific professionalization of the field. The bridge between administrative theory and practice is a strong one in The Netherlands. This is not only reflected in the structure and contents of course programs but also in research activities. A relatively large number of research projects are commissioned and financed by public organizations, such as ministries, municipalities, and other public bodies.

INSTITUTIONAL PROGRESS

The historical sketch above has shown the postwar institutional progress of public administration in The Netherlands. The field has separated from the

Table 2. Public Administration in The Netherlands, 1994.

University	Position within the Institution
Erasmus University Rotterdam and University of Leiden	Faculty of Social Sciences/Faculty of Law/Department of Public Administration
Technical University Twente	Faculty of Public Administration
Catholic University Nijmegen	Faculty Policy Sciences/Department of Administrative and Organization Science
Catholic University Brabant (Tillburg)	Faculty of Social Sciences/Department of Administrative and Policy Sciences
	Faculty of Law/Department of Administrative and Constitutional Law and Public Administration
University of Amsterdam	Faculty of Political and Social-Cultural Sciences/Department of Political Science
Free University (Amsterdam)	Faculty of Social-Cultural Sciences/Department of Political Science
University of Groningen	Faculty of Law/Department of Administrative Law and Public Administration
University of Utrecht	Faculty of Social Sciences and Faculty of Law/Center for Policy and Management
Technical University Delft	Faculty of Systems Engineering, Policy Analysis and Management
Open University (Heerlen)	Faculty of Business and Administrative Sciences

supporting disciplines and has created its own identity, which has become both substantially and institutionally distinct from other disciplines. It has developed into an integrative subject with a recognized scientific *raison d'être* of its own. The subject is taught at many places, and student interest has boomed in the last decade. The institutional identity of public administration is reflected by the appearance of academic journals. Beside the journal of *Administrative Sciences* founded in 1947, there are *Policy and Society* created in 1974, *Administration* (later called *Public Administration*) in 1982, *Policy Science* in 1984, and in 1992 the journal of the Dutch PA Association, *Public Administration.* The number of textbooks is also steadily growing. Its institutional identity is reflected in the existence of its own professional organization, the Dutch Association of Public Administration (*Vereniging voor Bestuurskunde*), which frequently organizes conferences, research seminars, and so forth.

TRENDS AND SCHOOLS IN ADMINISTRATIVE RESEARCH

Policy Science

Twente has from the beginning of the first full-degree program in 1976 been a research center with a strong policy-process orientation. Not long after the establishment in America of a distinct policy analysis movement with an identity separate from the traditional American public administration schools, similar developments took place in The Netherlands. In 1972, a journal, *Policy Analysis* was created, linked to the interdepartmental Committee for the Development of Policy Analysis (CODPA), which advocated a Planning Programming Budgeting Systems (PPBS)-like approach in the Dutch ministries, and in 1974, the journal *Policy and Society* appeared. Andries Hoogerwerf (1978) became the most prominent stimulator of the Dutch policy sciences. His special interest was the rationalization of policy design and the improvement of policy making by the use of scientific analysis. Hoogerwerf has successfully and systematically worked out a research program on the different aspects and dimensions of policy. A number of his followers have elaborated and extended his policy approach, particularly in the direction of policy implementation and effectiveness (Bressers, 1983; Maarse, 1983), thus supplementing Hoogerwerf's orientation on policy design and preparation with the development of an elaborate policy-evaluation approach (Herweijer, 1985).

Of course, Twente was not the only place where research into policy processes was carried out (Snellen, 1975; Ringeling, 1983; Hoppe, 1985). Also worth mentioning is the development (Bressers & Klok, 1988; Klok, 1991) of second-generation-type modern policy instruments (Bruyn & ten Heuvelhof, 1991), which leave the unrealistic assumption of mono-rationality and mono-centrism in governmental policy making and adopt the complexity of multi-actor and multi-rational networks. Note that the theoretical development of modern governmental policy instruments in The Netherlands seems to have progressed differently from, for example, the American development of new tools of government (Salamon, 1989). The area of policy sciences is rather well covered in Dutch research. Initially, the development of Dutch policy sciences was heavily influenced by American policy studies. There is, however, one remarkable difference with the American policy sciences. In the United States, the policy analysis school originated in the 1960s as a hard science separate from the soft science descriptive public administration school. In American public policy science, much attention is paid to facts and figures, to hard data, to mathematical and statistical methods, and to economic analysis. This hard data and hard science orientation has not conquered much ground in the Dutch scientific community.

LIMITS OF PLANNING AND GOVERNANCE

With the creation and expansion of the welfare state, the planning role of government became increasingly important. In many social fields, welfare arrangements had to be built, extended, and maintained, preferably in a coherent way, by means of integrated planning. The Socialist-Christian cabinet attempts at integrated planning reached a peak during the period 1973–1977. The possibilities of public governance seemed unlimited, but the first oil crisis in 1973 heralded the end of belief in planning. The economy could hardly be controlled, and despite all the beautiful plans, unemployment kept rising. Confidence in the beneficial effects of government planning faded, and the hard times of public budget retrenchments began. In 1977, the social democrats were replaced by the (conservative) liberals in the cabinet. A short intermezzo of a center-left cabinet, which was doomed no fail, led to the last unsuccessful socialist attempt to counter the economic tide by government planning. The 1980s were the period of the no-nonsense, center-right cabinets. The planning euphoria of the 1970s was replaced by a planning aversion in the 1980s. The developments within the academic community ran somewhat parallel. At the end of the 1970s, the development of a planning theory attracted more and more scientific attention. The rational planning model was increasingly considered inadequate, and modern, more refined planning models and theories were invented. Much effort was put into the search for "new" planning (Gunsteren, 1976; Kreukels, 1980; Veld, 1980; Vught, 1982).

In some European countries, the economic crisis and budget deficits led to a fundamental social and political debate about the future, restricted steering role of government, about the limits of governance. In Germany, a fundamental debate on "Steuerung" took place in the 1980s (Mayntz, 1987, 1988; Kaufmann, Majone, & Ostrom, 1986). In France, debate on the limitations of the traditionally top-down and centrally steering state called for a more modest state (Crozier, 1987). In The Netherlands, a debate on the limits of government steering arose in scientific as well as administrative and political circles. The Christian Democratic Party launched ideas on the retreat of government and the revitalization of social institutions in a plea for more self-responsibility of citizens in a responsible society. In the Social Democratic Party too, doubts arose about the steering capabilities of government and the possibility and desirability to "make and shape" society. In a publication of the Dutch Scientific Council for Government Policy (WRR), it was argued that government is not able to steer society as a deus ex machina and is unjustly ascribed a steering position above and apart from society (Hoed, Salet, & van der Sluys, 1983). Government is part of society, and is only one of the co-directing actors in the societal traffic among various other social actors. These changing views on government steering led to an emphasis on the limits and restrictions of the steering capacity of government in administrative research in the first-half of the 1980s. The Department of Public Administration at the Nijmegen Institute of Political Science in the early 1980s was the most outspoken representative of this school (Veld, 1978, 1980; Kickert, Aquina, & Korsten, 1985; Snellen, 1985). The Leiden Center for Societal Steering also played an important role in drawing attention to the study of the limits of governance in the "Rechnssnaat" and society (Bovens & Witteveen, 1985).

GOVERNANCE IN COMPLEX NETWORKS

At the end of the 1980s, another school of thinking emerged that attempted to stand up to the prevailing negative public and political opinion about the functioning of the public sector. Somewhat comparable to the 1987 Blacksburg Manifesto in the United States, where a number of public administration scientists from Virginia Polytechnic Institute tried to reverse the very negative anti-government tide of the bureaucrat-bashing period of the Reagan administration, Dutch administrative scientists became more aware of their responsibility for the public sector, both in teaching its future officials and in studying (Ringeling, 1983, 1994). Instead of mainly studying the limitations, boundaries, and failures of government, research became more and more oriented toward exploring the possibilities of new forms of government steering. Within the limits of complexity, new forms of public governance were to be sought. Insight in complex and dynamic public policy networks was considered as a possibility to improve government steering. This approach was adopted in the Rotterdam–Leiden research program on governance in complex networks (Hufen & Ringeling, 1990; Kickert, 1991; Koppenjan, Bruyn, & Kickert, 1993).

LOCAL AND REGIONAL ADMINISTRATION

Dutch administrative scholars have from the beginning been interested in local administration. The founding father of the field, G. A. van Poelje, was appointed in 1928 as professor in municipal administration. The traditionally anti-central orientation of the Dutch nation always has been strong. Central administration only originated early in the 19th century. The 1848 Dutch Constitution of the *decentralized unitary state* formed a sensitive balance between local autonomy and central authority. No wonder that central–local relations in Dutch home administration continues to interest scholars (Toonen, 1987; Derksen & Korsten, 1985).

In The Netherlands, an interesting process of regionalization is taking place. After more than 40 years of fruitless debates and experiments on many different forms of inner municipal cooperation, which all failed to bring about any substantial changes, since the end of the 1980s, a movement has started which finally seems to be succeeding. This movement started with the formation of new regional administrations around the large Dutch cities of Amsterdam, Rotterdam, The Hague, and Utrecht. Interesting developments at the regional meso-level between central and local administration are taking place in a number of other European states as well (Sharpe, 1993).

PUBLIC MANAGEMENT AND ORGANIZATION

The management and organization of Dutch administration has also been a subject of major interest, both in practice and in science. The organization

and functioning of the central government and administration has been the
subject of investigation by a number of advisory committees, some of which
have commissioned supporting studies by Dutch scholars. The 1980 advice
of the Vonhoff Committee on the structure of the civil service, which more
or less resembled the British 1968 Fuiton Report, was based on a number of
background studies, some of them performed by administrative scientists.
The 1993 report of the Wiegel Committee on departmental reordering,
which contained recommendations about the distinction between policy
making core-departments and executive agencies, was also partially based
on contributions by administrative scientists.

In the United States, public management scholars have increasingly succeeded in making a distinction between themselves and the generic management and organization sciences and have developed a specifically public-
sector-oriented approach (Bozeman, 1993). In The Netherlands, an explicit
school of thinking about public organization and management is lacking so
far. In the past, sporadic attempts were made to develop a distinct theory of
managing public organizations (Kooiman & Eliassen, 1987). It is remarkable that the few people interested in this topic all emphasize the importance
of public governance for public management and organization (Kooiman,
1993; Bekke, 1987, 1993; Kickert, 1993).

OTHER RESEARCH TOPICS

Some Dutch administrative scholars have specialized in national government and administration. An example is the Leiden–Rotterdam research
program on ministerial departments, which is producing a series of books
on all Dutch ministries (Hakvoort & De Heer, 1989). This research program
is in some respects a follow-up of the traditional research on civil service and
bureaucracy (Braam, 1957; Meer & Roborgh, 1993). Some Dutch scholars
are more interested in the subnational local, regional, and provincial level,
as mentioned before. And some scholars are more interested in the supranational level of European administration.

In view of the relatively strong policy science orientation, it is no surprise
that some scholars have sought their specializations in policy sectors. Owing
to the current importance of environmental policy making, both in the
political sense and in the availability of funds, many scholars work in that
area (Bressers, 1983; Glasbergen, 1989; Hanf, 1994). Education is a second
policy area that attracts the interest of Dutch scholars. Educational policy
analysis is carried out in The Netherlands at the Center of Studies of Higher

Education Policy (Vught, 1989). Besides these two sectoral examples, of course, almost any policy area can count on a number of administrative scholarly admirers.

Finally, three Dutch research programs are particularly embedded in the international scientific community. The Center for Studies of Higher Education Policy at Twenne plays an active and leading role on the international scene. Second, the Tilburg–Rotterdam cooperative program on informatization in public administration has many international contacts, has performed a number of international comparative studies (Snellen & Frissen, 1992) and has started an international journal, *Informatization and the Public Sector*. A third example is the Rotterdam–Leiden Crisis Research Team which has specialized in crisis decision making (Rosenthal, Charles, & Hart, 1989; Rosenthal & Pijnenburg, 1991).

CONCLUSIONS AND DISCUSSION

Welfare State and Policy Science

It is no coincidence that a distinct administrative science in The Netherlands originated in the 1960s after the postwar creation and expansion of the Dutch welfare state. Until then, administrative law was considered the only administrative science in Europe. Neither is it a coincidence that the postwar rise of administrative science in the welfare state started with the development of policy sciences. For the creation and expansion of the Dutch welfare state actually implied an enormous growth of public tasks and a steady increase in the role of the state in providing growing welfare programs such as in housing, health, education, social security, and welfare. The Dutch state became more and more involved in the growth of these and other sectoral policy fields. The expansion called for plans, strategies, and policies; legal expertise was no longer sufficient. The welfare state was in the need of other scientific support of sectoral policy making. Hence the origin of the Dutch policy sciences, the improvement of policy making by the use of scientific analysis, and the rationalization of policy design.

American and European Administrative Science

In the early days, Dutch public administration was strongly oriented toward U.S. literature. However, Dutch administrative science has recently reached a level of self-identity and self-confidence that has allowed Dutch policy scientists to recognize that the American state and its administration differs quite fundamentally from the Dutch. The Dutch state and administration are in many respects a special case and illustrative of the differences between the United States and Western Europe and between various European countries. The highly institutionalized, confessional form of corporatism in The Netherlands not only illustrates the difference with American pluralism but also with the many other European types of corporatism, such as the Social-Democrat Swedish type, the social market German type, and the language-based corporatism in Belgium and Switzerland. The decentralized unitary state of The Netherlands differs from the highly centralized French state, from the German federal state, and from the much more decentralized but still unitary Danish state. Such differences ought to be somehow re-flected in the models and theories of the administrative and policy sciences. It is hoped that the future development of Dutch administrative sciences might contribute to the resurrection of some kind of European thinking about administration.

NOTES

1. The usual Dutch equivalent word for the scientific study of public adminis-tration is *bestuurrkunde*. It contains the term "steer*ing*" – *besturen* – *and* the term "craft" – *kunde*. The Dutch term *besturen* has a broader meaning than sneering and control. The best Anglo-Saxon equivalent is the term "governance." The Dutch term *kunde* refers to the relationship between art, craft, and science. The Dutch word *bestuurskunde* – literally "the craft of governance" – reflects the bridge between administrative theory and practice.

REFERENCES

Becker, B. (1989). *Oeffenrliche Verwaltung*. Kempfenhausen: Verlag R.S. Schulz.
Bekke, A. J. G. M. (1987). *Public management in transition*. In: Kooiman & Eliassen (Eds).
Bekke, A. J. G. M. (1993). *Governance in interaction. Private tasks and public organizations.* In: Kooiman.
Bovens, M. A. P., & Witteveen, W. J. (Eds). (1985). *The ship of state. Reflections on law, state and steering*. Zwolle: Tjeenk Willink (in Dutch).
Bozeman, B. (Ed.) (1993). *Public management. The state of the art*. San Francisco: Jossey-Bass.
Braam, A. van. (1957). Officials and bureaucracy in The Netherlands. Zeist (in Dutch).
Bressers, J. Th. A. (1983). *Policy effectiveness and water quality policy*. Dissertation, Twente University (in Dutch).
Bresser, S. H., & Klok, P. J. (1988). Fundamentals for a theory of policy instruments. *International Journal of Social Economics, 15*(3/4), 21–41.

Bruyn, J. A. de., & ten Heuvelhof, E. F. (1991). *Steering instruments for government*. Leiden: Stenfert Kroese (in Dutch).

Crozier, M. (1987). *Etat Moderne, Etat Modeste* (ed.). Paris: Seuil.

Derksen, W., & Korsten, A. F. A. (Eds) (1985). *Local government in The Netherlands*. Alphen: Samson (in Dutch).

Gunsteren, H. R. van. (1976). *The quest for control*. London: Wiley.

Hemerijck, A. (1993). *Historical contingencies of Dutch corporatism*. Dissertation, Balliol College, Oxford.

Herweijer, M. (1985). *Evaluations of policy evaluation*. Dissertation, Twente University, Deventer, Kluwer (in Dutch).

Hoed, P. den, Salet, W., & van der Sluys, H. (1983). *Planning as enterprise*. The Hague: Staatsuitgeverii (in Dutch).

Hoogerwerf, A. (1978). *Government policy*. Alphen: Samsom (in Dutch).

Hoppe, R. (1985). *Trends in policy and design theory*. Amsterdam: VU Uitgeverij (in Dutch).

Hufen, J., & Ringeling, A. B. (Eds) (1990). *Policy networks*. The Hague: VUGA (in Dutch).

Kaufmann, F. X., Majone, G., & Ostrom, V. (Eds) (1986). *Guidance, control and evaluation in the public sector*. Berlin: De Gruyter.

Kickert, W. J. M. (1991). *Complexity, self-governance and dynamics*. Inaugural address, Erasmus University, Alphen, Samsom (in Dutch). Abridged version published in English in Kooiman (1993).

Kickert, W. J. M. (Ed.) (1993). *Changes in management and organization at central government*. Alphen: Samsom (in Dutch).

Kickert, W. J. M., Aquina, H. J., & Korsten, A. F. A. (1985). *Planning within bonds*. Zeist: Kerckebosch (in Dutch).

Klok, P. J. (1991). *An instrumental theory for environmental policy*. Dissertation, Twente University (in Dutch).

Kooiman, J. (Ed.) (1993). *Modern governance*. London: Sage.

Kooiman, J., & Eliassen, J. (Eds) (1987). *Managing public organizations*. London: Sage.

Koppenjan, J., de Bruyn, J. A., & Kickert, W. J. M. (Eds) (1993). *Management of policy networks*. The Hague: VUGA (in Dutch).

Kossmann, E. H. (1986). *The low countries*. Amsterdam: Elsevier (two volumes in Dutch. Originally published in English in 1978).

Kreukels, A. M. J. (1980). *Planning and planning process*. Dissertation, Utrecht University, The Hague, VUGA (in Dutch).

Lijphart, J. A. (1984). *Democracies: Patterns of majoritarian and consensus government in twenty-one countries*. New Haven: Yale University Press.

Lijphart, J. A. (1985). *The politics of accommodation: Pluralism and democracy in The Netherlands*. Amsterdam: De Bossy (in Dutch. Originally published in English in 1968).

Maarse, J. A. M. (1983). *Implementation and effects of labor market policy*. Dissertation, Twente University (in Dutch).

Mayntz, R. (1987, 1988). Political control and social problems. In: Th. Ellwein et al. (Eds), *Yearbook of government and public administration* (pp. 81–98). Baden: Nomos.

Meer, F. M. van der, & Roborgh, L. J. (1993). *Officials in The Netherlands*. Alphen: Samsom (in Dutch).

Raadschelders, J. (1994). Administrative history: Contents, meaning and usefulness. *International Review of Administrative Sciences*, *60*(1), 117–129.

Ringeling, A. B. (1983). *The instruments of policy*. Inaugural Address at Erasmus University. Alphen: Samsom (in Dutch).

Ringeling, A. B. (1994). *The image of government*. The Hague: VUGA (in Dutch).

Rosenthal, U., Charles, M. T., & Hart, P. T. (Eds). (1989). *Coping with crises. The management of disasters, riots and terrorism*. C. C. Springfield, IL: Thomas.

Rosenthal, U., & Pijnenburg, B. (Eds) (1991). *Crisis management and decision-making*. Dordrechn: Kluwer Academic.

Rutgers, M. R. (1993). *Between fragmentation and integration*. Dissertation, Leiden University, Delft, Eburon (in Dutch).

Salamon, L. M. (Ed.) (1989). *Beyond privatization. The tools of government action*. Washington: Urban Institute Press.

Sharpe, L. J. (1993). *Rise of meso government in Europe*. London: Sage.

Snellen, I. Th. M. (1975). *Approaches to strategy formulation*. Alphen aan den Rijn: Samsom (in Dutch).

Snellen, I. Th. M. (Ed.) (1985). *Limits of government*. Amsterdam: Kobra.

Toonen, The. A. J. (1987). *Thinking about home administration*. Dissertation, Erasmus University, Rotterdam, The Hague, VUGA (in Dutch).

Twist, M. van, & Schaap, L. (1992). The founding fathers of Dutch administrative science. *BB Management, 3–7*, (in Dutch).

Veld, R. J. in't. (1978). *Limits of administration*. Inaugural address at Nijmegen University, The Hague, VUGA (in Dutch).

Veld, R. J. in't. (1980). Planning and democracy. In: *Approaches to planning*. The Hague: Scientific Council for Government Policy (in Dutch).

Vught, F. A. van (1982). *Experimental policy planning*. Dissertation, Twente University, The Hague, VUGA (in Dutch).

Vught, F. A. van (Ed.) (1989). *Governmental strategies and innovation in higher education*. London: Jessica Kingsley.

Williamson, R. J. (1990). *Corporatism in perspective*. London: Sage.

FURTHER READING

Kickert, W. J. M. (1997). Public governance in The Netherlands. An alternative to Anglo-American managerialism. *Public Administration and International Quarterly*, *75*(4), 731–752.

Thieme, W. (1984). *Verwaltungslehre* (4th ed.). Cologne: C. Heymans Verlag.

CHANGING EUROPEAN STATES, CHANGING PUBLIC ADMINISTRATION:

FROM CONTINENTAL LAW TO ANGLO-SAXON BEHAVIORISM: SCANDANAVIAN PUBLIC ADMINISTRATION

Torben Beck Jorgensen

ABSTRACT

While Norway, Sweden, and Denmark share many historic, political, and cultural features, their state systems and public administration exhibit important differences. Likewise, Nordic administrative sciences reflect a significant degree of ethnocentric diversity. Although as a whole, since the 1960s, Scandinavian academic public administration has witnessed rapid growth, an emphasis on local–regional government, and highly sophisticated scientific-empirical research, as opposed to professional training or narrow application of technical–legal methodologies.

Comparative Public Administration: The Essential Readings
Research in Public Policy Analysis and Management, Volume 15, 811–830
Copyright © 2006 by Elsevier Ltd.
All rights of reproduction in any form reserved
ISSN: 0732-1317/doi:10.1016/S0732-1317(06)15038-1

Norway, Sweden, and Denmark[1]are, in many ways, like three siblings: closely linked, with a common heritage, but nonetheless very different and often in conflict with each other although nowadays in a peaceful way.[2]

The similarities are manifold. First, the three countries share many culturally determined features. The linguistic differences are minor. Since the middle of the 16th century, these countries have embraced the same religion: Protestantism. Hence, the common cultural heritage is significant and reinforced by the fact that none of the countries contains major ethnic or religious minorities.

Second, the three countries have uniform political systems and traditions: consensus-oriented democracies of many parties, a fairly strong social democratic dominance, well-established traditions of corporate pluralism, and low levels of labor market conflict. Especially since the Second World War, the three countries have developed extensive public sectors with an emphasis on the institutional welfare state.

Third, contemporary Scandinavia has historical development of great continuity. The monarchical form of government will soon celebrate its millennium, a centralized and – in Weberian terms – bureaucratic state apparatus has developed gradually since the 17th century, and there is a long tradition of local self-government and parliamentarian democracy well rooted in the 19th century. Breaks in this continuity have naturally occurred, but they typically have been nonviolent.

However, these common features tend to conceal a number of significant differences in state-building and political culture. First, certain minor but nonetheless important differences exist in the formal political system. Sweden has, as part of its constitution, highly independent public agencies. Government ministers have no direct responsibility for the agency's concrete decisions and cannot reverse these decisions. External control is exercised by administrative courts and the ombudsman. In contrast, public agencies in Denmark and Norway are subject to direct ministerial responsibility.

Norway and Sweden, unlike Denmark, have politically appointed state secretaries and parliamentary elections every four years, whereas the Danish prime minister can call a general election at any time. One result of these differences is that relations between politicians and civil servants develop in different ways.

The differences are more marked – and more difficult to describe and document – when it comes to the national political culture or policy style. In Sweden, the sense of collectivity seems stronger than in Denmark. There is a greater respect for public authorities in Sweden. The Swedish term *Folkehemmet* (the people's homeland), which expresses the state's care for its

Table 1. Scope of Research (Percentages in Parentheses).

Scope	Denmark	Norway	Sweden	1979–1985	1986–1993	Total (1979–1993)
National	105 (87)	115 (88)	55 (77)	110 (89)	165 (83)	275 (85)
Comparative	5 (4)	8 (6)	6 (8)	3 (2)	16 (8)	19 (6)
Review articles	11 (9)	8 (6)	10 (14)	10 (8)	19 (10)	29 (9)
Total	121 (100)	131 (100)	71 (99)	123 (99)	200 (101)	323 (100)

citizens, cannot be used in Denmark in a neutral sense, let alone in a positive sense. Its use in Denmark provokes, rightly or wrongly, an indulgent smile. Compared to Sweden, Denmark has a more pragmatic and liberal policy style.

These characteristic differences can be observed within many diverse policy areas, such as industrial policy and alcohol policies. This applies no administrative reform policies as well. Compared to Denmark, Sweden has a long tradition of systematic "official" analyses and diagnoses of administrative problems and well-established ties between the academic world and practitioners (Lægreid & Pedersen, 1994). And Sweden spends three times as much as Denmark on social science.

What does all this imply for an article on Scandinavian research on administration? Primarily that readers should not expect administration research in the three countries to be the same, despite the many obvious similarities. Nor should they expect to find close Nordic cooperation or a great number of comparative studies on the Nordic states. In fact, Anckar (1991), in a review of Nordic political science, claims that Nordic political science is marked by a high national ethnocentricity. There is no reason to believe that public administration research should be less ethnocentric than political science in general (Table 1).[3]

Although some growth in comparative studies can be identified, national studies clearly dominate the overall picture. As will be demonstrated later, national profiles are identifiable, and, although similarities do occur, they may be explicable to some extent in terms of a strong, international orientation.

THE INSTITUTIONAL LANDSCAPE OF SCANDINAVIAN PUBLIC ADMINISTRATION RESEARCH

Scandinavian research on public administration has one thing in common: all three countries have demonstrated a considerable growth in this field

Table 2.   The Overall Production of Articles (Percentages in
Parentheses).

Country	1979–1985	1986–1993	Total (1979–1993)
Norway	37 (26)	105 (45)	142 (38)
Denmark	64 (46)	80 (34)	144 (38)
Sweden	39 (28)	50 (21)	89 (24)
Total	140 (100)	235 (100)	375 (100)

since the Second World War.[4] This is reflected in Table 2, especially if one bears in mind that articles in new and sometimes specialized public administration journals have not been registered. Thus, in four of the five included journals, public administration articles will have to compete with comparative politics, international politics, political theory, and so forth. Norway and Denmark seem to be most productive, and Norway especially shows a remarkable expansion in public administration research (Table 2).

Denmark

Danish administration, administration research, and teaching have long had a strong legal emphasis, and administrative issues have often been viewed as synonymous with legal issues.[5] When the Nordic Administrative Association was founded in 1918, the Danish members were exclusively lawyers, and administrative research was synonymous with constitutional law and administrative law until the 1950s.

Poul Meyer paved the way for the political science-oriented study of public administration in Denmark. Ironically, Meyer was a lawyer, but he had stumbled across Herbert A. Simon's *Administrative Behavior.* Inspired also by American political science, Denmark's first political science department was established at the Aarhus University in 1959, with Poul Meyer as Denmark's first professor in public administration. His works include *Administrative Organization* (1957) and *Die Werwaltungsorganisation* (1962).

At the Department of Political Science, Aarhus University, the integration of public administration research in political science is emphasized. For example, a study on the central administration and its political base (Grønnegaard Christensen, 1981) views bureaucratic actors as political actors in their own right, which has led to a concentration on studies that incorporate public policy and public administration. This is shown in several studies: policy implementation (Winter, 1990), policy evaluation and the use of knowledge in policy making (Albæk, 1989–1990); technology policy (Munk Christiansen, 1989), and an analysis of the liberal–conservative government's regulatory and deregulatory policies during the 1980s (Grønnegaard Christensen, 1988).

The same linkage of public policy and public administration can be found at the Aalborg University Center. For several years, the Department of Politics, Economics, and Administration research has done research in the regional administration of labor market policies (Jorgensen, 1991). At the Department of Social Affairs and Organization, research has focused on the study of local welfare institutions (Hegland, 1994).

The Department of Commercial Law and Political Science, University of Odense, has a strong concentration on local government, specialties within this focus are, among others, the aspects of city management (Mouritzen, 1989) and the effect of fiscal stress on local decision-making and resource allocation (Mouritzen, 1991). Other research topics are local institutions and user-influence (Larsen, 1991) and voluntary organizations (Klaudi Klausen, 1991).

Like the University of Odense, the Department of Social Science and Business Administration, Roskilde University Center, concentrates on the local level. A number of aspects of the local politico-administrative system have been studied. Examples include the role of interest of organizations and local movements in the local welfare state (Villadsen, 1986) and local institutionalization in a bottom-up policy perspective (Bogason, 1992). The development of public policy and public administration in central government has been studied from a negotiated economy perspective including comparisons between different sectors and between the Scandinavian countries (Pedersen, 1993).

The Institute of Political Science, University of Copenhagen, has a tradition of studies in governance and control, emphasizing external control and internal management of public organizations (Antonsen & Foss Hansen, 1992), with the aim of contributing to the development of the theory of public organizations (Beck Jorgensen, 1991). Another important research field focuses on change, reform, and the history of public administration. The Institute of Political Science is engaged in the writing of the history of Danish public administration since the Middle Ages (Knudsen, 1991a, 1991b), and administrative reform and change are studied from a governance perspective (Beck Jorgensen, 1993a, 1993b). Finally, the institute has specializations in: informanization of the public sector (Hoff, 1991), gender and organization (Nexø Jensen, 1994), and research and education policy and administration (Foss Hansen, 1990).

Norway

Norway experienced a breakthrough in public administration research after the Second World War.[6] The pioneer work was done by Knut Dahl Jacobsen in the 1960s (1964). Dahl Jacobsen introduced behavioralism, empirical studies, and a combination of political science and organization theory into Norwegian research. In 1972, the Norwegian Power Study was launched, headed by, among others, Johan P. Olsen and Gudmund Hernes. A number of the Power Study's significant findings have been published by Olsen (1983).

In many ways, Dahl Jacobsen's studies and the Power Study influenced later Norwegian research in public administration to emphasize a special blend of political science and organization theory and, at the same time, a strong empirical orientation manifested through the establishment of a number of major databases.

The Department of Administration and Organization Theory, University of Bergen, is the only academic department in Scandinavia with a main responsibility for public administration research, and the department represents the strongest concentration of resources devoted to that field in Scandinavia. Historically, the department is tooted in organization theory – more explicitly the Carnegie-Tech School (the Simon and Match tradition). Classic works are *A Garbage Can Model of Organizational Choice* (Cohen, March, & Olsen, 1972) and several spin-off studies from that theoretical breakthrough (March & Olsen, 1976).

From the late 1980s, studies have focused on politics for the development of public administration, including issues such as tensions between central control and institutional autonomy (Baldersheim, 1989); sneering and management through goal formulation (Lægreid, 1991); reform in personnel policies (Lægreid, 1993b); reform in an institutional perspective (Brunsson & Olsen, 1993); and comparative studies on reform policies for public administration (Lægreid & Pedersen, 1994).

Beside studies on general public administration and central government, the department is engaged in research on local government. Examples are democratic leadership and the roles of elected politicians (Larsen & Offerdal, 1990), leadership and innovation (Baldersheim & Stava, 1993), and evaluation of the Nordic Free-Commune Experiments (Baldersheim & Stahlberg, 1994).

The Department of Political Science, University of Oslo, has in a number of publications treated decision-making and reorganization in central government as the steps of the Norwegian Power Study. In the 1980s, these studies led to an interest in the formulation of a constructive discipline of public administration (Egeberg, 1989, 1994), that is, to formulate research-based answers to the classic question: what are the effects of a specific way of organizing public administration? Modern reform policies for public administration have been studied by Christensen (1991), who has adopted instrumental and institutional perspectives on central sneering by goal formulation and strategic planning.

Since the early 1970s, the department specialized in local government studies. Research has included issues such as the adoption of the public policy perspective (Kjellberg, 1975), budgetary studies and resource allocation (Hansen, 1984), and organizational learning in municipalities through local experiments (Rose, 1990).

Comparative government is represented in the works of Lane (1993) and the internationalization of national public administration is dealt with in the newly established ARENA-project, with Johan P. Olsen as coordinator.

The Department of Public Policy and Administration, University of Tromso, also conducts studies on public administration from an institutional perspective. Rovik has studied whether the use of organizational consultants in public administration is best understood as rational diagnosis and problem solving, or as a vague phenomenon (Røvik, 1992a), Røvik (1992b) perceives organizational designs as institutionalized standards. The development of values and the normative basis of the state are discussed in Eriksen (1993).

Sweden

Contrary to Norway and Denmark, Sweden is characterized by a long tradition in political science.[7] The first Nordic political science journal was Swedish and has been published since 1897. However, as in Denmark and Norway, Swedish public administration research did not develop until after the Second World War. One of the pioneer works is Gunnar Heckscher's (1953) *Svensk statsforvaltning i arbete* (Swedish Central Administration at Work).

At the Department of Political Science, University of Gothenburg, a strong concentration on local government was established in the 1960s (Westerstahl, 1967), and the department later included many aspects of local government such as decision-making (Westerstahl, 1974), reform (Stromberg, 1980), fiscal austerity (Bokenstrand et al., 1992), and housing politics (Lundquist, Elander, & Danermark, 1990).

The Department of Political Science, University of Stockholm, focuses primarily on policy analysis, which has been studied in general (Premfors, 1992a), on higher education (Premfors, 1984), and on the connection between knowledge, science, and the state (Premfors, 1992b; Wirtrock, Peter, Carol, & Wollmann, 1991). Central administration and the Swedish tradition within core departments and executive agencies have also been studied in general (Linde, 1982).

At the Department of Political Science, University of Lund, local and regional politics and administration are the focus (Beckman, 1993; Gustafsson, 1991). Part of the interest in local matters is reflected in studies of, for example, schools and local leadership (Blom, 1990; Schartau, 1993). Another emphasis is on steering (Lundquist, 1987). In the last few years, an interest in the normative basis of the public sector has emerged, that is, an interest in the general values for which the public administration should be responsible, such as democratic responsibility (Lundquist, 1991) and bureaucratic ethics (Lundquist, 1993).

The Department of Political Science, Uppsala University, is mainly characterized by an interest in macrostudies and policy analysis. In a number of studies, Rothsnein (1991) has analyzed the broad structures of the state in terms of corporanism and the welfare state. Within policy analysis, evaluation and implementation studies dominate. In Vedung, Rist, and Bemelmans-Videc (1995), a general theory of evaluation is outlined, and Vedung (1993) analyzes the implementation of Swedish land-use policies. Public administration is also studied within the framework of policy analysis, that is, conceptualized as administrative policies (Petersson & Soderlind, 1993).

The Department of Political Science, Umeå University, has specialized in local and regional politics and has gradually adopted a policy perspective on the public sector, focusing on education, social affairs, environmental policies, and regional development of business and municipal planning (Khakee & Eckerberg, 1993). In the last few years, a number of research projects have focused on the Baltic countries (Eckerberg et al., 1994). The Umeå University has a long tradition of implementation studies (Hjern & Porter, 1981; Hjern & Hull, 1987; Eckerberg, 1987).

A description of Swedish research on public administration would be incomplete without mentioning the research at the Stockholm Business School and Department of Business Administration at the University of Lund. Since the early 1970s, a number of scholars have studied public administration from the perspective of organization theory. The point of departure has been a critique of rational decision-making (Brunsson, 1985) and a search for understanding organizations acting in complex worlds (Brunsson, 1989; Jacobsson, 1989), complex steering and decision-making processes (Czarniawska-Joerges, 1992; Sahlin-Andersson, 1992), and reform processes in organizations (Brunsson & Olsen, 1993).

STABLE FEATURES OF SCANDINAVIAN RESEARCH: CONTEXTUAL PUBLIC ADMINISTRATION RESEARCH

Public administration in Scandinavian research is rarely, if ever, seen as a purely technical matter. First, public administration is viewed as an academic discipline rather than as a profession, and university studies are thus oriented toward a scientific understanding of reality more than training for positions in the public administration. This applies to Denmark and Norway in particular.

Second, public administration is mostly understood as a part of a wider context, not as a technical matter. Naturally, the conceptualization of context differs significantly. The policy perspective may highlight political bodies and interest groups as the context (Universities of Stockholm, Uppsala, and Arhus), and organization theory may emphasize the importance of organizational environments in general (Universities of Bergen, Oslo, and Copenhagen). Even when a purely intraorganizational perspective is adopted, the focus is often on complex decision-making processes – conflicting internal values, and so forth.

The contextual identity and the academic orientation do not, however, imply that Scandinavian research is purely theoretical. In Table 3, public administration articles are categorized according to their empirical/theoretical content.

Two conclusions may be drawn from these figures. First, the empirical orientation in general is quite high, especially in Norway and Denmark. Second, there is a small but nevertheless notable growth in what is normally considered "healthy" research – articles with an explicit combination of theory and data.

Local Government

There is a quite strong emphasis on local and regional government. This is not surprising since the Scandinavian countries have perhaps the strongest local governments in the world.

Table 3. Theoretical/Empirical Orientation of Articles (Percentages in Parentheses).

Orientation	Denmark	Norway	Sweden	1979–1985	1986–1993	Total (1979–1993)
Theoretical	49 (34)	40 (28)	38 (43)	47 (34)	80 (34)	127 (34)
Empirical	68 (47)	66 (46)	30 (34)	68 (49)	96 (41)	164 (44)
Both	27 (19)	36 (25)	21 (24)	24 (17)	60 (25)	84 (22)
Total	144 (100)	142 (99)	89 (101)	139 (100)	236 (100)	375 (100)

Table 4.   Level of Jurisdiction Analyzed in Articles (Percentages in Parentheses).

Level	Denmark	Norway	Sweden	1979–1985	1986–1993	Total (1979–1993)
Nation-state	67 (47)	54 (38)	26 (29)	57 (41)	90 (38)	147 (39)
Municipality/ country	24 (17)	35 (25)	25 (28)	33 (24)	51 (22)	84 (22)
Relations between levels	14 (10)	13 (9)	8 (9)	16 (11)	19 (8)	35 (9)
General public administration	39 (27)	40 (28)	30 (34)	34 (24)	75 (32)	109 (29)
Total	144 (101)	142 (100)	89 (100)	140 (100)	235 (100)	375 (99)

It is interesting that the significance of local government research is not found in Table 4. The figures reveal more about the organization of research and the publication patterns. One hypothesis is that local government studies constitute a research community, distinct from public administration research and political science in general. In fact, several journals specialize in local government, and in all three countries nonuniversity institutes with a strong focus on local government, urban research, and so forth have been established.

TOPICS AND TRENDS FROM PLANNING TO CUTBACKS

In the 1970s, planning was quite a popular theme, be it spatial planning, sectoral planning, or expenditure planning. Following a number of "planning disasters," the rational approach was subject to increasing criticism, and studies on nonrational processes flourished. After the energy crisis in 1973 and the state's subsequent fiscal crisis, studies on the apparently inevitable growth in public expenditure and cutback studies took over.[8] This trend seems to have peaked.

Attempts to understand the autonomy and the effects of fiscal stress have evidently been a Swedish–Danish endeavor. This is hardly surprising. Because of the Norwegian oil revenues, the effects of steadily growing public expenditures were postponed. In fact, the growth in cutback studies in Sweden and Denmark demonstrates how closely the development in research sometimes is linked to emerging problems in practice – without any central control.

Table 5. Administrative Level Analyzed in Articles (Percentages in Parentheses).

Level	Denmark	Norway	Sweden	1979–1985	1986–1993	Total (1979–1993)
Context of administration	32 (28)	24 (29)	28 (47)	34 (31)	60 (33)	94 (32)
Central departments	58 (51)	45 (38)	22 (37)	57 (52)	68 (38)	125 (43)
Agency level	24 (21)	38 (32)	10 (17)	19 (17)	53 (29)	72 (25)
Total	114 (100)	117 (99)	60 (101)	110 (100)	181 (100)	291 (100)

THE RISE OF NEW INSTITUTIONALISM

The strong development of New Institutionalism in the Scandinavian countries is no coincidence. It is merely the logical consequence of the interest in how organizational factors affect people and politics (Rothsnein, 1993). With the strong ties between political science and organization theory in Norway, it is not surprising that the starting signal was Norwegian (Olsen, 1985). However, New Institutionalism soon spread epidemically to Denmark and Sweden. It has been presented as a coherent program in March and Olsen (1989). In general, New Institutionalism has created or at least supported a new interest in institutional history, reform, and the shaping of values, and it is perhaps also partly responsible for the renewed interest in normative issues (Table 5).

THE EUROPEAN DIMENSION

The European dimension has not been a prominent theme in Scandinavian research in public administration for many years.[9] However, following the development of further European integration and the possibility of the inclusion of Norway and Sweden in the European Union (EU), the European dimension has gained considerable interest. So far, studies have focused on the internationalization of national administration in general (Blichner & Sangolt, 1993) and on the future role of local government in the EU (Klaudi Klausen & Goldsmith, 1995). In Norway, a large research project on the Europeanization of the nation state (the ARENA project) has been launched (Table 6).

Table 6.   Organization/Environment (Percentages in Parentheses).

Unit	Denmark	Norway	Sweden	1979–1985	1986–1993	Total (1979–1993)
Organizational analysis	26 (20)	26 (27)	12 (18)	16 (13)	58 (29)	74 (22)
Environmental relations						
Citizens	17 (13)	18 (14)	8 (12)	14 (12)	29 (14)	43 (13)
Political bodies	27 (21)	31 (23)	19 (29)	23 (19)	54 (26)	77 (23)
Interest groups	19 (15)	10 (8)	6 (9)	22 (18)	13 (6)	35 (11)
International level	12 (9)	2 (1)	6 (9)	3 (2)	17 (8)	20 (6)
Ministries	25 (19)	30 (23)	14 (21)	35 (29)	34 (16)	69 (21)
Other administrative units	4 (3)	6 (5)	1 (2)	6 (5)	5 (2)	11 (3)
Total	130 (100)	133 (101)	66 (100)	119 (98)	210 (101)	329 (99)

FROM MACRO TO MICRO – AND BACK AGAIN?

The 1970s were characterized by a prevailing interest in the macrolevel, that is, an interest in general political/administrative patterns such as corporatism, centralized departments in ministries, and connections between administrative units and political bodies. During the 1980s, the microlevel attracted increased attention, with a growing interest in intraorganizational analysis, low-level public organizations producing services or imposing control on directly affected citizens, public management, and the relationship between public organizations and the users. The shift from macro- to microlevel also represents a shift in values from due process and democracy to efficiency.

This trend is most visible from the remarkable growth in studies on low-level producing organizations, although these studies are certainly not dominating the overall picture. With the Norwegian roots in organization theory, it is not a surprise that Norway seems to be the leading country of the micro wave ....

The microwave with its ideological flavor of new public management and neoliberalism has provoked a new discussion of what is meant by public values. A common theme has been the attempt to rethink the normative basis of the public sector and to relocate isolated producers of services within a larger structure in which, for example, solidarity, democratic responsibility, stability, ethics, and the notion of the *Rechtstaat* play a major role (Lundquist, 1991; Olsen, 1993).

What we are currently confronting is perhaps not so much "a return of the macro" as a renewed interest in normative issues in general. New publications and research initiatives, especially in Sweden, deal explicitly with value issues (Lundquist, 1994) and state responsibilities (Rothstein, 1994) and signal an interest in traditional judicial values as well ....

CONCLUDING REMARKS

Historically and intellectually, Scandinavian public administration research and practice are rooted in law, a fact that was evidenced in all three countries until the late 1950s. Today, public administration research is mainly anchored in political science and organization theory. However, one finds quite different patterns in the three countries.

Sweden has a long tradition in the field of political science and the growth in public administration research after the Second World War took place in political science departments. Studies in public administration based on organization theory have mainly been carried out at business schools (Stockholm) and in business administration departments at universities (Lund). Naturally, this institutional profile tends to keep political science and organization theory approaches separate. This is not a purely Swedish phenomenon. Harmon and Mayer (1986) tell the same story about the United States.

Norway represents the opposite case. For several years, organization theory has been the major route to the understanding of public administration and, to some extent, political institutions in general. One explanation is probably the combination of the lack of a political science tradition and the early ties between the United States and Norway in general social science. It is no coincidence that the Norwegian Power Study in the 1970s had a strong emphasis on public administration, whereas the recent Swedish Power Study tends to ignore public administration. Denmark is somewhat in between.[10]

Does separating political science and organization theory represent any risk? To a certain point the answer is yes. Public administration research located at political science departments is naturally regarded as a subdiscipline. When compared to international politics, comparative politics, and political theory, public administration more often than not is considered "low politics" and hence of less interest.

On the other hand, public administration research based on organization theory and located at business schools obviously may lose the sense of politics. Especially when adopting standard American organization theory, there is the risk of misinterpreting or simply bypassing the political environments of Scandinavian public organizations and of forgetting their institutional history.

Recent innovations may change this picture. First, in Copenhagen, Bergen, and Stockholm, research centers have been established as joint ventures between political science departments and business schools. Thus, disciplinary barriers between political science and organization theory may be partly overcome, and the renewed interest in normative issues may succeed in combining macro- and microperspectives.

Second, the rise of New Institutionalism is not only a negative reaction to behavioralism. It may also stimulate a new interest in administrative and constitutional law and history. This may, in turn, lead to a reconsideration of the intellectual roots of Scandinavian public administration research.

NOTES

1. This review excludes Finnish research despite the fact that the inclusion of Finland would be natural. The main reason for excluding Finland is that only a small part of Finnish research is written in Swedish or English.

2. For a general introduction to Scandinavian government and politics, see Penerston (1993), and for a discussion of Scandinavian state-building, see Knudsen and Rothstein (1994).

3. This and the following figures are based on a quantitative survey of all scientific articles on public administration published in 1979–1993 in five major Scandinavian journals (all published as a quarterly): *Nordisk Admtnistratjeit Tidsskrift* (Nordic Journal of Administrative Sciences), Scandinavian Political Studies, *Statsvetenskapligt Tidsskrift* (Swedish Journal of Political Science), *Norsk Statsvitenskaplig Tidsskrift* (Norwegian Journal of Political Science), and *Politica* (Danish Journal of Political Science). For a detailed description of the universe, methodological problems, and so forth, cf. Beck Jorgensen (1995).

4. A more extensive guide to Scandinavian research can be obtained by contacting the author of this article.

5. Guides to Danish public administration and Danish research in public administration can be found in Bogason (1988, 1990). For overall descriptions of Danish welfare administration, see Knudsen (1991a, 1991b).

6. For a description of the Norwegian public administration, major political institutions, and recent developments, see Christensen and Egeberg (1992), Laegreid (1993a), and Olsen (1983, 1991).

7. Guides to Swedish public administration and research can be found in Politologen (Vol. 1, 1986), Politologen (Vol. 2, 1993), Premfors (1984, 1991), and Lundquist (1994). For a general introduction to Swedish government and politics, see Petersson (1994b).

8. Studies include – besides the mentioned studies from Odense University – Mouritzen (1989), Baldersheim (1992), Bokenstrand et al. (1992), GrRnnegaard Christensen (1992), Kristensen (1980), Beck Jorgensen (1993a, 1993b), Magnusson (1992), and Tarschys (1975).

9. Not surprisingly, the European dimension is most visible in Danish research. For a review of Danish research on the EU, see Beukel and Klauds Klausen (1994).

10. This intellectual/institutional pattern is reflected in The Scandinavian Center of Organizational Research at Stanford University (SCANCOR). The major SCANCOR members from Norway are universities/political science departments in contrast to Sweden and Denmark, the major members being business schools/business administration departments.

REFERENCES

Albæk, E. (1989–1990). Policy evaluation: Design and utilization. *Knowledge and Society, 2*(4), 6–19.

Anckar, D. (1991). Nordic political science: Trends, roles, approaches. *European Journal of Political Research, 20*(3–4), 239–261.

Antonsen, M., & Foss Hansen, H. (1992). Central styring, selvstyring og omverdensstyring – balance eller konflit? *Nordisk Adminjstrativt Tidsskrift, 73*(3), 230–255 (Central control, self-governance and environmental pressures – balance or conflict?).

Baldersheim, H. (1989). *Sentral uyring og institusjonell autonomi.* Bergen: Alma Mater (Central control and institutional autonomy).

Baldersheim, H. (1992). Fiscal stress and political environments. In: P. E. Mouritzen (Ed.), *Managing cities in austerity.* London: Sage.

Baldersheim, H., & Stahlberg, K. (Eds) (1994). *Towards the self-regulating municipality.* London: Dartmouth.

Baldersheim, H., & Stava, P. (1993). Reforming local government. Policymaking and management through organizational learning and experimentation. *Policy Studies Journal, 21,* 104–114.

Beck Jorgensen, T. (1991). Theory of public organizations – demands and possibilities of development. In: T. Knudsen (Ed.), *Welfare administration in Denmark* (pp. 357–391). Copenhagen: Institute of Political Science.

Beck Jorgensen, T. (1993a). Modes of governance and administrative change. In: J. Kooiman (Ed.), *Modern governance. New government–society interactions* (pp. 219–232). London: Sage.

Beck Jorgensen, T. (1993b). Public resource allocation. In: K. A. Eliassen & J. Kooiman (Eds), *Managing public organizations: Lessons from contemporary European experience* (pp. 140–154). London: Sage.

Beck Jorgensen, T. (1995). Scandinavian research on public administration 1979–1993. Research report. Copenhagen: Institute of Political Science.

Beckman, B. (1993). Public policy transformation – regional policy in Sweden. In: M. Hill (Ed.), *New agendas in the study of the polity process.* Brighton: Harvester Wheatsheaf.

Beukel, E., & Klauds Klausen, K. (1994). Danish research on the EC. *European Journal of Political Research, 25*(4), 519–526.

Blichner, L., & Sangolt, L. (1993). Internasjonalisering av offentlig forvaltning. In: P. Lægreid & J. P. Olsen (Eds), *Organisering av offentlig sektor.* Oslo: Tano (The internationalization of public administration).

Blom, A. P. (1990). Roles and situations of chief officers in Swedish municipalities. *Local Government Studies, 16.*

Bogason, P. (1988). Denmark. In: D. C. Rowat (Ed.), *Public administration in developed de-mocracies* (pp. 133–146). New York: Marcel Dekker.

Bogason, P. (1990). Danish local government: Towards an effective and efficient welfare state. In: J. J. Hesse (Ed.), *Local government and urban affairs in international perspective. Analysis of twenty Western industrialized countries* (pp. 261–290). Baden-Baden: Nomos.

Bogason, P. (1992). Local collective choice without and with the state. In: R. Torstendahl (Ed.), *State theory and statehistory* (pp. 206–222). London: Sage.

Bokenstrand, C., et al. (1992). Choosing fiscal austerity strategies. In: P. E. Mouritzen (Ed.), *Managing cities in austerity. Urban fiscal cirisis in ten Western countries.* London: Sage.

Brunsson, N. (1985). *The irrational organization: Irrationality as a basis for organizational action and change.* New York: Wiley.

Brunsson, N. (1989). *The organization of hypocrisy. Talk, decisions and actions in organizations.* New York: Wiley.

Brunsson, N., & Olsen, J. P. (1993). *The reforming organization.* London: Routledge.

Christensen, T. (1991). *Virksomhetsplanlegging: Instrumentel problemløsning eller mysteskaping.* Oslo: Tano (Strategic planning: Rational problem solving or a ritual act?).

Christensen, T., & Egeberg, M. (Eds) (1992). *Forvaltningskunnskap. Forvaitningen i samfisnnet.* Oslo: Tano (Public administration. Administration in society).

Cohen, M. D., March, J. G., & Olsen, J. P. (1972). A garbage can model of organizational choice. *Administrative Science Quarterly, 17*(1), 1–25.

Czarniawska-Joerges, B. (1992). *Styrningent paradoxer.* Stockholm: Norstedts (Paradoxes of steering).

Eckerberg, K. (1987). *Environmental protection in Swedish forestry: A study of the implemen-tation process.* Umeå: University of Umeå.

Eckerberg, K., Mydske, P. K., Niemi-Iilathi, A., & Pedersen, K. H. (Eds) (1994). *Comparing Nordic and Baltic countries: Environmental problems and politics in agriculture and for-estry.* Copenhagen: Nordic Council of Ministers.

Egeberg, M. (Ed.) (1989). *Institusjonspolitikk og forvaltningsutvikling. Bidrag til en anvendt statsvitenskap.* Oslo: Tano (Developments of public administration. Contributions no a constructive political science).

Egeberg, M. (1994). Bridging the gap between theory and practice. The case of administrative policy. *Governance, 7*(1).

Eriksen, E. O. (1993). *Den offent/ige dimension.* Oslo: Tano (The public dimension).

Foss Hansen, H. (1990). Implementation of modernization: Pardoxes in the public control of higher educational institutions: The case of Denmark. *Scandinavian Political Studies, 13*(1), 37–56.

Grønnegaard Christensen, J. (1981). *Centraladministrationen: Organisation og politisk placering.* Copenhagen: Samfundsvidenskabelign Forlag (The central administration: Organization and political context).

Grønnegaard Christensen, J. (1988). Withdrawal of government. An administrative problem in ins political context. *International Review of the Administrative Sciences,* (1), 45–76.

Gustafsson, A. (1991). The case of Sweden: A way to decentralization. In: R. Barley & G. Stoker (Eds), *Local government in Europe: Trends and development.* London: Macmillan.

Hansen, T. (1984). Urban hierarchies and municipal finances. *European Journal of Political Research, 12.*

Harmon, M. M., & Mayer, R. T. (1986). *Organization theory for public administration*. Boston: Little, Brown and Company.

Heckscher, G. (1953). *Svensk statsförvaltning i arbete*. Stockholm (Swedish central administration at work).

Hegland, T. J. (1994). *Fra de tusind blomster til en målrettet udvikling*. Aalborg: Alfuff (From thousand flowets to a goal-conscious development).

Hjern, B., & Hull, C. J. (1987). *Helping small firms to grow: An implementation approach.* London: Croom Helm.

Hjern, B., & Porter, D. O. (1981). Implementation structure: A new unit of administrative analysis. *Organization Studies, 2*(3), 211–228.

Hoff, J. (1991). Information technology between citizen and administration. *Informatization and the Public Sector, 1*, 213–235.

Jacobsen, K. D. (1964). *Teknisk hjelp og politisk struktur*. Oslo: Universitetsforlaget.

Jacobsson, B. (1989). *Konsten att reagera. Intressen, institutioner och näringspolitik*. Stockholm: Carissons (The art of reacting. Interests, institutions and business policies).

Jorgensen, H. (1991). The administration of labor market policy in Denmark in the 1980s. In: T. Knudsen (Ed.), *Welfare administration in Denmark* (pp. 181–203). Copenhagen: Institute of Political Science.

Khakee, A., & Eckerberg, K. (Eds) (1993). *Process and policy evaluation in structure planning*. Stockholm: Swedish Council for Building Research.

Kjellberg, F. (1975). *Political institutionalization*. London: Wiley.

Klaudi Klausen, K. (1991). Private welfare provision. In: T. Knudsen (Ed.), *Welfare administration in Denmark* (pp. 243–269). Copenhagen: Institute of Political Science.

Klaudi Klausen, K., & Goldsmith, M. J. (1995). *Local Governments in the European Integration*. Cheltenham: Edward Elgar.

Knudsen, T. (1991a). State-building in Scandinavia: Denmark in a Nordic context. In: T. Knudsen (Ed.), *Welfare administration in Denmark* (pp. 9–105). Copenhagen: Institute of Political Science.

Knudsen, T. (1991b). *Welfare administration in Denmark*. Copenhagen: Institute of Political Science.

Knudsen, T., & Rothstein, B. (1994). State building in Scandinavia. *Comparative Politics, 26*, 203–220.

Kristensen, O. P. (1980). The logic of political–bureaucratic decision-making as a cause of government growth. *European Journal of Political Research, 8*, 249–264.

Lægreid, P. (1993a). *Trends in the development of the public sector: The case of Norway*. Bergen: Department of Administration and Organization Theory, Notat no. 17.

Lægreid, P. (1993b). *Salary policy reforms for high public office in Norway*. Bergen: LOS-Notat 9230.

Lægreid, P. (Ed.). (1991). *Milstyring og virksomhetsplanlegging i offentlig sektor* (Steering by Goals and Strategic Planning in the Public Sector).

Lægreid, P., & Pedersen, O. K. (Eds) (1994). *Forvaltningspolitik i Norden*. Copenhagen: Jurist- og økonomforbundets forlag.

Lane, J.-E. (1993). *The public sector: Concepts, models and approaches*. London: Sage.

Larsen, H. (1991). Brugerindflydelse i den offentlige sektor. Gør det nogen forskel? *Nordisk Administrativt Tidsskrift, 72*(3), 260–277 (Users influence in the public sector. Does it make a difference?).

Larsen, H. O., & Offerdal, A. (1990). *Demokrati uten deltakere? Arbeidsvilkår og lederroller i kommunalpolitikkeri*. Oslo: Kommuneforlager (Democracy without participants? Working conditions and managerial roles in local politics).

Linde, C. (1982). *Departement och verk*. Stockholm: Stansvetenskapiiga Institutionen (Core departments and executive agencies).

Lundquist, L. (1987). *Implementation steering: An actor-structure approach*. Lund: Studentlitteratur.

Lundquist, L. (1991). *Förvaltning och d.emokrati*. Stockholm: Norstedrs (Public administration and democracy).

Lundquist, L. (1993). Freedom of information and the Swedish bureaucrat. In: R. Chapman (Ed.), *Ethics in public service*. Edinburgh: Edinburgh University Press.

Lundquist, L. (1994). *Problem och trender i statsvetenskapliq fdrvaltningsanalys*. Lund: Studentlitteranur (Problems and trends in political science oriented studies in public administration).

Lundquist, L. J., Elander, I., & Danermark, B. (1990). Housing policy in Sweden – still a success story? *International Journal of Urban and Regional Research, 14*(3), 445–467.

Magnusson, H. (1992). Fiscal changes and policy responses – a comparison of ten countries. In: P. E. Mourirzen (Ed.), *Managing cities in austerity*. London: Sage.

March, J. G., & Olsen, J. P. (Eds) (1976). *Ambiguity and choice in organizations*. Bergen: Universitetsforlaget.

March, J. G., & Olsen, J. P. (Eds) (1989). *Rediscovering institutions: The organizational basis of politics*. New York: The Free Press.

Mouritzen, P. E. (1989). City size and citizen's satisfaction: Two competing theories revisited. *European Journal of Political Research, 17*, 661–688.

Mouritzen, P. E. (Ed.) (1991). *Managing cities in austerity: Urban fiscal stress in ten Western countries*. London: Sage.

Munk Christiansen, P. (1989). Danish technology policy: From market direction to structural change. In: J. L. Pedersen (Ed.), *Technology policy in Denmark* (pp. 31–60). Copenhagen: New Social Science Monographs.

Nexø Jensen, H. (1994). Gendered theories of organizations. In: J. de Bruijn & E. Cyba (Eds), *Gender and organizations – changing perspectives*. Amsterdam: VU Uitgeverij.

Olsen, J. P. (1983). *Organized democracy*. Bergen: Universitetsforiaget.

Olsen, J. P. (1985). Nyinstitusjonalismen og statsvitenskapen. *Statsvetenskaplig Tidsskrift*, (1), 1–14 (New institutionalism and political science).

Olsen, J. P. (1991). Modernization programs in perspective: Institutional analysis of organizational change. *Governance, 4*(2), 125–149.

Olsen, J. P. (1993). Utfordringer for offentlig sektor og for statsvitenskapen. *Norsk Sratsvitenskaplig Tidsskrift*, (1), 3–28 (Challenges for the public sector and for political science).

Pedersen, O. K. (1993). The institutional history of the Danish polity. From a market – and mixed – to a negotiated economy. In: S.-E. Sjostrand (Ed.), *Institutional change: Theories and empirical findings*. New York: Sharpe.

Petersson, O. (1994b). *Swedish government and politics*. Stockholm: Publica.

Petersson, O., & Soderlind, D. (1993). *Forvaltningspolitik*. Stockholm: Publica (Politics of Administration).

Politologen, Vol. 1. 1986 (Political Science in Sweden).

Politologen, Vol. 2. 1993 (A Guide to Political Science and Political Scientists in Sweden).

Premfors, R. (Ed.) (1984). *Higher education organization: Conditions for policy implementation.* Stockholm: Almquist och Wicksell.

Premfors, R. (Ed.) (1991). *Svensk forvaltningsforskning, PM till FOS-utredningen.* Stockholm: University of Stockholm (Swedish research in public administration).

Premfors, R. (Ed.) (1992a). *Policyanalys. kunskap, praktik och etik i offentlig verksamhet.* Lund: Studentlitteratur (Policy analysis. Knowledge, practice and ethics in the public sector).

Premfors, R. (Ed.). (1992b). Knowledge, power and democracy: Lindblom, critical theory and post-modernism. *Knowledge and Policy, 5*(2), 77–93.

Rose, L. (1990). Nordic free-commune experiments: Increased local autonomy or continued central control? In: D. S. King & J. Pierre (Eds), *Challenges to local government.* London: Sage.

Røvik, K.-A. (1992a). *Den "syke" stat.* Oslo: Universitetsforlaget (The "Sick" state).

Røvik, K.-A. (1992b). Instinunionaliserte standarder og multistandardorganisasjoner. *Norsk Statsvitenskaplig Tidsskrift, 8*(4), 261–284 (Institutionalized standards and multistandard organizations).

Sahlin-Andersson, K. (1992). The social construction of projects. A case study of organizing an extraordinary building project – the Stockholm globe arena. *Scandinavian Housing and Planning Research, 9,* 65–78.

Schartau, M.-B. (1993). *The public sector middle manager: The puppet who pulls the strings?* Lund: Wi.

Stromberg, L. (1980). Local government reforms in Sweden. In: D. C. Rowat (Ed.), *Handbook on local government reorganization* (pp. 308–320). London: Greenwood and Aldwych Press.

Tarschys, D. (1975). The growth of public expenditures: Nine modes of explanation. *Scandinavian Political Studies, 10,* 9–31.

Vedung, E. (1993). *Statens markpolitik, kommunerne och historiens ironi.* Stockholm: Forlag (The politics of land use, the municipalities and the irony of history).

Vedung, E., Rist, R. C., & Bemelmans-Videc, M. L. (Eds) (1995). *Policy instruments and evaluation.* New Brunswik: Transaction Books.

Villadsen, S. (1986). Local corporatism? The role of organizations and local movements in the local welfare state. *Politics and Policy, 14*(2), 247–266.

Westerstahl, J. (1967). Swedish local government research. *Scandinavian Political Studies, 2,* 276–280.

Westerstahl, J. (1974). Decision-making systems in thirty-six Swedish communes. In: T. N. Clark (Ed.), *Comparative community politics* (pp. 141–162). Beverly Hills: Sage Publications.

Winter, S. (1990). Integrating implementation research. In: D. Palumbo & D. Cal Ister (Eds), *Implementation and the policy process. Opening the black box* (pp. 19–38). New York: Greenwood Press.

Wirtrock, B., Peter, W., Carol, W., & Wollmann, H. (Eds) (1991). *Social sciences and modern states: National experiences and theoretical crossroads.* Cambridge: Cambridge University Press.

FURTHER READING

Grønnegaard Christensen, J. (1992). Hierarchical and contractual approaches to budgetary reform. *Journal of Theoretical Politics, 4*(1), 67–91.

Kjellberg, F. (1988). *The dynamics of institutional change*. London: Sage.

Lægreid, P., & Olsen, J. P. (Eds) (1993). *Organisering av offentlig sector*. Oslo: Tano (The organizing of the public sector).

Petersson, O. (1994a). *The government and politics of the Nordic countries*. Stockholm: Publica.

Premfors, R. (Ed.) (1985). *Forvaltningsforskning I Sverige*. Stockholm: University of Stockholm (Research in public administration in Sweden).

Ronhstein, B. (1991). State structure and variations in corporanism: The Swedish case. *Scandinavian Political Studies, 14*(2), 149–171.

Ronhstein, B. (1993). Institutional choices and labor market policy: A British–Swedish comparison. *Comparative Politics, 26*, 147–177.

Ronhstein, B. (1994). *Vadstaten bör gora? Om vä lfdrdsstatens politiska cch moraliska logic*. Stockholm: SNS Forlag (Oust institutions matter: The political and moral logic of the universal welfare state).

Vedung, E. (1992). Five observations on evaluation in Sweden. In: J. Mayne, M. L. Bemelmans-Videc, J. Hudson & R. Conner (Eds), *Advancing public policy evaluation. Learning from international experience* (pp. 71–84). Amsterdam: Elsevier.

INTERNATIONAL DEVELOPMENT MANAGEMENT IN A GLOBALIZED WORLD

Derick W. Brinkerhoff and Jennifer Brinkerhoff

Is development management, as a subfield of international and comparative administration, still relevant and applicable to the administrative problems facing today's managers in developing and transitional economies? The authors answer this question by exploring the implications of globalization for development management. They identify the global trends with the most direct impacts on governance and management in developing and transitional economies, and analyze how these relate to the theory and practice of development management. The analysis focuses on four facets of development management: as a means to foreign assistance agendas, as a tool kit, as values, and as process. While globalization has introduced many changes, much of what development management has to offer remains useful, appropriate, and valuable. Maintaining relevance and applicability hinges upon a closer integration between theory and practice; more cross-fertilization among development management, comparative analysis, and mainstream public administration; and clearer demonstration to policy makers of the timeliness of the subfield's concepts, tools, and approaches.

It is difficult to pick up a newspaper or turn on a television without reading or hearing commentary on the impact of global trends on the fate of nations and the lives of their citizens. Fukuyama (1990) tells us that we have

Comparative Public Administration: The Essential Readings
Research in Public Policy Analysis and Management, Volume 15, 831–861
Copyright © 2006 by Elsevier Ltd.
All rights of reproduction in any form reserved
ISSN: 0732-1317/doi:10.1016/S0732-1317(06)15039-3

entered an unprecedented period where history as we know it is over. Huntington (1996) lays out the parameters of an emerging new world order.

Commentators on the task of administration and management in the private, public, and nonprofit sectors, catalog and analyze the ways managers need to change the ways they think and act as a result of the penetration of global economic, political, technological, and social forces.[1] The field of international and comparative public administration (ICA) has not been immune from self-examination and reflection in the context of these global trends. Three recent articles in *Public Administration Review* (PAR), part of a symposium in celebration of the 25th anniversary of the founding of the Section on International and Comparative Administration (SICA) of the American Society for Public Administration (ASPA), offer perspectives on where international and comparative public administration has come from and where it needs to go in light of the changes underway around the world (Heady, 1998; Riggs, 1998; Welch & Wong, 1998).

This article constitutes a further contribution to the SICA symposium, and adds to the debate regarding ICA in today's world.[2] Our focus is on development management.[3] This term encompasses the set of ICA theory and practice that concentrates upon organizational and managerial problems, issues, and practices in the developing countries of Africa, Asia, and Latin America, and in the transitional economies of Eastern Europe and the former Soviet Union. For many years mainstream public administration and development management had – with a few exceptions – very little interchange or cross-fertilization.

However, since globalization has led to closer integration between industrialized countries and those in the developing/transitional world, the lines between these two realms of public management have been blurred, both in terms of analytics and praxis. This integration suggests that development management has applicability to poverty alleviation in the industrialized world. We think that it is an opportune time to take a fresh look at development management.[4]

We consider the current state of development management, and explore the implications of global trends for the subfield's continued applicability to critical administrative problems and its contribution to the broader field of ICA. In the discussion below, we (1) identify those global trends with the most direct implications for development management, (2) review the evolution and current status of the development management subfield, (3) explore the implications of the global trends for development management, (4) comment on development management theory and practice, and (5) reevaluate what development management has to offer in the global context.

GLOBAL TRENDS: A QUICK OVERVIEW

Tracking global trends has evolved into an analytic and prognostic industry in and of itself, and we do not pretend to offer a comprehensive overview of global trends and globalization. We offer a selective catalog of what we see as the major global trends that impact upon public managers in developing and transitional nations.[5]

Economic and Financial: The triumph of capitalism over socialist ideology has led to a veritable tidal wave of economic and financial reforms in developing and transitional economies. The International Monetary Fund (IMF), the World Bank as well as other multilateral and bilateral assistance agencies have preached the gospel of the free market, backed up by structural and sectoral adjustment packages with similar contents. Bolstered by these packages, private international capital has flowed into the developing world.[6] The features of this new economic order are well known: the dominance and independence of transnational corporate investment, interconnected markets, an emphasis on export trade and competitive advantage, unfettered international financial flows, and rapid communication. New contours have superseded the old boundaries. At the supranational level, trading arrangements, such as the GATT (General Agreement on Tariffs and Trade), WTO (World Trade Organization), and NAFTA (North American Free Trade Agreement) reconfigure economic relationships among nations. At the regional and local levels, free trade areas, economic empowerment zones, regional development authorities, direct overseas links, and so on shape new forms of public–private interaction.

A major component of structural adjustment has been the reduction of fiscal deficits and the downsizing of the public sector. Most developing/transitional countries cut back public expenditures drastically, with the effect of radically reducing basic services in public health, education, and social welfare. In some developing countries, communities were left almost entirely without national or state services. Particularly in Eastern Europe and the former Soviet Union, this downsizing was accompanied by government bashing, tax revolt, and distrust in public officials and public problem solving.[7]

Technological: The pace of technological innovation has accelerated. Coupled with the increased financial power of transnational corporations has been an increase in the search for new products, new production methods, and new markets. The East Asian miracle, now tarnished by the financial meltdown of Indonesia and other Asian tigers, was based in part on the combination of global capital and reengineered technologies that combined cheap labor with "high-tech" production methodologies in global commodity chains. Particularly in agricultural and natural resource-based products, developing countries have become, ready or not, integrated into the global technological marketplace.

Another global technological force is the ever-accelerating development of information technology. The ability to transmit and access information around the globe both easily and cheaply is a profound change. The evolution of the Internet, cellular telephones, fax machines, and increasingly inexpensive personal computers has made possible communications and transactions in quantities and at speeds heretofore unimagined.

Environmental: A powerful set of global trends that threaten the very basis of livelihoods and well-being around the world relate to the natural environment. Unsustainable resource utilization rates, increased incidence of resource shortages (e.g., water, arable land), environmental degradation of the natural resource base, decreased levels of food security, pollution and contamination of both urban and rural areas, and global warming are among the litany here. These trends do not respect national borders; witness the disastrous effects of Indonesia's forest fires, deliberately set by timber firms, on its neighbors in the region. Many of these environmental issues have been tackled at the international level and have led to collaborative efforts to address them: for example, the 1992 Earth Summit (United Nations Conference on Environment and Development), the International Convention on Global Warming, etc. Many developing countries are signatories to such international agreements, and with external assistance have engaged in a variety of planning exercises to address environmental problems (e.g., Tropical Forestry Action Plans, National Environmental Action Plans), yet have extremely limited capacity to implement them in any serious way. Further, their economic development policies often exacerbate environmental problems, as transnational corporations seek to invest where they are the least hampered by regulation.

Socio-Political: Three trends are especially important in this category. First is the emerging primacy of democratic forms of politics and government. The dominance of market liberalization has been accompanied by democratization and political liberalization. This trend has been fueled both by the triumph of global capitalism and by citizen expectations. One of the effects of the information revolution has been that citizens can discover what goes on around the world as well as in their own countries, and there is little the state can do to prevent this. The second socio-political trend is the rise of civil society citizens are increasingly coming together and organizing to represent their interests, express their views, and undertake actions to assist themselves, either independent of, or in partnership with, government. Civil society groups are at the forefront of increased demands on the state in developing/transitional countries, and take an active role in monitoring state actions and performance. The third trend is the intensification of ethnic, religious, and tribal conflict, which at times has exploded into mass slaughter in places like Bosnia, Rwanda, and ex-Zaire. Among the consequences have been unprecedented refugee flows, complex humanitarian emergencies, and strain and occasional collapse of existing state security and basic service delivery functions.

WHAT HAS NOT CHANGED

In thinking about the impact of global trends on developing/transitional countries, we also need to bear in mind the things that have not changed. These too shape the landscape for development managers and development management. The poor are still poor, and there are a lot of them. In most countries, economic gains have not been evenly distributed, and income disparities have worsened. In many countries, for those at the bottom of society, gains have been wiped out by population growth. For example, India has an economically powerful middle class, a vibrant software industry and nuclear capability, but huge numbers of India's citizens continue to eke out a living under conditions of extreme poverty.

Developing country's government capacity is still weak, for the most part. Civil servants are underpaid and underskilled. Government agencies operate inefficiently, infrastructures and operations are neglected and crumbling. Outreach is limited; in some areas, little effective public sector presence can be detected. Coupled with weak capacity, resources available for public investment and development are still scarce; tax systems are inadequate and/or nonfunctional. Local jurisdictions are particularly starved. Many countries are weighed down under a crushing burden of international debt that must be serviced, leaving little room for discretionary social investment. As a result, in many countries, critical basic needs in education, health, welfare, and infrastructure still go unmet. A short trip off the beaten path reveals that villages in rural China, India, or the Sahel, or urban slums in Rio or Djakarta look much the same today as they did 10 or 25 years back. Many of the poor are in fact worse off now than they were a decade ago or so.

DEVELOPMENT MANAGEMENT: YESTERDAY AND TODAY

Before turning to the question of what development management has to offer in today's globalizing world, we need a clearer understanding of what development management is. We start with some thoughts on development itself, because it is hard to separate discussion of development management from notions of development. Both have evolved in tandem.

Our rapid and, of necessity, highly compressed look backwards begins in the 1950s where the early post-World War II view of development saw a set of stages imitative of the growth path of Western industrialized societies. If countries could mobilize for take-off or the big push, then they would launch themselves on the road to economic growth. Development theory and practice was mainly concerned with economics. Experience soon revealed that economics and a focus on industrialization was insufficient, and analysts and practitioners in developing countries and in international development agencies expanded their focus beyond production to distribution, politics, basic human needs, and cultural values. Although variations in emphasis can be found, today there is relatively broad consensus that besides economic growth, development includes equity, capacity, empowerment, self-determination, and sustainability. Along with the evolution of the concept of development have been changes in thinking regarding how to achieve it. The primary trajectory here has been along a path that began with centrally planned, state-dominated strategies to market-led polycentric approaches with the state as coordinator and regulator rather than as the sole or predominant actor.

The evolution of development management, as an applied discipline like its parent field, public administration, has shifted along with changes in development strategies. The trend has been away from a technorational, universalist, public sector administrative model toward a context-specific, politically infused, multisectoral, multiorganizational model. From its initial focus on institution-building for central-level public bureaucracies and capacity-building for economic and project planning, development management has gradually expanded to encompass bureaucratic reorientation and restructuring, the integration of politics and culture into management improvement, participatory and performance-based service delivery and program management, community and NGO capacity-building, and policy reform and implementation.[8]

Currently, development management is a broadly eclectic applied discipline whose analytic and practical contents reflect four related facets, depending upon which perspective is emphasized. Development management has an explicitly interventionist orientation that derives from its instrumental affiliation with international assistance agencies and programs whose objectives address socio-economic development. So first, and most commonly understood, development management is a means to improving the efficiency and effectiveness of foreign assistance programs and to furthering international agencies' policy agendas. Second, development management is a toolkit; it promotes the application of a range of management and analytical tools adapted from a variety of social science disciplines, including strategic management, organization development, psychology, and political science. Third, development management incorporates a value dimension that emphasizes self-determination, empowerment, and an equitable distribution of development benefits. Fourth, development management is process intervention, where the application of tools in pursuit of objectives is undertaken in ways that self-consciously address political and values issues.

Each of these facets represents one essential aspect of development management as a field of theory and practice, and taken together they constitute a whole (Thomas, 1996). However, there can be inherent tensions among them and they can be contradictory. For example, while it is fairly straightforward to understand how its tools can promote foreign assistance agendas, less clear is whether or not their application in this context will promote espoused values of empowerment and self-determination, and whether or not the donor agency and its procedures can adequately support a genuine process approach. Such contradictions imply that development management means different things to different actors. The choice of balance among its four facets varies, contributing to what some might perceive as development management's ambiguity. An examination of each of the facets of development management illustrates their inter-dependencies and helps to answer the question of development management's continued relevance in the globalized world of today.

Development Management as Means to Foreign Assistance Agendas: Development management is most often sponsored by international aid agencies, all of which have their own priorities and corresponding agendas. Typically, development management professionals enter the scene upon request from a donor agency for a predetermined task. It is not always clear if the need for and the design of this task represent priorities of the ultimate client, a developing country actor. In this *sense*, development management is a means to enhancing the effectiveness and efficiency of projects and programs determined and designed by donor agencies (Rondinelli, 1987; Spector & Cooley, 1997).

This facet of development management is perhaps the most problematic to reconcile with its other facets. First and most obviously, foreign assistance agendas at a minimum compromise some degree of self-determination in pursuit of socio-economic reforms; and sometimes these externally derived reform agendas strongly limit the ability of countries to modify the reform package in ways that would support local empowerment. Second, donor programing requirements and incentives – such as loan disbursement schedules, project timetables, and compliance with predetermined indicators – can further inhibit the ability of groups in the recipient country, whether inside or outside of government, to play an active role in tailoring the assistance provided to their needs and their pace of change. These limitations can make it difficult to allow room to accommodate political realities, or to take a process approach.[9] What if, for example, the process leads to identified priorities and targets that significantly modify or contradict the foreign assistance package funding the effort? Third, these same pressures and incentives can also lead to superficial commitment to reform and pro forma meeting of targets. For example, development clients may go through the motions of complying with requirements and making changes without internalizing them. In recent years, development management specialists have had an impact on how international donor programs are designed and implemented to take more account of process considerations (see Brinkerhoff, 1996).

Development Management as a Toolkit: Development management promotes the application of a range of management and analytical tools adapted from a variety of disciplines, including strategic management, public policy, public administration, organization development, psychology, anthropology, and political science. These tools assist in mapping the terrain in which policy reforms, programs, and projects are designed and implemented, that is the political, socio-cultural, and organizational contexts of interventions. For example, strategic policy management might begin with SWOT analysis (identifying internal strengths and weaknesses and external opportunities and threats), which would then be followed by other tools to assess the actors involved. These latter tools include stake-holder analysis and political mapping (Crosby, 1997; Lindenberg & Crosby, 1981). The results of these exercises feed into the elaboration of potential response strategies that incorporate flexibility and adaptation.

Development management tools merge policy and program analytics with action. It is precisely the blending of the process and value facets with the tools that accounts for the distinctiveness of development management as a toolkit. On the analytic side, this means tools that explore the institutional and organizational incentive aspects of achieving results (see Brinkerhoff,

1997; Bryant, 1996), and that examine the psychology of change efforts (see Hubbard, 1997), focus on individual incentives and motivation. On the operational side, this means tools and approaches focus on data gathering, such as participatory rural appraisal (Kumar, 1993; Blackburn & Holland, 1998), flexible and adaptive design and planning (Brinkerhoff & Ingle, 1989; Delp, Thesen, Motiwalla, & Seshadri, 1977), and action-learning and experimentation (Kerrigan & Luke, 1987; Rondinelli, 1983).

Development Management as Values: This facet of development management recognizes that development-promoting activities of any sort constitute interventions in the status quo, and that any intervention advances some particular set of interests and objectives at the expense of others. Thus, helping to implement a policy reform or program more effectively or building managerial capacity in a particular agency or organization is a value-laden endeavor. Development management as values is expressed in two ways. First, development management acknowledges that managing is infused with politics; successful management takes account of this fact and therefore is both contextual and strategic (see, for example, White, 1987; Brinkerhoff, 1996; Crosby, 1997; Lindenberg & Crosby, 1981). Second, development management takes a normative stance on empowerment and supporting groups, particularly the poor and marginalized, to take an active role in determining and fulfilling their own needs. Development management should enhance the capacity of development actors to effectively pursue their own development: it should be people-centered (see, for example, Bryant & White, 1982; Korten & Klauss, 1984; Thomas, 1996).

Development management as values is closely related to development management as process, as the section below clarifies. The values orientation also links to tools and the donor-funded provision of external assistance. Management tools and technologies are meant to combine external expertise with local knowledge and skills in a process that employs outside resources in the service of indigenously directed endeavors (see Spector & Cooley, 1997). Thus, development management blends indigenous knowledge and norms as it seeks to promote sustainable change, whose contours are developed through a participatory dialog incorporating multiple perspectives (Joy, 1997).

Development Management as Process: The process facet of development management is most closely related to development management as values, both politics and empowerment. Development management as process operates on several levels, in terms of the individual actors involved, it builds on organizational development and process consultation; that is, starting with the client's priorities, needs, and values, development management specialists help to "initiate and sustain a process of change and continuous learning for systemic improvement" (Joy, 1997, p. 456). Because the process is client-driven, development management serves as handmaiden to (1) empowering individual actors to assert and maintain control, and (2) building their capacity to sustain the process into the future and in other situations.

At the organizational level – whether an individual agency or multiple organizations – development management as process is concerned with the interplay between policy, program, and project plans and objectives, and the organizational structures and procedures through which plans are implemented and objectives achieved. Here, development managers look for a balance among these factors and the broader setting where development intervention takes place. This is the contingency notion; that is, the best managerial solutions are context-specific and emerge from a process of searching for a fit among programmatic, organizational, and environmental factors.[10] At the sector level – public, civil society, and private – development management as process addresses broader governance issues, such as participation, accountability, transparency, responsiveness, and the role of the state. This brings in empowerment in its societal and political dimension, looking at how various socio-political groups interact in the policy and program implementation process. Development management's process facet considers the following types of illustrative questions: Who has a place at the policy table? What process mechanisms allow which groups to play a role, and exclude others? What managerial practices and capacities are required for effective democratic governance and socio-economic development? How can public sector agencies and *NGOs* best cooperate to achieve joint objectives?[11]

As these questions imply, the process facet of development management links with the tool and foreign assistance agenda facets. An important place in the toolkit is accorded to process tools, those that facilitate consultation, joint problem and solution identification, ownership and commitment building, participatory strategy development, and so on. Further, many of these questions arise in the context of evolving international assistance agendas.

IMPLICATIONS FOR DEVELOPMENT MANAGEMENT

We now turn to the globalization trends overviewed earlier and examine their implications for this subfield of ICA. These implications are presented in relation to the four facets of development management.

Development Management as a Means to Foreign Assistance Agendas

Today there is much questioning regarding development strategies and the role of donors. The head of the United Nations Development Programme, for example, has called for a "new architecture for development cooperation." At the World Bank, senior staff are questioning its effectiveness as a poverty-focused lending institution (Overseas Development Institute, 1996); at the IMF, economists are reflecting upon the effectiveness of its policy prescriptions; and at the U.S. Agency for International Development (USAID), staff and implementing partners are reviewing its comparative advantage in light of funding cutbacks. Further, the constituencies of these agencies have raised their voices in criticism. For example, the NGO community faults the World Bank for being insufficiently participatory and failing to respect the views and desires of local people.[12] The U.S. Congress faults USAID for being insufficiently concrete about the results it seeks to achieve, managing poorly, and failing to demonstrate impact and value.

What does this mean for development management? As long as international agencies, governments, and, increasingly, NGOs and corporations, continue to engage in efforts to enhance the management, services, enabling environments for economic growth, and quality of life in developing and transitioning nations, there will be a demand for methods by which these efforts can be made more efficient and effective. That said, international development agendas and assistance modalities are in flux – indeed we have seen this already throughout the evolution of development. This is revealed in a closer examination of the four areas of global trends noted above.

Economic and Financial Trends: The globalization of economic activity has perforated the jurisdictional boundaries along which public administration has been organized. National, regional, and local governments have seen their traditional functions, powers, and authority leak away as the new international economic order has become established as the dominant factor in the public as well as the private sector. Governments in developing and transitional countries, along with those in the industrialized world, are searching for efficient, effective, and equitable structures and processes to reconcile the core provision of public services in the new boundary-less era (Dobell & Steenkamp, 1993). Development management's focus on process and values, along with its toolkit, can help governments in this search, and holds the potential for a more situationally sensitive application of the so-called new public management, the one-size-fits-all managerial solution that has evolved out of the triumph of the free market and the drive to downsize the public sector.[13] In addition, development management can contribute to capacity-building for the new partners engaged in development.

The global economic and financial trends have brought new actors and new agendas onto the development scene. Predominant among them have been NGOs and civil society groups. As governments have been compelled to try to do more with less, and to cut back on state-supplied goods and services, NGOs have increasingly stepped in to fill the resulting gaps, both on their own and in partnership with the state (Coston, 1998a). One frequent observation is that NGO's managerial capacity is weak, thus development management has an important role in NGO capacity-building (see Fowler, 1997). This new set of actors generally has an agenda that stresses empowerment and people-centered development, which means that the value facet of development management emerges more strongly at the forefront.

The private sector constitutes a second set of new actors that has emerged as governments downsize and privatize, becoming more prevalent with the rise of corporate philanthropy. Multinational corporations are sponsoring and/or directly engaging in development activities, both independently and in partnership with donor agencies and national governments; for example, supporting infrastructure projects that benefit the operation of their factories, or providing infrastructure and/or health and education services in those communities that are sources of local labor (Tichy, McGill, & St. Clair, 1997). While the more limited agendas represented by corporate interests raise questions for development management's value facet, to the extent that development management can inject community empowerment and local control into those agendas as a function of assisting to implement them, the door is opened to broadening corporate philanthropy and deepening the commitment of multinational corporations to socially responsible actions in developing/transitional countries.

Technological Trends: New agendas also include the introduction of new technologies, specifically information technology. International assistance agencies are increasingly designing programs that transfer information and communications technology both in the service of sectoral objectives and broader democratization goals. For example, USAID's Leland Initiative supports Internet connectivity throughout Africa. Development management professionals can assist in a number of ways; for example, addressing the organizational and process aspects of implementing new communications and technology policies, helping decision-makers focus on the equity and distributional issues, and so on (see World Bank, 1998).

Environmental Trends: The agendas of foreign assistance agencies, international environmental NGOs, and national governments seek to tackle the environmental trends sketched above. Donors, NGOs, and their partner governments have moved from an initial focus on the technical dimensions of environmental problems to increasingly recognizing their social, organizational, and managerial dimensions. Development management has been, and will remain, instrumental to designing and implementing sustainable environmental and natural resources policies and programs in support of these agendas. New challenges for development management will be in the areas of conflict resolution, and advocacy support within the highly politicized arenas that characterize environmental concerns. Development management can usefully contribute at all levels, from the local to the transnational, the latter being particularly important in dealing with environmental trends.

Socio-Political Trends: One implication of these trends for development management is that as the programmatic mix of foreign assistance agencies' objectives shifts to respond to more numerous and more serious complex humanitarian emergencies, development management specialists may be called upon for assistance. Despite the potential relevance of development management's process approach and toolkit, this has not yet taken place because of the politics of international relief and the disconnect between short-term emergency assistance and long-term development support (Anderson & Woodrow, 1998; Bryant, 1999).

Another implication of these trends relates to the continuing importance of international NGOs, the growing importance of civil societies worldwide, and the promotion of democratization agendas. International NGOs have long been important actors in development. While their role has generally shifted from one of providing primarily humanitarian aid to supporting development, and from working independently to contracting and partnering with donors, the activities of NGOs continue to represent an important proportion of development assistance. Like corporations, as private institutions NGOs are empowered to be selective in the services they choose to provide and the clients they work with.

The range of NGO actors and their roles are evolving fast with the growth of civil society globally. New, creative partnerships are also emerging, including those between corporations and NGOs, and corporations and local governments (Tichy et al., 1997). Reconciling the interests of multiparty sponsorship will be a key challenge for development managers into the future. NGOs and other civil society actors are also increasingly important advocates for or against particular agendas. In fact, some argue that advocacy is the most appropriate role for international NGOs (see Korten, 1990). Accordingly, as the capacity of local NGOs and civil society grows, tensions emerge between international NGOs and their local counterparts or partners. Development management will be increasingly challenged to integrate the participation of a diverse body of implementers and advocates.[14]

More and more, development management is expected to contribute to foreign assistance agendas that promote values, particularly democratization. While at first glance such an application would appear to be entirely consistent with the values development management espouses, sometimes foreign assistance agendas, especially the bilaterals, have a more limited definition of democracy and/or choose to limit participation for political reasons, as for example, limiting support for and participation of potentially disruptive elements of civil society such as fundamentalist Islamic groups. These decisions are by nature subjective and can conflict with the other facets of development management. In addition, limited foreign assistance agendas, if pursued in isolation, can generate negative consequences. For example, Coston (1998b) highlights the potential danger of addressing the demand side of democratic governance promotion, without considering the ability of states to respond to that demand.

Development Management as a Toolkit

Are development management's tools still relevant given the trends identified? Projects and programs still exist. Policy implementation still poses thorny managerial problems. Attention to participation and empowerment has increased, not diminished. Governments are still wrestling with capacity limitations. Thus, it can be argued that a core administrative problem set remains for which the development management toolkit, with its combination of process and technical tools, continues to be useful and applicable. Process tools in particular are relevant – increasingly managers operate in settings where, as Bryson and Crosby (1992) say, no one is in charge.

The overarching implication of the global trends for development management as a toolkit will be the need to take into account far greater complexity and uncertainty in the administrative environment of development managers. This suggests the need for more attention to theoretical and conceptual integration with practice, so that the key variables affecting administrative capacity and performance are identified and targeted for intervention.[15]

Economic and Financial Trends: These trends are perhaps the major source of uncertainty and complexity that development managers face. The challenge for development management will be to sharpen and refine its analytic toolkit so as to usefully contribute to the debate on the appropriate role of the state, the trade-offs between economic and social development goals that have arisen more starkly in the wake of the current financial crisis in Asia, and the drive for ever more efficient public governance. Because development management's four facets explicitly address politics, values, and process in the context of development goals, and administrative tools and techniques to achieve them, the subfield has the potential to counter the tendency to look for quick solutions based on narrow economic criteria.

Technological Trends: Information technology advances represent an important opportunity for development managers to enhance existing tools and create new tools. Many of the standard project-planning tools already exist in computer form, and several tools specific to international projects, programs, and policies have been developed.[16] Tools that do more than computerize analysis, store the information, but that use information technology to facilitate participation and empower people are an innovative avenue for development management to explore. For example, the World Bank has been experimenting with "groupware" as a means to a more participatory process of designing its Country Assistance Strategies. This experimentation is in its infancy. Another area ripe for exploration is how information technology can contribute to organizational redesign for performance in developing country public agencies (see Peterson, 1997).

Environmental Trends: Environmental trends pose two particular challenges to development management's toolkit. First, existing and new tools will need to incorporate broader and increasingly diverse constituencies in environmental projects, especially those that cross national borders. This implies a stronger focus on reconciling opposing interests; thus the tools of conflict resolution, negotiation, and consultation will become more important. Further, refined analytic tools are needed for institutional design of feasible policy and program solutions. Second, environmental trends imply severe future consequences of current resource utilization practices that are difficult to envision. Again, new tools could be advanced, for instance, with the help of information technology, to more clearly demonstrate the salience of the issues to decision-makers. ... Negative consequences can be shown visually and quite dramatically, and alternative policy solutions can be graphically demonstrated using a simulated computer world.

Socio-Political Trends: Similar to the environmental trends, among the most important implications of socio-political trends will be the need for crisis management, conflict resolution, and negotiation tools. Development management's experience with such tools in situations of complex emergencies is relatively new and untested (Bryant, 1999). Similarly, with the expansion of democratic governance around the world, and the attendant growth and diversity of civil society, new tools and approaches will be needed to build effective state–civil society partnerships, both national and international (Coston, 1998a). The trends also suggest a need for new tools and approaches to address building constituencies and motivation for sustained reforms to deal with citizen demands for transparency, accountability, and responsiveness.[17] Also related to reforms is the need for methodologies that allow policymakers to better assess the political implications and trade-offs of policy alternatives in a democratic and/or politically unstable environment.

With respect to the growing importance of civil society, development management may need to borrow more from psychology and anthropology when considering the increasing diversity of development players. For example, how can the participation of the formerly voiceless be promoted in a newly democratic regime when there is no tradition or culture of democracy (see Coston & Butz, 1999)? How can the deeply internalized ethnic and religious conflicts be addressed?

Development Management as Values

Development management's self-consciousness about politics and values, plus its focus on empowerment, increases the subfield's relevance to managers coping with the impacts of global trends. Development management involves tools and approaches that (1) illuminate goal trade-offs and conflicts, (2) clarify who participates in decisions and who does not, and (3) build capacity for empowering managerial and decision processes. Hence, it can contribute to incorporating equity and sustainability into socio-economic development when the thrust of many of the trends may push toward a narrower focus on efficiency and the preservation of vested interests.

An important implication for development management specialists in regard to values is how, given global trends, to deal with the ethics of development intervention. This surfaces most starkly as a potential conflict between development management as an instrument of international assistance agendas versus the agendas of groups within developing/transitional countries, and in the conflicts among developing country groups. One response, related to development management's process facet, is to be very explicit about who the client is for any change intervention (see Joy, 1997; Cooke, 1997). In this regard, some development management professionals have shifted their efforts away from the public sector to focus on NGOs and civil society, and to opt for challenging existing power structures (Thomas, 1996).[18]

Economic and Financial Trends: These trends have essentially imported private business values into the public sector. Market principles applied to public management transform citizens into customers and emphasize the "bottom line" as a paramount objective (see Larson, 1997). Mainstream public administration is questioning the politics and ethics that support this perspective, and in developing and transitional countries, such questioning is raking place as well. Just as development management's process approach assists in reconciling diverse interests, so too it may contribute to identifying the appropriate balance between private-sector values of least-cost efficiency and public-sector values such as responsiveness, accountability, and equity. With development management's emphasis on capacity-building, and its recognition that politics and administration are inextricably linked, development management can assist both governments and nonstate actors to engage with each other on these issues.

Development management has traditionally acknowledged the importance of community self-determination and locally driven development (Esman, 1991). The interdependence inherent in a global economy suggests that the challenge for the future will be addressing how to manage an appropriate degree of integration and linkage such that local, regional, national, and international priorities and interests can be balanced. If its empowerment emphasis is directed only locally, development management will likely be sidelined and considered less relevant.[19]

Technological Trends: These trends raise a number of implications for development management as values. Technology can open up people's horizons and possibilities, but there are always trade-offs. Information technology, for example, can be empowering if it provides information and linkages to societal groups that previously were excluded; but it will favor those groups who have the potential to take advantage of it. For those without the necessary resources and capacities, the gaps between technology haves and have-nots can widen. Knowledge flows and intellectual property rights are other important technological issues (see World Bank, 1998). Development management could play a role in helping countries establish and implement equitable and politically feasible trade and technology transfer policies.

Environmental Trends: Given the increasing diversity of environmental actors, noted above, development management's greatest challenge and contribution will be to grapple with the question of whose rights take precedence and how to address the political dimensions of the environmental trends, locally, nationally, and internationally. For example, in natural resource management, whose interests should receive priority, those of local resources users, corporations whose investments bring in necessary foreign exchange, or national governments, who may or may not effectively pursue the public interest in regard to resource conservation? Development management can also help with designing and making operational the institutional structures and mechanisms that can be used to effectively implement policy priorities in the environment and natural resources sector.

Socio-Political Trends: As democratic forms of government spread, development management will be increasingly important in helping governments build the capacity to respond to citizen expectations and to put in place the institutional structures that allow democracy to function effectively. The promotion of democratization and its associated values is among the agendas of a number of foreign assistance agencies, but those values are frequently translated into a relatively narrow view of what constitutes democracy. Traditional village governance structures in Africa, for example, are not considered "democratic" due to perceived limits in representation in their consensual model. The notion of traditional benevolent leaders runs counter to Western ideals of democracy. Development management, as Riggs (1998) points out, needs to be at the forefront of exploring various institutional options for democratization that fit with particular country circumstances, recognizing that the U.S. model is but one path among many.

Concerning the rise of civil society and subnational conflicts based on ethnicity or religion, development management's value facet will need to address critical questions. Whose self-determination and empowerment should take precedence and who can legitimately speak for the constituencies involved? What organizational and procedural mechanisms can be used to develop sustainable solutions to problems of representation, participation, and conflict resolution among competing interests? In the search for answers, it will be important to confront the naiveté and mythologizing around civil society's homogeneity, harmoniousness, and civic-mindedness, and develop a realistic understanding of how societal interest groups actually behave.

Development Management as Process

In each of the categories of trends we have summarized, the importance of process, as a crucial adjunct to good technical solutions, stands out. To paraphrase the popular aphorism, the trends may be examined globally, but acting to address them means intervening locally. Someone, located in a particular place with particular constraints, capacities, history and so on, needs to determine what to do and then mobilize and organize to do it. Development management's process facet holds important lessons to help move from analysis to action, beginning at the individual level with its emphasis on client-driven change efforts (e.g., Joy, 1997), and extending to the organizational and sectoral levels with its concentration on understanding and building linkages and system-wide capacity (e.g., White, 1987; Brinkerhoff, 1996). All of the trends, as previously noted, heighten uncertainty, complexity, unpredictability, and interconnectedness.

Development management's focus on iterative solution design, testing and learning, and adaptation is highly salient to coping with these trends. As mentioned, an important set of development management tools and approaches are, in fact, process-focused. These trends highlight and reinforce the relevance of development management as process to helping developing/transitional countries to successfully cope with global trends. An important implication for development management will be the increasing use of cross-sectoral partnerships, multiorganizational networks, etc. When no one is in charge, the importance of process is heightened for several reasons: to bring to bear everyone's energies and ideas for solving problems, for generating widespread support for solutions adopted, for negotiating agreements on implementation, and for resolving conflicts and disputes throughout. Process changes can also result in shifts in power distributions and dynamics, important variables in shaping the politico-administrative environment.

Economic and Financial Trends: As already mentioned, these trends have increased the pressures on governments at all levels to increase efficiency and output, while at the same time pushing them to rethink their core functions. While evidence is accumulating that development management's process approaches can save money in the longer term, through contributing to the design of more feasible policies and programs and building commitment among stakeholders for their implementation, in the short term these approaches can prove costly and time-consuming. An important area for future development management attention is the cost-benefit analysis – broadly construed – of participatory process approaches. Development management needs to pursue questions that explore and clarify the connection between process inputs and policy and service delivery outputs (see, for example, Blackburn & Holland, 1998; Brinkerhoff, 1997).

Technological Trends: These trends affect development management as process in a number of ways. First, advances in information technology hold the potential for vastly expanding the possibilities for stakeholder consultation by government, for citizen participation, and for coordination and integration across organizations engaged in service delivery, as the tools discussion outlined. Information technology can facilitate the identification and mobilization of contributors to policy issues and solutions. The utilization of information technology for improving the organizational processes of public agencies is a burgeoning area of application, and relates to the worldwide drive for efficiency and decentralization. To remain relevant, development management's process facet will need to keep pace and contribute to learning and adaptation related to information technology and its links to process innovations, organizational effectiveness, and outcomes (see Peterson, 1997).

Beyond the public sector, information technology has served as an important vehicle through which civil society groups have developed processes of constituency mobilization, advocacy, and demand-making. In this sense, information technology can multiply the challenge to the state's capacity for, or commitment to, responsiveness, openness, and accountability. On the other side, as we mentioned previously, technology can create gaps between haves and have nots; there is the potential to create exclusionary processes as well. In developing/transitional countries to a greater extent than in industrialized ones, this gap can be a factor in keeping the poor both from advancing economically and/or participating in democratic governance. Development management's process facet, when combined with values and tools, can help address this issue.

Environmental Trends: As previously noted, the trends here suggest that countries need processes and consultative mechanisms that can deal with priority-setting, clarification of public–private–NGO sector roles, participation of resource users groups, regulatory development and enforcement, and sustainable resource utilization. Besides the need for such processes nationally, because of the transnational nature of environmental problems, they are required at the international level as well (e.g., Killick, 1992). This is a burgeoning area of application and refinement of development management's process component with much potential for theoretical and practical advances.

Socio-Political Trends: Democratization and the rise of civil society have made citizens hyper-attuned to issues of responsiveness, transparency, and accountability. George Orwell got it partially right: someone out there is watching. But in today's world it is not some government monolith that has its lens turned on its citizens, rather the lens is reversed – citizens are watching their governments. Being responsive, transparent, and accountable are basically procedural and process issues; developing/transitional country governance structures need process capacity in order to institutionalize democratic governance. Development management has an ongoing role to play in building this process capacity from the central to the local level.[20]

Development management's process perspective is also applicable to the other socio-political trends. It is clear that civil society groups need the same kind of process tools and approaches as public managers if they are to fulfill their potential. Regarding ethnic conflicts and complex emergencies, process interventions can be important for conflict resolution and negotiation, and as Bryant (1999) points out, for seeking to begin as soon as possible to institute processes that help former combatants build a basis for, at a minimum, peaceful co-existence, if not cooperation. Development management's process approaches also have the potential to build upon and mobilize local capacity in the context of emergency situations, thus speeding the transition from relief to development (see, for example, Anderson & Woodrow, 1998).

BRIDGING PRACTICE AND THEORY

In the preceding discussion we have sought to map, albeit roughly and rapidly, the implications of several categories of global trends for development management. The discussion has revealed that some of these implications lead to applications of existing development management knowledge and practice to areas where they have yet to be brought to bear, some suggest the continued relevance of their applicability for areas that are their traditional bailiwick, and still others suggest areas where further analytic work is called for. Bryant (1996) characterizes development management as largely an inductive field, where what is known "has often been learned experientially, and usually from the bottom up, with a focus on a project or a program" (p. 1540).[21] Thus, we can anticipate that as development management gains experience with the impacts of global trends on developing/transitional country public managers and their private and NGO sector partners, new knowledge will emerge. However, we think that it is critical to structure such learning so that it moves beyond the anecdotal and gains increased relevance across a range of settings and circumstances.

As globalization unifies the pressures facing public managers around the world, public administration scholars and practitioners are calling for more explicitly comparative investigation. Riggs (1998) advocates such investigation to combat what he sees as the ethnocentrism of American public administration. Heady (1998) argues for an integration of the analytic efforts of internationalists and comparativists to address the increasingly universal nature of administrative problems resulting from globalization, suggesting along the way that development management has been more international than comparative. How can the development management subfield move in this direction?

An important step is to build more robust bridges between theory and practice. This does not mean seeking to develop an all-encompassing and integrative theoretical and explanatory framework. We believe that such a search is ultimately counterproductive and can divert attention from what really counts in the applied field of development management: developing usable knowledge. Esman suggests that usable knowledge will emerge from interactively drawing upon three sources: (1) formal analytics from the professional and academic literature, (2) learning from concrete situations and interventions – that is, the experiential database referred to by Bryant (1996), and (3) experience and judgment of "front-line" development managers and the members of "client" publics (1991, p. 23). Combining these three sources, while not requiring an overarching theoretical framework, does call for some sort of mid-range analytic framework so as to allow for sufficient abstraction to reach generalizable lessons.

Development management, along with its parent discipline of public administration, has been criticized for lacking a unifying "grand theory." It is interesting to note that recent efforts in this direction have been undertaken by scholars under the disciplinary umbrella of the new institutional economics (NIE), which has evolved constructs and vocabulary to describe and analyze many of the same concepts and issues that the development management subfield has focused on for years.[22] However, across the diverse theoretical and analytic lenses that development managers have used, there are more common building blocks for mid-range frameworks than are usually perceived. For example, concepts such as nested and interactive systems, organizational learning and adaptation, and political economy provide the elements for constructing the kind of frameworks that can usefully bridge theory and practice.[23]

Bridging theory and practice will continue to be a key challenge for the development management subfield – a challenge exacerbated by development management's instrumental orientation to serving the needs of international assistance agencies and their developing/transitional country partners/clients. In the past, international agencies have provided the resources and the opportunities for development management applied research and analysis; with rare exceptions, they are now less willing or able to support such investigation.[24] In today's increasingly complex world, it is unfortunate that there is shrinking patience for understanding and learning, but this in itself is an outgrowth of the impact of the global trends on the realm of foreign assistance, where the constituencies of international aid expect quick results, efficiency, and immediate impacts.

CONCLUSIONS

Development specialists have a history of disillusionment and self-criticism; and, like public administration more generally but perhaps more acutely, development management has suffered a chronic identity crisis (see Esman, 1980). While painful and potentially demoralizing, the self-questioning of relevance and effectiveness among development management scholars and practitioners has yielded important advances in the field. Through iterative cycles of analysis and practice, development management has, for example, evolved past the blueprint to elaborate process approaches; and has come to better appreciate and incorporate cultural, institutional, and political factors into the organizational and managerial arena in developing/transitional countries. These innovations emerged from a process of trial and error, reflection, and learning. This openness to embracing error and willingness to draw upon diverse experience bases and analytic perspectives are among the strengths of the subfield, even as they make its boundaries hard to pinpoint or describe.

What, then, are the prospects for development management's contribution now and in the future? As our above discussion indicates, we argue that development management remains applicable to current management and governance issues in developing/transitional countries, and as global trends continue to exert their impacts development management may be increasingly important. Capacity-building is an ongoing and crosscutting need. Process approaches will be necessary to identify, mobilize, and incorporate diverse stakeholders and their viewpoints to develop policy solutions that can be successfully implemented and sustained. Around the world, attention to participation and empowerment has increased, not diminished, as core process elements of making democratic governance work. Development management's value facet is critical to reminding policymakers that development involves choices that advantage some societal groups and disadvantage others, and that how those choices are made affects the balance of winners and losers.

At the same time, our analysis points to several avenues to be pursued as the subfield of development management evolves. We single out just a few for mention here. As suggested above, development management needs to explore a closer integration between theory and practice through the development of mid-range analytic frameworks. This path involves, for example, bringing institutional analysis and design perspectives to bear more directly on development management's tool and process facets. Another avenue includes a continuation of development management's interdisciplinary approach, but with a different balance in the mix, giving more emphasis to the fields of comparative politics, anthropology, and psychology. Along this avenue are questions, for example, of path dependence and how the past shapes the present, of the interplay between culture and management, and of the complex interaction of politics and values in shaping discourse both about socio-economic development and its management. A third avenue, also previously touched upon, concerns the implications of information technology for new organizational forms and processes, state–society interactions, and knowledge management.

We see the boundaries between the subfield of development management, ICA, and mainstream public administration becoming fuzzier. As Mittelman (1996, p. 237) observes, "globalization is about opportunities arising from reorganizing governance, the economy, and culture throughout the world". In informing developing/transitional countries' search worldwide for best practices and lessons to deal with these opportunities – and challenges, development management needs to extend the subfield's scope. This means looking not simply at what has worked in other developing/transitional countries, but at industrialized nations as well. Conversely, industrialized nations have much to learn from developing/transitional nations' efforts.

However, beyond these responses, more is required to ensure development management's continued relevance. An important component to thinking about this question involves Schon's (1971) notion of "ideas in good currency". Those of us who see ourselves as development management professionals continue to see relevance in what we do and study, but often make assumptions about the perceptions of relevance of our discipline on the part of decision-makers and policymakers, both in international donor agencies and in developing/transitional countries. Yet the extent to which management and administration are in good currency varies. The Reagan/ Thatcher era in the 1980s of public sector bashing is a case in point.

Development management specialists need to hone in on the critical managerial features of the problems that are preoccupying decision-makers and demonstrate how the discipline is relevant and useful. It is these decision-makers who must be convinced of the fit between development management and current global issues. Development management has made a difference in the lives of citizens in the developing world, but continuing to contribute means remaining "in good currency". This is as much a challenge to the subfield as renewing and advancing development management's practical and applied research agendas.

NOTES

1. The management-related literature dealing with globalization is enormous and growing. To cite just a few examples related to public management: the role of nation-state (Guchenno, 1995; Panitch, 1996), the need for a theoretical reconceptualization of public administration (Baltadano, 1997), the detrimental effects on citizens of the global economic order (Korten, 1995), managing public affairs in a global economy (Dunning, 1997; Garcia-Zamor & Khator, 1994; Greider, 1998), and the new public management (Ferlie, Pettigrew, Ashburner, & Fitzgerald, 1996).

2. We build upon a dialog among scholars and practitioners initiated at a mini-plenary entitled, "Postcards from the Edge: Future Directions in Comparative and International Administration," held at the 59th ASPA National Conference, Seattle, WA, May 1998, convened by Derick Brinkerhoff and Tjip Walker.

3. The term development administration has been the traditional label for the subfield of public administration in developing/transitional countries. However, this has in many circles been gradually supplanted by the term development management. Although some consider the shift nothing more than semantics, we see the replacement of administration with management as signifying a stronger emphasis on strategy and proactive style, as opposed to the tasks and tools of routine administration. Also, development management is not restricted to the public sector; development managers can be staff of NGOs, members of community groups, or businesspeople, as well as civil servants.

4. Our inquiry builds on earlier work that has, over the years, reflected upon development management, where it has been, and where it might go. Besides Riggs (1998) and Heady (1998), see Esman (1980, 1988, 1991), Korten and Klauss (1984), Rondinelli (1987), Nicholson and Connerley (1989), and Brinkerhoff (1986, 1990, 1997).

5. This section summarizes the broader literature on global trends, and draws upon the "Postcards from the Edge" session at the 1998 ASPA National Conference in Seattle.

6. The flow of private capital to developing countries grew from $45 billion in 1990 to $244 billion in 1996 (World Bank, 1997).

7. Riggs (1997) elaborates on this trend and the threat to the legitimacy of public administration and public managers.

8. This overview obviously does not do justice to the evolution of development and development management. See the introductory chapters of Bryant and White (1982), the thematic overview of the development management field by one of its founders (Esman, 1991), the history of development management and U.S. foreign assistance (Rondinelli, 1987), the review of approaches to institutional development in Brinkerhoff (1986), the retrospective on policy analysis in Brinkerhoff (1997), and the framework-building effort in Thomas (1996).

9. The literature on the politics of reform is vast. See, for example, Haggard and Kaufman (1992) or Bates and Krueger (1994).

10. The contingency approach has been widely applied in development management analysis and practice. See Brinkerhoff (1991), Brinkerhoff et al. (1990), Hage and Finsterbusch (1987), and Israel (1987).

11. See, for example, Brinkerhoff (1998) and Coston (1998a).

12. See, for example, the monthly newsletter of the Bread for the World Institute's Development Bank Watcher's Project, "News and Notices for World Bank Watchers." This publication is available by e-mail at http://bankwatch@igc.apc.org

13. This statement is a bit of an oversimplification, but new public management (NPM) does have identifiable features that its proponents advocate as good for what ails government around the world. For an excellent overview of NPM, see Chapter 1 in Ferlie et al. (1996).

14. For example, a forthcoming symposium issue of the *International Journal of Organization Theory and Behavior* (Vol. 2, 1999), entitled "Grassroots Organizations and Public Policy Processes," addresses this challenge.

15. This gap is at the crux of Nicholson and Connerley's (1989) thesis regarding the crisis of development management, where they argue that the focus should be on larger issues of institutional choice rather than bandaid-like organizational improvement interventions. This argument is further elaborated in Nicholson (1997). See also Grindle (1997).

16. Microsoft Project exemplifies generic project planning software. Development project planning has been computerized (PCTeamUp), as has stakeholder analysis and political mapping (PolicyMaker) developed for the health sector (see Reich, 1996). Other tools include software for designing capacity-building interventions developed by the United Nations Development Program (http: Jlmagnet.undp.org/capbuild/Read 1 st.htm); and an analytic capacity assessment tool for NGOs, called DOSA (discussion-oriented self-assessment), developed by Private Agencies Collaborating Together (PACT) and Education Development Center, with USAID funding (http://www.edc.org/INT/CapDev/dosintr.htm).

17. See Brinkerhoff (1996) on the need for policy champions for reform, and Brinkerhoff (1999) for a preliminary effort to develop and assessment methodology for political will and anti-corruption efforts.

18. Perhaps the most well-known "defector" is David Korten, whose early work on bureaucratic reorientation, learning process organizations, and people-centered development has been very influential in shaping the development management

subfield (see, for example, Korten, 1984; Korten & Klauss, 1984). Korten sees development management professionals who work with international donor agencies or developing/transitional country governments as contributors to the problem, not the solution. His reasoning is laid out in Korten (1995) and in the various publications of the advocacy NGO he founded, the People-Centered Development Forum (http://iisdl.iisd.ca/pcdf).

19. Uphoff and Esman (1974) were among the first to demonstrate that local communities could not develop without linkages to larger administrative and economic entities. The same principle of linkages applies today in the larger sphere of nations and global economy.

20. Some interesting work is being done in helping to improve the functioning and effectiveness of cabinet offices to manage the policy formulation and implementation process. This is critical for governments to be able to respond to citizen expectations. See, for example, Garnett, Koenen-Grant, and Rielly (1997).

21. This characteristic of development management's knowledge base derives largely from the subfield's instrumental connection with foreign assistance agendas. Another perspective is that of Cooke (1998), who argues that development management is essentially organizational development (OD) where the theory–practice dichotomy does not apply because it is by nature a theory of practice.

22. NIE discusses public sector management with a near-total disregard for any of the development management literature. See, for example, Girishankar and Dc Silva (1998). Some observers consider that development management has been encroached upon by the disciplinary "imperialism" of the NIE due to donor agencies' relatively higher regard for economists as constituting a "harder" social science than that of management and organization specialists (Bryant, 1996).

23. For an example of an analytic framework explicitly developed to serve the purpose of organizing knowledge across experience to inform practice, see Brinkerhoff, Goldsmith, Ingle, and Walker (1990) and Oakerson and Walker (1997). Tendler (1997) uses the framework of industrial performance and workplace transformation in her cross-case study of good government.

24. The commitment of USAID to research and analysis on development management has been significant, beyond the agency's early support for work on institution-building. A series of centrally funded projects that began in the late 1970s and continue up to the present (Development Project Effectiveness, Performance Management, Decentralization: Financial Management, and Implementing Policy Change, Phases I and II) has underwritten an important segment of the subfield's applied research and literature base. Universities and foundations may have a role to play in supporting further inquiry.

REFERENCES

Anderson, M. B., & Woodrow, P. J. (1998). *Rising from the ashes: Development strategies in times of disaster.* Boulder, CO: Lynne Rienner Publishers.

Baltadano, A. P. (1997). The study of public administration in times of global interpenetration: A historical rationale for a theoretical model. *Journal of Public Administration Research and Theory, 7*(4), 615–638.

Bates, R. H., & Krueger, A. O. (1994). *Political and economic interactions in economic policy reform: Evidence from eight countries.* Cambridge, MA: Basil Blackwell.

Blackburn, J., & Holland, J. (Eds). (1998). *Who changes? Institutionalizing participation in development.* London: Intermediate Technology Publications.

Brinkerhoff, D. W. (1986). The evolution of current perspectives on institutional development: An organizational focus. In: D. W. Brinkerhoff & J.-C. Garcia Zamor (Eds), *Politics, projects, and people: Institutional development in Haiti* (pp. 259–273). New York: Praeger.

Brinkerhoff, D. W. (1990). Technical cooperation and training in development management: Trends, implications, and recommendations. *Canadian Journal of Development Studies, 11*(1), 139–149.

Brinkerhoff, D. W. (1991). *Improving development program performance: Guidelines for managers.* Boulder, CO: Lynne Rienner Publishers.

Brinkerhoff, D. W. (1996). Process perspectives on policy change: Highlighting implementation. *World Development, 24*(9), 1395–1403.

Brinkerhoff, D. W. (1997). Integrating institutional and implementation issues into policy decisions: An introduction and overview. In: D. W. Brinkerhoff (Ed.), *Policy analysis concepts and methods: An institutional and implementation focus* (Vol. 5, pp. 1–18). Policy Studies in Developing Nations Series. Greenwich, CT: JAI Press.

Brinkerhoff, D. W. (1998). *Democratic governance and sectoral policy reform: Linkages, complementarities, and synergies.* Washington, DC: American Society for Public Administration, Section on International and Comparative Administration.

Brinkerhoff, D. W. (1999). *Identifying and assessing political will for anti-corruption efforts.* Working Paper no. 13, Implementing policy change project, Washington, DC: U.S. Agency for International Development, Center for Democracy and Governance.

Brinkerhoff, D. W., Goldsmith, A. A., Ingle, M. D., & Walker, S. T. (1990). Institutional sustainability: A conceptual framework. In: D. W. Brinkerhoff & A. A. Goldsmith (Eds), *Institutional sustainability in agriculture and rural development: A global perspective* (pp. 19–49). New York: Praeger.

Brinkerhoff, D. W., & Ingle, M. D. (1989). Between blueprint and process: A structured flexibility approach to development management. *Public Administration and Development, 9*(5), 487–503.

Bryant, C. (1996). Strategic change through sensible projects. *World Development, 24*(9), 1539–1551.

Bryant, C. (1999). *Strategic management in complex emergencies: A role for international donors.* Working Paper no. 14, Implementing Policy Change Project. Washington, DC: U.S. Agency for International Development, Center for Democracy and Governance.

Bryant, C., & White, L. G. (1982). *Managing development in the Third World.* Boulder, CO: Westview Press.

Bryson, J., & Crosby, B. (1992). *Leadership for the common good: Tackling public problems in a shared-power world.* San Francisco, CA: Jossey-Bass.

Cooke, B. (1997). From process consultation to a clinical model of development practice. *Public Administration and Development, 17*(3), 325–340.

Cooke, B. (1998). Participation, 'process' and management: Lessons for development in the history of organization development. *Journal of International Development, 10*(1), 35–54.

Coston, J. M. (1998a). A model and typology of government–NGO relationships. *Nonprofit and Voluntary Sector Quarterly, 27*(3), 358–383.

Coston, J. M. (1998b). Administrative avenues to democratic governance: The balance of supply and demand. *Public Administration and Development, 18*(5), 479–493.

Coston, J. M., & Butz, J. L. (1999). Mastering information: The birth of citizen-initiated voter education in Mongolia. Symposium issue on grassroots organizations and public policy processes. *International Journal of Organization Theory and Behavior, 2*(1 & 2), 107–139.

Crosby, B. (1997). Stakeholder analysis and political mapping: Tools for successfully implementing policy reforms. In: D. W. Brinkerhoff (Ed.), *Policy analysis concepts and methods: An institutional and implementation focus* (Vol. 5, pp. 261–287). Policy Studies in Developing Nations Series. Greenwich, CT: JAI Press.

Delp, P., Thesen, A., Motiwalla, J., & Seshadri, N. (1977). *Systems tools for project planning.* Bloomington: Program of Advanced Studies in Institution Building and Technical Assistance Methodologies, Indiana University.

Dobell, R., & Steenkamp, P. (1993). Preface to the symposium on public management in a borderless economy: National governments in a world of trans-national networks. *International Review of Administrative Sciences, 59*(4), 569–577.

Dunning, J. H. (Ed.). (1997). *Governments, globalization, and international business.* New York: Oxford University Press.

Esman, M. J. (1980). Development assistance in public administration: Requiem or renewal. *Public Administration Review, 40*(5), 426–431.

Esman, M. J. (1988). The maturing of development administration. *Public Administration and Development, 8*(2), 125–134.

Esman, M. J. (1991). *Management dimensions of development: Perspectives and strategies.* West Hartford, CT: Kumarian Press.

Ferlie, E., Pettigrew, A., Ashburner, L., & Fitzgerald, L. (1996). *The new public management in action.* Oxford: Oxford University Press.

Fowler, A. (1997). *Striking a balance: A guide to enhancing the effectiveness of non governmental organisations in international development.* London: Earthscan Publications.

Fukuyama, F. (1990). Are we at the end of history? *Fortune, 121*(2), 75–78.

Garcia-Zamor, J.-C., & Khator, R. (Eds). (1994). *Public administration in the global village.* Westport, CT: Praeger.

Garnett, H., Koenen-Grant, J., & Rielly, C. (1997). Managing policy formulation and implementation in Zambia's democratic transition. *Public Administration and Development, 17*(1), 77–91.

Girishankar, N., & De Silva, M. (1998). *Strategic management for government agencies: An institutional approach for developing and transitional economies.* Discussion Paper no. 386, Washington, DC: World Bank.

Greider, W. (1998). *One world, ready or not: The manic logic of global capitalism.* New York: Free Press.

Grindle, M. S. (Ed.). (1997). *Getting good government: Capacity building in the public sectors of developing countries.* Cambridge, MA: Harvard University Press, for the Harvard Institute for International Development.

Guchenno, J.-M. (1995). *The end of the nation-state.* Minneapolis: University of Minnesota Press.

Hage, J., & Finsterbusch, K. (1987). *Organizational change as a development strategy: Models and tactics for improving Third World organizations.* Boulder, CO: Lynne Rienner Publishers.

Haggard, S., & Kaufman, R. R. (Eds). (1992). *The politics of economic adjustment: International constraints, distributive conflicts, and the state.* Princeton, NJ: Princeton University Press.

Heady, F. (1998). Comparative and international public administration: Building intellectual bridges. *Public Administration Review, 58*(1), 32–40.

Hubbard, R. (1997). People – hearts and minds towards rebirth of the public service. *Public Administration and Development, 17*(1), 109–114.

Huntington, S. P. (1996). *The clash of civilizations and the remaking of the world order.* New York: Simon and Schuster.

Israel, A. (1987). *Institutional development: Incentives to performance.* Baltimore, MD: Johns Hopkins University Press.

Joy, L. (1997). Developing a development practice: A commentary in response to cooke. *Public Administration and Development, 17*(4), 453–477.

Kerrigan, J. E., & Luke, J. S. (1987). *Management training strategies for developing countries.* Boulder, CO: Lynne Rienner Publishers.

Killick, T. (1992). Policy-making under extreme uncertainty: Developing country responses to global warming. *Journal International Development, 4*(1), 29–39.

Korten, D. C. (1984). Strategic organization for people-centered development. *Public Administration Review, 44*(4), 341–352.

Korten, D. C. (1990). *Getting to the 21st century: Voluntary action and the global agenda.* West Hartford, CT: Kumarian Press.

Korten, D. C. (1995). *When corporations rule the world.* West Hartford, CT: Kumarian Press.

Korten, D. C., & Klauss, R. (Eds). (1984). *People-centered development: Contributions toward theory and planning frameworks.* West Hartford, CT: Kumarian Press.

Kumar, K. (Ed.). (1993). *Rapid appraisal methods.* Washington, DC: World Bank.

Larson, P. (1997). Public and private values at odds – can private sector values be transplanted into public sector institutions? *Public Administration and Development, 17*(1), 131–139.

Lindenberg, M., & Crosby, B. (1981). *Managing development: The political dimension.* West Hartford, CT: Kumarian Press.

Mittelman, J. H. (1996). How does globalization really work? In: J. H. Mittelman (Ed.), *Globalization: Critical reflections.*(pp. 229–241). Boulder, CO: Lynne Rienner Publishers.

Nicholson, N. (1997). Analyzing bureaucracy and rural development policy implementation: The limits of hierarchy. In: D. W. Brinkerhoff (Ed.), *Policy analysis concepts and methods: An institutional and implementation focus* (Vol. 5, pp. 113–141). Policy Studies in Developing Nations Series. Greenwich, CT: JAI Press.

Nicholson, N. K., & Connerley, E. F. (1989). The impending crisis in development administration. *International Journal of Public Administration, 12*(3), 385–426.

Oakerson, R. J., & Walker, S. T. (1997). Analyzing policy reform and reforming policy analysis: An institutionalist approach. In: D. W. Brinkerhoff (Ed.), *Policy analysis concepts and methods: An institutional and implementation focus* (Vol. 5, pp. 21–53). Policy Studies in Developing Nations Series. Greenwich, CT: JAI Press.

Overseas Development Institute. (1996). *Rethinking the role of multilateral development banks.* Briefing Paper no. 4. London: Overseas Development Institute.

Panitch, L. (1996). Rethinking the role of the state. In: J. H. Mittelman (Ed.), *Globalization: Critical reflections* (pp. 83–113). Boulder, CO: Lynne Rienner Publishers.

Peterson, S. B. (1997). Hierarchy versus networks: Alternative strategies for building organizational capacity in public bureaucracies in Africa. In: M. S. Grindle (Ed.), *Getting good government: Capacity building in the public sectors of developing countries* (pp. 157–177).

Cambridge, MA: Harvard University Press, for the Harvard Institute for International Development.

Reich, M. R. (1996). Applied political analysis for health policy reform. *Current Issues in Public Health, 2,* 186–191.

Riggs, F. W. (1997). Modernity and bureaucracy. *Public Administration Review, 57*(4), 347–353.

Riggs, F. W. (1998). Public administration in America: Why our uniqueness is exceptional and important. *Public Administration Review, 58*(1), 22–32.

Rondinelli, D. A. (1983). *Development projects as policy experiments: An adaptive approach to development administration.* New York: Methuen and Company.

Rondinelli, D. A. (1987). *Development administration and U.S. foreign aid policy.* Boulder, CO: Lynne Rienner Publishers.

Schon, D. A. (1971). *Beyond the stable state: Public and private learning in a changing society.* London: Maurice Temple Smith Ltd.

Spector, B. I., & Cooley, L. (1997). *Consultant roles in the strategic management of policy change.* Technical Note no. 8. Implementing Policy Change Project. Washington, DC: U.S. Agency for International Development, Center for Democracy and Governance.

Tendler, J. (1997). *Good government in the tropics.* Baltimore, MD: Johns Hopkins University Press.

Thomas, A. (1996). What is development management? *Journal of International Development, 8*(1), 95–110.

Tichy, N. M., McGill, A. R., & St. Clair, L. (Eds). (1997). *Corporate global citizenship. Doing business in the public eye.* Lanham, MD: Lexington Books.

United Nations Development Programme. (1994). *Process consultation for systemic improvement of public sector management.* New York: UNDP.

Uphoff, N., & Esman, M. (1974). *Local organization for development: Analysis of Asian experience.* Ithaca, NY: Center for International Studies, Cornell University.

Welch, E., & Wong, W. (1998). Public administration in a global context: Bridging the gaps of theory and practice between Western and Non-Western nations. *Public Administration Review, 58*(1), 40–51.

White, L. G. (1987). *Creating opportunities for change. Approaches to managing development programs.* Boulder, CO: Lynne Rienner Publishers.

World Bank. (1997). *Background note on the World Bank's corporate citizenship program.* Corporate Citizenship Conference: Building Partnerships for Development. Washington, DC, May 21–22.

World Bank. (1998). *Knowledge for development.* World Development Report, Washington, DC: World Bank.

PUBLIC ADMINISTRATION IN POST-SOCIALIST EASTERN EUROPE

Eric M. Rice

Eastern European governments have been preoccupied with the grand questions of dismantling inherited socialist political structures and their command economies, rewriting their constitutions and laws to facilitate the emergence of democracy and free markets, and responding to the resulting shocks and crises. Understandably, little progress has been made to date in the overhaul of public administration, and no systematic evaluation has been done of the capacity of Eastern European governments to implement either the transformation or their future programs.

The transition to a market economy clearly requires both the elimination of a range of existing government institutions and practices and the introduction of new agencies with new goals, staffed with people having different attitudes and behavior. This article is a first effort to lay out the problem of capacity constraints in the key public institutions involved in the transition. It incorporates the following five principles that are likely to guide Eastern European societies in rebuilding their governments:[1]

Retreat from the discredited central government, as subnational governments and private enterprises assume many functions of central governments.

Comparative Public Administration: The Essential Readings
Research in Public Policy Analysis and Management, Volume 15, 863–881
Copyright © 2006 by Elsevier Ltd.
All rights of reproduction in any form reserved
ISSN: 0732-1317/doi:10.1016/S0732-1317(06)15040-X

Improved channels of communication between government and their citizens, as policy transparency and a voice for the public in the policy-making process are increasingly being demanded and institutionalized.

Creation of a hospitable business environment, including clarification of property rights, policy stability, consistency and accountability, low-cost provision of government services, and infrastructure and protection of agents from abuses in the marketplace.

Concern for public welfare and social justice, as citizens of postcommunist Eastern Europe are hoping to obtain the familiar basic securities (job security, subsidized consumption, and universal access to basic health care and education) as well as new freedoms and rights.

Efficient government administration at all levels, under the scrutiny of elected legislatures, citizens groups, and internal audit and review agencies in the new governments themselves.

These principles constitute political constraints on the formulation of a successful institutional reform strategy and so guide the analysis of this article.

The government in each country of Eastern Europe is uniquely defined by historical, cultural, and bureaucratic anomalies; by its prior level of contacts outside the Soviet bloc; and by the personalities and political shades of its reformers. All the same, public administration across these countries is more notable for similarities than differences both in its shortcomings and in the stages of its reform. This article not only concentrates on the issues of public administration which Eastern European governments have in common, but also attempts to point out salient differences, especially in the paths and status of their respective reforms.

POLICY-MAKING CAPACITY

The design and direction of economic reforms are heavily taxing the macroeconomic policy apparatus of every country of Eastern Europe. Government ministers and their senior staff tend to operate in relative isolation from other ministries. Few officials grasp the broad shape of their national reform program or can express the underlying motivations for the policies being enacted.[2]

The lack of a top-level focal point for promulgating, debating, and approving specific economic reform measures calls for governments to (1) develop a strategic vision of the transition and to manage its broad direction and (2) enhance policy coordination across ministries to ensure the quality, consistency, and prioritization of these measures. Yet substantial disagreement remains as to how these measures can best be achieved, both to conform to the particular circumstances in each country and to prevent this apparatus from becoming either large and bureaucratized or marginalized.

Several countries are evaluating alternative types of transition policy apparatuses. These may simply consist of formal and informal contacts among economic ministers (as in Poland), an interministerial coordination council such as the one Romania proposes to introduce, or a temporary transition office or ministry, possibly including a technical secretariat. The Czech and Slovak Federal Republic's (CSFR) new hybrid system shares the coordination function between a cabinet-level interministerial council for the economic transition and a financial council composed of the federal and republican ministers of finance plus the president of the central bank. Multilateral and bilateral advisors can help by advising governments about experiences outside the region stressing the importance of coordination and the impact of economic linkages.

It seems that all governments of Eastern Europe will have to expand their capacity to formulate economic projections and strategies. Few government mechanisms now exist for making multiyear estimates, and for laying out indicative strategies for the public and private sectors. One hopeful reform took place in Bulgaria, which has supplanted its large planning ministry with a new, small agency for indicative planning. Other countries that have experimented successfully with mechanisms for developing economic strategy (e.g., France, Japan, Korea, Taiwan, and Thailand) might offer Eastern Europe organizational models and technical assistance.[3]

In many critical areas, the ability of these governments to make sensible policy is also sorely hampered by a lack of information. For example, across the region these countries have essentially no data on goods' prices outside the public sector or on the changing condition of the poor. They also lack knowledge of economic policy alternatives and reform experiences elsewhere in the region and in the developing world. The governments' need for information demands activity in at least three areas: overhauling their statistical systems, exploiting nongovernnmental resources, and information sharing across the region.

The statistical systems of Eastern Europe were designed to serve the needs of a planned economy. There is broad agreement on the pressing need for Eastern European countries to develop statistical systems and new data series to serve the policy needs of business and of their new governments. Such efforts would include the adoption of modern international concepts, methods, and standards for statistical collection and reporting.[4] A loose confederation of multilateral donors currently coordinates a number of projects aimed at expanding statistical capabilities in Eastern Europe.

Given that governments are strapped for analytical expertise, they might make greater use of extragovernmental sources of information. Academic institutes of economics and finance – both inside and outside the government bureaucracy – already provide substantial policy analyses in Czechoslovakia, Hungary, and Poland. So do some university faculty and independent groups of eminent citizens and experts (such as Hungary's Blue Ribbon Commission and Bulgaria's Economic Transition Project). The governments of the CSFR and Hungary have been quite successful in their concerted efforts to attract expatriate advisors (both as short- and long-term advisors and as senior civil servants); some funded by external nongovernnmental foundations or bilateral assistance programs.

The governments of the region can learn from each other's experiences as well by increasing their information sharing. For instance, Poland's unfortunate experience with hyperinflation taught the rest of the region how to design better anti-inflation policies and the urgency of doing so. Not only would information sharing enable governments to borrow successful programs from their neighbors, but it would also help them sustain public support for difficult policies by showing that the policies worked elsewhere.

The governments of the CSFR, Hungary, and Poland continually exchange views and experiences among themselves. Many of these contacts take place informally, while others occur in regional or international conferences or through the intermediation of outside advisors or agencies with cross-country experience. Ideas borrowed from other countries in the region tend to embody "appropriate technology," involving policies that are likely to be relatively inexpensive and simple to manage.

CHANGING THE ROLE OF
GOVERNMENT IN SOCIETY

Transforming the Central Government from "Governor" of the people to "Servant" of its citizens' day-to-day interactions between the public and the government has not changed substantially. Burdensome administrative and regulatory procedures persist – evidenced by the numerous steps typically still required to register a small business – failing to reflect the changes at the level of macroeconomic policy. At the same time, newly emerging interest groups across the region are exercising an active voice concerning the environment, consumer protection, business opportunity, and occupational safety. The clamor to be heard seems to have grown faster than the governments' capacity to listen. Eastern Europe's transformations will require commensurate governmental changes on three fronts: replacing and retraining top managers; developing communication channels between citizens and their governments; and ensuring that civil servants are being held accountable for their actions.[5]

All governments have taken action on the first front, having replaced the top-most layer of ministry management (with some exceptions in Romania and Bulgaria). The replacement of a few more management layers is believed to be needed to change the culture of a ministry. This will be a major undertaking; however, given the lack of processes to identify qualified incumbent managers, the absence of a functioning labor market for managers, and a shortage of skilled replacements.

Communication channels both to and from the governments should eventually be developed. One part of this effort might be for the governments to adopt legal assurances granting citizens access to any unclassified information about government activities (a freedom of information code). Another might be to introduce the institution of parliamentary testimony under oath by government officials. Such measures would help parliamentarians, the media, and interest groups in their role as public watchdogs. Without such guarantees, information is obtained only haphazardly, as with the sensationalized news accounts of scandalous spontaneous privatization.

Governments will also need to institutionalize channels for receiving and responding to citizens' inputs. These enhance government accountability (both in fact and in appearance) and thereby help to alleviate potentially explosive political pressures. They can also help protect citizens from arbitrary actions by the government. One such channel might be a citizens' advocate, as was introduced in Poland back in 1988.

EVOLVING DECENTRALIZATION FROM CENTRAL TO SUBNATIONAL GOVERNMENTS

In Eastern Europe, subnational "governments" previously were structured as arms of the central government. The devolution of significant powers and responsibilities to subnational government has already advanced a great distance[6] even though their capacities and capabilities are uneven. This is widely viewed as a positive development: decentralization as a means of restoring democratic rights. Yet the radical shift from central to subnational governments complicates the reform process in a number of ways.[7]

Most governments have not yet resolved the question of what model of central–regional–local government relations they will adopt. This is necessarily a political process and so will take time to resolve. Meanwhile, some reforms and projects have been put on hold pending the designation of the appropriate authorities. Laws clearly defining the jurisdictions and responsibilities of each level of government could alleviate critical uncertainties for all concerned.

Decentralization complicates reform implementation in that measures approved by national legislatures risk derailment of subnational governments that are not "on board." Building local government institutions must have high priority across the region because the domain of local and regional governments will encompass communal services, housing, much of regulatory administration, the delivery of health care and poverty assistance, and parts of the education and transportation systems. Some forms of private-sector promotion will also take place at the local level.

Three broad deficiencies of subnational governments can be identified: rudimentary operating systems, insufficient and poorly trained staff, and an undeveloped capacity to raise revenue. Subnational governments will have to be strength-coded to enable them to handle their broad new responsibilities. Otherwise, the good intentions of central governments, evidenced by the flurry of reform legislation, will not reach the implementation stage.

Hungary and Poland have taken concrete steps to strengthen local government capacity. In Hungary, the central government consults the Association of Local Self-Governments on all relevant draft legislation. It has also introduced a sweeping comprehensive local government reform law, which will transfer subnational authority, assets, and taxing authority to local governments. Poland has established a new, high-profile office charged with reforms at the local level and has stepped up revenue sharing and asset transfers for municipalities.

The heavy demands likely to be placed on local governments warrant a study of their capacity, like those already prepared for Hungary (Davey, 1990) and Poland (Prud'homme, 1990). The World Bank also intends to initiate a cross-country study of local government issues in Poland, Hungary, and Romania.

Donor governments (national and subnational) are also beginning to participate. For example, the United States Agency for International Development has earmarked $5 million specifically for subnational government development in Eastern Europe. Donor countries may be called upon to impart their particular expertise in the areas of allocating administrative and political turfs, and of revenue-sharing arrangements. OECD governments' methods of local taxation and their interregional revenue arrangements might provide models (and technical assistance) for Eastern Europe. Hungary has relied on local government specialists from foreign academies of public administration for technical assistance and training. In addition, Hungary implemented local government reforms over the past few years and may itself be well positioned to offer advice that is tailored to the conditions of the region.

LIQUIDATING OBSOLETE
GOVERNMENT AGENCIES

It is encouraging that Eastern Europe's reformers have been able to shut down obsolete bureaucratic structures with relative ease. Throughout the region, central-planning ministries died along with the demise of command economies.[8] Nearly the entire region has enacted impressive and rapid price decontrol,[9] allowing governments to eliminate or shrink their price-setting offices.[10] Finally, under the old system, each branch (i.e., individual industry) ministry acted as the head office of its industry, managing enterprises as subsidiaries. With control devolving to the enterprises, the need for branch ministries evaporated. In response, every country in the region consolidated its branch ministries into a single much smaller Ministry of Industry[11] on the Western European model.

Even though the closing of these agencies had overwhelming popular support, one might have expected greater difficulty in shutting them down. For one thing, the functional vacuum left by the closure of a national-level agency (even one which performs badly) might have caused nationwide economic disruptions. For another, civil servants might have used their clout to prevent job loss, fighting the closing of these agencies through political channels.

Part of the explanation for the speedy liquidation of redundant agencies is that governments deferred the employment issue by limiting layoffs.[12] The exception is Poland, which has witnessed substantial layoffs of civil servants. However, a wide diversity of opinion exists about whether civil servants from liquidated government agencies can be recycled usefully into new government functions. Some governments outside the region have apparently succeeded in turning civil servants who formerly obstructed the market into functionaries who serve a promarket role.

Yet most observers of Eastern Europe are quite pessimistic, citing a gross mismatch of skills, experience, and attitudes. For instance, it has been suggested that former planners be used to develop longer-term macroeconomic and sectoral strategies. However, many doubt the possibility of convening former central planners from quantity allocators to advisors, promoters, and financial regulators. Similarly, some officials proposed putting pricing officers in charge of price liberalization and fair competition, but doubts that these staffs can be productively transformed have held sway.

Although governments have found it relatively painless to disband unneeded agencies, it should be noted that they have tended to have greater difficulty introducing new institutions and making them operate effectively. Among these relatively slow starter agencies are those concerned with privatization and state property management, social welfare programs, and overhauling the financial system.

REDESIGNING FUNDAMENTAL GOVERNMENT SYSTEMS

Designing new government systems risks conflicting with the popular desire to shrink the central government. For this reason, particular attention should be paid to initiating programs that minimize central government involvement. For instance, governments might consider the private provision of services that would otherwise be delivered by government. Also, local governments will increasingly provide public goods and services such as job training and unemployment benefits.

Given the severe constraints on Eastern European governments in their capacity to implement the required new system, they might look for explicit mechanisms to economize on implementation. For instance, governments should offer their employees incentive awards for suggesting innovations that enhance technical and managerial efficiency. Or where economic and legal expertise are limited, the wholesale adoption of a foreign country's system may sometimes make sense. This might help countries avoid both mistakes and the disruption caused by ensuing corrections.[13]

"Twinning" arrangements, whereby a public or private Eastern European institution is paired with a foreign analog, have begun on a limited and ad hoc basis.[14] Such arrangements are used to facilitate many types of technical assistance, exchanges, and training across a wide array of institutions. A major expansion of government institutional twinning might decentralize institutional development assistance and help speed its implementation.

PUBLIC FINANCE REFORM

Under the former system, the state enterprise sector served as the main source of government revenue. As a result, governments developed very little capacity to collect revenue or fight tax evasion. The process of economic transformation has brought about the collapse of traditional revenue sources without creating new ones. Moreover, it appears that the governments of the region do not fully recognize the urgency of initiating active efforts to overhaul and expand tax administration.

Simplicity and uniformity should rank among the foremost considerations in overhauling the system of taxes and oilier revenues (in order to assure both equity and ease of administration and enforcement). For example, collecting taxes from individuals may be difficult, and governments will certainly depend to some extent on tax withholding by employers. It has been suggested as well that income taxes might also be collected at the source for dividends, interest, and the fringe benefits of managers and employees.

Given the enormous new need for tax administration, attempts to impose complex Western European taxes may be misguided.[15] Rather many feel that governments should look more to model systems used in countries of a similar level of economic development. Technical assistance in tax administration might, therefore, be sought from the tax authorities and finance ministries of the newly industrialized economies. These foreign agencies might also serve as sources of training for civil servants to beef up their capacity to design tax policy to administer tax amidst other revenue systems, and to audit the private and state-enterprise sectors (Table 1).

To prevent income tax evasion, governments must ensure that they have access to the financial information of certain kinds of companies.[16] Yet

Table 1. Civil Service Employment Levels in Government Ministries.

Country	Thousands of Employees	Percentage of Labor Force
Bulgaria[a]	18	0.4
Hungary	8	0.2
Poland[b]	11	0.1
Romania	25	0.2

Note: Estimates for Eastern Europe are from 1989 unless otherwise noted and are World Bank calculations based on government statistics. Data for the CSFR are not available, although World Bank operations staff believe the pattern to be similar.
[a]1991 estimate.
[b]1988 estimate.

privatization weakens governments' direct information links to the economy. The governments of Eastern Europe intend to impose standard requirements for financial disclosure, reporting, and auditing on corporations that are traded on public stock exchanges. However, the need for public access to information argues in favor of extending these requirements to all corporations (Rice, 1990).[17]

Regarding the region's system for budget preparation, approval, and execution, little is known by donor countries (aside from those in Hungary and Poland). In Hungary and Poland, the International Monetary Fund (IMF) recently evaluated the budgeting methods being used at the time, finding them to be entirely incompatible with the modern systems used in capitalist economies. The IMF installed systems in Hungary and Poland that conform to international budgeting conventions. It appears that the IMF will eventually follow the same procedure of diagnosis and reform in the calmer countries.

Once accounting standards are in place and accountants trained (or foreign accounting firms contracted), the government can proceed to establish critical auditing and control mechanisms for their own finances and for the finances of state-owned enterprises and subnational governments. They will also need simple systems to audit their own operational effectiveness, so as to remedy program deficiencies and refer cases of malfeasance and nonfeasance to the appropriate authorities. For each of these auditing functions, the perception of objectivity and independence is critical.

Rudimentary financial auditing infrastructure exists in some countries. The parliaments of Hungary and Poland have a State Audit Committee and an Inspector General, respectively. However, the objectivity of their budgetary audits has been questioned, and their small staffs and lack of routine systems limit the quality and scope of their work. Poland's government auditor performs functional audits of government operations, which elicit both press attention and responsiveness from the rest of the government. Poland's attorney general investigates fraud. So far, such offices are highly political, and they need to be strengthened both in governments and elected legislatures.

Modern accounting and auditing systems are now being installed in Hungary and Poland, and the rest of the region will soon follow. It is likely that central governments will have to establish financial control over subnational governments and state enterprises through budgeting and accounting standards and financial disclosure requirements. Specific suggestions regarding budgetary reform include introducing a formalized system of competitive bidding for procurement (Vecchietti, 1990) and creating an independent procurement oversight department, perhaps located in a government auditor's office.

With respect to public investment, experts identify a regionwide failure of governments to apply standard rate-of-return criteria, and they question the project assessment capabilities of the governments of Eastern Europe. In addition, market forces are not capable of giving clear signals, given the regions' continuing price distortions, undeveloped capital markets, and foreign exchange shortages. Governments appear to be reacting with excessive caution in borrowing for investment. At the same time, they demonstrate a preference for large, state-of-the-art infrastructure projects (for which they hope to attract foreign equity investment) in lieu of coupling more modest investment with managerial improvements.

For the near term, governments will require technical assistance in setting a careful prioritization of investment projects. The most urgent priorities can readily be identified and should be targeted specifically to the identifiable needs of private enterprise. Given the extent of unutilized capacity of existing public investments, emphasis should be on the rehabilitation of existing assets. An evaluation of specific training needs should also be undertaken now to assist Eastern Europe's governments to develop independent capabilities in project design, assessment, and management.

CIVIL SERVICE REFORM

The governments of Eastern Europe have paid almost no attention to civil service reform, even though it is their civil servants who must implement planned reforms. They are relatively uninformed about the systems' operating methods and capacities as well as the current skills, knowledge, and attitudes of civil servants.[18]

Governments have apparently not conceived of their employees as a bureaucracy-wide civil service. They have yet to develop any comprehensive strategies for reorienting, retrenching, retraining, and redeploying their staffs, let alone for building an organized and nonideological civil service system. Currently, these civil services have four broad problem areas: staff and skills shortages, low and compressed salary scales, job mismatch, and demoralized bureaucracies.

Donor countries express unanimous concern about the ability of Eastern Europe's civil servants to manage their reform programs. Although the socialized sectors of Eastern Europe's economies are vast, their *central government* civil services are surprisingly small. Staffing levels in government ministries are low both in absolute terms (ranging from 8,000 in Hungary to 25,000 in Romania), and as a fraction of the overall labor force (from 1% in Poland to 4% in Bulgaria). This fraction is also small compared to that found in market economies (Heller & Tait, 1984).[19]

Moreover, higher wages in the region's emerging private sector are increasingly draining talent from their core civil services. Rather than looking for ways to streamline these core civil services, the countries of Eastern Europe may need to consider strategies to expand and improve them. In contrast, many government services are provided by agencies that are situated administratively outside of the civil service, and these agencies may indeed need dramatic staff cuts.

Eastern Europe's secondary schools, universities, and institutes have historically offered almost no education or training in economics and finance, public and private management, accounting and auditing, project assessment, or tax administration.[20] About the only civil servants who are trained for these functions are the few who have received a foreign education. Although these critical skills and knowledge appear to be virtually missing, governments have been slow in determining their training priorities and expressing their needs to external donors.

A related problem is the strain placed on the limited human resources of domestic bureaucracies by the international donor community itself. This comes in two forms: excessive and uncoordinated international contacts distract government officials from other matters of state and the generous salaries of aid agencies act to lure away some of the best domestic government staff.

The problem of missing skills is exacerbated by a tendency for low civil service salaries and salary compression in all off Eastern Europe.[21] As in the past, managers supplement their pay by teaching when they should be working in the ministries, while other civil servants moonlight or use government time and resources for private business sidelines. With the expansion of the private sector in Poland, Czechoslovakia, and Hungary, better private-sector remuneration has induced a brain drain of newly trained managers, financial technicians, and support staff. This same pattern is now developing elsewhere in Eastern Europe. To the extent that the government cannot match salaries in the private sector, even greater numbers of civil servants must be trained to compensate for this brain drain.

Another staffing problem arises from the governments' typical method of dealing with the civil servants of obsolete ministries: in order to avoid layoffs (or owing to personnel shortages), redundant staff are placed in institutions that will perform new economic functions – even when their skills and attitudes are entirely mismatched. For instance, long-time planning office staffs in Romania were transferred to the privatization office. In Poland and Romania, former price setters are now being asked to perform as price liberalization watchdogs in the new anti-trust offices. Even though both jobs involve prices, many employees may be incapable of switching to such a diametrically opposed role. Many skills and work attitudes are simply not fungible or would necessitate substantial retraining and reorientation.

Each of the personnel issues just mentioned also contributes to the over-arching civil service problem: Eastern Europe's demoralized bureaucracies. In part, the problem is that some of the debilitating *ancient regime* culture of Eastern Europe's civil services still pervades many government bodies. Its implications are a lack of toast and a fear of communication, a staff that achieved its positions via a highly politicized system of recruitment and promotion, and work attitudes and tightly directed operational methods that are incompatible with a market orientation. The tradeoff here is well-known: members of the old guard often have better training for government positions, but their intentions and modes of operation are suspect.

On top of this, bureaucracies now face an added layer of conflict, to the recent mixing of old-style incumbents with new reformers. Loyalties and commitment are constantly challenged, job security seems nonexistent, professional sabotage is an ever-present threat, and turf-battling managers send confused signals to their subordinates. In response, incumbents are increasingly fearful, reformers are increasingly frustrated, and many of both seem to have settled into an uneasy, unproductive paralysis.

The first step of governments might be to establish personnel administration capacity, introducing a formal civil service with a competent, reform-oriented, and high-level directorate. Such a government-wide personnel office would be capable of evaluating its human resource needs on a systemic basis. During the transition, this directorate would be charged with civil service reform: determining training needs and organizing training programs, and instituting structural changes and salary reform. Later, it would become the administrator for the civil service.

Other measures for immediate government action include quickly identifying the greatest needs for salary decompression, and then implementing the most critical pay increases needed to stern the outflow of personnel;[22] rapidly designing short courses to overcome shortages of key skills, in order to help alleviate bottlenecks; and establishing training institutes, since they take time to yield results.[23]

A comprehensive medium- and long-term national action plan for civil service development is also needed, and three broad types of systemic reform to overhaul the civil services have been identified: transforming the bureaucratic culture and organizational structure, introducing mechanisms to assure accountability, and expanding training capacity in a remarkable manner.

Although the challenge of changing the communist bureaucratic culture and organizational structure is unprecedented, governments elsewhere have dealt with analogous transformations in demoralized civil service and in moving from authoritarian to democratic political structures. Eastern Europe can learn from these similar experiences and can obtain technical assistance from those involved. Possible means of transforming the bureaucracy include: a study of the functional structure and priorities of the government bureaucracy; a survey of civil servants' attitudes in order to understand the kind of changes needed; replacement of the top few layers of bureaucracy; development of a professional, merit-based civil service corps; video and seminar presentations aimed at staff and system reorientation; new hiring of (undoctrinated) recent graduates; and reorganizing to assure improved horizontal and vertical communication.

Efficient government depends in part on the ability to give proper signals and incentives to civil servants – a difficult problem with which governments continue to wrestle even in the OECD countries. To this end, respondents recommend that civil service reforms include mechanisms to ensure that bureaucrats be held accountable for their actions. A first step would be to reassert clear hues of responsibility based on a study of the government's functional structure. This would enable one to trace and evaluate policy implementation.

The introduction of needed incentives could then follow via a formalized and transparent civil service review and promotion system – perhaps including merit testing for advancement, awards for meritorious service, rewards for innovative ideals that lead to efficiency improvements, and financial incentives for state enterprise managers. The civil service reform would also contain methods for identifying and punishing malfeasance and nonfeasance. In this, Poland has taken the lead, using its inspector general to audit government operations and its attorney general to prosecute fraud.

Finally, Eastern Europe faces an overwhelming need to train its civil servants, the magnitude of which government leaders do not appreciate. Fortunately, government employees are hungry for training, and the opportunity to enhance one's professional skills is seen as an enviable job prerequisite. Moreover, local schools and institutes are now rushing to respond to the new demand for certain occupational skills. Of particular note are new programs in business and public administration in the CSFR,

Hungary; Poland; and most recently; in Romania. These efforts might be expanded by initiating teaching seminars by foreign instructors in the areas of economics and management teaching, and teacher training.

For the medium term, donors could help quantify shortages of skills and specific training needs (i.e., their urgency and the amount and level of training necessary), on a government-wide basis (not ministry by ministry). Such an effort would probably use interviews or tests of civil servants in several ministries and agencies and managers in a range of state enterprises. Preferably, such tests would serve two purposes: to diagnose systematic needs and to root out untrainable employees.[24]

Eastern Europe will have to rely in large part on existing training facilities, although the capacity and capabilities of such facilities are yet to be determined. Foreign private and not-for-profit institutions are already playing a part in expanding training capacity and will certainly continue to do so. These include traditional educational institutions as well as less conventional sources of training – such as officials seconded from government ministries in industrialized economies, foreign chambers of commerce, liar and dither professional associations, and labor unions. However, it is widely believed that the scale of training activity by domestic and foreign-based private institutions will be insufficient and that their leach times will be too great.

Technical assistance and regional information sharing might assist Eastern European countries in linking up with potential external sources of training. In addition, the World Bank and the IMF are already directly involved in training, and there is a broad consensus for stepping up this commitment. Bilateral organizations have also begun limited programs of job training and twinning[25] of civil servants with their analogs in donor government ministries.

The enormous scale of the required training effort demands innovative delivery methods. For instance, Eastern Europe's civil servants are relatively computer literate, and so some types of computer-assisted courses might be economical. In addition, Western European and American public broadcasters are already involved in planning educational programs for these regions. They envision several types of mass media training such as television and radio programing to educate civil servants (and the population at large) about the nature of a market economy and of capitalist society,[26] and telecourses for more technical training. Multilateral and bilateral aid organizations might evaluate the cost effectiveness of such methods and, based thereon, consider financing the cost of course development.[27]

The parliaments of Eastern Europe have already passed an array of pro-democracy and promarket legislation. In addition, governments have reorganized some parts of their bureaucracies and have plans to do much more. It is apparent, however, that structural forms can be changed on paper much faster than can actual functions and capabilities down the line. Although institutional reform will be an intensely political process, foreigners can play a useful role as advisors, trainers, researchers, investors, and creditors, providing a menu of policy options and innovations to be debated via internal political mechanisms.

NOTES

1. These principles derive from an analysis of the following countries' strategy documents: Report of the Bulgarian Economic Transition Project; "Scenario of the Economic Reform" (CSFR, 1990); Hungarian Economic, Financial and Monetary Policies: Proposals for a Coherent Approach (Bagatelle-Geneva, 1990) and Hungary in Transformation to Freedom and Prosperity (the Blue Ribbon Commission Report, 1990); "Memorandum of the Government of Poland on Economic Reform and Medium-Term Policies, 1991–1993" (Government of Poland, 1990); Program of Working Out and Coordinating Reform Projects (Government of Romania, 1990).

2. Macroeconomic reform policy outcomes have, nonetheless, generally been bent from the perspective of the multilateral institutions.

3. An integral part of these mechanisms is the forging of stable coalitions among representatives of a fairly wide range of interests, including government, business, and labor. This is intended to ensure that government policy making in these countries accounts for the needs and concerns of the private sector and also to enhance popular support for policy. In this respect, Hungary's incipient National Reconciliation Council may prove to be a model for the region of such a tripartite advisory agency.

4. For instance, the Material Product System (MPS) found in socialist economies is being replaced by the System of National Accounts (SNA) used elsewhere. Because the former excludes service-sector activity, governments will have to install systems for collecting data relevant to this sector. Because the government will not automatically receive information from service-sector firms regarding their activities, it will be obliged to introduce a system of regular business surveys.

5. The last issue is discussed in this article under the heading, "Civil Service Reform."

6. Only Romania's government still manifests extreme reservations about the movement away from centralized jurisdiction. For example, the Romanian government's reform program retains food subsidies, central government administration of social programs, state investment in production, and a massive role for "state orders" from enterprises.

7. Consider the example of environmental protection policy. There are three main implications to having subnational governments become responsible: (1) because environmental concerns tend to arise at the local level, those affected will be well

positioned to assess them and give them priority; (2) local governments may have an even lesser capability than national governments to analyze the economic considerations of environmental policy; and (3) many environmental problems extend beyond local jurisdictions. Devolution of power to localities will thus still require national-level environmental coordination among localities, enforcement of clear property rights, and technical assistance from donors.

8. A (much diminished) planning apparatus still exists only in Poland, where it was downgraded from a ministry to an office. The World Bank recommended moving this office to the Ministry of Finance and charging it with multiyear fiscal planning.

9. Only in Romania has there been halting progress in and a lack of political commitment to price liberalization.

10. Civil servants from these offices now tend to serve the relatively minor role of price monitoring.

11. In Czechoslovakia, branch ministries were consolidated into a single ministry, but the republics have so far only succeeded in reducing slightly the number of branch ministries.

12. Many of these countries simply transferred redundant civil servants to other ministries. For example, the former planning staff typically dispersed to state enterprises, the Ministry of Industry (for sectoral planners) and the Ministry of Finance (for macroeconomic planners), and many retrenched employees of branch ministries went to enterprises in their former subsidiary sector. Nonetheless, large numbers of employees in obsolete agencies found employment in the private sector or in education and research.

13. Of course, the appropriateness of a foreign system depends on many characteristics of the country, and limited adaptations to local conditions will therefore often be necessary.

14. Among the many examples, Eastern European securities' regulators have been paired up with the U.S. SEC, broadcasters with West European television companies, local governments with municipal governments in the United States, management institutes with business schools in Europe and the United States, and social welfare agencies with the U.S. Department of Health and Human Services.

15. However, reforms must also be made with an eye to fiscal compatibility with Western Europe – particularly regarding the VAT and customs tariffs – to facilitate increasing integration with the European Community.

16. Additional reasons for guaranteeing information flows include fairness in labor relations and environmental, consumer, and investor protection.

17. It has been suggested that universal reporting requirements might be viewed as the price of having limited liability status.

18. Many issues that concern the civil service are also general labor market issues, which this section does not address. Instead, it looks only at explicit civil service issues.

19. The comparative countries from Heller and Tait (1984) include only central government employees working in administration, finance, and planning. Thus, the accurate comparator values may actually be greater.

20. In addition, Eastern Europe's engineering expertise tends to lag 20 years behind the OECD countries, and outside of Hungary, there are not enough lawyers to draft reform legislation or civil servants with necessary foreign language skills.

21. For example, the salary range in Romania's civil service appears to have a ratio of 1:3, only a small fraction of the ratio found outside the region (e.g., in the Asian Newly Industrialized Countries (NIC)).

22. A word of warning: the distributional effect of increased salary dispersion is a delicate social issue, and reform efforts must pay attention to its implications.

23. This is being done to a very limited degree for managers, public administrators, accountants, bankers, and economists in various parts of the region.

24. One example was the recent testing of East Germany's judges. If it is politically impossible to select out civil servants based on a test, governments may still wish to conduct anonymous tests that will serve only to diagnose systemic needs.

25. Training via twinning has the advantage of immersing the trainee in the foreign institutional culture at the same time as he or she receives training. In the United States, for example, counterpart civil servants have been placed in the Department of Justice, Environmental Protection Agency, Federal Reserve Board, Federal Trade Commission as well as in municipal governments. However, some of those interviewed expressed reservations about overseas training: that it is not cost effective and is itself a vehicle for international brain drain. Although it has the administrative advantage of being decentralized, it must be particularly well structured to have an impact.

26. For example, Czechoslovak radio broadcasted a series on entrepreneurship in 1990.

27. Telecourses can reach large groups of civil servants nationwide while economizing on scarce financing, classrooms, and teachers. Where professional course or training is needed for smaller groups or at different times, delivery can be made on the jobsite by video tape or closed-circuit television.

REFERENCES

Bagatelle-Geneva (1990). *Hungarian economic, financial and monetary policies: Proposals for a coherent approach.* Geneva.

Blue Ribbon Commission. (1990). *Hungary in transformation to freedom and prosperity.* Indianapolis, IN: Hudson Institute.

Davey, K. (1990). *Local government reform in Hungary.* Mimeograph. University of Birmingham Institute of Local Government Studies.

Government of Czech and Slovak Federal Republic. (1990). *Scenario of the economic reform.* Mimeograph. Prague.

Government of Poland. (1990). *Memorandum of the Government of Poland on economic reform and medium-term policies, 1991–1993.* Mimeograph. Warsaw.

Government of Romania. (1990). *Program of working out and coordinating reform projects.* Bucharest.

Heller, P., & Tait, A. (1984). *Government employment and pay: Some international comparisons.* Occasional Paper no. 24. Washington, DC: International Monetary Fund.

Prud'homme, R. (1990). *The rise of local governments in Poland.* Mimeograph. Laboratoire d'Observation de l'Economie et des Institutions Locales.

Rice, E. (1990). *Firms' reluctance to go public: The deterrent effect of financial disclosure requirements.* Unpublished chapter of Ph.D. dissertation, Harvard University, Cambridge.

Vecchietti, G. (1990). Steps to effective government contracting with private business. Mimeograph. New York: Institute of Public Administration.

FURTHER READING

Fischer, S., & Gelb, A. (1990). *Issues in socialist economy reform.* Policy, research and external affairs Working Paper No. 565. Washington, DC: World Bank.

Hardt, J. et al. (1990). *Strategies for facilitating East European and Soviet transformation.* Atlantic Council Consultation Policy Paper.

Kopits, G. (1991). *Fiscal reform in European economies in transition.* Mimeograph. Washington, DC: International Monetary Fund.

Kornai, J. (1990). *Vision and reality, market and state contradictions and dilemmas revisited.* New York: Routledge.

Lipton, D., & Sachs, J. (1990). *Privatizing in Eastern Europe: The case of Poland.* Mimeograph.

McLure, C. (1991). A consumption-based direct tax for countries in transition from socialism. *OECD conference on economies in transition: The role of tax reform in central and eastern European economies.* OECD Conference.

Milor, V. (1990). *An institutional analysis of the problems of transition to a market economy in Hungary.* Mimeograph. Washington, DC: World Bank.

Paul, S. (1991). *Strengthening public accountability: What can the bank do?* Mimeograph. Washington, DC: World Bank; *Poland: Economic management for a new era 1990.* Washington, DC: World Bank.

Rahn, R., et al. (1990). *Report of the Bulgarian economic transition project.* Washington, DC: National Chamber Foundation.

Renaud, B. (1990). *The framework for housing reform in socialist economies.* Mimeograph. Washington, DC: World Bank.

Rice, E. (1991). *Managing the transition: Enhancing the efficiency of eastern European governments.* Pre Working Paper no. 757. Washington, DC: The World Bank.

Rollo, J. (1990). *The new Eastern Europe: Western responses.* New York: Council on Foreign Relations Press.

Svejnar, J. (1990). *A framework for the economic transformation of Czechoslovakia.* PlanEcon Report.

Tsantis, A. (1991). *Public sector management in the transformation of the socialist economies: The case of Romania.* Mimeograph.

Vodopivec, M. (1990). *The labor market and the transition of socialist economies.* Policy, Research and External Affairs Working Paper no. 561. Washington, DC: World Bank.

ASSESSING PUBLIC MANAGEMENT REFORM STRATEGY IN AN INTERNATIONAL CONTEXT

L. R. Jones and Donald F. Kettl

INTRODUCTION

This article attempts to capture and extend the lessons rendered in the previous articles in this book. In overview we may observe that over the past three decades, criticisms about government performance have surfaced across the world from all points of the political spectrum. Critics have alleged that governments are inefficient, ineffective, too large, too costly, overly bureaucratic, overburdened by unnecessary rules, unresponsive to public wants and needs, secretive, undemocratic, invasive into the private rights of citizens, self-serving, and failing in the provision of either the quantity or quality of services deserved by the taxpaying public (See, for example, Barzelay & Armajani, 1992; Osborne & Gaebler, 1993; Jones & Thompson, 1999). Fiscal stress has also plagued many governments and has increased the cry for less costly or less expansive government, for greater efficiency, and for increased responsiveness. High profile members of the business community, financial institutions, the media, management consultants, academic scholars and the general public all have pressured politicians and public managers to reform. So, too have many supranational organizations, including OECD, the World Bank, and the European Commission.

Comparative Public Administration: The Essential Readings
Research in Public Policy Analysis and Management, Volume 15, 883–904
Copyright © 2006 by Elsevier Ltd.
All rights of reproduction in any form reserved
ISSN: 0732-1317/doi:10.1016/S0732-1317(06)15041-1

Accompanying the demand and many of the recommendations for change has been support for the application of market-based logic and private sector management methods to government (see, for example, Moe, 1984; Olson, Guthrie, & Humphrey, 1998; Harr & Godfrey, 1991; Milgrom & Roberts, 1992; Jones & Thompson, 1999). Application of market-driven solutions and business techniques to the public sector has undoubtedly been encouraged by the growing ranks of public sector managers and analysts educated in business schools and public management programs (Pusey, 1991).

Driving the managerial reform movement has been a notion that the public sector builds on the wrong principles and needs reinvention and institutional renewal (Barzelay & Armajani, 1992; Osborne & Gaebler, 1993; Jones & Thompson, 1999). The strategies have included caps on public spending, tax cuts, selling off of public assets, contracting out of many services previously provided by government, development of performance measurement, output- and outcomes-based budgeting, and business-type accounting (Guthrie, Olson, & Humphrey, 1999). The reforms produced all sorts of promises: a smaller, less interventionist and more decentralized government; improved public sector efficiency and effectiveness; greater public service responsiveness and accountability to citizens; increased choice between public and private providers of public services; an "entrepreneurial" public sector more willing and able to work with business; and better economic performance, among others.

The potential has lured many elected officials to what has become known as the "new public management" (NPM). However, academic observers, citizens, and public managers alike have wondered how many of these promises will produce genuine results – and how long any such results will endure. Some principles have already well established themselves. The financial management and accounting reforms have already proven successful. So, too, is the notion that public organizations should be better managed, more responsive, and held more accountable for results. Almost everything else about the NPM, though, is open for debate.

In both practice and study, NPM is an international phenomenon (see, for example, Hood, 1995, 2000; Olsen & Peters, 1996; Jones & Schedler, 1997; Borins, 1997; Gray & Jenkins, 1995; Kettl, 2000a). The OECD continues to monitor NPM developments across a range of countries (OECD, 1997; PUMA & OECD, 1999), and researchers report on developments in particular countries, especially New Zealand, which have drawn international attention (Boston, Martin, Pallot, & Walsh, 1996; Jones & Schedler, 1997; Guthrie & Parker, 1998; Pallot, 1998). In its early days in the 1980s, NPM was mostly strongly associated with right-leaning governments, like

Thatcher in the UK, Reagan in the U.S., and Hawke in Australia. Since then, however, it has lost its ideological stripes. Left-leaning governments like Clinton in the U.S. and Blair in the UK have embraced it as well, along with a democratic Swedish parliament and a conservative British parliament (Olson et. al., 1998).

Despite the rapid spread of these reforms, they have produced wide diversity in practice, even across countries widely regarded as active reformers (Olson et al., 1998; Guthrie et al., 1999). If financial management and accounting changes have been perhaps the most universal reforms, there has been little detailed analysis of the practical application and results of these techniques (Hood, 1995; March & Olsen, 1995). Indeed, analysts have found that the new public financial management has not been so much a uniform, global movement as a "reforming spirit" focused on instilling private sector financial practices into public sector decision-making. It has emphasized new standards in financial reporting, accrual accounting, debt and surplus management, and capital investment strategy that had previously been missing from much government decision-making. There has been broad application of these techniques, however, there has been little research about what results these strategies are likely to produce.

Attempts to understand the global public management reform movement suggest two general implications for research. First, there is a glaring need to understand the short- and long-term outcomes of the reforms where they have been implemented. Second, despite the importance of conducting this research, doing so is almost impossible in the short term and exceedingly difficult in the long term. It is hard enough simply to keep pace with management changes in each nation. It is even harder to make sound multi-country comparisons. Efforts to solve this problem sometimes have led researchers to use a particular nation's reforms – often New Zealand's – as a benchmark, but the particular problems facing each nation weaken the value of such comparisons (See, for example, Riley & Watling, 1999; Guthrie, Olson, & Humphrey, 1999). The paucity of "results about reforms" – and the need to assess whether management reforms have helped each nation solve its particular problems – should motivate researchers to press ahead.

LESSONS FROM REFORM IN AUSTRALIA AND NEW ZEALAND

Scholars have perhaps focused most on the Australian and New Zealand reforms. They were the vanguard of the NPM. Their strategies and tactics heavily influenced the broader scholarly debate as well as the practice in many other nations. Any understanding of the NPM, therefore, must begin there.

English and Guthrie (2001) for example, have analyzed the NPM in Victoria, Australia's second largest state, between 1992 and 1999. The reforms were far-reaching and aimed at a major shift in the role and accountability of government. The Victorian model grew on a well-articulated theoretical framework from classical economic theory, and it was well supported by a series of specific government directives and manuals. The reforms attempted to be comprehensive, tackling all components of the public sector and its subsystems. The output-management model developed to determine and report on expenditure, planning, financial management, control and evaluation were comprehensive in both scope and implementation. The reforms, however, promised more than they delivered. In particular, the speed and massive scale of contracting out and privatization proved difficult to implement.

In fact, Hughes and O'Neill (2001) argue, the public management reforms introduced in Victoria by the Kennett government led to somewhat contradictory consequences. While the government implemented arguably successful reforms, particularly in sale of government assets and privatization of services and balanced the budget after serious deficits, cuts in social services also appear to have contributed to Kennett's electoral defeat. The NPM may have some payoffs, but the political consequences can be significant and unanticipated.

Carlin and Guthrie (2001) have examined recent efforts in Australian and New Zealand public sectors to implement accrual output-based budgeting. While agreeing on the need for public sector accounting reform, the authors use two detailed case studies – Queensland, Australia and the New Zealand national government – to show that the reforms have not accomplished all that their governments had hoped. For example, there is little real difference between the old cash-based and the new accrual budgets. That led the authors to wonder about the effectiveness of management reforms if decision-making was unchanged. Carlin and Guthrie identify three conditions to be met if reforms in public sector accounting are to succeed. First, carefully defined and appropriately specified outputs that relate directly to the activities of the agency are needed. Second, appropriately specified and measurable outcomes must be identified to provide accountability as to the degree to which public resources are achieving public goals. Third, performance indicators and performance measures should provide a link between outputs and outcomes.

In New Zealand, Jonathan Boston (2001) has examined the hard questions of that nation's cutting-edge reforms. For example, at what stage of reform in the public sector does it become possible to conduct a thorough appraisal of results and how does one know when this stage has been reached? How should such an assessment be undertaken? Boston argues that most assessments have focused upon specific changes in management practice, including the introduction of performance pay, the move to accrual accounting, the growth of contracting-out, the separation of policy and operations or the devolution of human resource management responsibilities. Some studies have dealt instead with management changes in particular policy domains – such as health care, education, community services or criminal justice – or within a particular organization (department, agency or private provider). By contrast, there have been relatively few macro evaluations: comprehensive assessments of the impact of root-and-branch changes to the system. Boston provides broad reflections on the limitations to policy evaluation in the field of public management, and more particularly explores the obstacles confronted when assessing the consequences of systemic management reforms. Given his foundation in New Zealand's reforms, perhaps the most systematic and far-reaching in the world, his warnings underline the importance of the evaluation problem.

In his own study of New Zealand, Laking (2001) agrees that serious debate about the New Zealand reform is bedevilled by the limited evaluation. In fact, he concludes, the assessments of the successes and failures of reform in New Zealand to date seem not to be particularly concerned about the absence of comprehensive evaluation. Laking finds that most evaluations tend to assert that there have been overall gains in efficiency as a result of reform, but they are far less certain or negative about the consequences for effectiveness.

Despite the lack of clear evidence about the New Zealand reforms' impact, the elegant simplicity of the reforms has had a seductive quality for analysts. Gill (2001) finds that much of the elegance has been obscured in the intervening years, but that the yield from the reforms has been significant. The trick in evaluating the New Zealand experience with public management reform, he argues, is to compare it with real world alternatives. In using the existing reforms to guide future questions, Gill attempts to unravel the disparate threads about "what remains to be done" by distinguishing four categories of problems: (a) Political – problems that are inherent to the political arena, and are evident under a range of public management regimes; (b) Incompleteness – problems that provide evidence that the system is incomplete in some areas, but do not suggest inherent difficulties; (c) Implementation – problems the stem from the way the system has been implemented; (d) Inherent – problems that flow directly from the nature of the New Zealand regime, which might be different in other systems (Gill, 2001, p. 144).

Few observers write about the New Zealand reforms with more authority than Graham Scott, one of the movement's chief architects for more than 20 years. In looking carefully at the New Zealand experience and comparing it with reforms around the world, Scott (2001) has identified important lessons. Among other things, he concludes, the success of management reform depends on: (a) the clarity of roles, responsibilities and accountability in the implementation of management reform; (b) the importance of matching decision capacity to responsibility; (c) the significance of ministerial commitment and clarity of expectations; (d) the structural innovations within the New Zealand cabinet; (e) the need to analyze disasters carefully for what they teach; (f) approaches to embrace and foibles to avoid in implementing performance management; (g) problems caused by confusion over ownership and improper assessment of organizational capability; (h) the fact that actually doing strategic management in the public sector is hugely complicated; (i) that it is time to put an end to the notion that there is an "extreme model" of public management applied in New Zealand; and (j) that public management, government and governance innovations in New Zealand are no longer novel compared to those advanced in other nations. Scott concludes with an admonition to avoid too quickly drawing the conclusion from New Zealand's change in government that past reforms must be quickly and radically changed – or that the New Zealand model has failed.

A senior public servant in the New Zealand Treasury, Andrew Kibblewhite (2001), agrees with Scott on the need for detailed analysis of results and a careful consolidation of the lessons. He suggests that much of the initial energy for reform has faded, that it is time to assess what has and has not been achieved, and that it is important now to search for ways to move forward. The election of a new government in November 1999 stirred a sense of anticipation, as well as some apprehension, across the New Zealand public sector. As New Zealand moves into a new phase of reform, one of the key challenges is to take advantage of what has already been achieved to make government even more effective. Kibblewhite argues further that central agencies can sharpen the specification of outputs by being clearer about the basic management framework by being more flexible about how that framework is applied. Outcome measures should be refined and used along with outputs where feasible. However, he suggests, some outcome measures should be abandoned where they do not provide useful information.

The New Zealand reforms, however, have certainly drawn critics. Robert Gregory (2001) contents that a price has been paid for the overly narrow theoretical framework used to design state sector reforms. According to Gregory, the way ahead must be informed both by more eclectic theoretical input, as well as by closer dialogue between theory and practice. He argues that the state sector reforms in New Zealand, especially in their application to the public services, have been too "mechanistic" and too blind to the important "organic" dimensions of public organizations. They have focused too much on physical restructuring and they have tried too hard to reduce complex government practices to artificial dualities, such as "outputs" and "outcomes," "owner" and "purchaser," "founder" and "provider." They have tended to ignore the less quantifiable and more holistic elements that underpinned a strong culture of public service trusteeship in New Zealand prior to reform. Gregory argues that it is difficult to conclude that reform has all been for the good. There is too much evidence to the contrary, he asserts.

Tooley's (2001) analysis of the New Zealand school system helps identify those tensions. Despite the rhetoric about decentralization and democratization through devolution of governance and decision-making to the level of the individual school and principals as chief executives, there has been a concomitant strengthening of central control over curriculum and tighter monitoring by the Education Review Office. These changes have reduced citizen choice in school education, turned principals into managers instead of skilled leaders and, ultimately, wrested control over education from educators and into the control politicians. Tooley suggests that the educational "experiment" in New Zealand is being reversed because of its inability to deliver the outcomes promised from reform. Recent changes proposed by the government suggest its intent to rein back some of the more "market-oriented" elements of the educational reforms and, in particular, to soften some of the key features of the managerialist approach to education administration. Tooley concludes that the reforms failed almost completely, and that the coalition government elected in November 2000 has or will reverse many of the changes made under previous governments.

Newberry's (2001) study of the operation during 1996 of a public hospital emergency department likewise revealed serious problems. Hostility between the hospital's clinical staff and management escalated to the point that the hospital's Medical Staff Association released a report to the public titled, "Patients are Dying: A Record of System Failure and Unsafe Healthcare Practice at Christchurch Hospital." The report detailed the story of four patient deaths and alleged that deteriorating conditions within the hospital contributed to those deaths. The Medical Staff Association sought a public inquiry, but the Health and Disability Commissioner announced a more-narrow consumers' rights inquiry. Newberry revisits that inquiry and recast its findings in the context of the NPM. She finds that, although the hospital-based reforms were structurally sound and had real value, they did not address the broader issues of performance and accountability. She concludes that NPM as applied in New Zealand needed to create better structures, involve customers more directly in evaluation and decision-making, and be more accountable to the public for results.

Putterill and Speer (2001) likewise found problems in information technology. New Zealand benchmarked its IT innovation and development against its own policy aims and the achievements of a set of peer countries, chosen for similar size and technical sophistication. They concluded that peers nations have significantly outperformed New Zealand. The Zealand government maintained a "hands off" stance, while most of the peer countries actively promoted IT involvement. Putterill and Speer question past policy direction, call for more active industry involvement by the New Zealand government, and argue for more industry-friendly policies to advance competitiveness in the region.

In sum, the Australia and New Zealand reforms are the benchmarks by which reforms around the world have been judged. A careful look at those reforms – or, at least, at what analysts have written about them – reveals how much we have yet to learn about what truly has worked and why. Moreover, as the work of some analysts show, serious issues, both managerial and political, lurk just below the surface. Only more careful analysis and comparison can sort out the claims and counterclaims.

LESSONS FROM REFORM IN ASIA

Many Asian nations have worked energetically to reform their public management systems, but comparing their results has been handicapped by the relatively small collection of studies written in English. Moreover, since many of these reforms have occurred in developing nations, they present very different issues and require a different kind of analysis. Clay Goodloe Wescott (2001) poses a number of important questions concerning these Asian reforms. Is it possible, he asks, to measure the quality of overall governance in a developing Asian country? Are present measures robust enough to allow the ranking of countries along a continuum from well-governed to poorly governed? Should these rankings be used by donor agencies and private investors in making investment decisions? Wescott reflect on these questions and concludes that, despite the complexity and diversity of approaches of governance systems, qualitative and quantitative tools are being used reasonably well in the region.

In Hong Kong, for example, Kevin Yuk-fai Au, Ilan Vertinsky, and Denis Yu-long Wang (2001) chart a paradigm shift in NPM. They argue that, contemporary reform has its roots in the late 1960s and early 1970s, with periods of lull and renewal characterized by shifting powers and expectations among stakeholders. Early reforms, especially in the colonial period, sought social legitimacy. The transfer to sovereignty, adjustment of a both the economy and society, and diffusion of new ideas into public management all shaped Hong Kong. The authors investigate the conditions that shaped the reform process in each of Hong Kong's key episodes, the triggers that accelerated it, and the forces that emerged to dampen it. They conclude that, as with many nations, it is simply too early to determine whether reforms now under implementation will be successful.

Yu-Ying Kuo (2001) has explored public management reform in Taiwan in the 1990s. The apex of the movement was government reinvention. In 1998, Premier Vincent C. Siew announced, "the Executive Yuan is energetically planning for and promoting the national development plan for entering the next century, of which the Asia-Pacific Regional Operations Center (APROC) plan and the Taiwan Technology Island Initiative comprise the core." The author argues that the NPM developments are likely to determine the direction of Taiwan's government modernization over the next several decades. The government has launched an across-the-board reinvention to create a new, flexible and adaptable government and to raise national competitiveness. At this point there is no way to tell what the new government that took office in 2001 will do with these developments or where they may lead.

Roberts's (2001) work has explored the strategies that public officials use to cope with "wicked problems," especially in Afghanistan. Three coping strategies – authoritative, competitive, and collaborative – have been especially important. The strategies derive from a model based on the level of conflict present in the problem solving process, the distribution of power among the stakeholders, and the degree to which power is contested. Collaborative strategies, she believes, offer the most promise, as illustrated in a case study of the relief and recovery efforts in Afghanistan. Her paper, a revised version of the contribution that won the Frieder Naschold Best Paper Award at the International Public Management Network conference held in Sydney, Australia in March 2000, explores the implications of using collaborative strategies to deal with wicked problems around the world.

The imperatives of management reform have deeply affected the institutions working with Asian nations as well as the nations themselves. David Shand (2001), a senior official at the World Bank working in the East Asian region, has examined World Bank experience in public sector management reform in Asia. He argues that public sector management reform has stimulated a "new wave" of activity in his institution since the 1970s. Many of the World Bank's strategies to reinvigorate state institutions reflect the thinking of the new institutional economics – the importance of structures, incentives, rules and restraints, norms, and best practices. Recent public sector work has focused on three of the "East Asia five" – Thailand, Indonesia, and the Philippines (the other two of the five are Korea and Malaysia). The World Bank has also focused on smaller countries including Cambodia and Laos. It has made preliminary efforts in the transition economies of China (including Mongolia) and Vietnam. Shand concludes that recent fiscal and economic crises in Asia have created urgent pressures for public sector management reform.

Less clear, however, is how the broader lessons of the Asian experience add up. Research has been scanty and far less systematic than the admittedly rudimentary work on the Australian and New Zealand reforms. Moreover, the experiences of developing Asian nations are bound to be different from highly developed governments with rich administrative traditions, like Hong Kong. Research into these questions, however, is in its infancy, and we consequently know relatively little about the central questions.

LESSONS FROM TWO DECADES OF PUBLIC MANAGEMENT REFORM

What lessons spin from the two decades of reforms and transformations flying loosely under the banner of "the new public management"? A careful review of the experiences of nations around the globe suggests a series of propositions.

Public Management Reform is Never Done

Analysts and practitioners alike have sometimes been tempted to view the reforms with cynicism. For some, the lack of clear or full success led to the conclusion that the reforms had failed. For others, the evolution of new strategies led to the conclusion that earlier efforts had been abandoned. In fact, history shows that public management reforms recur, with each new piece woven – sometimes seamlessly – into the next. There are several reasons for this. First, no reform can ever fully solve the problems that led to its creation. Lingering issues tend to breed the next generation of reforms. Second, public management is not so much a problem-solving activity as a problem-balancing enterprise. Any reform strategy requires making choices at the margin that focus on some problems more than others and that emphasize some values more than others. Because no solution can ever be complete, each reform necessarily leaves problems unaddressed and under-addressed and every reform therefore breeds the next. Third, because management problems tend to recur and the bag of management tricks is relatively limited, reforms tend to cycle between accepted strategies – periods of centralization followed by episodes of decentralization, deregulation replacing bureaucratization. Careful observers of administrative reform can detect the recurring patterns.

The "New Public Management" has Proven a Fundamentally Different Approach to Reform

Some critics have therefore dismissed the NPM as worthless nostrums or old ideas dressed up in new clothes. The experience over the last two decades, however, shows that there truly has been something new in the "new" public management. To the dismay of some detractors and to the hopes of some reformers, the NPM has introduced a heavy dose of economic models and tactics into public management. From privatization to performance contracts, the NPM has sought to replace bureaucratic authority with economic incentives. Contracting out and other market-based strategies, of course, have been around for decades, if not centuries. But the NPM pursued them with a single-mindedness unseen previously. Moreover, the NPM reforms spread around the world with an energy and simultaneity never seen before with any kind of management reform. The rise of the internet and relatively inexpensive international air travel helped drive this movement. So too did the near universal rise of citizen discontent over the cost and performance of government. Never before have so many governments tried such similar things in such short order.

Political Reality Drives Management Reform more than
Management Concerns

Scholars in particular have examined the NPM and other management reforms, like America's reinventing government, for theoretical insights. Enduring analytical conclusions have proven elusive because the reforms have been so different. Different nations have gone down different paths because their high-level officials have been trying to solve different problems and cope with different political realities. Even relatively similar nations, such as the United Kingdom, Canada, Australia, and New Zealand, have produced markedly different strategies. Finding common ground with other nations' experiments has often proven difficult. In large part, this is because top officials launched the management reforms for fundamentally political reasons: to cope with budget crises, to sustain public services without increasing taxes, and to signal concern about citizens' disaffection with government. Top officials sustained the reforms as long as they had political value; they transformed them or backed away when political pressures demanded. When asked to comment on the New Zealand reforms, one careful observer immediately began discussing the proportional representation plan for the parliament – not the 15 years of management reforms that preceded it. A New Zealand official tells audiences of his mother's constant question about the management reforms: "Why does it still take so long to get a gall bladder operation?"[1] Politics lies at the core of the management reform, not vice versa. Management reforms have their genesis and sustenance in the degree to which they help solve political problems.

The Political Clout of the New Public Management has been Negligible

After the NPM's first 20 years, it has become clear that the effort provided little political clout in any nation. In the US, President Bill Clinton significantly downsized the bureaucracy and proudly proclaimed the smallest bureaucracy in 30 years, only to have Republicans win control of both houses of Congress for the first time in 40 years. Vice President Al Gore barely mentioned his reinventing government effort on the presidential campaign trail in 2000 and got no political credit for having led it. Prime Minister Tony Blair made little of his own management reforms in the 2001 elections. There simply is little evidence that management reforms have translated into electoral victories or, even, into modest political gains.

Despite the Lack of Traction from Management Reform as a Political Issue, it is a Puzzle with which Elected Officials Nevertheless Feel Obliged to Wrestle

Even if public management builds little political capital, management problems do have the potential to cause enormous headaches. Prime Minister Blair found himself struggling with the management of the foot-and-mouth outbreak as he geared up election campaign, and these struggles in fact shifted the timing of the elections. In the language of political consultants, management reform has little upside potential but can pose a tremendous downside threat. In other words, it might not help, but it certainly can hurt. Management problems have a recurring tendency to develop, and elected officials must deal with them effectively or risk serious political damage. Thus, management reform springs eternal.

With the New Public Management, Reforms are Moving Increasingly from Restructuring to Process Reengineering

In most countries, public management for generations had built on the traditions of hierarchy and authority. The Prussian influence was especially strong in European nations and in other countries, like the United States, that borrowed heavily on these ideas. As these nations developed their empire, the traditions spread as well. When these approaches encountered problems – as inevitably they did – the instinct was to reorganize the structure and reorient the authority. The launch of the NPM movement was a frank recognition that hierarchy and authority, in all their variations and reforms, had reached their limits. The NPM emphasized market incentives and contract-based approaches. The reforms, in short, sought either to supplement or replace traditional structure-based approaches with process-based reforms.

Despite Wide Variation in Reform Strategies, there is a Convergence of Reforms around General Themes

The enormous variation in reforms has long frustrated analysts, who have struggled to define what "the new public management" actually is. Assessing whether the NPM actually constitutes an identifiable set of ideas, let alone whether nations are increasingly pursuing more-similar ideas, is a daunting problem. No less an authority than Graham Scott, however, has observed, "For most of the world, the late twentieth century has been about reducing the scope of government. But this process must inevitably slow down." In time, he suggested, the pace of downsizing will inevitably slow down and governments will face the task of managing the programs that remain. That, in turn, will likely turn more governments to the American reform strategy of making government "work better and cost less." As Scott concluded, "Over time, the rest of us will look more and more like the United States, as the problems of what the government is going to do become less urgent and we deal with them by marginal adjustments rather than sudden and radical change, and focus more on the steady processes of improvement around the organizations that will persist" (Scott, 1999).

Developing Nations have Different Management Reform Problems than Developed Nations

For at least some observers, the convergence argument suggests that nations that are serious about performance pursue management reform and that most reforms are moving in at least loose synchronization. However, Allen Schick (1998) bluntly warns that "most developing countries should not try New Zealand reforms" or other "new public management" strategies. Indeed, facing a huge need to grow their economies and shrink their governments, many developing countries have found the reforms irresistible. Schick contends that the NPM-style reforms require a foundation of governmental rules, vigorous markets, and broadly accepted dispute–resolution processes that many developing countries lack. Seeking short cuts, Schick concludes, risks sending developing nations into dead ends. Different nations in different positions with different traditions, structures, and capacities need different strategies, even if they attempt to follow the NPM course.

The Pursuit of the New Public Management Strategy has Revealed a Mismatch among Practice, Theory, and Instruction

Unlike some previous reforms around the world, where scholars charted at least some of the course, the NPM has evolved with only modest theoretical foundation. Formal theory has suggested concepts like moral hazard and adverse selection, but most of the hard work has come from pragmatic officials cobbling together approaches to very hard problems. Theorists have struggled to determine just what the NPM is, how it differs from country to country, whether it has succeeded, how it might transform itself, and whether it will prove a lasting phenomenon. Public officials, pressed with high public demands and limited resources, have rarely stopped to ask such questions. Meanwhile, in public policy programs around the world, academic leaders have struggled to assess whether they need to transform their curricula to prepare students for the NPM. For the most part, these leaders have understandably taken a cautious approach. However, this has left public officials with an even greater problem of finding young managers with the skills to operate effectively in the new program strategies. Of all the options, the one sure bet probably lies in forecasting rapid change. The tensions at the core of the practice, theory, and instruction dilemma thus will only increase.

What Role will National Governments Play?

Osborne and Gaebler (1993) inspired some officials and enraged others by suggesting that the government of the future ought to steer, not row. Central governments around the world have found themselves in the midst of a fundamental transformation, with simultaneously more globalization and devolution of power (Kettl, 2000b). What role can and should central governments play in a world where their traditional roles have become more marginal yet their importance has only increased? Managers of central government agencies have sought greater leverage in the management of networks and the creation of information systems, among other tools. How to weave these new tools together into a freshly defined role, however, proved anything but clear.

CONCLUSIONS

Learning from the experience of public management reform strategy within and across national boundaries is daunting. The tendency is to say that context dominates all lessons. However, the lessons reviewed here and elsewhere suggest some interdependence. In many regions of the world, cross-national organizations, like OECD, the Asian Development Bank, the World Bank, and the International Monetary Fund, have encouraged management reform and have stimulated reform networks across national

borders. There are elements of isomorphic transference in the reform experiences of some countries: in Hong Kong, in Taiwan, and from New
Zealand to almost everywhere.

One nation's copying the reforms of others can help improve the effectiveness of public services and attract greater investment. Information technology has spurred the spread of reform ideas. The internet reveals, at least
to the computer literate, the success or failure of policy adventures
in different countries and analyses of reforms by academics and others.
The media play an important role in identifying policy problems and
comparing solutions among nations. Consultants have spread many ideas
among their clients. As a result, nations engage in far more rapid
policy reproduction and perhaps even learning than has been evident in
the past.

Public management reform invites evaluation of convergence: how much,
of what kind, and in what directions. Boston's assessment of New Zealand
invites questions about the degree of unisonance in reform. He finds clear
benefits, but the dearth of "before and after" studies, or even thoughtful
quasi-experimental designs, prevent genuine evaluation of the effectiveness
of public management reforms. Boston terms the broad nature of evaluations about reform as "counter-factual," because gauging the impact is
difficult without greater specificity. Similarly, Wescott's analysis reinforces
this picture of diversity with his analysis of methodological problems in
defining and introducing reforms. In Gregory's account, the "mechanistic"
adoption of reform in New Zealand created long-term implementation
problems, which proved especially notable compared with the enthusiasm
that first greeted the reform process.

Convergence versus divergence is a long-standing debate in public administration and management. Principles of economic efficiency and effectiveness, or choice and market forces would suggest that rhetorically one
would expect to see a more consistent picture of reform in the past decade
or so. There is ample evidence of a convergence in rhetoric. Reformers speak
eagerly of "reinvention," "entrepreneurial management," and "results-
based approaches." Indeed, the work reviewed here suggests that there indeed is some convergence. However, there clearly are instances of divergence
as well, because of the special circumstances of nations, regions, and the
developed-developing nations contrast. On balance, there appears to be a
convergence in the reform agendas and implementation efforts in the UK, in
most British Commonwealth nations, in selected OECD nations, and the
United States. The convergence emerges among developed nations. The
experience of developing nations is more diverse.

Even assessing the convergence/divergence question, however, requires far greater precision in defining the problem and developing a useful language for exploring it. Roberts' analysis of the inability to define "problems" accurately shows the underlying problems affecting both the formulation and implementation of management reform. That, she suggests, is why cooperative strategies can prove useful. Similarly, both Wescott and Shand suggest that while diversity exists, cooperative tools can assist in the reform process and are applicable across borders.

Nevertheless, application of the same or similar approaches in different nations may succeed or fail in different ways. Reform is about building capacity to do the old things in different ways and to discover new things that need doing. Reforming public organizations may provide institutional remedies, but traditional restructuring cannot eliminate the changes of retrograde tendencies or prevent problems from recurring. This comparison, moreover, suggests the need for more careful analysis about what constitutes "good reform." Is it merely locating the definition of a "problem" in the standard NPM lineup and finding the relevant "solution"? Is there greater need for refinement of interpretive and epistemological skills before nations embark to mimic what is done elsewhere? A significant lesson, thus, is this clear definition of the problems to be solved is the first step towards successful change.

From there nations need to move toward experimenting with various methods, and carefully gauging results, until the combination that best solves their problems emerges. This experimentation takes time, energy, patience and a commitment to be careful, and unbiased and unvarnished evaluation. It requires the will to ask questions when the answers could prove inconvenient or embarrassing. Then there is the question of building the political will to move in the direction the evaluation points. Politics plays the crucial role throughout this cycle in determining how the problem is to be defined, what methods may be tried, whether evaluation is to be done and by whom, and whether the results are to be heeded and followed.

Other lessons apply to the role of the state. English and Guthrie, and Hughes and O'Neill emphasize the importance of strengthening the institutions of governance. Accountability is a paramount virtue in governance. Reform *per se* is not sufficient to ensure greater accountability; it is necessary to strengthen the institutions of governance *and* management. Shand and Wescott concur in this observation. Neale and Anderson outline the challenges for the New Zealand performance reporting process with respect to parliamentary utility. Jones and Mussari (2001) suggest that the U.S. Congress and the Italian Parliament may not benefit from the accountability mechanisms they have enacted. Conversely, Schedler (2001) demonstrates the value of performance budgeting in Switzerland to result from a unique balance between freedom and regulation, between the rigidities of the law and the needs of politicians.

Institution building is not likely to be achieved by enlarging the role of the state, but by *rediscovering* the tasks and roles that governments are best suited – and most needed – to perform. Those tasks can include building critical capacity for planning and evaluation. Reform might well produce more effective service delivery institutions as well as governments that work more effectively with the private sector. It might also produce new forms of regulation that more productively shape market behavior.

The manifestations of public management reform are many and varied. Debate about its variations can be awkward because of widespread differences in governance problems, political cultures, and reform language. This reinforces the need for a conceptual framework and language for public management reform, allowing for contribution from different disciplines. Barzelay (2001) argues that without a common frame of reference and language, meaningful dialogue on public management reform cannot occur.

The public management reform movement has also framed new questions. What role should the nation-state play as but one player in a new architecture of governance where networks of organizations comprise more effective problem solving entities than single governments? How can public bureaucracy effectively solve complex governance problems without sacrificing the public interest? New organizational forms such as hyperarchies, flatter and more decentralized entities with greater delegation of authority and responsibility and faster learning-adaptation-action cycles (Jones & Thompson, 1999, pp. 3–4,174–176; see also Evans & Wurster, 1997, p. 75), appear likely to be more effective than traditional bureaucratic organizations to manage networked programs.

It is simply too early to tell whether NPM is or is not a new "paradigm," in the Kuhnian sense. Indeed, it is not clear whether the question has meaning and it certainly is clear that not enough information is available to try to answer it. Management reform, in fact, has proven a far more subtle enterprise that extends over the medium and long-term in order for any political or managerial regime to succeed relative to the ambitious agendas proposed and the need for assessment and feedback using an appropriately broad set of evaluative measures. The survival of governments, politicians, and managers advocating reform and attempting to implement comprehensive change appears to depend upon relatively slow and careful implementation. Moreover, any theory of public management by necessity is highly contingent.

Nevertheless, it is also clear that the "new public management" is no longer new. Many of the reforms labeled as NPM have been under implementation for 10, 20, or more years. Although academics can claim to have defined the techniques and terminology of the "new public management" with a reasonable degree of precision (see Jones & Schedler, 1997; Borins, 1997), much of the dialogue about NPM, pro and con, is confusing, disconnected, and in effect, a distraction that inhibits sincere attempts to determine the outcomes of change.

Out of this decades-long tradition have emerged criticisms by academics from a variety of social science disciplines. Indeed, NPM critics appear to out-number advocates in academe, if not in the practitioner environment. Some of this may be related to the fact that academics face professional and career incentives to find fault rather than to extol success. Additionally, some criticism of NPM may derive from the fact that it is perceived to draw conceptually too strongly from a business-driven perspective. This approach threatens the traditions of public administration and public policy programs, which build on the primacy of government aggressively pursuing the public interest. The NPM debate will – and should – continue, and as it does, it should move toward a better structured and more informed dialogue about reform more generally. Recently published works on NPM and public management reform attempt to clarify this dialogue (see, for example, Kettl, 2000a; Jones & Thompson, 1999; Barzelay, 2001).

At the core of the reforms lurks the issue of equity, which neither academics nor practitioners have considered carefully enough. In particular, public officials have not sufficiently addressed equity goals while pursuing managerial efficiency. It is surely the case that those who support increased public sector efficiency will (or wish to) ignore the risk of greater income disparity, impaired earning capability for many citizens, increased poverty, and worsening of health, social, and educational services. Much reform appears to be directed with a high degree of insularity of purpose to change governments internally without much attention to distributional consequences. Any careful review of the implications of management reform must address those linkages. As Frieder Naschold would warn, unless better government and improved services result from reform, why should change be undertaken?

NOTES

1. Interview with the author.

REFERENCES

Barzelay, M. (2001). *The new public management*. Berkeley, CA: University of California Press.

Barzelay, M., & Armajani, B. J. (1992). *Breaking through bureaucracy: A new vision for managing in government*. Berkeley: University of California Press.

Borins, S. (1997). What the new public management is achieving: A survey of commonwealth experience. In: L. R. Jones & K. Schedler (Eds), *International perspectives on the new public management* (pp. 49–70). Stamford, CT: JAI Press (1997).

Boston, J. (2000). The challenge of evaluating systemic change: The case of public management reform in New Zealand. In: L. R. Jones, J. Guthrie & P. Steane (Eds), *Learning from international public management reform* (Vol. 11A, pp. 103–132). Oxford: JAI – Elsevier.

Boston, J., Martin, J., Pallot, J., & Walsh, P. (1996). *Public management: The New Zealand model*. Auckland: Oxford University Press.

Carlin, T., & Guthrie, J. (2001). Lessons from Australian and New Zealand experiences with accrual output-based budgeting. In: L. R. Jones, J. Guthrie & P. Steane (Eds), *Learning from international public management reform* (Vol. 11A, pp. 89–100). Oxford: JAI – Elsevier.

English, L., & Guthrie, J. (2001). The challenge of evaluating systemic change: The case of public management reform in New Zealand. In: L. R. Jones, J. Guthrie & P. Steane (Eds), *Learning from international public management reform* (Vol. 11A, pp. 45–60). Oxford: JAI – Elsevier.

Evans, P. B., & Wurster, T. S. (1997). Strategy and the new economics of information. *Harvard Business Review, 75*(5), 71–82.

Gill, D. (2001). New Zealand experience with public management reform. In: L. R. Jones, J. Guthrie & P. Steane (Eds), *Learning from international public management reform* (Vol. 11A, pp. 143–160). Oxford: JAI – Elsevier.

Gray, A., & Jenkins, B. (1995). From public administration to public management: Reassessing a revolution? *Public Administration, 73*(Spring), 75–99.

Gregory, R. (2001). Getting better but feeling worse? Public sector reform in New Zealand. In: L. R. Jones, J. Guthrie & P. Steane (Eds), *Learning from international public management reform* (Vol. 11A, pp. 211–231). Oxford: JAI – Elsevier.

Guthrie, J., Olson, O., & Humphrey, C. (1999). Debating developments in new public financial management: The limits of global theorising and some new ways forward. *Financial Accountability and Management, 15*(3/4), 209–228.

Guthrie, J., & Parker, L. (1998). Managerialism and 'marketisation' in financial management change in Australia. In: O. Olson, J. Guthrie & C. Humphrey (Eds), *Global warning – debating international developments in new public financial management* (pp. 49–75). Bergen, Norway: Cappelen Akademisk Forlag.

Harr, D. J., & Godfrey, J. T. (1991). *Private sector financial performance measures and their applicability to government operations*. Montvale, NJ: National Association of Accountants.

Hood, C. (1995). Emerging issues in public administration. *Public Administration, 73*(Spring), 165–183.

Hood, C. (2000). Paradoxes of public sector managerialism, old public management and public service bargains. *International Public Management Journal, 3*(1), 1–20.

Hughes, O., & O'Neill, D. (2001). Public sector management in the state of Victoria: 1992–1999: Genesis of the transformation. In: L. R. Jones, J. Guthrie & P. Steane (Eds), *Learning from international public management reform* (Vol. 11A, pp. 61–76). Oxford: JAI – Elsevier.

Jones, L. R., & Mussari, R. (2001). Management control reform within a responsibility framework in the U.S. and Italy. In: L. R. Jones, J. Guthrie & P. Steane (Eds), *Learning from international public management reform* (Vol. 11B, pp. 499–530). Oxford: JAI – Elsevier.

Jones, L. R., & Schedler, K. (Eds) (1997). *International perspectives on the new public management*. Stamford, CT: JAI Press.

Jones, L. R., & Thompson, F. (1999). *Public management: Institutional renewal for the 21st century*. Stamford, CT: Elsevier.

Kettl, D. (2000a). *The global public management revolution: A report on the transformation of governance*. Washington, DC: The Brookings Institution.

Kettl, D. (2000b). The transformation of governance: Globalization, devolution, and the role of government. *Public Administration Review*, *60*(6), 488–497.

Kibblewhite, A. (2001). Effectiveness: The next frontier in New Zealand. In: L. R. Jones, J. Guthrie & P. Steane (Eds), *Learning from international public management reform* (Vol. 11A, pp. 177–192). Oxford: JAI – Elsevier.

Laking, R. (2001). Reflections on public sector reform in New Zealand. In: L. R. Jones, J. Guthrie & P. Steane (Eds), *Learning from international public management reform* (Vol. 11A, pp. 133–142). Oxford: JAI – Elsevier.

March, J. G., & Olsen, J. P. (1995). *Democratic governance*. New York: The Free Press.

Milgrom, P., & Roberts, J. (1992). *Economics, organization, and management*. Englewood Cliffs, NJ: Prentice-Hall.

Moe, T. M. (1984). The new economics of organization. *American Journal of Political Science*, *28*(4), 739–777.

Newberry, S. (2001). Network structures, consumers and accountability in New Zealand. In: L. R. Jones, J. Guthrie & P. Steane (Eds), *Learning from international public management reform* (Vol. 11A, pp. 257–278). Oxford: JAI – Elsevier.

OECD. (1997). In search of results: Performance management practices. Paris: OECD.

Olsen, J. P., & Peters, G. (1996). *Lessons from experience: Experiential learning in adminstrative reforms in eight democracies*. Oslo: Scandanavian University Press.

Olson, O., Guthrie, J., & Humphrey, C. (Eds) (1998). *Global warning – debating international developments in new public financial management*. Bergen, Norway: Cappelen Akademisk Forlag.

Osborne, D., & Gaebler, T. (1993). *Reinventing government: How the entrepreneurial spirit is transforming the public sector*. New York: Penguin.

Pallot, J. (1998). The New Zealand revolution. In: O. Olson, J. Guthrie & C. Humphrey (Eds), *Global warning – debating international developments in new public financial management* (pp. 156–184). Bergen, Norway: Cappelen Akademisk Forlag.

PUMA, OECD. (1999). *Performance contracting: Lessons from performance contracting case studies*. Paris: OECD.

Pusey, M. (1991). *Economics rationalism in Canberra: A nation-building state changes its mind*. London: Cambridge University Press.

Putterill, M. & Speer, D. (2001). Information policy in New Zealand. In: L. R. Jones, J. Guthrie & P. Steane (Eds), *Learning from international public management reform* (Vol. 11A, pp. 279–290). Oxford: JAI – Elsevier.

Riley, K., & Watling, R. (1999). Education action zones: An initiative in the making. *Public Money and Management*, *19*(3), 51–59.

Roberts, N. (2001). Coping with wicked problems: The case of Afghanistan. In: L. R. Jones, J. Guthrie & P. Steane (Eds), *Learning from international public management reform* (Vol. 11B, pp. 353–376). Oxford: JAI – Elsevier.

Schedler, K. (2001). Performance budgeting in Switzerland: Implications for political control. In: L. R. Jones, J. Guthrie & P. Steane (Eds), *Learning from international public management reform* (Vol. 11B, pp. 455–477). Oxford: Elsevier.

Schick, A. (1998). Why most developing countries should not try New Zealand reforms. *The World Bank Research Observer* (February), 123–131.

Scott, G. (1999). *Presentation at the global forum on reinventing government, plenary session 1*, Washington, DC (January 14).

Scott, G. (2001). Public management reform and lessons from experience in New Zealand. In: L. R. Jones, J. Guthrie & P. Steane (Eds), *Learning from international public management reform* (Vol. 11A, pp. 133–142). Oxford: JAI – Elsevier.

Shand, D. (2001). The World Bank and public sector management reform. In: L. R. Jones, J. Guthrie & P. Steane (Eds), *Learning from international public management reform* (Vol. 11B, pp. 377–390). Oxford: JAI – Elsevier.

Tooley, S. (2001). Observations on the imposition of new public management in the New Zealand state education system. In: L. R. Jones, J. Guthrie & P. Steane (Eds), *Learning from international public management reform* (Vol. 11B, pp. 233–255). Oxford: JAI – Elsevier.

Wescott, C. (2001). Measuring governance in developing Asia. In: L. R. Jones, J. Guthrie & P. Steane (Eds), *Learning from international public management reform* (Vol. 11B, pp. 295–310). Oxford: JAI – Elsevier.

Yu-Ying, K. (2001). New public management in Taiwan: Government reinvention. In: L. R. Jones, J. Guthrie & P. Steane (Eds), *Learning from international public management reform* (Vol. 11B, pp. 337–351). Oxford: JAI – Elsevier.

Yuk-fai Au, K., Vertinsky, I., & Yu-long Wang, D. (2001). New public management in Hong Kong: The long march toward reform. In: L. R. Jones, J. Guthrie & P. Steane (Eds), *Learning from international public management reform* (Vol. 11B, pp. 311–336). Oxford: JAI – Elsevier.

FURTHER READING

Giddens, A. (1998). *The third way: The renewal of social democracy*. Cambridge: Polity Press.

Guthrie, J., Humphrey, C., & Olson, O. (1997). Public financial management changes in OECD nations. In: L. R. Jones & K. Schedler (Eds), *International perspectives on the new public management* (pp. 255–269). Stamford, CT: JAI Press.

Jones, L. R. (2000). IPMN Newsletter No. 2, IPMN website http://www.willamette.org/ipmn

Naschold, F., & Daley, G. (1999). Modernizing local governments. *International Public Management Journal*, 2(1), 25–98.

GOOD GOVERNMENT: AN UNSTYLISH IDEA THAT WARRANTS A WORLDWIDE WELCOME

Nicholas Henry

The international watchword of public administration in the opening decade of the twenty-first century, at least among most developed countries and in many developing ones, is the new public management.

THE RISE OF "THE NEW PUBLIC MANAGEMENT"

In the United States, the new public management emerged in the 1980s at the local level, and since has been embraced by the federal and state governments as well. At root, the new public management is composed of the following five ideas (Denhardt & Denhardt, 2000; Henry, 2007; Light, 2005; US Government Accountability Office, 2005):

- *Alertness*. Government should anticipate problems and changes before they emerge, then deal effectively with them.
- *Agility*. Government should be entrepreneurial, open, and communicative. It should empower citizens and public employees alike.

Comparative Public Administration: The Essential Readings
Research in Public Policy Analysis and Management, Volume 15, 905–915
Copyright © 2006 by Elsevier Ltd.
ISSN: 0732-1317/doi:10.1016/S0732-1317(06)15042-3

- *Adaptability.* Government should continuously improve the quality of its programs and services, and it should do so by assessing its performance with measurable results. It should alter with changing circumstances and take advantage of new opportunities.
- *Alignment.* Government should saturate itself with knowledge by effectively managing its information technology. Governments should collaborate with other governments and the nonprofit and private sectors to achieve social goals.
- *Accountability.* Government should have a clear and compelling mission that focuses on the needs of people. Government should improve its accountability to the public interest, which should be understood in terms of law, community, and shared values.

These ideas lead to a much greater emphasis on certain kinds of public management that have been stressed only intermittently in the past, notably continuous quality improvement; electronic government; performance measurement; intersectoral and intergovernmental collaboration; coalition formation; benchmarking; citizen satisfaction studies; public program evaluation; strategic planning; training; team building; decentralization; devolution; downsizing; privatization; enhanced executive authority; and streamlining and innovating procurement, budgeting, and human resources.

Governments, certainly, have responded to these developments. One survey of the federal, state, and local governments in the United States found that only 10 percent "had no experience" with the bundle of concepts, approaches, and techniques that we associate with the new public management (Durst & Newell, 1999, p. 96).

In short, the new public management is "in," and this is, doubtless, good. But what is "out"?

THE FALL OF "GOOD GOVERNMENT"

What is out is that reformist phrase of yesteryear, good government. As a historic rallying cry for political reform, "good government" is unequalled, and its roots are surprisingly global, cultural, and deep. Some 1,400 years ago, Emperor T'ai-tsung (626–649) left his lasting legacy to China, known to this day as "The Era of Good Government." Nearly 700 years ago, the great Italian artist, Ambrogio Lorenzetti, plastered his superb murals, "Frescoes of the Good and Bad Government," on the walls of Siena's city hall, a theme replicated in the 1924 work, "Good Government," by the renowned Mexican muralists, Diego Rivera and Frida Kahlo. It silently admonishes educators in the administration building of the Autonomous University of Chapingo.

In the United States, the phrase fell out of favor with the slow demise of the National Civil Service League (formerly the National Civil Service Reform League, founded in New York in 1877), a shriveling that began in the mid-twentieth century and ended with its termination in the 1980s. Perhaps more than any other organization, the League is associated with the good-government reform movement (indeed, Good Government was the title of the journal that it sponsored), and during the late-nineteenth and early-twentieth centuries, the League was on the forefront of establishing civil services designed to replace corrupt party hacks with honest public administrators.

Ironically, the National Civil Service League forsook its good-government tradition with the issuance of its sixth and final model Public Personnel Administration Law in 1970, which, whatever its influential merits (and they were many), nonetheless represented a distancing from its founding values of good government in favor of those values that we now associate with the new public management. The League, in its ending days, was trying to be relevant. And it was. But, as with the public administration community in general, the League abandoned the concept of good government in the process.

Today, good government is dead, a victim of both its own success in largely achieving its goals, and of its own weaknesses, notably the stifling rigidities that remain its legacy in most governments. These governments are now facing new challenges and changes that demand flexibility and creativity, and the new public management is properly their escutcheon. Good government, by contrast, is seen as the underlying, if unwitting, cause of creaky, cranky, crusty, wrapped-in-red-tape, job-for-life government.

There are, inevitably, some remnants of good government, but they are sparse. There are: a collection of fewer than two dozen nonprofit associations that call themselves the "Good Government Groups," or "G3"; the Seasongood Good Government Foundation, based in (and oriented toward) Cincinnati; the Project on Government Oversight's occasional "Good Government" award for outstanding service; and a few other, smaller, and even more limited, leftovers. For all intents and purposes, however, good government long has been dismissed as a movement whose time came and went.

THE GLOBE'S GOVERNMENTAL REALITIES: AUTHORITARIANISM, CORRUPTION, INEPTITUDE

It is time to resuscitate good government. Why? Because good government asserts that, to be a good government, government must be good in every public sense of that word – politically, ethically, and professionally.

Good government embodies three core values of public administration that we have taken for granted in the past, but which elude most of the planets' populace. The values of good government are: democracy, honesty, and competency. I suggest that they are more important to human happiness than ever before.

Democracy, honesty, and competency are by no means the exclusive preserve of the developed world, and, in fact, these values are deteriorating in some developed nations, notably the United States. Often, this deterioration associates with the radically conservative agenda promoted by some political circles. This perspective holds that the best government is not merely the least government, a la Jefferson, but that the best government is no government – or, at least, ineffectual government. Consider this illustrative comment uttered by a prominent and powerful anti-government American ideologue: "I don't want to abolish government. I want to reduce it to the size where I can drag it into the bathroom and drown it in the bathtub" (Norquist, 2005).

Certainly, there are some governments that likely should be drowned in a tub, and the examples of pervasive governmental corruption and callousness are countless. Consider: the Cameroonian cops who stopped a traveler 47 times during a 300-mile journey to demand bribes (Guest, 2004). Or, in India, farmers who must pay baksheesh to their local governments' accountants to gain a clear title to their farms, or the rickshaw drivers who routinely sacrifice a sixth of their meager earnings to extortionist police (Das, 2004). Or the 15 percent of Americans who sometimes go hungry because they cannot afford food (Pew Global Attitudes Project, 2003), a proportion that is – in the richest economy on earth, one that controls over a third of the world's wealth (US Bureau of the Census, 2005, Table 1336) – larger than those in Canada, Japan, and Western Europe (Pew Global Attitudes Project, 2003).

The planet's people are profoundly aware that governments can be corrupt and callous, even cruel, and long have been united in their view that good government is crucial to a good life.

DEMOCRACY IS GOOD GOVERNMENT

Central to good government, in the majority opinions of all the world's people, is democracy. A massive and ongoing study, begun in the late 1970s, of citizens in 72 countries on six continents finds that "the basic ideas of democracy are virtually universally accepted around the world," regardless of culture, and that these ideas are "viewed as the only game in town," even by the residents of dictatorships (Norris, 2002).

The stirring, pro-democracy revolutions began in 1974 with the overthrow by the Portuguese people of their Fascist government, went into remission for 15 years, then broke out with a boom when the Berlin Wall tumbled (and with it, European Communism) in 1989. These revolutions have continued without let up, and dramatically demonstrate the global desire for democracy. We have heard this omnipresent cry from Kiev to Kyrghistan, from Beirut to Budapest, from Tblisi to Tiananmen.

HONESTY IS GOOD GOVERNMENT

There is more, however, to the universal longing for good government than just a desire for democracy. Clean, open, and honest government is equally longed for. The Orange, Rose, Velvet, and Cedar revolutions, plus many more national rebellions for democracy that went uncolored and untitled, that were victorious or vanquished, consistently have sounded a clarion leitmotif. That leitmotif is the exorcising of governmental corruption, and it matches in intensity the demand for democracy. Global polls find that political corruption ranks third in people's minds, after crime and AIDS, as a "very big" problem in their countries (Pew Global Attitudes Project, 2002).

People under the knout of authoritarian, undemocratic, and corrupt governments seem to viscerally understand that democracy and honest government are fraternal twins. And research indicates that these people are on to something. Healthy democracy – defined as large numbers of citizens voting repeatedly in open and competitive elections – associates with the relatively successful curtailment of corruption, and this correlation holds on a global scale (Bohara, Mitchell, & Mittendorf, 2004). There is, in brief, a pleasing link between robust democracy and governmental honesty.

THE COSTS OF CORRUPTION

So, introducing democracy is closely related to controlling corruption, and curtailing corruption is becoming essential, especially in the developing nations. Global corruption costs an estimated $2.3 trillion per year (World Bank), or approximately the same amount as the annual budget of the government of the United States. Political corruption appears to inflate the prices for goods by as much as 15 percent to 20 percent, and corrupt public officials who skim tax payments may cost their governments as much as 50 percent of their tax revenue (Stapenhurst & Kpundeh, 1999). ("Skim," in these instances, may not be the precisely accurate verb; perhaps "pour" is more to the point.)

Those benighted citizens who are saddled with pervasively corrupt governments must bribe officials to the tune of an additional 3 percent to 10 percent of the cost of government services as the price for assuring the reasonably prompt delivery of those services (Stapenhurst & Kpundeh, 1999). Of course, they already have paid for these government services, at least ostensibly, with their taxes.

But wait. There is more. Corruption and poverty stroll hand-in-hand. Countries seen as corrupt have lower levels of foreign investment, whereas countries that reduce corruption experience improved child mortality rates, higher per capita income, and greater literacy, among other benefits. Not one of the 19 impoverished nations that have been granted debt service relief through the Heavily Indebted Poor Countries Initiative is rated as anything better than having "serious to severe" governmental corruption (World Bank Institute, 2005).

OUT OF OSTRICHVILLE

In contrast to the globe's people, and despite corruption's colossal cost, much of the globe's officialdom has been slow, even recalcitrant, in recognizing the overweening importance of good government in bettering people's lives. The World Bank asserts, accurately, that corruption has been "treated as a taboo subject" by the international development community for decades (Stapenhurst & Kpundeh, 1999).

Fortunately, this ostrich-like view is changing. Thirty-five countries, including the United States, have agreed to the Organisation for Economic Co-operation and Development's Anti-bribery Convention, which was activated in 1999. In 2003, 95 nations, including the United States, signed the United Nations Treaty to Combat Corruption. The World Bank, whose mission is to assist in the economic development of poorer countries, has recognized that "corruption is one of the most serious obstacles to development," and has made fighting corruption "a central institutional priority" (Pradham et al., 2000, p. xiv). The United Nations Development Program, the world's largest aid agency, has made "good government" its "top priority in poverty fighting" on the grounds that "without good government, reliance on trickle-down economic development and a host of other strategies will not work" (Crossette, 2000; United Nations Development Program, 2000).

GOOD GOVERNMENT IS COMPETENCY

Encouraging as these developments are, we should remind ourselves that good government encompasses more than just democratic values and governmental honesty. There is our third component: Good government also includes professional competence.

As with democratic and uncorrupted government, well-managed government clearly enhances the daily lives of people. A study of the American states found that there was a solid and positive relationship between highly professional public administration in state government and a high quality of life for residents in those states. "Our results clearly indicated that the management of state governments also contributes directly to improving the overall quality of life for state citizens" (Coggburn & Schneider, 2003, p. 1337). It is at last dawning on scholars and policymakers (and here is where good government and the new public management merge) that good governments do not necessarily have to be big, but they do have to be strong, supple, and able (Fukuyama, 2004).

Katrina, Collapse, and Incompetence. The price of weak, brittle, and clumsy government can be steep. When Hurricane Katrina slammed into Alabama, Louisiana, and Mississippi on August 29, 2005, there appeared to be a collapse in governments' response that exemplified these dysfunctions.

State and local governments were slow off the mark. The governor of Louisiana requested federal aid only after the mayor of New Orleans had ordered mandatory evacuations, and highways were jammed with evacuees.

In the view of many, the mayor's evacuation order itself was too late in coming as, only 24 hours later, Katrina struck (Brookings Institution, 2005).

The city's mayor failed to mobilize the city's busses to rescue those citizens who had no other transportation. And there were many – some 57,000 households in the city owned no car ("Fix the Failures," 2005).

One of the more poignant instances of governmental failure occurred in assuring the public's safety. Although there were many acts of heroism by individual police officers, the New Orleans Police Department "as an institution ... disintegrated with the first drop of water ... a collapse that shocked even the department's oldest veterans." The chief of New Orleans' police was almost invisible during the first three days of the crisis, and about a third of the city's finest failed to report for duty six days after the hurricane made landfall (Baum, 2006, pp. 52, 55–56).

The federal government was especially tardy. Washington sent serious assistance to the region only after

- nine days had elapsed after Katrina was spotted in the Gulf of Mexico;
- eight days after it glanced off Florida, causing 14 deaths;
- seven days after Hurricane Katrina had attained Category 3 dimensions, was projected to hit Gulfport and New Orleans, and Louisiana declared a state of emergency;
- six days after Mississippi and New Orleans declared states of emergency;
- five days after Katrina registered as a Category 5 hurricane, the most destructive storm possible, Alabama declared a state of emergency, and a mandatory evacuation was ordered by the mayor of New Orleans;
- four days after Katrina made landfall as a Category 3 hurricane, and New Orleans began to flood;
- three days after 80 percent of New Orleans was flooded and widespread looting had erupted;
- two days after the evacuation of 25,000 people trapped in New Orleans' Superdome began; and
- one day after some rescue efforts in New Orleans were suspended because of sniper fire. Only on the next day did significant federal aid arrive (Brookings Institution, 2005).

Governments failed to clean up their act by failing to promptly clean up Katrina's mess. Congress had allocated $7.15 billion to house evacuees, and, only 70 days after Katrina struck, Washington had spent at least two-fifths, about $3 billion, of this substantial sum to do so (Katz, Liu, Fellowes, & Mabanta, 2005). Yet, five months after Katrina made landfall, some

750,000 displaced households still were living in, or moving to, rental or temporary housing (Brookings Institution, 2006).

Federal incompetence in finding permanent shelter for displaced people produced some sad outcomes for both victims and taxpayers. "For many families," the months following Katrina were "a series of frustrations and uncertainty, moving from one short-term venue to another in search of more stable housing options and more long-term financial aid and security. And the ad-hoc nature and multiple components of housing aid have only added to the confusion." One analysis found that, simply by using the federal government's existing Section 8 housing voucher program, Katrina's evacuees could have been housed far more humanely, quickly, and cost-effectively (Katz et al., 2005, p. 5).

Governments' response to Katrina was late, weak, and bumfuzzled, and people knew it. From over a fourth to more than three-fourths of the residents in the areas hit by Katrina rated governments' response to the hurricane and its aftermath as "only fair" or "poor," with the federal government receiving the greatest criticism, followed by state and local governments, respectively (Governments Get Poor Marks, 2005). Katrina's victims focused their ire on their public administrators. One local elected official accused, "The bureaucracy has murdered people in the greater New Orleans area" (Broussard, 2005, p. 515).

Governments' pathetic response was caused, in part, by a decline in professional talent in the Federal Emergency Management Agency (FEMA), the feds' central bureau for dealing with such crises. When Katrina made landfall, five of the eight highest executives in FEMA, including its director, had come "to their posts with virtually no experience in handling disasters," but they did have significant partisan backgrounds. Three of the Agency's five chiefs for natural disasters, and nine of its ten regional directors, were in acting positions because many of FEMA's seasoned professionals had quit over a deepening disgust with falling funding and promotion through patronage (Hsu, 2005).

COMPETENCE COUNTS

9/11: Catastrophe and Competence. Conversely, when government is strong, supple, and able, then government comes considerably closer toward fulfilling its fundamental duties. When terrorists murdered some 3,000 people on September 11, 2001, we were reminded, once again, why societies need competent government.

After 9/11, government was the core institution that responded to the horror. In contrast to the Katrina catastrophe, in 9/11 credit was given to government, and properly so, for courageous rescues and the restoration of order. Surveys indicated that Americans' trust in their government essentially doubled immediately following the attacks. In July 2001, 29 percent of respondents in a national survey said they trusted the government in Washington to do the right thing just about always or most of the time, compared to 57 percent in October 2001 (McKenzie & Labiner, 2002, p. 3).

As an astute observer noted, until that fateful day, "one idea took hold all along the political spectrum: Government was rapidly losing its relevance, its reach, and its right to make demands on the purses and practices of private citizens" (Hoagland, 2001). Following September 11th that relevance, reach, and right were accorded renewed legitimacy.

So, there is our point: Competent government is essential for the creation and delivery of public benefits, including the most rudimentary ones. And public safety is about as rudimentary as it gets.

The new public management is progress. Many, including me, applaud it. But our applause should not drown out older, if fustier, notions about what progressive public administration is. Those notions are the pillars of good government – democracy, honesty, and competency – and they have never been more important.

REFERENCES

Baum, D. (2006). Deluged. *The New Yorker*, January 9, pp. 50–63.

Bohara, A. K., Mitchell, N. J., & Mittendorff, C. F. (2004). Compound democracy and the control of corruption: A cross-country investigation. *Policy Studies Journal, 32*(4), 481–499.

Brookings Institution. (2005). *Hurricane Katrina timeline*, Washington, DC.

Brookings Institution. (2006). Measuring progress in New Orleans: A Katrina index update. *Update from Brookings Metro Program*, January 10, p. 1.

Broussard, A., President, Jefferspm Parish, Louisiana, September 7, 2005, as quoted in Saundra K. Schneider (2005). Special report: Administrative breakdowns in the governmental response to hurricane Katrina. *Public Administration Review, 65*(5), 515–516.

Coggburn, J. D., & Schneider, S. K. (2003). The relationship between state government performance and state quality of life. *International Journal of Public Administration, 26*(12), 1337–1358.

Crossette, B. (2000). U. N. says bad government is often cause of poverty. *New York Times*, April 5, p. 29A.

Das, G., former head of Procter & Gamble in India, writing in the Times of India, as cited in Thomas L. Friedman (2004). Think global, act local. *New York Times*, June 6, p. 13A.

Denhardt, R. B., & Denhardt, J. V. (2000). The new public service: Serving rather than steering. *Public Administration Review, 60*(6), 549–559.

Durst, S. L., & Newell, C. (1999). Better, faster, stronger: Government reinvention in the 1990s. *American Review of Public Administration, 29*(1), 67–76.

Fix the Failures. (2005). *Savannah Morning News*, September 10, p. 6A.

Fukuyama, F. (2004). *State-building: Governance and world order in the 21st century*. Ithaca, NY: Cornell University Press.

Governments get poor marks. (2005). *USA Today*, October 14, p. 15.

Guest, R. (2004). Africa earned its debt. *New York Times*, October 6, p. 29A.

Henry, N. (In press). Public administration and public affairs (10th ed.). Upper Saddle River, NJ: Prentice-Hall.

Hoagland, J. (2001). Government's comeback. *Washington Post*, September 26, p. B10.

Hsu, S. S. (2005). Leaders lacking disaster experience: 'Brain drain' at agency cited. *Washington Post*, September 9, p. A1.

Katz, B., Liu, A., Fellowes, M., & Mabanta, M. (2005). *Housing families displaced by Katrina: A review of the federal response to date*. Washington, DC: Brookings.

Light, P. C. (2005). *The four pillars of high performance: How robust organizations achieve extraordinary results*. Washington, DC: Brookings.

McKenzie, G. C., & Labiner, J. M. (2002). *Opportunity lost: The rise and fall of trust and confidence in government after September 11*. Washington, DC: Brookings.

Norquist, G., as quoted in T. L. Friedman (2005). Osama and Katrina. *New York Times*, September 7, p. 29A.

Norris, P., as quoted in Richard Morin (2002). Islam and democracy. *Washington Post*, April 28, p. B5.

Pew Global Attitudes Project. (2002). *What the world thinks in 2002*. Washington, DC: Pew Research Center for the People and the Press.

Pew Global Attitudes Project. (2003). *Most of the world still does without*. Washington, DC: Pew Research Center for the People and the Press.

Pradham, S., Anderson, J., Hellman, J., & Jones, G. (2000). *Anticorruption in transition: A contribution to the policy debate*. Washington, DC: World Bank.

Stapenhurst, R., & Kpundeh, S. (Eds). (1999). *Curbing corruption: Toward a model for building national integrity*. Washington, DC: World Bank, http://publications.worldbank.org/ecommerce/catalog/product-detail?product_id = 208301&

United Nations Development Program. (2000). *Overcoming human poverty: UNDP poverty report 2000*. New York.

US Bureau of the Census. (2005). *Statistical abstract of United States 2004–2005* (124th ed.). Washington, DC: US Government Printing Office.

US Government Accountability Office. (2005). *21st century challenges: Transforming government to meet current and emerging challenges, GAO-05-830T*. Washington, DC: US Government Printing Office.

World Bank Institute, as cited in Transparency International. (2005). *Perceived corruption index 2005*. Berlin: World Bank Institute.

FURTHER READING

Swope, C., & Patton, Z. (2005). In disaster's wake. *Governing, 19*(2), 48–58.

CONCLUSION: IMPACT OF GLOBALIZATION ON THE STUDY AND PRACTICE OF PUBLIC ADMINISTRATION

Fred W. Riggs

Although globalization may be seen as a long-term process, its acceleration in recent years is a result of the launching of the Internet, satellite communications and cell phones, the growth of the United Nations (UN) system and innumerable trans-national organizations, plus fast and easily available trade, transportation, and migration throughout the world. As a result the way we understand public administration needs to be reconsidered – especially its ramifications for comparative analysis.

The traditional unit of analysis for comparative purposes was the nation state, and public administration was understood as a governmental function. For most Americans, the term was understood by reference to public administration in the United States. Restrictive adjectives were added only when one thought of administration outside the American context and "Comparative Public Administration" came to be viewed, especially after World War II, as primarily the study of administration in the countries that had been liberated from imperial control. On the optimistic premise that these countries were uniformly in the process of "developing" modern institutions linked with their formal independence, the term "development" came to be a virtual synonym – thus to speak of "development administration" became a

Comparative Public Administration: The Essential Readings
Research in Public Policy Analysis and Management, Volume 15, 917–967
ISSN: 0732-1317/doi:10.1016/S0732-1317(06)15043-5

euphemism for talk about administration in new states. Moreover, constitutional governance was thought of in terms of the American Constitution as a model without critical assessment of its limitations or its deep-rooted implications for public administration.

In the context of globalization we need to re-think these parameters and it seems appropriate to conclude this collection of essays with some thoughts about the conceptual and constitutional implications of established practices, especially in the U.S., and what may be understood as a future scenario for comparative public administration. We will discuss the subject under the following headings:

1. Synarchy – Visualizing anarchy as a concomitant of synthesis
2. Transition – Historical perspective on the dynamics of change
3. Two constitutional models – Proto and ortho modern
4. Contemporary crises – Clash of models and the rise of dictatorships
5. Governance – Erasing the state/non-state divide

Section 1 is conceptual and sets the stage by discussing some key concepts needed for the analysis that follows. In Section 2 we take a broad historical look at forces that have set the stage for modern governments to evolve. The next two sections discuss the structures of governance and public administration that have emerged in the modern context: Section 3 primarily in Europe and the Americas, and Section 4 in the rest of the world. The final section offers a more futuristic look at evolving forces that have eroded the state/non-state distinction and posed new problems for public administration.

1. SYNARCHY – VISUALIZING ANARCHY AS A CONCOMITANT OF SYNTHESIS

To clarify our analysis, we start with a conceptual explanation of synarchy and the key terms that we need to use in this chapter. Synarchy is a neologism that combines *synthesis* with *anarchy*. We will first look at how these two contrasting ideas are linked. In juxtaposition, they provide a basis for understanding contemporary public administration in a global and comparative context.

A global synthesis is evolving in which a host of international organizations, public and private, voluntary, for-profit, and sectarian, participate. The UN is the core institution of global synthesis, but it is a weak core and a vast number of global and regional organizations do coordinate their activities in remarkably coherent patterns. The traditional purview of international administration has grasped the superstructure but largely ignored its vast underpinnings. The highly complex and extensive list of linked international organizations can be found at the UN's official web site.[1]

This explanation is adequate for present purposes, and more will be said about it in Section 5.

Anarchy, however, is an ambivalent and ambiguous term that requires some explanation. It may be viewed as a synonym for chaos and disorder, or a recipe for harmony and freedom. Both notions are manifest in the world today where anarchy has grown, partly because of resistance to the global synthesis and its salient organs, and partly also because new technologies, especially the Internet, now enable individuals and groups to promulgate their preferences and recruit followers anywhere in the world. Much anarchic activism takes harmless, even benign, forms as manifest in voluntarism and sportsmanship. However, the same opportunities are open to terrorists and criminals who can spread violence and death. To enable us to discuss this phenomenon clearly, we need to distinguish clearly between "malignant" and "benign" anarchy.

1.1. Malignant Anarchy

In everyday usage, "anarchy" typically refers to a malignant nightmare vision that implies no government, chaos and violence. This idea is supported by the two senses of the word offered in *The Encarta* Dictionary:[2]

1. Chaotic situation: a situation in which there is a total lack of organization or control.
2. Lack of government: the absence of any formal system of government in a society.

Interestingly, this definition fails to mention the positive concept intended by those who speak of philosophical anarchism which has a substantial literature. Because the world system and much public administration involve benign anarchy, we need to say more about this idea.

1.2. Benign Anarchy

In its positive sense, one may value anarchy as benign, enabling harmony among free people acting without the oppressive tyranny imposed by arbitrary rule. For a general discussion, see the classic essay on "Anarchism" from the 1910 edition of *Encyclopedia Britannica*, as reproduced for *Anarchism Archives*.[3]

It provides historical background information about various important writers and anarchist theories.

Dana Ward teaches a well-structured course on anarchy and the Internet.[4] He offers an extensive collection of URLs for texts from leading philosophers and writers on benign anarchy in his *Anarchy Archives*.[5]

Contemporary philosophical anarchism is taught by the Institute for Anarchist Studies. According to its web site, this organization is dedicated to:

> Promoting critical scholarship on social domination and the reconstructive vision of a free society.[6] Their humane goals and pacific orientation is surely opposed to the chaos and disorder we usually associate with anarchy. On the other hand, militant leftist or working class anarchism is espoused by authors and texts reported at numerous web sites.[7]

One way to distinguish between the positive and negative conceptions of anarchy is to use "anarchism" to refer to philosophical ideas of benign anarchy, and reserve "anarchy" for the negative senses identified in the *Encarta Dictionary*. A better way, however, might be to adopt a different word for the positive vision expressed in the definition of panarchy offered by James N. Rosenau in 1955:

> A new form of "anarchy" has evolved in the current period – one that involves not only the absence of a highest authority but that also encompasses such an extensive disaggregation of authority as to allow for much greater flexibility, innovation, and experimentation.

Christian Butterbach has compiled an extended annotated bibliography for the relevant literature.

He writes:

> as a panarchist, I do always stress that my primary aim is maximum tolerance for all tolerant actions, however much I may disapprove of them in their contents. As long as people are tolerant they can be tolerated.[8]

1.3. Polyarchy

A closely related term is "polyarchy." This word presupposes the need for government but stresses popular control and responsibility. The word expresses the idea of rule by many. Ideally speaking, all democracies are forms of polyarchy. Whereas panarchy and anarchy both imply the absence of government, the concept of polyarchy accepts the need for governance but stresses popular participation in the choice and monitoring of rulers. Dahl's definition of polyarchy in *Democracy and its Critics* (1989) is authoritative. It prescribes seven attributes:

1. elected officials
2. free and fair elections
3. inclusive suffrage
4. the right to run for office
5. freedom of expression
6. alternative information and
7. associational autonomy.[9]

More generally, "polyarchy" refers to any system of governance in which authority is widely dispersed among many actors, even if all the criteria mentioned by Dahl are not implemented. More diffuse and technologically oriented discussions of polyarchy identify technology and the Internet as factors that lead to the diffusion of power. An example can be found in Tiscali's extended treatise on polyarchy in which he writes:

> "Polyarchy is the organization/diffusion of power in the age of universal electronic communication and ubiquitous cybernetic regulation."[10]

This libertarian tradition does not advocate polyarchy, but it accepts the need for minimal regulation by government of a system that maximizes free choices in a market-controlled environment. The maintenance of such a system hinges on an effective ordering regime so it is not fully anarchic. However, its vision of minimalist governments reduces public administration to the maintenance of public order while assigning maximum scope to private enterprise and free market competition.

1.4. Dictatorship

A logical antonym for polyarchy is "monarchy." However, this term has historical connotations discussed below in Section 2. A more apt term for this discourse is "dictatorship" which connotes the use of force by rulers to dominate subject populations.[11]

In contemporary thought, the word has negative connotations and it is hard to think of any polity dominated by an unaccountable ruler that is seen as benign or beneficial. We may, however, make a couple of distinctions involving words that are often used as synonyms. A "tyranny," for example, refers to oppressive rule by a dictator, leaving open the possibility that some dictators are not oppressors. The word, "totalitarian" is also used synonymously. However, this term involves comprehensive control over everyone's life by a regime. In practice some dictatorships have more limited aims, and they may not succeed in their aspirations. This leaves open to empirical enquiry questions about the possibility of benevolent and limited dictatorships. No doubt dictators often present themselves as benevolent and set no limits on their efforts to control everyone. It is useful to use dictatorships – a concept to be elaborated below in Section 4 – as a broad term, and to consider "tyranny," "despotism" and "totalitarianism" as narrower concepts.

All of the terms discussed above apply to some degree to parts of to-day's world, yet none of them capture the contradictions inherent in the dynamics of today's synarchic system. The world today and many parts of it link synthesis and anarchy in complex ways that require further discussion.

1.5. Synarchy

The synarchic model, by definition, involves linked synthesis and anarchy. The model is therefore consistent with increased governmental functions, even including socialism and the welfare state. This implies, therefore, substantial growth of administrative structures and operations. However, the concept also includes the co-existence of vast areas of public interest in which a congeries of governmental and private organizations have overlapping jurisdictions and imperfect mechanisms for reconciling their activities or handling conflicts between them. Indeed, these mechanisms often fail and they enable individuals and groups to engage in anti-social conduct and even provoke such behaviors.

My own use of "synarchy" is based on the need for a term that clearly juxtaposes the ideas of cooperation among independent authorities and individuals with the notion of disorder and chaos as linked phenomena. The word has an early meaning reported in Webster's 1828 dictionary: "joint rule or sovereignty." In this early sense, "synarchy" has a meaning that is very close to polyarchy.[12]

Most dictionaries do not list the word so we may view it as a neologism. However, to avoid any possible ambiguity we might coin a truly new word like "synanarchy." However, we find this word awkward and unnecessary. The shorter form is easier to remember and use. Should anyone protest that the word already has another meaning, we might suggest that it now has a

new sense, and in cases of possible ambiguity, use synanarchy to disam-
biguate the new meaning from the earlier one.

1.6. Revisions

Writers about public administration often presuppose the existence of
a system of governance in which a congeries of bureaucratic structures
are formally organized and guided by a sovereign – or even a dictator – to
implement public policies. Although that image was somewhat valid in
the past, especially in monarchic regimes, modern democracies have substantially revised the foundational premises of public administration
to recognize the influence of public opinion and dispersed political forces
in the conduct of governance. However, this pluralistic expansion of the
administrative model is scarcely adequate for understanding our contemporary global system. We need to see the world as synarchic and base our
thinking about the design and problems of public administration on this
context.

Because this requires a fundamental revision of the foundational paradigm for our work, it seemed necessary to elaborate its conceptual premises
as given above. Now we can turn to the historical context in which the study
and practice of public administration has evolved. Comparisons are
needed not only between different contemporary regimes or countries, but
also between historical periods. As we shall see, historically, principles
of governance were first conceptualized as occurring in monarchic contexts.
In today's world, by contrast, the context of all governments should,
ideally speaking, be polyarchic. Our theories of public administration normally presuppose the existence of polyarchic regimes as the context – or,
especially in third world countries, they imagine that "development" will
lead in that direction. However, the reality of the contemporary world is
highly synarchic and in many parts of the world, synarchy also prevails as
transitions between past and present modes of conduct and administration
have become jumbled. One need only mention extreme cases like Iraq or
Sudan to make such generalizations concrete and specific.

Following this historical analysis, we will look more narrowly at the
American model and how it has shaped much of our thinking about public
administration despite the evidence of very different forces elsewhere in the
world. Finally, we will talk about how these synarchic conditions are erasing
the boundaries between public and private management and between the
domestic and international levels of governance and how that will affect the
theory and practice of public administration.

2. TRANSITION: HISTORICAL PERSPECTIVE ON THE DYNAMICS OF CHANGE

In the context of global synarchy, we are not thinking of a single administrative system but, rather, a vast array of entities, including many states, inter-national organizations and autonomous non-state organizations in each of which we can find organized bureaucracies. Ideally speaking, the global system would be a vast panarchy in which these independent entities and their bureaucracies work amicably together to reconcile conflicts and optimize the general welfare.

In fact, however, global *synarchy* prevails, which means that there are vast zones of anarchy marked by the absence of order and the prevalence of conflict between organized entities and their administrations. How can we best make sense of this disorder and develop strategies for understanding and working with it? Of course, public administration is a contingent perspective by which we mean administrative systems do not stand alone – they always hinge on a political context. There must be some embracing organization that contains any administration. Sad to say, our world system contains a vast number of synarchic organizations – this includes many countries as well as non-state entities.

To understand why this is so, we need to be clear about the macro-historical transition through which the world is now passing. Most writings about public administration presuppose the ubiquity of states, each organized according to Dahl's polyarchic model. Unfortunately, this model is rarely implemented though it is usefully imagined as an ideal type that no doubt is approximated in some cases. A more realistic picture of the current status of public administration in today's world can be formed if we think about the dynamics of the transition from pre-modern to modern forms of government and the transitional structures of organization – or disorganization – that have arisen in this process.

2.1. Monarchic Sovereignty

For most of human history, established polities have been organized under the aegis of sacred legitimacy as ritualized in the coronation of kings. Let me add that, archeologically speaking, humans lived on earth long before history began – "history" begins with civilizations that were able to leave records in their writings and artifacts from which we can learn something about how they were organized. We know that in these civilizations, state sovereignty was visualized as divine in character and "sovereigns" were their human deputies. Subjects accepted their human masters because they saw them as part of a divinely ordained order from which they benefited – no doubt force was also involved, but stable structures of governance hinged on supernatural forces as well depicted in the remains of ancient Egypt, China, India, Babylon, Greece, Rome and other ancient societies.

In these polities, all authority descended from above in hierarchic chains: superiors were viewed as rightful masters over those to whom they delegated power in hierarchies that extended down to the lowliest serfs and slaves. Humans were viewed as inherently unequal and legitimate power was exercised only by delegation from above. Public administration, therefore, could be viewed as fully and essentially *hierarchic*. The Indian caste system carried this concept to its logical extreme, but *caste-ism* in various degrees prevailed in all traditional polities: humans were not viewed as equals but as essentially unequal. Their rights and duties hinged on birth, including differences of gender, race, speech and especially occupational prerogatives marking status differences.

2.2. Contemporary Examples

The most familiar example of such a hierarchic structure that persists today can be found in the Roman Catholic Church which is organized, under the authority of a Pope vested with a sacred mandate and ranked office-holders extending down to individual congregations and parishioners to be found today throughout the world. Such a complete hierarchy includes everyone in the system, and derives its authority from super-natural forces as we have recently seen in the ordination of a new Pope. According to *Catholic Encyclopedia*, the Papacy is the "ecclesiastical system in which the pope as successor of St. Peter and Vicar of Jesus Christ governs the Catholic Church as its supreme head."[13] Readers of this Encyclopedia on the Web who click on the underlined terms will find official explanations of these terms as taught by the Roman Church.

Traditional civilizations organized their monarchies under similar principles. Sacred coronation rituals were employed to confer upon each new sovereign the sacred right to rule. Exceptionally, as in Tibet, a new Dalai Lama was to be discovered at birth as a sacred reincarnation.[14] It is noteworthy that much information on Tibet is vetted by the Chinese authorities.[15] However, the persistence in diaspora of a global Tibetan community provides evidence for the survivability of the traditional system of sacred rule.

Both the Catholic and Tibetan institutions are global and non-territorial except for the vestigial Vatican state. It is hard to find any contemporary state that retains the traditional form of sacred monarchy. Bhutan may be the nearest exception.[16]

2.3. Former Regimes

Historical and anthropological records are needed to provide information about former regimes. After eons of stateless anarchy, the institutions of divine kingship evolved. Usually they were monarchies where a single ruler, enthroned by coronation ceremonies in which a divine mandate conferred sovereignty on the person of a sovereign, presided over a hierarchy of office holders subject to the will and mandates of the ruler. From sovereign to subjects to slaves, everyone in a given domain was assigned a status and functions in the hierarchy as manifest in a caste-like social system. With many variations of details – no doubt with some exceptions where republicanism gained a foothold – the monarchic formula prevailed globally. Hierarchic order, imposed from above, had a supernatural ritual foundation. These regimes were typically accepted by their subjects because of the benefits they were thought to confer on all who accepted the sovereign's authority. A brilliant analysis of the traditional sacred structure of governance can be found in Arthur Hocart's *Kingship* (1927).[17]

In addition, an essay by David Livingston contains this quotation:

> Perhaps there never were any gods without kings, or kings without gods. When we have discovered the origin of divine kingship we shall know, but at present we only know that when history begins there are kings, the representatives of gods (our emphasis).[18]

2.4. Separation of Church and State

No doubt there were exceptions and we may trace notions of democratic equalitarianism to antiquity, but it was not until modern times that these principles became widely institutionalized in political regimes. For many different reasons, but especially the clash of competing religious doctrines and sects, secularism came to be widely accepted, leading to the separation of church and state in Europe and America. To legitimize authority, equalitarianism and popular sovereignty gained widespread acceptance, including polyarchic theories based on the people's right to elect representatives to create legitimate governments. The vast literature on this subject is widely known and scarcely needs bibliographic reinforcement. The founders embraced republicanism as an ideal, not as democracy. They derived this ideal from ancient Roman and more recent European thought as explained in *The Reader's Companion to American History*.[19]

Republicanism in 1776 meant more than eliminating a king and instituting an elective system of government; it set forth moral and social goals as well. Republics required a particular sort of egalitarian and virtuous people: independent, property-holding citizens who were willing to sacrifice many of their private, selfish interests for the res publica, the good of the whole community. Equality lay at the heart of republicanism; it meant a society whose distinctions were based only on merit. No longer would one's position rest on whom one knew or married or on who one's parents were.

The meanings of "democracy" are quite similar as shown by this definition in various documents. For example the *Encarta Dictionary* suggests that democracy connotes:

the free and equal right of every person to participate in a system of government, often practiced by electing representatives of the people by the majority of the people.[20]

Freedom and equality are important criteria in both concepts, but freedom is stressed more in the concept of republicanism whereas equality takes priority in the concept of democracy.

Together they show that the ideals and practices of republicanism and democracy do have ancient roots, but they came to prevail in Europe and America only in modern times. Today they are celebrated globally, in theory if not in practice. It is useful to make a broad distinction between the situation in Europe and the Americas where modern constitution-alism based on popular sovereignty replaced monarchism in the 18th and 19th centuries; and the situation in most of Asia, Africa and Oceania where this process is contemporary, i.e., in the 20th and 21st centuries. We usually do think of globalization as a contemporary process although it has been going on for a long time. However, it has greatly accelerated in modern times.

We may refer to the first modern phase of globalization in Europe and the Americas as *proto-modern* and the more recent phase as *ortho-modern*. The distinction is important because two different models for the design of a constitutional democracy evolved during these two periods and they have significant implications for their survivability and for public administration. In Section 3, we describe and compare these two models. Both of them are being spread around the world today, but the persistence of monarchic traditions and ways of thought seriously disrupts their application and leads to many lawless tyrannies and endemic violence for reasons to be explained in Section 4. Finally, in Section 5, we contemplate the future and speculate about some further implications of accelerated globalization as it erases many of the boundaries that have hitherto insulated states.

3. TWO CONSTITUTIONAL MODELS – PROTO AND ORTHO MODERN

Unfortunately, most of the American literature in Political Science and Public Administration is premised on the historical experience of the United States, and the word, "comparative" is really used to refer to studies based on experience elsewhere in the world. This practice blinds us to important realities that become apparent when we transcend this parochialism. Taking an historical perspective, we can first distinguish traditional monarchic polities based on supernatural sovereignty from modern polyarchic regimes based on popular sovereignty. We can use "polyarchy" to overcome some semantic perplexities raised by both "republicanism" and "democracy." As noted above, republics by definition have elected, not hereditary heads, but constitutional monarchies may be more democratic than some republics. The term, "polyarchy" is one of the technical terms political scientists try to avoid yet its use can be helpful. The International Political Science Association (IPSA) Committee on Concept and Methods has recently published a working paper by Frederic Schaffer on this question.[21] Its opening paragraph includes this question:

> Despite the importance of coining new terms to the scientific enterprise, political scientists continue to rely heavily on everyday terms like "politics," "freedom," "democracy," "power," and "interest." Why haven't political scientists invented more neologisms to replace these ordinary words, words that are arguably loose and unscientific?

Without going into the reasons for this terminological taboo, it is helpful to coin and use technical terms that convey intended concepts more precisely than our everyday language. Here we will use "polyarchy," as defined by Robert Dahl – see above. We may also define "modern constitutions" as basic charters for governance that embody polyarchic principles. The American Constitution, as originally promulgated, approximated the polyarchic norm, which is why it can be called "proto-modern." It was created in 1787 and did not accept the notion of full equality until the 19th Amendment (1920) gave women the right to vote. We can call it proto-modern because the principle of popular rather than royal sovereignty was accepted, even though its application was incomplete.

The basic structural difference between fully modern and proto-modern constitutions, however, involves the right of the elected legislature to name and remove the chief executive, thereby making public administration fully accountable to the sovereign people. The American proto-modern constitution retained the traditional principle of monarchic power by vesting the executive power in a surrogate king, an elected president who combined the ceremonial and executive authority for a fixed number of years and was not vulnerable to removal by a Congressional majority. Because all polities following this proto-modern model elect their presidents, we may conveniently and unambiguously call the systems "presidentialist."

We cannot use "presidential," however, because many non-presidentialist regimes also call their head of state a "president." In fully modern constitutions, these functions are divided so that the executive power can be rendered accountable by making it subject to removal by a vote of the elected assembly. The head of state may be a president or a king. Because the sovereign power is vested in a "parliament" we can unambiguously call these systems "parliamentarist." We cannot use the word, "parliamentary," however, because many polities have an assembly called "parliament" which is not able to hold the chief executive accountable. A regime is parliamentarist only if its parliament is able to exercise effective control over the chief executive.

To understand the virtues and limitations of the proto-modern constitutional model, one needs to compare all the polities that have accepted this polyarchic formula for governance. Sad to say, by separating the study of American government from that of other countries using the same design, we avoid recognizing the real problems the system creates. Because most of the world's presidentialist regimes have been in Latin America, research about them has been monopolized by Latin Americanists, and area specialists have also monopolized the study of presidentialist regimes in Africa, Eastern Europe and elsewhere. But area specialists do not link research about presidentialism in their region with the American case, and this means that the most important case for understanding presidentialism by comparative analysis is ignored. A global framework for studying all presidentialist (proto-modern) governments provides a more solid basis for understanding both politics and administration in these countries.

3.1. Proto-Modern Structure

The pioneer proto-modern system, articulated in the U.S. Constitution, was actually only semi-polyarchic because it excluded women, slaves and native Americans from suffrage. This abridges Dahl's definition of polyarchy, which stipulates "inclusive suffrage" and "the right to run for office." Since more than half the American population was excluded from suffrage and the right to seek office by the original Constitution, we see that the full implications of a polyarchic design were not accepted. Ironically, the privileges of slave-owners were enhanced by Article 1, Section 2 of the Constitution, which stipulated that slaves were to be counted as two-thirds of a person for purposes of representation and taxation.[22]

Thus even citizens were not to be treated with full equality – property qualifications denied suffrage to the poor, and women were excluded. The founders stressed the republican norm of freedom but looked with suspicion on democratic goals of equality. It took a civil war to end the slavery system and it was not until 1920 that the 19th Amendment finally gave equal representation to women including the right to run for office. More importantly, however, the executive power was vested in a surrogate monarch, the elected president, not subject to discharge by Congress. Like a king, the president would be both head of state and government. Because of the separation of powers, however, the actual powers of the president were limited and had to be shared with members and committees of Congress. This meant that effective control over the bureaucracy and public administration was shared between the two branches – actually three because the Supreme Court could invalidate legislation and therefore the nominal hierarchy of authority in the Federal government's bureaucracy was exercised under three competing jurisdictions. Moreover, because of its federal design, government operations had to be divided between levels – sometimes with seriously dysfunctional results as seen recently in the New Orleans disaster following Hurricane Katrina. The extreme complexity of relief activities following this monstrous disaster is revealed on the official page for the recovery efforts, which identifies a wide range of cooperating organizations.[23]

The Internet is now facilitating coordination to solve problems that often arise in the context of our presidentialist system as further complicated by overlapping federal, state and local jurisdictions.

Throughout Latin America the presidentialist model was replicated. Because of the power and wealth of the United States, its influence and example have induced other countries around the world to copy this 18th century constitutional model. Our unconscious suppositions based on the American model led to two fundamental misconceptions: the first involves our failure to recognize the basic fragility of the proto-modern constitutional design which almost certainly leads to the collapse of democracy and the rise of dictatorships; and the second relates to the difficulties that occur in the management of any republic based on "presidentialist" constitutional foundations, including the United States.

3.2. Fragility

Looking first at the difficulties faced by all presidentialist regimes, we need to compare the U.S. with virtually all Latin American countries and scattered polities throughout the world. Such comparisons highlight the fact that presidentialist regimes are extremely fragile and almost always experience periods of tyranny under dictatorships. Often this occurs when an elected president usurps power. However, presidents are often too weak to master serious emergencies and an unelected military officer, leading a coup group, seizes power. Because this has not happened in the United States, we tend to assume that the collapse of presidentialist regimes was not caused by any basic weakness in their design. Instead, we look for other reasons to explain political instability and dictatorships. Because Latin America is the main region where presidentialism has prevailed and so often failed, we easily fall into the trap of looking for an "area studies" answer. We assume there must be something about this region and its ecology, history, religion or culture that accounts for political tyranny. The literature is extensive, but let me just mention one example, a report by Mario Vargas Llosa, a novelist who in 1990 was an unsuccessful candidate for the presidency of Peru.[24]

His analysis of the terrible experiences of governance in Latin America are attributed to moral, social and historical forces without any mention of the constitutional rules that apply in all these countries. He writes, inter alia,

> It's not possible for countries to develop if those who govern, or those with political responsibilities, are Alemán (Nicaragua), Chávez (Venezuela), Fujimori (Peru), real gangsters, authentic bandits who go into government like thieves go into houses – to rob, to sack, to enrich themselves in the fastest and most cynical way possible. How can politics be an attractive pursuit for idealistic people? The young, naturally, look on politics as robbery. And the only way to clean up politics is to bring decent people into politics, people who don't steal, people who do as they say they will, people who don't lie or who lie only a bit, since some lying is probably inevitable.

Latin Americans who do talk about the United States are more likely to blame U.S. foreign policies and intervention for the failures in their region than they are to use the American case as a basis for comparison to identify the essential problems of presidentialism.

If presidents are popularly elected and checked by Congress, how can we account for this pathological behavior? Among the structural features of presidentialism, the basic principle of "separation of powers" was seen by the American founding fathers as providing protection against tyranny, a premise based on faith that presidents would respect the constitution and

Congress as an institution would be powerful. Unfortunately, however, when clashes between the executive and legislative branches escalate, Congress lacks the effective power to resist and presidents are often able to mobilize military force to dissolve or dominate Congress. Alternatively, when stalemates between the two branches arise, impatient officials, led by military officers, seize power and Congress is powerless to resist. The details in each case are, of course, unique but this basic weakness seems to pervade most presidentialist regimes.

3.3. The Exceptional Case

The U.S. experience has been exceptional. If this is so, then we must ask for an explanation of the American case. If we should expect presidentialist regimes to collapse, then should we not seek to explain the exception? Finding an answer to this question may shed light on the conditions needed to enable any presidentialist system to succeed – or show why a different kind of system is more likely to work properly.

The basic problem for public administration in all presidentialist regimes, therefore, is how to establish and maintain responsible and coherent political control over government bureaucracies, military and civil. We impede our ability to understand this problem because we fail to consider the U.S. system in our comparisons.

The first point involves the requisites of Congressional power. In many countries we find puppet legislatures easily dominated by a ruling party or the chief executive. Strong assemblies seem to require competing parties but not too many of them. When most members of a legislature belong to one party, the leaders of that party can dominate the assembly and it becomes a pawn – if the president is also leader of this party, presidential domination is assured. When too many parties are represented in an assembly, competition between them leads to instability, shifting coalitions and indecisiveness. The resulting frustrations, especially in times of crisis, lead to executive intervention or military coups.

Since members of Congress are typically loyal to the political party that nominated them and supported their election, it is understandable that they do not rush to support their opponents. Yet the survival of legislative power seems to require an understanding by members of any legislature that the maintenance of their institution's power hinges on the safeguarding of opposition. Indeed, legislatures are the only institution whose self-interest requires the protection of opponents. Presidents, courts of law, political parties and bureaucracies can all survive and exercise power without opposition. Of course, a powerful legislature aware of the need for opposition will also support laws and policies that protect the countervailing power of institutions such as the executive, courts and even bureaucracies. However, in the heat of daily controversies it is easy to forget the need for opposition and all political and administrative actors are tempted to prioritize the current issues that confront them.

The need for political opposition is most easily overlooked when current controversies escalate to a fever pitch. If the executive authority cannot manage effectively, the stage is set for a *coup d'etat*, the seizure of power by some group able to defeat rivals and impose order. The leaders in such a movement are normally military officers. Sometimes they may lead a militant political party.

At least one foundation for the maintenance of Congressional power seems to be a two-party system, which in turn requires single-member districts. Proportional representation and multi-party legislatures are inherently vulnerable to instability and polarization. However, the key to success for a two-party system is also a liability – it involves the need for centrist orientations, which make bi-partisan cooperation possible. This, in turn, hinges on financial arrangements that favor middle and upper class constituencies augmented by electoral rules that permit widespread abstention by alienated and indifferent citizens. Where compulsory voting has prevailed, as in several Latin American countries, extremist parties are likely to arise that can capture mass support and polarize views on truly divisive issues that seriously block compromise agreements. Ironically, the conditions favorable for survival of a presidentialist regime appear to be those that are intrinsically undemocratic.

No doubt there are other factors. For example, in order for military officers to succeed in staging a coup, they need to be concentrated in the capital city. One of the interesting effects of federalism in the United States has been the widespread distribution of military facilities in virtually every state, a response not just to security needs but even more to pressures in Congress designed to give every state some of the benefits of a military presence. In most countries, the centralization of power and large concentrations of troops in the capital have meant that during times of unrest and indecision, it is possible for coup leaders to mobilize overwhelming force in the nation's center of power.

As for dominant political parties, they often come to power during periods of extreme national trauma when a country is torn by civil and international wars. People become desperate and turn to leaders who promise solutions based on monopolizing power, especially in the legislature. Once in control, such parties are able to oust opponents and rule tyrannically. The executive authority may be exercised by party leaders – or their puppets.

3.4. Fully Modern Format

Democratic norms of equality play a dominant role in notions of democracy, a term that replace republicanism. Moreover, many democracies are constitutional monarchies, whereas every republic, by definition, has an elected head of state. Although expanding the suffrage to include all citizens is a major feature of the development of modern constitutional design, a feature that has even more decisive importance involves popular control over the chief executive. The presidentialist formula, as we have seen, does not empower the legislature to discharge the executive by a simple vote, a limitation on the exercise of democratic control of government. That right was created in England after the effective power of running the government was taken away from the king and given to a Cabinet headed by a prime minister, subject to parliamentary authority. Since there is no written Constitution in the UK, the process of making this change was gradual on the basis of historical events and evolving traditions. A series of reform acts, most notably in 1832 and 1867, extended the suffrage without making it universal. No such acts marked the parallel devolution of power from the king to parliament, but during the 19th century this process did occur in England and spread throughout Europe.[25] According to Wikipedia,

> By the mid 20th Century, the political culture in Europe had shifted to the point where all constitutional monarchs had been reduced to the status of effective figureheads, with no effective power at all. Instead, it was the democratically elected parliaments, and their leader, the prime minister who had become the true rulers of the nation.[26]

A summary of this process in England suggests:

> The office of Prime Minister is governed not by codified laws, but by unwritten and to some extent fluid customs known as constitutional conventions, which have developed over years of British history. These conventions are for the most part founded on the underlying principle that the Prime Minister and his fellow Ministers must maintain the support of the democratically elected component of Parliament, the House of Commons. The Sovereign, as a constitutional monarch, always acts in accordance with such conventions, as do Prime Ministers themselves...

> The Prime Minister's powers are also limited by the House of Commons, whose support the Government is obliged to maintain. The House of Commons checks the powers of the Prime Minister through committee hearings and through Question Time, a weekly occurrence in which the Prime Minister is obliged to respond to the questions of the Leader of the Opposition and other members of the House... a Member of Parliament

may be expelled from his or her party for failing to support the Government on important issues... In general, the Prime Minister and his or her colleagues may secure the
House's support for almost any bill.[27]

3.5. Comparisons

No doubt constitutional regimes of all kinds are vulnerable to collapse and
we cannot assume they will last forever. However, the record shows that
governments following the ortho-modern parliamentary model are less
likely to collapse than those adhering to the proto-modern presidentialist
model. We have made this case in earlier papers and shall not repeat the
argument here.[28]

In this paper, we offer an extended discussion of the history and experience of presidentialist and parliamentarist regimes, stressing the importance of parliamentary control over the government. This reform gave teeth
to the fundamental principle of polyarchy – it not only made the government more effectively accountable to democratic control, but it also improved public administration by enabling the government to exercise
integrated control over all branches of the bureaucracy. By contrast, under
the proto-modern format of presidentialism, administrative control has to
be divided between the President, Congress, and the Courts. Precisely because no President under presidentialist rules has an assured majority in
Congress, he (or she) needs to concede power to members on matters not
central to executive policy. Hopefully, in exchange, the President will garner
enough votes to win on core issues.

Because members of Congress can call the shots on so many matters, their
ability to favor the interests that support their election and re-election becomes crucial. These interested parties, through their lobbyists, act to support and finance the election of those who will favor them. The effective
dispersal of bureaucratic power also means that public officials who are
employed to implement these policies have a stake in their perpetuation and
revision. As a result they are far more responsive to policies set in legislative
committees than they are to over-all policies set by the administration. A
third force that sometimes overrides both Presidential and Congressional
control arises when Courts invalidate laws as unconstitutional – but since
proper discussion of judicial review will take too much space, let me just
mention it as another factor that disrupts coherent polyarchic control of
public bureaucracy in presidentialist regimes.

When we compare the features of proto-modern presidentialism with
ortho-modern parliamentarism, we discover a striking paradox. The first

involves the status of legislatures:

- PARLIAMENTS are strong but their members are weak.
- CONGRESSES are weak but their members are strong.

The second involves the position of chief executive:

- PRESIDENTS are weak but invulnerable.
- PRIME MINISTERS are strong but vulnerable.

3.6. Discussion

By way of further explanation, consider that because, in presidentialist regimes, the office of Head of State is ceremonial and therefore basic for political legitimacy, it cannot be effective if it is vulnerable to political forces – hence the office must not be vulnerable to legislative responsibility. Clearly monarchs hold office for life, and elected presidents for a fixed term. Reciprocally, since the President in presidentialist regimes cannot be accountable to Congress, he/she cannot count on Congressional support. The consequence is that the office is invulnerable (cannot be removed by act of Congress) but weak (cannot count on Congressional support). As noted above, under parliamentarist rules, governments are able to expel from their party any members of Parliament who fail to support their policies. This is a double-edged sword: it is a way to assure support for government policies, yet it also undermines any government that loses its majority and hence must resign. It means, however, that so long as a parliamentarist government has a majority in parliament, it is able to exercise strong power, while individual members of Parliament lack independent power over public policies.

In sum, by splitting the functions of chief executive, it is possible in parliamentarist regimes to combine an invulnerable Head of State possessed of ceremonial authority with a vulnerable Prime Minister (PM) who has great political power so long as he/she can count on parliamentary support. When that support evaporates, the PM is ousted by parliamentary vote and replaced by someone else who can succeed. This support enables a PM, with assured cabinet support also, to shape policy over a wide spectrum, making the office powerful though vulnerable.

3.7. Iron Triangles

The administrative consequences of presidentialism have often been noted but not really explained. Because presidents must share power with members of Congress, many autonomous "empires" arise, each controlled by a legislative committee exercising power within its "special interest" domain. They can make policy and reward supporters, in alliance with the officials who benefit and help create these "iron triangles." At one corner of the triangle are interest groups (constituencies). These are the powerful interests that buy Congressional votes in their favor and which guarantee re-election for supporting their programs, using well-paid lobbyists as intermediaries. At another corner members of Congress sit who seek to align themselves with a constituency for political and electoral support. These Congressional members support legislation that advances the interest group's agenda. Occupying the third corner of the triangle are bureaucrats, who are often captured by those they are designed to regulate. The result is a three-way, stable alliance that is sometimes called a sub government because of its durability, impregnability and power to determine policy. Dan Brody's expose of the Carlyle Group provides a popular exposition of a spectacular example.[29]

A current example involving the pharmaceutical industry is discussed in a letter from House Speaker, Dennis Hastert to Democratic Leader, Pelosi and others on January 25, 2006. It calls for a Congressional investigation into the role played by the Alexander Strategy Group, a lobbying firm closely linked to Tom DeLay and Jack Abramoff, in the passage of the Medicare Prescription Drug Act and the drafting of the budget reconciliation bill currently before the Congress. The letter alleges that:

> We know from lobby disclosure forms that the largest single client of the Alexander Strategy Group was the pharmaceutical industry, which paid the small firm over $2.5 million, including nearly $1 million in 2003 when the prescription drug law was being written.[30]

Sad to say, these accounts describe the symptoms and lament the pathology without recognizing their constitutional foundations. Recent publicity about the machinations of Jack Abramoff received cover page attention in *Time Magazine* on January 9, 2006. Administrative implications are rife but the whole scandal is explained as a result of immoral behavior by the individuals involved, not as a symptom of the complex constitutional process which invites such operations. Yet it is just because of the power the system gives to members of Congress and their ability to reward beneficiaries, including the President, that lobbyists and the special interests that fund them, in collaboration with their bureaucratic allies, are both motivated and empowered to create such triangles of power.

3.8. Budgets

The weakness of the presidency is revealed by the inability of the chief executive to manage a national budget full of pork barrel appropriations and "add-ons" or "ear-marks" that increase the costs of government and favor special interests.[31] An analysis of Defense Department appropriations passed at the end of 2005 is illustrative. The practice is old and, although often portrayed as partisan, in fact favors any party in power as an essay on "ear-marking" in 2003 shows.[32]

By contrast, since members of parliament (MPs) are obligated to support (or oppose) cabinet policies that include comprehensive budget management, they lack the power to earmark appropriations for favored clients and special interest communities. This makes MPs individually weak. However, they are institutionally strong because they have the collective power to retain or oust the government.

3.9. Parochialism and Compartmentalization

Our inability to grasp the constitutional foundations of such problems reflects mainly our parochialism as displayed in the way we equate "Political Science" with its American version, and pin the "Comparative" label on the study of foreign polities. This blinkering factor is compounded by the way we compartmentalize academic disciplines. The study of government has become partitioned. Studies of the Constitution and the judicial branch of government are lodged in Law Schools, Political Science departments analyze the polyarchic structures of governance as manifest in the election and performance of politicians, and public administration focuses on the operations of hierarchies of appointed public servants. We are like the blind men feeling an elephant who all "see" quite different unrelated phenomena.

The dichotomy between the polyarchic and hierarchic dimensions of governance is also reflected in the professional dualism manifest in the separate organization of the American Political Science Association (APSA) and the American Society for Public Administration (ASPA). Each association pays scant attention to the counterpart dimension. The sub-field of Public Administration (PA) is studied in just one of 37 organized sections sponsored by APSA, and Law and the Courts by another.[33] All the other sections are concerned with matters relating to polyarchic (political) matters – as, no doubt, the term "Political" science indicates. The holistic study of "Government" has virtually vanished in American universities.

ASPA, of course, reciprocates – none of its 21 organized sections look at links between politics and administration or considers constitutional matters. Moreover, it is not surprising that all but one of these sections generalizes about public administration on the basis of American experience. The rest of the world is left to Section #1, Section on International Comparative Administration (SICA), which seeks to combine the fields of Comparative and International Administration.[34]

Neither APSA nor ASPA has a section that studies constitutional design and its implications for politics or administration. Moreover, the persistence of the dichotomy that separates the study of "Public Administration" from "Comparative PA" leads to irrational generalizations from the exceptional American case and conclusions based on experience elsewhere are often wrong because they are not checked against the very different American experience.

3.10. Paradigm Change

A more objective look at the global problems and phenomena of "Public Administration" needs to be based on comparative analysis of all countries. In short, the study of "Public Administration" in America needs a paradigm change. To be truly worthy, it must be comparative. Indeed, outside the United States, this is already the case. No Indian, German or Egyptian, studying "Public Administration" would use the term to refer to "PA in America." Everywhere except in America, Public Administration, as a field of scientific or objective analysis, is already comparative. No doubt specialists in any country naturally, focus on administration in that country, with a nation-specific qualifier. If Americans would insist on adding a qualifier, then the study of "American Public Administration" could properly be recognized as one of the many fields of application of the general study of "Public Administration." It will become what we now call Comparative Administration.

Sadly, however, this field already needs another paradigm shift. In our discourse so far we have presupposed nation states under some kind of polyarchic constitutional governance as the basic unit of analysis. Today, in the context of accelerating globalization, we need to see that many so-called "states" are fields of conflict more than domains of order. To gain a proper understanding of the impact of globalization, we need to think not only about the different models – proto-modern and ortho-modern discussed above – but also the clash between traditional monarchic models based on supernatural sovereignty and the modern idea of governance anchored in popular sovereignty. Very often, this clash has led to dictatorships and civil wars, even where constitutional formulas have been promulgated as a legitimizing fiction. The next section, #4, focuses on this theme. The final section, # 5, will look at the spread of overlapping organizations outside the framework of nation states, leading to further complications for the study of public administration.

4. CONTEMPORARY CRISES – CLASH OF MODELS AND THE RISE OF DICTATORSHIPS

Some of the new states created by collapsed empires have established viable constitutional democracies. Not surprisingly their citizens are mainly immigrants from Europe as in Australia, New Zealand and Canada. For the most part, however, countries composed mainly of conquered peoples have experienced dictatorships. Exceptionally, India has avoided this fate and been able to maintain democracy since it obtained independence in 1947, despite serious internal crises and wars, as reported in a BBC Chronology.[35] Another former colony that has maintained democratic self-government despite serious troubles is Jamaica.[36] However, most Jamaicans were also immigrants, though more from Africa than Europe.

4.1. Disorder

For the most part, however, the new states of the world have experienced serious difficulties in their efforts to govern themselves. Neither modern democratic processes for self-government nor traditional kingships worked for them. Regardless of which constitutional formula – proto- or ortho-modern – was adopted, it presupposed a sense of shared national identity and commitment to democratic values based on the acceptance of popular sovereignty that had not been established. Nor could traditional kingships function because they also require beliefs that had eroded. Many newly independent countries were composed of diverse people who had been linked by imperial conquests and united only by their resistance to the conquerors. Although tribal and clan identities often remained, these tended to divide rather than unite a country, and new religions like Christianity and Islam were rarely shared by everyone. Where they were, especially in some Islamic countries, believers rallied around leaders whose teachings repelled non-believers and created deep schisms.

Under such conditions, it was difficult to gain consensus on any traditional or modern formula for legitimate government, creating political vacuums that were filled, temporarily, by brute force. Military men or demagogues were able to mobilize coup groups or political machines able to seize power by force and stay in power by tyrannical means. No doubt traditional loyalties and beliefs survived, especially those based on the supernatural premises underlying sacred kingships, as well as tribal or clan identities. However, new concepts and classes generated by imperial rule, urbanization and migrations also flourished, clashing with traditional views and practices. In the chaotic conditions generated by these overlapping forces and beliefs, it was difficult to create a viable constitutional system and neither traditional nor modern could prevail.

A third force often arose on the basis of the imperial bureaucracies that had been created to manage conquered territories. They often survived and served new bosses but not in a homogeneous way. Especially when dictators came to power, the old bureaucrats faced critical choices. Some climbed on the bandwagon and stayed in office, whether for expedient self-interest or as loyal followers. A few rejected the dictators and fled, some coming to Europe or America as refugees where, in some cases, they were able to find new employment using their knowledge of languages and culture in their former homelands. Some also entered contradictory double lives, posing as willing accomplices of dictators while secretly conspiring to undermine or overthrow them. The dictators who came to power were generally ruthless and ambitious men relied on their ability to use violence, wealth and their own shrewd organizational and political skills. They typically needed and sought the help of former officials while adding personal followers to the bureaucracy. In many cases the dictators were themselves bureaucrats, especially military officers, but in a few they were politicians able to manipulate mass sentiments and wealth to gain power. After a brief historical comment, we will examine several different types of dictatorship and offer some illustrative data.[37]

4.2. History

The concept of a dictatorship is quite old and was originally viewed as a constitutionally justifiable way to deal with emergencies. In ancient Rome, in times of emergency, dictators were appointed by the Senate to rule, with sweeping authority, but their terms of office were limited to 6 months and financial limits were imposed. Historically, however, many regimes have suffered under the brutal control of one man, whether called pharaoh, king, emperor or president.[38] In modern times we use *dictator* rather broadly to refer to any ruler who governs authoritatively without benefit of constitutional norms, whether traditional or modern. They may be "kings" whose rule is rejected as illegal and arbitrary by their subjects, or "presidents" whose election was stage-managed by a ruling party or simply appropriated by a usurper following a *coup d'etat*. Descriptive terms like "tyrant," "despot" and "totalitarian" are often used for dictators, but each of these words has negative connotations that may or may not apply. Thus a dictator might be benevolent and hence not a tyrant or despot, and many dictators are not totalitarians because they are unable or unwilling to exercise comprehensive control over all aspects of life within their domain. Qualitative judgments are needed when using these terms, so they will not be used here.

Among dictators a broad distinction can be made between traditional and modern forms. Historically, monarchs benefited from the sacred rituals that legitimized their rule and put them above the law. They were not subject to countervailing powers, however, and this meant that they were free to abuse their powers and, as hereditary offices, they were not subject to evaluations before taking office. This meant that those who wanted to abuse their powers and rule in an arbitrary way were often able to do so.

Modern dictators lack the legitimacy conferred upon kings, which means that, after seizing power they may feel compelled to take brutal measures to defend themselves from their enemies. The way they proceed to gain and use power, however, differs according to structural criteria we may call "populist" and "bureaucratic." Populist dictators gain power on the basis of mass mobilization and elections managed by a ruling party – they are likely to be seen as totalitarians who seek to mobilize mass support to stay in power. By contrast, bureaucratic dictators are public officials who rely on the support of fellow bureaucrats, mainly military officers. They are likely to be viewed as despots who rely more on money, brutality and intrigue to extend their rule. A few examples of each type are offered below. After that, we will examine three possibilities that qualify the way dictators operate and help determine whether or not they will succeed. First, failure of dictators to govern effectively can lead to chronic civil war and *failed states* as we see in Somalia today. Second, some dictators are able to manipulate elections and/ or traditional institutions to mask their dictatorial practices with legitimating fronts – a classic example occurred in Thailand after the absolute monarchy was overthrown in 1932. Third, a peculiar paradox can also arise when traditionalists discover that they can use elections to gain public support for their efforts to come to power. All these possibilities confront public administration with horrendous difficulties and social costs.

4.3. Populist Dictatorships

Classic examples are provided by the Fascist regime in Italy under Benito Mussolini, the National Socialist period in Germany under Adolph Hitler, and the Communist system in the Soviet Union under Josef Stalin. All are well known with a readily available literature so we need say no more about them. However, some contemporary regimes follow these examples but there are not many of them.

4.3.1. North Korea

A good example can be found in North Korea under Kim Jong II who boasts that the Chollima Movement, which he leads, has "become a great revolutionary movement of millions of workers."[39]

Kim Jong II does not accept any supernatural legitimation of the North Korean regime but he promotes a new secular "religion" called "Juche." According to him,

> The Juche viewpoint and attitude to the world are truly revolutionary in that they enable men to transform the world and shape their destiny independently, creatively and consciously, with a high degree of awareness that they are masters of the world and their own destiny.[40]

Generally speaking, populist dictatorships are secular, reject supernatural sovereignty and espouse the rhetoric of democratic equalitarianism and justice for all. Although Marxist premises are evident, Juche presents itself as an original doctrine or ideology. In general we may conclude that populist dictatorships can promulgate quasi-religious doctrines to legitimize their rule even though they reject the supernatural basis for royal sovereignty found in traditional societies.

4.3.2. Iraq

Saddam Hussein's Baathist Party regime in Iraq may also be seen as a populist dictatorship.[41] The ideology of this party is explained in these words:

> The Baath movement in one country was considered merely an aspect of, or a phase leading to, "a unified democratic socialist Arab nation."

However, just as Stalin broke with CP universalism to develop communism in one country, so Saddam found it necessary to abandon the pan-Arab ideology in order to focus on Iraq. However, he did so in a brutal way that is described in the Aljazeera account thus:

> In one display of his brutality, Saddam stood in front of an audience of party members where he named several high-ranking Baathists who were quickly ushered out of the

auditorium and executed for allegedly planning a coup. The infamous speech was videotaped and used to strike fear in anyone who dared consider challenging Saddam's authority.[42]

A parallel history of the Baath by the BBC contains this comment:

> Though the Baath party was formally the institution that ruled Iraq, actual power, even in the early days, was in the hands of a narrow elite united by family and tribal ties, not ideology.[43]

Everyone knows about the problems confronting contemporary Iraq since the overthrow of Saddam as it seeks to link Kurds, Sunnis and Shi'a and develop patriotic loyalties to this artificial creation of British Imperialism.[44]

4.3.3. Other Cases

More familiar examples include China under Mao Tse Tung; Vietnam under Ho Chi Minh; and Cuba under Fidel Castro. These cases are so well known that no documentation is needed here, but we might add the observation that, over time, even a one-party system may soften, as it did in the Soviet Union and Eastern Europe before the Communist regimes collapsed.

No doubt each individual case has its own distinctive properties but all share the myth of democratic constitutionalism and use elections to select leaders. However, since a dominant party compels everyone to vote for official candidates, these systems offer only a façade of democratic equalitarianism. Without viable opposition parties, these regimes are dictatorships wearing a constitutional mask.

Administratively, populist dictatorships blur the lines between partisan and administrative roles. Members of the ruling party infiltrate the bureaucracy at all levels and it is not easy for anyone to determine whether they are acting to support party or public interests. Moreover, corruption in office is endemic because there are no truly independent sources of authority to monitor and control the conduct of public officials. Sometimes the regime creates secret police forces to protect its interests and monitor bureaucratic conduct, but their very secrecy makes this device difficult to assess. Although one might assume that strict party control over a regime would enhance administrative efficiency, in practice the reverse is true: corruption and the need to follow a party line undermine performance.

4.4. Bureaucratic Domination

The most common form of contemporary dictatorship is bureaucratic. Without troubling to mobilize a mass following, a small group of public officials led by military officers is able to conspire secretly and use brute force to assassinate and replace whoever is currently running a country. A group that has seized power by a *coup d'etat* can often rule by fear and force without either traditional or modern forms of sovereignty and legitimacy. Sometimes the dictator comes to power after a civil war in which one of the contending forces triumphs. Civil servants, facing the choice of supporting the military regime or disaster, often go along to save their lives and income, thereby giving the dictator an organizational infrastructure able to govern, however, corruptly or inefficiently that may be. The regime relies on coercion and fear rather than popular support and legitimacy. This means, however, that such dictators live in fear of assassination and unseen opponents, justifiably so as the violent history of these regimes demonstrate. No doubt this is an oversimplification of a process that has varied greatly in details yet replicated itself in many countries. Consider an example.

4.4.1. Nigeria

The basic historical experience of Nigeria is narrated by the BBC in a country profile. It notes, this country received its independence from the UK in 1960 as a parliamentarist regime under a civilian president heading a negotiated coalition government but it promptly encountered insuperable problems.[45] The first of seven coups took place in 1966, a second following in the same year, and others in 1975, 1976, 1983, 1985 and 1999. Lieutenant-General Olusegun Obasanjo, who seized power in 1976, was subsequently elected president in 1976 and introduced an American-style presidentialist system. However, he was overthrown by a coup in 1983. Further coups followed in 1985 and 1993. However, efforts to legitimize the regime continued and in 1999, Obasanjo was elected president again, and he was re-elected in 2003. The experience of this country illustrates the instability of bureaucratic dictatorships. Throughout the period since independence citizen movements, with the help of friendly foreign powers and voluntary agencies have kept up a continuing effort to re-legitimize the regime by holding elections.[46]

Following nearly 16 years of military rule, a new constitution was adopted in 1999, and a peaceful transition to civilian government was completed. The president faces the daunting task of reforming a petroleum-based economy, whose revenues have been squandered through corruption and mismanagement, and institutionalizing democracy. In addition, the Obasanjo administration must defuse longstanding ethnic and religious tension if it is to build a sound foundation for economic growth and political stability. Although the April 2003 elections were marred by some irregularities, Nigeria is currently experiencing its longest period of civilian rule since independence.[47]

There are, of course, a great many other countries that have also experienced many coups and conflicts with unstable and inefficient government but enough has been said to illustrate the problem. Let us look next at some of the problems that arise when not even a dictator is able to impose any semblance of order on a fractured and conflicted society.

4.5. Endemic War

In some states born from the collapse of imperial rule the forces of integration are so weak that all efforts to create a viable new state structure seem doomed to fail. Indeed, the term "failed state" is often used to refer to these countries. An extreme case can be found in Somalia where an inclusive Somali state was planned on the basis of a union of the former Italian and British colonies. Sadly, not all Somalis were actually included, and internal differences between them were not understood or cared for. As with many other new states, they were constituted by international agreements with scant reference to the capacity of local people and their leaders to form a viable state.[48]

From this source we learn that Britain and Italy granted independence to their respective sectors, enabling them to join as the Republic of Somalia on July 1, 1960 with an agreed-upon government for the new state. However, there was dissatisfaction because Somalis in neighboring Ethiopia and Kenya were not included. In 1977 Somalia backed rebels in easternmost Ethiopia's Ogaden Desert. The new state was defeated after 8 months of fighting, having lost much of its 32,000-man army and most of its tanks and planes. President Siad Barre fled the country in late January 1991. His departure left Somalia in the hands of a number of clan-based guerrilla groups, none of which trusted each other. The area formerly under British rule broke away and formed an unrecognized state they called Somaliland.[49] Several warlords set up their own mini-states in Puntland and Jubaland. Although internationally unrecognized, these states are reportedly peaceful but it is not easy to get reliable information.[50]

In countries like Somalia, endemic civil war has continued for a long time and some localities have created sub-states or split off to become new states, like Somaliland, which claims independence but has not yet been internationally recognized.

According to a BBC report:

In 2004, after protracted talks in Kenya, the main warlords and politicians signed a deal to set up a new parliament, which later appointed a president. The fledgling administration, the 14th attempt to establish a government since 1991, has no civil service or government buildings. It faces a formidable task in bringing reconciliation to a country divided into clan fiefdoms.[51]

A number of other failed states, especially in Africa, retain international recognition yet do not have any effective governments. Warlords and tribal leaders war with each other and sometimes maintain order within their own domains. It is not possible to identify and discuss them here.[52]

No doubt there are many other good places to look for this information but these suffice for present purposes. They show how difficult it has been to establish peaceful and viable states in the countries that have evolved following the collapse of the great empires.

4.6. Parties of Traditionalists

To cope with anarchy and promote democratic self-government, the United States, the UN and many internationalists have provided technical assistance and financial subventions to facilitate the growth of political parties and electoral systems. No doubt they have often been successful, but sometimes they produce a surprising amalgam of traditional and modern ideas. Consider Palestine where recent (2006) elections have produced a victory for Hamas (the Palestine Liberation Movement). Its charter, published in 1988, provides an elaborate exposition of the religious basis for its activities.[53] The thrust of this movement can be learned from its opening paragraphs.

4.6.1. Hamas Charter (1988)
Article One: The Ideological Aspects

The Islamic Resistance Movement draws its guidelines from Islam; derives from it its thinking, interpretations and views about existence, life and humanity; refers back to it for its conduct; and is inspired by it in whatever step it takes.

Article Two: The Link between Hamas and the Association of Muslim Brothers

The Islamic Resistance Movement is one of the wings of the Muslim Brothers in Palestine. The Muslim Brotherhood Movement is a world organization, the largest Islamic Movement in the modern era. It is characterized by a profound understanding, by precise notions and by a complete comprehensiveness of all concepts of Islam in all domains of life: views and beliefs, politics and economics, education and society, jurisprudence and rule, indoctrination and teaching, the arts and publications, the hidden and the evident, and all the other domains of life.

Their opposition to international initiatives for peace that include acceptance of Israel is expressed in:

> Article Thirteen: Peaceful Solutions, [Peace] Initiatives and International Conferences
> [Peace] initiatives, the so-called peaceful solutions, and the international conferences to resolve the Palestinian problem, are all contrary to the beliefs of the Islamic Resistance Movement. For renouncing any part of Palestine means renouncing part of the religion; the nationalism of the Islamic Resistance Movement is part of its faith, the movement educates its members to adhere to its principles and to raise the banner of Allah over their homeland as they fight their Jihad... the Islamic Resistance Movement, which is aware of the [prospective] parties to this conference, and of their past and present positions towards the problems of the Muslims, does not believe that those conferences are capable of responding to demands, or of restoring rights or doing justice to the oppressed. Those conferences are no more than a means to appoint the nonbelievers as arbitrators in the lands of Islam.

On January 26, 2006, the *New York Times* reported:

> With discipline and a well-financed campaign to turn out its faithful, the Islamic group Hamas scored an overwhelming victory in legislative elections, taking 76 out of 132 seats, with the former governing faction, Fatah, winning only 43.

We see here a striking example of the clash between tradition and modernity: a movement fully committed to traditional sacred concepts of governance has accepted the polyarchic electoral process and won a popular victory. Will Hamas now move toward accommodations with Israel, the United States, the UN and the rest of the secularized world, or insist on its exclusive vision based on deeply held religious convictions? It is hard to see how a peaceful polyarchic regime can evolve when such contradictory positions confront each other.[54]

The perplexing seriousness of this development has caused global concern. It highlights what may be a growing phenomenon, the ability of traditional religious groups to manipulate modern technology and electoral processes to create regimes that support their agendas. The outcome antagonizes non-believers in their own countries and provokes ambivalent international responses. The results resemble the seizure of power by dictators, but when they are accomplished through popular elections, it is hard not to accept them as legitimate. Populist dictators, as noted above, learned long ago how to manipulate elections to bring their factions to power. Their ideologies were essentially secular, however, as most recently illustrated by North Korea's Juche movement explained above. The Hamas victory in Palestine repeats similar episodes in other Middle Eastern countries where mass support for religiously oriented parties have flourished, sometimes leading the United States and others to support dictators whose efforts to suppress dissent have, unfortunately, helped fuel the rise of religious opposition parties.

4.7. Complementary Facades

Dictators have often paid lip service to legitimate sources of authority to win popular support for their arbitrary rule. In an increasingly interlocked global context, political leaders whose local power is weak may depend on international support to maintain and extend their authority. To illustrate a variety of possibilities, three countries may be singled out for comment: Thailand, Iran and Afghanistan. All of them have retained their formal independence throughout the modern era's history of imperial conquests so their situations are exceptional.

A number of other third world countries also maintained their formal independence throughout all or most of the modern period: Ethiopia, Egypt, Bhutan, but the list is short. All of them were seriously affected by Western ideas and influences and have suffered disruptions and dictatorships as have the countries that came under imperial rule. Bhutan was the most successful in retaining its traditional institutions as mentioned above, but even this country is now experiencing global impacts as evident from its official web site.[55]

4.7.1. Thailand
An early and classic case can be seen in Thailand where, traditionally, an absolute monarch anchored in Buddhist beliefs ruled with sacred authority. The revolution of 1932 brought an end to absolutism but not to the monarchy which survived by accepting a compromise based on the acceptance of parliamentary principles. The result, however, was a military dictatorship created by coup leaders who proceeded to put up a double façade: retain the monarchy as a front to appease traditionalists and create an elected parliament to placate the secularized urban modernists. It was this example that led me to think of the prismatic model as a prototype for similar transitions taking place in many other new states of the third world.[56]

The Thai case was exceptional among third world countries in that it was never conquered. This meant that the monarchy was still loved and honored by most Thai people even after it lost its absolute power.

At the same time, the urban population, especially in Bangkok, was seriously influenced by Western ideas, and this was particularly true of public officials. The new military rulers who seized power in 1932 accepted these realities and so they compromised with the King and permitted him to retain the throne though without effective power, and at the same time they established an elected Parliament but appointed military officers and civil servants to fill half its seats. Thereby they knew they could also control the legislature. Thus, rather exceptionally, the Thai dictatorship set up a double façade to shield its arbitrary exercise of power: it appeased traditionalists by keeping the monarchy and it wooed modernists by creating a puppet assembly.

Nevertheless, military rule proved unstable and a series of dictators ruled the country. It experienced 17 coups before effective parliamentary rule was established in 1992. There were several aborted efforts to replace military with civilian rule during this period. Gradually, the forces favoring democracy came to prevail.[57]

4.7.2. Iran (Persia)

Quite a different scenario is reported for Iran. Under Mohammed Reza Shah Pahlavi, government pursued modernizing policies with strong support from the US and UK, but alienated growing numbers of Iranians. They finally revolted and a traditionalist regime was established in 1979 in the form of a republic dominated by clericals under the leadership of Ayatollah Khomeini. The electoral system, under strict controls, has produced reforms, but the latest round in 2005 brought to power an ardent traditionalist, Mahmoud Ahmadnejad. He is a religious conservative who links Islamist and populist views. Islamist movements seek to re-shape the state by implementing a conservative formulation of Sharia, views not shared by many Muslims who reject Islamist fundamentalism. Ahmadnejad also has modernist training as a civil engineer and he was an assistant professor at the Iran University of Science and Technology.[58] He combines western education with a Ph.D. in engineering, revolutionary activism and religious fervor.

Ahmadnejad's presidency constitutes a double-façade. In his presidential role, it is a façade using modernist electoral democracy to sustain a traditionalist autocracy while defying the outside world by developing nuclear power, allegedly for peaceful purposes. A report about him from the Arab point of view can be found in the Beirut-based *Dar Al-Hayat*. It reads, in part:

> Ahmadi-Nejad's campaign themes were social justice for the poor, the redistribution of Iran's oil wealth, a crackdown on corruption in high places and a return to the traditional values and the "spiritual purity" of the 1979 Islamic Revolution. His website was called mardomyar – "friend of the people."[59]

His effective power is constrained, however, because the Iranian presidency is also a façade for the higher authority of the "Supreme Leader of Iran," Ayatollah Ali Khamanei, whose constitutional powers surpass those of the elected president.

> His functions include commander-in-chief of the armed forces and control of the Islamic Republic's intelligence and security operations; he alone can declare war. He has the power to appoint and dismiss the leaders of the judiciary, the state radio and television networks, and he is the supreme commander of the Islamic Revolutionary Guard Corps.[60]

4.7.3. Afghanistan

This country was never annexed but it retained its independence as a buffer zone between the Russian and British spheres of interest and, as such, acquired artificial boundaries that patched together a set of incompatible tribal societies. After the Taliban "dictatorship" with traditionalist content, it now has a popularly elected president under U.S. tutelage with hopes of gaining power and coping with strong local factions based on clan and traditional loyalties.[61]

This is a multi-lingual expatriate web site with commercial funding that offers fairly objective information about Afghanistan. Whether or not the administration of President Hamid Karzai is an effective national government remains in question. An influential web site notes about his tribal affiliation:

> The Popolzai are the Pashtoon clan of Ahmad Shah Durrani, the Persian army commander who conquered the southern Afghan city of Kandahar and in 1747 became the first king of Afghanistan. Because tribal position is of great importance in Afghan society, the mujahideen always trusted the Westernized and moderate Karzai. The same went for the Taliban, who sought him out long before they seized power and later offered him the post of United Nations ambassador.[62]

Local and tribal identities remain entrenched in much of the country, but Karzai bridges many divides, internal and international. His administration seems as adept at managing facades as did that of the Thai rulers noted above.

4.8. Zones of Uncertainty

To summarize our argument in this section, we have argued that the collapse of global empires in the mid-twentieth century launched a period of wrenching transformations throughout the third world. A host of new countries gained their independence and joined the United Nations.[63]

The contemporary phase of globalization is spurred by the global extension of the UN system and the rise of American power (following the collapse of the Soviet Union) as the world's only super-power.

All these states are encouraged to adopt international standards and develop modern democratic institutions, but obviously many fail and dictatorships of various kinds, as noted above, have emerged.

Global influences are felt by every country, coming through many channels. Among them are many technical assistance and development programs that focus on administrative (bureaucratic) reform as an independent process divorced from its constitutional context. Dealing with political and constitutional structure is considered too sensitive for direct intervention. Yet, if a bureaucracy, especially its military components, is strengthened while the political system designed to direct and control its policies is not well formed, the unintended result may be that the polity collapses and in the power vacuum that results, public officials (especially military officers) are empowered. Not intentionally, no doubt, but unintentionally, and with dire consequences bureaucratic domination most assuredly leads to dictatorships. Moreover, when appointed officials rule a country, their ability to monitor and sanction other officials is inhibited and corruption and abuses flourish.

In our optimism, we have tended to visualize "development" as a universal process and imagined that the peaceful and incremental growth of democratic institutions, supported by efficient bureaucracies inherited from former imperial masters, would surely occur in most countries. In my own thinking about this process, after having studied events in several new states, I found the "prismatic model" helpful as a way of visualizing turbulent transitions from traditional "fused" systems of governance where religion, economy and politics were seen as mere aspects of a single gestalt or whole, to modern "diffracted" polities in which a host of separate but coordinated and functionally specific institutions could evolve and function autonomously.

In the prismatic model, a state is captured by ambitious cliques or tyrants ruling arbitrarily and violently with scant respect for the rule of law – i.e. as dictators. Usually, dictators come to power through the bureaucratic apparatus created under imperial rule, typically as part of its military component, although they are sometimes able to lead a single party to power on the basis of mass mobilization and totalitarian tactics. They manipulate both traditional and modern criteria of legitimacy to build support for their own arbitrary actions.[64]

As my research on Thailand revealed, when a regime is dominated by a bureaucratic coup group, appointed officials come to play a dominant role in policy making as well as implementation, generating huge conflicts of interest and many opportunities for corruption. Admittedly one cannot generalize from a single case study, but hypotheses based on this research have been tested elsewhere and found to have widespread validity. An evaluative essay by Howard McCurdy provides some background data on the origins of the prismatic theory and its relevance to understanding contemporary administrative problems in third world countries.[65]

Admittedly the prismatic model was an over-generalized image, but it seemed to capture key features of a global process in which every individual case has its own unique and highly variable characteristics. However, the main defect I now see in the prismatic model was that it presupposed the existence of states as relatively stable units of analysis. It failed to take into account the pervasive waves of globalization that have continuously penetrated contemporary states, many of which are merely imagined constructs or "failed states." The dynamics of change within each state were shaped by a combination of domestic and external forces. These pressures were complicated and often conflicted with competing domestic pressures based on the clash of traditional and modern values and practices.

So varied are these patterns that we abandon efforts to generalize about them and resort to idiographic case studies treating every case as truly exceptional and intelligible only on the basis of local forces and historical events. Yet, in the context of globalization, it seems necessary and possible to think about a broader global framework in which we can understand governance as a generic process that takes a wide variety of forms under the impact of overlapping and competing jurisdictions in today's world. We may close this essay by taking a quick look at some of these dimensions.

5. FUTURE GOVERNANCE – ERASING THE STATE/NON-STATE DIVIDE

Traditionally, we have been accustomed to think about public administration as a function of nation-states in which government employees were agents working under mandates from the political system. Globalization has erased the boundary between state and non-state actors in ways that confuse our understanding of what is "public" administration by contrast both with private administration and politics. Again, the American model and our presidentialist regime provide benchmarks and a basis for comparison. However, the phenomena are ubiquitous on a global scale and in all countries.

In the U.S., iron triangles epitomize the phenomenon inasmuch as government officials, working hand-in-glove with members of Congress and private corporations, form complexes in which the public-private divide can scarcely be found. Moreover, increasingly non-profit organizations are engaged in public service functions that complement or even duplicate governmental operations. The use of private contractors working for government as though they were state employees has also become endemic. The armed forces provide extreme examples where all kinds of operations that could have been performed by government are actually carried out by private enterprises working for government.

5.1. Military Administration

Speaking of the armed forces reminds us that even for American public administration, the scope of inquiry has normally been restricted to open civilian agencies. The military establishment is one of the largest and most powerful arms of public administration and needs to be included in any comprehensive framework for our field of study. True as this is for the U.S., it is even more important in most third world countries where, all too often, the armed forces dominate the government for reasons explained above in Section 2, dealing with historical perspectives. There is no shortage of information about the operations of agencies in the U.S. Department of Defense.[66] Thousands of resources provide information about the role of the military in public administration.

No doubt there are historical reasons for this blind spot in the American tradition of public administration studies, but if the field is to mature as a comprehensive comparative field of teaching and research, the role of military and security agencies need to be included.[67]

5.2. State Governments

Another essential limitation of American public administration has been its preoccupation with national government. In the federal system, there are, of course, 50 sovereign states and the word, "state" is used ambiguously to refer to them as well as to the whole federal system.[68] Dependent governments outside the federal system are listed separately and include: American Samoa, District of Columbia, Guam, Northern Mariana Islands, Puerto Rico, Tribal Governments, U.S. Virgin Islands. The category of "tribal governments" includes a host of sites for the regimes sustained by many different tribes in the U.S.[69]

5.3. International Comparisons

Most studies of American public administration are predominantly concerned with the administration of civilian agencies in the U.S. Federal Government. Thus they scarcely look at the widely diverse practices of sub-governments within the U.S. system. If we were to add comparisons with local governments at all levels in all countries of the world, the scope of comparison would be vastly increased – most of them have web sites with good starting points for analysis. Is that possible? A good place to look is the CIA's *World Factbook*.[70]

In addition, the U.S. State Department maintains in archival form a list of independent states with information about each, as of January 2001 – but it has not updated these data. However, they provide a good starting point that can be supplemented from other sources.[71]

Its definition of "countries" is broad and includes polities that are not internationally recognized – Taiwan, for example, is a de facto though not de jure state, and Somalia is listed, a de jure state that is actually a zone of anarchy. An interesting side-list includes all the dependencies administered by world powers from Australia to the U.S.[72]

5.4. World Organizations

At the international level, a highly complex and extensive list of linked organizations can be found in the UN System. All of them have complex administrative structures that are not well described. Each involves many linkages with other international organizations and with states and non-governmental organizations.

As for the NGOs, those that have an official relationship with the UN system are listed separately for each international organization, starting with the UN. A chart depicting their relationships in schematic form is widely available.[73]

The complex intermixture of public and private organizations, national and international, is well illustrated in emergency situations like the earthquake in Pakistan, tsunami off Sumatra or the hurricane that struck New Orleans. International organizations, private charities, government agencies and every kind of public/private mixture are all mixed up together. No doubt such intermingling or structures is an old phenomenon but globalization has intensified the phenomenon and made it more visible and pervasive. Consider a few examples or indicators. For example, the Group of 77 provides a starting point.

As the largest Third World coalition in the UN, the Group of 77 provides the means for the developing world to articulate and promote its collective economic interests and enhance its joint negotiating capacity. The year 2005 was loaded with continuous and intensive activity for the Group of 77 and China. The Group engaged in lengthy discussions and negotiations on important fundamental questions related to development co-operation, its place within the UN system, the institutions and focus of global management, the international policy environment, the flow of financial resources and institutional reform in the international system.[74]

5.5. Global Complexity

Another UN-based organization whose activities have generated widespread interest and criticism is the UN Oil-for-Food operation involving Iraq. This program has been widely criticized.[75] For example a harsh critic of the program's administration Stephen F. Hayes, writing in the *Weekly Standard*, May 27, 2005 charged:

> The details of the Oil-for-Food scandal – who participated, and what they apparently did – are jaw-dropping. Vladimir Putin's chief of staff, Alexander Voloshin, appears to have accepted millions of dollars in oil-soaked bribes from Saddam Hussein. The same appears to be true of the former interior minister of France, Charles Pasqua, a close friend of President Jacques Chirac. And the same appears to be true of three high-ranking U.N. executives including Benon Sevan, handpicked by Kofi Annan to administer the Oil-for-Food program. Oil-for-Food money even went to terrorist organizations supported by the Iraqi regime and, according to U.S. investigators, might be funding the insurgency today.[76]

5.6. Katrina Disaster

A purely domestic issue in the U.S. that generated international interest and involvement was created by the hurricane Katrina. Global interest stimulated many international organizations to offer assistance.[77] The organizations numbering above 30 reveal global connectedness. On their numerous Internet links, the organizations "network for good." For example, Oxfam has been widely influential in provision of relief services. Oxfam pronounced its role:

> In response to the tsunami that struck East Asia in 2004, Oxfam will assist more than one million people, providing both emergency aid and long-term assistance to rebuild their communities. Elsewhere, Oxfam will conduct relief operations as needed– across West Africa, in southern Africa, and in response to Hurricane Katrina, right here in the US.[78]

Any number of excellent examples could be selected from this list. They all suggest complex administrative problems of managing complexity, linking public and private agencies with overlapping concerns at national and international levels around the world.

5.7. Individual Initiatives

The proliferation of overlapping and interlocked organizations, public and private, is further compounded by the enhanced role individuals now play in the world. A major factor is the spread of the Internet. It is now possible for anyone to become a global actor, to use blogs and lists to mobilize others who share their concerns.[79] Blogs deal with a wide range of themes and topics but anyone looking for administrative implications can find them.

Here is an excerpt from a current blog posted on December 4, 2005 by A. Vinegas at:

> Senator Byron Dorgan said at the Democratic Policy Committee Hearing on Iraq Contracting Practices (Feb. 2004): ...what are we to make of reports that Halliburton charged $2.64 a gallon to import gasoline into Iraq from Kuwait – resulting in over-charges well over $100 million? Or that Halliburton employees took up to $6 million in kickbacks to funnel subcontracts to particular Kuwaiti companies? Or that Halliburton over-charged $28 million for meals served to troops in Iraq? That, in just one month, that same company billed the US Army for 42,000 meals per day, when it had served only 14,000 meals? It seems to me that these incidents may well reflect a broad mindset: one that was born on the day that these contracts were awarded without competition, and that was nurtured through a lack of oversight by this current Administration and majority-controlled Congress.[80]

Another example of an individual actor provoking widespread interest is Jack Abramoff. He became a key actor in a set-up described in a *Washington Post* article describing the origins of the K Street Strategy and how it relied on lobbyist funding to promote special interests through favorable legislation and partisan support and used money and favors to achieve its goals.[81]

A key player was Jack Abramoff whose activities and role are described at various blogs.[82] Without discussing the details, we may just note that they shed light on the complex interplay of money, politics and public administration as they enmesh each other in Washington, nationally, and globally. Media reports shed much light on these matters, but the new technology of blogs on the Internet permits many individuals with personal knowledge to share information – and, no doubt, personal biases. Blogs make extensive use of hyperlinks, which can guide readers to a wide range of interlocking news and comments also posted on the web. As a bibliographic tool, web links are far more efficient than paper-based documentation via footnotes that require users to hunt painfully through libraries of books and journals to find related information.

Of course, there are also great search engines that enable interested observers to retrieve a host of relevant sites on almost any matter. The most widely used these days is Google which lets any web master post its engine on their web site – or even on a cell phone to carry in one's pocket – thereby making global information instantly available to readers at any time.[83]

It is unnecessary to pursue this subject further but the main point should be clear: it is now possible for any individual concerned in any way about public events to reach wide audiences and to mobilize others with a shared interest and point of view. What, then, shall we conclude about the impact of all these organized entities and even individuals and informal groups as factors affecting public administration? Perhaps some concluding observations can help us see how this vast multiplicity of entities in the world today do and can interact with each other. Two concepts discussed above will help us: through polyarchy a host of actors can select representatives to coordinate and mediate their concerns and manage administrative bureaucracies to administer them; and simultaneously many autonomous actors can negotiate with each other through means discussed above under panarchy.

5.8. Polyarchy vs. Panarchy

The distinction between panarchy and polyarchy is not well understood yet it underlines a basic struggle that persists and helps explain a fundamental paradox in modern governance. The panarchic ideal recognizes the need for governance but seek to minimize its role, relying as much as possible on libertarian ideals count on market mechanisms and voluntary cooperation among people committed to non-violence and humane ideals. As Rosenau defined it, panarchy permits such an extensive disaggregation of authority as to allow for much greater flexibility, innovation, and experimentation.

The ideal of panarchy is well expressed in the design of the World Trade Organizations (WTO) whose

> ... agreements cover goods, services and intellectual property. They spell out the principles of liberalization, and the permitted exceptions. They include individual countries' commitments to lower customs tariffs and other trade barriers, and to open and keep open services markets.[84]

A host of serious problems have evolved because of the increased global flow of goods and services resulting from free trade. They have generated more interest in developing global polyarchy whereby, through global collective action and emphasis on social justice, programs designed to regulate markets and compensate those who have suffered will be enacted.

The International Labour Organization provides an expression of this polyarchic perspective. As announced on its web site, it formulates:

> ... international labour standards in the form of Conventions and Recommendations setting minimum standards of basic labour rights: freedom of association, the right to organize, collective bargaining, abolition of forced labour, equality of opportunity and treatment, and other standards regulating conditions across the entire spectrum of work related issues.[85]

In December 2004, the UN General Assembly unanimously endorsed the report of the ILO World Commission Report on Fair Globalization, which includes this paragraph:

> There is an urgent need to rethink current institutions of global economic governance, whose rules and policies it says are largely shaped by powerful countries and powerful players. The unfairness of key rules of trade and finance reflect a serious "democratic deficit" at the heart of the system. The failure of policies, it argues, is due to the fact that market-opening measures and financial and economic considerations have consistently predominated over social ones, including measures compatible with the prerogatives of international human rights law and the principles of international solidarity.[86]

These issues of polyarchy and panarchy are now globally pervasive and confront administrators, public and private, in all parts of the world and its many organized units. They can no longer be understood at a parochial or national level because they are global in extent and, of course they apply to private as well as public organizations.

5.9. Terrorism and Anarchy

Our reliance on both polyarchy and panarchy to effect cooperation among independent actors runs into a monumental problem when some individuals or groups become so angry and impatient that they resort to terrorism. Current events in Iraq have put this issue on central stage. The current bloody "war" against "terrorism" is not, like past wars, an inter-state conflict but a struggle against global forces that operate outside of any state and in any state.[87]

This site is maintained by the Terrorism Research Center Inc., a private organization founded in 1996 to conduct research on: *terrorism, information warfare and security, critical infrastructure protection, homeland security and other issues of low-intensity political violence and gray-area phenomena.*[88]

Malignant anarchy has now become a global phenomenon, but advocates of benign anarchy stress the potential for peaceful coexistence, both within states and internationally. An organized group promoting the reduction of administrative controls over individuals and organizations is the Libertarian Party.[89] Their views are expressed in this declaration of goals:

> we're in favor of lowering taxes, slashing bureaucratic regulation of business, and char-
> itable – rather than government– welfare. We're active in all 50 states, have more than
> 200,000 registered voters and more than 600 people in office, which is more than all other
> third parties combined.[90]

This is not to say that Libertarians will triumph politically, but rather to illustrate the appeal of anarchist ideas. Can they apply at the global level? In a synarchic world, is it possible to reconcile the need for order and social control with the appeal of individualism and autonomy?

5.10. Global Governance

For inter-state relations we have long had to deal with global anarchy, but the rise of the UN and its host of linked organizations is a giant move toward global governance. However, the system remains more panarchic than polyarchic. Nevertheless, democratic regimes do not make war against each other though they are drawn into wars against dictatorships. The spread of viable democratic governance is, therefore, a valid goal for creating a peaceful world. But it needs to have a polyarchic overhead system of governance. How can that be done?

In order to achieve this goal we need to think first about how to design democracies that are stable and effective. What fundamental rules or constitutional systems will be most likely to facilitate the organization of these efforts? The challenge for development is not just to find ways to manage affairs responsibly in third world countries but even in the most developed countries, like the United States, the world's most immense super-power. How can we re-shape its constitutional, political and administrative practices to best meet the growing problems of our world system? We surely need to think seriously about the problems inherent in the proto-modern presidentialist constitution that was designed in the 18th century and consider the experience of other democracies that have embraced a more modern parliamentary model.

This is not only important for Americans at home, but it poses issues in foreign affairs where the U.S. is actively engaged in promoting democratic governance and very often, without much critical assessment, also promotes constitutional designs that follow the American model. Further thoughts on this matter can be found in my paper on "The American Myth as a Global Model."[91]

Globalization now also confronts us with increasingly urgent problems created by global diasporization. Increasingly, citizens of any country are now living in many countries – or migrating among them. Absentee balloting is widely practiced which means that Americans living anywhere in the world can vote in U.S. elections – and citizens of other countries often do the same in their own nations. What implications does this have for the management of democratic governance? Elsewhere I have suggested that we use the bi-cameral principle to support group representation in one chamber while retaining individual representation in the other.[92]

This idea is grounded in the structure of the UN General Assembly, which represents states, not individuals, and efforts are being made to create a World Parliament for a Federation of Earth.[93]

They have not succeeded so far, but a successful prototype can be found in the design of the European Union. Its Council of Ministers (representing states) shares power with a Parliament (representing all the citizens of Europe).[94]

5.11. Glocalization

The goal of international organizations will increasingly be to encourage local diversity and uniqueness while also facilitating all forms of cooperation between states, localities, individuals and groups that move among them. "Localization" is sometimes used to refer to the development of local socio-political structures and practices, but this is an ancient process that globalization has profoundly affected, even transformed. We need, therefore, a new term to represent the development of localities in response to globalization. Actually, a word has already been proposed that can serve this purpose. It is "glocalization." This neologism was coined to refer to strategies adopted by global corporations to succeed in widely scattered domains by means of locally sensitive adaptations. This is a top-down version of glocalization, spinning from the global to the local. It refers to corporate policies that create products or services intended for the global market, but are customized to suit a local culture. The word was introduced to English readers by Roland Robertson on the basis of earlier Japanese usage.[95]

"Glocalization" can also have a related sense that recognizes countervailing pressure, which take the form of local responses to global forces, a bottom-up process. No doubt both the top-down and bottom-up process occur and they complement each other. Here, however we need to stress the latter: increasingly highly divergent but potent strategies (whether beneficent or malignant) are adopted by local leaders and tyrants, all of whom seek to carve out zones of autonomy for their own ambitions and also find ways to succeed or survive in the face of increasingly pervasive global forces. The outcome of glocalization is growing diversity. If globalization leads to homogenization, as many fear, we might anticipate a world system pervaded by sameness. However, a more realistic image of the globalized world is a highly heterogeneous system in which a wide range of local variations prevails precisely because of pressures generated by the world system.

Terrorism and anarchy can be seen as manifestations of glocalization. However, instead of relying on violence and power to overcome global pressures, a safer and more effective strategy can be based on the design of constitutional structures that respect and protect local diversity while assuring everyone a safe and respected place in the world system. The design of constitutional structures that go beyond simple parliamentarism to introduce group as well as individual representation, and provide support for diasporans living outside their homelands may be part of the solution. Thereby the contradictions of global synarchy will be resolved first by better administration of the polyarchy of overlapping international organizations, and second by converting malignant to benign anarchy through the evolution of global panarchy.

Increasingly administrators working for private as well as public organizations, at the international, national and local levels will all have to face these issues. They involve overcoming dictatorships and giving everyone a secure niche in regimes that are both polyarchically representative and panarchically peaceful in their willingness to cooperate globally. Public administration as it evolves in a global and comparative context will need to understand and confront the challenges posed by global synarchy.

NOTES

1. http://www.unsystem.org/
2. See encyclopedia, http://encarta.msn.com/encnet/features/dictionary/Dictionary Results.aspx?refid = 1861585434
3. http://dwardmac.pitzer.edu/anarchist_archives/kropotkin/britanniaanarchy.html
4. http://dwardmac.pitzer.edu/dward/classes/Anarchy/anarchyinternet98.html
5. List available at http://dwardmac.pitzer.edu/Anarchist_Archives/aboutus.html
6. http://www.anarchist-studies.org/

7. For a comprehensive list, please see http://www.anarkismo.net/docs.php?id = 1. An extended list of anarchist writings can also be found at: http://dmoz.org/Society/Politics/Anarchism/Theory/

8. http://www.butterbach.net/prolong.htm; Another comprehensive bibliography of web site that relate to anarchy and panarchy can be found at:http://www.panarchy.org/

9. http://www.iue.it/Personal/Researchers/Andreev/COD/zara/idem/polyarchy.html; Robert Alan Dahl, *Democracy and its Critics* (New Haven: Yale University Press, 1989).

10. Available at http://www.polyarchy.org/manifesto/english/present.future.html# polyarchy. Another perspective is illustrated by works cited by the Liberty Fund: http://www.libertyfund.org/about.htm

11. For a discussion by Gilbert Pleuger on the history and meanings of this word see: http://www.history-ontheweb.co.uk/concepts/dictatorship43.htm

12. For additional details, visit http://65.66.134.201/cgi-bin/webster/webster.exe? search_for_texts_web1828 = synarchy

13. The Catholic Encyclopedia is available at: http://www.newadvent.org/cathen/11451b.htm

14. Since Tibet today is under Chinese rule, we cannot find an independent web site in Tibet, but a Chinese explanation is available at: http://www.tibet-tour.com/tibet/reincarnation.html

15. Dalai Lama, in exile, posts a beautiful web site with much useful information but no account of the reincarnation tradition: http://www.dalailama.com/

16. No web site depicts Bhutan's traditional structure and outlook, but an official news site is available that provides a Westernized view of the contemporary scene: http://www.bhutannewsonline.com/monarchy.html; See also views from émigrés on Tourism in Bhutan available at: http://www.bootan.com/bhutan/bhutan.shtml

17. His work is evaluated and extended by reference to anthropological studies in many parts of the world in Sasaki Kokan's *Priest, Shaman, King*: http://www.nanzan-u.ac.jp/SHUBUNKEN/publications/jjrs/pdf/313.pdf. An essay on Sacred Kingship to be found in the *Encyclopedia Britannica* contains an extended bibliography on the subject reproduced at: http://www.britannica.com/eb/article-38733. My own reflections on this subject, drawing heavily on Hocart, can be found in a 1996 paper. http://www2.hawaii.edu/~fredr/6-lap9e.htm#top

18. http://www.ancientdays.net/sonsofgod.htm; A. M. Hocart, *Kingship* (Oxford University Press: H. Milford, 1927), p. 7.

19. An online version of the *Reader's Companion to American History* is available at: http://college.hmco.com/history/readerscomp/rcah/html/ah_074800_republicanis.htm. See Eric Foner and John Arthur Garraty, *The Reader's Companion to American History* (Boston: Houghton-Mifflin, 1991).

20. http://encarta.msn.com/dictionary_1861603633/democracy.html

21. Frederic Schaffer at: http://www.concepts-methods.org/working_papers/20050909_02_PC%207%20Schaffer.pdf

22. http://www.archives.gov/national-archives-experience/charters/constitution_transcript.html

23. http://www.firstgov.gov/Citizen/Topics/PublicSafety/Hurricane_Katrina_Recovery.shtml

24. http://www.cato.org/pubs/policy_report/v25n1/llosa.pdf

25. http://en.wikipedia.org/wiki/Constitutional_monarch#Constitutional_Monarchy

26. http://en.wikipedia.org/wiki/Constitutional_monarch#Constitutional_Monarchy

27. http://en.wikipedia.org/wiki/Prime_Minister_of_the_United_Kingdom#History

28. http://webdata.soc.hawaii.edu/fredr/taipei.htm

29. Dan Brody, http://www.wiley.com/WileyCDA/WileyTitle/productCd-0471281085.html

30. The full text can be found in: http://www.truthout.org/docs_2006/012506Q.shtml

31. http://www.elitestv.com/pub/2005/Dec/EEN43a8ccb8323be.html

32. http://www.commondreams.org/headlines03/1208-11.htm

33. http://www.apsanet.org/section_300.cfm

34. http://www.aspanet.org/scriptcontent/Index_listing_page.cfm

35. http://news.bbc.co.uk/1/hi/world/south_asia/country_profiles/3020583.stm

36. http://news.bbc.co.uk/1/hi/world/americas/country_profiles/1191049.stm

37. An excellent source of data for most countries of the world up to 1998 can be found in the handbooks posted by the U.S. Library of Congress as part of the Country Studies/Area Handbook Series. See, http://countrystudies.us/

38. A summary can be found in the *Encyclopaedia Brittannica* at: http://www.britannica.com/ebi/article-209000 and at http://dictatorship.biography.ms/

39. http://www.korea-dpr.com/history41.htm

40. This quotation is taken from a statement by Kim posted at: http://www3.cnet-ta.ne.jp/j/juche/pdf/e-works2.pdf; The philosophy of Juche is promoted internationally as a kind of religion. See: http://www3.cnet-ta.ne.jp/j/juche/DEFAULTE.htm

41. A history of the Baath Party is offered by Aljazeera.net, the Arabic language network posted at: http://english.aljazeera.net/NR/exeres/AFBF5651-45AF-45E7-910E-ECA0AFEA24C1.htm

42. http://english.aljazeera.net/NR/exeres/AFBF5651-45AF-45E7-910E-ECA0A-FEA24C1.htm

43. http://news.bbc.co.uk/1/hi/world/middle_east/2886733.stm

44. A chronology of events in Iraq can be found at: http://news.bbc.co.uk/1/hi/world/middle_east/737483.stm

45. BBC Web Site, http://news.bbc.co.uk/1/hi/world/africa/country_profiles/1067695.stm

46. An optimistic perspective on these events can be found in the CIA Factbook on Nigeria to be found at: http://www.cia.gov/cia/publications/factbook/geos/ni.html

47. The longer-term historical experience that created the country by conquest and brought unification under imperial control despite continuing conflicts with many disparate people and parties is recorded at: http://www.factmonster.com/ce6/world/A0860005.html. The Nigerian government maintains an official site that offers a somewhat euphoric account of its history and government. See, http://www.nigeria.gov.ng/government.aspx

48. The key events that followed Somali independence are summarized in "Fact Monster," a site offering information based on the Columbia Encyclopedia: http://www.factmonster.com/ipka/A0107979.html

49. They have no official web site, but one is maintained by friends and émigrés with support from advertisers. It can be viewed at: http://www.somaliland.org/aboutus.asp

50. A time-line reporting the chronology of events in Somalia can be found on the BBC site at: http://news.bbc.co.uk/1/hi/world/africa/country_profiles/1072611.stm. As for Puntland, it claims to be part of Somalia and operates a commercial web site, but offers precious little information about its situation: http://allpuntland.com/ A more informative Somali site, maintained by "Wardheernews," offers a continuing flow of current comments and information about the country. See: http://wardheernews.com/index.htm

51. A brief summary of Somalia's sad history can be found at: http://news.bbc.co.uk/1/hi/world/africa/country_profiles/1072592.stm

52. Information about all 191 members of the United Nations at: http://www.un.org/Overview/unmember.html. Other sources of information about the countries of the world include the CIA's *World Factbook*: http://www.cia.gov/cia/publications/factbook/geos/ni.html. The Columbia Encyclopedia offers a computerized "Fact Monster" database that includes a list of countries of the world, with appended lists of dependencies and hyperlinks to their Web sites: http://www.factmonster.com/countries.html

53. http://www.palestinecenter.org/cpap/documents/charter.html

54. http://newssearch.bbc.co.uk/cgi-bin/search/results.pl?scope = newsukfs&tab = news&q = Palestine + + + Hamas&go.x = 30&go.y = 11

55. http://www.kingdomofbhutan.com/

56. A detailed account of the Thai experience is offered in Fred Riggs, *Thailand: The Modernization of a Bureaucratic Polity* (Honolulu: East-West Center Press, 1966). An autobiographical account explaining the way this idea evolved can be found at: http://webdata.soc.hawaii.edu/fredr/autobio3.htm#thai

57. A time-line for the main events in modern Thai history is posted at: http://news.bbc.co.uk/2/hi/asia-pacific/country_profiles/1243059.stm

58. http://news.bbc.co.uk/1/hi/world/middle_east/4107270.stm and http://www.mardomyar.ir/aspx2/elamieh12p.aspx

59. http://english.daralhayat.com/opinion/commentators/06-2005/Article-20050630-cdd943f9-c0a8-10ed-00f8-0297dd62c078/story.html

60. A summary of Iran's history up to 2004, can be found on the U.S. Library of Congress profile posted at: http://lcweb2.loc.gov/frd/cs/profiles/Iran.pdf. The CIA Factbook for Iran, updated to January 2006, can be found at: http://www.cia.gov/cia/publications/factbook/geos/ir.html. The Iran Press Service, published outside Iran, is an international web site with comprehensive news coverage of current Iranian politics and problems. Its site is at: http://www.iran-press-service.com/

61. A good source of information about Afghanistan, its history and current events, can be found at:http://www.afgha.com/

62. http://www.afgha.com/?af = who&op = read&id = 243

63. A list of today's 191 member states can be found at: http://www.un.org/Overview/unmember.html

64. A personal account of how I developed the prismatic model while studying the Thai system of governance is offered in an autobiographical account posted at: http://webdata.soc.hawaii.edu/fredr/autobio3.htm#thai.

65. Howard McCurdy's text can be found at: http://www2.hawaii.edu/~fredr/mccurdy.htm

66. http://www.defenselink.mil/sites/ Here one can find an index to so many agencies and functions that they baffle the imagination.

67. Intelligence agencies, incidentally, operate under a mantle of secrecy that defies inquiry, but nevertheless a great deal of information about them is available as one can discover at: http://www.intelligence.gov/1-members.shtml

68. Information about all state and local governments in the U.S., plus those of American Indian tribes and much more can be found at: http://www.firstgov.gov/. A comprehensive source for information about state and local governments in the U.S. can also be found at: http://www.statelocalgov.net/index.cfm

69. Even this listing is not complete, however, it omits the Federated States of Micronesia, which has a general site at: http://www.fsmgov.org/

70. http://www.cia.gov/cia/publications/factbook/index.html. This site is maintained by the U.S. Central Intelligence Agency and provides a comprehensive list of more or less independent polities, plus a host of international and regional organizations. The data for each entity is offered in conveniently summarized outlines and there are no links to web sites. Consequently other information sources are needed. However, if one does a Google search on any of these entities, one will discover a host of relevant web sites to support one's inquiry.

71. http://www.state.gov/www/background_notes/afbgnhp.html

72. A convenient non-governmental source of comprehensive information about the countries of the world is INFOPLEASE: http://www.infoplease.com/countries.html and http://www.infoplease.com/ipa/A0762461.html

73. http://www.un.org/aboutun/chart.html

74. http://www.g77.org/Speeches/011206.htm

75. http://www.un.org/Depts/oip/background/index.html and Claudia Rosset, *Wall Street Journal*, May 3, 2005, http://www.meforum.org/article/716

76. http://www.weeklystandard.com/Content/Public/Articles/000/000/005/640mcodm.asp. A series of blogs exposing abuses in this program can be tracked from: http://acepilots.com/unscam/archives/002050.html. Recipients of Iraqi oil are listed at: http://acepilots.com/images/saddam270.xls

77. Links to international organizations are at: http://www.networkforgood.org/topics/animal_environ/hurricanes/. This "network for good" site lists a wide range of organizations participating in the rescue and re-development programs for New Orleans. Clicking on any category reveals a list of organizations and their global connections.

78. Oxfam is available at: http://www.networkforgood.org/

79. To see how the system works, take a look at the 'Globe of Blogs'site: http://www.globeofblogs.com/ See also: http://-30-.blogspot.com/

80. http://revolutionagainandagain.blogspot.com/2006/01/understanding-corruption-hell-in-dc.html

81. http://www.washingtonpost.com/wp-srv/politics/special/campfin/stories/cf112795.htm

82. See, for example, http://www.sourcewatch.org/index.php?title = Jack_Abramoff%27s_Criminal_Activities

83. http://www.google.com/

84. Further details can be found on the WTO site at: http://www.wto.org/english/thewto_e/whatis_e/tif_e/agrm1_e.htm

85. ILO details at: http://www.ilo.org/public/english/about/index.htm

86. http://www.ilo.org/public/english/fairglobalization/report/index.htm

87. A long list of countries facing terrorist attacks with information about them can be found at: http://www.terrorism.com/modules.php?op = modload&name = Countries&file = index

88. For details, see: http://www.terrorism.com/index.php

89. http://www.lp.org/

90. http://www.lp.org/article_85.shtml

91. Riggs, F. W. http://webdata.soc.hawaii.edu/fredr/AmMyth.htm

92. Riggs, F. W. http://webdata.soc.hawaii.edu/fredr/apctalk.htm#DEM

93. http://www.worldparliamentgov.net/

94. An overview of the EU can be found at: http://europa.eu.int/abc-en.htm. This page offers links to many sites at which its various component organs are described. To make such a system work, it clearly needs complex and linked structures such as the EU has created.

95. See: http://tcs.ntu.ac.uk/books/titles/g.html and Robertson, *Globalization: Social Theory and Global Culture* (Sage, 1992). The concluding chapter was prepared for use in this volume.

APPENDIX I: GLOBAL ORGANIZATIONS OF PUBLIC ADMINISTRATION

EUROPEAN ORGANIZATIONS

European Group of Public Administration, http://www.iiasiisa.be/egpa/agacc.htm
Austria, http://www.austria-cafe.com/gov.htm
Denmark, http://www.dspa.dk/
France, http://www.idheap.ch/idheap.nsf/vwBaseDocuments/IdActHomepage
Finland, http://www.suomi.fi/english/
Germany, http://www.bakoev.bund.de/
Greece, http://www.egov-project.org/partners.htm
Ireland, http://www.ipa.ie/
Italy, http://www.eurofound.eu.int/emire/ITALY/PUBLICADMINISTRATION-IT.html
Portugal, http://www.ina.pt/gb/ina.htm
Spain, http://www.ina.pt/gb/ina.htm
Sweden, http://www.sweden.gov.se/sb/d/2102/a/20613
United Kingdom, http://www.direct.gov.uk/

REGIONAL ORGANIZATIONS OUTSIDE OF EUROPE

Africa, http://www.cafrad.org/
Asia and the Pacific, http://www.unpan.org/asia.asp
Australia, http://www.ipaa.org.au/
Commonwealth, http://www.capam.org/
Caribbean, http://www.unpan.org/latin.asp

Central and Eastern Europe, http://www.nispa.sk/_portal/homepage.php
Hong Kong, http://www.hkpaa.org.hk/
South Africa, http://www.up.ac.za/academic/soba/SAAPAM/home.htm
New Zealand, http://www.ipanz.org.nz/SITE_Default/

LATIN AMERICA ORGANIZATIONS

Argentina, http://www.sgp.gov.ar/
Brazil, http://www.enap.gov.br/
Chile, http://www.modernizacion.cl/1350/channel.html
Colombia, http://www.esap.edu.co/esap/index.htm
Costa Rica, http://ns.mideplan.go.cr/
Mexico, http://www.ipn.mx/
Uruguay, http://www.onsc.gub.uy/

MIDDLE EAST ORGANIZATIONS

Saudi Arabia, http://www.ameinfo.com/db/92/
Israel, http://jointnet.org.il/elka/en/personal.php
Palestine, www.birzeit.edu/news/news-d?news_id = 80201
Egypt, http://www.escwa.org.lb/unpan/main/links.html

NORTH AMERICAN ORGANIZATIONS

Canada, http://www.ipaciapc.ca/
United States, http://www.aspanet.org/scriptcontent/index.cfm

Originally collected by Fred W. Riggs and updated by Nancy S. Lind

SUBJECT INDEX

971